lonely planet

Greece

Northern
Greece
p256

Central
Greece
p208

Evia & the
Sporades
p648

Northeastern
Aegean Islands
p588

Ionian
Islands
p678

Athens &
Around
p60

Peloponnese
p146

Saronic
Gulf Islands
p324

Cyclades
p346

Dodecanese
p510

Crete
p454

Simon Richmond, Andrea Schulte-Peevers, Andy Symington,
Kate Armstrong, Stuart Butler, Peter Dragicevich, Trent Holden,
Anna Kaminski, Vesna Maric, Hugh McNaughtan, Kate Morgan,
Isabella Noble, Zora O'Neill, Leonid Ragozin, Kevin Raub, Greg Ward

Contents

MONASTERY OF ST JOHN
THE THEOLOGIAN P583

GREEK SALAD P45

Contents

R07105 46982

UNDERSTAND

SURVIVAL GUIDE

COVID-19

We have re-checked every business in this book before publication to ensure that it is still open after the COVID-19 outbreak. However, the economic and social impacts of COVID-19 will continue to be felt long after the outbreak has been contained, and many businesses, services and events referenced in this guide may experience ongoing restrictions. Some businesses may be temporarily closed, have changed their opening hours and services, or require bookings; some unfortunately could have closed permanently. We suggest you check with venues before visiting for the latest information.

SPECIAL FEATURES

Right:
Meteora (p248)

JUSTIN FOULKES/LONELY PLANET ©

WELCOME TO

Greece

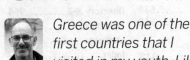

Greece was one of the first countries that I visited in my youth. Like many European travellers, I was drawn by its ancient culture, sunny skies, azure seas and general affordability. On arrival I also discovered that Greek cuisine was superb – all those fresh, healthy ingredients! – that its mountainous landscape meant you could downhill ski as well as waterski around islands, and that the locals were a superfriendly and sociable lot. Nothing has changed on all those scores: Greece remains the perfect holiday destination.

By Simon Richmond, Writer
🐦 @simonrichmond 📷 @simonrichmond
For more about our writers, see p800

Greece

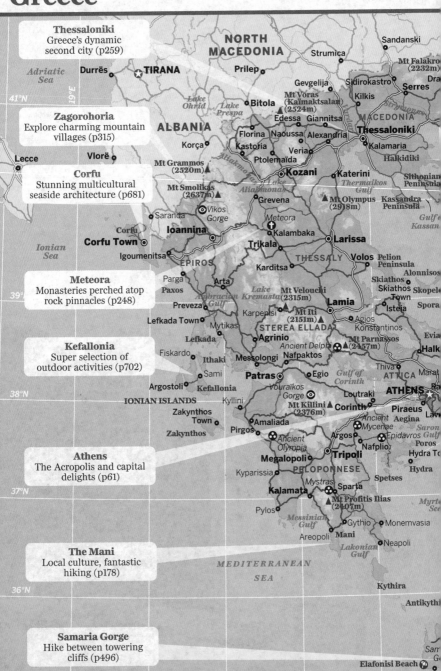

Thessaloniki
Greece's dynamic second city (p259)

Zagorohoria
Explore charming mountain villages (p315)

Corfu
Stunning multicultural seaside architecture (p681)

Meteora
Monasteries perched atop rock pinnacles (p248)

Kefallonia
Super selection of outdoor activities (p702)

Athens
The Acropolis and capital delights (p61)

The Mani
Local culture, fantastic hiking (p178)

Samaria Gorge
Hike between towering cliffs (p496)

ELEVATION

	4000m
	3000m
	2000m
	1000m
	500m
	0

0 — 100 km
0 — 50 miles

BULGARIA
Svilengrad
Edirne
Smolyan
Kârdzhali
Orestiada
Lüleburgaz
Didymotiho
Dadia-Lefkimi-Soufli
National Park
İstanbul
Xanthi
Komotini
THRACE
Keşan
Tekirdağ
Sea of
Marmara
Kavala
Alexandroupoli
Thasos
Thasos Town
Thracian
Sea
Gelibolu
The
Dardanelles
Bandırma
Samothraki
Gallipoli
Peninsula
Athos
Peninsula
Imvros
(Gökçeada)
Çanakkale
Halkidiki
Lovely beaches, sacred
monasteries (p277)
Mt Athos
(2033m)
Gulf of
Agion Oros
Limnos
Myrina
Bozcaada
TURKEY
Balıkesir
Edremit
NORTHEASTERN
AEGEAN ISLANDS
Agios
Efstratios
Molyvos
Lesvos
Ayvalık
Molyvos
Well-preserved medieval
Ottoman town (p627)
Mytilini
Town
Akhisar
Hydra
Car-free and arty
island (p335)
Skyros Town
Skyros
Psara
Manisa
Chios
Chios
Town
İzmir
Sardis
Aegean
Sea
Çeşme
Karystos
Kuşadası
Vathy
(Samos Town)
Aydın
Cyclades
Island-hopping in the
Aegean (p347)
Andros
Gavrio
Tinos
Ikaria
Samos
Kea
Hora (Tinos)
Fourni
Islands
Syros
Mykonos
Ermoupoli
Hora (Mykonos)
Patmos
Kythnos
Delos
Leros
Olymbos
Colourful, mountain-edge
village (p534)
Serifos
CYCLADES
Parikia
Hora (Naxos)
Bodrum
Sifnos
Antiparos
Paros
Naxos
Donousa
Kalymnos
Kimolos
Little Cyclades
Amorgos
Kos Town
Kos
Marmaris
Sikinos
Ios
Astypalea
Milos
Folegandros
Nisyros
Symi
Fethiye
Fira
Anafi
Tilos
**Rhodes
Town**
Santorini
(Thira)
Karpathian
Sea
Halki
Rhodes
Lindos
Kastellorizo
(Megisti)
DODECANESE
MEDITERRANEAN
SEA
Saria
Olymbos
Sea of Crete
Karpathos
Pigadia
Hania
Rethymno
Crete
Iraklio
Agios
Nikolaos
Kasos
Knossos
Explore the remains of a
Minoan palace (p466)
Moni Arkadiou
Knossos
Sitia
Preveli
Beach
Mt Psiloritis
(2456m)
Ierapetra
Gavdos

Greece's Top Experiences

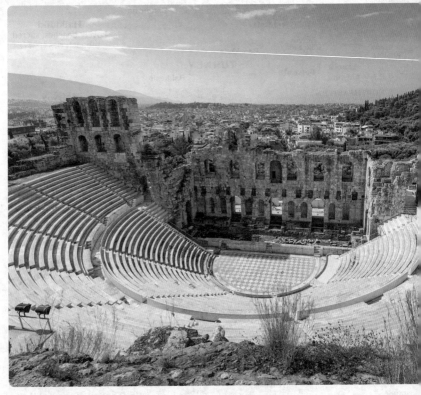

1 ANCIENT SITES

Greece is littered with World Heritage–listed ruins. Athens' Acropolis, Ancient Delphi and the Palace of Knossos come to mind first, but other standout sites include the ancient theatre of Epidavros, the Byzantine ruins of Mystras and Ancient Olympia, birthplace of the Olympic Games.

Athens' Acropolis

No matter how you experience the Acropolis (pictured left and right), you'll be mesmerised by its beauty, history and sheer size. The Parthenon is the star attraction, but don't overlook the exquisite Temple of Athena Nike and the Theatre of Dionysos. p72

Ancient Delphi

Early morning is a magical time at Delphi (pictured above), as the sun's rays pour over the Sanctuary of Athena Pronaia. Gazing out over the Gulf of Corinth, it's easy to understand why the ancient Greeks chose this as the centre of their world. Today, only three columns remain, but that's enough to let your imagination soar. p213

Knossos

Knossos was the capital of the mighty Minoan empire more than 4000 years ago. An extraordinary wealth of frescoes, sculptures, relics (storage jars pictured above) jewellery and structures lay buried under the soil here until the site's excavation in the early 20th century. p466

2 IDYLLIC BEACHES

Golden brown, pink, red, black and white: Greece's beaches come in a myriad of shades and styles, from unspoilt coves to party centrals. With thousands of miles of coastline, Greece has an absurd number of beautiful beaches, so you are bound to find one that fits your dreams.

Preveli Beach

With its heart-shaped boulder lapped by the bluest waves, this Crete beach (pictured above) is iconic. Bisected by a freshwater river and flanked by cliffs concealing sea caves, Preveli is a ribbon of soft sand on the Libyan Sea, with clear pools of water that are perfect for dips. p484

Myrtos Beach

One of the most breathtaking strands in Greece, Myrtos Beach (pictured at top) on Kefallonia is perhaps best viewed from above. Verdant hills and white cliffs astound. It's the white pebbles that turn the sea such a dazzling shade of turquoise. p709

Voidokilia Beach

Imagine the perfect beach and Voidokilia (pictured above) on the west coast of Messinia in the Peloponnese is what is likely to come to mind: a horseshoe-shaped cove of white sand and lush vegetation wrapping its arms around a lagoon of warm turquoise water. p194

3 MARVELLOUS MUSEUMS

You could spend a lifetime exploring Greece's museums and still want to come back for more. Athens' museums are superb, but you'll also encounter priceless antiquities and treasures in the collections on the islands.

Benaki Museum of Greek Culture

This expansive collection brings together precious works from all over Greece and the Ottoman Empire. The main event is the Benaki Museum (pictured below), but other key branches include 138 Pireos St and the Museum of Islamic Art. p94

Heraklion Archaeological Museum

Most famous for its Minoan collection, including the gob-smacking frescoes from Knossos, this museum (pictured above) is one of the largest and most important in Greece. p459

National Archaeological Museum

The world's foremost repository of ancient Greek artefacts occupies an enormous neoclassical building. Key pieces include the golden Mask of Agamemnon and the Artemision Jockey. p90

4 ISLAND LIFE

ROMAS_PHOTO/SHUTTERSTOCK©

SAIKO3P/SHUTTERSTOCK ©

STAVROS ARGYROPOULOS/SHUTTERSTOCK ©

Among the 6,000 Greek islands and islets scattered across the Aegean and Ionian Seas, 227 are inhabited. From Crete (the largest island) to Halki (just 28 sq km), each island has its own personality, culture and landscape.

Corfu

Stroll past Byzantine fortresses, neoclassical 19th-century British buildings, Parisian-style arcades and Orthodox church towers in the Venetian Old Town. Beyond the town, Corfu is lush green mountains, rolling countryside and dramatic coastlines. p681

Hydra

The stunningly preserved stone village of Hydra (pictured above) fills a natural cove and hugs the edges of the surrounding mountains. Sailboats, *caïques* (little boats) and megayachts float in the quays, while locals and travellers fill the cafes. p336

Milos

Arched around a central caldera, Milos and its offshore islets offer dramatic landscapes, surreal rock formations, over 70 splendid beaches and picturesque villages. p435

5 WINE & DINE

Greece is one the world's most sustainable food locales. Organic produce markets, prolific wild herbs and island seafood hauls are an integral part of the culinary scene. Marry that to wine producers with centuries of experience and you have the makings of a feast.

PIOTR KRZESLAN/SHUTTERSTOCK ©

MARIONTXA/SHUTTERSTOCK ©

Turkish Delight

The Turkish influence is felt strongly in the kitchens of northern Greece, from *yiaourtlou* (beef kebab on pitta with Greek yoghurt) to patisseries piled high with *loukoumi* (Turkish delight). p273

Local Cheeses

Crafted mainly from goat's and sheep's milk, there's a world of Greek cheese beyond feta: ricotta-like *myzithra*, provolone-style *kaseri* and nutty, mild, gruyère-like *graviera*, best sampled on Naxos. p384

Cretan Cuisine

A highlight of Crete is the island's delicious and distinctive cuisine. Visit village tavernas where you'll frequently find yourself presented with wholesome feasts at surprisingly reasonable prices. p455

6 GET ACTIVE!

As well as the beaches and waters surrounding Greece's islands, there's no shortage of dramatic cliff faces, mountains and gorges as well as flourishing forests and ancient walkways to experience. It's all perfect terrain for outdoor activities.

Samaria Gorge

This dramatic gorge – Crete's most-trodden canyon – is home to soaring birds of prey and a dazzling array of wildflowers in spring. It's a full-day's walk (pictured top), but the jaw-dropping views make it worth every step. p496

The Mani

With everything from rugged rocky highlands and hidden lush green oases to small fishing tavernas and severe rock-solid tower houses, this pocket of the Peloponnese (pictured bottom) is well worth exploring. p178

Kefallonia

Remarkably unflustered by tourism, Kefallonia is a paradise for outdoor enthusiasts. Kayak between white-sand beaches; scuba-dive in crystal-clear waters; and hike mountains that spiral high into the sky. p702

7 ARTS SCENE

The refined classical sculptures, frescoes and mosaics of Greece's ancient artists lay the foundations for the country's modern and contemporary art scenes. Exciting works can be found in museums and commercial galleries and even street walls.

Art on Rhodes

Landscapes of Rhodes by Valias Semertzidis are a highlight of the Modern Greek Art Museum in Rhodes Town. The collection also features works by some of Greece's greatest 20th century artists. p518

ARTWORK BY SONNE : TITOSLACK/GETTY IMAGES ©

Athens' Street Art

Athens' art scene is vibrant, with scores of galleries vying for attention, but it's the city's street art that is the most eye-catching, particularly the giant murals tackling serious political and social themes. p94

Teriade Museum

This astonishing Lesvos museum (pictured right) enshrines the collection of art critic and publisher Stratis Eleftheriadis and includes works by Picasso, Chagall, Miró, Le Corbusier and Matisse. p623

8 SPIRITUAL PLACES

Orthodox Christianity is a cornerstone of national identity and culture, with Easter the biggest festival on the Greek Orthodox calendar. Search out other religious sites around the country, including the synagogues of Athens and Thessaloniki, and the Catholic St George's Cathedral on Syros.

Meteora

Soaring pillars of rock jut heavenward, 24 of them complete with centuries-old monasteries perched on their summits (pictured above). It's a spectacular location that beckons both religious pilgrims and rock climbers. p248

Easter on Patmos

This Dodecanese island comes to life over Easter, with fireworks, dancing in the streets and plenty of ouzo. A candlelit processions of flower-filled biers winds its way through the capital on Good Friday. p578

Prodromos Monastery

Hike the 75km Menalon trail through the dramatic scenery of the Lousios Gorge to reach this memorable monastery that clings to the cliffs like a swallow's nest. p165

Need to Know

For more information, see Survival Guide (p763)

Currency
Euro (€)

Language
Greek

Visas
Generally not required for stays of up to 90 days; however, travellers from some nations may require a visa, so double-check with the Greek embassy.

Money
Debit and credit cards are accepted in cities, but elsewhere it's handy to have cash. Most towns have ATMs, but they may be out of order.

Mobile Phones
Local SIM cards can be used in unlocked phones. Most other phones can be set to roaming. US and Canadian phones need to have a dual- or tri-band system.

Time
Eastern European Time (GMT/UTC plus two hours)

When to Go

Dry climate
Warm summer, mild winter
Mild summer, very cold winter

Thessaloniki
GO May–Nov

Corfu
GO May–Sep

Athens
GO May–Sep

Rhodes
GO Apr–Sep

Iraklio
GO May–Oct

High Season
(Jun–Aug)

➡ Sights, tours and transport are running full tilt.

➡ Accommodation prices can double.

➡ Crowds swell and temperatures soar.

Shoulder
(Apr & May, Sep & Oct)

➡ Accommodation prices can drop by up to 20%.

➡ Temperatures are not as blazing.

➡ Internal flights and island ferries have reduced schedules.

Low Season
(Nov–Mar)

➡ Many islands shut up their tourist infrastructure and ferry schedules are skeletal.

➡ Accommodation rates can drop by as much as 50%.

➡ Expect chilly, wet weather; Athens and Crete may even see snow.

Useful Websites

EOT (Greek National Tourist Organisation; www.visitgreece.gr) Concise tourist information.

Greeka (www.greeka.com) Plenty of planning advice, photos and booking services.

Greek Travel Pages (www.gtp.gr) Access to ferry schedules and accommodation.

Lonely Planet (www.lonelyplanet.com/greece) Destination information, hotel bookings, traveller forum and more.

Ministry of Culture (www.culture.gr) For cultural events and sights.

Odysseus (http://odysseus.culture.gr) Portal for info on ancient sites and for booking tickets.

Important Numbers

In Greece, the area code must be dialled for ordinary numbers, meaning you always dial the full 10-digit telephone number. Emergency numbers are shorter, as detailed in the table below.

Country code	📞30
International access code	📞00
Ambulance	📞166
Police	📞100
Tourist police	📞171

Exchange Rates

Australia	A$1	€0.61
Canada	C$1	€0.67
Japan	¥100	€0.81
New Zealand	NZ$1	€0.58
UK	£1	€1.13
US	US$1	€0.88

For current exchange rates see www.xe.com.

Daily Costs

Budget: Less than €100

➡ Dorm bed and domatio (Greek B&B): less than €60

➡ Meal at markets and street stalls: less than €15

Midrange: €100–180

➡ Double room in midrange hotel: €60–150

➡ Hearty meal at a local taverna: around €20

➡ Entrance fee for most sights: less than €15

Top End: More than €180

➡ Double room in top hotel: from €150

➡ Excellent dining, some accompanied by Michelin stars: €60–100

➡ Activity such as diving certification: around €400

➡ Cocktail: around €12

Opening Hours

The following are high-season hours; hours decrease significantly for shoulder and low seasons, and some places close completely.

Banks 8.30am–2.30pm Monday to Thursday, 8am–2pm Friday

Restaurants 11am–11pm

Cafes 10am–midnight

Bars 8pm–late

Clubs 10pm–4am

Post Offices 7.30am–2pm Monday to Friday (rural); 7.30am–8pm Monday to Friday, 7.30am–2pm Saturday (urban)

Shops 8am–2pm Monday, Wednesday and Saturday; 8am–2pm and 5pm–9pm Tuesday, Thursday and Friday

Arriving in Greece

Eleftherios Venizelos International Airport (Athens) Express buses (€6, one hour) operate 24 hours between the airport, city centre and Piraeus. Half-hourly metro trains (€10, 50 minutes) run between the city centre and the airport from 5.30am to 11.30pm. Taxis to the city centre cost €38 (€50 at night) and take about 45 minutes.

Makedonia International Airport (Thessaloniki) Buses X1, N1, 45 & 79 (€2, 50 minutes) connect to the city every half hour around the clock. Taxis to the city centre cost €30.

Nikos Kazantzakis International Airport (Iraklio, Crete) Buses run to the city centre from 6am to midnight (€1.20, every 15 minutes). Taxis to the city centre cost €15.

Diagoras Airport (Rhodes) Buses run to Rhodes Town from 6.40am to 11.15pm (€2.60, 25 minutes). Taxis cost €25.

Getting Around

Air Domestic flights are abundant. In high season, flights fill up fast so book ahead.

Boat Ferries, including catamarans, well-equipped modern ferries and overnight boats with cabins, link the islands to each other and the mainland. Schedules change annually and can be announced as late as May. In high season it's smart to book ahead.

Bus Generally air-conditioned, frequent, and as efficient as traffic allows; good for travel between major cities.

Car & Motorcycle Rentals are reasonably priced and found on all but the tiniest islands. They give you the freedom to explore the islands, but some islands are becoming overrun with hire vehicles.

For much more on **getting around**, see p773

First Time Greece

For more information, see Survival Guide (p763)

Checklist

➡ Check your passport is valid for at least six months past your arrival date.

➡ Make reservations for accommodation and travel, especially in high season.

➡ Check airline baggage restrictions, including for regional flights.

➡ Inform credit-/debit-card company of your travel plans.

➡ Organise travel insurance.

➡ Check if you'll be able to use your mobile (cell) phone.

What to Pack

➡ International driving licence, if you don't hold an EU one

➡ Phrasebook

➡ Diving qualifications

➡ Phone charger

➡ Power adaptor

➡ Lock/padlock

➡ Lightweight raincoat

➡ Seasickness remedies for ferry trips

➡ Mosquito repellent

➡ Swimwear, snorkel and fins

➡ Clothes pegs and laundry line

Top Tips for Your Trip

➡ In late spring or early autumn the weather is softer and the crowds are smaller.

➡ Visit a few out-of-the-way villages to find traditional culture. Rent a car and explore. Stop for lunch, check out the local shops and test out your Greek.

➡ Go slowly. Greece's infrastructure doesn't befit a fast-paced itinerary. Visit fewer places for longer.

➡ Many sites (including the ancient sites in Athens) offer free entry on the first Sunday of the month, except in July and August.

What to Wear

Athenians are well groomed and the younger crowd is trendy, so keep your most stylish clothes for the city. Nevertheless, in Athens and other big cities such as Rhodes and Iraklio, you'll get away with shorts or jeans and casual tops. Bars or high-end restaurants require more effort – the scene is fashionable rather than dressy. Think tops and trousers rather than T-shirts and cut-offs. In out-of-the-way places you can wear casual clothing; in summer, the heat will make you want to run naked so bring things such as quick-drying tank tops and cool dresses. Sturdy walking shoes are a must for the cobbled roads and ruins.

Sleeping

If travelling in high season, reserve accommodation well in advance. Many hotels on islands are closed during winter.

Hotels Greece ranks all accommodation from one to five stars depending on how they meet 'minimum standards' (this includes allowances for guests in wheelchairs). As such, the stars may reflect the services offered, rather than quality.

Domatia The Greek equivalent of the British B&B, minus the breakfast. Many have equipped kitchens.

Campgrounds Found in the majority of regions and islands and often include hot showers, communal kitchens, restaurants and swimming pools.

Money

ATMs are widespread in tourist areas, and can usually be found in most towns large enough to support a bank. Most are compatible with MasterCard or Visa, while Cirrus and Maestro users can make withdrawals in major towns and tourist areas. If travelling to smaller islands, you may want to take a backup supply of cash, as many ATMs can lose their connection or (in remote areas) run out of cash at the end of the day!

It's always wise to notify your bank of your travel plans before you leave, to avoid them blocking the card as an antifraud measure after your first withdrawal abroad.

Bargaining

Bargaining is acceptable in flea markets and markets, but elsewhere you are expected to pay the stated price.

Tipping

Restaurants Tipping is not traditionally the culture in Greece, though it is appreciated. Locals tend to leave a few coins. Depending on where you are, you can round it up or leave around 10%.

Taxis Round up the fare. There's a small fee for handling bags; this is an official charge, not a tip.

Bellhops Bellhops in hotels appreciate a small gratuity of around €1.

Language

Tourism is big business in Greece and being good businesspeople, many Greeks have learned the tools of the trade: English. In cities and popular towns, you can get by with less than a smattering of Greek; in smaller villages or out-of-the-way islands and destinations, a few phrases in Greek will go a long way. Wherever you are, Greeks will hugely appreciate your efforts to speak their language.

 Does this ferry go to (Rhodes)?
Πηγαίνει αυτό το φέρι στη (Ρόδο)
pi·ye·ni af·to to fe·ri sti (ro·tho)

With over a hundred islands, it would be a shame not to get out there and explore.

 What is the local speciality?
Ποιες είναι οι τοπικές λιχουδιές
pies i·ne i to·pi·kes li·khu·thies

Most areas and islands in Greece have a local dish – and the locals love to talk food.

 Do you speak English?
Μιλάς Αγγλικά
mi·las ang·gli·ka

Given the tourist-oriented nature of Greece, the chance is the answer will be 'yes', but it's always polite to ask.

 I'd like to hire a car.
Θα ήθελα να ενοικιάσω ένα αυτοκίνητο
tha i·the·la na e·ni·ki·a·so e·na af·to·ki·ni·to

For some of the more remote areas and islands, travelling around is easier by car.

 What time does it open?
Τι ώρα ανοίγει
ti o·ra a·ni·yi

Avoid the crowds – especially if a cruise ship is in port – by getting to sites and museums as they open.

Etiquette

Eating Meals are commonly laid in the table centre and shared. Always accept a drink offer as it's a show of goodwill. Don't insist on paying if invited out; it insults your hosts. In restaurants, service might feel slow; dining is a drawn-out experience and it's impolite to rush waitstaff.

Photography In churches, avoid using a flash or photographing the main altar, which is considered taboo. At archaeological sites, you'll be stopped from using a tripod which marks you as a professional and thereby requires special permissions.

Places of worship If you visit churches, cover up with a shawl or long sleeves and a long skirt or trousers to show respect. Some places will deny admission if you're showing too much skin.

Body language 'Yes' is a swing of the head and 'no' is a curt raising of the head or eyebrows, often accompanied by a 'ts' click-of-the-tongue.

What's New

In 2019 over 33 million visitors flocked to Greece, stoking overtourism at key locations. The COVID-19 pandemic hit the pause button, allowing Greece time for a rethink and to formulate plans to reboot its tourism economy with a variety of sustainable initiatives.

Bicentennial

Events and initiatives to mark Greece's 200th anniversary of independence are being held throughout 2021 – details can be found at www.greece2021.gr. Celebrate in Nafplio, the first capital of modern Greece, and Spetses, home to the independence war heroine Laskarina Bouboulina. Among other projects are efforts to gain World Heritage status for the early-20th century leper colony of Spinalonga (p504) off the coast of Crete.

Wine Tourism

Greece's wine industry is booming, bringing global attention to unique, quality wines made from local varietals such as *assyrtiko* in Santorini. Kefallonia is particularly well set up for wine tourism, as is Evia. Also zone in on Greece's largest organic winery, Domaine Porto Carras (p279), in Macedonia's Sithonian Peninsula, Manousakis Winery (p491) on Crete and the Paneri Winery (p677) on Skyros.

Plastic Bans

Donoussa became the first Greek island committed to the reduction and gradual abolition of disposable plastics in 2019. This initiative is part of the **SeaChange Greek Islands** programme of projects across the Cyclades, including Santorini and Serifos. **Clean Blue Paros** (https://commonseas.com/countries/clean-blue-paros) also aims to make that island the first in the Mediterranean to become plastic-waste free.

LOCAL KNOWLEDGE

WHAT'S HAPPENING IN GREECE

Simon Richmond, Lonely Planet writer

Before COVID-19 hit in early 2020, Greece was finally shedding its image as the EU's weakest economic link. The centre-right New Democracy party, led by Kyriakos Mitsotakis, has been in government since July 2019, overseeing a rise in foreign investment and tempting skilled citizens who had left Greece during the years of austerity to return to establish new businesses.

Mitsotakis's government garnered praise for its handling of measures to quell the health impact of the first wave on the pandemic. There was little that Greece could do, however, about global travel restrictions – they dealt a severe blow to the country's tourism industry, which accounts for around 20% of the economy. The second wave of the pandemic in Greece has also proved far more deadly.

In November, the government set out its National Recovery and Sustainability Plan to reboot the economy with an injection of €32 billion from the EU. And moving into 2021, Greece is gearing up to celebrate the bicentennial of the beginning of the Greek War of Independence, a struggle that freed the country from the Ottoman Empire.

Athens Upgrades

Since October 2020, Athens' signature ancient site the Acropolis (p72) has been bathed in a new light show. The new 30m-wide fountain at the heart of the city's revamped **Omonia Square** is also eye-catching when illuminated at night. And head north of Metaxourgio to find the historic **Lenorman Street Tobacco Factory**, which has been turned into a new cultural venue by arts organisation Neon (https://neon.org.gr).

Paths of Greece

The social cooperative **Paths of Greece** (www.pathsofgreece.gr) has recently been creating new hiking routes across the country. Head to Samos to follow the 10km Muscat Vineyards Path dedicated to the island's production of muscat wine. Alternatively, make your way to the mountains and small lakes of Western Macedonia to follow the Paths of Peace multi-day hiking trail and cycling route.

Digital Museums

Some of Greece's leading museums have come up with digital solutions to lockdown hiatuses. Athens' Acropolis Museum (p78) was the first museum in Greece to go fully digital to showcase exhibits in high definition, with an array of multimedia applications, including games, videos and 3D images. Also offering 360° tours of exhibitions at several of its branches is the Benaki Museum (www.benaki.org).

Improved Regional Airports

A €440 million development programme of 14 airports was completed in February 2021. The upgraded Makedonia International Airport (p276) in Thessaloniki features a new terminal, restaurants and shopping facilities. Improved island airports include Corfu, Crete, Kefalonia, Kos, Lesvos, Mykonos, Rhodes, Samos, Santorini, Skiathos and Zakynthos.

High Speed Trains

White Arrow high-speed trains were put into service between Athens and Thessaloniki in March 2021. The trains, which travel at speeds of up to 160km per hour, will cut the journey time between Greece's top two cities by 45 minutes to 3¼ hours.

FAST FACTS

Food trend Eco-friendly dining

National drink ouzo

Number of populated islands 227

Population 11.2 million

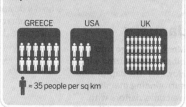

≈ 35 people per sq km

Underwater Museum

The Peristera shipwreck dating back to about 425 BCE can now be explored by recreational divers in Greece's first 'underwater museum' in the pristine National Marine Park of Alonnisos Northern Sporades (p670). Dives can be arranged via Triton Dive Center (p671) and Ikion Diving (p662).

Koons on Hydra

The Hydra Slaughterhouse Project, an annual contemporary art installation on Hydra organised by the Deste Foundation (p336), has been postponed until 2022, when it will feature the celebrated American artist Jeff Koons.

Month by Month

January

Most islands go into hibernation during winter. However, the capital and surrounding mainland welcome visitors with festivals that aren't really aimed at tourists. Expect local insight and warmth from hospitality (rather than the sun).

🎎 Feast of Agios Vasilios (St Basil)

The first day of January sees a busy church ceremony followed by gifts, singing, dancing and feasting. The *vasilopita* (golden glazed cake for New Year's Eve) is cut; if you're fortunate enough to get the slice containing a coin, you'll supposedly have a lucky year.

🎎 Epiphany (Blessing of the Waters)

The day of Christ's baptism by St John is celebrated throughout Greece on 6 January. Seas, lakes and rivers are all blessed, with the largest ceremony held at Piraeus.

🎎 Gynaikokratia

The villages of the prefectures of Rodopi, Kilkis and Seres in northern Greece hold a day of role reversal on 8 January. Women spend the day in *kafeneia* (coffee houses) while the men stay at home to do the housework.

February

While February is an unlikely time to head to Greece, if you like a party and can time your visit with Carnival, which starts three weeks before Lent, it's well worth it.

🎎 Carnival Season

Minor events from as early as late February lead to a wild weekend of costume parades, floats, feasting and traditional dancing. There are regional variations: Patra's Carnival is the largest, while Skyros features men and their male 'brides' dressed in goatskins.

March

The islands are sleepy but the weather is warming up, making March a relaxed time to visit. Although the national calendar is quiet, there are countless religious festivals celebrated with great gusto in towns.

🎎 Clean Monday (Shrove Monday)

On the first day of Lent (a day which is referred to as Kathara Deftera), people take to the hills throughout Greece to enjoy picnicking and kite-flying.

🎎 Independence Day

The anniversary of the hoisting of the Greek flag by independence supporters at Moni Agias Lavras is celebrated with parades and dancing on 25 March. This act of revolt marked the start of the War of Independence.

April

A great month to visit with the scent of orange blossom heavy in the air. Easter weekend is busy with vacationing Greeks; reserve accommodation well in advance. Some businesses shut up shop for the week.

Orthodox Easter

Communities commemorate Jesus' crucifixion with candlelight processions on Good Friday and celebrate his resurrection at midnight on Easter Saturday. Feasting follows on Easter Sunday.

Festival of Agios Georgios (St George)

The feast day of Greece's patron saint is celebrated on 23 April, but if it falls during Lent, it moves to the first Tuesday following Easter. Expect dancing, feasting and a general party atmosphere, particularly in Arahova, near Delphi.

May

If you're planning to go hiking, May is a great time to hit Greece's trails. Temperatures are relatively mild and wildflowers create a huge splash of colour. Local produce fills Greek kitchens.

May Day

The first of May is marked by a mass exodus from towns for picnics in the country. Wildflowers are gathered and made into wreaths to decorate houses. It's a day associated with workers' rights, so recent years have also seen mass walkouts and strikes.

Naxos Festivals

Between May and September various festivals take place on Naxos. Classical concerts are held in the Venetian kastro, art exhibitions are staged at the Bazeos Tower and celebrations of traditional food and music are held in several different venues.

June

For festival-goers looking for contemporary acts rather than traditional village parties, June is hopping on the mainland. Top national and international performers fill atmospheric stages with dance, music and drama.

Navy Week

Celebrating their long relationship with the sea, fishing villages and ports throughout the country host historical reenactments and parties in early June.

Nafplion Festival

Featuring Greek and international performers, this classical-music festival, which falls at the end of the month, uses Nafplion's Palamidi fortress as one of its atmospheric concert venues. (p161)

Feast of St John the Baptist

The country is ablaze with bonfires on 24 June as Greeks light up the wreaths they made on May Day.

Athens & Epidaurus Festival

The most prominent Greek summer festival features local and international music, dance and drama at the ancient Odeon of Herodes Atticus on the slopes of the Acropolis in Athens and the world-famous Theatre of Epidavros in the Peloponnese. Events run from June to August. (p100)

Miaoulia Festival

Hydra ignites in celebration of Admiral Miaoulis and the Hydriot contribution to the War of Independence. Witness a spectacular boat burning, fireworks, boat racing and folk dancing, usually held the third weekend of June.

Delphi Festival

With events scheduled for both June and August this cultural festival includes musical and theatrical events in a variety of spaces in and around Delphi and Dorida. See www.delphifestival.gr for details.

July

Guaranteed sunshine as temperatures soar and life buzzes on the islands' beaches. Outdoor cinemas and giant beach clubs draw visitors to Athens' nightlife.

Rockwave Festival

Rockwave has major international artists (with an emphasis on metal, most years) and is held over several weekends at Terra Vibe, a parkland venue on the outskirts of Athens in Malakasa. (p104)

☆ Skopelos Rembetika Festival

Held in Skopelos Town in mid-July, this musical jamboree is a three-day showcase for local folk-blues musicians. (p664)

August

Respect the high heat of August – do a little bit less and relax a little more fully. If you're travelling midmonth, reserve well ahead as Greeks take to the roads and boats in large numbers.

🎆 August Moon Festival

Under the year's brightest moon, historical venues in Athens open with free moonlit performances. Watch theatre, dance and music at venues such as the Acropolis or Roman Agora. The festival is also celebrated at other towns and sites around Greece; check locally for details. (p100)

🎆 Feast of the Dormition

Also called Assumption and celebrated with family reunions on 15 August; the whole population is seemingly on the move on either side of the big day. Thousands also make a pilgrimage to Tinos to its miracle-working icon of Panagia Evangelistria.

🎆 XLSIOR

One of the LGBT+ pride season's biggest party events is this week-long festival held at the end of the month on Mykonos. See https://xlsiorfestival.com for the full line-up.

🍷 Wine & Culture Festival

Held at Evia's coastal town of Karystos during the last week of August and the first week of September, this festival includes theatre, traditional dancing, music and visual-art exhibits as well as a sampling of every local wine imaginable. (p656)

September

The sun is high though less and less blazing, especially on the islands. The crowds begin to thin and some ferry schedules begin to decline midmonth. Fresh figs and grapes are in season and plentiful.

🎆 Gennisis Tis Panagias

The birthday of the Virgin Mary is celebrated throughout the country on 8 September with religious services and feasting.

October

While most of the islands start to quieten down, the sunny weather often holds in October. City life continues apace.

🎆 Ohi Day

A simple 'no' (*ohi* in Greek) was Prime Minister Metaxas' famous response when Mussolini demanded free passage through Greece for his troops on 28 October 1940. The date is now a major national holiday with remembrance services, parades, feasting and dance.

November

Autumn sees temperatures drop. Olive-picking is in full swing in places such as Crete and feta production picks up, giving you the opportunity to taste some seriously fresh cheese.

☆ Thessaloniki International Film Festival

Around 150 films are crammed into 11 days of screenings around the city in mid-November, alongside concerts, exhibitions, talks and theatrical performances. (p270)

🧗 Leonidio Climbing Festival

Climbers descend on this eastern Peloponnesian town in early November to scale the impressive cliffs of the Badron Gorge. See www.climbinleonidio.com.

December

The islands may be quiet but Athens and Thessaloniki are still in full swing. Expect cooler temperatures and a chilly sea. With fewer tourists, you're likely to meet more locals and not have to push through crowds at the major sights.

🎆 Christmas

Celebrated on 25 December and traditionally marking the end of a 40-day fast. Expect to see Christmas trees, children carolling and fishing boats decorated with lights. Families gather for a Christmas Day feast including a roasted hog and honey cookies.

Itineraries

 The Grand Tour

First trip to Greece? Here's a mixed bag of the country's top sights, most beautiful beaches, cultural highs, contemporary cities and laid-back island life.

Begin in **Athens**, visiting ancient sites, museums and markets, and sampling the contemporary-art scene and award-winning restaurants. Catch a ferry to chic **Mykonos**, with its fashionable bars and crowd-pleasing beaches. Day-trip to the sacred island of **Delos** for its fascinating ancient ruins. Hop a ferry to spectacular **Santorini** to watch the sun sink from the dramatic cliffs of its volcanic caldera.

Depending on your time, take a ferry or a flight to **Iraklio**, Crete's vibrant capital. Explore the magnificent Minoan ruins of **Knossos**. Continue to **Hania** with its charming harbour and labyrinth of backstreets, then go trekking through the famous **Samaria Gorge**, which spills out on to a beach lapped by the crystal-clear Libyan Sea.

Fly from Iraklio to **Thessaloniki** to lose yourself in Ottoman-style architecture, Turkish sweets and a vibrant arts scene. Scale **Mt Olympus** (2918m), Greece's highest peak, then visit the monasteries of **Meteora**, perched high on narrow pinnacles of rock. Your last stop is **Ancient Delphi**, former home of the mysterious Delphic oracle.

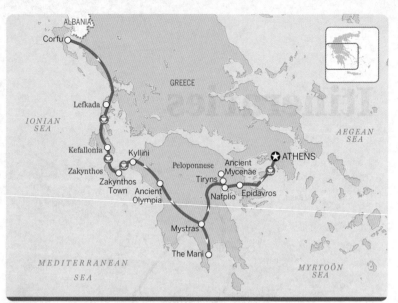

Ionians & the Peloponnese

A tour of the Ionian Islands and the neighbouring Peloponnesian peninsula delivers beautiful medieval towns, ancient historic sights, dramatic scenery and some great outdoor activities.

Begin on **Corfu**, spending a couple of days wandering through the amazing blend of Italian, French and British architecture in Corfu's Old Town, indulging in gourmet cuisine, exploring picturesque coastal villages and lounging on sandy beaches. Corfu is also great for windsurfing, or biking in the mountainous interior.

Hop across to Igoumenitsa on the mainland, and travel down to **Lefkada** where Lefkada Town is a charming place to spend a day or two, or you could head to villages in the mountainous interior. It's a short ferry ride from here to **Kefallonia**. Visit the picturesque village of Fiskardo, kayak to isolated beaches and sample the island's local wine.

If you have your own transport then you could use the ferry (mid-May to October) from Pesada to Agios Nikolaos on Zakynthos. Otherwise it's easier and cheaper to cross to mainland Kyllini and reach historic **Zakynthos Town** from there.

Return to Kyllini and make your way inland to **Ancient Olympia** where you can stand in the stadium that hosted the first Olympic Games. Stay overnight in the town and take in some of the excellent museums. Head south to the captivating World Heritage–listed ruins of **Mystras**. This massive ancient fortress town was the last stronghold of the Byzantine Empire.

If you have time and your own wheels to explore, continue south to the rugged **Mani** region, superb for hiking. Otherwise, head north to graceful **Nafplio** with its mansions, museums and lively port. From here, it's easy to do day trips to the impressive acropolis at **Tiryns** and the citadel of Ancient Mycenae. East of here is the ancient theatre of **Epidavros**, where it's well worth taking in some starlit classical performances. Then hop on a ferry from nearby Methana to end your journey in **Athens**.

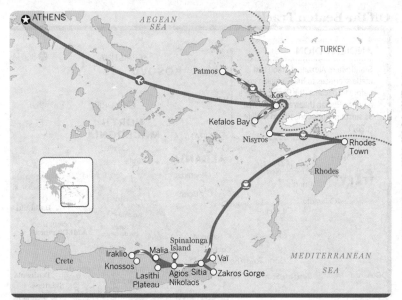

4 WEEKS Crete & the Dodecanese

Eastern Crete offers a tranquil side of the island with relaxed resorts and impressive sights. From here it's a short hop to the neighbouring Dodecanese, with their wealth of culture and speedy catamaran services that make island hopping a breeze.

Begin in **Iraklio**, taking in the excellent archaeological museum. Make a day trip to the captivating Minoan ruins of **Knossos** before sampling fine vintages in the Iraklio Wine Country, a mosaic of shapely hills, sun-baked slopes and lush valleys.

From Iraklio head east along the northern coast to the relaxed resort town of **Agios Nikolaos**, which radiates charm and chilled ambience. This makes a great base for exploring the surrounding region. Explore the massive Venetian fortress on **Spinalonga Island**, a leper colony until 1957 and just a short ferry ride across the Gulf of Mirabello. Visit the surrounding Minoan ruins, such as the **Palace of Malia**, still filled with mysteries, and rent a bike to explore the tranquil villages of the fertile **Lasithi Plateau**, lying snugly between mountain ranges and home to Zeus' birthplace.

Continue on to **Sitia**, from where you can head for the clear water and white sand of **Vaï**, Europe's only natural palm-forest beach. You can also head south from here to Zakros to hike through the dramatic, cave-honeycombed **Zakros Gorge** to Kato Zakros and its Minoan palace.

From Sitia, get settled on a twice-weekly, 12-hour ferry ride to **Rhodes**. Spend a couple of days exploring the atmospheric, walled medieval Old Town and checking out its burgeoning nightlife. Visit some of the surrounding beaches and stunning Acropolis of Lindos. Catch a catamaran to lush **Nisyros** to explore atop the alarmingly thin crust of its caldera and then carry on to **Kos** to spend a couple of days on gorgeous, sandy **Kefalos Bay** and to sip coffee and cocktails in Kos Town's lively squares. There still may be time to squeeze in a quick trip to **Patmos** to experience its artistic and religious vibe, and to visit the cave where St John wrote the Book of Revelations, before backtracking to Kos from where you can catch onward flights to **Athens**.

Off the Beaten Track

ANCIENT DION

Stand where Alexander stood and made sacrifices to the Olympian gods before he became 'the Great'. There's a ruined Roman theatre here, as well as surrounding woods rich in wildlife. (p287)

PYLI

Guarding the entrance to a spectacular gorge in the southern Pindos Range Pyli is the jumping off point for a short drive or hike to the stunning 13th-century Church of Porta Panagia. (p247)

KYPSELI

Escape touristy Athens by heading to this suburb offering pretty neo-classical and art-deco architecture, the promenade park of Fokionos Negri and a municipal market hosting a variety of social projects. (p104)

ARKADIA

Head to the rugged coastal region of Kynouria, between Leonidio and the village of Geraki in Lakonia, for one of the most scenic drives or bike rides in the Peloponnese. (p164)

KYTHIRA

This charming and time-forgotten Ionian island offers lush valleys, abrupt overgrown gorges, and flower-speckled cliffs tumbling into the vivid blue sea as well as picturesque villages with sugar-cube architecture. (p719)

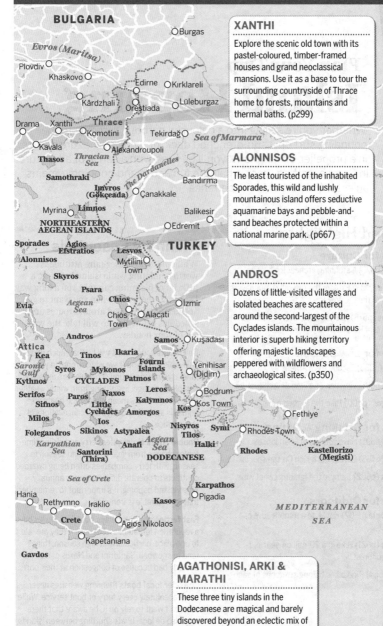

0 — 200 km
0 — 100 miles

XANTHI

Explore the scenic old town with its pastel-coloured, timber-framed houses and grand neoclassical mansions. Use it as a base to tour the surrounding countryside of Thrace home to forests, mountains and thermal baths. (p299)

ALONNISOS

The least touristed of the inhabited Sporades, this wild and lushly mountainous island offers seductive aquamarine bays and pebble-and-sand beaches protected within a national marine park. (p667)

ANDROS

Dozens of little-visited villages and isolated beaches are scattered around the second-largest of the Cyclades islands. The mountainous interior is superb hiking territory offering majestic landscapes peppered with wildflowers and archaeological sites. (p350)

AGATHONISI, ARKI & MARATHI

These three tiny islands in the Dodecanese are magical and barely discovered beyond an eclectic mix of yachties, artists and the occasional backpacker. (p582)

Plan Your Trip
Island Hopping

Whether you're sailing into a colourful harbour, listening to the pounding surf on a sun-drenched deck, or flying over azure waters in a propeller-driven plane, you'll be filled with a sense of adventure. In Greece, getting there is half the fun and island hopping remains an essential part of the experience.

Island Highlights

Best for Culture

Delos (p373) A stunning archaeological site.

Rhodes (p513) Explore the (literally) multilayered history of the Old Town.

Patmos (p578) See the cave where St John wrote the Book of Revelations.

Best for Low Season

Hydra (p335) Escape from Athens.

Corfu (p681) Venetian and French architecture.

Amorgos (p400) Hike the rugged trails.

Best for Drinking & Dining

Ikaria (p591) Have your fill of fresh lobster.

Crete (p455) Savour herb-rich Cretan specialities.

Samos (p602) Sample the famous sweet wine.

Best for Outdoors

Kefallonia (p702) Kayak to a remote cove or beach.

Lesvos (p621) Hike in a 20-million-year-old petrified forest.

Kos (p554) Ride bikes to long stretches of sand.

Planning Essentials

While the local laissez-faire attitude is worth emulating while island hopping, a little bit of planning can take you a long way. Deciding where and when you want to go and getting your head around routes and schedules before you go will take the work out of your holiday.

Be Flexible Your travels will be that much more enjoyable when you leave wiggle room in your itinerary. Transportation schedules are *always* vulnerable to change. Everything from windy weather to striking workers mean planes and boats are regularly subject to delays and cancellations at short notice.

Double check timetables Ferry and airline timetables change from year to year and season to season, with ferry companies often being awarded contracts to operate different routes annually. When island hopping, it's important to remember that no timetable is iron-clad.

Fast ferries are not always best Fast ferries have a reputation for lateness, because if they are late to one place, particularly in high season, things tend to snowball. Santorini and Naxos can be particularly bad because of congestion at their ports.

Consider local boats Planning websites never cover absolutely every ferry or boat service. While you don't want to rely on it, be aware that there may also be local boats shuttling between islands, including day excursion boats that may work for your itinerary. Check with contacts on an island (the hotel where you are staying for example) for up-to-date information.

GETTING YOUR SEA LEGS

Even those with the sturdiest stomachs can feel seasick when a boat hits rough weather. Here are a few tips to calm your tummy.

➡ Gaze at the horizon, not the sea. Don't read or stare at objects that your mind will assume are stable.

➡ Drink plenty and eat lightly. Many people claim ginger biscuits and ginger tea settle the stomach.

➡ Don't use binoculars.

➡ Sit towards the back of the boat, this is marginally more stable.

➡ If possible stay in the fresh air – don't go below deck and avoid hydrofoils where you are trapped indoors.

➡ Try to keep your mind occupied.

➡ If you know you're prone to seasickness, take seasickness medication and/or invest in acupressure wristbands before you leave.

When to Go

High Season

➡ Lots of ferries and transport links but book ahead.

➡ Water temperature is warm enough for swimming.

➡ The *meltemi* (dry northerly wind) blows south across the Aegean, sometimes playing havoc with ferry schedules.

Shoulder Season

➡ Transport is less frequent but still connects most destinations.

➡ Water temperature is still warm in September and early October, so great for diving.

➡ The best time for sea-life spotting begins in May and runs through to September.

Low Season

➡ Planning ahead is essential as transportation can be limited.

➡ Swimming in the sea is only for those immune to cold water.

➡ Most businesses offering water sports are closed for the winter.

Travelling by Sea

With a network covering every inhabited island, the Greek ferry system is vast and varied. The slow rust buckets that used to ply the seas are nearly a thing of the past. You'll still find slow boats, but high-speed ferries are increasingly common and cover most of the popular routes. Local ferries, excursion boats and tiny, private fishing boats called caïques often connect neighbouring islands and islets. You'll also find water taxis that will take you to isolated beaches and coves. At the other end of the spectrum, hydrofoils and catamarans can drastically reduce travel time. Hydrofoils have seen their heyday but continue to link some of the more remote islands and island groups. Catamarans have taken to the sea in a big way, offering more comfort and coping better with poor weather conditions.

For long-haul ferry travel, it's still possible to board one of the slow boats chugging between the islands and to curl up on deck in your sleeping bag to save a night's accommodation. Nevertheless, Greece's domestic ferry scene has undergone a radical transformation in the past decade and these days you can also travel in serious comfort and at a decent speed. Of course, the trade-off is that long-haul sea travel can be quite expensive. A bed for the night in a cabin from Piraeus to Rhodes can be more expensive than a discounted airline ticket.

Ticketing

As ferries are prone to delays and cancellations, for short trips it's often best not to purchase a ticket until it has been confirmed that the ferry is leaving. During high season, or if you need to reserve a car space, you should book in advance. High-speed boats such as catamarans tend to sell out long before the slow chuggers. For overnight ferries it's always best to book in advance, particularly if you want a cabin

Shipwreck Beach on Zakynthos (p717)

or particular type of accommodation. If a service is cancelled you can usually transfer your ticket to the next available service with that company.

Many ferry companies have online booking services or you can purchase tickets from their local offices and most travel agents in Greece. Agencies selling tickets line the waterfront of most ports, but rarely is there one that sells tickets for every boat, and often an agency is reluctant to give you information about a boat it doesn't sell tickets for. Most have timetables displayed outside; check these for the next departing boat or ask the *limenarhio* (port police).

Fares

Ferry prices are determined by the distance of the destination from the port of origin, and the type of boat. The small differences in price you may find at ticket agencies are the results of some agencies sacrificing part of their designated commission to qualify as a 'discount service'. (The discount is seldom more than €0.50.)

High-speed ferries and hydrofoils cost about 20% more than traditional ferries, while catamarans are often 30% to 100% more expensive than their slower counterparts. Caïques and water taxis are usually very reasonable, while excursion boats can be pricey but useful if you're trying to reach out-of-the-way islands. Children under five years of age travel for free while those aged between five and 10 are usually half price.

Classes

On smaller boats, hydrofoils and catamarans, there is only one type of ticket available and these days, even on larger vessels, classes are largely a thing of the past. The public spaces on the more modern ferries are generally open to all. What does differ is the level of accommodation that you can purchase for overnight boats.

A 'deck-class' ticket typically gives you access to the deck and interior, but no overnight accommodation. Aeroplane-type seats give you a reserved, reclining seat in which you will hope to sleep. Then come various shades of cabin accommodation: four-berth, three-berth or two-berth interior cabins are cheaper than their equivalent outside cabins with a porthole. On most boats, cabins are very comfortable, resembling a small hotel room with private bathroom. However, light sleepers should note that you are likely to be woken in the middle of the night by announcements over the loud speakers in each of the cabins.

ISLAND FINDER

ISLAND	FOOD	FAMILY FRIENDLY	OFF THE BEATEN TRACK	NIGHTLIFE	BEACHES	CULTURE	ACTIVITIES	EASY ACCESS
Aegina						X		X
Alonnisos			X			X	X	
Amorgos			X			X	X	
Andros			X			X	X	X
Chios	X	X			X	X	X	X
Corfu	X	X			X	X	X	X
Crete	X	X			X	X	X	X
Evia			X			X	X	X
Fourni Islands			X		X	X		
Hydra		X		X		X	X	X
Ios	X			X	X		X	X
Kalymnos		X		X		X	X	X
Karpathos			X			X	X	
Kefallonia	X	X			X		X	X
Kos		X		X	X	X	X	X
Lefkada					X	X	X	X
Leros		X	X			X	X	
Lesvos	X	X			X	X	X	X
Milos		X			X	X	X	X
Mykonos	X			X	X			X
Naxos	X	X		X	X	X	X	X
Paros	X	X		X	X	X		X
Patmos	X	X			X	X	X	X
Paxi			X			X	X	X
Rhodes	X	X		X		X		X
Samos	X	X			X	X	X	X
Samothraki			X		X	X	X	
Santorini	X			X	X	X	X	X
Sifnos			X			X	X	
Skiathos				X	X		X	X
Skopelos	X	X			X	X		X
Skyros	X				X	X	X	X
Small Cyclades			X		X		X	
Symi						X		X
Thasos		X			X	X	X	X
Tilos			X		X		X	
Zakynthos					X	X		X

Unless you state otherwise, you will automatically be given deck class when purchasing a ticket.

Taking a Car

While almost all islands are served by car ferries, they are expensive and, to ensure boarding, you'll generally need to secure tickets in advance. A more flexible way to travel is to board as a foot passenger and hire a car on each island. Hiring a car for a day or two is relatively cheap and possible on virtually all islands.

Resources

The comprehensive weekly list of departures from Piraeus put out by the EOT (known abroad as the GNTO, the Greek National Tourist Organisation) in Athens is as accurate as possible. While on the islands, the people with the most up-to-date ferry information are the local *limenarhio* (port police), whose offices are usually on or near the quayside.

You'll find lots of information about ferry services on the internet and many of the larger ferry companies have their own websites. Always check online schedules, or with operators or travel agencies for up-to-the-minute information.

A few useful websites:

Danae Travel (www.danae.gr) A good site for booking boat tickets.

Ferries.gr (www.ferries.gr) Listing all the information for all the boats.

Greek Travel Pages (www.gtp.gr) Has a useful search program and links for ferries.

Greekferries.gr (www.greekferries.gr) Allows you to search ferry schedules from countless providers, including accommodation options and multileg journeys.

My Ship Tracking (www.myshiptracking.com) Tracks boats in real time; a way to keep tabs on chronically late ferries.

Open Seas (www.openseas.gr) A reliable search engine for international ferry routes and schedules.

Day Trip Boats

At some mainland ports you'll find boats offering day trips to the islands (and vice versa), and there are also interisland day trips. Usually, you cannot use such day-tripping boats for a one-way journey – you have to return on the same boat the same day. If it's an island-to-island trip, some boats are permitted to drop off passengers and pick them up for the return leg on another day.

Some excursion boats, however, are also permitted to offer a 'one-way' trip, such as the *Kasos Princess*, a cruiser that runs day trips between Kasos and Kalymnos and can also drop people off in Kalymnos – useful on the days the ferries don't run. Make careful enquiries at boat booking offices before purchasing tickets.

Travelling by Air

A flight can save you hours at sea and offers extraordinary views across the island groups. Flights between the islands tend to be short and aeroplanes small, often making for a bumpy ride. The vast majority of domestic flights are handled by the merged Olympic Air and Aegean Airlines, offering regular domestic services and competitive rates. In addition to these national airlines, there are a number of smaller outfits running seaplanes or complementing the most popular routes.

Ticketing & Fares

The easiest way to book tickets is online, via the carriers themselves. You can also purchase flight tickets at most travel agencies in Greece. Olympic Air has offices in the towns that flights depart from, as well as in other major towns. There are discounts for return tickets when travelling midweek (Monday to Thursday), and bigger discounts for trips that include a Saturday night away. You'll find full details and information on timetables on the airlines' websites.

Resources

Up-to-date information on flight timetables is best found online. Airlines often have local offices on the islands.

Aegean Airlines (https://en.aegeanair.com) Domestic flights.

Astra Airlines (www.astra-airlines.gr) Thessaloniki-based carrier with domestic flights.

Olympic Air (www.olympicair.com) Aegean Airline's subsidiary with further domestic flights.

Sky Express (www.skyexpress.gr) Domestic flights based out of Crete.

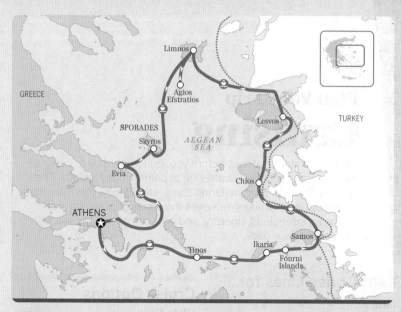

Island-Hopping Itinerary

3 WEEKS

For intrepid travellers without a tight time schedule, Greece's northeastern islands offer languid coasts, lush scenery and divine beaches, as well as some amazing historic sights. Scheduled ferries are regular but not always very frequent – thankfully you won't be in any hurry to leave.

From Athens, hop a ferry for **Tinos** to visit the sacred Church of the Annunciation and explore marble-ornamented villages dotted across the terraced hillsides and misty mountaintops. Head east via **Mykonos** to **Ikaria** for isolated stretches of soft sand. Join in the island culture of dancing, drinking and feasting during summer *panigyria* (all-night celebrations held on saints' days across the island). Afterwards take a short hop to the serene **Fourni Islands**, a former pirates' lair with surreal sunsets.

Ferry north to **Samos** where you can hike through lush forests to secluded waterfalls and laze on idyllic beaches. From Samos, head to **Chios** and get lost in the labyrinth of stone alleyways in the southern village of Mesta before venturing into the interior to hike through citrus groves under the shade of towering mountain peaks.

The next stop is **Lesvos**, birthplace of the poet Sappho and producer of some of Greece's finest olive oil and ouzo. Mytilini, the island's capital and port, offers a fantastic modern-art gallery as well as great eating and drinking. Also check out the well-preserved Ottoman-era town of Molyvos and the hilltop Byzantine monastery of Moni Ypsilou. Lesvos' landscape, with salt marshes, gushing hot springs, dense forests and variety of beaches, is as diverse as its cultural offerings.

From Lesvos, hop to **Limnos** to dine on the day's catch at Myrina's waterside seafood restaurants. Carry on to secluded **Agios Efstratios** to stretch out on volcanic-sand beaches. The village, flattened by an earthquake in 1968 and rebuilt by uninspired junta, draws few tourists meaning the beaches are all yours.

Continue to **Skyros** for its cobble-stoned village, Byzantine-Venetian fortress and many artist studios; if lucky, you may also spot an endangered Skyrian wild horse. Hop a ferry to **Evia** for a therapeutic dip in the thermal-fed bay at Loutra Edipsou before catching a final boat to Rafina on the mainland and returning to **Athens**.

Plan Your Trip
Cruising

The azure water stretches before you, punctuated by occasional dolphins and an endless scattering of palm-fringed islands. The Aegean will call to your seafaring spirit – thankfully, there are many cruising options. Cruising removes the stress of planning and booking an interisland itinerary, and gets you out on the sea with the breeze at your back.

Great Cruise Lines for...

Culture
Silversea (www.silversea.com) Runs exclusive tours with language and cooking classes, guest lectures and entertainment from local ports.

Freedom
Azamara (www.azamaraclubcruises.com) Offers cruises at a slower pace, with top service and few organised activities.

Luxury
Seadream Yacht Club (https://seadream.com) Ultrapampering with nearly as many crew as guests.

Small & Personalised Trips
Variety Cruises (www.varietycruises.com) Has a maximum of 50 guests and the sea as its swimming pool.

Unconventional Trips
Star Clippers (www.starclipperscruises.com) Runs cruises on the world's largest fully rigged tall ships.

Cruise Options
Ship Size

Forget what you've heard, size does matter – at least when you're choosing a cruise ship. A ship's size says a lot about the experience it's offering: megaships can seem more like floating resorts, with a few thousand people on board, while tiny liners cater to fewer than 50 passengers.

Large or Megaships
➡ Accommodate 1000-plus people.

➡ Nonstop activities and complete amenities.

➡ Casinos, restaurants, spas, theatres, children's clubs, discos, bars, cafes and shops.

➡ Often unable to squeeze into some of the smaller islands' harbours and so visit the largest, most popular ports.

➡ Can seem to dwarf an island, with its passengers more than doubling the destination's population.

Medium or Midsized Ships
➡ Cater for 400 to 1000 passengers.

➡ Usually more focused on the destination, with more port stops, more excursions and fewer on-board activities.

➡ Spa, pool, restaurants and bars.

➡ More often able to dock in small island harbours.

CRUISE COMPANIES

COMPANY	CONTACT	SHIP SIZE	CRUISE LENGTH	DESTINATIONS	PRICE RANGE
Azamara	www.azamaraclubcruises.com	medium	7-10 days	Greece, Turkey, Italy	€€€
Celebrity Cruises	www.celebritycruises.co.uk	mega	10-13 days	Greece, Italy, Turkey, Croatia, France	€€
Celestyal Cruises	www.celestyalcruises.uk	medium	3-7 days	Greece, Cyprus	€€
Costa Cruise Lines	www.msccruises.co.uk	large	7-9 days	Greece, Italy, Turkey, Croatia, Israel	€
Crystal Yacht Cruises	www.crystalcruises.com	small	9-15 days	Greece, Italy, Turkey, Spain, Portugal	€€€
Cunard Line	www.cunard.com	large	7-14 days	Greece, Croatia, Italy, Turkey, France, Spain	€
Golden Star	www.golden-star-cruises.com	medium	3-8 days	Greece, Turkey	€
Holland America Line	www.hollandamerica.com	large	6-12 days	Greece, Italy, Spain, Croatia	€
MSC	www.msccruises.co.uk	large	7-10 days	Greece, Turkey, Croatia, Italy, Egypt	€
Oceania Cruises	www.oceaniacruises.com	medium	10-12 days	Greece, Turkey, France, Italy, Spain	€€
Ponant	https://en.ponant.com	small & medium	8-9 days	Greece, Croatia, Italy, Montenegro, Turkey	€€€
Princess Cruises	www.princess.com	large & mega	7-21 days	Greece, Italy, Turkey	€€
Regent Seven Sea Cruises	www.rssc.com	medium	7-21 days	Greece, Italy, Turkey, France	€€€
Seabourn	www.seabourn.com	medium	7-26 days	Greece, Italy, Spain, Portugal, France, Israel, Jordan, Oman, UAE	€€€
Seadream Yacht Club	https://seadream.com	small	6-13 days	Greece, Turkey, Italy, Croatia	€€€
Silversea	www.silversea.com	small & medium	7-12 days	Greece, Spain, Turkey, Italy	€€€
Star Clippers	www.starclipperscruises.com	small	7-14 days	Greece, Turkey, Italy	€€€
Voyages to Antiquity	www.voyagestoantiquity.com	small	13-27 days	Greece, Italy	€€
Windstar	www.windstarcruises.com	small & medium	7-51 days	Greece, Turkey, Italy, Spain, Portugal, France, Croatia	€€€

Small Ships

➡ Itineraries tend to be more varied as they can stop at small, out-of-the-way ports.

➡ Often concentrate on a particular cruise niche, such as luxury or activity-based adventure.

➡ Don't expect a pool, spa, large cabin or plethora of dining options.

Local Cruise Lines

International cruises tend to visit Greece in combination with ports from other countries – usually Italy, Turkey and Croatia, often beginning at one port and ending at another. Greece-based cruises usually focus solely on ports within Greece and offer round-trips. These cruises are often

Above: Oia (p420), Santorini

Left: Yachting near Fira (p410), Santorini

CRUISING INDEPENDENTLY

Yachting offers the freedom to visit remote and uninhabited islands – but what if you can't afford to buy a yacht? The answer is yacht charter companies and there are several options:

Bareboat If two of your party have sailing certificates, you can hire a boat without a crew. Prices start at around €2000 per week; check out Bare Boat Yacht Charters (www.moorings.com).

Crewed yachts If you'd rather have someone else do the sailing for you, Odyssey Sailing (www.odysseysailing.gr) will add a skipper to your bare-bones boat for around an additional €150 per day.

Cabin cruises Book a cabin on a crewed yacht and sit back and enjoy the ride. However, on these trips you'll be tied into a generally pre-set itinerary. Offering all types of yachting experience is Yacht Cruising Holidays (www.we-yachting.com) known as World Expeditions in Greece.

Hellenic Yachting Server (www.yachting.gr) has general information on sailing around the islands and lots of links, including information on chartering yachts.

The sailing season is from April to October, although July to September is most popular. Unfortunately, it also happens to be when the *meltemi* (dry northerly wind) is at its strongest. This isn't an issue in the Ionian Sea, where the main summer wind is the *maïstros*, a light to moderate northwesterly that rises in the afternoon and usually dies away at sunset.

more destination-focused, with one or two stops each day. The crew are usually Greek, adding to the feel of authenticity, and cuisine and entertainment is more locally based with a bit of international flavour thrown in.

Among Greek-based cruise lines worth checking out are Golden Star, Variety Cruises and Celestyal Cruises.

Excursions

Excursions are often what make cruises worthwhile and are designed to help you make the most of your sometimes-brief visits ashore. They are generally most valuable when sights are not near the port or if a cultural expert is leading the tour. Where all the sights are near the harbour, it's often just as worthwhile and more relaxing to go exploring on your own. If you plan to explore alone, it's worth double-checking before you book; some larger cruise boats dock at distant ports and it's difficult to reach the island's sights or main towns independently.

Excursions are usually booked before you depart or when you first board the ship. They are offered on a first-come, first-served basis and are generally very popular, so if you're choosing your cruise based on the excursions on offer, it's important to

book as soon as possible. Tours generally range from €40 to €60 for a half-day, or €80 to €120 for a full day. Activity-based tours such as mountain biking or kayaking tend to be more, with a half-day around €100. Ensure that you factor in the cost of excursions from the get-go.

Budgeting

Cruise prices vary greatly depending on the time of year. Booking during the low season will get you good deals but it means you will probably only have the opportunity to visit the largest and busiest ports, as smaller islands virtually close out of season.

Budget cruises (€) can be anywhere from €100 to €200 per day, midrange (€€) from €200 to €400, and luxury liners (€€€) begin at around €400 and go up to as much as €650 per day. Prices on cruises include meals, on-board activities, entertainment, port fees and portage but there are sometimes additional fuel charges. You also need to budget for airfare, tips, alcohol, pre- and post-cruise accommodation and excursions. Deals to look out for include two-for-one offers, airfare- or hotel-inclusive deals, and early-bird rates.

Booking

If you know what you want from your cruise, booking online can be a straightforward option, and certainly worth it for the virtual tours and reviews. But a knowledgeable travel agent can help you through the plethora of options available and advise you on extra excursion charges and surcharges that you may miss when booking online.

There are often great rates for booking early and this allows you more choice in choosing cabins, excursions, dining options and so forth. While you can get great last-minute deals, you need to be willing to be flexible about dates and options. Booking your airfare through the cruise line may also mean you're collected at the airport and taken to the ship and if your flight or luggage is delayed, they will wait or transport you to the first port.

Choosing a Cabin

Standard cabins are akin to very small hotel rooms, with fully equipped en suites, a double bed and somewhere to unpack. The cheapest option is an 'inside cabin' (ie no window). If you get claustrophobic, you can pay significantly more for an 'outside cabin' where you get either a window or porthole. Prices tend to climb with each floor on the ship but so does the ship's movement. If you suffer from seasickness, choose a lower deck where it's less rocky.

Cabin pricing is for double occupancy; if you're travelling solo you pay a surcharge, and if you're travelling as a group of three or four and willing to share a cabin, you can receive substantial discounts. Bunks are referred to as upper and lower berths, otherwise there is a double bed or twin beds that can be pushed together to make a double. Family rooms are sometimes available via connecting cabins.

Things to check are how close your cabin is located to the disco and, if you're paying extra for a window, whether or not your view is likely to be blocked by a lifeboat.

Life on Board

Embarking: What to Expect

➡ Check-in time will be two or three hours before sailing.

➡ Your passport will be taken for immigration processing.

➡ The first day's program and a deck map can be found in your cabin.

➡ You'll be offered a tour of the ship.

➡ A safety drill is legally required on all ships.

➡ You'll be able to set up an on-board credit account.

➡ Your dining-room table will be assigned.

Meals

Set mealtimes and seating assignments are still the norm on most ships and you will be able to choose your preferred dinnertime and table size when you book. Many ships continue to have formal dining evenings with dress codes. Some smaller ships have an all-casual policy, while others have alternative dining options for those not interested in attending the formal evenings.

Tipping

Firstly, don't tip the captain or officers; it would be akin to tipping your dentist or airline pilot. On the final day of your cruise, you'll likely find tipping guidelines in your cabin, usually around €8 per person per day. Tipping is not required but makes up a huge part of the wage of service staff, and is expected.

Plan Your Trip
Eat & Drink Like a Local

Greeks love eating out, sharing impossibly big meals with family and friends in a drawn-out, convivial fashion. Whether you're eating seafood at a seaside table or sampling contemporary Greek cuisine under the floodlit Acropolis, dining out in Greece is never just about what you eat, but the whole sensory experience.

Food Experiences

Take a cue from the locals and go straight to the source, heading to seaside fishing hamlets for fresh fish or mountain villages for local meat. Seek out tavernas that produce their own vegetables, wine and oil, where the fried potatoes are hand-cut and recipes are passed down through generations.

Meals of a Lifetime

Marco Polo Cafe (p522) Idyllic garden courtyard with an ever-changing menu of delicious Greek and Italian-influenced dishes in Rhodes.

Peskesi (p464) Crete's finest culinary moment with dishes made from heirloom produce, organic meats and olive oil from the owner's farm.

Lauda (p420) Santorini fine dining that's a destination in its own right.

Yevsea (p552) In Nisyros and run by two former Masterchef contestants cooking gourmet cuisine, using local ingredients.

Taverna Mylos (p575) In a sublime setting in Leros this charming place is up there on the world's gastronomic scale.

Karamanlidika tou Fani (p114) Athens corner deli, reimagined as a casual restaurant serving delicious small plates of food.

Year in Food

Spring

Artichokes and other fresh vegetables abound while cheesemaking kicks into gear. Easter is celebrated with *tsoureki* (brioche-style bread flavoured with cherry kernels and mastic) and dyed-red hard-boiled eggs.

Summer

Watermelon, cherries and other fruit jam-pack markets. In August, Skala Kaloni on Lesvos celebrates its sardine festival, while in the Peloponnese you can attend Leonidio's Aubergine Festival in the same month.

Autumn

Nuts and figs are harvested and raki (Cretan firewater) is distilled. Aegina's pistachio industry celebrates Fistiki Fest mid-September. Raki or tsikoudia festivals are held in Voukolies and Cretan villages in November, when olive oil is produced.

Winter

Olive harvest peaks. Honey cookies are eaten at Christmas to end fasting. On New Year's Day, the golden-glazed cake vasilopita is shared.

Cheap Treats

Souvlaki Greece's favourite fast food, both the *gyros* (meat cooked on a vertical rotisserie) and skewered meat versions wrapped in pitta bread, with tomato, onion and lashings of tzatziki.

Pies Bakeries make endless variations of *tyropita* (cheese pie) and *spanakopita* (spinach pie), plus other pies.

Street food Includes *koulouria* (fresh pretzel-style bread) and seasonal snacks such as roasted chestnuts or corn.

Cooking Courses

Well-known Greece-based cooking writers and chefs run workshops on several islands and in Athens, mostly during spring and autumn.

Glorious Greek Kitchen Cooking School (www.dianekochilas.com) Diane Kochilas runs week-long courses (from US$3750) on her ancestral island, Ikaria, in spring and summer, as well as culinary tours to Athens, Nemea and Nafplion (from US$1560).

Kea Artisanal (www.aglaiakremezi.com/kea-artisanal) Aglaia Kremezi and her friends open their kitchens and gardens on the island of Kea for cooking workshops.

Crete's Culinary Sanctuaries (www.cookingin-crete.com) Nikki Rose combines cooking classes, organic-farm tours and cultural excursions around Crete.

The Greek Kitchen (www.greekkitchenathens.com) Runs half-day hands-on cooking classes in Athens (adult/concession €59/29) as well as food tours of the city's main market.

Other courses include **Selene** (☏22860 22249; www.selene.gr; Pyrgos; cooking class €85-100) on Santorini, FindinGreece (p406) in Amorgos, **Rodialos** (☏28340 51310; www.rodialos.gr; Vassilis Damvoglou) on Crete and Sifnos Farm Narlis (p445) on Sifnos.

Cook it at Home

Leave room in your baggage for local treats (customs and quarantine rules permitting) such as olives and extra virgin olive oil from small, organic producers; aromatic Greek thyme honey; dried oregano, mountain tea and camomile flowers; or a jar of spoon sweets (fruit preserves).

The Greek Kitchen

The essence of traditional Greek cuisine lies in seasonal homegrown produce. Dishes are simply seasoned. Lemon juice, garlic, pungent Greek oregano and extra virgin olive oil are the quintessential flavours, along with tomato, parsley, dill, cinnamon and cloves.

Mayirefta Home-style, one-pot, baked or casserole dishes. Prepared early, they are left to cool to enhance the flavours. Well-known *mayirefta* include *mousaka* (eggplant, minced meat, potatoes and cheese), *yemista* (vegetables stuffed with rice and herbs), *lemonato* (meat with lemon and oregano) and *stifadho* (sweet stewed meat with tomato and onion).

Grills Greeks are masterful with grilled and spit-roasted meats. Souvlaki – arguably the national dish – comes in many forms, from cubes of grilled meat on a skewer to pitta-wrapped snacks with pork or chicken *gyros* done kebab-style on a rotisserie. *Païdakia* (lamb cutlets) and *brizoles* (pork chops) are also popular.

Fish & seafood Fish is often grilled whole and drizzled with *ladholemono* (lemon and oil dressing). Smaller fish such as *barbounia* (red mullet) or *maridha* (whitebait) are lightly fried. Octopus is grilled, marinated or stewed in wine sauce. Popular seafood dishes include *soupies* (cuttlefish), calamari stuffed with cheese and herbs, and *psarosoupa* (fish soup). The best way to avoid imports is to seek out tavernas run by local fishing families.

Mezedhes These small dishes (or appetisers) are often shared. Classics include tzatziki (yoghurt, cucumber and garlic), *melidzanosalata* (aubergine), *taramasalata* (fish roe), fava (split-pea puree with lemon juice) and *saganaki* (fried cheese). Also watch for *keftedhes* (meatballs), *loukaniko* (pork sausage), grilled *gavros* (white anchovies) and dolmadhes (rice wrapped in marinated vine leaves).

Greek salad This ubiquitous salad (*horiatiki* or 'village salad') is made of tomatoes, cucumber, onions, feta and olives; however, it's often garnished with local greens, peppers, capers or nuts. Feta is sometimes replaced by a local cheese. Beetroot salad is also popular, often served with walnuts and cheese.

Cheese Greece's regions produce many different types of cheese, most using goat's and sheep's milk, with infinite variations in taste. Apart from feta, local cheeses include *graviera* (a nutty, mild Gruyere-like sheep's-milk cheese), *kaseri* (similar to provolone), *myzithra* (ricotta-like whey cheese) and *manouri* (creamy soft cheese from the north).

Traditional sweets These include baklava, *loukoumadhes* (spherical doughnuts drizzled with honey and cinnamon), *kataïfi* (chopped nuts inside angel-hair pastry), *ryzogalo* (rice pudding) and *galaktoboureko* (custard-filled pastry). *Ghlika kutalyu* (syrupy fruit preserves, also known as 'spoon sweets') are served on tiny plates as a welcome offering but are also eaten over yoghurt.

Local Specialities

From cheese and olive oil to the raw ingredients on your plate, you will find many regional variations and specialities on your travels. Crete is a popular foodie destination with distinct culinary traditions, but the islands and mainland offer their own culinary treats. Be sure to ask about local dishes, cheese and produce.

Northern Greece Influenced by eastern flavours, there's more butter, peppers and spices in this region's dishes, along with a strong *mezes* (small-plate) culture and Ottoman sweets.

Peloponnese Known for its herb-rich, one-pot dishes and *ladhera* (vegetarian, peasant-style dishes).

Cyclades A traditional reliance on beans and pulses led to the popularity of fava (split-pea puree) and *revythadha* (chickpea stew); you'll also find spaghetti with lobster and a strong sausage tradition.

Ionian Islands The Venetian influence is found in spicy braised beef, rooster *pastitsadha* (red-sauce pasta) and *sofrito* (braised veal with garlic and wine sauce).

Crete Herb-rich dishes include *anthoi* (stuffed zucchini flowers), *soupies* (cuttlefish) with wild fennel and *hohlioi bourbouristoi* (snails with vinegar and rosemary).

What to Drink
Coffee

The ubiquitous *kafeneio* (coffee house) is a time-honoured tradition, with older Greeks stationed over a cup of coffee, intensely debating local politics, football or gossip. They're often small and unchanged for generations, and it's well worth visiting at least one. The trendy cafes serving delicious iced coffees (*frappé*) are the modern answer to the *kafeneia* and are usually packed with a younger crowd.

Greek coffee is traditionally brewed in a *briki* (narrow-top pot), on a hot-sand apparatus called a *hovoli*, and served in a small cup. Order a *metrio* (medium, with one sugar) and sip slowly until you reach the mud-like grounds (don't drink them).

Ouzo & Other Spirits

Ouzo – Greece's famous liquor – has come to embody a way of eating and socialising, enjoyed with *mezedhes* (small plates) during lazy, extended summer afternoons. Sipped slowly and ritually to cleanse the palate between dishes, ouzo is usually served in small bottles or *karafakia* (carafes) with a bowl of ice cubes to dilute it (turning it a cloudy white).

Ouzo is made from distilled grapes with residuals from fruit, grains and potatoes, and flavoured with spices, primarily aniseed, giving it that liquorice flavour. The best ouzo is produced on Lesvos.

Tsipouro is a distilled spirit, similar to grappa, that is produced only in Greece. It's made using the leftover must from pressing wine and is usually enjoyed as an aperitif. *Tsikoudia,* also known as *raki,* is essentially the Cretian version of *tsipouro.*

If all of the above are too harsh a shot of alcohol for your tastes, you may well prefer the sweet sweet liqueur *mastika,* made with mastica resin grown on Chios. It's an excellent digestive.

Greek Wine

Greece's wine industry benefits from some age-old indigenous varietals with unique character. The contemporary generation of winemakers are producing great, award-winning wines from Greece's premier wine regions, including Nemea in the Peloponnese, the vineyards of Santorini, the Iraklio Wine Country on Crete and Naoussa in the Cyclades.

Greek white varieties include *moschofilero, asyrtiko, athiri, roditis, robola* and *savatiano;* the popular reds include *xinomavro, agiorgitiko* and *kotsifali.*

House or barrel wine varies dramatically in quality (white is the safer bet), and is ordered by the kilo/carafe or glass.

Greek dessert wines include excellent muscats from Samos, Limnos and Rhodes, Santorini's Vinsanto, Mavrodafni wine (often used in cooking) and Monemvasia's Malmsey sweet wine.

Retsina, white wine flavoured with the resin of pine trees, became popular in the 1960s and retains a largely folkloric significance with foreigners. It's something of an acquired taste but some winemakers make a modern version. It's popular in Thessaloniki (where the main brand, Malamatina, is made) and it goes great with salty *mezedhes* (share plates) and seafood.

How to Eat & Drink

When to Eat

Greece doesn't have a big breakfast tradition, unless you count coffee and a cigarette, and maybe a *koulouri* (pretzel-style bread) or *tyropita* (cheese pie) eaten on the run. You'll find English-style breakfasts in hotels and tourist areas.

While changes in working hours are affecting traditional meal patterns, lunch is still usually the big meal of the day, starting around 2pm.

Greeks eat dinner late, rarely sitting down before sunset in summer. This coincides with shop closing hours, so restaurants often don't fill until after 10pm. Get in by 9pm to avoid the crowds. Given the long summers and mild winters, al fresco dining is central to the dining experience.

Most tavernas open all day, but some upmarket restaurants open for dinner only.

Vegetarian Friendly

Vegetarians are well catered for, since vegetables feature prominently in Greek cooking – a legacy of lean times and the Orthodox faith's fasting traditions. The more traditional a restaurant you go to, the more vegetable options you get, because they follow more of these fasting rules. If you come during Lent, it's a vegan bonanza at these places.

Look for popular vegetable dishes such as *fasolakia yiahni* (braised green beans), *bamies* (okra), *briam* (oven-baked vegetable casserole) and vine-leaf dolmadhes. Of the nutritious *horta* (wild greens), *vlita* (amaranth) is the sweetest, but other common varieties include wild radish, dandelion, stinging nettle and sorrel.

Festive Food

The 40-day Lenten fast spawned *nistisima*, foods without meat or dairy (or oil if you go strictly by the book). Lenten sweets include *halva*, both the Macedonian-style version made from tahini (sold in delis) and the semolina dessert often served after a meal.

Red-dyed boiled Easter eggs decorate the *tsoureki*, a brioche-style bread flavoured with *mahlepi* (a species of cherry with very small fruit and kernels with an almond flavour) and mastic (the crystallised resin of the mastic tree). Saturday night's post-Resurrection Mass supper includes *mayiritsa* (offal soup), while Easter Sunday sees whole lambs cooking on spits all over the countryside.

A *vasilopita* (golden-glazed cake) is cut at midnight on New Year's Eve, giving good fortune to whoever gets the lucky coin inside.

Where to Eat

Steer away from tourist restaurants and go where locals eat. As a general rule, avoid places on the main tourist drags, especially those with touts outside and big signs with photos of food. Be wary of hotel recommendations, as some have deals with particular restaurants.

Tavernas are casual, good-value, often family-run (and child-friendly) places, where the waiter arrives with a paper tablecloth and plonks cutlery on the table.

Above: Dining in the Plaka district (p112), Athens

Right: *Mezedhes* (tapas-style dishes)

ETIQUETTE & TABLE MANNERS

➡ Greek tavernas can be disarmingly and refreshingly laid-back. The dress code is generally casual, except in upmarket places.

➡ Service may feel slow (and patchy), but there's no rushing you out of there either.

➡ Tables generally aren't cleared until you ask for the bill, which in traditional places arrives with complimentary fruit or sweets or a shot of liquor. Receipts may be placed on the table at the start and during the meal in case tax inspectors visit.

➡ Greeks drink with meals (the drinking age is 16), but public drunkenness is uncommon and frowned upon.

➡ Book for upmarket restaurants, but reservations are unnecessary in most tavernas.

➡ Service charges are included in the bill, but most people leave a small tip or round up the bill; 10% to 15% is acceptable. If you want to split the bill, it's best you work it out among your group rather than ask the server to do it.

➡ Greeks are generous and proud hosts. Don't refuse a coffee or drink – it's a gesture of hospitality and goodwill. If you're invited out, the host normally pays. If you are invited to someone's home, it is polite to take a small gift (flowers or sweets), and remember to pace yourself, as you will be expected to eat everything on your plate.

➡ Smoking is banned in enclosed public spaces, including restaurants and cafes, but this rule is largely ignored, especially on distant islands.

Don't judge a place by its decor (or view). Go for places with a smaller selection (where food is more likely to be freshly cooked) rather than those with impossibly extensive menus.

Restaurant Guide

Taverna The classic Greek taverna has a few specialist variations – the *psarotaverna* (serving fish and seafood) and *hasapotaverna* or *psistaria* (for chargrilled or spit-roasted meat).

Mayirio (cookhouse) Specialises in traditional one-pot stews and *mayirefta* (baked dishes).

Estiatorio Serves upmarket international cuisine or Greek classics in a more formal setting.

Mezedhopoleio Offers lots of *mezedhes* (small plates).

Ouzerie In a similar vein to the *mezedhopoleio*, the *ouzerie* serves a usually free round of *mezedhes* with your ouzo. Regional variations focusing on the local firewater include the *rakadhiko* (serving *raki*) in Crete and the *tsipouradhiko* (serving *tsipouro*) in the mainland north.

Menu Advice

➡ Menus with prices must be displayed outside restaurants. English menus are fairly standard but off the beaten track you may encounter Greek-only menus. Many places display big trays of the day's *mayirefta* (ready-cooked meals) or encourage you to see what's cooking in the kitchen.

➡ Bread and occasionally small dips or nibbles are often served on arrival (you are increasingly given a choice as they are added to the bill).

➡ Don't stick to the three-course paradigm – locals often share a range of starters and mains (or starters can be the whole meal). Dishes may arrive in no particular order.

➡ Salads and other side dishes can be large – if you're a single diner, it's usually alright to ask for half portions.

➡ Frozen ingredients, especially seafood, are usually flagged on the menu (an asterisk or 'kat' on Greek menu).

➡ Fish is usually sold per kilogram rather than per portion, and is generally cooked whole rather than filleted. It's customary to go into the kitchen to select your fish (go for firm flesh and glistening eyes). Check the weight (raw) so there are no surprises on the bill.

Plan Your Trip

Outdoor Activities

Greece is graced with blue water, warm winds, undersea life, dramatic cliff faces, flourishing forests and ancient walkways – making it perfect terrain for outdoor activities. If you're a novice kitesurfer or avid cyclist, if you want to hike deep gorges or ski from lofty heights, opportunities abound.

Water Activities

Diving & Snorkelling

Snorkelling can be enjoyed just about anywhere along the coast of Greece and equipment is cheaply available. Especially good spots to don your fins are Monastiri on Paros, Paleokastritsa on Corfu, Xirokambos Bay on Leros and anywhere off the coast of Kastellorizo (Megisti). Many dive schools also use their boats to take groups of snorkellers to prime spots.

Greek law insists that diving be done under the supervision of a diving school in order to protect the many antiquities in the depths of the Mediterranean and Aegean Seas. Until recently dive sites were severely restricted, but many more have been opened and diving schools have flourished. You'll find schools on the islands of Corfu, Evia, Leros, Milos, Mykonos, Paros, Rhodes, Santorini, Skiathos, Crete, in Glyfada near Athens, and in Parga and Halkidiki in northern Greece.

The Professional Association of Diving Instructors (PADI; www.padi.com) has lots of useful information, including a list of all PADI-approved dive centres in Greece.

Windsurfing

Windsurfing is a very popular water sport in Greece. Hrysi Akti on Paros and Vasiliki on Lefkada vie for the position of the best windsurfing beach.

Best Outdoors

Hiking

Samaria Gorge Trek among towering cliffs and wildflowers.

Andros Follow well-worn footpaths across hills to deep valleys.

Nisyros Hike amid lush foliage and down into the caldera.

Samos Wander through woods and swim under waterfalls.

Experts

Santorini Enjoy a pathway of canyons and swim-through sand caverns for divers.

Kalymnos Climb towering limestone cliffs.

Paros Shangri-La for kitesurfing.

Novices

Vasiliki Learn how to windsurf.

Santorini Dive schools catering to first-timers.

Poros Waterskiing beginners.

Paxi Walks through ancient olive groves.

Hiking in Zagorohoria (p315)

There are numerous other prime locations around the islands and many water-adventure outlets rent equipment. Check out Kalafatis Beach on Mykonos, Agios Georgios on Naxos, Mylopotas Beach on Ios, Cape Prasonisi in southern Rhodes, around Tingaki on Kos, Kokkari on Samos and Kouremenos Beach on Crete's east coast.

You'll find sailboards for hire almost everywhere. Hire charges range from €15 to €30, depending on the gear and the location. If you are a novice, note that most places that rent equipment also give lessons. Sailboards can be imported into Greece freely (one per passenger) provided they will be taken out of the country on departure, but always check customs regulations for your country.

Kitesurfing & Surfing

With near-constant wind and ideal conditions, Paros' Pounta Beach is a magnet for kitesurfing's top talent, attracting both the Professional Kiteboard Riders Association and the Kiteboard Pro World Tour. With a shallow side, this is also a great place to learn surfing. Mikri Vigla on Naxos is also an excellent spot, with courses off the gorgeous white-sand beach.

Waterskiing

Given the relatively calm and flat waters of most island locations and the generally warm waters of the Mediterranean, water-skiing is a very pleasant activity. August is sometimes a tricky month, when the *meltemi* (dry northerly wind) can make conditions difficult in the central Aegean. Poros is a particularly well-organised locale, with Passage (p335) hosting a popular school and slalom centre.

White-Water Rafting

The popularity of white-water rafting and other river-adventure sports has grown rapidly in recent years as more and more urban Greeks, particularly Athenians, head off in search of a wilderness experience. While spring and autumn are the best times, with high water levels and decent weather, many operators offer trips year-round on the larger rivers.

Athens Extreme Sports (www.athens extremesports.com) offers rafting on several rivers including the Nestos and Lusios Alfios. Also check out the rafting trips organised by **Trekking Hellas** (https://trekking.gr) and **No Limits** (☑6944751418; www.facebook.com/nolimits.rafting).

Land Activities

Hiking

Much of Greece is mountainous and, in many ways, a hiker's paradise. Popular routes are well walked and maintained; however, the EOS (p98) is underfunded and consequently many lesser-known paths are overgrown and inadequately marked. You'll find EOS branches and climbing associations in Ioannina (p311), Xanthi (p297), Halkida (p654) and **Hania** (EOS; ☑28210 44647; www.eoshanion.gr; Tzanakaki 90; ☺9-11pm Mon-Fri).

Northern Greece has plenty of rugged hiking terrain, especially around the Zagorohoria in the Pindos Mountains and the hill trails around Prespa Lakes. Beyond the mainland, the Lousios Gorge and the Mani, both in the Peloponnese, are two of the best places in Greece to explore on foot. Crete's Samaria Gorge is rightly a global favourite, but western Crete boasts many gorges suitable for hikers of different skill levels. If you're headed to Tilos, pick up a copy of *Exploring Tilos: a Walkers' Guide to the Island* by Jim Osborne.

On small islands you will encounter a variety of paths, including *kalderimia*, which are cobbled or flagstone paths that have linked settlements since Byzantine times. Other paths include *monopatia* (shepherds' or monks' trails) that link

PLAN YOUR TRIP OUTDOOR ACTIVITIES

TOP ISLAND HIKES

DESTINATION, ISLAND GROUP	SKILL LEVEL	DESCRIPTION
Alonnisos, Sporades	easy	A network of established trails that lead to pristine beaches
Hydra, Saronic Gulf Islands	easy	A vehicle-free island with a well-maintained network of paths to beaches and monasteries
Paxi, Ionian Islands	easy	Paths along ancient olive groves and snaking drystone walls; perfect for escaping the crowds
Samaria Gorge, Crete	easy to medium	One of Europe's most popular hikes with 500m vertical walls, countless wildflowers and endangered wildlife (impassable mid-October to mid-April)
Zakros & Kato Zakros, Crete	easy to medium	The trail through Zakros Gorge (also known as Gorge of the Dead) leads to a remote Minoan palace site
Tragaea, Naxos, Cyclades	easy to medium	A broad central plain of olive groves, unspoiled villages and plenty of trails
Sifnos, Cyclades	easy to medium	Monasteries, beaches and sprawling views abound on this network of trails, covering 200km of island terrain
Tilos, Dodecanese	easy to medium	Countless traditional trails along dramatic clifftops and down to isolated beaches; a bird-lover's paradise
Dimosari Gorge, Evia	easy to medium	A 10km trek through a spectacular gorge of shady streams and cobbled paths ending at a small bay
Ithaki, Ionian Islands	easy to medium	Mythology fans can hike between sites linked to the Trojan War hero Odysseus
Samos, Northeastern Aegean Islands	easy to medium	Explore the quiet interior of this island with its mountain villages and the forested northern slopes of Mt Ambelos
Nisyros, Dodecanese	medium to difficult	A fertile volcanic island with hikes that lead down steep cliffs to reach steaming craters
Steni, Evia	medium to difficult	Day hikes and more serious trekking opportunities up Mt Dirfys, Evia's highest mountain

settlements with sheepfolds or link remote settlements via rough unmarked trails. Shepherd or animal trails can be very steep and difficult to navigate.

If you're venturing off the beaten track, a good map is essential. Most tourist maps are inadequate; the best hiking maps for the islands are produced by Anavasi (www.anavasi.gr) and Terrain (www. terrainmaps.gr), both Greece-based companies. Be realistic about your abilities. Always inform your guesthouse or local hiking association of your planned route before setting out.

Spring (April to June) is the best time for hiking; the countryside is green and fresh from the winter rains, and carpeted with wildflowers. Autumn (September to October) is another good time, but July and August, when temperatures rise to around 40°C (104°F), are not much fun. Whatever the season, come equipped with a good pair of walking boots to handle the rough, rocky terrain, a wide-brimmed hat, a water bottle and a high-UV-factor sunscreen.

A number of companies run organised hikes. The biggest is Trekking Hellas (https://trekking.gr), which offers a variety of hikes ranging from a four-hour stroll through the Lousios Valley to a week-long hike around Mt Olympus and Meteora. The company also runs hikes in Crete and the Cyclades. Many of the treks require a minimum number of participants or the price hike is steeper than the trail. Also look into the Greece hiking offerings of UK-based On Foot Holidays (www.onfoot holidays.co.uk).

Long-Distance Hikes

Menalon Trail (https://menalontrail.eu) Along this 75km route, hikers can choose between short walks or the five-day trek along the Lousios Gorge, Mt Menalon's western slopes and scenic villages galore.

Corfu Trail (www.thecorfutrail.com) Crosses the whole island from Kavos to Agios Spyridon and can be completed in between eight and 12 days, offering a fantastic mix of scenery on the way.

E4 European long-distance path staring in Portugal that also makes it way through mainland Greece and Crete on its way to Cyprus. A great resource if you plan to follow this challenging route is *Trekking in Greece: The Peloponnese and Pindos Way* by Tim Salmon and Michael Cullen.

Cycling

Greece has recently established itself as a cycling destination both for mountain bikers and novices yearning to take a spin on its coastal roads. Bicycles can usually be taken on trains for free, though you may need a ticket. On ferries, mention your bike when booking tickets.

Much of Greece is very remote. Be sure to carry puncture-repair and first-aid kits with you. Motorists are notoriously fast and not always travelling in the expected lane; extra caution on corners and narrow roads is well warranted. In July and August most cyclists break between noon and 4pm to avoid sunstroke and dehydration.

CycleGreece (www.cyclegreece.gr) Runs road- and mountain-bike tours across most of Greece for various skill levels including some sail-and-cycle tours.

Hooked on Cycling (www.hookedoncycling. co.uk/greece) Offers boat – and bike – trips through the islands plus tours of the mainland.

Cyclists Welcome Hellas (http://cyclists welcomehellas.blogspot.com/) Local business network supporting the needs of cyclists and tourists on bicycles.

Skiing & Snowboarding

Greece's main skiing areas are Mt Parnassos (1600m to 2250m) 195km north-west of Athens and home to the country's biggest ski resort, and Mt Vermio (1420m to 2005m) 110km west of Thessaloniki. There's also great action in the north, with Metsovo, Konitsa and the Zagori villages all possible bases for snow sports around Vasilitsa in the Pindos Mountains.

Resorts are used mainly by Greeks and can be a pleasant alternative to western Europe's expensive resorts. If you want to combine city and snow, ski Vigla-Pisoderi as a day trip from Florina or head to Mt Vermio from Veria.

The season depends on snow conditions but runs approximately from January to the end of April. Get information from the Hellenic Skiing Federation (www.eox.gr) and check conditions and ski centres at Snow Report (www.snow report.gr).

Plan Your Trip
Family Travel

While Greece doesn't cater to kids the way that some countries do, children will be welcomed and included wherever you go. Greeks generally make a fuss over children, who may find themselves receiving many gifts and treats. Teach them some Greek words and they'll feel even more appreciated.

Children Will Love...

Ruins & Palaces

Ancient Olympia (p196) Go for a sprint in the ancient stadium that was the original location of the Olympic Games.

Palace of Knossos (p466) Spot dolphins on the frescos in the Queen's room at this imaginatively reconstucted Minoan complex.

Rhodes Town (p515) Explore the Old Town, a medieval time capsule behind a double ring of high walls and a deep moat.

Pandeli Castle (p574) Take in 360-degree views from the 14th century walls of this hilltop ruin on Leros.

Fun Museums

Acropolis Museum (p78) A great way to educate kids on the glories of ancient Greece.

Herakleidon Museum (p67) Split across two buildings this quirky Athens museum includes an exhibition on ancient types of robots and warships.

Volcanological Museum (p554) Learn about the history, mythology and environmental impact of Nisyros' volcano.

Noesis (Science Museum; ☎2310 483 000; www.noesis.edu.gr; Km 6 Thessaloniki–Thermi Rd; adult/child combined ticket €12/8; ⊙10.30am-3pm Tue-Fri, 6.30-9.30pm Sat & Sun; P⊞) Fascinating museum of science and technology outside of Thessaloniki, that includes a planetarium and a giant-screen cinema.

Keeping Costs Down

Accommodation

Many hotels let small children stay for free and will squeeze an extra bed or cot in the room. Larger hotels and resorts often have package deals for families.

Sightseeing

There are free or half price tickets for children and teens at most sights. Save time queuing at major sites such as the Acropolis by prepurchasing tickets online.

Eating

Ordering lots of *mezedhes* (small dishes) lets your children try the local cuisine and find their favourites. You'll also find lots of kid-friendly options such as pizza and pasta, omelettes, chips, bread, savoury pies and yoghurt.

Transport

Travel on ferries, buses and trains is free for children under four. For those up to age 10 (ferries) or 12 (buses and trains) the fare is half. Full fares apply otherwise. On domestic flights, you'll pay 10% of the adult fare to have a child under two sitting on your knee. Kids aged two to 12 travel with half-fare.

PLANETIX/GETTY IMAGES ©

Valley of the Butterflies, Rhodes (p530)

Wildlife Encounters

Saloon Park (☎22370 24606; www.saloonpark.gr; Karpenisi–Prousos; ⊙9am-midnight; 🛜🚹) Wild West theme park where all the family can enjoy horse riding.

Valley of the Butterflies (p530) Visit this top Rhodes attraction between mid June and September to wander through a forest alive with colourful butterflies.

Mouries Farm (p676) Call ahead to book tours, take riding lessons and dine at this breeding farm for rare Skyrian horses.

Aqua Adventures

Limni Vouliagmenis (p138) Have your feet tickled by tiny fish in the mineral rich and warm waters of this lake on the Apollo Coast.

Shakayak (p239) Lessons for kids on paddling a kayaking or using a stand-up paddleboard (SUP) in the Pelion Peninsula.

Acqua Plus (☎28970 24950; www.acquaplus.gr; adult/child €27/17; ⊙10am-6pm May, Jun, Sep & Oct, to 7pm Jul & Aug; 🚹) This Crete-based waterpark is good for a few hours of splashy fun.

Creta Semi-Submarine (☎28410 24822, 6936051186; www.semi-submarine.gr; adult/child €16/10; ⊙11am, 1pm & 3pm; 🚹) This yellow submarine in Crete allows all the family to go deep sea marine life spotting without getting wet.

Tasty Treats

Yemista Veggies (usually tomatoes) stuffed with rice.

Pastitsio Buttery macaroni baked with minced lamb.

Kolokithokeftedes Freshly made courgette (zucchini) fritters.

Loukoumadhes Ball-shaped doughnuts served with honey and cinnamon.

Galaktoboureko Custard-filled pastry.

Politiko pagoto Constantinople-style (slightly chewy) ice cream made with mastic.

Region by Region

Athens

With superb park playgrounds such as the ones at Stavros Niarchos Park (p114) and Flisvos Park (p85), ruins to clamber over and child-geared sights to explore, Athens is great for kids. Many museums make an effort to appeal to kids. Older children may like the War Museum (p95), where they can climb into the cockpit of a WWII plane and other aircraft. Come summer, there's no shortage of outdoor cinemas for evening entertainment.

Crete

The island's beaches are long and sandy, Knossos (p466) ignites kids' imaginations, and you can explore from a single base, side-stepping the need to pack up and move around.

Dodecanese

The magical forts and castles, glorious beaches, laid-back islands, and speedy catamarans linking the Dodecanese daily make it ideal for families. And the Italian influence means an abundance of kid-friendly pasta dishes. Rhodes, the largest island, is particularly good for family holidays.

Northern Greece

Offers slightly lower summertime temperatures, Ottoman patisseries and Halkidiki's beaches. Laid-back Ioannina makes a great base and Parga is popular with families. Sithonia is less crowded but also less family-friendly than the rest of Halkidiki.

Good to Know

Look out for the icon for family-friendly suggestions throughout this guide.

Pre-trip study Lots of younger children enjoy stories of Greek gods and Greek myths while slightly older kids will enjoy movies like *Mamma Mia*, *300* or *Lara Croft: Tomb Raider* for their Greek settings. You can also find children's books about life in Greece that include a few easy phrases that your kids can try out.

When to Go The shoulder seasons (April to May and September to October) are great times to travel with children because the weather is milder and the crowds thinner.

Pushchairs (strollers) Unless they are the sturdy, off-road style, pushchairs can a struggle in towns and villages with slippery cobblestones and high pavements. Consider a sturdy carrying backpack for your little ones instead.

Baby needs Fresh milk is available in large towns and tourist areas, but harder to find on smaller islands. Supermarkets are the best place to look. Formula is available almost everywhere, as is heat-treated milk. Disposable nappies are also available everywhere, although it's wise to take extra supplies of all of these things to out-of-the-way islands in case of local shortages.

Useful Resources

Lonely Planet (www.lonelyplanet.com/family-holidays) Articles, products, destinations and more. For an entertaining guide packed with information and tips, turn to Lonely Planet's *Travel with Children* book.

Santorini Dave (https://santorinidave.com/greece-with-kids) For plenty of recommendations and hearty discussion on visiting Greece with kids.

Travel Guide to Greece (www.greektravel.com) Matt Barrett's website has lots of useful tips for parents.

Greece 4 Kids (www.greece4kids.com) Matt Barrett's daughter Amarandi has put together some tips of her own.

Kids' Corner

Say What?

Hello.	Γειά σας. ya·sas
Goodbye.	Αντίο. an·di·o
Please.	Παρακαλώ. pa·ra·ka·lo
Thank you.	Ευχαριστώ. ef·ha·ri·sto
My name is ...	Με λένε ... me le·ne ...

Did You Know?

- There are 114 Greek Islands with people living on them.
- Greece's currency is the euro.

Have You Tried?

Souvlaki
Greece's favourite fast food

RAWF8/SHUTTERSTOCK ©

Regions at a Glance

Peloponnese

Ancient Ruins
Architecture
Activities

Citadels

The Peloponnese is packed with inspiring ancient sites. Visit the sanctuary of Ancient Olympia, explore the citadels of Mycenae and Tiryns, or take in a show at the Theatre of Epidavros.

Fortresses

From Byzantine cities to Venetian fortresses, this region is peppered with architectural gems. Cross the causeway to magical Monemvasia *kastro* (fort) or explore the Mani's tower houses from the 17th century.

Hiking Trails

The Mani, the peninsula's rugged and remote southern region, is a popular place to amble, with mountains tumbling down to gorgeous coastal views. Northwest of here, hike through the Lousios Gorge to find charming village monasteries.

p146

Central Greece

Ancient Sites
Activities
Beaches

Delphi & Meteora

Located on Mt Parnassos with views of the Gulf of Corinth, the sanctuary of Delphi has a serene and majestic air. Way to the north, Meteora's monasteries sit defiantly atop towering pinnacles of rock.

Trails & Waterways

Follow cobblestone trails past villages and through forests on the Pelion Peninsula, hug the coast in a kayak on the Aegean Sea, and follow in Hercules' footsteps to explore the green depths of Iti National Park.

Sandy Coves

Central Greece offers beautiful beaches. Low-key resorts dot the Gulf of Corinth and the Pelion Peninsula, where hidden, sandy coves and crystal-clear waters await the intrepid.

p208

Athens & Around

Ancient Ruins
Nightlife
Museums

Architectural Relics

The Acropolis is a must but there are many other superb ruins to visit; in Athens don't miss the Odeon of Herodes Atticus and the Ancient Agora, then head out to the dramatic Temple of Poseidon on Cape Sounion.

Bars & Clubs

This city refuses to snooze, with glamorous beachside clubs where thousands dance to international DJs, intimate *rembetika* clubs where you can soak up Greek blues and ouzo, and everything in between.

Ancient Treasures

The ultramodern Acropolis Museum and elegant Benaki Museum both houses priceless treasures. Also explore the expansive collection at the Byzantine & Christian Museum and the antiquities at the National Archaeological Museum.

p60

Northern Greece

Food & Wine
Activities
Beaches

Eastern Spice

This region's cuisine brings a spiciness from the Anatolian Peninsula in Turkey. Sample mussel pilaf, crayfish, lots of cheese and Macedonian wine as well as artful Ottoman sweets in Thessaloniki.

Mountain Hikes

The story of Zeus takes you hiking into the clouds atop Mt Olympus, Greece's highest peak. In Zagorohoria, hike between 46 preserved hamlets in the Pindos Mountains.

Resort Life

With sandy beaches, island getaways and strong Italian-village influences, Parga typifies the region's resorts – popular yet relaxed, good for families yet also great for nightlife. Alternatively, head for the remote sandy coves of Halkidiki.

p256

Saronic Gulf Islands

Activities
Architecture
Museums

Diving & Hiking

Encounter dolphins, sunken pirate ships and underwater caves when diving in the Gulf. On dry land, Poros, Hydra and Spetses have forests to explore and hilltops to climb.

Monasteries & Mansions

Tiers of traditional buildings sweep down to Hydra's pretty harbour, and serene, ancient monasteries dot nearby hilltops. Next door on Spetses, see traditional boatbuilding and impressive ancestral mansions.

Traditional Seacraft

Hydra's museums include a fully restored hilltop mansion and eclectic naval collections. At Spetses, see a traditional seafarer's home, and at Baltiza, a museum of sea craft, from caïques to yachts.

p324

Cyclades

Ancient Ruins
Cuisine
Nightlife

Delos & Ancient Thira

The sacred relics of Delos are protected on their own strictly regulated island. Ancient Thira on Santorini is a melange of Hellenistic, Roman and Byzantine ruins.

Traditional Meals

Sample smoked eel and ham, Mykonian prosciutto, handmade soft cheeses and local wild mushrooms. Kitchens are filled with creative culinary flair and modern takes on traditional foods.

Glamour Clubs

Mykonos' nightlife is glamorous and LGBT+ friendly. Ios is less swanky but very full-on, with wall-to-wall clubs and nonstop beach parties. Quieter Santorini has cocktail bars over the caldera with unparalleled sunset views.

p346

Crete

Ancient Ruins
Activities
Beaches

Minoan Palaces

The ruins of the ancient Minoan civilisation grace this island. Survey the palaces of Knossos, Malia, Phaestos and Zakros and pick up on a lingering sense of mystery at countless minor sites.

Gorge Hikes

The Samaria is Europe's longest gorge, and one of Crete's most popular draws. The island boasts other quieter, equally dramatic gorges for hiking and rock climbing, and a mountainous interior with caves and woodland to explore.

Sun Worship

Crete has some of Greece's top beaches, palm-fringed stretches of powder-soft sand. Others are backed by charismatic old towns or are lapped by the crystal-clear Libyan Sea. All are worth sinking your toes into.

p454

Dodecanese

Architecture
Activities
Cuisine

Byzantine & Medieval Architecture

Architectural eye candy is everywhere. See fairy-tale hilltop castles, frescoed Byzantine churches and Rhodes' medieval Old Town. Visit mountain villages, the ruins of ancient temples and Italian-inspired harbours.

Outdoor Adventures

Some of the world's top rock climbing, kitesurfing, beachcombing, diving and walking are packed into the Dodecanese. Ancient footpaths, endangered birdlife, a bubbling volcano and surfing too.

Culinary Mix

Mix Greek cuisine with long-term Italian influences for scrumptious results: pizzas, pastas, stews, local cheeses, honey, wild greens and herbs, seafood and grilled meats.

p510

Northeastern Aegean Islands

Activities
Cuisine
Beaches

Great Outdoors

The clear water lapping these islands is perfect for diving into. You'll be beckoned to hike to wooded waterfalls, wade through rivers and explore old-growth forests on foot or bicycle.

Seafood & Wine

Dining daily on fresh seafood is a way of life. Venus clams, sea urchins, crayfish, grilled cod and lobster are all washed down with plenty of ouzo and Samos' sweet local wine.

Aqua Aegean

From the remote, white-pebbled coast on Ikaria to hidden coves on the Fourni Islands, pristine sandy stretches on Chios and seaside resorts on Samos, you're never far from a beach on the aquamarine Aegean.

p588

Evia & the Sporades

Beaches
Activities
Food & Drink

Skiathos' Blonde Shores

Some of the Aegean's most seductive beaches grace Skiathos' sparkling shoreline, including the pine-fringed sands of Koukounaries. Skopelos' perfect coves are close behind.

Seaside Adventures

Seek out dolphins and rare birdlife in Alonnisos' pristine marine park; hike through olive groves, pine forests and shady gorges; or head out kayaking, snorkelling, paddle-boarding and scuba diving.

Local Produce

Try locally pressed olive oil and island-grown veggies. Also don't miss the Sporades' super-fresh seafood, *tyropita* (cheese pie) or honey, especially the *elatos* (fir) and *pefko* (pine) varieties.

p648

Ionian Islands

Architecture
Activities
Cuisine

Mansions & Windmills

Corfu Town is a symphony of pastel-hued Venetian mansions, French arcades and British neoclassical architecture. Neighbouring islands offer whitewashed villages and ancient windmills.

Kayak & Ramble

Kayak remote coves, sail the blue Aegean, wander ancient olive groves and hike the mountains. Continuous stretches of gorgeous coastline and quiet interiors on Kefallonia lure the adventurous.

Italian-Inspired Cuisine

Corfiot cuisine is distinctive and delicious. Plenty of garlic, homemade bread, seafood risottos and hand-rolled pasta allude to an Italian influence in the kitchen.

p678

On the
Road

AT A GLANCE

POPULATION
City 664,000; wider
municipality
3.1 million

WORLD'S FIRST
THEATRE
Theatre of Dionysos
(p75)

BEST CULTURAL
FESTIVAL
Athens & Epidaurus
Festival (p100)

BEST MARKET
Varvakios Agora
(p126)

BEST CORNER DELI
Karamanlidika tou
Fani (p114)

WHEN TO GO
May Perfect weather
for sightseeing and
outdoor cinemas and
restaurants.

Jun–Aug The Athens
& Epidaurus Festival
lights up venues with
drama and music.

Sep & Oct Weather
cools and the social
scene heats up as
residents return from
the islands.

Acropolis view from Monastiraki (p85)
MILAN GONDA/SHUTTERSTOCK

Athens & Around

With equal measures of grunge and grace, Athens (Αθήνα) is a heady mix of ancient history and contemporary cool. Cultural and social life plays out amid, around and in ancient landmarks. The magnificent Acropolis, visible from almost every part of the city, reminds Greeks daily of their heritage and the city's many transformations. The city is on the rise. There is crackling energy in galleries, political debates and even on the walls of derelict buildings. This creates a lively urban bustle, but at the end of the day, Athenians build their own villages in the city, especially in open-air restaurants and bars where they linger for hours.

Beyond Athens, down the Attica peninsula, are more spectacular antiquities, such as the Temple of Poseidon at Sounion, as well as very good beaches, such as those near historic Marathon.

Athens Highlights

1 Acropolis (p72) Visiting the awe-inspiring ancient site.

2 Acropolis Museum (p78) Enjoying the majesty of the Parthenon sculptures.

3 Ancient Agora (p82) Strolling in the historic centre.

4 Benaki Museum (p94) Admiring superb antiquities and cultural artefacts.

5 National Archaeological Museum (p90) Exploring the finest collection of Greek antiquities.

6 Odeon of Herodes Atticus (p75) Watching a performance in this ancient amphitheatre.

7 Stavros Niarchos Foundation Cultural Center (p114) Feeling the sea breeze at this wonderful arts hub and park.

8 Panathenaic Stadium (p95) Revelling in ancient feats of strength.

History

Early History

The archaeological record of Athens' early years is patchy. What is known is that the hilltop site of the Acropolis, with two abundant springs, drew some of Greece's earliest Neolithic settlers. When a peaceful agricultural existence gave way to war-orientated city-states, the Acropolis provided an ideal defensive position.

By 1400 BCE the Acropolis had become a powerful Mycenaean city. It survived a Dorian assault in 1200 BCE but didn't escape the dark age that enveloped Greece for the next 400 years. Then, in the 8th century BCE, during a period of peace, Athens became the artistic centre of Greece, excelling in ceramics.

By the 6th century BCE, Athens was ruled by aristocrats and generals. Labourers and peasants had no rights until Solon, the harbinger of Athenian democracy, became *arhon* (chief magistrate) in 594 BCE and improved the lot of the poor by establishing a process of trial by jury. Continuing unrest over the reforms created the pretext for the tyrant Peisistratos, formerly head of the military, to seize power in 560 BCE.

Peisistratos built a formidable navy and extended the boundaries of Athenian influence. A patron of the arts, he inaugurated the Festival of the Great Dionysia, the precursor to Attic drama, and commissioned many splendid works, most of which were later destroyed by the Persians.

In 528 BCE, he was succeeded by his son, Hippias, no less an oppressor. With the help of Sparta in 510 BCE, Athens rid itself of him.

Athens' Golden Age

After Athens finally repulsed the Persian Empire at the battles of Salamis (480 BCE) and Plataea (479 BCE) – again, with the help of Sparta – its power knew no bounds.

In 477 BCE Athens established a confederacy on the sacred island of Delos and demanded tributes from the surrounding islands to protect them from the Persians. The treasury was moved to Athens in 461 BCE and Pericles, ruler from 461 BCE to 429 BCE, used the money to transform the city. This period has become known as Athens' golden age.

Most of the monuments on the Acropolis today date from this period. Drama and literature flourished due to such luminaries as Aeschylus, Sophocles and Euripides. The sculptors Pheidias and Myron and the historians Herodotus, Thucydides and Xenophon also lived during this time.

Rivalry with Sparta

Sparta didn't let Athens revel in its newfound glory. Cooperation gave way to competition and the Peloponnesian Wars, which began in 431 BCE and dragged on until 404 BCE. Sparta gained the upper hand and Athens never returned to its former glory. The 4th century BCE did, however, produce three of the West's greatest orators and philosophers: Socrates, Plato and Aristotle.

In 338 BCE Athens, along with the other city-states of Greece, was conquered by Philip II of Macedon. After Philip's assassination, his son Alexander (soon to be known as the Great) favoured Athens over other city-states. But after Alexander's untimely death, Athens passed in quick succession through the hands of his generals.

Roman & Byzantine Rule

The Romans defeated the Macedonians, and in 86 BCE attacked Athens after it sided against them in a botched rebellion in Asia Minor. They destroyed the city walls and took precious sculptures to Rome. During three centuries of peace under Roman rule, known as the 'Pax Romana', Athens continued to be a major seat of learning. The Romans adopted Hellenistic culture: many wealthy young Romans attended Athens schools and anyone who was anyone in Rome spoke Greek. The Roman emperors, particularly Hadrian, graced Athens with many grand buildings.

In the late 4th century CE, Christianity became the official religion of Athens and worship of the 'pagan' Greek gods was outlawed. After the subdivision of the Roman Empire into east and west, Athens remained an important cultural and intellectual centre until Emperor Justinian closed its schools of philosophy in 529. Athens declined and, between 1200 and 1450, was continually invaded – by the Franks, Catalans, Florentines and Venetians, all preoccupied with grabbing principalities from the crumbling Byzantine Empire.

Ottoman Rule & Independence

Athens was captured by the Turks in 1456, and nearly 400 years of Ottoman rule followed. The Acropolis became the home of the Turkish governor, the Parthenon was converted to a mosque and the Erechtheion became a harem.

NEIGHBOURHOODS AT A GLANCE

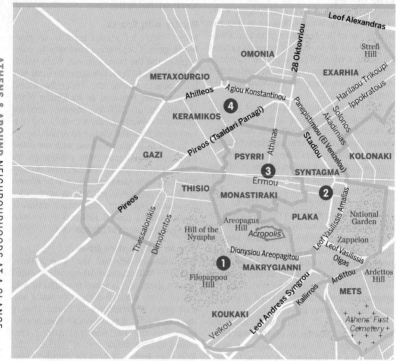

❶ Acropolis, Filopappou Hill & Thisio (p66)

Athens' crown is the Acropolis and its jewel is the Parthenon. This epic monument soars above the city, and on the hill's southern slopes, a fabulous modern museum holds its treasures. A pedestrian promenade links the two – it's a tourist throughway, but also a favourite spot for locals to enjoy a sundown stroll.

Further south, the neighbourhoods of Makrygianni and Koukaki deliver a slice of residential Athens life and offer reliable hotels, hip bars and restaurants, and cool craft shops and boutiques.

Filopappou Hill offers eye-level views of the Acropolis from the top, as well as some welcome green space, along with the Hill of the Pnyx to the north.

Just beyond, the sedate Thisio neighbourhood is cut through with two fine pedestrian routes, around which a pleasant cafe precinct flourishes. If you walk south to Petralona, you'll find even more low-key residential streets that make a nice change from the more heavily touristed centre.

❷ Syntagma & Plaka (p70)

Syntagma is the heart of modern Athens, a business and bar district with Plateia Syntagmatos (Syntagma Sq) its historical meeting point, political centre and transport hub.

Adjacent to the square is the National Garden; a short stroll southwest is Plaka, the heart of old Athens, virtually all that existed when the city was declared the new Greek nation's capital in 1834. With narrow streets winding by neoclassical mansions, Byzantine churches and telegenic tavernas, Plaka is ground zero for Athens tourism. Lifelong residents and splashes of graffiti keep its soul strong.

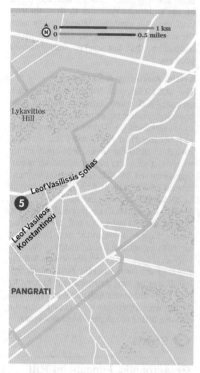

A decade passes, the edge becomes the centre, and the transformation continues in surrounding areas. Currently, adjacent Keramikos and Metaxourgio, east of Gazi, are where new scruffy-cool bars, theatres and cafes are popping up, alongside derelict mansions, moped dealerships and Chinese wholesalers. Come to this area at night, certainly, but also by day for the ancient cemetery of Kerameikos, as well as a couple of good museums.

Exarhia is famous for its squat scene and its vocal anarchists, but also offers a fascinating mix of students (it's near the universities), creative types, immigrants, families, old lefties and intellectuals, against a backdrop of graffiti, street art and ever-present riot police.

❺ Kolonaki, Mets & Pangrati (p94)

Kolonaki is an adjective as much as a district: chic, stylish, elite. The area, which stretches from near Syntagma to the slopes of Lykavittos Hill, is where old money mixes with the nouveau riche and wannabes. On a more practical level for visitors, it's also the location of several excellent museums and a delightfully green area. Its cool, tree-shaded streets make a lovely retreat after walking around sun-blasted ruins. Come here to sample Athens' good life...and maybe buy some shoes.

The attractive residential districts of Mets and Pangrati surround the Panathenaic Stadium, built into Ardettos Hill. Mets, to the southwest and named for a brewery once headquartered here, is characterised by some delightful neoclassical and prewar houses; Pangrati to the north is a diverse, unpretentious residential neighbourhood with low-key-cool places to eat.

❸ Monastiraki & Psyrri (p85)

Monastiraki's busy square is one of Athens' key hubs, a place where people meet before hitting nearby bars and souvlaki joints. To the south, the Ancient Agora was the city's original civic meeting place and remains a wonderful site to explore.

And to the north and west, Psyrri may look dilapidated, but it's the city's liveliest quarter, where restaurants and bars coexist with warehouse conversions and workshops.

❹ Gazi, Keramikos & Exarhia (p88)

Gazi's story is a typical contemporary urban one: abandoned industry – here, a former gasworks – is revived by artists and bar owners.

On 25 March 1821, the Greeks launched the War of Independence, declaring independence in 1822. Fierce fighting broke out in the streets of Athens, which changed hands several times. Britain, France and Russia eventually stepped in and destroyed the Turkish–Egyptian fleet in the famous Battle of Navarino in October 1827.

Initially the city of Nafplio was named Greece's capital. After elected president Ioannis Kapodistrias was assassinated in 1831, Britain, France and Russia again intervened, declaring Greece a monarchy. The throne was given to 17-year-old Prince Otto of Bavaria, who transferred his court to Athens. It became the Greek capital in 1834, though was little more than a sleepy town of about 6000, as so many residents had fled after the 1827 siege. Bavarian architects created imposing neoclassical buildings, tree-lined boulevards and squares.

Otto was overthrown in 1862 after a period of power struggles, including the British and French occupation of Piraeus, aimed at quashing the 'Great Idea' – Greece's doomed expansionist goal. The imposed sovereign was Danish Prince William, crowned as Prince George in 1863.

The 20th Century

Throughout the latter half of the 19th century and the beginning of the 20th, Athens grew steadily – and then quite suddenly in 1922 and 1923, when more than a million refugees arrived in the city, first from the burning of Smyrna (Izmir), then due to the population exchange mandated by the Treaty of Lausanne the next spring.

During the German occupation of WWII, Athens suffered appallingly. More Athenians died from starvation than were killed by the enemy. The suffering only continued during the bitter civil war that followed.

A 1950s industrialisation program, launched with the help of US aid, brought another population boom, as people from the islands and mainland villages moved to Athens in search of work. The colonels' junta (1967–74) tore down many of the old Turkish houses of Plaka and the neoclassical buildings of King Otto's time, but failed to tackle the chronic infrastructure problems resulting from the rapid growth of the 1950s. The elected governments that followed didn't do much better, and by the end of the 1980s the city had a reputation as one of the most traffic-clogged, polluted and dysfunctional in Europe.

In the 1990s, as part of an initial bid to host the Olympics, authorities embarked on an ambitious program to drag the city into the 21st century. Athens finally won the competition to host the 2004 Olympics, a deadline that fast-tracked infrastructure projects.

Crisis, Austerity & Recovery

The 2004 Olympics legacy was a cleaner, greener and more efficient capital, and booming economic growth. But the optimism and fiscal good times were short-lived, as it became clear the country had overborrowed. In 2010 the Greek debt crisis set in, with strict austerity measures including cutting pensions by half. The unemployment rate hit 28% in 2014 and banks closed briefly in 2015 amid dramatic elections.

With the worst of the financial crisis over, Athens appears to be on a roll. There's a new mayor, Kostas Bakoyannis, new businesses are starting up and the arts scene – particularly street art – is especially on fire. But the city is plenty more than the next trendy capital. It has its own struggles and history, its own fight-the-power attitude – as evidenced by the way Athenians have coped with the massive influx of refugees in recent years.

◉ Sights

◉ Acropolis, Filopappou Hill & Thisio

Areopagus Hill   PARK
(Map p86; Ⓜ Monastiraki) This rocky outcrop below the Acropolis has great views over the Ancient Agora (p82). According to mythology, it was here that Ares was tried by the council of the gods for the murder of Halirrhothios, son of Poseidon. The council accepted his defence of justifiable homicide on the grounds that he was protecting his daughter, Alcippe, from unwanted advances.

Filopappou Hill   PARK
(Map p80; Ⓜ Akropoli) Also called the Hill of the Muses, Filopappou Hill – along with the hills of the Pnyx (Map p102; Ⓜ Thissio) and the Nymphs (Map p102; Ⓜ Thissio) – is a somewhat wild, pine-shaded spot that's good for a stroll, especially at sunset. The hill also gives some of the best vantage points for photographing the Acropolis, and views to the Saronic Gulf.

The hill is identifiable by the **Monument of Filopappos** (Map p80) crowning its sum-s

ATHENS IN...

Two Days

Climb to the glorious Acropolis (p72) in the early morning, then wind down through the Ancient Agora (p82). Explore Plaka, looping back to the Acropolis Museum (p78) for the Parthenon masterpieces. Complete your circuit along the pedestrian promenade, then up to Filopappou Hill (p66) and the cafes of Thisio before dinner at a restaurant with Acropolis views – or grab a souvlaki and head to an outdoor movie.

On day two, watch the changing of the guard (p95) at Syntagma Sq before heading through the gardens to the Temple of Olympian Zeus (p70) or the Panathenaic Stadium (p95). Spend the afternoon at the National Archaeological Museum (p90), then head to the Plateia Agia Irini area in Monastiraki for dinner and nightlife.

Four Days

Take your pick from the Benaki Museum (p94), the Museum of Cycladic Art (p94) and the Byzantine & Christian Museum (p94) before lunch in Kolonaki. Take the *teleferik* (funicular railway) or climb Lykavittos Hill (p95) for panoramic views. Hit a *rembetika* club in winter, or bar-hop around Exarhia in summer.

On day four spend the morning exploring the Varvakios Agora and Kerameikos, then head in the afternoon to the Stavros Niarchos Foundation Cultural Center (p114), finishing the day with a show at the Greek National Opera (p124). Alternatively, trip along the coast to Cape Sounion's Temple of Poseidon (p141), saving some energy for nightlife at Glyfada's beach bars.

---

mit; it was built between 114 and 116 CE in honour of Julius Antiochus Filopappos, a prominent Roman consul and administrator. The marble-paved path, laid out in the 1950s by modernist architect Dimitris Pikionis, starts near the *periptero* (kiosk) on Dionysiou Areopagitou. After 250m, it passes the excellent Church of Agios Dimitrios Loumbardiaris (Map p80; www.facebook.com/agios dimitriosloumpardiaris; Ⓜ Thissio, Akropoli), which contains fine frescoes. There's a detour to Socrates' prison (Map p80; Ⓜ Thissio), and the main path leads to the Shrine of the Muses (Map p80), cut into the rock face just below the top of the hill.

Inhabited from prehistoric times to the post-Byzantine era, the area was, according to Plutarch, the area where Theseus and the Amazons did battle. In the 4th and 5th centuries BCE, defensive fortifications – such as the Themistoclean wall and the Diateichisma – extended over the hill, and some of their remains are still visible.

Herakleidon Museum Building B   MUSEUM
(Map p102; ☑ 210 346 1981; www.herakleidon -art.gr; Apostolou Pavlou 37, Thisio; adult/student/ child €7/5/free; ⊙ 10am-6pm Wed-Sun; Ⓜ Thisio) This eclectic private museum, split over two locations, examines the interrelation of art, mathematics and philosophy, explored through rotating exhibits on such diverse subjects as ancient robotic and computer

technology, and shipbuilding. Building B focuses on weapons of war, including triremes, the ancient warships that allowed the Greeks to conquer the Persians at the Battle of Salamis.

Around the corner in a restored mansion, the smaller Building A (Map p102; Iraklidon 16, Thisio) has an exhibition on automata, featuring an ancient type of robot including one of a moving servant girl. The museum also holds one of the world's biggest collections of MC Escher artworks (though it is not always on view).

Athens Pinball Museum   MUSEUM
(Map p80; ☑ 210 924 5958; www.facebook.com/ AthensPinballMuseum; Makri 2, Makrygianni; adult/ student/child €10/7/free; ⊙ 10am-10pm Mon-Fri, 9am-11pm Sat & Sun; Ⓜ Akropoli) Not so much a museum as an all-bleeping, flashing games arcade where you play pinball to your heart's content. It has more than 100 working pinball machines, with the oldest dating back to 1957; the fanciest is a gold-plated version of an *Addams Family*–themed machine.

Melina Merkouri Cultural Centre   MUSEUM
(Map p102; ☑ 210 345 2150; www.cityofathens. gr/node/676; Iraklidon 66, Thisio; ⊙ 10am-8pm Tue-Sat, to 2pm Sun; Ⓜ Thissio) FREE For anyone who loves the Greek tradition of *karagiozi* (shadow puppets), this free museum is a treat, packed with the creations of

Greater Athens

Kifissos
Terminal A
(300m)

Liossion
Terminal B (1.6km)

Ermonos

Petras

Ioanninon

Leof Konstandinoupoleos

Larissa Train Station

Larissa

Ioulianou

Ipirou

Aharnon

Plateia
Petroula
Sot

Alexandreias

Marathonomahon

Platonos

Argous

Lehorman

Palamidiou

Deligianni

Plateia
Ramnes

Plateia
Vathis

OMONIA

Plateia
Eleotrivion

Metaxourghio

Ahilleos

METAXOURGIO

Agiou
Konstantinou

Agiou Konstantinou

Iera Odos

Eleonas Flea
Market (850m)

See Gazi, Keramikos & Thisio Map (p102)

See Psyrri & Exarhia
Map (p96)

Agiou Polykarpou

Patsi Spyrou

Meg Alexandrou

Thermopylon

KERAMIKOS

Kolokinthous

Pireos (Tsaldari Panagi)

Deligeorgi

Sofokleous

Plateia Eleftherias
(Koumoundourou)

PSYRRI

Orfeos

Leof Konstantinoupoleos

Iera Odos

Kerameikos

GAZI

Technopolis

Pireos

Thisio
Park

Ermou

Plateia Agion
Asomaton

Thissio

See Syntagma,
Plaka & Monastiraki
Map (p86)

Monastiraki

MONASTIRAKI

ROUF

THISIO

Nileos

Apostolou Pavlou

Ralli Petrou

Alsos
Petralonon

Hill of the
Nymphs

Areopagus
Hill

Acropolis

Tsaldari Pan

Hill of the
Pnyx

Pireos

Petralona

Filopappou
Hill

Ionos

Thessalonikis

Dimofontos

KOUKAKI

Veikou

Dimitrakopoulou N

See Makrygianni, Koukaki &
Filopappou Hill Map (p80)

Carokopou

Lambraki Grig

Stavros Niarchos Foundation
Cultural Center (3km);
Piraeus (8km)

Leof Andreas Syngrou

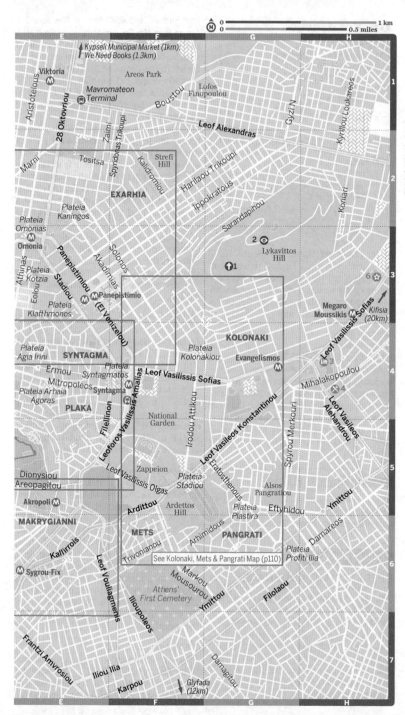

ATHENS & AROUND

N

0 ━━━━━━━━━━━ 1 km
0 ━━━━━━━━━━━ 0.5 miles

Kypseli Municipal Market (1km);
We Need Books (1.3km)

Viktoria Ⓜ

Areos Park

Mavromateon
Terminal

Boustou

Lofos
Finopoulou

Gyzi N

Kyrillou Loukareos

Aristotelous

28 Oktovriou

Zaimi

Spyridonos Trikoupi

Kalidromiou

Leof Alexandras

Marni

Tositsa

Strefi
Hill

Harilaou Trikoupi

EXARHIA

Ippokratous

Koniari

Plateia
Kaningos

Solonos

Akadimias

Sarandapihou

Plateia
Omonias
Omonia Ⓜ

Panepistimiou

Lykavittos
Hill

2 ◎

❶1

6 ★

Athinas

Plateia
Kotzia

Eolou

Stadiou

Panepistimio Ⓜ
(El Venizelou)

Megaro
Moussikis

Leof Vasilissis Sofias

Kifisia
(20km)

Plateia
Klafthmonos

KOLONAKI

Plateia
Agia Irini

SYNTAGMA

Plateia
Kolonakiou

Evangelismos Ⓜ

Ermou

Plateia
Syntagmatos

Leof Vasilissis Sofias

Mihalakopoulou

🚌3

Mitropoleos

Syntagma

Plateia Arhaia
Agoras

PLAKA

Filellinon

Leoforos Vasilissis Amalias

Irodou Attikou

🚌4

Leof Vasileos
Alehandrou

National
Garden

Leof Vasileos Konstantinou

Spyrou Merkouri

Dionysiou
Areopagitou

Zappeion

Eratosthenous

Akropoli Ⓜ

Leof Vasilissis Olgas

Plateia
Stadiou

Alsos
Pangratiou

Ymittou

MAKRYGIANNI

Ardittou

Ardettos
Hill

Plateia
Plastira

Eftyhidou

Damareos

Kallirrois

METS

Arhimidous

PANGRATI

Plateia
Profiti Ilia

Ⓜ Sygrou-Fix

Trivonianou

See Kolonaki, Mets & Pangrati Map (p110)

Leof Vouliagmenis

Athens'
First Cemetery

Markou
Mousourou

Ymittou

Filolaou

Ilioupoleos

Frantzi Amvrosiou

Iliou Ilia

Karpou

Glyfada
(12km)

Damagitou

Greater Athens

master puppeteer Haridimos (Sotiris Haritos). There's very little English signage, but the displays tell their own stories. Upstairs is a mock street scene of 'old Athens', with shop windows of the typesetter, the photo studio, the barber and more.

**National Museum of
Contemporary Art**   MUSEUM
(EMST; Map p80; ☑211 101 9000; www.emst.gr; Kallirrois & Frantzi, Koukaki-Syngrou; Ⓜ Sygrou-Fix) Set in the former Fix Brewery, this contemporary museum opened in 2015 but was closed for prolonged renovations at the time of research. In the past, it has exhibited Greek and international art in all media, from painting to video to experimental architecture

⊙ Syntagma & Plaka

★ Temple of Olympian Zeus   TEMPLE
(Olympieio; Map p86; ☑210 922 6330; http://odysseus.culture.gr; Leoforos Vasilissis Olgas, Plaka;

LOCAL KNOWLEDGE

PEDESTRIAN PROMENADE

You could skip all the sights in Athens and still feel you've got the city's pulse just by strolling along the pedestrian street of Dionysiou Areopagitou around sundown. Lights glow on the Acropolis above, and the road is filled with tourists, snack vendors, musicians and local couples out for an arm-in-arm promenade.

---

adult/student/child €6/3/free; ⊙ 8am-3pm Oct-Apr, to 8pm May-Sep; Ⓜ Akropoli, Syntagma) A can't-miss on two counts: it's a marvellous temple, once the largest in Greece, and it's smack in the centre of Athens. Of the temple's 104 original Corinthian columns (17m high with a base diameter of 1.7m), only 15 remain – the fallen column was blown down in a gale in 1852.

Begun in the 6th century BCE by Peisistratos, the temple was abandoned for lack of funds. Various other leaders took a stab at completing it, but it was left to Hadrian to finish the job in 131 CE, thus taking more than 700 years in total to build. In typically immodest fashion, Hadrian built not just a colossal statue of Zeus, but an equally large one of himself.

Admission to the site is included with the Acropolis combo ticket (€30), which permits entry to the Acropolis and six other sites (including this one) within five days.

Final admission is 30 minutes before closing.

★ Hadrian's Arch   MONUMENT
(Map p86; cnr Leoforos Vasilissis Olgas & Leoforos Vasilissis Amalias, Plaka; Ⓜ Akropoli, Syntagma) FREE The Roman emperor Hadrian had a great affection for Athens. Although he did his fair share of spiriting its Classical artwork to Rome, he also embellished the city with many temples and infrastructure improvements. As thanks, the people of Athens erected this lofty monument of Pentelic marble in 131 CE. It now stands on the edge of one of Athens' busiest avenues.

★ National Garden   GARDENS
(Map p110; ☑210 721 5019; www.cityofathens.gr; ⊙ 7am-dusk; Ⓜ Syntagma) FREE The former royal gardens, designed by Queen Amalia in 1838, are a pleasantly unkempt park that makes a welcome shady refuge from summer heat and traffic. Tucked among the trees are a cafe, a playground, turtle and duck ponds, and a tiny (if slightly dispiriting) zoo. The main entrance is on Leoforos Vasilissis Sofias, south of Parliament (p95); you can also enter from Irodou Attikou to the east, or from the adjacent Zappeion (p85) to the south.

**★ Museum of Greek
Popular Instruments**   MUSEUM
(Map p86; ☑210 325 4119; Diogenous 1-3, Plaka; ⊙ 10am-2pm Tue & Thu-Sun, noon-6pm Wed; Ⓜ Monastiraki) FREE A single avid ethno-

ℹ COMBINED TICKETS & ENTRY HOURS

➡ A €30 combo ticket covers entry to the Acropolis and Athens' other main ancient sites: the Ancient Agora, the Roman Agora, Hadrian's Library, Kerameikos, the Temple of Olympian Zeus and Aristotle's Lyceum. It pays off if you're planning to see the Acropolis (€20 alone) and at least two other sites. The ticket is valid for five consecutive days and can be purchased at any of the included sites.

➡ For museums, a €15 ticket covers the National Archaeological Museum, the Byzantine & Christian Museum, the Epigraphic Museum and the Numismatic Museum. It's valid for three days.

➡ A €25 pass covers entry to all branches of the Benaki Museum and is valid for three months.

➡ Hours for many sites and museums cut back in winter, closing sometimes as early as 1pm. Additionally, budget cuts occasionally curtail opening times. Double-check hours before making a special trip. Ticket offices close 15 to 30 minutes before the sites close.

➡ Check www.culture.gr for free-admission holidays.

musicologist collected almost 1200 folk instruments; the best are on display in three floors of this house-turned-museum. Headphones let visitors listen to the *gaïda* (Greek goatskin bagpipes) and the wood planks that priests on Mt Athos use to call prayer times, among other distinctly Greek sounds. Musical performances are held in the lovely garden in summer.

Anafiotika   AREA
(Map p86; Stratonos, Plaka; M Monastiraki, Akropoli) Clinging to the north slope of the Acropolis, the tiny Anafiotika district is a beautiful, architecturally distinct subdistrict of Plaka. In the mid-1800s, King Otto hired builders from Anafi to build a new palace. In their homes here, they mimicked their island's architecture, all whitewashed cubes, bedecked with bougainvillea and geraniums. The area now is a clutch of about 40 homes, linked by footpaths just wide enough for people and stray cats.

It's easy to completely miss the entrances to the district. On the west side, head uphill near the Church of the Metamorphosis on Theorias. On the east side, zigzag up Stratonos. On the way, you'll pass a surprise olive grove/local park.

Bath House of the Winds   MUSEUM
(Map p86; ☑210 324 5957; www.mnep.gr; Kyrristou 8, Plaka; adult/child €2/free; ☺9am-4pm Wed-Mon; M Monastiraki) One of the few remnants of Athens' Ottoman period, this 17th-century *hammam* (Turkish bath) is also the only intact public bath building in the city – though it unfortunately no longer functions as such. As a museum, though,

it's quite attractive and atmospheric, with music, sound and a few projections conjuring its glory days as you stroll through the various rooms. As part of the Museum of Greek Folk Art, this museum hosts displays secular and religious folk art, mainly from the 18th and 19th centuries. Typical exhibits include embroidery, pottery, weaving, puppets or Greek traditional costumes.

Museum of Greek Folk Art at 22 Panos   MUSEUM
(Map p86; ☑210 324 5957; www.mnep.gr; Panos 22, Plaka; adult/child €2/free; ☺9am-4pm Wed-Mon; M Monastiraki) Until the main Museum of Greek Folk Art reopens, this annexe houses the permanent collection *Men & Tools*, which is not quite as dry as it sounds. The small display, enhanced by music, is a loving tribute to Greeks' hard labour and refined skills in the pre-industrial era.

The museum also manages the **Mosque of Tzistarakis** (Map p86; Areos 1, Monastiraki; M Monastiraki), which is occasionally open for temporary exhibitions.

Church of Agioi Anargyroi   CHURCH
(Metochi of the Holy Sepulchre; Map p86; ☑210 322 5810; https://jerusalem-patriarchate.info; Erechtheos 18, Plaka; M Akropoli) Tucked away in Plaka, this 17th-century church is worth visiting any time for its peaceful courtyard and beautiful interior decoration. On the evening of Easter Saturday, a 'holy flame' is flown from the mother Church of the Holy Sepulchre in Jerusalem, and in ritual said to be over a millennium old, the faithful pack out the church to light their candles from it.

TOP SIGHT
ACROPOLIS

The Acropolis is the most important ancient site in the Western world. Crowned by the Parthenon, it's visible from almost everywhere in Athens. Its marble gleams white in the midday sun and takes on a honey hue as the sun sinks, then glows above the city by night. A glimpse of this magnificent sight cannot fail to exalt your spirit.

Parthenon

The Parthenon (pictured) is the monument that more than any other epitomises the glory of Ancient Greece. It is dedicated to Athena Parthenos, the goddess embodying the power and prestige of the city. One of the largest Doric temples ever completed in Greece, it was designed by Iktinos and Kallicrates to be the pre-eminent monument of the Acropolis and was completed in time for the Great Panathenaic Festival of 438 BCE.

Columns

The Parthenon's fluted Doric columns achieve perfect form. The eight columns at either end and 17 on each side were ingeniously curved to create an optical illusion: the foundations (like all the 'horizontal' surfaces of the temple) are slightly concave and the columns are slightly convex, making both appear straight. Supervised by Pheidias, the sculptors worked on the architectural detail of the Parthenon, including the pediments, frieze and metopes, which were brightly coloured and gilded.

DON'T MISS

➡ Parthenon

➡ Erechtheion

➡ Porch of the Caryatids

➡ Propylaia

➡ Temple of Athena Nike

➡ Beulé Gate and Monument of Agrippa

➡ Theatre of Dionysos

➡ Asclepieion and Stoa of Eumenes

➡ Odeon of Herodes Atticus

PRACTICALITIES

➡ Map p86; M Akropoli

➡ ☑ 210 321 4172

➡ http://odysseus. culture.gr

➡ adult/concession/child €20/10/free

➡ ⊙ 8am-8pm May-Sep, reduced hours in winter, last entry 30min before closing

Pediments

The temple's pediments (the triangular elements topping the east and west facades) were filled with elaborately carved three-dimensional sculptures. The west side depicted Athena and Poseidon in their contest for the city's patronage, the east Athena's birth from Zeus' head. See their remnants and the rest of the Acropolis' sculptures and artefacts in the Acropolis Museum (p78).

Metopes & Frieze

The Parthenon's metopes, designed by Pheidias, are square carved panels set between channelled triglyphs. The metopes on the eastern side depicted the Olympian gods fighting the giants, and on the western side they showed Theseus leading the Athenian youths into battle against the Amazons. The southern metopes illustrated the contest of the Lapiths and centaurs at a marriage feast, while the northern ones depicted the sacking of Troy. The internal cella was topped by the Ionic frieze, a continuous sculptured band depicting the Panathenaic Procession.

Erechtheion

The Erechtheion, completed around 406 BCE, was a sanctuary built on the most sacred part of the Acropolis: the spot where Poseidon struck the ground with his trident, and where Athena produced the olive tree. Named after Erechtheus, a mythical king of Athens, the temple housed the cults of Athena, Poseidon and Erechtheus. This supreme example of Ionic architecture was ingeniously built on several levels to compensate for the uneven bedrock.

Porch of the Caryatids

The Erechtheion is immediately recognisable by the six majestic maiden columns, the Caryatids (415 BCE), that support its southern portico. Modelled on women from Karyai (modern-day Karyes, in Lakonia), each figure is thought to have held a libation bowl in one hand, and to be drawing up her dress with the other. Those you see are plaster casts. The originals (except for one removed by Lord Elgin, now in the British Museum) are in the Acropolis Museum.

Temple of Poseidon

Poseidon's cella, the Erechtheion's northern porch, is accessible by a small set of stairs against the boundary wall. It consists of six Ionic columns; the fissure in the floor is supposedly left either by Poseidon's trident in his contest with Athena, or by Zeus' thunderbolt when he killed the mythical king Erechtheus.

TOP TIPS

➡ Visit at 8am or late in the day.

➡ Big tour groups tend to use the main entrance. The southeast entrance can be less crowded.

➡ Large bags must be checked in the cloakrooms – you'll find them at both entrances.

➡ Wheelchairs access the site via a cage lift; call ahead to arrange it (☑ 210 321 4172).

➡ Tickets can be bought online at https://etickets.tap.gr.

➡ Also avoid the ticket-booth lines at the Acropolis by buying the €30 combo ticket at other covered ancient sites.

➡ Check www.culture.gr for free-admission holidays and changing opening hours.

QUICK TOUR

It's possible to tour the site in about 90 minutes towards the end of the day. Enter from the less busy southeast entrance, and make a beeline up to the Parthenon. Site clearance starts up here about 45 minutes before closing time; then you can start making your way back down along the south slope, a little ahead of the exiting crowds.

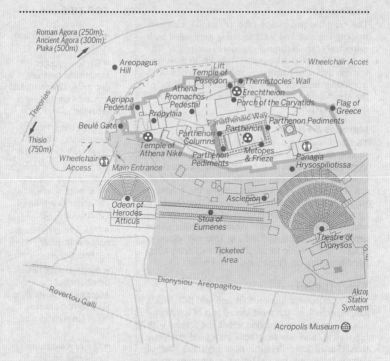

Themistocles' Wall

Crafty general Themistocles (524–459 BCE) hastened to build a protective wall around the Acropolis and in so doing incorporated elements from archaic temples on the site. When you're down the hill in Monastiraki, look for the column drums built into the wall on the north side of the Erechtheion.

Propylaia

The monumental entrance to the Acropolis, the Propylaia was built by Mnesicles between 437 BCE and 432 BCE, and consists of a central hall with two wings on either side. In ancient times its five gates were the only entrances to the 'upper city'. The middle gate opens onto the Panathenaic Way. The ceiling of the central hall was painted with gold stars on a dark-blue background. The northern wing was used as a *pinakothiki* (art gallery).

Temple of Athena Nike

This tiny but exquisitely proportioned Pentelic marble temple was designed by Kallicrates and originally built around 425 BCE; it has been restored three times, most recently in 2003. The internal cella housed a wooden statue of Athena as Victory (Nike), and the exterior friezes illustrated scenes from mythology, the Battle of Plataea (479 BCE) and Athenians fighting Boeotians and Persians. Parts of the frieze are in the Acropolis Museum, as are some relief sculptures, including the beautiful depiction of Athena Nike fastening her sandal.

Beulé Gate & Monument of Agrippa

Just outside the Propylaia lies the Beulé Gate, named after French archaeologist Ernest Beulé, who uncovered it in 1852. The 8m pedestal halfway up the zigzagging ramp to the Propylaia was once topped by the Monument of Agrippa. This bronze statue of the Roman general riding a chariot was erected in 27 BCE to commemorate victory in the Panathenaic Games.

Theatre of Dionysos

Originally, a 6th-century-BCE timber theatre was built here, on the site of the Festival of the Great Dionysia. During Athens' golden age, the theatre (Map p86; Dionysiou Areopagitou) hosted productions of the works of Aeschylus, Sophocles, Euripides and Aristophanes. Reconstructed in stone and marble between 342 and 326 BCE, the theatre held 17,000 spectators (spread over 64 tiers, of which only about 20 tiers survive) and an altar to Dionysos in the orchestra pit.

The ringside Pentelic marble thrones were for dignitaries and priests. The grandest, with lions' paws, satyrs and griffins, was reserved for the Priest of Dionysos. The 2nd-century-BCE reliefs at the rear of the stage depict the exploits of Dionysos. The two hefty men (who still have their heads) are *sileni*, worshippers of the mythical Silenus, the debauched father of the satyrs, whose favourite pastime was charging up mountains with his oversized phallus in lecherous pursuit of nymphs.

Asclepieion & Stoa of Eumenes

Above the Theatre of Dionysos, steps lead to the Asclepieion (Map p86), a temple built around a sacred spring. The worship of Asclepius, the physician son of Apollo, began in Epidavros and was introduced to Athens in 429 BCE at a time when plague was sweeping the city: people sought cures here.

Beneath the Asclepieion, the Stoa of Eumenes is a colonnade built by Eumenes II, King of Pergamum (197–159 BCE), as a shelter and promenade for theatre audiences.

Odeon of Herodes Atticus

The path continues west from the Asclepieion to the magnificent Odeon of Herodes Atticus (Herodeon; Map p86; ☑ 210 324 1807; Ⓜ Akropoli), known as the Herodion. It was built in 161 CE by wealthy Roman Herodes Atticus in memory of his wife Regilla. The theatre was excavated in 1857–58 and completely restored between 1950 and 1961. Performances of drama, music and dance are held here during the Athens & Epidaurus Festival (p100).

ATHENS & AROUND ACROPOLIS

GREEK FLAG

The one modern detail on the Acropolis (aside from the ever-present scaffolding and cranes) is the large Greek flag at the far east end. In 1941, early in the Nazi occupation, two teenage boys climbed up the cliff and raised the Greek flag; their act of resistance is commemorated on a brass plaque nearby.

STATUE OF ATHENA PARTHENOS

The statue for which the temple was built – the Athena Parthenos (Athena the Virgin) – was considered one of the wonders of the ancient world. It was taken to Constantinople in 426 CE, where it disappeared. Designed by Pheidias and completed in 432 BCE, it stood almost 12m high on its pedestal and was plated in gold. Athena's face, hands and feet were made of ivory, and the eyes fashioned from jewels.

The Acropolis

A WALKING TOUR

Cast your imagination back in time, two and a half millennia ago, and envision the majesty of the Acropolis. Its famed and hallowed monument, the Parthenon, dedicated to the goddess Athena, stood proudly over a small city, dwarfing the population with its graceful grandeur. In the Acropolis' heyday in the 5th century BCE, pilgrims and priests worshipped at the temples illustrated here (most of which still stand in varying states of restoration). Many were painted brilliant colours and were abundantly adorned with sculptural masterpieces crafted from ivory, gold and semiprecious stones.

As you enter the site today, elevated on the right perches one of the Acropolis' best-restored buildings: the diminutive ❶ **Temple of Athena Nike**. Follow the Panathenaic Way through the Propylaia and up the slope towards the Parthenon – icon of the Western world. Its ❷ **majestic columns** sweep up to some of what were the finest carvings of their time: wraparound ❸ **pediments, metopes and a frieze**. Stroll around the temple's exterior and take in the spectacular views over Athens and Piraeus below.

As you circle back to the centre of the site, you will encounter those renowned lovely ladies, the ❹ **Caryatids** of the Erechtheion. On the Erechtheion's northern face, the oft-forgotten ❺ **Temple of Poseidon** sits alongside ingenious ❻ **Themistocles' Wall**. Wander to the Erechtheion's western side to find Athena's gift to the city: ❼ **the olive tree**.

TOP TIP

The Acropolis is a must-see for every visitor to Athens. Avoid the crowds by arriving first thing in the morning or late in the day.

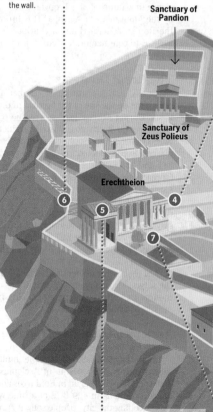

Themistocles' Wall
Crafty general Themistocles (524–459 BCE) hastened to build a protective wall around the Acropolis and in so doing incorporated elements from archaic temples on the site. Look for the column drums built into the wall.

Sanctuary of Pandion

Sanctuary of Zeus Polieus

Erechtheion

Temple of Poseidon
Though he didn't win patronage of the city, Poseidon was worshipped on the northern side of the Erechtheion, which is said to bear the mark of his trident-strike. Imagine the finely decorated coffered porch painted in rich colours, as it was in the past.

ALEXTRAVELERPHOTOGRAPHER/GETTY IMAGES ©

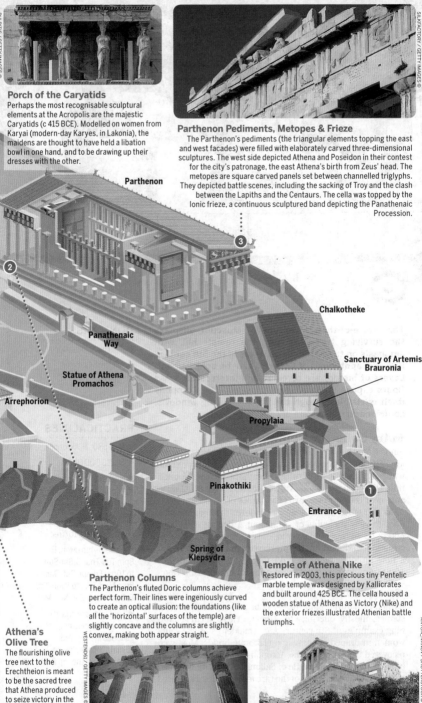

Porch of the Caryatids
Perhaps the most recognisable sculptural elements at the Acropolis are the majestic Caryatids (c 415 BCE). Modelled on women from Karyai (modern-day Karyes, in Lakonia), the maidens are thought to have held a libation bowl in one hand, and to be drawing up their dresses with the other.

Parthenon Pediments, Metopes & Frieze
The Parthenon's pediments (the triangular elements topping the east and west facades) were filled with elaborately carved three-dimensional sculptures. The west side depicted Athena and Poseidon in their contest for the city's patronage, the east Athena's birth from Zeus' head. The metopes are square carved panels set between channelled triglyphs. They depicted battle scenes, including the sacking of Troy and the clash between the Lapiths and the Centaurs. The cella was topped by the Ionic frieze, a continuous sculptured band depicting the Panathenaic Procession.

Parthenon

Chalkotheke

Panathenaic Way

Sanctuary of Artemis Brauronia

Statue of Athena Promachos

Arrephorion

Propylaia

Pinakothiki

Entrance

Spring of Klepsydra

Athena's Olive Tree
The flourishing olive tree next to the Erechtheion is meant to be the sacred tree that Athena produced to seize victory in the contest for Athens.

Parthenon Columns
The Parthenon's fluted Doric columns achieve perfect form. Their lines were ingeniously curved to create an optical illusion: the foundations (like all the 'horizontal' surfaces of the temple) are slightly concave and the columns are slightly convex, making both appear straight.

Temple of Athena Nike
Restored in 2003, this precious tiny Pentelic marble temple was designed by Kallicrates and built around 425 BCE. The cella housed a wooden statue of Athena as Victory (Nike) and the exterior friezes illustrated Athenian battle triumphs.

TOP SIGHT
ACROPOLIS MUSEUM

The state-of-the-art Acropolis Museum displays the surviving treasures from the temple hill, with emphasis on the Acropolis as it was in the 5th century BCE, the apotheosis of Greece's artistic achievement. Layers of history are revealed and interpreted: glass floors expose subterranean ruins, and the Acropolis itself is visible through the floor-to-ceiling windows, so the masterpieces are always in context.

Entry Gallery & Ruins

Finds from the slopes of the Acropolis fill the entryway gallery. The floor's slope echoes the climb up to the sacred hill, while giving glimpses of ruins beneath the museum foundation. Objects here include votive offerings from sanctuaries and, near the entrance, two clay statues of Nike.

As you enter the museum, look down through the glass floor to view the ruins of an ancient Athenian neighbourhood. These were uncovered during the museum's construction and had to be preserved and integrated into a new building plan. In 2019 the museum opened up a 4000-sq-metre section of these ruins for closer inspection.

Archaic Gallery

Bathed in natural light, the 1st floor is a veritable forest of statues, mostly offerings to Athena. These include stunning examples of 6th-century *kore* (maiden) statues: young women in draped clothing and elaborate braids. Most were recovered from a pit on the Acropolis, where the Athenians buried them after the Battle of Salamis. The youth bearing a calf, from 570 BCE, is one of the rare male statues discovered.

DON'T MISS

➡ Parthenon Gallery
➡ Archaic Gallery
➡ Caryatids
➡ Ancient ruins

PRACTICALITIES

➡ Map p80; Ⓜ Akropolis
➡ ☏ 210 900 0900
➡ www.theacropolis museum.gr
➡ Dionysiou Areopagitou 15, Makrygianni
➡ adult/child €10/free
➡ ⊙ 8am-4pm Mon, to 8pm Tue-Thur & Sat-Sun, to 10pm Fri Apr-Oct, 9am-5pm Mon-Thu, to 10pm Fri, to 8pm Sat & Sun Nov-Mar
➡ Last admission is 30 mins before closing; galleries are cleared 15 mins before closing, starting from the top floor

The Archaic Gallery also houses bronze figurines and interesting finds from temples predating the Parthenon, which were destroyed by the Persians. These include elaborate pedimental sculptures of Hercules slaying the Lernaian Hydra and a lioness devouring a bull.

On the mezzanine of the 1st floor are the five grand Caryatids, the world-famous maiden columns that held up the porch of the Erechtheion. (The sixth is in the British Museum.)

Parthenon Gallery

The museum's crowning glory, this top-floor glass atrium (pictured left) is built in alignment with the Parthenon (visible through the wraparound windows) and showcases the Parthenon's pediments, metopes and 160m frieze. When the museum opened in 2009, it marked the first time in more than 200 years that the frieze was displayed in sequence, depicting the full Panathenaic Procession. Interspersed between golden-hued originals are white plaster replicas of missing pieces – the controversial Parthenon Marbles taken to Britain by Lord Elgin in 1801.

Acropolis History

The earliest temples on the Acropolis were built during the Mycenaean era, in homage to the goddess Athena. People lived on the Acropolis until the late 6th century BCE, but in 510 BCE the Delphic oracle declared it the sole province of the gods.

In the 4th century BCE Pericles transformed the Acropolis into a city of temples, which has come to be regarded as the zenith of Classical Greece. It was a showcase of lavishly coloured buildings and gargantuan statues, some of bronze, others of marble plated with gold and encrusted with precious stones.

Foreign occupation, inept renovations, visitors' footsteps, earthquakes and, more recently, acid rain and pollution have all taken their toll on the surviving monuments. The worst blow was in 1687, when the Venetians attacked the Turks, opening fire on the Acropolis and causing an explosion in the Parthenon – where the Turks had been storing gunpowder – and damaging all the buildings. And in 1801, Thomas Bruce, Earl of Elgin, spirited away a portion of the Parthenon frieze, which is still on display in the British Museum, despite Greece's ongoing campaign for its return.

The Acropolis became a World Heritage–listed site in 1987. Major restoration programs are ongoing. Most of the original sculptures and friezes have been moved to the Acropolis Museum, so what you see now on the hill are replicas.

TOP TIPS

➡ Buy tickets online at www.theacropolismuseum.gr to skip the queue.

➡ EU students and under-18s enter free; non-EU students and youth, plus EU citizens over 65, get reduced admission. Bring ID.

➡ Leave time for the fine museum shop (ground floor) and the film describing the history of the Acropolis (top floor).

➡ You can visit the restaurant on the 2nd floor without paying, but you must get a special ticket at the desk. The ground-floor shop and cafe are open without admission.

TAKE A BREAK

For the splendid view it provides of the Acropolis, the museum's **restaurant** (Map p80; 210 900 0915; www.theacropolismuseum.gr; mains €8-34; 8am-4pm Mon, until 8pm Tue-Thu, Sat & Sun, until midnight Fri;) is already a winner. Even better is that the food, made using local seasonal ingredients, is excellent and very reasonably priced, given its location. Breakfast dishes are served up until noon, then a lunch menu continues until the end of the day.

Makrygianni, Koukaki & Filopappou Hill

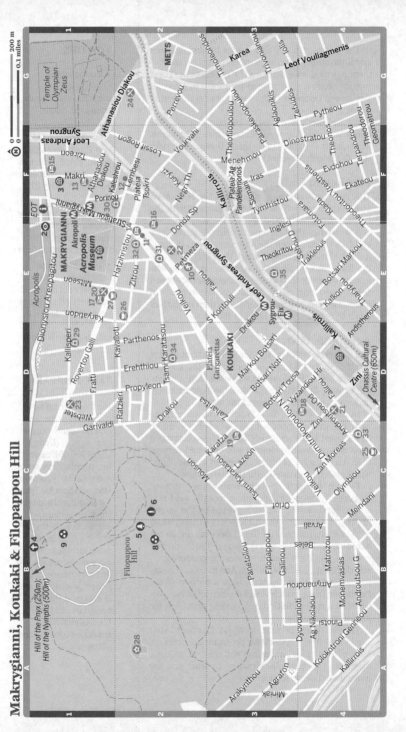

Makrygianni, Koukaki & Filopappou Hill

Plateia Syntagmatos SQUARE
(Syntagma Sq; Map p86; Syntagma; Ⓜ Syntagma) Generally considered the centre of Athens, this square is a transport hub and general hang-out spot, especially on warm summer evenings when young people and families lounge around the central fountain. Parliament (p95), where the *syntagma* (constitution) was granted in 1843, is directly across the road, so the square is also the epicentre for any demonstrations or strikes.

National Historical Museum MUSEUM
(Map p86; ☎ 210 323 7617; www.nhmuseum. gr; Stadiou 13, Syntagma; adult/child €3/free; ◔ 9am-2pm Tue-Sun; Ⓜ Syntagma) This grand old collection of swords, ship figureheads and portraits of moustachioed generals is a bit short on signage; it's best for people who already know something about modern Greek history and the many battles of the 19th century that built the nation, piece by piece. This includes the battle of Messolongi, where Lord Byron fought; the museum owns the camp bed on which he died of malaria, among other effects – though they are often out on loan.

Kanellopoulos Museum MUSEUM
(Map p86; ☎ 210 324 4447; https://pacf.gr; Theorias 12, Plaka; adult/child €4/2; ◔ 8am-3pm Tue-Sun, reduced hours in low season; Ⓜ Monastiraki) A neoclassical mansion contains the collection of Paul and Alexandra Kanellopoulos that was bequeathed to the Greek state in the 1970s. There's lovely classical and Byzantine art and jewellery, and especially transfixing terracotta and bronze classical figurines. Also note the ceilings in the Byzantine wing (the icons are great too). Signage is a bit sparse, and preservation conditions aren't ideal, but as the place is often empty of other visitors, it can feel like you're touring your own eclectic collection.

Church of Agios Nikolaos Rangavas CHURCH
(Map p86; ☎ 210 322 8193; http://enoria-ragkavas.blogspot.com; Prytaniou 1, cnr Epiharmou, Plaka; ◔ 8am-noon & 5-8pm; Ⓜ Akropoli, Monastiraki) This lovely 11th-century church was part of the palace of the Rangavas family, who counted among them Michael I, emperor of Byzantium. The church bell was the first installed in Athens after liberation from the Turks (who had banned them), and was the first to ring in 1833 to announce the freedom of Athens. Its facade is decorated

TOP SIGHT
ANCIENT AGORA

Starting in the 6th century BCE, this area was Athens' commercial, political and social hub. Socrates expounded his philosophy here, and St Paul preached here. The site today has been cleared of later Ottoman buildings to reveal only classical remains. It's a green respite, with a well-restored temple, a good museum and a Byzantine church.

Stoa of Attalos

In architectural terms, a stoa is a covered portico, but the ancient model, this stoa built by King Attalos II of Pergamum (159–138 BCE), was essentially an ancient shopping mall. The majestic two-storey structure, with an open-front ground floor supported by 45 Doric columns, was filled with storefronts. (Today, Greek still uses the word *stoa* for a shopping arcade.) The building, which was restored in the 1950s, holds the site museum.

Housed on both floors of the Stoa of Attalos is a museum (admission included with Ancient Agora ticket; ⊙ 10am-3.30pm Mon, from 8.30am Tue-Sun), which can get uncomfortably crowded when tour groups come through. Inside, you'll find neat relics that show how the *agora* was used on a daily basis: ancient voting ballots, coins, terracotta figurines and more. Some of the oldest finds date from 4000 BCE. If the crowds get too much, head to the upper part of the building, which provides panoramic views over the site.

DON'T MISS

➡ Stoa of Attalos and Agora Museum

➡ Temple of Hephaistos

➡ Council House and Tholos

➡ Church of the Holy Apostles

PRACTICALITIES

➡ Map p86;
Ⓜ Monastiraki

➡ ☑ 210 321 0185

➡ http://odysseus.culture.gr

➡ Adrianou 24, Monastiraki

➡ adult/student/child €8/4/free

➡ ⊙ 8am-8pm Apr-Oct, to 3pm Nov-Mar

Temple of Hephaistos

On the opposite (west) end of the agora site stands the best-preserved Doric temple in Greece. Built in 449 BCE by Iktinos, one of the architects of the Parthenon, it was dedicated to the god of the forge and surrounded by foundries and metalwork shops. It has 34 columns and a frieze on the eastern side depicting nine of the Twelve Labours of Hercules. In 1300 CE it was converted into the Church of Agios Georgios, then deconsecrated in 1934. In 1922 and 1923 it was a shelter for refugees from Asia Minor; iconic photos from that period show families hanging laundry among the pillars and white tents erected along the temple's base.

Stoa Foundations

Northeast of the Temple of Hephaistos are the foundations of the Stoa of Zeus Eleutherios, one of the places where Socrates spoke. Further north are the foundations of the Stoa of Basileios, as well as the Stoa Poikile, or 'Painted Stoa', for its murals of battles of myth and history, rendered by the leading artists of the day.

Council House & Tholos

Southeast of the Temple of Hephaistos, archaeologists uncovered the New Bouleuterion (Council House), where the Senate (originally created by Solon) met, while the heads of government met to the south at the circular Tholos.

Church of the Holy Apostles

This charming little Byzantine church, near the southern site gate, was built in the 11th century to commemorate St Paul's teaching in the *agora*. Following the style of the time, its external brick decorations mimic Arabic calligraphy. During the period of Ottoman rule, it underwent many changes, but between 1954 and 1957 it was stripped of its 19th-century additions and restored to its original form. It contains several fine Byzantine frescoes, which were transferred from a demolished church.

TOP TIPS

➡ The main (and most reliable) entrance is on Adrianou; the south entrance is open only at peak times.

➡ The Temple of Hephaistos is a key photo op: it's well preserved, and you can get quite close to it.

➡ Site clearing starts 30 minutes before closing, from each end. Late in the day, visit the Temple of Hephaistos and the Stoa of Attalos first, then more central spots.

➡ If you're interested in birds, come early: the many trees here harbour a lot of life.

➡ Hours change. Call ahead to check.

PANATHENAIC FESTIVAL

The biggest event in ancient Athens was the Panathenaic Procession, the climax of the Panathenaic Festival held to venerate the goddess Athena. The route cut through the whole city, including the Ancient Agora. Scenes of the procession are vividly depicted in the 160m-long Parthenon frieze in the Acropolis Museum (p78).

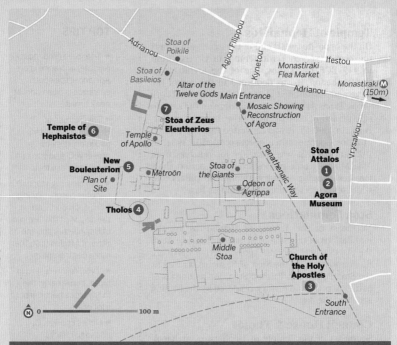

Site Tour
Ancient Agora

START STOA OF ATTALOS
END STOA OF ZEUS ELEUTHERIOS
LENGTH TWO HOURS

As you enter the Agora, make your way first to the magnificent **1 Stoa of Attalos**, a two-storeyed portico, replete with columns, built by the king of Pergamum in the 2nd century BCE as a shopping arcade. Originally its facade was painted red and blue. People gathered here to watch the Panathenaic Procession. The **2 Agora Museum**, inside the stoa, holds some of the site's best finds, and illustrates how the area was used. It is surrounded by ancient statues of the gods.

Continue to the southern side of the site to the charming **3 Church of the Holy Apostles**. The exterior brick patterns are an imitation of Islamic Kufic-style decoration, showing the cross-pollination of style in this period. Inside, it's decorated with 17th-century frescoes.

Walking northwest across the site, you'll pass the circular **4 Tholos**, where the heads of government met, and what was the **5 New Bouleuterion** (Council House), where the Senate met.

On the *agora*'s western edge is the striking **6 Temple of Hephaistos**, god of the forge, which was surrounded by foundries and metalwork shops. It was one of the first buildings of Pericles' rebuilding programme. The last service held there was in 1834, to honour King Otto's arrival in Athens.

Northeast of the temple, you'll pass the foundation of the **7 Stoa of Zeus Eleutherios**, one of the places where Socrates expounded his philosophy.

ATHENS WITH CHILDREN

Athens is short on playgrounds, but between ice cream and street musicians and stray cats, there's plenty to keep kids amused. It helps too that children are welcome everywhere; at casual restaurants they're often encouraged to run off and play together while the adults eat.

The shady National Garden (p70) has a playground, duck pond and small (if somewhat dismal) zoo; immediately south, Zappeion (Map p110; Leoforos Vasilissis Amalias; Ⓜ Syntagma) FREE also has an enclosed, shaded playground. Beside the coast there are much bigger facilities at Stavros Niarchos Park (p114) and Flisvos Park (☑ 210 988 5140; https://parkoflisvos.gr; Palaio Faliro; ⊙ 24hr; ⚡; ☐ Parko Flisvou) FREE.

The Museum of Greek Children's Art (Map p86; ☑ 210 331 2621; www.childrens artmuseum.gr; Kodrou 9, Plaka; €3; ⊙ 10am-2pm Tue-Sat, 11am-2pm Sun; Ⓜ Syntagma) has a room set aside where children can learn about modern Greece. The Hellenic Children's Museum (Map p110; ☑ 210 331 2995; www.hcm.gr; Leoforos Vasileos Georgiou B 17-19, Athens Conservatoire; ⊙ 11am-7pm Wed, to 3pm Thu-Sun; ⚡; Ⓜ Evangelismos) FREE is a good place to meet Greek kids. Older children may like the War Museum (p95), where they can climb into the cockpit of a WWII plane and other aircraft.

Younger children may enjoy Greece's traditional shadow-puppet tradition. Shows are in Greek, but are slapstick, with lots of music. In summer, visit Theatro Skion Tasou Konsta (☑ 210 322 7507; www.fkt.gr; Flisvos Park, Palaio Faliro; €3.50; ⊙ 8.30pm Fri-Sun Jun-Sep; ⚡; ☐ Park Flisvou); in winter, check the Melina Merkouri Cultural Centre (p67).

with faux-Kufic Arabic brick decoration, in vogue at the time among Byzantine artisans.

Church of Agia Ekaterini   CHURCH
(Map p86; Lysikratous 3, Plaka; ⊙ 8am-2pm Mon-Fri, to noon Sat, 7.30am-11pm Sun; Ⓜ Akropoli) One of the few very old Byzantine churches that are open regularly, this is definitely worth a peek inside to see how an 11th-century space is still in vibrant use and adorned with bright frescoes. For a time it was the property of the Monastery of St Catherine in the Sinai Peninsula, which is how it took on that saint's name. In the front yard are some Roman ruins.

◉ Monastiraki & Psyrri

★ Roman Agora   HISTORIC SITE
(Map p86; ☑ 210 324 5220; http://odysseus. culture.gr; Dioskouron, Monastiraki; adult/student/ child €6/3/free; ⊙ 8am-3pm Mon-Fri, to 5pm Sat & Sun, mosque from 10am; Ⓜ Monastiraki) This was the city's market area under Roman rule, and it occupied a much larger area than the current site borders. You can see a lot from outside the fence, but it's worth going in for a closer look at the well-preserved Gate of Athena Archegetis, the propylaeum (entrance gate) to the market, as well as an Ottoman mosque and the ingenious and beautiful Tower of the Winds (Map p86;), on the east side of the site.

The gate, formed by four Doric columns, was financed by Julius Caesar and erected sometime during 10 BCE. To the right of the entry, look also for the outlines of what was a 68-seat public latrine. Squatting atop one wing of the *agora* is the 17th-century Fethiye Mosque, now restored and housing temporary exhibitions. The mosque's interior frescoes have been lost – except for a tiny patch high on the back wall.

Admission to the site is included with the Acropolis combo ticket (€30), which permits entry to the Acropolis and six other sites (including this one) within five days.

Museum Alex Mylona   MUSEUM
(Map p96; ☑ 210 321 5717; http://mouseioalex mylona.blogspot.com; Plateia Agion Asomaton 5, Psyrri; adult/concession €4/2; ⊙ 11am-7pm Tue, Wed, Fri & Sat, to 10pm Thu, to 4pm Sun; Ⓜ Thissio, Monastiraki) The permanent collection here is superminimalist sculpture and paintings by Athenian grande dame Alex Mylona, who died in 2016. The creatively refurbished mansion also hosts contemporary shows, and often includes dynamic video and sculpture by Alex's daughter, Eleni. Make sure you go up to the roof for a great view of the area. Entrance is on Lepeniotou.

Church of Agios Eleftherios   CHURCH
(Little Metropolis; Map p86; Plateia Mitropoleos, Monastiraki; Ⓜ Monastiraki) This 12th-century

Syntagma, Plaka & Monastiraki

Sarri
Nika
Agion Anargyron
Aristofanous
Eshylou
Vyssis
Nikiou
Osygou
Agatharchou
Taki
Plateia
Iroön
Pallados
Plateia
Karamanou
56
Agathonos
Vasilikis
Limbona
Leokoriou
Lepeniotou
Mikonos
Protogenous
Athinas
Voreou
60
47
Ivis
Navarhou Apostoli
Esopou
Hristokopidou
PSYRRI
Miaouli
Agias Eleousis
Avramiotou
40
Karori
Eolou
78
Aviiton
Karaiskaki
Pittaki
Agias Theklas
80
Plateia
Agia Irini
Arionos
Agias Irinis
79
Ermou
Agion Apostoli
Ermou
59
97
Thisiou
Astingos
Plateia
Avyssinias
68
TAF
Ermou
Adrianou
53
99
75
8
Plateia
Monastikiou
Plateia
Dimopratiriou
57
103
100
Ifestou
95
91
98
Kynetou
Nisou
Monastiraki
26
Pandrosou
Adrianou
22
34
2
Ancient
Agora
11
MONASTIRAKI
Eolou
Kapnikareas
Hristopoulou
Vrysakiou
Kladou
Areos
Dexippou
Adrianou
Kalogrioni
Plateia Arhaia
Agoras
Peikilis
Epaminonda
Pelopida
Museum of Greek
Popular Instruments
4
7
Roman Agora
36
Polygnotou
Markou Aureliou
Kyrristou
15
Mnisikleous
Dioskouron
Panos
Mitroou
28
Tholou
Lyssiou
Thrasyvoulou
82
Erotokri
Aretousas
Klepsydras
Theorias
18
24
Prytaniou
Areopagus
Hill
12
13
Theorias
ANAFIOTIKA
21
16
31
1
Acropolis
33
6
Parthenon
10
Odeon of
Herodes Atticus
5
32
Apostolou Pavlou
35
Dionysiou Areopagitou
Filopappou
Hill
Rovertou Galli

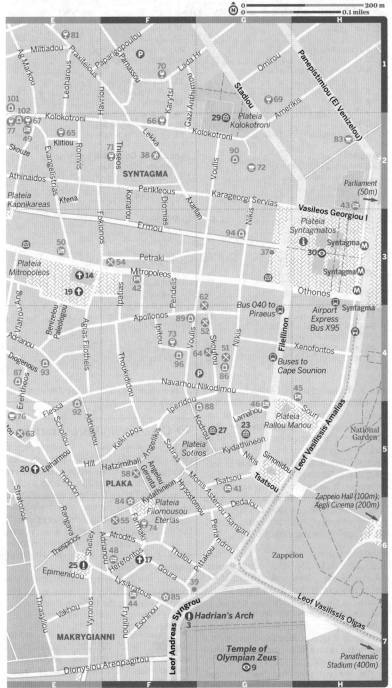

Syntagma, Plaka & Monastiraki

◉ Top Sights

◉ Sights

◉ Activities, Courses & Tours

◉ Sleeping

◉ Eating

church, dedicated to both Agios Eleftherios and Panagia Gorgoepikoos (Virgin Swift to Hear), is Athens' religious history in one tiny building. The cruciform-style marble church was erected on the ruins of an ancient temple and its exterior is a mix of medieval beasts and ancient gods in bas-relief, and columns appropriated from older structures. It was once the city's cathedral, but now stands in the shadows of the much larger new cathedral (Map p86; ☏210 322 1308; http://iaath.gr; Plateia Mitropoleos, Monastiraki; ☉7am-7pm; Ⓜ Monastiraki).

Hadrian's Library   RUINS
(Map p86; ☏210 324 9350; http://odysseus. culture.gr; Areos 3, Monastiraki; adult/child €4/ free; ☉8am-3pm; Ⓜ Monastiraki) These are the remains of the largest structure erected by Hadrian (2nd century CE). Not just a library, it also held music and lecture rooms. It was laid out as a typical Roman forum, with a pool in the centre of a courtyard bordered by 100 columns. The library's west wall, by the site entrance, has been restored. Beyond are only traces of the library, as well

as two churches, built in the 7th and 12th centuries.

◉ Gazi, Keramikos & Exarhia

★ **Kerameikos**   HISTORIC SITE
(Map p102; ☏210 346 3552; http://odysseus. culture.gr; Ermou 148, Keramikos; adult/child incl museum €8/free; ☉8am-8pm, reduced hours in low season; Ⓜ Thissio) This lush, tranquil site is named for the potters who settled it around 3000 BCE. It was used as a cemetery through the 6th century CE. The grave markers give a sense of ancient life; numerous marble *stelae* (grave markers) are carved with vivid portraits and familiar scenes.

The site was uncovered in 1861 during the construction of Pireos St; it once sat on the clay-rich banks of the Iridanos River.

There's an excellent small museum here.

★ **Museum of Islamic Art**   MUSEUM
(Map p102; ☏210 325 1311; www.benaki.org; Agion Asomaton 22, Keramikos; adult/student/ child €9/7/free; ☉10am-6pm Thu-Sun; Ⓜ Thissio) While not particularly large, this museum

houses a significant collection of Islamic art. Four floors of a mansion display, in ascending chronological order, exceptionally beautiful weaving, jewellery, porcelain and even a marble-floored reception room from a 17th-century Cairo mansion. Informative signage provides the detail on what you're seeing. In the basement, part of Athens' ancient Themistoklean wall is exposed. The rooftop cafe, with a great view of Keramikos, has a lovely mural: *Imagine a Palm Tree* by Narvine G Khan-Dossos.

Benaki Museum at 138 Pireos St MUSEUM
(Map p102; ☑ 210 345 3111; www.benaki.org; Pireos 138, Rouf; adult/concession from €6/3; ⊙ 10am-6pm Thu & Sun, until 10pm Fri & Sat, closed Aug; Ⓜ Kerameikos) While the main Benaki Museum of Greek Culture (p94) displays the classical and traditional, this annexe focuses on modern and inventive. Apart from a few canvases by contemporary painters that are portraits of founder Antonis Benakis, there are no permanent exhibitions here, rather several rotating temporary exhibits, which can be excellent. Also check

the schedule of musical performances in its atrium courtyard. It has a pleasant cafe and an excellent gift shop.

Industrial Gas Museum NOTABLE BUILDING
(Technopolis; Map p102; ☑ 210 347 5535; https://gasmuseum.gr; Pireos 100, Gazi; adult/child €1/free; ⊙ 10am-8pm Tue, Wed, Fri & Sat, to 9pm Thu & Sun mid-Oct–mid-Apr, to 6pm Tue, Wed, Fri & Sat, to 9pm Thu & Sun mid-Apr–mid-Oct; Ⓜ Kerameikos) It's fascinating to follow the walking route that runs through the old gasworks (Map p102; ☑ 210 346 7322; www.technopolis-athens.com; Pireos 100, Gazi; Ⓜ Kerameikos) in Gazi, in operation from 1862 until 1984. The preserved complex of furnaces and industrial buildings from the mid-19th century appear like giant art installations. Photos and interactive elements provide an idea of what the works were like when in operation. Make sure you go up the watchtower of the New Watergas building for a panoramic city view.

There's is also a pleasant cafe on-site as well as a kids' playground.

Note that the site is often used for music and other events.

 TOP SIGHT
NATIONAL ARCHAEOLOGICAL MUSEUM

The National Archaeological Museum houses the world's finest collection of Greek antiquities. The enormous 19th-century neoclassical building holds room upon room filled with more than 10,000 examples of sculpture, pottery, jewellery, frescoes and more. You simply can't appreciate it all in one go – but whatever you do lay eyes on will be a treat.

Prehistoric Collection & Mycenaen Antiquities

Directly ahead as you enter the museum is the prehistoric collection, showcasing some of the most important pieces of Mycenaean, Neolithic and Cycladic art, many in solid gold. The fabulous collection of Mycenaean antiquities (gallery 4) is the museum's tour de force.

A highlight is the great death mask of beaten gold is commonly known as the Mask of Agamemnon (pictured), the king who, according to legend, attacked Troy in the 12th century BCE – but this is hardly certain. Heinrich Schliemann, the archaeologist who set to prove that Homer's epics were true tales, and not just myth, unearthed the mask at Mycenae in 1876. But now some archaeologists have found the surrounding grave items date from centuries earlier. And one researcher even asserts that Schliemann, a master of self-promotion, forged it completely.

The exquisite Vaphio gold cups, showing scenes of men taming wild bulls, are regarded as among the finest surviving examples of Mycenaean art. They were found in a tholos (Mycenaean tomb shaped like a beehive) at Vaphio, near Sparta.

DON'T MISS

➡ Mask of Agamemnon
➡ Vaphio gold cups
➡ Sounion Kouros
➡ Artemision Bronze
➡ Varvakeion Athena
➡ Artemision Jockey
➡ Antikythera Mechanism

PRACTICALITIES

➡ Map p96
➡ 213 214 4800
➡ www.namuseum.gr
➡ Patision 44, Exarhia
➡ adult/child €10/free mid-Apr–Oct; €5/free Nov–mid-Apr
➡ ⊗ 8am-8pm Wed-Mon, 12.30pm-8pm Tue mid-Apr–Oct, reduced hours Nov–mid-Apr
➡ 🚊 2, 3, 4, 5 or 11 to Polytechneio, Ⓜ Viktoria

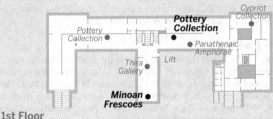

1st Floor

Pottery Collection

Pottery Collection

Thira Gallery

Lift

Minoan Frescoes

Panathenaic Amphorae

Cypriot Collection

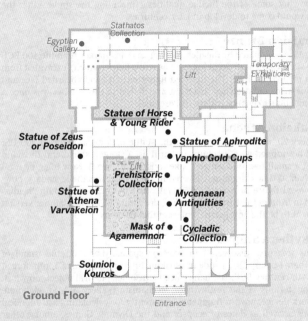

Ground Floor

Stathatos Collection

Egyptian Gallery

Lift

Temporary Exhibitions

Statue of Horse & Young Rider

Statue of Zeus or Poseidon

Statue of Aphrodite

Vaphio Gold Cups

Prehistoric Collection

Lift

Mycenaean Antiquities

Statue of Athena Varvakeion

Mask of Agamemnon

Cycladic Collection

Sounion Kouros

Entrance

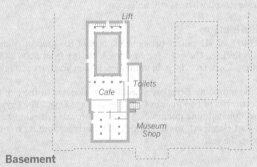

Basement

Lift

Toilets

Cafe

Museum Shop

Cycladic Collection

Gallery 6 contains some of the superbly minimalist marble figurines of the 3rd and 2nd millennia BCE that inspired artists such as Picasso. One splendid example measures 1.52m and dates from 2600 to 2300 BCE.

Sounion Kouros

The galleries to the left of the entrance house the oldest and most significant pieces of the sculpture collection. Galleries 7 to 13 exhibit fine examples of Archaic *kouroi* (male statues) from the 7th century BCE to 480 BCE. The best by far is the colossal 600 BCE Sounion Kouros (room 8), which stood before the Temple of Poseidon at Cape Sounion (p141). Its style marks a transition point in art history, starting with the rigid lines of older Egyptian carving but also showing some of the lifelike qualities – including the smile – that the Greeks would come to develop in later centuries.

Artemision Bronze

Gallery 15 is dominated by the incredibly precise, just-larger-than-life 460 BCE bronze statue of Zeus or Poseidon (no one really knows which), excavated from the sea off Evia in 1928. The muscled figure has an iconic bearded face and holds his arms outstretched, his right arm raised to throw what was once a lightning bolt (if Zeus) or trident (if Poseidon).

Varvakeion Athena

In Gallery 20, admire the details on the statue of Athena, made in 200 CE: the helmet topped with a sphinx and griffins, a Gorgon shield and the hand holding a small figure of winged Nike (missing its head). Now imagine it all more than 10 times larger and covered in gold – that was the legendary, now-lost colossal figure of Athena (11.5m tall) that the master sculptor Pheidias erected in front of the Parthenon in the 5th century BCE. This daintier version is thought to be the best extant replica of that colossus.

Antikythera Shipwreck

Precious treasures discovered in 1900 by sponge divers off the island of Antikythera (gallery 28) include the striking bronze Antikythera Youth, forged in the 4th century BCE. His hand once held some spherical object, now lost. More mysterious is the Antikythera Mechanism (gallery 38), an elaborate clockwork device, now in fragments, apparently for calculating astronomical positions as well as dates of eclipses and the Olympic Games, among other events. Who made it, and when, is still unknown.

Egyptian Collection

The two-room (40 and 41) gallery presents the best of the museum's significant Egyptian collection, the only one in Greece. Dating from 5000 BCE to the Roman conquest, artefacts include mummies, Fayum portraits and bronze figurines.

The bulk of the museum's Egyptian collection was donated in the late 19th and early 20th centuries by two wealthy Greek residents of Egypt. The Egyptian government also donated nine mummies. The relics provide critical historical context for Ancient Greek art, some of which took early inspiration from the culture just across the sea.

ATHENS & AROUND NATIONAL ARCHAEOLOGICAL MUSEUM

Attic black-figured pottery

Pottery Collection

The superb pottery collection (galleries 49 to 56) traces the development of ceramics from the Bronze Age through the Protogeometric and Geometric periods, to the famous Attic black-figured pottery (6th century BCE), and red-figured pottery (late 5th to early 4th centuries BCE). Other uniquely Athenian vessels are the Attic White Lekythoi, slender vases depicting scenes at tombs.

In the centre of gallery 56 are ceramic vases presented to the winners of the Panathenaic Games. Each one contained oil from the sacred olive trees of Athens; victors might have received up to 140 of them. The vases are painted with scenes from the relevant sport (wrestling, in this case) on one side and an armed Athena *promachos* (leading warrior) on the other.

Jockey of Artemision

In Gallery 21 is a find from the shipwreck off Evia excavated in 1928. This delicately rendered bronze horse and rider dates from the 2nd century BCE; only a few parts were found at first, and it was finally reassembled in 1972. Opposite the horse are several lesser-known but equally exquisite works, such as the statue of Aphrodite showing the demure nude goddess struggling to hold her draped gown over herself.

TOP TIPS

➡ A joint museum ticket is available for €15 (€8 for students), valid for three days here and at the neighbouring Epigraphical Museum, plus the Byzantine & Christian Museum and the Numismatic Museum.

➡ Arrive early in the day to beat the rush. If you come after tour groups are moving through, head upstairs first.

➡ Allow a few hours, and maybe more if you have a special interest.

➡ Entrance is free on 6 March, 18 April, 18 May, the last weekend of September, 28 October, and the first Sunday of the month from 1 November to 31 March.

MUSEUM CAFE

The self-service museum cafe, serving drinks, sandwiches and cakes, is in the basement and has seating in a lovely open-air internal courtyard with a garden and sculptures.

THE BUILDING

The museum was built between 1866 and 1889, with a facade designed by Ernst Ziller. The east wing was expanded during the 20th century. In total there's around 8000 sq metres of floor space.

⊙ Kolonaki, Mets & Pangrati

★ Benaki Museum of Greek Culture
MUSEUM

(Map p110; ☑210 367 1000; www.benaki.org; Koumbari 1, cnr Leoforos Vasilissis Sofias, Kolonaki; adult/student/child €9/7/free, 6pm-midnight Thu free; ⊙10am-6pm Mon, Wed, Fri & Sat, to midnight Thu, to 4pm Sun; Ⓜ Syntagma, Evangelismos) In 1930 Antonis Benakis – a politician's son born in Alexandria, Egypt, in the late 19th century – endowed what is perhaps the finest museum in Greece. Its three floors showcase impeccable treasures from the Bronze Age up to WWII. Especially gorgeous are the Byzantine icons and the extensive collection of Greek regional costumes, as well as complete sitting rooms from Macedonian mansions, intricately carved and painted. Benakis had such a good eye that even the agricultural tools are beautiful.

★ Byzantine & Christian Museum
MUSEUM

(Map p110; ☑213 213 9500; www.byzantine museum.gr; Leoforos Vasilissis Sofias 22, Kolonaki; adult/student/child €8/4/free; ⊙12.30-8pm Tue, from 8am Wed-Sun Apr-Oct, reduced hours Nov-Mar; Ⓜ Evangelismos) This outstanding museum, based in the 1848 Villa Ilissia, offers exhibition halls, most of them underground, crammed with religious art. The exhibits go chronologically, charting the gradual and fascinating shift from ancient traditions to Christian ones, and the flourishing of a distinctive Byzantine style. Of course there are icons, but also delicate frescoes (some salvaged from a church and installed on floating panels) and more personal remnants of daily life.

★ Museum of Cycladic Art
MUSEUM

(Map p110; ☑210 722 8321; https://cycladic. gr; Neofytou Douka 4, Kolonaki; adult/child €7/free, Mon €3.50, special exhibits €10; ⊙10am-5pm Mon, Wed, Fri & Sat, to 8pm Thu, 11am-5pm Sun;

FROM GRAFFITI TO STREET ART

The one thing you cannot miss in Athens, apart from the Acropolis, is how much graffiti there is across the city. It's not just walls that are blighted by tagging and general spray-paint scribbling, but practically any part of the urban fabric from trains to park benches. There's an age-old tradition to all this; the word 'graffiti' comes from the Ancient Greek word '*graphi*' meaning 'to write'.

The 2008 financial crisis was a particular spur to people venting their economic and political frustrations in spray-paint slogans and images. Recently, though, there has been a civic effort to work more creatively with street artists, so as to add some beauty and form to the general visual chaos. Projects such as Urban Act (https://urbanact.gr) have bequeathed Athens some giant and very impressive murals.

Particularly notable are the murals by INO (http://ino.net), who can be recognised by his trademark monotone paintings with splashes of vivid light blue. One of his most impressive creations, on the Pireos side of the Old OSY Depot (Map p102; www. osy.gr/ethelsite/pages/gazi_amax.php; Ermou, Keramikos; Ⓜ Keramikos), is a homage to famous Leonardo da Vinci images: take note of the rioter and policeman reflected in the Mona Lisa's eyes.

Manolis Anastasakos and Pavlos Tsakonas, along with students from the Athens School of Fine Arts (ASKT), are responsible for the giant Praying Hands Mural (Map p96; Pireos 20, Omonia; Ⓜ Omonia). Inspired by Albrecht Dürer's image, the hands have been inverted so that it appears that it is the Lord praying for the people rather than the other way around.

Exarhia is so plastered with graffiti that spotting the better pieces of street art can be a challenge. Standing out is the splendidly executed mural No Land For the Poor (Map p96; http://wdstreetart.com; Emmanuel Benaki 84, Exarhia; Ⓜ Omonia) of a sleeping homeless man, by Indonesian-born and Athens-based artist Wild Drawing. See the map on his website for the locations of more of his works around the city.

If you'd like to discover more prime pieces of street art, Alternative Athens (☑211 012 6544; www.alternativeathens.com; tours from €40) offers an excellent themed walking tour.

DON'T MISS

PARLIAMENT & THE CHANGING OF THE PRESIDENTIAL GUARD

Designed by Bavarian architect Friedrich von Gärtner, Greece's Parliament (Map p110; www.hellenicparliament.gr; Plateia Syntagmatos, Syntagma; ☉ tours 3pm Mon & Fri Jun, Jul & Sep; M Syntagma) FREE was originally the royal palace. From its balcony, the *syntagma* (constitution) was declared on 3 September 1843, and in 1935 the palace became the seat of parliament. For history and politics geeks, the building is open by guided tour a few months of the year; book at least five days ahead.

In front of Parliament, the traditionally costumed *evzones* (presidential guards) stand by the tomb and change every hour on the hour. On Sunday at 11am, a whole platoon marches down Vasilissis Sofias to the tomb, accompanied by a band. The *evzones* uniform of the *fustanella* (white skirt) and pom-pom shoes is based on the attire worn by the klephts, the mountain fighters of the War of Independence.

You can also see *evzones* outside the Presidential Guard (Map p110; 10 Irodou Attikou, Syntagma; M Syntagma) and nearby Presidential Palace. It's interesting to see them here, alone and away from tourist cameras, going through their ritual pomp even in the dead of night.

M Evangelismos) The 1st floor of this exceptional private museum is dedicated to the iconic minimalist marble Cycladic figurines, dating from 3000 BCE to 2000 BCE. They inspired many 20th-century artists, such as Picasso and Modigliani, with their simplicity and purity of form. Most are surprisingly small, considering their outsize influence, though one is almost human size. The rest of the museum features Greek and Cypriot art dating from 2000 BCE to the 4th century CE.

Lykavittos Hill   LANDMARK
(Map p68; www.lycabettushill.com; M Evangelismos) The 277m summit of Lykavittos – 'Hill of Wolves', from ancient times, when it was wilder than it is now – gives the finest panoramas of the city and the Attic basin, *nefos* (pollution haze) permitting. Perched on the summit is the little Chapel of Agios Georgios (Map p68), floodlit like a beacon over the city at night. Walk up the path from the top of Loukianou in Kolonaki, or take the 10-minute funicular railway (p132) from the top of Ploutarhou.

★ **Basil & Elise**
Goulandris Foundation   MUSEUM
(Map p110; ☎ 210 725 2895; https://goulandris.gr; Eratosthenous 13, Pangrati; M Akropoli) Opened in October 2019, this new museum showcases the collection of modern and contemporary artworks belonging to shipping magnate Basil Goulandris and his wife Elise. Alongside pieces from the likes of top European artists including Cézanne, Van Gogh, Picasso and Giacometti are works from pioneering Greek painters such as Parthenis,

Vasiliou, Hadjikyriakos-Ghikas, Tsarouchis and Moralis.

★ **Panathenaic Stadium**   HISTORIC SITE
(Kallimarmaro; Map p110; ☎ 210 752 2985; www.panathenaicstadium.gr; Leoforos Vasileos Konstantinou, Pangrati; adult/student/child €5/2.50/free; ☉ 8am-7pm Mar-Oct, to 5pm Nov-Feb; ☐ 2, 4, 10, 11 to Stadio, M Akropoli, ☐ Zappeio) With its serried rows of white Pentelic marble seats built into a ravine next to Ardettos Hill, this ancient-turned-modern stadium is a draw both for lovers of classical architecture and sports fans who can imagine the roar of the crowds from millennia past. A ticket gets you an audio tour, admission to a tiny exhibit on the modern Olympics (mainly eye-candy games posters) and the opportunity to take your photo on a winners' pedestal.

Numismatic Museum   MUSEUM
(Map p110; ☎ 210 363 2057; www.nummus.gr; Panepistimiou 12, Kolonaki; adult/student €6/3; ☉ 8.30am-3.30pm Tue-Sun; M Panepistimio, Syntagma) The collection of coins here, dating from ancient through to modern times, is excellent, but of more general interest is the dazzling 1881 mansion in which it's housed. Built by architect Ernst Ziller, it was the home of Heinrich Schliemann, the archaeologist who excavated Troy; fittingly, its mosaic floors and painted walls and ceilings are covered in classical motifs.

War Museum   MUSEUM
(Map p110; ☎ 210 725 2975; www.warmuseum.gr; Rizari 2, cnr Leoforos Vasilissis Sofias, Kolonaki; adult/child €4/2; ☉ 9am-7pm Apr-Oct, to 5pm

Psyrri & Exarhia

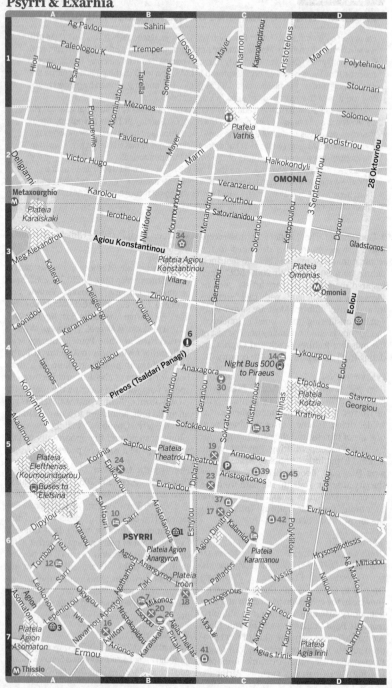

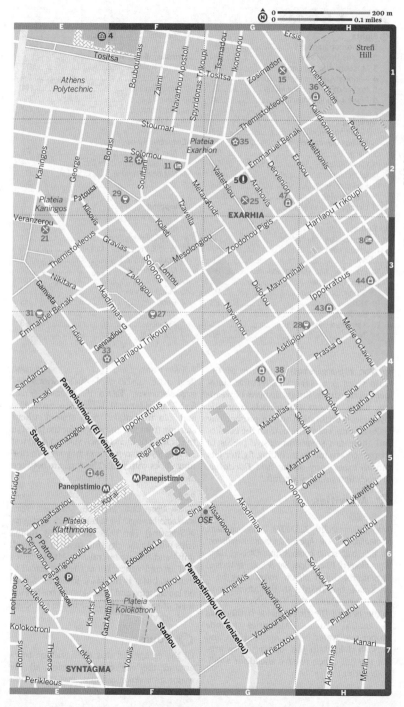

Psyrri & Exarhia

Nov-Mar; Ⓜ Evangelismos) This relic of the junta years is a stark architectural statement of the times. But its displays of weapons, maps, armour and models from the Mycenaean civilisation to the present day make an interesting break from the classics and there are some impressive pieces of kit parked around it, including fighter jets and an exact copy of the 1912 *Daedalus,* Greece's first military aircraft.

🏃 Activities

Hammam SPA
(Map p102; ☑210 323 1073; www.hammam. gr; Melidoni 1, cnr Agion Asomaton, Keramikos; 1hr €25, bath-scrub combos from €45; ⊘11am-10pm Mon-Fri, 10am-10pm Sat & Sun; Ⓜ Thissio) The marble-lined steam room may be a bit small, but thanks to the attention to detail throughout, this Turkish-style place is the best of the three major bathhouses in central Athens. Amenities include proper-size water bowls, and hot tea and Turkish delight in the lounge afterwards. For the full effect, reserve ahead for a full-body scrub.

Adidas Runbase RUNNING
(Map p80; ☑210 924 4073; www.adidas. gr/adidasrunners; Falirou 16, Koukaki; ⊘runs 6am-9pm; Ⓜ Akropoli) **FREE** Sign up online and join free guided runs around Athens starting from this showroom for the latest in the brand's trainers (which you can road test for free if you haven't brought your own running shoes with you). The runs are between 5km and 6km.

EOS HIKING
(Greek Alpine Club; Map p86; ☑210 321 3255; www.eosathinon.gr; 1st fl, Lekka 23-25, Syntagma; Ⓜ Syntagma) The EOS runs weekly hiking trips outside the city (information in Greek only) and maintains trails on Mt Hymettos and around Attica. It's not really geared to tourists, but it is the place to ask for advice on longer trips and lesser-known trails. Find their office on the 1st floor inside the shopping arcade.

☞ Tours

Of the companies that offer walking tours around the city centre, passing all the major archaeological sites, one of the best organised, and least expensive, is Athens

Adventures (Map p80; ☑210 922 4044; www.athensadventures.gr; Veïkou 3a, Makrygianni; Ⓜ Akropoli); Athens Walking Tours (☑6945859662, 210 884 7269; www.athens walkingtours.gr) is another long-established company. To do a similar route by bike, try Roll in Athens (Map p86; ☑6974231611; www.rollinathens.tours; Voreou 10, Monastiraki; half-day tours €40; Ⓜ Monastiraki) or, for the ease of an e-bike, Solebike (Map p80; ☑210 921 5620; www.solebike.eu; Lembesi 11, Makrygianni; 2hr/1 day €28/36; ☺9.30am-2.30pm & 4.30-8.30pm Mon-Fri, 9.30am-4.30pm Sat Apr-Oct, shorter hours Nov-Mar; Ⓜ Akropoli).

If you prefer to sit and not exert yourself at all, hop on the Athens Happy Train (Map p86; ☑213 039 0888; www.athenshappytrain. com; Plateia Syntagmatos, Syntagma; adult/child €5/3; ☺9am-11pm Jun-Sep, to 9pm Oct-May; Ⓜ Syntagma). You won't score cool points, but it's inexpensive and covers a useful loop, with on-and-off privileges.

The cushiest option is a city coach tour (from €78), but like the Happy Train, these are light on guiding (aside from an Acropolis visit) and more a way to get oriented in air-conditioned comfort. This is also an easy way to see major sights outside the city, such as Cape Sounion (€49), Delphi (€93), and Nafplio and Epidavros (€100). CHAT (☑210 323 0827; www.chat-tours.com; walking/ bus tour from €39/55), GO Tours (☑210 921 9555; www.gotours.com.gr; tours from €38) and Hop In Sightseeing (Map p86; ☑210 428 5500; www.hopin.com; Leoforos Vasilissis Amalias 44, Plaka; ☺6.30am-10pm; Ⓜ Akropoli) are the main operators, and they also run package boat trips to nearby islands.

This Is My Athens (http://myathens. thisisathens.org) is an excellent city-run program that pairs you with a volunteer local to show you around for two hours. You must book online 72 hours ahead.

Trekking Hellas
OUTDOORS

(☑210 331 0323; www.trekking.gr; Gounari 96, Marousi) Lovers of the outdoors can head out of Athens for action in the Attica region, including rock climbing and canyoning on Mt Parnitha. The guides are experienced and reliable, and offer activities for children too.

Pyrgos Vasilissis Winery
WINE

(Map p140; ☑210 231 3607; www.pyrgosvasilissis. gr; 67 Dimokratias Ave, Ilion; adult/child €27/13.50; ☺by appointment) Crops were first planted at this winery back in the 1850s. The stately property offers organic wines and one- to two-hour tours around the castle tower, vineyards, stables, gardens and the winery itself; the tour concludes with wine tasting. Reserve in advance.

For more information on the region's wineries, see www.winesofathens.com, which has a downloadable map. Cycle Greece (☑210 921 8160; www.cyclegreece.com) runs day-trip bike rides to some regional wineries.

JEWISH ATHENS

The Jewish community of Athens numbers nearly 3000 today but its roots go back thousands of years, perhaps even to before the 5th century BCE: some archaeologists believe there was a synagogue in Ancient Agora (p82). You can find out about the community's history at the Jewish Museum (Map p86; ☑210 322 5582; www.jewishmuseum.gr; Nikis 39, Plaka; adult/student/child €6/3/free; ☺9am-2.30pm Mon-Fri, 10am-2pm Sun; Ⓜ Syntagma), beginning with the Romaniotes of the 3rd century BCE, through to the arrival of Sephardic Jews in the 15th century and beyond the Holocaust.

There are two synagogues in Athens – the small Ets Hayim (Map p102; ☑210 325 2875; https://athjcom.gr; Melidoni 8, Keramikos; ☺8.30am-1.30pm Mon-Fri by appointment only; Ⓜ Thissio) FREE, a Romaniote synagogue built in 1904, and the larger Beth Shalom (Map p102; ☑210 325 2875; https://athjcom.gr; Melidoni 5, Keramikos; ☺8.30am-1.30pm Mon-Fri by appointment only; Ⓜ Thissio) FREE, dating from 1935; they stand opposite each other. A fascinating tour of the synagogues is by appointment only: send an email with a photocopy of your passport to sec@athjcom.gr.

Outside Beth Shalom look for the metal book memorial to the Righteous Gentiles – Greeks who helped save Jews during the Nazi German occupation of WWII. Nearby, shaded by trees next to Keramikos, is the city's Holocaust Memorial (Map p102; cnr Melidoni, Ermou & Evvoulou, Keramikos; Ⓜ Thissio), a Star of David made of large sculpted fragments of marble. Finish your tour of Jewish Athens with a hearty meal at the good kosher restaurant Gostijo (p115), part of the city's Chabbad centre.

✨ Festivals & Events

Athens & Epidaurus Festival
PERFORMING ARTS

(Hellenic Festival; ☎210 928 2900; www.greek festival.gr; ☉Jun-Aug) The ancient Theatre of Epidavros (p156) and Athens' Odeon of Herodes Atticus (p75) are the headline venues for Greece's annual cultural festival, running since 1955 and featuring a top line-up of local and international music, dance and theatre.

August Moon Festival
PERFORMING ARTS

(☉Aug) A reward for enduring the hottest month in Athens: on the night of the full moon, major historical sites such as the Acropolis (p72) and the Roman Agora (p85) are open all night and host musical performances.

Athens International Film Festival
FILM

(☎210 606 1413; www.aiff.gr; ☉Sep) Features retrospectives, premieres and international art films and documentaries.

Athens Pride
PARADE

(☎697 418 7383; www.athenspride.eu; ☉early Jun) Athens Pride is an annual LGBTQ event, usually celebrated in early June, culminating in a parade that usually starts on Syntagma.

Athens Biennale
ART

(☎210 523 2222; http://athensbiennale.org; ☉Oct-Dec) Every odd-numbered year, the Athens Biennale showcases top local and international artists across a range of media and locations around the capital.

Athens Technopolis Jazz Festival
MUSIC

(☎213 010 9300; www.technopolisjazzfestival.com; ☉late May-early Jun) Week-long early-summer jazz festival at Technopolis (p89), the converted gasworks in Gazi, as well as at the Onassis Cultural Centre (p124).

Athens Street Food Festival
FOOD & DRINK

(☎210 963 6489; https://athensstreetfoodfestival. gr; ☉May) Athenians have embraced this event with gusto since the first one in 2016. Over three weekends, the former tram depot next to the Kerameikos (p88) archaeological site is crammed with every delicious snack the capital has to offer. A great place to sample both traditional and supercreative parts of the food scene.

🏃 City Walk
Central Athens

START PLATEIA SYNTAGMATOS
END MONASTIRAKI FLEA MARKET
LENGTH 3.5KM; TWO HOURS

Start in ❶ **Plateia Syntagmatos** (p81). The square has been a favourite place for protests ever since the rally that led to the granting of a constitution on 3 September 1843. In 1944 the first round of the civil war began here after police, under British direction, opened fire on a communist rally.

The historical ❷ **Grande Bretagne** (p105), the most illustrious of Athens' hotels, was built in 1862. During WWII, the Nazis made it their headquarters; the British moved in afterwards. Resistance fighters laid dynamite to blow up the entire building but the operation was halted when Winston Churchill arrived unexpectedly; the fighters weren't willing to assassinate him. On the north side of the square is a section of the ❸ **Peisistratos aqueduct**, which was unearthed during metro excavations. Across the road, in front of ❹ **Parliament** (p95), the much-photographed *evzones* (presidential guards) stand sentinel at the ❺ **Tomb of the Unknown Soldier**. The changing of the guard takes place every hour on the hour.

Walk through the lush ❻ **National Garden** (p70) and exit to the ❼ **Zappeio Hall** (www.zappeion.gr), opened in 1888 in preparation for the first modern Olympic Games in 1896, for which part was used as a fencing venue.

Walk back along the south edge of the gardens to the striking ❽ **Temple of Olympian Zeus** (p70), the remains of the largest temple ever built. Teetering on the edge of the traffic alongside the temple is ❾ **Hadrian's Arch** (p70), the ornate gateway erected to mark the boundary of Hadrian's Athens.

Cross Leoforos Vasilissis Amalias and head right towards Lysikratous, where you turn left into Plaka. Ahead on your right, below street level, is the ❿ **Church of Agia Ekaterini** (p85), with the ruins of a Roman monument in the forecourt.

Ahead on the left is the ⓫ **Lysikrates Monument**, built in 334 BCE, the only remaining example of the monuments that once lined this street to the Theatre of

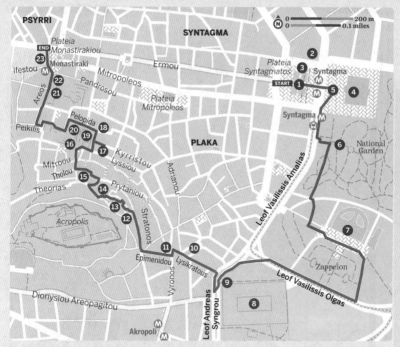

Dionysos, site of dramatic contests. The monument commemorates one chorus' victory, with reliefs showing Dionysos battling the Tyrrhenian pirates, transformed into dolphins. It's the earliest known monument using Corinthian capitals externally, a style imitated in many modern monuments. Later, the monument was made into a Capuchin convent library, where Lord Byron stayed in 1810–11 and wrote *Childe Harold*.

Facing the monument, turn left and then right into Epimenidou. At the top of the steps, turn right into Stratonos, which skirts the Acropolis. Just ahead you'll see the **12 Church of St George of the Rock**, which marks the entry to **13 Anafiotika** (p71). This picturesque maze of little whitewashed houses is the legacy of stonemasons from the Cycladic island of Anafi, who were brought in to build the king's palace after Independence in the mid-19th century. It's a peaceful spot, with brightly painted olive-oil cans brimming with flowers in the tiny gardens in summer.

Continue past the tiny **14 Church of Agios Simeon**. The street looks like a dead end but persevere and you'll emerge at the Acropolis road. Turn right, then left into Prytaniou, veering right after 50m into Tholou. The yellow-ochre building at Tholou 5 is the **15 old Athens University** (1837–41). Built by the Venetians, it was

used by the Turks as public offices; it's now a missable history museum.

Continue down to the ruins of the **16 Roman Agora** (p85). Jog right on Kyrristou to see the **17 Bath House of the Winds** (p71), a historical (but nonfunctional) Turkish *hammam*. On the next corner, Diogenous, the **18 Museum of Greek Popular Instruments** (p70) is a three-storey mansion filled with more than a thousand ways to make music. Turning on to Pelopida, skirting the edge of the Roman Agora, you'll see on the right the gate of a 1721 madrasa. It's a short walk across the road to the **19 Tower of the Winds** (p85), a classical weather station which was repurposed as a Sufi meeting house in the Ottoman period. Ahead on the left, the 17th-century **20 Fetiye Mosque** is inside the fence of the Roman Agora.

Follow the road around the *agora* to the ruins of **21 Hadrian's Library** (p88). Next to them is the 1759 **22 Mosque of Tzistarakis** (p71); after Independence it lost its minaret and was used as a prison – it is now occasionally open as a museum.

You're now in Monastiraki, the colourful, chaotic square teeming with street vendors. To the left down Ifestou is **23 Monastiraki Flea Market** (p127).

Gazi, Keramikos & Thisio

N

0   200 m
0   0.1 miles

The Breeder (200m)

Iasonos

Kolokinthous

Akadimou

Leoprion 27 26

Myllerou

Marathonos

Thermopylon

Germanikou

Keramikou

Gravias

Agisilaou

Salaminos

Plateon

Plateon

Mykalis

Leonidou

Mela Alexandrou

Paramythias

Keramikou

Plateon

KERAMIKOS

21

18 34

Ieratandon

Artemisiou

Evrymedondos

Efpatridon

Eleusinion

Enneidon

Iera Odos

25 Pireos (Tsaldari Panagi)

Plateia Eleftherias
(Koumoundourou)

Kalogirou
Samouil

Museum of
Islamic Art 2 Diplou

Agion Asomaton

Keramikos 1

Ermou

13

Technopolis

Voutadon

35

Iakhou

Eolmolpidon

Tiptolemou

Persefonis

PSYRRI

Meidani 5 4 14
4
10

Plateia Agion
Asomaton

Thisio

Plateia
Thisio

Agion Asomaton

Amfiktyonos 22 38

Poulopoulou

Akteou

Vasilis

THISIO

Eptachalkou

Fleston

Erysithonos

Dimofontos

Thessalonikis

Sikeliotou

Thisio
Park

Thessalonikis

Persefonis

11

Pireos

GAZI

Sofronion

Persefonis

Keramikos M

Dekeleon

Gargittion

Ikarieon

Zakyadon

Orfeos

Plateia
Irakildon 12

Plateia
Area

Vitonos

Evadnis

Iraklidon

Elasidon

Plateia
Koulouris

Stratoniki

Dekeleon

Ahniadon

Getyreon

Dyaleon

VOTANIKOS

Tzani

Iera Odos

Votanikos
Kipos

Kerytsas

Korytsas

Halkidikis

Pellis

Melenikon

Kastorias

Orous

Veras

Patsi Spyrou

Kassandras

Vonissou

Pydnas

Agiou Polykarpou

Amfipoleos

Edessis

Kozanis

Strymonos

Orfeos

Sperthiou

Praviou

Piniou

Rodopis

Greverion

Ag Markellas

Pangeou

Ermou

Eleo

Kadmias

Nevrokopiou

Angisis

Patsi Spyrou

Faleseis

Leof Konstantinoupoleos

Leof Konstantinoupoleos

Leof Konstantinoupoleos

Leof Konstantinoupoleos

24

33

32

20

28 Zagreos

17

Eleonas Flea
Market (1.4km)

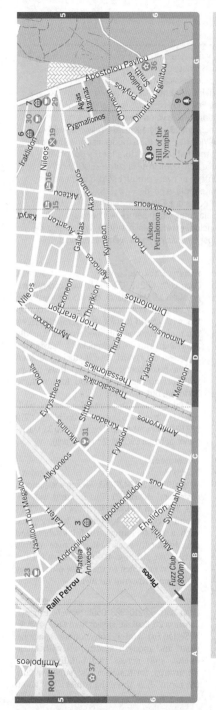

Gazi, Keramikos & Thisio

KYPSELI

Kypseli, a 15-minute walk north of Exarhia, was once one of the most desirable residential areas of Athens, on a par with Kolonaki. It's not so ritzy today, even though if you keep an eye out there's still the odd pretty neoclassical mansion or art deco block to be found among the dense streets of identikit five-storey Athens apartment blocks.

The neighbourhood's social centre is the Fokionos Negri pedestrian strip of park, lined with cafes. Here you'll find an interesting new development at the **Kypseli Municipal Market** (https://athens.impacthub.net/dimotiki-agora-kypselis; Fokionos Negri 42, Kypseli; ☉8am-8pm Mon-Fri, until 2pm Sat; Ⓜ Victoria). The 1935 modernist building now houses a range of social projects including the first physical store for the nonprofit business **Wise Greece** (www.en.wisegreece.com), which sells some 2500 good-quality food products from across the country. For every product sold, a percentage of the profit goes into a fund to buy food for people in need.

The NGO **We Need Books** (www.weneedbooks.org; Evias 7, Kypseli) has also set up nearby. This free library, play space and social integration centre has been set up to help marginalised and vulnerable people, including refugees in Athens. They welcome donations of books and they sometimes host discussions and events in English.

Rockwave Festival   MUSIC

(☎210 882 0426; www.rockwavefestival.gr; ☉Jul) Annual international rock festival (with an emphasis on metal, most years) held over several weekends at Terra Vibe, a parkland venue on the outskirts of Athens in Malakasa. Special buses run from town. Sometimes cheap camping is offered.

🛏 Sleeping

Athens' lodging covers the full range, from one- to five-star hotels plus plenty of short-term rental accommodation. In recent years there's been a mini-explosion of chic boutique developments, most with only a handful of rooms. To be sure your ideal choice is available, make bookings at least a couple of months ahead; for July and August, ideally aim for four months ahead.

🛏 Acropolis, Filopappou Hill & Thisio

Marble House Pension   PENSION €

(Map p80; ☎210 923 4058; www.marblehouse.gr; Zini 35a, Koukaki; d/tr/q from €45/55/69; ❄@☎; Ⓜ Sygrou-Fix) Tucked into a quiet cul-de-sac is one of Athens' best-value budget hotels. Rooms are well maintained, all with a fridge and a ceiling fan; some have small balconies. If you use the air-con it's €5 extra per night. It's a 15-minute walk to the Acropolis, but close to the metro. Breakfast available (€5).

Athens Backpackers   HOSTEL €

(Map p80; ☎210 922 4044; www.backpackers.gr; Makri 12, Makrygianni; dm incl breakfast from €27; ❄@☎; Ⓜ Akropoli) The popular rooftop bar with cheap drinks and Acropolis views is a major draw at this modern and friendly Australian-run backpacker favourite. There's a courtyard, a well-stocked kitchen and a busy social scene. Spotless dorms with private bathrooms and lockers have bedding, but towel use costs €1.

Management also runs the nearby, well-priced **Athens Studios** (Map p80; ☎210 923 5811; www.athensstudios.gr; Veïkou 3a, Makrygianni; apt from €90; @☎; Ⓜ Akropoli).

Chameleon Youth Hostel   HOSTEL €

(Map p102; ☎210 342 8053; www.chameleonyouth hostel.com; Nileos 25, Thisio; dm/d with private bathroom €19/40; ❄☎; Ⓜ Thissio) This friendly, colourful hostel is a homey place with a comfy lounge, useful kitchen and laundry facilities as well as a nice rooftop terrace for chilling. It's a short walk from the main entrance to the Acropolis; trendy Petralona is also not far away.

Tony   APARTMENT €

(Map p80; ☎210 923 0561; www.hoteltony.gr; Zaharitsa 26, Koukaki; studios from €65; ❄@☎; Ⓜ Sygrou-Fix) Hotel Tony offers spacious, clean and modern studios, all with kitchenette, split across two buildings. Great for groups; for instance, the 'superior family room' has three balconies. It's about

1km southwest of the Acropolis and has a great view of the monument from its roof terrace.

★ Be My Guest Athens
HOTEL €€

(Map p102; ☏ 213 044 9929; www.bemyguest athens.gr; Nileos 33, Thisio; d/tr/ste incl breakfast €102/126/150; ❄ 🛜; Ⓜ Thissio) Opened in 2017, this 14-room hotel is for those seeking calm: the minimalist monotone-and-turquoise colour scheme is soothing, and its residential location (about 15 minutes' walk to the Acropolis) is quiet. The cheapest double rooms don't have balconies, but it's not much to upgrade. The suites have kitchens, and there's a handy grocery store downstairs.

Hera Hotel
BOUTIQUE HOTEL €€

(Map p80; ☏ 210 923 6682; www.herahotel.gr; Falirou 9, Makrygianni; d/ste incl breakfast from €145/280; ❄ @ 🛜; Ⓜ Akropoli) Behind its elegant neoclassical facade, this boutique hotel has been totally rebuilt. But the formal interior design stays true to exterior style, with lots of brass and dark wood. It's a short walk to the Acropolis and Plaka. North-side rooms, away from an adjacent music bar, are preferable. The rooftop Peacock restaurant and bar have fine views and good service.

★ Athens Was
BOUTIQUE HOTEL €€€

(Map p80; ☏ 210 924 9954; www.athenswas.gr; Dionysiou Areopagitou 5, Makrygianni; d/ste incl breakfast from €390/465; ❄ @ 🛜; Ⓜ Akropoli) The location, a two-minute walk to the east gate of the Acropolis, couldn't be better. Staff are friendly, adding a warm touch to the minimalist decor, and standard rooms have big balconies overlooking the pedestrianised street. Breakfast is excellent and the terrace has a magnificent view. Suites on the 5th and 6th floors also have Acropolis views.

Herodion
HOTEL €€€

(Map p80; ☏ 210 923 6832; www.herodion.gr; Rovertou Galli 4, Makrygianni; d incl breakfast from €195; ❄ @ 🛜; Ⓜ Akropoli) At this pleasant, contemporary hotel, rooms are small but have super-comfortable beds and a not-trying-too-hard minimalist style. The roof terrace and two outdoor Jacuzzi baths have great Acropolis views.

🛏 Syntagma & Plaka

★ Phaedra
HOTEL €

(Map p86; ☏ 210 323 8461; www.hotelphaedra. com; Herefontos 16, Plaka; s/d/tr from €60/80/90; ❄ @ 🛜; Ⓜ Akropoli) Almost all the 21 rooms at this family-run hotel have balconies overlooking a church or the Acropolis. The rooms are basic and range from small to snug; a few have private bathrooms across the hall. Given the superb rooftop terrace, the friendly staff and the unbeatable location, it's one of the best deals in Plaka.

★ InnAthens
BOUTIQUE HOTEL €€

(Map p86; ☏ 210 325 8555; www.innathens. com; Souri 3, Syntagma; d incl breakfast €150; ❄ @ 🛜; Ⓜ Syntagma) This 37-room hotel is minutes from Syntagma, but you'd never know it once you're inside its cocoon, down the end of a shopping arcade. Most rooms look on to a pretty interior courtyard, and the restfulness is reinforced with soothing grey-and-white decor and excellent beds.

Home and Poetry Hotel
BOUTIQUE HOTEL €€

(Map p86; ☏ 210 322 3204; www.homeand poetry.com; Lysikratous 10, Plaka; d incl breakfast from €150; ❄ 🛜; Ⓜ Akropoli) A lovely neoclassical mansion has been converted to create this elegant and excellently located property. The 16 rooms – all with wooden floors and classical furnishings – come in a range of different sizes. A plus is the rooftop dining terrace with all-important Acropolis views.

Alice Inn
GUESTHOUSE €€

(Map p86; ☏ 210 323 7139; www.jjhospitality. net; Tsatsou 9, Plaka; d/tr/ste from €100/170/220; ❄ 🛜; Ⓜ Akropoli, Syntagma) On a blessedly quiet block, this big old town house fulfils the fantasy that you live in Athens, in old-time elegance: high ceilings, fans, marble floors, plus a shared kitchen and a comfy living room where you're welcome to crank up the gramophone. In addition to the three main suites, there is a cosy budget double.

★ Grande Bretagne
LUXURY HOTEL €€€

(Map p86; ☏ 210 333 0000; www.marriott.com; Vasileos Georgiou I 1, Syntagma; r/ste from €515/838; Ⓟ ❄ @ 🛜 ⓢ; Ⓜ Syntagma) If you aspire to the best, *the* most prestigious place to stay in Athens is – and always has been – the Grande Bretagne, right on Syntagma Sq. Built in 1862 to accommodate visiting heads of state, it was renovated some years ago, but still retains enough old-world grandeur.

ADRIANA IACOB/SHUTTERSTOCK ©

1. Architectural details, Church of Agios Eleftherios
2. Moni Kaisarianis 3. Church of the Holy Apostles
4. Mosaic, Moni Dafniou

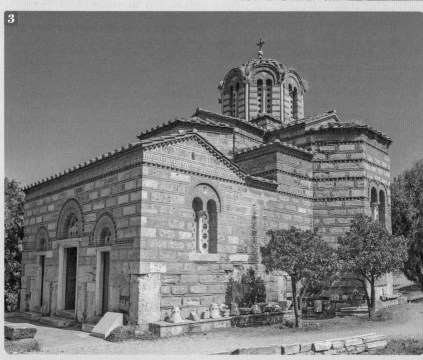

Byzantine Athens

The city is dotted with churches that just happen to be a thousand years old, dating from the high point of the Byzantine Empire. Few churches open regularly, but the ones that do are gold-bedecked portals to the past. Don't miss the outstanding Byzantine & Christian Museum (p94), as well as the great icons at the Benaki Museum (p94).

Moni Dafniou

The area's most important Byzantine building is the World Heritage–listed 11th-century **Moni Dafniou** (📞210 581 1558; http://whc.unesco.org/en/list/537; Dafni; ⊘9am-2pm Tue & Fri; 🚌811, 866 or A16 to Psychiatreion) FREE at Dafni, 10km northwest of Athens. Many of the church's elaborate mosaics, wrought by artisans from Constantinople, have been beautifully restored and more work is underway. The octagonal structure incorporates part of a wall from a 6th-century church.

Moni Kaisarianis

Nestled on the slopes of Mt Hymettos, 5km east of Athens, beautiful 11th-century **Moni Kaisarianis** (Monastery of Kaisariani; 📞210 723 6619; Mt Hymettos; adult/child €2/free; ⊘8.30am-2.45pm, grounds to sunset, Tue-Sun) is a peaceful walled sanctuary. The domed *katholikon* (main church), supported by four columns from an ancient temple, has well-preserved frescoes from the 17th and 18th centuries.

Church of the Holy Apostles

One of the oldest churches in Athens is the 11th-century Church of the Holy Apostles in the Ancient Agora (p83), a tribute to the place where St Paul once taught. It bears decorative details that are now seen as Islamic but were a product of artisans who worked across the eastern Mediterranean.

Church of Agios Eleftherios (Little Metropolis)

Look closely at this 12th-century **church** (Plateia Mitropoleos, Monastiraki), and you'll see it's a historical collage of medieval stonework and ancient Pentelic marble. Its facade sports both medieval lions and Classical athletes, a portion of a delicate ancient marble frieze. It was even built on the ruins of an ancient temple.

Ergon House
BOUTIQUE HOTEL €€€

(Map p86; ☑ 210 010 9090; https://house.ergon foods.com; Mitropoleos 23, Syntagma; d from €195; P ❊ @ ⏥; M Syntagma) Having created a sleek boutique hotel above their stylish deli and restaurant (p113), Ergon House offers communal kitchens in its hallways so you can prepare meals with all the goodies available to buy on the ground floor. The cheapest rooms are compact but are appealingly decorated with breeze (Besser) blocks, grey marble and wooden fittings in minimalist style.

NEW Hotel
DESIGN HOTEL €€€

(Map p86; ☑ 210 327 3000; www.yeshotels. gr; Filellinon 16, Plaka; d from €239; P ❊ @ ⏥; M Syntagma) Brazilian designers the Campana brothers melded their signature scraps-to-art style with Greek-folk touches and old Athens photos, creating a hip space that's full of fun eye candy. More practically, the rooms are cushy (lots of pillow options) and there's a good roof lounge and restaurant. Location is prime but can be noisy; upper floors are better.

🛏 Monastiraki & Psyrri

★ City Circus
HOSTEL €

(Map p96; ☑ 213 023 7244; www.citycircus.gr; Sarri 16, Psyrri; dm/d incl breakfast from €27/72; ❊ @ ⏥; M Thissio, Monastiraki) With its jaunty, colourful style and helpful staff, City Circus lifts the spirit more than most budget hostels. Its bright, well-designed rooms have modern bathrooms; some have kitchens. Book on its website for free breakfast at the chic bistro Zampano downstairs.

Cecil
HOTEL €

(Map p96; ☑ 210 321 7079; www.cecilhotel.gr; Athinas 39, Monastiraki; s/d/tw/tr/q incl breakfast €60/75/85/120/155; ❊ @ ⏥; M Monastiraki) This charming old hotel on busy Athinas has beautiful high moulded ceilings, polished timber floors and an original cage-style lift. The simple rooms are tastefully furnished, but don't have fridges. Two connecting rooms with a shared bathroom are ideal for families.

Small Funny World
HOSTEL €

(Map p86; ☑ 210 324 7167; www.sfwhostel.com; Kalamiotou 25, Monastiraki; dm €17; ❊ @ ⏥; M Monastiraki) Located in the most happening corner of Monastiraki, this laid-back hostel is an excellent budget option with 14 beds in each of the four large tiled dorm rooms. The communal kitchen is a plus and so is the rooftop terrace, a casual meeting place decorated with cushioned wooden sofas and mismatched tables facing out to the urban skyline.

18 Micon Street
BOUTIQUE HOTEL €€

(Map p96; ☑ 210 323 5307; www.18miconstr. com; Esopou 14, Psyrri; d/ste incl breakfast €138/151; ❊ ⏥; M Monastiraki) An old warehouse has been sprinkled with interior-designer fairy dust to emerge as this chic 14-room boutique hotel. Cement, wood and brick are the foundation blocks of the interior design, with pops of colour and pattern from wall art and tiles. Rooms also come equipped with smart phones for full internet access in and out of the hotel.

★ Foundry Hotel
APARTMENT €€€

(Map p96; ☑ 211 182 4602; www.thefoundry hotelathens.com; Sarri 40, Psyrri; apt incl breakfast from €170; ❊ ⏥; M Thissio) An old metalwork factory provides the base and inspiration for this industrial-chic apartment hotel. Rooms, which all have mini-kitchens, sport thematic steel-and-wood decor and favour analogue features such as books and vinyl LP players rather than TVs. Choose a wine from the wine cellar and enjoy it up on the beautiful roof garden.

★ Perianth Hotel
DESIGN HOTEL €€€

(Map p86; ☑ 210 321 6660; https://perianth hotel.com; Limbona 2, Monastiraki; d/ste from €198/351; ❊ @ ⏥ ⏥; M Monastiraki) Athens designers K-Studio have done a splendid job modernising this 1930s building into a gorgeous 38-room hotel, using natural materials such as marble, wood and metal alongside choice pieces of contemporary art. Splash out on the two-bedroom penthouse suite which includes a private Jacuzzi and swimming pool on a wrap-around roof terrace with stunning Acropolis views.

Zillers
BOUTIQUE HOTEL €€€

(Map p86; ☑ 210 322 2277; www.thezillersathens hotel.com; Mitropoleos 54, Monastiraki; r incl breakfast from €180; ❊ @ ⏥; M Monastiraki) This boutique hotel offers just 10 rooms in a handsomely converted neoclassical building right beside the metropolitan cathedral (p88). Six of the rooms overlook the Acropolis (the rest get light from an atrium). Breakfast is served at the excellent rooftop restaurant and bar, which is worth a visit even if you aren't staying at the hotel.

📍 Gazi, Keramikos & Exarhia

★**Athens Quinta Hostel** HOSTEL €
(Map p96; 📞213 030 5322; www.facebook.
com/athensquinta; Methonis 13, Exarhia; dm/d with
shared bathroom €25/55; 🕿; Ⓜ Panepistimio)
Set in an old mansion, complete with velvet
sofas and patterned tile floors, this friendly
place is pleasantly homey and a nice change
from slicker, busier hostels. There's a leafy
backyard for lounging.

The House PENSION €
(Map p102; 📞210 345 7765; www.thehouse
athens.com; lakchou 7, Gazi; d from €70; ❄@🕿;
Ⓜ Kerameikos) If you want to be close to the
Gazi nightlife, then this place hits the sweet
spot. It bills itself as a boutique hotel, but in
reality the rustic furnishings, whitewashed
walls and mock stone-flagged floors give
it the feel of a Greek island pension. Some
rooms have small kitchenettes, and the vibe
is relaxed and youthful.

Exarchion HOTEL €
(Map p96; 📞210 380 0731; www.exarchion.com;
Themistokleous 55, Exarhia; s/d/tr €45/58/70;
❄🕿; Ⓜ Omonia) What this 1960s high-rise
hotel lacks in character, the surrounding
neighbourhood of Exarhia makes up for.
Rooms are clean and comfortable; some
have balconies. There's a rooftop cafe-bar
and the management is friendly. There are
numerous nearby dining and entertainment
options.

Grecotel Pallas Athena DESIGN HOTEL €€
(Map p96; 📞210 325 0900; www.grecotel
pallasathena.com; Athinas 63, Syntagma; d from
€168; ❄@🕿; Ⓜ Omonia) The designers have
brought a playful touch to the rooms of this
63-room boutique hotel, filling them quirky,
colourful pieces of contemporary art, decor
and furnishings. Kids will love the superhe-
roes and other cartoon characters that feature in some of the wall murals.

Fresh Hotel BOUTIQUE HOTEL €€
(Map p96; 📞210 524 8511; www.freshhotel.
gr; Sofokleous 26, Omonia; r incl breakfast from
€144; ❄🕿; Ⓜ Omonia) A hip hotel in the
gritty south-of-Omonia area, this groovily
designed place offers modern rooms freshly
renovated in 2019 with new mock bleached-
wood floors and splashes of colour on the
walls. Pluses include a fantastic Acropolis-
view rooftop with small pool, bar and restaurant. Front rooms have balconies, but can
be noisy if you sleep with the window open.

APARTMENT RENTALS
....
Athens is awash with short-term apart-
ment rentals of the likes offered by
Airbnb. You'll pay a premium the closer
you are to the Acropolis. Pleasant and
generally safe areas of the city to look
for rentals include Plaka, Kolonaki, Mets
and Pangrati.

Book ahead for a superbly renovated,
spacious apartment or whole house
with **Boutique Athens** (📞6985083556;
www.boutiqueathens.com; 1-/2-/4-bedroom
apt from €40/59/134; ❄🕿). Prime locations around the centre offer excellent
value for the amenities. In Psyrri, for
example, one apartment's massive
roof garden with Acropolis views has
sunbeds, a barbecue and a beer fridge.
Two-night minimum.

📍 Kolonaki & Around

★**Coco-Mat**
Athens Jumelle BOUTIQUE HOTEL €€
(Map p110; 📞210 723 0000; www.cocomat
athens.com; Ypsilandou 2, Kolonaki; s/d incl breakfast from €150/165; ❄@🕿; Ⓜ Evangelismos)
Coco-Mat, the luxury mattress and bedding
company that has branched out into hotels,
has another winner on its hands with this
property. It cleverly combines a neoclassical
mansion with a modern block, linked by
a corridor with a cascading wall of water.
There's a gorgeous wooden staircase and
rooftop terrace for breakfast. The entrance
is on Irodotou.

St George Lycabettus BOUTIQUE HOTEL €€€
(Map p110; 📞210 741 6000; www.sglycabettus.
gr; Kleomenous 2, Kolonaki; s/d from €221/235;
❄@🕿🌊; Ⓜ Evangelismos, Syntagma) A high-
end clientele bunks here for excellent service and posh rooms. Newer 'eco-chic' rooms
have organic bedding and comfy Coco-Mat
beds; other floors are styled to focus on
young Greek fashion designers, photography and local composers. Up the hill in Kolonaki, it's a bit remote, but this pays off in
views of the city (Lycabettus greenery isn't
bad either).

Periscope BOUTIQUE HOTEL €€€
(Map p110; 📞210 729 7200; www.yeshotels.
gr; Haritos 22, Kolonaki; d/ste incl breakfast from
€318/393; ❄@🕿; Ⓜ Evangelismos) On a quiet
street lined with tiny, chic boutiques, this

Kolonaki, Mets & Pangrati

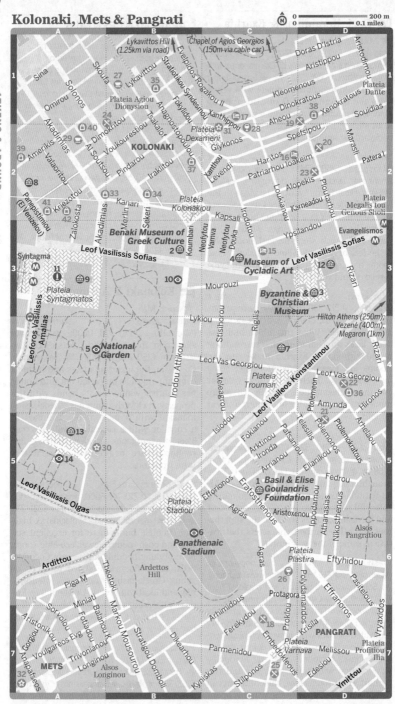

Kolonaki, Mets & Pangrati

sleek grey-tone hotel is the essence of new Kolonaki. Rooms are minimalist but have great beds and neat aerial shots of the city on the ceilings or walls. Complimentary snacks are available all day in the lounge.

Hilton Athens BUSINESS HOTEL €€€
(Map p68; ☑210 728 1000; www.hiltonathens.gr; Leoforos Vasilissis Sofias 46, Hilton; r from €196; ❄@ⓢ❄; ⓜEvangelismos) Swathes of polished marble greet you both in the lobby and rooms of the Hilton, occupying an iconic 1963 modernist building that's worth a look in its own right for its clean lines and facade relief mural by Yiannis Moralis, inspired by Greek themes. Rooms are spacious, many with splendid views, and there are plenty of facilities.

✕ Eating

Eating, drinking and talking is the main entertainment for Athenians. The vibrant restaurant scene is marked by a delightful culture of casual, convivial al fresco dining. *Ouzeries* and *mezedhopoleia,* both serving small plates with drinks, are popular for those with limited budgets. Some of the best food is found in just-slightly modernised tavernas that showcase fresh produce and regional ingredients.

✕ Acropolis, Filopappou Hill & Thisio

Gevomai kai Magevomai TAVERNA €
(Map p102; ☑210 345 2802; Nileos 11, Thisio; mains €4-13; ⊙1pm-midnight Tue-Sun; ☎; ⓜThissio) Stroll off the pedestrian way to find this small corner taverna with marble-topped tables. Neighbourhood denizens know it as one of the best for home-cooked, simple food with fresh ingredients – a boon in this high tourist-traffic area.

Veganaki VEGAN €
(Map p80; ☑210 924 4322; www.facebook.com/VeganakiGR; Athanasiou Diakou 38, Kynosargous; mains €3.50-6.50; ⊙8.30am-11.30pm; ☑; ⓜAkropoli) A fine addition to Athens' vegan dining options, this convivial spot may occupy a spot overlooking a busy road, but inside all is calm as customers enjoy falafel plates, sandwiches and traditional Greek pies, some of which are also gluten free. Also served here, a great cup of fair trade organic coffee.

★ **Ellevoro** GREEK €€
(Map p80; ☑ 210 924 6256; www.facebook. com/ellevoro; Rovertou Galli 2, Makrygianni; mains €17-28; ☉ 2pm-midnight Mon-Sat, 1-9pm Sun; 🖥; Ⓜ Akropoli) Three generations of a family work at this romantic homestyle restaurant that's decorated with wood beams, lacy white tablecloths, twinkling candles and chandeliers. Traditional Greek dishes – such as fava beans with smoked eel, and slow oven-baked lamb *kleftiko* – are superbly prepared and presented. A nice touch is the welcoming amuse bouche of a small cup of soup.

★ **Steki tou Ilia** TAVERNA €€
(Map p102; ☑ 210 345 8052; Eptachalkou 5, Thisio; mains €6-30; ☉ noon-1am, to 7pm Sun; Ⓜ Thissio) If there's a line to dine at this no-frills *psistaria* (restaurant serving grilled food), it's worth joining. The payoff is succulent lamb and pork chops, barrel wine and simple dips, chips and salads. In summer, the operation moves across the street into a hidden garden over the train tracks.

Fabrika tou Efrosinou GREEK €€
(Map p80; ☑ 210 924 6354; Zini 34, Koukaki; mains €14-18.50; ☉ 1-11pm Sun & Tue-Thu, to midnight Fri & Sat; Ⓜ Sygrou-Fix) Named for the patron saint of cooks, this 'factory' is really a two-level restaurant focusing on good ingredients and rarer Greek recipes. When everything is swinging, it's the perfect combination of bountiful, healthy food, including organic vegetables and farmstead cheeses, excellent Greek wines and great atmosphere. Book ahead on weekends.

Mani Mani GREEK €€
(Map p80; ☑ 210 921 8180; www.manimani. com.gr; Falirou 10, Makrygianni; mains €12-23; ☉ 2-11pm; Ⓜ Akropoli) Head upstairs to the relaxing, elegant dining rooms of this delightful modern restaurant, which specialises in herb-filled cuisine from the Mani region in the Peloponnese. Standouts include the ravioli with Swiss chard, the tangy sausage with orange, and the chicken stuffed with mushrooms and pecorino cheese.

Strofi GREEK €€
(Map p80; ☑ 210 921 4130; www.strofi.gr; Rovertou Galli 25, Makrygianni; mains €16-19; ☉ noon-1am, closed Mon Nov-Apr; Ⓜ Akropoli) Book ahead for a Parthenon (p72) view from the rooftop of this exquisitely renovated town house. Food is simple grilled meats and fish, but the setting, with elegant white linen and excellent service, elevates the experience to romantic levels.

Hytra MEDITERRANEAN €€€
(Map p68; ☑ 217 707 1118, 210 331 6767; www. hytra.gr; Onassis Cultural Centre, Leoforos Syngrou 107-109, Neos Kosmos; mains €34-39, 8-course tasting menu €62; ☉ restaurant 8pm-midnight Sun-Thu, to 1am Fri & Sat, bar to 3am; 🚌 10, 550 to Panteio, Ⓜ Sygrou-Fix) Hytra offers exquisitely presented Greek food with a hypermodern twist. Though portions can be small, the flavours and cooking techniques are spot on, which is how it earned its Michelin star. There's a 10-course vegetarian tasting menu (€58), and a lighter, more casual menu (mains €20 to €25) served in the bar area.

✕ Syntagma & Plaka

Damigos TAVERNA €
(Map p86; ☑ 210 322 5084; www.mpakaliarakia. gr; Kydathineon 41, Plaka; mains €9-12; ☉ 2pm-midnight; Ⓜ Akropoli) Hidden away and with an intimate feel, this traditional place, in business since 1865, specialises in *bakaliaros*, toothsome cod fried in pillow-light batter and spiked with garlicky sauce. Everything else is solid too, aided by quality house wine, naturally chilled in barrels set in the bedrock. A real treat in Plaka.

Avocado VEGETARIAN €
(Map p86; ☑ 210 323 7878; www.avocadoathens. com; Nikis 30, Plaka; mains €9-14; ☉ noon-11pm Mon-Fri, 11am-11pm Sat, noon-7pm Sun; 🖥🍴; Ⓜ Syntagma) This popular cafe offers a full array of vegan, gluten-free and organic treats with an international spin. Next to an organic market, and with a tiny front patio, here you can enjoy everything from sandwiches to quinoa with aubergine, or mixed-veg coconut curry. Juices and mango lassis are all made on the spot.

Kalderimi TAVERNA €
(Map p96; ☑ 210 331 0049; Plateia Agion Theodoron, Panepistimio; mains €6-12; ☉ 11am-8pm Mon-Thu, to 10pm Fri & Sat; 🖥; Ⓜ Panepistimio) This downtown taverna offers Greek food at its most authentic. Everything is freshly cooked and delicious: you can't go wrong. Hand-painted tables edge a pedestrian street, providing for a feeling of peace in one of the busiest parts of the city. (It helps that it closes just before nearby bars get rolling.)

Glykys MEZEDHES €
(Map p86; ☏210 322 3925; www.glykys.gr; Angelou Geronta 2, Plaka; mezedhes €4-8; ⊙10am-1am; Ⓜ Akropoli) In a quiet corner of Plaka, this low-key place with a shady front yard is mostly frequented by students and locals. It has a tasty selection of mezedhes, including traditional dishes such as *briam* (oven-baked vegetable casserole, only available in the evening) and cuttlefish in wine.

★**Ergon House Agora** GREEK €€
(Map p86; ☏210 010 9090; https://house. ergonfoods.com; Mitropoleos 23, Syntagma; mains €8-11.50; ⊙7.30am-midnight; 🛜; Ⓜ Syntagma) A superb addition to Athens' culinary landscape is this deli, cafe and restaurant occupying a gorgeously designed atrium space flooded with light. There are separate areas for a greengrocer, fishmonger, butcher and bakery, plus shelves packed with top-quality Greek products sourced from small-scale producers around the country. You'll dine well here and, most likely, leave laden down with goodies.

Birdman JAPANESE €€
(Map p86; ☏210 321 2800; www.facebook. com/birdmanathens; Skoufou 2, Syntagma; skewer €2.50-4, mains €15; ⊙6pm-midnight Mon-Fri, from 1pm Sat; 🛜; Ⓜ Syntagma) This part of Syntagma offers a cluster of Japanese restaurants, among which Birdman, which specialises in yakitori (charcoal-grilled skewers of meat) is a gem. The main ingredients – free-range organic chicken, grass-fed beef – are top quality, the cooking by Japanese chefs is totally authentic and the ambience relaxed and contemporary.

Cherche la Femme GREEK €€
(Map p86; ☏210 322 2029; Mitropoleos 46, Syntagma; mains €7.50-12.50; ⊙9am-11.30pm, until midnight Fri & Sat; Ⓜ Syntagma) Leafy wallpaper, a twinkling chandelier and Parisian brasserie-style furniture and bar set the chic tone for this all-day cafe. The atmosphere may scream France but the menu, with traditional dishes such as *mousakas* and *skioufichta* (a local pasta), is very much homegrown. It's a perfect spot to graze on mezedhes with a glass of wine or beer.

Nolan FUSION €€
(Map p86; ☏210 324 3545; www.nolan restaurant.gr; Voulis 31-33, Syntagma; mains €8.50-13; ⊙1pm-midnight Mon-Sat; 🛜; Ⓜ Syntagma) It's a good idea to make a reservation for this casual, chic and popular restaurant.

Chef Sotiris Kontizas has incorporated some Asian ingredients and influences into his fresh and flavoursome menu with dishes such as soba noodles with smoked salmon, and NFC (Nolan Fried Chicken). Everything is designed to be shared.

Palia Taverna tou Psara TAVERNA €€
(Map p86; ☏210 321 8734; www.psaras-taverna. gr; Erehtheos 16, Plaka; mains €12-24; ⊙noon-1am; Ⓜ Akropoli) A little above the main bustle of Plaka, this taverna fills tables cascading across the street and down the stairs. It's touristy, but respected by locals as one of the best seafood tavernas in the area. If fish (€65 per kilogram) isn't your thing, they have plenty of other dishes to choose from.

★**Sushimou** JAPANESE €€€
(Map p86; ☏211 407 8457; www.sushimou.gr; Skoufou 6, Syntagma; set menu €50-60; ⊙6.30-10.30pm; 🛜; Ⓜ Syntagma) Sushi in Athens doesn't get any better than this. Tell Antonis Drakoularakos, the Tokyo-trained chef who holds court behind the counter, your budget and he'll prepare a feast of local seafood sliced up as sashimi (raw fish) and nigiri (atop vinegared rice). It's a tiny place so book ahead at least a month to be sure of a spot.

🍴 Monastiraki & Psyrri

★**Diporto Agoras** TAVERNA €
(Map p96; ☏210 321 1463; Sokratous 9 & Theatrou, Psyrri; plates €5-7; ⊙7am-7pm Mon-Sat, closed 1-25 Aug; Ⓜ Omonia, Monastiraki) This charming old taverna is an Athens gem. There's no signage – look for two sets of doors leading to a rustic cellar. There's no printed menu, just a few dishes that haven't changed in years. Order the house speciality *revythia* (chickpea stew) and follow up with grilled fish, paired with wine from one of the giant barrels lining the wall.

Hoocut GREEK €
(Map p86; ☏210 324 0026; https://hoocut.com; Plateia Agia Irini 9, Monastiraki; souvlaki from €2.50; ⊙noon-1am; Ⓜ Monastiraki) The five Athenian chefs behind this upmarket snack joint have focused on the quality of the ingredients to create 'haute cuisine' souvlaki with a choice of meats beyond pork and chicken. The portions are a little smaller and the prices slightly higher than your run-of-the-mill *gyros*, but with the meat grilled to perfection it's totally worth it.

WORTH A TRIP

STAVROS NIARCHOS FOUNDATION CULTURAL CENTER

Sitting beneath an artificial slope above Faliro Bay, and shaded by a 'Magic Carpet' roof covered with solar panels, is the Stavros Niarchos Foundation Cultural Center (SNFCC; Map p140; 216 809 1001; www.snfcc.org; Leoforos Syngrou 364, Kallithea; 550 to Onasseio, 10 to Epaminonda) FREE. This stunning Renzo Piano–designed building, completed in 2016, is home to the Greek National Opera (p124) and the main branch of the National Library (216 809 1000; www.nlg.gr; Pisistratou 172, Kallithea; public areas 6am-midnight, exhibition fl 9am-10pm, library 9am-5pm Mon-Fri; 550 to Onasseio, 10 to Epaminonda) FREE.

Covering a hill that incorporates SNFCC's roof is the 21-hectare and sustainably designed Stavros Niarchos Park (216 809 1000; www.snfcc.org; Leoforos Syngrou 364, Kallithea; 6am-midnight Apr-Oct, to 8pm Nov-Mar; 550 to Onasseio, 10 to Epaminonda) FREE with paths cutting through plantings of lavender, olive trees and other Mediterranean flora. There are also kids' play areas, an outdoor gym and much more. A variety of free activities are laid on, but you can simply sit in a chair and soak up the sunshine.

In addition to regular public transport, you can also use a free shuttle bus, departing from Syntagma at Ermou. It runs several times a day on weekdays, and every 30 minutes from 9.30am to 9.30pm on weekends.

Bougatsadiko Thessaloniki PIES €

(Map p96; 210 322 2088; Plateia Iroön 1, Psyrri; pita €2; 7am-2am Sun-Thu, 24hr Fri & Sat; M Monastiraki) Unexpected for its location on a key nightlife square in Psyrri, this place makes excellent *pites* (pies), with filo crust that's 'opened' (rolled out by hand) every day – you can watch the baker at work. *Bougatsa* (filo with custard) is great for breakfast, the meat pies are a treat after drinks and *spanakopita* (spinach pie) hits the spot anytime.

Feyrouz TURKISH €

(Map p86; 213 031 8060; www.feyrouz. gr; Karori 23, Monastiraki; sandwiches from €3; noon-10pm Mon-Thu, to 11pm Fri & Sat;) M Monastiraki) *Lahmajoun* (flatbread topped with spiced meat and rolled up with vegetables) is the focus at this jewel box of a Turkish-Lebanese snack shop. The vegetarian option is a treat, with chewy whole-grain bread; there's also excellent lentil soup and bountiful salads. It's on a pedestrian street with benches, so you can eat outside if the tiny place is jammed.

Kostas GREEK €

(Map p86; 210 323 2971; Plateia Agia Irini 2, Monastiraki; sandwich €2.20; 9am-6pm; M Monastiraki) On a pleasant square opposite Agia Irini church, this old-style virtual hole-in-the-wall joint grills up tasty souvlaki and *bifteki* (Greek-seasoned hamburger), served on pitta with a signature spicy

tomato sauce. Go before the lunch rush, as it may close early if it runs out of meat.

Avli MEZEDHES €

(Map p96; 210 321 7642; Agiou Dimitriou 12, Psyrri; dishes €5-13; 1pm-midnight; M Monastiraki) Cheap, cheerful and borderline chaotic on weekend nights, Avli requires you to squeeze down a narrow hall to get in; you'll probably wait for service if it's busy. The whitewashed walls and outdoor seating give you an island feel in the city, and the *keftedhes* (fried meatballs) and the special omelette, filled with fries and sausage, are excellent drinking food.

★ Atlantikos SEAFOOD €€

(Map p96; 213 033 0850; Avliton 7, Psyrri; mains €6-13; 1pm-midnight; M Monastiraki, Thissio) Tucked down a little lane, this small, hip fish restaurant is easy to miss – look for happy people chatting over heaps of shrimp shells. The atmosphere is simple and casual, with low prices to match – but there's excellent-quality seafood, whether it's fried or grilled.

★ Karamanlidika tou Fani GREEK €€

(Map p96; 210 325 4184; www.karamanlidika. gr; Sokratous 1, Psyrri; dishes €6-15; 11am-midnight; M Monastiraki) At this modern-day *pastomageireio* (combo tavern-deli) tables are set alongside the deli cases, and staff offer complimentary tasty morsels while you're looking at the menu. Beyond the Greek cheeses and cured meats, there's good seafood, such as marinated anchovies, as well as rarer wines and craft beers. Service is excellent, as is the warm welcome, often from Fani herself.

Fouar
ASIAN €€

(Map p86; [📞] 210 321 1381; http://fouar-athens. gr; 1st fl, 6 Hristopoulou, Monastiraki; mains from €10; [🕐] 7pm-3am Tue-Fri, 1pm-3am Sat & Sun; [Ⓜ] Syntagma) Fouar is a central meeting point for Athens' fashionable crowd. The casual-stylish restaurant serves international cuisine with a strong Asian influence. Start with a signature cocktail at the bar, check out the running exhibition in the gallery, enjoy your meal under the atrium greenery and dance in the club (open only some nights) until the early hours.

Gostijo
JEWISH €€

(Map p96; [📞] 210 323 3825; www.gostijo.gr; Esopou 10, Psyrri; mains €8.50-17; [🕐] 1-10.30pm Sun-Thu Apr-Oct, from 4pm Nov-Mar; [📶]; [Ⓜ] Monastiraki) Convivial Israeli expat Ricky Vidal is the force of nature running this fully kosher restaurant that occupies a modern, pleasantly decorated space on the ground floor of Jewish outreach organisation Chabbad. Dishes are both traditional Sephardic and Mediterranean; the menu includes options such as beef stew with wine and prunes; falafel; and Moroccan chicken. Reservations are recommended.

Café Avissinia
MEZEDHES €€

(Map p86; [📞] 210 321 7047; https://cafeavissinia. net; Kynetou 7, Monastiraki; mains €10-16; [🕐] 11am-1am Tue-Sat, to 7pm Sun; [Ⓜ] Monastiraki) This antiques-bedecked place on Plateia Avyssinias, in the middle of the antique dealers, has been legendary since the 1980s for its live music and varied mezedhes. It's great for a midday break from the market (p127), or for a late supper on a weekend night. In summer, snag fantastic Acropolis views upstairs from their terrace.

Kuzina
GREEK €€

(Map p86; [📞] 210 324 0133; www.kuzina.gr; Adrianou 9, Monastiraki; mains €16-36; [🕐] 1pm-midnight; [Ⓜ] Thissio) This comfortably elegant restaurant does chic Greek, with creations such as fried dumplings filled with feta and olives. It's cosy in winter, as light streams in, warming the crowded tables. In summer, book ahead for a rooftop-terrace table for views all around. A fine second choice is an outside table on the pedestrian street.

Telis
TAVERNA €€

(Map p96; [📞] 210 324 9582; Evripidou 86, Psyrri; meal with salad €13; [🕐] noon-midnight Mon-Sat; [Ⓜ] Thissio) A fluorescent-lit beacon of good food and kind service on a grimy block, Telis has been serving up simplicity since 1978. There's no menu, just a set meal: a small mountain of charcoal-grilled pork chops atop chips, plus a side vegetable. Greek salad is optional, as is beer or rough house wine.

🍴 Gazi, Keramikos & Exarhia

⭐ Ama Lachei stis Nefelis
GREEK €

(Map p96; [📞] 210 384 5978; https://restaurant -47828.business.site; Kalidromiou 69, Exarhia; mezedhes €5.50-11.50; [🕐] 1pm-12.30am Thu-Sun, from 6pm Tue & Wed; [🚌] 2, 5, 9, 11 to Polytechneio) This modern *mezedhopoleio* (restaurant specialising in mezedhes) is a minor hike up Exarhia's hill, but you're rewarded with a lovely setting – an old school building, with tables outside in the vine-shaded playground – and super-savoury small plates that go well with drinks. Think pickled octopus, meatballs flavoured with cinnamon and cloves, and lamb kebabs.

Elvis
GREEK €

(Map p102; [📞] 210 345 5836; Plateon 29, Keramikos; skewers €1.70; [🕐] noon-3am, to 5am Fri & Sat; [Ⓜ] Kerameikos or Thissio) This souvlaki joint is mobbed, and not just because the counter staff slide you a shot of booze while you're waiting. The meat quality is high, the prices are right and the music is great. Every skewer comes with good chewy bread and fried potatoes.

⭐ Seychelles
GREEK €€

(Map p102; [📞] 210 118 3478; www.seycheles.gr; Keramikou 49, Metaxourgio; mains €8.50-14.50; [🕐] 2pm-12.30am Sun-Thu, until 1am Fri & Sat; [Ⓜ] Metaxourghiou) Gutsy fresh food, an open kitchen, friendly service, a handwritten daily menu and rock on the soundtrack: Seychelles may be the Platonic ideal of a restaurant. Dishes can look simple – meaty pan-fried mushrooms with just a sliver of sheep's cheese, say, or greens with fish roe – but the flavours are excellent. Go early or book ahead; it's deservedly popular.

Kanella
TAVERNA €€

(Map p102; [📞] 210 347 6320; www.kanellagazi. gr; Leoforos Konstantinoupoleos 70, Gazi; dishes €8.50-14; [🕐] 1pm-midnight Mon-Fri, to 1am Sat & Sun; [Ⓜ] Kerameikos) Housemade village-style bread, mismatched retro crockery and brown paper on the tabletops set the tone for this modern taverna serving regional Greek cuisine. Friendly staff offer daily specials such as lemon lamb with potatoes, and an excellent zucchini and avocado salad.

★ I Kriti   CRETAN €€
(Map p96; ☑210 382 6998; Veranzerou 5, Omonia; mains €6-12; ⊙ noon-midnight Mon-Sat; 🔊; Ⓜ Omonia) There is no shortage of Cretan restaurants in Athens, but this is the one that Cretans themselves recommend, especially for rare seasonal treats such as stewed snails, bittersweet pickled *volvi* (wild bulbs), and tender baby goat with nuts and garlic. It occupies several storefronts inside the arcade; on weekends it's a good idea to reserve.

★ Yiantes   TAVERNA €€
(Map p96; ☑210 330 1369; www.yiantes. gr; Valtetsiou 44, Exarhia; mains €9-15; ⊙ 1pm-midnight; 🖋; Ⓜ Omonia) This lovely restaurant with a central courtyard garden is upmarket for Exarhia, but the food is superb and made with largely organic produce. Expect interesting seasonal greens such as *almirikia* (sea beans), perfectly grilled fish or delicious mussels and calamari with saffron.

🍴 Kolonaki, Mets & Pangrati

Kalamaki Kolonaki   GREEK €
(Map p110; ☑210 721 8800; Ploutarhou 32, Kolonaki; souvlaki from €5; ⊙ 1pm-midnight; Ⓜ Evangelismos) Order your pork or chicken by the *kalamaki* (skewer), add some salad and pittas, and you have great quick bites at this standout souvlaki joint. It's small, but there's pavement seating for the requisite people-watching. And, because it's Kolonaki, it's just a little more chic than average.

Filippou   TAVERNA €
(Map p110; ☑210 721 6390; www.filippou.gr; Xenokratous 19, Kolonaki; mains €5-10; ⊙ 1-5pm & 7.30pm-midnight Mon-Fri, 1-5pm Sat; Ⓜ Evangelismos) Why mess with what works? Filippou has been dishing out Greek goodness – hearty meats, long-stewed vegetables – since 1923, and it's still a go-to for the neighbourhood. You can get this food elsewhere, but here you get white linen and a gracious, older, long-lunching clientele, in the heart of Kolonaki.

Ohh Boy   CAFE €
(Map p110; ☑211 183 8340; www.facebook.com/ohhboygr; Archelaou 32, Pangrati; sandwiches €6.50; ⊙ 8.30am-midnight, from 9am Sat & Sun; 🔊🖋; Ⓜ Evangelismos) Whitewashed tables and chairs nestle beneath olive trees at this cool cafe that has plenty of healthy eating options, including vegan cakes. It's a great spot for sandwiches and a coffee.

Colibri   PIZZA €
(Map p110; ☑210 701 1011; Embedokleous 9-13, Pangrati; pizzas €6.50-14, mains €7-9; ⊙ 1pm-12.30am; 🚌 2, 4, 11 to Plateia Plastira) Locals go here for the alleged best pizza in Athens. The pies range from classic Italian to creative vegetarian (seriously, the yoghurt works). Burgers and salads are also excellent. It's one of several fine eateries on a quiet tree-lined street.

★ Mavro Provato   MEZEDHES €€
(Black Sheep; Map p110; ☑210 722 3466; www. tomauroprovato.gr; Arrianou 31-33, Pangrati; dishes €6-17.50; ⊙ 1pm-1am Mon-Sat, to 7pm Sun; Ⓜ Evangelismos) Book ahead for this wildly popular modern *mezedhopoleio* (mezedhes restaurant) in Pangrati, where tables line the footpath and delicious small (well, small for Greece) plates are paired with regional Greek wines.

★ Philos Athens   INTERNATIONAL €€
(Map p110; ☑210 361 9163; www.facebook. com/philos.athens; Solonos 32, Kolonaki; mains €8-16; ⊙ 9am-5pm Mon-Fri, from 10am Sat & Sun; Ⓜ Panepistimio, Syntagma) Distressed walls, a beautiful old tiled floor and a cascade of paper cranes dangling from the tall ceiling set the shabby-chic tone for this delightful cafe. It's a lovely spot to browse style magazines while grazing on breakfast or lunch dishes such as macrobiotic bowls or bolognese ragu over pasta.

★ Oikeio   MEDITERRANEAN €€
(Map p110; ☑210 725 9216; www.facebook. com/oikeio; Ploutarhou 15, Kolonaki; mains €10-12; ⊙ 12.30pm-midnight Mon-Thu, to 1am Fri & Sat, to 6pm Sun; Ⓜ Evangelismos) With excellent homestyle cooking, this modern taverna lives up to its name (meaning 'homey'). It's decorated like a cosy bistro, and tables on the footpath allow people-watching without the usual Kolonaki bill. Pastas, salads and international fare are tasty, but try the daily *mayirefta* (ready-cooked meals), such as the excellent stuffed zucchini. Book ahead on weekends.

Benaki Museum Cafe GREEK €€
(Map p110; ☎210 367 1000; www.benaki.org;
Koumbari 1, Kolonaki; mains €10-24; ⊗10am-6pm
Mon, Wed, Fri & Sat, to midnight Thu, to 4pm Sun;
Ⓜ Evangelismos) Traditional Greek food gets
dressed up to match the museum (p94)
setting, with an open dining room and terrace
with a view of the National Garden (p70)
and the Acropolis. It feels a bit clubby, with
older locals meeting for lunch, and it's open
as late as the museum is, so you can have dinner or even just a late drink here.

★Spondi MEDITERRANEAN €€€
(Map p110; ☎210 756 4021; www.spondi.gr;
Pyrronos 5, Pangrati; mains €48-60, set menus from
€79; ⊗8-11.45pm; ☐209 to Plateia Varnava, ☐2,
4 or 11 to Plateia Plastira) Athenians frequently
vote two-Michelin-starred Spondi the city's
best restaurant, and its Mediterranean
haute cuisine, with a strong French influence, is indeed excellent. It's a lovely dining
experience, in a relaxed setting in a charming old house with a bougainvillea-draped
garden. Book ahead.

Vezené GREEK €€€
(Map p68; ☎210 723 2002; http://vezene.gr;
Vrasida 11, Hilton; mains €25-40; ⊗7pm-2am Mon-
Sat, 1-5.30pm Sun; ☎; Ⓜ Evangelismos) One of
Athens' best modern Greek bistros, Vezené
is a relaxed affair where the waiters will
bring to the table the catch of the day and
glistening cuts of prime steak to explain the
provenance and what goes into each dish.
The wood-oven-baked pies are very good, as
is the signature, deconstructed *pastitsio*, a
kind of Greek lasagne.

🍷 Drinking & Nightlife
In Athens the line between cafe and bar
is blurry. Most places segue from coffee to
drinks, and maybe music and a DJ, at night.
There is almost always food – although
places that serve only drinks are more common in the economic crisis (in which case,
you can bring your own snacks). The smoking ban is often ignored.

🍷 Acropolis, Filopappou Hill & Thisio

★Little Tree Book Cafe CAFE
(Map p80; ☎210 924 3762; www.facebook.
com/littletreebooksandcoffee; Kavalloti 2, Makrygianni; ⊗8am-11pm Tue-Thu, until 11.30pm
Fri, 9am-11.30pm Sat & Sun; Ⓜ Akropoli) This

friendly social hub is much beloved by
neighbourhood residents, who go for books
(they stock a small selection of translated
Greek authors here), but also excellent coffee, cocktails and snacks.

★The Underdog COFFEE
(Map p102; ☎213 036 5393; www.underdog.gr;
Iraklidon 8, Thisio; ⊗9am-11pm; ☎; Ⓜ Thissio) Far
from underdogs, the championship-winning
baristas here really know how to make a
decent cup of coffee. This speciality coffee
roaster and cafe-bar occupies a roomy location with a shaded courtyard to the rear and
industrial fittings throughout. If coffee isn't
your thing, they also serve craft beers and
have a decent brunch-style menu.

Drupes & Drips CAFE
(Map p80; ☎6970300404; www.facebook.com/
drupesdrips; Zitrou 20; ⊗7am-4pm Mon, until
10pm Tue-Fri, until 11pm Sat; Ⓜ Akropoli) A coffee
to speed your step up to the Acropolis in the
morning, or an Aperol spritz or glass of wine
to soothe you into the evening on the way
down – that's what this pocket-sized cafe/
wine bar is all about. Pair your drink with a
small plate of something, usually involving
the bread from Takis Bakery across the way.

Bel Rey CAFE
(Map p80; ☎213 032 6450; http://belraybar.gr;
Falirou 88, Koukaki; ⊗10am-2am; Ⓜ Sygrou-Fix)
Occupying the triangular corner of a former
car workshop, this is the go-to hang-out of
Koukaki's hipsters. It's a buzzy, casual scene
that works equally well for a quiet morning
coffee or late-night drinks against the background sounds of chatter and a DJ.

★Upoa Epops BAR
(Map p102; ☎212 105 5214; www.facebook.
com/upupaepopsthebar2016; Alkminis 7, Kato
Petralona; ⊗10am-2am, to 3am Fri & Sat; Ⓜ Petralona) This lovely bar-restaurant is one of
the reasons Petralona is considered a just-
the-right-amount-of-cool neighbourhood. It
has numerous rooms filled with vintage furniture and a pretty courtyard, the food and
drinks are great and there's often a DJ, but
there's always a place to have a conversation.
And the name? Latin for the hoopoe bird.

Sin Athina CAFE
(Map p102; ☎210 345 5550; www.sinathina.
gr; Iraklidon 2, Thisio; ⊗8am-1am, until 2am Fri
& Sat; Ⓜ Thissio) Location, location, location! This cafe-bar sits at the junction of
the two pedestrianised cafe strips and has

a sweeping view up to the Acropolis. The real magic is on the rooftop – though the menu up here is more elaborate and slightly higher priced.

 ## Syntagma & Plaka

The Clumsies
BAR

(Map p86; ☑ 210 323 2682; www.theclumsies. gr; Praxitelous 30, Syntagma; ☉10am-2am Sun-Thu, to 4am Fri & Sat; Ⓜ Syntagma) Look for the red neon in the hallway of this discreet bar that fills your coffee and creative cocktail needs. Founded by three award-winning bartenders, it's very serious about its drinks, but the atmosphere is definitely fun, and full of slick, handsome types on the weekends. From 6pm to 10pm you can order their degustation of four cocktails for €20.

★ Baba Au Rum
COCKTAIL BAR

(Map p86; ☑ 211 710 9140; www.babaaurum. com; Klitiou 6, Syntagma; ☉7pm-3am Sun-Fri, 1pm-4am Sat; Ⓜ Syntagma, Monastiraki) As the name implies, the focus here is on rum drinks, with an excellent selection of rarer Caribbean rums and a whole range of cocktails, from classic tiki drinks to new inventions. This is just one of a handful of good little bars on this strip.

★ Yiasemi
CAFE

(Map p86; ☑ 213 041 7937; www.yiasemi.gr; Mnisikleous 23, Plaka; ☉10am-3am; Ⓜ Monastiraki) Proof that Plaka is still very much a Greek neighbourhood despite the tourists, Yiasemi attracts a good mix of young Athenians, who set up for hours in the big armchairs or out on the scenic steps. It's better by day (especially for the great veg breakfast buffet) and on weeknights, when it's not overwhelmed by the scene at nearby restaurants.

L'Audrion
WINE BAR

(Map p86; ☑ 210 324 1193; https://laudrion.gr; Plateia Filomousou 3 & Farmaki 1, Plaka; ☉5pm-1am; Ⓜ Akropoli, Syntagma) Something of an oasis of Gallic calm in the midst of touristy Plaka, L'Audrion is a classy French wine bar and restaurant that sports more than 100 different labels in its cellar. As well as bottles you can order by the glass. The food is excellent. An added bonus is live music from 7.30pm on Wednesday.

Zonars
CAFE

(Map p86; ☑ 210 325 1430; Voukourestiou 9, Syntagma; ☉9am-3am, to 4am Fri & Sat; Ⓜ Syntagma) It's worth coming here for a coffee (from €4) or cocktail (€13) just to lounge in the sumptuous interior of this famous cafe, all velvet and brass and walnut panelling. In the 1950s and '60s, it claimed patrons such as Simone de Beauvoir and Sophia Loren; following a 2016 renovation, it still hosts a distinctly elegant scene.

Ippo
BAR

(Map p86; ☑ 213 005 4715; Thiseos 11, Syntagma; ☉7.30pm-2am Sun-Thu, to 4am Fri & Sat; Ⓜ Syntagma) This great little place caters to the slightly more mature bar-crawler, with pinball, David Bowie and old soul on the sound system, and better-than-average bar snacks. The bathrooms are a whole other world.

Barley Cargo
BAR

(Map p86; ☑ 210 323 0445; www.facebook. com/BarleyCargo; Kolokotroni 6, Syntagma; ☉11am-3am, from 5pm Sun; Ⓜ Syntagma) If you think Greek beer begins and ends with Alfa, head here to learn more. The big open-front bar stocks the products of many Greek microbreweries, as well as more than 100 international beers. Live music is a bonus.

Galaxy
BAR

(Map p86; ☑ 210 322 7733; www.facebook.com/ GalaxyBarAthens; Stadiou 10, Syntagma; ☉1pm-2am Mon-Sat; Ⓜ Syntagma) Once upon a time (1972 to be exact), this was a modern bar – the sort with an actual European-style *bar*. Now it's a worn-at-the-edges but atmospheric time capsule with gallant bartenders who respect the spirit of the place, which can be summarised in the framed photos of the Rat Pack and Franz Kafka. It's at the end of the arcade.

Brettos
BAR

(Map p86; ☑ 210 323 2110; https://brettosplaka. com; Kydathineon 41, Plaka; ☉10am-2am; Ⓜ Akropoli) Plaka is short on bars in general, but Brettos, both a bar and a distillery, makes up for it. More than a century old, its walls glow with stacks of multicoloured bottles and huge barrels. Sample its home brands of wine, ouzo, brandy and other spirits.

Kaya
COFFEE

(Map p86; Voulis 7, Syntagma; ☉7am-6pm Mon-Fri, 8am-3pm Sat; Ⓜ Syntagma) Serving the best coffee in the Syntagma area, Kaya is in an odd triangle of real estate, with just enough room for the baristas. Order to go, or sip your flat white while standing at the small

DON'T MISS

ART GALLERIES

Athens has a dynamic and vibrant contemporary arts scene. Download the Athens Contemporary Art Map (http://athensartmap.net) or pick up a paper copy at galleries and cafes around town. The following are some of our favourite spaces.

TAF (The Art Foundation; Map p86; ☑ 210 323 8757; http://theartfoundation.metamatic.gr; Normanou 5, Monastiraki; ⊙ noon-9pm Mon-Sat, to 7pm Sun, cafe-bar open late; Ⓜ Monastiraki) Whether you want a shot of art, a clever design morsel or a refreshing drink, stop in at TAF, a just-barely updated complex of 1870s brick buildings. The central courtyard is a cafe-bar that fills with an eclectic young crowd, and the surrounding rooms act as galleries, DJ space and an excellent souvenir shop. Events are usually free.

A.antonopoulou.art (Map p96; ☑ 210 321 4994; www.aaart.gr; 4th fl, Aristofanous 20, Psyrri; ⊙ 2-8pm Wed-Fri, noon-4pm Sat; Ⓜ Monastiraki) One of the original galleries to open in Psyrri's warehouses, this impressive art space hosts exhibitions of contemporary Greek and international art, including installations, video art and photography.

Bernier/Eliades (Map p102; ☑ 210 341 3935; www.bernier-eliades.gr; Eptachalkou 11, Thisio; ⊙ 10.30am-6.30pm Tue-Fri, noon-4pm Sat; Ⓜ Thissio) This gallery, established in 1977 and occupying this grand old home since 1999, showcases prominent Greek artists and an impressive list of international artists, from abstract American impressionists to British pop. Shows change roughly every six weeks and tend towards the minimalistic.

The Breeder (Map p68; ☑ 210 331 7527; http://thebreedersystem.com; Iasonos 45, Metaxourgio; ⊙ noon-8pm Tue-Fri, to 6pm Sat; Ⓜ Metaxourghiou) Press the buzzer to gain entry to this hip concrete warehouse-style art gallery that displays a variety of works over two levels. Every year they reinvent the exterior design of the gallery as an art project.

Allouche Benias Gallery (Map p110; ☑ 210 338 9111; http://allouchebenias.com; Kanari 1, Kolonaki; ⊙ 11am-8pm Tue-Fri, until 5pm Sat; Ⓜ Syntagma) Occupying the beautifully restored 1882 Deligeorgis Mansion, designed by Ernst Ziller, this gallery made a splash on the local art scene when it opened in 2018. There's usually a couple of different shows a year with contemporary pieces in all media by both international artists and local talents such as Filippos Kavakas and Elias Kafouros.

CAN (Map p110; ☑ 210 339 0833; www.can-gallery.com; Anagnostopoulou 42, Kolonaki; ⊙ noon-3pm & 5-8pm Mon-Fri, noon-4pm Sat; Ⓜ Syntagma) This fresh entry on the Kolonaki gallery scene, founded by art specialist Christina Androulidaki, has a stable of emerging and midcareer contemporary Greek and international artists. In August it's open by appointment only.

Zoumboulakis Gallery (Map p110; ☑ 210 363 4454; www.zoumboulakis.gr; Kriezotou 6, Kolonaki; ⊙ 10am-3pm Mon & Wed, to 8pm Tue, Thu & Fri, to 4pm Sat; Ⓜ Syntagma) An excellent selection of limited-edition prints and posters by leading Greek artists, including Yannis Tsarouchis, Dimitris Mytaras and Alekos Fassianos, plus other decorative objects. The curators also have a contemporary space on the *plateia* (square) in Kolonaki.

counter by the window. It's at the back of the shopping arcade.

Kiki de Grece　　WINE BAR
(Map p86; ☑ 210 321 1279; www.facebook.com/kikidegrece; Ipitou 4, Syntagma; ⊙ noon-1am, to 2am Sat; Ⓜ Syntagma) Man Ray's muse, Kiki de Montparnasse, declared that in hard times, all she needed was bread, an onion and a bottle of red wine. This pedestrian-street bar also takes her as its muse, and offers plenty more than a bottle of red. There's a huge range from Greece's vintners,

paired with seasonal dishes from various regions in Greece.

Gin Joint　　COCKTAIL BAR
(Map p86; ☑ 210 321 8646; Christou Lada 1, Syntagma; ⊙ 6pm-2am Tue-Thu & Sun, 7pm-3am Fri & Sat; Ⓜ Syntagma) Just what the name promises: there's an impressive 180 gins (but only one produced in Greece) as well as other fancy beverages to sample, some with historical notes on their origin. It's a tiny place but, like so many downtown bars, the crowd can expand into the adjacent arcade.

Melina CAFE

(Map p86; ☑ 210 324 6501; Lyssiou 22, Plaka; ⊙ 9am-2am; Ⓜ Akropoli, Monastiraki) A tribute to the great Mercouri, this cafe-bar is decorated with images of the actress and politician who lobbied for the repatriation of the missing Parthenon marbles. Mercouri's most famous for the film *Never on Sunday*, but in fact that's a great day to come, when it's very busy and prime outdoor seats offer a view of the Plaka parade.

🍸 Monastiraki & Psyrri

★ **Couleur Locale** BAR

(Map p86; ☑ 216 700 4917; www.couleurlocale athens.com; Normanou 3, Monastiraki; ⊙ 10am-2am Sun-Thu, to 3am Fri & Sat; Ⓜ Monastiraki) Look for the entrance to this rooftop bar down a narrow pedestrian lane, then inside the arcade. From there, an elevator goes to the 3rd floor and its lively all-day bar-restaurant. It's a go-to spot for Athenians who love a chill coffee or a louder evening, all in view of their beloved Acropolis.

★ **Noel** BAR

(Map p86; ☑ 211 215 9534; https://noelbar.gr; Kolokotroni 59b, Monastiraki; ⊙ 10am-2am Sun-Thu, to 4am Fri & Sat; Ⓜ Monastiraki) One of the best of Athens' breed of maximalist-designed cafe-bars, Noel's slogan is 'where it's always Christmas' – meaning the candlelit cocktail-party kind of Christmas, no Santa suits required. Under softly glimmering chandeliers, smartly suited bartenders serve some of the most creative cocktails in town. Music is a mix of 1980s, '90s and jazz.

★ **Six d.o.g.s.** BAR

(Map p86; ☑ 210 321 0510; https://sixdogs. gr; Avramiotou 6-8, Monastiraki; ⊙ 10am-late; Ⓜ Monastiraki) The core of this super-creative events space is a rustic, multilevel back garden, a great place for quiet daytime chats

---

ⓘ SUMMER CLUBBING

In summer, much of the city's serious nightlife moves to glamorous, enormous seafront clubs radiating out from Glyfada (p137). Many sit on the tram route, which runs to 2.30am on Friday and Saturday. If you book for dinner you don't pay cover; otherwise admission ranges from €10 to €20 and includes one drink. Glam up to get in.

---

over coffee or a relaxed drink. From there, you can head in to one of several adjoining buildings to see a band, art show or other generally cool happening.

Orea Hellas CAFE

(Map p86; ☑ 210 321 3023; Pandrosou 36, Monastiraki; ⊙ 8.30am-11pm; 🛜; Ⓜ Monastiraki) This lovely old-style coffee house is a perfect place to take a break from shopping on the Monastiraki strip. Head upstairs for a seat on an open balcony overlooking Mitropoleos, or, in cooler weather, an indoor spot with an Acropolis view. Pair your Greek coffee with sweets or a range of solid snacks and salads.

Little Kook CAFE

(Map p96; ☑ 210 321 4144; www.facebook.com/ littlekookgr; Karaïskaki 17, Psyrri; ⊙ 10am-midnight Mon-Fri, from 9am Sat & Sun; 📶; Ⓜ Monastiraki) Nominally, this place sells coffee and cake. But it's really about its dazzling decor, which conjures up childhood fantasies. Precisely which one depends on the season, as the theme changes regularly. Everywhere are dolls, props, paintings and table decorations. You'll know you're getting close when you see party streamers over the street. Kids will be dazzled; Instagrammers will swoon.

Playhouse CAFE

(Map p86; ☑ 210 382 1200; www.playhouse.gr; Skouze 3, Monastiraki; ⊙ 10am-midnight Sun-Thu, until 2am Fri & Sat; 🛜📶; Ⓜ Monastiraki) A great way to spend a rainy day with the kids once you've exhausted the museums is at this brightly decorated cafe that specialises in board games. The choice of some 500 different games is impressive, with expert staff on hand to explain rules if needed.

Booze Cooperativa BAR

(Map p86; ☑ 211 405 3733; http://boozecooper ativa.com; Kolokotroni 57, Monastiraki; ⊙ 11am-3am, until 4am Fri & Sat; 🛜; Ⓜ Monastiraki) By day this art mansion is full of young Athenians playing chess and backgammon and working on their laptops. Later it transforms into a happening bar that rocks till late. The basement hosts art exhibitions and there's a theatre upstairs.

🍸 Gazi, Keramikos & Exarhia

★ **Blue Parrot** CAFE

(Map p102; ☑ 211 012 1099; Leonidou 31, Metaxourgio; ⊙ 9am-2am Sun-Thu, until 3am Fri & Sat; Ⓜ Metaxourghiou) Lashes of hanging greenery and a laid-back vibe, both inside and outside, make the Blue Parrot one of the area's most pleasant spots to hang out over a drink.

★**Romantso** CLUB
(Map p96; ☑216 700 3325; www.romantso.gr; Anaxagora 3, Omonia; ☺9am-1am Mon-Fri, from 10am Sat & Sun; ⓜOmonia) Based in the former offices of famous, but now defunct, magazine *Romantso,* this diamond of a creative hub has multiple facets. It's an all-day cafe-bar, there are DJ dance parties pretty much every weekend and they stage regular exhibitions, live music events and activities such as social yoga and fun hula-hoop classes (hoopit.gr).

Bios ROOFTOP BAR
(Map p102; ☑210 342 5335; www.bios.gr; Pireos 84, Keramikos; ☺11am-2am Sun-Thu, until 4am Fri & Sat; ⓜThissio) Occupying a Bauhaus apartment building, this multilevel warren has a great rooftop bar, restaurant, basement club and tiny art-house cinema. Expect live performances, art and new-media exhibitions, or at the very least a solid DJ and fab Acropolis view. In colder months, most activity is in Tesla, the ground-floor bar.

Lotos BAR
(Map p96; ☑210 380 1380; Zoodohou Pigis 5; ☺3pm-3.30am; ⓜPanepistimio) This urban bar with an exotic feel is hidden in a backstreet of the laid-back Exarhia neighbourhood. Loved by a younger crowd and students, it's one of the few bars in Athens that's packed every weeknight until the early hours – not coincidentally it serves the cheapest alcohol in the city. There are different DJs and music genres every night.

Nabokov BAR
(Map p96; ☑211 111 0432; Asklipiou 41, Exarhia; ☺noon-2am Mon-Thu, to 3am Fri & Sat, 7pm-2am Sun; ⓜPanepistimio) Just what you expect in an Exarhia bar: literary leanings, retro music, a bit of food and customers who treat it like their lifelong haunt, even though it only opened in 2017. There's even a pinball machine squashed in the corner.

Taf Coffee COFFEE
(Map p96; ☑210 380 0014; www.cafetaf.gr; Emmanuel Benaki 7, Omonia; ☺7am-8pm Mon-Fri, 8am-5pm Sat; ⓜOmonia) One of the best of Athens' third-wave coffee roasters, with distribution around the country and a bit abroad. Sip a pour-over here, or grab a quick espresso at the front bar. A nice touch are

---

WORTH A TRIP

TRENO STO ROUF
....
Look for the glowing headlight on a steam locomotive behind Rouf station. Attached is **Treno sto Rouf** (Map p102; ☑210 529 8922; https://totrenostorouf.gr; Leoforos Konstantinoupoleos, Rouf; ☺7.30pm-1am Tue-Sun; ☐21 or B16 to Rouf, ⓜKerameikos), a string of old train cars converted into a restaurant, bar-cafe, music club and theatre. Even on a night when nothing's scheduled, it's a cool place to have a drink and a snack (€6 to €15) and imagine yourself on the *Orient Express* of old. Check online for slightly different hours from June to October.

---

tasting notes (in English) of the daily coffee blends.

Revolt BAR
(Map p96; ☑210 380 0016; Koletti 25-27, Exarhia; ☺10am-2am, to 3am Fri & Sat; ⓜOmonia) This small, simple bar with tables spilling out onto a pedestrian street anchors a few solid blocks of good nightlife. The vibrant murals out front are super. Start here and explore down Koletti as far as Mesolongiou, and the pedestrian blocks there.

🍸 Kolonaki, Mets & Pangrati

Chelsea Hotel BAR
(Map p110; ☑210 756 3374; Arhimidous 1, Pangrati; ☺8am-4am; 🛜; ☐2, 4, 11 to Plateia Plastira) When people talk about the cool-but-mellow scene in Pangrati, they're probably thinking of this busy cafe-bar on Plateia Plastira. By day it's about coffee and people reading or working on their laptops. When the sun sets every seat, inside and out, is filled with young Athenians aspiring to be as artistic and bohemian as residents of the bar's NYC namesake.

★**To Tsai** TEAHOUSE
(Map p110; ☑210 338 8941; www.tea.gr; Alexandrou Soutsou 19, Kolonaki; ☺9am-9pm Mon-Sat; 🛜; ⓜSyntagma) Get a Zen vibe as you sip from a vast range of teas from around the world at this minimalist tearoom and shop that's a calm respite in the midst of Kolonaki. Keep an eye on your blonde-wood table, though, as they rest on trestles and can shift about a bit unexpectedly.

Jazz in Jazz BAR

(Map p110; ☎210 722 5246; https://jazzinjazz.business.site; Dinokratous 4, Kolonaki; ⏰8pm-3am; Ⓜ Syntagma, Evangelismos) A good cool-weather destination, this cosy bar glows with candles and vintage brass instruments, and stays warm with the sounds of New Orleans bebop and neighbours chatting over a glass of wine or whisky.

Filion CAFE

(Map p110; ☎210 361 2850; www.filioncafe.com; Skoufa 34, Kolonaki; ⏰7am-12.30am; 📶; Ⓜ Syntagma) Holding strong against Kolonaki's modern glitz, Filion is a pleasantly old-school cafe-bar, frequented by older members of the intellectual establishment and the occasional younger artist or writer.

☆ Entertainment

Athenians consider every musical event an opportunity for a singalong, which can make the most formal concert venues feel wonderfully chummy (even if you don't know the words yourself). Options vary seasonally: most indoor venues close or scale back programming in the summer, when the open-air theatres and cinemas take over.

For comprehensive events listings, with links to online ticket-sales points, try the following.

www.thisisathens.org Athens tourism site

www.athensculturenet.com English listings of events and performances

www.viva.gr Major ticket vendor, including for the Athens & Epidaurus Festival

www.ticketservices.gr Range of events.

Cinema

One of the delights of Athens is the enduring tradition of open-air cinema, where you can watch the latest Hollywood or art-house flick in the warm summer air. The settings are old-fashioned gardens and rooftops, with modern sound and projection. Cinemas start up in early May and usually close in September.

★Cine Paris CINEMA

(Map p86; ☎210 322 2071; www.cineparis.gr; Kydathineon 22, Plaka; adult/child €8/6; ⏰May-Oct; Ⓜ Syntagma) The Paris was established in the 1920s and it's still a magical place to see a movie. On a rooftop in Plaka, it offers great views of the Acropolis from some seats.

Thission CINEMA

(Map p102; ☎210 342 0864; www.cine-thisio.gr; Apostolou Pavlou 7, Thisio; tickets €6-8; ⏰May-Oct; Ⓜ Thissio) Across from the Acropolis, this is a lovely old-style outdoor cinema in a garden setting. Sit towards the back if you want to catch a glimpse of the glowing edifice. Tickets are the lower price if you attend Monday to Wednesday shows.

Aegli Cinema CINEMA

(Map p110; ☎210 336 9300; www.aeglizappiou.gr; Zappeio Gardens; adult/child €8.50/6.50; ⏰screenings at 9pm & 11pm May-Oct; Ⓜ Syntagma) This historical open-air cinema showed its first film in 1903. Set in the verdant Zappeion (p85), it's a little quieter than others.

Cine Dexameni CINEMA

(Map p110; ☎210 362 3942; www.cinedexameni.gr; Plateia Dexameni, Kolonaki; adult/child €8/5; ⏰screenings around 9pm; Ⓜ Evangelismos) This classic open-air cinema is in a lovely spot in the quieter reaches of Kolonaki, adjacent to a very good all-day cafe and the ancient cistern of Hadrian's aqueduct. Settle in for the film in a deck chair, with a little table to rest your beer on. A wall of cascading bougainvilleas rounds out the view.

Vox CINEMA

(Map p96; ☎210 381 0727; www.facebook.com/vox.athens; Themistokleous 82, Exarhia; adult/child €7/6, Tue €5; ⏰7.30pm-1am; Ⓜ Omonia) Vox open-air cinema on Exarhia's main square has been around since 1938, and fortunately has received historic-building designation. Still, it has the rough-and-ready vibe you'd expect in this neighbourhood. Arrive early and have a drink at the ground-floor cafe.

Greek Film Archive CINEMA

(Tainiothiki tis Ellados; Map p102; ☎210 360 9695; www.tainiothiki.gr; Iera 48, Keramikos; tickets €7; ⏰varies; Ⓜ Kerameikos) There are two auditoriums at this art-house cinema. Check the website for special film series and festivals.

Live Music

Perivoli tou Ouranou TRADITIONAL MUSIC

(Map p86; ☎210 323 5517; www.facebook.com/toperivolitououranou; Lysikratous 19, Plaka; ⏰9pm-late Fri & Sat, noon-6pm Sun Oct-Jun; Ⓜ Akropoli) A favourite Plaka music haunt with dinner (mains €18 to €29).

LGBT+ ATHENS

Athens' LGBT+ scene is lively and increasingly becoming an international drawcard. Athens Pride (p100), held in June, is an annual event; there's a march and a concert on Syntagma.

For nightlife, Gazi is Athens' LGBT+ hub. Gay and gay-friendly clubs around town are also in Plateia Agia Irini, Metaxourgio and Exarhia. For more information, check out http://athens-real.com and www.athensinfoguide.com.

Rooster (Map p86; ☑210 322 4410; www.roostercafe.gr; Plateia Agia Irini 4, Monastiraki; ⊗9am-3am; ☎; ⓂMonastiraki) This always-busy LGBT+ cafe on lively Plateia Agia Irini is straight-friendly too, and so fills with chatting locals across the rainbow spectrum.

Loukoumi (Map p86; ☑210 323 4814; https://en.loukoumibar.gr; Plateia Avyssinias 3, Monastiraki; ⊗10am-3am Sun-Thu, to 4am Fri & Sat; ⓂMonastiraki) This creative, gay-friendly cafe and arts space occupies two buildings facing each other across Plateia Avyssinias. It covers everything from daytime coffee and snacks to night-time DJs to drag queens, plus a vintage shop and gallery space.

Shamone (Map p102; ☑210 345 0144; www.shamone.gr; Leoforos Konstantinoupoleos 46, Gazi; entry after midnight €8; ⊗10.30pm-6am Fri & Sat; ⓂKerameikos) Since it opens a bit earlier than other Gazi LGBT bars and clubs, this is usually where the rainbow dance-and-party crowd starts off the night. Check their Facebook page (www.facebook.com/shamoneclub) for details of events.

BeQueer (Map p102; ☑213 012 2249; www.facebook.com/bequeerathens; Keleou 10, Keramikos; ⊗midnight-6am Fri & Sat; ⓂKerameikos) Gazi's gay bar and club scene can be a little homogenous, but this quirkier, more casual club breaks that mould. The vibe is friendly and open, and there are occasional theme and drag nights.

Beaver Collective (Map p102; ☑211 210 3540; www.facebook.com/collectivebeaver; Vasiliou tou Megalou 46, Rouf; ⊗1.30pm-2am Mon-Thu, to 3am Fri & Sat, 11.30am-midnight Sun; ⓂKerameikos) This women-run cooperative cafe is of course lesbian-friendly, but also just generally friendly. Sunday brunch gets a good crowd and cocktails flow freely.

Myrovolos (Map p102; ☑210 522 8806; Giatrakou 12, Metaxourgio; ⊗noon-4am Mon-Fri, 11am-4am Sat & Sun; ⓂMetaxourghiou) Popular lesbian cafe-bar-restaurant on a somewhat unkempt square, with a motorcycle clubhouse (unrelated) upstairs. Archetypal Metaxourgio, in other words.

★**Gazarte** LIVE MUSIC
(Map p102; ☑210 346 0347; www.gazarte.gr; Voutadon 32-34, Gazi; tickets from €10; ⓂKerameikos) At this respected arts complex, you'll find largely mainstream music and a trendy 30-something crowd. A ground-level theatre hosts live performances and there's also a rooftop bar and restaurant.

★**Half Note Jazz Club** JAZZ
(Map p110; ☑210 921 3310; www.halfnote.gr; Trivonianou 17, Mets; tickets €10-25; ⊗varies; ⓂAkropoli) Athens' most serious jazz venue is a stylish place that hosts Greek and international musicians. Check the schedule ahead of your trip, as it's not open every night and closes entirely in summer.

Fuzz Club LIVE MUSIC
(Map p68; ☑210 345 0817; www.fuzzclub.gr; Patriarchou Ioakim 1, Moschato Tavros; tickets from €10; ⓂPetralona, ☒Tavros) One of the best midsize music venues in Athens, this place is a little out of the centre, but worth the trip for a band you like (they host plenty of international acts) and probably with cheaper admission than the equivalent venue in your home city. It also has occasional club nights.

Steki Pinoklis TRADITIONAL MUSIC
(Map p102; ☑210 577 7355; www.facebook.com/pinoklis; Megalou Alexandrou 102, Keramikos; ⊗5pm-3am Mon-Sat, 2pm-1am Sun; ⓂKerameikos) Although this taverna opened in 2017, its musical taste and style skews much older. This is an excellent place to hear *rembetika* (blues) songs from Smyrna plus other traditional Greek music, with a band playing most nights (starting at 10pm) and Sunday afternoons (usually from 4pm). Food is average, but not expensive.

SPORTING ATHENS

Greece's top football teams are the Athens-based Panathinaikos (www.pao.gr) and AEK (www.aekfc.gr), and Piraeus-based Olympiacos (www.olympiacos.org), all three of which are in the European Champions League. Check club websites, English-language press or www.ticketmaster.gr.

'Basket' (basketball) is one of Athens' most popular sports, with a number of men's and women's pro teams in Athens (Panathinaikos and AEK are the biggest) and Piraeus (Olympiacos). For schedules, see the website of the Hellenic Basketball Federation (EOK; www.basket.gr). Games are often held at the 18,000-seat stadium at the **Athens Olympic Complex** (OAKA; Map p140; ☑210 683 4777; www.oaka.com.gr; Marousi; Ⓜ Irini).

Feidiou 2 Music Cafe
LIVE MUSIC

(Map p96; ☑210 330 0060; www.facebook.com/Feidiou2; Fidiou 2, Exarhia; ⊙8am-2.30am Mon-Sat, from 5pm Sun; Ⓜ Omonia) Cosy little space on the edge of Exarhia. Traditional music, usually *rembetika* (blues songs) and other heartfelt tunes, starts around 10pm most nights, when there's a minimum charge of €8 for food and drinks. Attracts a nice mixed crowd of all ages.

AN Club
LIVE MUSIC

(Map p96; ☑210 330 5056; www.anclub.gr; Solomou 13-15, Exarhia; tickets from €6; Ⓜ Omonia) A small spot with a long history of live rock, featuring lesser-known international and local bands, especially metal.

Theatre & Performing Arts

Greek National Opera
OPERA

(Ethniki Lyriki Skini; ☑210 366 2100; www.nationalopera.gr; Leoforos Syngrou 364, Kallithea; tickets €10-90; ☎; ☐550 to Onasseio, 10 to Epaminonda) Having settled into state-of-the-art digs within the Stavros Niarchos Foundation Cultural Center (p114), the Greek National Opera is going from strength to strength. The season runs from November to June. Its main 1400-seat auditorium is a stunning space with superb sight lines throughout.

The season includes classic works, quirkier new ones and big international coproductions. Performances are top quality and tickets prices are very reasonable.

As well as the opera, the Greek National Ballet, Orchestra and Choirs perform here. The complex also includes the **Alternative Stage**, a flexible space that accommodates up to 450 people for more experimental and intimate productions.

During the Athens Festival (p100) each summer, the GNO stages performances at the Odeon of Herodes Atticus (p75).

Megaron
PERFORMING ARTS

(Athens Concert Hall; Map p68; ☑210 728 2333; www.megaron.gr; Kokkali 1, cnr Leoforos Vasilissis Sofias, Ilissia; tickets from €7; ⊙box office 10am-6pm Mon-Fri, to 2pm Sat, later on performance days; Ⓜ Megaro Mousikis) The city's premier performance hall presents an impressive program of entertainments, including classical concerts, opera, theatre and dance shows, featuring world-class international and Greek performers. There's often some sort of art exhibition on here, and between June and September concerts are also staged outdoors in the complex's back garden.

Onassis Cultural Centre
ARTS CENTRE

(Map p68; ☑info & tickets 210 900 5800; www.sgt.gr; Leoforos Syngrou 107-109, Neos Kosmos; ☎; ☐10 or 550 to Panteio, Ⓜ Sygrou-Fix) Housed in an eye-catching piece of architecture that livens up the dull urbanity of Leoforos Syngrou, this visual- and performing-arts centre is well worth a visit. Cloaked in a striped cage of white marble, the building glows at night when it hosts big-name productions, installations and lectures. Check the schedule for free events.

★ National Theatre
THEATRE

(Map p96; ☑210 528 8100; www.n-t.gr; Agiou Konstantinou 22-24, Omonia; Ⓜ Omonia) One of the city's finest neoclassical buildings hosts contemporary theatre and ancient plays. The organisation also supports performances in other venues around town and, in summer, in ancient theatres across Greece. Happily for tourists, some of the productions are surtitled in English, and tickets are reasonably priced.

Dora Stratou Dance Theatre
DANCE

(Map p80; ☑210 921 4650; www.grdance.org; Filopappou Hill, Thisio; adult/child €15/5; ⊙performances 9.30pm Wed-Fri, 8.15pm Sat & Sun late May-Sep; Ⓜ Petralona, Akropoli) Every summer this company of 75 singers and dancers performs Greek folk dances, showing off the rich variety of regional costume and musical traditions. Performances are held at its open-air theatre on the western side of Filopappou Hill. It also runs folk-dancing workshops.

🏠 Shopping

Central Athens is the city's original commercial district, and still one big shopping hub, with an eclectic mix of stores. The area is still organised roughly by category – lace and buttons on one block, light bulbs on the next. The main (if generic) shopping street is pedestrianised Ermou, running from Syntagma to Monastiraki.

🏠 Acropolis & Around

★ Athena Design Workshop
FASHION & ACCESSORIES

(Map p80; ☑ 210 924 5713; www.athenadesign workshop.com; Parthenonos 30, Makrygianni; ⊗ 11.30am-7pm Mon-Fri, until 5pm Sat; Ⓜ Akropoli) You can often find Krina Vronti busy woodblock printing her appealing graphic designs on T-shirts, cushion covers and paper at this combined studio and shop. The images are often inspired by ancient and classical themes but are given a contemporary twist.

★ Underflow
MUSIC

(Map p80; ☑ 211 403 9926; http://underflow.gr; Kallirrois 39, Kynosargous; ⊗ 11am-9pm Mon-Thu, until 1am Fri, 4pm Sat; Ⓜ Sygrou-Fix) Specialising in Greek avant-garde rock and obscure sounds, this is one of Athens' top record shops. It stocks a wide range of music genres on vinyl and CD, both new and secondhand. It's also an art gallery, cafe and, on Friday nights, a performance space – check the website to see who's playing.

El.Marneri Galerie
JEWELLERY

(Map p80; ☑ 210 861 9488; www.elenimarneri. com; Lembesi 5-7, Makrygianni; ⊗ 11am-8pm Tue, Thu & Fri, to 4pm Wed & Sat; Ⓜ Akropoli) Sample rotating exhibitions of local modern art and some of the best jewellery in the city. Handmade, unusual and totally eye-catching.

Me Then
FASHION & ACCESSORIES

(Map p80; ☑ 6947520477; https://methen athens.com; Odissea Androutsou 36, Koukaki; ⊗ 5-8pm Tue, Thu & Sat, 1-5pm Fri; Ⓜ Sygrou-Fix) There's a relative dearth of local designers creating contemporary menswear in Athens, so it's nice to see George Soumpasis filling in the gap at this boutique. Many of his designs are actually unisex; offerings include shirts

with bold Matisse-style prints, structural jackets and trousers.

Mon Coin
CERAMICS

(Map p80; ☑ 6976800244; www.facebook. com/moncoin.athens; Erehthiou 16, Koukaki; ⊗ 10am-2.30pm Mon-Fri, also 5-8pm Tue, Thu & Fri, 10am-6pm Sat; Ⓜ Sygrou-Fix) This branch of the ceramics, homewares and accessories boutique set up by former French lawyer Eleonore Trenado-Finetis stocks a traditional – but very appealing – range of designs from across Greece.

There's a second, larger branch in **Monastiraki** (Map p86; 7 Thisiou, Monastiraki; ⊗ 10am-3pm Mon, until 8pm Tue-Fri, until 6pm Sat; Ⓜ Monastiraki) that carries more contemporary designs.

Fabrika + Sonja Blum
FASHION & ACCESSORIES

(Map p80; ☑ 6946463657; https://fabrika -sonjablum.tumblr.com; Veïkou 9, Makrygianni; ⊗ 10.30am-2pm Tue-Fri, also 5-8pm Tue & Thu, 11am-4pm Sat; Ⓜ Akropoli) Sonja Blum's fabric mobiles, kids' clothes and knitted scarves in the shape of foxes are the star attractions in this cute little accessories boutique. It also stocks jewellery and artworks by a collective of other designers and artists.

Lovecuts
CLOTHING

(Map p80; ☑ 215 501 1526; Veïkou 2, Makrygianni; ⊗ 11am-8.30pm Mon-Fri, until 4pm Sat; Ⓜ Akropoli) Greek designer Maria Panagiotou makes all the cute, affordable cotton clothing here, such as reversible hoodies, skirts and blouses in fun prints. It's one of several creative small-scale boutiques on this street.

🏠 Syntagma & Plaka

★ Alexis Papachatzis
JEWELLERY

(Map p86; ☑ 210 325 4064; www.alexisp.gr; Erehtheos 6, Plaka; ⊗ 10am-4pm Mon, Wed & Fri, to 7pm Tue, Thu & Sat; Ⓜ Monastiraki, Syntagma) This charming jewellery store is a delight before you even enter: turn the handle on the window display and watch as gears and pulleys animate the scene. Papachatzis' designs have a storybook quality: small figures, clouds and animals rendered in sterling silver and enamel.

★ Forget Me Not
GIFTS & SOUVENIRS

(Map p86; ☑ 210 325 3740; www.forgetme notathens.gr; Adrianou 100, Plaka; ⊗ 10am-9pm Apr & May, until 10pm Jun, Sep & Oct, until 11pm Jul & Aug, until 8pm Nov-Mar; Ⓜ Syntagma, Monastiraki) This impeccable small store (two shops, one upstairs and one down around the corner) stocks super-cool gear, from fashion to housewares and gifts, all by contemporary Greek designers. Great for gift shopping – who doesn't want a set of cheerful 'evil eye' coasters or some Hermes-winged beach sandals?

Flâneur
DESIGN

(Map p86; ☑210 322 6900; www.facebook.com/flaneursouvenirsandsupplies; Adrianou 110, cnr Flessa, Plaka; ⊙11am-8pm; MSyntagma, Monastiraki) This cute shop has a tightly curated collection of souvenirs and travel gear. Get your hand-stamped 'φλανέρ' (that's 'flâneur' spelled in Greek) notebooks and your feta-tin patches and pins here. Even stocks vinyl by Greek indie bands.

Anavasi
MAPS

(Map p86; ☑210 321 8104; www.anavasi.gr; Voulis 32, cnr Apollonos, Syntagma; ⊙9.30am-5pm Mon & Wed, to 8.30pm Tue, Thu & Fri, 10am-4.30pm Sat; MSyntagma) Great travel bookshop with an extensive range of Greece maps and walking and activity guides.

Korres
COSMETICS

(Map p86; ☑210 321 0054; www.korres.com; Ermou 4, Syntagma; ⊙9am-9pm Mon-Fri, to 8pm Sat; MSyntagma) Many pharmacies stock some of this popular line of natural beauty products, but you can get the full range at the company's original location, where it grew out of a homeopathic pharmacy.

Amorgos
ARTS & CRAFTS

(Map p86; ☑210 324 3836; www.amorgosart.gr; Kodrou 3, Plaka; ⊙11am-8pm Mon-Fri, to 7pm Sat; MSyntagma) Charming store crammed with wooden toys, *karagiozi* (shadow puppets), ceramics, embroidery and other Greek folk art, as well as carved wooden furniture made by the owner.

Matalou at Home/Blanc
FASHION & ACCESSORIES

(Map p86; ☑211 184 5416; www.facebook.com/matalouathome; Ipitou 5, Syntagma; ⊙noon-9pm Tue, Thu & Fri, until 5pm Wed & Sat; MSyntagma) Two designers share the space here. Matalou at Home creates an appealing range of affordable bags and accessories from leather, cotton and natural fibres, with the designs inspired by Athens. Blanc (www.blanc.gr) is all about handmade hats.

Chat to the owner for recommendations and tips on other local designers and hip hang-outs, covered twice a year in their free *By Local* map.

Aristokratikon
FOOD

(Map p86; ☑210 322 0546; www.aristokratikon.com; Voulis 7, Syntagma; ⊙8am-9pm Mon-Fri, to 4pm Sat; MSyntagma) This shop has been making fine chocolates since 1928. One of its specialities is dried fruits and candied citrus peel dipped in dark chocolate.

Aidinis Errikos
ARTS & CRAFTS

(Map p86; ☑210 323 4591; www.facebook.com/Errikos.Aidinis; Nikis 32, Syntagma; ⊙10am-5pm Mon, Wed & Sat, to 8.30pm Tue, Thu & Fri; MSyntagma) Artisan Errikos Aidinis' unique metal creations are made in his workshop at the back of this charming store, including small mirrors, candlesticks, lamps, aeroplanes and his signature bronze boats.

Xylouris
MUSIC

(Map p96; ☑210 322 2711; http://xilouris.gr; Stoa Pesmatzoglou, Panepistimiou 39, Panepistimio; ⊙9am-4pm Mon, Wed & Sat, to 8pm Tue, Thu & Fri; MPanepistimio) Set in an arcade with several other music shops, this treasure trove is run by the family of legendary Cretan composer Nikos Xylouris. They can guide you through the comprehensive range of Greek music CDs and DVDs, as well help with a new bouzouki purchase.

🏠 Monastiraki & Psyrri

★Shedia
ARTS & CRAFTS

(Map p86; ☑213 023 1220; www.shediart.gr; Nikiou 2, Monastiraki; MMonastiraki) Meaning 'raft', *Shedia* is Greece's version of street-vendor magazines such as the *Big Issue*. Unsold copies are now being upcycled into an appealing range of homewares and accessories including papier-mâché lampshades and bowls, dainty earrings and necklaces. The space beneath their editorial offices has been reimagined as a shop and stylish cafe-bar.

★Varvakios Agora
MARKET

(Athens Central Market; Map p96; Athinas, btwn Sofokleous & Evripidou, Psyrri; ⊙7am-6pm Mon-Sat; MPanepistimio, Omonia) A wonderful sight in its own right, this huge old wrought-iron market hall is dedicated to fish and meat, especially row upon row of lamb carcasses, hanging in just-barely EU-compliant glass cases. Tavernas within the market, many open 24/7, are an Athenian institution for hangover-busting *patsas* (tripe soup).

LOCAL KNOWLEDGE

FLEA MARKETS

Athens' flea markets are not for everyone. The city's trash-pickers prefer the Eleonas Flea Market (Pazari; Agias Annis, Eleonas; ⊙dawn-2pm Sun; ⓂEleonas). In this industrial part of town, junk dealers, sellers of vegetables, new clothes and bulk items lay out their wares in several warehouses and parking lots. The brave of heart can find some bargains, collectables and kitsch delights among the junk. You may need to scout around a bit to find it. When you get out at the metro stop, walk south until you see parked cars and a church in a traffic circle. Vendors are usually set up in warehouses nearby.

The central Monastiraki Flea Market (Map p86; Plateia Avyssinias, Monastiraki; ⊙daily May-Oct, Sun-Wed & Fri Nov-Apr; ⓂMonastiraki) is easy to locate. Ifestou is signed as the 'Athens flea market', but the street mostly has souvenir shops. The true flea feel is on Plateia Avyssinias and in nearby small streets, where dusty *palaiopoleia* ('old-stuff sellers') rule. For the best rummaging, come Sunday mornings, when the bric-a-brac explodes out onto the pavements, including on Astingos and even across Ermou in Psyrri.

West across Athinas is the fruit and vegetable market (Map p96; Athinas, btwn Sofokleous & Evripidou, Psyrri; ⊙7am-6pm Mon-Sat; ⓂOmonia, Monastiraki). In the surrounding streets are olives, cheeses and spices.

To Rodakio & Fotagogos   BOOKS
(Map p86; ☑210 383 9355; www.facebook.com/ToRodakio; Kolokotroni 59b, Monastiraki; ⊙11.30am-9pm Mon-Sat; ⓂMonastiraki) This charming bookshop and gallery, run by Julia Tsiakiris and hidden at the back of cafe-bar Noel (p120), is a wonderful find. Browse locally published books and magazines (some in English), and quirky pieces of art.

Pan-Pol   HATS
(Map p96; ☑210 321 1431; Athinas 36, Monastiraki; ⊙10am-5pm Mon, Wed & Sat, to 7pm Tue, Thu & Fri; ⓂMonastiraki) Whether you want a moss-green fedora or a nontouristy Greek fisherman's cap, this shoebox of a shop will have it, along with many other felt hats in lovely colours and classic shapes. Most of the stock comes from a workshop upstairs, and prices start at just €10.

Fotsi   FOOD
(Map p96; ☑210 321 7131; www.fotsi.gr; Evripidou 39, Psyrri; ⊙8am-5pm Mon-Sat; ⓂMonastiraki) Evripidou is Athens' traditional street for spices, a couple of highly aromatic blocks of Mediterranean herbs and imported seeds, barks and other wonders. Three generations of the same family have run Fotsi, the most picturesque of half a dozen shops here, all overflowing with hundreds of ways to add flavour and fragrance to your life.

Yiannis Samouelian   MUSICAL INSTRUMENTS
(Map p86; ☑210 321 2433; www.musicshop.gr; Ifestou 36, Monastiraki; ⊙11am-8pm; ⓂMonastiraki) Wedged between more-modern, generic shops on Ifestou, this shop is the place to buy the bouzouki of your dreams; handmade ones cost around €180. It has been dealing in musical instruments from around the world since 1928.

Martinos   ANTIQUES
(Map p86; ☑210 321 2414; www.martinosart.gr; Pandrosou 50, Monastiraki; ⊙10am-3pm Mon, Wed & Sat, to 6pm Tue, Thu & Fri; ⓂMonastiraki) This Monastiraki landmark opened in 1890 and has an excellent, sometimes museum-quality selection of Greek and European antiques and collectables, including painted dowry chests, icons, coins, glassware, porcelain and furniture.

Center of Hellenic Tradition   ARTS & CRAFTS
(Map p86; ☑210 321 3023; Pandrosou 36, Monastiraki; ⊙10am-6pm Tue-Sat; ⓂMonastiraki) This organisation collects excellent traditional craftwork and stocks its shop with ceramics, sculpture and handicrafts from around the country.

It shares an upstairs space with the old-style coffee house Orea Hellas (p120) that makes a nice break from the Monastiraki shopping frenzy.

Monastic Art   HOMEWARES
(Map p86; ☑210 324 5034; http://monasticart.gr; Pandrosou 28, Monastiraki; ⊙10am-7pm Mon-Sat; ⓂMonastiraki) All of the products in this store are made by monks on Mt Athos: olives, wine, beauty products from wild and cultivated herbs, and beautiful gold and

ATHENS & AROUND SHOPPING

silver icons. Prices range from €5 to well over €25,000.

Olgianna Melissinos
SHOES

(Map p86; ☑210 331 1925; www.melissinos -sandals.gr; Normanou 7, Monastiraki; ⊙10am-6pm Wed, Sat & Sun, to 8pm Tue, Thu & Fri; Ⓜ Monastiraki) A scion of the legendary poet/sandalmaker Stavros Melissinos (along with brother Pantelis, who has a separate shop), Olgianna has a line of custom-fitted sandals as well as smart belts and bags. She can also make designs to order.

Melissinos Art
SHOES

(Map p96; ☑210 321 9247; www.melissinos-art. com; Agias Theklas 2, Psyrri; ⊙10am-8pm Tue-Sun May-Sep, to 6pm Oct-Apr; Ⓜ Monastiraki) Pantelis Melissinos continues the sandalmaking tradition started by his grandfather in 1920 and made famous by his poet/cobbler father Stavros, who built his reputation crafting Classical-inspired shoe designs for Hollywood stars and VIPs. The shop can get a bit crowded, as people come for charming Pantelis himself. Prices are reasonable - especially as the shoes are adjusted to your feet.

🏠 Exarhia

⭐ Free Thinking Zone
BOOKS

(Map p96; ☑210 361 7461; www.freethinking zone.gr; Skoufa 64, Exarhia; ⊙10am-9pm Mon-Fri, to 8pm Sat, noon-5pm Sun; Ⓜ Panepistimio) Billing itself as Greece's first activist bookshop, the Free Thinking Zone specialises in books on LGBT issues, refugees, violence in society and so on. However, rather than being earnest, it's quite a fun and creative place. It has a cafe and sells locally made souvenirs such as their multilingual board game Beat the Book Bug.

ℹ️ WEEKLY FOOD MARKETS

Most Athens neighbourhoods have a weekly *laïki agora*, a street market for fruit, veg, fish, olives, honey, handmade products and flowers. Even if you're not interested in grocery shopping, they are wonderful street theatre and very photogenic. Good ones include those in Kolonaki (Map p110; www.laikesagores. gr; Xenokratous, Kolonaki; ⊙7am-2pm Fri; Ⓜ Evangelismos) and Exarhia (Laïki Agora; Map p96; Kalidromiou, Exarhia; ⊙6am-2pm Sat; 🚌026, Ⓜ Omonia).

⭐ Zacharias
FASHION & ACCESSORIES

(Map p96; www.zacharias.es; Zoodohou Pigis 55, Exarhia; ⊙10am-5pm Mon-Sat; Ⓜ Omonia) A Greek-Spanish duo specialising in silk-screen designs inspired by classical motifs. Especially nice are their leather notebooks, wallets and more, where black ink on the natural hide echoes the colours of ancient pottery. Some of their work shows up in museum shops, but this storefront and workspace has the best selection.

Koukoutsi
FASHION & ACCESSORIES

(Map p96; ☑210 361 4060; www.koukoutsi.net; Skoufa 81, Exarhia; ⊙10am-5pm Mon, Wed & Sat, until 8.30pm Tue, Thu & Fri; Ⓜ Panepistimio) Niko and Taso design the simple, elegant Athens-and Greece-inspired graphics that adorn the T-shirts, accessories and art prints sold in this tiny shop. Their products are available in a few other boutiques and gift shops around the city, but this one has the largest selection in a full range of sizes and colours.

Plastikourgeio
GIFTS & SOUVENIRS

(Map p96; ☑213 044 3356; http://plastikourgeio. com; Asklipiou 51, Exarhia; ⊙10.30am-3.30pm Mon & Wed, until 7pm Tue, until 8pm Thu & Fri; Ⓜ Panepistimio) In a time when the world is worried about single-use plastics and waste, this store is there to help; it stocks products made from recycled plastic or goods that help avoid the use of plastic in the first place. There are a few nice local craft products to browse.

Redo
FASHION & ACCESSORIES

(Map p96; ☑215 501 7280; www.redo.gr; Asklipiou 67, Exarhia; ⊙3-8pm Mon-Fri, 11am-3pm Sat; Ⓜ Panepistimio) Cork fabric from Portugal and Italian leather are used for the striking range of handbags and backpacks made at this atelier by designer Maria Mavroudi. Come here to see the full range and have your bag customised as you like.

🏠 Kolonaki, Mets & Pangrati

Lemisios
SHOES

(Map p110; ☑210 361 1161; Lykavittou 6, Kolonaki; ⊙9am-3pm Mon, Wed & Sat, to 8.30pm Tue, Thu & Fri; Ⓜ Syntagma, Panepistimio) An Athens classic, open since 1912, with classic designs – T-straps, ballet flats, elegant Oxfords (their only style for men) – all custom-fit just for you. Bespoke designs are also possible. Considering the level of craft, this place is surprisingly affordable with shoes starting at €100.

Katerina Ioannidis JEWELLERY

(Map p110; ☑ 6932375717; www.katerina ioannidis.com; ⊙ 10am-4pm Mon, Wed & Sat, to 9pm Tue, Thu & Fri; Ⓜ Syntagma) From a family of goldsmiths, Ioannidis merges Greek and other global folkloric elements into jewellery that is light, bohemian and sometimes even a little funny: a pendant of, say, a gold-plated sheep's head set on a fuzzy black pompom, or a bean-shaped charm.

Mastiha Shop FOOD

(Map p110; ☑ 210 363 2750; www.mastihashop. com; Panepistimiou 6, Kolonaki; ⊙ 9am-8pm Mon & Wed, to 9pm Tue, Thu & Fri, to 5pm Sat; Ⓜ Syntagma) Mastic (*mastiha* in Greek), the medicinal resin from rare trees only found on the island of Chios, is the key ingredient in everything in this store, from natural skin products to a liqueur that's divine when served chilled.

Kombologadiko FASHION & ACCESSORIES

(Map p110; ☑ 212 700 0500; www.kombologadiko. gr; Amerikis 9, Kolonaki; ⊙ 10am-4pm Mon, Wed & Sat, to 9pm Tue, Thu & Fri; Ⓜ Syntagma) If you're in the market for a very special set of that old-school Greek accessory, *komboloï* (worry beads), check this oh-so-elegant showroom. It stocks ready-made designs, some from industrial materials as well as semiprecious stones and amber, starting from as little as €7. They can also string custom sets from their collection of beads.

Apivita COSMETICS

(Map p110; ☑ 210 364 0560; www.apivita.com; Solonos 6, Kolonaki; ⊙ 10am-9pm Tue, Thu & Fri, to 5pm Mon, Wed & Sat; Ⓜ Syntagma) Honey, propolis and other bee-made stuff are the wonder ingredients in many of Apivita's natural beauty products. You can also try Greek herbal teas or head upstairs to the hairdressers, barber shop and spa (which is closed Monday).

★ **Hallelujah** FASHION & ACCESSORIES

(Map p110; ☑ 210 723 5210; www.hallelujahdesign. gr; Archelaou 32, Pangrati; ⊙ 10.30am-2.30pm & 5.30-9pm Tue, Thu & Fri, 11am-6pm Wed & Sat; Ⓜ Evangelismos) Eleftheria Domenikou is the young designer whose minimalistic, elegant yet comfortable clothes and accessories are stocked here. She cooperates with jewellery designers and stocks some other cute accessories and gifts.

ℹ Information

DANGERS & ANNOYANCES

Since the financial crisis, crime has risen in Athens. But this is a rise from almost zero, and violent street crime remains relatively rare. Nonetheless, travellers should be alert. Stay aware of your surroundings at night, especially in streets southwest of Omonia and parts of Metaxourgio, where prostitutes and drug users gather.

EMERGENCY

If you are using a foreign mobile phone in Greece, the only three-digit emergency number that works is the main one (☑ 112).

Greece's country code	☑ 30
Emergency Assistance	☑ 112
Police	☑ 100 or 210 770 5711
Tourist Police	☑ 171 or 210 920 0724
Ambulance	☑ 116

MEDICAL SERVICES

Check pharmacy windows for details of the nearest duty pharmacy, or call ☑ 1434 (Greek only). There's a 24-hour pharmacy at the airport (p130).

SOS Doctors (☑ 210 821 2222, 1016; www. sosiatroi.gr; ⊙ 24hr) Pay service with English-speaking doctors who make house (or hotel) calls.

MONEY

Major banks have branches around Syntagma. ATMs are plentiful enough in commercial districts, but harder to find in more residential areas.

National Bank of Greece (☑ 210 334 0500; cnr Karageorgi Servias & Stadiou, Syntagma; Ⓜ Syntagma) Has a 24-hour automated exchange machine.

Onexchange Currency and money transfers. Branches include **Syntagma** (☑ 210 331 2462; www.onexchange.gr; Karageorgi Servias 2, Syntagma; ⊙ 9am-9pm; Ⓜ Syntagma) and **Monastiraki** (☑ 210 322 2657; www.onexchange. gr; Areos 1, Monastiraki; ⊙ 9am-9pm; Ⓜ Monastiraki).

POST

The Greek postal system is not entirely reliable and tends to be slow. Larger post offices sell boxes and the like for shipping.

Athens Central Post Office (Map p96; ☑ 210 321 6024; www.elta.gr; Eolou 100, Omonia; ⊙ 7.30am-8.30pm Mon-Fri, to 2.45pm Sat; Ⓜ Omonia)

Parcel Post Office (Map p86; ☑ 210 321 8143; www.elta.gr; Mitropoleos 60,

Monastiraki; ⊘7.30am-8.30pm Mon-Fri; Ⓜ Monastiraki)

Syntagma Post Office (Map p86; ☑ 210 324 5970; www.elta.gr; Mitropoleos 2, Syntagma; ⊘7.30am-8.30pm Mon-Fri, to 2.45pm Sat, 9am-1pm Sun; Ⓜ Syntagma)

TOURIST INFORMATION

Athens City Information Kiosk (Map p86; www.thisisathens.org; Plateia Syntagmatos, Syntagma; ⊘9am-6pm; Ⓜ Syntagma) Dishes out leaflets and advice. Also has a branch at the **airport** (☑ 210 353 0390; www.athensconventionbureau.gr/en/content/info-kiosk-athens-international-airport; Eleftherios Venizelos International Airport; ⊘8am-8pm; Ⓜ Airport).

Athens Contemporary Art Map (http://athensartmap.net) Download a PDF of art spaces and events; alternatively, pick up a paper copy at galleries and cafes around town.

EOT (Greek National Tourism Organisation; Map p80; ☑ 210 331 0347, 210 331 0716; www.visitgreece.gr; Dionysiou Areopagitou 18-20, Makrygianni; ⊘8am-8pm Mon-Fri, 10am-4pm Sat & Sun May-Sep, 9am-7pm Mon-Fri Oct-Apr; Ⓜ Akropoli) Free Athens map, current site hours, and bus and train information. Also has a branch at the airport (⊘9am to 5pm Monday to Friday, 10am to 4pm Saturday).

ⓘ Getting There & Away

AIR

Athens' **airport** (ATH; Map p140; ☑ 210 353 0000; www.aia.gr), at Spata, 27km east of Athens, is a manageable single terminal with all the modern conveniences, including 24-hour luggage storage in the arrivals hall (from €3.50 for six hours), a children's playroom and even a small archaeological museum above the check-in hall for passing the time.

It's served by many major and budget airlines as well as high-season charters, including **easyJet** (☑ 211 198 0013; www.easyjet.com).

Between Aegean Airlines and Olympic Air (which have merged but still run separate routes), there are flights to all islands with airports.

Aegean Airlines (https://en.aegeanair.com)

Astra Airlines (☑ 801 700 7466, 2310 489 390; www.astra-airlines.gr) Thessaloniki-based, but with a few flights from Athens to Kozani/Kastoria, Chios and Samos.

Olympic Air (☑ 801 801 0101, 21035 50500; www.olympicair.com)

Sky Express (GQ; ☑ 215 215 6510; www.skyexpress.gr)

BOAT

Most ferry, hydrofoil and high-speed catamaran services to the islands leave from the massive port at Piraeus (p136), southwest of Athens.

Purchase tickets online at **Greek Ferries** (☑ 281 052 9000; www.greekferries.gr), over the phone or at booths on the quay next to each ferry. Travel agencies selling tickets also surround each port; there is no surcharge.

BUS

Athens has two main intercity bus stations, plus a small bay for buses bound for south and east Attica. Pick up timetables at the tourist office, or see the relevant KTEL operator's website; find a master list of KTEL companies at www.ktelbus.com. **KTEL Attikis** (☑ 210 880 8000; http://ktelattikis.gr) covers the Attica peninsula; **KTEL Argolida** (☑ 275 202 7423; www.ktelargolida.gr) serves Epidavros, with dedicated buses during the summer festival season.

Advance tickets for services from **Kifissos Terminal A** (☑ 210 515 0025; Drakontos 76, Peristeri; Ⓜ Agios Antonios) can be purchased at the **ticket office** (☑ 210 523 3810; Sokratous 59, Omonia; ⊘7am-5.15pm Mon-Fri; Ⓜ Omonia) near Omonia.

For international buses (from Bulgaria, Turkey etc), there is no single station; some come to Kifissos, while others stop between Plateia Karaïskaki and Plateia Omonias. **Tourist Service** (www.tourist-service.com) is one operator from Piraeus and Athens to Bulgaria.

CAR & MOTORCYCLE

Attiki Odos (Attiki Rd), Ethniki Odos (National Rd) and various ring roads facilitate getting in and out of Athens.

Nationwide roadside assistance is available through **ELPA** (Elliniki Leschi Aftokinitou kai Periigiseon; ☑ 24hr roadside assistance 10400).

The airport has all major car hire companies, and the north end of Leoforos Syngrou, near the Temple of Olympian Zeus (p70), is dotted with firms. Expect to pay €45 per day, less for three or more days.

Avis (☑ 210 322 4951; www.avis.gr; Leoforos Syngrou 23, Makrygianni; ⊘7.30am-9pm; Ⓜ Akropoli)

Budget (☑ 210 922 4200; www.budget.gr; Leoforos Syngrou 23, Makrygianni; ⊘7.30am-9pm; Ⓜ Akropoli)

Hertz (☑ 210 922 0102; www.hertz.gr; Leoforos Syngrou 12, Makrygianni; ⊘8am-9pm; Ⓜ Akropoli)

Kosmos (☑ 210 923 4695; www.kosmos-carrental.com; Leoforos Syngrou 5, Makrygianni; ⊘8am-8.30pm; Ⓜ Akropoli)

Motorent (☑ 210 923 4939; www.motorent.gr; Kavalloti 4, Makrygianni; ⊘9am-5pm Tue-Fri, 9.30am-2pm Sat; Ⓜ Akropoli) From €20 per day; must have motorcycle licence (and nerves of steel).

TRAIN

Intercity (IC) trains to central and northern Greece depart from the central **Larisis train station** (Stathmos Larisis; [J] €1 per 1 min 6am-11pm 14511; www.trainose.gr; [M] Larissa), about 1km northwest of Plateia Omonias.

For the Peloponnese, take the **suburban rail** (Proastiakos; [J] 14511; www.trainose.gr) to Kiato and change for a bus there. The Patra train line is chronically closed for repairs, so OSE buses, via Kiato, replace its services. Because of this, it's easier to just take a bus from Athens' Kifissos Bus Terminal A to your ultimate destination.

Domestic schedules/fares should be confirmed online or at **OSE** ([J] 210 362 1039; www.trainose.gr; Sina 6, Panepistimio; ⊙ 8am-3pm Mon-Fri; [M] Panepistimio), where tickets can also be purchased.

For tips on international trains, consult www.seat61.com; all trains in and out of Greece go via Thessaloniki. International tickets must be purchased in person at the train station.

DESTINATION	TIME (HR)	FARE (€)	FREQUENCY
Alexandroupoli	14	38	1 daily (overnight, via Thessaloniki)
Alexandroupoli (IC)	15	63	1 daily (via Thessaloniki)
Corinth (suburban rail)	1	9	hourly 5.30am-11.30pm
Kalambaka (for Meteora)	5	18	1 daily direct, 5 via Paleofarsalos (€32)
Kiato (suburban rail)	1hr 20min	12	hourly 5.30am-11.30pm
Thessaloniki	6	25	1 daily (overnight)
Thessaloniki (IC)	5½	45	5 daily
Volos (IC)	5	35	4 daily (via Larissa)

❶ Getting Around

Central Athens is compact and good for strolling, with narrow streets and a lovely pedestrian promenade. From Gazi in the west to the Byzantine & Christian Museum in the east, for example, takes only about 45 minutes – so you may find you need a transit pass very little or not at all. In summer, however, take the punishing sun into consideration.

TO/FROM THE AIRPORT

Bus

Express buses operate 24 hours between the airport and key points in the city. At the airport, buy tickets (€6; not valid for other forms of public transport) at the booth near the stop.

Plateia Syntagmatos Bus X95 (Map p86; tickets €6; ⊙ 24hr), one to 1½ hours, every 20 to 30 minutes. The Syntagma stop is on Othonos St.

Kifissos Terminal A and **Liossion Terminal B bus stations** Bus X93, one hour (terminal B) to 1½ hours (terminal A), every 20 to 30 minutes (60 minutes at night).

Piraeus Bus X96, 1½ hours, every 20 minutes. To Plateia Karaïskaki.

Metro

Metro line 3 goes from the airport to the city centre. Trains run every 30 minutes, leaving the airport between 6.30am and 11.30pm, on the hour and half-hour. Coming from the centre, trains leave Monastiraki between 5.40am and 11pm; some terminate early at Doukissis Plakentias, so disembark and wait for the airport train (displayed on the train and platform screen).

Tickets from the airport are priced separately from the rest of the metro. The cost is €10 per adult or €18 return (return valid seven days). A €22 pass, good for three days, includes round-trip airport service and all other transit in the centre.

Suburban Rail

Suburban rail (one hour) is an option to the centre, if you're headed near Larisis train station (after a change at Ano Liosia) or a stop on metro line 1 (change at Neratziotissa). It's the same price as the metro. Trains to Athens run every 15 minutes from 5.10am to 11.30pm; to the airport, from 6am to midnight.

Suburban rail also goes from the airport to Piraeus (change trains at Neratziotissa) and Kiato in the Peloponnese (via Corinth).

Taxi

From the airport to the centre, fares are flat day/night €38/54 rates; tolls are included. The ride takes 30 to 45 minutes. For Piraeus (one hour), expect day/night €50/60.

To the airport, drivers will usually propose a flat fare of €40 from the centre. You can insist on the meter, but with all the legitimate add-ons – tolls, airport fee, luggage fees – it usually works out the same.

To prebook a taxi, contact **Welcome Pickups** (www.welcomepickups.com), at the same flat rate as regular taxis.

BICYCLE

Even experienced cyclists might find Athens' roads a challenge, with no cycle lanes, often reckless drivers and loads of hills – but some hardy locals do ride. A bike route runs from Thisio to the coast. A few outfits offer bicycle hire, such as **Funky Ride** (☑ 211 710 9366; www.funkyride.gr; Dimitrakopoulou 1, Makrygianni; 3hr/day €7/15; ☺10.30am-3.30pm & 5.30-8.30pm Mon-Fri, 10.30am-4pm Sat; Ⓜ Akropoli) and Solebike (p99).

CAR & MOTORCYCLE

Athens' notorious traffic congestion, confusing signage, impatient drivers and narrow one-way streets make for occasionally nightmarish driving.

Contrary to what you see, parking is actually illegal alongside kerbs marked with yellow lines, on footpaths and in pedestrian malls. Paid parking areas require tickets available from kiosks.

PUBLIC TRANSPORT

Tickets & Passes

The transit system uses the unified Ath.ena Ticket, a reloadable paper card available from ticket offices and machines in the metro. You can load it with a set amount of money or buy a number of rides (€1.40 each; discount when you buy five or 10) or a 24-hour/five-day travel pass for €4.50/9.

Children under six travel free; people under 18 or over 65 are technically eligible to pay half fare, but you must buy the Ath.ena Ticket from a person at a ticket office. If you're staying a while, you may want the sturdier plastic Ath.ena Card, also available at ticket offices; you must load at least €4.50 to start.

Swipe the card at metro turnstiles or, on buses and trams, validate the ticket in the machine as you board, and keep it with you in case of spot-checks. One swipe is good for 90 minutes, including any transfers or return trips.

Bus & Trolleybus

Local express buses, regular buses and electric trolleybuses operate every 15 minutes from 5am to midnight. In lieu of maps, use Google Maps for directions or the trip planner on the website of the bus company, **OASA** (Athens Urban Transport Organisation; ☑ 11185; www.oasa.gr; ☺call centre 6.30am-10.30pm Mon-Fri, from 7.30am Sat & Sun) (click 'Telematics'). The most useful lines for tourists are trolleybuses 2, 5, 11 and 15, which run north from Syntagma past the National Archaeological Museum (p90). For all buses, board at any door; swipe your ticket on validation machines.

Express buses from the airport (p130) run 24 hours, and also require a dedicated ticket, purchased from a kiosk by the stop.

Buses to Cape Sounion (Map p86; www.ktelattikis.gr)

Buses to Elefsina (Map p96)

Buses to Moni Kaisarianis depart from beside the **Athens University** (Map p96; www.uoa.gr; Omonoia 30, Panepistimio; ☺ closed to public; Ⓜ Panepistimio) building at Panepistimio.

Metro

The metro works well and posted maps have clear icons and English labels. Trains operate from 5.30am to 12.30am, every four minutes during peak periods and every 10 minutes off-peak. On Friday and Saturday, lines 2 and 3 run till 2.30am. Get information at www.stasy.gr. All stations have wheelchair access.

Line 1 (Green) The oldest line, Kifisia–Piraeus, known as the Ilektriko, is slower than the others and above ground. After hours, a **night bus** (Map p96) (500, Piraeus–Kifisia) follows the route, stopping outside the metro stations.

Line 2 (Red) Runs from Agios Antonios in the northwest to Agios Dimitrios in the southeast.

Line 3 (Blue) Runs northeast from Egaleo to Doukissis Plakentias, with airport trains continuing on from there. Transfer for line 1 at Monastiraki; for line 2 at Syntagma.

Train

Suburban rail (p131) is fast, but not commonly used by visitors – though it goes to the airport and as far as Piraeus and the northern Peloponnese. The airport–Kiato line (€14, 1½ hours) connects to the metro at Doukissis Plakentias and Neratziotissa. Two other lines cross the metro at Larisis station.

A short **funicular railway** (Teleferik; ☑ 210 721 0701; www.lycabettushill.com; Aristippou 1, Kolonaki; return/one way €7.50/5; ☺ 8.30-2.30am) runs up Lykavittos Hill.

Tram

Athens' trams are slow but can make for very picturesque journeys, particularly once you're following the lines along the coast to either Glyfada or Piraeus. There are three lines:

Line 1 (Red) Connects Kasomoule with Piraeus.

Line 2 (Green) Connects Kasomoule and Glyfada.

Line 3 (Blue): Connects Piraeus with Glyfada.

Trams run from 5.30am to 1am Sunday to Thursday (every 10 minutes), and to 2.30am on Friday and Saturday (every 40 minutes). Ticket-vending machines are on the platforms.

TAXI

Athens' taxis are excellent value and can be the key for efficient travel on some routes. But it can be tricky getting one, especially during rush hour. Thrust your arm out vigorously... you may still have to shout your destination to the driver to see if he or she is interested. Make sure the meter is on. It can be much easier to use the mobile app **Beat** (www.thebeat.co/gr) or **Taxiplon** (☑ 210 277 3600, 18222; www.taxiplon.gr) – you can pay in cash. Or call a taxi from dispatchers such as **Athina 1** (☑ 210 921 0417, 210 921 2800; www.athens1.gr), **Enotita** (☑ 6980666720, 18388, 210 649 5099; www.athensradiotaxienotita.gr) or **Parthenon** (☑ 210 532 3300; www.radiotaxi-parthenon.gr). For day trips, **Athens Tour Taxi** (☑ 6932295395; www.athenstourtaxi.com) comes recommended.

If a taxi picks you up while already carrying passengers, the fare is not shared: each person pays the fare on the meter minus any diversions to drop others (note what it's at when you get in). Short trips around central Athens cost about €5; there are surcharges for luggage and pick-ups at transport hubs. Nights and holidays, the fare is about 60% higher.

ATHENS PORTS

Piraeus   Πειραιάς

POP 163,688

Ten kilometres southwest of central Athens, Piraeus is dazzling in its scale, its seemingly endless quays filled with ferries, ships and hydrofoils. It's the biggest port in the Mediterranean (more than 20 million passengers pass through annually), the hub of the Aegean ferry network, the centre of Greece's maritime trade and the base for its large merchant navy. While technically its own city, it melds into the Athens sprawl, with close to half a million people living in the greater area.

Shabby and congested, central Piraeus is not a place where visitors normally choose to linger. Beyond its shipping offices, banks and public buildings are a jumble of pedestrian precincts, shopping strips and rather grungy areas. The most attractive quarter lies east around Zea Marina, Pasalimani and Mikrolimano harbours. The latter is lined with cafes, restaurants and bars filled with Athenians, locals and visitors.

⊙ Sights

Electric Railways Museum   MUSEUM
(Map p134; ☑ 210 414 7552, 210 412 9503; www.museum-synt-isap.gr; Loudovikou 1; ⊙ 9am-2pm Mon-Fri; M Piraeus) FREE Tucked inside the Piraeus station, this museum is a trove of old switches, nifty models and cool machinery, including a gleaming old wooden train

car. It's a passion project of a former railway employee, and he and the other staff are full of interesting facts.

Piraeus Archaeological Museum   MUSEUM
(Map p134; ☑ 210 452 1598; http://odysseus.culture.gr; Harilaou Trikoupi 31; adult/child €4/free; ⊙ 8am-3pm Tue-Sun; M Piraeus) The museum's star attraction is the magnificent statue of Apollo, the *Piraeus Kouros*, the larger-than-life, oldest hollow bronze statue yet found. It dates from about 520 BCE and was discovered buried in rubble in 1959. Other important finds from the area include fine tomb reliefs from the 4th to 2nd centuries BCE.

Hellenic Maritime Museum   MUSEUM
(☑ 210 451 6264; http://hmmuseum.gr; Akti Themistokleous, Plateia Freatidas, Zea Marina; €4; ⊙ 9am-2pm Tue-Sat; M Piraeus) As nautical museums go, this isn't one of the best, despite Greece's long maritime history. Still, it does have all the requisite models of ancient and modern ships, seascapes by leading 19th- and 20th-century Greek painters, guns, flags and maps, and even part of a submarine.

🛏 Sleeping

If you're catching an early ferry, it can make sense to stay in Piraeus instead of central Athens. The area closer to Pasalimani has the newer and more elegant hotels.

Phidias Piraeus   HOTEL €
(Map p134; ☑ 210 429 6480; www.hotelphidias.gr; Kountouriotou 189, Zea Marina; s/d/tr from €50/80/120; ❄ @ 🛜; 🚌 040 to Terpsithea) A far cry from standard Piraeus grunge, this place is also a bit far from the metro (20-minute walk) and the ferry port. But it runs a free shuttle and you're close to the prettier leisure port, for an evening's stroll. Rooms are simple and new, with cute wallpaper. Full breakfast is an extra €7.

Piraeus Dream City Hotel   HOTEL €
(Map p134; ☑ 210 411 0555; www.piraeusdream.gr; Notara 78; d/tr from €75/95; ❄ @ 🛜; M Piraeus) About a 10-minute walk from the metro, this modern hotel has spacious rooms in whites and creams. Quiet rooms start on the 4th floor. It has a rooftop restaurant.

Hotel Triton   HOTEL €€
(Map p134; ☑ 210 417 3457; www.htriton.gr; Tsamadou 8; s/d/tr from €58/94/95; ❄ @ 🛜; M Piraeus) This simple, conveniently located hotel with helpful staff is a treat compared

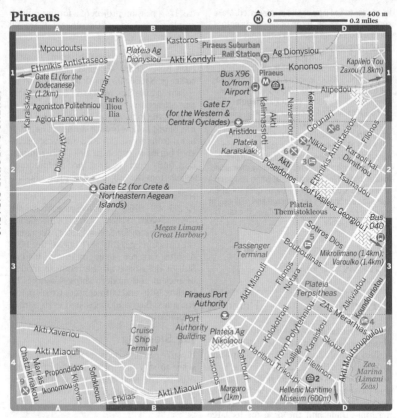

Piraeus

Sights
1 Electric Railways Museum C1
2 Piraeus Archaeological Museum D4

Sleeping
3 Hotel Triton...D2
4 Phidias Piraeus D4

5 Piraeus Dream City Hotel.....................D3

Eating
6 General Market C2
7 Mandragoras D2
8 Rakadiko D2
9 Yperokeanio A4

to some of the other run-down joints in Piraeus. Some rooms overlook the bustling market square. There's one family suite (€148) with a large terrace.

✗ Eating & Drinking

The Great Harbour is backed by lots of gritty cafes and fast-food joints; better food and ambience hide away in the backstreets or further afield around Mikrolimano, Zea Marina and along the waterfront promenade at Freatida.

★ **Yperokeanio**   MEZEDHES €
(Map p134; ☏ 210 418 0030; Marias Hatzikiri-akou 48; dishes €6-12; ⊗ noon-11.30pm) Grab a cab to this fantastic seafood *mezedhop-oleio*, where you can tuck into small plates of grilled sardines or steamed mussels. For dessert there's *kaimaki* ice cream – an old Asia Minor recipe made chewy with *sahlep* (orchid root) and flavoured with Chios mastic. Book ahead if possible; it's often packed.

★ **Mandragoras** DELI €

(Map p134; 210 417 2961; Gounari 14; ⊙7.45am-4pm Mon, Wed & Sat, to 8pm Tue, Thu & Fri; Ⓜ Piraeus) This superb delicatessen and spice shop offers a fine selection of gourmet cheeses, ready-made mezedhes, olive oils, Greek honey and preserved foods. It's a veritable museum of regional Greek foodstuffs and fantastic for snacks and food gifts.

General Market MARKET €

(Map p134; Dimosthenous; ⊙6am-4pm Mon-Fri; Ⓜ Piraeus) With the sea breezes blowing over the morning hustle and bustle, the Piraeus market is an excellent slice of life. There's a broad range of food and bric-a-brac, as well as cheap bars and cafes around the periphery, especially in the back alley behind.

To Kapileio Tou Zaxou TAVERNA €€

(210 481 3325; Komotinis 37; mains from €15; ⊙noon-1am; 16) It may be a bit inland, but this family-run Greek fish taverna still conveys the spirit of the sea. Choose from grilled catches of the day, calamari and octopus. House wine comes from the big barrels shelved above the tables, as it ought to in a traditional place. A favourite among locals for its reasonable prices and generous portions.

Margaro SEAFOOD €€

(210 451 4226; Marias Hatzikiriakou 126; mains €6-21; ⊙noon-midnight Mon-Sat, to 5.30pm Sun Sep-Jul; 904) This port restaurant is the picture of simplicity, with a menu that comprises exactly three things: salad, fried shrimp and fried red mullet. Although it's tucked away by the naval academy, it's no secret, and can be very crowded on weekends. Take the bus here from the Piraeus metro, or a taxi.

Rakadiko TAVERNA €€

(Map p134; 210 417 8470; www.rakadiko.gr; Karaoli kai Dimitriou 5, Stoa Kouvelou; mains €7-18; ⊙noon-midnight Mon-Sat, 1-6pm Sun; Ⓜ Piraeus) A spot of calm: head into this renovated old shopping arcade to dine under grapevines on mezedhes or classic dishes from all over Greece. There's live *rembetika* (blues) on weekends. If you're not hungry for a full meal, stop at the adjacent sweets shop for ice cream or very good orange-blossom-scented fried *loukoumadhes* (ball-shaped doughnuts served with honey and cinnamon).

ℹ️ **PIRAEUS BUSES**

The metro is preferable, but after it stops at midnight, you can still get to Piraeus on the bus:

From Syntagma Bus 040 (Map p86). On Filellinon just south of Syntagma to Akti Xaveriou (every 10 to 20 minutes from 6am to midnight, half-hourly after).

From Omonia Bus 500 (p132) Opposite the town hall south of Omonia to Plateia Themistokleous (hourly from midnight to 5am, starting in Kifisia).

★ **Varoulko** SEAFOOD €€€

(210 522 8400; www.varoulko.gr; Akti Koumoundourou 52, Mikrolimano; mains €45-65; ⊙1pm-1am; Nautiko Omilos) Chef Lefteris Lazarou, a Piraeus native, has been shaping Greek tastes since the 1980s, when he brought fish to the fine-dining menu. For years he had a Michelin-starred restaurant in Athens, but moved back to his roots in 2014. Michelin still approves, and his cooking remains elegant and creative. The setting in Mikrolimano, where sailboats bob, is lovely.

ℹ️ **Information**

There are luggage lockers at the metro station (€3 for 24 hours, maximum 15 days).

ATMs and moneychangers line the Great Harbour.

Alpha Bank (210 412 1721; Ethnikis Antistaseos 9; ⊙8am-2pm Mon-Fri)

National Bank of Greece (210 414 4311; cnr Antistaseos & Makras Stoas; ⊙8am-2.45pm Mon-Fri)

ℹ️ **Getting There & Away**

The metro and suburban rail from Athens terminate at the **E7 gate** (Map p134) of the Great Harbour on Akti Kalimassioti. A few ferry departure points are just across the road; for further gates, you'll need a port-run bus (free) or a taxi (cheap). The best place to catch the **airport bus X96** (Map p134; adult/child under 6 €6/free) is in front of the church, Agios Dionysios, four blocks north on Papastratou.

The Athens tramway is extending its line from Faliro to the harbour, with a terminus just south of the metro stop; it's expected to be completed in 2021.

BOAT

Piraeus is the busiest port in Greece, with daily service to most island groups. The exceptions are the Ionians, with boats only to Kythira (for the other islands, sail from Igoumenitsa) and the Sporades, plus Kea (Tzia) and Andros in the Cyclades (which sail from Rafina and Lavrio). Piraeus ferries also serve the Peloponnese (Methana, Ermioni, Porto Heli, Monemvasia and Gythio).

Always check departure docks with the ticketing agent.

For Crete, ferries for Iraklio and Hania leave from the western end of Akti Kondyli (Gates **E2** (Map p134) and E3).

Schedules & Tickets

Ferry schedules are reduced in April, May and October, and radically cut in winter, especially to smaller islands. Find schedules and buy tickets online (www.greekferries.gr, www.openseas.gr, www.ferries.gr or company websites), or buy in person at travel agents or at each ferry company's kiosk in front of the boat (open about two hours before sailing). **Piraeus Port Authority** (Map p134; ☎210 455 0000, €0.89 per 1min 14541; www.olp.gr) also has schedule information.

BUS

The X96 Piraeus–Athens Airport Express (p135) stops in front of Agios Dionysios on Papastratou. It runs around the outside of the port also, but stops rarely, so it's better to take the inside-port shuttle to your gate. **Bus 040** (Map p134) goes to Athens from Lambraki at the corner of Vasileos Georgiou II. Arriving, you'll come down Polytehniou; get off at Plateia Koraï.

METRO

The fastest and most convenient link between the Great Harbour and Athens is the metro (€1.40, 30 minutes, every 10 minutes, 5am to midnight), near the ferries at the northern end of Akti Kalimassioti.

You can get the metro to/from the airport (p130) all the way to Piraeus, changing at Monastiraki station.

SUBURBAN RAIL

Piraeus is connected to the suburban rail – the terminus is next to the metro station. To get to the airport or to Kiato in the Peloponnese, you need to change trains at Kato Acharnai.

Getting Around

The port is massive, so a free shuttle bus runs regularly along the quay inside the port from gate E7 to E1; cross over from the metro and you'll see it. For gate E9, look for buses outside the port, with route numbers starting with 8.

The Piraeus city buses most likely to interest travellers are 904 and 905 between Zea Marina and the metro station.

Athens tramway and metro extensions are under way (not completed at the time of research), and have made the port area a zoo of blocked streets and redirected traffic.

Rafina

POP 13,091

Rafina, on Attica's east coast, is a port town with passenger ferries to the northern Cyclades. If this is your destination, it's a good alternative to Piraeus, as it's smaller (hence, less confusing), and fares are about 20% cheaper. It's also a pleasant place to spend a night if ferry schedules require it.

Sleeping & Eating

Avra HOTEL €€

(☎22940 22780; www.hotelavra.gr; Arafinidon Alon 3; d from €75; ❄📶) Set on one end of Rafina's pretty crescent port, Avra is a big and functional hotel that helps make this town a pleasant stop midtransit. (It also runs a free shuttle to the airport, about 30 minutes away.) Rooms are modern and comfortable, with balconies for watching the ships come in.

Ta Kavouria Tou Asimaki GREEK €

(☎22940 24551; Akti Andrea Papandreou; mains from €8; ⏲9am-midnight) One of Rafina's oldest and most loved restaurants, this place sits right on the port and is handy for those waiting to catch a ferry. The food is excellent; fish is fresh and simply prepared, and there are delicacies such as sea-urchin salad. The grilled squid is tender and fragrant. Superfriendly service.

Getting There & Away

Rafina is close to Athens airport (p130), so if you're headed to the northern Cyclades (Mykonos, Naxos etc), consider coming here directly, bypassing Athens and Piraeus completely.

BOAT

Rafina Port Authority (☎22940 28888; www.rafinaport.gr; Akti Andrea Papandreou 10) and www.openseas.gr have information on ferries.

Fast Ferries and Golden Star ferries go to Andros (2½ hours, €19, four to six daily) and Mykonos (4½ hours, €29, two to three daily). Seajets has a high-speed service to Mykonos

(2¼ hours, €33, two daily). Golden Star takes you to Ios (six hours, €48, six weekly). Golden Star and Seajets provide a high-speed service to Naxos (four hours, €33, three daily). Fast Ferries gets you slowly to Naxos (six hours, €30, six weekly). Golden Star takes you to Santorini (Thira; 6¾ hours, €48, one daily). Get to Tinos by high-speed Seajets (two hours, €39, two daily) and regular service with Fast Ferries and Golden Star (3¾ hours, €27, six to nine daily).

BUS

Frequent KTEL buses (p130) run from Athens to Rafina (€2.60, one hour) between 5.45am and 10.30pm, departing from Athens' Mavromateon bus terminal. Buses from Athens airport (p130; €3, 45 minutes) leave from in front of the arrivals hall near the Sofitel, between 4.40am and 10.20pm; buy tickets on the bus. Both stop on the Rafina quay.

Lavrio   Λαύριο
POP 10,370

Lavrio, on the coast 60km southeast of Athens, is the port for ferries to Kea and Kythnos, and high-season catamarans to the western Cyclades. It is, unfortunately, not an exciting place to spend the night. The long beach north of the ferry port is a bit of a windsurfing scene, but that same wind is somewhat wearing if you're not on the water. It has a grand industrial past – from silver mining in antiquity to massive late-19th-century steam-powered mining works – but there's not much happening overall.

The sprawling ruins of the more recent industry are awesome, but open only to Athens Technical University students.

Other minor sights include the Mineralogical Museum (☑22920 26270; Iroön Polytechniou; adult/child €2/free; ⊗10am-noon Fri-Sun) with limited opening hours and a small Archaeological Museum (☑22920 22817; http://odysseus.culture.gr; cnr Agias Paraskevis & Leoforos Souniou; adult/child €2/free; ⊗8am-3pm Tue-Sun).

✖ Eating

Pezodromos   GREEK €
(☑22920 22670; Ermou 40; mains from €8; ⊗noon-midnight; ☑) Located in the old centre of Lavrio, this is a popular fish and seafood tavern – try the octopus in vinegar or stuffed squid. There are also meat dishes, such as spit-roast lamb, and a variety of salads and wild greens for vegetarians.

❶ Getting There & Away

BOAT
Lavrio Port Authority (☑22920 25249; Akti Andrea Papandreou) and www.openseas.gr have ferry information.

BUS
KTEL buses (p130) to Lavrio (€5.30, two hours, every 30 minutes) run from the Mavromateon terminal in Athens. Airport buses leave from the front of the arrivals hall near the Sofitel; you must change buses at Markopoulo. Both stop on the Lavrio quay.

TAXI
Taxi Posidon (☑22920 24200; www.taxiposeidon.gr) can run you to the airport (day/night €38/55, 30 minutes) and central Athens (€55/87, one hour); fares are higher for pick-up in Athens or the airport. Lavrio to Cape Sounion is €12.

AROUND ATHENS

An agricultural region with several large population centres, the southern Attica peninsula has some fine beaches, particularly along the Apollo Coast and at Shinias, near Marathon. It's also known for its wine production.

Until the 7th century, Attica was home to a number of smaller kingdoms, such as those at Eleusis (Elefsina; p145), Ramnous (p142) and Brauron (Vravrona). In pure visual terms, the remains of these cities pale alongside the superb Temple of Poseidon (p141) at Cape Sounion, but any of them can be nice to visit simply because you'll probably have the place to yourself.

Apollo Coast

Glyfada, about 17km southeast of Athens, is an upscale suburb of Athens that marks the beginning of the Apollo Coast (sometimes called the Athenian Riviera), a 48km stretch down to Cape Sounion of fine beaches, resorts and summer nightlife. It's a great place to get out of overheated Athens in summer, and easily reached by bus.

The coast road (Poseidonos Ave, often just called *Paraliaki*) leads from Glyfada to Voula, Kavouri and then bustling and popular Vouliagmeni and ritzy Astir Beach. The coast is a bit expensive, but the further south you go, the cheaper and less built-up it becomes. Of note are the natural mineral waters at Limni Vouliagmenis, and the gay and nudist beaches tucked in the rocky coves at Limanakia.

There's better (free) swimming northeast and east of Athens, at Shinias, Marathon and Vravrona; these take longer to get to and are best reached by car.

🏃 Activities

Most of the Apollo Coast beaches are privately run and charge admission (€5 to €15 per adult). They're usually open from 8am to dusk, May to October (later during heatwaves), and have sunbeds and umbrellas (additional charge in some places), changing rooms, children's playgrounds and cafes.

Limni Vouliagmenis   SWIMMING
(Map p140; ☎210 896 2239; www.limnivoul iagmenis.gr; Leoforos Vouliagmenis; adult/child Mon-Fri €13/6, Sat & Sun €14/7; ⊗7.30am-8pm; 🖔; 🚌114, 115 or 149, 🚌A2 or E2) This slightly salty lake, at the base of a huge cliff, is connected to the sea underground and fed by mineral-rich warm springs; its temperature never falls below 21°C. This makes it a friendly habitat for fish that nibble the dead skin from your feet – an exfoliating treat for some, or a nightmare for the ticklish.

The loyal clientele of bathing-cap-clad elderly citizens tout the water's healing properties. There's a modern spa-cuisine cafe (lunch from €12) at the edge, where you can eat without paying the lake admission, plus sunbeds, a playground and showers. Take the A2 bus (E2 express in summer) to

Plateia Glyfada (aka Plateia Katraki Vasos), then take bus 114, 115 or 149.

Limanakia   BEACH
(Map p140; 🚌117, 122) The rocky coves below the bus stop at Limanakia B (near Varkiza) are a popular nudist hang-out with a slight gay slant. Take the tram or A2/E2 express bus to Glyfada, then bus 117 or 122 to the Limanakia B stop.

Asteras Beach   BEACH
(☎210 894 1620; www.asterascomplex.com; Glyfada; adult/child Mon-Fri €6/3, Sat & Sun €7/3; ⊗beach 8.30am-8pm; 🚌790 from Syntagma, 🚃T5 to Asteria) Swanky Asteras, convenient to Glyfada and the tram, is a resort without the hotel: a complex of waterfront cafes, play zones, bars and the see-and-be-seen Balux (p139) restaurant. If the megabeach with sunloungers for thousands isn't enough, there's also a pool.

The restaurants are expensive for Greece (coffee €4.50, mains from €15), but if you don't take a seat, you can order from a basic menu of coffee, water and toasted sandwiches for less than €2.

Astir Beach   BEACH
(☎210 890 1621; Apollonos 40, Vouliagmeni; adult/child Mon-Fri €18/10, Sat & Sun €28/15 mid-Jun–mid-Sep, reduced prices rest of year; ⊗beach 8am-9pm, restaurants to midnight; 🚌114 from Glyfada or Voula tram stops) Astir is the most exclusive summer beach playground (giveaway: there's a helipad, for the most elite Athenian commuters). It has all the water sports, shops and restaurants you could want (plus, oddly, a TGI Fridays). It's 19.5km south of Athens, 7.5km south of Glyfada. If it all gets too flashy for you, there's a nice public beach across the road.

Yabanaki   BEACH
(☎210 897 2414; www.yabanaki.gr; Varkiza; adult/child Mon-Fri €5/3.50, Sat & Sun €6/3.50; ⊗8am-7pm Jun-Aug, 9am-5pm May; 🚌122) Slightly less flashy than the beach clubs near Glyfada, Yabanaki (21km south of Syntagma) nonetheless has a full complement of entertainment options, from a restaurant to beach volleyball. Great if you're travelling with kids.

Akti tou Iliou   BEACH
(☎210 985 5169; www.aktitouiliou.gr; Leoforos Poseidonos, Alimos; adult/child Mon-Fri €5/3, Sat & Sun €6/3; ⊗8am-8pm; 🚌Zefyros) Relatively laid-back, with a slew of sunloungers and

some reed-roofed beach bars. It's one of the closer beaches to Athens (just 7.5km south).

🛏 Sleeping

Villa Orion HOTEL €
(📞210 895 8000; www.villaorionhotel.gr; Ioanni Metaxa 4, Voula; d/tr incl breakfast €73/85; ❄ 🛜; 🅿A1, A2, 122, 🚌 Asklipiio Voulas) This simple hotel has been dressed up with a bit of creative interior decor, but the real attraction is its great value. It's a few blocks inland, yes, but convenient to all the beaches. Rooms have little balconies and breakfast is served outside in a small garden. Prices go down off-season.

Palmyra Beach Hotel HOTEL €€
(www.palmyra.gr; Leoforos Poseidonos 70, Glyfada; d incl breakfast from €125; 🅿❄🛜🏊) The Palmyra has large, sleek and modern rooms with balconies, plus big breakfasts and a swimming pool in a verdant garden. It's also super close to Glyfada beach and the marina.

Hotel Vouliagmeni Suites HOTEL €€€
(📞210 896 4901; www.vouliagmenisuites.com; Panos 8, Vouliagmeni; s/d incl breakfast from €172/183; 🚌122 to Agia Pantelimon) This posh pad a bit back from the beach has quirkily decorated luxe rooms, some with sea views.

🍴 Eating

Yi VEGAN €
(📞210 964 8512; Grigoriou Lambraki 69, Glyfada; mains €8-10; ⏰8.30am-midnight; 🛜🏊; 🚌A3 to Omiroi, 171 to Lambraki) Breezy, elegant Yi is a mostly open-air, all-raw vegan cafe where the food is bursting with colour and life. Go with a friend to share one of the delicious plates for two (€18), such as falafel in a flaxseed wrap, spiced with tahini-mustard sauce. Delectable vegan cheesecakes too.

Family AMERICAN €€
(📞21210 43411; www.family-voula.gr; Vasileos Pavlou 74, Voula; mains €9-15; ⏰9am-2am; 🚌Asklipiio Voulas) Affectionate service and a nice homey atmosphere in an old mansion. There is a wide-ranging family-friendly menu: eggs, burgers, pizzas and plenty more. It's on Voula's pleasant little downtown strip, calmer than Glyfada. It's about a 20-minute walk from the last tram stop.

Trigono TAVERNA €€
(📞22990 48540; Athinon 36, Kalyvia; mains €8-15; ⏰lunch & dinner) At this casual grill house,

the pork chops are flawless and flow nonstop – thanks to an in-house butcher, a rare feature in Greece. As it's just off the highway back to Athens, it's a popular family pit stop on weekend afternoons. Go early to avoid the epic post-lunch lull, when it feels like an army has just marched out.

Kohylia ASIAN €€€
(Map p140; 📞22910 76000; www.lagonissiresort.gr; Grand Resort Lagonissi, Km 40 Athens-Sounion Rd; mains €20-62; ⏰8pm-1.30am Tue-Sun; 🅿❄🛜🏊; 🚌Lagonissi 122) Kohylia offers a romantic, upmarket dining experience with elegant tables spread over a seaside veranda at the exclusive Grand Resort Lagonissi. The menu adds its own exotic touch in the form of Polynesian and Japanese cuisine; tasteful mains include the baked black-cod fillet with red miso sauce.

🍸 Drinking & Nightlife

Malabar LOUNGE
(📞210 892 9160; www.themargi.gr; Margi Hotel, Litous 11, Vouliagmeni; ⏰11am-2am; 🚌122 to Laimos, Ⓜ Elliniko) Drop in for a drink at the cushy poolside bar at the boutique hotel Margi (doubles from €441).

The hotel's restaurant, Patio, is known for its haute Greek food, with ingredients from the hotel's own organic farm, inland near Kalyvia.

Akanthus CLUB
(📞210 968 0800; www.akanthus.gr; Leoforos Poseidonos, Alimos; ⏰8am-late; 🚌Zefyros) Typical of the Glyfada day–night beach clubs, this is a restaurant-cafe for beachgoers and has a DJ at night. It's part of the Akti tou Iliou beach complex, at the south end. Dress smartly.

Balux LOUNGE
(📞210 894 1620; www.baluxcafe.com; Leoforos Poseidonos 58, Glyfada; ⏰10am-late; 🛜; 🚌T5 to Asteria) This glamorous club-restaurant-lounge right on the beach must be seen to be believed, with poolside chaises and four-poster beds with flowing nets.

Akrotiri CLUB
(📞210 985 9147; www.akrotirilounge.gr; Vasileos Georgiou II 5, Agios Kosmas, Alimos; ⏰10pm-4am; 🚌2nd Aghios Kosma) This massive beach club holds 3000 people in bars, a restaurant and lounges over different levels. Superbusy party nights bring top resident and visiting DJs.

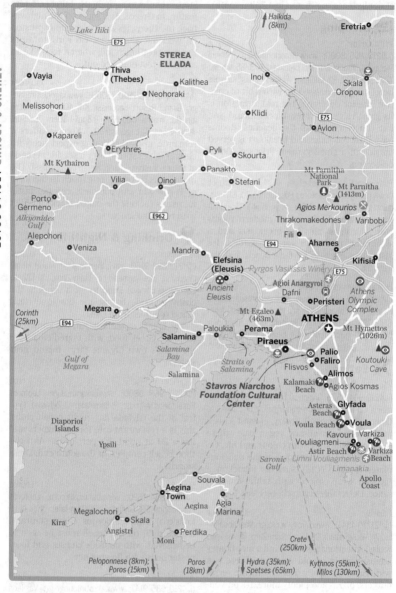

Halkida
(8km)

Eretria

Lake Iliki

E75

**STEREA
ELLADA**

Vayia

Thiva
(Thebes)

Kalithea

Inoi

Skala
Oropou

Neohoraki

Melissohori

Klidi

E75

Kapareli

Avlon

Erythres

Pyli

Skourta

Mt Parnitha
National
Park

Mt Kythairon

Vilia

Oinoi

Panakto

Stefani

Mt Parnitha
(1413m)

Porto
Germeno

*Alcyonides
Gulf*

E962

Agios Merkourios

Thrakomakedones

Varibobi

Alepohori

Veniza

Mandra

Fili

E94

Aharnes

Elefsina
(Eleusis)

Pyrgos Vasilissis Winery

E75

Kifisia

Agioi Anargyroi

Corinth
(25km)

E94

Megara

*Ancient
Eleusis*

Dafni

Peristeri

*Athens
Olympic
Complex*

Mt Egaleo
(463m)

ATHENS

Paloukia

Perama

Salamina

Mt Hymettos
(1026m)

*Salamina
Bay*

Piraeus

Palio
Faliro

Koutouki
Cave

*Straits of
Salamina*

Flisvos

*Gulf of
Megara*

Salamina

Kalamaki
Beach

Alimos

Agios Kosmas

**Stavros Niarchos
Foundation Cultural
Center**

Asteras
Beach

Glyfada

Voula

Diaporioi
Islands

Voula Beach

Kavouri

Varkiza

Ypsili

Vouliagmeni

Astir Beach

Limni Vouliagmenis

Varkiza
Beach

*Saronic
Gulf*

Limanakia

Apollo
Coast

Souvala

Aegina
Town

Aegina

Agia
Marina

Megalochori

Skala

Kira

Angistri

Perdika

Moni

Crete
(250km)

Peloponnese (8km);
Poros (15km)

Poros
(18km)

Hydra (35km);
Spetses (65km)

Kythnos (55km);
Milos (130km)

Island   CLUB

(☑ 210 965 3563; www.islandclubrestaurant.gr;
Km 27, Athens-Sounion Rd, Varkiza; ⏰ 9pm-4am;
🚌 117 or 122 to Camping Varkizas, Ⓜ Elliniko)
Dreamy, classic summer club-restaurant
at the seaside, with superb island decor.

A bit more grown-up than the clubs in
Glyfada.

🛈 Getting There & Away

The Athens tram (p132) runs all the way to
Voula, via Glyfada. For Vouliagmeni and beyond,

Cape Sounion
Ακρωτήριο Σούνιο

The Ancient Greeks knew how to choose a site for a temple. At Cape Sounion, 70km south of Athens, the **Temple of Poseidon** (Map p140; ☎22920 39363; http://odysseus. culture.gr; Cape Sounion; adult/child €8/4; ☺9am-sunset) stands on a craggy spur that plunges 65m to the sea. Built in 444 BCE – same year as the Parthenon – of marble from nearby Agrilesa, it is a vision of gleaming white columns. Sailors in ancient times knew they were nearly home when they saw the first glimpse of white; views from the temple are equally impressive.

On a clear day you can see Kea, Kythnos and Serifos to the southeast, and Aegina and the Peloponnese to the west.

It is thought that the temple was built by Iktinos, the architect of the Temple of Hephaistos in Athens' Ancient Agora. Sixteen of the slender Doric columns remain. The site also contains scant remains of a propylaeum, a fortified tower and, on a lower hill to the northeast, a 6th-century temple to Athena.

As with all major sites, it's best to visit first thing in the morning, or head there for sunset to enact Byron's lines from *Don Juan*: 'Place me on Sunium's marbled steep/Where nothing save the waves and I/ May hear our mutual murmurs sweep.'

Byron was so impressed by Sounion that he carved his name on one of the columns (sadly, many other not-so-famous travellers followed suit).

There is a decent cafe-restaurant at the site, and from the parking lot at the Athena temple, a steep path leads down to a small beach. If you want more room or variety, you'll need a car, or a short bus ride, to reach the nearby bigger beaches and tavernas. There is a pretty, if busy, beach near the site to the west, plus some nice wilder areas along the west-coast road towards Sounio town.

The site is a common package day trip from Athens; this is the easiest way to visit. KTEL also runs frequent buses from the Mavromateon terminal in Athens; the buses also stop near Syntagma. The ride along the coast road takes about two hours.

you can take buses from the end of the tram line or (faster but less scenic) buses direct from Athens.

To avoid heavy traffic on weekends in summer, set out by 9am; without much traffic, the drive from Glyfada to Sounion should take about an hour.

Mt Parnitha   Πάρνηθα

About 25km north of Athens, Mt Parnitha (☑ 210 243 4061; www.parnitha-np.gr/welcome. htm) comprises a number of smaller peaks, the highest of which is Karavola (1413m), tall enough to get snow in winter. The forest was badly burned in 2007 but has rebounded well. There are many caves and much wildlife, including red deer. The park is crisscrossed by hiking trails, with two large, full-featured hiking lodges. It's popular for mountain biking as well.

The easiest way to explore is on the path (about a 45-minute walk) through Tatoi, the 40-sq-km grounds of the former summer palace (closed); follow Tatoi Rd out of Varibobi and look for a small trail sign on the right. For other common trails, see 'Activities' on the park website, or contact EOS (p98) in Athens for current advice (the site is not well maintained).

For a meal with a view, wind past the posh country estates of Varibobi and up the foothills of Mt Parnitha to reach busy taverna Agios Merkourios (Map p140; ☑ 210 816 9617; Varibobi; starters €4-6, lamb per kg €33; ☺ 1pm-midnight Tue-Sun). Weekends, it's packed with Athenians making the pilgrimage for a big family meal. You'll see all sorts of meat on the menu, but charcoal-grilled lamb chops are the order of the day.

Marathon & Around

The town of Marathon (Μαραθώνας), northeast of Athens, may be small and unremarkable but, in 490 BCE, the surrounding plain was the site of the Battle of Marathon, one of the most celebrated battles in world history. All over the area, you can see traces of the event – even in the road signs that mark the historic route of Pheidippides, the courier who ran to Athens to announce victory, and thus gave the name to the 42km race. The Marathon battlefield (Map p140; ☑ 22940 55155; site & archaeological museum adult/child €6/3; ☺ 8am-3pm Tue-Sat), directly south of town, is where the Athens Marathon begins (www.athensauthenticmarathon.gr).

◎ Sights & Activities

Marathon Archaeological Museum   MUSEUM
(Map p140; ☑ 22940 55155; http://odysseus. culture.gr; Plataion 114; museum & Marathon Tomb site adult/child €6/3; ☺ 8.30am-3pm Tue-Sat)

South of Marathon town, this excellent museum displays local discoveries from various periods, including Neolithic pottery from the Cave of Pan and finds from the Tomb of the Athenians. The showpieces are several larger-than-life statues from an Egyptian sanctuary in nearby Brexiza. Next to the museum is a prehistoric grave circle site, which has been preserved under a hangar-like shelter, with raised platforms and walkways. Another hangar on the road to the museum contains an early Helladic cemetery site.

The admission fee covers entrance to the Marathon battlefield & tomb area, a few kilometres southeast.

Ramnous   RUINS
(Map p140; ☑ 22940 63477; http://odysseus. culture.gr; adult/child €4/2; ☺ 8.30am-3pm Tue-Sun) The evocative, overgrown and secluded ruins of the ancient port of Ramnous, about 10km northeast of Marathon, stand on a picturesque plateau overlooking the sea. Among the ruins are the remains of the Doric Temple of Nemesis (435 BCE). Another section of the site leads 1km down a track to a clifftop with the relatively well-preserved town fortress and the remains of the city, a temple, a gymnasium and a theatre. There is no public transport to the site.

Nemesis was the goddess of divine retribution and mother of Helen of Troy. There are also ruins of a smaller 6th-century temple dedicated to Themis, goddess of justice.

Shinias   BEACH
A long gold-sand beach, Shinias is backed by a brushy pine forest. There are sunloungers and a taverna, but no other major developments around, making it the most relaxed and prettiest place to swim in this part of Attica. It's very popular at weekends.

🛏 Sleeping & Eating

Ramnous Camping   CAMPGROUND €
(☑ 22940 55855; www.ramnous.gr; Leoforos Poseidonos 174, Shinias; camp sites per adult/child €6/4; ☺ Apr-Oct; 🅿 🛜) About 1km south of Shinias Beach, this is the most pleasant campground in Attica, with sites nestled among shrubs and trees. Long-stay residents maintain a calm atmosphere. There's a minimarket, playground, laundry and a nice bar-restaurant, Octopus (mains €4 to €14). Casual campers can rent a tent (€6 per night). Buses to Athens go right by out front.

DON'T MISS

MONI DAFNIOU

Lovers of mosaics will be dazzled by the glittering gold scenes in the 11th-century main church here, a listed Unesco site. The work was likely done by craftspeople from Constantinople, showing the fluidity of styles between here and what would become the Islamic Empire. In the apse are portions of geometric decoration of the kind popular in Islamic buildings further east – just as, say, the Umayyad Mosque in Damascus features Byzantine-style gold-backed mosaic scenes.

Restoration work is nearly complete. When the Ministry of Culture takes control of the finished project (at an unknown future date), the site is expected to be open six days a week, with an admission fee. Confirm details with the tourism office before you leave Athens.

It's possible to combine a visit to the monastery with one to Elefsina, as they are on the same A16 bus line (departs from Agia Marina metro stop); you can also take the 866 or 811 from Koumoundourou. On the access road to the monastery are a decent cafe and a free, shady botanical garden.

Isidora   SEAFOOD €€
(Map p140; ☎22940 56467; www.isidora.com.gr; Paralia Marathonos, Pesodromos Perikleous; Παραλία Μαραθώνος, Πεζόδρομος Περικλέους; mains from €12; ☉noon-midnight) Right on Marathon Beach, Isidora has beachfront tables and fresh fish and seafood – do check prices per kilo before ordering fish, as it can be quite expensive. Try the marinated anchovies or sardines in season, and enjoy the views.

❶ Getting There & Away

Given that most of the traces of ancient Marathon are spread around the area, it is easiest to visit by car (and you can also pass by the large dam at Lake Marathon). But the tomb and museum, at least, are a short walk from bus stops. Service is hourly (half-hourly in the afternoon), from Athens' Mavromateon terminal (€4.10, 1¼ hours).

Vravrona   Βραυρώνα

The **Sanctuary of Artemis** (Archaeological Museum at Brauron; Map p140; ☎22990 27020; http://odysseus.culture.gr; Vravron, Markopoulou; adult/child €6/free; ☉8am-2.45pm Tue-Sun), a partially restored temple to the goddess of the hunt, dates from approximately 420 BCE, with some earlier remains. Most remarkable is an ancient stone bridge over the river (now rerouted), cut through with wagon-wheel tracks. Entrance is via a very good museum, which shows remarkable votive gems and statues of children (Artemis was their protector). Then a pleasant path leads to the site through lush marshland with lots of birds. Another path leads to a quiet stretch of beach.

From Athens, take metro line 3 to Nomismatikopio, then bus 304 to Artemis (Vravrona). It's a 10-minute taxi ride from there.

Peania   Παιανία

Vorres Museum   MUSEUM
(☎210 664 2520; www.vorresmuseum.gr; Parodos Diadohou Konstantinou 4; adult/child €5/free; ☉10am-2pm Sat & Sun) This hodgepodge of a museum is set on a rambling 32-hectare estate, once the home of Ion Vorres. Vorres migrated to Canada as a young man, but built his home here in 1963 and began collecting contemporary art, furniture, artefacts, textiles and historical objects from around Greece to preserve the national heritage. Like many personal collections, it's a bit erratic, but a pleasant place to spend an hour or two.

Take bus 125 or 308 to Koropi-Peania from Athens' Nomismatikopio metro station.

Koutouki Cave   CAVE
(Σπήλαιο Κουτούκι Παιανίας; Map p140; ☎210 664 2910; http://odysseus.culture.gr; adult/child €2/free; ☉8.30am-3pm Mon-Fri, to 2.30pm Sat & Sun) This cave is not particularly large, but the winding path goes past some interesting formations and the whole place is tinged rust-red from iron deposits. The guided tour (included in entry) takes about half an hour.

The cave is best visited by car. Buses can take you as far as Peania (either the 125 or

Top
Odeon of Herodes Atticus
(p75)

Bottom
Panathenaic Stadium
(p95)

308 from outside Athens' Nomismatikopio metro station), but it's a further 4.5km to the cave. Best use your own wheels.

Elefsina Ελευσίνα
POP 29,902

Rusting hulks of ships and the chuffing towers of an oil refinery greet you on the quay in Elefsina. This port town west of Athens is gearing up to be the European Capital of Culture in 2021, but apart from the Ancient Eleusis ruins and the Old Oil Mill (Palaio Elaiourgeio; Kanellopoulou 1, Paralia Elefsinas) FREE, a rejuvenated industrial building that's now a rough-and-ready arts centre, a visitor might find Elefsina a little underwhelming. Once a soap factory, the Old Oil Mill features an outdoor theatre (Eleusis was the home town of Aeschylus, father of tragedy); it hosts artistic performances and a festival (210 556 5613; https://aisxylia.gr; Jun & Jul) in the summer months.

Elefsina is also home to a small pebble beach right off the *plateia* (main square) and an open-air cinema with interesting screenings.

Sights

Ancient Eleusis RUINS
(Map p140; 210 554 6019; Sotiriou Gkioka; adult/child €6/free; 8am-8pm Tue-Sun; 876 from Agia Marina metro, Agia Marina) Eleusis occupies a great site on the slopes of a low hill, close to the shore of the Saronic Gulf. Although little has been restored, the scale of its construction is impressive, as enormous pieces of columns and building blocks are scattered all over. The core of the site is the Sanctuary of Demeter, dating to Mycenaean times, when the goddess's cult was one of the most important in Ancient Greece.

By Classical times, until the 4th century CE, Demeter was celebrated with a huge annual festival that attracted thousands of pilgrims seeking initiation to the Eleusinian mysteries. They walked in procession from the Acropolis to Eleusis along the Sacred Way, which was lined with statues and votive monuments. Initiates were sworn to secrecy on punishment of death; during the 1400 years that the sanctuary functioned, its secrets were never divulged.

The museum, at the back of the site, with a good view of the bay, has models of the old city as well as some excellent marble statuary, including a caryatid bust that's great to see at eye level.

Eating & Drinking

Rakoun GREEK €
(210 554 7910; Nikolaidou 66; mezedhes from €4; 9am-2am) This excellent *tsipoura-dhiko* (*ouzerie* in the north) hugely popular with locals, serves good Greek mezedhes and specialises in *tsipouro* and raki. Traditional music is played here. The terrace overlooks the ruins of Ancient Eleusis and stays busy until the small hours. If you're visiting on a Sunday or during public holidays, book a table in advance.

Kapaki GREEK €
(210 554 4126; Plateia Iroon 2; mains from €6; 9am-2am) Right on Elefsina's main square, this popular taverna serves a fantastic fava-bean puree, grilled sardines and chilled wine on a terrace under a canopy of trees. There's also a variety of other traditional Greek dishes. Finish up with a Greek coffee and a baklava.

Gazoza CAFE
(210 554 5494; Nikolaidou 82; 9am-midnight) This pleasant cafe and bar on Nikolaidou is busy with families and youngsters who spend hours enjoying their cappuccinos under the shady canopies. Sit here and people-watch while overlooking the Ancient Eleusis ruins.

Getting There & Away

From Athens, take bus 876 from Agia Marina metro, the last stop on line 3.

AT A GLANCE

★

POPULATION
Patra: 167,300

REGIONAL CAPITAL
Patra

LOCAL CUISINE
Elies (p186)

**BEST TOWER
HOUSE**
Antares (p182)

**BEST ROCK
CLIMBING**
Leonidio (p167)

📅

WHEN TO GO
Easter The pomp
and ceremony of
religious festivities
during Orthodox
Easter week are
unforgettable.

Apr–Jun Perfect
hiking and beach
weather, without the
summer crowds.

Sep Take part in
the gruelling Spar-
tathlon...if you think
you're tough enough.

Corinth Canal (p151)
ALEXANDER TOLSTYKH/SHUTTERSTOCK ©

Peloponnese

T he Peloponnese (Πελοπόννησος) is the stuff of legends. It is here that Hercules fought the Nemean lion and gods walked the earth, meddling in mortal affairs; it's from here that Paris of Troy eloped with Helen and the Argonauts set sail in search of the Golden Fleece. Celestial and mythological charms aside, this region bears tangible traces of the many civilisations that once called it home, witnessed in its classical temples, Mycenaean palaces, Byzantine cities, and Ottoman, Frankish and Venetian fortresses.

The very topography that kept invaders at bay for centuries – lofty, snowcapped mountains, vast gorges, plus sandy beaches and azure waters – now draws visitors of a different kind. *Filoxenia* (hospitality) is as strong here as anywhere in the country; the food is among Greece's best; and the region's vineyards are contributing to Greece's wine renaissance.

Peloponnese Highlights

1 **Monemvasia**
(p175) Soaking up the past and present of an ancient walled city.

2 **Ancient Olympia**
(p196) Marvelling at this sanctuary, the birthplace of the Olympic Games.

3 **Mani** (p178) Hiking one of Greece's most remote and rugged regions, and spending a night in a traditional Maniot tower house.

4 **Menalon Trail**
(p165) Following this stunning trail through the Lousios Gorge and charming mountain villages Stemnitsa and Dimitsana.

5 **Mystras** (p172) Meandering through the magical World Heritage–listed ruins of the former Byzantine capital.

6 **Ancient Mycenae** (p154) Tapping into the ghost of Agamemnon at this incredible historic site.

7 **Vouraïkos Gorge**
(p204) Tackling the dramatic gorge via the unique rack-and-pinion train or on foot from the beautiful village of Kalavryta.

8 **Epidavros**
(p156) Checking out the acoustics in the best-preserved of all Ancient Greek theatres.

9 **Nafplio** (p158) Enjoying the excellent accommodation choices of one of Greece's most romantic towns.

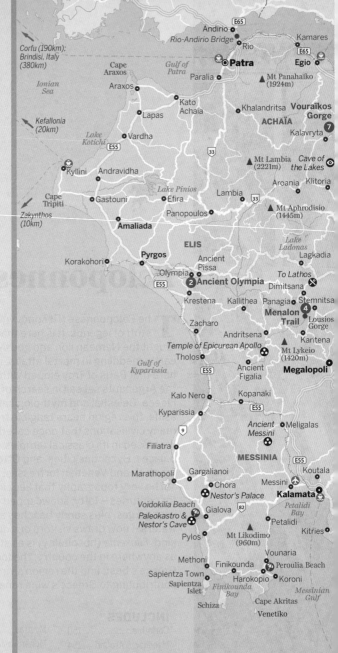

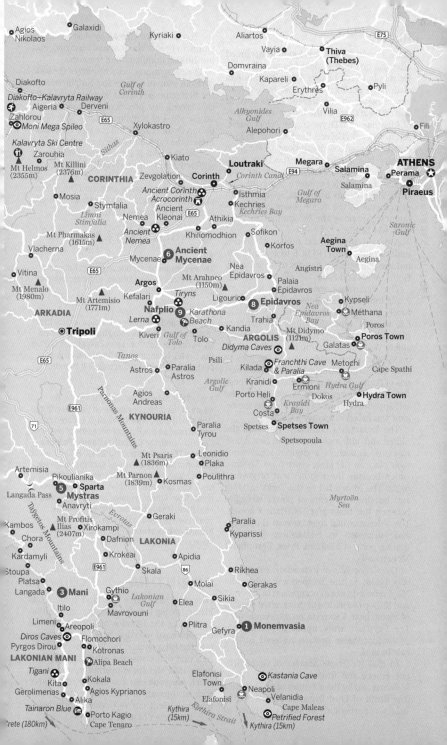

History

Since ancient times the Peloponnese (named after the mythical Pelops) has played a major role in Greek history. When the Minoan civilisation declined after 1450 BCE, the focus of power in the ancient Aegean world moved from Crete to the hill-fortress palaces of Mycenae and Tiryns in the Peloponnese. As elsewhere in Greece, the 400 years following the mysterious disruptions of the 12th century BCE are known as the Dark Ages. When the region reemerged in the 8th century BCE, Corinth became a powerful city-state. Then Athens' arch rival, Sparta, rose to prominence as the major power in the Peloponnese, sparking the Peloponnesian Wars (431–404 BCE).

A period of peace and prosperity ensued under Roman rule (146 BCE to around 250), but was shattered by a series of invasions by Goths, Avars and Slavs.

The Byzantines were slow to make inroads into the Peloponnese, only becoming firmly established during the 9th century CE. In 1204, after the fall of Constantinople to the Crusaders, the Frankish Crusader chiefs William de Champlitte and Geoffrey de Villehardouin divided the region into 12 fiefs, which they parcelled out to various barons of France, Flanders and Burgundy. These fiefs were overseen by de Villehardouin, the self-appointed prince of the Morea, as the region was called in medieval times.

The Byzantines gradually won back the Morea and, although the empire as a whole was now in decline, a glorious renaissance took place in the area, centred on Mystras, which became the region's seat of government. The Morea fell to the Turks in 1460, and hundreds of years of power struggles between the Turks and Venetians followed. The Venetians had long coveted the Morea and succeeded in establishing profitable trading ports at Methoni, Pylos, Koroni and Monemvasia.

The Greek War of Independence supposedly began in the Peloponnese, when the Mani rebelled against occupation in Areopoli and Bishop Germanos of Patra raised the flag of revolt near Kalavryta on 25 March 1821. The Egyptian army, under the leadership of Ibrahim Pasha, brutally restored Turkish rule in 1825.

In 1827 the Triple Alliance of Great Britain, France and Russia – moved by Greek suffering and by the activities of philhellenes (the death of Lord Byron at Messolongi in 1824 was particularly influential) – came to the rescue of the Greeks by destroying the Ottoman fleet at the Battle of Navarino, ending Turkish domination of the area.

The Peloponnese became part of the independent state of Greece, and Nafplio became the first national capital. Ioannis Kapodistrias, Greece's first president, was assassinated on the steps of Nafplio's Church of St Spyridon in October 1831, and the new king, Otto, moved the capital to Athens in 1834.

Like the rest of Greece, the Peloponnese suffered badly during WWII and the civil war (1944–49) that followed. During the 1950s many villagers migrated to Athens, and further abroad to Australia, Canada, South Africa and the USA.

ℹ Getting There & Away

AIR

The Peloponnese has one airport at Kalamata. Most visitors fly in to Athens, just over an hour away by car.

BOAT

Domestic and international ferries service the region, the main ones being from Patra (for Italy), Kyllini (for Kefallonia and Zakynthos), Gythio (for Crete), Neapoli (for Kythira) and various ports in Argolis for the Saronic Gulf Islands.

BUS

A good bus network services the region. Be aware of the difference between Corinth Isthmus (the canal) and Corinth (the city). Located on a main road on the Peloponnese side of the Corinth Canal, the **Corinth Isthmus (Peloponnese) KTEL bus station** (☑ 27410 83000; www. ktelkorinthias.gr) is a useful spot to change for buses travelling south to the rest of the Peloponnese. Few formal timetables are available; most buses from Athens heading to the Peloponnese stop here. Meanwhile, for Ancient Corinth, you'll need to head to Corinth City's **KTEL Korinthos bus station** (☑ 27410 75410; www. ktelkorinthias.gr; Dimocratias 4).

CORINTHIA   ΚΟΡΙΝΘΙΑ

Corinthia has had a rich and tumultuous history, owing largely to its strategic position controlling the Isthmus of Corinth. Several empires have wrestled here for dominance over the Peloponnese: the Romans constructed a vast wall across the isthmus; many centuries later the Turks overran it; and pretty much everyone else has attempted to carve a canal through it. Once dominated by the mighty ancient city of Corinth, Corinthia is now the keeper of its remains.

In the pretty hinterland southwest of Corinth you can take part in the resurrected Nemean Games, or travel the region's wine route in search of Greece's best vintages.

History

Ancient Corinth was an affluent and powerful city-state during its first golden age, which began in the 8th century BCE. Earthquakes and centuries of pillage, however, have left only the remnants of once-grand buildings, 7km southwest of the modern city, surrounded by the village of Ancient Corinth and overlooked by the Acrocorinth fortress.

During the 7th and 6th centuries BCE Corinth was one of Ancient Greece's richest cities, thanks to its strategic position on the Corinth Isthmus, where the Isthmian Games boosted its reputation. Its twin ports, one on the Aegean Sea (Kenchreai, near Kechries) and one on the Ionian side (Lecheon), enabled it to trade throughout the Mediterranean. Corinthian ceramics were notable, with an exotic array of Asian beasts featuring in the 7th century, which then merged into the iconic black figure style that was developed here and spread throughout Greece.

Corinth survived the Peloponnesian Wars and flourished under Macedonian rule, but it was sacked by the Roman consul Mummius in 146 BCE for rebelling against Roman rule. In 44 BCE Julius Caesar began rebuilding the city and it again became a prosperous port.

◎ Sights & Activities

Corinth Canal   CANAL
The Corinth Canal is an engineering marvel. A project that spanned many centuries, it was conceived by a ruler of Ancient Corinth, begun by Roman emperor Nero, and completed in the 19th century by the French. Cut through solid rock, the canal is more than 6km long and 23m wide, its vertical sides rising 90m above the water. The canal did much to elevate Piraeus' status as a major Mediterranean port and is particularly impressive when a ship is passing through.

The concept of cutting a canal through the Corinth Isthmus to link the Ionian and Aegean Seas was first proposed by Periander, tyrant of Ancient Corinth at the end of the 7th century BCE. The magnitude of the task defeated him, so he opted instead to build a *diolkos* (paved slipway), across which sailors dragged small ships on rollers, a method used until the 13th century.

In the intervening years many leaders, including Alexander the Great and Caligula, toyed with the canal idea, but it was Nero who struck the first blow himself, using a golden pickaxe in 67 CE before leaving it to 6000 Jewish slaves to do the hard work. The project was soon halted by Gallic invasions. The modern project was inaugurated in 1882 and, after numerous bankruptcies, the canal was finally completed in 1893.

The main bridge over the canal is packed with bus tours but offers an undeniably impressive view of the cutting. If you have your own transport, head to nearby Isthmia to the submersible bridge (Isthmias). The nearby banks are great vantage points to watch the procedure when a ship comes through.

Boat trips run along the canal from Loutraki. For the adventurous, Zulu Bungy Jump (☑ 27410 49465; www.zulubungy.com; €80; ☺ 10am-5.45pm Wed-Sun Jun-Sep, Sat & Sun only May & Oct, Sun only Apr), by the main bridge, offers the chance to see the canal walls from a unique angle.

All buses from Athens pass over the bridge and stop at the Corinth Isthmus KTEL bus station (p150), 200m from the canal.

★**Ancient Corinth**   ARCHAEOLOGICAL SITE
(☑ 27410 31207; http://odysseus.culture.gr; adult/concession €8/4; ☺ 8am-8pm Apr-Aug, reduced hours Sep-Mar) Within a modern village loom the extensive yet compact ruins of this ancient (mostly Roman) city. Home to legendary Jason of the Argonauts, stealer of the Golden Fleece, the streets of Ancient Corinth were once trodden by the likes of Pausanias, Roman traveller, and St Paul, who taught the gospel of Christ here. Follow in their footsteps by visiting the Temple of Apollo, the Peribolos of Apollo, the ancient theatre and other highlights. The excellent on-site museum puts everything into context.

An exception to the Roman ruins is the prominent 5th-century-BCE Doric Temple of Apollo. To the south of this temple is a huge agora (market) bounded on its southern side by the foundations of a huge 71-column stoa (long colonnaded building). This was likely built to accommodate the bigwigs summoned here in 337 BCE by Philip II to sign oaths of allegiance to Macedon. In the middle of the central row of shops is a bema, a marble podium from which Roman officials addressed the people. St Paul was supposedly tried for illegal preaching here.

At the eastern end of the *agora* are the remains of the Julian basilica. To the north is the Lower Peirene fountain – the Upper Peirene fountain is on Acrocorinth.

According to mythology, Peirene wept so much when her son Kenchrias was killed by Artemis that the gods, rather than let all the precious water go to waste, turned her into a fountain.

West of the fountain, steps lead to the Lecheon road, once the main thoroughfare to the port of Lecheon. On the east side of the road is the Peribolos of Apollo, a courtyard flanked by Ionic columns, some of which have been restored. Nearby is a public latrine, where some seats remain.

South of the museum are the columns of Temple E (Pausanias describes it as being dedicated to Octavia, sister of Augustus).

The site's excellent museum is a must-see and a good way to begin and end your visit. It has main rooms that contain finds from the area (including their prized pieces, two *kouros* statues that were stolen and retrieved). The next two rooms exhibit fine Greek and Roman statues, mosaics, figurines, reliefs and friezes. A smaller room houses the finds of excavations at the nearby Sanctuary of Asklepios (500 BCE); look out for the model body parts left as votive offerings. Don't miss the pretty courtyard with its fine reliefs from the 2nd-century-CE theatre.

Opposite the site entrance is the fairly ruinous ancient theatre, constructed in the 5th century BCE for up to 15,000 spectators, and the Roman odeion (indoor theatre), from the 1st century CE.

Note that closing times vary through the winter period according to sunset.

Acrocorinth   FORTRESS

(⟐27410 31266; http://odysseus.culture.gr; Ancient Corinth; ⊙8.30am-4pm) FREE High up above Ancient Corinth, crowning the sheer bulk of limestone known as Acrocorinth, are the ruins of one of the finest natural fortifications in Ancient Greece. Cast your eyes upwards and you'll give an involuntary gasp. Commanding wonderful views over the surrounding region, the fortress is a stiff but utterly worthwhile 4km uphill hike (or taxi ride) if you don't have your own wheels. It's a lovely spot up top, with buzzing bees and clover meadows.

The unparalleled vantage point controlling the Isthmus of Corinth, plus the availability of spring water, made this a powerful defensive position. The original fortress has been modified many times over the centuries by a string of invaders. Passing through the three gates, you can explore the medley of imposing Roman, Byzantine, Frankish, Venetian and Turkish ramparts, harbouring remains of Byzantine chapels, Turkish houses and mosques. The walls are some 3km long.

From the main path, the right fork leads to the remains of a Frankish keep, which is in fact mostly Ottoman. The central path leads you to the Fountain of Peirene, the favourite watering hole of Pegasus the winged horse. Accessible by the left-hand path, on the higher of Acrocorinth's two summits are the remains of the Temple of Aphrodite, where sacred courtesans catered to the desires of the insatiable Corinthians. All paths basically interconnect, so it doesn't much matter which way you ramble.

Wear sturdy shoes and take plenty of water. There's a small restaurant by the entrance.

★ Ancient Nemea   ARCHAEOLOGICAL SITE

(⟐27460 22739; http://odysseus.culture.gr; Stephanos Miller; adult/child €6/3; ⊙8am-8pm Apr-Aug, reduced hours Sep-Mar) Ancient Nemea was once the venue for the biennial Nemean Games, held in honour of Zeus. Three original columns of the imposing 4th-century-BCE Doric Temple of Zeus survive, and the on-site museum displays finds from the area. The atmospheric stadium is nearby; once connected to the sanctuary by a sacred road, it plays host to a resurrected version of the Games. It's located 31km southwest of Corinth and 4km northeast of modern Nemea.

Like Ancient Olympia, Nemea was not a city but a sanctuary of Zeus. The Nemean Games, held in the stadium here, were hosted by the nearby city of Kleonai and became one of the great Panhellenic festivals. It was also around here that Hercules carried out the first of his labours – the slaying of the lion that had been sent by Hera to destroy Nemea. After Hercules had killed the lion by lifting it off the ground and choking it to death, the lion became the constellation Leo (each of Hercules' 12 labours is related to a sign of the zodiac).

It's worth visiting the site's museum before seeing the remains of the temple. It has two models of the ancient site – the first shows what it would have looked like at the site's zenith around 300 BCE, the second in 500 CE, when a Christian basilica and community had developed around the ruined temple – as well as ancient paraphernalia from the Games and treasures from the area's Mycenaean tombs. The jewel of the collection, quite literally, is the Gold of Aidonia, an exquisite assortment of gold rings, seals and beads from the site of Aidonia, near

WORTH A TRIP

NEMEA WINE ROUTE

In the rolling hills southwest of Corinth, the Nemea region is one of Greece's premier wine-producing areas, famous for its smooth, full-bodied reds, many produced from the local *agiorgitiko* grape. Look out also for wine made from *roditis*, a local variety of white grape, and aromatic, lemony *moschofilero*, grown around Tripoli.

Nemea has been known for its fine wines since Mycenaean times, when nearby Phlius supplied the wine for the royal court at Mycenae.

There are 40-odd wineries in the region, signposted as part of a wine route. Many are open to the public, though some must be prebooked. Visits usually include a winery tour and a tasting with local cheese and bread.

Look out for the *anoichtes portes* (open doors) weekend in May, when most wineries are open and tastings are often free. A wine festival in early September marks the beginning of the vintage.

Wineries include:

➡ Seméli Estate (see below)

➡ Ktima Bairaktaris (see below)

➡ Ktima Palivou (p154)

➡ Ktima Skouras (☑ 27510 23688; www.skouras.gr; Argos-Sterna Rd Km 10; tastings €8-20; ⊘ 9am-3pm Mon-Fri, 10.30am-6pm Sat)

➡ Lafkiotis Winery (☑ 27460 31000; www.lafkiotis.gr; Ancient Kleonai; ⊘ 10am-3pm, must be prebooked)

➡ Gaia Wines (☑ 27460 22057; www.gaiawines.gr; Nemea-Stigmaka Rd, Koutsi; wine tastings €8-15; ⊘ by appointment)

➡ Domaine Spiropoulos (☑ 27960 61400; www.domainspiropoulos.com; Corinthos-Tripoli National Rd; tour and tasting €15; ⊘ by appointment)

Nemea. Don't miss the video that explains the extraordinarily advanced race-starting mechanism or the sad story of the last Christian inhabitant of the settlement.

At the temple site, the three original columns of the 4th-century-BCE **Temple of Zeus** have been joined by six more, reassembled by an American team. Other ruins include a hostelry and, under a roof, a bathhouse, which has some beautifully preserved washbasins. The athletes probably oiled up here before competition.

The **stadium** is 300m away along the road. There's a fantastic view of it in all its glory from the path that skirts it through the pine trees. Alternatively, enter it the way the athletes would have done, through the atmospheric and archaeologically important tunnel hidden behind the columns by the site entrance. The athletes' starting line is still in place, together with the distance markers. Look out for ancient graffiti in the tunnel. Resurrected in 1996, the two-day **Modern Nemean Games** (www.nemeangames.org) occur each Olympic year in June.

Buses to/from Corinth Isthmus (around €5, one hour, four to five daily, one Sunday)

stop on request outside the site on the way to modern Nemea, about 4km northwest of the site.

Note that closing hours alter substantially through the winter period according to sunset times.

Ktima Bairaktaris
WINERY

(☑ 27460 20455; www.bairaktariswines.gr; Eleftheriou Venizelou 83, Nemea; tastings 2/4/8 wines free/€5/10; ⊘ 9am-6pm) This modern family winery is set among spectacular craggy scenery on the outskirts of modern Nemea. Try their dry-as-a-bone *moschofilero* white or their excellent *agiorgitiko* reds. They age wines here, so you can taste how a wine improves over the years. A winery tour is usually thrown in.

Seméli Estate
WINERY

(☑ 27460 20360; www.semeliestate.gr; Nemea-Stigmaka Rd; tastings €8-20; ⊘ 10am-4pm Mon-Fri, 11am-5pm Sat & Sun) Seméli is a dramatically located modern winery that is well set up for visits. It produces several delicious *agiorgitiko* reds, as well as other varietals. Whites include *moschofilero* – try the one that has sat on the lees for extra complexity

– chardonnay and sauvignon blanc, and there are also rosés. Tastings include a winery tour. It's 7km north of Nemea.

Ktima Palivou WINERY
(☑ 27460 24190; www.palivos.gr; Ancient Nemea; tastings €5-10; ⊙ 9am-5pm Oct-Mar, 10am-6pm Apr-Sep) Third-generation winemaker George Palivos runs this boutique winery, which has a pretty vineyard running uphill, a cute barrel room and a range of interesting wines. Their *agiorgitiko* is good, and there are also intriguing blends of chardonnay and *malagouzia* and a powerful merlot.

🛏 Sleeping

Resort hotels line the strip of Loutraki, on the northeastern edge of the city of Corinth. Ancient Corinth makes for a quieter place to stay right by the ruins.

Pegasus Rooms GUESTHOUSE €
(☑ 27410 31366; www.pegasusrooms.gr; Ancient Corinth; r incl breakfast €35-55; P ⊝ ❋ 🤶) In the heart of Ancient Corinth, very close to the ruins, Pegasus offers simple, clean and well-equipped rooms with easy parking out back. Pleasant patio areas make lounging easy, but the highlight is the abundant breakfast, featuring homemade conserves and served in a roof space with super views of the local church and Acrocorinth looming behind.

ⓘ Getting There & Away

The KTEL Korinthos bus station (p150) in Corinth (City) has frequent services to Athens (€9, one hour, hourly or more). This is the departure point for buses to Ancient Corinth (€1.80, 20 minutes, regular Monday to Friday, seven Saturday), Nemea (€4.90, one hour, six Monday to Friday, three Saturday and Sunday) and Loutraki (for Corinth Isthmus; €1.90, 10 minutes, half-hourly).

ARGOLIS   ΑΡΓΟΛΙΔΑ

The Argolis peninsula, which separates the Saronic and Argolic Gulfs, is steeped in legend and history. The town of Argos is thought to be the longest continually inhabited town in Greece. Argolis was the foremost seat of power of the Mycenaeans that dominated Greece from around 1500 to 1200 BCE. Traces of this mighty civilisation lie scattered across the region in the shape of *tholoi* (beehive-shaped tombs), citadels and ancient theatres. The Venetian seafront town of Nafplio, the first capital of modern Greece, makes a handy base for exploring the surrounding countryside.

The southern knob of the peninsula proper, centred on the agricultural town of Kranidi, features the small resorts of Porto Heli, 4km south of Kranidi, and Ermioni, 4km east of Kranidi. Few travellers venture to the northeast, yet the zigzagging drive along the coast is spectacular.

Mycenae & Around

⊙ Sights

★ **Ancient Mycenae** ARCHAEOLOGICAL SITE
(☑ 27510 76585; http://odysseus.culture.gr; Mykines; adult/child €12/free; ⊙ 8am-8pm Apr-Aug, reduced hours Sep-Mar) On a hilltop backed by powerful mountains stand the sombre and mighty ruins of Ancient Mycenae, home of the legendary Agamemnon. For four centuries in the second millennium BCE, this kingdom was the most powerful in Greece, holding sway over the Argolid and influencing other Mycenaean cities.

Two to three daily buses (excluding Sundays) head to Mycenae from Nafplio (€3.20, one hour) via Argos (€1.80, 30 minutes). Buses stop in Mykines village, continuing the 1.3km to the site from April to October. A return taxi from Nafplio with waiting time is €70.

World Heritage–listed Mycenae is synonymous with the names Homer and Schliemann. In the 9th century BCE Homer told in his epic poems, *Iliad* and *Odyssey*, of 'well-built Mycenae, rich in gold'. These poems were, until the 19th century, regarded as no more than gripping and beautiful legends. But in the 1870s the amateur archaeologist Heinrich Schliemann (1822–90), despite derision from professionals, struck gold, first at Troy then at Mycenae.

In Mycenae, myth and history are inextricably linked. According to Homer, the city of Mycenae was founded by Perseus, the son of Danae and Zeus. By Agamemnon's time the Royal House of Atreus was the most powerful of the Achaeans (Homer's name for the Greeks). Whether Agamemnon and his family are real or mythical is uncertain. However, the archaeological facts are that Mycenae was first settled in the Neolithic period and came to prominence in the late Bronze Age, from about 1600 BCE. In the wake of the Indo-European wave that arrived in Greece between 2100 and 1900 BCE, and influenced by the Minoan and Cycladic civilisations, an advanced culture developed on the mainland. This new civilisation is now referred to as the Mycenaean, named after its most powerful kingdom. The other kingdoms included Pylos, Tiryns, Corinth and Argos, all in the Peloponnese. Evidence of Mycenaean civilisation has also been found at Thiva (Thebes) and Athens.

The city of Mycenae consisted of a fortified citadel and surrounding settlement, at its height from 1450 to 1200 BCE. Due to the sheer size of the 'Cyclopean' walls (13m high and 7m thick), formed by stone blocks weighing 6 tonnes in places, legend has it that Perseus enlisted the help of a Cyclops, one of the one-eyed giants described in the *Odyssey*, to build Mycenae.

Archaeological evidence indicates that the palaces of the Mycenaean kingdoms declined sometime around 1200 BCE and the palace itself was destroyed around 1180 BCE, possibly by fire. Whether the destruction was the work of outsiders or due to internal division between the various Mycenaean kingdoms remains unresolved.

Through the entrance gate, it's worth stopping by the Ancient Mycenae Museum for context.

Agamemnon's fortress is entered through the dramatic Lion Gate, a solid construction of stone blocks over which rear two large lions. This motif is believed to have been the insignia of the Royal House of Atreus.

Once inside the citadel, Grave Circle A is on the right. This was the royal cemetery and contained six grave shafts. Five shafts were excavated by Schliemann between 1874 and 1876, uncovering one of the richest archaeological hauls ever to be found, including a well-preserved gold death mask. Schliemann sent a telegram to the Greek king stating, 'I have gazed upon the face of Agamemnon', though the mask is thought to have belonged to a ruler who lived centuries before the era when the Trojan War might have taken place.

South of Grave Circle A are the remains of a group of buildings that probably had a religious purpose; many of the wall-painting fragments and votive offerings in the museum were found here. In one was discovered the famous Warrior Vase, regarded by Schliemann as one of his greatest discoveries because it offered a glimpse of what Mycenae's legendary warriors looked like.

Follow the main path up to Agamemnon's Palace, accessed through what was once a monumental doorway. The rooms on the north side of the palace were likely private royal apartments (where Agamemnon was supposedly murdered). On the palace's southeastern side is the megaron (reception hall where the great hearth would have been), with the column bases remaining. Beyond this are buildings that probably served as artisans' workshops. The valley views from the top of the hill here are phenomenal.

Head down to the northeast extension, and you'll find the entrance to the secret cistern in the corner. This marvellous vaulted tunnel, a masterpiece of engineering at the time, descends via dark steps (half-heartedly roped off) to a spring. Follow the main path anticlockwise and on the northern boundary of the citadel you'll come across the Postern Gate, through which, it is said, Orestes escaped after murdering his mother, Clytemnestra.

Until the late 15th century BCE the Mycenaeans interred their royal dead in shaft graves; later they used a new form of burial – the beehive-shaped *tholos* tomb. Back outside the Lion Gate, head down to the *tholos* tombs of Aegisthus, with its collapsed roof, and Clytemnestra, with its dramatic entrance and dome roof. Near the museum, the Lion Tomb is also impressive, while another Mycenae highlight, the Treasury of Atreus, also known as Agamemnon's Tomb, is found 500m down the road from the car park, beyond the main Mycenae site.

Treasury of Atreus
ARCHAEOLOGICAL SITE

(Agamemnon's Tomb; http://odysseus.culture.gr; Mykines; adult/child incl Mycenae €12/free; ⊘ 8am-8pm Apr-Aug, reduced hours Sep-Mar) Dating back to around 1300 BCE, this is the finest existing example of a domed *tholos*. It's wonderfully misnamed, since it probably has little to do with Atreus or Agamemnon, but the interior is truly awe-inspiring, with a 40m-long passage leading to the vast beehive-shaped chamber, with evidence of the powerful door that once sealed the tomb.

Ancient Mycenae Museum
MUSEUM

(☑ 27510 76585; http://odysseus.culture.gr; Mykines; adult/child incl site €12/free; ⊘ 8am-8pm Apr-Aug, reduced hours Sep-Mar) Part of the Ancient Mycenae complex, this museum is well worth visiting before seeing the rest of the site. It initiates you into the mysteries of Mycenae's construction, its various incarnations, and its excavation from 1841 onwards. The displays run the gamut from fine stirrup jars, fascinating fresco fragments and beautiful seals to ritual objects, written tablets in Linear B script, jewellery and bronze weaponry. Replicas of the most spectacular

PELOPONNESE MYCENAE & AROUND

Mycenae finds are also displayed; the originals are in Athens' National Archaeological Museum (p90).

Tiryns
ARCHAEOLOGICAL SITE

(🗒 27520 22657; http://odysseus.culture.gr; Argos–Napflio Hwy; adult/concession/child €4/2/free; ☺ 8am-8pm Apr-Aug, reduced hours Sep-Mar) The unfairly underrated Mycenaean acropolis, 4km north of Nafplio, is the apogee of Mycenaean architectural achievement. Legend has it that its massive walls, 7m thick in parts, were built by a Cyclops. You can stroll around the immense stonework and explore the Upper and Lower Citadels. Look out for the vaulted passageways, secret stairway and impressive gallery, though ongoing restoration means that parts of the ruins may be off limits.

Any Nafplio–Argos bus can drop you here. A return taxi from Nafplio with waiting time is €30.

★ Epidavros
ARCHAEOLOGICAL SITE

(🗒 27530 22009; http://odysseus.culture.gr; adult/concession/child €12/6/free; ☺ 8am-8pm Apr-Aug, reduced hours Sep-Mar) In its day Epidavros, 30km east of Nafplio, was famed and revered across the Mediterranean as a place of miraculous healing. Visitors came great distances to the tranquil Sanctuary of Asclepius, the god of medicine, to seek a cure for their ailments. Today the World Heritage Site's amazingly well-preserved theatre remains a venue during the Athens & Epidavros Festival for Classical Greek plays, first performed here over 2300 years ago.

Legend has it that Asclepius was the son of Apollo and Coronis. While giving birth to Asclepius, Coronis was killed by the jealous Apollo, who discovered she had been unfaithful to him. Apollo took his son to Mt Pelion, where the physician centaur Chiron instructed the boy in the healing arts. Asclepius became a healer of such great renown that he brought a man back from the dead, which angered Hades, the god of the underworld, who asked Zeus to strike Asclepius down. Zeus did so, provoking, in turn, the wrath of Apollo, and Asclepius was eventually deified.

Apollo was worshipped at Epidavros in Mycenaean and Archaic times, but by the 4th century BCE he had been superseded by his son. Epidavros became acknowledged as the birthplace of Asclepius. Although the afflicted worshipped Asclepius at sanctuaries throughout Greece, the two most important sites were at Epidavros and on the island of Kos. The fame of the Epidavros sanctuary spread, and when a plague raged in Rome, Livy and Ovid came to Epidavros to seek help.

It is believed that licks from snakes were one of the curative practices at the sanctuary. Asclepius is normally shown with a serpent, which – by renewing its skin – symbolises rejuvenation. Other treatments provided at the sanctuary involved diet instruction, herbal medicines and occasionally even surgery. The sanctuary also served as an entertainment venue and every four years, during the Festival of Asclepieia, Epidavros hosted dramas and athletic competitions.

There are buses from Nafplio to the theatre (€3.20, 45 minutes, four Monday to Friday, three Saturday, one Sunday) as well as direct Athens services. Off-season they only stop 1.5km away on the main road. A return taxi from Nafplio with waiting time is €70.

★ Theatre of Epidavros
ARCHAEOLOGICAL SITE

(🗒 27530 22009; http://odysseus.culture.gr; adult/concession/child €12/6/free; ☺ 8am-8pm Apr-Aug, reduced hours Sep-Mar) Built of limestone, yet one of the best-preserved Ancient Greek structures in existence, this late-4th-century-BCE theatre is the undisputed highlight of Epidavros. It's renowned for its amazing acoustics; a coin dropped in the theatre's centre can be heard from the highest seat. The theatre seats up to 14,000 people. Its entrance is flanked by restored pilasters and the foundations of the ancient stage building are beyond the circle. It's now used for performances during the annual Athens & Epidavros Festival.

Sanctuary of Asclepius
ARCHAEOLOGICAL SITE

(🗒 27530 22009; http://odysseus.culture.gr; adult/concession/child €12/6/free; ☺ 8am-8pm Apr-Aug, reduced hours Sep-Mar) The Sanctuary of Asclepius was dedicated to the god of healing. The ruins include the huge katagogeion, a hostelry for pilgrims and patients; the large banquet hall in which the Romans built an odeum (a room for musical performances); and the stadium, a venue for athletic competitions. Just beyond is the remarkable tholos, a circular cult building, the Temple of Asclepius and the abaton (dormitory), where cures were effected. Excellent information panels (Greek and English) make the site easy to navigate.

Didyma Caves
CAVE

(☺ 24hr) FREE Off the main road between Kranidi and Epidavros, near the village of Didyma, are the Didyma Caves – two extraordinary sinkholes. They collapsed thousands of years ago, leaving large craters in the earth. One hides an unexpected surprise – a tiny Byzantine church, Agios Georgios, constructed under a crevice. The other is a haven for nesting birds. The caves are well signposted.

Franchthi Cave & Paralia CAVE

(Killada; ⊙24hr) FREE Atmospheric Franchthi Cave is one of Greece's oldest and most significant Palaeolithic, Mesolithic and Neolithic sites, with occupation dating back over 40,000 years. The remarkable finds have revealed the transitions between all eras: the way hunter-gatherers lived from fishing, then organised themselves in groups, and finally transitioned to tool-using farmers. Many of the excavation's findings are in the archaeological museum (p158) in Nafplio. Offshore, you can snorkel among a submerged Neolithic settlement, Paralia; the shoreline was a further 7km away back then.

Signage in English is excellent and there's a small jetty. To get there, follow the signs to the cave for 4km (signs are 5km before Kranidi if coming from the north) to a beach. From here, you must walk along a trail over rocks for about 500m (these are marked by red painted arrows). At the time of research you could enter the cave freely. If this changes, access will be via the Municipality of Ermionida. You can get quite a good look through the security fencing.

Lerna ARCHAEOLOGICAL SITE

(⊉27910 47597; http://odysseus.culture.gr; Myli; adult/child €2/free; ⊙8am-3pm) This small site is worth a stop for its intriguing House of the Tiles, one of the most important Greek remains from the 3rd millennium BCE. It's very well preserved, conserving the base of staircases as well as plaster on the brick structure. Clay seals found here attest to a system of control over goods. Other remains include walls and a tower from earlier in the Helladic period, as well as later Mycenaean tombs. It's 7km west of Nafplio along the coast.

Lerna is also famous in mythology as the lair of the Hydra, which was slain by Hercules as one of his labours.

✷ Festivals & Events

Athens & Epidavros Festival THEATRE

(⊉21092 82900; www.greekfestival.gr; ⊙Jul & Aug) The Theatre of Epidavros stages both modern theatre and Ancient Greek dramas during the annual Athens and Epidavros Festival, part of the larger cultural Hellenic Festival (p100). Tickets can be bought in Epidavros at the theatre box office, online or from the Athens box office (⊉210 327 2000; Stoa Pesmazoglou, Panepistimiou 39, Panepistimio; ⊙10am-4pm Mon-Fri, to 3pm Sat; Ⓜ Panepistimio). There are special bus services available from Athens (around €25, two hours) and Nafplio (around €10, 45 minutes).

❶ Getting There & Away

Both Argos and Nafplio are hubs for the region and are well serviced by regional KTEL Argolis buses, including those from Corinth Isthmus (a transport hub to the Peloponnese).

There are **bus services** (⊉27540 21218; www.ktelargolida.gr) between Kranidi and Nafplio (€8.50, two hours, four weekdays, three on Saturday, one on Sunday), and local buses from Kranidi to Ermioni (€1.85, 10 minutes, several daily) and Porto Heli (€1.85, 10 minutes, several daily).

While you can reach major ancient sites by bus, your own wheels will give you far more flexibility.

BOAT

Regular **Hellenic Seaways** (⊉21089 19800; https://hellenicseaways.gr) high-speed passenger boats (three to four daily April to September, reduced service winter) depart from Porto Heli to Piraeus (€41.50, 3½ hours) via Spetses (€6.50, 10 minutes), Ermioni (also in the Peloponnese), Hydra (€17.50, 1¼ hours) and Poros (€22, two hours). Fares from Ermioni on this service are Hydra (€8.50, 25 minutes), Spetses (€8.50, 25 minutes), Poros (€17.50, 1¼ hours) and Piraeus (€33.50, 2½ hours). Some faster services cut out intermediary stops.

The cheapest and most frequent boats to Hydra from Argolis are **Hydra Lines** (⊉22980 52961; www.hydralines.gr; €6.50) from Metochi (€6.50, 15 minutes, hourly in summer, less frequently at other times); park for free by the waterfront or leave your car in a secure, shaded car park.

Caïques zip constantly between Galatas and Poros (€1, five minutes). Car ferries (passenger/car €1/6) also make this crossing.

Argos Αργος

POP 22,200

The ancient town of Argos has a past stretching back an astonishing 6000 years, though today most vestiges of its former glory lie buried beneath the bustling modern town. Overshadowed by its neighbour, Nafplio (12km away), Argos is worth a detour for its excellent Byzantine museum and the nearby ruins and fortress.

◉ Sights

Byzantine Museum of Argolis   MUSEUM

(☑ 27510 68937; www.byma.gr; Kapodistrias Barracks, Zouraphou; adult/child €4/free; ⊙ 8.30am-4pm Wed-Mon) It's worth visiting Argos for this fine museum alone. Opened in 2017, it provides an evocative insight into Byzantine history, within the context of the region of Argolis. Six rooms neatly showcase Byzantine life in Argolis from the 4th century CE onwards. 'An Empire is Born' explains the empire and then, through objects – mosaics to jewellery, household plates to smoking pipes – you follow themes: the Middle Ages, church life, home life, a market and a look at Argolis itself. It's housed in the restored former barracks of Ioannis Kapodistrias, Greece's first president.

Larissa Castle   CASTLE

(⊙ 24hr) FREE Looming over Argos, Larissa Castle is a crumbling conglomeration of purple-flower-studded towers, bastions and wall sections – contributed by Roman, Frankish, Venetian and Ottoman Turk conquerors – that stands on the foundations of the city's principal ancient citadel. Sections of original Mycenaean walls are visible. The all-encompassing views from the top are well worth the ascent.

Greek & Roman Ruins   ARCHAEOLOGICAL SITE

(☑ 27510 68819; http://odysseus.culture.gr; cnr Tripolis & Theatrou; adult/concession €2/1; ⊙ 8.30am-4pm Mar-Oct, to 3.30pm Nov-Feb) FREE A complex of impressive Greek and Roman ruins straddles both sides of the Tripoli road. The star attraction is the impressively large theatre, which originally seated 20,000 people. Dating from around 300 BCE, it was greatly modified by the Romans in the 2nd century CE. Next to it is the impressively preserved wall of a Roman bathhouse; beyond is the 1st-century CE odeion (smaller covered theatre), whose origins date back to the 5th century BCE. Across the road is the sizeable ancient agora.

ⓘ Getting There & Away

On the southeastern edge of Argos, the KTEL Argolis (☑ 27510 69323; www.ktelargolida. gr; cnr Nafpliou & Karamoutza) bus station has services to Nafplio (€1.80, 30 minutes, hourly) and Mycenae (€1.80, 30 minutes, two to three Monday to Saturday).

There are also bus services to Athens (€13, two hours, at least hourly), some via Corinth Isthmus (€5.70, 50 minutes), and to Tripoli (€7.70, one hour, two daily).

Nafplio   Ναύπλιο

POP 33,400

Nafplio is one of Greece's prettiest and most romantic towns. It occupies a knockout waterside location beneath the towering Palamidi fortress, and is graced with attractive narrow streets, elegant Venetian houses, neoclassical mansions and interesting museums. It's also chock-full of tavernas, posh boutiques, and comfortable hotels and guesthouses. Because it's a popular destination for locals from Athens, it fills up on weekends and gets overcrowded in high season.

Nafplio was the first capital of Greece after Independence (between 1833 and 1834) and has been a major port since the Bronze Age. So strategic was its position on the Argolic Gulf that it had three fortresses: the massive principal fortress of Palamidi, the smaller Akronafplia, and the diminutive Bourtzi on an islet west of the old town.

The town, though quite touristy, is still a charming and ideal base from which to explore many nearby ancient sites.

◉ Sights

★ Archaeological Museum   MUSEUM

(Map p160; ☑ 27520 27502; http://odysseus. culture.gr; Plateia Syntagmatos; adult/child €6/free; ⊙ 8.30am-4pm Wed-Mon, to 3.30pm Nov-Feb) Inside a splendid Venetian building, this museum traces the social development of Argolis, from the hunter-gatherers of the Franchthi Cave to the sophisticated Mycenaean-era civilisations, through beautifully presented archaeological finds from the surrounding area. Exhibits include a Palaeolithic hearth, Geometric-period pottery, a 6th-century-BCE amphora that was a prize from the Panathenaic Games, plus – a real highlight – the only existing bronze armour from near Mycenae (3500 years old, with a boar-tusk helmet). Excellent audio guides available in several languages (leave a government-issued ID).

Palamidi Fortress   FORTRESS

(Map p160; ☑ 27520 28036; http://odysseus. culture.gr; adult/child €8/free; ⊙ 8am-8pm Apr-Aug, reduced hours Sep-Mar) This vast, spectacular citadel, reachable either by steep ascent on foot or a short drive, stands on a 216m-high outcrop of rock that gives all-encompassing views of Nafplio and the Argolic Gulf. It was built by the Venetians between 1711 and 1714, and is regarded as a masterpiece of military architecture in spite of being successfully stormed in one night by

Greek troops in 1822, causing the Turkish garrison within to surrender without a fight.

Within its walls stands a series of independent, strategically located bastions. The most important, and best preserved, is the western **Agios Andreas Bastion**, which stands at the top of the steps from town. The former home of the garrison commander, it is named after the tiny church in the interior courtyard.

The **Miltiades Bastion**, to the northeast, is the largest of the bastions. It was used as a prison for condemned criminals from 1840 to 1920. War of Independence hero Theodoros Kolokotronis spent several years here after being condemned for treason.

There are two main approaches to the fortress. You can go via the road (a taxi one way will cost about €10) or tackle the steps that begin southeast of the bus station. It's 911 steps to the ticket office at the entrance to the castle (we've counted). Climb early or towards sunset and take water.

Peloponnesian Folklore Foundation Museum   MUSEUM

(Map p160; ☑ 27520 28379; www.pli.gr; Vasileos Alexandrou 1; adult/child €5/3; ☺ 9am-2.30pm Mon-Sat, 9.30am-3pm Sun) Nafplio's award-winning museum is a beautifully arranged collection of folk costumes and household items from Nafplio's 19th- and early-20th-century history. Be wowed by the intricate embroidery of traditional costumes and the heavy silver adornments; admire the turn-of-the-20th-century couture and look out for the cute horse-tricycle. The gift shop sells high-quality local crafts.

Arvanitia Beach   BEACH

(Map p160) This small pebble beach is just five minutes' walk south of town, tucked beside the Akronafplia fortress, past the Land Gate. It's a nice place for a sunset bathe, with great views. For a scenic stroll, take the blustery, cactus-adorned path that skirts the headland from the bottom of the promenade.

Bourtzi   FORTRESS

(☑ 6977716998; www.odysseycruises.gr; return cruise €4.50) Odyssey Cruises runs boat excursions to this island fortress. Built in 1473, it lies about 600m west of the town's port and has served variously as a pirate deterrent, a home for executioners and a hotel. Note that the battlements are identical in design to Moscow's Kremlin; both were built by 15th-century Venetians. Boats leave from the northeastern end of Akti Miaouli. You can buy tickets from where the boats depart.

Komboloi Museum   MUSEUM

(Map p160; ☑ 27520 21618; www.komboloi.gr; Staïkopoulou 25; adult/child €2/free; ☺ 9.30am-8pm Wed-Mon) Whether or not you wish to buy Greece's most popular souvenir item – *komboloï* (worry beads) – at the gift shop, it's worth popping into the incense-scented museum here to learn what distinguishes the *komboloï* from prayer beads and why the amber-mastic mix is so special. Among the collection of prayer beads belonging to assorted religions are tiny wooden skulls, and black coral beads inlaid with mother-of-pearl and carved ivory.

Akronafplia Fortress   FORTRESS

(Map p160; ☺ 24hr) **FREE** Rising above the old part of town, the Akronafplia fortress is the oldest of Nafplio's three castles. The lower sections of the walls date back to the Bronze Age, while the most recent were built by the Venetians in the 15th century; the town was restricted to within its walls at the time. There's a lift up to the hotel complex within the walls from Plateia Politikou Nosokomeiou, but most of the stuff to see is around the eastern end near the car park.

National Gallery – Nafplio Annex   GALLERY

(Map p160; ☑ 27520 21915; www.nationalgallery.gr; Sidiras Merarhias 23; adult/concession €3/1.50; ☺ 10am-3pm Mon, Thu & Sat, 10am-3pm & 5-8pm Wed & Fri, 10am-2pm Sun) This arm of the Athens National Gallery is housed in a stunningly restored neoclassical building (don't be deterred; the front door looks to be closed). It features numerous seascapes and different thematic takes on the 1821 Greek War of Independence, including paintings by Theodoros Vryzakis and Dionysios Tsokos, who are considered the most important Greek artists of the postwar years. Entry is free on Mondays.

Karathona Beach   BEACH

A gorgeous pine-tree-lined 3km path runs from the car park next to Arvanitia Beach to the long, sandy Karathona Beach. It's a flat, easy walk, though the beach could be cleaner. Don't feel like walking? Head your car along 25 Martiou east of town. It's 5km from the centre.

☞ Tours

Nafplio Bio-Farms   FOOD

(☑ 6944184703; www.nafpliobiofarms.gr; tours per person €15-40) This fun, hands-on cultural experience is also tasty and informative. Guests visit a small organic farm, located just outside Nafplio, that produces oranges

Nafplio

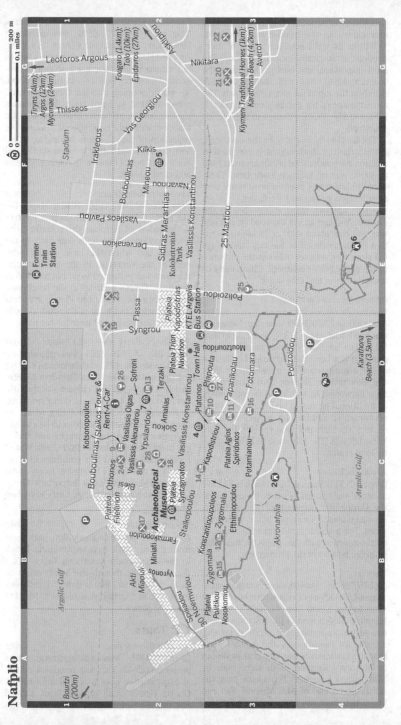

Nafplio

and olives and makes its own organic flour. Owners Petros and Panagiota run through the history of farming techniques that follow centuries-old practices; depending on the tour, you may sample and/or make local goodies.

Pegasus Cruises BOATING
(☑ 27250 59430; www.pegasus-cruises.gr; Tolo; adult/child €34/17; ☺ late Apr–late Sep) Pegasus Cruises offers popular full-day trips to the islands of Hydra and Spetses from Tolo, 10km southeast of Nafplio. The tour stops for a couple of hours in each place. You can get to/from Tolo by taxi (around €12) or bus, depending on the schedule. There are at least two weekly departures (more in July and August). Tickets are available at Staikos Tours (p164).

✯✦ Festivals & Events

Nafplion Festival MUSIC
(www.nafplionfestival.gr; ☺ Jun or Jul) This classical-music festival features Greek and international performers. Dates change annually.

🛏 Sleeping

There are numerous boutique hotels and midrange guesthouses, as well as some solid budget options scattered around. The old town is chock-full of accommodation but can book out in summer.

Pension Eleni PENSION €
(Map p160; ☑ 27520 27036; www.pensioneleni. gr; Zygomala 5; d/tr/ste incl breakfast €50/55/80; ❄ 🤖) One of Nafplio's oldest and most

traditional pensions, tucked away down a quiet street. It's clean and very well kept by the grandmotherly long-time owner. Some rooms have views and the suites have tiny balconies. Park in the nearby square.

★ Pension Marianna HOTEL €€
(Map p160; ☑ 27520 24256; www.hotelmarianna. gr; Potamianou 9; s/d/tr/q incl breakfast €55/80/90/105; ℗ ❄ 🤖) Vibrant Pension Marianna is one of Nafplio's long-standing and outstanding favourites; you can't get better for value, Greek authenticity, and setting (all fabulous). Many of the bright and airy, squeaky-clean rooms provide superb views from the hilltop position. The welcoming Zotos family epitomises Greek *filoxenia* (hospitality), and provides conviviality, travel advice and delicious breakfasts, using their own farm produce.

Klymeni Traditional Homes APARTMENT €€
(☑ 27520 96194; www.klymeni.gr; Karamanli; apt for 2 €105-125; ℗ ❄ 🤖) Set among citrus groves with lovely perspectives over the peaceful countryside, these traditional-style stone houses are perfect for families. They have proper kitchens, spacious living areas and offer respite from the hubbub of Nafplio, although the city is accessible by car. Helpful owner Alexander makes everything easy. Take 25 Martiou out of town for 1.5km towards the Palamidi fortress.

Nafplion 1841 PENSION €€
(Map p160; ☑ 27520 24622; www.nafplion1841. gr; Kapodistriou 9; s/d/tr incl breakfast from €50/55/95; ❄ 🤖) The five bright rooms (and

steep stairs) are crammed into this converted 19th-century mansion. Rooms are simple and white: expect good mattresses, superior bed linens, climate control, hydro-massage showers and flat-screen TVs. The hosts are a delight and so is the breakfast.

Grand Sarai
BOUTIQUE HOTEL €€
(Map p160; ✆27520 22563; www.grandsarai nafplio.com; Potamianou 3; incl breakfast s €100-140, d €120-160; ❇️🛜) A beautifully renovated pink mansion over three floors that's sleek and modern on the inside. Rooms are very stylish, decorated in soft neutral tones. Most have marvellous views, some have balconies, two rooms have spa baths. Extensive breakfasts using local produce are served in an intimate setting downstairs. There's also a lift; rare in the old town.

Aetoma
BOUTIQUE HOTEL €€
(Map p160; ✆27520 27373; www.aetoma.gr; Plateia Agios Spiridonos 2; r incl breakfast €90-125; ❇️🛜) Intimate and comfortable, the five rooms in Aetoma, a classic mansion, have dark, heavy and stylish furnishings, and hospitable owners who go out of their way to be helpful. All rooms have balconies with views to a pretty, traditional alley below, or to the Palamidi. Generous traditional breakfast.

Messini Pension
BOUTIQUE HOTEL €€
(Map p160; ✆27520 22102; www.messinipension. gr; Sofroni 7; r €60-80) In a great old-town location, right in the heart of things, this sweet little five-roomer has inviting chambers with very commodious beds and, in some rooms, balconies with red shutters. Some of the bathrooms are extremely compact. No breakfast, but numerous options within a minute's stroll.

Adiandi
BOUTIQUE HOTEL €€
(Map p160; ✆27520 22073; www.hotel-adiandi. com; Othonos 31; r incl breakfast €85-145; ❇️🛜) Rooms in this fun place are individually decorated by artists with bright colours, quirky painted-door bedsteads and marble sinks. There's a sizeable top-floor suite; the cheapest room is a small double. There's more space in the funky cafe-meets-breakfast-room downstairs.

Leto Nuevo
HOTEL €€
(Map p160; ✆27520 28093; www.letohotelnafplio. gr; Zygomala 28; d incl breakfast €95-110; ❇️🛜) This revamped hotel on a quiet street overlooks much of the old town, with spacious rooms decked out in contemporary creams and greys. The views are just fabulous from all of them and the excellent location, room to move and homemade jams at breakfast add appeal.

3Sixty Hotel & Suites
BOUTIQUE HOTEL €€€
(Map p160; ✆27525 00501; www.3sixtyhotel.gr; Papanikolau 26; ste incl breakfast €200-270; ❇️🛜) Ascend the spectacular spiral staircase, chandeliers all around, and you're faced with seven sumptuous suites of various sizes decked out in contemporary creams, charcoals and browns. They sport huge beds with Versace linen and quality mattresses, enormous ornately framed mirrors and designer furniture. Breakfast is cooked to order in the excellent restaurant.

✖️ Eating

Although it's full of reasonable, pleasant restaurants, Nafplio doesn't win the award for the world's best culinary destination. Avoid the places in tourist-filled Staïkopoulou to discover some surprises.

Pidalio
GREEK €
(Map p160; ✆27520 22603; www.pidalio.gr; 25 Martiou 5; mains €7-10; ⊙12.30pm-midnight Wed-Mon) One of several excellent spots in the new town frequented mainly by locals, Pidalio is a lovely taverna that serves excellent Greek fare at fair prices. It's warm and lively; you'll smell the cooking before you spot it.

Select from a huge range of appetisers, but leave room for the mains, like chicken with Roquefort and pork with lemon.

Pseiras
GREEK €
(Map p160; ✆27520 24117; www.pseiras.gr; 25 Martiou 33; dishes €6-9; ⊙6pm-midnight Mon, Wed & Thu, 11am-1am Fri-Sun; ✍️) Simple, good-value dishes (eg lamb with lemon) characterise this family-run restaurant in the new town. Venerable black-and-white images create an old-time ambience and there's streetside seating.

Antica Gelateria di Roma
GELATO €
(Map p160; ✆27520 23520; cnr Farmakopoulou & Komninou; ice cream from €2.50; ⊙8.30am-11pm, later in summer; ✍️) The only 'true' gelato shop in Nafplio is still holding back the competition. Italian gelati maestros Marcello, Claudia and Monica Raffo will tell you: 'This is no fantasy – it's the real thing!' Only natural and local ingredients are used and it's all made on the premises. Other Italian products lend enticing aromas to the place. Prepare to queue in summer.

★ **I Gonia Tou Kavalari** MEZEDHES €€
(Kavalaris Corner Mezedopoleio; Map p160;
☑ 27525 00180; cnr Amalias & Koleti; mezedhes
€4-9; ☺ 8am-1am Tue-Sun; ☑) Just off Plateia
Syntagmatos and nestled into a cosy corner,
this delightful spot whips, tosses and fries up
some of the best *mezedhes* (tapas-style dishes) around. You can watch the chef at work in
the open kitchen, though our guess is you'll
be too busy munching on everything from
spetsofaï (sausage) to *apaki* (fried pork).
Excellent vegetarian options too. Traditional
products but contemporary creations.

Menta GREEK €€
(Map p160; ☑ 27520 23603; 25 Martiou 7-19; dishes €8-15; ☺ noon-midnight Thu-Tue; ☎☑♨) On
an appealing eat street in the new town, this
contemporary place recreates a traditional
kafeneio (coffee house) and blends it with
millennial designer flair: mismatched chairs
and tables, exposed light bulbs and an industrial interior. Service is very welcoming and
the dishes – contemporary flair meets traditional ingredients – are delicious, though not
all the food pairings are thought through.

Karamalis GREEK €€
(Map p160; ☑ 27520 97999; cnr Bouboulinas &
Syngrou; mains €6-15; ☺ 11am-midnight) One of
Nafplio's most long-standing stalwarts rises above its location overlooking the port
car park. It's got a friendly boss, old-school
atmosphere and a decent mixture of locals
and visitors. Seafood is a speciality: bypass
the menu and ask what they've got fresh
that morning. Whether it's octopus, prawns,
shellfish or fish...delicious!

Taverna Aiolos GREEK €€
(Map p160; ☑ 27520 26828; Vassilissis Olgas 30;
mains €8-15; ☺ noon-midnight; ☑) A warm and
cosy traditional taverna where you come for
a well-cooked and hearty Greek meal...and
end up staying until three in the morning,
such is the convivial atmosphere. It serves
up reliable Greek classics with many ingredients grown by the owners. Cheery drawings
by satisfied customers plaster the walls.

Scuola PIZZA €€
(Map p160; ☑ 27520 99431; Bouboulinas 39; mains
€7-13; ☺ 8am-2am; ☎♨) Scuola ('school' in
Italian) teaches the locals, especially the
younger crowd, a thing or two about good
cuisine. Its quirky interior comprises a classroom setting, complete with a blackboard
and books. Pasta and pizza with Greek twists
break all the rules.

Fougaro CAFE, FUSION €€
(☑ 27520 47347; www.fougaro.gr; Asklipiou 98;
mains €12-16, sandwiches €4-6; ☺ 9am-1am Wed-
Sun; ☎☑) This cultural space sits 3km from
Nafplio (towards Epidavros) in a converted
canning factory. There's pleasant courtyard
seating to enjoy good coffee, tasty sandwiches, sweet and savoury crêpes, and waffles.
The menu also has serious culinary inten-
tions, with sous-vide meat dishes and elaborately sauced fish. It doesn't always succeed
but it's a nice break from the taverna scene.
Look for the *fougaro* (chimney).

🍷 Drinking & Nightlife

★ **Mavros Gatos** BAR
(Map p160; ☑ 27520 26652; Sofroni 1; ☺ 8am-3am)
Chilled-out cafe by day, buzzy bar by night,
the 'Black Cat' has live performers some
nights and DJs always. There are comfy seats
outside and an eclectic vintage vibe inside
and upstairs.

Kontrabasso BAR
(Map p160; ☑ 27520 27434; www.facebook.com/
kontrabassocafe; Arvanitias 1; ☺ 9am-midnight
or later; ☎) Just by the steps up to the Palamidi fortress, this welcoming cafe-bar is
an all-rounder that offers breakfasts and
brunches, all-day sandwiches and salads,
and pints of cold beer – just the thing after
the hot staircase walk. We like it best in the
evening, when a cocktail on the stepped
wooden terrace is pleasantly removed from
the centre's hubbub.

🛍 Shopping

Glykos Peirasmos FOOD
(Map p160; Plapouta 10; ☺ 9am-9pm Mon-Thu, to
10pm Fri-Sun) *The* place for delicious chocolate, baklava, *loukoumi* (Turkish delight)
and honey-sodden walnut cake.

Karonis WINE
(Map p160; ☑ 27520 24446; www.karoniswine
shop.gr; Amalias 5; ☺ 8.30am-2pm & 6-9.30pm
Mon-Sat) Wine enthusiasts can find a fine
selection of wines from all over the country,
including Nemean reds and spirits. Tastings
are offered. Well-read owner Ioannis has
a wide range of interests, from grapes to
politics.

❶ Information

Tourist Police (☑ 27520 98728; Eleftherias 2)
At Nafplio's police station.
Hospital (☑ 27523 61100; Kountouriotou 1)
Nafplio's general hospital.

Staikos Tours (Map p160; ☑ 27520 27950; www.rentacarnafplio.gr; Bouboulinas 50; ⊗ 8.30am-2.30pm & 5.30-8.30pm Mon-Sat, 10am-noon & 6-8pm Sun) Run by the personable, English-speaking Christos. Has full travel services, including ferry tickets, plus Sixt rental cars.

ⓘ Getting There & Away

The **KTEL Argolis bus station** (Map p160; ☑ 27520 27323; www.ktelargolida.gr; Syngrou) has buses to Athens (€14.40, 2½ hours, at least hourly), some via Corinth Isthmus (Peloponnese) KTEL bus station (€7.10, 1½ hours). Lockers available.

Other services include buses to Argos (€1.80, 30 minutes, half-hourly), Epidavros Theatre (€3.20, 45 minutes, four Monday to Friday, four Saturday, one Sunday), Galatas (€9, two hours, one Monday to Friday), Kranidi (€8.50, two hours, four Monday to Friday, three Saturday, one Sunday), Mycenae (€3.20, one hour, three Monday to Friday, two Saturday), Tolo (€1.80, 15 minutes, nine to 12 daily) and Tripoli (€7.70, 1½ hours, two daily).

ⓘ Getting Around

Head to the **taxi rank** (Map p160) on Syngrou, which has a list of official prices for excursions in the area. Car-hire agencies include **Hermes Car Rental** (☑ 27520 25308; www. hermestravel.gr; Syngrou 20; ⊗ 9am-9pm) and Sixt rentals at Staikos Tours.

ARKADIA   ΑΡΚΑΔΙΑ

The picturesque rural prefecture of Arkadia occupies much of the central Peloponnese. Its name evokes images of grassy meadows, forested mountains, gurgling streams and shady grottoes. According to mythology, it was a favourite haunt of Pan, the flute-playing, cloven-hooved god of nature.

Almost encircled by mountain ranges, Arkadia was remote enough in ancient times to remain largely untouched by the battles and intrigues of the rest of Greece, and was the only region of the Peloponnese that the Dorians did not penetrate. The region is dotted with crumbling medieval villages, remote monasteries and Frankish castles, and is popular among fresh-air fiends.

The heart of Arkadia (to the west of the regional capital, Tripoli) comprises a tangle of precipitous ravines and narrow roads that wind their way through the medieval-village-speckled valleys of the Menalon range. The breathtaking mountainous scenery is ideal

for excellent hiking opportunities and skiing in winter.

ⓘ Getting There & Away

Having your own wheels is advantageous here, as public transport to the main villages is limited to one or two buses per day.

KTEL Arkadia (☑ 27102 22560; www. ktelarkadias.gr; Nafpliou 50, Tripoli) in Tripoli is the departure point for buses to Stemnitsa (€4.50, one hour, one daily Monday, Thursday and Friday), Dimitsana (€6.30 to €7.10, 1½ hours, two Monday to Friday) and Andritsena (€9.40, 1½ hours, one to two daily).

It also handles buses to Athens (via Corinth Isthmus, €16.50, 2½ hours, almost hourly), Olympia (€13.50, 2¼ hours, one daily weekdays), Pyrgos (€15.50, 2¾ hours, one daily weekdays), Nafplio (€7.70, 1½ hours, one to two daily) and direct to Patra (€19.80, three hours, one to two daily except Saturday).

Buses also run to Sparta (€5.90, one hour, seven to nine daily) and Kalamata (€8.90, 1¼ hours, one daily on weekdays).

Stemnitsa   Στεμνίτσα

POP 200 / ELEV 1083M

Stemnitsa is a striking village of stone houses and Byzantine churches. If you want to peek into any of the churches, ask around for the keys. There are several monasteries in the area, in the Lousios Gorge along the riverbank to/from the site of Ancient Gortys.

The starting (or finishing) point for the Menalon Trail, Stemnitsa is a good base for hikers. It provides a useful base for a hike along the Lousios Gorge, accessed by Ancient Gortys and passing by monasteries including Prodromos, and the New and Old Filosofou.

Stemnitsa is also known for its silver and gold craftsmanship; even today, there is a silversmith school here. It's 26km northwest of Tripoli.

🛏 Sleeping & Eating

⭐ **Mpelleiko**   B&B €€
(☑ 6976607967, 27950 81286; www.mpelleiko. gr; s/d/tr incl breakfast €70/80/90; 🐾) The ultrahospitable and knowledgeable English-speaking owner, Nena, has converted her family home (dating from 1650) into a stylish guesthouse perched above the village. Each room's decor is unique and features tasteful, traditional local homewares. You can even sleep in the former 'donkey basement'. Breakfast includes homemade organic

THE MENALON TRAIL

The well-signposted, 75km Menalon Trail (www.menalontrail.eu) stretches from Stemnitsa to Lagkadia, passing the dramatic scenery of the Lousios Gorge, the western slopes of Mt Menalon, the Mylaon River valley and the Gortynian Mountains. The trail is divided into eight sections of varying difficulty; the Stemnitsa–Dimitsana section is the most popular for a day hike. The website has a trail outline and maps. See also the Anavasi Topo 25 map, *Lousios 8.51 1:22,000*.

You can also download the excellent Menalon Trail TopoGuide app for detailed offline maps and numerous points of interest.

Of the villages, Stemnitsa, Dimitsana, Valtesiniko and Lagkadia all have places to stay and eat, and you can pick up provisions at Vytina, Nymphasia and Magouliana.

There are eight trail sections:

Stemnitsa–Dimitsana (12.5km) A picturesque descent into the Lousios Gorge past Prodromos Monastery, followed by an ascent to the Old and New Filosofou Monasteries. The trail then follows the course of the river before leading up to the Open Air Water-Power Museum). From the Prodromos Monastery there's a worthwhile detour south to Ancient Gortys.

Dimitsana–Zygovisti (4.2km) A gentle ascent past St Apostoli Monastery, and along footpaths and dirt roads through fields.

Zygovisti–Elati (14.9km) This section ascends to the Bilali Pass over the Western Menalon massif, with some steep sections and an optional detour to Pliovouni Peak (1643m).

Elati–Vytina (8.5km) Partially paved, wooded trail that passes by some ancient ruins and abandoned windmills.

Vytina–Nymphasia (5.6km) The trail descends to a short gorge before ascending gently through a rock-and-shrub landscape.

Nymphasia–Magouliana (8.9km) Leading through oak and spruce forests, the trail descends to Kernitsas Monastery and passes by Sfyrida Hermitage and Gavros Spring.

Magouliana–Valtesiniko (6.6km) The path descends past an old sanatorium and follows a riverbed.

Valtesiniko–Lagkadia (13.9km) The path ascends to a Byzantine fortress, then passes through open country and traverses valleys before ending at a war memorial.

Monasteries

The Prodromos Monastery (🏠 27950 81385; ⊙ closed 1-5pm) clings to the cliff face in memorable fashion. The monastery church is adorned with frescoes, while up the hill where the road ends is a modern chapel offering spectacular gorge views. Monks are welcoming and may even offer coffee and sweets to visitors. The monastery is on the Menalon Trail network from Dimitsana or Stemnitsa and is also accessible by road from between the two towns.

The two Filosofou Monasteries (🏠 27950 81447; ⊙ new monastery closed 1-5pm) is perched on the west side of the Lousios Gorge. The 'new' monastery dates from the 17th century and its atmospheric, incense-laden church is magnificently frescoed from top to bottom. From the new monastery, it's a short but steep 800m to the incredible old monastery, built along a ledge in the cliff face with an amazing view over the gorge. The monasteries are 8km from Dimitsana, and also accessible from the Menalon Trail.

The old monastery, founded in the 10th century, is also said to have functioned as a subversive school in the 19th century under the Ottoman occupation. There are few structures left except the wall and a little church, often closed. From here you can continue by foot to the Prodromos Monastery on the other side of the gorge (30 minutes).

The monks request that you dress appropriately when visiting the new monastery, though they seem too polite to turn hikers away.

produce and is served in a beautiful room with an open fireplace.

There are no TVs; enjoy the charming common area instead.

I Stemnitsa
GREEK €

(☑ 27950 81371; mains €6-13; ☺ 10am-midnight; 🛜) The only taverna open year-round in Stemnitsa, and it's a solid one, just behind the bell tower. Eat inside or sit outdoors under giant umbrellas. The local butcher owns the establishment, so go for the grills and expect quality, hearty cuts of meat.

❶ Getting There & Away

There is one bus in each direction between Tripoli and Stemnitsa (€4.50, one hour, Monday, Thursday and Friday), continuing to Dimitsana (€1.80, 15 minutes). A taxi to Dimitsana costs around €12, to Prodromos Monastery €15, Ancient Gortys €20 and the Filosofou Monasteries €25.

Dimitsana   Δημητσάνα
POP 400 / ELEV 945M

Built like a choir of buildings across two hills at the beginning of the Lousios Gorge, Dimitsana, 11km north of Stemnitsa, is a delightful medieval village. This small place played a significant role in the country's struggle for self-determination. Its Greek school, founded in 1764, was an important spawning ground for the ideas leading to the uprisings against the Turks. Its students included Bishop Germanos of Patra and Patriarch Gregory V, who was hanged by the Turks in retaliation for the massacre in Tripoli. The village also had a number of gunpowder factories and a branch of the secret Filiki Eteria (Friendly Society), where Greeks met to discuss the revolution. Today, this sleepy village is hiker central in summer and full of skiing weekenders in winter.

❂ Sights

★ Open Air Water-Power Museum
MUSEUM

(☑ 27950 31630; www.piop.gr; adult/child €4/2; ☺ 10am-6pm Wed-Mon Mar–mid-Oct, to 5pm mid-Oct–Feb) This excellent little museum is an entertaining romp through the region's pre-industrial past. It occupies a complex 1.6km south of town (signposted), where a spring-fed stream once supplied power for a succession of mills spread down the hillside. The lush grounds are alive with rushing water powering a fully operational

fulling mill, flour mill and gunpowder mill (the last having provided ammunition during the Greek War of Independence). The tannery is equally fascinating, and videos and demonstrations bring the often complex procedures alive.

🛏 Sleeping

Some great little guesthouses are nestled around the narrow alleys of the village. Winter is high season here, so expect small discounts in summer.

Tsiapa Guesthouse
PENSION €

(☑ 27950 31583; www.xenonas-tsiapa.gr; d/tr €50/65; 🛜) One of the old-school budget options, with so-clean-you-could-eat-off-the-floor rooms that have fridges and hotplates. Some also have marvellous valley views. The communal living room has a fireplace – perfect for a cold evening. At time of research it was going to close for renovation, but it should be open by the time you read this.

★ Amanites
BOUTIQUE HOTEL €€

(☑ 27950 31090; www.amanites.gr; d/tr incl breakfast €85/105; 🅿🛜) This lovely place, a converted historic home, has eight elegant rooms with drapes and tasteful fabrics. All of them face the fabulous outlook over the valley, and half have balconies making the most of it. Kitchenettes and connecting rooms make for good family options. Delightful owners Chara and her parents, Aris and Elena, go out of their way to be helpful.

Enastron Guesthouse
B&B €€

(☑ 27950 31684; www.xenonasenastron.gr; d incl breakfast €70-80; 🛜) This appealing guesthouse with only three rooms is distinguished not just by the friendliness and helpfulness of its owners, but also by the meticulous attention to detail. The spacious wooden-beamed rooms come with contemporary fittings and excellent bathrooms, and the extensive breakfast buffet comprises fresh local produce. Rates are higher over weekends.

Proselinos
BOUTIQUE HOTEL €€

(☑ 27950 31675; www.proselinos.gr; d incl breakfast €85-130; 🛜) Managed by a friendly young couple who can offer good hiking info, Proselinos has been fitted out in keeping with the age of this traditional building. Creaky wooden floors, black-and-white photos, lacy table covers, brass beds and antique furniture give the exposed-stone rooms, which vary substantially in size and price, plenty of atmosphere. Breakfast is a generous affair, with allergies catered for.

Nerida
BOUTIQUE HOTEL €€

(☑ 27950 32700; www.nerida-hotel.gr; s/d/tr incl breakfast €85/95/110; P ❄ ☎) This upmarket, peaceful choice looks like it's modelling a designer homeware collection and, as such, is more contemporary than the average mountain-village accommodation. It's popular for romantic getaways and some rooms fit the bill with fireplaces, sofas and in-room tubs. Standard rooms are smaller but still high quality and breakfast is brilliant. Amazing valley views from most rooms.

Kazakou
B&B €€

(☑ 27950 31660; www.xenonaskazakou.com; d/f incl breakfast €80/100; ☎) This rambling stone house above central Dimitsana is one of the more casual options around. Host Ilias is ultrahelpful and the five varying rooms offer plenty of space (steep stairs to some). A vast breakfast is served in the vaulted lounge. The location is either a boon or a bane, depending on whether you enjoy the sound of church bells.

✗ Eating & Drinking

Most of the village tavernas serve seasonal mountain fare, such as game casseroles or roasts, rooster in red wine and *fasoladha* (bean soup).

Drymonas
GREEK €

(☑ 27950 31116; Lampardopoulou 65; mains €6.50-9; ☎ 11am-11pm Wed-Mon; ☎⁂) On the main road through town, this family-run taverna is a good pick for a pleasing no-frills meal. Dishes prepared daily might include soup, rabbit in olive oil and oregano sauce, meatballs, or stewed chicken with tomato. Salads are bright and fresh, grilled meats generously proportioned and prices very fair.

Taverna Margarita
GREEK €

(☑ 27950 31368; Zatouna; mains €7-12; ☎ 11.30am-10pm) This casual, ultratypical, family-run taverna in the quaint village of Zatouna is a far cry from the tourist haunts of nearby Dimitsana. The pine decor and souvenir paraphernalia look like they've been there since time immemorial. Don't expect silver service, but do expect some genuine kitchen cooking. It's known for its *pita* (pie), filled with fresh mountain *horta* (greens).

To Lathos
GREEK €

(☑ 27950 31709; Dimitsana–Karkalou Rd; mains €6-9; ☎ 11am-10pm Fri-Sun; ☎⁂) This country taverna makes a good weekend lunch excursion. Run by a mother and her two sons, it offers great value for traditional Greek home cooking, mostly based around grilled meats. The meat patties and rabbit in oregano sauce are delicious. The menu is in Greek only, but they'll help you order. It's 6km northeast of Dimitsana, about 1km before Karkalou.

Kids can romp safely on the grass and make some local friends while they eat.

★ Zerzova
GREEK €€

(☑ 27950 32452, 6932847358; Panagia; mains €8-14; ☎ 10.30am-9.30pm Fri-Sun Sep-May, longer hours Jun-Aug; ⁂) ✈ Zerzova ticks all the right boxes. Sustainable practices? The husband-and-wife team collects wild herbs and cultivates their own produce. Home cooking? Even Greek grandmothers are happy to come here. Traditional? The setting is in a lovely old building. However, as it's a social media star you may have to wait for a table. It's located 14km southwest of Dimitsana in Panagia.

Kato Apo To Roloi
WINE BAR

(☑ 27950 31195; www.undertheclock.gr; ☎ 10am-late; ☎) The Under the Clock cafe is *the* spot to unwind after a day's hiking. Look down at the gorge with a large glass of wine (€3.50) or an expertly mixed cocktail (from €8) in hand.

❶ Getting There & Away

There are two daily buses in each direction on weekdays only between Tripoli and Dimitsana (€6.30 or €7.10, 1½ hours). A taxi to Stemnitsa costs around €12, to Filosofou Monastery €16 and to Ancient Gortys €25.

Leonidio   Λεωνίδιο

POP 3800

Leonidio is dramatically located at the mouth of the Badron Gorge, 76km south of Argos along a spectacular winding road. In recent years the village has become a magnet for climbers who hang off the precipices and magnificent cliff faces. Culturally, it's famous for its Tsakonian aubergines (eggplants) and summer Aubergine Festival, Melizazz. Its tiny Plateia 25 Martiou is an archetypal, unspoilt, whitewashed village square. There are still living locals who speak the local dialect, Tsakonica, said to date back to the time of Sparta. Five kilometres north of Leonidio, the tiny fishing village of Plaka attracts those after stunning clear waters and excellent beachside tavernas.

CLIMBING IN LEONIDIO

Climbing is a major drawcard here, with hundreds of routes across a couple of dozen sites in the Badron Gorge; there's something for all levels. The website www.climbinleonidio.com has an excellent map with details of all the climbs and a forum for finding a climbing buddy. There are several gear shops in town, which gets busy in early November for the Leonidio Climbing Festival.

Some of the climbing hotspots, as well as several local hikes, are marked on the useful free tourist map that's available throughout town.

🛏 Sleeping & Eating

The local Tsakonian aubergine (eggplant) is a must-try here. You can buy *melitznaki gliko* (sweet aubergine) from village shops, or ask for the aubergine salad, served at the waterside tavernas in Plaka.

Semeli Camping   CAMPGROUND €
(✆27570 22995; www.camping-semeli.gr; Plaka; camp sites per tent/person €6/6; ⊙ Apr-Nov; Ⓟ 🛜) Near the Badron Gorge and set amid trees, this welcoming spot is camping as nature intended. Oh, and the ocean and beach are a quick stroll away. It's a little cheaper outside of high summer.

Archontiko Hatzipanayiotis   HOTEL €€
(✆27570 22476; www.hatzipanayiotis.gr; 21 Ianouariou; d €75-100; Ⓟ ✳ 🛜) In the heart of Leonidio, this hotel has a lovely paved courtyard with hammock chairs. The rooms surrounding it are just beautiful, with rough stone walls creating a grotto-like atmosphere. There's also a cafe-restaurant.

Agroktima Traditional Guesthouse   APARTMENT €€
(✆27570 23244; www.agroktima.com; Leonidio-Peleta Rd; apt for 2 €75) A cluster of traditional-style stone houses surrounded by green lawn, 1km before Plaka. They are attractively split-level and well equipped with kitchen and fireplace. Prices jump to €105 in high summer.

Dolphin   GREEK €
(✆27570 23036; Plaka; mains €7-15; ⊙10am-midnight; ✆) Owner Theodore's brother-in-law is a fisherman, so you get to eat the catch of the day. But have a look at the prepared dishes inside first – the aubergine creations are

fantastic. Kids can run amok, while parents sit on the terrace overlooking the water.

ℹ Getting There & Away

There are three daily buses to/from Athens (€22, four hours); change at Astros. The friendly **Café Bar 2Porto** (✆27570 22255; www.2porto.gr; Leonidio–Skala Rd; ⊙7am-1am) doubles as the KTEL bus ticket office.

LAKONIA   ΛΑΚΩΝΙΑ

The boundaries of Lakonia have changed little since King Menelaus ruled the powerful mountain-skirted realm in Mycenaean times. It is home to legends, including the city of Sparta, as well as the spectacular ruins of Mystras, the Byzantine Empire's last stronghold.

Dominating the landscape are two massive mountain ranges, the Taÿgetos Mountains in the west and the Parnonas Mountains in the east. These taper away to create the central and eastern fingers of the Peloponnese.

ℹ Getting There & Away

A motorway runs from Athens to Sparta (also branching to Kalamata). The local **KTEL Lakonia's bus services** (✆27340 23222; www.ktel-lakonias.gr; Leoforos Dimokratias, Neapoli) connect villages in Lakonia, if sometimes infrequently. It's easy to shoot up or down to/from Sparta (or Mystras) to Gythio or Monemvasia, so any of these makes a useful base.

Sparta   Σπάρτη
POP 16,200

Sparta, fearing no one, was without city walls or fortifications, which is probably why so few traces are left of a remarkable people. At the height of their power, Greece's toughest, incorruptible, legendary warriors triumphed over Athens and the rest of Greece in the Peloponnesian Wars (431-404 BCE). However, decisive defeat by Thebes at the Battle of Leuctra in 371 BCE was the beginning of the end; this was followed by successive subjugations by the Macedonians, Romans, Goths and Slavs.

The town was refounded in 1834 CE on the orders of King Otto. Mindful of history, Otto and his court felt that since Athens was to be rebuilt to reflect its former glory, so too should Sparta. He didn't succeed, though it's a pleasant country town. A few ruins attest to its ancient preeminence and its proximity to the Byzantine glories of Mystras makes it a handy stop.

Sights

★ Museum of the Olive & Greek Olive Oil
MUSEUM

(☑ 27310 89315; www.piop.gr; Othonos Amalias 129; adult/child €4/free; ⊗ 10am-6pm Wed-Mon Mar–mid-Oct, to 5pm mid-Oct–Feb) This beautifully designed museum initiates you into the mysteries of the olive from its initial appearance in the Mediterranean in 60,000 BCE to the present day. Immerse yourself in olive oil's many uses (cooking, fuel, ritual, perfume-making) and check out the magnificent reconstructions of olive presses in the courtyard, ranging from prehistoric to Byzantine. Finally, marvel at the minute working models (press the button) that demonstrate changes in pressing technology.

Archaeological Museum
MUSEUM

(Map p170; ☑ 27310 28575; http://odysseus. culture.gr; cnr Lykourgou & Agiou Nikonos; adult/ child €2/free; ⊗ 8.30am-4pm Wed-Mon Mar-Oct, to 3.30pm Nov-Feb) In a park, this likeable old-style archaeological museum hosts artefacts from Sparta's illustrious past. Look for the votive sickles of the kind that Spartan boys dedicated to Artemis Orthia. There are also reliefs perhaps featuring Helen and Menelaus (and Helen with Paris), bronze and lead votive figurines, heads and torsos of various deities, a head and torso dubbed King Leonidas, a brilliant razor-backed wild boar, votive terracotta masks and grave *stelae* (pillars). Fine mosaics from Hellenistic and Roman Sparta are also on show.

King Leonidas Statue
LANDMARK

(Map p170) The King Leonidas statue stands belligerently in front of a football stadium. When the Persians attacked at Thermopylae and told the Spartans and their allies to lay down their weapons, Leonidas' response, immortalised beneath his feet, was 'Molon labe' ('Come and get them').

Ancient Sparta
ARCHAEOLOGICAL SITE

(Map p170; ☑ 27310 28575; http://odysseus. culture.gr; ⊗ 8.30am-4pm Wed-Mon) **FREE** Though few buildings are standing that date back to the height of Sparta's greatness, it's an atmospheric stroll around this hillside, where the acropolis and agora made up the religious and administrative centre (8th century BCE until the Roman period). There's an ancient theatre, Sanctuary of Athena Halkioitou, stoas, the 'round building' and remains of later Byzantine churches. There are good information panels.

On the north side of the town of Sparta are remains of the Sanctuary of Artemis Orthia.

Courses

Mosaic Art Greece
ARTS & CRAFTS

(☑ 6978440119; www.mosaicartgreece.com; Xirokampi; workshop €50) Over the course of four hours, Dimitra teaches students how to make a mosaic: learn to mix the base then shape and place your tesserae, creating your own example of this millennia-old art. You'll need to book ahead. She also runs weekly workshops in Kardamyli and sells her own creations via the website.

Her workshop is located in the village of Xirokampi, 16km south of Sparta.

★ Festivals & Events

Spartathlon
SPORTS

(www.spartathlon.gr; ⊗ Sep) This gruelling annual foot race takes place over the 246km between Athens and Sparta. It follows in the footsteps of Pheidippides, the messenger

---

WORTH A TRIP

LANGADA PASS

If you have time and your own wheels, the 59km Sparta–Kalamata road is one of the most stunning, if time-consuming and winding, routes in Greece. The road crosses the Taÿgetos Mountains by way of the Langada Pass.

The climb begins in earnest at the village of Trypi, 9km west of Sparta, where the road enters the dramatic Langada Gorge. To the north of this gorge is the site where the ancient Spartans left to die those babies too weak or deformed to become good soldiers.

The road then follows the course of the Langada River before climbing sharply through a series of hairpin bends, fringed with plane trees and pines, to emerge in a sheltered valley. This is a good spot to stop for a stroll among the plane trees along the riverbank. The road then climbs steeply once more, to the high point of 1524m, crossing the boundary from Lakonia into Messinia on the way. The descent to Kalamata is equally dramatic.

Sparta

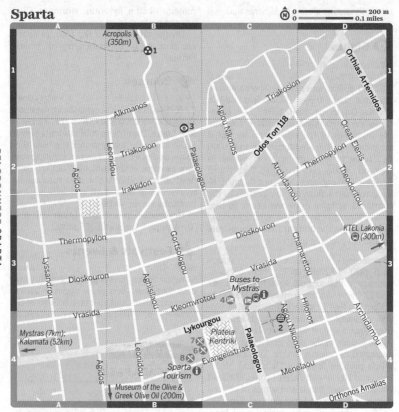

Sparta

◉ Sights

🛏 Sleeping

🍴 Eating

who ran from Athens to Sparta in a day and a half in 490 BCE, to ask the Spartans for assistance in the Battle of Marathon against the Persians. The record currently stands at 20 hours and 25 minutes (set in 1984 by Yiannis Kouros).

🛏 Sleeping

There are adequate business-style hotels in Sparta, and options for all budgets around the ruins of Mystras, 7km to the west.

Hotel Lakonia　　　　　　　HOTEL €
(Map p170; ☎ 27310 28951; www.lakoniahotel. gr; Palaeologou 89; d €55; ❈ 🛜) The compact rooms at the Lakonia are not particularly memorable, but they are far from spartan nonetheless. Boons include balconies, a super-central location and double-glazed windows that cut out street noise; the service is friendly and helpful. Breakfast is €5.

Hotel Maniatis　　　　　　　HOTEL €€
(Map p170; ☎ 27310 22665; www.maniatishotel.gr; Palaeologou 72; s/d incl breakfast €50/67; ❈ 🛜) Light and pleasant carpeted rooms with balconies and firm beds in a modern business hotel on a central corner. The upmarket Zeys restaurant (mains €9 to €14) is in the lobby.

Eating

★ **Tsipouradiko To Peninda** GREEK €
(Map p170; ☑ 27310 83585; Evangelistrias 50; mains €7-11; ⊙ noon-11pm; 🛜 🅿) This atmospheric spot has been renovated to look like an old-style shop and *tsipouradiko* (a taverna that specialises in *tsipouro,* the alcoholic spirit) – barrels, china pieces and old cans line the walls. There's an amazing backyard and all sorts of nooks and crannies. As for the food? Traditional *mayirefta* (ready-cooked meals) and grills.

Kechribári MEZEDHES €
(Map p170; ☑ 27313 02440; www.kexribari.com; Gortsologou 81; mezedhes €6-12; ⊙ 11.30am-1am; 🛜 🅿) On the main square, 'Amber' gets a green light from us with its nouveau-rustic interior and commodious outdoor tables. The menu offers punchy flavours and creative twists. Daily specials are invariably excellent and service is notably friendly.

Kápari GREEK €€
(Map p170; ☑ 27313 00520; www.kaparirestaurant.gr; Gortsologou 77; mains €9-15; ⊙ 11am-11pm) This friendly restaurant is one of Sparta's best, located on the square with a sociable outdoor terrace. Greek standards are well prepared, but there are also lovely salads, huge steaks and an extensive seafood menu; shrimp *saganaki* (prawns in a savoury tomato sauce with cheese) stands out.

ⓘ Information

Sparta Tourism (Map p170; ☑ 27310 28166; Evangelistrias 83-91; ⊙ 8am-3pm Mon-Fri) On the 3rd floor and in an office, this is an administrative centre that can provide information.

Tourist Information Kiosk (Map p170; ☑ 27310 25811; Lykourgou; ⊙ 9am-5pm Mon-Fri) Just off the principal intersection, this friendly kiosk is right by where buses stop for Mystras.

ⓘ Getting There & Away

Sparta's **KTEL Lakonia bus station** (☑ 27310 26441; www.ktel-lakonias.gr; cnr Lykourgou & Thivronos) has buses to Athens (€21.40, 3¼ hours, seven to nine daily) via Tripoli (€5.90, one hour) and Corinth (two hours, €14.10), and buses to Gythio (€4.70, one hour, five to six daily),

---

THE SPARTANS

Maybe you saw the gory and highly imaginative film *300*, based (very loosely) on the battle of Thermopylae in 480 BCE, one of the most talked-about battles in history? Three hundred elite Spartan soldiers held an entire Persian army (whose force numbered several thousand) at bay at the pass of Thermopylae (near today's Lamia). For three days, wave upon wave of Persian soldiers fell upon their deadly spears and unbridgeable tortoise-shell formation. What kind of soldiers could display such bravery? Ones raised in Sparta, where warfare was held to be the only occupation worthy of its men and where warriors embodied ferocious, self-sacrificing martial supremacy, living (and very often dying) by the motto 'return with your shield, or on it'.

If you were born male and deemed too weak and feeble to make it to adulthood, you would be left on the slopes of the Taÿgetos Mountains to die. Passed the first round? Then at the age of seven, you'd be plucked from the bosom of your family and sent to live in barracks with other boys, to undergo the military education system known as *agoge*, designed to build physical and emotional toughness. You'd be habitually underfed to encourage you to survive by living off the land and by stealing, but punished harshly if caught. You'd undergo brutal institutionalised beatings, which you'd be expected to bear without showing pain. At the age of 12, you'd form a sexual bond with an older mentor, who'd be responsible for your training. Upon turning 18, you'd become a member of the army until the age of 30, when you'd finally be granted Spartan citizenship, if you had proved yourself worthy.

Born a girl? Then you'd be better off than anywhere else in Greece at the time. You would eat the same food as your brothers, participate in sport and exercise nude. You'd be well educated and literate, and forbidden to marry until your early 20s, which would spare you from teenage pregnancies and miscarriages. Then when you finally did marry, your husband-to-be would 'abduct' you, and you'd have your head shaved and be dressed in men's clothing before the marriage could be consummated. That'd be to make your husband comfortable, since he wouldn't have spent much time around women.

Neapoli (€15.60, three hours, three daily) and Monemvasia (€11, two hours, four to six daily).

Buses (Map p170) run to Mystras (€1.80, 15 minutes, four to five daily except Sunday) from next to the tourist information kiosk on Lykourgou; a taxi costs around €12.

Travelling by bus to Kalamata (€6.30, 1¾ hours, one to two daily) involves changing at Artemisia on the Messinian side of the Langada Pass.

To the Mani peninsula, there are three daily buses to Gerolimenas (€11.30, 2½ hours), via Areopoli (€7.60, two hours).

Mystras Μυστράς

POP 850

The captivating ruins of churches, libraries, strongholds and palaces in the fortress town of Mystras, a World Heritage–listed site, spill from a spur of the Taÿgetos Mountains 7km west of Sparta. It's among the most important historical sites in the Peloponnese. This is where the Byzantine Empire's richly artistic and intellectual culture made its last stand before an invading Ottoman army, almost 1000 years after its foundation.

Traveller facilities are split between Neo Mystra, about 1km from the lower gate of ancient Mystras, and Pikoulianika village, 1.3km from Mystras' upper gate.

History

The Frankish leader Guillaume de Villehardouin built the fortress in 1249. When the Byzantines won back the Morea from the Franks, Emperor Michael VIII Palaeologos made Mystras its capital and seat of government. Settlers from the surrounding plains began to move here, seeking refuge from the invading Slavs. From this time until Dimitrios surrendered to the Turks in 1460, a despot of Morea (usually a son or brother of the ruling Byzantine emperor) lived and reigned at Mystras.

While the empire plunged into decline elsewhere, Mystras enjoyed a renaissance. Gemistos Plethon (1355–1452) founded a school of humanistic philosophy here and his enlightened ideas, including the revival of the teachings of Plato and Pythagoras, attracted intellectuals from all corners of Byzantium. Art and architecture also flourished, as seen in the town's splendid buildings and frescoes.

Mystras declined under Ottoman rule, but thrived again after the Venetians captured it in 1687 and developed a flourishing silk industry. The population swelled to 40,000.

The Turks recaptured the town in 1715 and from then it was downhill all the way; it was burned during the Orlov uprising in 1770 and Ibrahim Pasha torched what was left in 1825. By the time of independence it was a largely abandoned ruin, and the refounding of nearby Sparta in 1834 contributed to the decline, though Mystras remained inhabited until 1953. Much restoration has taken place since the 1950s (and continues to this day) and in 1989 it was declared a Unesco World Heritage site.

⊙ Sights

★ **Mystras** HISTORIC SITE

(☑ 23315 25363; http://odysseus.culture.gr; adult/child €12/free; ⊗ 8am-8pm Apr-Aug, reduced hours Sep-Mar) Spread over a steep mountainside and surrounded by verdant olive and orange trees, this former Byzantine capital and fortified city is the single most compelling set of medieval ruins in Greece. Treading the cobblestones, worn smooth by centuries of footsteps, you can walk with the ghosts, ducking into the ruins of palaces, monasteries and churches, most dating from between 1271 and 1460. Good information panels throughout focus on the background rather than specific details of buildings.

From the upper-entrance ticket office, the right-hand path (signposted 'Castle') leads up to the fortress; it's a 10-minute ascent. The fortress was built by the Franks and extended by the Turks; the views of the Lakonia plain, spread out below, are nothing short of fantastic. The left-hand path descends from the ticket office to Agia Sofia, which served as the palace church and burial ground for several emperors' wives; some frescoes survive in a side chapel, including a well-preserved *Birth of the Virgin Mary* over the doorway. Steps descend from here via the church of Agios Nikolaos to a T-junction.

A left turn leads to the huge and heavily restored Palace of Despots, under ongoing work. The complex was started by the Franks and finished by the Byzantines; various buildings were constructed between 1250 and 1450, and the main palace was built between 1350 and 1400. The right fork leads down to the Monemvasia Gate, the entrance to the lower town.

Through the gate, turn right for the well-preserved 14th-century Convent of Pantanassa. Featuring a beautifully ornate stone-carved facade, it is still maintained by nuns, Mystras' only inhabitants besides the motley crew of stray cats. The convent is an

Mystras

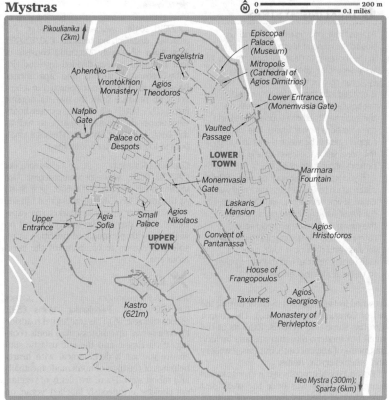

Pikoulianika (2km)

Evangelistria

Aphentiko

Vrontokhion Monastery

Agios Theodoros

Nafplio Gate

Palace of Despots

Episcopal Palace (Museum)

Mitropolis (Cathedral of Agios Dimitrios)

Lower Entrance (Monemvasia Gate)

Vaulted Passage

LOWER TOWN

Monemvasia Gate

Marmara Fountain

Upper Entrance

Agia Sofia

Small Palace

Agios Nikolaos

UPPER TOWN

Laskaris Mansion

Convent of Pantanassa

Agios Hristoforos

House of Frangopoulos

Kastro (621m)

Taxiarhes

Agios Georgios

Monastery of Perivleptos

Neo Mystra (300m); Sparta (6km)

0 ——— 200 m
0 ——— 0.1 miles

elaborate, perfectly proportioned building that's never overstated. The exquisite, richly coloured 15th-century frescoes here are among the finest examples of late-Byzantine art. Look out for the tiny stamped silver and gold votive offerings beneath the large icon of the Virgin. You'll find images of eyes, ears, legs, arms, breasts, babies, husbands and wives stamped onto these small tablets, depending on the problems for which the faithful have come seeking aid. It's a continuation of a long tradition going back to Classical Greece and beyond. The nuns may provide wraps to cover your legs.

The path continues down, via an impressive mansion house, to the exceptional Monastery of Perivleptos, which is built into a rock and tucked away in a pine grove at the far end of the site. Inside, the 14th-century frescoes, preserved virtually intact, equal those of Pantanassa. It's an extraordinary place. The marble-floored church has a dome in whose centre you'll find the Pantokrator

(depiction of Christ as the universal, all-powerful ruler) surrounded by the Apostles, and the Virgin flanked by two angels.

Continue down towards the Mitropolis and you'll pass Agios Georgios, one of Mystras' many private chapels. Further down, and above the path on the left, is the Laskaris Mansion, a typical Byzantine aristocratic house. It's currently being restored, along with the adjacent house, Chroni.

The Mitropolis (Cathedral of Agios Dimitrios) is a complex of buildings enclosed by a high wall. The original church was built in the 1200s, but was greatly altered in the 15th century. The church stands in an attractive courtyard surrounded by stoas and balconies. Its impressive ecclesiastical ornaments and furniture include a marble iconostasis, an intricately carved wooden throne, and a marble slab in the floor featuring a two-headed eagle (the symbol of Byzantium) located on the exact site where the last Byzantine emperor, Constantine XI, was

ℹ TACKLING MYSTRAS

At least half a day is needed to do justice to the ruins of Mystras. Start early in the morning to beat the tour groups, wear sensible shoes and bring water (you can refill at the convent). The site is divided into three interconnected sections – the *kastro* (the fortress on the summit), the *hora* (upper town) and the *kato hora* (lower town). The fortress (upper) gate is between the *kastro* and the *hora*, while the lower gate is at the bottom of the *kato hora*.

If you want to limit walking, you could catch a taxi to the fortress gate and walk down. If you have a car, you can cover the lower town first (enter and exit from the main gate) and then head separately up to the fortress gate to visit the fortress and the upper town ruins (or vice versa). You can use the same ticket to re-enter at either entrance.

crowned in 1449 (he died in battle during the fall of Constantinople in 1453). The church also has some fine frescoes. Exhibits at the small but modern museum upstairs include fragments of ancient cloth, buttons, jewellery and other everyday items.

Beyond the Mitropolis is the **Vrontokhion Monastery**. This was once the wealthiest monastery of Mystras, the focus of cultural activities and the burial place of the despots. Of its two churches, light-filled **Agios Theodoros** and **Aphentiko**, the latter is the most impressive, with striking frescoes.

🛏 Sleeping

Mystras Castle Town   PENSION €
(📞 27310 20047; www.mystras-castle-town.com; Neo Mystra; d/tr/q €45/50/55; 🅿🛜) Run by a friendly English-speaking Russian-Greek couple, these simple and spacious high-ceilinged rooms in a converted house are just off Neo Mystra's main square. Guests can use a communal kitchen. A separate apartment is ideal for families.

Hotel Byzantion   HOTEL €
(📞 27310 83309; www.byzantionhotel.gr; Neo Mystra; s/d/tr incl breakfast €50/60/70; 🅿❄🛜❄) Located in the centre of the modern village of Neo Mystra, this 26-room option is a sound choice. There's a delightful garden in the rear and the bright rooms have balconies with arresting valley or mountain views.

⭐ **Mazaráki Guesthouse**   BOUTIQUE HOTEL €€
(📞 27310 20414; www.xenonasmazaraki.gr; Pikoulianika; d/ste/apt incl breakfast €90/125/195; 🅿❄🛜❄) 🌿 Lovely Mazaráki consists of four beautiful houses divided into individually decorated studios and apartments. Breakfast arrives on your doorstep in a basket, with produce from the owners' organic farm. The hotel affords an extraordinary view across the plains to Sparta, as well as the *kastro* (fort) of Mystras. There's a small pool to lounge in after a long hike.

Euphoria Retreat   SPA HOTEL €€€
(📞 27313 06111; www.euphoriaretreat.com; Neo Mystra; d incl breakfast €300-500; 🅿❄🛜❄) At the top of Neo Mystra, this gated hillside complex offers a very upmarket spa experience. Your stay can be totally focused on wellness, with personalised nutrition available and classes to complement the enormous spa.

🍴 Eating

Taverna Pikoulianika   GREEK €
(📞 27310 82403; Pikoulianika; mains €8-12; ⏱noon-midnight; 🖋) This traditional roadside taverna serves up quintessential home cooking. It's a classic and the enthusiastic staff ensure you get a decent meal with hearty helpings of the likes of homemade meatballs and rabbit stew. There are plenty of vegetarian choices (erroneously labelled 'vegan' on the English menu).

⭐ **Ktima Skreka**   GREEK €€
(📞 27310 28298; www.facebook.com/ktimaskreka; Pikoulianika; mains €9-15; ⏱11.30am-11.30pm; 🛜🖋) A pleasant outdoor terrace and rustic stone-walled interior make for appealing surrounds here. The menu focuses on local produce but has influences from around Greece and plenty of inventiveness; daily specials back up the offering. The food is excellent: generously proportioned, richly flavoured and perfectly prepared.

Chromata   INTERNATIONAL €€
(📞 27310 23995; www.facebook.com/Chromata. Mystras; Pikoulianika; mains €9-14; ⏱noon-late Jun-Sep, reduced hours Oct-May) Pikoulianika shows its true colours *(chromata)* at this wonderful spot, set high on a hill behind the village. The gorgeous garden patio (open in summer) has a 180-degree view over the Sparta plains. Nikos, the owner-chef, creates both Greek and modern dishes, such as handmade ravioli with pumpkin and smoked pork.

ⓘ Getting There & Away

Buses run in both directions between Sparta and Mystras (€1.80, 15 minutes, four to five daily except Sunday). A taxi between Sparta and Mystras costs around €12.

Monemvasia   Μονεμβασία

POP 20

Surrounded by the teal waters of the Aegean Sea, imposing Monemvasia is an iceberg-like slab of rock, with sheer cliffs rising hundreds of metres from the sea, linked to the mainland by a single, highly defensible causeway.

These days Monemvasia incorporates both the rock, with its medieval village enclosed within the walls of its *kastro,* and the modern mainland village of Gefyra, just across the causeway. 'You can find everything you want in this city – except water', observed an 18th-century Turkish traveller. Monemvasia has remained inhabited to this day, though only around 20 people live in the *kastro* permanently – the rest go home to Gefyra after a day's work. In spite of Monemvasia's immense popularity, the extraordinary visual impact of the medieval village, and the delights of exploring it, override the effects of mass tourism.

◉ Sights

★ **Kastro – Medieval Village**   HISTORIC SITE

FREE Almost wholly surrounded by ocean, Monemvasia's fortified medieval village is divided into the lower town, bisected by a main cobbled street lined with souvenir shops, hotels and tavernas that leads to the main square, and the upper town, with its ruins and fortress. The greatest pleasure of visiting the site comes from wandering the labyrinth: exploring the tiny alleyways and winding stairways that weave between a complex network of stone houses and walled gardens, and ducking into atmospheric nooks and crannies.

In the lower town, the central square is dominated by the Cathedral of Christos Elkomenos, dating from the 13th century. Head up through the stone archway opposite the bell tower and you come across the handsome 17th-century Church of Myrtidiotissa. Down near the waterfront fortifications is the whitewashed 16th-century Church of Panagia Chrysafitissa.

The path to the fortress and the upper town is signposted off the main street in several locations. A steep walking path skirts the edge of the upper-town ruins all the way

to just above the main gate, affording great views of Monemvasia's cluster of rooftops against a cliff backdrop. Some of the upper town's extensive ruins – the central gate complex – have been restored and provide an evocative representation of how the entrance to the upper *kastro* operated (it's believed that the vaulted passages and spaces were used by the fort's garrison; excellent explanations in English). Don't miss the Church of Agia Sofia perched on the edge of a sheer cliff. Take care and keep to the paths, as the area is covered with overgrown cisterns.

Agia Sofia   CHURCH

(Upper Kastro; ◷9am-4pm Fri-Mon) FREE In a spectacular clifftop position in the upper town, this foursquare Byzantine church was built in the 12th century. Its interior is richly decorated with wall paintings. It was converted into a mosque during the Turkish occupation.

⌂ Sleeping

There are several character-packed places to stay within the *kastro,* and this is where you'll want to base yourself if you don't mind a bit of walking and lugging bags. Accommodation is cheaper in Gefyra.

A torch or headlamp is a good idea. Don't forget to plug in the mosquito repellent tablets (usually provided); mosquitoes seem to love this place.

Hotel Filoxenia   HOTEL €

(☑27320 61716; www.filoxenia-monemvasia.gr; Gefyra; d/tr €60/70; ▣⊛☎) Spotless cheapie off Gefyra's main street. It's a simple, family-run place that offers good value with its views of the Monemvasia rock from its balconies. It fills up fast in summer. Breakfast €6 per person.

Kellia   GUESTHOUSE €€

(☑27320 61520; www.keliamonemvasia.com; Kastro; d/apt incl breakfast €85/200; ⊛☎) In a wonderful location, near the front sea wall with unimpeded views over a church and the sea. Rooms are simple and unfussy but atmospheric (some have fireplaces), and it's more laid-back than other hotels. The friendly, English-speaking owner adds to the experience.

Poetry lovers can wax lyrical about the bedroom where Yiannis Rizsos was born.

Hotel Byzantino   HOTEL €€

(☑27320 61351; www.hotelbyzantino.com; Kastro; d incl breakfast €65-145; ⊛☎) This range of atmospheric rooms is a great way to experience the traditional *kastro*. Rooms occupy seven different buildings and come in varying shapes, sizes and prices, from cheaper rooms with no views to smarter digs with sea-facing balconies and vaulted stone ceilings. Most are decked out in antiques. Full buffet breakfast.

Bastione Malvasia HOTEL €€
(☏ 27320 63007; www.bastionemalvasia.gr; Kastro; r €85-145; ❋ ☎) Right at the end of the main street by the eastern walls, this has a wonderfully peaceful location. All but two of the 20 rooms have privileged views; they are compact but comfortable. A friendly boss makes your stay a pleasure.

Malvasia Traditional Hotel HOTEL €€
(☏ 27320 61160; www.malvasiahotel-traditional.gr; Kastro; d incl breakfast €65-130; ❋ ☎) The Malvasia makes the most of traditional architecture, though rooms vary in quality. Some of its renovated rooms feature heavy wooden beams and bright colour schemes; others are cosy nooks with vaulted stone ceilings. Pricier rooms come with sea views; some have balconies overlooking the water. The reception is on the left after entering the *kastro*.

Moni Emvasis
Luxury Suites BOUTIQUE HOTEL €€€
(☏ 27320 62122; www.moniemvasis.gr; Kastro; ste incl breakfast €180-340; ❋ ☎) Consisting of three individually conceived suites, Moni Emvasis aims for luxury, from rain showerheads and spa baths to oversized, sumptuous beds. The sea views from the balconies of the junior and deluxe suites are the best, but the Moni Emvasis suite has a decadent, neomedieval ambience with vaulted ceilings and marble fireplace. The extensive breakfast showcases local produce.

✖ Eating & Drinking

The tourist-focused restaurants on Monemvasia's main street serve similar fare, with a couple of notable exceptions.

Marianthi GREEK €
(☏ 27320 61371; Kastro; mains €8-12; ⊙ 10am-10pm) Forget the views just this once and concentrate on what's on your plate: hearty, honest fare. Marianthi is run by 70-something Magda, who has been preparing and dishing up wonderful traditional cuisine for as long as she can remember.

★ **Voltes Mezedopolio** MEZEDHES €€
(☏ 27320 61919; Kastro; mezedhes plates $4-9; ⊙ 6pm-1am Thu & Fri, 1pm-1am Sat & Sun,

extended hours summer) Named after the switchbacks leading to Monemvasia's upper *kastro* (the *voltes*), this wonderful place manages to link modernity and tradition with ease. Choose from a fabulous array of fresh mezedhes: the presentation is contemporary, the flavours are still old school.

★ **Chrisovoulo** INTERNATIONAL €€€
(☏ 27320 62122; www.chrisovoulo.gr; Kastro; mains €15-27, set menus €22-35; ⊙ 1-11pm Apr-Oct; ☎ ✐) Aiming higher than the other restaurants hereabouts, Chrisovoulo raises expectations. But it delivers: it prepares creative salads and various delicacies like veal with morel sauce or risotto with *siglino* (salted pork) from the Mani, all served in an intimate, stylish environment. Service is professional, the sea views fantastic, and there's a serious local wine list.

Enetiko CAFE
(☏ 27320 61352; https://enetiko.olympicbiz.com; Kastro; ⊙ 7am-3am; ☎) One of a new generation of cafes to rattle the medieval ambience of the Kastro, Enetiko has a lovely terrace with views, perfect for morning coffee, evening cocktails or both. They serve a brunch menu until 5pm.

❶ Information

Malvasia Travel (☏ 27320 61752; malvtrv@otenet.gr; Gefyra; ⊙ 7.30am-2.30pm & 5-8pm or 9pm Mon-Sat Apr-Oct, to 6.30pm Nov-Mar) Just over the causeway in Gefyra.

❶ Getting There & Away

Buses leave from outside Malvasia Travel just over the causeway in Gefyra. There are buses to Athens (€32.50, six hours, four to six daily) via Sparta (€11, two hours), Tripoli (€17, three hours) and Corinth Isthmus (€25.20, four hours).

❶ Getting Around

The medieval *kastro* is pedestrian only, but cars and motorcycles can cross the causeway. Parking is available on the left-hand side of the narrow road skirting the rock. Alternatively, park in the waterfront car park in Gefyra.

Cross the causeway and follow the curving road that skirts the cliff to the official entrance, a narrow tunnel in a massive fortifying wall. The tunnel is L-shaped, so the magical town is concealed until you emerge on the other side.

A **shuttle bus** (€1.10; ⊙ 8am-midnight) ferries visitors between Gefyra and the *kastro* every 30 minutes.

WORTH A TRIP

NEAPOLI

Neapoli, close to the southern tip of the eastern prong of the Peloponnese, is the departure point for the Ionian Island of Kythira, clearly visible across the bay. Also in Neapoli is the amazing Kastania Cave (27343 60100; www.kastaniacave.gr; Kato Kastania; adult/child €7/3; ☉10am-6pm daily Jun-Aug, to 4pm Sat & Sun Sep-May) and the impressive Archaeological Museum of Neapolis Voion (27340 22877; www.amnv.gr; Leoforos Dimokratias; adult/child €2/free; ☉8.30am-4pm Wed-Mon Apr-Oct, by reservation Nov-Mar) – but check ahead to see if the latter is open. Geologists, and anyone after quirky rocks, will love the petrified forest (Agia Marina; ☉24hr), trees that were fossilised several million years ago. It's located on the coast in a spectacular spot (perfect for a plunge and a picnic) around 16km southeast of Neapoli, the last 3km on a rough road.

From March to December, a daily ferry (sometimes two in summer) runs between Neapoli and Diakofti on Kythira (per person/car €12.50/44.50, 1¼ hours). Tickets are sold at Vatika Bay Shipping Agency (27340 24004; www.vatikabay.gr; ☉8am-3pm & 5.30-8pm Sep-May, 9am-9pm Jun-Aug), 350m before the small bridge.

KTEL Lakonias (p168) has buses from Neapoli to Athens (€37, six hours, three daily) via Sparta (€15.60, three hours) and Molai (€7.40, 1¼ hours). Change in Molai for Monemvasia.

Nearby, the small island of Elafonisi is renowned for its white beaches and loggerhead turtles. Regular ferries make the 10-minute trip (up to 15 daily) from Pounda, 8km west of Neapoli.

Gythio   Γύθειο
POP 7100

Once the port of ancient Sparta, Gythio is the gateway to the Lakonian Mani. This pretty fishing town, with its 19th-century pastel houses, makes a pleasant stopover if you're travelling between the Mani and Sparta or Monemvasia, or if you're taking a ferry to Kythira. As well as a handful of things to see in the village, including a recently opened folkloric museum, there's Mavrovouni Beach, a long sandy stretch 2km south of Gythio, and pine-shaded Marathonisi Islet. The islet is alleged to be ancient Cranae, where Paris of Troy and Helen consummated the affair that sparked the Trojan War. A visit here, however, is less about the attractions and more about soaking up a local way of life.

◉ Sights

Folkloric Museum   MUSEUM
(27330 23888; www.kpmanis.gr; Irakleous 1; ☉10am-1pm & 6-9pm) FREE It may be compact, but this museum does a wonderful job of bringing to life the past residents of Gythio and the surrounding Mani. Themed rooms exhibit everything from a historic classroom to objects relating to the trades, crafts and professions of the locals in what was a thriving port town. Music was

particularly important to Gythio, thanks to visiting Italian musician Giocondo Moretti (1863–1941), who established a philharmonic society. On the plaza at the northern end of town.

Shadow Theatre Museum   MUSEUM
(Giorgos Hassanakos; 27330 29128; Larissiou 2; ☉9am-8.30pm Mon-Sat, 10am-2.30pm Sun) FREE This beautiful little studio-museumshop is run by personable local artist Giorgos Hassanakos. The small upstairs gallery pays homage to traditional shadow puppets, and also has a range of the artist's own creations, including satirical puppets (Greek politicians). He's one of the few surviving creators who still make these puppets and will happily show you around. It's the first shop on the rising street at the northern end of town.

⌂ Sleeping

Domatia Matina Kontogiannis   PENSION €
(27330 22518; Pavlou 19; r €45-55; ❄ 🛜) Clean and comfortable rooms in a great location bang in the middle of town. Elderly owner Matina speaks no English but is very welcoming.

Saga Pension   PENSION €
(27330 23220; www.sagapension.gr; Kranais; s/d/tr €45/55/60; ❄ 🛜) This is a goodvalue, comfortable place that overlooks

Marathonisi Islet. The pleasant French owner speaks English and some of the small, simple rooms come with views and balconies. The upmarket restaurant downstairs specialises in seafood. Breakfast €5.

Camping Meltemi CAMPGROUND €
(☑27330 22833; www.campingmeltemi.gr; Mavrovouni; camp sites per tent/adult/car €5/6.50/4, bungalows €30-60; ☺Apr-Oct; Ⓟ🎏🏊) Very well organised and the pick of the three campgrounds at Mavrovouni. Three kilometres southwest of Gythio, it's right behind the beach and sites are set among 3000 well-tended olive trees. The bungalows include kitchen, air-con and TV. There's a cafe-restaurant here too. Buses to Areopoli stop outside.

 Eating

As you can imagine, fresh fish features prominently on the menus of tavernas that cluster along the seafront between the pier and the causeway to Marathonisi Islet. Wander along and take your pick; if you're lucky, racks of drying octopus will be out front.

Trata GREEK €€
(☑27330 24429; Kranais; mains €7-14; ☺noon-1am; 🅟) If it's not fresh, they don't have it at this excellent seafood taverna on the waterfront. Stellar calamari and octopus are highlights. Wash it down with retsina served in the classic coloured aluminium pitcher.

❶ Getting There & Away

BOAT

LANE Lines (www.lane.gr) has one weekly ferry on Wednesdays to Crete (person/car €24/80) via Kythira (person/car €13/31) and Antikythira (person/car €17/57). Buy tickets from **Rozakis Travel** (☑27330 22207; www.rozakistravel. gr; Pavlou 5; ☺9am-2pm & 5.30-8pm Thu-Tue, 9am-8pm Wed), on the waterfront.

BUS

The **KTEL Lakonia bus station** (☑27330 22228; www.ktel-lakonias.gr; Vasileos Georgios 55) is northwest along the waterfront. Services run north to Athens (€23.80, 4½ hours, five to six daily) via Sparta (€4.70, one hour) and Tripoli (€10.60); and south to Areopoli (€2.90, 30 minutes, three daily), Gerolimenas (€6.60, 1¼ hours, three daily), the Diros Caves (€4, one hour, one daily in summer, Friday only at other times) and Vathia (€7.50, 1½ hours, Wednesday).

For Kalamata or Monemvasia, change at Sparta.

THE MANI H MANH

Covering the central peninsula in the south of the Peloponnese, the Mani is a wild, rugged region. From the steep foothills of the snow-tipped Taÿgetos Mountains to the pristine coastal coves, and from the tiny villages nestling amid olive groves, connected by threads of walking trails, to the arid landscapes in the south of peninsula, speckled with abandoned stone towers, the Mani has some of the most dramatic and varied scenery in the Peloponnese, much of it still wonderfully under-explored.

The Mani is generally divided into the Messinian Mani (or outer Mani) and the Lakonian Mani (or inner Mani). The Messinian Mani starts southeast of Kalamata and runs south between the coast and the Taÿgetos Mountains, while the Lakonian Mani covers the rest of the peninsula south of Itilo.

History

The Maniots regard themselves as direct descendants of the Spartans. The legend goes that after the decline of Sparta, citizens loyal to the principles of Lycurgus (founder of Sparta's constitution) chose to withdraw to the mountains rather than serve under foreign masters. Certainly, over later centuries, many refugees from occupying powers filtered into this remote area. For centuries the Maniots were a law unto themselves, renowned for their fierce independence, resentment of attempts to govern them and for their bitter, spectacularly murderous internal feuds.

The Ottoman Turks failed to subdue the Maniots and largely left them alone, yet Mani became the cradle of rebellion that grew into the War of Independence. After the Greek victory, though there had been a fatal falling out with the first president of independent Greece over the spoils of victory bypassing the Maniots, they nevertheless reluctantly became part of the new kingdom in 1834.

Patrick Leigh Fermor's charming book *Mani* is an ideal introduction to this unique region.

◉ Sights

Grey rock, mottled with defiant clumps of green scrub, characterises the steep, forbidding mountains of the Lakonian Mani. Cultivable land is at a premium here, and supports little more than a few stunted olives and figs.

The indented coast's sheer cliffs plunge into the sea, and rocky outcrops shelter pebbled beaches. This wild and barren landscape is broken only by imposing stone towers, which still stand sentinel over the region. In recent years, many of these have been restored and are no longer the crumbling sights you'll see in many photographs.

Long known to locals as Kakavoulia (land of evil counsel), this tough, mesmerising land makes for a fantastic road trip if you have your own wheels. You can follow the loop that runs south along the west coast from the main town, Areopoli, detouring en route along narrow lanes into semi-deserted villages. Stop to peek into chapels (there are almost as many churches and chapels as there are towers), many of which are adorned with Byzantine frescoes, and walk to Mani's southernmost tip before returning via the east coast (or vice versa). For detailed exploration, arm yourself with a copy of the brilliant Anavasi Topo 25 map, *Mani 8.4; 1:30,000*.

The Messinian Mani, or outer Mani, lies to the north of its Lakonian counterpart, sandwiched between the Taÿgetos Mountains and the west coast of the Mani peninsula. The rugged coast is scattered with small coves and beaches, and backed by mountains that remain snowcapped until late May. Kardamyli features the region's best-organised hiking opportunities, and there are also some good options around Stoupa.

Cape Tenaro   AREA
(Cape Matapan) From the car park at the end of the road in Kokinogia, at the south of the Mani peninsula, it's a beautiful 2km walk along an uneven rocky path to one of Europe's southernmost points, Cape Tenaro, where a restored lighthouse stands. The cape has been an important location for millennia and was first mentioned in Homer's *Iliad*.

At the beginning of the path are the ruins of ancient Tainaron, once a thriving Roman city (the entire area is buried ruins; look out for the stunning wave-patterned, circular mosaic), while by the car park is a ruined church built on the foundations of a temple to Poseidon. Also nearby is a cave thought by ancients to be the entrance to Hades.

Diros Caves   CAVE
(🖉 27330 52222; adult/child €13/8; ⊙9am-4.15pm) These extraordinary flooded caves, inhabited since Neolithic times, lie 11km south of Areopoli and are signposted near the village of Pyrgos Dirou. The entrance is on the beach. Guides basically only speak Greek, so if your group doesn't you'll be treated to a half-hour's silent, eerie glide by boat through the cave's many passages, giving you time to admire the stalagmites and stalactites, many of the latter as fine as gossamer threads. You tackle the remaining 300m on foot.

Tigani   RUINS
This spectacular peninsula juts out of the Mani coast like an upside-down saucepan and, indeed, its Greek name means 'frying pan'. The high point of Tigani offers majestic views and is dominated by the ruins of a medieval fortress. Historians disagree as to whether this was the location of the famous Frankish crusader castle of Grand Maigne.

It's an exhilarating if shadeless walk to the castle from the village of Agias Kiriakis. From the end of the road (it gets quite rough and turning is limited at the end so you might want to leave the car at the cemetery along the way), you descend a path through scratchy bushes to the exposed peninsula itself – go carefully over the stony ground. Climb through the walls on the far right to reach the fortress, where you'll find the ruins of a Byzantine church among other buildings. Be careful, as there are uncovered cisterns around.

🛏 Sleeping

★ Citta dei Nicliani   BOUTIQUE HOTEL €€
(🖉 27330 51827; www.cittadeinicliani.com; Kita; d incl breakfast €120-160; 🅿❄🛜🖾) 🖉 A former stronghold of a preeminent Mani clan, this welcoming and elegant rural hotel has a historic ambience, fine stonework, exquisite beds, rustic furniture and heavy wooden beams. The extensive breakfast makes great use of fresh local produce, and guests can engage in wine tasting from an extraordinary wine collection. There are good options for families and half-board rates are available.

Rooms come in three categories; the grande rooms are particularly pleasing. The stylish communal lounge room, cleverly designed to link different buildings, is especially beautiful with artwork, coffee-table books and fascinating ornaments. The genial family owners prioritise guest comfort.

Sventoura Hotel   BOUTIQUE HOTEL €€
(🖉 6975798180; www.facebook.com/Sventoura Hotel; Pyrgos Dirou; r incl breakfast €85-130; 🅿❄🛜) Tucked away en route from Pyrgos Dirou to the Diros Caves, this handsome tower has just five unique, characterful

and arty rooms. Vaulted ceilings, an antler chandelier, antique chests, wrought-iron bedsteads, and bathroom sinks hewn out of stone all conspire to give the lodgings that 21st-century-meets-Maniot vibe. Breakfast is exceptional.

Akrotiri Domatia GUESTHOUSE €€

(☎27330 52013; www.porto-kagio.com; Porto Kagio; d incl breakfast €70-80; ☺Mar-Oct; P❈🛜) Set right on the waterfront, this is a cordial spot. Rooms have been nicely spruced up with distressed furniture and modern bathrooms. The best have balconies overlooking the glorious bay. The restaurant downstairs serves fresh fish.

Tainaron Blue BOUTIQUE HOTEL €€€

(☎27333 00461; www.tainaronblue.com; d/ste incl breakfast €260/380; ☺May-Oct; P❈🛜🏊) This impressive stone tower, 4km west of the turn-off to Porto Kagio, is a true retreat: there's nothing for miles around, except for breathtaking coastline views...which you can enjoy from the clifftop infinity pool. Designed by the architect-owners, the three luxurious rooms were squeezed into the existing construction following strict planning requirements.

The project has won design awards, and the rooms comprise beautiful unadorned stone and vaulted ceilings. Be aware that rooms in the top tower are reached by the original and extremely steep staircase. Every nook and cranny has been adapted ingeniously. The owners prioritise guest comfort and seclusion. An on-site chef is on hand to whip up gourmet cuisine at your whim.

❶ Getting There & Away

If there's one place in the Peloponnese where your own car is a boon, it's here. If driving, the motorway from Athens to Kalamata provides a handy link to the Mani.

It is nevertheless possible to take buses. There are two main routes.

KTEL Messinias (www.ktelmessinias.gr) run buses down the west coast from Kalamata to Itilo (€8.50, 2½ hours, one to two Monday to Saturday) via Kardamyli and Stoupa (two to four daily). From Itilo, traditionally regarded as the border between the outer and inner Mani, you can change for nearby Areopoli (€1.80, 20 minutes, travels via Limeni). Service beyond Stoupa is a bit erratic, with frequent timetable changes.

KTEL Lakonias (www.ktel-lakonias.gr) run three daily buses from Athens to Areopoli (€29, 4½ hours) and Gerolimenas (€32.70, 5¼ hours) via Sparta and Gythio.

🚗 Driving Tour
The Lakonian Mani

START AREOPOLI
END AREOPOLI
LENGTH 112KM; SIX TO EIGHT HOURS

Journeying south down Mani's west coast from Areopoli, you encounter a barren mountain landscape broken only by semi-deserted settlements with mighty towers.

In ❶**Pyrgos Dirou**, whose main intersection is bright with the wares of ceramics shops, you can detour to the ❷**Diros Caves** (p179). Four kilometres south of Pyrgos Dirou, stop at the ❸**Panagia Faneromeni Monastery**, where you can peer at weathered Byzantine frescoes in the church.

Return north for 500m, and take a right turn off the main road. This heads up through the picturesque villages of ❹**Drialos**, ❺**Vamvaka**, ❻**Briki** and ❼**Mina**, which have fine examples of Maniot stonework, before depositing you back on the main road, 3km north of Kita.

Head across the road to the one that leads down to the ❽**Bay of Mezapos**, sheltered to the east by the frying-pan-shaped ❾**Tigani peninsula** (p179). Bear left in Mezapos and continue on this road. A kilometre beyond, a small dirt road leads down to a ruined tower house and a tiny gem of a ❿**Byzantine chapel**.

The road ends at a T-junction; a right turn will lead you to Tigani if you want to explore it. Otherwise, turn left to reach ⓫**Stavri**, where a 'castle' tower house was an HQ of a powerful local clan. Bear left leaving the village to return to the main road, where you turn right, soon coming to ⓬**Kita**.

Kita has the lion's share of the west coast's war towers and fortified houses. It was the setting for the last great interfamily feud recorded in the Mani, which erupted in 1870 and required the intervention of the army, complete with artillery, to force a truce. Just west of Kita, ⓭**Nomia** also bristles with some superb tower remains. South of here, you soon reach ⓮**Gerolimenas**, a pleasant seaside village with plenty of eating options.

South of Gerolimenas, the road continues 4km to the small village of ⓯**Alika**.

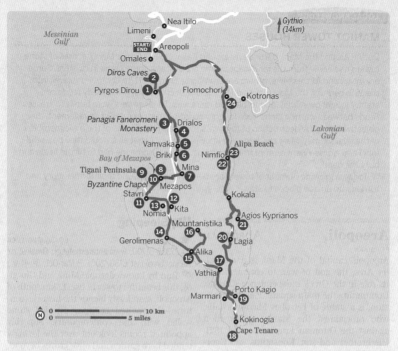

If you have nerves of steel and wish to see an impressive, generally deserted traditional village with practically no visitors, take the road into the mountains from Alika and then the turn-off to ⑯ **Mountanistika**. It's a spectacular spot, running along the high ridgetop, with special views. The road is very narrow, with a drop to one side and few places for passing, so pray there are no oncoming vehicles. It's 6.5km to get there; return via the same route.

From Alika, continue heading south. The road follows the coast, passing pebbly beaches. It then climbs steeply inland to ⑰ **Vathia**, the most photographed of the traditional Mani villages, comprising a cluster of closely packed tower houses perched on a rocky spur.

Turn right 3km south of Vathia, then bear right again, keeping on track to Kokinogia, a further 4km away. This is the end of the road, with a ruined basilica built atop the foundations of a temple to Poseidon, Roman ruins and an exhilarating walk to the lighthouse at ⑱ **Cape Tenaro** (p179).

Backtrack 3.5km and take the sharp right turn to the tiny east-coast fishing village of ⑲ **Porto Kagio**, set on a perfect horseshoe bay, popular with the international yachting set. It's a tranquil place to spend the night.

The waterfront tavernas there have similar menus (mains €8 to €17, fish per kilo €50 to €70) featuring seafood and local specialities, such as pie made with wild greens.

Head back north for nearly 2km then take a sharp right to head up the east-coast road. The east coast of the Mani peninsula is even more rugged and barren than the west. The main town is the formidable-looking ⑳ **Lagia**, 8km north of the turn-off. Perched some 400m above sea level, it was once the chief town of the southeastern Mani, and some of its towers stand derelict.

From Lagia, the road winds down with spectacular views of the little fishing harbour of ㉑ **Agios Kyprianos** – a 2km diversion from the main road. The next village is Kokala, a busy place with two pebbled beaches. The best beach is further north at ㉒ **Nimfio**, where a turn-off to the right leads to gorgeous, sheltered ㉓ **Alipa Beach**, backed by typical tower houses. Continuing north, bear left up the hill beyond tower-studded ㉔ **Flomochori** to cut west across the peninsula back to **Areopoli**.

Alternatively, you could bear right to the pretty little bay and beach of Kotronas, from where you can continue on the coast road towards Gythio.

LOCAL KNOWLEDGE

MANIOT TOWER HOUSES

Dotted around the Mani, particularly around Kakavoulia (or inner Mani), scores of stone towers rise eerily from the landscape. Some are solitary; some stand in clusters. Some are intact and fortress-like; others are crumbling. From the 17th century until well into the 19th century, the Mani was ruled by clans with chieftains, with bloody feuds constantly fought over what little fertile land there was. These towers were family fortresses. Feuds between warring clans were fought according to strict rules of engagement, the objective being the destruction of the rival's tower and the deaths of the male members of the rival's family. Male children were known as 'guns' (what else would they be useful for?) and women were exempt from the feuds; after all, someone had to till the fields and bury the dead.

Today, a growing number of towers are being restored beyond their former glory and turned into unique places to stay.

Areopoli   Αρεόπολη

POP 1000

Areopoli, capital of the Mani, is named after Ares, the god of war, to commemorate its role in the Greek independence struggle. Dominating the main square, Plateia Athanaton, is a statue of Petrobey Mavromichalis, who proclaimed the Maniot insurrection against the Ottoman Empire here in 1821. His brother and son, Konstantis and Georgios Mavromichalis, were responsible for the assassination of Ioannis Kapodistrias, the first president of independent Greece, in 1831. The town, formerly called Tsimova, retains many other reminders of its rumbustious past.

○ Sights

Church of Taxiarches   CHURCH

(Plateia 17 Martiou) On the southern side of Plateia 17 Martiou is this 18th-century church. Its picturesque five-storey bell tower marks it as the most important of Areopoli's many churches. The square is named after the day in 1821 when Mani leaders began the revolution against the Ottoman occupation at this very church.

Pikoulakis Tower House Museum   MUSEUM

(adult/child €2/free; ⊙ 8.30am-4pm Wed-Mon) Housed in a restored tower, this museum displays exquisite Byzantine pieces from Mani churches. These include a 12th-century marble *templon* (chancel screen) from the Church of Agios Ioannis in Mina, near Pyrgos Dirou. Upstairs is a clutch of well-preserved icons spanning five centuries. Take the westbound road from the southwest corner of the main square.

🛏 Sleeping

★ Antares   BOUTIQUE HOTEL €€

(☎ 27330 51700; www.antareshotel.gr; Omales; d/ste incl breakfast €130/200; ⊙ Mar-Oct; P 🅿 ❄ 🛜)
🍴 Run by knowledgeable Mina and Giorgios, this beautiful tower house, 1.5km south of Areopoli, seamlessly blends the historic (centuries-old vaulted ceilings, exposed stone walls) with the contemporary. Superbly appointed rooms look out over the lovingly tended herb garden and olive groves beyond. Breakfast is extraordinary with ingredients hand-picked from local suppliers. The tranquillity and care that guests experience inspire many to return.

The owners are a mine of information about the Mani region and can suggest walks, and villages and churches to visit in order to make the most of your stay in the area.

Areos Polis   HOTEL €€

(☎ 27330 51028; www.areospolis.gr; s/d/superior incl breakfast €42/64/72; ❄ 🛜) This central option on the main square blends old-world decor (cast-iron bedsteads, exposed stone walls) with hydro-massage showers and spa baths in some rooms. It's pretty good value and has courteous staff, a lift and a roof terrace. Rooms have a variety of outlooks. Breakfast buffet included.

✕ Eating & Drinking

I Palaiopolis   GREEK €

(☎ 27330 51345; Matapa 53; mains €7-12; ⊙ 6.30pm-12.30am; 🛜) 'Old Town' is in a beautifully restored building that once housed an incense maker followed by a cigarette workshop. These days the aromas and flavours are equally diverse, thanks to the eclectic selection of modern Greek dishes: salted pork salad, Mani spaghetti (local noodles), and more traditional vegetable concoctions. There's an atmospheric stone-vaulted dining area and lovely rear courtyard.

Bukka Home Bar COCKTAIL BAR
(🖉 27330 51003; ⊙9am-3am) A creeper-clad cafe by day, come evening this joint morphs into a sultry bar. Slip into the vaulted cavern and sip on their tasty cocktails or well-made mixed drinks.

❶ Getting There & Away

The **bus station** (🖉 27330 51229; www.ktel-lakonias.gr) is situated in the middle of the public car park at the town's northern end. There are three daily KTEL Lakonias buses from Athens (€29, 4½ hours) via Sparta (€7.60, two hours) and Gythio (€2.90, 30 minutes, three daily), continuing to Gerolimenas (€4, 45 minutes).

Buses to Itilo (€1.80, 20 minutes, two Monday to Friday, one Saturday) run via Limeni. From Itilo you can connect to services to Kardamyli and Kalamata.

Other destinations include the Diros Caves (€1.80, 15 minutes, departs 10.15am and returns 12.45pm) and Lagia (€4.10, 40 minutes, two on weekdays).

Limeni Λιμένι

POP 50
The tiny village of Limeni, on the southern flank of aquamarine Limeni Bay, benefits from a stunning outlook, some choice waterside restaurants and excellent accommodation. Its name derives from the Greek for 'harbour', and this was indeed once a port for Areopoli. Patrick Leigh Fermor described it as totally undeveloped in the 1950s, though now the little cove is buzzy with visitors. It's 5km north of Areopoli.

🛏 Sleeping

Vasilios Apartments Hotel APARTMENT €€
(🖉 27330 51934; www.vasilioshotel.com; d/studio/apt €90/95/130; ⊙Mar-Oct; 🅿❇🛜) This series of solid stone studios and apartments perched above Limeni Bay are excellent value for money. Both options are spacious, all have kitchenettes, and the views are so good you'd almost pay for them alone. Spyros, the host, is eager to make his guests happy. Furniture is of the dark and heavy wood variety, which suits the Maniot theme.

Mavromichalai BOUTIQUE HOTEL €€
(🖉 27330 52400; www.mavromichalai.gr; r/junior ste/ste incl breakfast €150/170/200;

⊙Easter–mid-Oct; ❇🛜) This 18th-century mansion was once home to the extravagantly moustachioed Petros Mavromichalis, Bey of the Mani and hero of the independence struggle. It's now a charming hotel with six rooms, featuring thick stone walls, cushy beds, wooden beams and small windows – what a view! Standard rooms are quite compact and reached via a narrow staircase.

Pirgos Mavromichali Hotel BOUTIQUE HOTEL €€€
(🖉 27330 51042; www.pirgosmavromichali.gr; d/superior d/ste incl breakfast from €160/195/270; ⊙Mar-Nov; ❇🛜) The owner has converted his family's 300-year-old tower house into 13 chic rooms. Delightful touches abound, from the vaulted lounge and little private beach to the luxurious split-level suite. Plus there's a lovely seafront area to relax in.

🍴 Eating

Teloneio GREEK €€
(🖉 27330 52702; www.teloneio-limeni.gr; mains €9-23; ⊙10am-midnight May-Sep; 🛜🍴) This colourful seafront restaurant and bar serves imaginative fare – traditional Greek with a modern twist – such as roasted *kritharaki* (rice-shaped pasta) with scampi, and grilled *talagani* cheese with prickly-pear marmalade.

I Oka GREEK €€
(🖉 27330 51595; www.facebook.com/Okalimeni; mains €9-15; ⊙noon-midnight; 🛜🍴) An offshoot of Teloneio opposite, this gets away from the seafood vibe of Limeni but still has top views over the water from its terrace. The menu is focused on high-class *mayirefta* (preprepared daily dishes) and grilled meats. There's a small produce shop downstairs.

Takis SEAFOOD €€€
(🖉 27330 51327; Limeni; fish per kg €45-60; ⊙10am-late Apr-Oct; 🛜) Takis lures in diners with simple yet beautifully prepared fresh fish – of course, the stunning setting, right over the turquoise water, helps. Take your pick of the day's catch at the counter. It's on the pricey side, but you're paying for the location.

❶ Getting There & Away

One to two buses Monday to Saturday drop in to Limeni on the way between Areopoli and Itilo. A taxi from Areopoli costs around €10.

Gerolimenas Γερολιμένας

POP 100

Gerolimenas is a tranquil fishing village built around a small, sheltered bay at the southwestern tip of the Mani peninsula. Its pebble beach overlooks teal waters and it's a popular weekend getaway for well-heeled Athenians.

🛏 Sleeping

Kyrimi Inn B&B €€
(☎ 27330 53078; www.kyrimi.com; r incl breakfast €100-120; ❈ 🛜) This lovely choice inside a traditional stone house consists of five luxurious rooms. Breakfast includes delicious homemade pies and produce. Each room has a patio overlooking the sea, perfect for sunbathing.

Hotel Kyrimai HOTEL €€€
(☎ 27330 54288; www.kyrimai.gr; incl breakfast d €160-240, ste €260-400; ❂ Mar-Oct & Christmas; ❈ 🛜 ❇) In an idyllic setting at the far southern end of the harbour, Kyrimai is a luxurious historic building with stone floors and timber beams. Rooms come in all shapes and sizes. Outside there's a massive restaurant terrace overlooking the water, open to nonguests. Breakfast is substantial.

❶ Getting There & Away

There are three buses daily from Gerolimenas to Areopoli (€4, 45 minutes), which head on to Athens (€32.70, 5¼ hours), Gythio (€6.60, 1¼ hours) and Sparta (€11.30, 2½ hours). The bus stop is in the square.

Kardamyli Καρδαμύλη

POP 400

It's easy to see why Kardamyli was one of the seven cities offered to Achilles by Agamemnon. This tiny village has one of the prettiest settings in the Peloponnese, nestled between the blue waters of the Messinian Gulf and the Taÿgetos Mountains. The Vyros Gorge, which emerges just north of town, runs to the foot of Mt Profitis Ilias (2407m), the highest peak of the Taÿgetos. Today the gorge and surrounding areas are very popular with hikers.

British writer Patrick Leigh Fermor lived in nearby Kalamitsi Bay for several decades until his death in 2011. Fermor wrote *Mani*, which is considered by many to be the definitive book on the region.

The surrounding mountain villages have wonderful nooks and crannies to explore, with ancient churches and excellent tavernas.

◉ Sights & Activities

Hiking is brilliant around this area. For something different, Mosaic Art Greece (p169) runs weekly mosaic workshops in Kardamyli from April to October.

Old Town Kardamyli MUSEUM
(☎ 27210 73638; http://odysseus.culture.gr; adult/child €2/free; ❂ 8am-8pm Tue-Sun Apr-Oct, 9am-4pm Tue-Sun Nov-Mar) Old Town Kardamyli consists of a fortified settlement with a handsome 18th-century church, plus restored tower, oil press and three-storey building. There are good information panels with explanations in English on traditional Maniot life. Follow the signs on the western edge of Kardamyli opposite the two supermarkets.

Patrick Leigh Fermor House HOUSE
(☎ 21036 71090; www.benaki.gr; tour €7; ❂ by appointment Tue, Thu & Sat) Larger-than-life Patrick Leigh Fermor (1915–2011), a Hellenophile and marvellously engaging writer, lived just outside Kardamyli for much of his later life with his wife, Joan. A scholar and soldier (involved in the Cretan resistance during WWII), he is known among other things for his marvellous travel book on the Mani. His stunning home is open to visitors by appointment three times a week, though this drops to once a week from June to August, when it becomes holiday accommodation.

★2407 Mountain Activities OUTDOORS
(☎ 27210 73752; www.2407m.com; ❂ 9am-10pm late Mar-Oct) Professional and friendly outfit offers a range of outdoor adventures, from half-day hikes (per person €60 to €70) to full-day assaults on Taÿgetos Peak (€110), bicycle tours (from €50) and cultural experiences. Located halfway along the main street. They can customise other trips too.

🛏 Sleeping

★Olympia
Koumanakou Rooms PENSION €
(☎ 27210 73623; s/d €35/40; ❈ 🛜) One of the Peloponnese's best budget options. Olympia loves her traveller guests (as they do her) and offers five clean rooms with bathrooms in the centre of the village. It's a stone's throw from the water, and has an appealing garden.

WALKING AROUND KARDAMYLI

Hiking is easily Kardamyli's biggest drawcard. The hills behind the village are criss-crossed with an extensive network of well-marked trails that consist of old stone paths, minor roads, dirt footpaths and a dry riverbed. A number of villages above Kardamyli and Stoupa are connected by winding, narrow paved roads, which make for fairly strenuous, scenic cycling.

To make sense of Kardamyli's colour-coded trails and to navigate your hike above Stoupa, invest in the excellent Anavasi Topo 25 map, *Mani: Kardamyli–Stoupa–Aghios Nikolaos 8.12/13; 1:25,000,* available from 2407 Mountain Activities and the local supermarkets. To avoid retracing your steps, you can get a taxi to drop you off in the village of your choice (book in advance via your lodgings) and walk back to Kardamyli or Stoupa. Some of the best trails:

Chora–Saidona Trail Follow the blue-and-white trail through Chora from Hotel Faraggi, then take the right-hand path (red with white cross), pass through Nikovo and follow the (green with white cross) trail, part dirt road, part old stone path, through the olive groves. The trail descends through lush vegetation to a dry river bed and then ascends gently to Saidona. The trail takes one hour and 15 minutes.

Chora–Kardamyli Trail This four-hour walk starts at the village of Chora. Follow the blue-and-white trail markers down through the picturesquely ramshackle village; take the right fork where the trails divide and continue your gentle descent through the olive groves until the trail meets a road. Head right. Follow the dry riverbed left through the striking canyon all the way to Kardamyli.

It's well worth making the slight detour to see the frescoes of the Likaki Monastery, signposted halfway down the canyon. You can also take the gently ascending, signposted path up to Agia Sofia through the woods from the same spot; this path joins the yellow-and-black trail.

Kardamyli–Petrovouni Trail This is a gorgeous two-hour loop walk. Follow the signs to Old Town Kardamyli, then take the old stone path that leads up to the Agia Sofia church. Follow the path down through an enchanted forest section (tangled vegetation, scent of pine) towards Petrovouni, with a fantastic view of the coast en route. Descend to Kardamyli along a zigzagging stone path.

★ **Vardia Hotel** BOUTIQUE HOTEL €€
(☑ 27210 73777; www.vardia-hotel.gr; studio/1-bedroom/2-bedroom €85/125/165; ☉ mid-Mar–early Nov; P ❋ @ ☎) This relaxing hotel sits amid a lovely garden high above Kardamyli. Studios and apartments have kitchenettes and balconies, and are tastefully attractive; it's a tranquil retreat. The huge bonus is the exceptional outlook over the Messinian Gulf: in a town of amazing views, this might be best of all. Staff are experienced and very helpful. There's a real magic to this place.

Elies APARTMENT €€
(☑ 27210 73140; www.elieshotel.gr; studio/apt/maisonette €130/160/240; ☉ Mar–Oct; P ❋ ☎) Live out your image of quintessential Greece (dreamy sigh): tasteful provincial-style stone studios, apartments (sleep four) and maisonettes (sleep six), with stylish 'haven't-missed-a-beat' interiors, all nestled within an olive grove. Breakfast includes fresh fruit, bread and eggs. You can enjoy lunch at Elies'

own taverna (p186), before wandering a few metres across the road – plop! – into the sea.

Kalamitsi Hotel HOTEL €€
(☑ 27210 73131; www.kalamitsi-hotel.gr; s/d/ste/f incl breakfast €80/130/180/250; ☉ mid-Mar–early Nov; P ❋ ☎) The Kalamitsi is a lovely stone-built hotel with serene, spacious rooms that are a touch bland but feature gorgeous balcony views over olive trees and the bay beyond. Within its shady grounds are paths leading to a secluded pebbly beach. Buffet breakfasts are a highlight, and home-cooked dinners (€22) are available. It's 1km south of town.

✖ Eating

Kritamos PUB FOOD €
(☑ 27210 64102; www.facebook.com/Kritamos Kardamili; mains €6-12; ☉ 7am-midnight; ☎ ✐) You don't come here for the view (it's off the road), but for a casual bar-restaurant experience and some tasty Greek pub grub. On

the menu are creative mezedhes, salads, risotti, burgers and wings. There's usually live music at weekends and it's a good spot for a coffee or drink any time of day.

★**Elies** GREEK **€€**
(☑27210 73140; www.elieshotel.gr; mains €8-14; ☺11am-midnight May-Aug, 1-6pm Apr, Sep & Oct; 🐾🚫) Right by Ritsa Beach, 1km north of town, and nestled in an olive grove, this pretty and popular eating venue has the atmosphere of a provincial Mediterranean private garden. Thanks to owner-chef Fani, it presents a fine selection of top-notch Greek and Mani fare, including numerous scrumptious veggie dishes.

Dioskouri GREEK **€€**
(☑27210 73236; mains $8-15; ☺11am-midnight Mar-Sep) This long-standing spot on the hill, overlooking the bay and with a terrace filled with umbrella pines, is glorious on a moonlit evening. It's been infused with a bit of youthful flair as the next generation is involved in the business, though still serves the old-school Greek cuisine: simple and good quality, from calamari to excellent grilled seafood dishes.

🍷 Drinking & Nightlife

1866 Beer Bar BAR
(☑27210 73479; ☺9am-5am Apr-Oct, 1pm-5am Nov-Mar; 🐾) This cosy bar, set back from the seafront, is renowned for its spirit shots and late nights. It's not raucous, but attracts a varied crowd who enjoy a chat, good company and a selection of the top-shelf stuff. And excellent beers. The friendly owner keeps it all buzzing.

Aquarella COCKTAIL BAR
(☑27210 75010; www.facebook.com/aquarella. kardamili; ☺8am-midnight; 🐾) This gorgeous flower-strewn spot is perched right over the bay and is perfect for a sundowner. Decent nibbles, including salads, are also served.

ℹ️ Getting There & Away

Kardamyli is on the bus route between Kalamata (€4, one hour, two to four daily) and Stoupa (€1.80, 15 minutes, four daily); one to two buses Monday to Saturday continue south to Itilo. The bus stops at the central square at the northern end of the main thoroughfare, and at the bookshop at the southern end.

Buses to the villages in the hills above Kardamyli are too sporadic to be useful. A taxi to Exohorio costs around €20.

MESSINIA ΜΕΣΣΗΝΙΑ

The southwestern corner of the Peloponnese has many attractions, from the peninsula's loveliest beaches to old Venetian towns, impressive castles and even underwater parks for divers.

Messinia's boundaries were established in 371 BCE following the defeat of Sparta by the Thebans at the Battle of Leuctra. The defeat ended almost 350 years of Spartan domination of the Peloponnese – during which time Messinian exiles founded the city of Messina in Sicily – and meant the Messinians were left free to develop their kingdom in the region stretching west from the Taÿgetos Mountains. Their capital was Ancient Messini, about 25km northwest of Kalamata on the slopes of Mt Ithomi.

ℹ️ Getting There & Away

Kalamata is Messinia's transport hub, with an international airport and good bus and road connections. There are limited bus services from Athens to other towns in the region.

Kalamata Καλαμάτα

POP 55,000

Kalamata, famous worldwide for its olives, is Messinia's capital and the second-largest city in the Peloponnese. Most travellers blitz through. Give it a chance and you'll discover a long beach, decent restaurants, good shopping, lively nightlife and some excellent museums.

Below the *kastro* is the small but attractive old town, which was almost totally destroyed by the Turks during the War of Independence, rebuilt by French engineers in the 1830s, then levelled again by an earthquake in 1986. The new town stretches south of here; after a couple of kilometres you reach the beachfront, lined with hotels and restaurants.

⊙ Sights & Activities

Archaeological Museum of Messenia MUSEUM
(Map p188; ☑27210 83485; www.archmusmes. gr; cnr Benaki & Agiou Ioannou; adult/child €4/ free; ☺8am-8pm Wed-Mon, 1.30-8pm Tue) This partially interactive, child-friendly museum focuses on treasures found in four regions – Kalamata, Pylia, Messini and Trifylia. Exhibits include everything from sculpture, pottery and funereal objects found in *tholos* tombs (Mycenaean tombs shaped like a

beehive) at Nestor's Palace (p194), to Roman mosaics, gold jewellery and votive offerings. It provides wonderful context to the surrounding areas.

Museum of Traditional
Greek Costumes   MUSEUM
(Map p188; ☎27210 86923; www.vgkarelias collection.com; Stadiou 64; adult/concession €5/3; ☺9am-2pm Tue-Sat, plus 5.30-8.30pm Wed & Sat, 10am-1pm Sun) Opened in 2017, this stunning museum features a remarkable collection of Greek costumes that was donated by Victoria Karelia. Far from moth-eaten old hand-me-downs, the clothing showcases male and female folk dress from the 18th to 20th centuries in beautifully curated, dramatically lit exhibits.

History & Folklore
Museum of Kalamata   MUSEUM
(Map p188; ☎27210 28449; Ioannou 12, cnr Kyriakou; adult/child €3/free; ☺9am-1pm Wed-Sat, from 10am Sun) This quaint eggshell-blue building holds an exquisite collection of donated local artefacts – from tools and looms to household items and clothes – that offer a thorough insight into Kalamata's bygone era.

Kastro   FORT
(Map p188; Vilardouinou; adult/child €2/free; ☺8am-8pm Wed-Mon Apr-Sep, to 3pm Oct-Mar) Looming over the town is the 13th-century *kastro*. Remarkably, it survived the powerful 1986 earthquake that levelled the city. The entry gate is its most impressive feature. Inside, the *kastro* is a lush haven of tranquillity and there are excellent views over Kalamata and beyond from the battlements.

Paragliding Kalamata   PARAGLIDING
(☎6947602339; www.paraglidingkalamata.gr; Filoxenia Hotel, Navarino 260; flight €80; ☺9am-8pm) If you're itching to jump off those hills beyond the beach, these guys will help you make the leap. Tandem flights run all year if conditions are suitable; morning departures are recommended for beginners. There's a 105kg weight limit. It's based at the Filoxenia Hotel at the end of the beach.

🎊 Festivals & Events

Kalamata International
Dance Festival   DANCE
(www.kalamatadancefestival.gr; ☺Jul) This annual festival draws crowds to its traditional music and dance performances. Venues include the amphitheatre of the *kastro*. See the website for dates and prices.

🛏 Sleeping

The majority of lodgings are located along the waterfront and vary from down-at-heel one-star jobs to resorts.

★Kalamata Art Rooms   GUESTHOUSE €€
(Map p188; ☎27210 27151; www.kalamatart rooms.com; Mitropetrova 12; s €50, d €60-80; ❄🐶🛜) This lovely spot is right on Kalamata's sociable pedestrian plaza, with eating and drinking options all around. Rooms, some of which have kitchenettes, are cute, with names like Sweet and Sunny describing their character. Bathrooms are stylish and exposed, though curtains can be drawn. Balconies overlooking the square are great. Ring ahead, as the helpful owners live off-site.

Pharae Palace Hotel   HOTEL €€
(☎27210 96000; www.pharae.gr; cnr Navarino & Feraiou; d incl breakfast €120; 🅿❄@🛜) Spacious chambers with balconies are modern and comfortable with gleaming white bathrooms in this seafront choice; go for a room with views out over the harbour. It's close to the beach and is quite a bargain off-season. Parking spaces are free but limited, so it's pot luck.

Hotel Rex   HOTEL €€
(Map p188; ☎27210 22334; www.rexhotel.gr; Aristomenous 26; s/d incl breakfast €80/101; ❄@🛜) The Rex has a superb central location and will appeal if you like unapologetically retro decor and a touch of faded grandeur (it's been here since 1899). The rooms are fairly bland, with varnished wood fittings. Some are better than others; corner rooms (ending in 03) are good choices. Not everything works as well as it should here.

🍴 Eating & Drinking

The beachfront has plenty of options, and the nearby marina is also lined with restaurants and tavernas. If you don't need water views, head for the cluster of modern and funky places located opposite the old train station. Across from the bus station, a lively food market (Wednesday and Saturday) sells Kalamata olives and other local produce.

Given Kalamata's youthful population, there's always drinking buddies to be found. Grab a tipple at one of the many bar-restaurants located around the former train station or the nearby Plateia Kentriki square; there's also a good rock-oriented pub scene around the southern end of the old town, along Amfias and surrounding streets.

PELOPONNESE KALAMATA

Kalamata

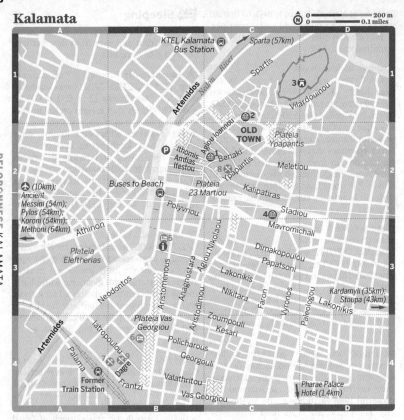

Kalamata

◉ Sights
1 Archaeological Museum of
  Messenia C2
2 History & Folklore Museum of
  Kalamata C1
3 Kastro D1
4 Museum of Traditional Greek
  Costumes C2

⌂ Sleeping
5 Hotel Rex B3
6 Kalamata Art Rooms B4

✕ Eating
7 Kardamo B4
8 O Thiasos C2
9 Tsipouradiko Therapeftirion B4

O Thiasos   CAFE €
(Map p188; ☎ 27210 88407; Ypapantis 7; mezedhes €4-7; ⊙8am-1am Tue-Sun; 🛜🍴) It's a real pleasure to sit out here on the leafy, shady terrace and sip a coffee in classic *kafeneio* (traditional cafe) style. But this isn't as traditional as it seems: it's a renovated centenarian establishment, and the young owners dole out delicious portions of creative market-driven Greek cuisine. There's often an evening gig or jam going on too.

Tsipouradiko Therapeftirion   MEZEDHES €
(Map p188; ☎ 6948530045; Dagre 2; mezedhes €3; ⊙8pm-midnight Mon-Sat; 🍴) Cheerful Vasilios is your personal food therapist in the downtown pedestrian zone. Grab a seat and he'll do the rest, selecting a range of small plates (you can guide him) to make up a meal. It's comfort food rather than gourmet and likeably casual. Wash it down with *tsipouro*, ouzo or the house red.

Kardamo   GREEK €

(Map p188; ☑ 27210 98091; www.kardamo.gr; Sidi-rodromikou Stathmou 21; mains €7-12; ⊙ 1pm-1am; 🐾🍴) Kardamo offers a tasty alternative to traditional Greek cuisine, without straying too far from its roots. The result? Greek dishes with a contemporary twist, like spinach salad with *manouri* (soft cheese) and cranberries. The good price-to-quality ratio pulls in a younger crowd who seek modern alternatives. The setting is pretty in a tasteful taverna with a twist.

ⓘ Information

Tourist Support Office (Map p188; ☑ 27213 60749; Aristomenou 28; ⊙ 10am-2pm & 5-9pm summer, reduced hours winter)

ⓘ Getting There & Away

AIR

Kalamata International Airport (KLX; ☑ 27210 22310; www.hcaa.gr; National Rd 82, Messini) is 10.5km west of the city, near Messini, and served by various airlines from several European cities, mostly in summer only. Aegean Airlines (www.aegeanair.com) operates flights between Kalamata and Thessaloniki.

BUS

KTEL Messinia bus station (Map p188; ☑ 27210 28581; www.ktelmessinias.gr; Artemidos) has buses to Athens (€24.30, 2¾ to 3¼ hours, eight to 10 daily), some express and some via Corinth Isthmus (€17.30, two hours).

It also has buses to Tripoli (€8.90, 1¼ hours), Patra (€24.90, four hours, two daily) via Kyparissia (€7.70, 1¼ hours) and Pyrgos (€14, two hours), where you can change for Olympia.

Heading west, there are buses to Koroni (€5.50, 1½ hours, four to six daily), Methoni (€6.80, 1½ hours, three to five daily) and Pylos (€5.50, 1¾ hours, four to seven daily).

Heading east across the Langada Pass, buses run to Sparta (€6.30, 1¾ hours, one to two daily) with a change at Artemisia. Two to four daily buses head to Kardamyli (€4, one hour) and Stoupa (€4.90, 1¼ hours), with some continuing to Itilo (€8.50, 2½ hours, one to two Monday to Saturday). There are also direct buses to Thessaloniki (€71.30, three weekly, 11 hours).

ⓘ Getting Around

TO/FROM THE AIRPORT

A taxi into Kalamata from the airport costs around €22. Local buses to Messini, Koroni and Pylos pass the airport (€1.80) and can drop you off on the main road, about 100m away from the entrance.

LOCAL KNOWLEDGE

KALAMATA OLIVES

Kalamata gives its name to the prized Kalamata olive, a plump, purple-black variety found in delicatessens around the world. The region's reliable winter rains and hot summers make for perfect olive-growing conditions.

The Kalamata tree is distinguished from the common olive (grown for oil) by the size of its leaves. Like its fruit, the leaves of the Kalamata are twice the size of other varieties and a darker shade of green.

Unlike other varieties, Kalamata olives can't be picked green. They ripen in late November and must be hand-picked to avoid bruising. You can buy and sample these famous olives at the markets in Kalamata.

BUS

Local buses leave from the KTEL Messinia bus station (p189). The most useful service is bus 1, which goes south to the seafront and then east along Navarinou as far as the Filoxenia Hotel. Buy tickets (€1.30) from kiosks or the driver. A handy **stop** (Map p188) is on the edge of the old town.

Ancient Messini
Αρχαία Μεσσήνη

POP 350

The name Ancient Messini is used to refer to both the historic site and the village, a cluster of attractive buildings 25km northwest of Kalamata that overlooks the ruins, which are extensive and very impressive.

Locals lobbied to drop the original name of Mavromati, which derives from the fountain in the central square whose water gushes from a hole that resembles a black eye *(mavro mati)*. Many residents, and bus schedules, still use the original name (don't confuse it with the Mavromati near modern Messini either).

◉ Sights

★**Ancient Messini**   ARCHAEOLOGICAL SITE
(☑ 27240 51201; http://odysseus.culture.gr; adult/child €12/free; ⊙ 8am-8pm May-Aug, reduced hours Sep-Apr) The remains of this vast ancient city are as extensive as those of Olympia and Epidavros, yet Ancient Messini receives only

a fraction of their visitors. Picturesquely situated on a hillside below the village of Mavromati and still undergoing excavation, the site comprises a large theatre, an *agora* (marketplace), a sizeable Sanctuary of Asclepius and one of the most impressive Ancient Greek stadiums. Entry includes the small museum at the site turn-off; don't miss the impressive Arcadian Gate 800m beyond, either.

Ancient Messini was founded in 371 BCE after the Theban general Epaminondas defeated Sparta at the Battle of Leuctra, freeing the Messinians from almost 350 years of Spartan rule. Built on the site of an earlier stronghold, the new Messinian capital was one of a string of defensive positions designed to keep watch over Sparta. Epaminondas himself helped to plan the fortifications, which were based on a massive wall that stretched 9km around the surrounding ridges and completely enclosed the town.

Apart from its defensive potential, Ancient Messini was also favoured by the gods. According to local myth, Zeus was born here – not in Crete – and raised by the nymphs Neda and Ithomi, who bathed him in the same spring that gives the modern village its name. The larger area is called Ithomi.

The first construction you come across is the large theatre, reconstructed for contemporary use. The path leads past the tiered Fountain of Arsinoe building, which supplied the ancient city with water. Next is the extensive agora, with remains of long stoas (columned porticoes), a public bathhouse, a Doric temple dedicated to the deified patron of the city, Messene, and a treasury. The Greek general Philopoemen was held prisoner by the Messinians here in 183 BCE and dispatched to the other world with poison.

Beyond is the Sanctuary of Asclepius, the spiritual centre that lay at the heart of the ancient city, consisting of a rectangular courtyard fringed with Corinthian columns. Unlike at Epidavros, this was not so much a healing centre as a repository of cult statuary. This extensive complex was centred on a Doric temple that once housed a golden statue of Ithomi. The modern awning west of the temple protects the Artemision, where fragments of an enormous statue of Artemis Orthia were found. The structures on the east side of the *Asclepion* include the ekklesiasterion, which looks like a small theatre but once acted as an assembly hall. Nearby are the remains of a Roman

villa, the steel roof protecting the mosaic remains.

Head downhill to the large stadium, which is surrounded by a forest of restored columns. You can see where the Romans closed off part of the athletics track, turning it into a gladiator arena. On the left-hand side, near the arena, are the VIP seats – the ones with backs and with lion paws for legs. On the right-hand side, near the rebuilt gate of the enormous gymnasium, are round holes in stone slabs – Roman public toilets positioned over a stream. The gymnasium itself includes a washroom with very well-preserved basins around it.

The curious building near the toilets is a grave memorial to an important Messinian family, and the Doric temple at the far end of the stadium is a mausoleum of the Saithidae, a prominent Roman family.

Museum of Ancient Messini
MUSEUM

(☑ 27240 51201; http://odysseus.culture.gr; adult/child €12/free; ⊗ 8am-8pm May-Aug, reduced hours Sep-Apr) The compact museum, by the turn-off for Ancient Messini, houses some wonderful statuary from the site – including a copy of one of the best-known statues in antiquity, Polykleitos' *Doryphoros,* and fine depictions of Hermes and Artemis Laphria. Those of Machaon and Podaleiros are assumed to be the work of Damophon, who specialised in oversized statues of gods and heroes and was responsible for many of the statues that once adorned Ancient Messini. Admission is included with the Ancient Messini entrance ticket.

Arcadian Gate
ARCHAEOLOGICAL SITE

(⊗ 24hr) FREE It's well worth heading 800m along the road from Mavromati village, past the museum to the celebrated Arcadian Gate. This unusual stone portal with a circular courtyard between the double gates and an immense, half-collapsed gatepost guarded the ancient route to Megalopoli – now a modern road – which runs through the gate. Flanking the gate is the finest surviving section of the mighty defensive wall built by Epaminondas. Through the gate are ornate columned tombs of notables: burials were not permitted within the city.

🛏 Sleeping & Eating

⭐ Messana Hotel
HOTEL €

(☑ 6974906832, 27240 51000; www.messana -hotel.gr; d with/without breakfast €60/50; ❉ @ 🛜) Ultrahospitable Messana successfully blends the traditional elements of stone, wood and clay with modern decor including contemporary coloured-glass screens, exposed stone and brightly painted walls. It has all the mod cons yet maintains a rustic and very romantic feel. All rooms have balconies and some have fireplaces. A perfect option for those who enjoy a remote village experience.

Likourgos Rooms GUESTHOUSE €
(☑6970052142, 27240 51297; roomslykourgos@yahoo.gr; s/d/tr €40/50/60; ℗✳☎) This simple budget spot has clean and spacious rooms. Front rooms afford glimpses of the ruins. The helpful owner, Victoria, speaks English; she lives opposite the fountain in the heart of the village, while the rooms are 100m or so further on.

Taverna Ithomi TAVERNA €
(☑27240 51298; www.ithomi.gr; mains €6-13; ☺9am-midnight Jun-Aug, to 6pm Sep-May; ☎☑) The pick of a handful of local *kafeneia* and tavernas, this one offers traditional cuisine with a superb view over the ruins. Friendly owner Nikos is the local 'man in the know', and besides grilled meats and superb roast pork he makes a mean *briam* (oven-baked vegetable casserole).

❶ Getting There & Away

Getting here without your own transport is difficult; there are only one to two weekly buses that run between the village and Kalamata. The easiest way to get here from Kalamata is to head for the airport and turn right just after passing it. The village is 19km from this turn-off and well signposted.

Koroni Κορώνη
POP 1700

Koroni is a lovely Venetian port town with medieval mansions and churches lining its narrow, winding streets. These lead up to a promontory, the site of an extensive castle and convent. Stroll the waterfront and admire the magnificent views across Messinia Bay to the Taÿgetos Mountains. Just south of town, Zaga Beach is a 2km sweep of golden sand.

◎ Sights

Kastro FORTRESS
(☺24hr) FREE The castle complex crowns a bluff overlooking the town. Much of it is occupied by the **Timios Prodromos Convent**, where a dress code applies. You can enter via the castle's impressive Gothic entrance. The small promontory beyond the castle is a tranquil place for a stroll, with lovely views over the bay to the Taÿgetos Mountains.

🛏 Sleeping & Eating

Hotel Diana HOTEL €
(☑27250 22312; www.dianahotel-koroni.gr; d €40; ✳☎) A friendly couple run this budget bargain, which books up fast. Rooms are simple and very compact but attractive. It's bang in the centre, just off the central square and almost on the harbour. Breakfast costs €5. They also have good-value apartments at Zaga Beach (€50; www.sipsas-villas.gr).

Camping Koroni CAMPGROUND €
(☑27250 22119; www.koronicamping.com; camp sites per adult/car/tent €8/4/5; ℗☎☀) Located only 500m from Koroni, near the beach, this year-round campground has can-do management and plenty of facilities. There's a poolside taverna that stocks fresh bread every morning, laundry, kitchen and shop. Popular with families.

★**Colonides Beach Hotel** HOTEL €€
(☑27250 41200; www.colonides.gr; Vounaria; d incl breakfast €134-154; ℗☎☀) This welcoming family-run resort is a cracking place. Apartments with kitchen and balcony are super spacious and have great outlooks over greenery, the pool and, not far away (a three-minute walk), the sea. At the time of our visit a spa and restaurant complex was under construction. It's situated 10km north of Koroni, near the village of Vounaria.

Sofotel HOTEL €€
(☑27250 22230; www.sofotel.gr; d €70-90; ✳☎) It's not a Sofitel, but it is much more charming. Modern, gold-trimmed and ornament-decorated digs at the entrance to the village are commodious with brilliant views. Lots of Greek hotels are spotless, but this takes it to another level. Some rooms have balconies; walls are on the thin side. Breakfast is an extra €7.50.

Peroulia GREEK €€
(☑27250 41777; www.peroulia.gr; Peroulia Beach; mains €8-15, fish per kg from €55; ☺9am-midnight May–mid-Oct; ☎) Overlooking the teal waters of the gorgeous Peroulia Beach, 6km north of Koroni, this waterfront restaurant has earned a loyal local following for its traditional Greek cuisine and fresh seafood. Fill up with delicious food, then take to a sunlounger to sleep it off to the sound of lapping waves.

Resalto GREEK €€
(27250 23064; mains €8-14; 1pm-midnight;) Opposite the pier, the terrace here has lovely evening views of the floodlit castle complex. Food is homemade and original in feel, with tasty sauces.

Getting There & Away

Buses will drop you in the central square outside the Church of Agios Dimitrios, one block back from the harbour. There are services to Kalamata (€5.50, 1½ hours, four to six daily) and one to Athens (€29.60, four hours, daily). For Pylos you must change at Rizomilos (two daily). Buy tickets on the bus.

Methoni   Μεθώνη
POP 1200

Methoni was one of the seven cities offered to Achilles by Agamemnon. Homer described it as 'rich in vines'. Today it's a pretty seaside town with a popular beach, next to which looms the most impressive example of a 15th-century Venetian fortress in the Peloponnese. It's 12km south of Pylos.

Sights

Kastro FORT
(adult/child €2/free; 8am-8pm Apr-Sep, to 3pm Oct-Mar) FREE This vast, crumbling *kastro*, a great example of 15th-century Venetian military architecture, is built on a promontory south of Methoni. It's surrounded on three sides by the sea and separated from the mainland by a dry moat. Enter the inner keep through the mighty gateway to discover a Turkish bath, a cathedral, a house, a cistern and underground passages. A short causeway leads from the fortress to the diminutive octagonal Bourtzi fortress on an adjacent islet.

Sleeping & Eating

Hotel Aris HOTEL €
(27230 31125; Plateia Sigrou; d/tr €60/70;) Two blocks from the sea and overlooking a tree-lined square, this immaculately clean, simple place is run by kind owners. Rooms have tiny balconies and breakfast is €5. Rates drop outside of summer.

★ **Apartments Melina** APARTMENT €€
(27230 31505; www.methoni-apartments.gr; d €60-70, tr/f €90/100; Mar-Oct;) This charming little gem speaks for itself – modern, spacious apartments across from the beach, with a perfumed garden of roses (over 300 varieties) and ultrafriendly English-speaking owners, Kathy, Spiros and Melina. It's a great summer retreat that's perfect for families and longer stays.

Hotel Achilles HOTEL €€
(27230 31819; www.achilles-hotel.gr; Plateia Eleftherias; d incl breakfast €70-100;) The smartest of a range of small hotels in town, Achilles has 13 comfortable modern rooms, all with balcony, and a pleasant outdoor terrace. There's an airy dining area too. The same owners run another hotel just north of town on the hillside.

Taverna Andreas Aléktor TAVERNA €
(27230 31838; www.facebook.com/Andreas Alektor; mains €7-12; 11am-3pm & 6pm-midnight mid-Feb–Dec;) Traditional Greek dishes are served with aplomb by the friendly and accommodating multilingual husband-and-wife team, Andreas and Irini. Often there's live music on Sundays; linger with a beer or carafe of house wine.

Getting There & Around

Buses depart Methoni from the fork at the Pylos end of town where the two main streets meet. Buses travel to Pylos (€1.80, 15 minutes, three to five daily) and on to Kalamata (€6.70, 1½ hours). Services also run to Finikounda (€2.60, 15 minutes, five to six Monday to Saturday, one on Sunday); change there for Koroni, though connections may not match up.

Methoni Bikes (6979163093; www. methonibikes.gr; per hour/day €2.50/12; 8.30am-2pm & 5.30-9pm Mon-Sat, 9am-2pm Sun) Has bicycles for rent.

Pylos   Πύλος
POP 2800

Coastal Pylos presides over the southern end of an immense bay. With its huge natural harbour that's formed by the Sfaktiria Islet, its castle and surrounding pine-covered hills, Pylos is not just picturesque, but is also one of the region's most historically significant towns.

Homer mentions 'sandy Pylos' and there was a substantial Mycenaean kingdom based in this area, centred on Nestor's Palace (p194). Classical-era Pylos lay a short distance from the modern town, near Gialova Lagoon, and was one of the few places where the Spartans suffered defeat to the Athenians. In 1827 the British, French and Russian navies, under the command of Admiral Codrington, attacked Ibrahim Pasha's

Ottoman fleet, sinking dozens of ships and effectively destroying Ottoman sea power. This Battle of Navarino (Navarino being the Venetians' name for the town) was a decisive moment in the War of Independence. It's 51km southwest of Kalamata.

◉ Sights

Neo Kastro
MUSEUM

(☑27230 22955; http://odysseus.culture.gr; adult/concession €6/3; ☺8am-8pm Wed-Mon Apr-Aug, reduced hours Sep-Mar) The more intact and accessible of two castles that lie on either side of Navarino Bay, Neo Kastro was built by the Turks in 1573 on the hilltop at the southern edge of town. It affords excellent views. Within its formidable walls is a mosque converted into a church, plus the hexagonal acropolis, used as a prison until the 1900s. The complex now houses Pylos' impressive **archaeological museum** and interesting displays on **underwater archaeology**.

In the museum, a selection of modern exhibits relate interesting finds from around the Pylos area, testifying to human presence from the Palaeolithic period to Roman times, and the Mycenaean past in the hinterland and at Voidokoilia. Highlights include the late-Roman bronze Diaskouri sculptures of two men, fine Mycenaean-era ceramics and jewellery, a stunning glass bowl, a Linear B tablet and fragments of wall paintings.

The underwater archaeology exhibition stretches across two buildings and the alcoves of the acropolis, covering finds from various shipwrecks around the Peloponnese as well as submerged settlements. The role of the amphora is given detailed treatment. A good video gives an introduction to this crucial field.

🛏 Sleeping & Eating

★ Karalís Beach Hotel
HOTEL €€

(☑27230 23021; www.karalisbeach.gr; Paralia; d/f incl breakfast €150/190; ☺Easter-Oct; ❄🅿) Pylos' best hotel is this intimate place with 14 beautifully renovated rooms in a brilliant setting under the castle walls and right over the water. Those at the front have balconies and a real wow factor, with waves lapping below. There's an excellent family suite with huge private balcony, and a memorable upstairs chamber with double window and a stateroom feel.

The luminous breakfast area is also pleasant and there's a swimming platform with beach bar. Rates are significantly lower outside high season.

To Kastro
APARTMENT €€

(☑27230 28292; www.hotelkastro-pylos.gr; d/tr €75/85; ☺Mar-Oct; ❄🅿) Opposite the entrance road to the castle, these delightful studio apartments are run by Panagiotis, who likes his guests to feel like they are 'in a small house'. He's referring to the sense of family and hospitality, though the apartments themselves are large enough to call home. In high season there's a three-night minimum.

Hotel Miramare
HOTEL €€

(☑27230 22751; mmpylos@otenet.gr; Tsamadou 3; s/d/tr/f incl breakfast €50/80/90/100; 🅿❄🅿) Rooms here are a little dated and bathrooms are a squish. But add the position, the light (all have sea-facing balconies) and the extensive buffet breakfast, and you can hardly complain.

Aetos
GREEK €€

(☑27230 22783; mains €7-18, fish by kg €50-60; ☺11am-midnight; 🅿🖉) On a harbourside corner, this is the best of the restaurants in this zone, with a decent line in fresh fish as well as a wide range of everything from salad to seafood. Service is a cut above most other places. Gas heaters keep the terrace warm even on chilly evenings.

Koukos
GREEK €€

(☑27230 22950; www.tavernaokoukos.gr; Kalamatas 6; mains €8-15; ☺11.30am-midnight; 🅿🖉) The Cuckoo serves hearty portions of grills and oven-baked dishes on a changing menu to a local clientele. It's about 100m up the coastal hill from the plaza. There's some decorative flair here, but traditional taverna values apply.

ℹ Getting There & Away

The **KTEL Messinia bus station** (☑27230 22230; www.ktelmessinias.gr; Plateia Trion Navarhon) is on the inland side of the central square. From the bus station, there are services to Kalamata (€5.50, 1¾ hours, four to seven daily), Gargaliani (€6, one hour, two to four daily) via Nestor's Palace (€2, 30 minutes) and Chora (€2.30, 35 minutes), Methoni (€1.80, 20 minutes, three to five daily) and Athens (€31, five hours, one daily). For Patra you must catch a connection from Kalamata or Kyparissia, accessible by regular connection from Gargaliani.

Two to four daily buses (sometimes more in summer) ply the route between Pylos and Gialova (€1.80, 15 minutes).

ⓘ Getting Around

Rent & Ride (☏ 6947322730; Kalamatas 6; scooters per day €15-25) rent scooters. For bikes, hit their Gialova branch.

Gialova   Γιάλοβα

POP 300

The well-kept little tourist village of Gialova lies 8km north of Pylos on the northeastern edge of Navarino Bay. There's a fine sandy beach and safe swimming in the sheltered waters of the bay. The Gialova Lagoon is a prime birdwatching site in winter.

🛏 Sleeping & Eating

Zoe Resort   HOTEL €€

(☏ 27230 22025; www.zoeresort.com; r incl breakfast €120-220; P ❄ 🛜 ☲) 🏊 This once-small family-run place on the seafront has morphed into an appealing midrange resort. Older hotel rooms with small front balconies (and the tiniest of bathrooms) are fine, though the modern superior rooms in the connecting building are a worthwhile upgrade. The apartments in the resort area out the back are very spacious and well equipped. Prices vary substantially by season.

★ Kochili   SEAFOOD €€

(☏ 27230 23259; www.kochiligialova.com; fish per kg €46-63, mains €8-20; ⊙11am-midnight; 🛜) Just along the beach from the main taverna strip, this upmarket spot has tables on boards over the sand and fresh fish cooked simply and beautifully. Take your pick from the selection out front and bolster the meal with quality salads or other dishes. The spacious interior is also pleasant.

Eliá   GREEK €€

(☏ 27230 23503; www.elia-gialova.gr; mains €8-17; ⊙4-10pm Feb & Mar, noon-midnight Apr-Oct; 🛜 ✏) Gourmet Greek meets contemporary Mediterranean on the seaside strip. The menu changes seasonally but is generally matched by the funky ambience, designer lights and flower boxes. A 'stayer' is Dimitris' version of moussaka, which has an Italian twist here.

ⓘ Getting There & Around

There are two to four buses a day south to Pylos (€1.80, 15 minutes) and two to four daily north to Gargaliani via Nestor's Palace and Chora. A taxi between Gialova and Pylos costs around €15.

Based at Martin's store, **Rent & Ride** (☏ 27230 23114; bikes €10-12 per day, scooters €15-25 per day) rent bikes and scooters.

Around Gialova

Voidokilia Beach   BEACH

This perfect sandy crescent with clear waters is presumed to be Homer's 'sandy Pylos', where Telemachus was warmly welcomed when he came to ask wise old King Nestor the whereabouts of his long-lost father, Odysseus, King of Ithaca.

Follow the signs to Paleokastro and walk the lagoon-side track labelled 'Nestor's Cave' from the Paleokastro car park (20 minutes) or approach by road from the village of Petrohori, 6km north of Gialova off the road to Chora.

Paleokastro & Nestor's Cave   RUINS

The ruins of this ancient castle, which the Franks built in the 13th century on the site of the acropolis of Ancient Pylos, lie 5km west of Gialova on rugged Koryphasion Hill, a formidable natural defensive position overlooking the northern entrance to Navarino Bay.

The castle (officially closed) can be explored, but with care; avoid falling down cisterns hidden by overgrowth. The views from the top are magnificent. The road to the castle is signposted on the northern edge of Gialova.

Follow signs to Paleokastro, where the road ends in a little car park. From there you'll find two ways of reaching the castle: the left-hand path (20 minutes) skirts Koryphasion Hill and gradually leads up to the entrance. The other route (40 minutes) is signposted 'Nestor's Cave': the path (officially closed) skirts the lagoon before leading towards Voidokilia Beach through the sand dunes; a fork in the path leads up towards atmospheric, bat-heavy Nestor's Cave where, according to legend, Hermes hid Apollo's cattle. From the cave, it's a tough scramble up to the castle's crumbling battlements, rewarded by views of the perfect crescent of Voidokilia Beach. Combining the two routes makes a great loop.

★ Nestor's Palace   ARCHAEOLOGICAL SITE

(☏ 27630 31437; http://odysseus.culture.gr; adult/child €6/free; ⊙8am-8pm Wed-Mon Apr-Aug, reduced hours Sep-Mar) The best preserved of all Mycenaean palaces lies 17km north of Pylos and is a thrilling sight. It's described in Homer's 'Odyssey' as the court of the hero Nestor, who took part in the voyage of the Argonauts and sent 90 ships to fight in the Trojan War. Originally a two-storey building, the palace's walls stand up to 1m high, and from the raised walkways and explanatory text you get a good idea of the layout of a Mycenaean palace complex.

The main palace was a building of many rooms. The largest, the throne room, was where the king dealt with state business. In its centre was a large circular hearth surrounded by four ornate columns that supported a balcony. Surrounding the throne is the sentry box, pantry, waiting room, a vestibule and, most fascinating, a bathroom with a terracotta tub still in place. In this tub, according to legend, Polycaste, Nestor's youngest daughter, bathed the hero Telemachus. Archaeologists found small ceramic cups used for bathing and ladling aromatic oils still in place. The palace was destroyed by fire in around 1200 BCE and burned ceramic debris in another room clearly reveals where a shelf of crockery collapsed.

The remains of an earlier palace are alongside, as are buildings revealed to have been workshops and a wine cellar. In an information kiosk on your way to the ticket office is good background, including information about the famous decipherment of Linear B, which was revealed to be an ancient form of Greek.

Many of the finds, including fragments of the palace frescoes and copies of some of the Linear B script tablets – the first to be discovered on the mainland – are housed in the museum in the nearby village of Chora.

Near the car park is an impressively reconstructed *tholos* (Mycenaean beehive-shaped tomb).

Chora Archaeological Museum   MUSEUM
(☑ 27632 31358; http://odysseus.culture.gr; Chora; adult/child €2/free; ☺ 8.30am-4pm Wed-Mon) This old-style museum houses finds from the palace site and other Mycenaean weaponry, jewellery and pottery from tombs around Messinia. The prize pieces are the fragments of frescoes from the throne rooms at Nestor's Palace and the Linear B tablets (the latter are copies). A new museum is in the planning stages.

It's located in the village of Chora, 4km northeast of Nestor's Palace. Buses from Pylos to Kyparissia stop at Chora. If driving, follow signs for Kalamata.

Ionian Dive Center   DIVING
(☑ 27630 61551; www.ioniandivecenter.gr; 1-/2-/3-dive packages €40/70/90) Based in Marathopoli, this reputable outfit offers dives in coastal sites in Messinia. PADI courses are also offered.

ELIS   ΗΛΕΙΑ

Most people come to the Elis (Ileia) region for one reason: to visit the historically important and impressive site of Ancient Olympia, birthplace of the Olympic Games. The surrounding region is largely agricultural, though it includes the lovely hill town of Andritsena and its stunning nearby temple of Apollo, as well as some excellent west-coast beaches.

The region originally took its name from the mythical King Helios. Its ancient capital was the city of Elis, now a forgotten ruin on the road from Gastouni to Lake Pinios. When the Franks arrived, they made Andravida the capital of the principate of Morea. Pyrgos is the region's underwhelming modern capital.

❶ Getting There & Away

From the KTEL bus terminal (p199) in Pyrgos, there are services to Athens (€30.10, four hours, seven to nine daily) via Tripoli (€15.50, 2½ hours, four to five daily), Patra (€10.60, two hours, eight to 10 daily), Andritsena (€6.40, two hours, two daily except Friday and Sunday), Kalamata (€13.50, two hours, two daily) and Olympia (€2.30, 30 minutes, eight to 13 daily).

There's also a small train that runs on the branch line from the cruise port of Katakolo to Pyrgos and on to Olympia (€10 return, 45 minutes).

From the port of Kyllini, **Levante Ferries** (Map p201; ☑ 26102 40000; www.levanteferries.com; ☺ kiosk 9am-8pm) run three to five times daily to Poros on Kefallonia (adult/car €9.80/38.70, 1½ hours) and four to six times daily to Zakynthos (adult/car €9.10/29.90, 1¼ hours). You can book online.

Olympia   Ολυμπία
POP 1000

The compact village of Olympia, lined with souvenir shops and restaurants, caters to the coach-loads of tourists who arrive to visit the most famous sight in the Peloponnese: Ancient Olympia. This is where myth and fact merge. According to one (of many different) legends, Zeus held the first Olympic Games to celebrate beating his father Kronos at wrestling. This is the birthplace of the ideal that still brings states together, differences aside, for the sake of friendly athletic competition, just as it did some 2800 years ago.

The ruins of Olympia are 500m south of the village, across the Kladeos River. As you walk around, or stand at the starting line of the ancient stadium, contemplate the influence of this site through millennia. This is where they light the Olympic flame every four years. This is where the Games began.

◉ Sights

★ **Ancient Olympia**　　ARCHAEOLOGICAL SITE
(☑ 26240 22517; http://odysseus.culture.gr; adult/child €12/free; ⊘ 8am-8pm Apr-Oct, to 3pm Nov-Mar) This is where the Olympic Games took place every four years for over 1100 years, until their abolition by Emperor Theodosius I in 393 CE. The Olympic flame is still lit here for the modern Games. Thanks to the destruction ordered by Theodosius II in 420 CE and various subsequent earthquakes, little remains of the magnificent temples and athletic facilities, but enough exists to give you a hint of the sanctuary's former glory. It is one of Greece's most evocative ancient sites.

Wandering amid the tree-shaded ruins, you can almost picture the blood and smoke of oxen sacrificed to Zeus and Hera, the sweaty, oiled-up athletes waiting inside the original stadium, the jostling crowds, and the women and slaves watching the proceedings from a nearby hill. It's worth remembering that some structures precede others by centuries; a visit to the archaeological museum before or after will provide context and help with visualising the ancient buildings.

On your right as you descend, the first ruin encountered is the gymnasium, which dates from the 2nd century BCE. South of here are the columns of the partly restored palaestra (wrestling school), where contestants practised and trained. Beyond is Pheidias' workshop, where the gargantuan ivory-and-gold Statue of Zeus, one of the Seven Wonders of the Ancient World, was sculpted by the Athenian sculptor. The workshop was identified by archaeologists after the discovery of tools and moulds; in the 5th century CE it was converted into an early-Christian church. Next is the leonidaion, an elaborate structure that accommodated dignitaries, built around 330 BCE.

The Altis, or Sacred Precinct of Zeus, lies on the left of the path you came down. Its most important building was the immense 5th-century-BCE Doric Temple of Zeus, which enshrined Pheidias' statue, later removed to Constantinople by Theodosius II (where it was destroyed by fire in 475 CE). One column of the temple has been restored and re-erected, and helps put into perspective the sheer size of the structure. To the east of the temple is the base for the Nike (Victory statue) that you can admire in the archaeological museum.

South of the Temple of Zeus is the bouleuterion (council house), which contains the altar of oaths, where competitors swore to abide by the rules decreed by the Olympic Senate and not to commit foul play. Here were kept the official records of the Games and its champions.

East of the temple is the echo stoa, with a Doric colonnade leading towards the stadium. Its remarkable acoustics meant that a sound uttered within was repeated seven times. Just east of the portico are the remains of a lavish villa used by Emperor Nero during his participation in the Games in 67 CE; it replaced the original Sanctuary of Hestia.

The stadium lies to the east of the Altis and is entered through a stone archway. It is rectangular, with a track measuring 192.27m; the stone start and finish lines of the sprint track and the judges' seats still survive. The stadium could seat at least 45,000 spectators; slaves and women, however, had to be content to watch from outside on the Hill of Kronos. The stadium was used again in 2004, when it was the venue for the shot put at the Athens Olympics.

To the north of the Temple of Zeus was the pelopion, a small, wooded hillock with an altar to Pelops, the first mythical hero of the Olympic Games. It was surrounded by a wall containing the remains of its later Classical-period Doric portico. Many artefacts now displayed in the museum were found on the hillock. There's also a large 3rd-millennium-BCE burial site here.

Further north is the late 7th-century-BCE Doric Temple of Hera, the site's oldest temple. An altar in front of the temple would have maintained a continuous fire during the Games, symbolising the fire stolen from the gods by Prometheus; today, the Olympic flame is lit here.

Near the altar is the nymphaeum (156–60 CE), erected by the wealthy Roman banker Herodes Atticus. Typical of buildings financed by Roman benefactors, it was grandiose, consisting of a semicircular building with Doric columns flanked at each side by a circular temple. The building contained statues of Herodes Atticus and his family, though Zeus took centre stage. Despite its elaborate appearance, the nymphaeum had a practical purpose; it was a fountain house supplying Olympia with fresh spring water.

Beyond the nymphaeum and up a flight of stone steps, a row of 12 treasuries stretched

Ancient Olympia

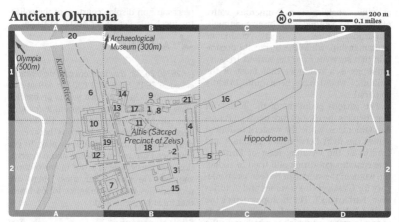

Ancient Olympia

to the stadium, each erected by a city-state for use as a storehouse for offerings to the gods; these were mainly used to advertise the city-state's prestige and wealth.

At the bottom of these steps are the scant remains of the 4th-century-BCE **Metroön**, a temple dedicated to Rhea, the mother of the gods. Apparently the ancients worshipped Rhea in this temple with orgies.

The foundations of the **philippeion**, west of the Temple of Hera, are the remains of a circular construction with Ionic columns built by Philip of Macedon to commemorate the Battle of Chaironeia (338 BCE), where he defeated a combined army of Athenians and Thebans. The building contained gold-and-ivory-covered statues of Philip and his family, including his son, Alexander the Great.

North of the *philippeion* was the 5th-century-BCE **prytaneum**, the magistrate's residence. Here, winning athletes feasted and were entertained. This was also where the fire of Hestia burned eternally, symbolising the common hearth of all Greeks.

It is worth visiting first thing in the morning or in the late afternoon; it's a magical experience to be there without the crowds. Information panels are in Greek, English and German. The entrance ticket also gives access to the superb archaeological museum and excellent museum of the ancient Games.

★ **Olympia**
Archaeological Museum MUSEUM
(☑ 26240 22742; http://odysseus.culture.gr; adult/child €12/free; ☉ 8am-8pm Apr-Oct, to 3pm Nov-Mar) This superb museum features finds from the adjacent archaeological site of Olympia. Visiting it in conjunction with the ruins helps to put the ancient site into perspective. The museum's exhibits span the Olympic sanctuary's past, from the prehistoric to the Roman periods. Artefacts include increasingly sophisticated ceramics, votive offerings to Zeus and Hera, sacrificial cauldron adornments and statuary from the Temple of Hera.

The main hall dramatically displays the biggest highlight: reassembled pediments and metopes from the Temple of Zeus.

The quality of finds is remarkable, with far more bronze artefacts recovered than at other ancient sites. Numerous votive offerings – ceramic and bronze animals, cauldrons, statues – display remarkable craftsmanship, while the terracotta decoration that survives from the various treasury buildings is a reminder that most of the buildings would have been quite brightly coloured.

The eastern pediment of the Temple of Zeus depicts the chariot race between Pelops and Oinomaos, while the western pediment shows the fight between the centaurs and Lapiths at the wedding feast of Pirithous (the centaurs got drunk and tried to abduct the women; the story can be seen as an allegory for Classical Greek values and victories over 'barbarians'). The metopes depict the Twelve Labours of Hercules; half the fun is trying to work out which is which from the remains alone.

Another highlight, in a room of its own, is the majestic 4th-century Parian marble statue of Hermes carrying baby Dionysus, carved by Praxiteles. The imposing Nike by Paionios (around 420 BCE) is another stunner.

Information panels are in Greek, English, French and German.

Museum of the History of the Olympic Games in Antiquity   MUSEUM
(☑26240 29119; http://odysseus.culture.gr; adult/child €12/free; ⊙8am-8pm Apr-Oct, to 3pm Nov-Mar) Beautifully presented displays depict the history of the world's most prestigious sporting competition. Learn about its core original events (foot racing, wrestling, boxing and chariot racing), why it's associated with Hercules (or Pelops), and what fate befell women who tried to watch the Games despite prohibitions. The sculptures, mosaics, pottery art and votive offerings all pay tribute to athletes and athleticism, while bronze strigils were used by the athletes themselves to scrape down. Other Games of Ancient Greece also get a mention.

★Kotsanas Museum   MUSEUM
(☑6931831530; www.kotsanas.com; Praxitelous Kondyli; by donation; ⊙10am-8pm) This extraordinary private collection gets into the literal nuts and bolts behind the technological achievements of the Ancient Greeks. Marvel at the mechanics of the crane used to build the Parthenon, the Antikythera Mechanism (the 'first laptop'), and a statue servant that serves holy water, touted as the 'world's oldest vending machine'. Fascinating, educational and marvellous for kids, both young and old. Excellent English explanations. The

pieces are on display courtesy of the collector, mechanical engineer Kostas Kotsanas.

🏃 Activities

Dig It!   EDUCATIONAL
(☑26240 26232; www.facebook.com/digitolympia; individual €9-15, family of 4 €30-50; ⊙9am-3pm Mon-Fri, 10am-2pm Sat) Two young archaeologists run this fabulous programme for kids and parents designed to bridge the knowledge of what actually happens between a ruin discovery and museum display. To get your head around excavation and conservation, you participate in a 'dig' in one of three simulated archaeological sites. There are programmes from 45 minutes to 1½ hours that must be prebooked.

Klio's Honey Farm   FOOD
(☑6977714530; www.klioshoneyfarm.com; ⊙10am-6pm Jun-Aug, from 10.30am Mon-Sat May-Sep, 11am-4pm Mon-Sat Mar-Apr & Oct-Nov) Enterprising Klio, a professional beekeeper, has opened up the family home to provide a very local experience. She'll talk you through the beekeeping and honey-making process, before you sit at one of the lace-cloth-covered tables in the flower-filled garden, converse with Klio's mother and try honey drizzled over *diplas* (fried pastry curls). It's 500m from the centre, well signposted from the station.

Entry is free; honey and other goodies are for sale. You can book a visit on Sundays or out of season.

👉 Tours

To really make the Ancient Olympia site come alive, it's worth considering a guide, especially if there are a few of you. Tours usually include both the site and the Archaeological Museum, but any preference will be catered for. Tours start at around €120 for two or three people. Recommended guides include Marieta Kolotourou (☑6977526146), who speaks English and Spanish, and Niki Vlachou (☑6972426085; www.olympictours.gr; Stefanopolou), who speaks English and French.

🛏 Sleeping

★Hotel Pelops   HOTEL €
(☑26240 22543; www.hotelpelops.gr; Varela 2; s/d/tr incl breakfast €45/60/75; ✳@🛜) This is among the town's most welcoming choices, with comfortable rooms (all with balconies and many recently renovated) and a delightful, sunny lounge. The Greek-Australian

owners, Susanna and Theo, provide knowledgeable service and a decent breakfast. Guests are treated like family and also have free use of the swimming pool at Hotel Europa.

Susanna might offer an impromptu cooking class too (price depends on numbers).

Prytanio
HOTEL €

(☑26240 26307; www.prytanio.gr; Bakopanou; d €40-55; ❄️🔊) At the northern end of the main drag, Prytanio has rooms named after gods and painted in battleship grey. On the ground floor, all are modern, spacious and have an outdoor patio space. It's run by a welcoming young couple and a good continental breakfast is available for €5.

Hotel Kronio
HOTEL €

(☑26240 22188; www.hotelkronio.gr; Tsoureka 1; s/d/tr incl breakfast €44/50/65; 🅿️❄️@🔊) The helpful, multilingual owner, Panagiotis, is a bonus at this pleasant spot, which has 23 warm-hued and airy rooms. It has good mattresses and spotless bathrooms; all have balconies.

Pension Posidon
PENSION €

(☑26240 22567; www.pensionposidon.gr; Stefanopoulou 9; s/d/tr incl breakfast €35/40/45; ❄️🔊) A helpful couple runs this centrally located, cosy spot where rooms are simple but pleasant; most have balconies. Snug roof terrace.

★Hotel Europa
HOTEL €€

(☑26240 22650; www.hoteleuropa.gr; Drouva 1; s/d/f incl breakfast €75/95/120; 🅿️❄️@🔊🏊) This family-run hotel on the hill above town is popular with groups and families. Smart renovated rooms have blonde wood and a modern ambience; traditional rooms in the adjacent building are larger. All have sofas and balconies, and are great for kicking back. A large pool, lovely taverna with olive-shaded tables, and excellent service seal the deal.

✕ Eating

Olympia's many tavernas cater largely to the lunchtime coach crowds, and as such most lack incentive to strive for excellence. Having said that, there are a few worth visiting.

Symposio
GREEK €

(☑26240 23620; mains €6-12; ⊙9am-midnight; 🍴) Warm-hearted taverna at the ruins end of town with checked tablecloths and a genuine welcome. Prices are fair for large portions of dips, salads, Greek favourites and grilled meats.

Anesis
GRILL €

(☑26240 22644; cnr Avgerinou & Spiliopoulou; mains €6-9; ⊙7pm-midnight May-Sep) No-frills grills. And excellent ones at that. Run by a hard-working family, Anesis is a fabulous budget option and will even deliver to your hotel for no charge. Look for hearty homemade dishes including *pastitsio* (baked pasta) and stuffed tomatoes. We love the *kontosouvli* (spit-roasted pork).

★Garden Taverna
GREEK €€

(☑26240 22650; www.hoteleuropa.gr; Hotel Europa; mains €10-17; ⊙noon-2pm & 7-10.30pm May-Sep; 🔊) Nestled under olive trees in a tranquil rose garden that overlooks the valley, this restaurant is the most original in Olympia. Alongside the excellent grilled meats you'll find the likes of pasta in vodka cream sauce with smoked salmon and dill. A great spot to come for sunset drinks.

❶ Getting There & Away

Buses depart from the train station, located in the middle of town one block east of the main street. There are services to Pyrgos (€2.30, 30 minutes, eight to 13 daily), with three handy Athens connections (€30.10, four hours), and to Tripoli (€15, 2¼ hours). Note that for tickets to Tripoli, you should reserve your seat with **KTEL Pyrgos** (☑26210 20600; www.ktelileias.gr; Erithrou Stavrou 6, Pyrgos) one day prior to travel; hotels will call on your behalf.

Andritsena   Ανδρίτσαινα
POP 800 / ELEV 705M

The birthplace of Panayotis Anagastopoulos, one of the leaders in the War of Independence, the charming mountain town of Andritsena overlooks the valley of the Alfios River, 65km southeast of Pyrgos. Crumbling stone houses, some with rickety wooden balconies, flank the village's narrow cobbled streets and a stream bubbles its way through the central square, Plateia Agnostopoulou. Keep an eye out for the fountain emerging from the trunk of a huge plane tree. Andritsena is a handy springboard for visiting the magnificent Temple of Epicurean Apollo, a World Heritage–listed site, located 14km south.

◉ Sights

★Temple of Epicurean Apollo
ARCHAEOLOGICAL SITE

(☑26260 22275; http://odysseus.culture.gr; Vassai; adult/child €6/free; ⊙8am-8pm Easter-Oct, 8.30am-3pm Nov-Easter) Situated on a wild, isolated spot overlooking rugged mountains and hills, this World Heritage–listed temple is one of Greece's most atmospheric archaeological sites. The striking, well-preserved temple is robbed of some of its splendour and immediate visual impact by the giant steel-girded tent that's been protecting it from the elements since 1987 (for restoration purposes), but it's magnificent all the same. It's located 14km southwest of Andritsena at Vassai (Bassae).

🛏 Sleeping & Eating

Archontiko Hotel   HOTEL **€€**
(☑ 26260 22401; www.archontiko-andritsenas.gr; s/d incl breakfast €60/75; P 🛜) With two rows of rooms sharing wooden balconies with a peaceful outlook over the village to the hills beyond, this dark and atmospheric historic building is at the western end of the main drag. Rooms are cosy and comfortable with an old-time feel.

ℹ Getting There & Away

Buses run to Athens (€26.50, two hours, one daily) via Megalopoli, Tripoli and Corinth Isthmus. Buy tickets from the *kafeneio* (coffee house) near the tiny main square.

ACHAÏA   ΑΧΑΪΑ

The northern Peloponnesian region of Achaïa (or Achaea) comprises some high and skiable mountain country (reached via a historic rack-and-pinion railway), a swathe of small coastal resorts and a bustling port city, Patra.

Achaïa owes its name to the Achaeans, one of the original ethnic groups that comprised Ancient Greece and were possibly the founders of the Mycenaean civilisation. Legend has it that the Achaeans founded 12 cities, which later developed into the powerful Achaean Federation that survived until Roman times. Principal among these cities were the ports of Patra and Egio (on the coast of the Gulf of Corinth).

ℹ Getting There & Away

The modernised Corinth–Patra motorway that spans the northern Peloponnese provides excellent access across northern Achaïa. From the road, there are turn-offs to both Diakofto **train station** (☑ 26910 43206) – for the rack-and-pinion train (p204) to Kalavryta – and Kalavryta. Public buses are more reliable and frequent than trains (many trains use bus replacement services in any case). Patra is the principal bus hub for the region.

Patra   Πάτρα

POP 167,400

Greece's third-largest city, Patra is named after King Patreas who ruled Achaïa around 1100 BCE. Little is evident of this busy port's 3000 years of history, during which it was an important trade centre under the Mycenaeans and the Romans. Though there's a gritty side to the city, it has attractive squares and lively pedestrian streets, and a great bar and restaurant scene filled with the young and the trendy.

Though most travellers come here to hop on a ferry or cross the Rio–Andirio suspension bridge, an engineering feat that links the city with western continental Greece, it's well worth spending a day or two, visiting Patra's wonderful castle and museum, and making the most of the diverse eating choices and nightlife, fuelled by the presence of Patra's 20,000 university students.

◉ Sights

Patra was an important Roman city and a brick-built **odeion**, built in the 2nd century CE, is one of several remains scattered about the centre.

★ Archaeological Museum of Patras   MUSEUM
(☑ 26106 23820; http://odysseus.culture.gr; Patra–Athens National Rd 38-40; adult/child €6/free; ⊙ 8.30am-4pm Mar-Oct, to 3.30pm Wed-Mon Nov-Feb) This fabulous museum should be shouting its existence from its space-age rooftop. Its exhibits comprise regional objects from prehistoric to Roman times arranged across three themed halls: Private Life, Public Life and Cemeteries. Displays largely focus on two eras: there are excellent Mycenaean ceramics from a variety of grave sites in the region, and some fine sculptures and mosaics from Roman villas and other sites excavated around town. Most extraordinary, though, are four moving Hellenistic-era skulls complete with beautiful, delicate funerary wreaths. The museum is 4km northeast of the centre.

Church of Agios Andreas   CHURCH
(Church of St Andrew; Agiou Andreou) Seating 5500 people, this church is one of the largest in the Balkans. Tradition holds that the Romans crucified St Andrew here in Patra (on the diagonal cross represented on the Scottish flag). The church houses religious icons and paintings, as well as relics including the apostle's skull and part of the cross.

Patra

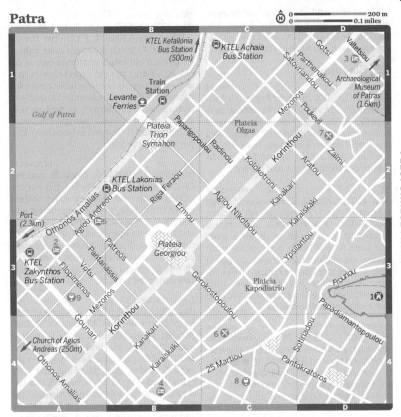

Patra

⊙ Sights
1 Kastro D3

🛏 Sleeping
2 Castello City Hotel A3
3 City Loft Boutique Hotel.......................D1
4 Maison Grecque B4
5 Pension Nicos...A3

🍴 Eating
6 Aptaliko C4
7 Labyrinthos D2

🍸 Drinking & Nightlife
8 Banana Moon C4
9 Bodegas...A3

Kastro CASTLE
(Map p201; ☏ 26106 23390; http://odysseus.
culture.gr; Panachaidos Athinas; ⊙ 8.30am-4pm
Wed-Mon Apr-Oct, to 3.30pm Nov-Mar) FREE
Patra's castle stands on the site of the acropolis of ancient Patrai. The Romans were the
first to build a fort here around 550 CE, but
the present structure is of Frankish origin,
remodelled many times over the centuries by
the Byzantines, Venetians and Turks. Set in
an attractively maintained pencil-pine park,
it is reached by climbing the 193 steps at the

southeastern end of Agiou Nikolaou, then
continuing and turning left. Great views of
the mainland, Zakynthos and Kefallonia are
the reward.

★ Festivals & Events

Patras Carnival CARNIVAL
(www.carnivalpatras.gr; ⊙ Feb/Mar) Patra's citizens party hard during the annual Patras
Carnival. The program features a host of
minor events from the opening on 17 January leading up to a wild weekend of costume

parades, colourful floats and celebrations seven weeks before Orthodox Easter. The event draws big crowds, so hotel reservations are essential if you want to stay overnight.

🛏 Sleeping

Pension Nicos PENSION €
(Map p201; ☑26106 23757; cnr Patreos 3 & Agiou Andreou 121; s/d/tr €25/30/40, without bathroom €22/25/35; ❄☎) One of the few good budget options, this 1960s-style walk-up on a busy street doesn't look much from outside, but Nicos runs a tight ship with clean bargain-priced rooms, plus a roof terrace.

★City Loft Boutique Hotel APARTMENT €€
(Map p201; ☑26102 23552; www.cityloft.gr; Valtetsiou 6; 1-/2-/3-person apt incl breakfast €80/100/120; P❄☎) Sleek and stylish apartments in white or black, on a quiet side street several blocks north of the main square, are slightly incongruous compared with the surrounding grittiness. Perks include high-quality bed linens, king-sized beds with orthopaedic mattresses, balconies and a small, attractive garden.

Castello City Hotel HOTEL €€
(Map p201; ☑26102 25000; www.castello cityhotel.gr; cnr Agios Andreou 118 & Filopoimenos 3; s/d/tr incl breakfast €59/69/85; P❄☎) The 17 rooms in this central business-style hotel are compact, but they are ultramodern and decked out in lots of taupes and greys. As such, it lacks any real Greek personality, but it's a drink's spit from the bars on the main drags and is convenient to everything. The cable TV has programs in lots of languages.

Maison Grecque BOUTIQUE HOTEL €€
(Map p201; ☑26102 41212; www.mghotels.gr; 25 Martiou 116; s/d/ste incl breakfast €70/90/150; ❄☎) This smart boutique spot has individually styled rooms in dark hues with metallic touches (with an original ceiling fresco or two thrown in). Some of the standard rooms are quite compact for the price. It's a five-minute walk from the pedestrianised centre and close to the Ifaistou eating strip.

🍴 Eating & Drinking

Trendy cafes, bars and restaurants line the pedestrianised Riga Fereou, Patanassis, Agiou Nikolaou and surrounding alleys. Cheap student eats are along Gerokostopoulou. Up against the remains of the Roman stadium, Ifaistou can be hard to find but it's a great pedestrian food street that's buzzy until late.

★Labyrinthos GREEK €
(Map p201; ☑26102 26436; Poukevil 44; mains €6-12; ⊙noon-5.30pm & 8.30pm-1am Mon-Sat Sep-Jun; ☎☑) Inside the rough stone walls of this 85-year-old family restaurant (one of the oldest in Patra), you can expect classics such as *briam* (oven-baked vegetable casserole), dolmadhes and beef casserole in *tentoura* (Patra's traditional sauce), as well as delicious if not-for-everyone *gardoumba* (roasted lamb innards wrapped in intestines). Plus plenty of hospitality.

Aptaliko MEZEDHES €€
(Map p201; ☑26140 00138; Ifaistou 36; mezedhes €4-10; ⊙8pm-1am; ☎☑) We love Ifaistou, the hidden eating and drinking street wedged under the hillside, with an alternative vibe and lively terrace scene. Aptaliko is our favourite spot on it, with views of the ruins of the Roman stadium, hospitable service and a pleasing menu of creative bites, from grilled cheeses to foraged greens, tasty sausage and succulent roast pork.

Banana Moon BAR
(Map p201; ☑26103 33876; www.facebook.com/PregoPatra; cnr Germanou & Charalambi; ⊙10am-3am; ☎) 🍴 An extension of the Prego cafe across the road, the broken doors, graffiti and crumbling concrete here meld into the tropical garden vibe, all plants and fairy lights. It adds up to an enchanting two-level space, with a roof terrace overlooking the Roman *odeion*. It's good for coffee, brunch and more, but comes into its own for cocktails at night.

Bodegas WINE BAR
(Map p201; ☑26102 21113; www.facebook.com/bodegaspatra; Riga Fereou 147; ⊙7am-5am; ☎) Whether you're nursing a margarita or a glass of wine from a great selection of Greek vintages, this stylish bar is a spot worth lingering. Salads come in an enormous bowl. It's in the heart of the pedestrian strip and is good for an early coffee too.

ℹ Getting There & Away

BOAT
The international passenger port is 1km south of town, though services occasionally still use the northern port, 500m north of the train station. Domestic ferry services currently use the dock in the centre of town, by the train station.

Ferry offices are located at the port, and a few agencies that sell ferry tickets are sprinkled along Othonos Amalias and Iroön Polytechniou. **Rota Shipping** (☑26102 79057; www.rotashipping.gr; Othonos Amalias 57;

⊙ 9am-9pm Mon-Fri, to 3pm Sat) is one that is handy. Ferry schedules and prices change seasonally; call ahead.

Domestic

At time of research, there were services from Patra to Kefallonia and Ithaki. There are also services from Kyllini, 76km southwest of Patra, to Kefallonia and Zakynthos. Bus-ferry combinations run from Patra for Kyllini services.

Always check the ferry situation before making plans: companies and routes change like the tides.

From Patra: Levante Ferries (p195) run once daily to Sami on Kefallonia (adult/car €15.10/49.80, 3½ hours) and on to Pisaetos on Ithaki (adult/car €15.10/52.90, four hours). You can book online; ferries leave from near the train station in the middle of town.

From Kyllini: Levante Ferries (p195) run three to five times daily to Poros on Kefallonia (adult/car €9.80/38.70, 1½ hours) and four to six times daily to Zakynthos (adult/car €9.10/29.90, 1¼ hours). You can book online.

International

Patra is Greece's main port for ferry services to Italy, with departures to Brindisi, Bari, Ancona and Venice. Note that while some ferries may stop at Igoumenitsa and Corfu en route, you cannot disembark.

ANEK/Superfast Ferries (Map p201; ☑ 21041 97470; www.anek.gr; cnr Othonos Amalias & Aratou) runs trips to Bari (adult/car €68/82, 16 hours, daily), Ancona (adult/car €75/108, 20 to 22 hours, six weekly) and Venice (adult/car €75/122, 32 hours, two to three weekly).

Minoan Lines (☑ 26104 26000; www.minoan.gr) heads to Ancona (adult/car €71/99, 22 hours, four weekly) and Venice (adult/car €71/99, 31 hours, two weekly).

Grimaldi Lines (www.grimaldi-lines.com) sails to Brindisi (adult/car €49/49, 15 hours, three weekly).

Prices given here are for deck seats in summer, but not the peak fortnight in August, when rates skyrocket. Rates are higher for airline seats and cabins, and they drop in the off-season. Check up-to-date schedules online.

BUS

Patra has four bus stations arrayed along the waterfront strip.

Services from the main **KTEL Achaia bus station** (Map p201; ☑ 26106 23886; www.ktelachaias.gr; Othonos Amalias 4):

Athens (€20.70, 2½ to three hours, every 30 minutes), some via Corinth Isthmus (€13.80, 1¾ hours)

Ioannina (€25.30, 4½ hours, two daily)

Kalamata (€25, four hours, two daily)

Kalavryta (€8.60, two hours, two to four daily)

Pyrgos (€10.60, two hours, eight to 10 daily). Change here for Olympia.

Thessaloniki (€48.50, seven hours, two to three daily)

The **KTEL Lakonias bus station** (Map p201; ☑ 26102 74938; www.ktel-lakonias.gr; Othonos Amalias 58; ⊙ 8am-8pm) has services to the Ionian island of Lefkada (€17.60, three hours, twice weekly), to Amfissa for Delphi (€14.80, three hours, two daily) and Tripoli (€20, one daily).

The **KTEL Zakynthos bus station** (Map p201; ☑ 26102 20993; www.ktel-zakynthos.gr; Othonos Amalias 84; ⊙ 8am-7pm) has services to Zakynthos, via the port of Kyllini (including ferry €17, 3½ hours, three daily).

The **KTEL Kefallonia bus station** (☑ 26104 20400; www.ktelkefalonias.gr; Iroön Polytechniou 42; ⊙ 9.30am-7.30pm) in the northern passenger terminal has two to three daily bus-ferry combinations to Kefallonia via Kyllini. The ferry goes to Poros (€17.80 including ferry, three hours); you can continue by bus to Argostoli on a single ticket (€22.10 total, four hours).

CAR

Avis (☑ 26102 75547; www.avis.gr; cnr Othonos & Amalias 33; ⊙ 8am-8.30pm Mon-Fri, 9am-3pm & 6-8pm Sat & Sun)

Hertz (☑ 26102 20990; www.hertz.gr; Othonos Amalias 33; ⊙ 8am-9pm)

TRAIN

Trains depart from the centrally located **Patra train station** (☑ 26102 74180; www.trainose.gr; ⊙ 6am-10pm). There are 10 trains a day to Athens (€17). At the time of writing, a replacement bus goes as far as Kiato (1¼ hours), from where you take the *proastiako*, Athens' local train service (another 1¼ hours). On arrival in Athens you can use your *proastiako* ticket for 1½ hours on the metro (validate it first).

❶ Getting Around

Buses run hourly between the KTEL Achaia Bus Station and the international passenger port. Incoming bus services will often stop at the port too.

An urban train service runs from north to south of the city (€1.40) but is not particularly handy for travel needs.

Kalavryta · Καλάβρυτα

POP 1800 / ELEV 758M

Perched high above sea level, Kalavryta is a delightful little town with fresh mountain air, gushing springs and a square that nestles under giant plane trees. Though in existence for centuries, the present-day town came into being on the ruins of ancient Kinaitha in the mid-19th century. The town is a popular ski-season destination among Athenians, who also come for weekend getaways year-round. In spring and summer, visitors from abroad come here to hike and visit the nearby monasteries as well as to try out the famous rack-and-pinion railway journey.

History

Two relatively recent historical events have assured Kalavryta a place in the hearts of all Greeks. First, despite plenty of evidence that fighting had already begun elsewhere, the official version of the War of Independence states that the revolt against the Turks began here on 25 March 1821, when Bishop Germanos of Patra raised the Greek flag at Moni Agias Lavras, a monastery 5km from town. Second, on 13 December 1943, in one of the worst single atrocities of WWII, the Nazis massacred most of the village's male inhabitants, nearly 500 people, as part of their scorched-earth Operation Kalavryta, designed to punish Kalavryta partisans, in particular, for the deaths of German prisoners of war. The hands of the old cathedral clock stand eternally at 2.34pm, the time the German guns finally fell silent.

◉ Sights

★ **Museum of the Kalavryta Holocaust** MUSEUM
(☑ 26920 23646; www.dmko.gr; 1-5 Syngrou; adult/teen/child €3/1.50/free; ⊙ 9am-4pm Tue-Sun) This is a powerful tribute to the residents of Kalavryta who perished in the 13 December 1943 slaughter perpetrated by the German army. It's a dignified, understated, yet extremely evocative account of the struggle between the occupying forces and partisan fighters in the area, and the events running up to the massacre. The immensely moving and sobering visit is brought to life by personal video testimony from survivors.

Martyrs' Monument MONUMENT
A huge white cross on a cypress-covered hillside just east of town marks the site where the German army machine-gunned nearly 500 men and boys from Kalavryta on 13 December 1943. Only 13 survived the massacre. Beneath this imposing monument is a poignant little shrine to the victims. It's signposted off Konstantinou.

★ **Cave of the Lakes** CAVE
(☑ 26920 31001; www.kastriacave.gr; Kalavryta–Klitoria Rd; adult/child €9/4.50; ⊙ 9.30am-4.30pm Sep-Jun, to 5.30pm Sun-Fri, to 6.30pm Sat Jul & Aug) The remarkable Cave of the Lakes lies

16.5km south of Kalavryta near the village of Kastria. A 500m boardwalk snakes its way through the cave, through the vast entrance chamber (home to five species of bats) past spectacular cauliflower-like rock formations, and over the deep, crystal-clear subterranean pools – the 13 stone basins formed by mineral deposits over the millennia. The most impressive formations are in the final chamber, where delicate, ribboning curtains cascade down the wall.

Moni Mega Spileo MONASTERY
(Monastery of the Great Cavern; ☑ 26920 23130; Diakofto–Kalavryta Rd; ⊙ 8am-1pm & 2-7pm) FREE
Ten kilometres north of Kalavryta, this is believed to be one of the oldest monasteries in Greece (though the current building dates from the 20th century). Its prized relic is a wax icon of the Virgin Mary, said to have been made by St Luke and supposedly discovered in the nearby cavern by St Theodore and St Simeon in 362 CE (though it most likely dates to around 1000 CE). It's popular with pilgrims; a strict dress code applies.

🏃 Activities

★ **Diakofto–Kalavryta Railway** RAIL
(☑ Diakofto 26910 43206, Kalavryta 26920 23050; www.odontotos.com; one way/return €9.50/19) One of the unmissable journeys to make in the Peloponnese is aboard the tiny train running along the vintage rack-and-pinion railway between Diakofto and Kalavryta. It takes travellers on a remarkably scenic ride through the dramatic Vouraïkos Gorge, its reddish cliffs seemingly closing in on the train. The line switches back and forth under a leafy canopy of plane trees, clinging to a narrow ledge overhanging the rushing rapids below, and passing through seven curving tunnels along the way.

To reach Kalavryta, the train climbs over 700m in 22.5km, using a rack-and-pinion (cog) system for traction on the steep sections, effectively clamping itself to the notched girder you can see running between the rails. Built by an Italian company between 1889 and 1895, the railway was a remarkable feat of engineering for its time, with only a handful of equivalents around the world (most notably in the Swiss Alps). Between 2007 and 2009 the entire rails and cog sections were completely replaced, and four new modern trains were constructed to replace the former carriages. The original steam engines that first plied the route can still be seen outside Diakofto and Kalavryta stations.

The journey takes just over an hour, and stops en route at the picturesque hamlet of Zahlorou and two other tiny stations on demand, in case you want to be dropped off at one and walk to another. The railway makes an even more scenic hike, as you have more time to appreciate your surroundings.

Hiking the 22km down from Kalavryta to Diakofto takes around five hours; train drivers are used to hikers along the tracks and give them plenty of warning. Take a torch for the tunnels.

At the time of writing there were three departures on weekdays and five on weekends in each direction; confirm times at respective train stations.

Kalavryta is linked by regular buses to Athens and Patra. To get to Diakofto, catch the only 'working' train line, Corinth–Patra, with OSE replacement buses running in place of trains along the Diakofto–Kiato section. On leaving Diakofto, you can catch the same replacement bus service west to Patra or, to head east, take this service to Kiato, from where you catch the *proastiako* train (Athens suburban train line), either to Corinth or as far as Athens airport.

Kalavryta Ski Centre
SKIING

(✆26920 24451; www.kalavrita-ski.gr; half-/full day €15/20; ⏰9am-4pm Dec-Apr) Head 14km east of Kalavryta on Mt Helmos (2355m) to the Ski Centre (elevation 1700m to 2340m), which has 12 runs and seven lifts (two chairlifts). There's no overnight accommodation but it rents skis and snowboard equipment (€20/15 for a full/half-day at peak period). The season lasts from December to April, snow permitting. A taxi costs around €20.

🍴 Sleeping & Eating

While ski lodges abound on the outskirts, good hotel options are in the village. Peak period is the ski season (December to April), when reservations are essential. Prices are slashed on weekdays. Alternatively, look inside the hotel information kiosk in front of the train station where accommodation options are listed; those with vacancies are lit up. Also check www.kalavrita-hotels.gr.

★Archontiko Zafeiropoulou
APARTMENT €€

(✆26920 24500; www.archontiko.gr; Striftompala; d/tr/ste incl breakfast €85/100/140; P❄🐕) All options are essentially spacious, spotless studios and apartments, all with kitchenettes. The real treasure here is the friendly South African–Greek owner, George, who has an outstanding knowledge of the town and surrounding attractions, and useful maps to hand. The excellent breakfast includes local sheep's milk yoghurt, preserves and cheeses.

Hotel Filoxenia
HOTEL €€

(✆26920 22422; www.hotelfiloxenia.gr; Ethnikis Andistaseos 10; s/d incl breakfast €50/70; P❄🐕) Kind of like an old-fashioned ski lodge with its handsome stone exterior, the long-running Filoxenia has had a modern spruce-up. Its 28 rooms are individually decorated with bright, fresh colours and contemporary fabrics. It offers an expansive buffet breakfast and there's a small spa complex.

Kelari
GRILL €

(✆26920 23301; Kapota 19; mains €6-8; ⏰9am-11.30pm) There's something life-affirming about this place, where locals come for a hearty feed of souvlaki, roast chicken or spit-roasted pork. It's great value; balance out the meat with some *horta* (boiled wild greens). The house red could pass for a rosé.

To Spitiko
GREEK €€

(✆26920 24260; Paleon Patron Germanou 15; mains €8-15; ⏰9am-11.45pm; 🐕🍽) This cosy place with a ski-lodge feel serves up great-quality traditional taverna meals and fabulous mezedhes. Expect the likes of veal with tomato sauce, chicken baked with vegetables, spinach and feta soufflé and scrummy tzatziki. Mikhaela is a delightful, multilingual host.

ℹ Information

For bargain sightseeing in and around Kalavryta, the Kalavryta CityPass discount card (www.trainose.gr) covers a return trip on the Diakofto–Kalavryta railway and entrance to the Cave of the Lakes, the Kalavryta Holocaust Museum and Kalavryta Ski Centre, saving you 40% overall. The card costs €24.80, is valid for a month and can be purchased at Kalavryta, Diakofto and Patra train stations.

ℹ Getting There & Away

The rack-and-pinion train to/from Diakofto via Zahlorou runs to a changing timetable.

There are buses to Patra (€8.60, two hours, three to four daily on weekdays, two on weekends) and Athens (€18.40, three hours, two Monday to Saturday, one Sunday). The **bus station** (✆26920 22224) is 200m before the entrance to town (from the Diakofto approach road), beside the Shell petrol station.

Kalavryta's **taxi rank** (✆26920 22127) is in front of the train station.

Most of the attractions are out of town, so it's very handy to have your own transport.

The Olympic Games

The Olympic Games were undoubtedly the ancient world's biggest sporting event and remain for most athletes today the ultimate dream. Then, as now, the Games made warring states temporarily halt their squabbles, and victorious competitors won great fame.

Origins of the Games

Some Ancient Greek texts attribute the founding of the Games to the hero Pelops; others name Hercules as the founder who made Zeus the patron god of the Olympic sanctuary. The first official quadrennial Olympic Games were declared in 776 BCE by King Iphitos of Elis, took place around the first full moon in August, and continued occurrng for over 1100 years.

During the ancient Games, writers, poets and historians read their works to large audiences; lavish sacrifices were made to the gods; traders clinched business deals; and city-state leaders attempted to resolve differences through diplomacy.

Olympic Qualifications

In Ancient Greece only free-born Greek males were allowed to compete in the Games; the Romans changed the rules to include Roman citizens. Slaves and women were not allowed to enter the Olympic sanctuary even as spectators; women trying to sneak in were thrown from Mt Typaion. Today's Summer Olympics include athletes from 206 countries, with 92 countries competing in the Winter Olympics.

Demise & Rebirth

During Roman times the Games declined. Held for the last time in 393 CE, they were banned by Emperor Theodosius I as part of a purge of pagan festivals.

1. Lighting the Olympic flame, Ancient Olympia (p196)
2. Ruins of the Temple of Hera (p196), Olympia
3. Statue of a discus thrower

The modern Olympic Games were instituted in 1896 and, except during WWI and WWII, have been held every four years around the world ever since. The Olympic flame is lit at the ancient site and carried by runners to the city where the Games are held.

Scandal & Controversies

Throughout history the Olympics have been marred by scandals. These range from the farcical – Emperor Nero entering the chariot race in 67 CE with 10 horses, ordering that other competitors could only have four, falling off and still being declared winner – to the serious, including Israeli athletes being murdered by Palestinian group Black September in 1972, and Hitler refusing to award gold medals to African American sprinter Jesse Owens in 1936.

ANCIENT OLYMPICS VS MODERN OLYMPICS

➡ Contemporary opening ceremonies may involve such displays as James Bond parachuting in. In Ancient Greece, it was all about sacrificing oxen to Zeus.

➡ Ancient Greek events included wrestling, chariot and horse racing, the pentathlon (three foot races, the long jump and the discus), javelin, boxing and pankration (few-holds-barred fighting). Today's Summer Olympics have been joined by the Winter Olympics; a total of around 50 events across both games include modified sprinting, equestrian, boxing and wrestling.

➡ Victorious ancient Olympians were crowned with sacred olive branches and enjoyed tax exemption and other privileges. Modern Olympians receive medals, TV fame and sponsorship fortune.

AT A GLANCE

★

POPULATION
Larrisa: 144,600

**GREECE'S APPLE
CAPITAL**
Zagora (p237)

TOP MONASTERY
Moni Osios Loukas
(p222)

**BEST
CHARACTERFUL
STAY**
Lost Unicorn Hotel &
Restaurant (p240)

BEST SEAFOOD
Skeletovrachos
(p224)

📅

WHEN TO GO
Apr & May Wild
chamomile and red
poppies mingle in
alpine meadows.

Sep Warmer seas,
sunny weather and
fewer crowds.

Orthodox Easter
Villages follow tradi-
tional customs, with
parades, dancing and
copious food.

Moni Agias Varvaras Rousanou and Moni Agiou Nikolaou, Meteora (p249)
PHOTO BY DIMITRIOS TILIS/GETTY IMAGES ©

Central Greece

C entral Greece holds three utterly unmissable destinations. To the ancient Greeks, Delphi was the centre or 'navel' of the earth. It remains as magical as ever, with its superb archaeological site (p213) and magnificent scenery. The Meteora region is similarly breathtaking, with towering rocky outcrops topped by teetering monasteries (and rock climbers). And the beautiful Pelion Peninsula is criss-crossed with cobblestone paths that link lush mountain hamlets with beaches to rival the finest islands.

Elsewhere, central Greece holds many surprises. Alpine meadows and valleys, perfect for breezy summer hikes and winter skiing, cover the Evritania mountain range, while Thessaly holds lively cities and charming villages. Above all, the region's good-natured inhabitants serve up hospitality, superb experiences and great cuisine.

INCLUDES

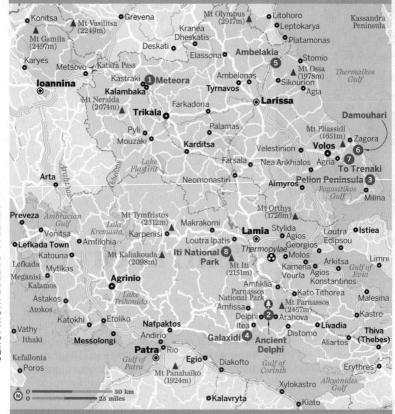

Central Greece Highlights

1 Meteora (p248) Gazing up, and up, to the Byzantine monasteries perched atop their stony thrones.

2 Ancient Delphi (p213) Meditating over the last light of day at the Sanctuary of Athena Pronaia.

3 Pelion Peninsula (p234) Wandering down the *kalderimia* (mule paths) to the sea.

4 Galaxidi (p223) Basking or feasting beside a pretty harbour facing the Gulf of Corinth.

5 Ambelakia (p229) Seeking out spectacular murals in the mansions of a time-forgotten village.

6 Damouhari (p239) Sea-kayaking beyond the exquisite bay to small coves in the blue Aegean.

7 To Trenaki (p242) Riding the 'little train' along the flanks of Mt Pelion.

8 Iti National Park (p228) Hiking the high-mountain trails or exploring Agathon Monastery.

ℹ Getting There & Away

Regular flights reach Athens for easy access to Delphi and Sterea Ellada, and Thessaloniki for access to Meteora and Thessaly. Bus service to the entire region is excellent, and daily excursion buses from Athens run to and from Delphi.

The roads in central Greece are generally very good, with the national toll road between Athens and Thessaloniki as the fastest north–south artery. However, mountain roads – in the Pelion Peninsula and between Nafpaktos and Karpenisi in Sterea Ellada, for example – can be winding and narrow. Fortunately, they're also extremely beautiful.

Rapid trains connect Athens and Thessaloniki via Lamia and Larissa, and there are good connections to Kalambaka (for Meteora).

DELPHI &
STEREA ELLADA
ΔΕΛΦΟΙ & ΣΤΕΡΕΑ ΕΛΛΑΔΑ

The rugged and scenic landscape of Sterea Ellada has borne witness to the full drama of Greek mythology and history – and nowhere more so than Delphi, where the slopes of Mt Parnassos were home to Apollo's all-seeing oracle. From fabled Thebes, north of Athens, this region stretches west along the Gulf of Corinth to Messolongi – where British poet Lord Byron died during the Greek War of Independence – and the Ionian Sea. It acquired the name Sterea Ellada, meaning 'Mainland Greece', in 1827, when it became part of the newly formed nation.

❶ Getting There & Away

BOAT

To Sporades from Agios Konstantinos

The workaday village of Agios Konstantinos, 50km southeast of Lamia on the main Athens–Thessaloniki route, is one of the three mainland ports (along with Volos and Thessaloniki) that serve the islands of Skiathos and Skopelos in the northern Sporades.

Between early June and early September, ANES Ferries sail from Agios Konstantinos at 9.15am daily, heading to and from Skiathos (per person/car €30/49, 3½ hours), and Glossa on Skopelos (same price, 4¼ hours).

Two English-speaking agencies, facing the port, advise on ferry travel and sell tickets: **Alkyon** (✆ 22350 32444, 210 383 2545; http://alkyontravel.gr; Riga Ferraiou 1, Agios Konstantinos; ◷ 8am-8pm) and **Bilalis Travel** (✆ 22350 31614; www.bta.gr; Karaiskaki 4, Agios Konstantinos; ◷ 8am-8pm).

From the **KTEL bus station** (✆ 22350 32223; www.ktelfthiotidos.gr; Agios Konstantinos) in Agios Konstantinos, 200m south of the ferry landing, there are buses to Athens (€19, 2¼ hours, eight to nine daily) and Lamia (€5.60, 50 minutes, 12 daily). For Patra and Thessaloniki, change at Lamia.

To Ionian Islands from Astakos

The only reason to head to Astakos (Αστακός), 50km northwest of Messolongi, is to catch the **Ionian P Lines** (Tsarpali Athina; ✆ 26460 38020; www.ionionpelagos.com; Vasileos Pavlou 1, Astakos) ferry to the Ionian Islands. Once or twice daily, the *Ionio Pelagos* sails to/from the port of Sami on Kefallonia (per person/car €12/42, three hours), and Pisa Aetos on Ithiki (per person/car €10/33, two hours). Check schedules in advance, as days and hours vary seasonally. Cafes and tavernas along the small waterfront in Astakos help to while away any waiting time.

Delphi   Δελφοί

POP 2370

For the ancient Greeks, Delphi (from *delphis,* womb) marked the very centre of the world, a sacred space where human beings could communicate directly with the gods. To this day, the home of the all-seeing oracle retains a magical sense of standing apart, not least because the ancient site (p213) stands in beautifully preserved splendour on a pristine mountainside 750m east of (and out of sight of) the modern village.

Located just 150km northwest of Athens, Delphi is now a major tourist destination. In summer especially, it's well worth spending at least one night here, to experience the site before or after it's deluged with day-trippers. Despite heavy commercialisation, the nearby village makes a pleasant place to stay, with hotels and restaurants to suit all budgets, and great views down to the Gulf of Corinth.

History

The Greeks told many stories to explain the origins of Delphi. The site was originally sacred to Gaia (also known as Ge), the 'Mother Goddess' whose cult centred on the Korykeon Cave, high on Mt Parnassos. After slaying a snake or she-dragon (known as Pytho) here, Apollo took the local name of Apollo Pythios.

For a thousand years, pilgrims flocked to his sanctuary for guidance. The height of its fame came between the 6th and 4th centuries BCE, after the Amphictyonic League, a federation of 12 tribal states, took control of the sanctuary following the First Sacred War (595–586 BCE). As an autonomous state, Delphi earned great prosperity from benefactors including the kings of Lydia and Egypt, and the Roman emperor Hadrian. Nominally neutral, it was a locus of political power.

After surviving fire in 548 BCE and earthquake in 373 BCE, the sanctuary was conquered by the Aetolians around 300 BCE, and by the Romans in 191 BCE. Although the Roman general Sulla plundered Delphi in 86 BCE, later emperors kept the oracle's rituals alive well into the 2nd century CE. Ultimately its influence waned with the spread of Christianity, and the sanctuary was abolished by the Byzantine emperor Theodosius in the late 4th century CE.

Sterea Ellada

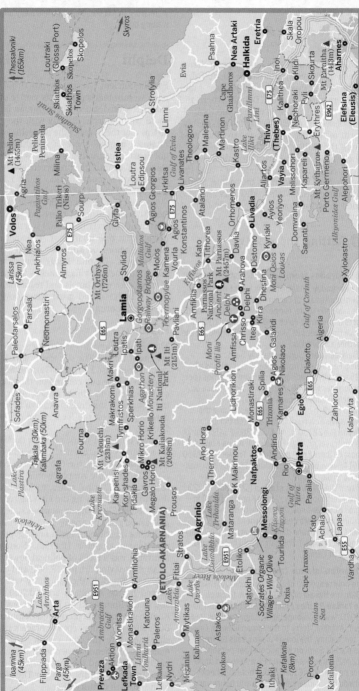

THE DELPHIC ORACLE

The Delphic oracle ranked high among the sacred sites of Ancient Greece. Devotees flocked from far and wide to ask for the guidance of Apollo in making decisions. Wars were fought, colonies created, marriages sealed, leaders chosen and journeys begun on the strength of the oracle's advice.

Surprisingly little is known about how the oracle actually functioned. Apollo's instrument of communication, the Pythia (priestess), was usually an older woman, and sat on a tripod in his temple. Although there's no evidence for the suggestion that she inhaled vapours from cracks or chasms in the rocks below the sanctuary, she certainly made her prophesies in a trance-like state.

The Pythia's pronouncements were notorious for their ambiguity, which left recipients to choose how they should be interpreted. Thus Croesus of Lydia was told that he would 'destroy a great empire' if he invaded Persia, but the empire that was destroyed was his own. Similarly, the Athenians were advised to trust their 'wooden walls' to defend against the Persians, but it took Themistocles to decide that the 'walls' in question were actually their ships.

One priestess suffered for her vagueness. When Alexander the Great dropped by, hoping to learn that his destiny was to conquer the world, the priestess refused direct comment, and asked that he return later. Enraged, he dragged her from the chamber by the hair, until she screamed, 'Let go of me; you're unbeatable!' He quickly dropped her, saying, 'I have my answer.'

By the 7th century, a new village, Kastri, had taken over the site. It remained atop the ruins until late in the 19th century, when its inhabitants were paid to relocate to the newly constructed village of Delphi, allowing archaeologists to unearth the ancient site.

◉ Sights

Ancient Delphi   ARCHAEOLOGICAL SITE
(Map p215; http://ancient-greece.org/history/delphi.html) Of all Greece's archaeological sites, Ancient Delphi has the most potent spirit of place. Centring on the mountainside Sanctuary of Apollo, home to the ancient world's most renowned oracle, this sacred spot was never a city. To this day, the haunting ruins – a short walk east of the modern town – look out over an unbroken expanse of olive trees, sloping down to the Gulf of Corinth.

As well as the sanctuary itself, the site also includes the Delphi Archaeological Museum (p214; entry is by the same ticket, on successive days if you prefer), and the nearby Sanctuary of Athena Pronaia (p214; to which access is free.

★ **Sanctuary of Apollo**   ARCHAEOLOGICAL SITE
(Map p215; ☑ 22650 82313; http://odysseus.culture.gr; combined ticket for site & Delphi Archaeological Museum adult/student/child €12/6/free; ⊙ 8am-8pm May-Sep, 8.30am-7pm Apr & Oct, 8.30am-3pm Nov-Mar) The hillside Sanctuary of Apollo, 750m east of the village, was the heart of the Delphic oracle. The Sacred Way, the path that climbs to its centrepiece

Temple of Apollo, was lined in ancient times by treasuries and statues, erected by city-states including Athens and Sparta to thank Apollo and assert their own wealth and might. Some stand complete, most lie in ruins, but together they form a magnificent spectacle.

To avoid the summer heat (and year-round crowds), aim to visit early morning or late afternoon, allowing at least an hour to explore the site in full. Whenever you visit, be sure to check opening times ahead, as hours can vary.

After entering the sanctuary at its lowest point, beside the main road, you set off up the Sacred Way, laid out in its modern form by 19th-century archaeologists. The first of several stone pedestals you reach, on your right, held the Bull of Kerkyra (Corfu). Just beyond it, on the left, are the remains of the Spartan Victory Monument (an offering to the admiral Lysander). The next two semicircular structures, to either side of the path, were erected by the Argives (people of Argos), while the Kings of Argos Monument stood to their right. Further on sits a small conical stone known as the Omphalos, the navel of the ancient Greek world.

Northeast of the reconstructed Athenian Treasury stands a portion of the column that supported the Sphinx of Naxos, displayed in the museum (p214). Near it, find the Rock of the Sibyl, where Delphi's earliest prophetess made her predictions. A few steps away, behind three columns from the

Stoa of the Athenians, the remarkable Polygonal Wall once supported the terrace of the second Temple of Apollo (548 BCE). Look closely, and you'll realise it's covered with minutely carved inscriptions.

As the home of Apollo himself, the **Temple of Apollo** dominated the entire sanctuary. Its surviving incarnation, from the 4th century BCE, contained a statue of the god, guarded by an eternal flame, and was where the Pythia, the god's mouthpiece, delivered her pronouncements. Its vestibule bore the so-called Delphic Maxims, including 'Know Thyself' and 'Nothing in Excess', which Socrates mentioned in Plato's *Protagoras*. Congregations gathered not inside the temple, but out in the open air.

Immediately east, the replica of the **Serpentine Column**, or Tripod of the Plataeans, was erected in 2015. The original bronze column commemorated the Greeks who defeated the Persian Empire at the Battle of Plataea (479 BCE). Removed by Constantine the Great in 324 CE, it now resides at the Hippodrome of Constantinople, in modern İstanbul.

Above the temple, the well-preserved 4th-century-BCE **theatre** was restored by Pergamene king Loukumenes II during the 2nd century BCE. Plays were performed here during the Pythian Festival, staged every four years. The views from the top row are breathtaking.

A path continues up to the **stadium**, but access is currently closed due to recent rockslides. Etched-in-stone starting blocks still stand at the eastern end of the 200m sprinting track, levelled out from the mountainside.

East of the Sanctuary of Apollo, a paved path parallel to the main road leads to the **Castalian Spring**, where pilgrims cleansed themselves before consulting the oracle.

★ **Delphi Archaeological Museum** MUSEUM
(Map p215; ☑22650 82312; http://odysseus. culture.gr; combined ticket for museum & site adult/student/child €12/6/free; ☉8am-8pm May-Sep, 8.30am-4pm Apr & Oct, 8.30am-3pm Nov-Mar) Delphi's magnificent modern museum, 500m east of town, perfectly complements the ancient site (p213) alongside. Which you visit first doesn't matter, but the treasures collected here will bring your image of ancient Delphi to life. Rich and powerful petitioners flocked to Delphi from the 8th century BCE onwards, bringing fabulous gifts and erecting opulent monuments. Unearthed by archaeologists, these now fill a succession of mind-blowing galleries.

Be sure to check the museum's opening times ahead, as hours can vary.

Standout highlights include the matching pair of *kouroi* (larger-than-life statues of young men) in room 3, known as the **Twins of Argos**; and the **Sphinx of the Naxians**, which towers over room 5. Bearing the face of a woman, the body of a lion, and the wings of a bird, the sphinx was donated by the island of Naxos, and originally topped a mighty column near the Athenian Treasury. Nearby, the well-preserved marble frieze from the Siphnian Treasury depicts the battle between the gods and the giants in extraordinary three-dimensional detail.

Look for the tall **Coiumn of Dancers** in room 11, with three women dancing around its top. The **omphalos** alongside, a cone sculpted as though wrapped in a woollen net, may have stood at the summit of the column, and takes the form of the Delphi omphalos that marked the centre of the world.

The greatest wonder of all is reserved for the final room (13). Focused yet calm, the **Bronze Charioteer** commemorates a victory in the Pythian Games of 478 or 474 BCE. Very few such life-size bronze statues have survived; this one did because it was buried by an earthquake a century later.

Sanctuary of Athena Pronaia ARCHAEOLOGICAL SITE
(☉24hr) FREE For ancient pilgrims, Delphi's first stop was the Sanctuary of Athena Pronaia, now set just below the road 800m east of the Sanctuary of Apollo. This lovely spot is best known as home to the superbly photogenic **Tholos**, a graceful circular structure of unknown purpose that dates from the 4th century BCE. Three of the 20 columns that stood on its three-stepped podium were re-erected in the 1940s; the white portions are original marble, the darker are new. Fragments of the Tholos are on display in room 10 of the Delphi Archaeological Museum.

Immediately west, only the foundations now survive of the **Temple of Athena Pronaia** itself.

Folklore Museum of Chrisso MUSEUM
(☑22650 83203; Chrisso; ☉Tue-Sun 9am-3pm) FREE An imposing mansion and former school in the traditional village of Chrisso, 6km southwest of Delphi by road, now holds an enjoyable museum of local life. Fronted by colourful citrus trees, it shows off 19th-century costumes including a man's skirt with 400 pleats to symbolise 400 years of Ottoman rule, along with jewellery, pistols, paintings and photographs.

Delphi Town

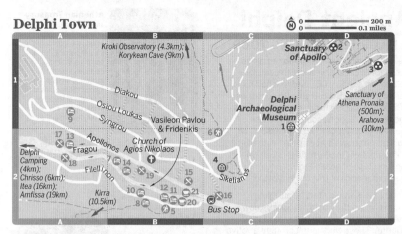

N 0 — 200 m
0 — 0.1 miles

Delphi Town

◎ Top Sights
1 Delphi Archaeological Museum C1
2 Sanctuary of Apollo D1

◎ Sights
3 Ancient Delphi D1
4 Sikelianos Museum C2

⊙ Activities, Courses & Tours
Christina Stoli .... (see 3)
5 Delphi to Ancient Kirra Walk B2
6 Delphi to Kroki Viewpoint Walk C2
George Malissos .... (see 3)
Georgia Hasioti .... (see 3)
Penny Kolomvotsou .... (see 3)

⊖ Sleeping
7 Fedriades Hotel B2

8 Hotel Acropole B2
9 Hotel Apollonia A1
10 Hotel Hermes B2
11 Hotel Sibylla B2
12 Kastalia Hotel B2
13 Nidimos Hotel A2
14 Rooms Pitho B2

⊗ Eating
15 Dionysos Souvlaki B2
16 In Delphi C2
17 Taverna Gargadouas A2
18 Taverna To Patriko Mas A2
19 Taverna Vakhos B2

◎ Drinking & Nightlife
20 Café Apollon B2
21 Melopoleio Cafe B2

Sikelianos Museum   MUSEUM
(Delphic Festivals Museum; Map p215; ☎ 22650 82175; www.eccd.gr; cnr Sikelianos & Diakou; €1; ⊗8am-3pm; P) Fans of Greek drama should head to this intimate 1920s mansion-turned-museum, which overlooks Delphi both ancient and modern. It's dedicated to Greek poet Angelos Sikelianos and his American-born wife Eva Palmer, who jointly reinvented Delphi as a modern Greek centre for drama and the arts. The museum displays intriguing photos of their attempts to recreate ancient festivals.

🕴 Activities

Three popular day hikes, all following segments of the E4 European long-distance path, start and end at Delphi. Choose between walking all the way up to the mysterious Korykeon Cave; just going as far as the dramatic Kroki Viewpoint (p218); or heading downhill to the sea and the ancient port of Kirra (p218). Local guides offering hiking tours include Giorgos Korodimos at Trekking Hellas (p221) in Arahova.

Korykeon Cave Walk   HIKING
The Korykeon Cave, 800m above Delphi on the Parnassian slopes, is probably where the ancient prophetic cult first originated. The exhilarating E4 trail climbs all the way up, but it's a gruelling all-day hike – four hours up, perhaps less to come down – so many visitors take a taxi to a point 2km from the cave (around €30), then hike back.

While the entrance to the cavern is surprisingly small, it opens into a vast natural amphitheatre, filled with stalactites and stalagmites, that was sacred to Pan and his nymphs. Look out for eerie formations and ancient inscriptions carved into the rock.

Ancient Delphi

A PILGRIM'S WALKING TOUR

Delphi's **Sanctuary of Apollo** remained in use for over 1200 years (8th century BCE to 4th century CE), and reached its height between the 6th and 4th centuries BCE. While the site today consists of ruins and reconstructions scattered across the beautiful slopes of Mt Parnassus, our illustration shows it at its peak. With a bit of imagination, modern visitors can walk in the footsteps of past pilgrims, and re-create their experience of this ancient place.

Worshippers would start by purifying themselves in the Castalian Spring (now closed to the public), then pay a pelanos (tribute). Those who hadn't brought a votive offering would buy one from ❶ **The Roman Market**, before setting off up the the ❷ **Sacred Way** towards the Temple of Apollo.

The sanctuary was adorned throughout with statues, sculptures and monuments dedicated to Apollo. In particular, victorious city-states would erect temple-like structures such as the ❸ **Athenian Treasury**, and fill them with the spoils of war. The nearby ❹ **omphalos** (navel stone), symbolising Delphi's status as the centre of the earth, was left by archaeologists where it was found.

Next, visitors pass the ❺ **Rock of the Sibyl** before arriving at the Stoa of the Athenians, behind which rises the amazing ❻ **polygonal wall**. Finally, they arrived at the ❼ **Temple of Apollo** at the sanctuary's core. It was here that consultations with the oracle took place, and the chants of the Pythia (priestess) were interpreted by the priests of Apollo. The ❽ **theatre** above the temple staged drama, music and poetry competitions.

TOP TIPS

➡ Visit in the morning or late after-noon to beat the heat and crowds.

➡ Wear comfortable shoes and a hat, and bring drinking water.

➡ Opening hours are subject to change, so check ahead.

➡ Don't miss the Delphi Museum, which helps to contextualise the site.

➡ Your ticket allows you to visit the sanctuary and museum on successive days.

Athenian Treasury
The impressive Athenian Treasury is among the sanctuary's most important buildings. Built to commemorate the Athenians' victory against the Persians at the battle of Marathon in 490 BCE, it was reconstructed in the early 1900s.

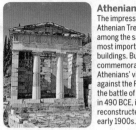

Omphalos
Delphi was considered the omphalos (navel) of the world. There was another omphalos in the adyton (temple chamber) where the Pythia pronounced her oracles.

Siphnian Treasury

The Bouleuterion

The Sacred Way
The Sacred Way (so-named by modern archae-ologists) leads to the Temple of Apollo. It was lined with monuments, statues and treasuries that commemorated victories (usually in war, sometimes the Pythian Games).

To Delphi Museum

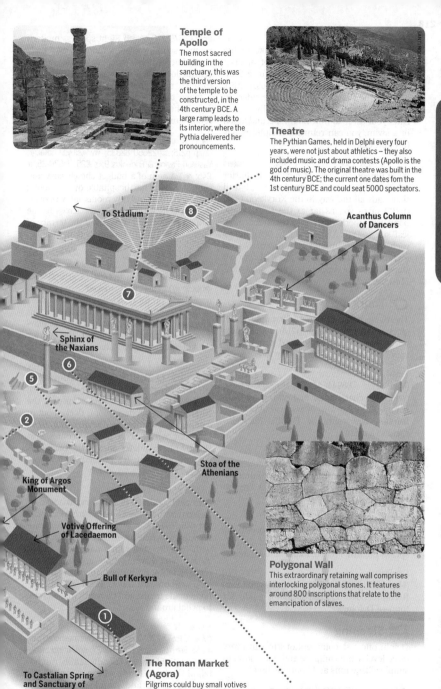

Temple of Apollo
The most sacred building in the sanctuary, this was the third version of the temple to be constructed, in the 4th century BCE. A large ramp leads to its interior, where the Pythia delivered her pronouncements.

Theatre
The Pythian Games, held in Delphi every four years, were not just about athletics – they also included music and drama contests (Apollo is the god of music). The original theatre was built in the 4th century BCE; the current one dates fom the 1st century BCE and could seat 5000 spectators.

To Stadium

Acanthus Column of Dancers

Sphinx of the Naxians

King of Argos Monument

Votive Offering of Lacedaemon

Stoa of the Athenians

Bull of Kerkyra

Polygonal Wall
This extraordinary retaining wall comprises interlocking polygonal stones. It features around 800 inscriptions that relate to the emancipation of slaves.

To Castalian Spring and Sanctuary of Athena Pronaia

The Roman Market (Agora)
Pilgrims could buy small votives and offerings here. Wealthier and more powerful visitors, however, brought statues and valuable items from afar. The remains of many of these are in the Delphi Museum.

Rock of the Sibyl
Legend has it that this marks the spot where the first sibyl (an elderly prophetess, not to be confused with the later Pythia), stood to declare Delphi's earliest oracle.

Delphi to Ancient Kirra Walk HIKING

(Map p215) The 14km downhill hike to the ancient port of Kirra, just east of modern Itea, starts from the E4 long-distance trailhead 100m east of the Hotel Acropole (p219). Skirting the village of Crissa, it meanders to the gulf through Greece's largest olive grove. After your three-to-four-hour hike, and lunch or a swim, you can return to Delphi by bus (around €2).

Delphi to Kroki Viewpoint Walk HIKING

(Kroki Observatory Walk; Map p215) A shorter hike up the same well-signposted E4 trail that leads all the way to the Korykeon Cave (p215) takes you as far as the Kroki Viewpoint for superb views over the archaeological site (p213). Allow roughly 90 minutes each way (4km up and 4km down). Set off – carrying water – up the *kako skala* (evil steps) opposite upper Delphi's Sikelianos Museum (p215).

Tours

There's no better way to understand the full glory of Ancient Delphi (p213) than to take a tour with an expert licensed guide. Rates vary with tour length and group size.

Penny Kolomvotsou WALKING

(Map p215; ☑ 6944644427; kpagona@hotmail. com) The charismatic and ultrapassionate Penny Kolomvotsou offers excellent English-language tours of Delphi. She also speaks German.

George Malissos WALKING

(Map p215; ☑ 6948181084; www.delphilocaltours. gr) A trained archaeologist, this recommended guide for tours of Delphi speaks English and French.

Georgia Hasioti WALKING

(Map p215; ☑ 6944943511; www.delphi-guide.gr) Recommended guide for tours of Delphi; speaks English, French, Italian and Japanese.

Christina Stoli WALKING

(Map p215; ☑ 6944987411; xristolh@gmail.com) Recommended English-speaking guide for tours of Delphi.

🛏 Sleeping

Delphi offers sleeping options to suit every price level, from camping and bungalows to simple village inns and boutique hotels.

★ Rooms Pitho PENSION €

(Map p215; ☑ 22650 82850; www.pithohotel.gr; Vasileon Pavlou & Friderikis 40a; s/d/tr incl breakfast from €45/55/70; ☒ 🛜) Eight spotless modern rooms, soundproofed windows, extremely charming owners, excellent service and a central location – halfway along the main through road, above the family's gift shop – make these peaceful homestyle lodgings a great budget pick. The cheaper 'economy' rooms are on the small side.

★ Hotel Sibylla HOTEL €

(Map p215; ☑ 22650 82335; www.sibylla-hotel.gr; Vasileon Pavlou & Friderikis 9; s €25, d €30-35, tr €45; 🛜) A gem of a budget choice, cosy and central, Sibylla has hospitable owners along with eight light and tidy rooms, all with overhead fans. Several have views across to the gulf. Breakfast isn't served, but the terrace of Café Apollon (p220) is directly downstairs.

Delphi Camping CAMPGROUND €

(☑ 22650 82209; www.delphicamping.com; camp sites per person/tent/car €7.50/5.50/4.50; 🄿@🛜🏊) This well-stocked campground occupies a pretty wooded setting 4km west of Delphi, with a swimming pool looking out over the olive trees to the gulf, plus safe playground equipment. Watch out, though, for the killer entrance on a sharp corner.

Nidimos Hotel HOTEL €

(Map p215; ☑ 22650 82056; www.nidimoshotel. gr; Dimou Fragkou 10; s/d/tr from €41/52/71; 🄿❄🛜) One of Delphi's sleeker options, the Nidimos offers modern rooms decked out in contemporary taupes and whites. Rooms at the front, which boast large balconies, cost slightly more; quieter ones at the back look out onto wall art. It's popular with school groups.

Fedriades Hotel HOTEL €

(Map p215; ☑ 22650 82370; www.fedriades.com; Vasileon Pavlou & Friderikis 46; s/d/tr/ste incl breakfast €45/55/65/130; @🛜) Smart modern hotel with balconies over Delphi's main road, with friendly staff and small, neat, bright rooms, plus a swank suite and a spacious, relaxing lobby. Enthusiastic owner Babis will help with onward routes. Breakfast includes homemade treats, and there are free bicycles to pedal around.

Hotel Hermes HOTEL €

(Map p215; ☑ 22650 82318; www.hermeshotel.com. gr; Vasileon Pavlou & Friderikis 27; s/d/tr incl breakfast €40/45/55; ❄🛜) Friendly family-run hotel, in the heart of the village, where all the wood-shuttered and marble-floored rooms have balconies facing the gulf. Views from the breakfast room and terrace are splendid. Book direct for the best rates.

WORTH A TRIP

PARNASSOS NATIONAL PARK

Towering northwards above Delphi and Arahova, Mt Parnassos was sacred to the gods Dionysos and Apollo. The modern Parnassos National Park (☎22340 23529; http://en.parnassosnp.gr) holds three peaks more than 2300m high: Parnassos itself (2457m), Tsarkos (2416m) and Gerondovrachos (2396m). The slopes support Kefallonian fir, spruce and juniper, interspersed with yellow-flowered shrubs, plum trees and the rare purple-flowered Daphne jasminea. Kouvelos (1882m) is a popular rock-climbing face.

The Parnassos Ski Centre, 24km by road from Arahova, handles ski and snow-board operations on Kelaria (1950m) and the steeper slopes of Fterolakkas, popular with extreme skiers. For more information, see www.snowreport.gr/parnassos/indexen.html and www.skiresort.info/ski-resorts/mount-parnassos.

The E4 European long-distance path (*orivatiko monopati*), which leads from Gibraltar to Cyprus, crosses Mt Parnassos; the path is administered by the European Ramblers Association (www.era-ewv-ferp.com).

For accommodation, it's best to stay in Arahova. No public transport connects Arahova with the ski centre, but a taxi from Delphi or Arahova costs around €50.

CENTRAL GREECE DELPHI

Kastalia Hotel   BOUTIQUE HOTEL €€

(Map p215; ☎22650 82205; www.kastaliahotel.gr; Vasileon Pavlou & Friderikis 13; s/d/tr/ste incl breakfast from €50/75/85/110; ❄@🛜) Named for the ancient spring nearby, the Kastalia is a recent addition to Delphi's upscale lodging scene. Rooms are large and smartly decorated, with comfortable beds, modern bathrooms and balconies overlooking the gulf. The hotel has its own restaurant (Elia) where the owner's Cypriot roots show up in several recipes.

Hotel Acropole   HOTEL €€

(Map p215; ☎22650 82675; www.delphi.com.gr; Filellinon 13; s/d/tr incl breakfast €52/60/88; ❄🛜) On the quiet street that runs parallel to the main drag, the Acropole has decent, spacious rooms with wooden and wrought-iron fittings. Most rooms are at the back; the higher you go, the better the uninterrupted views down to the gulf and over the hiking path that sets off downhill to ancient Kirra from nearby.

Hotel Apollonia   HOTEL €€

(Map p215; ☎22650 82919; www.hotelapollonia.gr; Syngrou 37-39; s/d/ste incl breakfast from €90/100/200; 🅿❄🛜) Tucked away on Delphi's upper Syngrou street – a bit of a climb if you're on foot – this relatively upscale option has an intimate feel. Rooms are on the dated-modern side, with dark-wood furnishings, carpet, large bathrooms and balcony views across Delphi.

Eating

Delphi has a wide assortment of restaurants. Some of the lazier places settle for doling out unremarkable food to busloads of day-trippers, but several worthy exceptions serve tasty local cuisine.

Dionysos Souvlaki   GREEK €

(Map p215; Apollonos 28; mains €2.50-7; ⏱11am-11pm) Great-value budget diner run by a family that conscientiously and efficiently whips up tasty dishes such as well-prepared souvlaki and Greek salads, to eat in or take away.

Taverna Gargadouas   TAVERNA €

(Map p215; ☎22650 82488; Vasileon Pavlou & Friderikis; mains €6-9.50; ⏱1-11pm) Welcoming, no-frills traditional taverna at the west end of the village; it makes a snug retreat from the tourist crowds. Daily specials can include *provatina* (slow-roasted lamb), but on the whole it's the grilled meats that keep bringing the locals back. Good value, but slightly disorganised.

★Taverna Vakhos   TAVERNA €€

(Map p215; ☎22650 83186; Apollonos 31; mains €8-16; ⏱noon-10.30pm; 🛜🅿) Delphi's best restaurant, this exceptional place uses fresh local ingredients and mountain herbs. Along with generous salads and hearty lamb and rooster dishes, the menu includes delicious veggie options ranging from *horta* (wild greens) to *trachanopita* (a savoury 'frumenty pie' of cracked wheat, zucchini and feta). Reserve for dinner; lunch tends to be less busy.Located on the upper one-way road.

Taverna To Patriko Mas   GREEK €€

(Map p215; ☎22650 82150; Vasileon Pavlou & Friderikis 69; mains €9-21; ⏱lunch & dinner; ❄🛜) Set in a 19th-century stone building, this smart restaurant opens into a large rear room with

ANCIENT THEBES

Modern **Thiva** stands on the site of ancient Thebes, the birthplace of Hercules and Dionysos. Emerging as the dominant power in the Boeotia region after the Trojan War, Thebes occupied a crucial strategic location between northern Greece and the Peloponnese, and grew by 400 BCE to rank among the greatest city-states of all. It's famed as the setting for the tragedy of Oedipus, fated to kill his father and marry his mother. The city's glorious run ended in 335 BCE, however, when it was sacked by Alexander the Great for siding with the Persians.

Thiva today has little to show for its past glory, apart from the exhibits in its excellent **archaeological museum** (☑22620 23559, 22620 27913; www.mthv.gr; Plateia Keramopoulou, Threpsiadon 1, Thiva; adult/student/child €6/3/free; ⊙8am-8pm Tue-Sun mid-Apr–Oct, to 3pm Tue-Sun Nov–mid-Apr; Ⓟ). The town centre though, filled with cafes, is an enjoyable place to explore.

Buses operate to Athens (€8.80, one hour, hourly until 8.30pm) from Thiva's **central bus station** (☑22620 27511; www.ktelthivas.gr; Estias 10, Thiva), 1km south of the museum. Trains from **Thiva station** (☑22620 27531; www.trainose.gr; Tiresiou & Kiriakou, Thiva; ⊙7am-11pm), 800m north of the museum, depart for Athens (normal/Intercity €8.10/15.20, 65 minutes/one hour, six or seven daily) and Thessaloniki (€27.80/48.10, 4½/3½ hours, four or five daily).

panoramic views, and also has an outdoor patio. Something of a place to linger in, it offers unusual salads and generous mezedhes, plus dishes including savoury pie with leek and pork, and rabbit with mustard and tarragon. Fine all-Greek wine list.

🍷 Drinking & Nightlife

Melopoleio Cafe　　　　CAFE
(Map p215; ☑22650 83247; Vasileon Pavlou & Friderikis 14; ⊙7am-midnight; 🛜) Smart little cafe on the inland side of the main through road, with a cosy interior plus streetside watch-the-world-go-by seating. Over the course of the day, it morphs from serving espresso drinks, teas from local herbs and fresh juices, via savoury pies, into an afternoon sandwich and ice-cream stop, and then an evening wine bar with signature cocktails.

Café Apollon　　　　COFFEE
(Map p215; ☑22650 82842; Vasileon Pavlou & Friderikis 9; ⊙7am-late; 🛜) A happy blend of old and new, Apollon is a charming, traditional *kafeneio* (coffeehouse) on the inside, coupled with a broad tiled terrace with stunning views. Linger over a great-value breakfast, coffees and snacks.

❶ Information

Delphi has no tourist office, but there's a staffed exhibition space at the town hall.

Amfissa Hospital (☑22650 72010, 22650 22222; www.gnamfissas.gr; 112i) The nearest hospital to Delphi (20km west).

Pharmacy (☑22650 82700; Apollonos 18; ⊙9am-1.30pm & 6-9pm) For first aid and minor medical matters.

❶ Getting There & Away

Buses (Map p215; ☑22650 82317; www.ktel-fokidas.gr; Vasileon Pavlou & Friderikis) depart from the eastern end of Vasileon Pavlou and Friderikis, outside the **In Delphi** (Map p215; ☑22650 82230; http://indelphi.weebly.com; Apollonos 8; mains €5-12.50; ⊙breakfast, lunch & dinner; 🌂🛜) restaurant, which sells tickets daily between 9am and 8pm (the time of the last bus). Buy tickets for early buses the day before, especially in high season. It's best to travel to Kalambaka/Meteora via Lamia and Trikala, rather than Larissa.

DESTINATION	DURATION	FARE (€)	FREQUENCY
Amfissa	30mins	2.20	6 daily
Arahova	20mins	1.80	4 daily
Athens	2½hrs	16.40	4 daily
Galaxidi	45mins	3.80	2-3 daily
Itea	30mins	2	6-7 daily
Lamia	2hrs	9.90	daily
Larissa	3½hrs	23.70	daily
Livadia	55mins	4.50	4-5 daily
Nafpaktos	2½hrs	13.40	1-2 daily
Patra	3½hrs	14.80	daily (except Sat)
Thessaloniki	4½hrs	38	daily

For Thiva, take the bus to Athens and change at Livadia.

ℹ Getting Around

The main road through Delphi divides into two one-way sections. The lower route, running west–east and named Vasileon Pavlou and Friderikis, holds most of the village's commercial activity; more hotels and restaurants line the east–west Apollonos, parallel and slightly higher. Steep stairways connect these two roads, and also the much quieter Filellinon just below.

The ancient site (p213) and museum (p214) are an enjoyable 500m walk east of the village, around a curve in the road.

Arahova   Αράχωβα

POP 3300

The small town of Arahova, just 8km east of Delphi, is largely geared towards Greek winter travellers, especially skiers hitting the slopes of Parnassos National Park (p219). Set on a rocky spur of Mt Parnassos at an altitude of 960m, it's a charming little place that makes a good alternative base for Delphi visitors. Stepped alleyways lead away from the commercialised through road into cobbled backstreets, while the historical 'clock on the rock', an impressive stone clock tower, surveys the mountainside from below the imposing former town hall.

Touristy shops along the main road sell embroidery, bags and *flokati* (shaggy woollen rugs), while Arahova is also noted for its *formaela* cheese, honey, *hilopites* (fettuccine-style pasta) and hearty red wine.

☞ Tours

Trekking Hellas   HIKING
(☑ 22670 31901; www.trekking.gr) Contact multilingual local hiking expert Giorgos Korodimos for guided treks around Parnassos, including Delphi's legendary Korykeon Cave (p215).

⛷ Festivals & Events

Festival of Agios Georgios   CARNIVAL
(☑ 22670 32091; ⊕ Apr) Known locally as 'Panigiraki', this joyous three-day celebration takes place around 23 April (though if that date falls during Lent, it's postponed until Easter Tuesday). Almost everyone in town wears traditional Greek dress. Highlights include dancing and singing, a tug-of-war contest and, on the last day, feasting on roasted lamb, all compliments of the town, wine included.

🛏 Sleeping

During ski season, the peak time to visit Arahova, room rates can be as much as double those in summer.

Hotel Likoria   HOTEL €€
(☑ 22670 31180; www.likoria.gr; Venizelou; s/d/tr incl breakfast from €60/75/95; P ✳ @ 🔊) The plush Likoria has the feel of a country inn. Its traditional rooms have carpets, huge soft beds and French windows opening to large balconies. The quiet location, sweeping valley views from the breakfast terrace, and friendly English-speaking staff are pluses. It's located one block above the main road, near the Spar supermarket 250m northwest of the town centre.

Alexandros Guesthouse   B&B €€
(☑ 22670 32884; www.alexandrosgr.com; r from €90; ⊕ Sep–mid-May; ✳ 🔊) Each of the five rooms in this upscale mansion, just off the main square, is named and themed for a constellation, and comes with a high-tech spa-type shower. Targeted primarily at ski-season visitors, rooms are kept cosy by open fireplaces.

Pension Maria   PENSION €€
(Xenonas Maria; ☑ 6976879205, 22670 31803; Solomou; d €55-75, tr €75; 🔊) This backstreet pension spreads through two charming but somewhat faded old houses, located up an alleyway that leads off the main road near Zampas (☑ 22670 31048; Delphon; ⊕ 8am-midnight; 🔊) cafe. There are seven split-level rooms filled with red carpets, antiques and stonework. Expect a warm welcome from Yiannis and Nikos, Maria's sons.

🍴 Eating

★ Dasargiris Taverna   TAVERNA €€
(☑ 22670 31291; Delphon 56; mains €7.50-16; ⊕ lunch & dinner) Outstanding traditional taverna, with a big open kitchen and vintage skis on the wall. House favourites include *hilopites* (local pasta), *horta* (wild greens), aubergine with garlic, and slow-roasted lamb with lemon and rosemary. Nothing is frozen.

Parnassos Taverna   TAVERNA €€
(☑ 22670 32569; Plateia Xenias; dishes €7-14; ⊕ lunch & dinner Thu-Tue; P ✳) Popular and dependable taverna on Plateia Xenias, alongside the post office (Plateia Xenias; ⊕ 7.30am-2pm Mon-Fri) and slightly above the taxi rank. Open year-round, with well-prepared *mayirefta* (ready-cooked dishes), good grills and jug wine.

❶ Getting There & Away

The daily buses that run between Athens' Liasion station and Delphi (€16.40, 2½ hours) stop at Arahova's **KTEL Bus Station** (www.ktel-fokidas. gr; Plateia Xenias). The direct Delphi–Arahova bus costs €1.80 and takes 20 minutes.

Amfissa   Άμφισσα

POP 6900

The town of Amfissa sits in the foothills 21km northwest of Delphi, on the road towards Lamia. A significant centre in antiquity, it was sacked in 338 BCE by Philip of Macedon. Under the Turks it became known as Salona, but reverted to its original name after playing a crucial role during the Greek War of Independence against Ottoman rule. Now the capital of the Municipality of Delphi, it's a sleepy but charming place that lies off the usual tourist path.

◎ Sights

Moni Profiti Ilia   CONVENT

(☉8am-2pm & 4pm-sunset; P) **FREE** East of Amfissa towards Delphi, the 19th-century convent of Moni Profiti Ilia rests on a hillside with superb views across the olive groves to the Gulf of Corinth. Essaeas, the bishop of Salona (Amfissa), raised the flag of revolution here on 24 March 1821. The turn-off is marked with a small cross and '3KM' sign, which also serves as a makeshift bulletin board. Sunday-morning masses are highlighted by the singing of the nuns.

Note: the convent has a strict dress code. Definitely no shorts for men or women.

Archaeological Museum of Amfissa   MUSEUM

(☑22650 23344; http://odysseus.culture.gr; Kechagia 2; adult/child €2/free; ☉9am-4pm Wed-Sun; P) This handsome museum, housed in an impressive mansion, holds a wonderful assortment of local finds dating from the Bronze Age to the early Byzantine period. Besides regional history, focusing on the ancient port of Kirra, it provides good coverage of all aspects of ancient life. Highlights include miniature marionettes, coin and precoin exchange displays, and a super Corinthian helmet from around 500 BCE.

⏹ Sleeping & Eating

Amfissa only offers limited accommodation; nearby alternatives include Delphi, or Galaxidi on the coast.

Steki tou Kalofaga   TAVERNA €

(☑22650 23322; Plateia Kehagia; pitta snacks €2-7.50; ☉5pm-1am; ✺) This popular evening-only restaurant on Amfissa's upper square serves up tasty souvlaki and other meaty snacks, plus good salads.

Kaisaras   GREEK €

(Caesar's; ☑22650 22007; Salonon 2; souvlaki & snacks €2-7; ☉lunch & dinner) Amfissa's go-to option for souvlaki, char-grilled meat, fresh potatoes and salads. Half a block off Plateia Isaia, west of the taxi rank.

🍷 Drinking & Nightlife

Although the central Plateia Isaia holds some decent cafe-bars, it's more rewarding to walk 200m northwest to Plateia Kehagia (aka *plateia pano,* or upper square), which

---

DON'T MISS

A MAGNIFICENT MONASTERY

The Moni Osios Loukas (Μονή Οσίου Λουκά; Monastery of St Luke; ☑22670 22228; www. osiosloukas.gr; €4; ☉8.30am-4pm), a World Heritage site, overlooks a remote valley 23km southeast of Arahova, between the villages of Distomo and Kyriaki.

Dedicated to a 10th-century hermit canonised for his healing and prophetic powers, its principal church, Agios Loukas, is a glorious symphony of marble and mosaics, with icons by Michael Damaskinos, the 16th-century Cretan painter. Opaque marble screens create striking contrasts of light and shade, while fine frescoes adorn the crypt where Loukas lies entombed.

The monks' former living quarters hold historical displays, while a shop adjoining the spacious scenic terrace outside sells simple snacks. Modest dress is required (no shorts).

To get here from Delphi, you'll need your own transport or a taxi. Taxis from Delphi cost €50 return (20 minutes each way); they're €20 return from Distomo or €30 from Livadia. Taxis will normally wait one hour; arrange the price before you set off.

has a lively mix of cafes and *ouzeries* (places serving ouzo and light snacks) and plenty of outside seating.

★ **Megalo Kafeneio 1929**　　　CAFE
(☑ 6948245729; Plateia Kehagia; ⏰ 24hr; 🛜) Now a round-the-clock bohemian hang-out, often cloudy with cigarette smoke, this grand vintage cafe featured in the classic 1975 Greek movie *The Travelling Players*. Its small stage features live jazz and comedy.

❶ Getting There & Away

The **bus stop** (KTEL; ☑ 22650 29900; www. ktel-fokidas.gr; Karaogiorgou at Karamanli) connects Amfissa to Delphi (€2.20, 30 minutes, six daily), Athens (€18.70, three hours, four daily), Lamia (€7.70, 1½ hours, two daily) and Patra (€14.10, three hours, one to two daily).

Galaxidi　　　Γαλαξίδι

POP 2010

The prettiest resort along the Gulf of Corinth, little Galaxidi curves around a seafront hillock, with narrow cobblestone streets connecting the well-sheltered harbours to either side. The older harbour was a major shipbuilding centre during the 19th century, a prosperous era when the town acquired its fine crop of stone mansions. It's known locally as Hirolakas, or 'Widows' Port', remembering the wives who waited in vain for seamen husbands whose ships never came home.

The other harbour, to the south, is lined with bars, cafes and fish restaurants. These look across a narrow channel to a forested headland, opposite the waterfront, that's fringed by walking paths and pebbled coves popular with swimmers.

Galaxidi makes an excellent – and cooler – alternative to staying in Delphi in summer. That said, its charm and tranquillity can be strained when carloads of Athenians descend during peak periods and holiday weekends.

◉ Sights

Nautical Historical Museum　　　MUSEUM
(☑ 22650 41795; Mouseio 4; adult/student/child €3/1/free; ⏰ 9am-3.30pm Tue-Sun) This small hillside museum documents Greek maritime history and Galaxidi's once-flourishing shipbuilding industry, via logbooks, archaeological finds, lots of paintings and miniature models, and some splendid carved wooden figureheads from the 19th century.

Downstairs you'll find a huge collection of naval-themed stamps from all over the world, plus a strange diorama depicting an underwater shipwreck.

Moni Metamorfosis of Sotiras　　　MONASTERY
The little 13th-century Byzantine-era Moni Metamorfosis of Sotiras stands amid olive groves and cypress trees, 4km directly inland from Galaxidi. This vantage point commands terrific views down to the Gulf of Corinth. To reach it, go under the flyover and continue straight ahead.

🛏 Sleeping

Galaxidi holds hotels and rentals to suit all budgets, with many of the finest located well back from the sea. In summer, several waterfront cafes also let rooms, but they're not great value, and tend to be noisy.

Hotel Galaxidi　　　HOTEL €
(☑ 22650 41850; www.hotelgalaxidi.gr; Sigrou 11; s/d/tr incl breakfast €40/60/70; 🅿 ❄ 🛜) Custard-coloured 32-room hotel in a sleepy backstreet 60m inland from the port, and thus lacking views. Friendly service, decent breakfast with homemade extras, plus balconies and basin sinks.

★ **Hotel Ganimede**　　　BOUTIQUE HOTEL €€
(☑ 22650 41328, 6937154567; www.ganimede.gr; Nikolaou Gourgouris 20; s/d incl breakfast €60/80, studios from €120; ❄ 🛜) Spreading through two buildings across a cosy courtyard, this friendly hotel offers large, tastefully decorated rooms. The nicest, in the original 19th-century mansion, have high ceilings, shiny wooden floors and period furniture. Owner Chrisoula lays on magnificent breakfasts, with homemade lemon curd and chutneys, and fresh pies from the family bakery. She also offers cooking classes.

Anneta House　　　APARTMENT €€
(☑ 6975869605; www.anneta-galaxidi-apartment. com; Nikolaou Mama 37; d/tr/q €75/80/85; 🅿 ❄ 🛜) Handsome, spacious rooms plus appealing touches including antiques and fresh flowers make Anneta an inviting spot. Owners Aspa and George are keen hosts. A common patio stays cool in summer; one apartment has its own private patio. Two-night minimum stay.

To Spitaki　　　PENSION €€
(☑ 22650 41257, 6977512238; www.tospitaki.com; 35 Nikolaou Mama; d/tr/f/ste incl breakfast €60-95/115/130/145; 🅿 ❄ 🛜) Its name meaning 'little house' in Greek, this converted 1830s stone *ouzerie* (ouzo bar) lends its name to three neighbouring properties of differing

sizes, halfway between the port and the main square. Each has a fully outfitted kitchen and pretty flower garden. Lovely ambience and a delightful, helpful owner, Stella.

Eating

Galaxidi is known for its excellent seafood. Start by comparing the enticing menus of the waterfront tavernas, but don't be afraid to go off piste to find some excellent back-street alternatives.

★ Skeletovrachos
TAVERNA €
(☑ 6987877263, 22650 41303; Akti Oianthis; mains €7.50-18; ⊙ lunch & dinner) Unassuming but outstanding restaurant towards the mouth of the port, where creative seafood dishes include shrimp with frumenty (cracked wheat); moussaka with cod; and truffle oil and their own smoked eel. The grilled fish, fairly priced by the kilo, is excellent too. Ask Dinos, the convivial and philosophical owner, about cooking lessons.

Albatross
TAVERNA €
(☑ 22650 42233; Konstadinou Satha 36; mains €6-8; ⊙ lunch Mon, lunch & dinner Tue-Sun) We love this little place, just along from Agios Nikolaos church, run by a long-standing, young-at-heart couple. Prices haven't changed in years and the generous offerings of mezedhes (try the dolmadhes, and *taramasalata*), along with a few oven-ready dishes, are always tasty.

★ Bebelis
GREEK €€
(☑ 22650 41677; Nikolaou Mama 20-22; mains €8-17.50; ⊙ 1-10.30pm Dec-Oct) Vintage village taverna with fresh flowers and lace curtains. Proud and convivial owner Bebelis offers a lovely go-slow dinner experience. There's a full bar, good wine, exceptional mezedhes, and local dishes including *lavraki* (sea bass) and *kelemnia* (stuffed onions).

Zygos
TAVERNA €€
(☑ 6945171359, 22653 01071; Akti Oianthis 115; mains €6.50-13; ⊙ 11am-late) The German beer mugs seem a little incongruous until you realise this small and inviting taverna, near the end of the port, serves more than 40 beers, plus assorted spirits. The food is good too, with fresh fish always on offer, as well as 'drunk pork hock', the priciest item on the menu; cooked slowly in beer, it's delicious.

Drinking & Nightlife

Ouzeries (places serving ouzo and light snacks) are sprinkled along the waterfront, while popular bars with later hours dot

Nikolaou Mama, the main street leading to the commercialised harbour.

ℹ Getting There & Away

Buses (☑ 22650 42087; www.ktel-fokidas.gr; Plateia Iroon, cnr Manousakia) connect Galaxidi with Delphi (€3.80, 45 minutes, three to four daily), Nafpaktos (€8, one hour, three to four daily), Athens (€20.30, 3½ hours, two to three daily) and Patra (€10.80, 1¾ hours, two to three daily).

Nafpaktos   Ναύπακτος
POP 13,400

Centring on a delightful, all-but-circular walled harbour built by the Venetians, the busy town of Nafpaktos stands 66km west of Galaxidi, just 11km east of the bridge (Rio–Andirio) that crosses the Gulf of Corinth to Patra in the Peloponnese. With a beach to either side – Psani, to the west, is better for swimming – it spreads up a hillside to a fine old castle, while the harbour area is scattered with trendy cafes and restaurants. There's a market every Saturday.

◉ Sights

Kastro
CASTLE
(€2; ⊙ 8am-3pm Tue-Sun) The well-preserved fortress and Venetian *kastro* that overlook Nafpaktos consist of a series of five terraced stone walls, built by successive conquerors (Doric, Roman, Byzantine, Venetian and Turk), that curl all the way down to the waterfront. It's well worth the climb, for both the walk and the views from the hill.

Fethiye Mosque
MOSQUE
(Fethiye Tzami; ⊙ open for special exhibitions only)
FREE The stunning Fethiye ('Conquest') Mosque, on the waterfront near the eastern side of the port, was built in 1499, shortly after the Ottoman Sultan Beyazid II captured Nafpaktos from the Venetians. It's only open for occasional temporary exhibitions.

Botsari Tower Museum
MUSEUM
(☑ 26340 29779; Botsareon; ⊙ 9am-1.30pm Mon-Fri) **FREE** The white-painted Venetian-style Tower of Botsaris, 100m northwest of the port square, holds this museum devoted to the 1571 Battle of Lepanto. It's a handsome mansion, but the displays are disappointing, consisting largely of low-quality reproductions of paintings and engravings by contemporary artists including Vasari and Tintoretto. Diagrams trace the course of the battle, while the prevailing imagery stresses

the role of divine intervention in the Christian victory. Ring the bell during opening hours; call ahead for weekend visits.

🛏 Sleeping & Eating

Hotel Akti
HOTEL €

(📞 26340 28464; www.akti.gr; Koridaleos 3, Gribovo Beach; s/d/tr/ste incl breakfast €40/45/55/110; 🅿 ❄ 🛜) The exterior of the Akti, in a leafy spot facing Nafpaktos' east-side beach, resembles a pastel colour chart with balconies. Inside this delightful surprise you'll find rooms that are high, wide and comfortable, plus beautiful rugs and antiques. Delightful English-speaking owner Giorgos offers continental breakfast with homemade produce.

Perigiali Mezedopoleio
GREEK €

(Ouzerie Perigiali; 📞 26343 03454; Navmahias 20, Psani Beach; mains €4-9.50) Part timeless taverna, part beach restaurant, this large place stretches back from the western waterfront road, just west of the Plaza Hotel. Its simple menu features typical mezedhes including anchovies, sardines and grilled squid, plus the odd local speciality such as fresh mussels in mustard sauce.

Ev Oinos
MEDITERRANEAN €

(📞 26340 28266; Sismani 3; mains €7.50-10.50; ⊙ noon-midnight, Sun-Thu, to 1am Fri & Sat) Attractive, lively taverna in a busy little pedestrian precinct not far back from the port. Its cuisine blends Greek-style appetisers and salads with more general Mediterranean dishes such as pastas and risotto, often using fresh seafood and given a gourmet twist, as with the *haloumi torta* (briny fried cheese sandwich).

❶ Getting There & Away

The magnificent Rio–Andirio suspension bridge connects mainland Andirio and Rio in the Peloponnese, a crossing previously only possible by ferry.

Despite the steep toll (€13.50 each way), getting to Patra and beyond couldn't be easier. If you're not in a hurry, a ferry (€7) also departs from beneath the bridge every 20 minutes, and gives great views of its underbelly.

BUS

Nafpaktos has two bus stations: the **KTEL Nafpaktos station** (Aitoloakarnania long-distance station; 📞 26340 27224; www.ktel-aitolnias.gr; Megalou Alexandrou), 1.5km east of the port, beyond the Church of Agios Georgios, and the **KTEL Fokidas station** (📞 26340 27241; www.ktel-fokidas.gr; Asklipiou 1, cnr Kefalourisou) 400m further east.

THE BATTLE OF LEPANTO

Nafpaktos was known as Lepanto in medieval times. On 7 October 1571, in the offshore Battle of Lepanto, the combined navies of the Vatican, Spain and Venice decisively defeated those of the Ottoman Empire. It was a turning point that marked the end of the Turkish naval domination of the Mediterranean.

A small, dramatic statue on the waterfront honours *Don Quixote* author Miguel de Cervantes, who fought in the battle and lost an arm. Another, up on the ramparts, commemorates a later Greek hero: during the Greek War of Independence in 1821, Giorgos Anemogiannis tried to burn a Turkish fleet moored in the harbour, but failed and was executed.

Buses from Nafpaktos:

DESTINATION	DURATION	FARE (€)	FREQUENCY
Athens (via Rio–Andirio bridge)	3hrs	28	2 daily
Delphi	3hrs	12	3-4 daily
Galaxidi	1½hrs	8	3-4 daily
Lamia	3½hrs	20	2-3 daily
Messolongi	50mins	6	3 daily
Patra	30mins	5	2-8 daily (Mon-Sat)
Thessaloniki	8hrs	50	daily

Buses from Fokidas:

DESTINATION	DURATION	FARE (€)	FREQUENCY
Athens (via Rio–Andirio bridge)	3hrs	28	2 daily
Delphi	3hrs	12	3-4 daily
Galaxidi	1½hrs	8	3-4 daily

Messolongi   Μεσολόγγι

POP 12,800

Messolongi is young by Greek standards, having started out as a small fishing settlement just a few centuries ago. It might feature on few travel itineraries had it not sprung to world fame in the 19th century, after poet Lord Byron – memorably characterised as

BYRON AND THE WAR OF INDEPENDENCE

In January 1824, the much-mythologised British poet Lord Byron arrived in Messolongi, hoping to rally international support for the Greek War of Independence (1821–30), and potentially organise the troops himself. After three unproductive months, Byron contracted a fever, and died on 19 April.

His death did spur international forces to come to the aid of the Greeks, and he remains a national hero to this day. Most Greek towns have a street named after Byron ('Vyronas'), and many men bear his name. Messolongi itself is home to the Byron Society, an international research group (www.messolonghibyronsociety.gr).

Messolongi was captured in 1826 by Ottoman forces, under Egyptian general Ibrahim Pasha. The year-long siege ended on the night of 22 April 1826, when 7000 of the town's 9000 men, women and children attempted to escape through what's now called the Gate of Exodus. A smaller group remained behind to detonate explosives as the Turks approached. Only 1000 survived in total. Most were massacred, while others took refuge on nearby Mt Zygos, only to be caught or killed by Albanian mercenaries. The tragic exodus was immortalised in Dionysios Solomos' epic poem 'I Eleftheri Poliorkimeni' (The Free Besieged).

'mad, bad and dangerous to know' – died here during the Greek struggle for independence.

Although modern Messolongi has been hit hard by the economic crisis, it's a lively little place, with pedestrians and cyclists bustling around the central Plateia Markou Botsari and the nearby lanes, busy with bars and tavernas. What's most striking, however, is its dramatic natural setting, at the edge of the motionless Klisova Lagoon, the largest natural wetland in Greece.

◎ Sights

Garden of the Heroes　　　　GARDENS
(⊙8am-8pm summer, dawn-dusk rest of year) **FREE** Just inside the Gate of Exodus, where Ottoman forces massacred escaping Greeks in 1826, this memorial garden contains a prominent statue of Lord Byron (look for the inscription BYPONA). After Byron died, his embalmed body was returned to England for burial in Hucknall, Nottinghamshire, but his lungs lie beneath the statue.

Museum of History & Art　　　MUSEUM
(Municipal Art Gallery; ☑26310 22134; Plateia Markou Botsari; ⊙9am-1.30pm & 4-6pm) **FREE** The ground floor of this neoclassical mansion on the central square holds a fine collection of Byron memorabilia. Treasures range from statues and paintings to pictures of Byron's sword and helmet (now in Athens); there's also a cricket bat signed by Nottinghamshire County Cricket Club. Upstairs the theme extends to the Greek War of Independence in general, with a large copy of a painting by Delacroix commemorating the sufferings of Messolongi.

⌸ Sleeping

Hotel Liberty　　　　　　　HOTEL €
(☑26310 28050; www.hotelliberty.gr; Iroön Polytechniou 41; s/d/tr/ste incl breakfast from €25/33/42/80; P❄@⊕) Ignore the drab exterior of this central Messolongi lodging so you don't miss the 1970s-era time warp that awaits inside. In its favour are spotless rooms (those on the 1st floor are marginally more up to date), funky wood decor, breakfast buffet, bicycle rental and small gym.

Socrates Organic
Village – Wild Olive　　　BUNGALOW €€
(☑26310 23732; http://socratesorganicvillage wildolive.reserve-online.net; Agrilia; bungalow €68; P❄⊕☷) A great alternative to staying in Messolongi itself, this attractive little complex is set in an olive grove 5km directly inland. It consists of five well-equipped bungalows, each sleeping two adults and potentially two kids, arrayed around a pool.

✕ Eating

★**Tourlida Restaurant**　　　　GREEK €€
(☑26310 25360; www.tourlis.gr; Tourlida; mains €7-17; ⊙9am-11pm) Even without such good food, it'd be worth the 5km trek to enjoy this lagoon setting, inches from bobbing boats and with stunning sunset views. Chairs and tables are paintbox-bright, the welcome friendly, and the fresh-caught fish enticing. Try one of their wonderful salads, and the cured fish they call 'Messolongi sushi'.

To Avgo Tou Kokora　　　　TAVERNA €€
(Egg of the Rooster; ☑26310 24377; Razi Kotsika 15; mains €7-16; ⊙lunch & dinner; ❄⊕) This

friendly taverna – a short walk southwest from the main Plateia Markou Botsari – offers up the day's catch of fresh fish (sold whole, by weight) plus well-prepared salads and pasta dishes.

Dimitroukas TAVERNA €€
(🖉26310 23237; Razi Kotsika 11; mains €6-18; ⊙noon-late Tue-Sun; ❇🛜) On a largely pedestrianised street southwest of the central square, this friendly spot has been pleasing locals since 1975. As well as no-nonsense seafood – from grilled eels to clams and octopus – they serve fine charcoal-grilled meats.

❶ Getting There & Away

The **KTEL Messolongi station** (🖉26310 22371; www.ktel-aitolnias.gr; Nafpaktou) is outside the walled town, near the arched Gate of Exodus. Regular buses run to Athens (€28, 3½ hours, nine or 10 daily) via the Rio–Andirio bridge, Patra (€6, one hour, nine or 10 daily), Nafpaktos (€6, 50 minutes, three daily) and Mytikas (€11, 1½ hours, one daily).

Lamia Λαμία

POP 52,000
Lamia, halfway between Delphi and Meteora, is the capital of the prefecture of Fthiotida. It figures on few travellers' itineraries, but it's a vibrant and lively place year-round. Daily life revolves around several rambling neighbouring squares, and the town is famous for foods such as *kokoretsi* (lambs' intestines), *kourabiedes* (almond shortcake) and *xynogalo* (sour milk). Lamia is also the gateway to Iti National Park.

◉ Sights

Thermopylae HISTORIC SITE
(🖉22310 93054; museum adult/child €3/free; ⊙site 24hr, museum 9am-5pm) One of the greatest military feats of antiquity, still legendary 2500 years on, took place at Thermopylae, signposted off the road to Athens 17km southeast of Lamia. In this narrow pass, in 480 BCE, Leonidas and 300 brave Spartans sacrificed their lives to halt Xerxes' vast Persian army long enough to secure an ultimate Greek victory. A large statue of Leonidas marks the battle site, while a modern museum alongside shows a short 3D movie but holds few other exhibits.

Sea levels have dropped considerably since Leonidas' time; Thermopylae now stands at the edge of a broad coastal plain. However, the thermal springs that gave the

site its name – 'Hot Gates' – are still here, down a short lane on the left roughly 200m north of the museum. A rushing sulphur hot spring fills a small natural pool, where you can relax in water that reaches up to 40°C.

Archaeological Museum MUSEUM
(🖉22310 29992; Melina Merkouri; €2; ⊙8am-3pm Tue-Sun; 🅿) Lamia's medieval castle commands great views atop a wooded hill directly above the centre, a steep 1km hike or longer drive up. Within its walls, the city's old-school Archaeological Museum displays local finds from Neolithic to Roman times. Look out for an amazing wreath of golden myrtle leaves from the early Hellenistic era, around 200 BCE.

Individual items are labelled in English, but the general information is in Greek only.

Gorgopotamos Railway Bridge BRIDGE
On 25 November 1942, in one of the greatest acts of sabotage of WWII, a combined Greek and British guerrilla force blew up the Gorgopotamos Railway Bridge, 10km southwest of Lamia. Designed to delay the German advance, the spectacular attack brought the Greek Underground to world attention, and forced the Germans to divert resources away from the Russian front. A reconstructed bridge now spans the deep ravine.

🍴 Sleeping & Eating

If you have your own transport, the village of Loutra Ipatis (p228) makes a cheaper and far more tranquil alternative to staying in Lamia. Along with the nearby villages of Ipati and Kastania, it's a good base for exploring Iti National Park.

Fitilis Restaurant TAVERNA €€
(🖉22310 26761; www.fitilis.com; Plateia Laou 6; mains €7-13; ⊙lunch & dinner; ❇🛜) With outdoor seating on a lively central square, Fitilis serves classic *mayirefta* (ready-cooked) dishes at value-for-money prices. If you're lucky, there might be slow-cooked goat, which sizzles over an open antique wood oven.

❶ Getting There & Away

All buses depart from the **KTEL bus station** (🖉22310 51345; www.ktelfthiotidos.gr; Taygetou 74), just over 2km southeast from the centre (around €5 by taxi).

For Iti National Park, head to Ipati (€2.40, 40 minutes, five to seven daily) via Loutra Ipatis (€1.90).

BUS

DESTINATION	DURATION	FARE (€)	FREQUENCY
Agios Konstantinos	50mins	5.60	hourly
Amfissa	1½hrs	7.70	2 daily
Athens	3hrs	22.30	hourly
Delphi*	2hrs	9.90	daily
Karpenisi	1½hrs	9	3 daily
Larissa	1½hrs	13.90	4-5 daily
Patra	3hrs	20.50	2-3 daily
Thessaloniki	4hrs	28.10	4-7 daily
Trikala**	1¾hrs	12.90	7 daily
Volos	2hrs	13.90	2-3 daily

* change in Amfissa
** change for Meteora and Kalambaka

TRAIN

Lamia's main train station, named Lianokladi though not actually in Lianokladi itself, is 6km west of the town centre. Buy tickets from Lamia's **OSE ticket office** (☑ 22310 22233; www.trainose.gr; Konstadinopoleos 351), linked with the Lianokladi station by an OSE shuttle bus. Normal and Intercity (IC) trains run to Athens (€16.80 to €26.70, 2½ to four hours) and Thessaloniki (€34.80, 2¾ hours to 4½ hours).

Iti National Park
Εθνικός Δρυμός Οίτης

Iti National Park, one of Greece's most beautiful but least developed parks, stretches across the higher slopes of graceful Mt Iti (2151m), 25km southwest of Lamia. A verdant expanse of forests of fir and black pine, upland meadows, wild mushrooms and snow-melt pools fringed by marsh orchids, it's home to butterflies, woodpeckers, eagles, deer and boar. According to mythology, Hercules built his own funeral pyre on Mt Iti, near the village of Pavliani, before joining his divine peers on Mt Olympus.

◉ Sights

The hillside village of Ipati, 22km west of Lamia and 8km south of the Karpenisi–Lamia road, holds the remains of a fortress and is (along with Pavliani to the south) a starting point for hikes on Mt Iti. Its tree-shaded central square, Plateia Ainianon, is circled by a roundabout and flanked by a few cafes and restaurants.

The village of Loutra Ipatis, an appealing if rather faded spa resort at the edge of the plains below Ipati, holds a year-round thermal spa, plus a surprising number of hotels that have grown far quieter since recession hit Greece.

Agathon Monastery   MONASTERY

(⊙ sunrise-sunset; P) FREE A tortuous mountain road climbs 7km west from Ipati to reach the lovely, still functioning Byzantine Agathon Monastery, into which visitors can freely wander. Dating from the 15th century, it's a fascinating complex, with the remains of older structures scattered amid charming mosaics of more recent origin, and catacombs burrowing beneath it. The setting is absolutely stunning, clinging to the slopes of Mt Iti more than 550m above sea level.

✦ Activities

Trails criss-cross Iti National Park. Ipati, where noticeboards illustrate potential routes, makes a good starting point. For great day hikes, trek for around four hours (8km) each way to the often-locked refuge (Trapeza at 1850m) near the Pyrgos summit (2151m), or to the villages of Kastania and Kapnohori. Shorter strolls include the 2.4km Farmakides Path to the Kremastos Waterfall, or the 4.4km trail to Arsali monastery.

Keen hikers should check out www.oiti.gr: click on 'Visitor's Guide' and then choose the drop-down option 'Hiking Routes – Footpaths'. Useful maps include *Anavasi Map No 2.3, Central Greece/Giona, Oeti, Vardoussia* (www.anavasi.gr); *Map of Mt Oiti – Routes & Paths,* published by the Mt Iti National Park administration; and *Road Editions Map No 43, Iti.*

Loutra Ipatis Thermal Spa   SPA

(☑ 22310 59526; Loutra Ipatis; €4; ⊙ 7am-8pm Jun-Sep, 9am-5pm May & Oct) The modern village of Loutra Ipatis is home to a low-key and well-managed thermal sulphur spa, which also holds mineral baths. You can see the 'eye' of the source in the nearby national park.

🍴 Sleeping & Eating

The village of Loutra Ipatis, at the foot of the mountain, offers the best lodgings in the vicinity. Ipati holds a handful of cafes and restaurants, while Loutra Ipatis has a single taverna.

★ Hotel Alexakis   HOTEL €

(☑ 22310 59380; www.hotelalexakis.gr; Loutra Ipatis; s/d/tr incl breakfast €35/45/55; P ❄ @ 🛜) The immaculate, newly renovated Alexakis boasts contemporary rooms, a lovely terrace with breakfast to match and broad views of Mt Iti. The delightful, friendly owners, Julia and Sofia, epitomise *filoxenia* (hospitality).

I Mouries TAVERNA €€
(Mulberry; ☑22310 59488; www.lymouries.gr; Loutra Ipatis; mains €7-13; ☺lunch & dinner; ℗☑) With a terrace shaded by its namesake mulberry trees, this village taverna offers meat specials (usually lamb) along with locally sourced *horta* (wild greens) and *briam* (oven-baked veggies). Before ordering from the short English-language menu, ask to see the day's *mayirefta* (ready-cooked meals) selection.

❶ Getting There & Away

With your own transport, it's easy to move between the villages that surround Mt Iti, or drive into the park as far as Neochori. Frequent local buses connect Lamia with Ipati via Loutra Ipatis (€2.40, 40 minutes, five to seven daily).

THESSALY ΘΕΣΣΑΛΙΑ

Stretching from the Pindos Mountains to the Aegean Sea, the region of Thessaly occupies much of east-central Greece. Always a crucial centre of civilisation, the fertile and river-fed Thessalian plain supported two of Europe's earliest Neolithic settlements, Sesklo and Dimini. These days it holds several likeable cities, including Trikala and Larissa, but is most renowned for being home to two of Greece's most compelling scenic attractions: the towering, monastery-capped rock columns of Meteora, and the lush, wooded sea-view slopes of the Pelion Peninsula.

Larissa Λάρισα
POP 144,600

Set at the heart of the great agricultural plain of Thessaly, on the east bank of the Pinios River, the city of Larissa has been inhabited for almost 10,000 years. Although the remnants of its layered Byzantine and Ottoman pasts lie scattered to all sides, Larissa is very much a modern metropolis. A major transport, military and service hub, it's also a vibrant university town, where lively cafes surround the central squares, shops galore line the pedestrianised streets and fine museums lurk in the suburbs.

◉ Sights

Larissa is an enjoyable city to explore on foot. Activity centres on two squares in particular; the more formal Plateia Sapka, and the hectic Tachydromeon a little way southeast. The latter is circled by cafes, busy both day and night; it's also known as the 'post office square' because, confusingly, the post office used to be here. The remains of the city's ancient theatre (☑24102 50232; www.larissa-theatre.com; Venizelou) FREE, and the acropolis (Agios Ahillios) where Larissa originated, stand nearby, but the main museums are out on the periphery.

Diachronic Museum of Larissa MUSEUM
(Archaeological Museum; ☑24135 08242; http://dml.culture.gr; Trikalon, Mezourlo; adult/student/child €4/2/free; ☺8am-8pm Apr-Oct, 9am-4pm Wed-Mon Nov-Mar; ℗) Filled with exquisite artefacts that range from stone arrowheads and Neolithic effigies to ancient Greek tombstones and 19th-century wall paintings,

---

WORTH A TRIP

AROUND LARISSA

An easy drive 32km northeast of Larissa will bring you to the Vale of Tembi. This dramatic gorge – cut between Mt Olympus and Mt Ossa by the Pinios River, and narrowing to as little as 25m – was sacred to Apollo in ancient times. Just past Tembi itself, the E75 highway burrows through successive tunnels. A clearly signposted side road leads down to a car park, where a footbridge crosses the river to the 13th-century Agia Paraskevi church. The ruins of a medieval fortress stand 2km further on.

Delightful little Ambelakia, 5km up a winding road from Tembi, was a prosperous textile centre in the 18th century. Walking its cobbled streets is a joy, and several of its original 600 mansions still survive. One holds a colourful folklore museum, while another chronicles the destruction of the village by Nazi troops during WWII. An especially attractive mansion, with superb murals, is now home to the lovely Archontiko (☑6947522337; www.archontiko-ampelakia.gr; Ambelakia; mains €7-15; ☺10am-midnight; ☒☎), which serves fine food indoors or on a mountain-view terrace. Nearby, the tree-shaded village square holds more cafes.

Thessaly

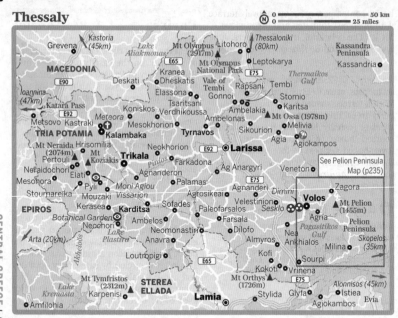

Larissa's history museum is not to be missed. Set in large grounds just across the city's ring road 4km southwest of the centre, it consists of a single large hall, divided by screens into galleries devoted to specific eras or topics.

Municipal Art Gallery of Larissa   GALLERY
(Katsigras Museum; ☑ 24106 21205; www.katsigras museum.gr; Papandreou 2; €3; ☉10am-2pm & 6-9pm Tue-Sun Oct–mid-Jun; 10am-2pm & 6-9pm Tue-Fri, 10am-2pm Sat & Sun mid-Jun–Sep; ℗) This stunning contemporary edifice stands 3km southwest of the centre, towards the history museum (p229). As well as housing a high-quality private collection of Greek art from 1850 to 1950, it hosts temporary exhibitions.

🛏 Sleeping

Larissa's hotels tend to cater more to business travellers than to tourists, but there are some reasonable central options.

Hotel Park   HOTEL €€
(☑ 24102 57071; www.parkhotellarisa.gr; 31 Augoustou 1; s/d/tr incl breakfast €68/73/90; ❄ 🛜) This crisp modern hotel stands at the northwest edge of a small central square that conveniently holds an underground car park. As well as comfortable rooms, attractively decorated in contemporary styles, it has friendly, helpful staff and a smart lobby cafe.

🍴 Eating & Drinking

Akamatra   MEDITERRANEAN €
(Vyronos 5; mains €8-10; ☉12.30pm-12.30am Tue-Sun; ❄ 🛜) From the outside, Akamatra looks like all the tavernas in the lanes east of the ancient theatre (p229). Inside, though, it's a veritable Aladdin's cave, festooned with fairy lights and colourful artwork. Settle into the cosy interior or garden courtyard and relax over fine food – from pasta with mushrooms and truffle oil to Greek grills and burgers – at very reasonable prices.

Just Winebar   WINE BAR
(☑ 24105 34240; www.justwinebar.com; Protopapadaki 6; ☉9am-2am; 🛜) Most evenings, deciding which Plateia Tachydromeon bar to drink in can be a question of finding one that's not already filled with students. Just is a good bet for its menu of fine wines from Thessaly and beyond, comfortable seating indoors or on the square, and high-class food menu if you never get around to moving on.

ℹ Getting There & Away

BUS

Buses leave Larissa's **KTEL station** (☑ 24105 67600; www.ktellarisas.gr; cnr Georgiadou & Olympou) for Athens (€32, four hours, nine daily), Thessaloniki (€15.50, two hours, nine daily) and Volos (€5.60, one hour, hourly until 9pm).

From the branch **KTEL Trikalon station**
(☑ 24106 10124; www.ktel-trikala.gr; Iroön Poly-techn101), on Iroön Polytechniou just west of the junction with Gazi Anthimou, buses run hourly to/from Trikala (€6.90, one hour, hourly until 9.30pm). To get to Meteora, change at Trikala for Kalambaka.

Trains pass through Larissa's **train station** (☑ 24102 36250; www.trainose.gr; 28 Octovriou, off Iroön Polytechniou) to/from Athens (Intercity €41.40, four hours, five daily), Thessaloniki (express €14, 1¾ hours; Intercity €21.60, 1½ hours, hourly) and Volos (normal €5.10, one hour).

Volos   Βόλος

POP 86,050

The large bustling city of Volos lies cradled within a bay at the northern end of the Pagasitikos Gulf, a superb natural harbour that's sheltered by the long arm of the Pelion Peninsula, curving to the east. Both a lively university town and a major Greek port, Volos is not in itself a tourist destination, but many travellers do pass through en route to the Pelion or the Sporades. Volos is believed to have originated as ancient Iolkos, the mythic starting point of Jason and his Argonauts; the precise site of the Mycenaean settlement has been unearthed in Dimini nearby.

◉ Sights

Volos is home to a handful of interesting museums. The finest of them display treasures unearthed in the nearby sites of Sesklo and Dimini, both of which are open to visitors and date from the earliest days of Greek civilisation in Thessaly.

Volos Museum of the City   MUSEUM
(☑ 24210 29878; www.vmoc.gr/en; Feron 15; ⊙ 10.30am-1.30pm Tue, Thu, Sat & Sun, 10.30am-1.30pm & 6-9pm Wed & Fri; ℗) FREE This smart modern museum, in a former tobacco warehouse in the Palaia district, tells the story of Volos through beautiful black-and-white photos from the 1800s to the present day. One riveting section covers the population exchange in 1923 between Greece and Turkey.

Dimini   ARCHAEOLOGICAL SITE
(☑ 24210 95172; adult/child €4/2; ⊙ 8.30am-4pm Wed-Mon) The remains of a walled Neolithic settlement, where perhaps 250 people lived 7000 years ago, stand atop a low mound just north of the village of Dimini, 6km

west of Volos. Follow the trail to the rear to see – and enter – a wonderful *tholos* (bee-hive-shaped tomb).

The *tholos* was constructed centuries later by the inhabitants of the larger Mycenaean settlement alongside. Identified, complete with a royal palace, as ancient Iolkos – the mythic starting point of Jason and his Argonauts – the settlement is still under excavation, and closed to visitors.

Sesklo   ARCHAEOLOGICAL SITE
(☑ 24210 95172; adult/child €2/1; ⊙ 8.30am-4pm Wed-Mon; ℗) First inhabited before 6000 BCE, and thus the oldest acropolis in Greece, this Neolithic site occupies a gently sloping hillside 14km west of Volos. Well signposted off the highway, and staffed by a helpful curator (and his dog), it's divided into two parts, and may have held as many as 5000 people. Individual buildings, including the so-called 'Potter's House', have been identified and partly reconstructed in Sesklo A. Sesklo B, slightly higher, consists of low ruined walls.

Archaeological Museum   MUSEUM
(☑ 24210 25285; Athanasaki 1; adult/child €4/2; ⊙ 8.30am-4.30pm Wed-Mon; ℗) Set behind a pretty rose garden, this excellent museum is just back from the seafront at the southeastern limit of Volos. As well as some amazing Neolithic pots and figurines from Dimini and Sesklo, it holds an impressive collection of painted grave *stelae* (pillars) from the nearby Hellenistic site of Dimitrias. Sadly, few captions are translated into English.

Tsalapatas Brickworks Museum   MUSEUM
(☑ 24210 29844; Notia Pyli, Palaia; €4; ⊙ 10am-6pm Wed-Mon Mar–mid-Oct, to 5pm Wed-Mon mid-Oct–Feb) From 1926 until 1975, Tsalapatas Rooftile and Brickworks, 1.5km west of the port at the Old Town's South Gate, formed part of the cultural fabric of Volos. The factory reopened in 2006 as a handsome and surprisingly interesting museum, displaying brickmaking machinery, grinding mills and massive kilns, plus frequent art exhibits.

🛏 Sleeping

Hotel Jason   HOTEL €
(☑ 24210 26075; Pavlou Mela 1, cnr Argonafton; s/d/tr incl breakfast €40/50/60; ❈ 🖳) Nicely positioned budget hotel, directly across the street from the ferry terminal. The simple modern edifice holds no-frills, decent-sized rooms with perfectly acceptable bathrooms. The basic breakfast is served in the bright lobby.

DON'T MISS

TSIPOURADHIKA

Volos is famous throughout Greece for its *ouzeries* and *tsipouradhika*. If you don't already know what to expect, an *ouzerie* (strictly speaking, called a *tsipouradhiko*) is a small restaurant that serves assorted plates of mezedhes (appetisers) along with tiny bottles of *tsipouro*, a distilled spirit, like ouzo but stronger. You can pour it over ice or dilute it with water if you prefer it weaker. When you've finished one round of mezedhes or *tsipouro*, you keep ordering until you've had your fill (or can't stand up). The basic rule: don't expect a drink without a plate. Typical mezedhes include grilled *ohtapodi* (octopus), *saredeles* (grilled sardines) and fried calamari. Traditional *tsipouradhika* were open during the day only, and many still stick to those hours. Some of our old-time favourites in Volos include:

Kyklos Tsipouradhiko (24210 20872; Mikrasiaton 85; ☺noon-midnight; ☏) Very simple, very friendly bar, with tables out in an alleyway that leads off the northeast corner of the large Plateia Riga Fereou. Inside, you'll find small marble-topped tables and, usually, plenty of students from the nearby university.

Food-wise, the house favourite is potatoes baked in a wood-fired oven, plus grilled sardine mezedhes.

MeZen Tsipouradhiko (24210 20844; www.mezen.gr; Alonissou 4; ☺noon-midnight) The name of this hip and hugely popular central *tsipouradhiko*, the flagship of a small Greek chain, is a pun on zen and mezed, short for mezedhes. Little bottles of *tsipouro* – choose anise-flavoured (which turns milky when poured over ice) or *choris* ('without') – come with tasty little plates of seafood, salad or whatever you fancy.

Kavouras Tsipouradhiko (24210 28520; Gatziagiri 8; drink & mezedhes plate €4-6; ☺11am-5pm Mon-Sat) Tucked into a tiny street between the shopping thoroughfares of Dimitriados and Iasonos, this is one of the oldest *tsipouradhika* (bars serving *tsipouro* and light snacks) in Volos. Bustling with locals, it's a no-nonsense, hard-drinking and eating experience with a heavy dose of testosterone, but all are welcome.

Kerasia Tsipouradhiko (Cherry Tree; 24210 27920; Krokiou 16, Palaia; drink & mezedhes €4-6; ☺1-7pm Mon-Sat) For more than 30 years, a husband-and-wife team have kept their heads down and clients happy at this veteran Palaia-district *tsipouradhiko*. Locals trek across town for their Greek coffee; language skills will help if you're here to try snacks such as sardines and mussels. Old photos attest to former times, though little has changed.

★**Hotel Aegli** HOTEL €€

(24210 24471; www.aegli.gr; Argonafton 24; s/d/tr/q incl breakfast from €83/91/123/160; ❄☏) This sleek, well-managed century-old hotel, facing the ferry terminal across the seafront road, has been given a modern face. The rooms are austere but comfortable, with high ceilings and modern bathrooms. Note that the cheapest doubles, labelled 'superior', do not have sea views. Helpful staff can advise on local travel plans.

Hotel Domotel Xenia Volos HOTEL €€

(24210 92700; www.domotel.gr/hotel/4/Xenia-Volos; Plastira 1; s/d incl breakfast from €125/140; P❄☏⊠) A sleek modern edifice, Volos' most upmarket option stands apart from the bustle, in a superb waterfront location at the eastern end of the harbour. Half of its smart rooms face the sea, the other half the city, and it also holds a spa, two pools and a *hammam* (Turkish bath). Parking is plentiful, and the breakfast lavish.

✗ Eating

Volos is renowned among Greek foodies, with recipes from the Pelion mountain villages finding their way onto many menus. Be warned, though, that the eye-catching seafood places along the waterfront tend to be consistently poor. The best restaurants are located a few blocks back from the sea, or in the older Palaia district to the west.

★**Brighton Gastronomiko** GREEK €

(24210 75012; Krokiou 34, Palaia; mains €6-12; ☺8pm-late Tue-Fri, 1-6pm Sat & 8pm-late, 1-5pm Sun; ❄☏) The old Palaia warehouse district is home to this handsome open-kitchen eatery started by two Greek friends who met at university in Brighton, England. Elias and Dimitris use organic produce and serve local craft beer, Greek wine and cocktails. Expect a subtle twist on old favourites, including fava-bean dip with leek, braised octopus, and pasta with zucchini and goat's cheese.

Palios Fournos
BAKERY €

(Palaia Bakery; ☑ 24210 33703; Krokiou 56; breads & pastries €1.50-5; ☺ 7am-midnight) Open late, in the Palaia district, this is the best bakery for miles around. Pelion residents think nothing of driving here from outlying villages to get authentic breads and pastries, and the pies are out of this world.

Stafylos
TAVERNA €€

(☑ 24210 38458; Melounas 6; mains €8-12; ☺ 7pm-2am Mon-Thu, from noon Fri-Sun; ❄ 🛜) Hidden away on a side street in the Palaia district, very close to the train station (p234), this friendly taverna serves lovely dishes from all over Greece, and Crete in particular, including a delicious *apaki* (Cretan cured pork), snails and more. Before you even order, you're welcomed with a small glass of *tsipouro* (distilled spirit of grape must) with some olives and a tomato dip.

🍷 Drinking & Nightlife

For a summer's evening of music, drinking and dancing, head to the revitalised old industrial district known as the Palaia, the hang-out for local university students. The narrow lanes around Krokiou here – and also, in the city centre, around Koumoundourou and Kontaratou, and along Ermou west of Agiou Nikolaou church – swarm with cafes, live-music and jazz bars.

★ Poco Pico Cafe Bar
CAFE

(☑ 24210 22922; Koumoundourou 6; ☺ 7am-late; 🛜) Big Coffee may be encroaching on Volos, like everywhere else, but with its comic artwork – check out the unbelievably smutty glass-topped table – this hole-in-the-wall cafe-bar is still proudly flying the flag for independent outlets. Local students especially congregate here for an evening drink, but it's also great for early risers who need a cheap, quick high-powered java fix.

ℹ Information

Volos Info Centre (☑ 24210 30940; www.volosinfo.gr; Sekeri 1; ☺ 8.30am-3.30pm Mon-Fri; 🛜) Across from the KTEL bus station at the west end of town, this modern facility offers hotel information, maps and transport schedules, along with travel tips for the Pelion Peninsula.

ℹ Getting There & Away

BOAT

Volos is a gateway to the northern Sporades isles of Skiathos, Skopelos and Alonnisos. Ferries arrive at and depart from the far end of the dock; hydrofoils come and go from the near end.

In July and August there is often a biweekly ferry service from Alonnisos to Skyros.

The following are high-season schedules, which change regularly.

DESTINATION	DURATION	FARE (€)	FREQUENCY
Alonnisos	4¾hrs	30	1-2 daily
Alonnisos*	3¼hrs	39	daily
Skiathos	2¼hrs	25	1-2 daily
Skiathos*	1¾hrs	32	1-2 daily
Skopelos (Glossa)	3hrs	26.50	1-2 daily
Skopelos (Glossa)	2¼hrs	35	daily
Skopelos (Skopelos Town)	4hrs	30	1-2 daily
Skopelos (Skopelos Town)*	2¾hrs	39	daily

* high-speed service

BUS

From the **KTEL Volos bus station** (☑ 24210 33254; www.ktelvolou.gr; cnr Zachou & Sekeri), opposite the tourist info centre, buses head to Athens (express, €30, four hours, five daily), Larissa (€5.10, one hour, hourly until 9pm), Thessaloniki (€21, 2¼ hours, eight daily), Trikala (€14.90, two hours, four daily) and Ioannina (€27.50, 4½ hours, three daily).

The following buses connect Volos with villages in the Pelion Peninsula.

DESTINATION	DURATION	FARE (€)	FREQUENCY
Agios Ioannis	2hrs	7.50	1-2 daily
Kala Nera	50mins	2	15 daily
Makrinitsa (via Portaria)	45mins	2	6-8 daily
Milina (via Argalasti & Horto)	1½hrs	5.20	5-6 daily
Pinakates	1hrs	2.80	3 daily (Mon-Fri only)
Platanias	2hrs	7.50	2-3 daily
Pouri	1¾hrs	5.50	2-3 daily
Trikeri	3hrs	8.50	1-2 daily
Tsagarada	1½hrs	5.80	1-3 daily
Vyzitsa (via Milies)	1¼hrs	3.30	3-5 daily
Zagora (via Hania)	1½hrs	5	2-3 daily

TRAIN

The atmospheric Volos **train station** (☑24210 24056; www.trainose.gr; Papadiamanti) is 200m northwest of Plateia Riga Fereou, and 1km from the ferry terminal. Twelve trains run daily to Larissa (€5.10, one hour), where you can connect to Athens (Intercity €42.80, five daily) and Thessaloniki (normal/express €19.10/26, hourly). You can also buy tickets at the **OSE outlet** (Dimitriados 186; ☺7.30am-2pm Wed, to 8.30pm Tue, Thu & Fri, 8am-2pm Sat, closed Sat Jun-Aug) near the university, at the southeast end of the city centre.

ⓘ Getting Around

Cars can be hired from a friendly team at **Hertz** (☑24210 22544; www.hertz.gr/en/volos; Port K-27; ☺9am-9pm Mon-Fri, 9am-2pm & 6-9pm Sat, 10am-1pm & 6-8pm Sun), conveniently located at the corner of Plateia Riga Fereou, close to the railway station.

Parking in Volos can be tricky. Head straight for a parking lot: the one on the quay (€1.50 per hour, with price decreasing to €1 after two hours) is the most convenient.

Pelion Peninsula
Πήλιον Ορος

Formed by a dramatic mountain range, collectively known as Mt Pelion, the Pelion Peninsula curves south and east from Volos, cradling the Pagasitikos Gulf within its protective arm. Its higher slopes are a green wonderland, where trees heavy with fruit vie with wild olive groves and forests of horse chestnut, oak, walnut, fir and beech to reach the light of day.

On both flanks, the mountain is peppered with delightful villages, linked by age-old trails, and holding whitewashed, half-timbered mansions that serve as guesthouses or tavernas. Down at sea level, several former fishing ports have become beach destinations. Those on the gulf-facing west coast grow more peaceful and attractive the further south you go. The east-coast shoreline, where high cliffs plunge into the Aegean, is often inaccessible, but some wonderful little resorts squeeze in nonetheless.

History

In Greek mythology, the Pelion was the summer home of the 12 gods of Mt Olympus. It was also the homeland of the centaurs (*kentavri*) – half-man, half-horse creatures who took delight in drinking wine, deflowering virgins and generally ripping up the countryside. Not all were random reprobates, however – Chiron, the wisest of the group, was renowned for his skill in medicine.

As the Turkish occupation failed to penetrate into the inaccessible central and eastern regions of the Pelion, the western coastal towns were largely abandoned in favour of mountain villages. In these remote settlements, culture and the economy flourished – silk and wool were exported throughout Europe. Like many such remote areas, the Pelion became a spawning ground for ideas that culminated in the Greek War of Independence. Locally, the Orthodox Church was instrumental in maintaining *Kryfa Skolia* (Hidden Schools).

✖ Eating

The cuisine of the Pelion hill villages has always drawn on mountain herbs. Local specialities include *fasoladha* (bean soup), *kouneli stifadho* (rabbit stew), *spetsofaï* (stewed pork sausages and peppers) and *tyropsomo* (cheese bread). Along the coast, seafood is very much the order of the day.

ⓘ Getting There & Away

Buses set off to villages throughout the Pelion from the Volos bus station (p233). Volos in turn is connected by train with Athens and Thessaloniki, via Larissa.

Northwest Pelion

Volos is known not only for its port, but also its *balkoni* (balcony), the nickname for the striking village of Makrinitsa. Along with neighbouring Portaria, Makrinitsa is a prime destination for escapees from Volos' hot summer days. The mountainside is popular for hiking and gathering the wild herbs so prominent in local recipes.

PORTARIA & MAKRINITSA
ΠΟΡΤΑΡΙΑ & ΜΑΚΡΙΝΙΤΣΑ

Reached by a slow-go switchback road that runs 12km up the mountain from Volos, Portaria has long offered an easy escape for sweltering city-dwellers. These days it's bursting with swish restaurants, cool cafes and luxurious lodgings. Its charming *plateia* (square) is still adorned with several splendid old plane trees, while the little 13th-century Church of Panagia holds some fine frescoes.

Clinging to the mountainside, 2.5km along a side road north of Portaria, Makrinitsa (Μακρινίτσα) is aptly known as the Balcony of Pelion. Among the loveliest of the Pelion villages, it's also, thanks to its proximity to

Pelion Peninsula

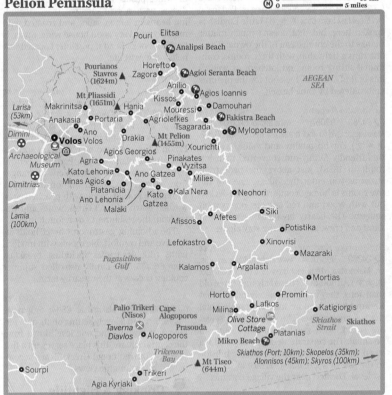

Volos, the most visited. While it's heavily commercialised and gets very crowded in summer, it remains as beautiful as ever. From a distance, its traditional houses appear to be stacked on top of one another. Up close, the whitewashed structures are linked with steep stairs crowded with geraniums, hydrangeas and roses.

Makrinitsa is a pedestrian zone; the approach road from Portaria ends at a car park and bus stop. Its central square, 250m west along a cobbled path, holds a couple of enormous plane trees, one of which is hollowed out to create a kid-friendly hideaway, plus there's a marble fountain and the tiny chapel of Agia Panagia.

To find out what the Pelion's historical mansions looked like in their prime – before being transformed into luxurious guesthouses – follow a circuitous 100m footpath down from the main square to reach the fascinating Museum of Folk Art (☐ 24280 99505; Makrinitsa; €2; ☺ 9am-2.30pm Wed-Sat,

11am-2.30pm Sun). Each of the three floors focuses on their original uses – the topmost as summer quarters, the middle for winter, and the lowest for the grandparents – while photos and artefacts recall village life and local history.

🛏 Sleeping

Both Portaria and Makrinitsa are popular overnight destinations in both winter and summer, and hold a fine array of *arhontika* (mansions), hotels and guesthouses.

Arhontiko Sisilianou GUESTHOUSE €
(☐ 24280 99556; sisilianou@gmail.com; Makrinitsa; s/d/tr/f incl breakfast from €45/55/65/80; P❄🛜) Just above the central square, this eight-room traditional *arhontiko* (mansion) is a bargain. Rooms are basic with old wood floors, high ceilings and a nice airy feeling throughout. Manager Anna makes a spectacular breakfast, served on a small terrace overlooking the village.

Dryanouvaina
GUESTHOUSE €

(☑ 24280 99238; www.dryanoybaina.gr; Portaria; d incl breakfast from €55; P ❄ 🛜) Little English is spoken here, but that doesn't much matter thanks to the enthusiasm of the owner, Dina. She runs a tight ship, with three rooms, communal sitting room and kitchen. As well as lots of fluffy carpets, look out for the pictures embroidered by Dina herself.

Arhontiko Repana
GUESTHOUSE €

(☑ 24280 99067; www.archontikorepana.gr; Makrinitsa; s/d/tr incl breakfast from €40/50/62; P ❄ 🛜) For hospitality and value, we love this friendly family-run converted mansion (built in 1858), just above the pedestrian street as you enter the village. Each of the five rooms is homey, comfortable and decked out with wood and red carpets; one is a bit squeezy. The hearty breakfasts, courtesy of Dimi and crew, are worth the stay alone.

Archontika Karamarlis
HOTEL €€

(☑ 24280 99570; www.archontikakaramarlis. gr; Makrinitsa; d/ste incl breakfast from €63/110; P ❄ 🛜) Although it's based around three old mansions, they're so completely rebuilt that Karamarlis feels more like an upscale hotel than a guesthouse. The rooms themselves are smart, with good bathrooms, but can be small. The separate tiers are accessed via steep stairways, stretching down the hillside to the sea-view breakfast terrace at the lowest level. Located near the village entrance.

Hotel Despotiko
BOUTIQUE HOTEL €€

(☑ 24280 99042; www.despotiko.gr; Portaria; r incl breakfast from €110, ste €215; P ❄ 🛜 🏊) For an upmarket experience, try this handsomely converted 'Egyptian-style' mansion. More than 30 gleaming white rooms are spread among four buildings, set amid immaculate grounds and centring on an infinity pool. Rates drop significantly in low season.

✖ Eating

Makrinitsa and Portaria are renowned as gourmet destinations, close enough to entice diners up from Volos for a special evening. Menus favour stews and soups, along with unusual starters such as grilled mushrooms, wild greens, and savoury pies with zucchini and leek.

★ Kardamo
TAVERNA €€

(Cardomom; ☑ 24280 90131; Makrinitsa; mains €8-20; ⊙ lunch & dinner; 🛜 🍴) Makrinitsa's finest restaurant enjoys a beautiful perch towards the end of the village. You'll find solid Greek grills, very tender rooster stewed in wine, pastas and well-prepared veggie dishes with a real creative twist, including beans in lemon sauce and roasted wild mushrooms. Very good house wine. Space is limited; book ahead if possible. Located just below the Art Cafe.

★ Kritsa Hotel Restaurant
MEDITERRANEAN €€

(☑ 24280 99121; www.hotel-kritsa.gr; Portaria; mains €8-20; ⊙ 7.30am-late; P ❄ 🛜 🍴) A favourite with foodies – more the kind of place you'd expect to find in Provence than in the Pelion – this outstanding restaurant spreads beneath the plane trees in Portaria's central *plateia* (square). Sumptuous cuisine ranges from slow-cooked lamb or boiled octopus with pasta to wild greens with poached eggs, washed down with all-Greek wines and water from the restaurant's own fountain.

The adjoining 'gastronomy hotel' holds attractive and comfortable rooms with modern baths (doubles/triples including breakfast from €65/75). The family also offers summer cooking classes at their nearby farm.

Apolafsi
GREEK €€

(☑ 24280 90085; Makrinitsa; €8-14; ⊙ 1pm-late Thu-Mon; 🛜) In a lovely setting on its own terrace, just beyond and one level down from the central square, this place serves up a fine selection of traditional Greek dishes accompanied by panoramic views.

🍷 Drinking & Nightlife

Art Cafe
CAFE

(Spiros; ☑ 6974384488; Makrinitsa; ⊙ 10am-midnight; 🛜) Unwind over a coffee or Greek mountain tea – served in cast-iron Japanese teapots – while admiring the gulf views as you sit outside this delightful cafe at the western end of the village. The small main building sells souvenirs and art by local craftworkers. Not to be confused with the nearby Paschalis Art House Cafe.

ANAKASIA
ΑΝΑΚΑΣΙΑ

The hillside village of Anakasia, 4km uphill northeast of Volos towards Portaria and Makrinitsa, is effectively a suburb of the city. It's worth pausing here, though, to visit the intriguing **Theophilos Museum** (☑ 24210 47340; Theofilou 211, Anakasia; ⊙ 8am-2.30pm Tue-Fri; P) **FREE** This inconspicuous and faded mansion in little Anakasia preserves fanciful and colourful murals by Theofilos Hatzimihail (1866–1934). A wandering self-taught artist from Lesvos, he earned his food and keep painting the interiors of cafes and houses, including, in 1912, this mansion. The rooms are a riot of whimsical and even humorous figures – modern, mythological and historical.

Call ahead to be sure the museum is open. It's not easy to find, so ask for directions at the local pharmacy when you reach the village.

Northeast Pelion

Mountain and sea intertwine to dramatic effect in the northeast Pelion. High on the hillside, tucked into the forests, charming villages stand sentinel over the blue Aegean far below. Here and there, endlessly twisting roads and steep mule paths cut down to the sea, ending at small bays that hold some of the finest beaches on the peninsula.

ZAGORA ΖΑΓΟΡΑ

The largest of the Pelion villages, Zagora stands 8km up from the sea on the eastern slopes of the mountain; it's reached by a road that zigzags down through the chestnut trees from Hania. Until blight ruined the silk industry in 1850, Zagora exported fine silk around the continent. It's now a major fruit-growing centre that ranks as the apple capital of Greece. The village is also home to two landmarks from the War of Independence – the museum (☑24260 23708; by donation; ☉10am-2pm & 6-9pm Tue-Sun; P) and the Library of Zagora (☑24260 22591; www.library-zagora.gr; ☉9am-1.30pm Mon, Tue, Thu & Fri, to 5pm Wed; P) FREE, which started with just 48 schoolbooks in 1762 and now holds one of the largest collections of rare books and manuscripts in Greece, including 10th-century publications.

🛏 Sleeping & Eating

Arhontiko Dhrakopoulou PENSION €
(☑24260 23566, 24260 23460; www.arxodiko.gr; Plateia Agios Georgios; r incl breakfast from €55; P ✲ 🕸) This century-old village house, next to the charming cobblestoned Plateia Agios Georgios, has been converted into an ever-so-cosy guesthouse by the local women's agritourism cooperative. A local flower designates each of five simply furnished rooms.

Arhontiko Stamou GUESTHOUSE €€
(☑24260 23880; www.stamou-hotel.com; s/d/tr/q incl breakfast from €60/70/90/120; P 🕸) In a quiet but central location, this stately and spacious villa (c 1863) holds six comfortable double rooms plus three larger suites that sleep three to four. Run by the gracious and

THE LITTLE APPLE OF ZAGORA

Zagora's famous orchards supply much of Greece with apples. One variety stands out from its larger cousins. Only cultivated in the Pelion, the *firiki* is known especially for its tempting aroma. You'll recognise it as the smallest apple in the bin; it has an elongated shape, is yellow and green with splotches of red and has a sweet taste.

Despite challenges from apples of a heavier weight (read: more profitable), the little *firiki* carries on, as popular, if not plentiful, as ever. It's also been designated as a Protected Designation of Origin (PDO) product, such as French cognac, feta cheese and balsamic vinegar.

In early September, a weekend apple festival (☑24263 50101; Plateia Agios Georgios; ☉early Sep) FREE in Zagora celebrates the *firiki* and other hangers-on.

knowledgeable George, it shares a courtyard with the mellow Cafe Anemella (Greek for 'silkworm'), up the garden steps to your left.

⭐ **Taverna Niki** TAVERNA €
(Meintani; ☑24260 22626; www.meintani.gr; mains €6.50-10; ☉noon-late; P 🕸) Enter this roadside taverna, set beneath a profusion of flowers 1km north of the Horefto turn-off, and Niki herself reels off a list of *mayirefta* (ready-cooked meals), fresh seafood and delicacies such as eggs baked with green vegetables and *kritama* (sea herbs) salad, hand-picked along the Pelion coast. Expect a convivial atmosphere, good wine and *tsipouro*, and stunning long-range views.

🛍 Shopping

Women's Agritourism Cooperative Zagora FOOD & DRINKS
(☑24260 23566; www.agrosweet.gr; Plateia Agios Georgios; ☉11am-7pm) The oldest women's cooperative in Greece is renowned for its delicious jams and sweet products. Stop in for a coffee and to see what's available, including jam made from the small *firiki* apple, found only in the Pelion.

KISSOS ΚΙΣΣΟΣ

The hydrangea-draped village of Kissos is built on steep terraces roughly 17km south of Zagora, halfway to Tsagarada along a spectacular road that's lined with similarly picturesque villages. A pleasant stop for a coffee or meal, it centres on the 18th-century **Church of Agia Marina** (⊙8am-2pm) FREE, home to some superb frescoes.

The seaside resort of Agios Ioannis is 8km downhill from Kissos. En route, the village of **Anilio** ('sunless' in Greek) rests in the shadow of a ridge of chestnut and walnut trees.

Taverna 5F
TAVERNA €

(O Makis; ☑ 24260 31266; mains €5-10; ⊙lunch & dinner) Village taverna serving the usual Greek standards, plus some Pelion touches such as *spetsofaï* (stewed pork sausages and peppers) and superb home-baked bread. The 5F name refers to *fili, fere filous, fae, fiye* (friends bring friends, eat and depart at leisure). Not fancy, but fine.

HOREFTO
XOPEYTO

Eight kilometres downhill from Zagora, Horefto is a low-key resort with palm trees and a long sandy beach. It's also the mythical home of Chiron, a roving centaur who healed the sick in the days when doctors still made house calls. The main beach is broad and very pleasant, but can fill up on summer weekends; isolated **Agioi Seranta** beach fills a beautiful cove 2km south.

🏃 Activities

Pelion Scout
OUTDOORS

(☑ 6986974815; www.pelionscout.com; 🔄) This family-run operator, based at the Marabou Hotel, offers outdoor activities in the Pelion ranging from hiking (€30), mountain biking and horse riding to boat trips (€60), kayaking and canyoning (€65). They also offer cooking lessons (€55) in a beautifully situated disused chapel.

🛏 Sleeping & Eating

★ Marabou Hotel
HOTEL €€

(☑ 24260 23710; www.marabouhotel.gr; s/d incl breakfast €55/65; P ❋ 🛜) Comfortable, very friendly hotel with 17 sizeable sea-view rooms perched amid the olive groves on the green hillside above Horefto. By road it's almost 1.5km short of the beach, but via a footpath it's only 200m from the sea. Special facilities are available for partially sighted guests. The Marea restaurant on the expansive terrace serves all meals in high season.

Hotel Aeolos
HOTEL €€

(☑ 24260 22910; www.aeolos.com.gr; studios/apt from €110/170; ⊙May-Sep; P ❋ 🛜 ♨) Centring on an elegant white-painted edifice on the beachfront road in the middle of town, this hotel offers split-level studios and

apartments in half a dozen separate buildings dotted around a 2-acre garden that's enclosed by an old stone wall. All the smart, comfortable rooms are equipped with modern bathrooms, and there's a large pool and helpful staff.

Taverna O Petros
TAVERNA €€

(Sogambros; ☑ 24260 22995; mains €7-15; ⊙lunch & dinner May-Oct; P 🛜) This much-loved seaside restaurant sets out its tables beside the sand in the centre of Horefto beach. Diners are greeted with a complimentary shot of local *tsipouro* and mezedhes, then can choose from fine fish grills or traditional oven-baked dishes including okra, zucchini and leeks, and cheesy local favourite *hortopita* (pie made with wild greens and cheese).

POURI
ΠΟΥΡΙ

The laid-back village of Pouri spills down a steep mountainside 5km north of Zagora. It's home to a few tavernas clustered beneath the church, while two fine swimming beaches – pebbly **Elitsa** and **Analipsi** – lie at the foot of the hill below. Enjoy a meal at the delightful **Taverna Plimari** (☑ 6977706151; Analipsi; mains €7-12; ⊙lunch & dinner, Easter-Oct; P 🛜), where the road ends.

Popotech Workshop
GALLERY

(☑ 6945447878; www.popotech-eng.blogspot.com; ⊙varies; P) FREE At the wonderful Popotech Workshop, a couple of kilometres south of Pouri, Irish and Dutch transplants Gemma and Gary create unique jewellery, ceramics and found-metal sculpture. You'll spot their quirky sculptures from the road, and the sign reading 'Orchard of Fools'.

Polidroso Cafe
CAFE

(☑ 6938882207; Plateia; ⊙11am-late; 🛜) Hip little cafe on the large four-level *plateia* (square) of Pouri, managed by the convivial Anna and Dimitris. As well as good coffee and drinks, and live Greek music on summer weekends, they offer a very decent menu.

AGIOS IOANNIS
ΑΓΙΟΣ ΙΩΑΝΝΗΣ

Agios Ioannis, the busiest of the eastern coastal resorts, is not in itself a particularly pretty place. A row of mostly small-scale hotels, cafes and tavernas stand facing a reasonable beach along its waterfront, though, while two lovely beaches lie within easy walking distance. Sandy **Papa Nero** is immediately south, via a footbridge across a small stream, while pebbly **Plaka** is just north, around the headland beyond the small harbour.

🛏 Sleeping

★ Katerina's Apartments APARTMENT €

(📞24260 31159; www.pilio-katerina.gr; d/tr/f from €45/55/85; ☉Apr-Oct; ❋🛜) This welcoming family-run gem is such a joy thanks to hostess Katerina, who, with her thoughtfulness, epitomises *filoxenia* (hospitality). The rooms are light, tidy and charming, with balconies and kitchenettes. Katerina provides a sumptuous homemade breakfast. It's reached via a short staircase that climbs to the tier of houses just behind the central seafront.

To Pelagos Studios APARTMENT €€

(📞24260 31404; www.topelagos.gr; Papa Nero; d & tr €90; ☉May-Oct; ❋🛜) This sublime spot sits in solitary splendour in front of Papa Nero beach. All of its eight light, breezy rooms have small kitchenettes and balconies overlooking the sea. You need only cross 10m of green lawn to reach the beach.

Hotel Anesis HOTEL €€

(📞24260 31123; www.hotelanesis.gr; s/d/tr incl breakfast €50/70/90; ☉May-Oct; ❋@🛜) This 60-year Agios Ioannis veteran surveys the waterfront atop a short flight of stone steps. The pleasant pastel-toned rooms have modern if smallish bathrooms. The great breakfast, served on a vine-shaded terrace, features fresh-squeezed juice, homemade yoghurt and jam. Ever-helpful owner Miltos can lead you on a lovely three-hour walk to Tsagarada.

🍴 Eating & Drinking

★ Taverna Poseidonas SEAFOOD €

(📞24260 31222; mains €8-12; ☉noon-late; P❋🛜) Seafood restaurant with a large seaview terrace at the heart of Agios Ioannis' waterfront strip. The owners proudly serve only their own fresh catch. Their cod, especially, and also their bream, is tasty, beautifully cooked and great value. You can also get the usual oven-ready standbys.

O Christos TAVERNA €

(O Xristos; 📞24260 31227; mains €7.50-11; ☉11am-midnight; P) Friendly little *psarotaverna* (fish taverna) and *ouzerie*, on a terrace at the north end of the waterfront (turn left at the foot of the road). Look in the fridge at today's fresh catch (sold by the kilo at reasonable prices) and order red mullet, squid or whatever else catches your fancy. Standard meat dishes also available.

Taverna Orea Ammoudia TAVERNA €€

(📞24260 31965; www.papanero.gr; Papa Nero Beach; mains €8-15; ☉9am-late May-Sep; P🛜) Spread through the lush foliage towards the southern end of Papa Nero beach, this breezy open-air taverna serves excellent oven-ready mains such as baked cod, plus unusual salads including *kritama* – tomatoes with sea herbs gathered in small rocky coves. An outdoor bar plies beachgoers with cool drinks and ice cream in summer.

Taverna Akrogiali SEAFOOD €€

(📞24260 31112; www.akrogialipelion.gr; mains €8-15; ☉noon-late May-Oct; P❋🛜) Prominent in Agios Ioannis' central row of seafood restaurants, Akrogiali is a favourite with day-trippers from Volos, who love dishes such as *rizi tou psara* (seafood risotto, or a Greek version of paella; €9). Owner Apostolos says 'our food is honest'; it's cooked by the matriarch, Elefteria, and realistically priced.

DAMOUHARI ΔΑΜΟΥΧΑΡΙ

Curving around an exquisite little cove, the hamlet of Damouhari – also transliterated as Ntamouchari – is arguably the most photogenic spot in the Pelion. Small wonder it served as a location for the 2008 movie *Mamma Mia!*.

Although Damouhari is little more than 1km south of Papa Nero beach, the coastal road from Agios Ioannis is precarious and narrow; the 14km road down from Kissos is less alarming. Both end at a car park amid the olive groves, near crumbling little Agios Nikolaos church, home to some remarkable frescoes. A short trail from there leads down to the bay itself, where a handful of tavernas and guesthouses circle the stony waterfront. The headland to the right is topped by a ruined castle, while the footpath continues to a longer shingle beach scattered with green-veined boulders. Beyond that in turn, a beautiful 4km walk leads to Fakistra Beach.

🤿 Activities

Shakayak KAYAKING

(📞24260 49872, 6934054169; www.shakayak.gr; short/half-day/full-day tour €18/30/60; ☉Apr-Oct; 🚘) Damouhari is the perfect spot from which to launch kayaks and stand-up paddleboards (SUPs). Excellent guided trips range from short jaunts to full-day journeys to hidden coves, caves and beaches. Kayak and SUP rental costs €10/30 per hour/half-day. SUP two-hour beginner or kids' lessons are €30.

The outfit also maintains a very nice domatia terrace, with four tidy rooms overlooking Damouhari bay.

🛏 Sleeping & Eating

Ghermaniko GUESTHOUSE €€
(☑24260 31644; www.gopelion.com; s/d/tr incl breakfast €75/80/85; ❄ 🐾 🛜) This former fisherman's cottage, burrowing into the hillside just above the seafront at the north end of the bay, was German-owned until 2001 – the name stuck. Three of its five simple, snug, whitewashed rooms share a wood-railing terrace on the upper storey, with magnificent views.

Hotel Damouhari HOTEL €€
(☑24260 49840; www.damouhari.gr; r from €65, apt €110; 🅿❄🛜🏊) Sprawling down the hillside to the cove, this lovely little hotel offers bright, well-furnished rooms with exposed-stone walls, filled with quirky antiques and paraphernalia. Rooms are clustered around a garden that also holds a good-sized swimming pool. The eye-catching, beach-facing Kleopatra Miramare bar, shaped around the prow of a boat, is a great spot for a post-swim drink.

Victoria Guesthouse GUESTHOUSE €€
(☑6946510004, 24260 49872; www.gopelion.com; d/apt incl breakfast €70/95; 🅿❄🛜) Very pleasant little guesthouse in the heart of tiny Damouhari, run by the brother of the owner of the nearby Ghermaniko. A cafe on the lower floor serves fresh lemonade and smoothies with up-close views of the bay. Book early: it only has three rooms.

Taverna Karagatsi TAVERNA €
(☑24260 49840; mains €8-12; ☺lunch & dinner; 🛜) In an idyllic setting, right above the sea in exquisite little Damouhari bay, this laid-back place serves up wonderful Pelion taverna standards. Fresh fish is the real speciality, complemented by large Greek salads, red-bean soup and tasty mezedhes such as *taramasalata*. Faded photos recall the time when Meryl Streep was a regular, while filming *Mamma Mia!* in the noughties.

MOURESSI ΜΟΥΡΕΣΣΙ
Famed for its cherries, chestnuts and *mouries* (mulberries), the mellow village of Mouressi nestles just below the main road, 5km up from either Agios Ioannis or Damouhari, and 3km north of Tsagarada. Its lime-tree-shaded *plateia* (square) offers great views of the Aegean.

★ Old Silk Store GUESTHOUSE €€
(☑6937156780, 24260 49086; www.pelionet.gr/OldSilkStore; d from €65; ☺Apr–mid-Oct; 🅿🛜) This neoclassical 19th-century gem stands in a leafy garden complete with a cherry tree. Behind this smart cream-and-blue trim, the cosy interior holds five traditional-style rooms. Personable British owner Jill Sleeman serves an €8 breakfast of homemade goodies on request, and can provide information on Pelion hikes and excursions.

TSAGARADA ΤΣΑΓΚΑΡΑΔΑ
Rather confusingly, the rambling and spread-out village of Tsagarada – also written as Tsangarada – consists of four semiseparate communities. From north to south, scattered through the oak and plane forests of the Pelion mountainside, these are Agia Kyriaki, Agios Stefanos, Agia Paraskevi and Agio Taxiarhes. The plane tree that dominates the main square in the biggest of the group, Agia Paraskevi, is said to be one of the largest and oldest in Greece.

Serpentin Organic Garden GARDENS
(☑24260 49060; www.serpentin-garden.com; Agio Taxiarhes; by donation; ☺by appointment) A one-woman, one-of-a-kind labour of love, Serpentin Organic Garden is the brainchild of Doris Schlepper, who, over 30 years, has created a virtual museum of all things green and flowering, including rare trees and scented roses, along with sustainable vegetable, berry and herb gardens. Call ahead. Seeds for planting and yummy homemade jams available.

🛏 Sleeping & Eating

Hotel Filoxenia HOTEL €
(☑6995192135, 24260 49392; filoxeniapilio@gmail.com; Agia Paraskevi; s/d/tr incl breakfast from €40/50/60, apt €80; ☺year-round; 🅿❄🛜) Head down a few flowery steps from the hand-painted roadside sign to reach this pretty, pastel-pink and exceptionally cosy 10-room lodging in the heart of Tsagarada. Rooms have high ceilings and large, bright and airy bathrooms. Daniella is the hospitable and hands-on manager. Open year-round.

★ Lost Unicorn Hotel & Restaurant HOTEL €€
(☑24260 49930; www.lostunicorn.com; Agia Paraskevi; s/d incl breakfast from €65/95; ☺Apr-Oct; 🅿❄@🛜) In a beautiful glade below the main road, the Lost Unicorn is an elegant, well-appointed 19th-century mansion where the antique-furnished rooms feature Persian carpets and slow-swirling fans. Anglo-Greek owners Christos and Clare make a breakfast worthy of the scenery, complete with a soundtrack of singing nightingales. Nightly

in August, and at weekends otherwise, the indoor/outdoor restaurant serves high-quality international cuisine.

Aleka's House GUESTHOUSE €€
(📞24260 49380; www.alekas-house.gr; Agia Paraskevi; d/tr incl breakfast €85/95; 🅿 ❄ 🛜) This attractive, rambling village hotel remains open year-round. Has 10 very comfortable rooms, all with wood and stained-glass touches and modern bathrooms (each has some form of spa bath). The upper level is home to a cafe-bar, while the lovely terrace restaurant serves local produce (mains €8 to €14), including specials such as Aleka's spice-tinged chicken.

Taverna To Agnanti TAVERNA €€
(📞24260 49210; www.agnantitsagarada.gr; Agio Taxiarhes; mains €8-15; ⊗ lunch & dinner May-Oct; 🅿 🛜) This atmospheric restaurant stretches across Plateia Taxiarhes, facing the church and luxuriating beneath the massive cover of the plaza's ancient plane tree. It's a great place to linger over dishes such as pork leg, slow-cooked lamb and risotto with shrimp.

MYLOPOTAMOS ΜΥΛΟΠΟΤΑΜΟΣ
Scenic, seafront Mylopotamos, 7km downhill by road from Tsagarada's Agia Paraskevi, is split in two by a rocky outcrop. A natural tunnel connects its two small, beautiful beaches.

🛏 Sleeping & Eating

Hotel Faros HOTEL €€
(📞24260 49994, 6946897965; d incl breakfast €75-85; ⊗May-Oct; 🅿 ❄ 🛜) As the name suggests – *faros* is Greek for 'lighthouse' – this place is a shining beacon. Ideal for anyone who likes peace and quiet, it's surrounded by olive groves and holds 17 simple, spotless rooms, with balconies overlooking the Aegean Sea. Although it's just beyond the south end of Mylopotamos Beach, access is via a somewhat rough 3km road from Xourichti.

Diakoumis Rooms GUESTHOUSE €€
(📞24260 49203; www.diakoumis.gr; s/d/tr from €50/70/80, apt €90; 🅿 ❄ 🛜) Energetic and welcoming owners Stathis and Athina have made the most of their dramatic cliffside setting in the last lodging option along the road to wonderful Mylopotamos Beach, less than 1km up from the sea. All nine airy, colourful stone-floored rooms have clear views of the bay and Skiathos beyond. There's also four self-catering apartments.

Taverna Aggelika TAVERNA €
(📞24260 49588; mains €7-14; ⊗daily May-Oct, Sat & Sun winter; 🅿 ❄ 🛜) With its to-die-for

setting, perched at the far southern end of ravishing Mylopotamos beach, and warm, welcoming atmosphere, Taverna Aggelika encapsulates all the appeal of the Pelion. Relax on the roomy terrace over exceptional seafood, mezedhes and salads, and bask in those views.

❶ Getting There & Away

It's easy to reach the northeast flank of the Pelion by car or bus from Volos; it takes about an hour and a half to get to Zagora or Tsagarada. If the prospect of driving hereabouts alarms you, stick to the main two-lane roads that connect the mountain villages with the coast, rather than attempting to follow the narrower tracks that link some shoreline settlements.

West-Central Pelion

The west-central Pelion is much the most developed portion of the peninsula, especially along the busy seafront road that heads southeast from Volos to reach the locally popular resorts of Kato Gatzea, Ano Gatzea and Kala Nera. There's some good camping by the sea, but otherwise it's best to fork away uphill from touristy Ano Lehonia, along the branch road that climbs inland to the handsome villages of Agios Vlasios, Agios Georgios, Pinakates, Vyzitsa and Milies. The terrain is relatively gentle hereabouts, so the roads are not as tortuous and narrow as in the eastern Pelion.

PINAKATES ΠΙΝΑΚΑΤΕΣ
High on the Pelion slopes 25km east of Volos, Pinakates is a pristine little village where the grand Agios Dimitrios church stands just below a curve in the main road. The central square, only accessible on foot and anchored by a colossal plane tree, holds a couple of tavernas, a seasonal pottery shop, and a fountain flanked by stately columns.

VYZITSA ΒΥΖΙΤΣΑ
In handsome Vyzitsa, 3km east of Pinakates and 2km west of Milies, cobbled pathways wind between fine slate-roofed *arhontika* (mansions). To reach the shady main square and its two tavernas, climb the short stony path from the main road, alongside Cafe Baraki and opposite the church.

MILIES ΜΗΛΙΕΣ
The enchanting village of Milies stretches for several hundred metres down the west Pelion hillside, from a broad terrace beside the Agioi Taxiarhes (p242) church (next to the main

CENTRAL GREECE PELION PENINSULA

road) down to the century-old terminus of the To Trenaki train line. It's a delightful place to explore on foot, along steep footpaths that connect fine old guesthouses. A three-hour, 11km round-trip hike can even take you all the way to coastal Kala Nera and back, following ancient *kalderimia* (mule paths).

Milies played a major role in the intellectual and cultural awakening that led to Greek independence; it was the birthplace of Anthimos Gazis (1761–1828). He organised revolutionary forces in Thessaly in 1821 and toured the Pelion mountain villages, inspiring local resistance and leadership.

◉ Sights & Activities

Agioi Taxiarhes
CHURCH

(Milies; ℗) This church, on Milies' central square, is noteworthy for its beautiful 18th-century frescoes, all painted over 33 years by a single monk, and for the 48 ceramic 'jars' that enhance its internal acoustics.

★ To Trenaki
RAIL

(Little Train; ☑ 24210 39723; www.trainose.gr; Ano Lehonia & Milies stations; adult/child 4-14 yr one way €10/6, return €18/10; ⊙ daily Aug, Sat & Sun late Mar-Jul & Sep-Oct) In 1896 a 13km-narrow-gauge (60cm) railway line was completed from Volos to Ano Lehonia. By 1903 it had reached Milies, bringing the village new prosperity. Services ended in 1971, but were revived as a tourist attraction in 1997. Although To Trenaki now uses a diesel engine rather than steam, it's still affectionately known as 'Moudzouris' ('the smudger').

Daily in August (less frequently otherwise), four-carriage trains sets off from Ano Lehonia, on the lower Pelion slopes 12km east of Volos, at 10am. They take 95 minutes to reach Milies, with a short stop at Ano Gatzea. The return trip leaves Milies at 3pm, allowing time to stroll around the village and have lunch. Check schedules and departure times, which change annually.

🛏 Sleeping

Each of the mountain villages of Milies, Vyzitsa, Pinakates and Agios Georgios holds a cluster of small hotels and guesthouses, along with some superbly restored *arhontika*, traditional mansions that now offer luxurious lodgings. If you prefer to camp, best head for the seashore instead.

Iliovolo Guesthouse
GUESTHOUSE €

(☑ 24230 86777; www.iliovolo.gr; Milies; d/tr incl breakfast from €61/75; ℗❄🖥) In an attractive hillside setting 300m northwest of Milies' central church, Iliovolo offers 10 well-equipped rooms with superb balcony views. Add in the hospitality of owners Maria and Andreas, and the homemade breakfast, and you've got a great spot from which to explore the Pelion.

Arhontiko Filippidi
GUESTHOUSE €€

(☑ 6972539233, 24230 86087; www.archontiko-filippidi.gr; Milies; d/tr/q incl breakfast from €60/75/100; ❄🖥) This stately old mansion, a short walk down a cobbled footpath from the central square, glories in a broad terrace that commands wonderful views over the gulf. So too do most of the rooms, along with the wood-framed gallery. The shared public spaces are superb, and they serve a good breakfast with village breads and espresso.

Mansion Karagiannopoulou
GUESTHOUSE €€

(☑ 24230 86717; www.karagiannopoulou.com; Vyzitsa; d/tr incl breakfast from €65/70; ℗❄🖥) An extraordinary specimen of Pelion architecture, this beautiful guesthouse (1791), towering above lush gardens, ingeniously combines the traditional with the contemporary. It boasts a range of stunning sitting rooms and bedrooms, elaborate ceilings included.

Palios Stathmos
Hotel & Restaurant
GUESTHOUSE €€

(Old Station; ☑ 24230 86425; www.paliosstathmos.com; Milies; s/d/tr/f incl breakfast €50/60/80/100; ℗❄🖥) This imposing 1903 wood-and-stone hotel stands near the narrow-gauge railway station, amid the plane trees; it's 800m down steep footpaths from the village square. Its balconied rooms are simple but comfortable. Both its indoor-outdoor restaurant – which serves good Greek standards (mains €7 to €12) – and espresso cafe stay open all day, and fill up when the Little Train is running.

Hotel Stoikos
HOTEL €€

(☑ 24230 86406; www.hotelstoikos.gr; Vyzitsa; d/tr incl breakfast from €61/81; ℗❄🖥) Ranging through two modern buildings built in traditional style, Stoikos has beamed ceilings, handsome furnishings, stained glass adorning its spacious upper-floor rooms, and great views of the gulf. Dynamic owner Stella prepares a breakfast of local and homemade goodies. It's at the eastern approach to the village.

Hotel Ta Xelidonakia
HOTEL €€

(Little Swallows; ☑ 6976215187; http://pinakates.com; Pinakates; d/tr incl breakfast €100/120;

P @ 🛜 ⛵) Beautifully restored by its charming Flemish owners, this mid-19th-century mansion balances history with comfort in grand style. Each of its 10 plush rooms is named for an ancient Greek deity, while the veranda is anchored by a 3000L chestnut wine barrel. Check out the wonderful slate roof.

Mansion Sakali   BOUTIQUE HOTEL €€€

(✒ 24230 86560, 6932429150; www.sakalihotel. gr/en; Pinakates; d incl breakfast from €150; P ✳ 🛜 ⛵) Old-world charm, including exposed-stone walls and wooden beams galore, meets contemporary conveniences. This atmospheric restored mansion would make a perfect honeymoon spot. It offers spa treatments too.

🍴 Eating

★Taverna Panorama   TAVERNA €

(✒ 24230 86128; Milies; mains €6.50-10.50; ☺ lunch & dinner; ✳ 🛜 ✒) This much-loved taverna occupies a wedge-shaped building 100m north of Milies' central square, and spreads in summer from the cosy interior to a terrace across the road. It's renowned for Pelion mountain favourites such as baked wild boar, oregano fritters, *spanakopita* (spinach pie) and pickled vegetables.

Tavern Aggeliko   TAVERNA €

(Angelikon; ✒ 24230 23042; Plateia, Ano Gatzea; mains €6.50-12; ☺ lunch & dinner; P ✳ 🛜) Drive 18km southeast from Volos to find this little gem in the main square of Ano Gatzea, serving very good Greek standards and wine at very decent prices. Sit on a lovely terrace in summer, or on a cosy balcony for two, with views to the gulf.

Stefanis   TAVERNA €

(✒ 24280 93000; Agios Georgios; mains €6-11; ☺ lunch & dinner; P) This little *ouzerie* in Agios Georgios, on your left as you enter the village from Volos, is best for traditional *mayirefta* (ready-cooked meals), all cooked in a wood oven. Good wine and *tsipouro*, and good prices too.

O Pileas   TAVERNA €€

(✒ 24230 86873; Pinakates; mains €6-13; ☺ lunch & dinner; P) Now relocated in smart new premises at the southern end of the village, Pinakates' best restaurant remains popular with locals and Volos folks for traditional rural dishes, including *mayirefta* (ready-cooked meals), grills and good *tsipouro* and regional wine.

Taverna Drosia   TAVERNA €€

(✒ 6971618757; Pinakates; mains €7-13; ☺ noon-late; 🛜) Beside the main road at the north end of the village, this restaurant is an extension of the family's house, and is one of the few places in Pinakates that's open all year. Look for Pelion favourites such as baked goat and *spetsofaï* (stewed pork with peppers), with good local wine always on hand.

Georgaras Restaurant   GREEK €€

(✒ 24230 86359; Vyzitsa; mains €7-16; ☺ 9am-late May-Sep, 6pm-late Sat & Sun Oct-Apr; P ✳ 🛜) Veteran taverna, with its sea-view tables spreading across the main square in the shade of the plane trees. Highlights on the mountain-flavoured menu include delicious stuffed pork with orange and feta, and *kouneli stifadho* (rabbit stew), along with salads, stews and rich soups.

🍷 Drinking & Nightlife

Pinakoti Pinakoti   CAFE

(✒ 24230 86712; Pinakates; ☺ 10am-11pm; 🛜 👣) It's hard to imagine a more perfect location for an all-day cafe than Pinakates' pedestrian-only village square. It's just below the main road in front of the church, and centres on a magnificent plane tree. Relax over coffee or evening drinks, eat good taverna food and let the kids run free. The lugubrious Polish manager is a hoot.

Anna Na Ena Milo   CAFE

(✒ 24230 86889; Milies; ☺ 8.30am-late; 🛜 👣) Snug cafe where the quirky interior is decorated with children's book covers (including the one that gave the cafe its name, *Anna Na Ena Milo* – Anna Have an Apple), classic movie stills and old posters. The twin specialities are fine coffees from around the world and crêpes served with jam.

🔒 Shopping

Esperides   FOOD

(Women's Agrotourism Cooperative; ✒ 24230 86838; Vyzitsa; ☺ 10am-2pm & 5-7pm Mon-Fri, 10am-7pm Sat & Sun) A great place to pick up edible souvenirs, this little bakery/shop alongside the car park draws on the combined skills of 13 local women. They create and sell traditional jams, biscuits, baklava and other irresistible sweet delights. Call ahead; hours vary each year.

ℹ Getting There & Away

Getting to the coastal and mountainside villages from Volos is easy by bus or car. A taxi to Kala Nera will cost around €25.

CENTRAL GREECE PELION PENINSULA

South Pelion

Southeast of Volos, the coastal road passes through successive resorts that fill in summer with local day-trippers and weekend visitors. While places such as Kala Nera and Afissos can be very lovely, if you're looking for an idyllic seaside stay, it's well worth continuing further to south Pelion.

Beyond Afissos, the road veers inland and winds up to the attractive farming community of Argalasti before descending once again to the twin resorts of Horto and Milina. The scenery here is quite magnificent, with sparsely forested hills, sweeping views across the bay, and lovely beaches. Beyond Milina lies even more remote and spectacular territory, whether you branch southwest to Trikeri or southeast towards Platanias.

HORTO & MILINA   ΧΟΡΤΟ & ΜΗΛΙΝΑ

The delightful little resorts of Horto and Milina, 46km and 48km southeast of Volos respectively, mark the point where the south Pelion road returns to the sea after detouring inland via Argalasti. Both can become overcrowded in high summer, but for most of the year they're a total joy. The languid, sheltered waters of the Pagasetic Gulf lap against pebble-and-sand beaches, while laid-back cafes and tavernas bask in the majestic views.

Horto is marginally the more peaceful of the two, with its pedestrianised waterfront, and has broader beaches within easy walking distance. The road through Milina runs right beside the sea, so the cafes on the inland side set their tables along the quayside.

LAFKOS   ΛΑΥΚΟΣ

The hillside village of Lafkos, a 1km detour off the road between Milina and Platanias, centres on a shady lost-in-time *plateia* (square) that's home to a few *kafeneia* (coffeehouses), one dating from 1720, and the Old Radio Museum ([☑] 6970374922; Lafkos; ⊙ daily 16 May-14 Sep, by appointment 15 Sep-15 May; [P]) FREE.

PLATANIAS   ΠΛΑΤΑΝΙΑΣ

Of the various charming villages scattered along the Pelion's southernmost shore, little Platanias, a 16km drive southeast from Milina, really has it all. Said to have sheltered an invading Persian fleet from a storm 2500 years ago, it's set at the mouth of a small stream, with a handful of cafes, studios and tavernas to either side. There's a small sandy beach to the left (east) of the foot of the road,

and a longer sand-and-rock beach to the west, fringed by olive trees.

An absolutely ravishing footpath leads further west over a low headland to Mikro Beach, which is itself also accessible by a separate road down the hillside.

AGIA KYRIAKI   ΑΓΙΑ ΚΥΡΙΑΚΗ

As the coastal road continues southwest beyond Milina, the landscape takes on an end-of-the-world feel. Residents pride themselves on their tradition as seafarers, fighters in the War of Independence, and upholders of traditional customs and dress.

The final stop on the Pelion Peninsula, the fishing village of Agia Kyriaki, is a steep 4km drive off the main road from Trikeri, or a quick 1.5km walk down a cobblestone path. Few tourists come this far, and the bright, orange-coloured boats here are put to good use by a hard-working population of around 200. A 20-minute stroll can lead you past tiny Milos to a lighthouse, while a longer trail gradually ascends 10km east from Agia Kyriaki to Mt Tiseo (644m), with views of both the Aegean to the south and Trikeri Bay to the north.

PALIO TRIKERI   ΠΑΛΙΟ ΤΡΙΚΕΡΙ

If you really must go that one step further to get away from it all, then head for the little island of Palio Trikeri, just off the coast at the southwest tip of the Pelion. Home to a year-round population of 15, it's often referred to as I Nisos (The Island). Taxi boats (€3) take five minutes to get here from the fishing village of Alogoporos. Alternatively, telephone Nikos at Taverna Diavlos – he's also the man to ask about guesthouse accommodation on the island – or take a cruise with Milina Holidays (p246).

The main activities on Palio Trikeri are explaining to locals why you're there, and then explaining to yourself why you're leaving.

🛏 Sleeping

Good little pensions and guesthouses, plus self-catering options and the occasional sizeable hotel, pepper the south Pelion coastline. Don't expect, though, to find the *arhontiko* (mansion) lodgings that characterise the mountain villages of the Pelion.

Studios Charoula   APARTMENT €

([☑] 24230 65020, 6948179977; www.charoula.com; Platanias; d/tr/q from €55/60/80; [P][❄][🛜][🛏]) Welcoming and comfortable whitewashed studios and fully outfitted apartments, in a garden setting 250m back from the beach beside the main road. All have balconies overlooking the pool and deck.

Hotel des Roses
HOTEL €

(☑ 24230 71268; www.peliondesroses.gr; Platanias; s/d/tr/q incl breakfast €30/55/58/62; ❋ 🛜) Framed by rose bushes, Platanias' first-ever hotel still stands proud at the foot of the road down the hillside, 100m inland from the beach. Quiet, spotless and affordable, it holds three floors of large rooms with kitchenettes.

Owner Nikos makes soaps from olive oil and donkey milk, and you can learn the art at an on-site class; milking optional. There are also regular 'ecowalking' and wild-herb-collecting excursions.

Hotel Nicolas
GUESTHOUSE €

(☑ 24230 65296, 6934624292; www.nicolaspelion. gr; Horto; d/tr from €45/50; ☺ May-Oct; 🅿 🛜) Set in a superb location, just south of Horto towards Milina, this no-frills hotel stands right beside a tiny beach. The actual rooms are very plain, but those at the front seem to dangle directly above the turquoise water. The friendly hosts speak German.

Agia Kyriaki Guesthouse
GUESTHOUSE €

(☑ 24230 91112, 6978771831; http://agiakyriaki.gr; Agia Kyriaki; s/d incl breakfast €35/50; ☺ May-Sep; 🅿 ❋ 🛜) Exactly what you need for a quaint stay in a quaint spot, this lovely little five-room guesthouse has a stunning setting just behind the main strip, plus clean polished-wood doubles and a friendly owner.

Ikosimo
HOTEL €€

(☑ 24230 65217; www.ikosimo.com; Milina; d/ste €60/70; 🅿 ❋ 🛜) A few metres from the seafront, up a peaceful side street at the northern end of Milina, this simple hotel offers brightly furnished double rooms as well as studios that sleep two to four and are equipped with kitchenettes. The owners run the neighbouring Paris taverna. Bikes are available for guests' use.

Diplomats' Holidays
APARTMENT €€

(☑ 24230 65497; www.diplomatsholidays.com; Horto; ste/apt from €100/160; 🅿 ❋ 🛜 🏊) Opulent by Pelion standards, this complex of smart stand-alone self-catering studios and two-room apartments spills down the hillside to its own little beach, immediately north of Horto. It's all very comfortable and suits those who prefer a resort-style experience. Rates drop enormously in low season.

Olive Store Cottage
VILLA €€

(☑ 6945575360; www.holidaylettings.co.uk/rentals/pelion/347420; Platanias; 2-person cottages

€140; 🅿 🛜) Head 4km north of Platanias for this beautiful self-catering cottage run by two enthusiastic expats and keen walkers.

🍴 Eating & Drinking

Each of the coastal villages of south Pelion holds at least one irresistible waterfront taverna, where you can linger over a fine meal of fish and more fish (red mullet, grilled octopus, squid and sardines).

★Petrino
TAVERNA €

(☑ 24230 65184; Horto; mains €6-12; ☺ lunch & dinner; 🛜 🍴) Quintessential seafront taverna that plants its tables in the gravel of the beach, shaded by palm-fringed awnings. As well as good fresh fish, they serve local staples such as rabbit stewed in wine, and excellent veggie dishes including courgette fritters and baked aubergines.

★Drosero Akrogiali
TAVERNA €

(☑ 24230 71480; Platanias; mains €7.50-12; ☺ 8.30am-3.30pm & 7-11pm; 🅿 🛜) With its tables on the quayside and friendly service, this taverna is exactly what you'd hope to find on the seafront. Ask about the daily catch – fresh fish such as mullet or cod comes perfectly grilled to order and is priced by the kilo – or opt for the usual meats or ready-made *mayirefta*.

Argentina
TAVERNA €

(☑ 6942953959; Milina; mains €5-12; ☺ 8am-late; 🅿 🛜 🍴) The pick of the seafront tavernas ranged along Milina's one through road. Its brightly painted tables stand right on the quayside, so only the occasional kitten squeezes in between you and the sea. Besides well-priced fresh fish specials, plus meat and pasta dishes, they have plenty of veggie options. Breakfast features omelettes and fresh orange juice. Cheerful service, open late.

Three simple, spotless rooms share a nice sea-facing terrace above the restaurant itself; they rent for around €30.

Taverna Diavlos
TAVERNA €€

(☑ 6976851056, 24230 55210; www.diavlos-tavern. gr; Palio Trikeri; mains €6-14; ☺ Feb-Nov) There's not a whole lot of choice for where to eat on little Palio Trikeri, but it doesn't matter – Diavlos, right on the quayside, is pretty much perfect. It's all about good fresh fish, with some unusual shellfish options on the menu too, along with veggie favourites.

★Casablanca
CAFE

(☑ 24230 65250; Horto; ☺ 8am-11pm; 🛜) A hand-painted sign, just north of Horto, points out the 200m path down to this delightful cafe alongside the Diplomats' Holidays (p245) complex. Themed for the classic Bogart–Bergman movie, it has a languid feel, complete with cushioned seats and slow-turning ceiling fans. Charming French-German-Moroccan expat Marie serves perfect sweet and savoury crêpes, along with fresh juices and a full bar.

ℹ Information

Milina Holidays (☑ 24230 65020; www.milina-holidays.com; Milina; ☺ 9am-2.30pm & 6-9pm May-Oct) This waterfront agency in Milina can help with accommodation and bike hire, and offers day cruises to nearby Palio Trikeri (p244) (adult/child €30/15), plus less frequent excursions to Skiathos and the other Sporades islands in midsummer.

ℹ Getting There & Away

The only access to south Pelion is by road. From Volos, five or six daily buses run to Milina (€5.20), via Horto. One or two continue to Trikeri (€8.50), and two to Platanias (€7.50).

Trikala   Τρίκαλα
POP 61,650

Straddling the narrow, tree-lined Lithaios River at the western edge of the plain of Thessaly, the lively and attractive city of Trikala makes a great base for visits to the Meteora region, just 20km northwest. It centres on a matching pair of squares, set to either side of the river. To the north, Plateia Iroön Polytechniou is more formal, but adjoins the busy Manavika district, a former red-light neighbourhood that's now bursting with bars and tavernas. Plateia Riga Fereou on the south bank is prettier and pedestrianised, while a footbridge connecting the two holds a statue of Asclepius, the god of healing, held in legend to have been born in Trikala. Down below street level, lovely footpaths wind beside the river itself.

◉ Sights

Tsitsanis Museum   MUSEUM
(☑ 24310 77977; www.mouseiotsitsani.gr; Karditsis 1; ☺ 9am-3pm; ℗) **FREE** Trikala's best museum, housed in the city's former Ottoman baths (later a prison), houses an intriguing and unusual mixture of exhibits. Displays downstairs explain how the baths operated, exploring gender roles and architectural intricacies, while the upstairs galleries pay homage to the city's favourite 20th-century

son, composer Vassilis Tsitsanis. The museum is 600m southeast of the centre.

Fortress of Trikala   CASTLE
(Frourio; ☺ 9am-3.45pm) Trikala's castle crowns a hilltop just back from the northern side of the river, 400m west of the central squares. Although it stands on the site of Trikala's ancient acropolis, its surviving incarnation dates from the Ottoman era. You can't enter the castle itself or the 16th-century clock tower that's set slightly apart, but the surrounding gardens make for a pleasant stroll, and there's a good cafe on a terrace immediately below.

Osman Shah Mosque   MOSQUE
(Koursoun Tzami; cnr Davaki & Kavrakou; ☺ 8am-2pm Mon-Fri) The amazing brick-built dome of this imposing mosque, built in the 16th century for the nephew of Süleyman the Magnificent, rises above the southern riverbank 750m south of central Trikala. The architect responsible, Sinan Pasha, also designed the Blue Mosque in İstanbul. Displays inside tell of the building's history, and it also holds archaeological finds from the Meteora region, mostly labelled in Greek only.

🛏 Sleeping

Hostel Meteora   HOSTEL €
(☑ 6975949554; www.nomads.gr; Tiouson 51, cnr Papagou; dm/d €12.50/35; ✱ 🛜) This small hostel, on a street corner 400m north of the Manavika nightlife district, offers three dorm rooms plus four private doubles with small balconies, and a cosy basement lounge. Friendly Trikala-born owner Dimitris is full of tips on getting around, and can arrange tours. Free bikes available.

★ Hotel Panellinion   HOTEL €€
(☑ 24310 73035; www.hotelpanellinion.com; Plateia Riga Fereou; s/d incl breakfast from €50/60; ✱ 🛜) Dominating the main square on the southern riverbank, this neoclassical beauty dates from 1914. Rooms vary in size, but the best are large, comfortable and well equipped, with fine views. The long corridors are filled with antiques and memorabilia, from old telephones to Nazi helmets. There's a good indoor/outdoor cafe downstairs, and the staff are extremely welcoming.

🍴 Eating

The busy Manavika district, just north of the river, is alive with restaurants, bars and nightspots, while more laid-back cafes

WORTH A TRIP

PYLI & AROUND

The small modern town of Pyli, which means 'gate' in Greek, guards the entrance to a spectacular gorge in the southern Pindos Range, 18km southwest of Trikala. It's home to the absolutely stunning 13th-century **Church of Porta Panagia** (Pyli; €2; ⊙ 8am-3pm; Ⓟ). To reach it on foot or by car, cross the bridge in Pyli, then continue 1km upstream (left).

Turn right instead after crossing the river and follow the first road on the left up the slopes of Mt Koziakas, and after 5km you'll come to the 16th-century monastery of **Moni Agiou Vissarion** (Dousikou; Pyli); note that only men are allowed to enter.

Three wonderful driving routes start from Pyli (or Trikala, if that's your base). The first makes a half-day (36km) circuit around each side of the gorge, heading in an anticlockwise direction by way of the mountaintop village of **Elati**. A summer retreat for Trikala residents, Elati was known as Tierna until the Germans burned it to the ground for harbouring resistance fighters in WWII.

The second itinerary heads north from Pyli all the way to the **Meteora**. Allow a full leisurely day to complete this full 80km route, which starts with a steady climb through breathtaking alpine scenery to reach Elati. Detour upwards there to visit the smaller alpine outposts of **Neraidochori** and **Pertouli** (a ski centre). Then return to the main road and continue north via successive mountain villages to reach Kalambaka.

A third route takes you 32km south of Pyli to the fascinating **botanical garden** (☑ 24413 52200; www.plastiras-ota.gr/en/building/botanical-garden; Neohori; ⊙ 10am-1pm & 5-8pm; Ⓟ) **FREE** just northeast of **Neohori**, on the shores of beautiful **Lake Plastira**.

---

congregate around Plateia Riga Fereou on the south bank.

Taverna Kapileio GREEK €
(☑ 24310 36444; Pangalou 14; mains €6-10; ⊙ lunch & dinner) Spreading from an old cottage into the adjoining garden, this small taverna faces a small park a few minutes' walk north of the Manavika district. As well as beautifully prepared mezedhes, they also serve fine grills.

To Tsikali CRETAN €€
(☑ 24315 51199; cnr Ypsilantou & Chatzipetrou; mains €8-13; ⊙ noon-late; 🖾) Friendly and very welcoming Manavika-district taverna that's on a mission to introduce Trikala to the joys of Cretan cuisine. Highlights on the handwritten menu include melt-in-your-mouth pork shin, baked with orange and rosemary, plus some substantial salads.

Taverna Katogi TAVERNA €€
(☑ 24310 20150; Kariskaki 58; mains €8-15; ⊙ 12.30pm-late; 🖾) With its rustic wooden fittings, this crumbling old orange-brick house in the Manavika district (entered from either of two parallel streets) is a big hit with both businesspeople and families. All want what this spot does best: grills. There's plenty of roast pork, chicken, lamb and *loukaniko*, a village sausage comprising leek and fat, plus wine to wash it down.

Drinking & Nightlife

Fairydust Coffee CAFE
(☑ 24310 25525; Othonos 14; ⊙ 7am-2am Mon-Fri, from 8am Sat & Sun; 🖾) Cheerfully celebrating the Mad Hatter's Tea Party, this charming cafe is kitted out with all sorts of Lewis Carroll references. The real appeal of joining the locals here is the large conservatory-like tearoom, perched on the southern riverbank just east of Plateia Riga Fereou; the cafe itself stands just across the street.

Sonar Jazz & Blues COCKTAIL BAR
(☑ 24310 38521; cnr Kariskaki & Nikotsara; ⊙ 9am-3am; 🖾) Music is very much the mainstay in this cavernous, high-ceilinged corner bar in the Manavika district, with exposed-stone walls, framed pop-culture memorabilia, and a fine menu of cocktails and whiskies. The impeccably cool playlist ranges from soul classics via Jim Morrison to Greek reggae band One Drop Forward.

Klimataria LIVE MUSIC
(Rembetika mezedhopoleio; ☑ 24311 01576; Asklipiou 46; ⊙ 11.30am-4am; 🖾) Once reserved for underground hideaways and speakeasies, *rembetika*, the mournful Greek equivalent of the blues, is alive and well at this late-night Trikala hang-out, 600m south of the central river bridge. Live music typically starts around 10.30pm, with good food (perfect mezedhes) and plenty of spirits to go around.

ℹ Getting There & Away

BUS

Trikala's main **KTEL bus station** (☑ 24310 73137; www.ktel-trikala.gr; Rizario; ☺ 6.30am-10.30pm) is 3.2km southwest of the centre. If you're heading for Delphi, change buses in Lamia. You can also catch buses to Kalambaka from KTEL's more central bus stop, on the south bank of the river 400m southwest of Plateia Riga Fereou, where Othonos meets Koukoulari. There's a **ticket office** (☑ 24310 73137; www.ktel-trikala.gr; cnr Othonos & Koukoulari; ☺ 6.30am-9.15pm Mon-Fri, 8am-4.30pm Sat, 10am-5pm Sun) alongside, and it's connected with the main bus station by €0.60 shuttle buses.

DESTINATION	DURATION	FARE (€)	FREQUENCY
Athens	4hrs	30.50	7 daily
Elati	1hrs	3.90	1-2 daily
Ioannina	2¾hrs	15.90	2 daily
Kalambaka	35mins	2.60	hourly
Lamia	1¾hrs	12.90	7 daily
Larissa	1hr	6.90	hourly
Patra	5¼hrs	33	3 weekly
Thessaloniki	2½hrs	20.40	5 daily
Volos	2hrs	14.90	4 daily

TRAIN

Trains from Trikala **train station** (☑ 24310 27529; www.trainose.gr; Euripidou; ☺ 5am-9pm), 1km south of the centre, run to Kalambaka (€1.80, 15 minutes, four to five daily), Larissa (€5.80, one hour, five daily), Athens (Intercity €24.90, 4½ hours, two daily) and Thessaloniki (€14.10, three hours, two daily).

Meteora   Μετέωρα

The extraordinary rock formations of the Meteora region would be an unmissable tourist attraction even if they weren't crowned by Byzantine monasteries. However, the sheer spectacle of those monasteries – somehow glued atop slender stone pinnacles by medieval masons and now collectively listed as a World Heritage site – makes this one of the most visited attractions in all Greece. This strange and beautiful landscape also offers wonderful opportunities for walkers and climbers.

While there's abundant food and lodging nearby in the modern town of Kalambaka and the pretty village of Kastraki, there's almost no infrastructure among the actual monasteries themselves, around 5km further up the road. Parking is minimal, so ideally you'd explore (p253) them on foot, by bus or on a tour with a local operator.

History

The name Meteora is derived from the Greek adjective *meteoros,* meaning 'suspended in the air' (the word 'meteor' comes from the same root).

Hermit monks (known as *meteorites*) began to make their homes in the scattered natural caverns of Meteora during the 11th century. By the 14th century, the power of the Byzantine Empire was waning, and with Turkish incursions into Greece on the rise, monks started to seek safe havens away from the bloodshed. The inaccessibility of the rocks of Meteora made them an ideal retreat.

At their peak, a total of 24 monasteries graced these remote pinnacles. As you explore the region, you'll spot the ruins of abandoned communities in sites that now seem utterly inaccessible. Only six now remain active, inhabited by monks or nuns and visited by the faithful and curious alike.

The earliest monasteries could only be reached by climbing removable ladders. Later on, windlasses were used to haul the monks up in nets. A famous story relates that when curious visitors asked how frequently the ropes were replaced, the monks' straight-faced reply was 'when the Lord lets them break'. These days, access is via steps that were hewn into the rocks in the 1920s, and a convenient road passes nearby.

◉ Sights

The prime destinations in the Meteora are the monasteries, with their exquisitely decorated churches and stunning viewpoints, but there's plenty more to see. The scenery is consistently jaw-dropping, with traces left by former inhabitants everywhere you look. The cliffs around Kastraki in particular are pockmarked with hollows and cavities. Many of these *askitiria* (cave hermitages), complete with hanging ladders and nesting doves, were occupied by solitary monks until as recently as last century.

★ **Moni Agias Triados**   MONASTERY
(Holy Trinity; Map p250; ☑ 24320 22220; €3; ☺ 9am-5pm Fri-Wed Apr-Oct, 10am-4pm Fri-Wed Nov-Mar) Of all the Meteora monasteries, Moni Agias Triados, which featured in the 1981 James Bond film *For Your Eyes Only,* feels the most remote. A long down-then-up footpath reaches it from the road, with the final climb following a staircase beneath an overhang cut into the rock. Apart from some

beautiful frescoes in the small church, the monastery buildings hold little to see, but the bare rocks beyond, topped by a white cross, offer stunning views over Kalambaka.

A well-marked 1km trail breaks away from the monastery footpath to head directly down to Kalambaka.

★ Moni Agias Varvaras Rousanou
MONASTERY

(Map p250; ☑24320 22649; €3; ⊙9am-5pm Thu-Tue May-Oct, to 2pm Thu-Tue Nov-Apr) Dramatically perched atop a steep pinnacle and accessed via a high narrow wooden bridge, Rousanou convent has an intimate atmosphere. Its small community of nuns engage with visitors by selling their jam and honey, and leading group tours. Their beautiful chapel, lit by stained glass, holds superb frescoes of the *Resurrection* (to the left) and *Transfiguration* (right). There's little outdoor space, but it feels as though you could almost reach out across the abyss to touch the neighbouring monasteries.

Moni Agiou Nikolaou
MONASTERY

(Monastery of St Nikolaou Anapafsa; Map p250; ☑24320 22375; http://agiosnikolaosanapafsas. blogspot.gr; €3; ⊙9am-4pm Sat-Thu) The 15th-century Moni Agiou Nikolaou is the first monastery you reach from Kastraki, 1km from the village square. Many visitors, keen to press on to the top of the massif, skip it altogether, but it's well worth making the steep climb up. Inside, it's very cosy and snug. Its small church, scooped into the rock, holds exceptional frescoes painted by the Cretan monk Theophanes Strelizas, including a gorgeous depiction of *The Naming of Animals by Adam in Paradise*.

Moni Megalou Meteorou
MONASTERY

(Grand Meteoron; Map p250; ☑24320 22278; €3; ⊙9am-3pm Wed-Mon Apr-Oct, to 2pm Fri-Mon Nov-Mar) The Meteora's largest monastery looks down on Kastraki from the highest rock in the valley (613m). Founded by St Athanasios in the 14th century, it grew rich and powerful after Serbian emperor Symeon Uroš donated his wealth to the monastery. Visitors can view the large *katholikon* (church) topped by a magnificent 12-sided dome, and the unchanged 16th-century kitchen, plus a museum devoted to the struggle for Greek independence and WWII.

Moni Varlaam
MONASTERY

(Map p250; ☑24320 22277; €3; ⊙9am-4pm Sat-Thu Apr-Oct, to 3pm Sat-Wed Nov-Mar) Beside the road a few hundred metres short of Moni Megalou Meteorou, Moni Varlaam was first occupied by the hermit Varlaam around 1350. It's now noteworthy for a small museum of monastic history; an original rope-basket of the kind used until the 1930s for hauling up monks and provisions; and fine late-Byzantine frescoes by Frangos Kastellanos. Beyond the buildings, you'll come to a walled, paved clifftop terrace with sweeping views.

Moni Agiou Stefanou
MONASTERY

(St Stephen's; Map p250; ☑24320 22279; €3; ⊙9am-1.20pm & 3.30-5.30pm Tue-Sun Apr-Oct, 9.30am-1pm & 3-5pm Tue-Sun Nov-Mar) High above Kalambaka, at the end of the road, Moni Agiou Stefanou suffered considerable damage during and after WWII, and is less architecturally interesting than its neighbours. Nonetheless, the combination of having a large parking lot and no stairs means it's usually thronged with tour groups; inconveniently, it also closes for lunch. It does however have a fine museum of ecclesiastical treasures, and Greek iconographer Vlassios Tsotsonis has in recent

---

METEORA: GEOLOGY OF A ROCK FOREST

The stark pinnacles and majestic cliffs of the Meteora originally formed part of sediments on the floor of an inland sea. About 10 million years ago, vertical tectonic movements pushed the entire region out of the sea, at a sloping angle. That same uplift caused the flanking mountains to move closer, exerting extreme pressure on the hardened sedimentary deposits.

The rocks of the Meteora were conglomerates of many types – limestone, marble, serpentinite and metamorphic, interspersed with layers of sand and shale – and began to develop netlike fissures and cracks.

As the sandstone and shale washed away, blocks of rock and cliffs became isolated, and were shaped and moulded into vast rounded boulders and towering spindles. By the dawn of human civilisation, the rocks had weathered and eroded into all sorts of fantastic formations. Where erosion was less extreme, caves and overhangs appeared in the rock face.

Meteora, Kastraki & Kalambaka

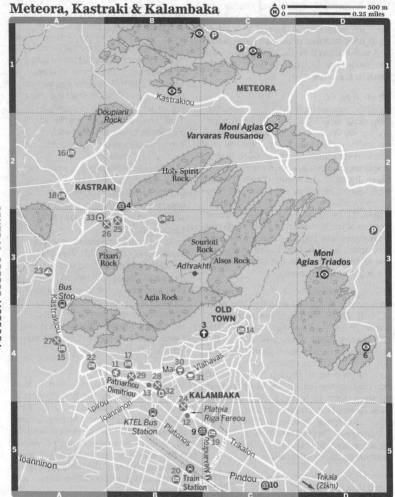

CENTRAL GREECE METEORA

years been repainting the church with splendid murals.

🏃 Activities

Rock climbers travel from all over the world to tackle the mind-boggling peaks, boulders and towers of the Meteora. Visit Meteora (p252) offers guided climbs as well as introductory sessions for beginners.

With around a thousand *monopatia* (monks' footpaths) lacing their way through Meteora, hikers and walkers can spend several superb days exploring the region. April and May are perhaps the best time to come, with the wildflowers out in force.

ℹ️ Getting There & Away

All public transport access to the Meteora is via Kalambaka, which is served by both trains and buses. Once there, you can pick up local buses to Kastraki and the monasteries.

ℹ️ Getting Around

The complete loop by road from Kalambaka to Kastraki, up onto the massif to see all the monasteries, and back down to Kalambaka, is just under 20km in length.

If you drive it yourself, it's just about possible to see all the monasteries that are open within a single day. Plot your route carefully, and start as early as you can; especially in summer,

Meteora, Kastraki & Kalambaka

and around Easter, the Meteora fills up with day-trippers from further afield.

Alternatively, a bus makes the circuit three times daily, making several stops along the Kalambaka–Kastraki road (one way/all day €1.80/5.50); check with your accommodation for the current timetable. There's a handy **stop** (Map p250; Kastrakiou) near Vrachos Camping (p254). By bus, there's enough time to see perhaps three monasteries in one day. Many visitors take the bus to the top, then work their way down and around on foot, finishing at either Moni Agiou Nikolaou (p249) on the Kastraki side, or at Moni Agias Triados (p248) on the Kalambaka side.

Kalambaka   Καλαμπακά

POP 8320

Kalambaka, the town that guards the approach to the Meteora, was burned to the ground by the Nazis in WWII, and is now almost entirely of recent construction. While not especially attractive in itself, it does occupy a stunning location immediately in front of some gigantic rock formations. It also holds a magnificent old Byzantine church (p252), plus a couple of enjoyable museums – one devoted to old schoolbooks and another to mushrooms – and hosts a bustling market (To Pazari; Map p250; Plateia Dimarhiou; ⊙8am-2pm Fri) every Friday.

As it takes at least a day to see all the nearby monasteries, most visitors spend a night or two either in Kalambaka or the nearby village of Kastraki.

◉ Sights

Museum of Hellenic Culture   MUSEUM
(Map p250; ☑24320 75219; www.bookmuseum.gr; cnr M Alexandros & Chatzipetrou; adult/student €5/4; ⊙9am-5pm Mon-Fri, from 11am Sat & Sun) This enjoyable museum focuses on a beautifully displayed collection of antiquarian books, from versions of *Aesop's Fables* to a 1567 edition of Homer. The emphasis on children's literature and schoolbooks is brought to life in a reconstructed Greek classroom from a century ago. You can also try your hand at some fun science experiments, and see old films and photos of the Meteora monasteries.

Natural History &
Mushroom Museum   MUSEUM
(Map p250; ☑24320 24959; www.meteoramuseum.gr; Pindou 20; adult/child €5/4; ⊙9am-5pm Mon-Fri, 10am-6pm Sat & Sun) Once you pass its forbidding modern exterior, this museum comes as a quirky surprise. Downstairs, dioramas display stuffed birds and animals ranging from beavers to flamingos, but the real joy comes upstairs, with a downright dotty collection of wax model mushrooms. Look out for the lurid *phallus*

impudicus! You can also buy all sorts of dried and pickled mushrooms, with free tastings if you're lucky.

Church of the Dormition of the Virgin Mary
CHURCH

(Map p250; €2; ☉8am-1pm & 3-8pm) The 14th-century frescoes in this Byzantine basilica, at Kalambaka's highest point where the footpath sets off to Moni Agias Triados (p248), are a match for anything you'll see in the Meteora monasteries. This is the world's only Orthodox church to centre on a free-standing pulpit, a relic of its 7th-century predecessor. Vespers are sung at 6.30pm.

☞ Tours

Visit Meteora
ADVENTURE SPORTS

(Map p250; ☑24320 23820; www.visitmeteora. travel; Patriarhou Dimitriou 2; ☉8am-9pm) Besides running monastery van tours (€30), this sharp, friendly crew specialises in guided hiking and walking excursions (€25 to €35) of varying difficulties; the most popular, especially with photographers, is the Sunset Tour. They also offer fully equipped rock-climbing sessions; a three-hour beginners' course costs €60.

Their office doubles as a centre for general visitor advice, as does the branch they open in neighbouring Kastraki village between April and October.

Meteora Thrones
HIKING

(Map p250; ☑24320 78455; www.meteora.com; Trikalon 28, Plateia Riga Fereou; ☉8am-8pm) Very enthusiastic local operator offering four-hour hiking tours, either in the morning or to coincide with sunset, as well as a morning-only van tour of the monasteries. All cost €25. They also arrange Meteora tours by train from Athens (day trip €93, overnight €139) or Thessaloniki (€96/143).

🛌 Sleeping

Kalambaka holds plenty of places to stay, at all budget levels. While it's convenient for transport connections, it's larger and noisier than neighbouring Kastraki, and doesn't offer such good views.

★Meteora Central Hostel
HOSTEL €

(Map p250; ☑6977809016; meteoracentral@gmail. com; Trikalon 86; dm/d €18/60; Ⓟ🟥🛜) With its welcoming and superhelpful owners, this sharp, well-managed spot in the heart of Kalambaka is one of the best hostels we've come across. The four dorm rooms (one has 10 beds, three have six) are spotless, with good

lockers; they also have private doubles. The common kitchen is well stocked, and there's even a slim view of the rocks.

Alsos House
GUESTHOUSE €

(Map p250; ☑24320 24097; www.alsoshouse.gr; Kanari 5; s/d/tr incl breakfast €45/50/65, f incl breakfast €75-80, apt €90-100; Ⓟ🟥🛜) This small, nicely renovated guesthouse stands at the upper end of Kalambaka, a steep 800m walk up from the centre near the start of wonderful hiking paths. All the comfortable modern rooms face the rocks. Newer sleek apartments sleep from four to six guests. Hospitable multilingual owner Yiannis Karakantas can offer useful advice on seeing the Meteora.

Hotel Meteora
PENSION €

(Map p250; ☑24320 22367; www.hotel-meteora. gr; Ploutarhou 14; d/tr incl breakfast from €55/90; Ⓟ🟥🛜) This friendly little hotel has nine simple, colourful rooms. Hosts Dimitris and Victoria serve a great breakfast for early starters. It's almost hidden on a quiet cul-de-sac 200m up from the west end of town, just below the rocks.

Theatro Hotel Odysseon
HOTEL €€

(Map p250; ☑24320 94444; www.theatrohotel odysseon.com; Patriarhou Dimitriou 54; d/ste incl breakfast €93/156; Ⓟ🟥🛜) Smart hotel located where the road rises just west of central Kalambaka. As the twin comedy/tragedy masks on the exterior suggest, the decor is inspired by stage musicals, including *The Three Musketeers*, *The Sound of Music* and *Phantom of the Opera* (a plush crimson suite). All rooms have balconies – half face the rocks – and there's a good buffet breakfast.

Monastiri Guest House
BOUTIQUE HOTEL €€

(Map p250; ☑24320 23952; www.monastiri-guesthouse.gr; Nea Dimotiki; s/d/tr/q/ste incl breakfast €80/95/110/125/155; Ⓟ🟥@🛜🟥) Behind the railway station, this converted stone mansion has colourful decorations, long poster-beds and light, airy bathrooms. The handsome wood-and-stone lobby sports a fireplace and bar. A small pool is ringed by rose bushes, and there are panoramic views of the rocks. Service is outstanding.

Guest House Elena
BOUTIQUE HOTEL €€

(Map p250; ☑24320 77789; www.elena-guest house.com; Kanari 3; s/d/tr incl breakfast from €60/70/80, ste €120; Ⓟ🟥🛜) Five attractive rooms, each individually styled to a different theme and sharing an intimate atmosphere.

VISITING THE MONASTERIES

Kalambaka lies at the edge of the plain of Thessaly, with Kastraki slightly higher up in the rocks. Above them looms the main Meteora massif, with a couple of roads skirting the rim, and the monasteries themselves perched on detached outcrops just beyond the edge. Visitors don't have to climb the full height of each pinnacle; access to almost every monastery is via a path and staircase from the adjoining upper level of the massif, and involves a typical ascent of between 140 and 300 steps.

Each monastery charges €3 admission, and has its own opening hours. Each closes on one or more weekdays, varying seasonally, while all six are open on weekends. Hours change so frequently that it's essential to check current schedules locally before you set off.

Only parts of each monastery are open to visitors. You can always expect to see the principal church or chapel, known as the *katholikon*, painted with exquisite medieval frescoes. Several monasteries also hold museums of ecclesiastical treasures and documents, some of which cover more general history. Some display fascinating old refectories, kitchens and communal areas; some have shops. All open onto clifftop terraces that reveal stupendous Meteora views. You won't, however, see where today's monks or nuns actually live.

Strict dress codes apply: no bare shoulders are allowed, men must wear trousers and women must wear skirts below the knee (wraparound skirts are provided as you enter).

Up at the top of town, it's next door to Alsos House, run by Elena's brother; when either is full, guests are referred to the other.

🍴 Eating

Taverna Archontariki   TAVERNA €
(Map p250; ☑ 6973767385; Trikalon 13, Plateia Riga Fereou; mains €6-10; ☺lunch & dinner; ✖) Roomy traditional taverna at the corner of Plateia Riga Fereou, with some outdoor tables. *Mayirefta* (ready-cooked dishes) such as *mousakas* are the mainstay, along with pasta, lamb chops, grilled feta and seasonal vegetables.

Taverna To Paramithi   TAVERNA €
(Map p250; ☑ 24320 24441; Patriarhou Dimitriou 14; mains €7.50-11; ☺noon-11pm Mar-Dec; ✖ ☎) This verdant taverna, slightly west of Plateia Dimarhiou, offers a tourist-friendly menu of Greek favourites, with nightly musical accompaniment from a guitar/bouzouki duo. Service can be perfunctory, as the place is usually packed, while the appetisers tend to taste better than the generally unremarkable mains.

Taverna Panellinion   TAVERNA €€
(Map p250; ☑ 24320 24735; Vlahavas 3, Plateia Dimarhiou; mains €8-13; ☺lunch & dinner) The parasol-shaded tables of the popular Panellinion sprawl across Plateia Dimarhiou alongside the fountain, while the original taverna nearby is filled with antique bric-a-brac. As well as mezedhes including roasted feta and red peppers, they serve fine traditional dishes such as *pastitsio* (macaroni and meat bake), *briam* (mixed eggplant and veggies) and chicken fillet.

🍷 Drinking & Nightlife

Fortounis   BAR
(Map p250; ☑ 24320 22555; Vlahavas 23; ☺noon-midnight; ☎) A favourite for snacks and drinks, with low-key music most evenings, this long-standing *ouzerie* (places serving ouzo and light snacks) attracts a young crowd that stays late.

Kafeneio Mikas   CAFE
(Map p250; ☑ 24320 22048; Vlahavas 32; ☺8am-midnight; ☎) The older generation of locals congregate at the simple pavement tables of this old-fashioned cafe, sipping coffee or ouzo and watching the modern world go about its business. Inside, the walls are clad with black-and-white photos of days gone by.

ℹ Information

Info Tourist Centre (☑ 24323 50245; www.infotouristmeteora.gr; Plateia Dimarhiou; ☺8am-8pm Mon-Fri, to 2pm Sat) The town tourist office provides maps as well as recommendations for lodging and transport; much material can also be downloaded from their website.

Visit Meteora (p252) This local tour operator has up-to-date information on opening hours and public transport.

❶ Getting There & Away

BUS

Kalambaka's **KTEL bus station** (Map p250; ☑ 24320 22432; www.ktel-trikala.gr; Ikonomou 9), 150m down Roudou from the roundabout at Plateia Dimariou, is the arrival/departure point for regular Trikala bus connections. To reach Delphi, change first at Trikala, and then at Lamia. Two buses from Trikala each day connect at Lamia with direct onward services to Delphi, while another two connect with buses to Amfissa, where you'll have to change again for Delphi.

DESTINATION	DURATION	FARE (€)	FREQUENCY
Athens	4½hrs	31.50	6 daily
Ioannina	2¾hrs	13.60	2 daily
Lamia (change in Trikala)	3hrs	15.50	2 daily
Thessaloniki	2½hrs	21.40	5 daily
Trikala	35mins	2.60	hourly
Volos (change in Trikala)	3½hrs	17.50	daily

TRAIN

Trains depart from Kalambaka's **train station** (☑ 24320 22451; www.trainose.gr; Pindou). To reach Athens and Thessaloniki, you may need to change at Paleofarsalos; for Volos, you must change at Larissa.

DESTINATION	DURATION	FARE (€)	FREQUENCY
Athens (intercity)	5hrs	38.30	2 daily
Athens (normal)	7hrs	25.60	daily
Thessaloniki	3-4½hrs	15.20-30.40	4 daily
Volos (via Larissa)	3½hrs	12-19.50	3 daily

❶ Getting Around

BICYCLE

Hobby Shop (Map p250; ☑ 6973743747, 24320 25262; www.meteora-bike-rentals.gr; Patriarhou Dimitriou 28; per 24hr bike €8-18, motorcycle & scooter €18-25; ⏰8am-9pm Mon-Sat, to 2pm Sun) Helpful service for bike and motorbike hire (helmets included); electric bikes available.

BUS

Every two hours, buses leave for Kastraki (€1) from beside the **Plateia Dimariou fountain** (Map p250; Plateia Dimariou). Three daily Meteora-bound buses (one way/all day

€1.80/5.50) depart from the KTEL station, with additional pick-ups at the fountain and Kastraki en route, between April and September.

CAR & TAXI

Each of Kalambaka's squares has a taxi rank. Taxis can take you to Kastraki (€4) or the monasteries (Moni Megalou Meteorou (p249), for example, will cost around €10). Some drivers speak English, German or Italian, and offer tours for around €20 per hour.

Meteora Car Rental (☑ 24320 75682; www.meteora-carrental.com; Patriarhou Dimitriou 12; ⏰8am-8pm) Useful car rental outlet.

Kastraki   Καστράκι

POP 560

Although the village of Kastraki stands less than 2km beyond bustling Kalambaka, you've now left the plain and found yourself amid the mighty rocks of the Meteora; it feels like another, very verdant world. Apart from the church in its sleepy central square, and the geology museum (Map p250; ☑ 24323 22523; Plateia Pavlou; ⏰9am-5pm) FREE that faces it, almost every building here is a hotel, cafe or taverna. But it's all very laid-back, and the scenery is utterly breathtaking.

🛏 Sleeping

Kastraki makes a lovely, peaceful base for Meteora visitors, especially walkers. Several of its hotels have amazing close-up views of the formations.

Vrachos Camping   CAMPGROUND € (Map p250; ☑ 24320 22293; www.camping kastraki.com; Kastraki; camp sites per person/tent €8/3; ⏰Mar-Oct; P 🖥 🏊) Well-run campground, just before the road from Kalambaka enters Kastraki. *Mouries* (mulberry trees) provide the shade, while the excellent facilities include barbecues, nightly movies and a pool. Owner George cooks up a great grill outside the on-site shop and taverna (open to the public; mains €6 to €10).

★**Pyrgos Adrachti**   BOUTIQUE HOTEL €€ (Map p250; ☑ 24320 22275; www.hotel-adrachti.gr; d/tr incl breakfast from €90/111; 🌐 🖥) This 10-room gem, a 300m walk up a very steep lane from the village church (follow the signs), stands face-to-face with the rocks. The rooms are nice, with their polished-wood floors and fittings, but you'll be spending your idle moments out on the balconies, where nothing stands between you and the majesty of the Meteora.

★**Doupiani House**   HOTEL €€
(Map p250; ☑ 24320 77555; www.doupianihouse.gr;
d/tr incl breakfast from €60/80; P ❄ @ ⚡) This
delightful hotel, perched in peaceful splendour 200m up a side road at the northern
end of the village, has the lot: comfortable
and tasteful rooms with balconies or garden
access, plus unrivalled Meteora views. In
summer, hosts Toula and Thanasis serve a
super breakfast on the terrace; a lovely fireplace blazes in winter; and there's birdsong
year-round.

Hotel Tsikeli   HOTEL €€
(Map p250; ☑ 24320 22438; www.tsikelihotel.
gr; Kastrakiou; d/ste incl breakfast from €76/140;
P ❄ ⚡) Set slightly below the main road,
near the centre of Kastraki, the Tsikeli has
crisply decorated rooms and modern bathrooms to complement large balconies. The
grassy front garden is a nice spot to enjoy a
drink, and the service is excellent. Unusually,
it's open to adults only; no children allowed.

Dellas Boutique Hotel   HOTEL €€
(Map p250; ☑ 24320 78260; www.dellasboutique
hotel.com; Kastrakiou; d/tr/ste incl breakfast
€77/90/125; ⊘ Closed Nov– late Dec; P ❄ ⚡)
This smart hotel is poised beside the road
that connects Kastraki and Kalambaka,
within easy walking distance of both. Ideal
for drivers, it has friendly staff and comfortable spacious rooms with good modern bathrooms, plus a big breakfast spread.

✕ **Eating**

Taverna Harama   TAVERNA €
(Xarama; Map p250; ☑ 24320 23976; Kastrakiou;
mains €7-12; ⊘ lunch & dinner, closed Mon & Tue in
low season; P ❄ ⚡) Good traditional taverna
in a lovely rural setting a few steps down
off the main Kalambaka–Kastraki road; it's
a 10-minute walk from either village. All the
usual standards, baked and grilled, are prepared with care, making this a fine spot to
linger over a leisurely meal.

Taverna Bakaliarakia   GREEK €€
(Map p250; ☑ 24320 23170; mains €6-12; ⊘ lunch
& dinner; P ⚡ �℘) This long-time local favourite, below the church in the village centre,
has reopened better than ever. Eat in the
simple interior or on the garden terrace
(heated in winter). As well as an excellent,
chunky country sausage (one serving comfortably feeds two), they offer good veggie
alternatives, and it's one of the few Kastraki
places to serve fresh fish.

Taverna Batalogianni   TAVERNA €€
(Map p250; ☑ 24320 23253; Kastrakiou; mains
€7-13; ⊘ 8am-late; ❄ ⚡) Set on a terrace below the side road into the village centre,
just before the church, this charming little
spot serves up delicious 100% homemade
mayirefta (ready-cooked meals), along with
lemon-flavoured dolmadhes, grilled meats
and fabulous views of the nearby rocks. All
the fish is frozen, though.

🛍 **Shopping**

Maro Theodorou   CERAMICS
(Map p250; ☑ 24320 22760, 6974483782; www.
maro-theodorou.gr; Kastrakiou; ⊘ 9am-8pm)
Kalambaka-born ceramicist Maro Theodorou runs this delightful shop in the heart of
Kastraki village, selling her own distinctive
pottery as well as works by other local artists.
Drop in to check out her tableware and one-
off sculptures.

ℹ **Getting There & Away**

The only buses that serve Kastraki are the shuttles that run to and from Kalambaka every two
hours (€1), and the three daily services that stop
here en route between Kalambaka and the Meteora monasteries (one way/all day €1.80/5.50).
All long-distance buses start from Kalambaka.

AT A GLANCE

POPULATION
754,566

GREECE'S SECOND CITY
Thessaloniki (p259)

BEST FOOD FESTIVAL
Thessaloniki Street Food Festival (p270)

BEST HERITAGE HOTEL
Kokkino Spiti (p289)

BEST BEAR SANCTUARY
Arcturos Bear Sanctuary (p291)

WHEN TO GO
May–Aug Sizzle on beaches and swim in perfect waters in Parga and Halkidiki.

Sep–Nov Bask in lower coastal prices then hit Thessaloniki's restaurants and film festivals.

Dec–Apr Snuggle at a ski lodge near Florina or by a fireplace in the Zagorohoria.

Church of Agios Dimitrios (p266)
SIAATH/SHUTTERSTOCK

Northern Greece

Diversity should be northern Greece's second name – the region stretches across more cultures and terrains than any other in the country. Mighty civilisations, including Macedonians, Thracians, Romans, Byzantines, Slavs and Turks, have left traces here and this is nowhere more apparent than in Greece's second city, Thessaloniki – a magnetic place that breathes history and character, and has the best food in the country.

Border influences add to the region's distinctive character. Northern Greece boasts beautiful beaches too – especially in Halkidiki and around Parga, along the golden Ionian coast. The plains and woodlands of Thrace offer rich birdlife. Ruins at Ancient Dion and Vergina will astound you, and if they don't, Epiros, to the west, will, with its distinctive mountain culture, grey-stone villages and one of Europe's biggest canyons.

Northern Greece Highlights

1 Thessaloniki (p259) Regaling your senses with the cuisine of Greece's gastronomic capital.

2 Halkidiki Peninsula (p277) Swimming in clear waters.

3 Zagorohoria (p315) Village hopping between little-populated settlements in a breathtaking mountain setting.

4 Vikos Gorge (p315) Being in awe at one of Europe's grandest canyons.

5 Ioannina (p309) Strolling around the relaxed old quarter and visiting a tranquil lake island.

6 Xanthi (p299) Roaming Old Xanthi's winding streets and visiting the unique villages in the Pomakohoria hills.

7 Dadia-Lefkimi-Soufli National Park (p304) Pointing your binoculars at wheeling birds of prey.

8 Mt Olympus (p286) Conquering Greece's highest peak and viewing the Aegean coast from the summit.

9 Parga (p321) Relaxing and swimming in this picture-perfect town.

ℹ Getting Around

TRAIN

Trains connect Thessaloniki with Thrace, via Serres and Drama; they also run west across Macedonia as far as Florina, via Veria. They are comfortable and affordable, but most routes run only two or three times daily. There is also train service to Athens (four hours), five times a day, plus a slower overnight train (five hours).

MACEDONIA ΜΑΚΕΔΟΝΙΑ

Travellers lured automatically to Greece's islands and southern charms risk missing out on one of the country's most fascinating regions: Macedonia. Forever associated with Alexander the Great, it's littered with ancient cities, holy places and natural wonders that bridge the years between ourselves and the ancients who once revered them. And then there's Thessaloniki: Greece's second city, a cultural dynamo of ancient pedigree and the country's acknowledged gastronomic capital.

Traces of successive conquerors and cultures can be seen everywhere, from the Macedonian treasures of Pella and Vergina, to Thessaloniki's Roman fora and palaces, ubiquitous masterpieces of Byzantine church-building and the extravagant bathhouses that arose during the centuries of Turkish power. Even deeper and older is Mt Olympus, a cloud-piercing wonder that makes perfect sense as the home of the gods. Add beaches, wineries, lakes and the ebullient culture of today, and you have a place not to be missed.

History

Although human life in Macedonia goes back 700,000 years, it's best known for the powerful and expansionist Macedonian civilisation that peaked with Alexander III. Known to history as Alexander the Great, he conquered a great part of the known world before his death, at just 32, in 323 BCE. Deemed barbarians by cultivated Athenians, the Macedonians subjugated Greece under Alexander's father, Philip II, yet adopted Greek mores. Alexander spread the Greek culture and language widely, creating a Hellenistic society that would in turn be absorbed by the Romans. Later, after their empire split in half in the 4th century CE, the Greek-speaking Byzantine Empire emerged.

Thessaloniki became Byzantium's second city, a vital commercial, cultural and strategic centre on the Balkan trade routes. However, 6th- and 7th-century-CE Slavic migrations brought new populations and challenges. The empire frequently battled with the Bulgarian kingdom from the 9th century to the 11th century. In 1018 Emperor Basil II finally defeated Bulgarian Tsar Samuel, who had ruled much of the southern Balkans from Macedonia's Mikri Prespa Lake.

After Serbian rule in the 14th century, Macedonia and the Balkans were overrun by the Ottoman Turks. The Ottoman system distinguished subjects by religion, not race, causing unrest that peaked in the late 19th century. Greek partisan movements arose to fight the Turks, pledging to annex Macedonia for Greece, Bulgaria or even an independent 'Macedonia for the Macedonians'. Prior to WWI, great powers such as Britain favoured the latter.

Ottoman atrocities against Macedonia's Christian populations presaged the First Balkan War of 1912, in which Greece, Bulgaria and Serbia drove the Turks from Macedonia. However, the Bulgarians were unhappy with their share, and in 1913 declared war on their former allies to inaugurate the Second Balkan War. Bulgaria's quick defeat lost it allotted portions of eastern Macedonia and Thrace, and Greece was the big winner, taking half of geographical Macedonia, with Serbia taking 38%. Bulgaria was left with 13%. Newly created Albania received a sliver around Ohrid and the Prespa Lakes.

In 1923, with the massive Greek–Turkish population exchanges, the government resettled many Anatolian Greek refugees in Macedonia, displacing the indigenous (non-Greek) populations. A vigorous program for assimilating non-Greeks was already under way, primarily through education and the Church. During WWII Greece was occupied by the Nazis, who deported and killed most of Macedonia's significant Sephardic Jewish population. Afterwards, during the Greek Civil War (1944–49), authorities targeted 'communist supporters' – often a label for ethnic minorities – causing the expulsion of thousands of (Slavic) Macedonians, many of them children, as well as Bulgarians and others. Greek Macedonia today is thus cut from a very different social fabric than that which prevailed even 60 years ago.

Thessaloniki Θεσσαλονίκη

POP 754,566

Thessaloniki is easy to fall in love with – it has beauty, chaos, history and culture, a remarkable cuisine and wonderful, vast sea views. This is Greece's second city, which, like

NORTHERN GREECE THESSALONIKI

Macedonia

the rest of the country, has suffered the hit of the economic crisis, but the streets remain full of life and vibrancy.

The different neighbourhoods are little worlds unto themselves, and when you climb up to the Byzantine walls and take in the whole of Thessaloniki at sunset, you see what a sprawling, organic city it is. Old and new cohabit wonderfully: the Arch of Galerius, an intricate 4th-century monument, overlooks the busy shopping drag of Egnatia, while Thessaloniki's most famous sight, the White Tower, anchors a waterfront packed with cocktail bars. The revamped waterfront area breathes life and is great for walking and cycling. By night, the city reverberates with music and nightlife.

History

With the help of remarkable Thessalian horsemanship, Philip II achieved a spectacular victory over a Phoenician tribe. To celebrate, he named his daughter Thessalonike (literally, 'victory of Thessalians'). Later, when Thessalonike married the Macedonian general Kassandros, her name was chosen for the city of Thessaloniki, founded in 315 BCE.

In 168 BCE the Romans conquered Macedon. Thessaloniki's importance was enhanced by its ideal location on the Thermaic Gulf, the east–west Via Egnatia and the Axios/Vardar River valley leading north. Under Galerius, Thessaloniki became the eastern imperial capital; with the empire's division in 395 CE, it became Byzantium's second city, a flourishing Constantinople in miniature.

However, it was also frequently attacked by Goths, Slavs, Saracens and Crusaders. Still, Thessaloniki remained a cultural centre. It bore the 9th-century monks Cyril and Methodius (creators of Glagolitic, precursor to Cyrillic), who expanded Orthodox Byzantine literary culture among the Slavs. The city also nurtured great 14th-century theologian St Gregory Palamas, who became Archbishop of Thessaloniki.

In 1430 the Ottoman Turks captured Thessaloniki; after 1492 they resettled Sephardic Jews fleeing the Inquisition here, adding to the city's diversity.

With the 1821–27 War of Independence only a partial success, 19th-century Thessaloniki became a lurid hub for intrigue, secret societies and mutually antagonistic rebels and reformers. Along with Greek revolutionaries, these included the pro-Bulgarian Internal Macedonian Revolutionary Organisation (IMRO), and the Young Turks, who wanted Western-style reforms for the empire. Indeed, one Young Turk and Thessaloniki native, Mustafa Kemal (Atatürk), would become modern Turkey's founding father.

Thessaloniki suffered successive tragedies over the following four decades. The August 1917 fire burned two-thirds of it, and ethnic diversity shrank with the 1923 population exchanges. During the WWII Nazi occupation, Thessaloniki's Jews were deported to concentration camps and other non-Greeks were expelled following the Greek Civil War.

Recent decades have brought cultural acclaim, including the city's 1997 reign as European Capital of Culture and its hosting of sporting events during the 2004 Athens Olympics. In 2014 Thessaloniki was European Youth Capital, thanks to having one of the largest student populations in Southern Europe.

◉ Sights

◉ White Tower & Waterfront

White Tower TOWER
(Lefkos Pyrgos; Map p262; ☑ 2310 267 832; www.lpth.gr; Leoforos Nikis; adult/concession €4/2; ⊙8am-8pm Apr-Oct, 9am-4pm Nov-Mar) Thessaloniki's iconic landmark, the 34m-high White Tower has a harrowing history as a prison and place of execution. Built by the Ottomans in the 15th century, it was here in 1826 that Sultan Mahmud II massacred the garrison of rebellious janissaries (forcibly Islamicised elite troops). One story goes that the structure was known as the Tower of Blood until a prisoner painted the tower white in exchange for his liberty in 1883, when it was renamed Lefkos Pyrgos (White Tower).

★**Archaeological Museum** MUSEUM
(Map p262; ☑ 2313 310 201; www.amth.gr; Manoli Andronikou 6; adult/concession €8/4, 1st Sun of month Nov-Mar free; ⊙8am-8pm Apr-Oct, 9am-4pm Nov-Mar) Macedonia's prehistory, Hellenistic and Roman periods are charted in this wonderful museum, home to many of the region's major archaeological discoveries. Highlights include goldwork from various hoards and graves, and the Derveni Krater (330–320 BCE), a huge, ornate Hellenistic bronze-and-tin vase marked by intricate relief carvings of Dionysos, along with mythical figures, animals and ivy vines. The Derveni Papyrus, Greece's oldest surviving papyrus piece (320–250 BCE), is recognised by Unesco as Europe's oldest 'book'.

Thessaloniki

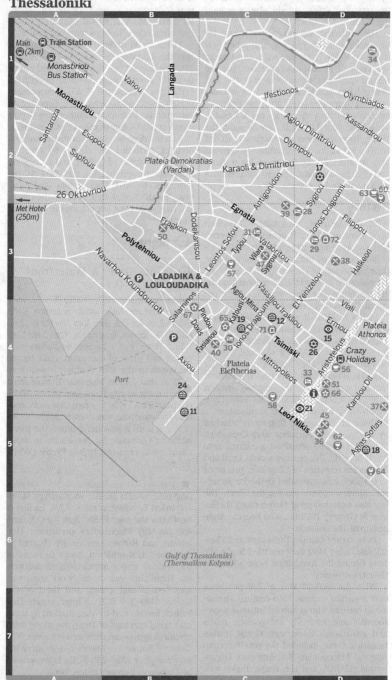

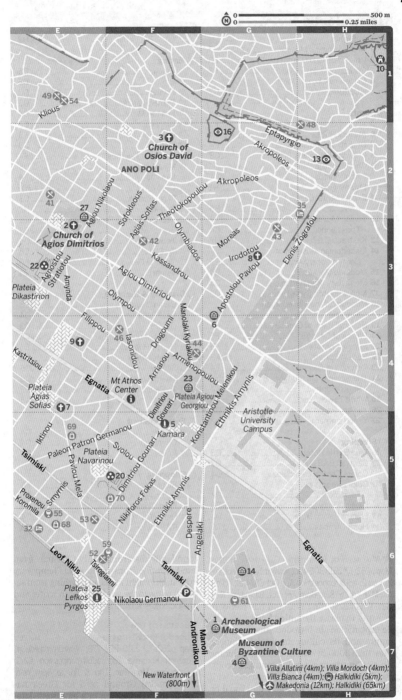

N ⬆ 0 ———————— 500 m
0 ———————— 0.25 miles

Klious
49 ✕ 54

3 ✝
**Church of
Osios David**

ANO POLI

⊙ 16

Eptapyrgio
Akropoleos

✕ 48

13 ⊙

🏛 10

Akropoleos

41 ✕

27 🏛

2 ✝
**Church of
Agios Dimitrios**

Agiou Nikolaou

Sorokleous

Agias Sofias

Theotokopoulou

Olymbiados

42 ✕

Kassandrou

Moreas

Irodotou

8 ✝

35 🏛

Elenis Zografou

43 ✕

22 ✕

Agnostou
Stratiotou

Amynda

Agiou Dimitriou

**Plateia
Dikastirion**

Olympou

Filippou

9 ✝

46 ✕ Iasonidou

Manolaki Kyriakou

Dragoumi

Apostolou Pavlou

🏛 6

44 ✕

Armenopoulou

23 🏛

Kastritsiou

Egnatia

Mt Athos
Center ℹ

Arianou

Plateia Agiou
Georgiou

**Plateia
Agias
Sofias**

✝ 7

Iktinou

69 🔒

Paleon Patron Germanou

Dimitriou
Gounari

5 🏛

Kamara

Konstantinou Melenikou

Ethnikis Amynis

**Aristotle
University
Campus**

Tsimiski

Pavlou Mela

**Plateia
Navarinou**

Syolou

Dimitriou Gounari

20 ✕

70 🔒

Nikiforos Fokas

Ethnikis Amynis

Despera

Egnatia

Proxenou
Koromila
Smyrnis

55 🏠

32 🏛

68 🔒

53 ✕

59

52

Tsirogianni

Tsimiski

Angelaki

🏛 14

Leof Nikis

25 ℹ

**Plateia
Lefkos
Pyrgos**

Nikolaou Germanou

🅿

🏛 61

🅿

Manoli
Andronikou

1 🏛 *Archaeological
Museum*

**Museum of
Byzantine Culture**

4 🏛

*New Waterfront
(800m)* ↓

*Villa Allatini (4km); Villa Mordoch (4km);
Villa Bianca (4km);* 🚌 *Halkidiki (5km);*
✈ *Makedonia (12km); Halkidiki (65km)*

Thessaloniki

★ **Museum of Byzantine Culture** MUSEUM
(Map p262; ☑ 2313 306 400; www.mbp.gr; Leoforos Stratou 2; adult/concession Apr-Oct €8/4, all tickets Nov-Mar €4; ⊗ 8am-8pm Apr-Oct, 9am-4pm Nov-Mar) This fascinating museum has plenty of treasures to please Byzantine buffs, plus simple explanations to introduce this long-lived empire and its culture to total beginners. More than 3000 Byzantine objects, including mosaics, intriguing tomb paintings, icons, jewellery and glassware, are showcased with characterful asides about daily life. You'll be confidently discerning early-Christian from late-Byzantine icons in no time. Temporary exhibitions might focus on anything from satirical maps to the work of Cretan writer and mystic Nikos Kazantzakis.

Museum of the Macedonian Struggle
MUSEUM
(Map p262; ☑ 2310 229 778; www.imma.edu.gr; Proxenou Koromila 23; adult/concession €2/1; ⊗ 9am-2pm Mon, Tue, Thu & Fri, to 8pm Wed, 10am-2pm Sat) Ground zero for Greek nationalism, this museum in a handsome late-

19th-century mansion recounts how heroic Hellenes wrested Macedonia from both Turks and Bulgarians. The building, which was the Greek Consulate in Ottoman times, contains intriguing examples of obscure maps, documents, accoutrements and fire-arms belonging to key players in the struggle, plus photos, uniforms and more.

New Waterfront WATERFRONT

(Nea Paralia) Thessaloniki's New Waterfront is evidence that architecture can improve urban life through intelligent redesign of the space in which it is lived. Recipient of numerous awards for its architects Prodromos Nikiforidis and Bernard Cuomo, this 3.5km walkway extends from the White Tower to the Thessaloniki Concert Hall. Completed in 2013, it has been embraced by Thessalonikans with absolute delight as the perfect place to promenade, rollerblade, bike, play, eat ice cream or just enjoy peripatetic conversation.

Thessaloniki Concert Hall ARCHITECTURE

(Megaro Mousikis/M1 & M2; ☑ 2310 895 800; www.tch.gr; 25 Martiou, cnr Paralia; ☺box office 10am-6pm Mon-Sat & 2hr before every event) **FREE** Japanese architect Arata Isozaki created the M2, one of two waterfront buildings that house Thessaloniki's high-brow music scene. It's a strikingly contemporary structure with impeccably simple geometry, using glass, stone and steel, and making the most of the city's sea views and natural light. The neighbouring M1 is a red-brick structure; yet the two work oddly together, the M1 solid and dense and the M2 transparent and light. International and domestic artists perform here. Check the website for details.

⊙ Egnatia & Central

Following the path of the 2nd-century-BCE Roman road between the Adriatic and Byzantium, Egnatia is still Thessaloniki's main drag, and much of the city is divided as above and below Egnatia. Three major Roman monuments of early-4th-century emperor Galerius spill across Egnatia at Plateia Navarinou: the ruined Palace of Galerius, the Arch of Galerius and the now-renovated Rotunda to its north. This central Thessaloniki neighbourhood also has some of the city's most fascinating churches.

Rotunda of Galerius HISTORIC BUILDING

(Map p262; ☑ 2310 204 868; Plateia Agiou Georgiou; €2; ☺8am-9.30pm Mon & Wed-Fri, 9am-4.30pm Sat & Sun) **FREE** In 306 CE Roman emperor Galerius built this harmonious 30m-high dome, comparable to Rome's Pantheon and possibly intended as his mausoleum. Marking the momentous arrival of Christianity as the religion of Empire, the Rotunda became Thessaloniki's first church (Agios Georgios; observe dragon-slaying St George above the door). The Ottomans in turn made it a mosque (hence the restored minaret), but since the Greek reconquest of 1912 it has served both sacred and secular purposes.

Arch of Galerius MONUMENT

(Map p262; Egnatia) **FREE** South of the Rotunda on Egnatia, the Arch of Galerius (303 CE) celebrates the eponymous emperor's victory over the Persians in martial scenes carved into the marble panels that face its masonry core. Known locally as Kamara, this landmark is also the city's main meeting spot. The Arch originally had four main and four supporting pillars, with eight gates and arches, and a dome – only two of the central arches and one supporting arch can be seen today.

Palace of Galerius RUINS

(Map p262; http://galeriuspalace.culture.gr; Plateia Navarinou; ☺8am-3pm Tue-Sun) **FREE** Sprawling in splendid incongruity amidst the souvenir shops and crêperies of Plateia Navarinou, the ruins of this 3rd- to 4th-century palace remain impressive in scope. You can descend into it, or just peer over the handrail to see the surviving mosaics, columns, walls and infrastructure. What most brings the site to life is the Arched Hall, where exhibits, videos and digital recreations convey something of the nature and scope of not just the palace, but the nearby triumphal arch and rotunda.

Roman Forum RUINS

(Ancient Agora; Map p262; ☑ 2310 221 260; btwn Olimpou, Fillippou, Makedonikis Aminis & Agnostou Stratiotou; adult/concession €4/2; ☺8.30am-4pm Wed-Mon) **FREE** As immaculately laid out as you'd expect of the Romans, this rectangular site was the centre of public and commercial Thessaloniki from the 1st to the 4th centuries. Understandably much reduced, you'll nonetheless be able to make out streets, shops, baths, cloisters, an amphitheatre, fountains and more. Underground is the small but very-worthwhile museum, which adds considerably to the understanding of the site you'll take away.

★ Church of Agios Dimitrios CHURCH

(Map p262; ☑ 2310 270 008; www.inad.gr; Agiou Dimitriou 97; ☺6am-10pm, crypt 8am-2pm

JEWISH THESSALONIKI

Thessaloniki's Jewish community swelled following the arrival of exiled Sephardic Jews from Spain in the 15th century. The city enjoyed a golden age of Jewish industry and culture, including crafts such as weaving and silk dyeing, in the 16th century.

The flourishing Jewish community was brutally cut down in 1943 when 43,850 Jews were deported to their deaths at Auschwitz. The history is movingly conveyed at the city's Jewish Museum (see next page).

In the city centre, find Thessaloniki's principal synagogue, Monastirioton (Map p262; ☑ 2310 275 701; www.jmth.gr; Sygrou 35; ☉ 9am-2pm Mon-Fri & 5-8pm Wed, 10am-2pm Sun), used as a Red Cross centre during the WWII Nazi occupation and therefore spared. Services are held at the newer Yad Lazikaron (Map p262; www.jct.gr; Vassiliou Irakliou 26).

Find other traces of this rich history at 19th- and 20th-century former Jewish mansions Villa Allatini (Leoforos Vasilissis Olgas 198), Villa Bianca (Municipal Art Gallery; ☑ 2310 427 555; Themistokli Sofouli 3; ☉ 10am-5pm Tue-Fri, 11am-3pm Sat) FREE – now the Centre for Contemporary Art – and Villa Mordoch (Leoforos Vasilissis Olgas 162), a 15-minute bus ride along Leoforos Vasilissis Olgas. To dig deeper into Thessaloniki's Jewish heritage, buy a copy of *Jewish Sites in Thessaloniki: Brief History and Guide* by Rena Molho and Vilma Hastaoglou-Martinidi (Lycabettus Press) from bookshops or the Jewish Museum.

Wed-Mon) This enormous 7th-century basilica honours Thessaloniki's patron saint. A Roman soldier, Dimitrios was killed around 306 CE at this former Roman bath site by order of Emperor Galerius, infamous persecutor of Christians. The martyrdom site is now a crypt; Dimitrios' remains occupy a silver reliquary inside. The Ottomans made Agios Dimitrios a mosque, and plastered over frescoes that were again revealed after the 1913 Greek reconquest. While the city's fire of 1917 was very damaging, five 8th-century mosaics survive.

Church of the Panagia Achiropiitos
CHURCH

(Map p262; Agias Sofias 56; ☉ 8am-noon & 5-7pm) This basilica-style 5th-century Byzantine church, built over Roman baths and one of the oldest in Greece, has notable mosaics and frescoes. The name, meaning 'made without hands', refers to a miraculous 12th-century appearance of an icon of the Virgin. The first of Thessaloniki's churches to be transformed into a mosque under Ottoman rule, its transition is marked by a marble column on the western side bearing the inscription 'Sultan Murad Conquered Thessaloniki in 833', recounting Murad II's victory in 1430.

Atatürk House
HISTORIC BUILDING

(Map p262; ☑ 2310 248 452; Apostolou Pavlou 17; ☉ 10am-5pm Tue-Sun) FREE Modern Turkey's illustrious founder, Mustafa Kemal Atatürk (1881–1938), was born here. Along with displays tracing Atatürk's life and career you'll see numerous original furnishings, clothing and memorabilia (some supplied from Atatürk's mausoleum in İstanbul, but most

belonging in situ). Built in 1870 and gifted to Turkey in 1935, the house is part of the Turkish Consulate complex.

Church of Agia Sofia
CHURCH

(Map p262; Plateia Agias Sofias; ☉ 7am-1pm & 6-7.30pm) Candlelight on gold chandeliers pierces the gloom in this stunning 8th-century church, modelled on its İstanbul namesake. Among many striking 8th- and 9th-century mosaics is an image of the Ascension of Christ in the central dome, while the 11th-century frescoes are masterpieces of Byzantine devotional art. Built over a previous 3rd-century church, it's notable for the cross-basilica style associated with middle-Byzantine architecture. The narthex and south aisle were used as a burial place for dignitaries from the 10th century.

⊙ Ladadika & Port

Former bazaar neighbourhood Ladadika has Thessaloniki's most concentrated dining and social scene, and is bordered to the east by the former Jewish neighbourhood along Mitropoleos. Opposite, the old port area's bulky pier supports three hip museums and is a favourite evening haunt for students.

Thessaloniki Museum of Photography
MUSEUM

(Map p262; ☑ 2310 566 716; www.thmphoto. gr; Warehouse A, Port of Thessaloniki; adult/concession €2/1; ☉ 11am-7pm Tue-Thu, Sat & Sun, to 10pm Fri) This 1910 port warehouse presents thought-provoking exhibitions of historic and contemporary photography in Greece's only dedicated photography museum. Temporary exhibitions rotate every four months or so, and the museum organises PhotoBiennale (p270), an international photography festival every even-numbered year.

Macedonian Museum of Contemporary Art
MUSEUM

(MOMus; Map p262; ☑ 2310 240 002; www.mmca.gr; Egnatia 154, TIF-Helexpo; ⊙ 10am-6pm Tue-Sun) FREE One of the most respected modern-art institutions in Greece, MOMus grew from an initial bequest of 30 modern masterpieces in 1979, and now exhibits over 2000 examples of painting, sculpture, photography and other visual art. While Greek artists such as Opi Zouni and Angelos Skourtis are given plenty of attention, there are many treasures from other countries and schools. A rich program of temporary shows augments the permanent collection.

Experimental Center for the Arts
MUSEUM

(Map p262; ☑ 2310 593 270; www.cact.gr; Warehouse B1, Port of Thessaloniki; adult/concession €4/2; ⊙ 10am-6pm Tue, Wed & Fri-Sun, to 10pm Thu) The wonderful programming at this old harbour space features fine art, video, installations, photography and all other forms of expression. Exhibitions range from reflections on radical humanist John Berger to the economic crisis, gender and identity issues, Greek art since 1960, and many more fascinating themes.

Modiano Market
MARKET

(Map p262; btwn Ermou & Vassiliou Irakliou; ⊙ 8.30am-2.30pm Mon, Wed & Fri, 8.30am-1.30pm & 5.30-8.30pm Tue, Thu & Sat) The city's largest indoor market sits on the ashes of former Jewish neighbourhood Kadi, which burned down in the 1917 fire. The architect Eli Modiano designed the market, which opened in 1930 and has carried his name ever since. Covered by a glass roof, there are several shops and tavernas here, and it's a charming place to wander around. It's partially closed for renovation until 2022.

Jewish Museum of Thessaloniki
MUSEUM

(Map p262; ☑ 2310 250 406; www.jmth.gr; Agiou Mina 13; ⊙ 9am-2pm Mon-Fri & 5-8pm Wed, 10am-2pm Sun) FREE This touching museum is housed in one of the few Jewish buildings to survive the great fire of 1917, the former office of Jewish newspaper L'Independent. The museum traces the city's Jewish heritage through the 15th-century Sephardic immigrations and its peak period of creativity in the 16th century, before the community was brutally annihilated during the Holocaust.

The upper floor has a timeline of Jewish life in Thessaloniki. The ground floor is split between a collection of photos and Jewish gravestones on one side, and a moving hall of remembrance on the other.

◉ Ano Poli

The labyrinthine, steep streets of Ano Poli, Thessaloniki's upper town, have magnificent ruins, lesser-visited churches, and a wonderful atmosphere. Only Ano Poli (then, the Turkish Quarter) largely survived the citywide devastation of the 1917 fire – although the fire originated here, the wind swept the flames towards the sea.

★ Church of Osios David
CHURCH

(Map p262; Epimenidou 17; ⊙ 10am-5pm Wed-Sun) This serene little 5th-century church, once the *katholikon* (major church) of the Monastery of Saviour Christ of Latomos, is one of the most significant early-Christian sites in Thessaloniki. It contains rare 12th-century frescoes and an even-more extraordinary 5th-century mosaic of Christ and the prophets Ezekiel and Habakkuk. Utterly glorious, it was covered up by the Turks during the church's time as a mosque, and only rediscovered in 1920.

Eptapyrgion
FORTRESS

(Yedi Kule; Map p262; ☑ 2313 310 400; ⊙ 8am-5.45pm Mon-Fri, to 3.45pm Sat & Sun) FREE A former Byzantine fortress repurposed as a prison by the Ottomans and only decommissioned in 1989, the Eptapyrgion ('Seven Towers') is a grim reminder of Thessaloniki's penal past, recounted in the Greek blues songs known as *rembetika*. Reached by a steep walk to the heights of Ano Poli, it's perfectly preserved, allowing access to some towers (of which there are actually 10), communal blocks and isolation cells, and displaying historical information and scattered artworks. The views from the Byzantine walls are the best in the city.

Kastra
HISTORIC SITE

(Map p262) FREE The *kastra* (castle) encloses Byzantine churches and timber-framed houses with overhanging upper storeys. Enjoy panoramic views from the tower by the eastern edge of the Byzantine Walls, built to survive sieges in the late 4th century BCE. Emperor Theodosius fortified the

NORTHERN GREECE THESSALONIKI

walls; in places they were 10m high and 5m thick. They stood until the 19th century when the Ottomans demolished large stretches. Enjoy the views of the sunset over the city, along with students and locals.

Monastery of Vlatadon
MONASTERY

(Map p262; Eptapyrgio 64; ⊙ 7.30am-8pm) **FREE** Believed to have been founded around 1351 on the place where Paul preached in Thessaloniki, this secluded monastery blends fascinating history with some of the best views of the city. Listed by Unesco, it is thought to have been significant for Hesychasm, a controversial movement whose foremost 14th-century proponent, St Gregory Palamas, is depicted in a fresco here. You can explore the grounds, the ancient church, a museum of icons, and an aviary filled with peacocks.

A now-lost imperial *chrysobull* (gold-sealed decree) indicates the Byzantine Empress Anna Paleologina endowed Vlatadon, which still preserves a rich archive of documents dating to the 15th century.

Church of Nikolaos Orfanos
CHURCH

(Map p262; Apostolou Pavlou; ⊙ hours vary) This early-14th-century church, one of the most beautiful in a city heavy with stunning examples, has superb (though age-darkened) frescoes, many dating to the church's earliest days. The 'orphan' in the church's name remains a mystery: it may be a nod to an anonymous benefactor or be linked to a former orphanage nearby.

☞ Tours

Thessaloniki Walking Tours
WALKING

(☑ 6798186900; www.thessalonikiwalkingtours. com) Started by a Thessaloniki journalist, who enlisted architect, archaeologist and historian friends to work as guides, this is a great opportunity to go on specialised walks with expert locals. There are themed tours, such as a sailing tour exploring the city's bay as well as specific buildings, or a music tour that takes you around famous *rembetika* bars. Call for details.

★彡 Festivals & Events

Thessaloniki Documentary Festival
FILM

(☑ 2310 378 400; www.filmfestival.gr; 10-screening tickets €25; ⊙ Mar) Celebrating its 23rd iteration online in 2021 and adding a podcast competition section, this 10-day festival generally sees a rich program of short and feature-length documentary films screened at various Thessaloniki venues.

🚶 City Walk
Thessaloniki

START EPTAPYRGION
END PORT
LENGTH 8KM; SIX HOURS

Start around 9am, as many churches close by noon. Avoid Mondays, when most sites are closed.

Begin at the city's highest and most scenic point, the grimly fascinating Byzantine-fortress-turned-Turkish prison ❶ **Eptapyrgion**. From here, go downhill to the ❷ **Kastra** at the easternmost end of the Byzantine Walls, admiring the mighty Alysseos Tower and the handsome Anna Palaiologina Gate. Once inside the walls, and in Ano Poli, follow them west on the main road, Eptapyrgio. Crossing Akropoleos, look on your left for the entrance to the lofty ❸ **Monastery of Vlatadon**.

Rejoin Eptapyrgio and continue west, following more ragged Byzantine walls. Turn left at Argonafton, and immediately left again to follow the stairs on Sthenonos. At the bottom of the stairs, veer right along Dimitriou Poliorkitou. Look out for the easy-to-miss narrow way Lycia, branching to the left, and follow it down to Unesco-listed ❹ **Church of Osios David** (p265) – a sign for the church marks the stairway. This 5th-century gem has many rare frescoes.

From here, wander labyrinthine Ano Poli eastwards along its small and charming streets. The most direct route follows Fotiou across Akropoleos, turning left onto Krispou. The road wiggles over Theotokopoulou into Eolou, and then hits Moreas. Dogleg right down Moreas, then left into Kodrou to find the 14th-century ❺ **Church of Nikolaos Orfanos** Take Irodotou south; once you cross Olympiados and reach Kassandrou, you're well and truly back in the big city.

Dodge the pedestrian bustle for a few blocks west along Kassandrou and turn south on Agiou Nikolaou. You'll see the bulging red-domed roof of ❻ **Yeni Hammam** (Map p260; ☑ 2313 059 024; Agiou Nikolaou 3; ⊙ bar 7am-3pm), a restored 17th-century Turkish bath, in front of you. A few steps south of Yeni Hammam is the burly 7th-century ❼ **Church of Agios Dimitrios** (p263), occupying its own square and sheltering relics of St Dimitrios within.

Venture south on Agnostou Stratiotou across Olympou and you'll see the ruin of

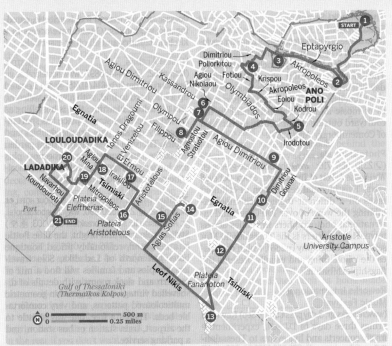

the **8 Roman Forum** (p263), with a backdrop of modern tower blocks. After marvelling at the contrast of ancient and new, double back to Agiou Dimitriou and proceed east 10 blocks to **9 Atatürk House** (p264) on your left, inside the Turkish consulate.

A block further east on Agiou Dimitriou, turn right on Dimitriou Gounari; at the end you'll find the imposing and newly renovated **10 Rotunda of Galerius** (p263). Amble downhill along the path towards the statue-studded 3rd-century **11 Arch of Galerius** (p263), created to commemorate Galerius' victory over the Persian army. After crossing busy Egnatia, meander down the pedestrianised street until you see a square dominated by low, excavated walls. The ruins may look scant, but they are remnants of the once-vast **12 Palace of Galerius** (p263).

Continue following gravity's pull downhill. Cross Tsimiski and, at Plateia Fanarioton, veer left to see the iconic **13 White Tower** (p258). Thessaloniki's waterfront icon was once a notorious prison, but now harbours a multimedia museum. Next wander west for a waterside stroll on Leoforos Nikis, a strip graced with some of the swankiest bars in the city.

Leave the water by turning right up Agias Sofias towards the impressive **14 Church of Agia Sofia** (p264). If your energy is low after craning your neck at its mosaic-decorated

inner dome, double back down Agias Sofias for a quick sugar rush at **15 Blé** (p271), before returning to Tsimiski to proceed west.

Soon you'll hit Aristotelous; **16 Plateia Aristotelous** (Map p260) is to the left. After exploring the square, head north on Aristotelous, then turn left on Irakliou: between here and Ermou you'll discover **17 Modiano Market** (p265), full of fish on ice and trays of olives and cheese.

Nibble your way through Modiano before rejoining Ermou. You'll cross busy main drag Venizelou. Next turn towards the sea once more by pacing down Ionos Dragoumi, through the former florists' market, the Louloudadika district, now overflowing with clothes shops, bars and restaurants. If your feet are sore, end here with a visit to the excellent **18 Jewish Museum** (p265), to the left on Agiou Mina.

Further down Ionos Dragoumi, at the Tsimiski intersection, note the splendid **19 National Bank of Greece** (Map p260; Tsimiski 11; ⊙ 8am-2pm Mon-Fri) building; after it, turn right onto Mitropoleos and zigzag your way into the **20 Ladadika district**, once comprising olive-oil warehouses and now home to atmospheric restaurants and bars. Complete the tour with a well-deserved late lunch at one of Ladadika's eateries. Otherwise, finish with sea views by walking south to Kountouriotou towards the beautified **21 port**.

anchovies with Cretan rusk and pickles is a stunning combination. While local producers are a focus, you can try cheeses and wines from across the country.

★ I Nea Follia   GREEK €€

(Map p262; ☑ 2310 960 383; cnr Aristomenous & Charitos; mains €7.50-12; ☺ 2pm-midnight Sep-Jun; 🛜🖲) This charismatic little backstreet joint, decorated with herb garlands, utensils, event posters and even a vintage jukebox, is locally loved for its outstanding food and convivial atmosphere. The grilled octopus with fava-bean puree and sea fennel is superb, and you can taste unique cheeses from islands such as Naxos, Andros and Ios.

✖ Ladadika & Port

Full tou Meze   MEZEDHES €

(Map p262; ☑ 2310 524 700; www.fullmeze.gr; Katouni 3; mezedhes €4-6, mains €7-9; ☺ 1pm-midnight; 🛜) This Ladadika favourite sees families, friends and workmates pack bread tables to order mezedhes and mains such as *marathopita* (Cretan fennel-and-cheese pie), grilled sardines and fava-bean puree with caperberries. In prime position on Plateia Katouni, it's tempting to let the hours just drift past between jugs of wine.

Omikron   GREEK €

(Map p262; ☑ 2310 532 774; Oplopiou 3; mains €7-15; ☺ noon-midnight Tue-Sat; 🛜) Beneath walls strikingly decorated with classical-painting mash-ups (think Botticelli's Venus emerging from a piece of aerosol art), this charming little place dishes up heart-warming plates such as homemade pasta with mushrooms and pureed fava beans with chilli oil. Bounteous seasonal salads, expertly grilled meat and super-fresh seafood complete the picture.

Pizza Poselli   PIZZA €

(Map p262; ☑ 2314 019 687; Vilara 2; pizza slices €2.30; ☺ noon-5am Sun-Thu, to 6am Fri & Sat) Many locals will agree that this is the best pizza place in town. Simple decor, with chic touches in the way of elegant wooden tables and vintage lamps, Poselli has mozzarella and truffle-oil pizzas, margheritas and the classic standards done to perfection. It also does a roaring trade in pizza by the slice for the Valaoritou bar crowd.

★ Sempriko   GREEK €€

(Map p262; ☑ 2310 557 513; Fragkon 2; mains €9-15; ☺ noon-11pm; 🛜) Just inside the western Byzantine Walls, Sempriko has become a by-word for excellent food. Enormous steaks

immersed in truffle oil are expertly grilled, while a salad of just wild greens, fresh curd, olives and tomatoes is unimprovable. Friendly, competent service and a good range of cheeses and wines from across Greece are the last pieces of a delightful puzzle.

✖ Ano Poli

Tsinari   GREEK €

(Map p262; ☑ 2310 284 028; Papadopoulou 72; mains €5-7; ☺ 1pm-midnight) This convivial *ouzerie* (a taverna serving food that complements ouzo) sits on a quiet crossroads in Ano Poli. In operation since the 19th century, it boasts a tile-floored, stove-heated dining room, a flower-scented deck for warm weather, and a great way with grilled sardines, roast aubergine, meatballs and other *ouzerie* staples. Tea, wine and other nonouzo drinks are easily obtained.

Rediviva Cucina Povera   GREEK €

(Map p262; ☑ 2313 067 400; Papadopoulou 70; mains €5-8; ☺ 1pm-midnight; 🛜) This earthy Ano Poli restaurant sources many of its ingredients locally and from its own back garden. Using what's in season, it serves a diverse range of Greek dishes with particular emphasis on the food of Crete and Lesvos. Try the Cretan herb *pita* (pie), sun-dried fish and fantastic salads, then perhaps buy a jar of their marmalade to take away.

Igglis   TAVERNA €

(Map p262; ☑ 2313 011 967; Irodotou 32; mains €7; ☺ 1pm-midnight; 🛜) This Ano Poli taverna's ordinary looks hide some extraordinary food. Slow-cooked pork shank in thyme, anything grilled, and daily specials such as mushrooms with cured pork and Cretan cheese all testify eloquently to the know-how in the kitchen. The excellent salads make use of whatever's in season, and there are local beers and *tsipouro* (pomace brandy) to wash things down.

Radikal   GREEK €€

(Map p262; ☑ 2310 202 007; http://radikal.gr; Stergiou 61; mains €8-12; ☺ 6pm-midnight Tue-Thu, 1pm-midnight Fri & Sat, 1-6pm Sun; 🛜) Up in the heights of Ano Poli, beneath one of the best-preserved stretches of the city's Byzantine walls, Radikal is a handsomely styled restaurant where the kitchen more than plays its part. From huge, spanking-fresh salads to slow dishes such as rooster stewed in wine with small pasta and sheep's cheese, the food's all seasonal and expertly handled. Great wines, too.

THE BEST THESSALONIKI DESSERT STOPS

Thessaloniki's historic ties with the Ottoman East have bequeathed it a rich tradition of sweets. In between traditional Greek pastries, fire your taste buds with *soutzouk loukoum* (aromatic rolls of Turkish delight and pistachio), as well as halva and refreshing gelato.

Trigona Elenidis (Map p262; ☎ 2310 257 510; www.elenidis.gr; cnr Dimitriou Gounari & Tsimiski; trigones €2.50; ⏱ 9am-11pm) A veritable institution since 1960, Elenidis specialises in Thessaloniki's favourite pastry, the *trigona*. This sweet, flaky triangular cone, filled with tasty custard cream, is legendary in these parts, and was first created here. Locals emerge with 2kg boxes, but you might want to save room for the Greek halva (made with semolina) or homemade ice cream.

Chatzis (Map p262; ☎ 2310 279 058; http://chatzis.gr; Venizelou 50; sweets €1.40-4; ⏱ 8am-1am; 🛜) Glistening syrup-soaked treats have been luring dessert fans into Chatzis since 1908, back when Thessaloniki was still an Ottoman city. Try the moist, sugar-rush-inducing *revani* (syrupy semolina cake), chickpea and raisin halva, or *rizogalo* (rice pudding) scented with cinnamon.

Terkenlis (Map p262; ☎ 2310 271 148; www.terkenlis.gr; cnr Tsimiski 30 & Aristotelous 4; cakes & sandwiches from €2; ⏱ 7am-11pm Tue-Fri, to midnight Fri & Sat; 🛜) This upmarket patisserie chain has temptations including freshly baked *tzoureki* (brioche-style bread) and macarons, as well as confectionery and honey-glazed fruit salads.

Blé (Map p262; ☎ 2310 231 200; www.ble.com.gr; Agias Sofias 19, cnr Georgiou Stavrou; cakes €2-5; ⏱ 24hr; 🛜) This chic patisserie chain (the name is French for 'wheat') offers a tooth-tingling range, from traditional Cretan baked goods to dainty cupcakes, at all hours. The Thessalonikians crowd here in the afternoons, choosing from creamy millefeuille or small bites of chocolate cake topped with berries. Get a coffee, too, and watch the world go by through the large windows.

Kokkinos Fournos (Map p262; ☎ 2310 206 337; www.kokkinosfournos.gr; Apostolou Pavlou 1; ⏱ 7am-8.30pm Mon-Sat) Just above the Rotunda of Galerius, this classic bakery does great breads as well as Thessaloniki's best *koulourakia vanilias* – crunchy, slightly sweet golden cookies perfect for dipping in Greek coffee.

NORTHERN GREECE THESSALONIKI

Drinking & Nightlife

If you are after varied and lively drinking spots, Thessaloniki won't disappoint. Each area has its own character and the bars follow suit. Prepare to stay up until the early hours.

★**Chatzi Bahtse**　　　　　　BAR
(☎ 2310 541 786; www.chatzi-bahtse.gr; Georgiou Tsontou 9; ⏱ 9pm-2am Thu-Sat, 8pm-midnight Sun) A little out of the way, this is the place to go for *rembetika* (urban 'blues') and other unamplified strains of traditional Greek song. Three brothers started it in the 1958 house of their father, and they ensure everything – the home-cooked food, the carafes of juicy wine, the tables draped with wine-splattered cloths, and the music – stay perfect.

Georgiou Tsontou is accessed via a slip road from the multilane highway heading northwest from the centre. Taking a cab the 3.6km from Plateia Aristotelous should take 15 minutes and cost no more than €10.

White Tower & Waterfront

West of the White Tower, pedestrianised Iktinou is bursting with boutique bars and charismatic cafes. Along the waterfront, most bars offer little to distinguish between them, except perhaps the stylishness of their interiors and the quality of their cocktails.

★**Café Palermo**　　　　　　CAFE
(Map p262; ☎ 2310 279 958; 1st fl, Plateia Aristotelous 8; coffee €2.50; ⏱ 10am-midnight; 🛜) A lovely oasis of potted plants, geometric tiles, slanting coloured light and vintage ephemera awaits those who find Palermo, up an unpromising flight of stairs within Plateia Aristotelous 8. The coffee, tea and cake are all excellent, and the calm contrasts deliciously with the throng of the square below.

Vogatsikou 3　　　　　COCKTAIL BAR
(Map p262; ☎ 2310 222 899; http://vogatsikou3.gr; Vogatsikou 3; cocktails €9-10; ⏱ 9am-3am; 🛜) Locals consider this darkly stylish cocktail bar

to be the best in town. If you like your drinks fancy and shaken, you'll enjoy poring over a long menu of classic and inventive cocktails. Whisky drinkers are very well catered to as well, and the nonsmoking policy comes as a great relief to many.

Thermaïkos
BAR

(Map p262; ☎2310 239 842; Leoforos Nikis 23; cocktails €7; ⊙10am-2am Mon-Thu, to 3am Fri-Sun; ☎) A marvellously mixed crowd plies this unpretentious waterfront bar, named after the gulf that forms the view. The chequerboard-tiled interior embraces cheeky vintage flourishes to create an effect somewhere between *Happy Days* and the Arabian Nights. An electronic soundtrack, sometimes provided by visiting DJs, intoxicates as much as the cocktails do.

Hoppy Pub
CRAFT BEER

(Map p262; ☎2310 269 203; Nikiforou Foka 6; ⊙5.30pm-1.30am Tue-Sun; ☎) With 18 beers on tap, and many more behind glass, Hoppy is Thessaloniki's most dedicated purveyor of craft and obscure froth. Beers change every week, quality rock plays on the stereo, and the smoke-free policy makes your cheese, charcuterie and other bar snacks taste all the better.

Skyline
BAR

(Map p262; ☎2310 265 460; Egnatia 154; ⊙10am-1am Sun-Thu, to 2am Fri & Sat; ☎) **FREE** A tacky yet thoroughly enjoyable throwback, this revolving bar-and-restaurant sits atop the OTE Tower, a 76m-high spired statement of the 1960s from which the first Greek TV broadcasts emanated. A full rotation, sweeping in the sea, city and hills, takes an hour, and is accompanied by live piano from 7pm to midnight. Expect to pay roughly double for drinks.

Berlin
BAR

(Map p262; www.facebook.com/berlinbarthessal oniki; Smyrnis 10; ⊙midnight-9am) Berlin has operated since 1979, and still welcomes a crowd of bleary-eyed party people seeking a grunge or Gothic fix to see them through until morning. As it doesn't open before the witching hour, you can assume your night's already gone off the rails if you find yourself here.

North of Egnatia

North of Egnatia you'll have to look harder for nightlife, though Olimpou, running west from the northwest corner of the Roman Forum, has a clutch of quality bars.

To Pikap
CAFE

(Map p262; ☎2310 271 499; www.topikap.gr; Olimpou 57; ⊙noon-1am Tue-Sun, from 6.30pm Mon; ☎) This grab-bag of groovy businesses, anchored on a gregariously smoky cafe-bar, also accommodates a record shop, a few racks of designer T-shirts and even a radio station over two levels of clean lines and funky furniture.

Mpate Skyloi
BAR

(Map p262; Olympou 61; ⊙noon-late; ☎) This punk- and alternative-oriented dive bar is the place to come for beer, good company and three-minute, three-chord rock songs. If you're not there when a live performance or party's on, just prop up the long red-wood bar and raise a glass to the picture of the sainted Lemmy that hangs above.

Valaoritou

The last decade has seen this former commercial district, north of Ladadika between Tsimiski and Egnatia, metamorphose into an alternative nightlife district. Graffiti and dive bars sit next to mushrooming cocktail bars.

Gorílas
COCKTAIL BAR

(Map p262; ☎6977590306; Verias 3; ⊙9am-3am Sun, Tue & Wed, to 4am Thu, to 5am Fri & Sat; ☎) This ultrapopular cocktail bar is all industrial interiors and serious attitudes – when it comes to cocktails. Thankfully the welcome comes without attitude, the music is eclectic and tasteful, and DJs select on weekend nights. Check out Gorílas' special cocktail mixes, which change seasonally.

Ladadika & Port

Competition from Valaoritou inspired a comeback for Ladadika, a historic quarter of old tobacco houses and brothel buildings; now its narrow spoking streets are lined almost exclusively with tavernas, bars and music venues. Facing it, the port area has trendy cocktail bars and student-driven cafes, and several art venues.

High School Pizza Bar
COCKTAIL BAR

(Map p262; ☎2310 286 161; Leoforos Nikis 9a; ⊙9am-2am) This nostalgic bar and pizzeria has some of the best cocktails in Thessaloniki's port area. The decor evokes school days past with pencil candleholders, exam-room chairs and arithmetic on the walls, and the mixed drinks are truly top of the class.

⭐ Entertainment

Olympion CINEMA
(Map p262; ☑ 2310 378 400; Plateia Aristotelous 10) Inside the Olympion complex in Thessaloniki's Plateia Aristotelous, this ornate, crimson-hued cinema was built in 1950 and hosts the Thessaloniki International Film Festival (p270), as well as the Thessaloniki Documentary Festival (p268). Check out the views from the 5th-floor cafe.

Rover LIVE MUSIC
(Map p262; ☑ 2310 544 304; Salaminos 6; ⊘ 4.30pm-4am Tue, Thu & Sun, 2.30pm-4am Wed, 4.30pm-6am Fri & Sat) Live music and arts events form an eclectic calendar at Rover bar. But while the soundtrack could be anything from Slovenian dubstep to rock 'n' roll, the cocktail quality is thirst-quenchingly consistent.

Kismet LIVE MUSIC
(Map p262; ☑ 2310 548 490; Katouni 11; ⊘ 10pm-4am) Set right among Ladadika's restaurants, Kismet is a fine, though crowded, spot for live bands, ranging from rock and pop to Greece's most popular *rembetika* acts.

🔒 Shopping

Modiano Market (p267), excellent for food shopping, is undergoing redevelopment due for completion in 2022. There are still abundant food vendors and delis in the markets and streets surrounding it. West Egnatia has bargain-basement shopping, while Tsimiski has more upscale clothing and electronics stores. Clothing boutiques and swanky design stores cluster around Proxenou Koromila, Mitropoleos and the connecting streets, east of Vogatsikou.

⭐ From Thessaloniki ARTS & CRAFTS
(Map p262; ☑ 2310 272 298; www.fromthessaloniki.gr; Dimitriou Gounari 21; ⊘ 10.30am-8.30pm Mon-Sat) Architect Evangelia and set designer Athanasia, two wonderfully creative and warm women, started this little shop that makes and sells the most original and beautiful souvenirs in town. Choose from painted tiles, Greek god and goddess pillows, T-shirts, tote bags, mugs, jewellery, notebooks – all original and locally produced, and all useful objects that you can enjoy for years.

⭐ R2 Rebelou 2 ARTS & CRAFTS
(Art Store Cafe; Map p262; ☑ 2310 265 999; Rempelou 2; ⊘ 9am-1am) It's difficult to categorise this place – it includes a workshop, a shop, an exhibition space and a cafe-bar. Run by agriculturist Christos and the graphic designer Nikos, who is also a marvellous carpenter, the pair find old furniture and decoration and turn them into something new and original.

⭐ Ergon Agora FOOD
(Map p262; ☑ 2310 288 008; www.ergonproducts.gr; Pavlou Mela 42; ⊘ 9am-1am) Fresh fish and meat, cheeses, top-notch fruit and vegetables, bread, oils, honey, vinegars – you name it, it's all to be found in this high-end 'closed market'. If you're overwhelmed by all you might create, you can simply put yourself in the hands of the central kitchen, which pumps out mainly Greek food from 10am to midnight.

Bientôt WINE
(Map p262; ☑ 2310 253 781; Morgentaou 5; ⊘ 11am-4pm Mon, Wed & Sat, 11am-3pm & 5-9pm Tue, Thu & Fri) This passionate little wine shop is the ideal place to learn more about the varied, expanding and ever-refining world of Greek wine. The staff, who cultivate close relationships with producers working with indigenous Greek grape varieties, are happy to talk visitors through prebooked tastings.

Herbs Olympos SPICES
(Map p262; ☑ 2310 533 591; https://votana-olympos.gr; Agiou Mina 18; ⊘ 7.30am-4pm Mon-Fri, 8am-3.30pm Sat) A fantastic place to shop and learn – Alkiviadis Grigoriadis, the store owner and botanist, will give you an insight into all the properties of the herbs, spices and essential oils you want to buy. He also makes herbal drinks and oregano oil for dribbling onto salads.

ℹ️ Information

MEDICAL SERVICES

Whenever closed, Thessaloniki pharmacies must list nearby working pharmacies.

If going to hospital, bring an ID card/passport and insurance information (if possible). If you are an EU citizen, bring your EU health card.

Farmakeio Gouva (☑ 2310 205 544; Agias Sofias 110; ⊘ 8.30am-9pm Mon-Fri, 9am-3.30pm Sat) Pharmacy in Ano Poli with experienced staff.

Farmakeio Sofia Tympanidou (☑ 2310 522 155; Egnatia 17; ⊘ 8am-8pm) Well-stocked pharmacy on west Egnatia.

Ippokrateio (☑ 2310 892 000; Kostantinoupoleos 49; ⊘ 24hr) Some 2km east of the city centre, this is Thessaloniki's largest public hospital.

POLICE

Police Station (📞 2310 502 720; Dodekanisou 6)

TOURIST INFORMATION

For local happenings and other info, visit the frequently updated www.enjoythessaloniki.com website, run by local enthusiasts.

Mt Athos Pilgrims' Bureau (Map p262; 📞 2310 263 308; www.agioritikiestia.gr; Egnatia 109, Thessaloniki; ⏱ 9am-4pm Mon-Fri) Issues permits for Mt Athos monasteries (p282) to male pilgrims.

Tourism Office (Map p262; 📞 2310 229 070; www.thessaloniki.travel; Plateia Aristotelous 10; ⏱ 10am-6pm) The tourist office on Plateia Aristotelous can assist with hotel bookings, local information, and arranging tours and excursions beyond Thessaloniki.

🛈 Getting There & Away

Thessaloniki is northern Greece's transport hub and gateway to the Balkans. Major European airlines and budget airlines fly to Thessaloniki and within Greece.

AIR

Besides Greece's **Aegean Airlines** (https://en.aegeanair.com), many foreign carriers use Thessaloniki airport for domestic and international flights. Prices and routes are fluid, so ascertain which companies are currently flying from the **Makedonia International Airport** (SKG; 📞 2310 985 000; www.thessalonikiairport.com) website. Then visit a travel agent or book online.

If you're visiting Thessaloniki briefly, you can store luggage with Sky Bag at the airport.

BOAT

Ferries from Thessaloniki port are limited and change annually. To access the Sporades, you must depart from Volos (all year) or Agios Konstantinos further south during the summer period only. With private yacht charters you can sail to Italy, Turkey and Albania.

Consult www.ferries.gr or **Karacharisis Travel** (📞 2310 513 005; www.thesferry.gr; Salaminos 10; ⏱ 10am-6pm Mon-Fri, to 2pm Sat) for details and booking options for ferries from Thessaloniki.

BUS

Thessaloniki's main bus station, **Macedonia Intercity Bus Station** (📞 2310 595 400; www.ktelmacedonia.gr; Giannitson 244), is 3km west of the city centre. Each destination has its own specific ticket counter, signposted in Greek and English.

For Athens *only*, avoid the trip by going instead to **Monastiriou bus station** (Map p262; 📞 2310 500 111; http://ktelthes.gr; Monastiriou 67) – next to the train station – where Athens-bound buses start before calling in at KTEL Makedonia.

Buses leave for Halkidiki from the eastern Thessaloniki **Halkidiki bus terminal** (📞 2310 316 555; www.ktel-chalkidikis.gr; Km 9 Thessaloniki-Halkidiki Rd). The terminal is out towards the airport, reached via city buses 45A or 45B. From the main bus station, buses stop en route at the train station and Plateia Aristotelous. With waiting time and traffic, this 'express' service to the bus terminal can take more than an hour. Then there's the trip to Halkidiki itself. The whole production can take three to six hours. Consider renting a car for your Halkidiki trip or at least take a taxi (around €15) to Halkidiki bus terminal.

International

KTEL offers international services to Bulgaria and Albania. Direct services reach Tirana (€30, nine hours, twice daily), Sofia (€23, five hours, eight daily), Plovdiv (€30, 7½ hours, five daily) and Blagoevgrad (€20, four hours, eight daily).

Weekly overnight buses set out to the Slovak and Czech Republics (€80, 19½ hours), through Bratislava, Brno and Olomouc.

Small bus companies, such as **Simeonidis Tours** (📞 2310 540 970; www.simeonidistours.gr; 26 Oktovriou 14; ⏱ 9am-6pm Mon-Fri, to 2pm Sat), serve Turkey, Romania, Hungary, Serbia, the Czech and Slovak Republics, and Germany. **Crazy Holidays** (Map p262; 📞 2310 231 545; www.crazy-holidays.gr; 1st fl, Aristotelous 10; ⏱ 9am-4pm Mon-Fri, to 2pm Sat) operates three daily buses to İstanbul. It also goes to Skopje, Belgrade, Budapest and Tirana.

Services from Macedonia Intercity Bus Station

DESTINATION	DURATION	FARE (€)	FREQUENCY
Alexandroupoli	3¾hrs	32	8 daily
Arta	4½hrs	37	3 daily
Athens	6hrs	45	hourly
Didymotiho	5½hrs	41	8 daily
Drama	2hrs	15	hourly
Edessa	1¾hrs	9.70	15 daily
Florina	3¼hrs	17	5 daily
Igoumenitsa	4hrs	38	2 daily
Ioannina	3½hrs	31	6 daily
Kastoria	3hrs	19	7 daily
Kavala	2¼hrs	15	15 daily
Komotini	3hrs	28	6 daily
Litihoro	1¼hrs	8.50	13 daily
Orestiada	6hrs	43	8 daily
Serres	1½hrs	8.20	half-hourly
Veria	1hrs	7	15 daily
Volos	2hrs	20	8 daily
Xanthi	2½hrs	20	11 daily

TRAIN

International

Daily international (also known as intercity; IC) trains serve Sofia (€17, six hours) and in summer only, Blagoevgrad (€12, 4½ hours) in Bulgaria. A service also goes to Skopje (€13, six hours) and Belgrade (€34, 14 hours). Check ahead at Thessaloniki **train station** (www.trainose.gr; Monastiriou) or consult the OSE website (www. trainose.gr).

Domestic

Direct ICE trains serve Athens (€5, four to five hours, six daily), Paleofarsalas (for Meteora; €25, 1¾ hours, eight daily) and Larissa (€14 to €22, 1½ to two hours, 17 daily). Regular trains also serve Veria, Edessa and Florina (mostly via Platy). Only two daily trains currently serve Xanthi, Komotini and Alexandroupoli in Thrace.

❶ Getting Around

TO/FROM THE AIRPORT

Bus X1 (during the day) and N1 (at night) runs half-hourly from the airport (17km southeast of town), heading west through the city to the main bus station (KTEL Makedonia) via the train station. Tickets cost €2 from the airport to the bus station; €1 for short journeys.

Taxis to the airport cost €20 to €30, depending on the distance – it is a set rate, even if the meter reads a lower fee (this allows for airport charges and the differences in central locations). Call in advance if you need them to pick you up from town; the operator speaks English.

BUS

Dependable city buses have electronic rolling signs listing the next destination, accompanied by an audio announcement in Greek and English. Screens above most bus stops note how many minutes until the next buses.

Bus X1 connects the main bus station (KTEL Makedonia) and the train station, while buses 45A and 45B stop at both (plus Plateia Aristotelous and Kamara) en route to the Halkidiki Bus Terminal. From the train station, major points on Egnatia are constantly served by buses such as bus 10 and 14.

Buy tickets on *periptera* (street kiosks), or from on-board blue ticket machines (€1). Validate the former in the orange machines. Machines neither give change nor accept bills; when boarding, be sure you have the right change and buy your ticket immediately. Thessaloniki's ticket police pounce at any sign of confusion. If they nab you, you'll pay €60.

CAR

If driving, take note that Ano Poli's streets are steep and can be rather narrow, so avoid driving there if you're not used to such conditions. If you can't find free parking (a common problem in hectic Thessaloniki, where double parking is de rigueur), try the municipal parking at the port (per hour €2). For rental cars try:

Avance Rent a Car (☑ 2310 279 888; www.avance.gr; Agelaki 7)

Budget Rent a Car (☑ 2310 888 100; www.budget.gr; Papandreou 5; ⊙ 8am-9pm Mon-Sat)

TAXI

Thessaloniki's blue-and-white taxis carry multiple passengers, and only take you if you're going the same way. The minimum fare is €3.40. A more expensive 'night rate' takes effect from midnight until 5am. To book a cab for an airport transfer, try **Taxi Way** (☑ 18 300, 2310 866 866; www. taxiway.gr).

Halkidiki   Χαλκιδική

The popular Halkidiki Peninsula has three tendrils stretching into the Aegean Sea. Kassandra and Sithonia draw crowds to their blissful beaches and growing adventure travel scene. Meanwhile, Athos is the mysterious monks' republic.

Kassandra Peninsula
Χερσόνησος Κασσάνδρας

Attractive beaches and proximity to Thessaloniki bring no shortage of tourists to Kassandra; its roads are clogged with city-based weekenders, Balkan families and Australian backpackers during the summer. But its rippling forested interior is a delight for road trips, mountain-bike tours draw visitors away from the shade of their beach umbrellas, and unfussy thermal baths are an antidote to the resort gloss.

Kallithea is a great base if you want nightlife; Polyhrono is crammed with fast-food places and souvenir stands but has great beaches; and Pefkohori is quieter with even more resplendent sands. You'll find the less-busy south coast has more cultural draws, such as snoozy villages and a thermal spa near Loutra.

🏃 Activities

★ **Possidi Cape**   BEACH

(Poseidi) An absolute beauty of a beach lies hidden at Possidi Cape. Kilometres of sand are lapped by crystal-clear waters, and it's a rare place to find peace and quiet (though little shade) in the summer months. It's a joy year-round, though, backed as it is by a lighthouse and a pine forest.

THE AMPHIPOLIS TOMB

In 2012 excavations at Amphipolis, an Athenian colony founded 100km east of modern-day Thessaloniki in 437 BCE, revealed the 497m-perimeter of a huge tomb. Made of limestone faced with marble, the circular walls rose to 3m and enclosed the largest ancient burial mound yet uncovered in Greece. Inevitable speculation that the tomb might belong to Alexander the Great, subsequently quashed by experts, has been replaced by suggestions it might belong to his mother, son, or even his wife Roxanne. It certainly dates to the period immediately after Alexander's death.

Three separate chambers have been uncovered, yielding five human skeletons, a splendid pebble mosaic depicting the abduction of Persephone by Hades, a set of magnificent marble doors and two marble sphinxes. The colossal Lion of Amphipolis, discovered and reconstructed several kilometres distant, once sat atop the tomb, and is thought to be the work of the master sculptor who produced the sphinxes found inside. Excavations at the site are ongoing, and it is hoped it may be accessible to the public by 2022. In the meantime, portable exhibits can be seen at the nearby **Archaeological Museum of Amphipolis** (☑ 23220 32474; http://odysseus.culture.gr; Amphipoli; adult/concession €6/3; ☉ 8am-3pm Nov–mid-May, to 8pm late May–Oct; ℗).

🛏 Sleeping

Polyhrono, Afytos and Pefkohori all have a wealth of hotels to stay in, but expect them to be very busy indeed in the summer months.

Blue Bay Hotel
HOTEL €€

(☑ 23740 91645; www.bluebayhotel.com.gr; Afytos; d/ste from €75/138; ☉ May-Oct; ℗ ✳ 🛜 ≋) This serene hotel, five minutes' drive north of Kallithea through narrow country lanes, has lively modern decor on the inside, and a delightful blue mosaic pool outside. With beach access, 69 clean-and-comfy rooms, a Greek and international breakfast spread, and a lavish *hammam,* it's family-friendly and a lovely spot to unwind. Four-night minimums apply at most times.

Flegra Beach Boutique Apartments
APARTMENT €€

(☑ 23740 61832; www.flegrahotels.com; Pefkohori; d/tr from €60/85; ☉ May-Oct; ℗ ✳ 🛜) The opulent Flegra Beach in Pefkohori village has luxury apartments with nautical and modern trimmings, and a snazzy beach bar and restaurant. Towards the southern end of the beach strip, it's a very appealing choice. Minimum stays of three or more nights apply for much of the season.

Akrogiali Exclusive Hotel
BOUTIQUE HOTEL €€

(☑ 6944503920; www.hotelakrogiali.com; Polyhrono; d incl breakfast from €80; ℗ ✳ 🛜) This sleek, technologically forward, adults-only hotel in a backstreet gives easy access to Polyhrono's seaside strip together with the peace of a quieter locale. There's a good restaurant, and a bar and lounge should you wish to maximise time here.

Flegra Palace Hotel
HOTEL €€€

(☑ 23740 61702; www.flegrahotels.com; Pefkohori; d from €140; ☉ May-Oct; ℗ ✳ 🛜 ≋) Spacious doubles and suites surround a refreshing pool at this family-friendly four-star hotel with breezy charm, just west of Pefkohori on Kassandra's north coast. The drawback is its roadside location, although the beach is very close. Three- and five-night minimums apply in busy times.

🍴 Eating

There are waterfront tavernas and restaurants in Polyhrono, Afytos and Pefkohori, all catering to tourists and serving fish and seafood.

Restaurant Bakalis
GREEK €

(☑ 23740 63060; www.bakalis-restaurant.com; Pefkohori; mains €8-10; ☉ 11am-1am; 🛜) A good seafood taverna with tables on the waterfront, just above the beach at the southern end of the strip. Try the grilled fish, big refreshing salads, or specials such as *htapodi me kofto makaronaki* (octopus with pasta). It's a busy place in the summer, but the service is always attentive.

ℹ Getting There & Away

Kassandra by bus from Thessaloniki requires a transfer: take city bus 45, 45A or 45B to Thessaloniki's KTEL Halkidiki bus terminal (p276), from where connections run to northeast-coast centres Kalithea (€9.70, two hours, 11 daily), Polyhrono (€12, 2¾ hours, eight daily) and Pefkohori (€13, three hours, eight daily) via Kryopigi (€12, 2½ hours) and Hanioti (€13, 2¾ hours). Buses also reach Agia Paraskevi Thermal Baths near Loutra (€14, three hours, three daily) and Nea

Skioni (€13, 2½ hours, three daily) on the south coast. Discounts apply for 15-day open-return tickets.

To return from Kassandra, check timetables with **KTEL Kallithea** (☑ 23740 23714; ☺ 7am-10pm May-Oct).

ℹ Getting Around

Hiring a car is the best way to explore the largely public-transport-free Kassandra Peninsula.

Sithonian Peninsula
Χερσόνησος Σιθωνίας

Of the two touristic 'fingers' of Halkidiki, the Sithonian Peninsula is one that is loved by families and those in search of a more low-key summer option – though the beaches still get rather packed in the high season and on weekends. Endless olive groves blanket large portions to the north, while pine forests stubble a wild interior, fringing cliffsides that plummet towards tranquil coves. Sunsets are remarkable; diving and water-sports opportunities are excellent; and dozing on a beach might seem a little enticing after all.

Along the west coast you'll find Sithonia's largest resort, Neos Marmaras. The east coast's beaches have a little more sparkle; further south the terrain gets wilder. Social holidaymakers might head to Sarti for a 1970s vibe, an escapist feel and good nightlife. Kalamitsi, at Sithonia's southernmost tip, is also an excellent base – a good starting point for diving excursions and water sports.

◉ Sights

Domaine Porto Carras   WINERY
(☑ 23750 77437; www.portocarraswines.gr; Imeri Elia; ☺ 9am-8pm; P) Greece's largest organic winery, Porto Carras was founded in 1970, and now grows 28 different grapes across 47.5 hilly square kilometres on Sithonia's west coast. Tastings begin at €6, and delectable chocolates and oils are also sold. Visits to the plantings and the spectacular Villa Galini, one-time home to Salvador Dalí, can be prearranged.

🏃 Activities

Along the west coast you'll find well-loved beaches, including Paradisos, Kalogria and Lagomandra. On the east coast, where your deep-blue water usually comes with splendid views of Mt Athos to the west, Karydi has ruggedly rocky views (though it's sometimes not the cleanest) and Zografou has stunning sands.

Sarti-based Sithon Travel (☑ 23750 94040, Oct-Apr 23104 25921; www.sarti.gr; Sarti; ☺ 10am-2pm & 6-10pm May-Sep) can assist with arranging excursions and activities.

Dolphin Diving Centre   DIVING
(☑ 23750 41565; www.kalamitsi.com; Kalamitsi; ☺ May-Oct) Right at the tip of the Sithonian Peninsula, Dolphin offers twice-daily dives from May to mid-October. Prices for boat dives start at €35 for accomplished divers with their own kit or €60 if you need to hire gear.

Atlantis Diving Center   DIVING
(☑ 6992757107,   6978165361;   www.atlantis-scubadiving.com; Nikiti; ☺ 9am-7.30pm May-Oct) The range of diving programs at this safety-conscious PADI outfit includes dives for absolute beginners and children. A one-day boat-diving trip including transport, tanks and weights, drinks, a barbecue and two dives costs €75. Look for the sign on the southern side of Nikiti's main road, on the western edge of town.

🛌 Sleeping

On the east coast the range of lodgings is more glamorous and extensive. In the south there are fantastic campgrounds tucked into hidden bays. Kalamitsi has comfortable guesthouses and campgrounds.

**Thalatta Kalimitsi
Village Camp**   CAMPGROUND €
(☑ 23750 41410; www.thalattacamp.gr; Kalamitsi; camp sites per adult/tent €7.50/8.50, motorhomes from €110; ☺ May-Sep; P 🛜 🏊) Surrounded by woodland and close to the beach about 1km south of central Kalamitsi, this great campground has top-notch facilities and on-site bars and restaurants. Staff help organise activities and water sports, plus there's a pool, fitness facilities, playgrounds and a store – in fact almost all you need for a self-contained family holiday.

**Armenistis Camping
& Bungalows**   CAMPGROUND €
(Map p282; ☑ 23750 91487; www.armenistis.gr; camp sites per person/tent €7.80/8.80, glamping €95, beach house €170; ☺ May-Sep; P 🛜) Set on 50 hectares shading from pine forest to attractive beach, this large, popular camp site between Sarti and Zografou offers a restaurant, bars, grocery, a cinema, sports grounds and even a medical centre. Summer sees frequent concerts and DJ parties. Kids will love the playgrounds, organised activities, and freedom of the beach.

NORTHERN GREECE HALKIDIKI

★ Porto Elea

Camping CAMPGROUND €€

(Map p282; ☑6984625581; www.portoelea.com; Zografou; camp sites per adult/child/tent €8/4/12, d incl breakfast €95, caravan from €110; ⊘May-Sep; P🅿🛜) Porto Elea is nestled in woodland shade by a glowing cove, down a dirt road 9km east from Vouvourou. The luminous water, fancy beach bars and excellent taverna explain why it's the favourite place of Balkan celebs. Apart from caravans, there is also the converted convent of Porto Elea, which is now a hotel featuring minimalist rustic rooms.

Sarti Vista Bed & Breakfast Resort RESORT €€

(☑23750 94651; www.sartivista.com; Sarti; r incl breakfast €120; ⊘Apr-Oct; P❄🛜⊠) This rural resort, with a great view over the sea to Mt Athos, is a collection of modern, self-catering apartments with balconies set amid olive groves above Sarti. The outdoor barbecue area, pool and gardens add to the friendly, relaxed vibe, and the helpful owners can advise on local activities.

Porto Kalimitsi RESORT €€

(☑23750 41565; www.kalamitsi.com; Kalamitsi; ⊘May-Sep; P❄🛜) Affiliated with the nearby Dolphin Diving Centre (p279), Porto Kalimitsi offers 10 spanking-new studios and five bungalows just back from Kalimitsi's winning beach strip. Expect tiled floors, muted decor, full comfort, and an appealing beach-bar and restaurant.

Karidi Beach Apartments APARTMENT €€

(☑23750 91102; www.karidibeach.gr; Vourvourou; apt from €85; ⊘May-Sep; P❄🛜) This family-run place offers simple, one- or two-room apartments 50m from lovely Karidi Beach, among peaceful foliage and lawns. It can be a good place to self-cater, but check that your specific apartment has a kitchenette.

Ekies All Senses Resort RESORT €€€

(☑23750 91000; http://ekies.gr; Vourvourou; d/ste €228/376; ⊘end Apr–mid-Oct; P❄🛜⊠) This sumptuous resort is a fantasy of sculpted grounds, spa amenities, and top-notch restaurants and bars, all just steps from a private beach. Themed rooms give a modernist nod to local nature and myth, while honeymooners and hedonists alike will delight in the shady alcoves and hammocks. Peak periods and online discounts require minimum stays of up to three nights.

Eating

Kivotos TAVERNA €

(Noah's Ark; ☑23750 94143; Sarti; mains €8-12; ⊘7am-1am mid-Apr–Sep; 🛜) This gloriously situated taverna in Sarti has tables right on the sand and an excellent seafood-dominated menu. Choose from the day's catch, but don't ignore thoughtful specialities from across Greece, or the mouth-watering mezedhes. Effusive owner Daniel is a man who relishes conversation, especially if you catch him over a double espresso during a morning lull.

Navagos SEAFOOD €

(☑6977193183; Vourvourou; mains from €8; ⊘lunch & dinner Jul-Sep) Yorgos, the fisherman who runs this driftwood beach bar and 'restaurant', lives here year-round; in the summer he prepares his catch for guests on an open fire on the beach. It's really quite spontaneous – he cooks what he's caught, and doesn't do requests. Core months are July to September, but you may be lucky anywhere between May and November.

There are no set hours beyond 'lunchtime' and 'dinnertime', and the ramshackle set-up is hard to find: look for Restaurant Gorgona on the beach side of the main strip, then walk 50m west along the sand.

Paris Restaurant GREEK €€

(☑23750 91312; www.parisrestaurant.gr; Vourvourou; mains €9-12; ⊘10am-2am May-Oct; P🛜) The broad decking and engaging service at this wonderfully situated waterside restaurant provide the ideal setting to enjoy a long summer-evening repast. Happily, Paris' broad repertoire of Greek classics, local seafood and seasonal treats, plus uniformly stunning sunsets, follow through on the early promise. The Dionysos Supermarket on the main road is a useful landmark to the beachward turning you'll take.

🍷 Drinking & Nightlife

Goa Beach Bar BAR

(☑6977995220; Sarti; ⊘Jun-Sep) This famed beach bar on a sheltered cove 4km south of Sarti pours drinks day and night in the season. It's reached via a rough and steepish track, so you may want to take advantage of the free shuttle from Sarti. Check ahead for DJ sets and themed parties.

❶ Getting There & Away

Driving is the best way to navigate around Halkidiki in general, and that includes Sithonia. Budget plenty of time to account for transfers and traffic if travelling from Thessaloniki to Halkidiki by public transport. Buses to the Sithonian centres depart from Thessaloniki's Halkidiki bus terminal (p276), reached via city bus 45, 45A or 45B.

Buses serve Nikiti (€12, 1¾ hours, five daily), Neos Marmaras (€14, 2¼ hours, three daily), Sarti (€20, 3¼ hours, three daily) and Kalamitsi (€18, 3½ hours, three daily). Check at the bus station for other villages served en route. The discounted return ticket is valid for 15 days.

Crossing to Sithonia from Kassandra by bus requires changing at Nea Moudania, at Kassandra's northern end. Halkidiki's buses do not go east to Kavala (or anywhere else); it's back to Thessaloniki for everyone.

ℹ Getting Around

Driving is by far the best way to reach and explore Sithonia. The coastal road loops around the peninsula; driving through the forested interior often takes more time than the long way around, but both are scenically rich. From mainland Halkidiki, the road divides at Nikiti to the east and west coasts.

Villages are widely dispersed, so choose your base village carefully.

Athos Peninsula

Athos offers an unforgettable, immersive experience into a 1700-year-old spiritual tradition – if you're an adult male, that is. While the main town of Ouranoupoli is open to all, just south is a strictly policed border sealing off the semi-autonomous and all-male monastic community of Mt Athos from the rest of the world. Twenty monasteries, the oldest dating back 1000 years, and smaller hermetic dwellings dot a gorgeous, forested finger of land that culminates in the looming Mt Athos itself.

Male visitors hoping to bunk with monks must apply for permits well in advance, the reward being access to the peninsula's rugged terrain and dazzling religious architecture. Meanwhile, women travellers in Ouranoupoli might feel alienated or bemused by the whirl of spiritual activity. Women and mixed groups can take boat trips to get a glimpse of the splendid terrain and ancient monasteries, but even these must remain hundreds of metres from the shore.

OURANOUPOLI   ΟΥΡΑΝΟΥΠΟΛΙ
POP 826

A thriving tourist industry has sprung up around Athos's monasteries. Consequently the pretty seaside town of Ouranoupoli, founded in the 4th century BCE, now feels rather commercial. Expect souvenir stands overflowing with monk-made soaps, high-end jewellery shops and touts guiding you into competing waterfront tavernas. It's a dramatic contrast to the untouched terrain and ongoing spiritual activity across the border on the holy peninsula itself. Nonetheless, it's a pleasant, friendly place with a lively centre and some excellent tavernas and guesthouses.

◉ Sights

Monastery of Zyrgou   MONASTERY
(Map p282) The only Athos monastery accessible by women (it sits just beyond the border), the quiet, atmospheric ruins of 10th-century Zyrgou are a short drive (or 45-minute walk) east of Ouranoupoli, along a dusty coastal road. Abandoned in the 12th century, plundered for stone and used for agricultural purposes, it nonetheless retains some mosaics, murals and recognisable structures.

🛏 Sleeping

Ouranoupoli Camping & Bungalows   CAMPGROUND €
(Map p282; ☑ 23770 71171; www.camping-ouran oupoli.gr; camp sites per adult/tent €7.90/7.90, bungalows from €65; ☺ late May-Oct; P 🐕) This well-run, extensive coastal camping ground on Ouranoupoli's northern beach side offers sites for tents and caravans (powered and unpowered), glamping and cosy little bungalows. Plus there's an on-site supermarket and restaurant, a cellar with organic wine, olive-oil honey and *tsiporou* (like grappa). Opportunities to explore the nearby islands and ancient sites can also be arranged.

Xenios Zeus   HOTEL €
(☑ 23770 71274; www.ouranoupoli.com/zeus; s/d/tr €45/60/70; 🕸 🐕) Perfectly central and perfectly pleasant, this thankfully unfashionable family-run hotel has accommodated luminaries such as Frankfurt School philosopher Herbert Marcuse over the years, yet treats guests of less renown with equal warmth. Private balconies, air-conditioning, a decent breakfast and good levels of cleanliness confirm it as a good cheap bet.

Hotel Filoxenia   HOTEL €€
(☑ 23770 71158; s/d incl breakfast €60/81; P 🕸 🐕) Perched in a tranquil location at the top of Ouranoupoli, this hospitable hotel has well-kept rooms, satisfying breakfasts, a scattering of photogenic palm trees and beautiful views of the Aegean from its terrace. Look out for signs for Filoxenia

Athos Peninsula

shortly after entering Ouranoupoli; it's left, up a steep driveway, 1km before you reach central Ouranoupoli.

Pension Antanakis PENSION €€
(☑ 6978233931; www.pension-antonakis.gr; s/d €55/70; ❄ 🖥) These airy, pine-furnished rooms, some with harbour views, are 50m from the Pilgrims' Office, just beyond the strip of seaside tavernas that branches off from the main pier. Accommodation is comfy, the welcome is warm, and some of the larger rooms have sea-facing balconies draped in greenery.

✖ Eating

The waterside has some good fish restaurants, while the town centre hosts more traditional tavernas.

★ Kritikos SEAFOOD €€
(☑ 23770 71222; www.okritikos.com; mains €14-18; ⏰ 11am-midnight Apr-Nov; 🖥) Set just back from the portside tavernas and their ingratiating hucksters, gleaming-white Kritikos is the place for seafood in Ouranoupoli. Freshness is assured by the tanks full of live bivalves at the front door, while if you'd care to talk fish, waiters are happy to bring clear-eyed, pink-gilled specimens to your table to discuss your needs.

There's also an attached bar and 'gallery', which in this case means a women's clothing boutique.

Lemoniadis TAVERNA €€
(☑ 23770 71355; mains €10-14; ⏰ 10am-midnight Mar-Nov; 🖥) This waterside taverna has been sizzling sensational seafood since 1960. With a rousing *rembetika* (blues songs) soundtrack and outdoor seating with views of the Aegean, an atmospheric feast is assured. Seafood is hard to decline, but if it's cooler and you have the appetite, consider dishes from Mt Athos like spoon-tender veal with orzo and cheese, baked in a ramekin.

❶ Getting There & Away

Buses to Ouranoupoli leave Halkidiki bus terminal (p276) in Thessaloniki (€13.70, 3½ hours, five or six daily), arriving in central Ouranoupoli, by the tower (Pyrgos Prosforeiou).
 The last Ouranoupoli–Thessaloniki bus leaves at 6pm.

MT ATHOS ΑΓΙΟΝ ΟΡΟΣ

This isolated peninsula has been spiritually significant for millennia: early-Christian communities settled here in the 4th century, and the mountain figured in classical mythology far before then. Access is granted to male visitors only, on whom traipsing the quiet Athonite forest paths and marvelling at monastic architecture will leave a strong impression.

An enormous World Heritage site, 56km long and 8km wide, Mt Athos is formally Greek, though ecclesiastically it's under the Orthodox Patriarchate of Constantinople (İstanbul). Athos has 20 working monasteries, and *skites* (monastic dependencies), plus *kelli* (ascetic hermitages). The north is thickly forested, and the more inaccessible south is dominated by soaring Mt Athos (2033m). With neither industry nor hunting in the region, it's essentially a nature reserve.

History

Unorganised ascetic life is thought to have begun on Athos as early as the 4th or even 3rd centuries. It was consolidated by Emperor Basil I's 885 CE *chrysobull* (sealed decree) and the 958 arrival of the monk Athanasios, who brought organisation to Athos' spiritual activity by framing daily life around communal food, work and prayer. In 963 the Holy Mountain was formally dedicated when Emperor Nikoforos II Fokas funded Megistis Lavras, still Athos' biggest monastery.

In 1060, acting on fears that Athos' traditions were being diluted, Constantine IX Monomahos banned women, female domestic animals, beardless persons and eunuchs. Women and female animals (except birds) are still refused access to Athos. Legend attests that the Virgin Mary visited and blessed Athos; considered the Garden of the Virgin, it's dedicated to her – hence no room for other women. Though controversial to European human-rights activists and frustrating to would-be women visitors, the 1000-year-old decree has stood firm.

By the 11th century, 180 monasteries had been built on Athos, though periodic pillaging and burnings by pirates necessitated ongoing investment and repair.

When the Ottomans arrived in 1430, Athonites pledged allegiance to Murad II in return for retaining their semi-independent status. During the War of Independence (1821–29), Turks plundered and burned monasteries and their libraries. During the WWII Nazi occupation, Hitler agreed to place Athos under his personal protection. It survived the war unscathed.

Athos' 1927 Constitution was guaranteed in Greece's 1975 Constitution. Each of the 20 surviving monasteries has one representative on the Holy Council (Iera Synaxis), which oversees Athos' 2300 monks. The Julian calendar is still followed by most monasteries.

Getting a Permit

Male visitors should book up to six months ahead for summer and Orthodox holidays. Only 10 non-Orthodox and 100 Orthodox men are admitted daily. Those under 18 years must be accompanied by their father or, if with a group or guardian, need their father's written permission.

First call Thessaloniki-based Mt Athos Pilgrims' Bureau (p276) before emailing or faxing them a copy of your passport and your preferred visit dates. They will inform you when you can pick up your permit. Otherwise, if not passing through Thessaloniki, print the confirmation email or retain the fax. Clergymen need written permission from the Ecumenical Patriarchate of Constantinople (☑ in Turkey 90 21253 19670; İstanbul; ⊘ 8.30am-6pm). Next, phone monasteries to reserve specific nights; free accommodation and food is generally offered for one night.

Finally, take your written/printed confirmation to Ouranoupoli for the *diamonitirion* (final permit). Show your passport and booking confirmation at Ouranoupoli's

---

ATHOS DAY TRIPS BY BOAT

Regular boat trips from Ouranoupoli skirt Athos, allowing both male and female visitors a peek at Athos' spectacular clifftop monasteries – while carefully keeping to the legal 500m distance from shore, of course.

Athos Sea Cruises (☑ 23770 71606, 23770 71370; www.athos-cruises.gr; Ouranoupoli; adult/child cruise from €20/10; ⊘ 10.30am Apr-Oct, 10.30am & 2pm mid-May–mid-Oct) runs daily three-hour excursions, passing major west-coast monasteries and giving good views of Athos' peak. There's a recorded running commentary in English, German and Greek, which explains Athos' turbulent history and the monks' unchanged lifestyle: work, prayer, sleep (and, occasionally, wine).

If you're based on Halkidiki's Sithonian Peninsula, similar tours run from Ormos Panagias – try Ormos Travel (☑ 23750 31522; http://halkidiki.com/ormos-travel; Ormos Panagias; ⊘ 7am-10pm Apr-Oct), whose cruises depart around 9.30am and return by 5pm. A lunch stopover in Ouranoupoli is often included.

AMMOULIANI ISLAND

Just off Athos' northwestern coast, Ammouliani is a small island with fine beaches, pensions, camping, tavernas and 600 year-round inhabitants. Up to 11 daily ferries (€2.50) travel here from Trypiti, 7km north of Ouranoupoli. Tickets can be bought on the ferry.

Ammouliani's best beach, Alykes, is a 20-minute stroll southwest of the dock. Walking to more distant beaches and accommodation can take over an hour, and the shadeless island has no taxis, so call ahead for a free lift if staying overnight. Above the ferry dock, waterfront restaurant Tzanis (Map p282; ☑ 23770 51322; Ammouliani; fish €8-15; ⊙ 9am-midnight May-Oct; ☎) is an excellent excuse to linger for fresh seafood and fine sunsets.

---

small Pilgrims' Office (☑ 23770 71422; ⊙ 5.30am-1pm Mon-Fri, from 6am Sat, from 8am Sun), on a side street near Jet Oil station, to get the three-night (four-day) *diamonitirion:* students pay €10, Orthodox believers €25, everyone else €30. There's a parking lot (per day €7.50) on Ouranoupoli's south side, though street parking is free, if you can find it.

The *diamonitirion* can be extended in Karyes for another two days at the Local Government Office (see next page).

◉ Sights

Dress modestly; don't take photos during church services; and if you must bathe, do it out of sight of monasteries.

KARYES TO THE SOUTHEAST-COAST MONASTERIES

From Karyes, walk southeast through the Kapsala woods to coastal Moni Stavronikita or, just under it, Moni Iviron (Map p282; ☑ 23770 23643; www.imiviron.gr). This Georgian-founded monastery contains more than 2000 manuscripts, including 100 rare Georgian-language parchments.

From Iviron, coastal paths reach hospitable Moni Filotheou, also accessible from Karyes along a shady path with spring water (3½ hours). Beyond Moni Karakallou, the Byzantine-era path becomes a road leading (after 5½ hours) to Moni Megistis Lavras. Alternatively, buses from Karyes go there.

Magnificent Megistis Lavras (Great Lavra; Map p282; ☑ 23770 23754) is Athos's biggest monastery and houses founder St Athanasios' tomb. From here, a small boat sometimes serves the hospitable west-coast Agias Annis Skiti. Alternatively, a very tough trail leads around the peninsula's southern tip, passing the Romanian Prodromou Skiti, then coastal Agias Kavsokalyvion.

KARYES TO THE SOUTHWEST-COAST MONASTERIES

If heading southwest from Karyes, you will first encounter Moni Koutloumousiou. Further west, coastal Moni Xiropotamou is said to hold the largest-known fragment of the True Cross. The path southward accesses Dafni; either walk the coastal path or take the boat, which leaves at 12.30pm, calling at Simonos Petras, Osiou Grigoriou, Dionysiou and Agiou Pavlou.

Spectacular Moni Simonos Petras (Simopetra; Map p282; ☑ 23770 23254), fronted by wooden balconies over a cliff, is Athos' most-photographed monastery. From here the coastal path branches off towards the *arsanas* (monastery port/dock) at a small shrine, accessing Moni Osiou Grigoriou (Map p282; ☑ 23770 23668), Athos' most populous monastery with a community of 100 monks.

The hilly coastal path south reaches Moni Dionysiou (Map p282; ☑ 23770 23687), another tranquil cliff-hanging monastery. Dionysiou's *katholikon* (principal church) contains a unique wax-and-mastic icon of the Virgin and Child.

After Dionysiou, the coastal path continues to the architecturally magnificent Moni Agiou Pavlou and Agias Annis Skiti.

KARYES TO THE NORTHERN MONASTERIES

Northward from Karyes, the road passes sprawling Skiti Agiou Andreou. The main route continues to coastal Moni Pandokratoros; an alternative two-hour forest path reaches coastal Moni Vatopediou, the only monastery to follow the modern Gregorian calendar.

From Vatopediou, a coastal path leads to Moni Esfigmenou, and further on is Moni Hilandariou, a hospitable Serbian monastery (also accessible from Dafni by a south-coast boat, and then a connecting bus ride). The UK-based Friends of Mt Athos (FOMA; www.athosfriends.org) donated towards rebuilding structures here that were destroyed in a 2004 fire. The FOMA website has detailed information in English on the monasteries, their history and tips on visiting them.

The humble, pretty Moni Konstamonitou is worth visiting, as is the Bulgarian Moni Zografou further north. Its name, meaning 'painter', comes from a miraculous icon believed not to have been painted by human hands. The northern west-coast monastery, Moni Dochiariou (Map p282), slopes towards the sea and boasts remarkable architecture.

Next down the coastal path, venerable Moni Xenofondos (Map p282; ☑ 23770 23633) was first mentioned in 998, but probably dates to the 6th century. Although loot-seeking pirates often plundered it, impressive mid-Byzantine marble and wood-carved iconostases survive in its 10th-century *katholikon*. Finally, Moni Agiou Panteleimonos, further on, is a typically grand and friendly Russian monastery.

ℹ️ Information

Karyes has an ATM.

Local Government Office (☑ 23770 23224; http://mountathosinfos.gr; Karyes; ⊙ 8.30am–1pm Mon-Sat) In Karyes, oversees local matters (including extensions of official visitors' permits).

ℹ️ Getting There & Away

If you have arranged an Athos pilgrimage, either take the first bus (5.30am) from Thessaloniki to Ouranoupoli on the date you'll enter Athos, or stay over the night before in Ouranoupoli, which lets you rest, buy supplies and store unnecessary luggage. Get your *diamonitirion* and ticket before the next morning's 9.45am boat, and make sure to bring your passport.

Slow ferries, stopping at all monasteries from Ouranoupoli to Dafni, leave every day at 9.45am; speed boats sail express to Dafni at 8am, 8.45am, 10.40am and 11.45am Monday to Saturday, and 8.30am, 8.45am, 10.40am and 11am on Sundays. Early-morning boats leave Ouranoupoli for Dafni at 6.30am on weekdays, 7am on Saturdays and 10am on Sundays. Get tickets in advance from the **ticket office** (☑ 23770 71248; Ouranoupoli) on the waterfront in Ouranoupoli. In Dafni a bus serves Karyes, the administrative capital (€2.60). For monasteries further down the coast, change boats at Dafni.

The Athos–Ouranoupoli ferry leaves Dafni at noon, after a customs check to prevent antiquities theft. The morning boat from monasteries south of Dafni is timed to catch this ferry, which also collects passengers from the coastal monasteries north of Dafni.

ℹ️ Getting Around

Twice-daily boats from Dafni (around €2.50) serve west-coast monasteries such as Dionysiou, Simonos Petras, Agiou Pavlou and Agias Triados/Kavsokalyvion.

While monastic vehicles, buses and boats operate, walking is ideal for experiencing Athos' serenity. Paths can be overgrown and ravines steep, so watch your step and prepare as you would for any hike (wear decent boots, bring water and use a map).

Litohoro   Λιτόχωρο
POP 6995

Sitting on the eastern approach to mythical Mt Olympus, facing the broad Thermaic Gulf, Litohoro offers the rare combination of splendid beaches and highland wilderness. It's also within striking distance of the ancient city of Dion (p287), sacred to the Macedonians. The town itself has a small centre with brick bell towers and wooden-balconied houses, and steep, winding streets.

Six kilometres east, Plaka Litohoro's stretch of coastal hotels and campgrounds springs to life during summer. The general area is known as Pieria, and nearby beaches such as Leptokarya and Skotina are very popular with Greek and foreign tourists. If you don't have a car, think carefully about where to base yourself; public transport is scant between town and coast, so you'll be reliant on taxis.

🕴️ Activities

EOS   CLIMBING
(Greek Mountaineering Club; ☑ 23520 82444; http://eoslitohorou.blogspot.com; ⊙ 9.30am–12.30pm & 6-8pm Mon-Sat Jun-Sep) Hikers and climbers should head to EOS, below the public parking lot, which distributes pamphlets with general and Olympus-specific hiking information, and runs the 15 refuges on the mountain. Noticeboards detail the locations of emergency huts and general hiking conditions.

🎉 Festivals & Events

Festival Olympou   CULTURAL
(www.festivalolympou.gr; ⊙ Jul-Aug) During this summer festival, concerts, plays and artistic events unfold at venues around Litohoro, including the ancient theatre at Dion, with its stunning Olympian backdrop, and the picturesque peninsular castle of Platamonas. Many events are free, or accessible at €5 to €20 full admission.

🛌 Sleeping

Litohoro village has plenty of accommodation options, including atmospheric rustic digs. Six kilometres away, the broad beaches around Plaka Litohoro offer campgrounds, hotels and an upscale resort.

★ **Xenonas Papanikolaou**　　GUESTHOUSE €

(☎ 23520 81236; www.xenonas-papanikolaou.gr; Nikolaou Episkopou Kitrous 1; s/d €50/55; P ❄ 🛜) This romantic guesthouse in a flowery backstreet garden has 18 spacious self-catering rooms, with uplifting views of Litohoro's terracotta rooftops. The downstairs lounge has a fireplace and couches. From the square, take 28 Oktovriou uphill and turn left on Nikolaou Episkopou Kitrous. Breakfast is an extra €5.

Olympos Beach　　CAMPGROUND €

(☎ 23520 22111; www.olympos-beach.gr; Plaka Litohorou; camp sites per adult/tent €7.50/7.50, bungalows €45; P 🛜) This pine-shaded, well-run camping option on the Plaka Litohorou strand has a restaurant, minimart, well-stocked bar and villas with wi-fi.

Hotel Olympus Mediterranean　　HOTEL €€

(☎ 23520 81831; www.mediterraneanhotels.gr; Dionysou 5; d/tr/ste incl breakfast €99/119/171; P ❄ 🛜 ❄) This four-star hotel occupies a neoclassical building with ornate balconies, luxurious, conservatively furnished rooms and suites, plus an indoor pool and sauna. Some rooms have fireplaces and spas.

Cavo Olympo Luxury Resort & Spa　　RESORT €€€

(☎ 23520 22222; www.cavoolympo.gr; Plaka Litohorou; r/ste from €157/330; P ❄ @ 🛜 ❄) On Plaka Litohorou's seafront, this minimalist masterpiece consists of 49 rooms and suites overlooking either Mt Olympus or the sea, some with spas or private pools. All are airy, spacious and relaxing, with big balconies. The hotel's centrepiece is an enormous infinity pool sloping towards the bluff overlooking the water. Different minimum stays apply, depending on seasonal demand.

🍴 Eating

Meze Meze　　GREEK €

(☎ 23520 82271; Agiou Nikolaou 40; mains €6-8; ◷ noon-11.30pm; 🛜) Justifiably popular, Meze Meze offers an unchallenging selection of Greek favourites, distinguished by freshness, generosity and a sure instinct for the diner's pleasure. The Greek salad is spot-on, spicy meatballs come with flatbread and yoghurt, and the service is welcoming and attentive.

★ **Gastrodromio Olympus**　　GREEK €€

(☎ 23520 21300; www.gastrodromio.gr; Agiou Nikolaou 36; mains €16-22; ◷ 1-11.30pm; 🛜) The most experimental kitchen in Litohoro, Gastrodromio doesn't forget the basics of good Greek cuisine, merely adding a little flair in dishes such as scallops with lentils, mushrooms, wheat cream and fish roe, or venison 'bolognese' with saffron pasta and sheep's cheese. The charcuterie, sourced from artisanal producers around Greece, is a highlight.

To Pazari　　GREEK €€

(☎ 23520 82540; 25is Martiou 1; mains €7-15; ◷ noon-midnight; 🛜) Named for the bazaar that flourished near here under Turkish rule, To Pazari is an unpretentious, tile-floored little place where the owner is usually in gregarious attendance and piscine artwork adorns the walls. Expect classic Greek fare (grilled sardines, stuffed fish in garlic sauce, souvlaki) in the knowledge that local meat and fresh fish are carefully sourced and prepared.

ℹ Information

Tourist Information Booth (Agiou Nikolaou; ◷ 8.30am-2.30pm & 5.50-9pm Jun-Sep)

ℹ Getting There & Away

From the **bus station** (☎ 23520 81271; Agiou Nikolaou) in Litohoro town, buses serve Katerini (€2.50, 25 minutes, 14 daily), Thessaloniki (€8.50, 1¼ hours, 13 daily) and Athens (€36, 7½ hours, three daily via Katerini). Buses from Thessaloniki to Volos and Athens drop you on the highway to catch a Katerini–Litohoro bus.

Litohoro's **train station** (☎ 23520 22522) is 4km north of Plaka Litohoro and serves Thessaloniki (€9, one hour, 11 daily). For Florina and Edessa, travel via Platy (€11, two to three hours, 10 daily).

Around Litohoro

★ **Mt Olympus**　　MOUNTAIN

(Όρος Όλυμπος) The cloud-covered lair of the Ancient Greek pantheon, awe-inspiring Mt Olympus is simply spectacular. It fires visitors' imaginations today, just as it did for the ancients who venerated it. Greece's highest mountain, Olympus hosts more than 1700 plant species, some rare and endemic, as well as wolves, jackals, deer and more than 100 bird species. Its slopes are thickly forested and its peaks often shrouded in fog.

The first known mortals to reach Myti-kas (2918m), Olympus' highest peak, were Litohoro local Christos Kakalos and Swiss climbers Frédéric Boissonnas and Daniel Baud-Bovy in August 1913. Olympus became Greece's first national park in 1938.

Although you can drive up Olympus, many people hike; consult the Litohoro-based hiking associations for maps and current conditions, or check with the Olympus National Park Information Center (Olympus National Park Management Agency; ☑23520 83000; www. olympusfd.gr; Litohoro; ☺9am-6pm Mon-Fri, to 4pm Sat & Sun May-Oct, 9am-4pm daily Nov-Apr), which also lists the hiking routes and the regulations for visitors. Both provide info on the mountain's 15 refuges, where hikers can sleep.

Ancient Dion   HISTORIC SITE
(Δίον; ☑23510 53484; www.ancientdion.org; Dion; adult/concession incl Archaeological Museum €8/4; ☺8am-8pm; ℗) Dating to the 5th century BCE, Dion was sacred to ancient Macedonians worshipping the Olympian gods, especially Zeus, thought to reside on the awesome heights of nearby Olympus. Before his world-binding conquests, Alexander the Great made sacrifices here. Signs and stone footings indicate extant sights including sacred springs, villas and a ruined Roman theatre. This watery, wooded area is also rich in wildlife: look out for frogs tumbling into often-flooded sanctuaries, and the snakes and kingfishers that hunt them.

The ruins of the 6th-century-BCE Sanctuary of Demeter are the first you'll see and are the site's oldest. Further along is the leafy Sanctuary of Zeus Hypsistos, which bears copies of statues and column bases (the originals are in the on-site museum). Other replicas adorn the remnants of Dion's (usually flooded) Sanctuary to Isis, goddess of childbirth, across a small bridge. As elsewhere in the Hellenistic world, worship of this Egyptian goddess was merged with that of Artemis and Aphrodite. Later constructions include 4th-century-CE Christian basilica ruins and public baths once paved with mosaics.

The park has a small visitor centre with cafe. Entry includes the Archaeological Museum of Dion (☑23510 53206; www. ancientdion.org; Dion; adult/concession incl Ancient Dion site €8/4; ☺8am-8pm), a 10-minute walk from the site and well worth the effort for its splendid statuary and mosaics. Taxis from Litohoro to Dion cost around €14.

Castle of Platamonas   CASTLE
(Κάστρο Πλαταμώνα; ☑23250 44470; Platamonas; adult/child €2/free; ☺8am-4pm) Looming from an imposing coastal bluff near Platamonas village, 20km south of Plaka Litohorou, this well-preserved stronghold assumed much of its present shape in the 13th century thanks to Crusaders. Later used by Byzantines to defend the coast from pirates, today it's inhabited by handymen with weed whackers and the occasional lumbering turtle. Taxis from Litohoro town cost about €22.

From the parking area, pass the (un-staffed) booth and take the hilly path 150m to the castle and ticket booth. From here, follow the walls counterclockwise to understand the development of the fortress over time. The first small tower on the right dates from the 6th-century emperor Justinian, and predates much of the existing structure. The ruined Byzantine Church B was rebuilt in the 17th century.

The more extensive Church A ruins, protected by a wooden enclosure, were built over a 2nd-century-CE Hellenistic warehouse. Squint through the gloom to see faint fresco remains. At the castle's nearby northeastern edge, drink in magnificent views of sandy Skotina Beach below and Mt Olympus in the distance.

Skeletal outlines of oikous (medieval dwellings) and shops are signposted further down the walls. The final upwards turn into the archway leads to the acropolis, where the castle's deep cistern lies, under a grate. This well-protected space contains the castle's most magnificent tower, the pyrgos; unfortunately closed, it dates from the 14th century and the last Byzantine (Palaeologan) dynasty. Archaeologists believe that Late Antique Herakleion was originally here. The castle hosts concerts during the Festival Olympou (p285).

Veria   Βέροια
POP 43,158

Around 75km west of Thessaloniki, Veria is a small but ancient city, founded in the 5th century BCE, and possibly settled for 500 years before that. It definitely merits a day's exploration – the old Jewish quarter, Barbouta, is atmospheric and its history fascinating, and the small but lush Tripitamos River that runs through it is a beauty. The two town museums are well presented, and it's a proximate base for the magnificent

DON'T MISS

SPLENDOURS OF ANCIENT MACEDON: VERGINA AND PELLA

Northern Greece boasts two remarkable sites of the ancient Macedonian dynasty. The royal burial site at Vergina lies 11km southeast of Veria. Between Thessaloniki and Edessa lies Alexander the Great's birthplace, the former royal capital Pella.

With a car, it's possible to see both sites in a single day trip from Thessaloniki. Matching up bus connections can be a jigsaw, so if you don't have wheels consider exploring Pella and Vergina on separate days or staying overnight: hospitable **Olympia Guesthouse** (📞 23310 68052; www.xenonasolympia.gr; Aristotelous, Vergina; s/d/tr €35/50/65; 🅿️ 🛜) is five minutes' walk from Vergina's archaeological site.

Buses from Thessaloniki to Palia Pella (€3.30, 45 minutes, seven daily) stop by the main road, 20 minutes' walk from the museum. From Thessaloniki to Vergina, take the bus to Veria (€7, one hour, 15 daily), from where you can then catch a bus to Vergina (€1.80, 20 minutes, up to seven daily).

Vergina Royal Tombs Museum (📞 23310 92347; www.aigai.gr; Vergina; adult/child €12/6, combined ticket incl Byzantine Museum & Veria Archaeological Museum €14/7; ⊙ 8am-8pm Wed-Mon, from noon Tue; 🅿️) A grass-covered *tumulus* (burial mound) has been converted into a truly spine-tingling museum where visitors can descend into unspoiled royal Macedonian tombs from the time of Alexander the Great and his dynast-warrior king father Philip II. The showpiece is the marble 336-BCE tomb of Philip II: buried with silver chalices, an ivory and gold shield, a gold-plated quiver, a full suit of gilded armour and countless other treasures, the grave was never robbed, and everything is on display here.

Elsewhere in the museum, Tomb I and Tomb IV boast mythic friezes, while Tomb III, the prince's tomb, is thought to be the final resting place of the son of Alexander the Great. About 400m past the Royal Tombs lie extensive palace ruins of 3rd-century-BCE king Antigonos Gonatas, while other burial grounds, urban remains and other fascinating archaeology are strewn lavishly about the town and hills above. Not all are accessible, and nothing comes close to the splendour of Philip's grave goods and tomb.

Archaeological Site of Pella (📞 23820 31160; www.pella-museum.gr; Pella; adult/child incl museum €8/4; ⊙ 8am-8pm Wed-Mon, from 12.30pm Tue; 🅿️) Pella rose to fame when dynastic King Archelaos (413–399 BCE) made it Macedon's capital. While not much rises above carefully excavated footings and low sections of wall, it's atmospheric and easy to imagine the dimensions of the Classical, Hellenistic, Roman and Byzantine cities. Resurrected columns, a broad *agora* (market) surrounded by uniform shops, two larger villas and various sanctuaries, walls and workshops all attest to the former importance of the city, which once commanded direct access to the Thermaic Gulf. Entry includes the on-site museum.

Archaeological Museum of Pella (📞 23820 31160; www.pella-museum.gr; Pella; adult/concession incl archaeological site €8/4; ⊙ 8am-8pm Wed-Mon, from 12.30pm Tue; 🅿️) Overlooking the northern end of the ancient city, Pella has been provided with a modern, meticulously curated museum that befits the site's importance and the quality of the artefacts discovered there. Two stately floors tell the area's prehistory and history, from Bronze Age bones in urns to well-preserved 300-BCE mosaics and phallic drinking vessels. Burial treasures include helmets, swords, and the mauve garb and remarkable gold jewellery of the 'Lady of Aigai', wife of Amyntas I.

This is a great place to appreciate the sophistication and character of Macedonian society at the time of Alexander's birth.

Vergina tombs (see box on this page), Macedonia's preeminent ancient site. Add to that some fantastic accommodation options and some decent restaurants, plus the nearby ski areas at Mt Vermio, and you have a real little treat.

🔘 Sights

Old Metropolis BASILICA
(Vasileos Konstantinou 32; ⊙ 10am-6pm Wed-Sun) **FREE** One of the largest Byzantine buildings in the Balkans, this basilica has a chequered past. Dedicated to St Paul in the 11th century,

it was remade as a mosque by conquering Turks in 1430 (they added a minaret and plastered over 13th-century frescoes), reconsecrated by the Greeks during the Balkan War (1912), used as a stable by WWII German occupiers, then left in near-ruin. Following extensive restoration, it's again accessible, its austere three-aisled architecture and fabulous frescoes the undoubted highlights.

Barbouta
AREA

(synagogue €3; ⊙ synagogue noon-3pm) Walk from Plateia Antoniou down Vasileos Konstantinou to find Veria's atmospheric former Jewish quarter. The synagogue (with the bright blue-and-yellow facade) dates back to 1850 and is the region's oldest. Plenty of architecturally significant houses in the traditional style remain, in various states of repair. The area around the Tripitamos River is leafy and lush, beautiful for a stroll.

Archaeological Museum
MUSEUM

(☑ 23310 24972; http://odysseus.culture.gr; Leoforos Anixeos 45; adult/concession €2/1, combined ticket incl Byzantine Museum & Vergina €14/7; ⊙ 8am-8pm Wed-Mon) Browse an impressive haul of Neolithic artefacts from the settlement of Nea Nicomedia, treasures from the Vergina tombs and other Classical, Hellenistic and Roman finds at this museum, located at Anixeos' northern end. You'll find iron swords, delicate jewellery, doe-eyed portrait heads and a charming statue of Aphrodite slipping out of her sandals. A combined ticket (€14) for Veria's Archaeological and Byzantine Museums, plus the royal tombs at Vergina, saves €4.

Byzantine Museum
MUSEUM

(☑ 23310 25847; www.byzantine-museum-veria.gr; Thomaidou 26; adult/concession €4/2, combined ticket incl Archaeological Museum & Vergina €14/7; ⊙ 8am-8pm Wed-Mon, from noon Tue) This museum in a restored mill will turn you from novice to nerd in all things Byzantine. Splendorous icons, huge 5th-century floor mosaics and ornate sarcophagi fill all three floors of the beautifully lit space. A film on the bottom floor gives the history of the mill and Veria's Barbouta quarter.

🛏 Sleeping

Barbouta has the best (if not cheapest) sleeping options – you might want to book early if you're visiting on a weekend.

⭐ Kokkino Spiti
BOUTIQUE HOTEL €€

(☑ 23310 74440; www.kokkinospiti.gr; Olganou 10; r from €78; P ❄ 🤝) 'Red House' is an absolute gem – a restored 1840 mansion with six uniquely decorated bedrooms in its main room and three more in the adjacent building. Wrought-iron bed frames, wood-beamed ceilings, fantastic details and mesmerising river views. It's nestled in the heart of Veria's old Jewish quarter, and is as comfortable as it is elegant. Breakfasts are lavish arrangements with pastries, fruit, preserves and eggs.

Olganos VL
BOUTIQUE HOTEL €€

(☑ 23310 72226; www.olganos.com; Merarchias 7; apt €80-120; ❄ 🤝) In the old Jewish quarter, this is a beautiful place to stay – a family-run boutique hotel with seven luxurious, spacious rooms. The suites have Jacuzzis in the bathroom, and a glass fireplace that you can watch as you bubble in the bath. There are solid timber fittings throughout, views of the neighbourhood are lovely, and one room has a terrace.

🍴 Eating

Out of the Blue
TAVERNA €

(Στα Καλά Καθούμενα; ☑ 6986046110; Kontogeorgaki 18; mains €8-10; ⊙ 1-11pm; 🤝) Steaks, traditional sausage, souvlaki and other meaty Greek favourites are all good at this gregarious little stone-walled taverna, which spills out onto the cobbles when the weather permits.

⭐ 12 Grada
GREEK €€

(☑ 23311 00112; Dimosthenous; mains €9-16; ⊙ 1pm-midnight Tue-Sun; 🤝) Backed by tumble-down traditional stone houses and overlooking the Tripitamos River, 12 Grada is a lovely little find. Try dishes such as sous-vide pork fillet with black garlic or traditional pasta with wild greens and local cheese, all washed down with a list of wines drawn substantially from the surrounding regions.

Bergi⬜tiko
GREEK €€

(Vergiotiko; ☑ 23310 74133; Thomaidou 2; mains €8-15; ⊙ 1pm-midnight; 🤝) They take their meat seriously at Bergi⬜tiko, selecting well-marbled and aged steaks for the grill, or stewing it to spoon-ready tenderness with homemade orzo and basil. There's even an in-house drying rack to bring the meat slowly to perfection. Vegetables are never unrepresented in any Greek kitchen, but meat is definitely the star here.

🍷 Drinking & Nightlife

A large population of young people and caffeine enthusiasts means that the cafes and bars are busy both day and night. The area around Elias in particular brims with life.

★**Bátrachos**   CAFE
(☑23310 20282; Karakosti 13; bar food €5-6, cocktails €7.50; ☺7am-1am Mon-Fri, from 8am Sat, from 9am Sun; ☏) Follow the scent of freshly brewed coffee to this welcomingly off-kilter little cafe-bar, festively decorated in most of the primary colours. There is a range of chocolate-slathered cakes and cookies for daytime socialisation; burgers and sandwiches for midday (including vegan choices); and a well-stocked bar for the evenings.

❶ Getting There & Away

Veria's two central adjoining **bus stations** (☑23310 22988; www.ktel-imathias.gr; near cnr Trempesina & Kinitsis) serve Thessaloniki (€7, one hour, up to 15 daily), Athens (€37, seven hours, two daily), Edessa (€5, 1½ hours, two per weekday) and Vergina (€1.80, 20 minutes, up to seven daily).

The **train station**, 3km north of town, has trains for Thessaloniki (€5, one hour, five daily) and Florina (€9, 1¾ hours, three daily).

Edessa   Εδεσσα
POP 18.229

Edessa's strategic location atop a prominence commanding the Via Egnatia, the Roman road between Byzantium and the Adriatic, is the basis of a long historical importance. Its long-existing Slavic name, Voden ('Place of Water'), evokes its other notable feature – it's woven through with water, in the form of rivers, streams, fountains and the famous waterfalls on the edge of town. The old quarter and a handsome Byzantine bridge add a further touch of charm to this generally pleasant town, where you can spend a night resting if you've been hiking or exploring archaeological parks in the surrounding area.

Until the 1977 discovery of Vergina's royal tombs (p288), Edessa was thought to have been ancient Macedonian Aigai. With the government's Hellenisation project following the 1923 Greek–Turkish population exchanges, the town's name was changed back to the archaic Edessa.

⊙ Sights

Edessa's old quarter, **Varosi**, lies south of Waterfalls Park. Brightly coloured traditional houses and churches make it a lovely area for a stroll. Edessa's **Byzantine Bridge** is beautiful; take Ir Polytechniou from central Plateia Timenidon until you reach the river fork.

Waterfalls Park   WATERFALL
(☑info 23810 20300) FREE Located at the eastern side of town, Waterfalls Park offers several viewing points allowing you to gaze at Edessa's star attraction, and even get quite close to the thunderous flow. The larger of the two falls, **Karanos**, is quite impressive at 70m high. A path winds downwards to a second, smaller waterfall.

🛏 Sleeping

Edessa has some truly lovely sleeping options; the best are in Varosi. Since all of them are quite small, book in advance.

★**Varosi Guesthouse**   PENSION €
(☑23810 21865; www.varosi.gr; Arhiereos Meletiou 45-47, Varosi; s/d incl breakfast €55/60; ᴘ❈☏) This gorgeous pension occupies a restored traditional wood-and-stone house in Edessa's old quarter. Rooms have double-wood doors, fine linen, colourful embroidery and antique brass beds. In winter a fireplace heats the lounge room, while the flower-filled balcony is superb for a relaxing coffee in summer. Stylish, inviting and fantastic value.

Hagiati   PENSION €
(☑23810 51501; www.hagiati.gr; Makedonomachon 30, Varosi; s/d incl breakfast €50/60; ᴘ❈☏) This wonderfully tranquil guesthouse in the old quarter, within earshot of the gentle chatter of water, has a tasteful, traditional feel with wooden furnishings, a rustic lounge room and a serene open courtyard. Rooms are all individually furnished with care and taste, and the breakfast (which you can opt out of for a €7 refund) is generous.

★**Varosi Four Seasons**   BOUTIQUE HOTEL €€
(☑23810 51440; www.varosi4seasons.gr; Arhiereos Meletiou, Varosi; s/d incl breakfast €70/90; ᴘ❈☏) This old-town hotel's 10 unique rooms work hard to banish modern anxieties, bringing together wooden furnishings, stone details, handmade curtains and plenty of antique comforts to help you recharge aesthetically as well as physically. There are great views from the six rooms with balconies, a lovely rooftop terrace and top-notch breakfasts.

✕ Eating & Drinking

Ousies   GREEK €
(☑23815 02414; 25th Martiou 4; mains €7-9; ☺noon-midnight; ☏) A wonderfully convivial *ouzerie* (taverna that serves ouzo, amongst other drinks) a little way from Edessa's busier spots, Ousies is a place where younger locals love to linger over small plates and drinks, and it's easy to see why. The atmosphere is energised yet laid back, the staff are all smiles and the food is very good.

Irtha & Edessa
TAVERNA €€

(☑23813 00660; cnr Karaoli & Tsmiski; mains €12-14; ☺1-11.30pm; 🛜🚗) A short walk from the waterfalls, this local favourite, set in a glass construction, has spit-roasted lamb and grilled meat specialities, as well as a great choice of vegetable dishes and innovative, heaped salads. The locals pour in on weekend evenings, making for a lively atmosphere full of families – luckily there's plenty of space.

The Jam
BAR

(☑6973775100; Thessalonikis 2; coffees €2; ☺10am-midnight; 🛜) There are more animated spots within earshot, but this relaxed little cafe-bar plays good music, makes good coffee and serves stronger stuff for the latter part of the day. The charm of its few canal-side tables is compromised by the narrow road you'll be equally close to, but there are usually seats inside.

❶ Information

Tourist Information Office (☑23810 20300; www.edessacity.gr; Tsimski 2; ☺10am-4pm Mon-Fri, to 6pm Sat & Sun)

❶ Getting There & Away

Edessa bus station (KTEL Pellas; Pavlou Mela 13) serves Thessaloniki (€9.70, 1¾ hours, up to 15 daily), Veria (€5, one hour, five daily) and Athens (€46, 6½ hours, two daily). The bus to Florina (€8, 1¾ hours, three daily) departs from 30m away.

The **train station** (☑23810 23510; Leoforos Nikis) is on the Thessaloniki–Athens line and also serves Florina (€7, 1¼ hours, three daily).

Find **taxis** (☑23810 23392, 23810 22904; cnr Dimokratias & Monastiriou) on the corner of Dimokratias and Monastiriou.

Florina
Φλώρινα

POP 17,686

Florina is the springboard to remarkable natural spaces further west, including the ski slopes of Vigla-Pissoderi (19km away) and the wild Prespa Lakes (45km away). Snug within a lush valley, it's a typical student town, with a lively social life, and good access to hiking and winter sports.

Florina also serves as a crossroads for further Balkan travel: southwest of Prespa Lakes lies Krystallopigi, the border crossing into Albania, and lively Bitola is only 35km to the north, across the international border to North Macedonia.

While Florina itself doesn't overflow with attractions, it has an abundance of cafes and

GREECE'S ELUSIVE BROWN BEAR

Twenty minutes' drive up the eastern flank of the mountains separating Kastoria and Florina is the Arcturos Bear Sanctuary (☑23860 41500; www.arcturos.gr; Nimfeo; adult/child €6/4; ☺10am-5pm Thu-Tue; 🅿), a sanctuary for the brown bears native to the Pindos Mountains, the Peristeri Range and the mountains that lie along the Bulgarian border. The ursine inhabitants have only 20 hectares to roam unmolested up here, but enjoy conserved natural habitat and an agreeably cool altitude of 1350m. This place is all about the bears: you can observe them, but no more. The brown bear, Europe's largest land mammal, survives only in very small numbers.

restaurants, and a short stop will allow you to taste distinctive local produce, including its famous sweet red peppers, and Prespa beans.

History

Florina was the northernmost town occupied and annexed by Greek troops during the Balkan Wars of 1912–13; its location just south of the mountains kept it near the front in subsequent wars. The existence of Greece's (Slavic) Macedonian minority, denied outright by the government and Greece's latter-day fascists, has always been sensitive in the Florina, Edessa and Prespa regions, where the Macedonian language is still spoken by many locals. Pressure from Greek society, media and government has suppressed it, but you'll still hear Macedonian spoken – usually in villages and by older people.

🛏 Sleeping

Hotel Hellinis
HOTEL €

(☑23850 22671; www.hotel-hellinis.gr; Pavlou Mela 31; s/d €40/50; 🛜) Despite some pretensions to being the kind of place where busy professionals hold high-powered breakfast meetings, Hellinis actually appeals as cheap and central. The rooms are clean, basic and somewhat cosy – there's a bar, individual balconies and wi-fi – and it's handy for restaurants, the museum and the bus and train stations.

Hotel Veltsi
HOTEL €€

(☑23850 46555; www.hotel-veltsi.gr; Km 6 Florina-Prespes Rd; d/ste €70/120; 🅿❄🛜🏊) A boutique hotel 6km west of Florina, Veltsi

GREECE'S FORGOTTEN WATERWAYS:
THE PRESPA LAKES ΛΙΜΝΕΣ ΠΡΕΣΠΩΝ

West of Florina, the twin Prespa Lakes are a breathtaking beauty spot, rich in wildlife and history. Megali Prespa and Mikri Prespa (Great Prespa and Small Prespa) are the Balkans' highest tectonic lakes and among Europe's most ancient, at one million years old. Once a single lake, today they are separated by a narrow isthmus formed by sediment churned up over centuries. Greece shares Megali Prespa with North Macedonia and Albania, and Mikri Prespa with Albania alone.

The wildlife is abundant: 40 mammal species include brown bears, wolves and wild pigs; 31 reptiles and amphibians include the bulky Hermann's tortoises; 260 bird species include the world's largest colony of Dalmatian pelicans at Mikri Prespa, as well as great white pelicans, great white egrets and the EU's largest colony of pygmy cormorants. A clutch of sleepy, atmospheric highland villages act as springboards to this majestic wilderness.

Driving allows you to make the most of Prespa Lakes, and it's quite hard to explore the area without your own wheels. Two buses from Florina take a circuitous route each Monday, Wednesday and Friday at 7am and 3pm (€5.70, 1½ hours), returning the same day at 8.30am and 3.30pm. Mention to the driver which village you want to get to. Taxis from Florina cost €60 to €80.

Agios Ahillios

The island of Agios Ahillios (Saint Achillius) attached to the shore by a causeway, is Mikri Prespa's main attraction and is superb for birdwatching. The grand, concave outer wall of the ruined Basilica of Agios Ahillios stands on its eastern shore, with some half-toppled walls, columns and a stone floor. It's a legacy of the 10th-century Bulgarian tsar Samuel, who expanded his empire across much of the southern Balkans, chronically sparring with Byzantium.

Driving west from Agios Germanos or Lemos, cross the connecting strip between the two lakes and turn immediately left onto a 1km-long wooden bridge. A signposted path to the left hugs the east coast and leads to the basilica and other church ruins. Alternatively, turn right off the bridge for the shop and taverna. Agios Ahillios is sparsely inhabited, though August's Prespes Festival features a headlining concert in the amphitheatre-like basilica.

Agios Germanos

With its wealth of melancholy stone houses, many derelict and used for stabling goats, and austere upland setting, Agios Germanos is the region's most visually appealing town. The highlight is 11th-century Agios Germanos church, an extraordinary work of ecclesiastic

has woodland views, well-furnished rooms, a pool and a playground. It is perfectly positioned for winter adventures at Vigla-Pissoderi Ski Area (Vigla-Pissoderi; ⊙Dec-Mar), 13km further west.

✖ Eating

Traditional tavernas are dotted around the centre of town, all serving good traditional food. Florina's famous red peppers, roasted and dressed with oil, vinegar and garlic, are delicious.

★ **Gentéki** GREEK €
(☑23853 00599; Georgiou 2; mains €6-9; ⊙noon-midnight Tue-Sun) Don't doubt the commitment to 'slow food' at this cosy corner restaurant on the Sakoulevas River. The telltale snail isn't for show: the owner (who found fame with Greek *Masterchef*) makes his own goat-feta, sausages and other treats, and doesn't cut corners. Salads are enormous, meat is local and ethically raised, and Florina's famous red peppers are roasted before your eyes.

Prespa TAVERNA €
(☑23850 23973; www.tavernaprespa.gr; Tirnavou 12; mains €5-8; ⊙7pm-midnight Mon-Fri, from noon Sat & Sun) A proper local taverna that is as frill-free as it is authentic – go for the beetroot salad with feta, grilled peppers, shrimp *saganaki* (fried with cheese), or any of the grilled meats. Gustatory explorers might try the spleen stuffed with offal – a Florina speciality.

mid-Byzantine architecture with a domed brick structure and separate bell tower. Also appealing is the watermill (☉10am-2pm Sat) FREE, meticulously restored to working order by local angels the Society for the Protection of Prespa. This tiny town, with excellent tavernas and some superior accommodation, makes a good base for exploration. For emergencies, there's a police station in the village and a health centre (☎23850 46284) further south in Lefkonas.

While so many of Agios Germanos' 19th-century stone houses are derelict, and/or housing goats, Hotel Agios Germanos (☎23850 51397; http://prespa.com.gr; s/d incl breakfast €55/70; P@🖥) is a delightful, heritage-protected homestead has been reborn as a truly beautiful and atmospheric hotel. Some of the 10 en-suite rooms have working fireplaces, all have traditional wood fittings and sensitively selected furniture. A simple breakfast of homemade Greek treats is provided, and the kitchen turns out a few basic traditional dishes, chalked up on a blackboard each day (dinner per person is €12 to €15).

The humble Taverna To Prespeiou (☎23850 51442; mains €7-8; ☉11am-7pm) is bang in the centre of Agios Germanos and has some of the best homemade Greek food in the region. Pies filled with nettles or other wild greens show the resourceful robustness of Greek mountain fare, while simple dishes such as stewed gigantes (giant beans) and grilled mutton ribs are as locally appropriate as they are delicious.

Psarades

Out on Lake Megali Prespa's promontory, friendly Macedonian-speaking villagers inhabit Psarades (population 83), while 1m-tall dwarf cattle meander in its surrounds. Fishers offer boat trips to Megali Prespa's isolated Byzantine askitiria (hermitages). These include the 13th-century cave Metamorfosi, where scant remnants survive of paintings and two sections from a wood-carved temblon (votive screen); the 15th-century Mikri Analipsi; and the early-15th-century rock Church of Panagia Eleousa, tucked above a ravine on the southern shore, and boasting beautiful frescoes.

Vrontero

South of Psarades and close to the Albanian border, ramshackle farming village Vrontero has little to detain you other than access to excellent walking trails. Kokkalis Cave, used as a partisan hospital during the Greek Civil War, is a 30-minute hike from Vrontero or a short drive if you have a 4WD. For maps and information, contact the Society for the Protection of Prespa (☎23850 51211; www.spp.gr; ☉9am-5pm Mon-Fri) in Lemos village, just west of Agios Germanos.

Drinking & Nightlife

★ **Magio** CAFE
(☎6947520477; Tagmatarchi Fouledaki 28; ☉10am-10pm; 🖥) A wonderland of judiciously assembled kitsch, this two-storey cafe-bar in an arcade in central Florina is a great alternative to the smoke-filled caffeine palaces that proliferate here in numbers unusual even for Greece. Breakfast pancakes, great coffee, cocktails when the hour strikes and pastries at any hour make it easy to linger in this offbeat little refuge.

Women's Cafe CAFE
(☎23850 24647; Kallergi 4; cakes from €1.50; ☉10am-2pm & 6-10pm Mon-Fri, 6-10pm Sun) A superfriendly cake shop run by the wonderful Flora, where you can sip tea and coffee by day and enjoy drinks by night, and eat homemade sweets. The decor is homey and rustic (think scuffed wooden tables and an apron of threadbare astroturf leading out the door), and occasionally there are live music events and book readings.

Getting There & Away

BUS

Florina bus station (KTEL Florinas; ☎23850 22430; www.ktelflorinas.gr; Makedonomahon 10) serves Athens (€51, 10 hours, one daily) and Thessaloniki (€17, 3¼ hours). Two serve Thessaloniki direct via the Egnatia Odos Hwy, the others go through Edessa (€8, 1½ hours, three daily).

For Prespa, buses leave on Monday, Wednesday and Friday at 7am and 3pm, returning at 8.30am and 4.30pm (€5.70, one hour). Tell the driver your destination when you board, as they may skip some villages. For Kastoria, head to Amyntaio (€4.10, 35 minutes, eight daily) and change buses there. Amyntaio has buses for Kastoria at 7.45am on Monday and 4pm on Friday and Sunday (€9, 1½ hours). Four buses per week also reach Ioannina (€21, two hours); alternatively, take a bus to Kozani and change there.

TRAIN

Florina's **train station** (☑ 23850 22404) connects with Edessa (€7, 1¼ hours, three daily) and Thessaloniki (€10, 2¾ hours, three daily).

Kastoria   Καστοριά

POP 13,387

Founded on the ruins of ancient Keletron by the Emperor Justinian, Kastoria enjoyed political and commercial prestige for many centuries, particularly from the 10th to the 14th. It's situated on Lake Orestiada, with a pretty old town covering a high peninsula protruding into the glassy waters. Orestiada remains Kastoria's focus – locals sip coffee in the many lakeside cafes, or get their exercise along a 9km waterfront circuit, while white swans, ferruginous ducks and noisy frogs are equally at home in the reeds and still waters.

Kastoria's steep and winding old-town lanes hide a surprising wealth of Byzantine and post-Byzantine churches, plus lively local squares lined with traditional houses and tavernas. You'll also notice an abundance of fur sellers: the town was historically dependent on the fur trade, and even takes its name from the Greek for 'beaver' – *kástoras*. Today, however, the furs are imported.

◉ Sights

Most charismatic is Kastoria's historic Doltso neighbourhood. This romantically undulating quarter has several restored 18th- and 19th-century *arhontika* (mansions) housing museums and tavernas, arranged around lively squares and twisting lanes. Notable, colourful, timber-and-stone *arhontika* include the splendid Skoutaris and Picheon houses. Signposting around the old town provides insight into the buildings and their former resident families.

Church of Agioi Anargyroi   CHURCH

(Anargiron 23; ⊙ 8.30am-3pm Tue-Sun) Best guesses date this three-aisle Byzantine basilica, perhaps Kastoria's most beautiful, to the late-10th or early-11th centuries. The external walls are composed of bricks decorated with diamonds,

suns and other patterns, while the interior is adorned with fine frescoes of the Passion of Christ and the martyrdom of saints.

Church of Agios Stefanos   CHURCH

(Paleologou; ⊙ 8.30am-3pm Tue-Sun) One of Kastoria's oldest Byzantine churches, St Stephen's is a triple-aisled basilica retaining frescoes dating back to its construction in the 9th century, augmented by sublime 12th- and 13th-century additions.

Church of the Taxiarchis of the Metropolis   CHURCH

(Mitropoleos 140) Dedicated to the Archangel Michael and built in the 9th century over earlier Christian ruins, this precious (but irregularly open) Byzantine church boasts stunning 10th- and 14th-century frescoes inside. A delightful 13th-century fresco of the Madonna and Child, however, can be seen above the entrance. Also inside is the sacrosanct tomb of Pavlos Melas, leader of the 1904–08 'Macedonian Struggle' against the Ottomans.

Byzantine Museum of Kastoria   MUSEUM

(☑ 24670 26781; www.bmk.gr; Plateia Dexamenis; adult/concession €4/2; ⊙ 8.30am-3.30pm Wed-Mon) FREE Testament to Kastoria's importance as a Byzantine city, this museum holds some 400 Byzantine and post-Byzantine icons. Many are displayed, alongside sanctuary doors, frescoes and mosaics from local churches. Pottery and coins from the city and region and across the Byzantine period are also exhibited.

☆ Festivals & Events

Nestorio River Festival   MUSIC

(☑ 6938639444; https://nestorio-riverparty.gr; 7-day ticket €60; ⊙ late Jul-early Aug) Burgeoning from humble beginnings in 1978, when it was essentially friends enjoying music and midsummer by the banks of the Aliakmon River, this annual event has grown into a popular seven-day festival of music (Greek and international), art, games and parties. Four camping areas are designed to suit different hedonism tolerance thresholds. Nestorio is around 25km southwest of Kastoria.

KTEL Kastoria runs special festival buses to Nestorio.

⌂ Sleeping

Vergoulas Mansion   B&B €

(☑ 24670 23415; www.vergoulasmansion.gr; Edithras 14; s/d/tr incl breakfast €50/60/70; ☎) Cleverly restored, but retaining the pleasing

NORTHERN GREECE KASTORIA

rusticity of its 1857 origins, this handsome Doltso mansion comes with soothing lake views and a plumb place in Kastoria's historical heart. The traditional rooms, with some stunning wood-carving decorations, plus cosy breakfast/dinner salon, make it a great choice.

★ **Hotel Doltso** BOUTIQUE HOTEL **€€**
(☑ 24670 22022; www.doltsohotel.gr; Riga Fereou 5; d from €75; ❋ ☏) Making great use of a renovated, stone-built Doltso mansion, this 10-room hotel has an intimate atmosphere, cosy communal spaces, and stylishly presented rooms with indulgent double beds and spacious bathrooms. Upstairs rooms have balconies, the service is friendly and the breakfast plentiful.

Katerina Suites APARTMENT **€€**
(☑ 24670 24645; www.katerinastudioskastoria. com; Leoforos Megalou Alexandrou 127; d/tr incl breakfast €70/80; ☐ ☏) These modern, family-friendly studios lie 15 minutes' walk from the bus station, east along the waterfront. Panoramic lake views unfurl from the balconies and the thoughtful owners can provide baby cots, a laundry service and even a boat tour on the lake.

✕ Eating

Palia Poli GREEK **€**
(☑ 24670 21401; www.paliapoli.webnode.gr; Orestiados 51; mains €6-8; ☺ noon-midnight; ☏) 'Old Town' is a lovely restaurant inside a waterfront mansion opening onto a spacious courtyard, where you can spend hours over your food and wine as the frogs sing in the nearby lake. The fare is classic Greek – try the meatballs, prawn *saganaki* (pan-fried with cheese and tomato) or the veal liver in wine. The service is attentive and friendly.

★ **Ntoltsó** GREEK **€€**
(☑ 24670 23377; www.ntoltso.gr; Tsakali 2; mains €9-13; ☺ noon-midnight; ☏) Overlooking a photogenic and always-lively square in the city's most handsome district, Ntoltsó is a family restaurant of long pedigree where you can be sure to find excellent Kastorian cuisine. Inside under timber ceilings, or outside watching the world busy itself, you'll enjoy *gigantes* beans with homemade sausage, wild greens, seasonal game and plenty more.

Grada BISTRO **€€**
(☑ 24670 29615; Oresteion 37; mains €9-13; ☺ 1-5pm & 8pm-midnight Tue-Sun; ☏) First there's the dining room: extravagantly colourful, with murals that could be Mexican, Indian,

Russian, or none of the above, and an unabashed fondness for zebra-skin. Then there's the equally experimental food: risotto with strawberries and black chocolate, and salmon with cream and anise. While these do work, there are plenty more-conventional options at this endearingly individual place.

❶ Information

Tourist Information Kiosk (☑ 24670 26777; ☺ 10am-6pm Wed-Sun) Brochures, maps and information in the lakeside Park of the Olympic Flame. Not much English is spoken.

❶ Getting There & Away

Kastoria bus station (KTEL Kastorias; ☑ 24670 83455; www.ktel-kastorias.gr; Athanasiou Diakou 14) is on the southern waterfront, facing the Park of the Olympic Flame. Buses serve Thessaloniki (€19, three hours, up to seven daily), Ioannina (€21, 2½ hours, four weekly) and Athens (€53, 7½ hours via Kozani, three daily).

Kavala   Καβάλα

POP 54,027

Founded in the 7th century BCE by settlers from the nearby island of Thasos, Kavala is often treated as a gateway to the northeastern Aegean Islands, yet has plenty of attractions itself. Historical highlights include the nearby remains of ancient Philippi, the aqueduct of Sultan Süleyman the Magnificent, quality museums, and the Byzantine castle and Ottoman buildings of its pastel-hued, peninsular old town, Panagia. You'll also find beach resorts nearby, and plenty of quality restaurants in its narrow central streets.

Modern Kavala was once ancient Philippi's port. More infamously, Ottoman Pasha Mehmet Ali (1769–1849), eventual founder of Egypt's last royal dynasty, was born here. He ordered his fleet to slaughter tens of thousands of Christian Greeks on islands such as Kassos and Psara during Greece's independence struggle. Islanders still commemorate these events annually.

◉ Sights

The peninsular old town district, Panagia, holds the greatest concentration of sights – principally Ottoman. A 280m-long aqueduct, Kamares, built by the Ottomans in the 16th century and still in beautiful condition, overlooks central Kavala. For swimmable shores, Rapsani Beach, 1.5km west of town, is popular, while young people flock to Batis

NORTHERN GREECE KAVALA

Beach, a further 3km southwest along the coastal road. For something quieter and more family-friendly, continue for another 2km to Tosca Beach.

★Philippi
Archaeological Site   ARCHAEOLOGICAL SITE
(☑25105 16251; Krinides; adult/concession €6/3; ☺8am-8pm Tue-Sun, 1-7.30pm Mon Apr-Oct, 8am-3pm Tue-Sun Nov-Mar; ℗) Founded in 356 BCE by the energetic Macedonian dynast Philip II, father of Alexander the Great, this evocatively sited ancient city is on Unesco's World Heritage list, and lies just 16km northwest from Kavala. Its strategic importance, commanding a principal trade route between Europe and Asia, saw it grow powerful and splendid in the Hellenic period that followed Alexander's death. That prominence persisted through subsequent Roman, Byzantine and post-Byzantine Christian periods, accounting for the palimpsest of stone remnants visitors walk amongst today.

Highlights include the Hellenistic theatre, set dramatically against the hill, the forum, and later remains of the basilicas that rose here once Philippi became an important centre of early Christianity. There's a very worthwhile museum, too, where more delicate finds are displayed and the overall story of Philippi can be better understood.

Mohamed Ali House   HISTORIC BUILDING
(☑25106 20154; Plateia Mehmet Ali; adult/concession €3/2; ☺10am-2pm Thu-Sun) Dating to around 1770, this superb example of late-Ottoman architecture was birthplace and home to Pasha Mohamed (or Mehmet) Ali, wali of Egypt and an important figure in that nation's modern history. Displays across two floors recreate how the Pasha would have lived in the late-18th century: there is a women's room, the Pasha's own quarters, plenty of swords and knives, and lovely Ottoman wood carvings and rugs. An equestrian statue of the man keeps watch outside.

Panagia Quarter   HISTORIC SITE
Named for the Panagia church, this historic peninsula's narrow, tangled streets are lined by pretty pastel houses. A calf-stiffening walk leads up to the castle (☑25108 38602; www.castle-kavala.gr; Isidorou 28; adult/child €2.50/1.50; ☺8am-9pm May-Sep, to 8pm Apr & Oct, to 4pm Nov-Mar; ▣), while other highlights include the restored ruby Halil Bey Mosque and Mohamed Ali House. The enormous 18-domed Imaret (1817), now a wonderful hotel, was Ottoman Pasha Mohamed Ali's hostel for Islamic theology students.

🛏 Sleeping

Hotels can be found along the seafront, mostly of the high-rise, business variety.

Oceanis Kavala   HOTEL €€
(☑25102 21981; www.oceaniskavala.gr; Leoforos Erythrou Stavrou 32; s/d/tr incl breakfast €50/70/80; ℗✳🛜🏊) This smart, modern hotel behind the western waterfront has 168 comfortable, well-maintained rooms with balconies. There's a serviceable fitness centre, in-house restaurant and bar, and even a rooftop pool.

★Imaret   BOUTIQUE HOTEL €€€
(☑25106 20151; www.imaret.gr; Poulidou 30-32; r/ste incl breakfast from €300/630; ✳🛜🏊) Occupying a former Islamic seminary built in 1817 by Pasha Mohamed Ali, this stunning hotel complex in Panagia blends original stone features such as vaulted ceilings and large fireplaces with every modern comfort. The restored Turkish hammam, a muscle-melting array of spa treatments and a candlelit indoor pool complete an exceedingly decadent picture.

The in-house restaurant brings Turkish, Greek and western European traditions into delightful concordance (mains €26 to €28).

🍴 Eating

Kavala is blessed with an abundance of good restaurants: look for them in the lanes off Doiranis and Kriezi, and on the waterfront along Erythrou Stavrou.

Soúsouro   BARBECUE €
(☑25102 26111; Agiou Nikolaou 4; mains €7-8; ☺noon-1am; 🛜) The laneways bordering Panagia and the portside parts of town are rich with ouzeries and tavernas where Kavalans congregate for lingering weekend lunches. Soúsouro, which focuses on grilled and rotisseried meats such as kokoretsi (lamb innards), kontosouvli (mixed pork) and spicy, coarse-textured sausages, is one of the best. Salads and less meaty appetisers are available.

To Araliki   TAVERNA €
(☑6984718521; Poulidou 33; mains €6-8; ☺noon-midnight; 🛜) This cheerful family-run taverna in Panagia isn't expensive, yet delivers an expertly cooked menu of meaty Greek favourites. Locals come for the barbecued souvlaki, lamb chops, kebabs and meatballs, and the jolly atmosphere.

Drinking & Nightlife

★ **Briki** CAFE
(⚑ 6944333220; Poulidou 76; coffee/cocktails €2/7; ⊘ 9am-1am; ⚶) Hands-down Kavala's best-situated cafe, Briki sits pretty at the southern end of the Panagia peninsula, its wood-and-stone, bric-a-brac–crammed interior giving onto a delightful, light-filled terrace that encourages lingering over Greek coffee, conversation and memorable views.

Nouvelle Vague BAR
(⚑ 25102 25067; Leoforos Erythrou Stavrou 18; coffee/cocktails €2/6; ⊘ 8am-1am; ⚶) Another of Kavala's linger-worthy cafe-bars, Nouvelle Vague entices with eclectic decor, a (nearly) portside terrace, and good coffee and cocktails. It's occasionally host to cinema nights, while DJs inject more life into Friday and Saturday nights.

❶ Information

Tourist Office (⚑ 25102 31011; www.kavala greece.gr; cnr Venizelou & Dragoumi; ⊘ 8am-9pm Mon-Sat)

❶ Getting There & Away

AIR
Kavala International Airport (Alexander the Great Airport; ⚑ 25910 53400; www.kva-air port.gr; Hrysoupoli) is 31km east of Kavala and 41km southwest of Xanthi. **Olympic Air** (www. olympicair.com) flies daily to Athens (from €52, 50 minutes); island flights go via Athens or Thessaloniki.

BOAT
Ferries serve Skala Prinos in Thasos (adult/child/car €5/2.50/19, 1½ hours, five daily during summer) from Kavala's eastern waterfront, a brisk 15-minute walk along the waterfront from the bus station. A small building on the left sells tickets for Thasos; tickets for other islands are sold by **Euro Kosmos Travel Agency** (⚑ 25102 21960; www.eurokosmos.gr; Leoforos Erythrou Stavrou 1; ⊘ 8.30am-2pm Mon-Fri, 6-8.30pm Tue, Thu & Fri, 9am-1.30pm Sat) and **Maritime Agency Miliadis** (⚑ 25102 26147; www.miliadou.gr; Kavala Passenger Port). Ferries to Limenas in Thasos (adult/child/car €4/2/18, 45 minutes) depart from Keramoti, 12km from the airport. Ferries from Kavala to Limnos run weekly during summer.

Timetables for ferry routes and information about weather-related route suspensions are available from the **Port Authority** (⚑ 25102 23691; www.portkavala.gr; Averof 1).

BUS
Kavala bus station (⚑ 25102 22294; www. ktelkavalas.gr; cnr Filikis Eterias & Mitropolitou Chrisostomou) serves Athens (€55, 8¾ hours, two daily), Xanthi (€5.40, one hour, 14 daily), Keramoti (€4.70, one hour, 17 daily), Serres (€9.30, two hours, four daily), Alexandroupoli (€15, two hours, five daily) and Thessaloniki (€15, 2¼ hours, 15 daily). The *apothiki* (storeroom) stores luggage.

THRACE ΘΡΑΚΗ

With relatively few beaches and no blockbuster archaeological sites, Thrace (Thraki) draws few foreign tourists, and not many Greeks, either. What Thrace does have is dramatic natural scenery, from the lush delta of the Evros River to the deeply forested Rhodopi Mountains, and a unique mix of cultures, religions and languages, forged by centuries of various empires and migration flows.

In Thrace, modern national borders are abstractions laid over the stronger, deeper roots of the Pomak people, Slavic Muslims who live on both slopes of the mountains that now demarcate Greece and Bulgaria. The border between Greece and Turkey is likewise arbitrary, cutting down the middle of the vast Thracian plain, with its fertile fields of sunflowers, wheat and tobacco. In many villages, people speak Greek as a second language, and the skylines are studded with church domes and minarets alike.

History

The ancient Thracians, a non-Greek tribe, were warlike sorts, at least according Greek sources such as the *Iliad,* and devoted to mystery religions such as the Great Gods cult. The supreme temple was on Samothraki island, where ancient Macedonian, Roman and Egyptian rulers were initiated. Secret rituals were associated with Orpheus, the mythical, tragic Thracian father of music.

Powerful Greek city-states vied with the Persians for Thrace's coast. Athens prevailed at the Battle of Plataea, though Philip II of Macedon took over in 346 BCE. Later, with the Roman Empire's 395 CE division, Thrace's strategic positioning on the Via Egnatia trade route made it important.

Constantinople's defensive zone was the Thracian plain, though its flatness made it vulnerable to marauding Goths, Huns, Vandals, Bulgars, Pechenegs, Cumans and poorly behaved Latin Crusaders – relatively few historic structures predating the Ottomans' 14th-century invasion thus remain.

In the 19th century Thrace's turbulent past reawakened. The 1877 Russo–Turkish War, the 1912–13 Balkan Wars, WWI and

Thrace

finally Greece's failed 1922 invasion of Anatolia saw the territory change hands frequently. A mess of treaties and tragedies resulted in its final tripartite division.

The Turks of Greek Thrace were exempt during the 1923 population exchanges. While İstanbul's Greek population was largely expelled after a 1955 pogrom, the Turks of Greek Thrace remain, mixing with Pomaks, the Bulgarian Muslims who live on both sides of the Rhodopi range.

Xanthi & Around

POP 63,083

Xanthi is the gateway to Thrace, and the most scenic town in the region. To Greeks, it has a mildly exotic reputation: its skyline is spiked with minarets, its food skews Eastern, and Turkish and Pomak (a dialect of Bulgarian) are spoken on the street. The old quarter showcases the grand homes of Ottoman-era tobacco barons, in various states of repair, while local university students bring life.

It's worth settling here for at least a couple of days, to explore the old town, as well as surrounding natural attractions. To the north, the inky-green Rhodopi Mountains rise to the Bulgarian border: go for forest hikes and thermal baths, and a glimpse of the Muslim Pomak culture in the villages. To the west, take a pretty walk along the Nestos River, or a kayak ride. South of Xanthi, the ports of Keramoti and Kavala have ferries to Thasos and other islands.

◉ Sights

Xanthi's old town is fantastic for strolling, as is the little stretch of river that cuts through town. Cross the river to the Samakov district, settled in 1923 by refugees from eastern Thrace, for good views of the old town, and interesting architecture – what was newly built then looks traditional now. If you're travelling by car, the archaeological site of Abdera, plus two interesting religious sites, make good breaks on the southeastern route to Komotini.

Old Xanthi   AREA
(Antika, Xanthi) Stacked up on the hillside on the north side of the city, Xanthi's picturesque historic district is a web of winding lanes and stairs lined with pastel-coloured timber-framed houses and grand neoclassical mansions. Although some of the buildings could use a bit more restoration, it is scenic. It's a functioning neighbourhood, not an outdoor museum with public schools, grocery stores, a 16th-century mosque and a lively bar scene.

Kioutouklou Baba Teke   ISLAMIC TOMB
(Selino) FREE Set amid fields of cotton and mustard seed on the plain southeast of Xanthi, this is the burial spot of a dervish of the Bektashi order, the primary Islamic sect in Thrace. What's striking is how the place functions as both a Muslim and a Christian site: in the antechamber are an Orthodox icon of St George and candles; in the main domed room is the Baba's tomb, draped in green cloth.

Moni Agiou Nikolaou   MONASTERY
(Porto Lagos; ⊙9.30am-8pm Wed-Sun) In the marshlands between Lake Vistonida and the sea, this monastery, associated with Vatopedi on Mt Athos, is set on two islets linked by a pedestrian causeway. It's a beautiful natural spot, and a minor pilgrimage destination; there's a gift shop for all your icon needs. The churches are lovely, but don't miss the uncannily realist mosaics in the parking area.

Archaeological
Site of Abdera   ARCHAEOLOGICAL SITE
(☑museum 25410 51003; Kavala-Alexandroupoli Rd, Skala Avdiron; €4; ⊙8.30am-4pm Wed-Mon) About 6km south of modern Abdera lies the acropolis of the ancient town, inhabited in the 7th century BCE but wracked by various invasions, until it was abandoned in the early 4th century CE. You can walk only along the perimeter of excavated areas, making it hard to see the details. Still, you can see a portion of the city wall, as well as the orderly block-style urban plan, including a paved courtyard of a Roman-era house.

🏃 Activities

Galani Beach   BEACH
(Toxotes) Not a beach as one typically imagines in Greece, but a big sandy spot and shallow water at a bend in the Nestos River, just on the edge of Toxotes. It's busy on the weekends, but quieter midweek. Stroll up the river path, alongside the train tracks, or just relax with a coffee at the obligatory cafe.

EOS Xanthi   HIKING
(Greek Mountaineering Club of Xanthi; www.eosx. gr) Check the website of the local branch of the national hiking club for scheduled group hikes (many Sundays, nearly year-round) or simply ideas on where to hike. It maintains a 'forest village' near the Livaditis waterfall, near the border with Macedonia and a great hike destination if you have time.

Riverland OUTDOORS

(☑25410 62488; www.riverland.gr; Toxotes) This outfitter runs rafting and kayaking trips on the Nestos River; the typical run is Stavroupoli to Toxotes. It can also provide transport and support for the hike to Livaditis waterfall (northwest of Xanthi), or along the river.

⚡ Festivals & Events

Xanthi Carnival CULTURE

(www.carnivalofxanthi.gr; ⊙ Feb-Mar) A mix of folk and pop culture instituted in 1966, this celebration is nationally famous for colourful parades, music, masked merrymaking and pyrotechnics. It's in the three weeks preceding Orthodox Lent, and worth planning around if you're travelling then.

🛏 Sleeping

Xanthippion HOTEL €

(☑25410 77061; www.hotelxanthippion.gr; 28 Oktovriou 212, Xanthi; s/d/tr incl breakfast €50/60/70; P ❄ 🛜) A short walk from the old town, this midrange hotel has a velvety-chic style that hasn't reached all the rooms, so it's worth the additional €10 for a deluxe renovated one. Still, all the fundamentals are solid: great breakfast, ample space, strong wireless internet and enormously helpful staff.

Elisso HOTEL €€

(☑25410 84400; www.hotelelisso.gr; Vasilissis Sofias 9, Xanthi; d/ste from €95/183; P ❄ @ 🛜) Built by the Greek government in the early 1970s, this blocky hotel has been updated to current hip-minimalist standards and functions as a town social hub, with a wine bar and a big outdoor lounge. Rooms are large and have balconies. It has zero old-city ambience, but it is by the historic district and the river.

★Boutique Hotel 1905 BOUTIQUE HOTEL €€€

(☑25410 77362; www.1905.gr; Hasirtzoglou 3, Xanthi; ste incl breakfast €100-140) Built for the last Ottoman deputy in Xanthi, this two-storey home now houses a delightful hotel with six suites with gorgeous ceiling frescoes, marble bathrooms and wood floors. The smallest are cosy but quieter; fortunately the quality windows help seal out bar noise. Mattresses are super-comfy Coco-Mat, the all-natural bed brand that has its factory in Xanthi. Breakfast is excellent.

🍴 Eating

★Palaia Polis TAVERNA €

(☑25410 68685; Hasirtzoglou 7, Xanthi; mains €8-13; ⊙1pm-midnight) This wood-and-stone taverna has some of the most sumptuous cuisine around, especially from the 'Oriental dishes' page of the menu: *hunkar begendi* (tender beef on mashed aubergine and cheese), for instance, and *bougiourdi,* feta baked with tomato and a little chili. The wine list is extensive, the service excellent, and the atmosphere lovely in winter and summer.

★Papaparaskevas SWEETS €

(☑25410 22677; www.papaparaskevas.gr; 28 Oktovriou 186, Xanthi; sweets from €0.50; ⊙10am-6pm) This cake shop has been satisfying Xanthi's sweet tooth since 1926. It's a good place to try Thrace's festive *karioka* – cakes of light walnut-studded fudge, enrobed in chocolate. Individually wrapped in various sizes (€17 per kilo), they're a great souvenir to take home or as gifts elsewhere in Greece, as the place is known countrywide.

Sofi SOUP €

(☑25410 72712; Mihail Karaoli 58-60, Xanthi; dishes €4-6; ⊙11am-midnight Mon-Fri, noon-8pm Sat & Sun) This cheery cafe is good for a lighter meal, coffee or a drink. Order at the counter from the day's selection of soups, a few hot lunch options (meatballs with rice, for example) or pasta cooked to order. The sign and menu are in Greek, but it's easy to point to what you want.

🍷 Drinking & Nightlife

★Ntili Ntili BAR

(☑25415 50575; Pygmalionos Hristidi 1, Xanthi; ⊙8am-late) Cosy and always busy, this '*diskokafeneio*' does coffee, drinks and DJs. The crowd skews young, but the schedule includes a big variety of cultural events and parties. A major local favourite. This is the start of a small bar zone: just head up Pygmalionos and see what looks good, whether traditional or pop.

Bahamas CAFE

(☑25415 52602; Stoa Bahtsegi, Xanthi; ⊙11am-3am Tue-Sun) This cool little bar-cafe is hidden behind the main street. In good weather, it basically takes over the whole interior courtyard; it's popular for brunch on weekends. The passage leading to it off Mihail Karaoli is lined with mod pastel posters, a hint of the retro style of the place.

Ermis BAR

(☑25410 83514; Orfeos 37-39, Xanthi; ⊙10am-3am) This bar in a restored old-town mansion has a fun vibe, an old *avli* (courtyard) with secluded tables and a colourful upstairs for winter. The owners, siblings Theodota and Georgios, serve homemade

POMAKOHORIA

For a road trip far from the tourist track, drive north of Xanthi to the fascinating Pomakohoria (Pomak villages), the 25 or so tiny towns tucked into the forested Rhodopi Mountains near Bulgaria.

The Pomaks are a Muslim Slavic people spread across Turkey, Greece and Bulgaria. In Greece, they are officially classified as 'Greek Muslims', for whom the 1923 Treaty of Lausanne requires education in Turkish. Pomaks receive this – even though their native language is Pomak, a very old dialect of Bulgarian. This accidental policy makes them some of the more polyglot people in Greece.

During the Cold War, the Pomak villages were suspect, and its residents kept behind a military cordon. The tanks and fences were removed only in the mid-1990s. Decades of neglect and exclusion took their toll: these villages are noticeably poorer, with rougher roads and erratic trash collection. In the less remote villages, concrete construction has replaced more traditional whitewashed buildings. Still, it's a very interesting corner of the country, and the natural scenery is majestic. Kapka Kassabova's book *Border* (2017) puts these villages in the context of greater Thrace, at the confluence of Turkey, Bulgaria and Greece.

Echinos village, 30km north of Xanthi, has remarkable mountain views, a shining metal-topped minaret that seems to glow across the valley and a fascinating multicultural cemetery. The best-known destination is Thermes, for its mineral baths (☑ 6973672230; Thermes; €3; ☉ 8am-8pm), in a tidy bathhouse east of town. A free outdoor bath, below the entry road, is less well tended, but worth a look to see the steaming, mineral-encrusted rocks. The water is known for treating skin conditions such as eczema.

If you have the nerve to drive your car on 5km of dirt road, press on past Medousa to near the village of Kottani, for the eponymous Taverna Kottani (☑ 6945009855; Km 9 Thermon-Kottani Rd, Kottani; mains €7-8; ☉ lunch & dinner Fri-Sun), a magical, end-of-the-world place where a kindly couple serves perfect mountain food in a cosy stone house trimmed with traditional Pomak textiles. (Call ahead to confirm opening times.)

It's possible to get as far as Thermes by bus (€4.60, 90 minutes), though the schedule is hardly ideal. Departure is 5.15am weekdays, with a return at 4pm. If you want to stay overnight, an afternoon bus leaves at 2.50pm. The owner of the baths rents rooms for €25, which includes bath access, and there is a taverna, Kalemtzis (☑ 6977597500; Thermes; lunches €7; ☉ lunch & dinner), across the road. Adventurous hikers could take the same bus farther, to Medousa, and walk to Kottani, then back to Thermes.

Greek-meets-international mezedhes and good cocktails.

🛍 Shopping

Bazaar of Xanthi　　　MARKET
(Pazari; Plateia Emporiou, Xanthi; ☉ 8am-4pm Sat)
Every Saturday at the base of Old Xanthi, a massive market converges, drawing a great cross-section of the city and surrounding villages. Vendors of giant cabbages, live snails and homemade booze all holler about their wares at once. There's also lots of cheap clothing and household goods.

ⓘ Getting There & Away

AIR

The closest airport to Xanthi is Kavala International Airport (p297), 44km southwest, near Hrysoupoli.

Only **taxis** (☑ 25410 72801) serve the airport (approximately €50) from Xanthi. Alternatively,

take a Kavala-bound bus to Hrysoupoli (€3.20, 30 minutes, 13 Monday to Saturday, nine on Sunday), and from there take a taxi 12km to the airport.

BUS

The **bus station** (KTEL Xanthis; ☑ 25410 27200; www.ktelxanthis.gr; Dimokritou 6, Xanthi) is 700m south of Kentriki Plateia. Arriving, follow Dimokritou (later Mihail Karaoli) to the centre.

Buses travel to Komotini (€5.20, one hour, eight Monday to Saturday, five on Sunday), Thessaloniki (€20, 2½ hours, seven daily), Athens (€65, nine hours, one daily at 8.30pm) and Alexandroupoli (€8.60, one hour, five daily). Buses also serve Thermes (€4.60, 1½ hours, two daily on weekdays) and other Pomak villages to the north, Toxotes (€1.80, 45 minutes, five daily on weekdays, two on Saturdays) to the southwest and Stavroupoli (€2.90, 45 minutes, four daily on weekdays, two on Saturdays) to the west.

Buses (€90) leave daily at 9.30am and 5.30pm for Bulgarian destinations Svilengrad, Harmanli, Haskovo and Plovdiv (Philippopouli in Greek).

TRAIN

Xanthi's **train station** (☎ 25410 22581; Terma Kondyli, Xanthi) connects Alexandroupoli and Komotini with Thessaloniki twice daily. Although the bus is more frequent, it's worth taking the train from points west, just to pass through the beautiful Nestos gorge between Stavropouli and Toxotes (where the train also stops).

🛈 Getting Around

Xanthi is small enough to be walkable, though you may want to take a taxi from the bus station to Old Xanthi. From the train station, a taxi to the centre costs less than €5.

Komotini   Κομοτηνή

POP 60,648

The draw for a curious visitor in Komotini is the town's multicultural character and the vibrant Turkish street life: spend a little time reading Greek signs, and they'll spell out Muslim names, such as Jamil and Hussein. From the piles of sugary *soutzouk loukoum* (sweet 'sausages' of Turkish delight studded with nuts) in sweet-shop windows, the scent of flame-seared kebabs, and merchants luring passers-by with bright silks and silverware, you might feel like you're much farther east on the map.

The town is spread wide, but most of it is fairly workaday, but the centre is both walkable and scenic, especially in the narrower streets around Yeni Camii (New Mosque). It's a lovely place to spend a day or stop for an afternoon.

◉ Sights

Turkish Quarter   HISTORIC SITE

Across Orfeos north of Plateia Eirinis, Komotini's Ottoman-era neighbourhood, still predominantly Turkish, has old homes, barber shops and teahouses. Its key landmarks are the Eski Camii (Old Mosque), built in 1608, and the Yeni Camii (New Mosque), which, paradoxically, predates the old mosque by 23 years. (Eski Camii is thought to be built over an even older mosque.) An 1884 clock tower adds to the skyline next to the minarets.

🛏 Sleeping

Most hotels in town are located on or near Plateia Eirinis. If coming by car, call to ask for advice on parking, as some are accessible on foot only, and parking on Orfeos is limited.

Orpheus Hotel   HOTEL €

(☎ 25310 37180; www.hotelorfeas.gr; Paraseiou 1; s/d/tr €47/57/67; ❊ ☎) Well positioned in an eight-storey concrete block on the *plateia* (square), Orpheus doesn't have any distinctive style, but its rooms are spacious and well maintained. And because it's so big, it's great for noncommittal travellers, as there's almost always a vacancy.

Chris & Eve Mansion   HOTEL €€

(☎ 25310 33560; www.chris-eve.com; Km 4 Komotini-Alexandroupoli Rd; s/d/ste incl breakfast from €45/65/100; ℗ ❊ ☎ ⊛) On the edge of town, with easy highway access, this place is much more than a generic motorists' crash pad. Its balconied rooms were all redone in late 2018, and there's a taverna and an enormous pool, complete with water slide. For cyclists, there's special bike parking. The attentive staff takes great pride in the place, and rightly so.

Hotel Astoria   HOTEL €€

(☎ 25310 35054; www.astoriakomotini.gr; Plateia Eirinis 28; s/d €52/65; ❊ ☎) This 'traditional' hotel has a faintly historic air, with peach walls and dark furniture. Rooms are a bit cramped, but they have more character than other options in town. Front balconies overlook Plateia Eirinis; opt for the back if you prefer quiet. It is in a pedestrian-only section; you'll need to park and walk in.

🍴 Eating

Good traditional restaurants can be found on the wisteria-shaded pedestrian streets north of Orfeos. There is a small strip of snack joints on Komninou, off the west end of Plateia Eirinis.

★ Petrino   TAVERNA €

(☎ 25310 73650; Mpizaniou 4; mains €7-9; ⊙ lunch & dinner) One of several enticing old-fashioned restaurants in the shady lanes off Ermou, Petrino serves Greek-Turkish mezedhes such as garlicky aubergine and mussels stuffed with rice, as well as the local spicy red sausage.

Fabrica-Farma Kreaton   GRILL €

(☎ 25310 20000; Adrianoupoleos 4; mains €6-10; ⊙ lunch & dinner) This friendly, modern restaurant has an excellent selection of meat, as the name suggests, but also great fresh salads and other veggie dishes to round out your meal. Its outdoor 'farm' area is open in summer.

Nedim SWEETS €
(☑ 25310 22036; Kriton 15; sweets €2-4; ⊙ 8am-11pm) Nedim has been serving some of the best baklava west of İstanbul since 1950. Sample *kadayif* (bird's nests of pistachio and pastry), Turkish delight in a range of flavours, and *soutzouk loukoum* (sweet 'sausages' of Turkish delight studded with nuts).

❶ Getting There & Away

BUS
From **Komotini bus station** (KTEL Rodopis; ☑ 25310 22912; www.ktelrodopis.gr; Georgiou Mameli 15) buses serve Xanthi (€5.20, one hour, eight Monday to Saturday, five on Sunday) and Alexandroupoli (€6.80, 70 minutes, 10 to 12 daily). Buses also serve Thessaloniki (€27.50, 3¼ hours, seven daily) and Athens (€76, 8¾ hours, two daily).

TRAIN
The **train station** (☑ 25310 22650; Panagi Tsaldari) connects Komotini with Xanthi (€4.70, 30 minutes, twice daily) and Thessaloniki, and, to the east, Alexandroupoli (€5.80, 80 minutes, twice daily). The train station is a little over 1km southwest of town.

❶ Getting Around

Komotini sprawls, but the town centre is walkable. There are **taxis** (☑ 25310 37777; http://radiotaxikomotini.gr) available, and **Evros Car Rental** (☑ 6945107712, 25310 32905; www.evroscar.gr; Orfeos 37; ⊙ 9am-7pm) has cars (from €45) and jeeps (€60) for hire.

Alexandroupoli
Αλεξανδρούπολη
POP 57,812

Most people rush through eastern Thrace's largest town and transit hub on their way to somewhere else: Samothraki island, Turkey or Bulgaria, or the relative wilds of the Evros Delta and Dadia National Park. The summer heat can be paralysing, and there are no big sights to plan around.

But a few hours or even overnight in Alexandroupoli is hardly a waste of time. Join the crowds on a *volta* (stroll) on the harbourfront at sundown, or settle in for snacks and drinks in the pleasant pedestrian-friendly streets close to the water. There are also two quality museums, as well as an excellent long, clean beach immediately west of town.

◉ Sights & Activities

Ethnological Museum of Thrace MUSEUM
(☑ 25510 36663; www.emthrace.org; 14 Maiou 63; adult/child €3/free; ⊙ 9am-3pm Tue-Sat, 10am-3pm Sun Oct-Feb, 9am-3pm Tue, Wed & Sat, 10am-3pm & 6-9pm Thu & Fri, 10am-3pm Sun Mar-Sep) Inside a grand sandstone mansion, this museum with backyard cafe packs its displays with colourful Thracian costumes, musical instruments, oil presses, and tools for beekeeping and tobacco production. You'll learn how many silkworms are needed to make 25g of silk and which Greek sweet is made by slamming the ingredients against a wall.

Ecclesiastical Art Museum MUSEUM
(☑ 25510 82282; Plateia Agiou Nikolaou; adult/student €3/2; ⊙ 9am-2pm Tue-Fri, to 1pm Sat) Next to the custard-coloured Agios Nikolaos cathedral, this excellent museum contains priceless icons, many brought by refugees in 1923, plus early printed Greek books. Look for the heart-rending realism of the lamenting Mary paintings in between embroidered priestly vestments, dragon-dispatching St George and delicate silverwork. Ask for an English-language pamphlet.

EOT Beach BEACH
(Alexandroupoli Beach) Just west of the centre (take city bus 7), Alexandroupoli's public beach is a wide swath of yellow sand, lined with umbrellas and loungers, plus cafes. It has Blue Flag status, meaning it's exceptionally clean. The water is shallow and usually calm.

⏿ Sleeping

★ **Sali** BOUTIQUE HOTEL €€
(☑ 25510 25000; Ioakeim Kavyri 16; d/ste from €80/120; ❋❂⊛) Sweet and personal, this labour of love opened in 2018 in a former boarding house. The 10 rooms are homey but plush, with a little retro flair; the Forest and Sea suites each have a private back terrace. Breakfast is an additional €10; the little restaurant also does creative dinners.

Santa Rosa Beach HOTEL €€
(☑ 25510 25551; www.santa-rosa.gr; Km 1 Alexandroupoli-Chili Rd; d/tr incl breakfast €91/106; ⓟ❂❋⊛) This family-run hotel on Alexandroupoli's main long beach is simple and welcoming. Rooms are well kept, and it's great value for the waterfront. It's 3km west of the centre. City bus 7 runs past on the main road; the closest stop is at the turn for the Delfini beach bar.

Eating

Ai Giorgis
TAVERNA €

(St George; ☑ 25510 71777; www.aigiorgis.com; Makri; mains €7-13; ☺ 10am-1am) Tucked among old olive groves and overlooking Demir Ali Beach, this sleek restaurant-lounge is expert in higher-end seafood, from sizzling shrimp *saganaki* to steamed cockles. Wash it down with ouzo and the salty breeze.

Nea Klimataria
TAVERNA €

(☑ 25510 26288; Plateia Kiprou 18; mains €5-8; ☺ noon-9pm) All the classics are done well at this *estiatorio* (restaurant serving ready-made food as well as à la carte), a block back from the harbourfront hubbub. The ready-made day's specials are on display in a visitor-friendly glass case, then you can add on enormous Greek salads, rich with feta, and succulent meats grilled to order. The service is friendly and considerate.

❶ Information

Leon Tours (☑ 25510 27754; www.leontours. gr; Konstantinou Paleologou 4; ☺ 9am-3pm & 6-9.30pm Mon-Sat) Arranges ferry tickets and international tours, including weekly trips to İstanbul and a combo trip to Ayvalik, via Lesvos island.

❶ Getting There & Away

AIR
Alexandroupoli's **Dimokritos Airport** (☑ 25510 89300; Alexandroupoli-Kipon Hwy) is 7km east. **Aegean Airlines** (☑ 25510 89150; www. aegeanair.com; Dimokritos Airport), based at the airport, serves Athens (from €69). Sky Express (www.skyexpress.gr) serves Athens and Sitia in Crete (from €99, three flights weekly).

BOAT
Ferries serve Samothraki only. There is usually one boat daily, but the schedule can change; always check locally, at the portside kiosk of SAOS (www.saos.gr), or through travel agencies such as Leon Tours, and book in advance.

BUS
From **Alexandroupoli bus station** (KTEL Evrou; ☑ 25510 26479; www.ktelevrou.gr; Eleftheriou Venizelou 36) at least 10 buses daily head northeast to Soufli (€6, 1½ hours), Didymotiho (€8.60, 1½ hours) and Orestiada (€10.60, two hours). For Kipi, the main Turkish border crossing (€4.10, 35 minutes) due east of the city, the bus runs four times on weekdays, and twice on Saturday and Sunday.

Buses serve Athens (€78, 10 hours, one daily), Thessaloniki (€31.80, 3¾ hours, 10 daily) and Komotini (€6.80, 70 minutes, 10 to 12 daily). For Kavala (€16.40, two hours, nine daily), buses travel via Xanthi (€11.60, 1¾ hours).

Leon Tours can assist with bus travel to Turkey.

TRAIN
The **train station** (☑ 25510 26395; www. trainose.gr; Dimitriou Karaoli) at Alexandroupoli Port has services west to Xanthi (€9, 1½ hours) and Thessaloniki (€22.50, seven hours) twice a day. To Orestiada (€6.60, two hours) and intervening towns, scheduled service is three times daily, but at the time of research, only the morning train was operating; the afternoon and late-night trains had been replaced with buses.

❶ Getting Around

Central Alexandroupoli is walkable, but a rental car makes exploring the delta and the Dadia forest more feasible; **Evros Car Rental** (☑ 25510 36996; Leoforos Dimokratias 67) is a local company with branches in Komotini and Kavala as well. For the airport, take a Loutra-bound bus from Plateia Eleftherias, or a **taxi** (☑ 25510 33500; www.alexpolistaxi.gr) (approximately €10).

Around Alexandroupoli

⊙ Sights & Activities

★ Dadia-Lefkimi-Soufli National Park
NATURE RESERVE

This large patch of protected forest is on a major bird migration route and home to three of Europe's four vulture species. Visits are best in spring or in July, when giant vultures pop from their nests. The Info Centre (☑ 25540 32202; www.dadia-np.gr; ☺ 8am-4pm) runs a shuttle 3km in to the bird observatory, which is furnished with telescopes to spot the giant raptors feeding; the excursion takes about an hour. You can also rent a mountain bike or take an easy hike in.

Farther south, near Lefkimi, there is a patch of petrified forest that is, unlike most examples of this phenomenon, in a pleasantly shaded patch of living forest, making a nice short hike (with advance notice to the gatekeepers there; ask at the info centre). Thanks to Forest Inn (☑ 25540 32263; www. forestinn.eu; d from €65; ⓟ❋☎) ☞, a fine guesthouse next to the park info centre, Dadia is a pleasant base for exploring the towns between Alexandroupoli and Orestiada. Of course you can drive, but for those who have time, forest trails also run to nearby villages; you can walk to Soufli in less than three hours. There are also two solid tavernas in the village of Dadia.

SOUFLI SILK AND DIDYMOTIHO

Some 66km north of Alexandroupoli, the village of Soufli was once a wealthy cultural centre, fuelled largely by silk production in the 19th century. When the borders shifted in 1923, the vital mulberry orchards that fed the silkworms fell on the Turkish side. Today Soufli has three small silk-weaving units, with only Tsiakiris processing silk from start to finish.

Located in Tsiakiri House, a silk producer of 60 years' pedigree, the Art of Silk Museum (☑25540 22371; www.artofsilkmuseum.gr; Vasileos Georgiou 199, Soufli; ⊙9.30am-8.30pm) FREE is fascinating and informative. Enthusiastic, multilingual staff take you through the history of Soufli's sericulture industry and the process of silk production, starting with the tiny worms (live, and actually munching on mulberry leaves) that grow to make the soft cocoon made of silk thread. The front has a shop where you can buy silk products. Displays include hand looms and silk-reeling machines, as well as elaborate traditional costumes.

Skip over impostor silk 'museums' on Soufli's main street, which are simply shops.

North of Soufli, Didymotiho is a sleepy place with some striking ruined buildings that speak to its colourful history. Break up a drive with lunch here, or get off the hourly Alexandroupoli–Orestiada bus to stretch your legs.

Looming over the town are the remnants of a Byzantine fortress that gives the town its name: twin (didymo) wall (tihos). Numerous eminent Byzantines were born in Didymotiho, and in 1341 Emperor John Kantakouzenis was crowned here. You can walk up the steep streets to the Princess Tower for a fine view of the Erythropotamos and the patchwork farmland – then up higher, past a hillside dotted with churches, such as the Church of Agios Athanasios, and many abandoned cave dwellings.

What you'll likely see first, however, is the enormous Bayezit Mosque, commissioned by Turkish sultan Murad I when he conquered the town in 1361 and briefly made it the Ottoman capital (it later shifted to Adrianoupoli, now Edirne, and eventually to İstanbul). The mosque was the first of its kind on the European continent. While it was undergoing needed renovation in 2017, a welding torch sparked a fire that destroyed its centuries-old wooden roof. Unfortunately, the huge shell of a building is now concealed by construction fences – but what you can see of the building's ornamentation is striking nonetheless. Just uphill from the mosque is a good lunch spot, Thrakiotissa (☑25530 22285; www.thrakiotissa. gr; Ipsilantou 7, Didymotiho; mains €4-6; ⊙7am-6pm); the parking area out front hosts a public market every Tuesday. Another historic sight, Erythropotamos, the 16th-century *hammam* known as the 'baths of love and whispers', is also destined for renovation.

In Prangi, 8km east of Didymotiho, Boufes kai to Masali (☑25530 92320; Prangi; mains €6-9; ⊙8pm-midnight Wed-Sat) is well worth seeking out. Grilled meats, bountiful salads, house-made *tsipouro* (pomace liquor) and the feeling you stumbled onto a secret hideaway: this quirky taverna has everything you want in a destination restaurant, not to mention its location in a decommissioned train station house. In winter, there's a cosy fire; in summer, there are seats out by the tracks (and Sunday hours, but call to confirm).

Evros Delta   NATURE RESERVE
(Δέλτα Εβρού) Just southeast of Alexandroupoli, where the Evros River reaches the Aegean, 188 sq km of coastal lakes, lagoons, sand dunes, swamps and reed beds harbour an immensely rich amount of wildlife. In the spring migrations, thousands of wader birds pause here to feed in the nutrient-packed waters. The protected western section, including the Anthia Marshes and Drana Lagoon, is accessible via the visitor centre (p306) in Loutra Traianoupolis. The eastern portion is reached via Feres, but is sometimes closed by the military.

Gushing from Bulgaria's Rila Mountains, the 530km-long Evros (Maritsa) River winds through Turkey into Greece's Evros prefecture, where it forms part of the Greece–Turkey border. The delta came under threat in the 1950s due to drainage works that attempted to prepare the land for cultivation. Fortunately, since 1974 half of the delta has come under Ramsar protection, allowing its fauna to flourish.

OFF THE BEATEN TRACK

EUROTHIRAMA

Perched on a hill in the Thracian countryside, Eurothirama (☑25560 61202, 6978890861; www.eurothirama.com; Pentalofos; mains €7-10; ☺lunch & dinner Fri-Sun, extra days summer; P ✳ ♿ 🏊) is a destination restaurant has a lord-of-the-manor feel, all stone walls and antler chandeliers. The estate raises game animals, served in dishes such as boar stewed with lemon. A pool is open to diners, and there are apartments for rent (from €50).

The place is a great base for a whole network of walking trails that criss-cross this northern part of Thrace, covering rolling terrain among vineyards as well as the more challenging foothills of the Rhodopi range.

An incredible 325 bird species have been observed here. Three species of European swan glide through these waters, while geese forage through meadows, including endangered lesser white-fronted geese, who winter here. Meanwhile eagles (spotted, white-tailed and imperial) wheel overhead along with more common buzzards and hen harriers.

There's more to the delta than just feathered friends. Forty species of mammal live around the delta, including prowling wild cats and boar in winter, and sousliks (European ground squirrels) scamper along the banks in summer. The waters are also home to 28 reptile species, including terrapins and water snakes.

To freely explore the eastern section, near Turkey, you should have a police and army permit, arranged two weeks in advance by the visitor centre. Fax or email with your full name, date of birth, passport number and expiry date. In practice, some boat captains based in Feres offer unofficial tours, but it helps to have some Greek.

Evros Delta Visitor Centre   BIRDWATCHING
(☑tel/fax 25510 61000; www.evros-delta.gr; Loutra Traianoupolis; ☺8am-4pm) Gather maps and wildlife-spotting tips at this visitor centre, a 20km-drive east of Alexandroupoli. The dirt access road is slow going and hard on hire cars, so it's preferable to joing a group tour (€10 per person, €30 if you're the only visitor). They run in late spring and summer at 9am, 11am and 1pm. Call ahead to confirm.

✕ Eating

Folia tou Pelargou   TAVERNA €
(☑25540 32482; Dadia; mains €7-9; ☺noon-8pm Fri-Wed) One of two tavernas in the village of Dadia, this one has a menu that excels both in local game meats and more standard basics, such as a supremely comforting chicken soup. Look for it on hill above the football field.

Orestiada   Ορεστιάδα

POP 23,600

With wide boulevards and a tidy grid layout, Orestiada has a different feel to most other Greek cities. Other towns boast of their ancient roots, but Orestiada was created after the 1923 Greek–Turkish population exchanges, when it was called Nea Orestiás. Ironically, though its bones are new concrete, the town now feels a bit more old-fashioned and traditional, simply because some of its wood-panelled groceries and bakeries look much as they did a century ago.

That said, aside from an excellent museum devoted to the town's recent history, Orestiada doesn't brim with attractions. Visitors from countries other than Bulgaria and Turkey may be greeted with a mix of astonishment and delight by down-to-earth locals. It is an agreeable stopover on your way from or to Bulgaria or Turkey – the latter is accessible from nearby Kastanies village.

◉ Sights

Orestiada's *plateia* is all modern: a huge open pedestrian plaza between the train station and Leoforos Konstantinou. The main attraction, the city's excellent museum, is just south.

Historical and Ethnographical Museum   MUSEUM
(☑25520 28080; www.musorest.gr; Agion Theodoron 103; €2; ☺10am-1pm Tue-Sun) Learn all about the Greek–Turkish population exchange at this excellent museum with an equally excellent and dedicated staff. The exhibits tell the stories of the broader regional culture, and the stories of the displaced communities, especially their pluck and ingenuity in rebuilding their lives anew.

🛏 Sleeping

Estia   MOTEL €
(☑25520 81198; www.hotel-estia.gr; Km 1 Pyrgos-Orestiada Rd; s/d/tr €31/41/46; P ✳ 🛜 🛁) Less central and geared to travellers with cars, Estia is a tidy roadside hotel about 3km

southwest of the centre. Rooms are basic but have kitchenettes. The real selling point is the large swimming pool – a true blessing in summertime.

Given the price and the pool, budget travellers without cars might make the trip too. It's a 30-minute walk, or a 20-minute ride on the city bus that runs six times a day; look for the stop near the corner of Emmanouil Riga and Konstantinoupoleos.

✖ Eating

Horiatiko BAKERY €
(☑ 25520 29282; Leoforos Vasileos Konstantinou 80; baked goods €1-3.50; ⊗ 5am-10pm Mon-Sat, 8am-4pm Sun) Go with an appetite to sample all the local Turkish-inflected forms of *pites* (pies) here, from flaky layered *giozlemes* filled with greens to creamy open-face *galatopita* (sweet milk pie). The giant sepia-tone photos that decorate the place aren't just for ambience – they're of the actual woman who does all the baking herself.

Agios Giorgos TAVERNA €€
(☑ 25520 92554; mains €7-12; ⊗ 1-11pm Mon-Sat, noon-11pm Sun) Considered one of the best tavernas in the area, Agios Giorgos sits by a chapel of the same name, on a hill above Lepti, about 10 minutes' drive west of Orestiada. Try pickled cabbage rolls and *gioulbasi*, a meaty casserole. It gets very busy on weekends with families and Turkish tourists; kids take to the playground outside.

❶ Information

Hatzigiannis Tours (☑ 25520 28333; Konstantinoupoleos 216, cnr Emmanouil Riga; ⊗ 9am-6pm Mon-Sat) Sells plane, boat and train tickets.

❶ Getting There & Away

BUS

From Orestiada's **bus station** (☑ 25520 22550; www.ktelevrou.gr; Andrianoupoleos 128), buses serve Didymotiho (€1.80, 20 minutes, 12 daily) and Soufli, many continuing to Alexandroupoli (€10.60, 1¼ hours, 13 daily) and Thessaloniki (€43.40, six to seven hours, seven daily).

Other buses go north as far as Ormenio (€5.70, 40 minutes, two daily), close to the Bulgarian border. For Turkey, take the bus to Kastanies (€1.80, 20 minutes, four daily); it's a short walk to the border crossing.

TRAIN

From the **train station** (☑ 25520 28984), three trains are scheduled daily to Alexandroupoli (€6.60, two hours), though at the time of research, the later two were replaced with buses. The early-afternoon service connects in Alexandroupoli for onward service to Thessaloniki (€23.50, 10 hours). The train also runs north to Ormenio (€2.20, 45 minutes), close to the Bulgarian border crossing.

EPIROS ΗΠΕΙΡΟΣ

Epiros (EE-per-os) boasts the magnificent 1km-deep Vikos Gorge, part of the larger Northern Pindos National Park, all forests, waterfalls and ice-cold mountain lakes. Add the entrancingly beautiful Zagorohoria (Zagori villages) and the alpine charm of Metsovo, and it's no wonder these mountains draw loyal repeat visitors. Greece's third-largest city, Ioannina, is the gateway, and a lovely lakeside destination in its own right.

Epirus' lowlands aren't bad either. The turquoise Ionian Sea laps at long sandy beaches, and beautiful Parga, sporting a Venetian castle, poses on a hillside above it all. Farther south, Preveza's yacht harbour is a low-key international scene, and the massive ruins of Nicopolis sprawl casually by the road.

Reaching Epiros is an event in itself. The road from Kalambaka winds over the Pindos Mountains; from Macedonia, the Egnatia Odos cuts straight through, via massive tunnels. Leave by sea, on a ferry to Italy or Corfu from Igoumenitsa.

History

The Dorian invasion (1100–1000 BCE) left three main Greek-speaking tribes: the Thesproti, the Chaones and the dominant Molossi. The marriage of Molossi princess Olympias to powerful Macedonian king Philip II brought conflict with emerging Rome. King Pyrrhus (319–272 BCE) famously defeated the Romans at Ausculum, at a heavy cost; hence the concept of a 'Pyrrhic victory'.

After the Roman Empire split in 395 CE, Epiros was ruled from Constantinople. Centuries later, it became important after the 1204 Latin sack of Constantinople; Byzantine nobles escaped here and established a key successor state, what historians call the Despotate of Epiros (after a standard Byzantine title, not the modern meaning of despot). It finally fell in 1479, when the Ottomans, having conquered Constantinople in 1453, took the region into their empire. Eminent Byzantines retreated to Epiros' mountain fastnesses, and negotiated tax exemptions for their region.

Epiros

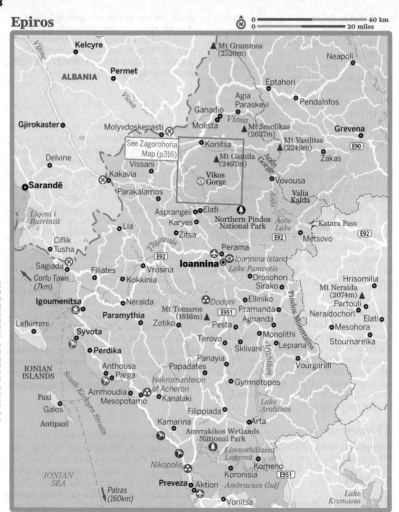

Infamously linked with Epiros is 18th-century Albanian ruler Ali Pasha, very much a despot in the modern sense, as he ransacked much of Albania and western Greece, while wheeling and dealing with Turks, Brits and even Napoleon. Ali's remorseless mass killings and torture made him infamous, while Europeans were titillated by tales of his hundreds-strong harem. Nevertheless, until he was killed in 1822, Ali had some local supporters because he shrugged off the Ottoman state, and aided Greek freedom fighters elsewhere by wearing down and distracting the Turks. In 1912 Epiros was divided when newly created Albania got

a northern chunk. Mussolini's 1940 invasion was repelled in Epiros, which became a communist resistance stronghold, first against the Nazis and then against the right-wing army in the Greek Civil War (1944–49).

🏃 Activities

Hiking in Epiros, especially the high mountains of the Northern Pindos National Park (p314), is a major attraction. Keep an eye on the developing Epirus Trail (www.epirustrail.gr), a long-distance route that showcases the region's most dramatic scenery.

Eating

In the mountains of Epiros, expect game meats, mushrooms and trout, as well as excellent *pites* (pie), including a crustless egg-and-feta version called *alevropita*. Sparkling wine from Zitsa is common, and Metsovo does good reds. Near the coast, look for eel farmed in the Ambracian Gulf, as well as the other usual seafood. The best selection of restaurants is in Ioannina, Preveza and Parga, as well as the Zagorohoria.

❶ Getting There & Away

Preveza Airport (Aktion International Airport; ☑ 26820 26113; www.pvk-airport.gr), known as Lefkada or Aktio, serves numerous destinations in the summer months.

Ioannina Airport (King Pyrros Airport; ☑ 26510 83600; Leoforos Grammou 135) has year-round connections with Athens (on Aegean/Olympic and Sky Express), but flights are often delayed or cancelled due to fog. Corfu's airport can be more reliable, and has flights from elsewhere in Europe.

❶ Getting Around

Driving is the best way to get around the region. Tiny mountain roads are mostly paved and go everywhere, and a fast toll road runs from Igoumenitsa to Thessaloniki, via Ioannina and Metsovo.

If you prefer not to drive, buses can take you between bigger destinations. Service to villages is infrequent, though; to explore in detail, you must allot time, and money for taxis.

Ioannina Ιωάννινα

POP 80,400

Set on the western shore of the lovely Lake Pamvotis, Ioannina is one of northern Greece's most atmospheric cities, and one of its more cultured and wealthy, as it was famous throughout the Ottoman Empire for its silver artisans. The walls of its old fortified city, the Kastro, enclose a tranquil quarter, spiked with minarets, and an island in the lake is a quiet, car-free escape. At sunset the lake turns silver and the impressive mountains behind turn lilac. Ioannina is a beautiful place in every season, and worth at least a couple of days in a larger tour of Epiros; many Athenians visit as a romantic long weekend away. If you come by car, or don't mind hiring a taxi, you can also visit the impressive ancient site of Dodoni (p311), a short drive southwest of town.

History

Byzantine emperor Justinian founded Ioannina in the 6th century, and it became an important commercial and cultural outpost with a significant community of Romaniote Jews. In 1204, when Latin Crusaders sacked Constantinople and dismembered Byzantium, Ioannina was where the Byzantine rulers regrouped and established the Despotate of Epiros, first ruled by Michael I Komnenos Doukas. Ottomans conquered in 1430, and a Sephardic Jewish population arrived after 1492. Between the silversmiths and the 'Epirot School' of icon painters, the city became a leading cultural and artistic centre by the 16th and 17th centuries.

In 1787 Albanian warlord Ali of Tepelene, who had worked his way up from highway banditry, was named pasha of Trikala, and promptly claimed Ioannina as his capital. This began a period of relative independence and stability for Epiros, as Ali Pasha ruled the region as his private fiefdom, ironically putting an end to the banditry that had served him so well. The drawback was the man's staggering cruelty, incidents of which grew into regional legends, and both fascinated and repulsed visiting western Europeans, such as philhellene and poet Lord Byron. But Ali enforced the law and Ioannina flourished – albeit with brutal mass drownings and torture along the way. In 1822, trapped at the Agios Panteleimon monastery on the island in Lake Pamvotis, octogenarian Ali was killed by the Ottomans, who paraded his severed head around İstanbul.

In the 1912–13 Balkan Wars, Greeks expanded the border of Greece north from Arta, claiming Ioannina. The 1923 population exchanges saw Turks replaced by Anatolian Greek refugees. In 1943 the Nazis deported the Jewish population to concentration camps.

◉ Sights

All of the city's museums are closed on Tuesdays, except for the Ali Pasha Museum on Ioannina Island.

Silversmithing Museum MUSEUM
(Map p310; ☑ 26510 64065; www.piop.gr; Its Kale; €4; ⊙10am-6pm Wed-Mon Mar–mid-Oct, to 5pm mid-Oct–Feb) Although the centre of Ioannina no longer rings with the distinctive tapping hammers of the city's famous artisans, that sound and their trade are preserved in this excellent museum. Built into the wall of the citadel, the two-level exhibit space

Ioannina

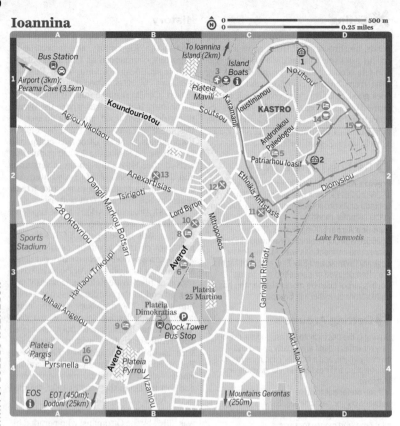

Ioannina

◎ Sights

✈ Activities, Courses & Tours

🛏 Sleeping

✗ Eating

🍷 Drinking & Nightlife

🛍 Shopping

shows the whole process of silver work and tells the story of how Ioannina came to supply the Ottoman Empire and beyond.

The museum is in the lower section of the citadel; you must enter through the main gate in the north wall and walk south, then west.

Ioannina Island   ISLAND

(To Nisi; www.nisi-ioanninon.gr) In the middle of the lake, the reed-encircled patch of land locals just call To Nisi (The Island) is a pretty, peaceful destination, whether you just want a boat ride and a stroll on some car-free streets, or you're up for sightseeing, at the interesting little Ali Pasha Museum, the **Lake Pamvotis Information Center** (☑ 26510 21834; ⊗10am-4pm Wed-Sun) FREE and a fresco-bedecked Moni Filanthropinon. (The island is Greece's third-largest monastic community, after Mt Athos and Meteora). Boats leave frequently from near Plateia Mavili; the ride takes about 10 minutes.

In the 17th century, refugees from the Mani, in the Peloponnese, built the little settlement where boats arrived; about 200 people still live here. Away from this little town area, the island is a little wilder, and a walking path leads around the circumference. Traditionally, the island was a destination for a meal of fish and eels from the lake. Pollution has dampened the local appetite for these dishes, but the tanks still feature outside restaurants. The real treat is the baklava and other nut snacks hawked at a lot of the shops.

Moni Filanthropinon · MONASTERY

(Μονή Φιλανθρωπινών; Ioannina Island; ⊗9am-2pm, plus 5-8pm summer) FREE This monastery, active at least since the 13th century, bursts with flowers and is tended by kindly nuns – in stark contrast with its church, in which one wall is filled floor to ceiling with severed limbs, rolling heads and every other grisly mode of martyrdom in Christian history. Just as intriguing (and easier on the eye) is a separate section of frescoes of Greek philosophers Plato, Aristotle and Plutarch, installed during a 16th-century renovation.

Perama Cave · CAVE

(Σπήλαιο Περάματος; ☑ 26510 81521; www.spilaio-perama.gr; Perama; adult/child €7/3.50; ⊗9am-9pm summer, to 5pm winter) Just around the edge of the lake from central Ioannina, this cave is among Greece's largest and most impressive. Discovered by accident in 1940 by residents fleeing bomb attacks, 1100m of its fairy-tale passageways can be explored on hourly guided tours (45 minutes, in Greek and English). Knowledgeable guides come armed with fascinating facts about geology and unique cave fauna. The cave is usually colder than outside, so dress accordingly.

Buses 8 and 16 from Ioannina's clock tower run regularly to Perama, 250m south of the cave.

Municipal Ethnographic Museum · MUSEUM

(Map p310; ☑ 26510 26356; Alexandrou Noutsou 18, Kastro; adult/student €2/1; ⊗8.30am-4.30pm Mon-Fri, 9am-3pm Sat & Sun, to 8pm in summer) Set inside the Aslan Pasha Mosque (1619), the museum exhibits local costumes and

period photographs, along with tapestries and prayer shawls from Ioannina's Jewish community, which numbered some 7000 people at its peak in the 19th century. The grounds of the mosque (free to enter during museum hours) include a ruined madrasa and idyllic lake views from this high point.

Ali Pasha Museum · MUSEUM

(☑ 26510 81791; Ioannina Island; €3; ⊗8am-10pm Jun-Sep, 10am-9pm Oct-May) On Ioannina's idyllic island, the monastery where Ali Pasha made his last stand (or recline, really) in 1822 is now a small, cheerfully morbid museum, highlighting the bullet holes in the floorboards. Also on display are various personal effects and etchings of the portly Pasha in full repose, sitting fat and happy with his favourite consort. To get there, walk up the hill from the dock, then bear left in the first square.

Dodoni · RUINS

(Δωδώνη; ☑ 26510 82287; http://odysseus.culture.gr; €6; ⊗9am-4pm, later in summer) Set in a wildflower-carpeted valley 21km southwest of Ioannina, Dodoni was the religious capital of the ancient Epirote Alliance. It is most famous for its massive **theatre**, built in the 3rd century BCE. The north-side acropolis has wall remnants, and east of the theatre are foundations of the **bouleuterion** (council house) and the small **Temple of Aphrodite**. As described in *The Odyssey*, Greece's oldest oracle functioned here, centred on an oak tree whose rustling leaves were interpreted by priests.

Activities

Take a relaxing **boat trip** (Map p310; one way €2; ⊗8am-10pm) to Ioannina Island, or, if you want a longer water outing, go for a one-hour **lake cruise** (Map p310; ☑ 6944470280; cruise €5; ⊗11am-midnight daily summer, Sat & Sun winter); both leave from the lakefront by Plateia Mavili.

For Anavasi's *Pindus-Zagori* 1:50,000 hiking map (€9), enquire at local *periptera* (kiosks), **Public** (Map p310; ☑ 26510 70087; Pyrsinella 4; ⊗9am-9pm Mon-Fri, to 8pm on Sat) or **Mountains Gerontas** (☑ 26510 38222; www.mountains-gerontas.com; Hristou Katsari 42; ⊗8.30am-2.30pm & 5.30-9.30pm Mon-Fri, 8.30am-2.30pm Sat). Hikers should consult EOS (p313) about mountain conditions.

🛏 Sleeping

The best sleeping options are inside the Kastro, where there are small and quiet hotels.

Hotel Astoria HOTEL €
(Map p310; ☑ 26510 20755; www.hotelastoria.
gr; Paraskeuopoulou 2, cnr Averof; s/d €40/50;
P ※ ☎) Basic, no frills, clean rooms – pretty
much all you need in a budget hotel. You may
even get a balcony. The preferable rooms are
on the side street, rather than on noisier
Averof. There's a parking lot at the end of the
street; the archaeology museum and adjacent park are just a block away.

★**Hotel Kastro** PENSION €€
(Map p310; ☑ 26510 22866; www.hotelkastro.gr;
Andronikou Paleologou 57; d from €66; P ※) This
restored mansion adjacent to the citadel
is immaculately decorated in antique style
that's still light and airy. The seven rooms,
set around a little courtyard, are all very quiet; rest is all but guaranteed. Follow signs
for the Byzantine Museum after you enter
the Kastro.

Metropolis BOUTIQUE HOTEL €€
(Map p310; ☑ 26510 30004; www.metropolis
hotel.gr; Averof 33; d incl breakfast from €120;
P ⊖ ※) Open since 1934 and now run by the
grandson of the founder, the Metropolis has
historic cachet (first hot and cold running
water in Epiros!) and has been modernised
very nicely. There are only nine rooms, all
with Coco-Mat beds and other comforts; deluxe rooms (€160) have bathtubs. Very good
breakfast too.

Saz City Life BOUTIQUE HOTEL €€
(Map p310; ☑ 26510 78888; www.saz-hotel.com; 28
Oktovriou 7; d incl breakfast from €95; P ⊖ ※ ☎)
Opened in 2018, this 23-room hotel brings
earth-toned minimalist chic to Ioannina.
(The breakfast buffet is, fortunately, full
maximalist.) The upper floors have views of
the water – worth the €20 premium. At the
time of research, a small rooftop pool was
planned as well.

Archontariki BOUTIQUE HOTEL €€
(Map p310; ☑ 26510 78010; www.hotel-archon
tariki.gr; Zalokosta 50; d incl breakfast from €75;
P ⊖ ※ ☎) In case the Kastro hotels are full,
this is a great alternative, tucked away on
a silent street that's still walking distance
to everything. There are just six rooms, all
done in a lavish historical style of ornate ceilings and dark-wood furniture. (If you prefer
an airier style, also check the same owner's
other property, Kamares, around the corner).
Breakfast also spares no detail.

Filyra BOUTIQUE HOTEL €€
(Map p310; ☑ 6932601240; www.hotelfilyra.gr; Andronikou Paleologou 18; d/studio €70/80; P ※ ☎)
Filyra is one of three sweet, flower-bedecked
small hotels under the same management,
all tucked into historic old courtyard houses in Ioannina's castle district. With a range
of room configurations, you're sure to find
a set-up that suits. Platanos in the Castle is
across the small *plateia* from Filyra; Dafni is
on Ioustinianou, facing the *kastro* wall.

Eating

★**Magazaki pou Legame** GREEK €
(Map p310; ☑ 26510 33106; Ethnikis Antistaseos
44; mains €8-9; ⊙ 2-11pm Tue-Thu, from 1pm Fri-
Sun) Fresh, imaginative food comes from
the open kitchen at this little restaurant.
The printed menu is small, to leave room for
daily and seasonal specials. Expect hearty
housemade sausage, tender ravioli and local
cheeses.

★**Fisa Roufa** GREEK €
(Map p310; ☑ 26510 26262; Averof 55; mains €6;
⊙ 24hr; ☎) This classic all-hours restaurant
has a visitor-friendly format: pick from
the dazzling array of prepared dishes on
the steam table (soups, roast lamb, stuffed
vegetables and more classics) and settle in
for a hearty meal. The staff is friendly and
efficient, and there's a great cross-section of
people to watch while you 'blow and slurp',
as the name translates.

Metsovotiki Folia GRILL €
(Map p310; ☑ 26510 22033; Averof 101; skewers
from €3; ⊙ 1-11.30pm Mon-Sat) Wood panelling
and embroidered curtains cosify what's essentially a cheap-and-cheerful charcoal-grill
restaurant, with a menu of souvlaki and
(thanks to the Metsovo connection) cheese,
cheese and more cheese. The *metsovone saganaki* (fried cheese) is deliciously smoky
and a tiny bit spicy.

Stoa Louli TAVERNA €€
(Map p310; ☑ 26510 71322; Anexartisias 78; mains
€10-15; ⊙ 10am-3am) Fronted by grand arches, this atmospheric place is set in a passage
between 19th-century stone buildings. The
solid, somewhat modernised Greek menu
includes dishes like beetroot salad bejew-
elled with pistachio, roast aubergine with
feta and garlic, and *hunkar beyendi* – tender pieces of beef on a bed of aubergine
mash. There's live music Thursday to Saturday nights, and Sunday afternoon.

🍷 Drinking & Nightlife

A large university student population keeps Ioannina lively. Cafes facing the lake by Plateia Mavili are popular for coffee. At night, crowds flock to the pedestrian strip of Kallari and Lord Byron, the old bazaar and silversmith area, and stoas (shopping passages) off Anexartisias also hold bars. Plateia Pargis has some scenic outdoor drinking spots too.

★ **Arte Povera**   CAFE
(Map p310; ☑26510 22656; Paleologou 66; ⊘9.30am-12.30am) This sweet house-turned-cafe is so relaxed and welcoming, you could easily spend hours here – there's coffee, homemade sweets, salads and a lovely garden to enjoy them in.

★ **Its Kale Cafe**   CAFE
(Map p310; ☑26510 64206; Kastro; ⊘9.30am-midnight Wed-Mon) This lovely cafe in a stone house inside the citadel draws just as many locals as visitors. It serves food, but most people come for a coffee and chat in the gorgeous setting. Occasionally there's music at night.

ℹ️ Information

An **info kiosk** (Map p310; ☑23105 55444; www.travelioannina.com; ⊘Jun-Aug) on the lakeshore is open in summer. For year-round service:

EOS (Greek Alpine Club; Map p310; ☑26510 22138; www.orivatikos.gr; Smyrnis 15; ⊘7-9pm Mon-Sat) Hiking information; also organises group hikes.

EOT (Greek National Tourist Organisation; ☑26510 48866; Dodonis 39; ⊘7.30am-2.30pm Mon-Fri) Good for basic maps and info on Ioannina, but not located in the centre.

ℹ️ Getting There & Away

AIR

Aegean/Olympic (A3; ☑801 112 0000; https://en.aegeanair.com) and Sky Express (p130) serve Athens. The airport (p309) is 4km west of town. Don't plan a tight itinerary, as fog commonly causes delays or cancellations.

BUS

Ioannina's **bus station** (KTEL Ioanninon; Map p310; ☑26510 25014; www.ktelioannina.gr; Georgiou Papandreou 45) serves Arta (€7, two hours, five daily on weekdays, four on weekends), Athens (€42.50, five to 6½ hours, seven daily, including two express), Igoumenitsa (€10.60, 1½ hours, six daily), Konitsa (€6.20, 1¼ hours, six daily on weekdays, three on weekends), Preveza (€10.40, two hours, six daily on weekdays, four on

weekends) and Thessaloniki (€30.50, 3½ hours, six daily). Direct service to Metsovo is limited (€5.80, 1½ hours, two daily on weekdays, once in the afternoon on weekends), but other intercity buses can drop you on the highway below the village. Zagorohoria service is very limited (one bus weekly in some cases) and changes by season.

Buses from Ioannina serve the Albanian border post at Kakavia (€6.10, 1¼ hours, seven daily).

ℹ️ Getting Around

City bus No 2 runs from the **clock tower** (Map p310; www.astiko-ioannina.gr; Mpizaniou & Plateia Dimokratis) to the airport every 20 minutes (€1.50). Coming from the airport, cross the main road and wait just before the traffic light.

Taxi (Map p310; ☑26510 46777, WhatsApp 6988046777) Taxis wait near Plateia Pyrrou, by the lake and at the bus station. A taxi to/from the airport costs approximately €7.

Metsovo   Μέτσοβο

POP 2500

The name Metsovo makes many Greeks sigh with delight. It's a singular village, thriving on tourism but still naturally charming, full of friendly people and tasty food, and fairly bursting with alpine-perfect scenery. Skiing is a draw in winter; in summer, the hiking is good; and year-round it's a pretty place to stop for a night or two and take in the distinct culture, bounteous cheeses and interesting history. The hospitable locals are mostly Vlachs (*armani* in Greek), descendants of a nomadic sheep-herding people who speak Aromanian, a Romance language. For centuries, in the Byzantine and Ottoman empires, they were hired to guard the Katara Pass (1705m), the only route across the Pindos Mountains.

◉ Sights

Old Metsovo houses have been polished to their former glory, some transformed into museums. There is centuries-deep wealth here, from Vlach families that moved and worked abroad. In the 1940s, an Averoff (Evangelos, one-time foreign minister and minister of defence) convinced a long-gone Tossizza (Baron Michael) to establish a foundation, which still funds local development, including the dairy and winery.

Folk Art Museum   MUSEUM
(☑26560 41084; www.metsovomuseum.gr; adult/student €3/2; ⊘10am-4pm Fri-Wed) The Tossizza family mansion conjures life in this mountain town: a cosy dream of fireplaces

and gorgeous carpets, and the reality of being snowbound for half the year. The guided tour, about 45 minutes, explains details like why Agia Paraskevi is the village's patron saint, and what the big wool pompoms on the shoes of Vlachs (and Athens' military guards, the *evzones*) are really for. All along are treasures you'd expect in far grander museums, such as 17th-century icons.

Averoff Gallery

GALLERY

(Museum of Modern Greek Art; ☑ 26560 41210; www.averoffmuseum.gr; adult/student €3/2; ☺ 10am-4pm Wed-Mon, to 6.30pm mid-Jul-mid-Sep) Founded by Evangelos Averoff to fulfil a long-held wish to crown his family's town with a quality gallery, this three-storey space exhibits works of Greek artists from the 19th century to the present day. There are some especially beautiful portraits and usually some interesting temporary exhibit on local culture, as well as a kids' art space. Look for the gallery on the south side of the park in the centre of town; it's just below street level.

🏃 Activities

In winter, Metsovo is a good base for skiing and snowboarding, with three small ski areas nearby. The rest of the year, the Ursa Trail system (www.ursatrail.com) is a pleasant way to explore, with four day hikes centred on the town. You can also head farther afield, into the Valia Kalda section of the Northern Pindos National Park (Map p316), north of town.

Metsovo Ski Centre

SKIING

(☑ 26560 41095, 26560 41211; Averof 17; ☺ 9.30am-3.45pm Dec-Mar) In winter, this office in town can advise on conditions at the three nearby ski areas. If you need to hire gear or arrange lessons, the staff can help with that too.

The three ski areas are Anilio (☑ 6980 760850, 26512 00520; www.anilioadventurepark. gr; lift ticket weekend/weekday €13/10; ☺ lifts 9am-3.15pm Mon-Fri, 8am-4pm Sat & Sun), the largest, to the south; Profitis Elias (also called Politsies or Mavrovouni), about 4km north; and tiny Karakoli on the highway just above town.

🛏️ Sleeping

Anax

GUESTHOUSE €

(☑ 26560 42003; www.hotelanax.com; Mpalatinou 1; d/tr incl breakfast €50/65; P 🛜) If you're here for a view, Anax is your best bet – it sits at the top of town with vistas all around.

Rooms have the requisite cosiness, from fluffy wool rugs to pine panelling. The only drawback, of course, is that it's a hike back up from the centre of town, but the staff can pick you up.

Arka Rooms

PENSION €

(☑ 26560 42086; www.arkametsovo.com; Stanou 1; d/studio €30/40; 🛜) A helpful family runs this great-value little guesthouse with a few spacious rooms and studio apartments with kitchenettes. Some have balconies, and one studio even has a fireplace.

★ Katogi Averoff Hotel & Winery

HOTEL €€

(☑ 26560 42554; www.katogiaveroffhotel.gr; d/ste incl breakfast from €80/120; P 🛜) A night at this luxury hotel includes a wine-tasting session, as well as an excellent breakfast. The rooms have a subdued Greece-meets-Morocco style, with painted stucco walls. In winter, step up to a suite to have a fireplace. It's a little bit north of the centre of town, but an easy level walk.

🍴 Eating

Metsovo is famous for its smoked cheese, as well as other varieties made by the Tossizza-funded cheese facility. Also don't miss the bakeries, still run on wood-fired ovens. On weekends, there is a public market near the main square.

★ Fournos me Ksyla

BAKERY €

(Tositsa 24; pies €2; ☺ 8am-5pm Mon-Sat) A cheerful couple has been running this bakery since 1969, with deserved pride. The excellent spinach-and-cheese pies are flaky, buttery and completely satisfying. As the name says, everything's baked in a wood oven. Look for the yellow door.

ℹ️ Information

Northern Pindos National Park Information Centre (☑ 26530 22241; www. pindosnationalpark.gr; ☺ 8.30am-3.30pm Wed-Sun) For details on outdoor exploring.

ℹ️ Getting There & Away

Metsovo is a 45-minute drive from Ioannina. From the *plateia* **bus stop** in Metsovo, there is limited service to Ioannina (€10, 1½ hours, two daily on weekdays, once in the afternoon on weekends). More frequent intercity services pass the **highway bus stop** (☑ 26560 41280) below the village; you'll need to take a **taxi** (☑ 265604858, 6946580979, 6945742607) there (€5).

Zagorohoria

Τα Ζαγοροχώρια

Northwest of Ioannina, the road leads over a steep ridgeline and into the Zagorohoria (Zagori villages). More than 40 tiny settlements built of the local grey stone, right up to the slate roofs, blend almost seamlessly into the flanks of the heavily forested mountains. Most of their streets are too narrow for cars, and they're linked to other villages by old stone paths and staircases and graceful arched bridges, all built in the 18th and 19th centuries. Although many of the villages are less than an hour's drive from Ioannina, the area feels much more remote, and it delivers on silence, quality hiking and nature, plus breathtaking views at every turn. The main attraction is the dramatic Vikos Gorge, nearly 1km deep, but snow-capped peaks to the north compete; the whole area is inside the Northern Pindos National Park.

◉ Sights & Activities

From Papingo in the west to Leptokarya in the east, all of the Zagorohoria are scenic, but each village has a slightly different character. The most visited, with the most services, are on the region's western side, around the Vikos Gorge.

In the relative lowlands, romantic Dilofo has a handful of inhabitants and an uncanny quiet; it's close enough to Ioannina that you could easily day-trip to the city. Very near the gorge's edge, Monodendri is a hub on hiking routes and draws the most road-trippers; nearby Vitsa is a calmer alternative. Over a ridge from the gorge, Elafotopos, Kato Pedina and Ano Pedina are less visited, and set in what feels like their own private valley. Active travellers flock to Aristi for rafting. Many visit Megalo Papingo and its tinier sibling, Mikro Papingo, at the end of the road, for an overnight hike to pristine glacial Drakolimni (Dragon Lake) on Tymfi Massif. Papingo also has the most guesthouses and restaurants.

East of the gorge, Kipi, split by a wide road, is less scenic, but good hikes start from here, and it's a short drive from Ioannina. Tiny Kapesovo is the starting point for several good day hikes, including the landmark Vradeto Steps. Tsepelovo is the largest village, with a year-round population of approximately 250; from here there's another approach to the Tymfi Drakolimni.

The eastern Zagori villages, many damaged in WWII, are far less populated, with few services. But if you like mountain driving, pack a paper map (phone service is weak) and head for lost-in-time villages like Dipotamos.

★ Vikos Gorge   CANYON

(Map p316) The Voïdomatis ('Good Water' in its Slavic roots) River, a tributary of the Aoös, carved the 12km-long, 900m-deep Vikos Gorge over millions of years. Per *Guinness*, it's the world's deepest canyon in proportion to its width. The cliffs begin near Vitsa and run north to near Papingo; the river's springs are below the village of Vikos, where there is also an impressive viewpoint. Several other overlooks on either side of the gorge are accessible by short trails.

The gorge and the Tymfi mountain range to the northwest comprise a special protected zone called the Vikos-Aoös Geopark, itself part of the much larger Northern Pindos National Park. Hiking routes around and in the gorge are mostly well tended and blazed; get guidance for your experience level from EOS (p313) in Ioannina. The most typical, if quite challenging, route starts in Monodendri, where a steep path heads down; at canyon's end, a right-hand trail leads to Mikro Papingo; the walk takes more than six hours. The only water is at Klima Spring, halfway along the gorge. Check the weather forecast and kit yourself out with sturdy hiking boots and drinking water. Always let someone local (such as your guesthouse) know your departure time and planned route, so they can raise the alarm if necessary.

Kokkori Bridge   BRIDGE

(Noutsou Bridge; Map p316) `FREE` Set between two sheer cliffs below the village of Koukouli, this is one of the most picturesque of the Zagorohoria's stone bridges. It was first built in 1750, and has been kept in excellent repair ever since. The small arch cut into one side of the bridge is for water overflow if the river runs high; otherwise the water pressure would weaken the structure.

Beloï Viewpoint   VIEWPOINT

(Map p316; Vradeto) `FREE` All the views of Vikos Gorge are stunning, but this one might be the best. It's reached from outside the village of Vradeto. You must park and walk about 1km (level ground) out to the edge.

Plakida Bridge   BRIDGE

(Kalogeriko Bridge; Map p316; Kipi) A stone-paved trail leads down from the roadside parking area to this stone bridge, one of the prettiest

Zagorohoria

in the Zagori region and a rarity in its triple-arched design, which makes it look a bit like a caterpillar inching over the Voïdomatis. It was built in 1814.

Moni Evaggelistria
MONASTERY

(Map p316; Ano Pedina; ⊙10am-5pm) **FREE** Built in 1630, this little monastery has a church that glows like a box of jewels: its vivid 18th-century frescoes have never been retouched, but simply preserved with care over the centuries. The attendant nun (who speaks French as well as Greek) will let you in, using an impressive key.

Moni Agia Paraskevi
MONASTERY

(Map p316; near Monodendri) From near the lower *plateia* in Monodendri, by Hotel Ark-touros, a stone path leads about 1km to this small, now-disused monastery perched on the edge of Vikos Gorge. The church here is the oldest in the Zagorohoria, founded in 1413. Some of the frescoes, including a portrait of the local man who paid for the

church, date to the 15th century. A truly alarming cliff-edge path leads from the monastery up to a small cave once used by hermits.

Vradeto Steps
HIKING

(Skala Vradetou; Map p316) Until a road was built in the 1970s, this mountainside stone staircase was the only way to reach the village of Vradeto. A loop walk starting in Kapesovo and returning on the road takes between four and five hours; in summer, a *kafeneio* (coffee house) opens in Vradeto. The best photos are from near the top, with the switchbacks all visible below.

Papingo Rock Pools
SWIMMING

(Ovires Rongovou; Map p316; Megalo Papingo) **FREE** A short walk from the road between Megalo and Mikro Papingo, these natural pools in a canyon are in summertime lightly dammed to create deep blue swimming holes. The rest of the year it's still a scenic diversion to see how the rushing water has smoothed natural bathtubs into the limestone.

Rafting Athletic Center OUTDOORS
(☑ 6942015143, 26530 41888; www.rafting-athletic-center.gr; Hotel Taxiarches, Aristi; per person €30) One of several rafting operations in and around Aristi, offering a range of trips, geared for different skill levels and seasons; some are farther afield in Epiros. The most popular, and closest, one is down the Voïdomatis River, starting just below Aristi and ending in Klidonia.

☞ Tours

Bikewise CYCLING
(☑ 6942620746; www.bikewise.gr; day tour from €60) Electric-assist bikes make cycle touring in the Zagori much more feasible, and this company can handle all the details, from the gear to the itinerary to general advice. There are day tours of varying levels, and two-, three- and six-day routes around the area.

Compass Adventures OUTDOORS
(☑ 6978845232; www.compassadventures.gr; Elati) Established in 2006, this company runs trips such as one-day mountain-biking tours and guided family hikes to multiday ski touring. It also has a six-day, self-guided hiking itinerary in the Vikos Gorge and up Mt Tymfi.

🛏 Sleeping

The region's beautiful old stone mansions lend themselves naturally to boutique lodging. Every village around the Vikos Gorge has a few, in a range of prices; even those on the lower end are comfortable. You don't need to prebook, except during holidays, but do call ahead in winter, as not every operation stays open all the time. Camping is not permitted in the national park; you must use the mountain shelters.

En Chora Vezitsa GUESTHOUSE €
(☑ 26530 71449; www.vezitsa-zagori.com; Vitsa; d/tr/ste incl breakfast from €40/55/70; P ❄ 🛜) Tiny Vitsa village makes a quieter alternative to Monodendri, just up the road, and this family-owned guesthouse with 10 rooms is all the more reason to stay. Rooms are simple but comfortable (many have fireplaces). There's also a restaurant with good traditional food, with seats right on the *plateia*, with one of the grandest plane trees in the area.

Archontiko Dilofou GUESTHOUSE €
(Map p316; ☑ 26530 22455; www.dilofo.com; Dilofo; s/d/tr incl breakfast from €54/60/95; 🛜) This restored 1633 mansion in placid Dilofo

offers peace and natural harmony. Each of its 10 rooms (several larger ones are great for families) features traditional decor and furnishings; some have fireplaces. There's a charming courtyard and views over the slate rooftops. The hosts are friendly and helpful. Be prepared to park at the edge of the village and walk in.

★Papaevangelou GUESTHOUSE €€
(☑ 26530 41135; www.hotelpapaevangelou.gr; Megalo Papingo; d/studio incl breakfast from €100/150; P ❄ 🛜) One of the first guesthouses in the area and still one of the best, this place has all the details right, from big-enough showers to comfortable beds to soothing lighting. A few studios, with kitchenettes, are available too. Cosy traditional style is a given; breakfast is a bonanza of homemade preserves and pastry.

Porfyron B&B €€
(☑ 26530 71579; www.porfyron.gr; Ano Pedina; d incl breakfast from €65; P 🛜) A Greek-Dutch couple run this eight-room guesthouse in a 19th-century mansion. With fireplaces in many of the antique-furnished rooms and a half-board option (excellent fresh home cooking, starting at €100), it's very cosy year-round, even when the rest of the village is quiet. The Trapezitsa room has the best view over the valley. Also runs workshops on cookery and yoga.

Aristi Mountain Resort RESORT €€€
(☑ 26530 41330; www.aristi.eu; Aristi; d incl breakfast from €190; P ❄ 🛜 ♨) ⊘ Perched at the top of Aristi, this tasteful luxury lodge blends in with the hillside, with spacious, serene rooms (book 'superior' for a fireplace). Families can opt for rooms with a loft, or a whole villa. With a pool, spa and excellent restaurant, you could stay in – but it's also an easy walk down the hill to the village centre.

🍴 Eating

Each village has a taverna or a restaurant, and since the distances are so short between the villages, it's quite easy to drive out for lunch or dinner. Game and meats are omnipresent, as are wonderful vegetable dishes, plentiful salads and excellent *pites* (pies). Another local speciality is *galotiri*, a sour soft cheese, almost like yoghurt. Distilling *tsipouro* (pomace brandy) is nearly every local's hobby

★Pita tis Kikitsas GREEK €
(Monodendri; pita €5) The *plateia* of Monodendri may be the geographic centre of *pita*

THE LAMENTS OF EPIROS

The music of Epiros, particularly in the Zagorohoria, is famous across Greece and Albania for its intensely haunting clarinet *mirologia* (laments). The music was traditionally played only once a year in each village, in a kind of group healing ritual. The Epirotic clarinet can now be heard round-the-clock on Radio Epirus (94.5 FM and www.radioepirus. gr), but to really experience the music, you should see it live at one of the village *panigyria* (festivals). Most *panigyria* occur from spring (starting the Friday after Easter, in Aristi) to autumn (8 September in Mikro Papingo). The best attended, by locals and visitors, is Vitsa's, on 15 August. The *panigyria* on off dates or in smaller villages can be very intimate and are best attended with Greek-speaking friends. For more on the music, see Christopher King's excellent book, *Lament from Epirus* (2018).

excellence in Greece. This wood-panelled restaurant serves a big slab of seasonal pie – leek, greens, cheese, and so on – that's a perfect balance of filling and flaky hand-rolled filo. Frossas, on the opposite side of the square, is equally delicious. Try them both!

Mikri Arktos
TAVERNA €

(Little Bear; ☑6977079871; Tsepelovo; mains €5-10; ☉1-10pm) Next to the town hall on the *plateia* in Tsepelovo, in the shade of a giant plane tree, this restaurant is a friendly place beloved by locals for miles around. Food is simple, hearty, well-prepared Epiros mountain fare, from the potato pie to the stewed wild boar.

★Thoukididis
GREEK €€

(☑6979983798; www.thoukididis.gr; Kapesovo; mains €8-12; ☉noon-9pm) Local historian Thoukididis Papageorgiou restored this building, and his daughter Joanna runs the kitchen. The short menu makes use of only seasonal ingredients, and everything, from simple boiled vegetables to more elaborate stews, is flawlessly prepared. A fireplace keeps it cosy in winter, and upstairs is a six-room guesthouse (doubles from €80), if you decide you never want to leave.

Astra
GREEK €€

(☑26530 42108; www.astra-inn.gr; Megalo Papingo; ☉1.30-10pm) This traditional restaurant and guesthouse (rooms from €105) is everything delightful about Papingo in one place. The owners are passionate about local, organic ingredients and preserving traditional foodways. Nearly everything changes by the season, but year-round the *pita* pastry is hand-rolled, the trout is fresh and the *tsipouro* is smooth.

Kanella & Garyfallo
GREEK €€

(☑26530 71671; www.kanela-garyfallo.gr; Vitsa; mains €8-14; ☉1-10pm Fri-Sun) Love mushrooms? Head straight for this restaurant devoted to woodland fungus in all its delicious forms. The menu celebrates foraged chanterelles, berries and other local bounty. The restaurant's sign is in Greek only; look for the painted mushroom and heart.

Salvia
GREEK €€€

(☑26530 41330; www.aristi.eu; Aristi Mountain Resort, Aristi; mains €12-17; ☉11am-10pm) Sink into a velvet chair and savour both the view – mountains wreathed in clouds – and local-inspired dishes like beet salad with smoked trout. Portions are smaller ('to share or not', as the menu puts it), good for solo diners or tasting plenty. Some produce is grown right at the resort; ask to see the greenhouse.

🛍 Shopping

Sterna
GIFTS & SOUVENIRS

(☑26530 25090; www.sternashop.gr; Megalo Papingo; ☉10am-5pm) Packed to the rafters with delightful toys, jewellery and home goodies, this shop has the feel of entering a fairy tale. The cellar is a wonderland of local preserves and surprising liqueurs (try the mushroom!). The place is also a charming cafe, with housemade sweets, coffee and craft beer.

ℹ Information

The Northern Pindos National Park (p314) (of which the Vikos-Aoös park is a part) maintains two offices with good details about the wilderness:

Asprangeli (☑26530 22241; www. pindosnationalpark.gr; Asprangeli; ☉8.30am-3.30pm Mon-Sat, also Sun Jun-Aug) Convenient location in the lowlands before the Zagori road divides.

Mikro Papingo (Map p316; ☑26530 25096; www.pindosnationalpark.gr; Mikro Papingo; ☉8.30am-3.30pm Mon-Sat, also Sun Jun-Aug) In the village's old school.

❶ Getting There & Away

BUS

For most villages, KTEL bus service is once a week only, with one early-morning departure and another in the early afternoon. Schedules can change seasonally, so always confirm with the Ioannina bus station and/or your hotel.

At last check buses were running from Ioannina on the following routes and schedules: Megalo and Mikro Papingo via Aristi (Tuesdays); Ano Pedina and Kato Pedina via Vitsa and Monodendri (Wednesdays); Kipi via Dilofo (Thursdays); Skamneli via Kapesovo and Tsepelovo (Mondays and Fridays). The longest trip and most expensive ticket is two hours and €5.10 for Mikro Papingo.

Additionally, for getting back to Ioannina, school buses are open to visitors, but the route ends in Karyes, where you must wait for a KTEL bus to Ioannina (they will be coming from Konitsa or Kakavia). School bus routes change every year. Ask your hotel for details.

For Aristi, Papigo and Ano and Kato Pedina, you can save money with a KTEL bus to Kalpaki (€3.70, 30 minutes, 13 daily on weekdays, 10 daily on weekends), which is on the Konitsa and Kakavia routes. Then take a taxi (about €20 to Aristi or Ano Pedina); you may need to call when you get off the bus, as there is not always a car waiting.

The dedicated car-free traveller can take a Konitsa-bound bus to Klidonia (€4.20, one hour, six daily on weekdays, three on weekends), then hike in on along the Voïdomatis River and up the road to Aristi, in three to four hours.

CAR

The most leisurely and flexible way to see the Zagorohoria is by car; rental agencies are all based in Ioannina.

If you don't want to rent your own car, taxis are available, if expensive. As sample fares, from Ioannina to Papingo is €90; to Kapesovo, €50.

Taxi Van Zagorohoria (☑ 6943491300; www.taxizagorohoria.gr) Has two large vans, good for groups.

Kalpaki Taxi (☑ 6945769887, 6945502138; Kalpaki) Handy for Aristi, Ano Pedina and Papingo.

❶ Getting Around

To enjoy the Zagorohoria by car, you must fundamentally enjoy driving. The roads here have every possible hazard: they are narrow, beset by blind curves and edged with alarming sheer drops. You'll need to look out for herds of goats and cows, sleeping dogs or even lumbering tortoises. Check weather conditions before you set out, and if at all possible, avoid driving at night. Also fill up the tank before you leave Ioannina; the closest petrol station to the Zagorohoria is in Asprangeli, before climbing into the mountains.

Preveza   Πρέβεζα

POP 22,853

Perched at the edge of the Ambracian Gulf, Preveza is a scenic town that, like Corfu, has a vaguely Italian style, thanks to centuries of connection. And thanks to a large international yacht harbour, the town is livelier and more stylish than its small size would suggest, with a lovely waterfront and old quarter, nice hotels and good restaurants. Nearby are the massive ruins of Nikopolis, and up the coast, en route to Parga, are a whole stretch of impeccable (if sometimes windy) beaches.

◉ Sights

The waterfront and a few streets inland are all given over to pedestrians. The major landmark is the 1792 Venetian clock tower (north end of Ethnikis Antistasis). There are no less than three old forts, all left to ruin; the northern one, Agios Andreas, is a former army base turned car park and occasional squatted arts zone.

Nikopolis   RUINS
(Nicopolis, City of Victory; ☑ 26820 41336; http://odysseus.culture.gr; Km 6 Preveza-Ioannina National Rd, E951; adult/child incl museum entry €8/4; ⊙ 8am-8pm Wed-Mon summer, to 4pm winter) The ruins of Nikopolis, built in 28 BCE by Octavian (later Augustus), after he defeated Mark Antony and Cleopatra in the naval Battle of Actium (Aktion), include Roman walls, Byzantine walls and churches, a stadium and two theatres. Much was destroyed by Bulgarians in the 11th century, but the scale of the ruined 'City of Victory' remains breathtaking, even if it requires a little imagination to conjure. It helps to visit the museum (☑ 26820 89892) first.

The main site entrance, 5km north of Preveza, leads to a Byzantine church and, a bit north, the Roman odeon. Farther north along the road are long stretches of the walls erected by Emperor Justinian in 540 CE. Around another bend is the Roman stadium and a larger theatre, with seating for 5000. These are all by the roadside and accessible for free. Allow a couple of hours to hike the site on foot, if you come by bus (take any bound for Filippiada or Ioannina). With a car you can cover the whole area more quickly, and also follow the signs for the farther-flung 'Actium Trophy', the massive monument Octavian built after the battle. The huge wall here once displayed the battering rams from the conquered warships.

⚡ Activities

Kiani Akti BEACH
(Eleftheriou Venizelou) At the southern end of town, Preveza's public beach is actually a series of smaller patches of sand, shaded with pine trees and umbrellas. At the east end, on the inland side of the road, is a shady city-run cafe and public baths (open mornings and late afternoon, June to October); in the centre is the ruined Fort of St George; and on the west end is **Pantokrator Castle**, a scenic sunset spot.

🛏 Sleeping

Avra HOTEL €
(📱26820 21230; www.hotelavra.net; Eleftheriou Venizelou 19; s/d €45/55; ❈ 🌐) Rarely do sea views come this inexpensively, and with such nice surroundings. Rooms in this tower block are small but very clean and functional, with mini fridges and little balconies for watching the harbour below. (Windows seal well too, if summer party noise intrudes.) Service is friendly, and there's free parking in a lot a couple of blocks south.

Dioni Boutique Hotel BOUTIQUE HOTEL €€
(📱26820 27381; www.masthotels.gr/boutiquehoteldioni; cnr Kalou & Parthenagogiou; s/d/ste incl breakfast from €110/120/155; 🅿❈🌐) Tucked a bit out of the noisy fray of the centre, Dioni is plush and elegant in a modern way: lots of velvet, and excellent Coco-Mat beds. The rooms are comfortable, with little balconies overlooking the small square, the service is friendly, and breakfast is served in a rooftop cafe with sea views.

🍴 Eating

★Amvrosios SEAFOOD €
(📱26820 27192; Patriarhou Grigoriou V; fish €6-11; ⊙11am-2pm Tue-Sun) There are an almost overwhelming number of seafood tavernas to choose from in Preveza, and although Amvrosios looks a great deal like all the others (checked tablecloths, wicker chairs, etc), it does distinguish itself with a reputation for especially fresh fish. Feel free to go to the kitchen to pick yours. Everything is well prepared, and the service is good.

🍷 Drinking & Nightlife

★Botilia sto Pelago BAR
(📱26824 00432; Theofanous 9; ⊙9am-3am) This 'art cafe' is a pretty place to enjoy a morning or afternoon coffee or, by night, a Belgian beer and some acoustic music.

🛍 Shopping

Roubou ALCOHOL
(📱26820 22274; www.ouzoroubou.gr; Adrianoupoleos 17; ⊙9am-3pm Mon-Sat) Established in 1949 by a family from Lesvos, this distillery and shop has barely changed since. Its fan-cooled interior is a dreamworld of grey-and-white barrels and orderly shelves of ouzo. You can also buy ouzo 'loose', by the litre, direct from the barrels, and you may be able to peek at the still set-up next door.

ℹ Information

Preveza's **tourism office** (📱26823 60600; www.discoverpreveza.gr; Bahoumi 2; ⊙8am-3pm Mon-Fri) has limited hours, but it has details about the surrounding beaches, villages and wetlands.

ℹ Getting There & Away

An underwater tunnel (vehicles €3) links Preveza with Aktion. Cyclists and pedestrians can be transported through for free.

AIR

Preveza Airport (p309), also known as Lefkada or Aktion, is a summer-only airport for European airlines and charters, as well as domestic flights to Athens (with Aegean; p313) and to Crete, Kefallonia and Zakynthos (with Sky Express; p130). A **taxi** (📱26820 28470, 26820 28030) to/from Preveza costs about €25; the bus costs €1.80.

BUS

Preveza bus station (📱26820 22213; www.ktelprevezas.gr; Leoforos Ioanninon 205a), 2km north of the centre, serves Arta (€5.60, one hour, twice daily on weekdays), Athens (€40, 5½ hours, five daily), Igoumenitsa (€10.60, 2½ hours, one daily), Ioannina (€10.40, two hours, six daily on weekdays, four on weekends, more in summer), Lefkada (€2.80, 45 minutes, six daily, two on Sunday), Parga (€7.10, two hours, three daily, more in summer) and Thessaloniki (€39.50, five hours, two daily).

Arta Άρτα
POP 27,300

The hub of a major citrus-growing region, Arta was historically important (ancient Ambracia, or Amvrakia, founded in 625 BCE, was the capital of Pyrrhus's kingdom), but today the relics are mixed into a midsize modern town tucked in a bend of the Arahthos River. It's usually a stop on a drive, rather than a destination in itself.

The centre of town is all pedestrianised, and the major landmarks are at the edges: the Byzantine castle on the north side, and on the west, a 17th-century stone bridge that steps delicately over the river. There's also an interesting archaeological museum and a unique church.

If you have a car, you can head south into the orange orchards and the Amvrakikos Wetlands National Park, and out along a narrow causeway to the windswept island of Koronisia, in the middle of the gulf.

◉ Sights

In addition to specific museums, you can see some ancient traces of Ambracia around town. The foundations of the Temple of Apollo are on the south end of Pyrrou, and around the corner on Agiou Konstantinou is Greece's smallest ancient theatre. Sections of Roman wall are visible in a few spots.

Old Bridge   BRIDGE
(Gefiri tis Artas; Thiakogianni) This stone bridge, likely built in the early 1600s, spans the Arahthos River in four elegant arches. (The windows in the pedestals are for water overflow if the river runs high.) Between 1881 and 1912, Arta was the northern edge of independent Greece; the high point of the bridge marked the border with the Ottoman Empire.

Archaeological Museum   MUSEUM
(☑ 26810 71700; www.efaart.gr; Trigono; adult/child €3/2; ⊙ 8am-3pm Tue-Sun; ℗) This museum is a gem: a fine collection, clearly presented, in a manageable space that's seldom busy. It focuses primarily on the ancient city of Ambracia, from its foundation in the 7th century BCE to 29 BCE, when Nikopolis became the new capital of Epiros. Displays cover the ancient city's musical traditions and burial practices, including elaborately carved marble slabs from graves.

🛏 Sleeping

Cronos   HOTEL €
(☑ 26810 22211; www.hotelcronos.gr; Plateia Kilkis; s/d €40/50; ℗ ❋ 🛜) This big blocky 55-room hotel in central Arta is perfectly functional and modern, if not bursting with character. Balconies give you a bird's-eye view onto the city below; rooms on the front have a nice vista on the trees on the *plateia*.

❶ Getting There & Away

Direct buses from the **main bus station** (☑ 26810 27348; www.ktelartas.gr; Plateia Kristalli) connect Arta with Thessaloniki (€36.80, 4½ hours, two daily), Athens (€34, 5½ hours, five daily), Preveza (€5.60, one hour, twice daily on weekdays) and Ioannina (€7, 1½ hours, six daily on weekdays, four on weekends).

Parga   Πάργα
POP 3900

If there is a picture-perfect beach town in northern Greece, Parga is it: an amphitheatre of a village, dominated by a Venetian castle, opening onto a clear turquoise bay pierced with islets. It's small and gets crowded in summer, but it's an undeniable beauty. If you stay overnight, it makes a base for swimming at beaches just north and south, as well as boat excursions to the Ionian Islands. After the sun sets, a slew of seafront tavernas and bars (blessedly untroubled by cars) give Parga plenty of fizz. For day trips, many visitors head to equally scenic beaches nearby, or south to the dramatic archaeological site known as the Nekromanteion of Acheron, as well as trips on the river of the same name. The season is May to September, but some tourist businesses open as early as March.

◉ Sights

At Parga's east edge, Krioneri Beach is sandy with shallow waters. To the west, a 15-minute walk or short water taxi ride, is 2km-long Valtos Beach. Both are solid with umbrellas and loungers. Four kilometres east of Parga, Lichnos Beach is quieter and isolated-feeling, though a little pebbly; drive, water taxi or walk two hours through olive groves. Northwest is Sarakiniko Beach, an exceptionally scenic pebble beach in a little bay.

Venetian Castle   CASTLE
(Kastro) 🆓 Centuries of turbulent history have made Parga's castle a romantic ruin facing the sea. The site was used for defence since the 11th century; the existing ramparts were built by the Venetians in the early 15th century. In 1819 the British sold it (along with the whole town) to Ali Pasha. Pine needles make everything slippery; wear grippy shoes and hang on to any kids with you. The cafe (open from 11am until late) is a lovely shady spot to watch ferries.

Nekromanteion of Acheron   RUINS
(Ephyra; ☑ 26840 41206; http://odysseus.culture. gr; Mesopotamos; adult/child €8/free; ⊙ 8.30am-4pm; ℗) This ancient complex is small but comes with a gripping backstory. According to Homer and Herodotus, it was a place to consult with an oracle (*nekromanteio*) who channelled dead ancestors for advice. Pilgrims took an elaborate ritual meal, then processed through a labyrinth into a hall where ghosts appeared. A 1998 study posited

a duller hypothesis (fortified farmhouse, yawn), but the site is still evocative, with massive walls of hewn boulders and access to the cool, shadowy underground hall.

Per ancient sources, the site was in use from at least the 8th century BCE, and the extant walls and labyrinth date from the late 4th century BCE. The Romans burned the place in 167 BCE. Sometime after the 15th century, a small monastery was built over the old temple ruins. In the 19th century, a *koulia* (an actual fortified farmhouse) was built; it was fully restored in 2015. The site ticket includes admission to the acropolis of Ephyra, a short walk to the north. Established in the Late Bronze Age (14th century BCE), the site is now only rubble, with a few stretches of wall that are rougher, more ancient versions of the ones at the *nekromanteio*. If it's not too hot, it's worth a stroll just for the view over the lush river valley.

The site is about 20km south of Parga, on the hill on the east side of Mesopotamos. In high season, you must park a few hundred metres away and walk up to the gate and ticket office. Alternatively, book a guided excursion through International Travel Services in Parga, or take a taxi, starting at €30 one way. This way (or in your own car), you can combine it with a boat excursion up the Acheron (the river the dead were said to cross) in nearby Ammoudia, on the coast.

🛏 Sleeping

Parga has a good range of accommodation, from campgrounds to simple hotel rooms, apartments and luxury options. But note that most places don't open until at least March, and beach spots often not until May. Moreover, in July and August, many hotels have a two- or three-night minimum.

★ Utopia   APARTMENT €€

(☑ 26840 31133; www.utopia.com.gr; Agiou Athanasiou 5; apt incl breakfast from €100; ❈ ⊜) Directly facing Krioneri Beach, these seven studio apartments couldn't be in a better spot – you can go for a swim before breakfast! The furnishings are simple and the balconies huge. Each studio has a kitchenette and a fridge. On the ground floor is a cafe, where breakfast and good coffee await.

Acrothea   HOTEL €€

(☑ 26840 32442; www.acrotheahotel.com; Agias Marinas; d incl breakfast from €70; ❈ ⊜) Perched at the top edge of town, Acrothea has several levels stepping down the steep hillside, giving nearly all of its rooms an excellent view

of the bay. The style is vaguely Italianate (tassels and taffeta) but very clean and comfortable. The same family runs Byzantio on Valtos Beach, another nice option. If driving, park on the main road.

Acropol   HOTEL €€

(☑ 6942018005, 26840 31239; www.acropolhotel.com.gr; Agion Apostolon 4; d/ste incl breakfast from €94/127; ❈ ⊜) Tucked in among the shady alleyways of Parga's old town, Hotel Acropol occupies an old home, with eight lovely rooms. From fine wrought-iron balconies to rustic handmade furniture, the details are well chosen, and the kindly owner ensures a relaxing stay. The only drawback is the lack of a view, but it's great for those who like a historic atmosphere.

🍴 Eating

The waterfront is lined with tavernas, most of which serve traditional Greek fare. A couple of options in the old quarter experiment with a wider range of Mediterranean cuisines.

Tzimas   GREEK €

(☑ 26840 32337; Parga-Perdikas Rd; mains €6-10; ⊙noon-late; 🖉 🖘) A great little taverna on the main highway, Tzimas is open year-round and recommended by locals for Greek standards such as roast aubergine with feta, beetroot salad and meatballs. The service is friendly, and although you're not near the water, the flower-laden terrace is shady and pleasant (go later, after traffic dies down).

★ Eden   BISTRO €€

(☑ 26840 31409; www.facebook.com/edenbistroparga; Vasila 26; mains €10-15; ⊙9am-1.30am) An array of Italian-inspired dishes are served with a smile at this refreshing bistro in Parga's old town. Try the seafood tagliatelle, or grab crêpes and juices for a quick bite. It's not on the water, but there are seats outside.

ℹ Information

International Travel Services (ITS; ☑ 26840 31833; www.parganet.travel; Spyrou Livada 4; ⊙9am-5pm Apr-Sep) Helpful for all kinds of travellers' needs, including excursions and maps.

ℹ Getting There & Away

Parga bus station (☑ 26840 31218; Perdikas-Pargas Rd) serves Igoumenitsa (€5.90, 1½ hours, three daily on weekdays), Preveza (€7.10, two hours, four daily), Thessaloniki (€44, seven hours, one daily) – or travel via Preveza for more services – and Athens

(€41.20, seven hours, three daily). Some services are cut October to May. In summer, buses also go south to Ammoudia, Vrahos and Kanali beaches (up to one hour, three daily).

ⓘ Getting Around

From the pier in the harbour, water taxis serve Valtos Beach (€2) and Lichnos Beach (€10 return) frequently, as late as midnight in July and August. Farther away is Sarakiniko (€11 return), with just enough service for a full-day outing.

Igoumenitsa   Ηγουμενίτσα

POP 17,902

If you're heading to Italy by ferry, you'll have to pass through Igoumenitsa, in Epiros' far northwest. This port city also serves the Ionian islands of Corfu (Kerkyra) and Paxi. The town itself doesn't have much going on beyond the promise of sailing to lovelier shores.

🛏 Sleeping

Acropolis Hotel   HOTEL €

(☑ 26650 28346; www.hotel-acropolis.gr; Ethnikis Andistasis 58; s/d €30/40; ❈ 🕿) At the far north end of Igoumenitsa's waterfront, the Acropolis feels a bit out of the way since the ferry ports shifted south. But it's worth the longer walk up here for the exceptionally cheerful and clean rooms, and the nice staff.

ⓘ Getting There & Away

BOAT

For departure times for all destinations within the coming week, call the automated **Igoumenitsa Port Authority information line** (☑ 26650 99400); press 9 for English. You can also speak to an operator for booking.

Corfu & Paxi

Boats for Greek destinations depart from the port in the centre of town. Vehicles enter at the traffic circle opposite Hotel Astoria, and **ticket kiosks** are set up inside the port fence just to the north.

Services to Corfu Town (€11, one hour) run as frequently as hourly; to Lefkimmi (€7, one hour), on the south end of the island, services run every few hours. Vehicle prices start at €25 for Lefkimmi and €40 for Corfu. With several ferry companies – **Lefkimmi Lines** (☑ in Lefkimmi 26620 23200; www.lefkimmilines.gr), **Kerkyra Lines** (☑ 26650 25908; www.kerkyralines. com), **Corfu Ferries** (Kerkyra Seaways; ☑ 26650 21000; www.corfuferries.gr) – and schedules that change frequently, the best strategy is simply to turn up and buy a ticket for the next available sailing. You can avoid the scrum at the kiosks (intense in summer) by visiting a travel agent or

booking online, although note that travel agents do not necessarily sell for all companies.

Paxi (passenger/vehicle €11/42.30, 1½ hours) is served directly by Kerkyra Lines, once daily in summer, and less frequently the rest of the year, when it's easier to take a ferry to Corfu, then continue to Paxi.

Italy

Ticketing and boarding are from the **International Ferry Terminal** (New Port, T1; ☑ port authority 26650 99300; www.olig.gr; Agiou Apostolon; 🕿), at the far south end of town. Plan ahead, as some destinations are not served every day, or have inconvenient departure times. Whether on foot or by car, you must check in at the port two hours before sailing.

Ferry companies have consolidated, so although many have desks in the terminal, in reality only one or two boats operate each day. **Grimaldi** (☑ 26650 24404, 26650 23077; www.grimaldi-lines.com) and **Minoan** (☑ 26650 26715, in Crete 2810 399899; www.minoan.gr) together serve Ancona, Brindisi and Venice. **ANEK** (☑ 26650 29063, in Piraeus 21041 22180; www.anek. gr) and **Superfast** (☑ 26650 29200; www. superfast.com) run to Ancona, Bari and Venice. July to September only, **European Seaways** (☑ in Piraeus 21095 61630; www.europeanseaways. com; ☺ Jul-Sep) serves Brindisi, and **Ventouris** (☑ 26650 23565, in Piraeus 21048 28001; www. ventourisferries.com; ☺ Jul-Sep) goes to Bari.

Prices are all similar, but vary by season. Fares spike in August. More typical prices for deck-class are: €41 to Brindisi (six to 9½ hours), €68 to Bari (8½ to 10½ hours), and €75 to Ancona (15 hours) and Venice (24 hours). A passenger ticket in a four-bed cabin with shower is generally twice as expensive. Vehicle prices for Bari and Brindisi start from €50, and from €82 for Ancona and Venice. If you have a campervan, you're permitted to sleep in it on most ferries, but air quality in the car hold can be poor.

To sort out the various options, including seasonal round-trip deals, and which ships have better facilities, such as power for campervans, it can be simpler to visit a travel agency, such as **Milano Travel** (☑ 26650 24237; milantvl@ otenet.gr; Ioniou Pelagous 35; ☺ 9am-7pm), directly across the road. If you're planning ahead from Parga, try International Travel Services.

BUS

From **Igoumenitsa bus station** (KTEL Thesprotias; ☑ 26650 22309; www.ktel-thesprotias.gr; Martiron 49), two blocks behind the Corfu ferry docks, buses serve Ioannina (€10.60, 1½ hours, six daily), Parga (€5.90, 1½ hours, three daily on weekdays), Athens (€48.50, eight hours, three daily), Preveza (€10.60, 2½ hours, one daily, en route to Lefkada) and Thessaloniki (€37.70, four hours, two daily, also stopping in Veria). Buses on some routes are less frequent from October to May.

AT A GLANCE

POPULATION
Aegina: 13,056

LEONARD COHEN'S HOUSE
Kamini, Hydra

BEST POSH STAY
Poseidonion Grand Hotel (p344)

BEST BISTRO
Oraia Hydra (p340)

BEST FASHION BOUTIQUE
Kashish (p341)

WHEN TO GO
Apr & May The islands awake after winter; come for flower-filled Easter.

Jun Celebrate Miaoulia in Hydra with sparkling waters and warm weather.

Sep Enjoy the clear skies, thinning crowds and Spetses' Armata celebration.

Omilos, Hydra Town (p341)
IMAGIN GR PHOTOGRAPHY/SHUTTERSTOCK

Saronic Gulf Islands

The Saronic Gulf Islands (Νησιά του Σαρωνικού) dot the waters nearest Athens and offer a fast track to Greek island life. As with all Greek islands, each of the Saronics has a unique feel and culture, so you can hop between classical heritage, resort beaches, exquisite architecture and remote escapism.

Aegina is home to a spectacular Doric temple (p330) and ruined Byzantine village (p331), while nearby pine-clad Angistri feels protected and peaceful outside of the booming midsummer months. Further south, Poros, with its beautiful old town and forested hinterland, curves only a few hundred metres from the Peloponnese. The Saronic showpiece, Hydra, is a gorgeous car-free island. Deepest south of all, pine-scented Spetses has a vibrant nautical history and pretty town architecture.

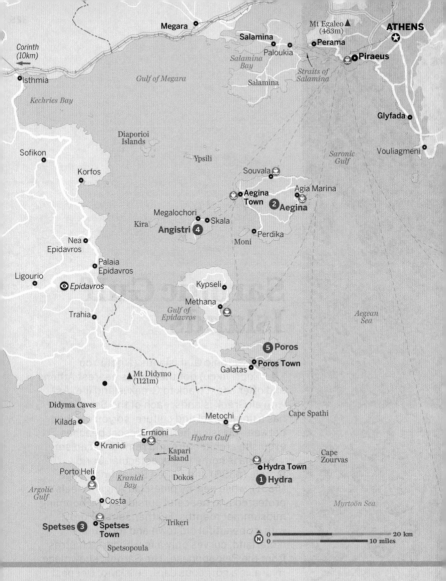

Saronic Gulf Islands Highlights

1 Hydra (p335) Taking in the gorgeous port, with its excellent museums and stylish scene, and the island's deserted trails and ubiquitous swimming rocks.

2 Aegina (p327) Delving into ancient history at the beautiful Temple of Aphaia and the Byzantine village of Paleohora, then sipping seaside cocktails.

3 Spetses (p342) Taste-testing your way through top restaurants, tracing the region's history in Spetses Town's museums, or cycling the island's ring road to dip into sparkling bays.

4 Angistri (p331) Getting away from it all in the low season, when the beaches are at their most tranquil.

5 Poros (p332) Exploring the peaceful, forested interior and wandering the colourful narrow lanes of Poros Town.

🛶 Tours

Evermore Cruises   CRUISE
(☑ 21118   82220;   www.evermorecruises.com;
cruise adult/child €100/60, with transfers €112/72)
Day trips from Piraeus (Marina Flisvos) to
Hydra, Poros and Aegina.

Athens One Day Cruise   CRUISE
(☑ 21045   16106;   www.athensonedaycruise.
com; cruise adult/child €100/60, with transfers
€112/72) Day trips from Piraeus (Marina
Flisvos) to Hydra, Poros and Aegina. Transfers from central Athens also available.

ℹ️ Getting There & Away

Ferries and high-speed hydrofoil services for the
Saronic Gulf Islands leave from Piraeus. It's also
possible to reach several of the islands from the
Peloponnese. Small boats connect Poros with
Galatas, Hydra with Metochi and Spetses with
Costa. Hellenic Seaways has high-speed servic-
es that stop en route to/from Poros, Hydra and
Spetses in Ermioni and Porto Heli.

ℹ️ Getting Around

No direct ferries connect Aegina and Angistri
with Hydra and Spetses; go via Piraeus or Poros.
For day trips, take the Hydra–Poros–Aegina
cruise from Piraeus with Athens One Day Cruise
or Evermore Cruises (see above). Pegasus
Cruises (p161) goes from Nafplio to Spetses and
Hydra.

AEGINA   ΑΙΓΙΝΑ

POP 13,056

Beyond its bustling port, Aegina has the
seductive, easy-going character of a typical
Greek island, but with the added bonus
of more than its fair share of prestigious
ancient sites. Weekending Athenians
spice up the mix of laid-back locals and
island-dwelling commuters who use the island like an Athens suburb. Special Aegina
treats include a fabulous sort of pistachio
nut, the splendid 5th-century Temple of
Aphaia (p330) and the magical Byzantine
Paleohora (p331) ruins.

History

Aegina was the leading maritime power
of the Saronic Gulf during the 7th century
BCE, when it grew wealthy through trade
and political ascendancy. The island made
a major contribution to the Greek victory over the Persian fleet at the Battle of
Salamis in 480 BCE. Despite this solidarity
with the Athenian state, the latter invaded in 459 BCE out of jealousy of Aegina's
wealth and status, and of its liaison with
Sparta. Aegina never regained its glory, although in the early 19th century it played
a bold part in the defeat of the Turks and
was the temporary capital of a partly liber-
ated Greece from 1827 to 1829.

ℹ️ Getting There & Away

Aegina's main port, Aegina Town, has conventional ferries that are booked online at www.
saronicferries.gr. They are operated by **Hellenic Seaways** (☑ conventional ferry 22970
22945, high-speed ferry 22970 26777; www.
hsw.gr), **Nova Ferries** (☑ 22970 24200; www.
novaferries.gr) and **Agios Nektarios** (ANES
Ferries; ☑ Aegina 22970 25625, Piraeus 21042
25625; www.anes.gr). Book high-speed hydrofoils with Hellenic Seaways and **Aegean Flying
Dolphins** (☑ 22970 25800) to/from Piraeus
and Angistri. Ferries dock at the large outer
quay, with hydrofoils at the smaller inner quay.

Evoikos Lines (☑ Agia Marina 22970 32234,
Piraeus 21048 21002, Souvala 22970 52210;
www.evoikoslines.gr) serves Aegina's smaller
ports Agia Marina and Souvala, and Piraeus in
high season only.

Even in winter, high-speed ferries from Piraeus get fully booked for weekends: book ahead.

Angistri Express (☑ 6934347867) makes
several daily trips in high season to Skala and
Mylos on Angistri. It leaves from midway along
Aegina harbour, where timetables are displayed.

Water taxis (☑ 6944535659, 6972229720,
22970 91387) to Piraeus cost about €40
one way, regardless of the number of people
travelling.

Ferries to Piraeus are plentiful from Aegina
Town throughout the year, ranging from regular,
slower ferries (€8 to €10, 70 minutes, hourly),
to high-speed services (€14, 40 minutes, six
daily). From Agia Marina, you can reach Piraeus
in summer only (€10, one hour, three to four
daily).

There are several daily boats that run to Angistri's Skala from Aegina Town, including large
ferries (€2.80, 20 minutes, one to two daily)
and faster catamarans (€6, 10 minutes, four to
six daily). You can also reach Mylos easily (€6,
10 minutes, five daily).

Getting to Poros from Aegina Town is easy
(€8.50, one hour and 50 minutes, two to three
daily).

Note that there are no direct ferries to Hydra
from Aegina; you must go back to Piraeus and
take a Hydra-bound ferry from there.

Aegina & Angistri

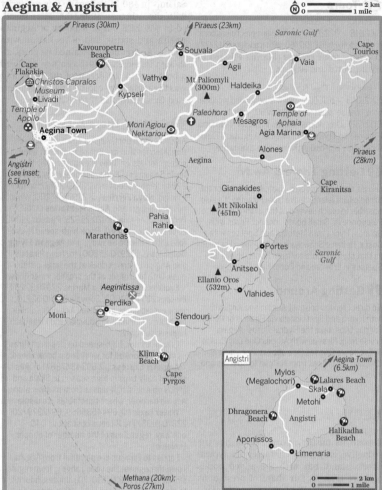

N
0 ————— 2 km
0 ————— 1 mile

Piraeus (30km)
Piraeus (23km)
Saronic Gulf
Cape Tourlos
Kavouropetra Beach
Souvala
Agii
Vaia
Cape Plakakia
Vathy
Mt Paliomyli (300m)
Haldeika
Christos Capralos Museum
Kypseli
Livadi
Temple of Apollo
Paleohora
Temple of Aphaia
Moni Agiou Nektariou
Mesagros
Agia Marina
Aegina Town
Alones
Aegina
Piraeus (28km)
Angistri (see inset; 6.5km)
Gianakides
Cape Kiranitsa
Mt Nikolaki (451m)
Pahia Rahi
Marathonas
Portes
Saronic Gulf
Anitseo
Aeginitissa
Ellanio Oros (532m)
Vlahides
Perdika
Moni
Sfendouri
Klima Beach
Cape Pyrgos
Methana (20km); Poros (27km)

Angistri
Aegina Town (6.5km)
Mylos (Megalochori)
Lalares Beach
Skala
Metohi
Dhragonera Beach
Angistri
Halikadha Beach
Aponissos
Limenaria
0 ————— 2 km
0 ————— 1 mile

ⓘ Getting Around

BUS

Buses from Aegina Town run several times a day on three routes across the island. Departure times are displayed outside the ticket office on Plateia Ethnegersias (Ethnegersias Sq); you must buy tickets there. Visit www.aeginagreece.com for details.

Agia Marina (€2, 30 minutes) via Paleohora (p331; €2, 15 minutes) and Temple of Aphaia (p330; €2, 25 minutes)

Perdika (€1.80, 15 minutes)

Vagia (€1.80, 25 minutes) via Souvala (€1.80, 20 minutes)

CAR, MOTORCYCLE & BICYCLE

Numerous outfits hire out vehicles. Prices start from €35 per day for cars, €17 for a 50cc motorcycle and €8 for bicycles.

Karagiannis Travel (☎22970 28780; www.aeginatravel.gr; Pan Irioti 44; ⊙9am-2pm & 5-9pm) Rents vehicles and arranges tours.

Sklavenas Rent A Car (☎22970 22892; Kazantzaki 5; ⊙9am-2pm & 5-9pm) For cars, 4WDs, scooters, quads and bikes. In Aegina Town, located on the road near the Temple of Apollo. Also has a branch in **Agia Marina** (☎22970 32871; ⊙9am-2pm & 5-9pm).

Taxi (☎Aegina Town 22970 22010, Agia Marina 22970 32107) Taxis around Aegina island.

Aegina Town   Αίγινα
POP 8905

The sparkling harbour of Aegina Town is backed by a buzzing promenade of people, motorbikes and restaurants. As you wander back into the narrow town streets, with kids riding bikes and laundry strung from balconies, Greek island life takes over again.

The parallel streets backing the harbour, Irioti and Rodi, are crammed with shops of every kind and a few 19th-century neoclassical buildings intermix with whitewashed houses – make sure you explore away from the main drag. The impressive ruins of the Temple of Apollo are just north of the harbour.

◉ Sights

Temple of Apollo   RUINS
(Kolona; Map p328; ☏22970 22248; http://odysseus.culture.gr; adult/child €3/free; ☉8.30am-3pm Tue-Sun May-Oct, reduced hours Nov-Apr) Northwest of the port, ruined walls and broken pillars in honey-coloured stone are lorded over by a solitary column. It's all that's left of a 5th-century-BCE temple that was once part of an ancient acropolis (built on a prehistoric site). The informative Sanctuary Museum has translations in English and German.

✪ Festivals & Events

Aegina Fistiki Fest   FOOD & DRINK
(www.facebook.com/AeginaFistikiFest; ☉Sep) *Fistiki* means 'pistachio' and this three-day brouhaha celebrates Aegina's famous Protected Designation of Origin (PDO) pistachio through music, art and culinary contests.

⌂ Sleeping

Aegina offers a range of solid, simple guesthouses, apartment complexes and a handful of hotels. Book ahead at weekends.

Electra Pension   PENSION €
(☏22970 26715; www.aegina-electra.gr; Leonardou Lada 25; r from €45; ❄☎) There are no views from this small whitewashed pension, but rooms are impeccable and comfy in a quiet corner of the town centre. It outclasses nearby hotels by a long way. Rates go down off-season.

Marianna Studios   PENSION €
(☏22970 25650; Kiverniou 16-18; s/d €35/40, d/tr with kitchen €40/45; ❄) Simple, basic rooms and very friendly owners create a top-notch budget choice. Some rooms have balconies

or overlook a quiet, leafy garden alongside an interior courtyard. One room has a kitchen. Not to be confused with Marianna Studios in Agia Marina.

★Hotel Rastoni   HOTEL €€
(☏22970 27039; www.rastoni.gr; Stratigou Dimitriou Petriti 31; d/tr/q incl breakfast from €80/120/130; ❄❄@☎) The rooms are spacious, with four-poster beds and exposed-stone walls. Top-floor rooms overlook the lovely garden and the Temple of Apollo from their balconies, while those on the ground floor open straight onto the fragrant garden. Generous breakfasts and friendly staff round out the experience. Find it in a residential neighbourhood a few minutes north of the harbour.

Aegina Hotel   HOTEL €€
(☏22970 28501; www.aeginahotel.gr; Stratigou Dimitriou Petriti 23; d/tr from €60/70; ❄☎) This 19-room hotel sits about 500m back from the harbour and has clean, well-appointed rooms with refrigerators and TVs.

Aeginitiko Archontiko   PENSION €€
(☏22970 24968; www.aeginitikoarchontiko.gr; cnr Ag Nikolaou & Thomaidou 1; s/d/tr/ste incl breakfast from €50/60/70/100; ❄☎) This centrally located old mansion is full of character, with period 19th-century features, a charming salon, lush courtyard and a splendid breakfast. First-floor rooms are better (some have balconies) than those on the ground floor, which can be a bit cramped and worn. Bathrooms are basic. Sea views from the rooftop.

Fistikies Holiday Apartments   APARTMENT €€
(☏22970 23783; www.fistikies.gr; Logiotatidou 1; studios from €90, 4-person apts €120; ℙ❄☎❄) This complex of tidy family-friendly apartments sits on the southern edge of town, inland from the football field. Spacious apartments have DVD players, and terraces overlooking the pool.

✗ Eating

The harbourfront restaurants make for lazy world-watching, but are not particularly outstanding, unless you hit the unvarnished *ouzeries* (places serving ouzo and light snacks).

Aegina's pistachio nuts are on sale everywhere (from €7 for 500g, depending on quality).

Gelladakis   MEZEDHES €€
(☏22970 27308; Pan Irioti 45; dishes €7-12; ☉lunch & dinner) Ensconced behind the noisy midharbour fish market, this vibrant joint is always thronged with people tucking into

PERDIKA

The quaint fishing village of Perdika lies about 9km south of Aegina Town on the southern tip of the west coast and makes for a relaxed sojourn.

Perdika's harbour is very shallow; for the best swimming, catch one of the regular caïques (little boats; return adult/child €5/free) to the small island of Moni, a few minutes offshore. A nature reserve, it has a tree-lined beach and summertime cafe.

Tavernas line Perdika's raised harbourfront terrace, and sultry sunset relaxation makes way for buzzing nightlife when late-night music bars rev into gear during summer.

charcoal-fired octopus or sardines, plus other classic mezedhes. If you want to get a table, get there a little early.

Elia   MEDITERRANEAN €
(22975 00205; Koumoundourou 4; mains €6-9; noon-4pm & 6-11pm, reduced winter hours) Burrow into the backstreets to find this excellent restaurant that's popular with locals. Imaginative, fresh specialities include Aegina's pistachio pesto and the *pites* (pies) of the day.

Tsias   TAVERNA €
(22970 23529; Dimokratias 47; mains €7-10; lunch & dinner) Harbourside eating at its best. Try shrimps with tomatoes and feta, the *horta* (wild greens) and sardines, or one of the daily specials.

Kriton Gefsis   CRETAN €€
(22970 26255; www.facebook.com/kritongefsis; cnr Pan Irioti & Damanos; dishes €5-15; 10am-2am) Cretan ingredients and flavours are the order of the day at this lively taverna featuring fresh seafood. Also has live music.

Bakalogatos   MEZEDHES €€
(22975 00501; cnr Pan Irioti & Neoptolemou; mains €7-13; lunch & dinner Tue-Sun) Marked out by a canopy of colourful umbrellas, Bakalogatos has fresh, well-crafted mezedhes in an elegant setting, with faux-finished tables and traditional products on the walls.

Drinking & Nightlife

Tortuga   BAR
(6983437913; www.facebook.com/tortugaegina; Pan Irioti 43; 10am-midnight) This lovely one-room bar, full of artistic knick-knacks, spills onto the busy Irioti street. This is the place for good coffee in the day and cocktails in the evening. There is live music too.

International Corner   BAR
(22970 26564; cnr I Katsa & S Rodi; noon-late) Get off the main strip and head to this bohemian wood-panelled bar room. The gregarious owner takes requests, from top 40 to fantastic Greek music.

Information

Aegina has no tourist office. Check Karagiannis Travel (p328) for car hire, tours and non-Aegina boats.

Getting There & Away

Aegina's main port is located in Aegina Town: it's served by both conventional ferries (book online at www.saronicferries.gr) and high-speed hydrofoils operated by Hellenic Seaways (p327) and Aegean Flying Dolphins (p327).

Getting Around

There is a hub of local buses and water taxis at the main port.

Around Aegina

Sights

Aegina is lush and wildflower-laden in spring, and year-round offers some of the best Archaic sites in the Saronic Gulf. The interior hills and mountains add drama to the small island, but beaches are not its strongest suit. The east-coast town of Agia Marina is the island's main package resort. It has a shallow-water beach that is ideal for families, but it's backed by a fairly crowded main drag. A few thin, sandy beaches, such as Marathonas, line the roadside between Aegina Town and Perdika.

★ **Temple of Aphaia**   TEMPLE
(Map p328; 22970 32398; http://odysseus. culture.gr; adult/child €4/free; 9.30am-4.30pm, museum 10.30am-1.30pm Tue-Sun) The well-preserved remains of this impressive temple stand proudly on a pine-covered hill with far-reaching views over the Saronic Gulf. Built in 480 BCE, it celebrates a local deity of pre-Hellenic times. The temple's pediments were originally decorated with splendid Trojan War sculptures, most of which were stolen in the 19th century and now decorate Munich's Glyptothek. Panels throughout the site are also in English.

Aphaia is 10km east of Aegina Town. Infrequent buses to Agia Marina stop here (20 minutes); taxis cost about €12 one way.

★**Paleohora** CHURCH
(Παλαιοχώρα; Map p328) FREE This enchanting remote hillside is dotted with the remains of a Byzantine village. More than 30 surviving churches punctuate the rocky heights of the original citadel, linked by a network of paths that is carpeted with wildflowers in spring. The ancient town of Paleohora was Aegina's capital from the 9th century through the medieval period and was only abandoned during the 1820s.

Paleohora is 6.5km east of Aegina Town, near enormous modern monastery Moni Agiou Nektariou (Map p328; ☑22970 53800; ☺hours vary). Buses from Aegina Town to Agia Marina stop at the turn-off to Paleohora (10 minutes); taxis cost €8 one way.

Christos Capralos Museum MUSEUM
(Map p328; ☑22970 22001; Nikou Kazantzaki/Coast Rd, Livadi; €2; ☺10am-2pm & 6-8pm Tue-Sun Jun-Oct, 10am-2pm Fri-Sun Nov-May) The home and studio of acclaimed sculptor Christos Capralos (1909–93), on the coast near Livadi, 1.5km north of Aegina Town, has been made into a museum displaying many of his fluid, powerful works. Monumental sculptures include the 40m-long *Pindus Frieze*.

🛏 Sleeping & Eating

Villa Rodanthos APARTMENT €
(☑22970 61400, 6944250138; www.villarodanthos.com; Perdika; studios from €55; ✳🐾🛜) A gem of a place, not least because of its charming owner. Each room has its own colourful decor and a small kitchen, and there's an excellent roof terrace for afternoon drinks with sea views.

O Thanasis SEAFOOD €
(☑22970 31348; Seafront, Portes; mains €7-8; ☺lunch & dinner, reduced hours winter) On the east coast of the island in Portes, 13km northeast of Perdika, a charming family welcomes you to a seafront terrace festooned with flowerpots. It serves up top seafood and Greek classics.

★**Miltos** SEAFOOD €€
(☑22970 61051; Perdika; mains €12-15; ☺noon-4pm & 6pm-late) The most locally popular of Perdika's quayside tavernas, known for the highest-quality seafood and no-nonsense Greek staples.

Aeginitissa SEAFOOD €€
(Map p328; ☑22970 61546, 6944651699; mains €6-15; ☺noon-late May-Sep) Plan for a sunset

meal at this simple seafood taverna, 1.5km north of Perdika (6km south of Aegina Town). It's a favourite with locals for its beautiful waterfront setting. If ordering fish, have it weighed first to avoid sticker shock when you get the bill.

ANGISTRI ΑΓΚΙΣΤΡΙ
POP 1142
Tiny Angistri lies a few kilometres off the west coast of Aegina and, out of high season, its mellow lanes and azure coves make a rewarding day trip or a worthwhile longer escape.

⊙ Sights

The port-resort village of Skala is crammed with small hotels, apartments, tavernas and cafes, but life, in general, still ticks along gently. A right turn from the quay leads to the small harbour beach and then to a church on a low headland. Beyond lies the best beach on the island (it's unnamed), but it disappears beneath sun loungers and broiling bodies in July and August. Turning left from the quay at Skala takes you south along a dirt path through the pine trees to the pebbly and clothing-optional Halikadha Beach.

About 1km west from Skala, Angistri's other port, Mylos (Megalochori), has an appealing traditional character, rooms and tavernas, but no beach.

Aponissos has turquoise waters, a small offshore island and a reliably tasty taverna. Limenaria has deeper green waters. The island as a whole gets super-sleepy in low season.

🛏 Sleeping

Book ahead, especially for August and summer weekends. A board on Skala's quay lists a range of small guesthouses and hotels.

Alkyoni Inn PENSION €
(☑22970 91378; www.alkyoni-agistri.com; Skala; s/d/maisonettes from €30/45/60; ☺Easter-Sep; ✳🛜) This lovely, elegant pension offers some sea-facing rooms with fabulous, unobstructed views. Two-storey family maisonettes sleep up to four. Its taverna (p332) is very popular too.

★**Rosy's Little Village** PENSION €€
(☑22970 91610; www.rosyslittlevillage.com; Skala; s/d/tr/q from €65/73/83/108; ✳🛜) A complex of simple Cycladic-style cubes steps gently

down to the sea, a short way east of Skala's quay. Full of light and colour, with built-in couches and tiny balconies with sea views, Rosy's also offers mountain bikes, summer courses, weekly picnics and live-music evenings. Its restaurant emphasises organics.

 Eating

Toxotis GREEK €
(☑ 22970 91283; Skala; mains from €7; ☺ lunch & dinner) A popular restaurant in Skala, with good meat and fish dishes, a decent wine selection and a busy terrace.

Petite Restaurant GREEK €€
(☑ 22970 91610; www.rosyslittlevillage.com; Rosy's Little Village; mains €8-18; ☺ lunch & dinner; ☑) Part of Rosy's Little Village (p331), this small restaurant focuses on organic produce and vegan and vegetarian options, in addition to the traditional Greek staples. Vegetarians and vegans should try the excellent tabbouleh and stuffed tomatoes, while meat and fish eaters can have fish roe salad, fresh fish or baked lamb with rosemary.

Alkyoni Inn TAVERNA €€
(☑ 22970 91378; www.alkyoni-agistri.com; Skala; mains €7-15; ☺ 8am-10pm Easter-Sep; ✱ ⛭ ⛲) The welcoming, family-run Alkyoni is a 10-minute stroll southeast of Skala's quay. The popular taverna dishes up well-prepared fish and meat, while the elegant pension (p331) offers sea-facing rooms and family maisonettes.

ⓘ Information

Visit www.agistri.com.gr for island information.

ⓘ Getting There & Away

Fast Aegean Flying Dolphins (p327) and Hellenic Seaways (p327) hydrofoils and car ferries (www.saronicferries.gr) come from Piraeus (hydrofoils €14.50, 55 minutes; ferry €10.90, 1½ hours) via Aegina (hydrofoils €6, 10 minutes, four to six daily; ferry €2.80, 20 minutes, one to two daily) to either Skala or Mylos. Angistri Express (p327) serves Aegina several times daily, Monday to Saturday.

Water taxis (p327) cost €45 one way between Aegina and Angistri.

ⓘ Getting Around

Several **buses** (☑ 6973016132, 22970 91244; Skala) a day during summer run from Skala and Mylos (Megalochori) to Limenaria and Dhragonera Beach. It's worth hiring a scooter (€15) or sturdy bike (€7) to explore the coast road.

You can also follow tracks from Metohi overland through cool pine forest to reach Dhragonera Beach. Take a compass; tracks divide often and route-finding can be frustrating.

Kostas Bike Hire (☑ 22970 91021; Skala)

Takis Rent a Bike & Bicycles (Logothetis; ☑ 22970 91001; www.agistri.com.gr/logothetis; Mylos)

Taxi (☑ 6977618040, 22970 91455; Skala)

POROS ΠΟΡΟΣ

POP 3800

Poros is separated from the mountainous Peloponnese by a narrow sea channel, and its protected setting makes the main settlement of Poros Town seem like a vibrant lakeside resort. The sight of its pastel-hued houses stacked up on the hillside around a clock tower is as romantic as it gets.

Poros is made up of two land masses connected by a tiny isthmus: Sferia, which is occupied mainly by the town of Poros; and the much larger and mainly forested Kalavria, which has the island's beaches and seasonal hotels scattered along its southern shore. Poros still maintains a sense of remoteness in its sparsely populated, forested interior.

The Peloponnesian town of Galatas lies on the opposite shore, making Poros a useful base from which to explore the ancient sites of the Peloponnese.

ⓘ Getting There & Away

Daily ferries (www.saronicferries.gr; €11.50 to €14, 2½ hours, two to three daily) or zippy catamarans (€24.50, one hour, four to five daily) connect Piraeus to Poros in summer (reduced timetable in winter). High-speed Hellenic Seaways (p327) ferries continue south to Hydra (€13.50, 30 minutes, two to five daily), Spetses (€16, 1½ hours, four daily), Ermioni and Porto Heli. Conventional ferries connect Aegina (€8.50,1¼ hours, two to five daily) to Poros and Methana on the mainland.. Travel agents (p334) sell tickets.

Caïques (little boats) shuttle constantly between Poros and Galatas (€1, five minutes). They leave from the quay opposite Plateia Iroön, the triangular plaza near the main ferry dock in Poros Town. Hydrofoils dock about 50m north of here. Car ferries to Galatas (per person/car €1/6, from 7.30am to 10.40pm) leave from the dock several hundred metres north again, on the road to Kalavria.

You can also do a one-way rental between branches of **Pop's Car** (☑ in Galatas 22980 42910; www.popscar.gr) at Athens Airport and Galatas (or Ermioni).

Poros

N 0 ——————— 2 km
   0 ——————— 1 mile

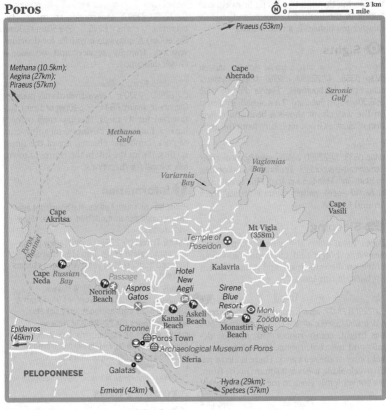

Piraeus (53km)

Methana (10.5km);
Aegina (27km);
Piraeus (57km)

Cape
Aherado

Saronic
Gulf

Methanon
Gulf

Vagionias
Bay

Variarnia
Bay

Cape
Akritsa

Cape
Vasili

Mt Vigla
(358m)

Temple of
Poseidon

Poros
Channel

Kalavria

Cape
Neda

Russian
Bay

Passage

Hotel
New
Aegli

Sirene
Blue
Resort

Moni
Zoödohou
Pigis

Neorion
Beach

Aspros
Gatos

Askeli
Beach

Kanali
Beach

Citronne

Monastiri
Beach

Epidavros
(46km)

Poros Town

Archaeological Museum of Poros

Galatas

Sferia

PELOPONNESE

Hydra (29km);
Spetses (57km)

Ermioni (42km)

ℹ Getting Around

BOAT

Caïques (little boats) go to beaches around the
island during summer.

BUS

A bus (€3) operates mid-June to October every
hour from 7am until midnight from the **Galatas
KTEL Bus Station** (☑ 22980 42480; www.
ktelargolida.gr; Galatas) on a route that starts
next to the kiosk at the eastern end of Plateia
Iroön. It crosses to Kalavria and goes east along
the south coast for 10 minutes as far as Moni
Zoödohou Pigis (p334), then turns around and
heads west to Neorion Beach (15 minutes). Buy
tickets from the kiosk.

MOTORCYCLE & BICYCLE

Several places on the road to Kalavria rent out
bicycles, scooters and all-terrain vehicles (ATVs;
per day from €6/20/30).
Moto Fotis (☑ 22980 25873; http://moto
rentalfotis.com.gr; Kanali; ⊙ 9am-9pm) Rents
bicycles, motorbikes and ATVs.

Moto Stelios (☑ 22980 23026; www.moto
stelios.gr; Harbour, Poros Town; ⊙ 9am-9pm)
Rents ATVs, scooters and bicycles in Poros
Harbour and Askeli Beach.

TAXI

Standard taxi fares are posted at the main stand
on the quay.
Taxi (Poros) (☑ 22980 23003)
Taxi (Galatas) (☑ in Galatas 22980 42888)

Poros Town   Πόρος

POP 3651

Poros Town's lively harbour area faces the
narrow channel at Galatas and the shapely
mountains of the Peloponnese, giving it a dynamic atmosphere – sailing boats bob along
the lengthy quay, while ferries glide through
the channel and smaller vessels scurry to and
fro. Behind the harbour, *plateies* (squares)
and tavernas hide from view and a rocky
bluff rises steeply to a crowning clock tower.

Wandering through the steep alleyways and taking in the beautiful colours and slightly dilapidated houses is a true delight.

◎ Sights

Archaeological Museum of Poros   MUSEUM
(Map p333; ☑22980 23276; http://odysseus.culture.gr; Harbourfront, Plateia Koryzi; €2; ⊙8.30am-3pm Tue-Sun) This small museum on the waterfront shows a beautiful collection of classic Greek sculpture from the area.

Citronne   GALLERY
(Map p333; ☑22980 22401; www.facebook.com/citronne.athens.poros; Leoforos Papadopoulou; ⊙10am-3pm Mon-Sat Jun-Aug) This bright and cheerful local gallery shows artists from around Greece.

⊨ Sleeping

Poros Town offers the gamut: simple business-style hotels and charming old-school hotels on the waterfront, and rooms for rent set back on tiny lanes.

★ Seven Brothers Hotel   HOTEL €
(☑22980 23412; www.7brothers.gr; Poros Harbour; s/d/tr €50/55/60; ❋ ⓢ) This charming hotel has bright, comfy rooms with antique details and neat bathrooms. Some have small balconies, some sea views. There is also a patio overlooking the small square in the front. It's conveniently close to the hydrofoil quay.

Georgia Mellou Rooms   PENSION €
(☑22980 22309; http://porosnet.gr/gmellou; Plateia Georgiou; d/tr €40/45; ❋ ⓢ) Simple old-fashioned rooms are tucked into the heart of the old town, next to the cathedral, high above the harbour. The charming owner keeps everything shipshape. Book ahead for fantastic views from west-side rooms.

Sto Roloi   APARTMENT €€
(☑22980 25808, 6932427267; www.storoloi-poros.gr; studio/apt/houses from €65/110/170; ❋) Roloi is a good source for stylish, tidy apartments and houses around Poros Town.

✗ Eating

Taverna Karavolos   TAVERNA €
(☑22980 26158; Dalakou; mains €6-12; ⊙7-11pm) Karavolos means 'big snail' and snails are indeed a house speciality at this quaint eatery on a backstreet. Friendly proprietors also offer classic Greek meat dishes and some fish, as well as rooms (double/triple €37/45) upstairs.

Poseidon   SEAFOOD €€
(☑22980 23597; www.poseidontaverna.gr; Harbourfront; mains €7-15; ⊙9.30am-12.30am Easter-Oct) A quayside favourite for delicious seafood, friendly service and occasional Greek dancing.

Dimitris Family Taverna   TAVERNA €€
(☑22980 23709; www.dimitrisfamily-poros.gr; Giannousi; mains €6-14; ⊙6-10pm or 11pm) Renowned for its meat, this taverna's owners have a butchering business, meaning cuts of pork, lamb and chicken are of the finest quality. It's up the hill in the centre of town; ask a local for directions.

❶ Information

Poros has no tourist office. Harbourfront agencies arrange accommodation, car hire, tours and cruises.

Askeli Travel (☑22980 25857; www.poros-accommodation.gr; ⊙8am-11pm Jun-Sep, reduced hours rest of year) Arranges studios for rent.

Family Tours (☑22980 23743; www.familytours.gr; Harbourfront; ⊙9am-2pm & 5-10pm) Sells conventional-ferry tickets.

Marinos Tours (☑22980 23423; www.marinostours.gr; Harbourfront; ⊙7am-9.30pm Apr-Oct, to 7pm Nov-Mar) Across from the hydrofoil quay; sells hydrofoil tickets.

Around Poros

◎ Sights

Temple of Poseidon   RUINS
(Map p333; ☑22980 23276; ⊙8.30am-3pm) FREE There's very little left of this 6th-century temple. Once it was a magnificent building giving sanctuary to fugitives and wrecked sailors, but in the 18th century it was mostly dismantled and the materials used to build a monastery on Hydra. Still, the walk or drive to the site gives superb views of the Saronic Gulf and the Peloponnese.

With your own wheels, from the road near Moni Zoödohou Pigis, head inland to reach the ruins. Then you can continue along the road and circle back to the bridge onto Sferia. It's about 6km in total.

Moni Zoödohou Pigis   MONASTERY
(Map p333; ⊙9am-noon & 2.30-6pm) FREE The 18th-century 'Monastery of the Life-giving Spring', well signposted 4km east of Poros Town, has a beautiful gilded iconostasis (a screen bearing icons) from Asia Minor.

🏃 Activities

Poros' best beaches include the pebbly **Kanali Beach**, on Kalavria islet 1km east of the bridge, and the long, sandy **Askeli Beach**, about 500m further east.

Neorion Beach, 3km west of the bridge, has waterskiing, and banana-boat and air-chair rides. The best beach is at **Russian Bay**, 1.5km past Neorion.

Passage   WATER SPORTS
(Map p333; ☑ 22980 42540; www.passage.gr; Neorion Bay; lesson from €45) A popular water-skiing school and slalom centre. Beginner lessons are available.

🛏 Sleeping & Eating

⭐ **Sirene Blue Resort**   RESORT €€
(Map p333; ☑ 22980 22741; Monastiri Beach; d incl breakfast from €140; ✴ 🛜 🌊) Sirene Blue Resort offers a deluxe seaside vacation, from the sparkling pool to crisp linens. Find it at Monastiri Beach, near Moni Zoödohou Pigis.

Hotel New Aegli   HOTEL €€
(Map p333; ☑ 22980 22372; www.newaegli.com; Askeli Beach; d from €95; ☺ Apr-Oct; ✴ @ 🛜 🌊) Poros' best beaches include the long, sandy Askeli Beach. Hotel New Aegli, across the road from the beach, is a decent resort-style hotel and offers good modern rooms, many with sea views.

⭐ **Aspros Gatos**   SEAFOOD €€
(Map p333; ☑ 22980 24274; Labraki 49; mains €6-15; ☺ noon-11pm Easter-Oct) A short walk from town, 400m west of the bridge on the road to Neorion Beach, Poros' best seafood taverna sits smack out over the water. Watch the local kayaking team do its thing as the jolly owner provides anything from bolognese to the catch of the day.

HYDRA   ΥΔΡΑ

POP 1966

Breathtaking Hydra is one of the only Greek islands that is free of wheeled vehicles. No cars. No scooters. Just tiny marble-cobbled lanes, donkeys, rocks and sea. Artists (Brice Marden, Nikos Chatzikyriakos-Ghikas, Panayiotis Tetsis), musicians (Leonard Cohen), actors and celebrities (Melina Mercouri, Sophia Loren) have all been drawn to Hydra over the years. In addition to the island's exquisitely preserved stone architecture, divine rural paths and clear, deep waters,

you can find a good cappuccino along the harbour, which is great for people-watching.

History

Hydra was sparsely populated in ancient times and is just mentioned in passing by Herodotus. The most significant evidence of settlement dates from Mycenaean times. But in the 16th century, Hydra became a refuge for people fleeing skirmishes between the Venetians and the Ottomans. Many hailed from the area of modern-day Albania.

By the mid-1700s the settlers began building boats and took to the thin line between maritime commerce and piracy with enthusiasm. They travelled as far as Egypt and the Black Sea, and ran the British blockade (1803–15) during the Napoleonic Wars. As a result of steady tax paying, the island experienced only light interference under the Ottoman Empire. By the 19th century, Hydra had become a full-blown maritime power, and wealthy shipping merchants had built most of the town's grand mansions. At its height in 1821, the island's population reached 28,000. Hydra supplied 130 ships for a blockade of the Turks during the Greek War of Independence, and the island bred such leaders as Admiral Andreas Miaoulis, who commanded the Greek fleet, and Georgios Koundouriotis, president of Greece's national assembly from 1822 to 1827.

ℹ Getting There & Away

High-speed **Hellenic Seaways** (www.hsw.gr) ferries link Hydra with Poros, Piraeus and Spetses, and Ermioni and Porto Heli on the Peloponnese. Service is greatly reduced in winter. Buy tickets from **Hydreoniki Travel** (☑ 22980 54007; Port; ☺ 7am-10pm or around ferry departures), up the lane to the right of the Alpha Bank in Hydra Town.

Freedom (Map p338; ☑ 6944242141, 6947325263; www.hydralines.gr) boats run between Hydra and Metohi (little more than a car park) on the mainland (€6.50, 15 minutes, five to 11 daily). The schedule is posted on the quay and online.

High-speed catamarans run to Piraeus throughout the year (€28, 1¾ hours, four to six daily), stopping at Poros on the way (€13, 30 minutes, four to six daily). You can also get to Spetses (€11.50, 40 minutes, four to six daily).

ℹ Getting Around

Generally, people get around Hydra by walking.

The island is vehicle-free, and mules and donkeys are the main means of heavy transport. Donkey owners are clustered around the port;

Hydra

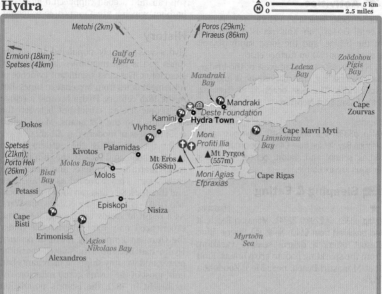

Metohi (2km)

Poros (29km);
Piraeus (86km)

Ermioni (18km);
Spetses (41km)

Gulf of
Hydra

Zoödohou
Pigis
Bay

Ledeza
Bay

Mandraki
Bay

Mandraki

Cape
Zourvas

Deste Foundation
Kamini Hydra Town

Dokos

Vlyhos

Moni
Profiti Ilia

Limnioniza
Bay

Cape Mavri Myti

Spetses
(21km);
Porto Heli
(26km)

Kivotos

Palamidas

Mt Pyrgos
(557m)

Molos Bay

Mt Eros
(588m)

Bisti
Bay

Molos

Moni Agias
Efpraxias

Cape Rigas

Petassi

Cape
Bisti

Episkopi

Nisiza

Myrtoön
Sea

Erimonisia

Agios
Nikolaos Bay

Alexandros

they transport luggage to the hotels and provide quick donkey rides around the port. Note that animal rights groups urge people to consider whether the animals are maltreated before deciding to take a ride.

In summer, caïques (little boats) from Hydra Town go to the island's beaches. **Water taxi** (Map p338; ☑ 22980 53690) fares are posted on the quay (Kamini €10, Vlyhos €15).

Hydra Town   Ύδρα

POP 1900

Whether you sail or ferry into Hydra, the sparkling boat-filled harbour and the bright light striking the tiers of carefully preserved stone houses make for a scene you'll never forget. The harbour in high season is an ecosystem of its own, with yachts, caïques (little boats) and water taxis zipping in and out. The marble quay is a surging rhythm of donkeys, visitors, cafe denizens and boat-taxi hawkers. By night the scene becomes a promenade: grab a chair, order a drink and watch the world go by.

If you head back into the warren of portside houses, to the steep slopes banking away from the town centre, you get a different view on Hydriot life. By the deep-blue-and-white houses and quiet lanes, grandmothers chat about what's for dinner, and roads peter out into dirt paths that head into the mountains, ever-changing in colour, depending on the time of day.

◉ Sights

★ Kimisis Tis Theotokou Cathedral   CHURCH

(Metropolis; Map p338; Harbour; ⊙7am-7pm) Within the peaceful monastery complex on the harbour, this lovely cathedral dates from the 17th century and has a Tinian-marble bell tower. Its **Ecclesiastical Museum** (Map p338; ☑22980 54071; www.imhydra.gr/mouseio_main.htm; Harbour; adult/child €2/free; ⊙10am-5pm Tue-Sun Apr-Nov) contains a collection of icons and vestments. The monastery complex is also known as Faneromeni. Dress appropriately (covered shoulders, long skirts or trousers) to enter.

★ Deste Foundation   GALLERY

(Map p336; ☑21027 58490; www.deste.gr; Harbour; ⊙11am-1pm & 7-10pm Wed-Mon Jun-Sep) **FREE** Deste Foundation hosts an annual Hydra exhibit at the small former slaughterhouse on the sea.

★ Lazaros Koundouriotis Historical Mansion   MUSEUM

(Map p338; ☑22980 52421; www.nhmuseum.gr; adult/child €3/free, Sun free; ⊙10am-4pm Tue-Sun Mar-Oct) Hydra's star cultural attraction is this handsome ochre-coloured *arhontiko* (stone mansion) high above the harbour. It was the home of one of the major players in the Greek independence struggle and is an exquisite example of late-18th-century traditional architecture. It features original furnishings, folk costumes, handicrafts and a painting exhibition.

Historical Archives
Museum of Hydra
MUSEUM

(Map p338; ☑22980 52355; www.iamy.gr; Harbour; adult/child €5/3; ☉9am-4pm) This fine harbourfront museum houses an extensive collection of portraits and naval artefacts, with an emphasis on the island's role in the War of Independence. It hosts temporary exhibitions in summer, and concerts on the rooftop terrace.

🏃 Activities

Vasilis Kokkos
BOATING

(☑6977649789; bkokkos@yahoo.com) Vasilis Kokkos, proprietor of **Caprice** (Map p338; ☑22980 52454; Sahtouri; mains €9-15; ☉6pm-midnight Apr-Oct) restaurant and boat captain, rents speedboats (per day €80 to €250) and a sailing boat (by prior arrangement; one-week minimum from €900). Licence required.

☞ Tours

Harriet's Hydra Horses
HORSE RIDING

(☑6980323347; www.harrietshydrahorses.com; 1/2/8hr tour €30/55/175) Harriet, a friendly bilingual British-Greek local, guides licensed horse-riding tours (anywhere from one to eight hours) around the island, to the monasteries and to the beaches. Note that the eight-hour tour is not available between May and September because of the heat.

✨ Festivals & Events

The Melina Mercouri Exhibition Hall and Deste Foundation host high-season art shows.

Miaoulia Festival
CULTURAL

(☉weekend around 21 Jun) Celebration of Admiral Miaoulis and the Hydriot contribution to the War of Independence, with a spectacular boat burning (with fireworks) in Hydra harbour.

Easter
RELIGIOUS

(☉Mar/Apr) Week-long extravaganza including a famous parade of a flower-festooned epitaph into the harbour at Kamini.

🛏 Sleeping

Accommodation in Hydra is of a high standard, but you pay accordingly. Most owners will meet you at the harbour and organise luggage transfer.

Piteoussa
PENSION €

(Map p338; ☑22980 52810; www.piteoussa.com; Kouloura; d €50-85; ※☎) Jolly owners maintain beautiful rooms in two buildings on a quiet, pine-tree-lined street. Rooms in the restored corner mansion drip with period character and also have all the modern amenities you need; the upstairs rooms in the second building have a contemporary feel, tea- and coffee-making facilities and balconies.

Hotel Sophia
BOUTIQUE HOTEL €€

(Map p338; ☑22980 52313; www.hotelsophia.gr; Harbourfront; d incl breakfast €85-115; ☉Apr-Oct; ※☎) Gorgeous small rooms sit right on the harbour; some have balconies. Each has been painstakingly outfitted with all the mod cons, and bathrooms are luscious marble. Some rooms are spread over two storeys.

Angelica Hotel
BOUTIQUE HOTEL €€

(Map p338; ☑22980 53202; www.angelica.gr; Miaouli; d/tr/q incl breakfast from €130/180/220; ※☎) An attractive boutique hotel in a quiet location, the Angelica is popular for its comfortable rooms and spacious, impeccable bathrooms. Superior rooms have balconies. Relax in the spa or courtyard.

Greco
HOTEL €€

(Map p338; ☑22980 53200; www.grecohotel.gr; Kouloura; d incl breakfast from €90; ※☎) Set in a former bakery, this atmospheric hotel has a gorgeous garden, big breakfasts and comfortable, simply designed rooms. There is a small library for reading in the lush garden.

Mastoris Mansion
BOUTIQUE HOTEL €€

(Map p338; ☑22980 29631; www.mastoris-hydra.gr; off Oikonomou; d/tr from €100/150; ※☎) This renovated stone building in the centre of town offers plush doubles and triples, with exposed stone walls and colourful decor. While convenient to harbour action, rooms don't have views.

Amaryllis Hotel
HOTEL €€

(Map p338; ☑22980 53611; www.amarillishydra.gr; Tombazi 15; s/d €50/65, with balcony €70; ※☎) Simple rooms, a friendly owner and a super location right in the heart of town make this a safe midrange bet. Good views can be had from the roof terrace. Shared kitchen and laundry.

Hydra Town

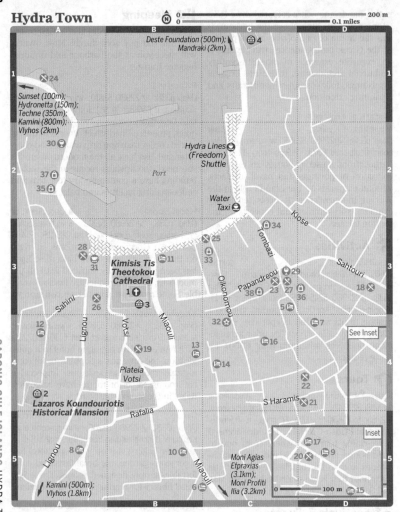

Deste Foundation (500m);
Mandraki (2km)

⊡ 4

0 200 m
0 0.1 miles

⊗ 24

Sunset (100m);
Hydronetta (150m);
Techne (350m);
Kamini (800m);
Vlyhos (2km)

30 ⊙

37 ⓐ

35 ⓐ

Port

Hydra Lines ⊙
(Freedom)
Shuttle

Water
Taxi ⊙

Kiose

⊗ 34

Tombazi

⊗ 25

28 ⊗
31 ⊡

⊡ 11

33 ⓐ

Sahtouri

**Kimisis Tis
Theotokou
Cathedral**

Oikonomou

Papandreou

⊡ 29

18 ⊗

Sahini

⊗ 26

1 ⓖ

⊡ 3

38 ⓐ 23 27 ⓐ
36

5 ⊡

12 ⊡

Lignou

Votsi

Miaouli

32 ⭐

⊡ 7

⊗ 19

13 ⊡

⊡ 16

See Inset

14 ⊡

**Plateia
Votsi**

22 ⊡

ⓐ 2

**Lazaros Koundouriotis
Historical Mansion**

Rafalia

S Haramis

21 ⊗

Inset

17 ⊡

Lignou

8 ⊡

10 ⊡

20 ⊗

9 ⊡

Kamini (500m);
Vlyhos (1.8km)

Miaouli

6 ⊡

Moni Agias
Efpraxias
(3.1km);
Moni Profiti
Ilia (3.2km)

0 100 m
⊡ 15

Pension Alkionides　　　PENSION **€€**
(Map p338; ☑22980 54055; www.alkionides
pension.com; off Oikonomou; d/studio €70/85;
❄️🛜) Hidden in a central, peaceful cul-de-
sac, rooms here are smart (though some are
quite small) and have tea- and coffee-making
facilities. There's a pretty courtyard. One studio has a private terrace. Owners are friendly.

Nereids　　　PENSION **€€**
(Map p338; ☑22980 52875; www.nereids-hydra.
com; Kouloura; d from €70; ❄️🛜) This carefully
restored stone house contains lovely rooms
of exceptional value and quality. Spacious,
peaceful and with elegant decor, they have

open views to Hydra's rocky heights; top-
floor rooms have sea views.

Hotel Miranda　　　HOTEL **€€**
(Map p338; ☑22980 52230; https://mirandahotel.
gr; Miaouli; d/tr/apt incl breakfast from
€130/145/260; ⏱️Mar-Oct; ❄️🛜) Pretend
you're a 19th-century sea captain in this an-
tique-laden jewel with spacious, lush rooms.
Public spaces are decked out in vintage
prints, carved woodwork and rotating exhibitions. Gaze at your inlaid ceilings or, in the
higher-end rooms, from your balcony. Apartments are available, too.

Hydra Town

★ **Cotommatae**   BOUTIQUE HOTEL €€€

(Map p338; ☎22980 53873; www.cotommatae.gr; d/f incl breakfast from €170/250; ❄) This restored mansion has retained the character and some of the memorabilia of the home's original family while adding impeccable modern touches. There's a wonderful sense of understated luxury throughout. Some suites have private terraces or a Jacuzzi.

★ **Hydra Hotel**   APARTMENT €€€

(Map p338; ☎22980 53420, 6985910717; www.hydra-hotel.gr; Petrou Voulgari 8; studio incl breakfast €175-265, maisonettes €255; ❄🛜) Climb high on the south side of the port to swishy, top-of-the-line apartments in an impeccably renovated ancient mansion with kitchenettes and sweeping views. Get room 202 for a tiny balcony with panoramas to die for.

Leto Hotel   HOTEL €€€

(Map p338; ☎22980 53385; www.letohydra.gr; Rigillis 8; d/ste from €177/485; ❄🛜) This proper hotel is family-owned with formal, comfortable rooms and all the services. It also offers a rarity in Greece: a wheelchair-accessible room, served by ramps all the way from the harbour.

Bratsera Hotel   HISTORIC HOTEL €€€

(Map p338; ☎22980 53971; www.bratserahotel.com; off Kouloura; d incl breakfast €173-290, ste from €290; ❄@🛜⌨) The Bratsera is Hydra's most venerable hotel, filling a renovated sponge factory with a complex of quaint rooms, a conference hall and a swimming pool, plus a well-regarded and peaceful restaurant (mains €9-30; ⊙7am-11pm Apr-Oct).

🍴 Eating

Tavernas and restaurants in Hydra Town line the harbour and dot the backstreets of town. The emphasis is on local Greek fare, with a couple of excellent Italian options as well.

★ **Flora's**   SWEETS €

(Anemoni; Map p338; ☎22980 53136; Plateia Votsi; sweets from €1; ⊙9am-late) Flora's sweets shop on inland Plateia Votsi makes *galaktoboureko* (custard slice), rice pudding and ice cream from local goat's milk.

Ke Kremmidi   GREEK €

(Map p338; ☎22980 53099; Tombazi; gyros €2.50, mains €6-9; ⊙noon-late) This friendly souvlaki joint has tables spilling out onto a busy pedestrian way and offers up good salads and grilled-meat plates as well.

LEONARD COHEN IN HYDRA

Hydra's pull on the artistic soul is well documented, but there is no more famous former inhabitant of this mesmerising island than the bard of the bedsit himself, Leonard Cohen (1934–2016).

Depressed by the cold weather of his native Canada and adopted UK, Cohen made his way to Greece, after allegedly asking a man in the street where he got his tan – the man answered: 'Greece!' Prompted by artistic expats already living on the island, the 26-year-old Cohen landed on Hydra, and bought a house only a few days later. The five-room house, which sits in Kamini, was whitewashed, dishevelled and charming; Cohen published the poetry collection *Flowers for Hitler* (1964), and the novels *The Favourite Game* (1963) and *Beautiful Losers* (1966) while living and writing there.

Young, and not quite the star he became later, Cohen shared his Hydra house with Marianne Ihlen, whom he met on the island; Ihlen is the subject of Cohen's well-known song 'So Long, Marianne'.

Some say that the years on Hydra were Cohen's most productive and tranquil – and no wonder, considering the beauty and simplicity of life that must have surrounded him. He wrote the poem 'The Days of Kindness' about his days in Hydra.

Cohen loved the Greek way of life, and the port cafe, Rolo, then known as the Kafenion o Katsikas, is apparently where he held his first public performance, with a few friends for an audience.

Cohen left Hydra for pastures new in the mid-1960s but kept returning whenever life and stardom, and increasingly ill health, allowed him. The house remains the property of his two sons. Cohen fans go to leave offerings and read his poetry at the door to this day; ask for directions locally if you want to find it for yourself.

Ostria
TAVERNA €

(Stathis & Tassoula; Map p338; ☑ 22980 54077; off Lignou; mains €5-8; ☺ noon-4pm & 6.30pm-late) Often referred to by just the gregarious owners' names 'Stathis and Tassoula' – Tassoula is the larger-than-life hostess – this year-round taverna serves only what's fresh: put the menu to one side and ask. You might be served grilled fish, or fava-bean or zucchini balls. Stathis catches his own sweet and delicious calamari.

Giasemi
GREEK €

(Map p338; ☑ 22980 52221; Kouloura; mains from €6; ☺ lunch & dinner) Opened in 2019, Giasemi comes highly recommended by locals. It has a nice canopised terrace and a decent range of Greek staples – from fava-bean puree to aromatic meatballs. The service is attentive.

★ Oraia Hydra
GREEK €€

(Map p338; ☑ 22980 52556; Harbourfront; mains €9-25; ☺ noon-midnight) Oraia Hydra translates as 'Beautiful Hydra' and this small bistro lives right up to its name. You'll dine on the harbour with sailboats bobbing alongside and enjoy Greek dishes elevated by top ingredients and creative twists – try the sea urchin pasta or orzo with shrimp and mussels.

★ Il Casta
ITALIAN €€

(Map p338; ☑ 22980 52967; Tombazi; mains €10-22; ☺ noon-11pm) Dine al fresco and enjoy authentic Italian food like owner Pietro's Neapolitan grandmother used to make. Menus change daily. Reserve in high season.

★ Sunset
MEDITERRANEAN €€

(☑ 22980 52067; Kamini path; mains €9-25; ☺ noon-11pm Easter-Oct) Famed for its splendid panoramic spot near the cannons to the west of the harbour, Sunset also has fine, fresh cuisine. Tasty salads, inventive pastas and local fish are prepared with flair and a hint of elegance.

Gitoniko
TAVERNA €€

(Map p338; ☑ 22980 53615; Haramis; mains €7-25; ☺ noon-3pm & 6-11pm Easter-Oct) Having recently changed owners, Gitoniko remains popular for its broad range of good Greek dishes, and its (pricey) fresh fish. The setting, on a lovely alley, is particularly atmospheric and relaxing.

Paradosiako
TAVERNA €€

(Map p338; ☑ 22980 54155; Tombazi; mains €5-15; ☺ noon-11.30pm Easter-Nov) This little streetside spot is traditional Greek personified. Sit on the corner terrace to watch the people parade as you dig into classic mezedhes – perhaps beetroot salad with garlic dip – or meats and seafood such as fresh, filleted and grilled sardines.

Psarapoula
TAVERNA €€
(Map p338; ✑22980 52630; Harbourfront; mains €7-14; ☺noon-late) Look just above the quay, near the Pirate bar and main bakery, to find this reliable taverna with lovely harbour views. Visitors and locals dig into daily specials at this historical eatery, which was established in 1911.

Omilos
MEDITERRANEAN €€€
(Map p338; ✑22980 53800; www.omilos-hydra. com; Seafront, Kamini path; mains €16-25; ☺noon-late Easter-Oct) This chic, all-white waterside restaurant is Hydra Town's gourmet entry. It turns into a night-time dance venue.

Drinking & Nightlife

Prices are high, but lively people-watching comes with your coffee or cocktail. The harbour revs up after midnight.

★Pirate
CAFE
(Map p338; ✑22980 52711; https://thepiratebar. gr; Harbourfront; ☺8am-late) During the day, friendly Wendy and Takis and their kids run this cafe with first-rate coffee, some of the island's most delicious breakfasts and home-cooked lunches (9am to 5pm), then morph it into a raging party place at night. Music changes with the crowd and the mood.

★Hydronetta
BAR
(✑22980 54160; www.facebook.com/hydronetta; Kamini path; ☺noon-11pm Easter-Oct) You can't beat this gorgeous waterfront location on the swimming rocks to the far west of the harbour. Brothers Andreas and Elias provide snazzy cocktails and lunch (high season only) with a smile.

Papagalos
BAR
(Map p338; ✑22980 52626; Harbourfront; ☺9am-late) Papagalos is just that bit away from the madding crowd, on the quieter side of the harbour. By day, it offers coffee and basic food, and by night, cocktails and a clear view of the moonrise.

☆ Entertainment

Cinema Club of Hydra
OUTDOOR CINEMA
(Map p338; ✑22980 53105; http://cineclub hydras.blogspot.com; Oikonomou) In July and August the open-air cinema screens blockbusters and indie flicks. It also organises excursions to plays at the ancient theatre of Epidavros (p156).

Shopping

Kashish
CLOTHING
(Map p338; ✑22984 00774; https://kashish.gr; Tombazi 8; ☺9.30am-midnight May-Sep, reduced hours rest of year) Athens- and Hydra-based Kelly Fotopoulou designs a range of women's and kids' clothing, jewellery and kaftans – perfect for the beach and summer lounging – using Indian block printing and traditional Greek motifs. The colours and patterns are mesmerising.

Sirens
CLOTHING
(Map p338; ✑22980 53340; Harbourfront; ☺10am-10pm Easter-Oct) Charming owner Elena offers unique island-friendly, high-end fashion and Greek-designed jewellery.

Sugarfree
CLOTHING
(Map p338; ✑22980 53352; www.sugarfree shops.com; Tombazi; ☺11am-11pm May-Nov) Youthful beach- and loungewear created by Greek designers fill this sparkling white shop just back from Amalour (Map p338; ✑22980 53800; Tombazi; ☺7pm-late Jun-Aug, reduced hours Sep-May), on the way to the Bratsera Hotel (p339). Prices are reasonable by local standards and the colours are dazzling.

Svoura
ARTS & CRAFTS
(Map p338; ✑22980 29784; Harbourfront; ☺10am-11pm Apr-Oct) Carefully curated ceramics from all over Greece plus a smattering of fashion make this one of Hydra's top shops.

Elena Votsi
JEWELLERY
(Map p338; ✑22980 52637; www.facebook. com/ElenaVotsiOfficial; Harbourfront; ☺10am-11.30pm) Hydra native Votsi is renowned for her original, bold jewellery designs using exquisite semiprecious stones, which sell in New York and London. She designed the Athens Olympic Games medal. A great souvenir to remember Hydra by.

Turquoise
FASHION & ACCESSORIES
(Map p338; ✑22980 54033; www.turquoise.gr; off Tombazi; ☺10am-10pm Jun-Aug, reduced hours Sep-May) Local designer Dimitris creates an annual line of womenswear and accessories using intricate Indian block prints.

Getting There & Away

Hydra Town is the main port on the island; all ferries (p335) dock here.

Around Hydra

Hydra's coastal road turns into a partially cobbled, beautiful trail about 1.5km west of the port, after Kamini. Kamini has a tiny fishing port, several good tavernas, swimming rocks and a small pebble beach. In fact, Hydra's shortcoming – or blessing – is its lack of sandy beaches to draw the crowds. People usually swim off the rocks, but if you go as far as Vlyhos, 1.5km after Kamini, this last little hamlet before the mountains offers two slightly larger pebble beaches (one called Vlyhos and the other, the more pristine Plakes), tavernas and a restored 19th-century stone bridge.

The coastal road leads 2.5km east from the port to a pebble beach at Mandraki.

Boats run from the harbour to all of these places, and you certainly need them to reach Bisti Bay or Agios Nikolaos Bay, in the island's southwest, with their remote but umbrella-laden pebble beaches and green waters.

Walking & Hiking

Hydra's mountainous, arid interior makes a robust but peaceful contrast to the clamour of the quayside. A useful map for walkers is Anavasi's *Hydra* map. A map is posted on the quay, and several marked trails extend across the island. Once you leave the villages of Hydra/Kamini/Vlyhos there are no services. Take plenty of water. Springtime is perfect for flower-strewn hillside walks.

An unbeatable experience is the long haul up to Moni Profiti Ilia. The wonderful monastery complex contains beautiful icons and boasts endless, dramatic views. It's a solid hour or more through zigzags and pine trees to panoramic bliss on top.

A smaller monastery, Moni Agias Efpraxias, sits just below Profiti Ilia and is run by nuns.

Other paths lead to Mt Eros (588m), the island's highest point, and east and west along the island spine, but you need advanced route-finding skills or reliable directions from knowledgable locals.

✖ Eating

To Pefkaki   SEAFOOD €
(📞 6973535709; Kamini; dishes €5-10; ⊗ noon-4pm & 6.30-10pm Thu-Tue Easter-Oct) Worth the short walk along the coast to Kamini for a laid-back lunch of mezedhes and fresh seafood (delicious fried anchovies).

★ **Techne**   INTERNATIONAL €€
(📞 22980 52500; www.techne-hydra.com; Coast Rd, Avlaki; mains €13-23; ⊗ 10am-midnight) Spread across several terraces and overlooking a broad sweep of sea and sunset, this elegant cafe and restaurant serves lighter fare by day and full, well-conceived, delicious meals at night. Book ahead on weekend evenings to nab a table, perfect for date night.

Four Seasons   TAVERNA €€
(📞 22980 53698; www.fourseasonshydra.gr; Plakes Beach; mains €6-15; ⊗ noon-10pm Easter-Oct; 📞) This tasty seaside taverna offers a different face of Hydra: the sound of the breeze and the waves instead of the portside buzz. Don't miss the *taramasalata* (fish-roe dip) with bread. It also has handsome suites (from €240, including breakfast).

Christina   TAVERNA €€
(📞 22980 53516; Kamini; mains €6-12; ⊗ noon-4pm & 6-10pm Thu-Tue Easter-Oct) Just inland from the port in Kamini, Mrs Christina and her kids dish out some of the island's best Greek dishes and fresh fish.

Enalion   TAVERNA €€
(📞 22980 53455; www.enalion-hydra.gr; Vlyhos; mains €6-12; ⊗ noon-10pm Easter-Oct) Perhaps the best seaside option at Vlyhos Beach, with traditional fare. Try the fried shrimps, *horta* (boiled wild greens) and a Greek salad.

Pirofani   INTERNATIONAL €€
(📞 22980 53175; www.pirofani.com; Kamini; mains €10-16; ⊗ 7.30pm-midnight Wed-Sun late May-Sep) Gregarious Theo creates an eclectic range of dishes, from a beef fillet with rose-pepper sauce to a spicy Asian curry.

Castello   MEDITERRANEAN €€€
(📞 22980 54101; www.castellohydra.gr; Kamini; snacks €7-15, mains €15-30; ⊗ 8am-1am Jun-Sep) In a renovated 18th-century bastion and spilling onto the beach, Castello offers snacks at its daytime beach bar, gourmet seaside dining at its refined restaurant and sunset cocktails at its bar. Amazing views.

SPETSES   ΣΠΕΤΣΕΣ

POP 4027

Spetses stands proudly just a few kilometres from mainland Peloponnese, but there is a stronger sense of carefree island Greece here than in other Saronic Gulf destinations. The lively, historical old town is the only village on the island; the rest, ringed by a simple road, is rolling hills, pine forests and crystal-clear coves. Relaxed Spetses Town, though not as picturesque as other towns on the Saronic Gulf, has great nightlife, some great restaurants and gorgeous, easily accessible swimming spots. With a rich naval history, it is still incredibly popular with yachties, and its vibrant culture attracts artists, intellectuals and lovers of a good island party.

History

In Spetses Town there's evidence of early Helladic settlement near the Old Harbour and around the Dapia Harbour. Roman and Byzantine remains have been found in the area behind Moni Agios Nikolaos, halfway between the two. From the 10th century, Spetses is thought to have been uninhabited for almost 600 years, until the arrival of Albanian refugees fleeing the fighting between Turks and Venetians in the 16th century.

Spetses, like Hydra, grew wealthy from shipbuilding. Island captains busted the British blockade during the Napoleonic Wars and refitted their ships to join the Greek fleet during the War of Independence. In the process they immortalised one local woman (albeit originally from Hydra), the formidable Laskarina Bouboulina, ship commander and fearless fighter.

The island's hallmark forests of Aleppo pine, a legacy of the far-sighted philanthropist Sotirios Anargyros, have been devastated by fires several times in the past 20 years. The trees are steadily recovering.

◉ Sights

Bustling Spetses Town stretches along a meandering waterfront encompassing several quays and beaches. The main Dapia Harbour, where ferries arrive, and the area around adjacent Plateia Limenarhiou and inland Plateia Orologiou (Clocktower Sq) teem with chic tourist shops and cafes.

As you head further inland on the quieter lanes – or go left along the harbourfront road of Sotiriou Anargyriou, past the town beach and Plateia Agiou Mama – impressive old *arhontika* (mansions) illustrate Spetses' historical (and ongoing) wealth.

Passing the church of Moni Agios Nikolaos, you arrive at the attractive Old Harbour (Palio Limani) and the interesting Baltiza yacht anchorage and boatbuilding area.

From the north side of Dapia Harbour, a promenade and road lead through the seafront Kounoupitsa area.

Bouboulina's Museum　　　MUSEUM
(Map p344; ☑22980 72416; Spetses Town; adult/child €6/2; ⊙10.30am-6pm Apr-Oct) The mansion of Spetses' famous daughter, the 19th-century seagoing commander Laskarina Bouboulina, has been converted into a museum. Entry is via 40-minute guided tours (billboards around town advertise starting times, also posted online). The museum hosts occasional concerts. There's an impressive statue of Bouboulina on the harbour, opposite the Poseidonion Grand Hotel (p344).

Spetses Museum　　　MUSEUM
(Map p344; ☑22980 72994; http://odysseus. culture.gr; Spetses Town; adult/child €3/free; ⊙8am-3pm Tue-Sun) Small, fascinating collections are housed in the old mansion of Hatzigiannis Mexis (1754–1844), a shipowner who became the island's first governor. They include island artefacts, traditional costumes and portraits of the island's founding fathers.

✯ Festivals & Events

★ Armata　　　CULTURAL
(⊙early Sep) This week-long celebration culminates on 8 September in a commemoration of Spetses' victory over the Turks in a key 1822 naval battle, with an enormous waterborne re-enactment and fireworks.

🛏 Sleeping

Spetses has high-quality lodgings, with many chic, small hotels, a grand historical hotel and many pensions. Most places offer discounts outside August.

Villa Christina Hotel　　　PENSION €
(☑22980 72218; www.villachristinahotel.com; Dapia; s/d/tr/f incl breakfast from €50/55/70/90; ❋🛜) Located about 200m uphill on the main road inland from the harbour, these well-kept rustic rooms and lovely garden are back from the worst traffic noise. A great budget choice.

Villa Marina　　　PENSION €
(☑22980 72646; www.villamarinaspetses.com; Agios Mamas; d €55-60; ❋🛜) Super-basic, clean rooms have refrigerators; there's is a well-equipped communal kitchen downstairs. Just to the right of Plateia Agiou Mama.

Economou Mansion　　　PENSION €€
(☑22980 73400; www.economouspetses.gr; Spetses Town; d incl breakfast from €130; ❋🛜🛝) This beautiful pension on the ground floor of a restored captain's mansion sits right on the waterfront, about 500m north of Dapia Harbour. It offers a homey, relaxed hideaway combining antique decor and modern amenities such as swimming pool, TV, hairdryer and safe. Breakfast is bountiful.

Spetses

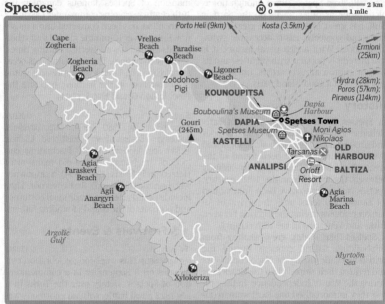

Kastro Hotel
APARTMENT €€

(☑ 22980 75319; www.kastrohotel-spetses.gr; Spetses Town; studios/4-person apt incl breakfast €120/165; ❊ ❈ ☎) A private, quiet complex encloses these studios and apartments close to the centre of town. Low-key decor and modern amenities combine with extensive terraces.

Klimis Hotel
HOTEL €€

(☑ 22980 73725; www.klimishotel.gr; Dapia Harbour; s/d/apt incl breakfast from €75/95/170; ❊ ❈) Sleek rooms, some with seafront balconies, at this standard hotel sit above a ground-floor cafe-bar and patisserie. Breakfast is served in the downstairs bar.

★ Poseidonion Grand Hotel
LUXURY HOTEL €€€

(☑ 22980 74553; www.poseidonion.com; Dapia Harbour; d/ste incl breakfast from €280/670; ❊ ❈ ☎) Here's your chance to live like a wealthy dame or gent in the roaring '20s. Every centimetre of this grand old hotel, from the chic rooms to the gracious lobby bar and fabulous pool, drips with luxury. Oh, and it also has two of the island's best restaurants, including the high-end On the Verandah.

★ Orloff Resort
BOUTIQUE HOTEL €€€

(Map p344; ☑ 22980 75444; www.orloffresort.com; Old Harbour; d/studios/apt incl breakfast from €210/225/410; ⊙ Mar-Oct; ❊ ❈ ☎) On the edge of town, along the road to Agia Marina and near the old port, the pristine Orloff hides behind high white walls. Enjoy stylish rooms, private patios and a crystal-clear pool.

Zoe's Club
APARTMENT €€€

(☑ 22980 74447; www.zoesclub.gr; Spetses Town; studio incl breakfast from €220; ❊ ❈ ☎) Free-standing spacious apartments surround a decadent pool and courtyard. It's behind a high stone wall in the central part of town, near the Spetses Museum (p343).

Nissia
APARTMENT €€€

(☑ 22980 75000; www.nissia.gr; Dapia; studio incl breakfast from €245; ⊙ Apr-Oct; ❊ ❈ ❈ ☎) Studios and maisonettes are arranged around a spacious courtyard with swimming pool and soothing greenery in this exclusive seafront oasis. It has a fine restaurant.

✖ Eating

★ Nero tis Agapis
MEDITERRANEAN €€

(☑ 22980 74009; https://ntarestaurant.com; Kounoupitsa; mains €9-22; ⊙ 11am-midnight) The sweetly named 'Water of Love' offers gourmet meat as well as fish dishes. The crayfish tagliatelle is worth every bite, as is the *zarzuela* (fish stew). There's a selection of creative salads. Book ahead for the romantic tables with the best sea views.

Akrogialia
TAVERNA €€

(📞22980 74749; Kounoupitsa; mains €9-17; ⏰11am-midnight) On the Kounoupitsa seafront, Akrogialia matches its delicious food with friendly service and a bright setting. Tasty options include *melidzana rolos* (eggplant with cream cheese and walnuts). Enjoy the fish risotto or a choice steak. All accompanied by a thoughtful selection of Greek wines.

Patralis
SEAFOOD €€

(📞22980 75380; www.patralis.gr; Kounoupitsa; mains €7-15; ⏰10am-midnight Jan-Oct) Operating for more than 70 years and known island-wide for its outstanding seafood, Patralis sits smack on the seafront in Kounoupitsa.

⭐ On the Verandah
MEDITERRANEAN €€€

(📞6957507267; www.poseidonion.com/en/On-the-Verandah; Poseidonion Hotel; 4-course dinner €38; ⏰7.30pm-midnight Jul & Aug, reduced hours May, Jun & Sep) One of the Saronic Gulf's top dining experiences, the Verandah at the Poseidonion Grand Hotel is the dining space for the refined, high-concept cuisine of chef Stamatis Marmarinos. Ingredients are locally sourced and comprise exquisitely presented creative Mediterranean dishes. Book ahead.

⭐ Tarsanas
SEAFOOD €€€

(Map p344; 📞22980 74490; www.tarsanasrestaurant.com; Old Harbour; mains €17-26; ⏰11am-midnight) A hugely popular *psarotaverna* (fish taverna) on the water at the Old Harbour, this family-run place deals almost exclusively in fish dishes. It can be pricey, but the fish soup (€7) alone is a delight and other starters, such as anchovies marinated with lemon, start at €6.

🍷 Drinking & Nightlife

Head straight for the Old Harbour–Baltiza area, the epicentre of Spetses' vibrant nightlife. Bars and clubs rise and fall in popularity, but the party's always here. Most bars are open May to October only.

Bar Spetsa
BAR

(📞22980 74131; www.barspetsa.org; Agios Mamas; ⏰8pm-late Mar-Oct) A great little bar, this Spetses institution never loses its easy-going atmosphere. Find it 50m beyond Plateia Agiou Mama, on the road to the right of the kiosk.

🛍 Shopping

Sox Art Shop
ARTS & CRAFTS

(📞22980 77166; https://soxartshop.com; Agora; ⏰10.30am-2pm & 6-10pm, Apr-Nov) A lovely boutique specialising in Greek-made arts and crafts, with sculpture and paintings, plus the specially designed Armata festival (p343) posters that make for great souvenirs.

ℹ Information

Municipal Information Kiosk (www.spetses.com.gr; Dapia Harbour; ⏰10am-9pm May-Sep) On the quay; seasonal staff provide answers to general questions about the island.

Bardakos Tours (📞22980 73141; hswbarda@yahoo.gr; Dapia Harbour; ⏰8am-9pm Jun-Aug, reduced hours Sep-May) Sells ferry tickets and assists with other arrangements.

ℹ Getting There & Away

High-speed ferries link Spetses with Hydra, Poros and Piraeus, and Ermioni and Porto Heli on the Peloponnese. In summer, caïques (little boats; per person €4) and a car ferry (€2) go from the harbour to Kosta on the mainland. Note: only locally owned cars are allowed on Spetses. Park yours in Kosta. Get tickets at Bardakos Tours.

There are high-speed services to Piraeus (€38.50, two hours and 10 minutes, five daily), Hydra (€11.50, 40 minutes, four to five daily) and Poros (€16, 1½ hours, four to five daily).

ℹ Getting Around

BICYCLE

Bike Center (📞22980 72209; http://spetsesbikecenter.blogspot.com; Dapia Harbour; ⏰10am-3.30pm & 5.30-10pm) Behind the fish market; rents out bikes (per day €8), including baby seats.

BOAT

In summer, caïques (small boats) serve the island's beaches (return €13). **Water taxi** (📞22980 72072; Dapia Harbour; ⏰24hr) fares are displayed on a board at the quay. All leave from the quay opposite Bardakos Tours.

BUS

Two routes start over Easter and increase in frequency to three or four daily from June to September. Departure times are displayed on boards by the bus stops and around town.

One goes from Plateia Agiou Mama in Spetses Town to Agia Paraskevi (€6, 40 minutes), travelling via Agia Marina and Agii Anargyri.

The other leaves from in front of Poseidonion Grand Hotel, going to Vrellos (€4) via Ligoneri.

CAR & MOTORCYCLE

Only locally owned autos are allowed on Spetses, and those are not permitted in the centre of town. The transport of choice tends to be scooters. Motorbike- and quad-bike-hire shops abound (per day €15 to €35). Taxis are another option.

AT A GLANCE

POPULATION
Ermoupoli: 11,400

LARGEST ISLAND
Naxos (p384)

**BEST SEAFOOD
TAVERN**
Armeni (p421)

BEST CAVE HOTEL
Iconic Santorini
(p414)

BEST ART & WINE
Art Space (p423)

WHEN TO GO
Apr–Jun Catch
early-season sun
without overheating,
and boats without
overcrowding.

Jul & Aug Pros: sun,
sea, sand, balmy
nights and lively
company. Cons: peak
crowds and prices.

Sep & Oct Quieter
beaches, warm seas,
the sweet scent of
herbs and walks on
island hills.

Oia (p420)
BABATE DORIN/SHUTTERSTOCK

Cyclades

Rugged, sun-drenched outcrops of rock, anchored in azure seas and liberally peppered with snow-white villages and blue-domed churches, the Cyclades (Κυκλάδες) is Greece straight from central casting, with stellar archaeological sites and dozens of postcard-worthy beaches. Throw in a blossoming food scene, some renowned party destinations and a good dose of sophistication, and you have the best of Greece's ample charms.

The biggest surprise may be the variety found within this island group. Chase hedonism on Mykonos or Ios, history on Delos, hiking trails on Andros or Amorgos. Try Santorini for a romantic break. Or escape reality on Donousa or Anafi. You can ferry-hop to your heart's content, enjoy lazy lunches at waterside tavernas, or simply lay claim to a sunbed by a spectacular beach. You're living the dream.

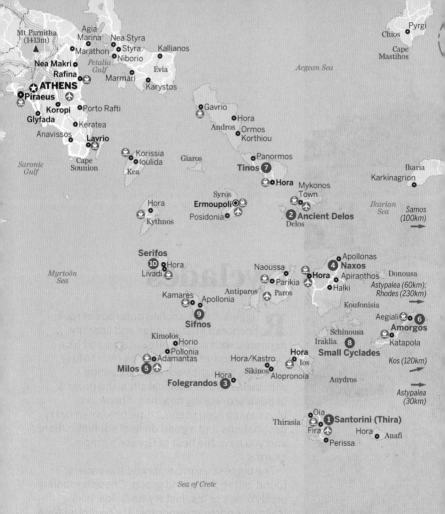

Cyclades Highlights

❶ Santorini (Thira)
(p410) Being mesmerised by dramatic volcanic cliffs.

❷ Ancient Delos (p374)
Immersing yourself in this spellbinding archaeological site.

❸ Folegandros (p430)
Wandering the leafy streets of atmospheric Hora.

❹ Naxos (p384) Exploring traditional villages before

relaxing on white-sand, beaches.

❺ Milos (p435) Sunning yourself on stone cliffs or lazing in sandy coves.

❻ Amorgos (p400) Marvelling at a monastery that clings to a cliffside, and hiking rugged trails.

❼ Tinos (p354) Exploring marble villages and dovecote valleys.

❽ Small Cyclades (p394)
Discovering the unique character and hidden beaches of four tiny islands.

❾ Sifnos (p441) Admiring the juxtaposition of natural beauty with classic Cycladic architecture.

❿ Serifos (p445) Seeking out remote beaches, then gazing over the landscape from the heights of the ancient capital.

History

The Cyclades are said to have been inhabited since at least 7000 BCE. Around 3000 BCE there emerged a cohesive Cycladic civilisation that was bound together by seagoing commerce and exchange. During the Early Cycladic period (3000–2000 BCE), the tiny but distinctive Cycladic marble figurines, mainly stylised representations of the naked female form, were sculpted. Recent discoveries on Keros, an uninhabited island near Koufonisia in the Small Cyclades, indicate that the island was a possible pilgrimage site where figurines that had been broken up in rituals were deposited.

In the Middle Cycladic period (2000–1500 BCE), many of the islands were occupied by the Minoans, who probably branched out from Crete. At Akrotiri, on Santorini, a Minoan town has been excavated, and artefacts from the site have all the distinctive beauty of those from Crete's Minoan palaces. At the beginning of the Late Cycladic period (1500–1100 BCE), the archipelago came under the influence of the Mycenaeans of the Peloponnese, who were supplanted by northern Dorians in the 8th century BCE.

By the mid-5th century BCE the Cyclades were part of a fully fledged Athenian empire. In the Hellenistic era (323–146 BCE), they were governed by Egypt's Ptolemaic dynasties, and later by the Macedonians. In 146 BCE the islands became a Roman province, and lucrative trade links were established with many parts of the Mediterranean.

The division of the Roman Empire in 395 CE resulted in the Cyclades being ruled from Byzantium (Constantinople), but after the fall of Byzantium in 1204, they came under a Venetian authority that doled out the islands to opportunistic aristocrats. The most powerful of these was Marco Sanudo (the self-styled Venetian Duke of Naxos), who acquired a dozen of the larger islands – including Naxos, Paros, Ios, Sifnos, Milos, Amorgos and Folegandros – introducing a Venetian gloss that survives to this day in island architecture.

The Cyclades came under Turkish rule in 1537, although the empire had difficulty in managing, let alone protecting, such scattered dependencies. Cycladic coastal settlements suffered frequent pirate raids, a scourge that led to many villages being relocated to hidden inland sites. They survive as the 'Horas' (capitals, also often written as 'Chora') that are such an attractive feature of the islands today. Ottoman neglect, piracy and shortages of food and water often led to wholesale depopulation of more remote islands, and in 1563 only five islands were still inhabited.

The Cyclades played a minimal part in the Greek War of Independence, but became havens for people fleeing from other islands where insurrections against the Turks had led to massacres and persecution. Italian forces occupied the Cyclades during WWII. After the war, the islands emerged more economically deprived than ever. Many islanders lived in deep poverty, while many more gave up the struggle and headed to the mainland, or to America and Australia, in search of work.

The tourism boom that began in the 1970s revived the fortunes of the Cyclades. The challenge remains, however, of finding alternative and sustainable economies that will not mar the beauty and appeal of these remarkable islands.

ⓘ Information

Terrain (http://terrainmaps.gr) maps are an invaluable resource for travellers wishing to get off the beaten track in the Cyclades and do some exploring on foot or on wheels. History, myths, sights, geography and walking trails are covered, and the maps are regularly updated. Available in most bookshops and souvenir stores.

ⓘ Getting There & Away

AIR

Of the 24 Cyclades islands, six have airports – Mykonos, Syros, Paros, Naxos, Santorini and Milos – all with daily links to Athens. Some have direct links with European cities in summer (charter flights, plus scheduled services to Mykonos and Santorini). There are rarely direct links between islands, so to fly from Mykonos to Santorini, you'll almost certainly need to go via Athens.

BOAT

The key to sculpting an itinerary through the islands is knowing which ferries go where – and when they're going. The peak ferry services run in July and August, but in winter services are reduced or nonexistent on some routes.

A host of companies offer connections throughout the Cyclades. They depart from the main ports of Attica: Piraeus (the largest port, with services to most islands), Rafina (particularly good for Mykonos, Andros and Tinos) and Lavrio (for Kythnos and Kea).

Three extremely useful websites are:

ferries.gr (http://ferries.gr) For checking dates and times, and buying tickets online.

Ferries in Greece (www.ferriesingreece.com/live-boat-traffic.htm) See ferry locations in real time and check if they are running on time.

Vessel Finder (www.vesselfinder.com) If you know your ferry's name, check here to see where exactly it is at any given time.

ANDROS ΑΝΔΡΟΣ

POP 9220

The second-largest island of the Cyclades, Andros has a long and proud seafaring tradition and, conversely, is a walker's paradise. Its wild mountains are cleaved by fecund valleys with bubbling streams and ancient stone mills. A lush island, springs tend to be a feature of each village, and waterfalls cascade down hillsides most of the year. It's worth renting a car to get out to the footpaths, many of them stepped and cobbled, which will lead you through majestic landscapes and among wildflowers and archaeological remnants. The handsome main town of Hora, also known as Andros, is a wealthy shipowners' enclave packed with neoclassical mansions.

ⓘ Getting There & Away

Gavrio is the island's ferry port. Up to four boats a day head to Andros from the mainland port of Rafina (€19 to €25, two hours), continuing south to Tinos (€13 to €16, 1½ hours) and Mykonos (€15 to €35, 2¼ hours). In the high season there are also direct boats to Naxos (€38, 3¼ hours, daily) and Paros (€35, 2½ to four hours, two daily). See www.ferries.gr for details.

ⓘ Getting Around

➡ **KTEL Andros** (☑ 22820 22316; www.ktelandrou.webnode.gr) has at least four buses a day linking Gavrio and Hora (€4, 55 minutes) via Batsi (€2, 15 minutes), continuing south between Gavrio and Korthi (€5, 1¼ hours) and at least two on weekdays between Hora and Korthi (€4, 40 minutes). Schedules are posted at the bus stops in Gavrio and Hora; services are much more frequent in the high season.

➡ **Taxis** (☑ Batsi 22820 41081, Gavrio 22820 71561, Hora 22820 22171) from Gavrio to Batsi cost about €12, and to Hora €40.

➡ Roads can be rough and narrow, but many walking paths and sights are only accessible by car. **Escape in Andros** (☑ 22820 29120; www.escapeinandros.gr) can arrange to meet you at the port with a rental car. Scooters and quad bikes can be hired from **Dino's Rent-a-Bike** (☑ 22820 41003; www.rent-bike-andros.gr; per day from €16; ☺ 9am-9pm) in Batsi.

Gavrio Γαύριο

POP 810

Gavrio is the main ferry port of Andros and often resembles an oversized car park, especially when a boat is due. The waterfront is lined with services (ATMs, ticket agencies, car and scooter hire), but it's not the most interesting or attractive part of the island in which to base yourself.

🛏 Sleeping & Eating

Standard tavernas and lacklustre cafes line Gavrio's waterfront.

Andros Camping CAMPGROUND €
(☑ 22820 71444; www.campingandros.gr; camp site per adult/tent/car €7.50/4/2; ☺ May-Sep; ☞ ⛺) This small and rustic site is set among olive trees about 400m behind the harbour. There's a decent toilet block, and the attractive pool area is a major bonus. Follow the signs from the road to Batsi, turning at the Escape in Andros agency.

Perrakis HOTEL €€
(☑ 22820 71456; www.hotelperrakis.com; Kipri; s/d from €68/76; ⊞ ☞ ⛱) Across the road from the blissful sweep of Kipri Beach, about 3km south of Gavrio, this large resort-style hotel offers super views and swell rooms, some with big balconies. A dive centre is based here, and there's a restaurant and selection of bars.

★ **O Kossis** GRILL €
(Map p351; ☑ 6972002975; mains €7.50-12; ☺ 2-11pm daily Jun-Sep, Fri-Sun Oct-May; ☞) Renowned throughout Andros as the island's best 'meatery', O Kossis is located in the middle of nowhere, in the hills above Gavrio, signposted beyond Epano Fellos. Attached to a farm and festooned with vines, this family-run taverna's speciality is melt-in-your-mouth lamb chops, though diners swear by its other meaty delights as well.

ⓘ Information

Kyklades Travel (☑ 22820 72363) and **Batis Travel** (☑ 22820 71489) sell ferry tickets and can arrange accommodation.

ⓘ Getting There & Away

In low season, buses from Hora and Batsi are timed to meet the ferries. By May there are four daily, climbing to up to nine in high season. There are also buses to Korthi (two to three daily, one hour).

Batsi Μπατσί

POP 1010

The island's main resort town lies 6km southeast of Gavrio, gathered around a handsome bay with a golden-sand beach. Despite its modest size, there's a vibrant stretch of restaurants, cafes and bars that starts to rev up

Andros

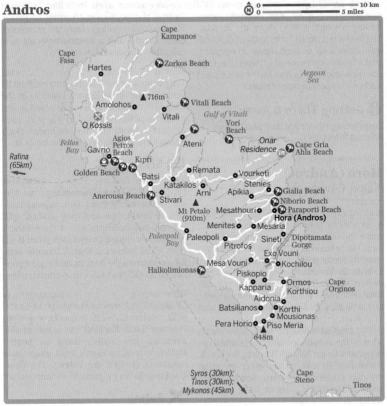

from May. If you tire of the main beach, there are further small bays a short walk south of the town, including sandy Anerousa.

Sleeping

Cavo D'Oro
GUESTHOUSE €

(☑22820 41776; www.andros-cavodoro.gr; d €50; [P][❄][📶]) Tucked above a popular waterfront restaurant, these four simple, pleasant, en suite rooms are excellent value. Each has a balcony with views over the beach, which lies directly across the road.

★ Paradise Design Apartments
BOUTIQUE HOTEL €€

(☑22820 41328; www.paradisedesignapartments. gr; r/ste from €75/131; [❄][📶]) Tastefully decorated rooms and suites gaze out to sea from this elegant little block, above a grocery shop and cafe at the southern end of the waterfront strip. Comfy beds, multinozzle showers, smart TVs and balconies all come as standard.

Krinos Suites Hotel
BOUTIQUE HOTEL €€€

(☑22820 42038; www.krinoshotel.com; s/d from €140/200; ◷Jun-Sep; [❄][📶]) One of Andros' most luxurious options, this former silk-weaving school on the slopes above the waterfront has nine well-kitted-out suites; some have sea-view balconies.

Eating

Oti Kalo
SEAFOOD €€

(☑6939844603; www.facebook.com/OtiKalo Andros; mains €9.50-16; ◷noon-midnight; [📶]) There's no better place to watch the sunset than the covered terrace of this relaxed restaurant, just up from the harbour. There are a couple of token meaty mains, but the focus is mainly on seafood: grilled sea bass, octopus carpaccio, stuffed and grilled squid, seafood risotto, prawn linguine and the like.

Stamatis Taverna
TAVERNA €€

(☑22820 41283; www.facebook.com/stamatis tavern; mains €7-18; ◷noon-11pm; [📶]) Founded in 1965, Batsi's longest-standing eatery is a charming time warp, with colourful tables spilling out onto a lane above the harbour. The food is renowned for its authenticity, with specialities such as lamb shank on eggplant, goat *kleftiko* (slow-cooked in paper), beef *sofrito* (slow-cooked in a white-wine sauce), and Andros *chilopita* (a type of pasta).

❶ Getting There & Away

Buses between Gavrio and Hora pass through Batsi (up to nine daily).

Hora (Andros)
Χώρα (Ανδρος)

POP 1430

Andros' classy capital perches dramatically on a rocky peninsula and has surprising views through the neoclassical mansions to large sandy bays on either side. The old town owes its pretty pastel mansions and squares to both its Venetian heritage and the shipowners who came to inhabit it. Hora's cultural pedigree is burnished by an impressive archaeological museum and art gallery, and several important churches.

The rarefied ambience is let down somewhat by the abandoned hotel and shabby development lining Niborio Beach to the north. You're best to turn in the other direction towards gorgeous Paraporti Beach, where green hills provide a much more pleasant backdrop.

◉ Sights

★ Andros
Archaeological Museum   MUSEUM
(☑ 22820 23664; Plateia Kaïri; adult/child €4/free; ⊙ 8.30am-4pm Wed-Mon) The unquestioned highlight of this excellent little museum is an exquisite 2nd-century BCE marble copy of the bronze *Hermes of Andros* by Praxiteles, the handsome life-sized god standing naked but for a robe draped nonchalantly over one shoulder. A Roman-period marble Artemis manages to be extraordinarily dynamic in her shimmering dress despite being headless and nearly limbless.

Museum of Contemporary Art   GALLERY
(☑ 22820 22444; www.moca-andros.gr; Vasili & Elizas Goulandri; Jul-Sep €5, Oct-Jun €3; ⊙ 11am-3pm & 6-9pm Wed-Sun, 11am-3pm Mon Jul-Sep, 10am-2pm Wed-Mon Apr-Jun & Oct, 10am-2pm Sat-Mon Nov-Mar) Split across two buildings, MOCA has earned a reputation in the international art world for its outstanding summer exhibitions

of world-famous artists, including the likes of Picasso, Matisse, Toulouse-Lautrec and Miró. The sculpture gallery features prominent Greek artists, and a summertime sea-view cafe offers homemade sweets.

Venetian Fortress   RUINS
The picturesque ruins of this fortress, built by Venice's doge (duke) Enrico Dandolo in the early 13th century, stand on an island linked to the tip of the headland by the worn remnants of a steeply arched stone bridge. Don't attempt to scramble over like the locals do.

⨼ Sleeping

Anemomiloi Andros   APARTMENT €€
(☑ 22820 29067; www.anemomiloi.gr; apt from €86; ⊙ Mar-Nov; ❉ ⏾ ⛱) This popular complex of bright, spic-and-span studios, split between two buildings, sits at the southern end of town enjoying views over green fields from all its balconies. There's friendly, helpful service from the owners, and a quiet poolside patio. Off-peak rates drop considerably.

Micra Anglia   BOUTIQUE HOTEL €€
(☑ 22820 22207; www.micra-anglia.gr; MI Goulandri 13; r/ste from €129/286; ⊙ Apr-Oct; ℗ ❉ ⏾ ⛱) Five-star 'Little England' has a raft of chic amenities and stylish decor in neutral shades, as well as Hora's most imaginative restaurant (Dolly's, see below). The clear-sided plunge pool is particularly impressive.

✕ Eating

Ta Skalakia   TAVERNA €
(☑ 22820 22822; 28 Oktovrio 1940; mains €8-9; ⊙ 6-11pm; ⏾) Tables spill down the eponymous stairs from this charming bric-a-brac strewn taverna run by a mother-and-daughter team on a fairy-lit lane. There's a short, tasty menu offering the likes of Greek salad, tzatziki, oregano-flavoured pork, meatballs and fennel pie.

Endochora   MEDITERRANEAN €€
(☑ 22820 23207; www.endochora.com; G Empirikou; mains €9-18; ⊙ 6pm-1am Mon-Thu, 1pm-1am Fri-Sun May-Oct, 1pm-1am Fri-Sun Nov, Dec, Mar & Apr; ⏾) Endochora is a stylish hotspot on the main drag, offering a fresh twist on Greek and Italian classics and a great vantage point for people-watching. Salads showcase prime local produce like capers, tomatoes, figs and cheeses. The pearl barley with mushrooms is a vegetarian showstopper.

Dolly's Bar & Restaurant   MEDITERRANEAN €€
(☑ 22820 22207; www.micra-anglia.gr; MI Goulandri 13; mains €13-20; ⊙ 7-11pm; ❉ ⏾) Poolside,

at the rear of the Micra Anglia hotel, Dolly's manages to be both stylish and relaxed, delivering a menu rich in Cycladic, mainland Greek and Italian influences. Go for the impeccably grilled steak or, for something a little different, try the lamb, vegetable and cheese pie. It's open at lunchtime but only for snacks.

ⓘ Information

Ploes Travel (☑ 22820 29220; G Empirikou) Sells ferry tickets and arranges guided hikes and vehicle rental.

ⓘ Getting There & Away

Buses run to Gavrio via Batsi (at least four daily) and Korthi (at least two on weekdays). Timetables are posted at the bus station, up from Plateia Goulandri.

Around Andros

It's well worth renting a car or scooter to explore Andros' panorama-filled mountain roads and picturesque villages. The north of the island, with the lush watershed around **Arni**, gives way to raw, windswept hills as the road zigzags to **Vourkoti** and **Agios Nikolaou** with its sweeping views.

The island is cleaved by a sweeping agricultural valley, and loads of small villages with springs, often marked by marble lions' heads and the like, surround Hora. The road winds through **Apikia**, **Stenies**, **Mesathouri**, **Strapouries** and **Menites** – all fun to explore.

In the south, visit quaint agricultural villages like **Livadia**, **Kochilou**, **Piskopio** and **Aidonia**, which has ruined tower houses. The area's charming landscape of fields and cypresses encircle **Ormos Korthiou**, a relaxed beach town with a picturesque church.

◉ Sights & Activities

Beaches

There are some excellent large and easily accessible beaches on the main road between Gavrio and Batsi, including built-up **Agios Petros** (St Peter's), tucked away but popular **Golden Beach** (Hrisi Ammos) and long, sandy **Kipri**.

Attractive **Halkolimionas** – with grey sand and a tiny church – sits 2km down a stone-terraced valley near the junction for Hora. A small beach bar sets up here in summer. Near Hora, check out the clear waters of pebbly but gorgeous **Gialia**.

Many of the best beaches, such as **Ahla**, **Vori** and **Vitali** (all in the northeast), are only reached by 4WD, ATV or boat. Boat trips can usually be arranged (or boats hired) from Batsi and from Hora's Niborio beach.

Walking

There are 19 wonderful waymarked trails criss-crossing Andros, marking walks that range in duration from 30 minutes to six hours, labelled in difficulty level from easy to average. Wear hiking boots and trekking pants, as there are some (shy) snakes.

The best investment you can make is the *Andros Hiking Map* (€6) published by the marvellous Andros Routes (www. androsroutes.gr) project, in conjunction with the Anavasi mapping company. It's available at bookshops and gift shops on the island. The Andros Routes website outlines the paths they maintain and has good advice for hiking on the island.

Locals recommend the areas north of Hora for great walks, including the villages of Stenies and Apikia. For a lovely short walk, **Pithara** is a shady glade of streams accessed from Apikia. For a longer ramble, hike up the dramatic **Dipotamata Gorge**, signposted as you drive inland, after Sineti (southeast of Hora). The trail is cobbled part of the way and leads past ancient bridges and water mills and through vivid foliage, with water burbling below.

Better yet, book a guided walk with **Trekking Andros** (☑ 22820 61368; www. trekkingandros.gr; guided walk from €25), a company that arranges and guides a menu of activities on the island, including hiking, mountain biking, boat trips, diving, rock climbing and more.

🛏 Sleeping & Eating

Onar Residence   COTTAGE €€€
(Map p351; ☑ 21180 02912; www.onar-andros.gr; Ahla Beach; house from €260; ☉ May-Oct; ❋ 🐾) 🐾 These ecofriendly, unique and luxurious secluded cottages are hidden within wetlands behind the gorgeous remote beach at Ahla. It's really in the middle of nowhere, so the organic onsite restaurant is a lifesaver. Details on how to reach the resort are on the website (access road is 4WD only; transfers can be arranged).

Sea Satin Nino   MEDITERRANEAN €€
(☑ 22820 61196; www.facebook.com/Sea.Satin. Nino.Andros; Ormos Korthiou; mains €7-16; ☉ 9am-late; 🐾) On a tiny leafy square, this hip cafe-cum-bistro uses local ingredients to great effect. Homemade pasta, fish dishes and a

smattering of beautifully done *mezedhes* (snacks) grace the short but sweet menu. Excellent coffee and French toast with bacon make it the island's best breakfast choice, too.

Gialia
GREEK €€

(☑ 22820 24452; mains €8-15; ⊗ noon-10pm Apr-Oct; ☎) A few kilometres from Hora is the delightful crystal-clear blue of Gialia Beach, where this excellent restaurant serves snacks and Greek classics to hungry beachgoers or island explorers. Try the delicious Andros salad topped with local *kopanisti* cheese.

TINOS
ΤΗΝΟΣ

POP 8640

Tinos is one of those sleeper hit islands. It's known widely for its Greek Orthodox pilgrimage site: the Church of the Annunciation, in the port and main town, Hora.

But as soon as you leave the throngs in town, Tinos is a wonderland of natural beauty, dotted with more than 40 marble-ornamented villages found in hidden bays, on terraced hillsides and atop misty mountains. Also scattered across the brindled countryside are countless ornate dovecotes, a legacy of the Venetians.

There's a strong artistic tradition on Tinos, especially for marble sculpting, as in the sculptors' village of Pyrgos in the north, near the marble quarries. The food, made from local produce (cheeses, sausage, tomatoes and wild artichokes), is some of the best you'll find in Greece.

❶ Getting There & Away

Year-round ferries serve the mainland ports of Rafina (€27 to €36, two to four hours, up to eight daily) and Piraeus (€52, 5¾ hours, daily) and the islands of Syros (€4.50 to €8.50, 50 minutes, up to two daily), Andros (€13 to €16, 1½ hours, up to four daily) and Mykonos (€8 to €15, 30 minutes, up to nine daily). Summer high-speed services include Tinos on their passage south from Rafina to major islands such as Paros, Naxos, Ios and Santorini; see www.ferries.gr for details.

Hora has two ferry departure quays. The New (or Outer) Port is located 300m to the north of the main harbour and serves conventional and larger fast ferries. The Old (or Inner) Port, at the northern end of the town's main harbour, serves smaller fast ferries. Check which quay your ferry is leaving from.

❶ Getting Around

Between May and September, **KTEL Tinos** (☑ 22830 22440; www.kteltinou.gr) has at least two buses a day from Hora to nearby Kionia (€1.80, 10 minutes), and northwest to Panormos (€4.50, one hour) via Kampos (€1.80, 15 minutes) and Pyrgos (€3.60, 50 minutes). Services are much more frequent in July and August. The Hora bus station is on the harbour near the port. Buy tickets on board.

The best way to explore the island is with your own wheels; you can see a lot with a one-day rental. **Vidalis Rent a Car & Bike** (☑ 22830 23400; www.vidalis-rentacar.gr; Leoforos Stavrou Kionion) has four outlets in Hora.

Alternatively, phone for a **taxi** (☑ 22830 22470).

Hora (Tinos) Χώρα (Τήνος)

POP 4760

Hora (also known as Tinos) is the island's modest capital. For the nondevout, its most appealing aspect is the little warren of narrow lanes, peppered with bars and cafes, set back from the waterfront. However, the town's biggest drawcard by far is the Church of the Annunciation, one of the most important Orthodox pilgrimage sites in Greece.

Two main streets lead up to the church. Evangelistria is lined with shops and stalls crammed with souvenirs and religious wares, while Leoforos Megalocharis has a carpeted strip down the side, used by pilgrims crawling towards the church and pushing long candles before them. Religion certainly takes centre stage here; woe betide the unwitting tourist looking for a room on one of the main feast days.

◉ Sights

Church of the Annunciation
CHURCH

(Panagia Evangelistria; ☑ 22830 22256; www.panagiatinou.gr; Leoforos Megalocharis; ⊗ 8am-8pm) **FREE** Tinos' religious focus is this large church and icon of Our Lady of Tinos. It was uncovered in 1823 in the ruins of a chapel beneath the current church, after a nun, now St Pelagia, received visions from the Virgin instructing her where to find it. From the start, the icon was said to have healing powers but the timing of its discovery also inextricably linked it with the rebirth of the Greek nation, thus encouraging mass pilgrimage.

As you enter the church, the icon is to the left of the aisle, the image almost completely obscured by jewels. Hundreds of silver lamps hang from the ceiling, each dangling a votive offering: a ship, a cradle, a heart, a pair of lungs, a chainsaw.

The frilly Renaissance-style church, built in 1830 of marble from the island's Panormos

Tinos

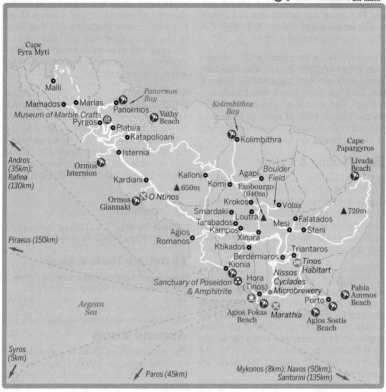

N 0 ▬▬▬▬ 5 km
  0 ▬▬▬▬ 2.5 miles

Cape
Fyra Myti

Malli

Mamados● ●Marlas
Museum of Marble Crafts
Pyrgos●

Panormos
Bay
Panormos●
        ●Vathy
        Beach
●Plateia
●Katapolioani

●Isternia

Andros
(35km);
Rafina
(130km)

Ormos
Isternion
Kardiani●
Ormos
Giannaki

Kolimbithra
Bay

Kolimbithra●

Cape
Papargyros

Kalloni●   Agapi
              ●
          Komi●
▲650m   Exobourgo
O Ntinos   (640m)
          Krokos●
Smardaki●
Tarabados● Loutra
Agios   Kampos● ▲
Romanos●   Xinara
Ktikados●
Berdemiaros●
Kionia●
Hora
Sanctuary of Poseidon (Tinos)
& Amphitrite

Boulder
Field

●Volax

▲729m

●Falatados
Mesi
●Steni

Triantaros

Tinos
Habitart
Nissos
Cyclades
Microbrewery

Pahia
Ammos
Beach

Livada
Beach

Porto●

Agios Fokas *Marathia*
Beach
Agios Sostis
Beach

Aegean
Sea

Piraeus (150km)

Syros
(5km)

Paros (45km)

Mykonos (8km); Naxos (50km);
Santorini (135km)

quarries, lies within a pleasant courtyard flanked by cool arcades. A disconcerting amount of graffiti is etched into the marble balustrades, some of it dating back well over 100 years. Beneath the church is a baptistery comprising three interconnected vaulted chapels, marking the site where the famous icon was discovered.

The complex has sweeping views all around and museums (with variable hours and poor signage) that house collections of religious artefacts, icons and secular art.

Respectful attire must be worn.

Cultural Foundation of Tinos   GALLERY
(☑ 22830 29070; www.itip.gr; Akti G. Drosou; adult/child €3/free; ◷ 9am-3pm Mon-Fri) This excellent cultural centre in a handsome neoclassical building on the waterfront houses a superb permanent collection of the work of famous Tinian sculptor Yannoulis Chalepas (1851–1938). A second gallery has rotating exhibitions. Musical events are staged here in summer.

**Sanctuary of Poseidon
& Amphitrite**   ARCHAEOLOGICAL SITE
(Map p355; ☑ 22830 22670; Kionia; €2; ◷ 8.30am-3pm Wed-Mon) From the 4th century BCE to the 3rd century CE, the area adjacent to the beach at Kionia (3km northwest of central Hora) was a major religious sanctuary devoted to sea god Poseidon and his wife Amphitrite. Now all that remains are the excavated foundations of temples, altars, fountains and baths. You can see a lot from the road but to make sense of it you really need the pamphlet that comes with admission.

Also helpful is the scale model at the **Tinos Archaeological Museum** (☑ 22830 29063; Leoforos Megalocharis; adult/child €2/free; ◷ 8.30am-3.30pm Wed-Mon).

☞ Tours

Poseidon Travel   BUS
(☑ 22830 22440; www.poseidontravel-tinos.com; Leoforos Stavrou Kionion; full-day tour €12; ◷ Jun-Aug) In summer, ask at the bus station about

the daily tour that takes in St Pelagia's Convent and the villages of Volax, Loutra, Pyrgos, Panormos and Tarambados. It's a great way to see the sights in a day. Tours depart at 11am, returning around 5.30pm.

Nissos Cyclades Microbrewery BREWERY
(Map p355; ☎ 22830 26333; www.nissos.beer; Tinou-Agiou Ioanni Porto, Vagia; tour €6; ⏱5pm & 6pm Tue & Thu, 10am, 11am & noon Sat mid-Jun–mid-Sep) Join a tour of this microbrewery on the eastern edge of town to familiarise yourself with the mysteries of brewing and to sample four Nissos beers.

🛏 Sleeping & Eating

Nikoleta Rooms GUESTHOUSE €
(☎ 22830 25863; www.nikoletarooms.gr; Kapodistriou 11; r/apt from €45/60; ⏱Mar-Nov; ❇ 🅿 🛜) Little Nikoleta is one of Hora's best-value options, tucked away in a side street down the southern end of town. There's a lovely garden, and some rooms have kitchens.

Voreades GUESTHOUSE €€
(☎ 22830 23845; www.voreades.gr; Nikolaou Foskolou 7; s/d/apt from €63/78/123; ❇ 🛜) Just up from the port, this friendly place offers plenty of local character both in terms of the building and the personalities of the Greek mother-and-son team who run it (he speaks good English, she speaks French). While the decor's a little old-fashioned, the rooms are comfortable and spotless.

Studios Eleni II APARTMENT €€
(☎ 22830 24352; www.studio-eleni.gr; Ioannou Plati 7; d/tr €90/120; ❇ 🛜) A stone's throw from the main church, this beautiful complex has whitewashed walls, pale linen and a supremely photogenic Cycladic courtyard. Eleni also runs Studios Eleni I, which is of an equally high standard, close to Agios Fokas Beach. Port transfer is offered.

Marathia GREEK €€
(Map p355; ☎ 22830 23249; www.marathiatinos.gr; Iroon Polytechneiou, Agios Fokas; mains €10-25; ⏱8.30am-midnight; 🛜 🅿) Slow-cooked octopus with giant beans; a glass of crisp white; waves lapping at the beach – pretty flawless, as far as combinations go. Superfresh ingredients, family recipes and a deep appreciation for Tinian cuisine make this stylish contemporary restaurant on Agios Fokas Beach a special place indeed.

Itan Ena Mikro Karavi MEDITERRANEAN €€
(☎ 22830 22818; www.mikrokaravi.gr; Trion Ierarchon; mains €12-19; ⏱noon-11.30pm; 🛜) Named

for the opening line of a well-known children's tale ('There was a little boat...'), this elegant indoor-outdoor eatery serves Greek fare with creative Mediterranean flair. Dishes like slow-cooked veal and rabbit ravioli are made with impeccable locally sourced ingredients, and the internal-courtyard setting and service are first class.

San To Alati TAVERNA €€
(☎ 22830 29266; www.facebook.com/santoalati; Iroon Polytechneiou, Agios Fokas; mains €10-20; ⏱noon-midnight; 🛜) Meaning 'like salt', this cute seaside taverna takes its name from a royal-themed fairy tale (hence the crowns and salt shakers). The place lives up to its Aegean cuisine label, with extensive use of local produce.

ⓘ Information

Malliaris Travel (☎ 22830 24242; www.malliaristravel.gr; ⏱9am-9pm) Sells ferry tickets.

ⓘ Getting There & Away

Buses depart from the harbourside bus station and serve numerous destinations around the island.

Around Tinos

The countryside of Tinos is a glorious mix of broad terraced hillsides, mountaintops crowned with crags, unspoilt villages, fine beaches and fascinating architecture that includes picturesque dovecotes. Rent wheels to see it all.

North of Hora, beautiful Ktikados perches in a hanging valley, with a good taverna and a skyline punctuated by a blue-domed church with an elegant campanile.

Kampos sits atop a scenic hill surrounded by fields and is home to the Costas Tsoclis Museum (☎ 22830 51009; www.tsoclismuseum.gr; Kampos; ⏱10am-6pm Wed-Mon Jun-Sep) FREE, displaying works by the renowned contemporary artist.

Don't miss Tarabados, a maze of small streets roamed by village dogs and decorated with marble sculptures, leading to a breezy valley lined with dovecotes.

About 17km northwest of Hora, lovely Kardiani perches on a steep cliff slope enclosed by greenery. Narrow lanes wind through the village, and the views towards Syros are exhilarating.

The gorgeous church-dotted settlement of Pyrgos is the highlight of Tinos and one of the prettiest of all the Cyclades towns.

Narrow whitewashed lanes wind towards a perfect little square lined with cafes, which looks just like a film set. Marble has been quarried from the encircling hills for millennia and during the late 19th and early 20th centuries, the town was the centre of a remarkable sculpture enclave. A trio of interesting museums celebrates this legacy.

Further north of Pyrgos the main road ends at Panormos, a popular excursion destination for its photogenic fishing harbour lined with fish tavernas.

About 12km north of Hora on the north coast is emerald Kolimbithra, where surfers enjoy two excellent sandy beaches.

A worthwhile detour inland takes you to Agapi, a pretty village set in a lush valley of dovecotes. Ethereal and romantic, it lives up to its name (meaning 'love' in Greek).

Pass eye-catching Krokos, with its enormous Catholic monastery and school, to reach Volax, about 6km directly north of Hora. This hamlet sits at the heart of an amphitheatre of low hills festooned with hundreds of enormous, multicoloured boulders. The ruins of the Venetian fortress of Exobourgo lie 2km south of Volax, on top of a mighty 640m rock outcropping.

The northeast coast beach at Livada is spectacular, but the ones east of Hora, like Porto and Pahia Ammos, can seem comparatively built-up.

🛏 Sleeping & Eating

★Tinos Habitart   COTTAGE €€€
(Map p355; ☑ 22830 41675; www.tinos-habitart. gr; Triantaros; house €180-400; P❄🞇❄) This cleverly designed complex lies in a village 6km northeast of Hora, and gives you a taste of traditional island life. The seven houses incorporate local stone and marble and are fully equipped with kitchen, living spaces and outdoor areas (most with private pool). Our favourite is the dovecote irresistibly transformed into a three-bedroom villa.

★O Ntinos   TAVERNA €€
(Map p355; ☑ 22830 31673; Ormos Giannaki; mains €9-22; ◔12.30-11.30pm Apr-Sep; 🞇) Set on a sunny terrace overlooking Giannaki Bay, this friendly taverna offers superlative home-cooked island specialities, including a particularly good selection of mezedhes; try the mackerel in oil with basil and fennel, or the eggplant with spicy Tinian cheese.

Drosia   TAVERNA €€
(☑ 22830 21807; www.facebook.com/taverna.dros ia.tinos; Ktikados; mains €9-13; ◔noon-3pm & 6-

WORTH A TRIP

MUSEUMS OF PYRGOS

Museum of Marble Crafts (Map p355; ☑ 22830 31290; www.piop.gr; Pyrgos; adult/child €4/2; ◔10am-5pm Wed-Mon) On the slopes above Pyrgos, this modern, well-curated complex creatively explains the quarrying and sculpting techniques that have been used on the island since antiquity. It includes beautifully illustrated displays with English translations, along with top examples of artefacts and architectural features shaped from Tinian marble. The films of some of the last traditional quarrymen plying their trade are fascinating.

Museum House of Yannoulis Chalepas (Pyrgos; adult/child €3/free; ◔11am-6pm Thu-Sun Apr–mid-Oct) This absorbing museum lets you see the troubled sculptor's rooms and workshop as they once were. The ticket includes admission to the neighbouring Museum of Panormos Artists.

10pm Easter-Oct; 🞇) Dine on fish or lamb and take in the magnificent views.

SYROS   ΣΥΡΟΣ

POP 21,500

Endearing little Syros merges traditional and modern Greece. One of the smallest islands of the Cyclades and relatively rural outside the capital, it nevertheless has the highest population since it's the legal and administrative centre of the entire archipelago. It's also the ferry hub of the northern islands and home to Ermoupoli, the grandest of all Cycladic towns, with an unusual history. As the Cyclades' capital, it pays less heed to tourism, and its beaches never get as crowded as those of the neighbouring islands. It buzzes with life year-round, has great eateries and showcases the best of everyday Greek life.

History

The island has been inhabited since at least the Neolithic era, with an early Cycladic fortified settlement and burial ground at Kastri in the island's northeast dating from 2800 to 2300 BCE.

The Venetians seized control of the island from the Byzantines in 1204 and remained until 1522, during which time most of the Greek islanders adopted Catholicism. Even

Syros

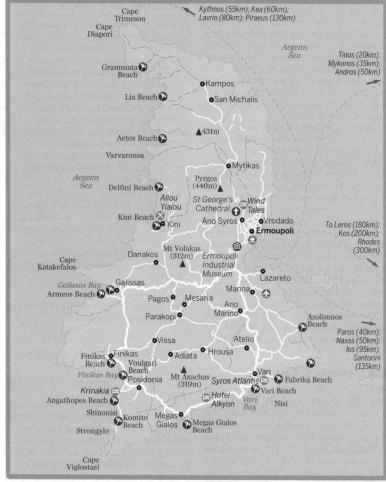

Kythnos (55km); Kea (60km);
Lavrio (80km); Piraeus (130km)

Cape Trimeson

Cape Diapori

Aegean Sea

Tinos (20km);
Mykonos (35km);
Andros (50km)

Grammata Beach

Lia Beach

Kampos

San Michalis

▲431m

Aetos Beach

Varvarousa

Mytikas

Aegean Sea

Delfini Beach

Pyrgos (440m) ▲

Allou Yialou

St George's Cathedral

Wind Tales

Kini Beach

Ano Syros

Vrodado

Ermoupoli

To Leros (180km);
Kos (200km);
Rhodes (300km)

Mt Volakas (312m) ▲

Danakos

Ermoupoli Industrial Museum

Cape Katakefalos

Galissas Bay

Galissas

Armeos Beach

Lazareto

Manna

Pagos

Mesaria

Ano Manno

Parakopi

Azolimnos Beach

Vissa

Atelio

Hrousa

Paros (40km);
Naxos (50km);
Ios (95km);
Santorini (135km)

Finikas Beach

Finikas

Adiata

Voulgari Beach

Finikas Bay

Posidonia

Mt Axachas (319m) ▲

Vari

Syros Atlantis

Fabrika Beach

Vari Beach

Krinakia

Hotel Alkyon

Vari Bay

Nisi

Angathopes Beach

Shinonisi

Komito Beach

Megas Gialos

Megas Gialos Beach

Strongylo

Cape Viglostasi

during the centuries of Ottoman rule that followed, the island maintained a largely Catholic identity.

During the War of Independence, thousands of Orthodox refugees from islands ravaged by the Turks fled to Syros. They brought an infusion of Greek Orthodoxy and a fresh entrepreneurial drive that made Syros the commercial, naval and cultural centre of Greece during the 19th century. Syros' position declined in the 20th century, but you still see shipyards, textile manufacturing, thriving horticulture, a sizeable administrative sector, a university campus and a continuing Catholic population.

ℹ Information

A useful website for general info on the island is www.syrosisland.gr.

ℹ Getting There & Away

AIR

Sky Express (www.skyexpress.gr) flies from Athens (€109, 35 minutes) to **Syros Island National Airport** (JSY; Map p358; ☑ 22810 81900), 5km south of Ermoupoli. There's no public transport but taxis congregate around flight times.

BOAT

As the island group's capital, Syros theoretically has fair to good year-round ferry links with all the Cyclades islands, and to Piraeus on the mainland.

High season services to Ermoupoli include Piraeus (€27 to €33, two to 3¾ hours, three daily), Kythnos (€9, 2¼ hours, three daily), Naxos (€29 to €35, 1¼ hours to 2¾ hours, two daily), Mykonos (€20, 40 minutes, three daily) and Tinos (€4.50 to €8.50, 50 minutes, two daily); see www.ferries.gr for details.

ⓘ Getting Around

BUS

KTEL Syros (☑ 22810 82575; www.ktel-syrou. gr) buses loop from Ermoupoli bus station beside the ferry quay, taking in Galissas, Finikas, Posidonia, Megas Gialos, Vari and Azolimnos. The full loop takes an hour, and buses run in both directions (at least three daily, increasing to hourly in the peak season), with a maximum fare of €1.70.

Three to five buses also go to Kini (€1.60, 20 minutes), some of which join the main island loop.

There are also regular minibuses to Ano Syros (€1.60, 15 minutes) from the waterfront end of El Vanizelou street.

CAR & MOTORCYCLE

You can hire cars and scooters at agencies such as Vassilikos (p361) on the Ermoupoli waterfront. Avoid driving in central Ermoupoli, as there are lots of stairs, pedestrian-only lanes and one-way streets.

TAXI

From the port, taxis charge around €4 to Ano Syros, €12 to Galissas and €12 to Vari.

Ermoupoli Ερμούπολη

POP 11,400

As you sail into striking Ermoupoli (literally Hermes' City, named after the messenger god), its two hilltops emerge, each topped by a dazzling church, with even taller hills rising behind. Buildings spread in a pink and white cascade in between, and the centre is a maze of stepped lanes and shopping streets all radiating out from the grand main square.

Catholic Ano Syros (Upper Syros) was the original hilltop settlement; catch a bus to the top and stroll down through its hive of medieval churches, monasteries and white-washed houses.

During the Greek Revolution, Orthodox refugees from the Turkish-held islands founded the modern town on the flat, spreading up Vrondado, the other hill, and capping it with their own grand church. In the 19th century, Ermoupoli was briefly Greece's principal port. The wealth of its shipowners is evident when wandering through Vaporia, a pleasant neighbourhood of palm-lined squares and elegant mansions.

◉ Sights

Church of the Dormition of the Virgin CHURCH
(Map p360; Proiou; ⊙ hours vary) After being badly bombed during WWII, it's a wonder anything survived in this stately 1820s Orthodox church – which made the discovery, in 1983, of a signed icon painted by El Greco even more extraordinary. The work dates from the 1560s, before the artist left his native Crete to become a leading light of the Spanish Renaissance. It's now proudly displayed in the porch, to the right of the main door.

St George's Cathedral CHURCH
(Map p358; Agios Georgios, Ano Syros; ⊙ 8.30am-9.30pm) Proudly capping the medieval hilltop settlement of Ano Syros, this pretty cathedral is the mother church of the Cyclades' significant Roman Catholic minority. Call in to admire the pastel-hued interior and star-fretted barrel roof.

Plateia Miaouli SQUARE
(Map p360) This great square is perhaps the finest urban space in the Cyclades. Once situated immediately upon the seashore, today it sits well inland and is dominated by the dignified neoclassical town hall (Map p360). Flanked by palm trees and lined along all sides with cafes and bars, the square and accompanying statue are named for Hydriot naval hero Andreas Miaoulis.

Ermoupoli Industrial Museum MUSEUM
(Map p358; ☑ 22810 84762; www.ketepo.gr; Georgiou Papandreou 11; adult/child €2/1.50; ⊙ 10am-3.30pm Sun-Fri, 10am-3.30pm & 6-8pm Sat Apr-Aug, 9am-5pm Mon, Tue, Thu & Fri, 9am-2pm Sun Sep-Mar) This excellent chronicle of Syros' industrial and shipbuilding traditions occupies a restored factory packed with more than 300 well-labelled items relating to sewing, printing, spinning, engines, ships and more. Ask if the neighbouring Aneroussis lead shot factory is open – it's fascinating. The museum is opposite the hospital, on the southwestern edge of town.

Syros Archaeological Museum MUSEUM
(Map p360; ☑ 22810 88487; Benaki; adult/child €2/1; ⊙ 8.30am-4pm Mon-Mon) The town's small archaeological museum is housed in the rear of the town hall (enter from the side). Founded in 1834 and one of the oldest in Greece, it houses a modest collection of ceramic and marble vases, grave *stelae,* a black-granite Egyptian statuette from 730 BCE, and some very fine Cycladic figurines.

Ermoupoli

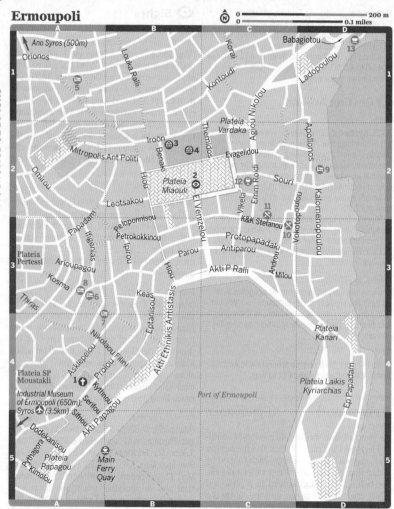

🛏 Sleeping

Most budget options cluster above the ferry quay, while boutique hotels in renovated mansions dot the Vaporia district. Much accommodation is open year-round, with discounts in low season.

Hermoupolis Rooms   GUESTHOUSE €
(Map p360; ☑ 6937135880; www.hermoupolis-rooms.gr; Kosma; r €50; ❉ 🐾) There's a cheerful welcome at these well-kept, self-catering en-suite rooms, a short climb from the waterfront. Front rooms open onto tiny, bougainvillea-cloaked balconies.

Wind Tales   B&B €€
(Map p358; ☑ 6946771400; www.windtales.gr; Agiou Aloisiou 4, Ano Syros; r from €96; ❉ 🐾) If you wish to linger after the madding crowd has gone and wander Ano Syros' labyrinthine lanes at your leisure, then try the Wind Tales' gorgeous, individually designed rooms, one of them carved into natural rock. The service is wonderfully personalised and sipping cocktails on the terrace overlooking Ermoupoli is pure magic.

Lila Guesthouse   B&B €€
(Map p360; ☑ 22810 82738; www.guesthouse.gr; Kosma; r/ste from €90/126; ❉ 🐾) In the former French consulate, these elegantly renovated

Ermoupoli

rooms and suites are kitted out with modern decor and top-notch bathrooms. Suites are spacious, with dining tables and antiques. A bumper breakfast is served by the genial proprietors in the airy common area.

1901 Hermoupolis Maison B&B €€
(Map p360; ✉6959990275; www.1901.gr; Palaion Patron Germanou 37-39; r/ste from €90/229; ❋ 🛜) Occupying a 19th-century house, this delightful place comprises just five rooms with supercomfortable beds, Molton Brown toiletries and quirky objects scattered throughout – antique telephones, an olive press, a Singer sewing machine. Terrific breakfast, too.

Ethrion HOTEL €€
(Map p360; ✉22810 89066; www.ethrion.gr; Kosma 24; apt/r/ste from €66/73/109; ❋ 🛜) The eight rooms, suites and apartments at this family-run hotel are comfortable and well equipped; opt for a sea view if you can. The ground-floor studio is on the dark side but it's priced accordingly and has its own kitchenette.

Ploes BOUTIQUE HOTEL €€€
(Map p360; ✉22810 79360; www.hotelploes.com; Apollonos 2; d/ste from €220/600; ❋Apr-Oct; ❋🛜) Unremitting elegance and attention to detail are hallmarks of this boutique beauty, inside a 19th-century mansion. Soaring ceilings, Venetian chandeliers, original artworks and designer furniture make the seven rooms here shine, and there's a private pavilion giving direct sea access to swimmers.

🍴 Eating & Drinking

Restaurants and cafe-bars throng the waterfront, especially along Akti Petrou Ralli. Another great area for dining is the bougainvillea-garlanded lanes of Emmanouil Roidi and Klonos & Kyparissou Stefanou.

⭐**Kouzina** MEDITERRANEAN €€
(Map p360; ✉22810 89150; www.facebook.com/kouzinasyros; Androu 5; mains €10-28; ❋7-11pm Thu-Tue; 🛜🍴) In a colourfully lit, intimate

dining room and spilling out onto Ermoupoli's main eat street, Kouzina makes use of fresh local ingredients to construct creative Mediterranean cuisine, from slow-cooked osso buco on parmesan risotto to smoked *mousakas*. There's a decent wine list, craft beer and excellent service to boot.

Seminario MEDITERRANEAN €€
(Map p360; ✉22813 01339; www.seminariosyros. wixsite.com/seminariosyros; Klonos & Kyparissou Stefanou 7; mains €8.80-16; ❋noon-midnight Fri-Wed, from 6pm Thu; 🛜🍴) Friendly and fun, this street taverna with a minty interior serves tasty traditional grills and seafood dishes. Vegetarians will find plenty of joy in the likes of the delicious Cycladic fennel pie, and the vegan-friendly baked eggplant topped with *fava* puree and smoked paprika.

Kouchico COCKTAIL BAR
(Map p360; ✉22813 00880; www.facebook.com/kouchico; Ioannou Lavrentiou Ralli 15; ❋7am-3am Mon-Fri, from 9am Sat & Sun; 🛜) A cool spot to sip a coffee by day, Kouchico turns into a buzzy cocktail bar at night, with a hip young crowd spilling out of its doors.

Sta Vaporia CAFE
(Map p360; ✉22810 76486; www.facebook.com/StaBaporia; Athanasíou Krinou 2; ❋10am-3am; 🛜) Down a set of stairs behind St Nicholas' Church, this perfectly positioned all-day cafe/restaurant offers postcard panoramas and a menu of coffee, cocktails, homemade lemonade and snacks, large and small. Down below are popular seaside swimming platforms (so bring your swimsuit).

ℹ Information

Vassilikos (✉22810 84444; www.vassilikos.gr; Akti Papagou 10; ❋9am-9pm) Sells ferry tickets and tours, and rents cars.

ℹ Getting There & Away

The island's **main ferry quay** (Map p360) is right in front of the town.

From the nearby **bus station** (📞 22810 82575), buses loop around Galissas, Finikas, Posidonia, Megas Gialos, Vari and Azolimnos (at least three daily in each direction). There are also buses to Kini (20 minutes, at least three daily). Services are much more frequent (usually hourly) in summer.

Around Syros

Outside Ermoupoli, Syros comprises a series of hills and valleys folding down to small bays and beaches, most well served by buses.

Kini, on the west coast, is a sandy beach in a horseshoe bay with a small strip of bars and tavernas. It's popular with families due to its shallow waters.

Popular with French travellers, Galissas has an appealing beach, a smattering of white-and-blue-trim Cycladic buildings, some good tavernas and a cute little white church on the headland. On the other side of the church is Armeos, a pretty little pebbly nudist beach.

Further south, Finikas sits on a large bay with a marina at one end and a narrow strip of pebbles and sand. It's more built up than most of the others, with a somewhat shabby feel. Further along the bay is Voulgari Beach, near the village of Posidonia. South of the headland is tiny but popular Agathopes Beach, with calm waters and a taverna. Another 10-minute walk south brings you to Komito, a sheltered bay backed by olive groves.

The south-coast town of Megas Gialos has a couple of beaches hard up against the main road. Gorgeous (and sheltered) Vari, further east, is the better bet with its sandy beach, though the waterfront and tavernas get packed with families in high season.

🛏 Sleeping & Eating

Krinakia　　　　　　　　　　APARTMENT €
(Map p358; 📞 22810 42375; www.krinakia.gr; Agathopes Beach, Posidonia; apt from €55; ☉ Apr-Oct; P ❄ 🕸) These eight quiet, spacious, well-equipped apartments occupy a classic blue-trimmed white block overlooking Agathopes Beach. Each sleeps up to four people in two separate bedrooms, making it popular with families.

⭐ Syros Atlantis　　　　　　　HOTEL €€
(Map p358; 📞 22810 61454; www.syrosatlantis.com; Vari; r €110; ☉ Apr-Oct; P ❄ 🕸) Professionally run by a charming pair of brothers, this hotel on a quiet lane near Vari Beach has 15 spacious and spotless rooms, each with a terrace or balcony. Some can be joined together for

family use. Delicious Greek-style breakfasts are served in the garden courtyard, featuring homemade pies, dolmadhes (stuffed vine leaves), jams and sweets.

Hotel Alkyon　　　　　　　　HOTEL €€
(Map p358; 📞 22810 61761; www.alkyonsyros.gr; Megas Gialos; r from €60; ☉ Apr-Oct; P ❄ 🕸 ☎) Set back from the water about 1.5km from Megas Gialos, this peaceful hotel is run by a charming French-Greek couple and has a large pool and spotless rooms. The hosts arrange seminars and activities (usually in French) that include painting and philosophy.

Allou Yialou　　　　　　　　SEAFOOD €€
(Map p358; 📞 22810 71196; www.allouyialousyros.gr; Kini; mains €11-24; ☉ noon-10pm Easter-Sep; 🕸) Tops for eats on Kini Beach, this elegant white-linen waterfront restaurant focuses mainly on seafood (the prawns in ouzo are well worth trying), along with the odd meat dish such as lamb and pork chops. It's a prime spot to watch the sunset.

MYKONOS　　　ΜΥΚΟΝΟΣ

POP 10,100

Mykonos is the great glamour island of Greece and flaunts its sizzling St-Tropez-meets-Ibiza style and party-hard reputation. The high-season mix of hedonistic holiday-makers, cruise-ship crowds, buff gay men and posturing fashionistas throngs Mykonos Town (aka Hora), a gorgeous whitewashed Cycladic maze, delighting in its cubist charms and its chi-chi cafe-bar-boutique scene.

The island is maxed out with cashed-up (or spendthrift) visitors, hip hotels, beach bars and restaurants. There are a few provisos about visiting here. Come only if you are prepared to pay. And are intent on jostling with street crowds. And sitting bum cheek to cheek with oiled-up loungers at the packed main beaches. Oh, and partying relentlessly. Out of season, devoid of gloss and preening celebrities, Hora basically closes, with nothing but the occasional person and pelican wandering the empty streets.

Mykonos is the jumping-off point for the archaeological site of the nearby island of Delos (p373).

ℹ Getting There & Away

AIR

Mykonos Airport (JMK; Map p364; 📞 22890 79000; www.mykonos-airport.com), 3km southeast of Hora, has flights year-round from Athens with Aegean and Olympic Air (who also offer seasonal flights from Thessaloniki). Numerous airlines offer seasonal flights from May to September, including Alitalia, British Airways, easyJet, Qatar Airways and Sky Express.

BOAT

Year-round ferries serve mainland ports Piraeus (€40, five hours, up to three daily) and Rafina (€29 to €48, 2½ to 4½ hours, up to nine daily) – the latter is usually quicker if you are coming directly from Athens airport – and nearby Tinos (€8 to €15, 30 minutes, up to nine daily). In the high season, Mykonos is well connected with all neighbouring islands, including Syros (€20, 40 minutes, three daily), Naxos (€29 to €39, 30 minutes to 1¾ hours, up to 11 daily) and Santorini (€52 to €68, 1¾ to four hours, seven daily); see www.ferries.gr for detailed information. Hora is loaded with ticket agents.

Mykonos has two ferry quays: the Old Port, 400m north of town, where a couple of small fast ferries dock, and the **New Port** (Map p364), 2km north of town, where the bigger fast ferries and all conventional ferries dock. When buying outgoing tickets, double-check which quay your ferry leaves from.

Excursion boats for Delos depart from the quay just off the waterfront at Hora.

① Getting Around

TO/FROM THE AIRPORT

Buses run between Mykonos' airport and Hora's **Fabrika bus station** (Map p366; Fabrika Sq) (€2). Some hotels and guesthouses offer free airport and port transfers. Otherwise, arrange airport transfer with your accommodation (around €10) or take a taxi (around €15).

BOAT

Mykonos Sea Transfer (Map p364; ☑ 22890 23995; www.mykonosseatransfer.com; ☺ 8am-7pm Apr-Oct) An association of sea-taxi operators offering services to the island's best beaches; see the timetables online. The main departure point is Platys Gialos, with drop-offs and pickups at Ornos, Paraga, Paradise, Super Paradise, Agrari and Elia beaches. Cruises and personalised itineraries can also be arranged.
Sea Bus (Map p366; ☑ 6978830355; www. mykonos-seabus.gr; one way €2) This water-taxi service connects the New Port to Hora in eight minutes, running at least hourly from 7.30am to 10.30pm (every 30 minutes from 10.30am to 6.30pm).

BUS

The **KTEL Mykonos** (☑ 22890 26797; www. mykonosbus.com) bus network has two main terminals in Hora. The **Old Port Bus Station** has services to the northwest and east of the island, including the New Port/Tourlos, Agios Stefanos,

Ano Mera, Elia and Kalafatis. The Fabrika Bus Station has services to the southwest, including Mykonos Airport, Ornos, Agios Ioannis, Platys Gialos, Paraga and Paradise Beach. The shuttle bus to Super Paradise also departs from here.

Low-season services are much reduced, but buses in high season run frequently; the fare is from €1.80 to €2.30, depending on the distance travelled; timetables are on the website. In July and August, some buses run until 2am or later from the beaches.

CAR & MOTORCYCLE

A regular 2WD car will get you most places on the island, but some of the more isolated beaches (notably Mersini and Fokos) are better with a 4WD or ATV.

Avis, Hertz and Sixt are among the rental agencies at the airport, and there are dozens of hire places all over the island, particularly near the ports and bus stations (which is where the large public car parks are found – you can't drive into Hora proper). Local options include **OK Mykonos** (☑ 22890 23761; www.okmykonos.com; Agios Stefanos), **Apollon** (☑ 22890 24136; www. apollonrentacar.com; Periferiaki; ☺ 9am-8pm) and **Anemos** (☑ 22890 24607; www.mykonos rentcar.com; Peri), which has the advantage of a large free car park for customers, just above Hora's pedestrian-only town centre.

TAXI

Taxis (☑ 22890 22400, 22890 23700) queue near the bus stations and ports, but waits can be long in high season. All have meters but beware: they can be fiendishly expensive. Approximate fares from Hora include New Port (€14), airport (€15), Ornos (€12), Platys Gialos (€14), Paradise (€15), Kalafatis (€22) and Elia (€22).

Hora (Mykonos)
Χώρα (Μύκονος)

POP 3780

Hora (also known as Mykonos), the island's well-preserved port and capital, is a warren of narrow lanes and whitewashed buildings overlooked by the town's famous windmills. In the heart of the medieval maze – which was intentionally designed to be confusing so as to baffle raiders – tiny flower-bedecked churches jostle with glossy boutiques, and there's a cascade of bougainvillea around every corner.

This 'Greek-island village by central casting' scenario comes at a price: people. In the high season, multiple cruise ships disgorge slow-moving phalanxes of flag followers, joining the catwalk cast of wannabe Instagram influencers, celebrity spotters and party boys squeezing past the chic stores, cafes and bars.

Mykonos

Tinos (15km);
Syros (30km);
Andros (70km);
Rafina (135km);
Piraeus (175km)

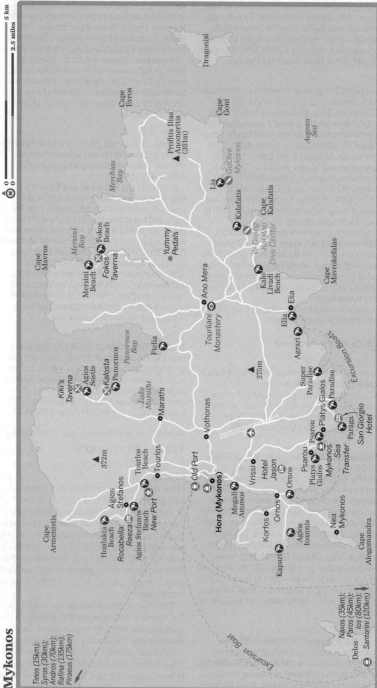

5 km
2.5 miles

Dragonisi

Cape Evros

Cape Goni

Profitis Ilias
Anomeritis
(351m)

GoDive
Mykonos

Lia

Aegean
Sea

Kalafatis

Cape
Kalafatis

Merchias
Bay

Yummy
Pedals

W-Diving
Kalafati
Dive Center

Cape
Mavros

Mersini
Bay

Fokos
Beach

Fokos
Taverna

Mersini Beach

Ano Mera

Kalo
Livadi
Beach

Cape
Mavrokefalas

Tourliani
Monastery

Elia

Elia

Panormos Bay

Kiki's
Taverna

Agios
Sostis

Kalosta

Panormos

Felia

275m

Agrari

Excursion
Boats

Lake
Marathi

Super
Paradise

Paradise

Marathi

Vothonas

Psarou

Platys Gialos

San Giorgio
Hotel

Parága

372m

Tourlos
Beach

Tourlos

Old Port

Vrissi

Hotel
Jason

Psarou
Platys
Gialos

Mykonos
Sea
Transfer

Agios
Stefanos

New Port

Hora (Mykonos)

Ornos

Cape
Armenistis

Houlakia
Beach

Rocabella
Reeza

Agios Stefanos
Beach

Megali
Ammos

Ornos

Korfos

Agios
Ioannis

Nea
Mykonos

Cape
Alogomandra

Kapari

Delos

Naxos (35km);
Paros (45km);
Ios (80km);
Santorini (120km)

Excursion Boat

◉ Sights

Despite its tiny size, without question, you'll get lost in Hora. It's entertaining at first, but can become frustrating amid throngs of equally lost people and fast-moving locals. For quick-fix navigation, head to the water and trace around the periphery of the maze before diving back in – even if there's a more direct route. It's also worth familiarising yourself with Plateia Manto Mavrogenous (Taxi Sq), and the three main streets of Matogianni, Enoplon Dynameon and Mitropoleos, which form a horseshoe through the centre.

Megali Ammos   BEACH
(Map p364) The best beach within easy walking distance of the centre of town, Megali Ammos has a couple of upmarket resorts and an excellent taverna right on the golden sands. It's a 10-minute walk south from the windmills.

Rarity Gallery   GALLERY
(Map p366; ☑22890 25761; www.raritygallery.com; Kalogera 20-22; ⊙10am-11pm) FREE This excellent little gallery is well worth a peek for its temporary exhibitions that showcase contemporary paintings, sculpture and photography.

Windmills   WINDMILL
(Map p366; off Plateia Alefkandra) Constructed in the 16th century by the Venetians for the milling of wheat, seven of Mykonos' iconic windmills are picturesquely situated on a small hill overlooking the harbour.

Archaeological
Museum of Mykonos   MUSEUM
(Map p366; ☑22890 22325; Agiou Stefanou; adult/child €4/2; ⊙9am-4pm Sun, Mon & Wed, to 9pm Thu-Sat Apr-Oct, 9am-4pm Tue-Sun Nov-Mar) A headless, almost limbless 2nd-century BCE statue of Hercules in Parian marble is the highlight of this small, well-presented collection. Otherwise it's very heavy on pottery and funerary *stelae* (carved monuments), much of it sourced from Delos and the neighbouring island of Rineia, which served as its cemetery. Periodic exhibitions incorporate contemporary art and design into the displays.

Panagia Paraportiani   CHURCH
(Map p366; Paraportianis) Built between the 15th and 17th centuries, Mykonos' most famous church comprises four small chapels – plus another on an upper storey reached by an exterior staircase. It's usually locked,

but the fabulously photogenic whitewashed, rock-like exterior is the drawcard.

Aegean Maritime Museum   MUSEUM
(Map p366; ☑22890 22700; www.aegean-maritime-museum.gr; Enoplon Dynameon 10; adult/student €4/2; ⊙10.30am-1pm & 6.30-9pm Apr-Oct) Amid the barnacle-encrusted amphorae, ye olde nautical maps and navigation instruments, there are numerous detailed models of famous sailing ships and paddle steamers. You can also learn the difference between an Athenian trireme, a Byzantine dromon and an ancient Egyptian seagoing ship. There's an enormous Fresnel lighthouse lantern in the courtyard.

🛏 Sleeping

In July and August, a midrange double room with a private bathroom costs anything from €110 (for something fairly average) to €250. The sky's the limit for the top-end category. It's best not to arrive in July or August without a reservation, as there will be few vacancies. Many places insist on a minimum stay during the peak period.

MyCocoon   HOSTEL €
(Map p366; ☑22890 78924; www.hostelmykonos.com; Kaminaki; dm/q €72/320; ⊙May-Sep; ❋⚛🏊) A lot of thought has gone into this stylish hostel including custom-made bunks, which are like Cycladic houses in miniature, allowing dorm dwellers some privacy. The 46-person dorm is tightly packed, though, and it's extremely pricy for a hostel but, hey, this is Mykonos, baby! It's a block from the Old Port.

Portobello Boutique Hotel   BOUTIQUE HOTEL €€
(Map p366; ☑22890 23240; www.portobello-hotel.gr; Agios Georgiou; s/d/ste from €160/220/560; ⊙Easter-Oct; P❋⚛🏊) In an elevated location on the edge of Hora, overlooking a ruined windmill, this welcoming hotel is a prime sunset-viewing spot. The delicious breakfast includes homemade yoghurt, and the obliging staff are more than happy to help you plan your stay.

Mykonos Town Suites   APARTMENT €€
(Map p366; ☑22890 23160; www.mykonostownsuites.com; apt from €240; ⊙Apr-Oct; ❋⚛) This hidden complex of bright, high-beamed studios and whole houses (the largest sleeping six in two bedrooms) makes for a splendid choice. Each has a well-equipped kitchen and sunny outdoor space. There's no staffed reception; directions will be provided when you book.

Hora (Mykonos)

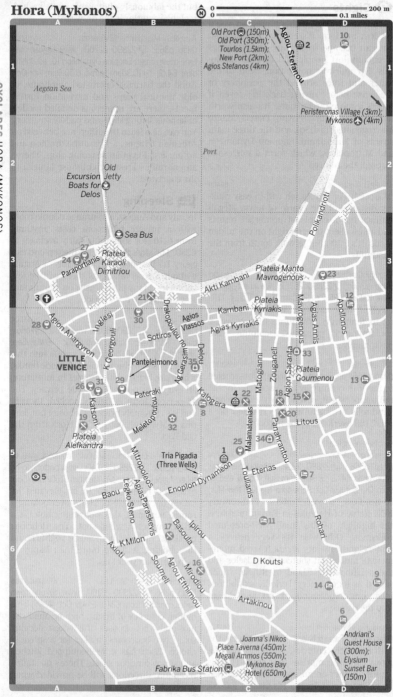

0 ——— 200 m
0 ——— 0.1 miles

Aegean Sea

Old Port (150m);
Old Port (350m);
Tourlos (1.5km);
New Port (2km);
Agios Stefanos (4km)

Agiou Stefanou

Peristeronas Village (3km);
Mykonos ✈ (4km)

Port

Excursion
Boats for
Delos

Old
Jetty

Sea Bus

Plateia
Karaoli
Dimitriou

Paraportianis

Plateia Manto
Mavrogenous

Polikandrioti

Akti Kambani

Agios
Vlassos

Kambani
Agias Kyriakis

Plateia
Kyriakis

Agias Annis

Apollonos

Sotiros

Agion Anargyron

Inglesi

K Georgouli

Drakopoulou

Mavrogenous

LITTLE
VENICE

Panteleimonos

Ag Gerasim

Delou

Matogianni

Zouganeli

Agias Saranta

Plateia
Goumenou

Kalogera

Paraportiani

Paterakì

Meletopoulou

Litous

Panahrantou

Katsoni

Plateia
Alefkandra

Malamatenias

Tria Pigadia
(Three Wells)

Enoplon Dynameon

Toulianis

Eterias

Rohari

Baou

Mitropoleos

Legko Steno

Agias Paraskevis

Ipirou

Basoula

Axioti

K Milon

Soumeli

Agiou Efthimiou

Mirodiou

Artakinou

D Koutsi

Joanna's Nikos
Place Taverna (450m);
Megali Ammos (550m);
Mykonos Bay
Hotel (650m)

Andriani's
Guest House
(300m);
Elysium
Sunset Bar
(150m)

Fabrika Bus Station

Hora (Mykonos)

Hotel Rochari   HOTEL €€
(Map p366; ☑22890 23107; www.rochari.com; Periferiaki; r/ste from €162/510; ⊘Easter-Oct; P⊛🛜⊠) Founded in 1976 by the present managers' parents, this well-established hotel has more than kept up with the times. Quietly stylish, it offers comfortable rooms, excellent breakfast spreads, attentive staff and an irresistible swimming pool. It's on the main peripheral road, just up the hill from the centre, so the free transfers will drop you right to the door.

Pension Joanna   APARTMENT €€
(Map p366; ☑22890 27117; www.pensionjoanna. com; Apollonas 9; apt from €212; ⊛🛜) Veteran traveller Kostas used to run neighbouring Hotel Lefteris, but has moved directly next door and now owns this striking white-and-plum complex of apartments, each sleeping four to six people. The decor is no-frills but comfy, and there's a roof terrace.

Fresh   BOUTIQUE HOTEL €€
(Map p366; ☑22890 24670; www.hotelfresh mykonos.com; Kalogera 31; s/d from €145/150; ⊘Easter-Oct; ⊛🛜) In the heart of town, with a lush and leafy garden and highly regarded on-site restaurant, Kalita, Fresh has compact and stylishly minimalist rooms with a bit of design attitude.

Carbonaki Hotel   BOUTIQUE HOTEL €€
(Map p366; ☑22890 24124; www.carbonaki.gr; Panahrantou 23; s/d from €170/178; ⊘Easter-Oct;

⊛🛜⊠) This family-run hotel is a pleasant garden oasis with bright but comfortable rooms (of various price categories). Some open directly onto the sunny central courtyard, with its Jacuzzi and tiny plunge pool.

Mykonos Bay Hotel   RESORT €€€
(☑22890 23338; www.mykonosbay-hotel.com; Megali Ammos; r/ste from €252/666; ⊘Apr-Oct; P⊛🛜⊠) Sitting right on the Megali Ammos Beach, 10 minutes' walk south of Mykonos Town, this appealing, whitewashed hotel curves around a saltwater pool, with outdoor whirlpool tubs and risqué art in some of the rooms and suites.

Belvedere Hotel   LUXURY HOTEL €€€
(Map p366; ☑22890 25122; www.belvederehotel. com; Periferiaki; r/ste from €585/900; ⊘Easter-Oct; ⊛🛜⊠) Effortlessly chic but extravagantly expensive, the Belvedere offers charming service, a first-class on-site restaurant (taken over in summer by culinary superstar Nobu Matsuhisa) and a magazine-worthy pool area. It's the kind of place where cocktails cost the equivalent of a nice meal and the honeymoon room has its own private plunge pool.

Semeli Hotel   HOTEL €€€
(Map p366; ☑22890 27466; www.semelihotel.gr; Rohari; r/ste from €315/567; ⊘Jan-Nov; ⊛🛜⊠) Expansive grounds, a glamorous restaurant terrace and swimming pool, and dozens of stylish, contemporary rooms combine to

make this one of Mykonos' loveliest top-end hotels. It's open nearly all year, too.

✖ Eating

Mykonos Town has an excellent dining scene, with high-end and 'top-dollar' fusion restaurants sitting alongside tavernas serving Greek standards and souvlaki shops feeding the partygoers.

Gioras Wood Bakery
BAKERY €

(Map p366; ☑ 22890 27784; Agiou Efthimiou; items €1-3; ☺ 7am-3pm) When the wood ovens first fired up in this basement bakery, the Byzantines still ruled Constantinople and Christopher Columbus' father was a toddler. Founded in 1420 and operated by the same family for the last 200 years, it's a great place to stock up on mini spinach pies, baklava and all manner of traditional biscuits. Avoid the coffee, though.

Sakis Grill House
GRILL €

(Map p366; ☑ 22890 24848; www.sakisgrill.com; Kalogera 7; mains €3.80-13; ☺ noon-2am) A welcome alternative to Mykonos' pricey restaurants, Sakis is perpetually crammed with hungry budgeteers tucking into heaped portions of pork or chicken souvlaki, or *gyros* spilling out of pita bread. It's particularly popular with squiffy night owls.

Taste Diaries
CRÊPES €

(Map p366; ☑ 22890 29117; www.facebook.com/ TheTasteDiaries; Akti Kambani; mains €5.80-11; ☺ 8am-3am May, Jun, Sep & Oct, 24hr Jul & Aug; ☎) If you've got a craving for sweet or savoury crêpes, waffles or creamy yoghurt – any time of the day or night in peak season – this is the place to come. It's a satisfying breakfast option, and it serves sandwiches and salads as well.

Joanna's Nikos Place
TAVERNA €€

(☑ 22890 24251; Megali Ammos; mains €9-16; ☺ 10am-11pm; ☎) Run by the delightful Joanna herself and overlooking the beach just a few minutes' walk south of the windmills, this taverna focuses on Greek standards and it does them very well, particularly the zucchini fritters, Mykonian egg and fennel pie, *mousakas* and the mixed grill.

Nice n Easy
CAFE €€

(Map p366; ☑ 22890 25421; www.niceneasy.gr; Plateia Alefkandra; mains €15-23, breakfasts €9-15; ☺ 10am-12.30am; ☎✐) With a great view of Mykonos' windmills from its seafront terrace, this Athenian outpost is Mykonos' best brunch option, serving hangover-assuaging eggs Benedict and healthier options such as avocado on toast, egg-white omelettes, quinoa salad and various vegan offerings. As the day progresses, burgers, sandwiches and quesadillas vie with traditional Greek fare.

Eva's Garden
GREEK €€

(Map p366; ☑ 22890 22160; www.evas-garden.gr; Plateia Goumenou; mains €12-25; ☺ 6.30pm-midnight; ☎) Its patio shaded by hanging grapevines, this tempting corner of Eden focuses on traditional Greek home cooking, such as 'Mama's *soutzoukakia*' (oblong meatballs in a tomato sauce), *spanikopita* (spinach pie), *mousakas* and plenty of grilled fish.

★ Funky Kitchen
EUROPEAN €€€

(Map p366; ☑ 22890 27272; www.funkykitchen. gr; Ignatiou Basoula 40; mains €21-26; ☺ 6pm-late May-Oct; ☎) The open kitchen of this contemporary restaurant brings forth beautifully presented dishes marrying Mediterranean flavours with French techniques. Dishes such as octopus carpaccio with pink peppercorns, or grilled fish in a *buerre blanc* sauce might tempt you back for a repeat visit. The chocolate nirvana is heavenly.

M-Eating
MEDITERRANEAN €€€

(Map p366; ☑ 22890 78550; www.m-eating.gr; Kalogera 10; mains €24-42; ☺ 7pm-1am; ☎) Attentive service, soft lighting and relaxed luxury are the hallmarks of this creative restaurant specialising in fresh produce prepared with flair. Options might include Cycladic fish soup, tuna cakes served on mashed fava beans and sous vide lamb, but save room for the dessert of Mykonian honey pie.

To Maereio
GREEK €€€

(Map p366; ☑ 22890 28825; Kalogera 16; mains €17-30; ☺ 7pm-1am; ☎) With a well-judged menu of Mykonian favourites, this cosy place is popular with locals and foodies in the know. It's heavy on meat – try the meatballs, local ham and spicy sausage. No reservations.

☐ Drinking & Nightlife

Night action in town starts around 11pm and warms up by 1am. From posh cocktail spots to the colourful bars of Hora's Little Venice (where there are also some hip clubs), Hora has the lot. Another prime spot is the Tria Pigadia (Three Wells) area on Enoplon Dynameon.

★ JackieO'
GAY

(Map p366; ☑ 22890 77298; www.jackieomykonos. com; Old Harbour; ☺ sunset-sunrise) The mainstay of Mykonos' gay party scene since Apollo was a lad, this waterside bar is wall-to-wall writhing bodies after 11.30pm, with the wait-staff shimmying around them delivering drinks with considerable panache. It's a lot of fun, with drag shows adding to the chaos in peak season.

Lola Bar
GAY

(Map p366; ☑ 22890 78391; Zanni Pitaraki 4; ⊙ 8pm-3.30am; ☜) Screen divas line the walls, tasselled lampshades shimmy along to torch songs, and a dragged up mannequin stares endlessly into a mirror at Mykonos' best gay cocktail bar. The vibe is relaxed and friendly, and the staff couldn't be more charming. It's the perfect post-dinner, pre-dancefloor rehy-dration station. If you can find it within the Mykonos maze.

@54
GAY

(Map p366; ☑ 22890 28543; www.facebook.com/at54Club; Plateia Manto Mavrogenous; ⊙ 9pm-4am; ☜) With mirror balls cascading from the ceiling and an artsy jungle theme to the decor, this large upstairs space is a stylish spot for an early evening cocktail or a late night boogie. Smokers hog the coveted front balcony, enjoying views along the waterfront.

Cosi
BAR

(Map p366; ☑ 22890 27727; www.facebook.com/cosi.gr; Enopion Dynameon; ⊙ 10am-6am; ☜) This, erm, cosy nook is a stylish cafe by day, with a few al fresco tables. By night it morphs into a lively little bar with occasional DJ sets.

Semeli
COCKTAIL BAR

(Map p366; ☑ 22890 26505; www.semelithebar.gr; Little Venice; ⊙ 9am-late) This slick cocktail bar in the heart of Little Venice draws the bold and the beautiful with its signature cocktails and DJ sets.

Babylon
GAY

(Map p366; ☑ 22890 25152; www.facebook.com/babylonmyk; Akti Kambani; ⊙ 7.30pm-6am) When JackieO' next door looks set to burst at the seams, the overflow heads here. In summer there are regular drag shows.

Katerina's Bar
COCKTAIL BAR

(Map p366; ☑ 22890 23084; www.katerinaslittlevenicemykonos.com; Agion Anargyron 8; ⊙ 9am-3am; ☜) Katerina's makes no effort to be glamorous or, heaven forbid, cool – INXS is likely to be played at some point in the night – but it consequently manages to have more fun than most places in Little Venice. What is unbelievably cool is that it's owned by the first female Greek naval captain. Plus there's an ace little balcony.

LGBT+ MYKONOS

Mykonos is one of the most popular beach-holiday destinations in the world for gay men. Days are spent at glitzy Super Paradise or cruisy Elia Beach before heading back to Hora for a disco nap and a costume change. The first stop of the evening is traditionally Elysium Sunset Bar for views, extortionately priced drinks and hit-and-miss drag shows before hitting the bars in town: Lola for camp and cocktails, or Porta for flattering lighting and a more blokey vibe. Everyone inevitably ends up wiggling their hips at JackieO' (but don't think of arriving before 11pm), switching to Babylon or @54 occasionally for a change of scene.

Party people should visit in late August for XLSIOR (www.xlsiorfestival.com), a huge gay clubbing festival that draws some 30,000 revellers.

Elysium Sunset Bar
GAY

(☑ 22890 23952; www.elysiumhotel.com; School of Fine Arts District; ⊙ 6-10pm Apr-Oct) Attached to the 'straight-friendly' Hotel Elysium, this poolside bar has long been the first port of call for the gay party crowd. Drag queens perform nightly from mid-May to September, although the real star of the show is the sun sinking over the horizon.

Galleraki
COCKTAIL BAR

(Map p366; ☑ 22890 27188; www.galleraki.com; Little Venice; ⊙ 10am-5am; ☜) Choose waterfront seating or the balcony at this friendly cafe-bar, and order a fresh-fruit cocktails (like the signature 'katerinaki', made with melon) or a classic champagne concoction.

Porta
GAY

(Map p366; ☑ 22890 27807; www.portabar-mykonos.com; Ioanni Voinovich 5; ⊙ 10pm-5am) The black sheep of the gay herd, Porta's cruisey ambience fills small-scale rooms bedecked in Tom of Finland imagery. Things get crowded and close towards midnight.

☆ Entertainment

Cine Manto
CINEMA

(Map p366; ☑ 22890 26165; www.cinemanto.gr; Meletopoulou; adult/child €9/7; ⊙ 9pm & 11pm Jun-Sep) Need a break from the bars and clubs? Seek out this gorgeous open-air cinema in a garden setting. There's a cafe here, too. Movies are shown in their original language; view the programme online.

🛍 Shopping

Fashion boutiques and art galleries vie for attention. Mavrogenous St is good for art, Matogianni is best for luxe brands and Greek designers, while the streets of Little Venice mix fashion with jewellery and tat. Most stores close in the winter (November to Easter).

True Image   FASHION & ACCESSORIES
(Map p366; ☑ 22890 78588; www.trueimage.gr; Kalogera 11; ☺10am-11pm) Digitally print images onto T-shirts and Converse sneakers while you wait – either from the store's vast digital library or bring in your own image.

Art & Soul   ART
(Map p366; ☑ 22890 27244; www.mykonosgallery. com; Mavrogenous 18; ☺10am-11pm) Run by the Rousounelos family for over 30 years, this gallery is for serious collectors. On display you'll find sculpture and paintings by renowned Greek artists, each sold with a certificate of authenticity.

HEEL Athens Lab   FASHION & ACCESSORIES
(Map p366; ☑ 22890 77166; www.heel.gr; Panahrantou; ☺11am-2am Apr-Oct) 🌿 Ecologically friendly women's garments made from organic cotton and other sustainable fibres, as well as one-of-a-kind jewellery made from recycled materials.

Muse   GIFTS & SOUVENIRS
(Map p366; ☑ 22890 77370; Dilou 8; ☺11am-3pm & 5-11pm) Pick up a fluoro Greek god, a marble figurine modelled on the blank-faced Cycladic originals or a replica of the classical art, jewellery and ceramics that fill the nation's museums.

ℹ Information

Mykonos has no tourist office; visit travel agencies instead. Online, visit **Mykonos Traveller** (☑ 69869 93013; www.mykonostraveller.com), www.inmykonos.com and www.mykonos.gr for more information.

Delia Travel (☑ 22890 22322; www.facebook. com/delia.travel.mykonos; Akti Kambani; ☺9am-9pm) Sells ferry and Delos tickets, and books accommodation and hire cars.

Sea & Sky (☑ 22890 28240; www.seasky.gr; Akti Kambani; ☺8.30am-9.30pm) Information, aeroplane, ferry and Delos tickets.

ℹ Getting There & Away

Hora is the transport hub of the island. The Old Port Bus Station (p363) has services to the northwest and east of the island, while the airport and beaches to the southwest are served by the Fabrika Bus Station (p363).

There are various car-rental agencies around town, including Apollon (p363) and Anemos (p363).

Excursion boats for Delos (Map p366) leave from the pier directly in front of the town; tickets can be purchased from a nearby kiosk.

Around Mykonos

Tourliani Monastery   MONASTERY
(Map p364; Ano Mera; €1; ☺10am-1pm & 3.30-7pm) Located in the centre of Ano Mera, the island's other main settlement, this castle-like monastery (founded in 1537 but rebuilt in 1767) has a gorgeous domed church with an ornate, gilded iconostasis, and a small museum displaying vestments, historic documents and icons.

🏖 Beaches

Mykonos' golden-sand beaches in their formerly unspoilt state were the pride of Greece. Now most are jammed with umbrellas and backed by beach bars, but they do make for a hopping scene that draws floods of beachgoers. Moods range from the simply hectic to the outright snobby, and nudity levels vary.

Without your own wheels, catch buses from Hora or boats from Ornos and Platys Gialos to further beaches. Mykonos Sea Transfer (p363) has an online timetable of its sea-taxi services.

Elia   BEACH
(Map p364) This beautiful stretch of golden sand has craggy cliffs on either side and an excellent waterfront restaurant. It's backed by some large resorts and, consequently, rows of recliners line the sand. A rainbow flag down the western end (to the right facing the water) marks the gay section. Just past here is the beginning of the nude area; most of the guys head to a tiny cove a little further along the path. Buses head here, via Ano Mera, from the Old Port station.

Agios Sostis   BEACH
(Map p364) This gorgeous, wide strip of golden sand receives far fewer visitors than the south coast. There's no shade and only limited parking but there's a popular taverna with a little sheltered cove directly below it.

Paradise   BEACH
(Map p364) Clear waters and golden sands make this one of the island's most famous beaches. It's completely lined with noisy beach bars and rows of umbrellas, but the

service (particularly at Tropicana) is friendly and attentive. There's a camping resort here, a dive centre, an excellent Indian restaurant and the island's most highly rated club. Regular buses head here from Hora's Fabrika station.

Super Paradise
BEACH

(Map p364) Flashy, trashy and great for people-watching – Super Paradise is Mykonos' most popular gay-friendly beach. The action is split between the glitzy JackieO' Beach Club on the southern headland and the Super Paradise beach bar on the sands. During the season, a private bus service connects the beach to Hora's Fabrika bus station.

Paraga
BEACH

(Map p364) This beautiful crescent-shaped cove became popular in the hippy era and is still known for its beach parties. There's a good selection of tavernas, plus a party hostel, a small gay section and a nudist area. Buses head here from Hora's Fabrika station.

Agrari
BEACH

(Map p364) There's lots of free sand to spread out on at this lovely sandy cove, and a beach bar to retreat to if you get parched. There are no buses but it's easily reached via a short walk from Elia Beach.

Panormos
BEACH

(Map p364) A chunk of this gorgeous sandy beach is given over to a pretentious beach-bar complex, but that still leaves a large expanse of golden sand to spread out on. There's a good taverna here as well.

Kapari
BEACH

(Map p364) Scooped out of the surrounding cliffs, this very appealing sandy cove is reached via a short walk along an unpaved track from the western end of Agios Ioannis.

Platys Gialos
BEACH

(Map p364) One of Mykonos' most popular beaches, this broad stretch of white sand is lined with restaurants and has an excellent water sports centre. Buses head here from Hora's Fabrika station.

Psarou
BEACH

(Map p364) A long stretch of white sand and teal waters, favoured by local cognoscenti. It's a short walk from Platys Gialos.

Activities

There's good diving to be had around Mykonos, with wrecks, caves and walls to explore, and scuba diving operators on Parad-

ise, Kalafatis (Map p364) and Lia (Map p364) beaches. Kalafatis and Ftelia (Map p364) beaches are good for windsurfing, while Platys Gialos is the place to try flyboarding or rent a stand-up paddleboard or kayak.

GoDive Mykonos
DIVING

(Map p364; ☑ 6942616102; www.godivemykonos. com; Lia Beach; 1-/2-tank dives €80/130; ☺ 9.30am-6pm; ☀) This highly professional operator is based on Lia Beach and offers a full range of activities below the waves, from multiday scuba safaris to night dives, PADI courses, snorkelling trips and Bubblemaker inductions for kids over seven.

Mykonos Diving Centre
DIVING

(☑ 22890 24808; www.dive.gr; Paradise Beach; 1-/2-tank dive €75/120; ☀) Based at Paradise Beach, this reputable operator offers a range of PADI courses, as well as night dives, guided snorkelling (€50), Discover Scuba outings (€120), and Bubblemaker for kids over eight (€120).

Platis Gialos Watersports
WATER SPORTS

(☑ 6977279584; www.mykonoswatersports.gr; Platys Gialos Beach; ☺ 9am-9pm Mon-Fri) This operator specialises in adrenalin-packed water sports and arranges flyboarding, wakeboarding, wakeskating, waterskiing and wakesurfing sessions. It also rents sea kayaks and stand-up paddleboards.

Mykonos On Board
BOATING

(☑ 69324 71055; www.mykonosonboard.com) Highly recommended private or small-group yachting excursions around Mykonos and to nearby islands Delos and Rineia.

W-Diving Kalafati Dive Center
DIVING

(Map p364; ☑ 22890 71677; www.mykonos-diving. com; Kalafatis Beach; 1-tank dive €65; ☺ 8am-4pm) Full range of diving courses and packages from a 'discover scuba diving' session (€80) to 10 boat dives with full gear (€470).

Tours

Yummy Pedals
CYCLING

(Map p364; ☑ 22890 71883; www.yummypedals. gr; 4hr tour from €50) A world away from the beach bars, multilingual Dimitra offers guided mountain-biking tours through the backroads of Mykonos. The duration and route is personalised to fit differing skill levels, but may take in farms, villages and quiet beaches (with swimming and snacking stops). Tours begin and end at Dimitra's family's vineyard, with the option of food and wine.

🛏 Sleeping

Mykonos Town may have the greatest variety of accommodation, but hotels, apartments and domatia are scattered throughout popular locations, such as Platys Gialos and Ornos. Paraga and Paradise Beach both have party hostels.

Hotel Jason   HOTEL €€
(Map p364; ☑ 22890 23481; www.hoteljason-mykonos.gr; Glastros; s/d from €65/120; 🅿 ❄ 🛜 🌊) This friendly midpriced hotel, with spotless, tiled rooms (some with heavy wooden beams, some with kitchenettes) is in an odd location. Hora and three beaches (Ornos, Psarou and Platys Gialos) are within a half hour's walk and there's a bus stop nearby. Doubles are nicer than the triple rooms.

Artemoulas Studios   APARTMENT €€
(☑ 22890 25501; www.artemoulas-mykonos.gr; Platys Gialos; apt from €180; ☺ May-Sep; 🅿 ❄ @ 🛜 🌊) With a hillside location a few minutes' walk from two of Mykonos' most popular beaches, these spacious, self-contained apartments are a solid midrange choice. Options range from studios with kitchenettes to two-bedroom apartments.

★ Rocabella   BOUTIQUE HOTEL €€€
(Map p364; ☑ 22890 28930; www.rocabella-hotel-mykonos.com; Agios Stefanos; r/ste from €361/532; ☺ Easter-Oct; 🅿 ❄ 🛜 🌊) Nothing screams relaxation more than the day beds projecting over the sea-gazing pool at this sophisticated retreat, 3km north of Hora. Rotary telephones and tiny Marshall speakers bring a quirky retro element to the otherwise contemporary decor of the 21 rooms, all of which have decks with sea views, and some have Jacuzzis on them.

Nissaki   BOUTIQUE HOTEL €€€
(☑ 22890 27666; www.hotelnissaki.gr; Platys Gialos; d/ste from €485/502; ☺ Apr-Oct; 🅿 ❄ 🛜 🌊) With its pool overlooking the bay, this is one of Mykonos' loveliest retreats. Whitewashed rooms are livened up with touches of contemporary art, floor-to-ceiling windows let in plenty of light, and suites come with hot tubs. A spa, romantic dining and the pearly light dancing on the water make this an ideal place to canoodle with your sweetie.

Branco Mykonos   RESORT €€€
(☑ 22890 25500; www.brancohotel.com; Platys Gialos; r/ste from €900/1070; ☺ Apr-Sep; ❄ 🛜 🌊) Ambient beats from the beachfront DJ station drift over the deckchairs and pool of this modern hotel that has commandeered the eastern half of Platys Gialos Beach. All rooms come with sea views, the restaurant serves contemporary Greek dishes and an excellent range of water sports is on offer.

San Giorgio Hotel   BOUTIQUE HOTEL €€€
(Map p364; ☑ 22890 27474; www.sangiorgio-mykonos.com; Paraga Beach; r from €410; ☺ May–mid-Oct; ❄ 🛜 🌊) Let your biggest holiday dilemma be where to recline: by the pool at this luxe, laid-back hotel, at Paradise Beach (seven minutes' walk) or at Paraga Beach (three minutes' walk).

🍴 Eating

Indian Palace   INDIAN €€
(☑ 22890 78044; www.jaipur-palace.gr; Paradise Beach; mains €8.60-16; ☺ 1-11pm; 🛜 🍴) An offshoot of Athen's renowned Jaipur Palace, this breezy place overlooks Paradise Beach, offering a fresh and fragrant take on the greatest hits of Indian cuisine. Given the location, ordering the fish curry is a no-brainer.

Bowl   CAFE €€
(☑ 22890 77659; www.bowlmykonos.co; Nea Periferiaki, Ornos; mains €9-25; ☺ 9am-6pm Mon-Sat, daily Jul & Aug; 🍴) A big pink sequinned disk provides an Instagrammable backdrop to this breezy health-focused cafe, especially popular with those who will later be dancing at the beach clubs in the skimpiest bikinis. Options include delicious breakfast bowls, açai berry smoothies, 'health' shots and plenty of 'superfood', raw and vegan dishes.

Kiki's Taverna   TAVERNA €€
(Map p364; ☑ 69407 59356; Agios Sostis; mains €10-25; ☺ 1-7pm; 🛜) Every day around noon, customers begin lining up outside Kiki's, helping themselves to complimentary cask wine as they wait. Their prize? Enormous portions of simple local food off the grill: marinated pork chops, chewy octopus, swordfish or cheese, accompanied by salads and served beneath a shady vine trellis on a terrace overlooking the sea.

Kalosta   MEDITERRANEAN €€
(Map p364; ☑ 22890 78589; www.facebook.com/KalostaRestaurantPanormos; Panormos Beach; mains €12-22; ☺ noon-10pm; 🛜) Drunk with sunshine and skin tangy with sea salt, beachgoers make their way up to Kalosta's shady terrace overlooking Panormos Beach. Bask in the afterglow of a long, lazy day and feast on the seafood-heavy selection of Greek and Italian dishes.

Fokos Taverna
TAVERNA €€

(Map p364; ☑ 6944644343; www.fokosmykonos. com; Fokos Beach; mains €9-22; ☺ 1-7pm; ☏) The smell of grilled lamb chops, sizzling burgers and grilled calamari wafts down from this long-standing taverna and over Fokos Beach. It's been attracting locals and visitors alike with its creative take on local dishes, including imaginative salads, along with a few exotic touches (ceviche, 'Oriental' rice). You'll need an ATV to brave the rutted road.

Nikolas Taverna
TAVERNA €€

(☑ 22890 25264; www.nikolas-taverna.com; Agia Anna Beach; mains €8-17; ☺ 10am-10pm; ☏) 🌱 This seaside taverna has been run by the same family for three generations. The current proprietor, Nikolas, goes fishing for fresh catch of the day to go with the locally sourced meats and vegetables from the family farm. Solid and satisfying.

★ Reeza
MEDITERRANEAN €€€

(☑ 22890 28930; www.rocabella-hotel-mykonos. com; Agios Stefanos; mains €18-38) Sophisticated yet deceptively simple contemporary Greek cuisine is served poolside at this exceptional restaurant attached to the Rocabella Hotel. Playful takes on classics include 'crab vs dolmas' and 'prawn carpaccio *saganaki*', and there's a range of set tasting menus if you're in the mood to splurge (€55 to €125). Vegans have a couple of options, too.

🍸 Drinking & Nightlife

JackieO' Beach Club
GAY

(☑ 22890 77298; www.jackieomykonos.com; Super Paradise) Occupying the western headland of Super Paradise Beach, this slick puppy is wall-to-wall buffed bodies in itsy-bitsy swimsuits, posing and prancing around the swimming pool – in other words, the people-watching is priceless. Prices are high, but there's free valet parking, a restaurant and drag shows in the peak season.

Super Paradise Beach Club
CLUB

(☑ 6985919002; www.superparadise.com.gr; ☺ 9am-late; ☏) Dominating its namesake beach, this beach bar and club is synonymous with hedonism. Celebrity sightings, a crush of scantily clad young bodies heaving to the DJs' beats, cocktails by the sea – yep, it's got all that. Music kicks off in the afternoons and pumps until the wee hours. Numerous free shuttle buses from Hora.

Paradise Beach Club
CLUB

(☑ 6973016311; www.paradiseclubmykonos.com; Paradise Beach; ☺ 4pm-5am Apr-Oct) By day it's a place to sip cocktails around a saltwater pool but afternoon parties kick off at 4pm, with the second shift starting from 10pm. Big-name international DJs such as Tiësto and Erick Morillo have played here.

Cavo Paradiso
CLUB

(☑ 22890 26124; www.cavoparadiso.gr; Paradise Beach; ☺ 11.30pm-7am) The only Mykonos venue to currently appear in DJ Mag's prestigious international Top 100 Clubs list, this open-air clifftop megaclub consistently showcases top international DJs. Look out for its regular Full Moon parties.

DELOS
ΔΗΛΟΣ

POP 24

The Cyclades fulfil their collective name (*kyklos* means circle) by encircling the sacred island of Delos. The mythical birthplace of twins Apollo and Artemis, splendid Ancient Delos was a shrine turned sacred treasury and commercial centre. This Unesco World Heritage Site is one of the most important archaeological sites in Greece. Cast your imagination wide to transform this sprawling ruin into the magnificent city it once was.

The island, just 5km long and 1300m wide, offers a soothing contrast to Mykonos, its main access point. Overnight stays are forbidden, so visits are at the mercy of the boat schedules. Aside from the museum, there's very little shelter; a hat, sunscreen and walking shoes are sensible precautions.

At the time of writing, there was no cafe operating on the island; it pays to bring water and food.

History

Delos has a special place in Greek mythology. When Leto was pregnant with Apollo and Artemis, she was relentlessly pursued by vengeful Hera, before finally finding sanctuary and giving birth to the twins on the island.

Delos was first inhabited in the 3rd millennium BCE. From the 8th century BCE it became a shrine to Apollo, and the oldest temples on the island date from this era. The dominant Athenians had full control of Delos – and thus the Aegean – by the 5th century BCE.

In 478 BCE Athens established an alliance known as the Delian League, which maintained its treasury on the island. A cynical decree ensured that no one could be born or die on Delos, thus strengthening Athens' control over the island by expelling the native population.

Delos reached the height of its power in Hellenistic times, becoming one of the three most important religious centres in Greece and a flourishing centre of commerce. Many of its inhabitants were wealthy merchants, mariners and bankers from as far away as Egypt and Syria. They built temples to their homeland gods, but Apollo remained the principal deity.

The Romans made Delos a duty-free port in 167 BCE. This brought even greater prosperity, due largely to a lucrative slave market that sold up to 10,000 people a day. During the following century, as ancient religions diminished and trade routes shifted, Delos began a long decline. By the 3rd century CE there was only a small Christian settlement on the island, and in the following centuries the ancient site was a hideout for pirates and was looted of many of its antiquities. It wasn't until the Renaissance that its antiquarian value was recognised.

Every now and then fresh discoveries are unearthed: in recent years a gold workshop was uncovered alongside the Terrace of the Lions.

◎ Sights

★ Ancient Delos ARCHAEOLOGICAL SITE
(Map p374; ☑ 22890 22259; museum & site adult/concession €12/6; ⊗ 8am-8pm Apr-Oct, to 2pm Nov-Mar) Delos has a special place in Greek mythology. When Leto was pregnant with twins Apollo and Artemis, she was relentlessly pursued by a vengeful Hera – the wife of their father, Zeus – before giving birth on this sacred island. The ancient town that sprang up here was a bustling commercial centre as well as shrine. Within the extensive ruins of this Unesco World Heritage Site, it's not difficult to imagine Ancient Delos in all its original splendour.

Boats for Delos leave Hora (Mykonos) at 9am, 10am, 11.30am and 5pm from May to October, returning at noon, 1.30pm, 3pm

Ancient Delos

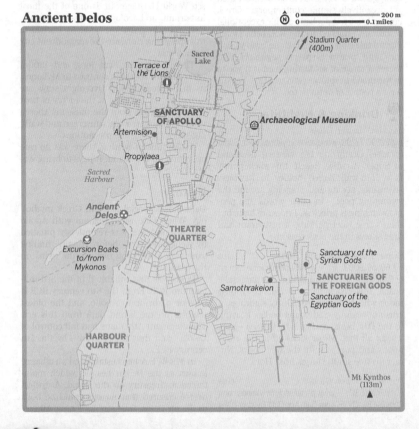

and 7.30pm. On Mondays throughout the year, and daily from November to April, only the 10am boat operates, returning at 1.30pm. The journey takes 30 minutes. Tickets are sold from the Delos Boat Ticket Kiosk, located at the foot of the jetty at the southern end of Mykonos' old harbour. When buying tickets, find out which boat you can return on.

On the island, the ticket office sells Delos guidebooks but there are also detailed information boards scattered around the site. Visitors are given a map with three walking routes marked on it, taking from 1½ to five hours.

While many significant finds from Delos are in the National Archaeological Museum in Athens, the island's museum retains an interesting collection, including the originals of many of the frescoes, mosaics and statues that were removed from the site and replaced with replicas in situ.

The key areas to explore are the Sanctuary of Apollo, the spiritual heart of the complex, to the left of the ferry dock. Two large stoas (colonnaded porticos) lined the Sacred Way leading to the Propylaea, the monumental entrance to a complex of magnificent temples and treasuries. Three temples to Apollo stood side by side, facing a colossal 9m-high statue of the god. Also within the compound is the Artemision, containing the Temple of Artemis. Beyond here is the much-photographed Terrace of the Lions. These proud marble beasts were offerings from the people of Naxos, presented to Delos in the 7th century BCE to guard the Sacred Lake (drained since 1925 to prevent malarial mosquito-breeding) where Leto gave birth to her twins.

To the right of the dock is the Theatre Quarter, where Delos' wealthiest inhabitants lived in houses built around peristyle courtyards, with intricate, colourful mosaics. Beyond this are the Sanctuaries of the Foreign Gods and the path leading up Mt Kynthos (113m); it's worth the steep climb for the terrific views of the encircling islands.

★ Archaeological Museum   MUSEUM
(Map p374; ◷ 8am-8pm mid-Apr–Oct) FREE A vast haul of artefacts has been protected from the elements and displayed in this must-see museum, including the originals of many of the frescoes, mosaics and statues that were removed from the site and replaced with replicas in situ. In the left-hand hall, look for the eye-opening cabinet of erotic items including large stone phalluses.

SANCTUARIES OF THE FOREIGN GODS

Delos was a place of worship for many cultures beyond the Greeks, and their temples are concentrated in the area called the Sanctuaries of the Foreign Gods on the slope of Mt Kynthos. The remains of a 1st-century BCE synagogue have also been uncovered near the stadium.

Samothrakeion (Map p374) The Kabeiroi, a mysterious group of Samothracian deities, were worshipped here.

Sanctuary of the Syrian Gods (Map p374) Built in around 150 BCE, this complex was dedicated to the Syrian gods Atargatis and Hadad, who were popular in the Greek world.

Sanctuary of the Egyptian Gods (Map p374) Honoured deities including Serapis and Isis.

ⓘ Information
Excellent information boards make it easy to do without one, but licensed guides can help provide context to the various neighbourhoods and buildings. An added bonus is that they can sometimes speed you past the queues at the entrance gates. Guided tours, including the boat trip and site admission, cost €50 – an extra €18 than if you were going it alone.

ⓘ Getting There & Away
Boats (Map p364) for Delos leave Hora (Mykonos) at 9am, 10am, 11.30am and 5pm from May to October, returning at noon, 1.30pm, 3pm and 7.30pm. On Mondays throughout the year, and daily from November to April, only the 10am boat operates, returning at 1.30pm. The journey takes 30 minutes. Tickets are sold from the Delos Boat Ticket Kiosk (☏ 22890 28603; www.delostours.gr; adult/child return ticket €20/10), located at the foot of the jetty at the southern end of Mykonos' old harbour. When buying tickets, find out which boat you can return on.

PAROS   ΠΑΡΟΣ
POP 12,853
Successively occupied by Cretans, Minoans, Ionians, Arcadians, Macedonians, Romans, Byzantians and others, who've all made their mark on this large, hilly and fertile island, Paros has been tagged as primarily a ferry hub in recent times. Yet Paros' bustling

Paros & Antiparos

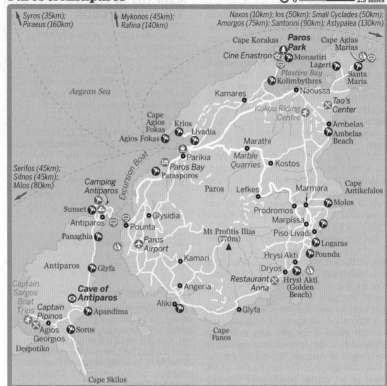

Syros (35km); Piraeus (160km)

Mykonos (45km); Rafina (140km)

Naxos (10km); Ios (50km); Small Cyclades (50km); Amorgos (75km); Santorini (90km); Astypalea (130km)

Aegean Sea

Serifos (45km); Sifnos (45km); Milos (80km)

capital with its ancient remains, the resort town of Naoussa and sweet rural villages are all the more charming for their relative lack of crowds, and there's plenty to do, with good walks, plus excellent windsurfing, kitesurfing and diving.

Geologically speaking, Paros has long been a Greek star; white marble drawn from the island's interior made the island prosperous from the Early Cycladic period onwards. Most famously, the *Venus de Milo* was carved from Parian marble, as was Napoleon's tomb.

For further information, check out www. parosweb.com.

The smaller and more laid-back island of Antiparos (p382), 1km southwest of Paros, is easily reached by car ferry or excursion boat.

ⓘ Getting There & Away

AIR

From **Paros Airport** (Map p376; ☑ 22840 44070), a few kilometres south of Parikia, there

are half a dozen daily flights to Athens (€75, 40 minutes) with Olympic Air (www.olympicair.com) and Sky Express (www.skyexpress.gr). Taxis from the airport to Parikia/Naoussa cost around €20/35.

BOAT

Boat services from Paros:

DESTINATION	DURATION	FARE (€)	FREQUENCY
Aegiali (on Amorgos)	3¼-5½ hrs	13-21.50	5 weekly
Anafi	7 hrs	16	2 weekly
Astypalea	5 hrs	37	4 weekly
Donousa	2¼-2½ hrs	11-17.50	5 weekly
Folegandros	3½-6¼ hrs	9-60	1-2 daily
Ios	50 mins	11-27	3-5 daily
Iraklia	1¼-6 hrs	11-17	4 weekly
Iraklio	4-6½ hrs	55-75	2-4 daily
Koufonisia	1¼-3¼ hrs	19-35	2-3 daily

Katapola (on Amorgos)	2-6 hrs	13-32	1-3 daily
Mykonos	40mins-1¼ hrs	18-32	6-8 daily
Naxos	30mins-1½ hrs	6-24	5-7 daily
Piraeus	3¼-5¼ hrs	33-40	3-6 daily
Rafina	3¼-6¼ hrs	31-46	3 daily
Santorini	2-3½ hrs	20-46	4-5 daily
Schinousa	2¾ hrs	7-35	1-2 daily
Syros	1½-2¼ hrs	7-35	1-2 daily
Tinos	1½-2½ hrs	34-39	4-5 daily

❶ Getting Around

BOAT

Sea taxis leave from the Parikia quay for beaches around Paros and to Antiparos. Tickets range from €8 to €15 and are available on board.

BUS

Parikia is the island's bus hub, and frequent **buses** (☑ 22840 21395; http://ktelparou.gr) link Parikia and Naoussa. It's also easy to reach popular destinations such as the Golden Beach, Prodromos and Marmara from both towns. Buses also link Parikia to Pounta (for the Antiparos ferry) and the airport.

Tickets can be purchased from machines at the bus terminals, and at kiosks and minimarkets island-wide, or from the driver at a slightly higher rate.

CAR & MOTORCYCLE

There are numerous rental outlets along the waterfront in Parikia, Naoussa and all around the island. In peak season the minimum cost is about €45 per day for car hire, €30 for a quad and €20 for a scooter. A good outfit is **Acropolis** (Map p378; ☑ 22840 21830; www.acropolisparos.com; Waterfront, Parikia).

TAXI

Taxis (☑ 22840 21500) gather beside the roundabout in Parikia. Fares include €20 to the airport, €15 to Naoussa, €13 to Pounta, €15 to Lefkes and €24 to Piso Livadi. Add €1 if going from the port. There are extra charges for booking ahead, and for luggage.

Parikia   Παροικιά

POP 3000

For its small size, Parikia packs a punch. Its labyrinthine Old Town is pristine and filled with boutiques, cafes and restaurants. You'll also find a handful of impressive archaeological sites, a waterfront crammed with tavernas and bars, first-class accommodation, and sandy stretches of beach – particularly popular is Livadia, a short walk north of town.

◉ Sights & Activities

★ Panagia Ekatontapyliani   CHURCH

(Map p378; www.ekatontapyliani.gr; Ekantondapylianis; ◷ 8am-9pm) The Panagia Ekatontapyliani, which dates from 326 CE, is one of the finest churches in the Cyclades. The building is three distinct churches: Agios Nikolaos, the largest, with superb columns of Parian marble and a carved iconostasis in the east of the compound; the ornate Church of Our Lady; and the ancient Baptistery. The name translates as Our Lady of the Hundred Doors. The Byzantine Museum (Map p378; €2; ◷ 9am-10pm Apr-Oct), within the compound, has a collection of icons and other artefacts.

★ Archaeological Museum   MUSEUM

(Map p378; ☑ 22840 21231; €2; ◷ 8am-3pm Wed-Mon) Fronted by four intricately carved stone sarcophagi, this museum harbours some important pieces, including a 5th-century BCE Nike on the point of alighting and a 6th-century BCE Gorgon, as well as the first known Greek depiction of a seated figure (8th century BCE). A major exhibit is a fragment slab of the 264 BCE Parian Chronicle, which lists the most outstanding personalities and events of Ancient Greece.

Frankish Kastro   RUINS

(Map p378) Check out the outer walls of this fortress, built by the Venetian Duke Marco Sanudo of Naxos in 1260 CE. Built with the stones from ancient buildings that once stood on this site, you can find remnants from the archaic temples of Athena and an Ionic temple from the 5th century BCE.

Paros Hikes   HIKING

(☑ 6972288821; www.paroshikes.com) Christoforos and Lambos guide ecotours to explore the lesser-known sides of Paros and Antiparos, ranging from countryside walks to mountain hiking adventures. Tours can be tailor-made, or you can join them for scheduled walks. Upcoming events are outlined on the website, along with route details, departure info and prices. There are also Bike & Hike and Sail & Hike combos.

🛏 Sleeping

★ Pension Sofia   PENSION €€

(Map p378; ☑ 22840 22085; http://pension-sofia.gr; d/tr €80/120; ◷ Apr-Oct; ❄ 🗟) A few blocks behind the waterfront, Sofia's verdant garden

Parikia

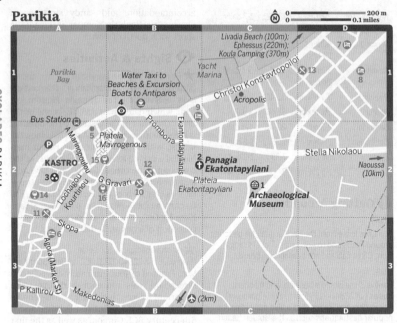

Parikia

alone makes it worth the stay. Rooms are immaculate, and some are decorated with the owner's artwork. Breakfast is available for €8; take it on your balcony or in the garden. Sofia is inland, 400m east of the ferry quay.

★ Paros Bay   RESORT €€
(Map p376; ☎ 22840 21140; www.parosbay.com; s/d/tr from €100/119/140; ❄ 🌐 ▩) A five-minute drive from town yet with all the seclusion and comfort of a beach resort, Paros Bay consists of airy, whitewashed rooms surrounding a saltwater pool and fringed by lush grounds. You're sufficiently near Parikia's dining and nightlife, but there's a good

Mediterranean restaurant and bar on-site if you want to stay put.

Hotel Dina   HOTEL €€
(Map p378; ☎ 22840 21325; www.hoteldina.com; Agora (Market St); s/d/tr €80/90/120; ⊙ May-Oct; ❄ 🌐) Smack-bang in the heart of the Old Town, these eight family-run rooms are a find. They have whitewashed walls and wrought-iron beds, and are spotless and comfortable. Each room has a small balcony, some looking out over Market St, with shared courtyards and verandas in the traditional building's centre. Hostess Dina is a mine of information.

Rooms Mike
PENSION €€

(Map p378; ☑22840 22856; http://roomsmike.
com; studio €100; ※ 🖱) A popular and friendly place, Mike's has a great location within
view of the ferry quay. Your only option here
are recently renovated, self-contained, two-
person studios with kitchens. Mike's sign is
easy to spot from the quay – away to the left.

La Selini
GUESTHOUSE €€

(Map p378; ☑22840 23106; www.laselini.com;
s/d/tr €75/95/120; ☺Apr-Oct; ※🖱) La Selini
shines under the care of its North American
owner, Lou Ann. A short walk from Livadia
Beach, the cheerful complex offers bright,
comfy rooms and studios sleeping up to four.
It's a block back from the water, but upper
rooms have a sea view.

✖ Eating

★ Cafe Distrato
CAFE €

(Map p378; ☑22840 25175; G Gravari; mains €5-
12; ☺8am-late) Dine outside under a leafy
canopy at this friendly place that will draw
you back time and again. This casual all-day
cafe exudes wholesomeness, and is attached
to a shop selling local food products. The
crowd-pleasing menu lists crêpes, sandwiches, burgers, pastas and salads, plus superb
milkshakes, cocktails and local wines.

Symposium
CAFE €

(Map p378; ☑22840 24147; http://cafesympos
ium.gr; mains from €8; ☺9am-3.30pm & 6pm-mid-
night) A gorgeous location under a massive
bougainvillea tree adds to the delicious light
meals, sophisticated atmosphere and tasteful
jazz and classical music to make this a top
place to hang out in Parikia. Head into the
back of town to find this haven away from
the full-on hustle and bustle. The salads here
are wonderful.

★ Trata Fish Taverna
SEAFOOD €€

(Map p378; ☑22840 24651; mains €12-20;
☺noon-3am) A five-minute walk from the
port, this family-run place has been going
strong for two decades. You come here for
one thing only: some of the best fish and seafood on Paros, from octopus stew and crispy
fried prawns, eaten in their shells, to freshly
grilled squid and catch of the day. Simple
and satisfying.

Ephessus
GREEK €€

(☑22840 22520; www.parosweb.com/ephessus;
Livadia Beach; mains €8-15; ☺10am-late) Sit in
the beachfront, lantern-filled garden, then
dig into a dish of Greek or Anatolian cuisine
from Ephessus' wood-fired oven, and you'll

DINING OFF THE BEATEN TRACK

Parikia and Naoussa don't have the monopoly on Paros' best dining. It's worth
travelling to the tiny villages of Prodromos and Dryos to seek out the best in
traditional local cooking, with most ingredients sourced from the families' own
farms and there being plenty of inexpensive barrel wine to wash it down with.

Taverna Tsitsanis (☑22840 41375; www.
facebook.com/tavernatsitsanis; Prodromos;
mains €8-14; ☺noon-3pm & 6.30-10pm) 🥗
Paros' oldest tavern, going strong since
1969 and serving terrific meatballs, cuttlefish stewed in wine and more.

Restaurant Anna (Map p376; ☑22840
41015; http://restaurant-anna.com; Dryos;
mains €8-13; ☺noon-3pm & 6.30-11pm; ☑)
🥗 Serves up goat with lemon sauce, as
well as rabbit casserole, artichoke stew,
or whatever happens to be fresh from
the family farm.

understand why this restaurant is so popular.
Try the *manti* (Anatolian ravioli) or take a
look at the specials.

Levantis
GREEK €€

(Map p378; ☑22840 23613; www.levantisrest
aurant.com; Agora (Market St); dishes €13-22; ☺7-
11pm May-Oct) A vine-covered courtyard and
whitewashed interior with splashes of modern art create a polished setting for some of
the Cyclades' finest contemporary Greek cuisine. Choose from inspired flavour combinations like chicken and pistachio dolmadhes;
slow-braised honey-spiced lamb and fennel;
and orange risotto with garlic prawns.

🍷 Drinking & Nightlife

★ Sativa Music Bar
COCKTAIL BAR

(Map p378; ☑22840 28307; www.facebook.com/
sativaparos; G Gravari; ☺10am-3am) On the
main pedestrian street in Old Town, this bustling cafe and brunch spot by day transforms
into a popular cocktail bar by night, with the
sultry Moroccan decor providing the ideal
backdrop for imbibing original cocktails and
twitching to live music.

★ Bebop
BAR

(Map p378; ☑22840 28075; ☺9am-4am) Climb
the steps up to this waterfront spot beneath
the *kastro* with no shortage of outdoor areas,

including a sunset-primed rooftop terrace. Go for one of many original cocktails such as Spicy Clown (bergamot liqueur, cucumber juice, pink peppercorns) or come for brunch and coffee. Keep an eye out for live-music events, especially jazz.

Koukoutsi BAR
(Map p378; ☑ 6933020592; Plateia Mavrogenous; ⊗ 8am-late) This traditional hangout is a gem. Small and lively, with walls covered in posters and wooden benches filled with cushions, come here to mix with older locals, nibble on mezedhes and sip juices, coffees, beer or a shot of ouzo.

ⓘ Information

On the waterfront opposite the bus terminal, **Travel to Paros** (Map p378; ☑ 22840 24245; http:// traveltoparos.gr) sells ferry tickets, can advise on accommodation and car hire, and has luggage storage. You can also book various tours here.

Naoussa Ναούσα
POP 2850

Naoussa has gradually turned from a quiet fishing village into an increasingly stylish resort and visitor destination. Perched on the shores of the large Plastira Bay, there are good beaches nearby, excellent restaurants and an ever-expanding number of chic beachside hotels, cafes and bars. Behind the waterfront is a maze of narrow, whitewashed streets, dotted with bars, cafes and intimidating fashion boutiques in stark white.

◉ Sights & Activities

The fun of Naoussa is to get lost wandering the streets of Old Town, and admire the crumbling remains of the 15th-century Venetian *kastro* guarding the port area.

The best beaches in the area are **Kolimbythres**, set among fabulous rock formations, and **Monastiri**, which has some good snorkelling. Low-key **Lageri** is also worth seeking out. **Santa Maria**, on the other side of the eastern headland, is ideal for windsurfing. These beaches can all be reached by road, but caïques run from Naoussa during July and August.

★**Moraitis Winery** WINE
(☑ 22840 51350; www.moraitiswines.gr; tastings €6-8; ⊗ 10am-3pm, to 10pm Jun-Sep) Pressing grapes since 1910, the Moraitis family has it down to a fine art. Sidle up to the bar for a taste of six or more wines out of 15. Their bestseller is the Paros White, made with the

island's indigenous grape, Monemvasia, also used to make the Malvasia dessert wine. It's an easy walk southeast of the centre.

Michael Zeppos BOATING
(☑ 6947817125; www.mzeppos.gr) Operating primarily from Naoussa (and also from Aliki), this company offers three full-day sailing itineraries taking in the beaches of Paros, Antiparos and potentially calling in at Naxos. There are also fishing options. See the website for details; prices depend on numbers.

Kokou Riding Centre HORSE RIDING
(Map p376; ☑ 22840 51818; www.horseriding paros.com) The well-established Kokou has 2½-hour morning rides (€60), venturing into the sea, and 1½-hour evening rides (€40). Pickup is available from Naoussa's main square for €5.

🛏 Sleeping

★**Sea House** GUESTHOUSE €€
(☑ 22840 52198; r €107; ❄ 🛜) Secluded enough to be away from Naoussa's bustle yet only a stroll away, the aptly named Sea House sits right on the water. Rooms are decked out in classic Cycladic blue-and-white, come with rain showers and – best of all – seafront terraces for sunset-watching.

Katerina Mare APARTMENT €€
(☑ 22840 51642; www.katerinamare.com; d/tr incl breakfast €120/140, apt from €160; ❄ 🛜) In a word: lovely. Light-filled suites are classy and pristine, each with a great view and every convenience, including kitchenettes. Service is stellar. It's on a hillside southwest of the town centre.

★**Mr & Mrs White** BOUTIQUE HOTEL €€€
(☑ 22840 55207; https://mrandmrswhiteparos. com; d/q from €180/220; ❄ 🛜 🏊) On a hillock overlooking Naoussa from a short distance and surrounded by three pools, this wonderful boutique place combines spacious, airy, whitewashed rooms with quirky wicker features with contemporary Cycladic design and personalised service. A tranquil retreat.

★**Lilly Residence** BOUTIQUE HOTEL €€€
(☑ 22840 51377; www.lillyresidence.gr; ste incl breakfast €331-873; ⊗ May-Oct; 🅿 ❄ 🛜 🏊) Naoussa's most stylish hotel, where stone, wood and wicker combine to great effect and white is the unifying theme. The place is discreetly luxurious (eg Hermes toiletries) and grownup (no kids under 12). Just back from the water, all 11 suites have sea views (and

some have private plunge pools or Jacuzzis), or you can enjoy the eye-candy pool area.

✗ Eating

There's plenty of waterfront dining and a superbly convivial atmosphere just inches from moored boats or the beach. The streets of Old Town offer more imaginative options than traditional tavernas, as well as simple *gyros* joints.

★ Sousouro   CAFE €
(☑ 22840 53113; www.facebook.com/Sousouro CafeBar; breakfast €4-6; ☺ 9am-3am) Occupying a small corner in Old Town, this cafe is big on flavour. One of the islands' best breakfast menus awaits: superfood smoothies and shakes, a selection of home-made granola with sheep's-milk yoghurt and thyme honey, and toast topped with smashed avocado or cacao hazelnut butter and banana. At night the wholesomeness makes way for killer cocktails.

★ Souvlakia Kargos   KEBAB €
(☑ 22840 53503; www.facebook.com/Kargas Paros; mains from €3; ☺ noon-1am) This souvlaki joint is a model of its kind: the pork and chicken *gyros* meat rotates enticingly rather than forlornly on their respective spits, the pitas are filled with chips as well as the nicely seasoned meat, doubling your carb-fest, and there are nice Greek salads to boot. Sit in the tiny alleyway or get the food to go.

To Paradosiako   SWEETS €
(loukoumadhes €4-5; ☺ 6pm-midnight) An essential evening stop for a serve of To Paradosiako's legendary fresh doughy balls of goodness known as *loukoumadhes* (Greek doughnuts). It's a self-service operation: add honey, chocolate sauce and/or ice cream.

★ Tao's Center   THAI €€
(Map p376; ☑ 22840 28882; www.taos-greece. com; Ambelas; mains €10-14; ☺ Apr-Dec; ☑) 🍃 This wellness retreat and meditation centre has an excellent restaurant open to nonguests, serving authentic Thai curries courtesy of the Thai chef, plus a supporting cast of pan-Asian dishes, such as gyoza.

Taverna Glafkos   MEDITERRANEAN €€
(☑ 22840 52100; mains €9-18; ☺ 1pm-midnight) With tables practically on the sand on Agios Dimitrios Beach, this tucked-away place specialises in Mediterranean seafood with global touches. Try steamed mussels and grilled calamari, or dig into shrimp

PAROS PARK

The 80-hectare **Paros Park** (Map p376; ☑ 22840 53573; www.parospark.com; Agios Ioannis Detis Peninsula) north of Naoussa features impressive rock formations, caves, hidden coves and gorgeous beaches. There's a lot going on here, with three established walking trails, a museum, monastery, an ancient theatre that now hosts festivals and the extremely popular open-air **Cine Enastron** (Map p376; ☑ 22840 53573; www.parospark.com/cine-enastron; ☺ 9.30pm Jul-Sep). There's also a lot of history – the Russian fleet was based here during the Russo-Turkish War (1768–74). The park is a 10-minute drive west, then north from Naoussa on the Agios Ioannis Detis Peninsula.

saganaki or black risotto with cuttlefish – all are great paired with local white wine.

🍷 Drinking & Nightlife

★ Santé   COCKTAIL BAR
(☑ 22840 51747; www.santecocktailbar.com; ☺ 10am-3.30am) Several tiny blocks south of the waterfront, in the shade of a huge eucalyptus tree, Santé is a good spot for coffee during the day, but things only really kick off come nightfall. Come for the signature Aegean Mist of Caramel Passion, expertly mixed from high-quality ingredients, and chill out to a soundtrack of mellow beats.

★ Sommaripa Consolato   BAR
(☑ 22840 55233; www.facebook.com/Sommaripa Consolato; ☺ 9.30am-late) The owner opened this elevated cafe-bar in the former home of his grandparents – how fortunate that it's right in the hub of Naoussa's small port (above Mario's restaurant), making for great people-watching from the terraces. First-class drinks, snacks and service, too.

To Takimi   BAR
(Music Cafe; ☑ 22840 55095; www.facebook.com/ takimiparos; ☺ 5pm-late) Just south of the main square, this is where locals come to drink beer or ouzo and listen to live music, often played on the traditional string instruments waiting on the walls. Everything from *rembetika* (blues) to rock goes down here.

ℹ Information

Erkyna Travel (☑ 22840 53180; www.erkyna travel.com) Sells ferry tickets and can help with accommodation, car hire, excursions, water sports and boat trips to other islands. It's on the main road into town.

❶ Getting There & Away

Naoussa is 8km north of Parikia. Frequent buses (p377) link the two towns directly (€2). The **bus stop** is some way inland from the waterfront, where there's a large public car park (most of the Old Town area is pedestrian-only). Old Town is east of here.

If you've got rental wheels, there is free public parking on the way into town.

Around Paros

On the southeast coast is Paros' top beach, Hrysi Akti (Golden Beach) (Map p376), with good swimming, windsurfing and diving operations.

Paros' west coast, around Pounta, is the hub for top water sports activities: a long shallow-water shoreline and perfect side-shore wind conditions make it perfect for all skill levels of kiteboarder or windsurfer.

Paros is also moderately popular with hikers.

🏃 Activities

Force7 Surf Centre   WINDSURFING
(☑ 22840 41789; www.force7paros.gr) Force7 Surf Centre is a well-run centre on Hrysi Akti (Golden Beach) offering windsurfing lessons (€40 per hour; kids' classes available) and rental (€16 per hour), plus kayak (€15 per hour), stand-up paddleboard (€20 per hour) and catamaran (€50 per hour) rentals.

Paros Kite   KITESURFING
(☑ 22840 93018; www.paroskite.com; 90min intro €90) At this slick, professionally run complex at Pounta it's all about the wind: kitesurfing and windsurfing instruction (four-hour beginner course costs €250) and gear rental are offered, plus there's a surf shop, beach bar-cafe, massage and yoga.

Aegean Diving College   DIVING
(☑ 22840 43347; shore dive from €80; ☺ 9.30am-7pm) At Hrysi Akti (Golden Beach), the Aegean Diving College has been well established since the 1990s and offers a range of dives. Dive courses are also available.

🛏 Sleeping

⭐ **Golden Beach Hotel**   HOTEL €€
(☑ 22840 41366; www.goldenbeach.gr; Hrysi Akti; d incl breakfast €130, 4-person apt €260;

☺ Apr–mid-Oct; ❇ 🎇) Right on Hrysi Akti (Golden Beach), this top spot offers simple, appealing rooms and apartments in pastel colours. More important is what's outside the rooms: a splendid grassy lawn down to the shore, plus restaurant, beach bar and oodles of beach activities. Lots of fun to be had on Paros' east coast. Two-night minimum in August.

ANTIPAROS ΑΝΤΙΠΑΡΟΣ

POP 1211

Antiparos lies dreamily offshore from Paros. As soon as your ferry docks, there's a distinct slowing down in the pace of things. The main village and port (also called Antiparos) are relaxed. There's a touristy gloss around the waterfront and main street, but the village runs deep inland to quiet squares and alleyways that give way suddenly to open fields.

The rest of the island runs to the south of the main settlement through quiet countryside. There are several decent beaches, especially at Psaralyki near town, and further south at Glyfa and Soros, plus one of Greece's most celebrated caves. Having run through the typical Greek gamut of civilisations during millennia of human habitation (Hellenic, pirate, Venetian, Turk...), Antiparos has recently acquired a 'secret getaway' factor that puts it on the radar of those who don't like to be disturbed: Euro royalty, Hollywood stars and A-list rock stars holiday here.

◉ Sights & Activities

⭐ **Cave of Antiparos**   CAVE
(Map p376; http://antiparos.gr; adult/child €6/3; ☺ 10am-5pm Jul & Aug, to 3pm Apr-Jun & Sep) Signposted off the main coastal road some 10km south of the port, this huge and atmospheric cave remains impressive despite much looting of stalactites and stalagmites in the past. In December 1673, Marquis de Nointel held Christmas Mass here. He and other luminaries (including King Otto and Queen Amalia of Greece) have left their graffiti on the rock formations over the centuries. Descending the 400-plus steps will give you thighs of steel. A bus runs here from the port (€1.80).

⭐ **Antiparos Town**   VILLAGE
The long pedestrianised main street of this enchanting village is lined with services and a whole lot of stylish boutiques, bars

and restaurants. Follow it to the end, to the distinctive, giant plane tree of Plateia Agios Nikolaou. From here, a narrow lane leads to the intriguing remnants of the old Venetian *kastro,* entered through an archway. This old fortified settlement – defence against pirates – dates from the mid-15th century; the surviving keep is a terrific place for sunset-viewing.

Anti Art Gallery
GALLERY

(☑22840 61544; www.antiartgallery.gr; ☺7pm-12.30am Jun-Sep) The 'anti' Art Gallery by the *kastro* entrance has an excellent run of scheduled exhibitions, including cutting-edge photography. The brainchild of curator Mary Chatzaki, it plays an entertaining, educational role in island life. In July, the gallery takes over the *kastro* and hosts an outdoor photo exhibition.

Captain Sargos Boat Trips
BOATING

(Map p376; ☑6973794876; www.sargosanti paros.gr; per person €30) Operating out of Agios Georgios, Yorgos runs three- to four-hour boat trips that include a visit to the archaeological site on nearby Despotiko Island, time to swim or laze on the island's spectacular beach, and a cruise through local sea caves. Also available for local charters.

Blue Island Divers
DIVING

(☑22840 61767; www.blueisland-divers.gr; 1-/2-tank dive €65/85, PADI certification from €240) On the northern waterfront, this well-regarded operator and its knowledgeable, enthusiastic instructors introduce you to the wrecks, reefs and caves of Antiparos. Fun dives, night dives and all manner of PADI courses on offer.

🛏️ Sleeping & Eating

Camping Antiparos
CAMPGROUND €

(Map p376; ☑22840 61221; www.camping-anti paros.gr; campsite per adult/child/tent €8/4/3; ☺May-Sep; 🛜) This chilled-out beachside campground is planted with bamboo 'compartments' and cedars. There's a restaurant and minimarket and Greece's first designated nudist beach is just a couple of minutes' walk away. It's a 10-minute walk north of the port (pickup is available).

★ Casa Flora
GUESTHOUSE €€

(☑6937970452; https://casaflora.gr; s/d/apt €63/70/90; 🛜) Near the Kastro, an Athenian couple run a clutch of spotless, spacious rooms and studios. Their knowledge of the island and its history is superb (Flora is a historian) and as a bonus (if you love felines), they look after 16 beautiful cats.

★ Artemis Hotel
HOTEL €€

(☑22840 61460; www.artemisantiparos.com; r incl breakfast €100-110, apt €200; ☺Apr–mid-Oct) The family-run, elegant, marble-lined rooms at Artemis (at the far northern end of the harbour) are compact but well priced, and have lovely private terraces (pay a bit extra for a sea-view room). The common areas are stylishly appealing, and the apartments comfortably sleep a family of four.

Taverna Yorgis
GREEK €

(☑22840 61362; mains €7-12; ☺noon-10pm) To locals, this food speaks of quintessential Greek cooking: classic recipes executed with flair and attention to detail. The crisp, fresh Greek salad, topped with a herb-sprinkled slab of feta, is exemplary, and you'll find yourself chasing the last morsels of the *pasticcio* (Greek lasagne) around your plate with a sigh of pleasure. On the main street.

5F Taverna
KEBAB €

(☑22840 61347; www.facebook.com/Taverna.5F; mains from €3; ☺noon-2.30am) Run with love and attention by Yorgis and Chrysoula, this souvlaki joint is Antiparos' finest. The pillow-soft pitta bread stuffed with smoky, moreish pork *gyros* is deeply satisfying, the souvlaki is on the right side of spiced and crisped meat and you can fill your boots for under €10.

★ Kalokeri
GREEK €€

(☑22840 63037; mains €14-20; ☺6.30-11.30pm) This imaginative restaurant on the main street executes modern Greek dishes with flair and a real understanding of seasonal ingredients. There's the tang of red mullet tartare with the pop-pop-pop of tobiko roe, the high notes of lemon against the earthiness of the dolmadhes and Naxos potatoes stuffed with Paros Gruyère and Andros' smoked ham – an instant crowd-pleaser.

Captain Pipinos
TAVERNA €€

(Map p376; ☑22840 21823; http://captainp ipinos.com; mains €8-15; ☺11am-10pm) In the island's south, right on the water at Agios Georgios and with panoramas of neighbouring uninhabited Despotiko, Captain Pipinos is a gloriously old-school fish taverna. Octopus dishes are a top pick (you'll see them drying), as is anything with fresh fish (sold by the kilo).

ⓘ Getting There & Around

In summer, frequent small passenger boats depart for Antiparos from Parikia (€5), and numerous operators offer day cruises taking in the beaches of both islands, departing from Parikia, Pounta, Aliki and Naoussa.

There's also a regular car ferry that runs from Pounta on the west coast of Paros to Antiparos (one way €1.20, per scooter €1.60, per car €6, one or two services hourly from 7am until midnight, 10 minutes). You can take a vehicle rented on Paros to Antiparos on this ferry.

Oliaris Tours (☏ 22840 61231; www. antiparostravel.gr) runs a bus service from the port to the cave, and another to the east-coast beaches as far as Agios Georgios; tickets cost €3 one way. The schedule varies with the season; in theory, buses run from April to September.

Wheels can be hired from **Aggelos** (☏ 22840 61626; http://antiparosrentacar.com; ⊗ 9am-8pm), the first office as you come from the ferry quay. Cars start at about €50 per day (high season), scooters €20 and bicycles €5 to €10.

Dimitris (☏ 22840 61286; ⊗ 8am-8pm) rents brand new mountain bikes (€5), electric bikes (€12), plus scooters (from €15) and ATVs (from €20).

NAXOS ΝΑΞΟΣ

The largest of the Cyclades, Naxos packs a lot of bang for its buck. Its main town of Hora has a gorgeous waterfront and a web of steep cobbled alleys below its hilltop *kastro* and fortified Venetian mansions – testament to three centuries of Venetian rule. You needn't travel far, though, to find isolated beaches, atmospheric mountain villages, ancient sites and marble quarries.

Naxos was a cultural centre of Classical Greece and Byzantium, and Venetian and Frankish influences also left their mark. Its high mountains form rain clouds, and consequently Naxos is more fertile and green than most of the other Cyclades islands. It produces olives, grapes, figs, citrus fruit, corn and potatoes. Mt Zeus (also known as Mt Zas; 1004m) is the Cyclades' highest peak and is the central focus of the island's mountainous interior, where you will find enchanting villages such as Halki and Apiranthos.

ⓘ Getting There & Away

BOAT

Like Paros, Naxos is something of a ferry hub in the Cyclades, with a similar number of conventional and fast ferries making regular calls to/from Piraeus, plus links to/from the mainland port of Rafina via the northern Cyclades. Boat services from Naxos:

DESTINATION	DURATION	FARE (€)	FREQUENCY
Aegiali (on Amorgos)	2¼-5hrs	12	1-2 daily
Anafi	7½hrs	13	2 weekly
Astypalea	4hrs	20	3 weekly
Donousa	1¼-3¾hrs	7	8 weekly
Folegandros	2¾-3¼hrs	11-43	2-3 daily
Ios	45mins-1¾hrs	16-43	2-3 daily
Iraklia	1-5hrs	7	1-2 daily
Iraklio	4hrs	78	daily
Katapola (on Amorgos)	1¼-3¼hrs	11-30	2-3 daily
Koufonisia	45mins-2½hrs	8-26	2-4 daily
Milos	2¼-6hrs	17-42	3-4 daily
Mykonos	35mins-1½hrs	28-39	6-10 daily
Paros	45mins-1½hrs	6-23	6-8 daily
Piraeus	4-8½hrs	37-57	4-8 daily
Rafina	3½-5hrs,	42-46	4-6 daily
Santorini	1¼-2¼hrs	22-44	5-7 daily
Schinousa	1¼-1¾hrs	7	8 weekly
Sikinos	3hrs	7	3 weekly
Syros	1¼-3hrs	9-35	2-3 daily
Tinos	1¼-2½hrs	35-42	4-5d d

AIR

There are several daily flights to/from Athens (around €81, 40 minutes) with Olympic Air (www.olympicair.com) and Sky Express (www. skyexpress.gr).

ⓘ Getting Around

TO/FROM THE AIRPORT

The **airport** (JNX; Map p385; www.naxos.net/ airport) is 3km south of Hora. There's no shuttle bus, but buses to Agios Prokopios Beach and Agia Anna pass close by. A taxi costs around €15; luggage costs extra.

BUS

Frequent buses run to Agios Prokopios Beach (€1.80) and Agia Anna (€1.80) from Hora. Seven buses daily serve Filoti (€2.50) via Halki (€2.2); five serve Apiranthos (€3.30) via Filoti and Halki; and at least two serve Apollonas (€6.40), Pyrgaki (€2.50) and Melanes (€1.80). There are less frequent departures to other villages.

Buses leave from the end of the ferry quay in Hora; timetables are posted outside the bus information office (p391), diagonally left and

Naxos

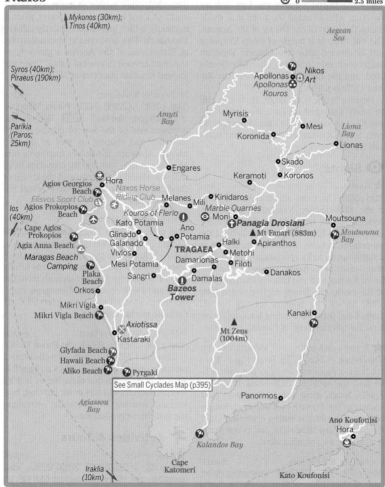

Mykonos (30km);
Tinos (40km)

Syros (40km);
Piraeus (190km)

Parikia
(Paros;
25km)

*Aegean
Sea*

Apollonas
Apollonas
Kouros

*Nikos
Art*

Myrisis

Koronida

Mesi

*Liona
Bay*

Lionas

Engares

Skado

Keramoti

Koronos

Agios Georgios
Beach
Flisvos Sport Club
Agios Prokopios
Beach

*los
(40km)*

Hora

*Naxos Horse
Riding Club*

Melanes

Kinidaros

Mili

Marble Quarries

Moni

Panagia Drosiani

Moutsouna

Cape Agios
Prokopios

Kato Potamia

Ano
Potamia

▲ Mt Fanari (883m)

*Moutsouna
Bay*

Agia Anna Beach

Glinado
Galanado

Halki

Apiranthos

*Maragas Beach
Camping*

Vivlos

TRAGAEA

Metohi

Plaka
Beach

Mesi Potamia

Damarionas

Filoti

Orkos

Sangri

Damalas

Danakos

**Bazeos
Tower**

Mikri Vigla
Mikri Vigla Beach

Axiotissa

Kanaki

Kastaraki

▲ Mt Zeus
(1004m)

Glyfada Beach
Hawaii Beach
Aliko Beach

Pyrgaki

See Small Cyclades Map (p395)

*Agiassou
Bay*

Panormos

*Ano Koufonisi
Hora*

Kalandos Bay

Iraklia
(10km)

Cape
Katomeri

Kato Koufonisi

across the road from the bus stop. You have to buy tickets from the office or from the machine outside (not from the bus driver).

CAR & MOTORCYCLE

Rates for hire cars during peak season range from about €45 to €65 per day, quad bikes from €30 and scooters from €20. Hire from **Naxos Auto Rent** (22850 41350; http://naxosautorent.com; 9am-7pm), **Rental Center** (22850 23395; www.rentalcenter.com.gr; Aristidi Protopapadaki; 9am-8pm), **Auto Tour** (22850 25480; www.naxosrentacar.com; 9am-7pm) or **Fun Car** (22850 26084; www.funcarandrides.com; 9am-8pm). **Moto Art** (22850 23511; Kiprou; 9am-8pm) rents out brand new scooters (from €25 per day) and ATVs (from €30 per day).

TAXI

Due to its large size, most visitors to Naxos rely on buses or their own wheels to travel around. **Taxis** (22850 22444) are an option for shorter trips (eg Hora to Agios Prokopios Beach or Agia Anna for around €10). Taxis cluster at the port, or you can call one.

Hora (Naxos) Χώρα (Νάξος)
POP 7070

Hora, or Naxos Town, feels different from other Cycladic island capitals. It's bigger and busier, for starters, with the remnants of the fortified Venetian *kastro* looming above the waterfront buildings. This was the seat of power for Marco Sanudo, the 13th-century Venetian who founded the town and made Naxos the heart of the Duchy of the Aegean. The old town is a tangle of steep footpaths and is divided into two historic Venetian neighbourhoods: Bourgos, where the Greeks lived, and the hilltop Kastro, where the Roman Catholics lived.

Despite being fairly large, Hora can still be easily managed on foot. It's almost impossible not to get lost in the old town, however, and maps are of little use. And that's half the fun.

⊙ Sights

★ Kastro
AREA

(Map p388) The most alluring part of Hora is the 13th-century residential neighbourhood of Kastro, which Marco Sanudo made the capital of his duchy in 1207. Behind the waterfront, get lost in the narrow alleyways scrambling up to its spectacular hilltop location. Venetian mansions survive in the centre of Kastro, and you can see the remnants of the castle, the Tower of Sanoudos (Map p388). To see the Bourgos area of the old town, head into the winding backstreets behind the northern end of Paralia.

★ Temple of Apollo
ARCHAEOLOGICAL SITE

(The Portara; ⊙ 24hr) FREE From Naxos Town Harbour, a causeway leads to the Palatia islet and the striking, unfinished Temple of Apollo, Naxos' most famous landmark (also known as the Portara or 'Doorway'). Simply two marble columns with a crowning lintel, it makes an arresting sight, and people gather at sunset for splendid views.

Petalouda Art Gallery
GALLERY

(Map p388; ☑ 6950427064; www.petalouda-art. com; ⊙ 10am-11.30pm) Next to the walkway to the heart of the *kastro*, this French-run art gallery features up-and-coming young artists, as well as established international ones. You may find haunting paintings by the likes of Isabelle Malmezat alongside antique ceremonial masks from Gabon and the Congo.

Agios Georgios Beach
BEACH

(Map p388) Conveniently located just south of the waterfront is sandy Agios Georgios, Naxos' town beach. It's backed by hotels and tavernas at the town end (where it can get crowded), but it runs for some way to the south, where you can spread out a little. Its shallow waters make it great for families.

Grotta Beach
BEACH

(Map p388) This pebbly, stony beach to the north of town is pounded by waves when a northerly is blowing, but is relatively calm in a southerly. This is where the Mycenaean city of Naxos, one of the Aegean region's most significant, stood in ancient times. There are ancient remains underwater off the beach.

Mitropolis Museum
MUSEUM

(Map p388; ☑ 22850 24151; Plateia Mitropolis; ⊙ 8.30am-3pm Wed-Mon) FREE Behind the northern end of the waterfront are several churches and chapels, as well as the Mitropolis Museum. It features fragments of a Mycenaean city (13th to 11th centuries BCE) that was abandoned because of the threat of flooding. Glass panels underfoot reveal ancient foundations.

Archaeological Museum
MUSEUM

(Map p388; ☑ 22850 22725; Kastro; adult/child €3/free; ⊙ 8am-3pm Wed-Mon) This museum in Kastro is housed in the former Jesuit school where novelist Nikos Kazantzakis was briefly a pupil. It contains fascinating finds from the Ionic and Doric eras, plus Mycenaean vases, but the most startling are the splendid Early Cycladic marble figurines.

Folk Museum Collection
MUSEUM

(Map p388; ☑ 22850 25561; Old Market St; €3; ⊙ 10am-2pm & 7-10pm) This small, well-curated, privately owned collection gives a digestible account of elements that make Naxos' history special: succinct displays cover farming, beekeeping, weaving, bread-making, winemaking and cheese production.

🏃 Activities & Tours

★ Naxos Bike
CYCLING

(Map p388; ☑ 6932795125, 22850 25887; www. naxosbikes.com; bike hire per day from €10) Get all your equipment at this place near the port, from electric (€35 per day), road, mountain and trekking bikes to children's seats. Local expert Giannis knows everything there is to know about bikes, and can set you up with maps to get you exploring. He also leads three-hour tours (per person €30, minimum two people).

Flisvos Sport Club
WINDSURFING

(Map p385; ☑ 22850 24308; www.flisvos-sport club.com; Agios Georgios Beach) Well-organised beach club offering a range of windsurfing courses (one-hour private lesson from €50, three-day course €225), catamaran sailing (one-hour rental from €48) and mountain-bike rental (from €18 per day). It also has a cool cafe, accommodation and the option of beach volleyball, a fitness centre and yoga.

Naxos Horse Riding Club
HORSE RIDING

(Map p385; ☑ 6948809142; www.naxoshorse riding.com; 2/3hr ride €50/60; ☺ Mon-Sat) Organises daily morning, afternoon and sunset horse rides inland and on beaches. Staff can arrange pickup and return to and from the stables. Beginners, young children and advanced riders are all catered for.

Naxos Tours
TOURS

(Map p388; ☑ 22850 24000; www.naxostours.net; island bus tour adult/child €30/15; ☺ 8am-10pm) This waterfront agency organises an island tour by bus, guided walks in more remote villages such as Melanes, Potamia, Tragaia and Moni (prices depend on number of participants) plus daily cruises. There are frequent excursion boats to Delos and Mykonos, Santorini, and Iraklia and Koufonisia, plus sailing explorations of southern Naxos.

✨ Festivals & Events

★ Domus Festival
MUSIC

(☑ 22850 22387; www.naxosfestival.com; Kastro; event admission varies; ☺ June) Special evening cultural events are held inside the Venetian Castle in June. Posters around town advertise what's on the horizon. It may be traditional music and dance concerts, classical piano recitals, bouzouki, or jazz and blues. There may even be screenings of *Zorba the Greek*. There's an inside venue on the off-chance it rains.

🛌 Sleeping

Hora has plenty of accommodation (much of it open year-round), particularly midrange hotels and studios, including numerous options backing the town beach, Agios Georgios. Book early for July and August.

The best campgrounds are at the beaches south of Hora (Agia Anna and Plaka); minibuses meet the ferries.

★ Venetian Suites
APARTMENT €€

(Map p388; ☑ 22850 23057, 6906389291; venetian suites.naxos@gmail.com; apt €125; ※ 🛜) Hidden in the maze of tiny medieval streets, these are among the most atmospheric of Naxos' lodgings. In spite of the heavy wooden beams, these studios seem light and bright, and bedroom nooks are accessed through medieval stone arches. Mod cons abound, including rain showers and fully equipped kitchenettes and plasma-screen TVs.

★ Hotel Grotta
HOTEL €€

(☑ 22850 22215; www.hotelgrotta.gr; off Kontoleontos; d incl breakfast €125; ※ 🛜) Located on high ground overlooking the *kastro* and main town, this excellent family-run hotel has immaculate rooms in soothing creams and baby blues, great sea views from the front, spacious public areas and a cool indoor Jacuzzi area. It's made even better by the cheerful atmosphere. A rooftop garden bar and private terraces are extra boons.

★ Panos Studios
HOTEL €€

(☑ 22850 26078; www.studiospanos.com; d/tr/apt/ ste €115/155/160/250; ☺ May-Oct; ※ 🛜) Decked out in chic whites and charcoals, these stylish, well-equipped rooms and apartments sit a block back from Agios Georgios Beach and come with kitchenettes and balconies. There are free port and airport transfers and a friendly welcome, including complimentary welcoming wine from the barrel at reception.

Hotel Glaros
BOUTIQUE HOTEL €€

(Map p388; ☑ 22850 23101; www.hotelglaros. com; Agios Georgios Beach; d/ste from €70/225; ☺ Apr-Oct; ※ @ 🛜) Edgy yet homey, simple yet plush, this well-run and immaculate 13-room hotel has a seaside feel in its boutique fit-out. Service is thoughtful, there's an indoor Jacuzzi, the beach is only a few steps away and it's adults only. Breakfast is €10. Two-night minimum in July and August.

Pension Sofi
PENSION €€

(☑ 22850 23077; www.pensionsofi.gr; d/tr from €70/90; ※ 🛜) Run by members of the friendly Koufopoulos family, guests at Pension Sofi are met with family-made wine or cake and immaculate rooms, each with a freshly renovated bathroom and a basic kitchen. Sofi is a short walk back from the waterfront. Let them know your arrival details for a complimentary pickup at the port. Rates halve out of high season.

Nikos Verikokos Studios
HOTEL €€

(Map p388; ☑ 22850 22025; www.nikos-verikokos. com; d/tr €100/130; ※ 🛜) Friendly Nikos maintains immaculate rooms in the heart of the old town, and is handy to everything. Some have balconies and sea views, all have little kitchenettes. It offers port pickup with prearrangement. A rooftop veranda provides further vistas.

Xenia Hotel
HOTEL €€

(Map p388; ☑ 22850 25068; www.hotel-xenia. gr; Plateia Pigadakia; s/d/tr incl breakfast from €92/117/125; ※ 🛜) Sleek and minimalist,

Hora (Naxos)

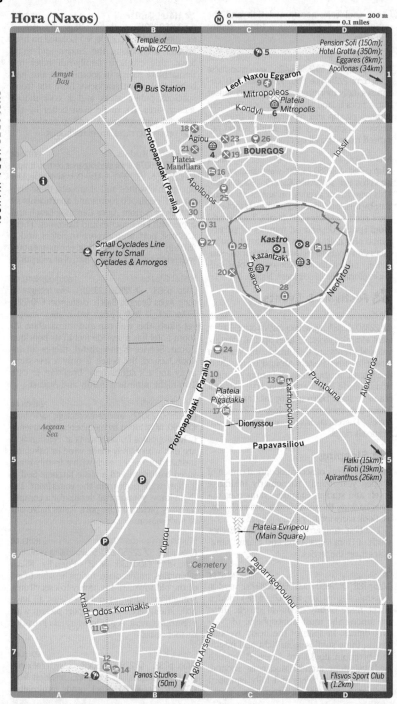

N 0 ———————— 200 m
   0 ———————— 0.1 miles

Amyti Bay

Temple of Apollo (250m)

Bus Station

Pension Sofi (150m);
Hotel Grotta (350m);
Eggares (8km);
Apollonas (34km)

Leof. Naxou Eggaron

9

Mitropoleos

Plateia
Mitropolis

Kondyli

6

18
Agiou
21
23
4
19
26
BOURGOS
Plateia
Mandilara
16
Apollonos
25
30

Protopapadaki (Paralia)

Iossif

31
27
29

Kastro
1
Kazantzaki
8
15
3
20
Delaroca
7
28

Nechytou

Small Cyclades Line
Ferry to Small
Cyclades & Amorgos

24

Protopapadaki (Paralia)

10
Plateia
Pigadakia
17
Dionyssou

13
Exarhopoulou
Prantouna

Alexinoros

Papavasiliou

Halki (15km);
Filoti (19km);
Apiranthos (26km)

Aegean
Sea

P

P

Kiprou

Plateia Evripeou
(Main Square)

Cemetery

22

Paparrigopoulou

Ariadnis

Odos Komiakis

11

Agiou Arseniou

12
14
2

Panos Studios
(50m)

Flisvos Sport Club
(1.2km)

Hora (Naxos)

this hotel is in the heart of the action in the old town, close to everything, and the staff are attentive. While the neutral tones and blonde-wood furnishings are not exactly unique, balconies overlook the old town and thick glass keeps the noise out. Superb central location. Restaurants and cafes are right outside the front door.

Hotel Galini HOTEL €€
(Map p388; ☑ 22850 22114; www.hotelgalini.com; s/d incl breakfast from €70/120; ❄️🌐) A nautical theme lends this superfriendly, family-run place loads of character. Updated, spacious rooms have small balconies, plus some rooms have creative decor fashioned from seashells and driftwood. The location is first rate – close to the old town and the beach – and the breakfast is hearty. Prices drop significantly outside high season.

★ **Traditional Castle House** RENTAL HOUSE €€€
(Map p388; ☑ 6986686493; house €160; 🌐) There are few more atmospheric lodgings in Naxos than this beautifully restored Venetian house, right in the heart of the *kastro*. The heavy wooden beams, exposed stone wall and heavy dark-wood furniture blend seamlessly with modern conveniences, the copper pans of the fully equipped kitchen, nautically themed paintings and a playful scattering of traveller paraphernalia.

Nissaki Beach Hotel HOTEL €€€
(Map p388; ☑ 22850 25710; www.nissaki-beach.com; Agios Georgios Beach; d/ste incl breakfast from €285/355; ❄️🌐🏊) Hard to beat on the island for luxury and locale, Nissaki Beach Hotel offers up a seaside restaurant and gorgeous pool area right on Agios Georgios Beach. The rooms are elegant, with colourful splashes of contemporary art; the suites have large sea-view terraces. A very good breakfast is included in the rates.

🍴 Eating

Hora has fantastic, varied dining. For the freshest seafood, head to the tavernas on the waterfront. Naxian cheeses, sausages and potatoes are also well worth taste-testing and are found in menus of traditional tavernas and fusion restaurants alike.

★ **Maro's Tavern** GREEK €
(Map p388; ☑ 22850 25113; mains €7-16; ⊙ lunch & dinner) There's no sea view or old-town romance here, but the locals don't care. They're too busy tucking into mammoth portions of delicious, good-value food. The zucchini balls (fritters) are tasty, and the *mousakas* and *pastitsio* (layers of buttery macaroni and seasoned minced lamb) will get you through a siege. It's just south of Plateia Evripeou.

★ **Doukato** GREEK €€
(Map p388; ☑ 22850 27013; www.facebook.com/doukatonaxos; Old Town; mains €9-17; ⊙ 6pm-1am May-Oct, weekends only rest of year) One of

the Cyclades' best eating experiences, in a magical setting that was once a monastery, church and a school, Doukato is rightly deserving of accolades. Owner Dimitris grows much of the produce, or sources it locally. The result? Top Naxian specialities such as *gouna* (sun-dried mackerel), *kalogeras* (beef, eggplant and cheese) and the unbelievably delicious Doukato 'Special' souvlaki.

★ L'Osteria ITALIAN €€
(Map p388; ☎ 22850 24080; www.facebook.com/osterialenuovestorie; mains €11-18; ☺ 6.30pm-1am Tue-Sun) This authentic Italian eatery is tucked away in a small alley uphill from the harbour, beneath the *kastro* walls. Grab a table in the cute courtyard and prepare to be impressed with the likes of gnocchi stuffed with goat's cheese and pork cheek and octopus with mash and red lentils. Excellent wine list, plus delectable antipasti and Greek craft beer.

Metaxi Mas GREEK €€
(Map p388; ☎ 22850 26425; mains €8-14; ☺ 12.30pm-2am) Sit on the tiny, vine-shaded terrace or in the wood-and-stone, cavern-like interior, and join the locals for a feast of flash-fried catch of the day, tender, slow-cooked veal with lemon sauce, platters of local cheeses and heaped portions of superlative *mousakas* and *pastitsio*. Near the northern entrance to the old town.

Lucullus GREEK €€
(Map p388; ☎ 22850 22569; Palia Agora; mains €9-14; ☺ 11am-11pm) Tucked into a tiny, vine-shaded lane off Old Market St, Lucullus has been around since 1908 and claims to be Naxos' oldest taverna. Greek staples in this atmospheric place are the way to go, with excellent versions of veal *limonata* (on mashed potatoes in a lemon sauce), lamb *kleftiko* (backed with cheese) and octopus *stifado* (stewed with onions and sauce).

Labyrinth GREEK €€
(Map p388; ☎ 22850 22253; www.facebook.com/Labyrinth.Naxos; mains €11-18; ☺ 6pm-midnight) It's a toss-up as to which is more welcoming here: the warm interior or pretty, private courtyard. Munch through marinated veggies with grilled *manouri* (soft cheese from northern Naxos), swordfish with herbs, or seafood risotto with ouzo sauce. The name is apt: it has a sign, but is easiest to find if you enter the winding alleys from the north.

♥ Drinking & Nightlife

There are a few large, loud clubs at the southern end of the waterfront, and some lovely, mellow bars offering big views and cocktails from upper floors in the *kastro* neighbourhood.

★ La Vigne WINE BAR
(Map p388; ☎ 22850 27199; www.lavignenaxos.com; ☺ 7pm-1am) The only true wine bar in Naxos is hidden in a tiny alley just behind Plateia Mandilara. It's run by two congenial French ladies who'll tell you a thing or two about their carefully selected wines (mostly from around Greece and France). Excellent fusion food, too.

★ Rum Bar BAR
(Map p388; ☎ 6948592718; www.facebook.com/therumbarnaxos; ☺ 8pm-4am) Perched upstairs above Hora's busy waterfront, this sleek place has lovely sunset views looking out over the yacht harbour. Open year-round, Rum Bar plays rock classics and occasionally features live music. Original cocktails are the name of the game here – try the Isla Tropical, which includes a healthy dose of Naxos *kitron* (liqueur made from the leaves of the citron tree).

Naxos Cafe BAR
(Map p388; ☎ 22850 26343; Old Market St; ☺ 8pm-2am) If you want to drink but don't fancy the club scene, here's your answer. This atmospheric, traditional bar is small and candlelit and spills into the cobbled Bourgos street. Drink wine with the locals and listen to the occasional live music.

Kitrón CAFE
(Map p388; ☎ 22850 27055; Protopapadaki; ☺ 8am-late) You can begin your day here, with coffee and a harbour view, and end it with one of the wonderful cocktails featuring *kitron* from Halki's distillery (p392). Try the *kitron* sour or the one with Prosecco and strawberries.

⌂ Shopping

★ Antico Veneziano ANTIQUES
(Map p388; ☎ 22850 22702; Dellaroca; ☺ 10am-1pm & 5-9pm) Inside the *kastro*, this remarkable antique shop hides inside a restored 800-year-old Venetian mansion. Even if you're not a collector who'll salivate at the treasure trove of Veneziana inside, the ancient temple pillars that prop up the shop are worth the visit alone.

⭐**Octopus Naxos** CLOTHING
(Map p388; Palia Agora; ⊘10am-10pm) If you're looking for something uniquely Naxian, you could do worse than these colourful T-shirts, designed in Naxos since 1988. The octopus appears in various guises.

Kohili Jewels GIFTS & SOUVENIRS
(Map p388; ☑22850 22557; ⊘10am-11pm) Hidden in the maze of small streets behind the waterfront, this is a good spot to purchase jewellery made from the Eye of Naxos, the hard shell that develops in the hole of a shellfish. The eye in the beautiful rings, necklaces, earrings and bracelets is said to bring good luck and fortune.

Papyrus BOOKS
(Map p388; ☑22850 23039; ⊘10am-2pm & 6-10pm) What began as a box of books left by a traveller has turned into a shockingly organised collection of over 10,000 second-hand books, covering multiple languages and genres. It's uphill from the port, behind Meze 2.

ⓘ Information

Information Booth (Map p388; ⊘hours vary) At the ferry quay in summer. Opens when ferries arrive.

Handy online resources include www.naxos.gr.

Naxos Tours (☑22850 24000; www.naxostours.net; Paralia; ⊘8am-10pm) Sells ferry tickets and organises excursions and car hire.

Zas Travel (☑22850 23330; www.zastravel.com; ⊘9am-9pm) Ferry tickets, tours and car hire. Located on the harbourfront.

ⓘ Getting Around

Hora is the bus hub for the island, with regular departures for various villages and beaches from the **bus station** (Map p388; ☑22850 22291; www.naxosdestinations.com; Harbour) next to the port.

The North

Heading north along the coast from Hora, the road winds and twists past the **Tower of Ayia**, the majestic ruins of a castle with a spectacular ocean backdrop, passing through Engares, where the **Engares Olive Press** (☑22850 62021; www.olivemuseum.com; ⊘10am-6pm May-Sep) **FREE** is a worthwhile stop – check out the equipment, sample various foodstuffs and stock up on olive products. Further north, the road eventually takes you to the pleasant fishing village of

ⓘ ROAD TRIP

Naxos is a big island. If you have limited time and want to see it all, we recommend renting some wheels and heading out on a road trip. It's feasible to visit Halki, Filoti, Apiranthos and Melanes in a big loop in a day, and even head further afield to Apollonas or Lionas.

Apollonas. Signposted in an ancient quarry on the hillside above the village is a colossal 7th-century BCE **kouros** (Map p385; Apollonas; ⊘24hr), much larger and easier to find than the **Kouros of Flerio** (Map p385).

Apollonas' pebble-and-sand beach is decent and tavernas line the waterfront, serving the freshest of fish. Swing by **Nikos Art** (Map p385; ☑22850 67202; Apollonas; ⊘10am-6pm May-Sep) for very reasonably priced ceramics in Japanese Raku style.

Take the main road south from Apollonas towards Apiranthos and you pass a turnoff to **Lionas**, where a scenic 8km drive past old emery mines leads you to a lovely stony beach and a couple of tavernas, including superfriendly **Delfinaki** (☑22850 51290; www.delfinaki.gr; Lionas; mains €8-14), serving up great home cooking and farm- and sea-fresh ingredients.

Further south of the Lionas turnoff, the road splits in two at Stavros Keramotis church; take the right fork to Moni, with its woodcarving workshops, stellar views of Mt Zeus, and the 7th-century **Panagia Drosiani** (Map p385; Halki–Moni Rd; entry by donation; ⊘10am-7pm) that attracts pilgrims from far and wide.

From Moni you can return to Hora via the marble quarries on the road between Kinidaros and Melanes, and the Kouros of Flerio, two marble statues dating back to the 7th and 6th centuries BCE, signposted in an ancient marble-working area near Mili.

Southwest Beaches

Beaches south of Agios Georgios (Hora's town beach) include beautiful **Agios Prokopios**, which is sandy and shallow and lies in a sheltered bay to the south of the headland of Cape Mougkri. It merges with **Agia Anna**, a stretch of shining white sand, quite narrow but long enough to feel uncrowded towards its southern end. Development is fairly solid at Prokopios and the northern end of Agia Anna.

Sandy beaches continue as far as Pyrgaki, passing the beautiful turquoise waters of the long, dreamy Plaka Beach and gorgeous sandy bays (some popular with naturists) punctuated with rocky outcrops. You'll find plenty of restaurants, accommodation and bus stops along this stretch – it's an idyllic place for a chilled-out beach stay. Maragas Beach Camping (Map p385; ☑22850 42552; www.maragascamping.gr; Agia Anna Beach; camp sites per adult/tent €9/3, d/studio from €55/€80) has a good setup across from a long sandy strand south of Agia Anna: camping, studios and rooms, a supermarket and a taverna. There's a regular bus from Hora that stops out front.

At Mikri Vigla (http://mikrivigla.com), golden granite slabs and boulders divide the beach into two. This beach is becoming an increasingly big fish on the kitesurfing scene, with reliable wind conditions. Flisvos Kite Centre (☑6945457407; www.flisvos-kitecentre.com; equipment rental per day/week €90/350) offers kite- and windsurfing classes and rents equipment to certified surfers, as does Naxos Kitelife (☑6906205807; https://naxoskitelife.com; Mikri Vigla; lessons per hour €60). You can stay next door at Orkos Beach Hotel (☑22850 75194; www.orkosbeach.gr; r/tr/f incl breakfast €81/95/126; ☺mid-May–Sep; ❋ 🛜 🛋), where rooms are clean and comfy.

There is more windsurfing and kitesurfing action in Pyrgaki, south of Mikri Vigla, reachable via an unpaved road past the Aliko promontory. Look out for Hawaii

Beach, just north of the promontory, known for its limpid blue waters.

Heading back north via Kastaraki and Vivlos villages, stop by the Axiotissa (Map p385; ☑22850 75107; www.facebook.com/Axiotissa; Kastraki–Vivlos Rd; mains €7-14; ☺2-11pm) taverna for one of the best meals on the island.

Halki   Χάλκη
POP 500

This village is a vivid reflection of historic Naxos, with the handsome facades of old villas and tower houses a legacy of its wealthy past as the island's long-ago capital. Today it's home to a small but fascinating collection of shops and galleries, drawing creative types. Halki lies at the heart of the Tragaea mountainous region, about 20 minutes' drive (15km) from Hora.

The main road skirts Halki, with parking areas near the entry (from Hora) and exit of town (by the schoolyard). Pedestrian lanes lead off the main road to the picturesque square at the heart of Halki.

Paths radiate from Halki through peaceful olive groves and flower-filled meadows. The atmospheric 11th-century Church of St Georgios Diasorites lies a short distance to the north of the village. It contains some splendid frescoes.

◉ Sights

★ Fish & Olive   GALLERY
(☑22850 31771; www.fish-olive-creations.com; ☺May–mid-Oct) This gallery displays the exquisite work of Naxian potter Katharina Bolesch and her partner, artist and jewellery designer Alexander Reichardt. Each piece of work reflects ancient Mediterranean themes of fish and olives, motifs that grace the blue-and-white plates, elegant jugs, bowls and platters. and appear on Alex's prints and his delicate silver tiepins, pendants and earrings. The artists' work has been exhibited nationally and internationally. There's also a boutique selling their works a few metres from the gallery.

★ Vallindras Distillery   DISTILLERY
(☑22850 31220; www.facebook.com/vallindras.kitrondistillery; ☺10am-10pm Jul & Aug, to 5pm Apr-Jun, Sep & Oct) The Vallindras Distillery on Halki's main square has been distilling the *kitron* liqueur in the same way since 1896, passing from one generation to the next. It's made from the eponymous citrus

TRAGAEA & MT ZEUS

Naxos' lovely inland Tragaea region is a vast plain of olive groves and unspoilt villages high in the mountains, harbouring numerous little Byzantine churches. The Cyclades' highest peak, Mt Zeus (1004m; also known as Mt Zas), dominates the landscape. Filoti, on the slopes of Mt Zeus, is the region's largest village.

To climb Mt Zeus from Filoti, walk 40 minutes up to Aria Spring, a verdant fountain and picnic area, carry on another 20 minutes to the Cave of Zeus, and then climb to the summit in another hour for 360-degree views of the Cyclades.

Alternatively, if you have own wheels and want to shorten the walk, there's a junction signposted to Aria Spring and Zeus Cave, about 800m up from Filoti on the main road. This side road ends after 1.3km. From the road-end parking it's a very short walk to Aria Spring, and you can carry on to the cave and summit from there.

An option for the descent, if you hike up via the cave, is to walk down via the little chapel of Agia Marina to Filoti. You can walk down this route on waymarked track Number 2 in about 1½ hours. Make sure to take good walking shoes, water and sunscreen.

fruit that looks like a large, lumpy lemon, and the distillery makes three varieties varying in colour and strength, as well as a spice-infused liqueur. While the exact recipe is top secret, visitors can check out the museum-like facilities, sample the wares and stock up on supplies.

Phos Gallery GALLERY
(☑ 22850 31118; www.phosgallery.gr; ⊙ 11am-4pm May-Oct) See the island through the lens of talented photographer Dimitris Gavalas. Stunning black-and-white landscapes – mostly of Naxos – grace the walls of this gallery, along with witty conceptual prints.

✖ Eating

Dolce Vita BAKERY €
(☑ 6981467240; snacks €3-7; ⊙ 9am-8pm) Cool and inviting, with dark wood and a gramophone daring to be wound, this is the place to lounge over the amazing orange cake, coffee and ice cream.

Giannis Taverna TAVERNA €
(☑ 22850 32294; www.yannistavern.gr; dishes €7-14; ⊙ 12.30-10pm) With tables filling Halki's pretty central square under a trellis of vine leaves, Giannis is well known for traditional fare. Try *moussakas*, pork souvlaki, *pasticcio* (macaroni pie) or village sausage.

🛍 Shopping

Penelope ARTS & CRAFTS
(☑ 22850 31754) The know-how has been passed down to Penelope through at least four generations – one of two such families of weavers in Halki – and her fingers and feet fly on the loom. Watch her incorporate traditional designs into hats, scarves, bags

and tablecloths to make fab souvenirs. You'll notice a lot of red and blue – the traditional colours of Naxos.

ℹ Getting There & Away

Halki can be visited by public bus (€2), but if you are keen to explore the mountainous regions of central Naxos, you're better off renting your own wheels.

Apiranthos Απείρανθος

POP 711

Apiranthos seems to grow out of the stony flanks of rugged Mt Fanari (883m), about 25km east of Hora (or 10 winding kilometres from Halki). The village's unadorned stone houses and marble-paved streets reflect a rugged individualism that is matched by the villagers themselves. Many of them are descendants of refugees who migrated from Crete, and today the village's distinctive form of the Greek language has echoes of the 'Great Island'. Apiranthos people have always been noted for their spirited politics and populism, and the village has produced a remarkable number of academics. These days, the village is known for its crafts (traditional weaving, ceramics) and has some excellent tavernas in which to while away an afternoon.

👁 Sights

Natural History Museum of Apiranthos MUSEUM
(☑ 22850 61725; €2.50; ⊙ hours vary) This museum specialises in local flora and fauna and has a marvellous collection of shells. It is split into two sections, one focusing on the

sea, the other on the land. It's signposted off the pedestrian street.

Archaeological Museum of Apiranthos   MUSEUM

(☑22850 61725; ☉ hours vary) FREE This museum is part-way along the main street. It has a marvellous collection of small Cycladian artefacts collected by mathematics professor Michael Bardani and donated to the museum.

Geological Museum of Apiranthos   MUSEUM

(☑22850 61725; €2; ☉ hours vary) The Geological Museum is near the village entrance and exhibits over 2500 rare rocks from the villages of Naxos, the Cyclades, the rest of Greece and around the world.

✖ Eating

Taverna O Platanos   GREEK €

(☑22850 61192; mains €8-15; ☉11.30am-10pm) Set beneath the shade of its namesake plane tree, this lively family restaurant is deserving of its Aegean Cuisine certification. The chunky hamburger comes filled with gooey Naxian Gruyère, the Naxian potato fries are moreish and the *platanos* (grilled pork chunks) come with a back note of oregano and thyme, and with a side of valley views.

★ Lefteris   GREEK €€

(☑22850 61333; mains €10-22; ☉noon-10pm May-Oct) With an outdoor terrace beneath a walnut tree, this charming, well-regarded family taverna has the feel of an old country kitchen and serves the best food in the village. Grilled meats are a speciality here (try the lamb, cheese-stuffed burger or homemade sausages), along with moreish cheese pie, and seasonal greens with lemon.

🔒 Shopping

Apiranthos Art   CERAMICS

(☉10am-8pm May-Oct) Gun-metal amphorae with a twinkle of mica line the street by this ceramics shop on the main pedestrian drag. They are locally made, as are the beautiful utilitarian dishes of varying styles that you find inside. Also on display are a few select pieces and masks by Giannis Nanouris, an internationally renowned artist who happens to live nearby.

ℹ Getting There & Away

There are five daily public buses from Naxos Town to Apiranthos (€3.10), but if you are keen to explore the mountainous regions of central Naxos, you're best off renting your own wheels.

SMALL CYCLADES
ΜΙΚΡΕΣ ΚΥΚΛΑΔΕΣ

The six tiny islands that lie between Naxos and Amorgos have gone through millennia of civilisation and upheaval, from being densely populated trading centres in the days of antiquity and then fortified Venetian outposts to pirate havens and impoverished fishing backwaters during WWII before recently re-emerging in the spotlight as increasingly fashionable getaways. Today, only four have permanent populations – Iraklia, Schinousa, Ano Koufonisi (Koufonisia) and Donousa – and they remain very distinct from one another in character and topography, with Koufonisia in particular welcoming sun-worshippers, Schinousa and rugged Donousa appealing to hikers, and Iraklia famous for its cave pilgrimage.

Donousa is the northernmost of the group and the furthest from Naxos; the others are clustered near the larger island's southeast coast.

ℹ Information

Terrain (http://terrainmaps.gr) has an excellent map titled *Minor Cyclades,* which covers all the islands, including walking tracks.

ℹ Getting There & Away

There are several connections a week between Piraeus and the Small Cyclades via Naxos, and daily connections to/from Naxos to Koufonisia (less frequent to the other islands). For ferry schedules, visit http://ferries.gr.

Blue Star Ferries (www.bluestarferries.gr) serves the Small Cyclades year-round from Piraeus via Paros and Naxos. From Naxos, three times a week the ferry calls at Donousa, then Amorgos (Aegiali) and terminates at Astypalea (in the Dodecanese). Three times a week, from Naxos the ferry stops at Iraklia, Schinousa and Koufonisia before terminating at Amorgos (Katapola).

The Small Cyclades Line runs the mainstay service, weather permitting in winter. Its sturdy little *Express Skopelitis* leaves from Naxos in the afternoon daily Monday to Saturday, and calls at the Small Cyclades and Amorgos (often to both Aegiali and Katapola), returning to Naxos early the following morning.

Iraklia   Ηρακλεία

POP 150

Sparsely inhabited, Iraklia only shakes off its soporific air in July and August, when yachts dot the island's sheltered Livadi Bay and the main village grows lively. Sitting

Small Cyclades

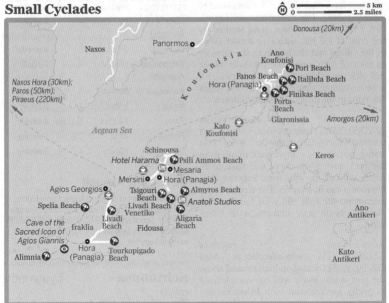

amid the olive groves, ruins of Hellenic-era temples, Venetian fortifications and mysterious *speires* (spiral petroglyphs, believed by some to be markers of pirate treasure) are enduring memorials of the island's long and venerable history.

Iraklia rewards hikers who explore its hilly topography on foot with secluded bays and thyme-scented solitude. There are also a couple of excellent beaches.

The port and main village of Iraklia is Agios Georgios. It has an attractive cove-like harbour, complete with a sandy beach.

Sights & Activities

A surfaced road leads off to the left of the ferry quay, and after about 1km you'll reach Livadi, the island's best beach. A steep 2.5km further on is Hora (also called Panagia). From Hora, a surfaced road carries on to Tourkopigado Beach.

There are seven well-marked hiking trails of varying length that cover the island. Get a map, make sure to wear decent walking shoes and take plenty of water.

Follow consecutive trails 7, 4 and 3 from Agios Georgios to get to the Cave of the Sacred Icon of Agios Giannis (Map p395) in less than two hours. Passing by olive groves, this route takes you through the deserted hamlet of Agios Athanasios before ascending fairly steeply to the top of the hill, from where a rocky path leads down to the cave. Alternatively, follow trail 3 from Hora to get there in one hour, ascending steeply from the village to the spot where trails 3 and 4 meet on the hilltop.

Beyond the cave, trails 5 and 6 make a loop, leading to the beach at Alimina, which is also served by boat from Agios Georgios in summer (offering a shortcut to the cave), and offering a picturesque seaside route back to the hamlet of Agios Athanasios.

For a shorter walk from Agios Georgios, take trail 8 for 30 minutes to reach the gorgeous cove of Vorini Spilla and a refreshing swim.

Sleeping

Maïstrali GUESTHOUSE €
(☑ 22850 71807; r/apt €50/85; ☜) Up the main road through the village from the port, Maïstrali offers a range of simple, good-value rooms and apartments with rates that tumble to €30 out of high season. It also features a shady elevated terrace taverna that has all the Greek standards covered and is open for breakfast, lunch and dinner. A good budget option.

★ **Alexandra Studios** GUESTHOUSE €€

(☑22850 71482; http://alexandrarooms.blogspot.
com; r €80; ❄☎) Spotless, snug studios on
the crest of the hill, with epic sunset views
of the village and the bay from the terraces
in front of each room. The convivial owner
will pick you up from the port; otherwise it's
a seven-minute uphill walk through Agios
Georgios in the direction of Livadi Beach.

Speires Hotel BOUTIQUE HOTEL €€

(☑22850 77015; www.speires.gr; d/tr/ste incl
breakfast €66/96/112; ☺May-Oct; ❄☎) This
stylish boutique is a short walk uphill from
the port, with white decor and flash bathrooms with all the mod cons. Superior double rooms can fit a family. The terrace at the
elegant on-site cafe and wine bar is a fine
place to begin your immersion in Greek
wine.

Anna's Place PENSION €€

(☑22850 74234; www.annasplace.gr; d/apt
€65/90; ❄☎) Located on high ground above
the port is this lovely, well-run complex, set
in pretty gardens and with balconies taking in sweeping views. Inside, each super-
clean, comfortable room has a kitchenette;
the two-room apartments are a boon for
families. Transfers from and to the port are
complimentary.

🍷 Drinking & Nightlife

★ **Surfin Bird** COCKTAIL BAR

(☑6936000295; www.facebook.com/surfinbird.
irakleia; Livadi Beach; ☺4pm-2am) A favourite
gathering spot at sunset, this chilled-out outdoor bar overlooking Livadi Beach has great
appeal for cocktail lovers: its original concoctions feature homemade thyme and other herbal syrups, plus fruit juices and Greek
liqueurs. It also has considerable appeal for
fans of 'Family Guy'. Have you heard...?

★ **En Lefko** CAFE

(☑22850 77027; www.facebook.com/en.leuko.
irakleia; ☺8am-2am May-Sep) This rooftop bar
right on top of Perigiali Supermarket is lovingly run by local couple Nikos and Anna.
There are brunch menus plus cocktails,
drinks and snacks until the wee hours. One
of few options in Iraklia if you feel the urge
to have a late night.

ℹ️ Getting There & Away

Ferry services are significantly reduced out of
season. Differences in journey durations are
because of routing or vessel type.

Ferry services from Iraklia:

DESTINATION	DURATION	FARE (€)	FREQUENCY
Aegiali (on Amorgos)	2¼-3¾hrs	9	4 weekly
Donousa	2¼hrs	8	4 weekly
Katapola (on Amorgos)	1¾-4¾hrs	8	1-2 daily
Koufonisia	50mins	5	1-2 daily
Naxos	1-5hrs	7	1-2 daily
Paros	1¼-6hrs	11-17.50	4 weekly
Piraeus	8hrs	20	3 weekly
Schinousa	10mins	4	9 weekly

ℹ️ Getting Around

There are buses in July and August only linking
Agios Georgios, Livadi Beach and Hora. You can
also hire **scooters** (☑6972755850, 6977168139;
scooters/ATVs per day from €20/30; ☺hours
vary) in summer.

Schinousa Σχοινούσα
POP 256

The undulating, hilly topography of small,
laidback Schinousa is a palimpsest of fields,
secluded coves, ancient stone walls, Byzantine chapels, and ruins of Venetian fortifications, reflecting the ebb and flow of
many civilisations. During three centuries
of Turkish rule, the island sheltered pirates
from the Mani, but these days it attracts
sunseekers after a slower pace of life, and
due to the sheer number of beaches, it
doesn't feel as crowded as its neighbours
even at the height of summer.

The main settlement, Hora (Panagia),
has a long, narrow main street lying along
the breezy crest of the island. Ferries dock
at the fishing harbour of Mersini. Hora is a
steepish 1km walk uphill from there.

◎ Sights & Activities

Dirt tracks lead from Hora to no less than
16 beaches all over the island. The nearest
are sandy Tsigouri (Map p395) (seven-minute walk) and the wide sweep of Livadi (Map
p395) (15-minute walk), both south of Hora
and uncrowded outside August. A 20-min-
ute walk southeast and downhill brings you
to the smaller, sand-and-pebble bays of Ali-
garia and Almyros with its shallow water.
Thirty minutes' walk, just east of Mesaria
in the north is the sheltered cove of Psili
Ammos. Tsigouri, Livadi and Almyros have
tavernas and/or beach bars; Hotel Harama (Map p395; ☑22850 76015; r €65; ❄⊠)

provides sustenance to beachgoers at Psili Ammos.

Aeolia
BOATING
(☑ 6979618233, 6982002327; boat trip €20-40) From June to September, Captain Manolis runs various daily trips on the *Aeolia*, including around the beaches of the island (€20), or to Iraklia (€20) and Keros and Koufonisia (€40). Private trips can also be arranged. Ask about the week's schedule where you are staying.

🛏️ Sleeping & Eating

There are rooms down at Mersini (the port), several hotels and domatia in Hora, and a handful of excellent options in remoter locations (near Almyros, Livadi, Tsigouri and Psili Ammos beaches). Domatia owners, with transport, meet ferries from about May onwards and will always meet booked guests. Book ahead in July and August.

Anatoli Studios
HOTEL €€
(Map p395; ☑ 6932371036; www.anatolistudio. com; Almiros Beach; r €100; ❋ 🎧 ≋) In the southeast part of the island and reachable via a 20-minute walk from Hora, this delightful, family-run property consists of a neat cluster of airy, whitewashed rooms with mozzie nets and kitchenettes, surrounding the pool and looking out over the undulating coastline. Four beaches are an easy walk away and the on-site restaurant serves terrific sea urchin spaghetti.

Meltemi
PENSION €€
(☑ 22850 71947; www.pension-meltemi.gr; d €75-85; ❋ 🎧) Genuinely warm hospitality is the hallmark of this family-run pension and restaurant in the heart of Hora. Rooms are comfy and simple. You have a choice between older rooms in the Meltemi 1 building or newer rooms in Meltemi 2. Both are good. The on-site restaurant serves up delicious homemade meals. Free port and beach transfers, too.

Iliovasilema
HOTEL €€
(☑ 22850 71948; www.iliovasilemahotel.gr; Hora; d incl breakfast €90; ❋ mid-May–Sep; ❋ 🎧) In Hora, but perched at the port end of town with king-of-the-castle sunset views ('*iliovaselima*' means sunset), rooms here are small, simple and spotless. The views out towards Iraklia from the balconies are fab, and the service is warm. Rates include a good buffet breakfast.

★ Deli Bistro-Bar
GREEK €€
(☑ 22850 74278; mains €13-25; ❋ noon-11pm Mar-Oct) Deli consists of a top-notch restaurant with views out to Ios and Iraklia, plus a cool ground-floor cafe-bar. The Cretan owner-chef's menu is the most inventive in Schinousa, with Schinousa cheese in filo pastry with tomato marmalade and slow-cooked prawns with ouzo sitting alongside Greek-style fish carpaccio. Excellent Greek wine list and a fine selection of craft beers, too.

Fish Tavern & Rooms Mersini
SEAFOOD €€
(☑ 22850 71159; www.mersini.gr; mains €9-20; ❋ May-Sep; ❋ 🎧) Down at the port, 'Aegean Cuisine' flag bearer Mersini woos diners in a garden setting with great harbour views and traditional Greek dishes and seafood (particularly lobster spaghetti and local squid) with a contemporary twist, and hand-picked wild herbs and organic vegetables from its own garden.

ℹ️ Information

Paralos Travel (☑ 22850 71160; ❋ hours vary) Sells ferry tickets and also doubles as the post office on the main street in Hora.

ℹ️ Getting There & Around

Ferry services are significantly reduced out of season. Differences in journey durations are due to routing or vessel type.

Destinations are: Aegiali on Amorgos (€8.50, 3½ hours, six weekly), Katapola on Amorgos (€8, 1½ to 4½ hours, one to two daily), Donousa (€8, two hours, three weekly), Iraklia (€4, 10 minutes, nine weekly), Koufonisia (€4, 30 minutes, one to three daily), Naxos (€14.50, 1¼ to 1¾ hours, eight weekly), Paros (€14.50, 2¾ hours, four weekly) and Piraeus (€37.50, 6½ hours, three weekly).

There are buses in July and August only, linking the port, Hora and the main beaches. Otherwise, walk or hire a scooter or ATV in summer from **Faros Bikes** (☑ 6977366853, 22850 71920; Hora; scooter/ATV €20/30 per day; ❋ hours vary).

Koufonisia Κουφονήσια

POP 399

At the heart of a mighty Cycladic civilisation in millennia past, and an impoverished backwater following the Axis occupation during WWII, the smallest of the inhabited Cyclades has been transformed in recent years into a fashionable destination – 'the Mykonos of the Small Cyclades', a place to wind down after the frenetic action of Mykonos and Santorini.

It's made up of three main islands, two of which, Kato Koufonisi and Keros, are uninhabited. You'll arrive at the populated, low-lying **Ano Koufonisi**. It sees a flash flood of tourism each summer season thanks to its superb beaches, good hotels and chic restaurants, and its narrow, bougainvillea-fringed main street is a joy to wander along.

⊙ Sights

Koufonisia's only settlement spreads out behind the ferry quay. The older part of town, the **Hora**, sits along a low hill above the harbour, parallel to the coast, and consists of a small grid of whitewashed streets dotted with restaurants, lodgings and cafes.

At the western end of the main street, you'll reach **Loutro**, with a stony cove, small boatyard, windmill and whitewashed church.

⊙ Beaches

The village has the white-sand **Ammos Beach**, though nicer beaches are found further east and south. A 1.2km (15-minute) walk along the sandy coast road east of the settlement brings you to the sandy **Finikas Beach** (Map p395), with calm waters and a taverna, passing a couple of rocky coves en route. **Fanos Beach** (Map p395), a five-minute walk east around the headland, has a beach bar and some shade. Another five minutes along the coast is **Italihda Beach** (Map p395), a favourite with naturists (though nudity generally becomes more overt the further east you go).

Beyond Italihda, the path skirts another headland and passes several rocky swimming places, including the deep and clear **Piscina** (10-minute walk), a swimming hole surrounded by rock that is linked to the sea. From there it's another 10 minutes to the yacht-dotted bay at **Pori** (Map p395), where a long crescent of sand slides effortlessly into the clear sea and there's a taverna and a cafe. Pori can also be reached by an inland road from Hora.

⌒⋝ Tours

Prasinos Boat Tours   BOATING
(☑ 22850 71438, 6945042548; www.roussetoshotel. gr; ☺ May-Sep) Hop on Captain Kostas' boat to transfer to/from various beaches around the island (€3 to €5 return depending on the beach) and Kato Koufonisi (€5 return). In peak season there's a dozen or so departures per day. There's a ticket kiosk at the port, or enquire at Prasinos travel agency (p399).

Koufonissia Tours   BOATING
(☑ 22850 74435; www.koufonissiatours.gr) Based on the main street (and also at Villa Ostria), Koufonissia Tours organises recommended sailing, diving and sea-kayaking trips around Koufonisia and the rest of the Small Cyclades.

⊨ Sleeping

★**Apollon Studios**   GUESTHOUSE €€
(☑ 22850 74464; www.apollonkoufonisia.gr; r from €60; ❋ 🖛) Decked out in blues and whites, these whitewashed, round-edged Cycladic cubes sit uphill from the port and come with small kitchenettes and snug little terraces overlooking the sea, and shaded by bamboo awnings. The friendly proprietor makes guests feel at home.

★**Ermis Rooms**   PENSION €€
(☑ 6972265240, 22850 71693; www.koufonisia. gr/?page_id=1255&lang=en; d €75-85; ❋ 🖛) These immaculate rooms are in a quiet location, behind a pretty white-and-lilac exterior and a flowering garden. Ask Sofia for a balcony with sea view. At the port end of the beach, take the road uphill to the left of Roussetos Hotel. Ermis Rooms is next to the pale green post office, also run by Sofia.

Villa Ostria   HOTEL €€
(☑ 22850 71671; www.ostriavilla.gr; r/studio from €85/120; ❋ 🖛) On the high ground east of the town beach, the flowering, creeper-clad classic Cycladic cubes of Ostria hide attractive rooms and studios with quirky decor made from seashells and driftwood. Rooms have kitchenettes; spacious studios have kitchens.

Anna Villas   PENSION €€
(☑ 22850 71697; www.annavillas.gr; d incl breakfast €100; ❋ 🖛) These fresh, bright studios with kitchenettes are charming and run with warmth. All have balconies overlooking either the town beach or the countryside. It's a family-friendly spot, with a lovely reading nook and summertime cafe. Take the first left after the bike-rental sign at the eastern end of the beach and climb the hill.

✕ Eating

★**Kalamia**   CAFE €
(☑ 22850 74444; www.facebook.com/kalamiabar; mains €7-12; ☺ 9am-4am; 🖛) A chilled-out cafe and lively bar, Kalamia does many things well. Grab a seat under the thatched roof and dig into eggs florentine for brunch, epic burgers and quesadillas the rest of the day,

and wash them down with award-winning Greek craft beers (Voria stout, 56 Isles pilsner, Chios smoked porter...). On the main street up the from town beach.

★**Mikres Cyclades** GREEK **€€**
(☑22850 74500; https://mikrescyclades.com; mains €10-15; ☺5pm-1am; 🛜☑) Showcasing the best of Cycladic produce with pride, Mikres serves a short and sweet menu of mezedhes, fish and meat dishes under a stylish bamboo awning on the main street. The Schinousa *fava* is earthy and moreish, the cheese selection spans Naxos, Syros and Sifnos, and the seafood tastes as if it just leapt out of the water.

Capetan Nikolas SEAFOOD **€€**
(☑22850 71690; Loutro; mains €7-25; ☺dinner May-Oct) A local seafood institution, this cheerful restaurant overlooks the harbour at Loutro. Bearded Captain Nikolas may greet you at the door – you may have seen him spearfishing around the island. The lobster salad is famous and the seafood pasta delicious. Locally caught fish, such as red mullet and sea bream, are priced by the kilo.

ℹ️ Information

Prasinos (☑22850 71438; ☺7am-11pm Jun-Aug) sells tours and ferry tickets on Hora's main street.

ℹ️ Getting There & Away

Koufonisia has a growing number of July and August high-speed connections to plenty of Cyclades islands.
Ferry services from Koufonisia:

DESTINATION	DURATION	FARE (€)	FREQUENCY
Amorgos	20mins-3½hrs	7-14	2-4 daily
Donousa	1¼hrs	6	3 weekly
Folegandros	2½hrs	70	6 weekly
Iraklia	50mins	5	1-2 daily
Milos	3-4hrs	69	1-2 daily
Mykonos	2¼hrs	56	daily
Naxos	45mins-2½hrs	9-26	2-4 daily
Paros	1¼-8½hrs	19-35	1-3 daily
Piraeus	4¼-8½hrs	38-70	2-4 daily
Santorini	2hrs	47	daily
Schinousa	30mins	4	1-3 daily
Serifos	5½hrs	65	daily
Sifnos	4-5hrs	65	2 daily

ℹ️ Getting Around

Bike hire (☑6973354991; www.thoosa.gr; per day €5-10; ☺9am-9pm Jun-Aug) is available from a shop at the eastern end of the town beach. Koufonisia is largely flat and cycling is easy. The island is also small enough to be easily walkable.

An hourly bus (€2, 10am to 8pm) operates between Hora and Pori Beach via Finikas Beach in July and August only.

Donousa Δονούσα
POP LESS THAN 150

According to Greek mythology, it was here that Dionysus, the god of wine, brought Ariadne to hide her from Theseus. As well he might – Donousa is still wonderfully out-on-a-limb and the remotest of the Small Cyclades. Stavros is Donousa's main settlement and port – a cluster of whitewashed buildings around a handsome church, overlooking the ferry quay and a decent sandy beach.

Late July and August sees crowds of holiday-making Greeks and sun-seeking northern Europeans, but out of season, fresh air fiends are likely to have the sandy beach coves and the rocky trails that traverse the hilly, arid landscape all to themselves.

◉ Sights

Kedros, 1.25km southeast of Stavros, reached by a steep, stepped track, is a large, gorgeous sandy crescent with a seasonal taverna, free camping and calm cerulean waters. Limenari, a 40-minute walk along the coast from Kedros, is a more secluded cove; both Kedros and Limenari are popular with naturists. Accessible both from the hamlet of Messaria (Charavgi) via a 25-minute hike and the largest village of Mersini via a steep, 25-minute descent, the white-sand sweep of Livadi sees even fewer visitors.

At the end of the road on the northeast coast, the tiny village of **Kalotaritissa** has three little beaches – two pebble beaches closest to the village and a sandy cove a 10-minute hike away. Get here by minibus, hike, or on the boat *Margissa* in summer.

🛏️ Sleeping & Eating

★**Argalios Guesthouse** GUESTHOUSE **€**
(☑22850 79008, 6982953374; www.argalios guesthouse.gr; r €50; 🛜) 🍽 This delightful guesthouse higher up in the village consists of four snug, individually styled apartments, all with heavy wooden beams, characterful reclaimed furniture and superior Cocomat

HIKING AROUND DONOUSA

Donousa has five numbered and well-marked hiking trails, four of which are old trails that connect the villages. They are:

#1: Stavros to Kalotaritissa (4.4km, 1¼ hours) The longest and toughest of the trails, with steep sections and terrific views.

#2: Kedros to Messaria (1.1km, 30 minutes) Connecting the most popular beach with the hamlet.

#3: Mersini to Livadi (0.9km, 30 minutes) Steep trail down to one of the lovelier beaches.

#4: Kedros to Kato Mylos/Vathy Limenari (2km, 45 minutes) Coast-hugging trail connecting Kedros Beach to the Limenari Beach via a ruined windmill.

#5: Kampos to Limni/Aspros Kavos (2.1km, 40 minutes) Trail starts near Stavros and leads to the tip of a remote cape.

It is a rocky and dry island covered in scrubland and with very little shade, so be prepared with decent shoes, plenty of liquids and sunscreen. The main beaches of Kedros, Limenari, Livadi and Kalotaritissa can all be reached on foot on these marked tracks.

mattresses. Your hosts, Iliad and Ploumissa, are committed to sustainable living and can organise traditional loom weaving classes.

★**Makares** APARTMENT €€
(☑ 22850 79079; www.makares-donoussa.gr; r & apt €80-140; ☺ May-Oct; ❋ 🛜) Loukas is an excellent host at Makares, a clutch of self-catering studios and apartments at the far end of Stavros Bay (across the beach from the port). It's a short walk to the village hub, the views are fabulous, the decor simple and elegant, and the feeling of seclusion is first-rate. Pickup offered from the port.

★**Avli** GREEK €€
(☑ 22850 51557; www.facebook.com/avlidonoussa; mains €10-15; ☺ noon-late) There's a lot to love about this innovative little restaurant above the quayside, run by a Greek-Czech couple: the sea views, Donousa's best wine list, plus classy Aegean cuisine (black-eyed pea salad, sardines stuffed with parsley and garlic, calamari stuffed with *graviera* cheese).

★**I Kori tou Mihali** TAVERNA €€
(☑ 6984618807; Mersini; mains €9-18) At this welcoming taverna in Mersini village, 6km from Stavros by road, Koula conjures up excellent Greek cuisine with a modern twist: wild goat from the island, pork in honey and yoghurt, and smoky eggplant dip. The knockout views are a bonus.

ℹ Information

Sigalas Travel (☑ 22850 51570; ☺ hours vary Mon-Sat) sells ferry tickets and is open in the mornings and evenings on ferry days, plus 40 minutes before ferry arrivals.

ℹ Getting There & Around

Ferry services are significantly reduced out of season. Differences in journey durations are due to routing or vessel type.

Destinations from Donousa are: Aegiali on Amorgos (€7, 45 minutes to 1¼ hours, seven weekly), Katapola on Amorgos (€7, 2¼ to 4¾ hours, three weekly), Astypalea (€15, 2¾ hours, four weekly), Iraklia (€8, 2¼ hours, four weekly), Koufonisia (€6, 1¼ hours, three weekly), Naxos (€7, 1¼ to 3¼ hours, eight weekly), Paros (€11 to €18, 2¼ to 2½ hours, five weekly), Piraeus (€30, 8¼ hours, four weekly) and Schinousa (€8, two weekly, three weekly).

There are no cars or scooters for hire. A minibus connects Stavros with the tiny hamlet of Kalotaritissa on the far side of the island via Donousa's only road (€2, early June to late August).

Bicycle hire should be up and running in the near future and the island is very walkable.

The island's only **taxi** (☑ 6971774696) can drop you off in Kalotaritissa (€13) and elsewhere.

The small boat *Margissa* takes visitors to island beaches (€5) from June to September with a schedule based on weather and wind direction.

AMORGOS ΑΜΟΡΓΟΣ

POP 2000

Dramatic Amorgos is shaped like a seahorse swimming its way east towards the Dodecanese, while the ribbon of road that winds its way along the long ridge of mountains, connecting the main villages, is among the most beautiful drives in the Cyclades.

Amorgos remains relatively off the beaten track – even the fast ferry from Athens takes seven hours to get here! Free-diving aficionados and fans of Luc Besson's cult classic *The*

Big Blue come to play in the Aegean, while walkers spend days exploring the numerous trails that zigzag across the rugged terrain, leading to secluded beaches, cutting across hillsides and abandoned stone terraces and meandering past ruined Cycladic windmills and remnants of ancient settlements.

Of the three main settlements, Katapola is more favoured by families, while Aegiali attracts a younger crowd and the enchanting capital of Hora is all maze-like, marble-paved alleyways and tumbling bougainvillea.

Three good websites on the island are www.amorgos.gr, www.amorgos.guide and www.amorgos-island-magazine.com.

❶ Getting There & Away

Connections from Naxos are good, with the Small Cyclades Line (www.ferries.gr/smallcycladeslines) operating each day (except Sunday), connecting Naxos with the two Amorgos ports by way of the Small Cyclades.

Blue Star Ferries (www.bluestarferries.gr) has three useful routes: two run regularly from Piraeus via Paros, Naxos and the Small Cyclades, ending at either Aegiali or Katapola port. The third route sails weekly from Piraeus to Katapola and eastwards to Patmos, Leros, Kos and Rhodes.

Purchase your tickets from **Nautilos** (☑ Aegiali 22850 73032, Katapola 22850 71201; nautilos@amorgos.net), a ticket agency with offices close to both harbours.

Boat services from Aegiali:

DESTINATION	DURATION	FARE (€)	FREQUENCY
Astypalea	1¾hrs	13	4 weekly
Donousa	45mins-1¼hrs	7	7 weekly
Iraklia	2¼-3¾hrs	9	4 weekly
Koufonisia	2½hrs	7	3 weekly
Naxos	2¼-5hrs	12	1-2 daily
Paros	3½hrs	13-21	5 weekly
Schinousa	3½hrs	8.50	6 weekly
Syros	5¼hrs	16	weekly

Boat services from Katapola:

DESTINATION	DURATION	FARE (€)	FREQUENCY
Donousa	2¼-4¾hrs	7	3 weekly
Folegandros	2¼hrs	70	daily
Ios	3hrs	12	weekly
Iraklia	1¾-4½hrs	8	1-2 daily
Koufonisia	40mins-3½hrs	7-14	2-4 daily
Milos	5½hrs	70	daily
Mykonos	2¼hrs	55	3 weekly
Naxos	1¼-3¼hrs	11-30	2-3 daily
Paros	4-4¼hrs	13-29	1-2 daily
Piraeus	5-10hrs	33-70	1-2 daily
Rhodes	8½hrs	33	weekly
Schinousa	1½-4¼hrs	8	1-2 daily
Santorini	1½-3¼hrs	12-50	1-2 daily

❶ Getting Around

The Amorgos Bus Company (http://amorgosbuscompany.com) has timetables and ticket prices online. Summer buses go regularly from Katapola to Hora (€2) and Moni Hozoviotissis and Agia Anna Beach (€2), and less often to Aegiali (€3, 45 minutes). There are also buses from Aegiali up to Langada and Tholaria. Schedules are posted at the main stop in each village.

Without doubt, the easiest way to get around is with your own wheels. Cars, ATVs and scooters are available for hire from **Thomas Rental** (☑ Aegiali 22850 73444, Katapola 22850 71777; www.thomas-rental.gr) or **Evis Cars** (☑ 22850 71066; www.eviscars.gr; Aegiali). Expect to pay from €40/30/20 per day for a car/ATV/scooter in August; less the rest of the year. There are only two petrol stations: one 1.5km inland from Katapola, the other in Aegiali.

Katapola   Κατάπολα

POP 634

Katapola sprawls round the curving, yacht-filled shoreline of a picturesque bay in the most verdant part of the island. It's a bustling port, divided into three villages: Katapola on the port, Rahidhi in the centre and Xylokeratidhi on the north side of the bay.

The remains of the ancient city of Minoa lie above the port and can be easily reached by footpath or a steep concrete road; although there is no information by the ruins, the views are magnificent. Amorgos has also yielded many Cycladic finds: the largest figurine in the National Archaeological Museum in Athens was found in the vicinity of Katapola.

⌂ Sleeping

⭐ **Big Blue**   GUESTHOUSE €€
(☑ 22850 73471; www.thebigblue.gr; apt €91-120; ❄🐾) Located uphill from the port, past the Botanical Garden, this clutch of spacious studio apartments in Cycladic blues and whites benefits from excellent sea views – from most of the lodgings, as well as the two communal terraces. Each room comes with its own little terrace and you're guaranteed a very warm welcome.

Amorgos

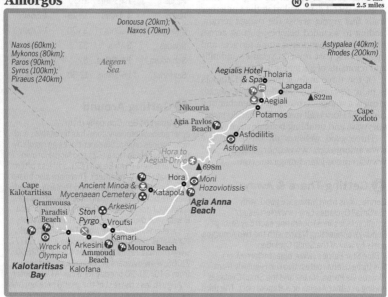

Pension Amorgos PENSION €€

(☑ 22850 71013; www.pension-amorgos.com; d €80; ❋ 🛜) There's a good deal of character in this traditional guesthouse, with bright and well-kept rooms right on the waterfront. It has the same owner as Emprostiada in Amorgos' Hora, and a similarly high quality. As a bonus, Katapola's tavernas are only a short stumble away.

Villa Katapoliani PENSION €€

(☑ 22850 71664; www.villakatapoliani.gr; d/tr/f €85/120/140; ❋ 🛜) Owner Stamatia has a high-quality collection of rooms, studios and apartments, handily located behind the waterfront and ferry quay. The balconies at Villa 1 overlook a garden filled with bougainvillea and the scattered ruins of the ancient temple of Apollo. Or scoot upstairs to the rooftop terrace for sea views. Apartments sleep up to four.

Minoa Hotel HOTEL €€

(☑ 22850 74055; www.hotelminoa.gr; s/d/tr €55/85/95; ❋ 🛜) Right near the waterfront, this family-run place couldn't be more convenient for early-morning ferries. Service is friendly, and the sweet, neat rooms have tidy bathrooms and balconies overlooking a tree- and bird-filled garden. The foyer shares space with the family's Sweets by Pothiti cafe and patisserie.

🍴 Eating

Tavernas and cafes line the waterfront. Most serve traditional seafood and Greek standards, but there are more imaginative options in Xylokeratidhi, on the opposite side of the bay from Katapola port.

Honey & Cinnamon BAKERY €

(☑ 22850 71485; snacks from €3; ☉ 9am-11pm) Look for the bright red window shutters and follow your nose. This tiny patisserie, a block back from the waterfront, bakes up cakes, pastries and lots of local cookies. Try the ones made with the local liquor, *psimeni raki,* or simply grab a coffee or a gelato.

★ Youkali GREEK €€

(☑ 22850 71838; www.facebook.com/youkali amorgos; mains €8-14; ☉ noon-2am; 🖉) Wander over to the opposite side of the bay from the port to Katapola's most imaginative cooking. That ingredients are fresh and locally sourced goes without saying; try them in combos such as orzo with beetroot and zucchini, meatballs with leek sauce, and linguine with shrimps. Friendly service, beautiful presentation.

Mouragio SEAFOOD €€

(☑ 22850 71011; mains €10-19; ☉ 11am-1am) An 'Aegean Cuisine' label bearer, this port-side tavern has been going strong since 1980.

Fish soup and lobster spaghetti are specialities here, along with grilled catch of the day.

❶ Getting There & Away

Boats dock right on the waterfront. The **bus station** is a few minutes' walk along the water. From Katapola, buses run to Aegali (€3, one hour, five times daily), Chora (€2, 20 minutes, 16 times daily) and Agia Anna Beach (€2, 30 minutes, eight times daily) from mid-June until the end of August; less frequently the rest of the year.

N Synodinos (☑ 22850 71201; synodinos@nax. forthnet.gr) Sells ferry tickets and has a money exchange on the waterfront.

Hora (Amorgos)
Χώρα (Αμοργός)

POP 414

Capped by a 13th-century *kastro* (castle) and guarded by windmills that stand sentinel on the hill above it, the historic capital of Hora is a wonderfully atmospheric village. Wandering the timeless streets is a joy, and there's a touch of sophistication in the handful of fashionable bars, clothing and offbeat jewellery stores run by local designers along the pedestrian main drag that enhance Hora's appeal without eroding its timelessness.

The bus stop is on a small square at the edge of town. There's an ATM next to a minimarket right at the entrance to Hora, and local preserves and tipples for sale along the main street.

Archaeological Museum   MUSEUM
(⊙ 8.30am-3pm Wed-Mon (reduced in winter)) Hora's archaeology museum has some interesting pieces excavated on the island, including remnants of the Minoan civilisation that existed on Amorgos more than 4000 years ago. It's signposted off the main pedestrian street.

🛌 Sleeping

★ Emprostiada   GUESTHOUSE €€
(☑ 22850 71814; https://emprostiada.com; d €110, ste €140-160; ⊙ Mar-Nov; ❄🛜) There's charm in abundance at this traditional guesthouse, where private, characterful suites are housed in an old merchant's home. It's a picture-perfect scene in a peaceful setting at the back of the village. Choose from spacious doubles, maisonettes and suites. Doubles are a bargain €60 outside the July and August peak. Free port transfers are available from Katapola or Aegiali.

Pension Ilias   PENSION €€
(☑ 22850 71277; www.iliaspension.gr; d/apt €60/100; ❄🛜) Tucked away amid a jumble of traditional houses not far from the bus stop is this friendly, family-run place with pleasant, comfortable rooms. The apartments can accommodate four people. Two-night minimum stay in July and August.

🍴 Eating

★ Kastanis   GREEK €
(☑ 22850 72048; mains €7-13; ⊙ noon-late; 🍴) In the shade of some trees on the main street, this family-run taverna excels at traditional dishes, such as *patatato* (lamb with potatoes in tomato sauce), *fava* with capers, superlative Greek salad topped with local cheese, and seasonal specialities, such as boiled local greens with a squirt of lemon.

Jazzmin   CAFE €
(☑ 22850 74017; breakfast €6.50-13, snacks €3-6; ⊙ 9am-2am) Down some steps from the main pedestrian street, Jazzmin spreads through the cosy rooms of a traditional home. Perch in a window seat or lounge on the roof deck. Breakfast choices are good, as are smoothies, juices and herbal teas. The list of cocktails hints at the impressively stocked bar, and jazz and other smooth tunes provide a chilled-out soundtrack.

Triporto   CAFE €
(☑ 22850 73085; www.facebook.com/3porto; breakfast from €8, snacks €3-5; ⊙ 8am-4am) Once the village bakery, this colourful, hip cafe doubles as a breakfast joint and a mellow late-night bar. Create an omelette from ingredients like olive sauce and hot paprika cream, snack on salads, sandwiches and sweets, or nurse a glass of wine while talking to the friendly owner – a virtual encyclopaedia of local knowledge.

❶ Getting There & Away

The **Amorgos Bus Company** (☑ 6936671033; http://amorgosbuscompany.com) has timetables and ticket prices online. Buses link Katapola to Hora (€2) and onwards to Aegiali (€2).

Some accommodation options offer free port transfers to/from Katapola and Aegiali. Check when you book.

Picking up a rental car, scooter or ATV at either of the ports is a good option. Or rent a car from Evis Cars (p401).

Aegiali   Αιγιάλη

POP 430

Amorgos' second port sees fewer yachts and more of a younger traveller scene. A sweep of white sand lines the inner edge of the bay on which the village stands, and it's a good place for water sports. Walkers use it as a base for hiking up to the lovely villages of Langada and Tholaria that nestle amid the craggy slopes above the town, each about 3km away, and linked both to each other and other parts of the island by walking trails. On the far side of the bay, a path leads over headlands to three sand-and-pebble beaches, the furthest popular with naturists.

🏃 Activities

Amorgos Diving Center   DIVING
(☑6932249538, 22850 73611; www.amorgos-diving.com) Enthusiastic and friendly instruction can be had at this well-run centre right on the beach. Dives (with equipment) start at €55, with night dives, wreck dives and PADI courses available. It also offers a Bubblemaker class for kids, snorkelling tours (€25), and rents SUPs and sea kayaks.

🛏 Sleeping & Eating

Apollon Studios   GUESTHOUSE €
(☑22850 73297; www.apollon-amorgos.com; studio d/tr €55/66; ❉🗦) With a nautically themed entrance, this guesthouse in the heart of the village has studios with well-equipped kitchens and harbour-view balconies. Rooms aren't fussy, but they're comfortable and reasonably priced. This place draws lots of repeat guests and families. Lots of places to eat right out the front door.

Yperia   HOTEL €€
(☑22850 73084; www.yperia.com; incl breakfast d €135-145, f €188; ⊙Apr-Oct; ❉🗦🏊) Yperia's modern rooms have warm, artsy touches, handmade wood-and-iron furnishings, big bathrooms and excellent sea views (pay €10 extra). The pool overlooks the ocean, and the hotel is just a block from the beach. Staff are friendly and accommodating.

Aegialis Hotel & Spa   HOTEL €€€
(Map p402; ☑22850 73393; www.amorgos-aegialis.com; d/ste from €222/548; ❉🗦🏊) High on a hill and with magical views over Aegiali Bay and village, this is the island's only five-star hotel. Rooms are classic Cycladic minimalism with a modern art accent, but it's the facilities that make this place shine: pool and pool bar, a bliss-out day spa, restaurants

– oh, and did we mention the view? Decent off-peak rates; book online.

Amorgis   CAFE €
(☑22850 73606; mains €4-10; ⊙9am-late; 🗦) On the steps leading up from the ferry quay, Amorgis is all pastel colours and hanging pot plants overlooking the bay. Good at any time – for fresh juices, classic cocktails and light bites such as tortillas, salads and baguettes.

★Taxidi Gefsis Apo Ti Kriti Sto Aivali   CRETAN €€
(☑22850 73342; mains €7-15) Near the south end of the beach, this Cretan restaurant is exceptional in terms of hospitality and the quality of its homemade dishes. Slow-cooked goat, shrimp *saganaki*, Cretan pasta and mixed mezedhes are all on the menu, served to a mellow jazz soundtrack.

★Falafel   INTERNATIONAL €€
(☑6936808038; dishes €6-14; ⊙11am-1am) Up an alley from the waterfront, grab a seat at a communal table or perch on a stool to dig into *shakshuka* or a falafel wrap for brunch, and a grab-bag of world cuisines (spring rolls, curries) the rest of the day. The carbonara comes with home-smoked Cretan pork and there are Ora microbrews to quench your thirst.

To Limani   TAVERNA €€
(☑22850 73269; http://tolimani.weebly.com; mains €8-18; ⊙8am-midnight) This popular restaurant, up from the main street, carries its traditional atmosphere comfortably. Using homegrown produce, the cooks whip up hefty portions of great local dishes: try the fish soup, *patatato* (lamb with potatoes in tomato sauce), or anything with local cheese. And save room for some homemade orange pie.

🍷 Drinking & Nightlife

★Embassa Bar   COCKTAIL BAR
(☑6932547187; ⊙8am-4am) Facing the tiny quayside windmill, this skull-emblazoned bar is arguably Amorgos' best cocktail bar, with a hefty menu of original tipples. Sip a cucumber martini with a side of killer sunset or come for a morning coffee to mix with the all-night crowd.

ℹ Information

If you're interested in organised walking holidays, try the Special Interest Holidays website, www.walkingingreece.com. It's run by Paul and Henrietta Delahunt-Rimmer, an English couple who

> **LOCAL KNOWLEDGE**
>
> ## WALKING ON AMORGOS
>
> Amorgos is a very popular walking destination, and the island has over a dozen hiking trails, eight of them numbered and well marked. Check these routes out online at www. amorgos.gr. Cartography company Terrain (http://terrainmaps.gr) produces an excellent hiking map for Amorgos.
>
> The most scenic trails include the following:
>
> **#1:** (13.4km; four to five hours) The longest trail runs from Hora, down to Moni Hozoviotissis, then ascending and meandering among the hills before descending to Aegiali.
>
> **#2:** (3.5km, one hour) Scenic descent from Hora to Katapola.
>
> **#3:** (14km; five hours) Relatively demanding trail from Katapola to Kato Kampos, via the coastal ruins of Minoa and Arkesini, plus the village of Vroutsi and Aghia Triada tower.
>
> **#4:** (8km; three hours) Horseshoe-shaped trail that starts and ends in Aegiali, connecting it to the lovely villages of Langada and Tholaria, with a gentle walk between the two.

have written the excellent resource *Amorgos: A Visitor's and Walker's Guide,* copies of which can be found at an Aegiali gift shop.

Aegialis Tours (☑ 22850 73393; http:// amorgos-aegialis.com/services), based at Aegialis Hotel & Spa, can help arrange local tours and experiences (hiking, cultural excursions, cooking classes etc).

❶ Getting There & Away

There are fewer boat departures from Aegiali than from the other port of Katapola; check the schedule ahead of time.

There are several car/scooter/ATV rental places on the waterfront.

The Amorgos Bus Company (p403) links Aegiali with Katapola (€3, 45 minutes) via Hora (five daily), Langada (€2, 10 minutes, six daily) and Tholaria (€2, 10 minutes, six daily) from mid-June until late August; less frequently the rest of the year.

Around Amorgos

◎ Sights

★ Kalotaritisas Bay
BEACH

(Map p402) On the western tip of the island, this is Amorgos' loveliest beach. Yachts and fishing boats bob on the cerulean waters of the protected bay. In July and August, boat trips (€4) run from this sand-and-pebble stretch to the uninhabited island of Krambousa.

★ Agia Anna Beach
BEACH

(Map p402) Agia Anna Beach is tiny and rocky, but with calm waters for swimming and rocks to leap off. It's popular for its starring role in the French film *The Big Blue,* and is known for its dramatic location and

photogenic chapel. On the other side of the car park there's a larger, sandy beach.

Moni Hozoviotissis
MONASTERY

(Μονή της Χοζοβιώτισσας; Map p402; donations appreciated; ⊗ 8.30am-1pm & 5-7pm) This iconic 11th-century monastery is a dazzling white structure seemingly embedded into the cliff face high above the sea on the precipitous east coast below Hora. It's also high above the car park, with 350 steps to get to it. With any luck, a custodian will be there to explain the significance of the monastery and its icons. The dress code is modest and strict. No shorts, no miniskirts, no bare shoulders and no women in trousers. No exceptions.

Tholaria
VILLAGE

A 3km ride along the looping road or a 30-minute hike from Aegiali, the mountain village of Tholaria sits near the ruins of ancient Aegiali, with millennia-old ruins of the yet-to-be-excavated settlement an easy 10-minute walk away. Stop by Kali Kardia (p406) for the best meatballs in the Cyclades and stargaze at night at the Seladi (p406) cocktail bar. There's a good hike from Tholaria to Langada across the valley, too.

Asfodilitis
VILLAGE

(Map p402) Reachable via a paved, steep and narrow road from the main Hora–Aegiali road, the handful of slate houses in this hamlet seems deserted at first glance. Then you spot the single taverna, the Greek Communist Party flag, the odd battered vehicle. It's a silent place, ideal for watching the sunrise, and a handy spot for breaking up the Hora–Aegiali hike. The turnoff for Asfodilitis is around 6km southwest of Aegiali.

Langada
VILLAGE

Some 3km east of Aegiali, the small village of Langada is a picturesque maze of narrow whitewashed streets. There are several excellent tavernas here, plus shops selling beautiful, locally produced ceramics. Stop by FindinGreece to learn about walking and cultural tours of the island. It takes around 30 minutes to hike up from Aegiali, though there are buses as well.

⚡ Activities & Tours

★ Hora to Aegiali Drive
SCENIC DRIVE

(Map p402) It's well worth driving the 16km between Hora and Aegiali – among the most scenic roads in the Cyclades. The road zigzags with the scrubland-covered mountains looming to one side and the land falling away gradually towards the sea on the other, with the uninhabited islands of Nikouria and Grabonisi clearly visible.

★ FindinGreece
WALKING

(☑ 6944326036; www.findingreece.com; Langada; ⊙ 9am-8pm) In Laghada village, Alix and Semeli are enthusiastic operators who offer guided walking tours of Amorgos, as well as all manner of cultural activities – whether you want to take part in ceramic classes, learn about local wild herbs, go scuba diving or learn to cook the local way. Get in touch in advance.

🛏️ Sleeping & Eating

Pagali Hotel
HOTEL €€

(☑ 22850 73310; www.pagalihotel-amorgos.com; Langada; s/d/tr €64/73/135; ❄️ 🛜) Pagali Hotel is tucked away in Langada village, and has superb views. Rooms and studios are comfortable, and the year-round hotel offers alternative agritourism activities like grape or olive harvesting and winemaking, as well as activities including rock climbing, hiking, yoga and art workshops.

The hotel sits in a cute family-run pocket of Langada, next to the excellent Nikos Taverna and Vassalos Bakery.

★ Ston Pyrgo
TAVERNA €

(Map p402; ☑ 22850 72258; Arkesini; mains €7-12; ⊙ 11am-10pm) Turn off from the village of Arkesini towards the signposted Tower of Agia Triada (also well worth a visit) and you find this traditional *mezedhopoleio* (cafe-restaurant specialising in mezedhes), run by young chef Vangelitsa. Terrific home-cooked food, from *patatato* (slow-cooked goat and potato stew), boiled local greens with lemon, and grilled catch of the day, all shine here.

★ Kali Kardia
GREEK €

(☑ 22850 73347; Tholaria; mains €5-8; ⊙ 8am-10pm) On the tiny square next to the church, this wonderful, family-run place, decorated with family photos and retsina jugs, cooks up the best meatballs in the Cyclades, plus hearty portions of other Greek classics.

🍷 Drinking & Nightlife

★ Seladi Cafe-Bar
COCKTAIL BAR

(☑ 22850 73197; Tholaria; ⊙ 10am-2pm & 6pm-2am) Its cosy terrace overlooking the valley, Seladi is a just a few minutes' walk from the ruins of the ancient settlement. It's a mellow place for a coffee and brunch, while in the evenings it morphs into an intimate cocktail bar. On clear nights, you can stargaze through its telescope.

IOS
ΙΟΣ

POP 1754

Ios' image has long been linked to a reputation for nonstop, booze-fuelled partying. It's partly true: there's no denying that from June to August, the island is the much-loved stomping ground of youth and hedonism. But it's so much more – if you want it to be – and the partying doesn't infiltrate every village or beach.

Spend your days exploring the winding footpaths of the traditional hilltop old town or ensconced on a sandy beach. Discover the isolated interior or sandy beaches such as Manganari in the south, or hike the little-trodden trails to the island's hilltop monasteries. Or visit in the shoulder season for a quieter pace, when Ios draws families and more mature travellers. It's pretty easy to escape the crowds: simply rent some wheels and venture into the countryside of goat farms, honey boxes and dramatic views.

◉ Sights

★ Panagia Gremiotissa
VIEWPOINT

(Map p407; Hora) Head up the alleyway behind Sally's Rooftop Garden and then proceed upwards by trial and error, along cracked steps and through ancient archways, and eventually you'll emerge by the top of Hora, next to the Panagia Gremiotissa church, with its superb sunset views. For even better views, climb a few minutes more to the three small chapels above it.

Homer's Tomb
ARCHAEOLOGICAL SITE

(Map p407) A remote and beautiful 13km drive northeast of Hora lies what is locally

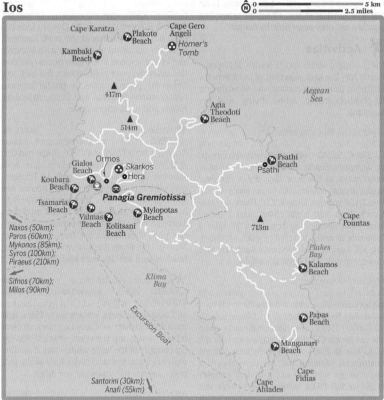

0 — 5 km
0 — 2.5 miles

Cape Karatza
Plakoto Beach
Cape Gero Angeli
Homer's Tomb
Kambaki Beach
417m
Aegean Sea
514m
Agia Theodoti Beach
Gialos Beach
Ormos
Skarkos
Hora
Psathi Beach
Psathi
Koubara Beach
Panagia Gremiotissa
Tsamaria Beach
Valmas Beach
Kolitsani Beach
Mylopotas Beach
Naxos (50km); Paros (60km); Mykonos (85km); Syros (100km); Piraeus (210km)
Cape Pountas
713m
Plakes Bay
Kalamos Beach
Sifnos (70km); Milos (90km)
Klima Bay
Excursion Boat
Papas Beach
Manganari Beach
Santorini (30km); Anafi (55km)
Cape Fidias
Cape Ahlades

believed to be the final resting place of Homer, Greece's greatest poet, who wrote the epics *Odyssey* and *Iliad*. While there are various legends surrounding Homer's Ios connections, and the Dutch archaeologist Pasch van Krienen declaring this tomb to be Homer's in 1771 may have little historical evidence behind it, Hellenic coins from Ios do bear Homer's likeness and name. And the drive is stunning.

Skarkos ARCHAEOLOGICAL SITE
(The Snail; Map p407; €4; ⊙8am-3pm Tue-Sun May-Sep) Crowning a low hill just north of Hora, this Early Bronze Age settlement is one of the Aegean's most significant prehistoric sites. There are restored walled terraces that follow the relief of the hill and the low ruins of several Cycladic-style buildings to explore; visiting the Archaeological Museum in Hora first is good for context. If driving, take the signed turnoff between Ormos and Hora, or walk the traditional stone footpath from the back of Hora (15 minutes). Great views.

Archaeological Museum MUSEUM
(☑22860 91246; Hora; €2; ⊙8.30am-4pm Wed-Mon) This musuem, on the main road that passes by Hora, is a must for those interested in antiquity. It displays a wealth of finds from the early Bronze Age settlement of nearby Skarkos, from ceramics and marble figurines to obsidian wares, bone tools and funereal *stelae*, providing an illuminating glimpse into the early Cycladic civilisation and its social structure.

⊙ Beaches

Ios is well known for its beaches. Those reachable by paved road include Manganari – a wide sweep of white sand on the south coast, reached by your own wheels (45 minutes from Hora), bus or by caïque in summer. Mylopotas is equally beautiful and is a major water sports centre as well. Agia Theodoti has the bluest of blue water and is favoured by Greek families. Nearby Psathi is quieter with a popular taverna and is an ace windsurfing venue. Plenty of other fine beaches are only accessible by caïque.

🏃 Activities

Ios is a major water sports centre. Mylopotas Beach has the best selection of outfitters for anything from waterskiing and windsurfing to paddleboarding, scuba diving, and sea kayaking.

Mylopotas Watersports & New Dive
WATER SPORTS

(📞 22860 92340; http://mylopotas-watersports. gr; Mylopotas Beach; ⊙ May–mid-Oct) A thousand ways to fill your day: try a discover scuba-diving session (€55) or more intensive PADI courses from €270. There are also wreck dives and night dives. Join a three-hour boat snorkelling trip for €35, take a tube ride or rent a long list of gear: windsurfing kit, kayaks, paddleboards, sailboats and more. Friendly and helpful staff, too.

Meltemi Watersports & Dive Centre
WATER SPORTS

(📞 6980386990; www.meltemiwatersports.com; Mylopotas) Based at the Far Out Beach Club (📞 22860 91468; www.faroutclub.com; camp site per person €12, dm €20, glamp tent €40, d/q €100/190; @ 🛜 🏊), with a ready flow of keen customers, Meltemi has a smorgasbord of ways to get wet: try out a diving sampler (€55) or full PADI courses, then check out wreck, cave and night dives. Learn to windsurf, waterski, wakeboard or paddleboard, join a canoe safari or go on a Hell Ride (tube ride; €18).

🛌 Sleeping

Ormos has the fewest pensions/hotels. Hora has a wide range of lodgings, from a legendary hostel to guesthouses and boutique hotels on the outskirts, with some places close to the centrally located bars and clubs. There are camp sites, dorms and private villas around Mylopotas. Book early for July and August.

⭐ Windmill
GUESTHOUSE €

(📞 22860 91482; r from €50; ❄🛜) Sadly, not inside one of Hora's beautiful yet somewhat dilapidated windmills, this guesthouse is the next best thing to it: right at the top of Hora, with great views of said windmills and the village. Simple, spotless rooms are attentively run by the father-and-son team Pavlos and Giorgios, and you're a couple of minutes' walk from the nightlife.

Avra Pension
PENSION €

(📞 22860 91985; www.avrapension.gr; Ormos; s/d €40/50; ⊙ Apr–mid-Oct; ❄🛜) Down a lane behind the yacht marina at the port, Katerina runs this delightful guesthouse with warmth and efficiency, and at bargain prices (outside the short summer peak, rooms fall to €30). Colourful potted plants, a restful terrace, homey common areas and fresh, appealing rooms add up to super value.

⭐ Francesco's
HOSTEL €€

(📞 22860 91223; www.francescos.net; Hora; dm/s/d/tr from €20/65/80/120; ⊙ Apr–mid-Oct; ❄@🛜🏊) Former backpackers are now sending their own 18-year-olds to Francesco's, which is still going strong. Rooms are spotless, hillside views are great and it's within stumbling distance of Hora's nightlife. There's a roll call of happy-traveller features: bar, pool, cheap breakfast, free entry to Blue Note (p410). From the square near Astra Bar, head up and left. It's near Midnight Cafe.

⭐ Kritikakis Village Hotel
HOTEL €€

(📞 22860 91100; www.kritikakis.gr; d/tr/q €120/140/158; ❄🛜🏊) Set back from the port and next to the steps leading up to Hora, this multilevel cluster of Cycladic cubes attracts mostly young, hip travellers who like the extra comfort of the large whitewashed studios with brick accents, and perks such as the two pools, on-site bar and welcome drink.

Aegeon Hotel
HOTEL €€

(📞 22860 91007; www.ios-aegeon.com; Mylopotas; r €105-115; ❄🛜🏊) Providing a higher level of comfort to a younger crowd than surrounding beachside places, this smart little hotel offers simple whitewashed rooms alongside such perks as a pool, hot tub and hammocks to laze in. A place to relax rather than to party; head down the street for the latter.

Yialos Ios Hotel
HOTEL €€

(📞 22860 91421; www.yialosioshotel.gr; Ormos; incl breakfast s/d from €90/105, studio from €210; ⊙ May-Sep; ❄🛜🏊) Just a block back from the port, this 200-year-old stone building feels like the home you wish you had. Crisp, characterful rooms, wood-beamed ceilings, traditional beds and a flower-filled poolside give it the edge. The owners are attentive, and the breakfast room is just like your Greek grandma's kitchen. Off-peak rates are excellent (doubles around €50).

⭐ Liostasi
BOUTIQUE HOTEL €€€

(📞 22860 92140; www.liostasi.gr; Hora; d/ste incl breakfast from €160/295; ⊙ May-Sep; ❄@🛜🏊)

Step into the foyer of this place and you may never want to leave. This contemporary, on-point place is an effortless blend of chic and comfort. The on-site spa, restaurant and pool area are top quality, and the rooms are crisp with splashes of colour and gorgeous sea views. Service is impeccable. It's halfway between Ormos and Hora.

✕ Eating

⭐**Hellenic Social** CAFE €

(☑ 22860 92663; www.facebook.com/Hellenic Social; mains €6-12; ⊙ 11am-midnight) On any given morning, this place is filled mostly with visitors to Ios, some slumped over their poached eggs, others perkily downing filled bagels, green smoothies and blended juices. Hellenic Social is very hipster, very now, with organic kombucha and dishes involving chia seeds and smashed avo. Evening events and parties frequently break out. It's off the main road.

Katogi MEZEDHES €

(☑ 6983440900; www.facebook.com/katogios; Hora; dishes €5-12; ⊙ dinner) Entering Katogi feels like you've walked into a party in someone's quirky house, full of hidden nooks and plants and clamour. The original cocktails hit the spot, while the meze can be hit and miss: the grilled *talagani* cheese with figs and pasta purses filled with cheese and pear rock, while the *saganaki* meatballs are merely okay. Great atmosphere, though.

⭐**Salt** FUSION €€

(☑ 22860 92217; www.facebook.com/SaltRestau rantBar; Mylopotas; mains €10-14; ⊙ 9am-2am; ☏) One of those rare restaurants that get everything right, Salt is a light-filled, breezy outdoor space under a canopy of white-washed bamboo overlooking the beach. Service is friendly and prompt, the dishes – from fish tartare and shrimp-and-leek risotto to slow-roasted spare ribs and salted caramel banoffee – are spot on, and it's wallet-friendly to boot.

⭐**Lord Byron** MEDITERRANEAN €€

(☑ 22860 92125; dishes €7-14; ⊙ dinner) Near the main square in Hora, coming here is like entering a curiosity shop, filled with masks, vintage ads, and other quirky memorabilia from the owner's travels. The dishes also tap into a global smorgasbord of delights, from bacon-wrapped scallops and a cracking Caesar salad to bouillabaisse and Moroccan-Mexican quesadilla crossovers. Service gets five stars.

⭐**Harmony Ios** MEXICAN €€

(☑ 22860 91613; https://harmonyios.com; mains €9-13; ⊙ 9am-2am; ☏) Harmony wears many hats and we like all of them. It's a mellow spot for pancakes, coffee and avo on toast in the morning, a place to laze about in a hammock or on giant cushions while nursing a frozen margarita at sunset, or an al fresco dinner venue for consuming nachos, tacos and quesadillas, accompanied by decent live music.

☆ Entertainment

⭐**Cine Liostasi** CINEMA

(☑ 22860 92140; www.liostasi.gr/cine-liostasi; ⊙ hours vary) FREE Outside at Liostasi Hotel & Suites, halfway between Ormos and Hora, this lovely setting hosts a nightly outdoor cinema under the stars. The aim is to become the top outdoor cinema in Greece and, indeed, this spot is hard to beat. Watch classic and modern movies in loungers while sipping signature cocktails with gorgeous views as background to the screen.

ℹ Information

Acteon Travel (☑ 22860 91343; www.acteon. gr; ⊙ 8am-10pm) Buy your onward ferry tickets at the port.

ℹ Getting There & Away

Boat services from Ios. Differences in journey durations are because of routing or vessel type.

DESTINATION	DURATION	FARE (€)	FREQUENCY
Anafi	3½hrs	9	2 weekly
Folegandros	1¼-1¾hrs	6-45	3-5 daily
Iraklio	3hrs	70	5 weekly
Katapola (on Amorgos)	3hrs	12	weekly
Kimolos	3hrs	11	3 weekly
Milos	3-4hrs	16-50	2-3 daily
Mykonos	1¾-2½hrs	48-54	2-3 daily
Naxos	45mins-1¾hrs	16-34	2-4 daily
Paros	50mins-5¼hrs	11-27	3-5 daily
Piraeus	45mins-6hrs	39-60	3-4 daily
Santorini	30mins-1½hrs	7-39	4-9 daily
Serifos	5-6hrs	14-60	1-2 daily
Sifnos	4½-5¼hrs	12-55	1-2 daily
Sikinos	25mins	4	4 weekly
Syros	6¾hrs	16	4 weekly

IOS' TOP NIGHTLIFE

Astra (6976953624; www.facebook.
com/Astra.ios.greece; ⊗10pm-3.30am)
Scandi-cool decor with fresh fruit-based
cocktails.

Blue Note Club (22860 92271; www.
facebook.com/bluenoteofficial; ⊗11.15pm-
late May-Oct) Legendary venue pumping
out Top 40 tracks.

Coo Bar (6982063864; www.facebook.
com/CooBarIos; ⊗11pm-5.30am) R'n'B
beats, cave-like decor, original cocktails.

Free Beach Bar (22860 28357; http://
freebeachbar.gr; Mylopotas Beach; ⊗10am-
1am May-Sep) DJ sets and pool parties.

Orange Bar (⊗8pm-4am) Originally
flavoured shots and a rock and alternative soundtrack.

ⓘ Getting Around

In summer crowded **buses** (22860 92015;
www.ktel-ios.gr) run between Ormos, Hora and
Mylopotas Beach (all fares €2) about every 20
minutes. Schedules are posted at the main village
bus stops and online. In summer, additional buses
run frequently to Koubara, and less frequently to
beaches at Agia Theodoti, Psathi and Manganari.
For taxis call **Ios Taxi Service** (6977760570);
it's €5 from the port to Hora and €5 from Hora to
Mylopotas.

Summertime caïques travel from Ormos to
Manganari via Mylopotas and cost about €12 per
person for a return trip.

Ormos, Hora and Mylopotas Beach all have
multiple car, motorcycle and four-wheeler rental
outlets.

SANTORINI ΣΑΝΤΟΡΙΝΗ

POP 11,400

If you approach Santorini from the water,
it's hard not to be awed by the sheer cliffs
that soar above a turquoise sea, by the fact
that you're sailing in an immense crater of a
drowned volcano and that before you lies an
island shaped by an ancient eruption cata-
clysmic beyond imagining.

High above, the main villages of Fira and
Oia are a snowdrift of white Cycladic houses that line the clifftops and spill like icy cornic-
es down the terraced rock. And then there
are the sunsets, with crowds breaking into
applause as the sun disappears below the
horizon.

In peak season, Santorini becomes a playground for the very wealthy, and while this

has resulted in some stellar restaurants and
superb wineries, the strain on the infrastructure is a concern. Still, there's relative seclusion found at the island's ancient sites, on
hiking trails and beneath the waves.

History

Minor eruptions have been the norm in
Greece's earthquake-prone history, but Santorini has a definite history of overachieving
– eruptions here were genuinely earth-shat-
tering, and so wrenching they changed the
shape of the island several times.

Dorians, Venetians and Turks occupied
Santorini, but its most influential early in-
habitants were Minoans. They came from
Crete some time between 2000 BCE and 1600
BCE, and the settlement at Akrotiri dates
from the peak years of their great civilisation.

The island was circular then and was
called Strongili (Round One). Thousands
of years ago, a colossal volcanic eruption
caused the centre of Strongili to sink, leaving
a caldera with towering cliffs along the east
side – a truly dramatic sight. The latest theory, based on carbon dating of olive-oil sam-
ples from Akrotiri, places the event 10 years
either side of 1613 BCE.

Santorini was recolonised during the 3rd
century BCE, but for the next 2000 years sporadic volcanic activity created further physical changes that included the formation of
the volcanic islands of Palia Kameni and Nea
Kameni at the centre of the caldera.

As recently as 1956, a major earthquake
devastated Oia and Fira, yet by the 1970s the
islanders had embraced tourism as tourists
embraced the island, and today Santorini is
a destination of truly spectacular global appeal, drawing honeymooners, backpackers,
the jet set, cruise-boat passengers, Chinese
bridal parties (in part due to the success of
Beijing Love Story, filmed partly on Santorini) and everyone else, too.

For better or worse, Santorini and
Mykonos have become the poster children
for the Greek islands. As well as bigger
crowds, that also means considerably higher
prices.

ⓘ Getting There & Away

AIR

Santorini Airport (JTR; Map p412; 22860
28400; www.santoriniairport.com) has flights
year-round to/from Athens (from €60, 45
minutes) with Olympic Air (www.olympicair.
com), Ryanair (www.ryanair.com) and Sky
Express (www.skyexpress.gr). Seasonal European connections are plentiful with some budget

carriers from London, Rome, Geneva, Milan and Toulouse.

Give yourself plenty of time when flying back out as tourism infrastructure hasn't kept up with the island's growing popularity and the small airport terminal can be mayhem.

BOAT

There are plenty of ferries each day to and from Piraeus and many Cyclades islands.

Santorini's main port, Athinios, stands on a cramped shelf of land at the base of sphinx-like cliffs. It's a scene of marvellous chaos (that works itself out), except when ferries have been cancelled and arrivals and departures merge. Advice? Be patient. It clears, eventually. Buses (and taxis) meet all ferries and then cart passengers up the towering cliffs through an ever-rising series of S-bends to Fira. Accommodation providers can usually arrange transfers (to Fira per person is around €10 to €25).

Ferries from Santorini:

DESTINATION	DURATION	FARE (€)	FREQUENCY
Amorgos	1½-4hrs	50	1-2 daily
Anafi	1½hrs	8	4 weekly
Folegandros	45mins-3¼hrs	7-45	3-4 daily
Ios	30mins-1½hrs	7-39	4-8 daily
Iraklio	1¾hrs	60	2 daily
Kimolos	4¼hrs	15	3 weekly
Kos	4½hrs	37	4 weekly
Koufonisia	2hrs	47	daily
Milos	2-4hrs	18-59	3-4 daily
Mykonos	2-3½hrs	45-69	5-7 daily
Naxos	1¼-2¾hrs	22-43	5-6 daily
Paros	2-3½hrs	20-46	4-5 daily
Piraeus	4¾-9hrs	38-80	6-8 daily
Rafina	5¾-9½hrs	35-45	2 daily
Rhodes	8½-17¾hrs	39	5 weekly
Serifos	3½-7¼hrs	19-60	2-3 daily
Sifnos	3-7hrs	14-68	2-3 daily
Sikinos	2hrs	7.50	3 weekly
Tinos	3½-5hrs	42-58	7 weekly

ⓘ Getting Around

TO/FROM THE AIRPORT

There are frequent bus connections between Fira's bus station and the airport, located 5km east of Fira (€1.80, 20 minutes, 5.30am to 10.15pm). Most accommodation providers will arrange paid transfers.

BUS

KTEL Santorini Buses (Map p416; ☑22860 25404; http://ktel-santorini.gr; Mitropoleos) has a good website with schedules and prices. Tickets are purchased on the bus. Fira is the island's bus hub, with departures for most villages, as well as the airport and ferry port.

CAR & MOTORCYCLE

Having your own wheels is the most convenient way to explore the island during high season, when buses are intolerably overcrowded and you'll be lucky to get on one at all. Be very patient and cautious when driving – the narrow roads and heavy traffic, especially in and around Fira, can be a nightmare.

There are representatives of all the major international car-hire outfits, plus dozens of local operators in all tourist areas. Good local hire outfits include **Damigos Rent a Car** (☑6979968192, 22860 22048; www.santorini-carhire.com; 25 Martiou, Fira) and **Tony's Rent a Car** (☑22860 22863; Firostefani; scooter/ATV rental per day from €20/30; ⊙8am-8pm). You'll pay from around €50 per day for a car and €25/30 for a scooter/four-wheeler in high season, but it pays to shop around. Note: scooter hire requires you to have an appropriate licence, while four-wheelers require a regular car licence. Check this website for details: www.santorini.com/rentals/motorbikes.

TAXI

Fira's **taxi stand** (Map p416; ☑22860 22555, 22860 23951) is on Dekigala just around the corner from the bus station. A taxi from the port of Athinios to Fira costs €10 to €15, and a trip from Fira to Oia about €15. Expect to add €2 if the taxi is booked ahead or if you have luggage. A taxi to Kamari is about €15, to Perissa €18 and to Ancient Thira about €25 one way.

Santorini Transport (☑6984637383; www.santorinitransport.com) is a good option for arranging fixed-price transfers to/from the airport or Athinios port.

Fira   Φήρα

POP 1900

Santorini's main town of Fira is a vibrant place, having bounced back since the 1956 earthquake. Its caldera edge is layered with swish hotels, cave houses and infinity pools, all backed by a warren of narrow streets packed with shops, more bars and restaurants. And people.

Admittedly, the admiring masses cannot diminish the impact of Fira's stupendous landscape beyond. Views over the multi-coloured cliffs are breathtaking, and come sunset, crowds gather at the caldera edge for the greatest free show on earth. Behind

Santorini (Thira)

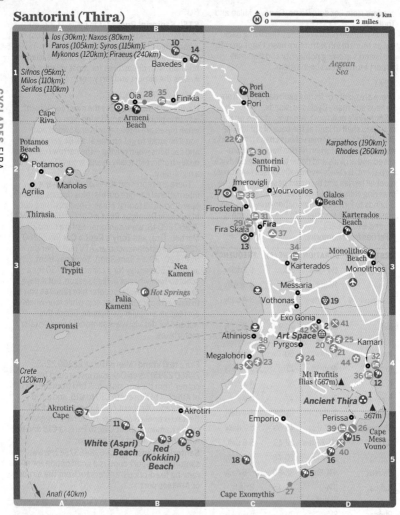

the cliffs, however, the prices of fame are exposed: frenetic vehicular activity, meandering pedestrians along the roads (there are few pavements), and frenzied development.

Fira sprawls north and merges into two more villages: Firostefani (about a 15-minute walk from Fira) and posher Imerovigli (about a half-hour walk from Fira).

◉ Sights & Activities

★ Museum of Prehistoric Thera   MUSEUM
(Map p416; ☎ 22860 22217; www.santorini.com/museums; Mitropoleos; adult/under 18 €6/3; ⊗ 8.30am-3pm Wed-Mon) Opposite the bus station, this well-presented museum houses extra-

ordinary finds excavated from Akrotiri, which has been settled since neolithic times. Check out the wealth of wall paintings, ceramics with a heavy Minoan influence and the glowing gold ibex figurine, dating from the 17th century BCE and in mint condition. Also look for fossilised olive tree leaves from within the caldera, which date back to 60,000 BCE. It's worth visiting this museum first, before heading out to Ancient Akrotiri (p423).

Skaros Rock   LANDMARK
(Map p412) From Imerovigli, a sign points west for the track to Skaros, the conical peninsula jutting out into the caldera. Not

Santorini (Thira)

only geologically interesting, it is also historically important, as it was the first of five *kasteli* (fortresses) built on Santorini in the 15th century to protect the islanders from pirate attacks. Earthquakes put an end to that, however, and the inhabitants moved to Fira. Walk out for great views and a perfectly situated church, but expect plenty of steps.

Old Port   PORT
(Map p412) Sitting 220m below Fira – three minutes by cable car, or 587 steps by foot – the Old Port, also known as Fira Skala, is now mainly used by cruise ship passengers visiting Fira for the day. They generally arrive in the morning, then head back in the afternoon. The little port has restaurants, tavernas and small shops, and presents a stunning view from the foot of the caldera cliffs.

Gyzi Megaron   MUSEUM
(Map p416; ☎ 22860 23077; www.gyzimegaron. gr; Erythrou Stavrou; adult/child €3/free;

⊙10am-9pm Mon-Sat, 10.30am-4.30pm Sun May-Oct) At the north end of Fira, this museum displays fascinating before-and-after photographs of the 1956 earthquake, along with centuries-old maps of the Cyclades, paintings, striking photography by Christos Simatos and 15th-century manuscripts.

Santorini Cable Car   CABLE CAR
(Map p416; https://scc.gr/cablecar.htm; one way €6; ⊙7am-9.20pm May-Sep, reduced hours Oct-Apr) Fira's efficient cable car links the caldera-top town with the Old Port, 220m below, in three minutes. It can be totally swamped with cruise ship passengers coming up in the morning and heading back down in the afternoon. One option: walk the 587 steps down, then come back up by cable car.

The Steps   WALKING
(Map p416; Marinatou) Fira and the Old Port are linked by 587 steps that zigzag down the cliff face and make a fun walk...down. You can also head back by the cable car.

🛏 Sleeping

There are plenty of upmarket and midrange boutique hotels in Fira; be prepared to pay a premium for a caldera view. Budget places without views are on the eastern side of town and offer some great deals out of the high season. Book well ahead, especially for July and August.

★ Aroma Suites
BOUTIQUE HOTEL €€

(Map p416; ☑ 22860 24112; www.aromasuites.com; Mitropoleos; d/ste from €240/280; 🌬🛜) Overlooking the caldera at the quieter southern end of Fira, and more accessible than similar places, this boutique hotel has charming service and six cave house rooms and suites. Built into the side of the caldera, the traditional interiors are paired with monochrome decor, smooth stone bathrooms and seaview balconies. Breakfast is an extra €12 per person.

Ersi Villas
HOTEL €€

(Map p412; ☑ 22860 24719; www.ersivillas santorini.com; Agiou Athanasiou 19, Firostefani; d/ tr €120/150; 🌬🛜🌊) Friendly and spotless, this wallet-friendly hotel clusters around an appealing dipping pool. Simple rooms come with terraces and the owner is always around to offer guidance and information, and will arrange transport from the port for late arrivals.

Kavalari Hotel
HOTEL €€

(Map p416; ☑ 22860 22455; www.kavalarihotel santorini.com; Ypapantis; s/d from €145/202; 🌬🛜) One of Fira's top-value hotels, Kavalari is at the heart of the action and offers standard rooms (which are nothing special) and

atmospheric cave rooms and apartments. The central location and views make this a desirable option when surrounding hotel rates are taken into consideration. An excellent breakfast is included.

Pension Petros
PENSION €€

(Map p416; ☑ 22860 22573; www.hotelpetros santorini.gr; r/tr from €172/226; 🌬🛜🌊) Three hundred metres east of the square in Fira, Petros offers decent rooms at good rates, but no caldera views. This is an ultrafriendly, family-run operation and makes an affordable option, especially outside high season, when rates are less than half. Cute Grecian-Roman pool, too.

Villa Soula
HOTEL €€

(Map p416; ☑ 22860 23473; www.santorini villasoula.gr; Fira; d/tr/apt from €125/160/180; 🌬🛜🌊) Cheerful and spotless, this hotel is a great deal. Rooms aren't large but come with small, breezy balconies. Colourful public areas and a small, well-maintained undercover pool give you room to spread out a little. It's a short walk from the town centre.

Keti Hotel
HOTEL €€

(Map p416; ☑ 22860 22324; www.hotelketi.gr; Agiou Mina, Fira; d/ste from €198/261; 🌬🛜) Hotel Keti is one of the smaller 'sunset view' hotels in a peaceful caldera niche. Its attractive traditional rooms are carved into the cliffs, half of which have Jacuzzis. Two-night minimum in high season.

★ Iconic Santorini
BOUTIQUE HOTEL €€€

(Map p412; ☑ 22860 28950; www.iconicsantorini. com; Imerovigli; r €545, ste €650-1245; 🌬🛜🌊) This five-star cave hotel is something special,

---

ℹ **SANTORINI ACCOMMODATION**

Things to know about Santorini accommodation:

➡ Few lodgings in Fira, Oia, Imerovigli and Firostefani are cheap. For a caldera view, expect to pay a premium.

➡ The sky is the limit, particularly in Oia and Imerovigli: luxury accommodation is everywhere, with all the trimmings (private terrace, plunge pool etc).

➡ Consider accommodation off Agiou Athanasiou on the east side of Fira if you want to be close to the action but are on a budget. Firostefani tends to be a bit cheaper than Fira, and is only a 10-minute walk into town.

➡ Many hotels on the caldera rim cannot be reached by vehicle and may involve several flights of steps. Many hotels have porters who can help with luggage.

➡ Some domatia touts at the port may claim that their rooms are in town, when they're actually a long way out; ask to see a map showing the exact location.

➡ Some places may offer free transfer to the port or airport; other places may charge €15 upwards for a transfer.

with great attention paid to tiny details. Terraces look out over the caldera, the Cliff Suite comes with a gorgeous grotto pool, all suites are endowed with private hot tubs, and the saltwater infinity pool seems to melt into the horizon. Spa and exceptional service are among the perks. Over 14s only.

★ **Cavo Tagoo** BOUTIQUE HOTEL €€€
(Map p412; ☑22890 20100; www.cavotagoo.com/santorini; Imerovigli; ste €1180-1600 mid-Apr–Oct; ❄ ⚹ ⛱) If money is no object or you're celebrating a once-in-a-lifetime occasion, it's hard to do better than these sleek, monochromatic suites with copper accents, all with secluded terraces and private plunge pools (though you can lounge by the infinity pool for a change of scenery). Terrific restaurant on-site.

★ **Anteliz Suites** BOUTIQUE HOTEL €€€
(Map p412; ☑22860 28842; www.anteliz.gr; d/ste from €310/665; ❄ ⚹ ⛱) North of Fira on the path that runs to Firostefani, Anteliz offers an amazing pool, sun terrace and, oh, those views. Relax in the open-air hot tub and take it all in. The suites feature white-marble floors, the pool suites come with private plunge pools and the Anteliz master suite is a masterpiece of luxurious minimalism.

Aria Suites BOUTIQUE HOTEL €€€
(Map p416; ☑22860 28650; http://ariasuites.com; ste/villa from €635/1000; ❄ ⚹ ⛱) With a mix of individually styled villas (some with private plunge pools or cave house Jacuzzis) and suites, Aria Suites is one of the top spots to stay in Fira. Just south of the Orthodox Cathedral, this is just outside the noise, yet close enough to the action. Dazzling Cycladic white walls, superb pool, sun terrace and views. Two-night minimum.

Cosmopolitan Suites BOUTIQUE HOTEL €€€
(Map p416; ☑22860 25632; www.cosmopolitan-santorini.com; ste from €699; ❄ ⚹ ⛱) This is about as good as it gets in the heart of Fira, with a spectacular, undulating infinity pool overlooking the caldera. This member of the Small Luxury Hotels of the World group consists of 10 understated, individually furnished suites, with plenty of natural light, a neutral colour palette and doorways of rough-hewn stone. Perfect location to boot.

✖ **Eating**

Fira has plenty to offer in terms of traditional Greek cuisine and stellar fusion food, though overpriced, indifferent food geared towards tourists is still present.

There's a price hike for a caldera view, while cheap eats surround the central square. For smart places, book ahead in July and August.

Lucky's Souvlaki GREEK €
(Map p416; ☑22860 22003; gyros from €3; ⊙11am-11pm) A top spot for cheap eats on Fira's main street. Perch on a bar stool and demolish a tasty *gyros* pitta (pork, chicken or lamb), or attack a plate of souvlaki, fries and tomatoes for €11. Quality inconsistent and service irascible.

Aktaion TAVERNA €€
(Map p412; ☑22860 22336; www.aktaionsantorini.com; Firostefani; mains €13-23; ⊙1pm-midnight; ✐) Just off the tiny Firostefani square, this taverna has been around since 1922 and continues to specialise in traditional island recipes, such as octopus with *fava* and capers, *skordomakarona* (homemade pasta with garlic), steamed seasonal greens and *mousakas*. Sit in the atmospheric cavern or on the outside terrace.

Volkan on the Rocks CAFE €€
(Map p412; ☑22860 28360; https://ergonfoods.com; mains €10-13; ⊙9am-midnight May-Oct; ✐) With a breezy clifftop terrace overlooking the caldera, this cafe is the home of Volkan craft beer, which is nicely paired with Santorini's fire in the sky. Come for breakfast, swing by for the selection of imaginative hot and cold mezedhes made from local produce, or visit in the evenings for the open-air movie screenings.

Parea Traditional Greek Restaurant GREEK €€
(Map p416; ☑22860 25444; https://parearestaurant.gr; mains €9-15; ⊙12.30-11pm) There's nothing fancy or fussy about Parea, which pairs traditional, wallet-friendly, home-cooked Greek dishes with rooftop dining and views out to the eastern coast of Santorini. The seared octopus has bite to it without being rubbery, and when you peel the parchment paper back from the lamb *kleftiko*, the meat is wonderfully tender.

Fanari GREEK €€
(Map p416; ☑22860 25107; www.fanari-restaurant.gr; dishes €8-40) On the steps down to the Old Port, Fanari offers a mix of traditional Greek dishes, plus pastas and pizzas, with a free helping of superlative views of the caldera. The mixed seafood platter is a good bet, plus there are local dessert favourites such as Santorini pudding and *meletinia*, made

Fira

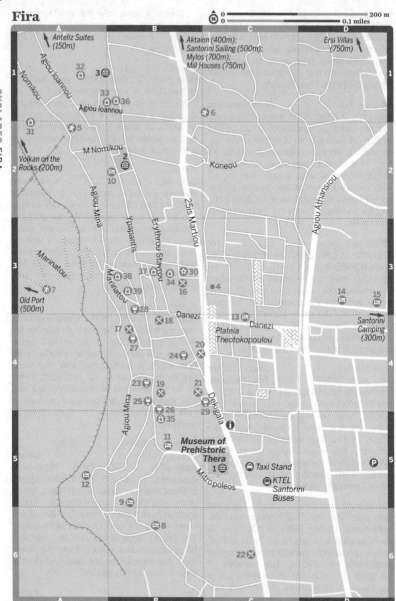

of skimmed-milk cheese and scented with mastic and vanilla.

Theoni's Kitchen
GREEK €€

(Map p416; ☎ 22860 25680; www.facebook.com/theoniskitchen17; Dekigala; mains €10-24; ◎noon-midnight) Theoni's isn't fancy and you

won't be gazing out over the caldera, but this 'mumma's kitchen' restaurant does its thing with grace, humour and enthusiasm. Expect decent-sized portions of Greek classics, such as *mousakas*, grilled mackerel and grilled white Santorini aubergine with feta. The Greek salad here is exceptional.

Fira

Camille Stefani
GREEK €€

(Map p416; ☑22860 22762; www.camillestefani.com; Erythrou Stavrou; mains €10-20; ☺noon-11pm) This old-school rooftop restaurant with views across to the east coast, has perfected its craft since the late '70s. Its authentic, traditional atmosphere matches its meals. Dig into countless mezedhes like *saganaki* and stuffed vine leaves or opt for *mousakas*, chicken souvlaki or swordfish fillet. This place is as popular with locals as it is with tourists.

★Ovac
FUSION €€€

(Map p412; ☑22860 27900; http://ovac.gr; Imerovigli; mains €35-52; ☺1pm-midnight) Helmed by one of Greece's hottest chefs, this Greek-Asian fusion place is all rough slate-grey rock and caldera views. The flavour combinations are bold and the presentation is impeccable; try the beetroot salmon tartare with roasted fennel or the bao buns with chilli jam. The original cocktails are terrific but the wine list is only for those with deep pockets.

★Idol Restaurant Bar
FUSION €€€

(Map p416; ☑22860 23292; https://idolsantorini.gr; Ypapantis; mains €22-35; ☺11am-11pm) This caldera-edge, three-level restaurant and bar serves up stupendous views and intelligent

dishes full of depth, fire and vivacity. The chef dares combine squid with kimchi, raisins and chickpeas, alongside the more classic slow-cooked pork belly with sweet potato puree. And what could be more Greek than *mastika* (mastic liqueur) ice cream?

★Mylos
GREEK €€€

(☑22860 25640; www.mylossantorini.com; Firostefani; mains €24-29; ☺5.30pm-midnight) Located in a converted windmill on the caldera edge in Firostefani, this uber-glam venue has upscale food that's ambitious in its techniques and beautifully presented. Try crispy fish 'covered with sea snow', or lamb with Greek coffee and shellfish powder. Book ahead.

★Koukoumavlos
GREEK €€€

(Map p416; ☑22860 23807; www.koukoumavlos.com; mains €28-36; ☺7pm-late Apr–Oct) Award-winning fresh, modern Aegean cuisine (including a worthwhile degustation at €82), with obligatory caldera views from the terrace. Daring pairings of ingredients include sea bass with passionfruit and Jerusalem artichoke, and tiramisu with white Santorini aubergine. Excellent selection of local wines (including by the glass). It's located 30m north of the cathedral.

♟ Drinking & Nightlife

After midnight, Erythrou Stavrou fires up as the clubbing caldera of Fira, while Marinatou is lined with chic cocktail bars and beer bars. The real action in clubs kicks off late and some places party all the way until morning.

MoMix Bar Santorini   BAR
(Map p416; ☑ 6974350179; www.momixbar.com; Agiou Mina; ⊙ 8pm-3am) It might take a minute to get your head around this, but MoMix is short for Molecular Mixology. This popular party spot offers innovative cocktails (to help your mind travel) and cool interior colours in its cave-like bar. Head outside for stunning caldera views.

Kira Thira   BAR
(Map p416; ☑ 22860 22770; Erythrou Stavrou; ⊙ 8pm-3am daily) The oldest bar in Fira and one of the best. Dark wood and vaulted ceilings give it an intimate, cave-like atmosphere, with smooth cocktails and smoother jazz, and there's a huge viola hanging on the ceiling, this tiny bar is so popular it. This often gets swamped, especially when there is live music on offer.

Crystal Cocktail Bar   COCKTAIL BAR
(Map p416; ☑ 22860 22480; www.crystal-santorini.gr; Marinatou, Loucas Hotel; ⊙ 10am-1am) Relax at Crystal, and its views to die for, with coffee in the morning and cocktails as your day evolves. This is one of those spots that you won't want to leave. Part of Loucas Hotel, Crystal is a top spot, with stupendous sunsets.

Two Brothers Bar   BAR
(Map p416; ☑ 22860 23061; www.2brothersbarsantorini.com; Dekigala; ⊙ 10am-6am) Originally started by brothers Dimitris and Giannis in 1983, this cosy cave bar is now run by their sons, Jack and Leuteris. Expect a party vibe and, when things really wind up, little room to move. Two-for-one cocktails from 4pm to 7pm and 9pm to midnight.

PK Cocktail Bar   COCKTAIL BAR
(Map p416; ☑ 22860 22430; http://paliakameni.com; ⊙ 10am-late) Open year-round and into its fifth decade of business, PK Cocktail Bar offers three tiered outdoor terraces on which to nurse your cocktail while admiring the sunsets over the caldera rim. Cocktails made with fresh fruit are the speciality here. Opposite the cathedral.

Tango   COCKTAIL BAR
(Map p416; ☑ 6947453999; www.tangosantorini.gr; Marinatou; ⊙ 8pm-5am) This is edge-of-the-caldera stuff, with stupendous views, delicious cocktails – its champagne cocktails are a speciality – a fashionable crowd and brilliant tunes that get louder and funkier as the sun goes down. Come for sunset and stay for hours and hours – or until your wallet is empty.

Tropical   BAR
(Map p416; ☑ 22860 23089; Marinatou; ⊙ 11am-4am May-Oct) Nicely perched just before the caldera edge, Tropical draws a vibrant traveller crowd with a long list of classic (and some original) cocktails, distinguished by their fresh fruit content. Try the strawberry daiquiri or the Jean Genie against a rock music backdrop, plus unbeatable balcony views. It's on the steps down to the Old Port.

☆ Entertainment

White Door Theatro   THEATRE
(Map p416; ☑ 22860 21770; www.whitedoorsantorini.com; €55; ⊙ 9pm May, Sep & Oct, 9.30pm Jun-Aug) Fira's popular *Greek Wedding Show* is a hit with visitors, featuring lots of traditional music, dance, fun and audience participation. Small plates (mezedhes) and local wine are included in the ticket, which can be booked online – advisable in the high season. The show is in an atmospheric open-air courtyard surrounded by whitewashed buildings.

🛍 Shopping

★ Ergon Deli   FOOD & DRINKS
(Map p416; ☑ 22860 28360; www.ergonfoods.com; Erythrou Stavrou; ⊙ 9.30am-9pm) Not only do these guys produce some of Santorini's hottest craft beer (Volkan, served at their caldera-edge cafe; p415), but this deli is also a terrific place to shop for island edibles (superb olive oil, preserves, pickled caper leaves) and drinkables, including Vinsanto dessert wine.

★ Ceramic Art Studio   CERAMICS
(Map p416; ☑ 22860 24750; next to the conference centre; ⊙ 9am-9pm) Ceramics artist Andreas Alefragkis has been perfecting his craft over the course of three decades and the results are striking. Behold the hanging amphorae in an aquamarine or artfully cracked cream glaze and the one-of-a-kind vases, as well as utility drinking vessels and platters.

★ Eduart Gjopalaj Gallery   ART
(Map p416; ☑ 69424 39225; www.facebook.com/gjopalajeduart; Agiou Ioannou; ⊙ 10am-9pm) This

LOCAL KNOWLEDGE

SANTORINI ON A BUDGET

Santorini is not a cheap destination, but it needn't completely blow your budget. Here are some tips to make your euros go further.

➡ If you don't need caldera views from your room, consider staying in Perissa on Santorini's southeast coast, or taking advantage of inexpensive lodgings in Fira, such as Santorini Camping (Map p412; ☑ 22860 22944; www.santorinicamping.gr; Fira; dm/d €25/80, camp site per person €15; ☺ Mar-Nov; ❋ ☎ ☎) or Fira Backpackers Place (Map p416; ☑ 22860 31626; www.firabackpackers.com; dm/d €49/218; ☎), or staying in Katerados Caveland Hostel.

➡ Take the frequent public buses. Prices range from €1.80 to €2.40 and the buses will get you to most places of interest. For more remote locations, renting a car for a day (€40 to €50) is reasonable if there's three or four of you.

➡ Ancient Thira (p423), Akrotiri (p424), the Archaeological Museum (Museum of Akrotiri; Map p416; ☑ 22860 22217; M Nomikou; adult/concession €6/3; ☺ 8.30am-4pm Wed-Mon), the Museum of Prehistoric Thera (p414) and the Collection of Icons and Ecclesiastical Artefacts at Pyrgos all sell a five-in-one ticket that allows discounted entry to the five sites for €14.

➡ Boat tours of the caldera cost as little as €20 for three hours, and snorkelling excursions start from €30, so you needn't deprive yourself of aquatic adventure.

➡ Eat cheaply. There are inexpensive tavernas and gyros joints in most locations, including Fratzeskos Fish Tavern (p426) in Perissa, Lucky's Souvlaki (p417) in Fira and PitoGyros (p421) in Oia.

➡ Take advantage of happy hours in the many bars and pubs; many do two-for-one drinks specials between certain hours.

gallery is filled with the sinuous, surreal woodwork of Albanian-born sculptor Eduart Gjopalaj: delicate, lattice-like platters, serene faces seemingly floating out of undulating waves of wood. If you're lucky, you'll catch the artist at work.

★ **Mati Art Gallery** ART
(Map p416; ☑ 22860 23814; www.matiartgallery. com; Cathedral Plateau; ☺ 10am-9.30pm) The shark-head installation piece outside is sure to catch your attention. This is the main exhibition space of Yorgos Kypris, an internationally celebrated artist who takes much of his inspiration from Santorini and the sea. From the larger pieces featuring bright silver darts of sardine shoals to glass-and-metal denizens of the deep, his work is striking and unique.

Tzamia-Krystalla Art Gallery Santorini ART
(Map p416; ☑ 22860 21226; www.tzamia-krystalla gallery.gr; Marinatou; ☺ 10am-10pm) Near the top of the steps leading down to the Old Port, this gallery specialises in Greek contemporary art, both from established artists and up-and-coming young talent. All the ceramic sculptures – including ones inspired by Santorini's volcanic origins and created especially for this gallery – are made by Manousos

Chalkiadakis, one of the most distinguished ceramic artists in Greece.

Theta 8 FASHION & ACCESSORIES
(Map p416; ☑ 22866 72935; Marinatou; ☺ 9am-midnight) This chic boutique in a white-cave shop on the steps down to the Old Port is a friendly family business. It offers colourful leather bags handmade in Greece (including some made to look like snakeskin). Owned and operated by the designer and her partner; expect friendly smiles and service.

Orion Art Gallery ART
(Map p416; ☑ 22860 21616; www.artoftheloom. gr; Kamares; ☺ 9am-10pm) This gallery next to the Gyzi Megaron museum (p413) at the northern end of town displays gorgeous pieces by some of the island's top artists. Expect everything from fusion glass to modern bronze statues, handmade jewellery and colourful ceramics.

AK ART
(Map p416; ☑ 22860 23041; www.ak-galleries.com) Just north of the Orthodox Cathedral, Santorini's first art gallery (and a former flour mill) was founded in 1980 by local painter Christophoros Asimis and his wife, sculptor

Eleni Kolaiti. On display are Santorini landscapes by Christophoros and more abstract paintings by his son Katonas, as well as jewellery and sculpture by Eleni.

the White, Santorini FASHION & ACCESSORIES
(Map p416; ☑ 22860 36217; www.thewhitesantorini.com; Ypapantis; ⊘ 9am-10pm) This small fashion boutique, run by designer Sophia Hatzigeorgiou, draws inspiration from Santorini's unique landscapes, colours and lifestyle. The clothing is hand-sewn in Greece and, as the name suggests, collections feature plenty of white. There's a second store out at Kamari Beach.

Art of the Loom ARTS & CRAFTS
(Map p416; ☑ 22860 21190; www.artoftheloom.gr; Nomikou; ⊘ 9am-10pm) A block north of the cable car, this gallery features colourful glasswork from the prioprietor, Mary, as well as silver jewellery, paintings and ceramics by some of the island's top artists.

ℹ Information

Information Kiosk (Map p416; Dekigala; ⊘ 9am-8pm Mon-Fri May-Sep) Seasonal information.

Dakoutros Travel (☑ 22860 22958; www.dakoutrostravel.gr; Fira; ⊘ 8.30am-midnight Jul & Aug, 9am-9pm Sep-Jun) Helpful travel agency and de facto tourist office on the main street, just before Plateia Theotokopoulou. It sells ferry and air tickets, and provides assistance with excursions, accommodation and transfers.

ℹ Getting There & Away

There are frequent bus connections between Fira's bus station and the airport, located 6km east of Fira. The first leaves Fira around 5.30am and the last leaves around 10.15pm (€1.80, 20 minutes).

In summer buses leave Fira twice hourly for Oia (€1.80), Akrotiri/Red Beach (€2), and Kamari (€1.80), plus Perissa and Perivolos Beach (€2.40) and Kamari via Messaria (€1.80).

Buses leave Fira for the port of Athinios (€2.30, 30 minutes) seven times per day, but it's wise to check times in advance.

Oia   Οία

POP 1550

Perched on the northern tip of the island, this once centre of trade in antiquity now reflects the renaissance of Santorini after the devastating earthquake of 1956. Restoration work has restored the beauty overwhelmingly enjoyed by visitors, though signs imploring visitors to be quiet and respectful remind

you that for some, Oia is home year-round and a functioning village. You will struggle to find a more stunning spot in the Cyclades. Built on a steep slope of the caldera, many of its dwellings nestle in niches hewn into the volcanic rock.

Not surprisingly, Oia draws enormous numbers of tourists, and overcrowding is the price it pays for its good looks. Try to visit in the morning or spend the night here; afternoons and evenings often bring busloads from the cruise ships moored in the bay. At sunset the town feels like a magnet for every traveller on the island.

◉ Sights & Activities

Ammoudi PORT
(Map p412) This tiny port of colourful fishing boats lies 300 steps below Oia. It's a steep haul down and up again but well worth it for the views of the blood-red cliffs, the harbour and back up at Oia. Once you're down there, have lunch at one of the excellent, if pricey, fish tavernas right on the water's edge.

In summer, boats and tours go from Ammoudi to Thirasia daily; check with travel agencies in Fira for departure times.

Maritime Museum MUSEUM
(☑ 22860 71156; €3; ⊘ 10am-2pm & 5-8pm Wed-Mon) This museum is located along a narrow lane that leads off north from Nikolaou Nomikou. It's housed in a renovated and converted 19th-century mansion and has endearing displays on Santorini's maritime history. Oia's prosperity was based on its merchant fleet, which serviced the eastern Mediterranean, especially between Alexandria and Russia.

★ Atlantis Oia DIVING
(☑ 22860 71158; https://atlantisoia.com; 1 dive €70, PADI course from €230; ⊘ 8am-10pm) Helmed by stellar diving instructor Apostolos, this five-star diving outfit has been going strong for years and is the first of its kind – a member of Cousteau Divers – in all of Greece. Its deep commitment to marine conservation and enthusiastic, professional divemasters make Atlantis Oia a top pick for all manner of dives. Snorkelling outings also (€45). Off main road.

🛏 Sleeping

Oia is known for its proliferation of luxury villas and suites cascading down the caldera. Book well ahead. There are several midrange options, but if you're on a budget, consider staying elsewhere.

Maria's Place HOTEL €€
(Map p412; ☑22860 71221; www.mariasantorini.
com; d studio €200; ❋🛜🌊) This cluster of
snug studio apartments, some split-level and
all with outdoor spas for sunset viewing, is
inland from town on the road to Finikia and
a 10-minute walk to the caldera. Peaceful (no
kids under 16), great hosts and a lovely pool.
Three-night minimum in July and August.

Marcos Rooms HERITAGE HOTEL €€
(☑22860 71012; www.marcosrooms.com.gr; r
€140-165; 🛜) This traditional cave house is
among the very few midrange options in
Oia. Run by hospitable Marcos, it consists
of an atmospheric subterranean double and
studio apartment, as well as a couple of cosy
standard rooms with partial sea views. A decent Greek breakfast is thrown in and you're
a couple of minutes' walk from the caldera
rim.

★**Zoe Aegeas** APARTMENT €€€
(☑22860 71466; www.zoe-aegeas.gr; studio/4-per-
son cave house €351/504; ❋@🛜) Traditional,
split-level cave houses built into the caldera's
edge with all the comforts of home. Classy
decor, amazing views and unrivalled hospitality mean that this place gets a lot of happy
return guests. Book ahead. Each suite is different; some (including the private villa) can
sleep up to six.

★**Chelidonia
Traditional Villas** APARTMENT €€€
(☑22860 71287; www.chelidonia.com; Nikolaou
Nomikou; studio €324, villa from €450; ❋🛜) Traditional cliffside dwellings that have been in
the owner's family for generations. It offers
beds in cosy alcoves, mod cons offset with
traditional wooden furniture, and private
patios with uninterrupted caldera views.

🍴 Eating

PitoGyros KEBAB €
(☑22860 71119; https://pitogyros.com; mains €3-
11; ⏲11am-11pm) You'll rarely find 'cheap' and
'Oia' in the same sentence, yet both apply to
this souvlaki joint, a model of its kind. Go for
a pitta filled with smoky, crisped meat with
notes of tangy tzatziki and the crunch of onion, or fill your belly with a mixed grill platter, washed down with a Donkey craft beer.
Near the bus station.

★**Armeni** SEAFOOD €€
(☑22860 71053; http://armenisantorinirestaurant.
gr; mains €13-27; ⏲10am-11pm) With the seashore literally at your table, this gem of a

tavern is worth the steep ascent on foot to
Armeni Bay (though you can also catch a
boat from Amoudi Bay). This is an altar to
seafood with a short and brilliantly executed menu of grilled sardines, calamari stuffed
with local cheese, and fresh catch seared on
the grill.

Karma GREEK €€
(☑22860 71404; www.karma.bz; mains €13-18;
⏲dinner) With fountains, flickering candles,
golden-coloured walls and wine-coloured
cushions, this courtyard restaurant feels
rather royal and august. The food is traditional and hearty (eg *fava* beans with caramelised onions and grilled sea bream with
capers), and what you lack in caldera views
you make up for with reasonable prices.

★**Lauda** MODERN GREEK €€€
(☑22860 72182; www.laudarestaurant.com; mains
€48-135; ⏲1-4.30pm & 6.30-10pm) One of the
top fine dining experiences in Santorini –
natch, in Greece! – Lauda morphed from
Oia's humble first restaurant into a destination in its own right. Chef Emmanuel Renaut
combines local produce with international
cooking techniques, with stellar results.
Splurge on a tasting menu or go for fish
marinated with caper leaves, or slow-cooked
lamb with gnocchi.

★**To Krinaki** TAVERNA €€€
(☑22860 71993; Finikia; mains €17-27; ⏲noon-
late) All-fresh, all-local ingredients, such as
wild greens, white aubergine, hand-crushed
fava, caper leaves and wild asparagus go into
top-notch taverna dishes at this homey spot
in tiny Finikia, just east of Oia. Local beer
and wine made from grape varieties grown
in Santorini since antiquity, plus a sea (but
not caldera) view looking north to Ios.

Catch FUSION €€€
(☑22860 72063; https://catchrestaurant.gr; mains
€26-39; ⏲6.30pm-2am) This new kid on the
block stands out among Oia's other fusion
offerings because it gets everything right.
Service is efficient, ingredient-driven dishes
– from sea bass tartare and grilled asparagus
with Myconian cheese to wild mushroom
risotto – are spot on, with beautiful presentation. There are terrific original cocktails,
divided into four elements, plus sunset views
from the terrace. Near the bus station.

1800 GREEK €€€
(☑22860 71485; www.oia-1800.com; Nikolaou Nomikou; mains €15-38; ⏲noon-midnight) Housed
in a restored sea captain's mansion, the

SANTORINI'S BEACHES

Santorini's best beaches are on the east and south coasts. Some of the beaches have no facilities at all, whereas others come fully equipped with sunbeds, beach bars and the odd water-sports operator.

The long stretches of black sand, pebbles and pumice stones at Perissa (Map p412), Perivolos and Agios Georgios (Map p412) are backed by bars, tavernas, hotels and shops and remain fairly relaxed. Perissa has a 24-hour bar that plays DJ sets on summer nights, so that's the place if you're looking to party.

Red (Kokkini) Beach (Map p412), near Ancient Akrotiri in the south, has particularly impressive red cliffs. Caïques from Akrotiri Beach can take you there and on to the sheltered cove of White (Aspri) Beach (Map p412) and the sunbed-studded sand at the Black (Mesa Pigadia) Beach (Map p412) for about €5 return. Mesa Pigadia has a beach-side tavern, and there are several restaurants up from Kokkini Beach.

Vlihada (Map p412), also on the south coast, has a beach backed by weirdly eroded cliffs as well as tavernas; it also has a photogenic fishing harbour with an excellent restaurant above it. The further along the beach you go, the less clothes you see; it's a favourite with naturists.

Kamari (Map p412) is Santorini's best-developed resort, with a long beach of black sand. The beachfront road is dense with restaurants and bars, and things get extremely busy in high season. Boats connect Kamari with Perissa in summer.

On the north coast, a short drive from Oia, there is the long, narrow stretch of sand that is the Baxedes Beach that flows seamlessly into Paradisos Beach. There are no facilities there, and the water isn't as sheltered for swimming as their brethren on the south coast, but there are relatively few people as well.

---

artistically prepared modern Greek cuisine has won this restaurant accolades for years. Sea bass with an aromatic spell of quinoa, artichoke and fennel puree or grilled lamb with sweet-and-sour green apple sauce give you a glimpse at the creative menu. Dine inside or on the caldera-view rooftop. Book ahead.

Shopping

★ Atlantis Books   BOOKS
(☑ 22860 72346; www.atlantisbooks.org; Nikolaou Nomikou; ☺ 11am-8pm) Follow quotes and words that wind their way down the steep stairs into a little cavern with floor-to-ceiling shelves of books: fiction, philosophy, history, art and more. Staff are friendly and knowledgeable, and musicians and other events are hosted on the rooftop.

B.Loose   CLOTHING
(☑ 22860 27309; https://b-loose.gr; Pliarchon; ☺ 10am-9pm) Going strong for almost a decade, this is the Oia outlet of the Athens casual fashion label that specialises in comfortable, loose-fitting streetwear handmade from high-quality cotton and linen.

Information

Travel agencies such as **NS Travel** (☑ 22860 71199; www.nst-santorinitravel.com;

☺ 9am-9pm) are found by the bus area; purchase ferry tickets here.

Getting There & Away

In summer, buses leave Fira twice-hourly for Oia, with more services pre-sunset (€1.80). From the bus terminal, head left and uphill to reach the rather stark central square and the beautiful marble-lined main street, Nikolaou Nomikou, which skirts the caldera.

It takes around three hours to walk from Fira to Oia on a spectacular, well-trodden path along the top of the caldera.

Around Santorini

Santorini is not all about the caldera edge. The island slopes gently down to sea level on its eastern and southern sides and here you'll find black beaches of volcanic pebbly sand at popular resorts such as Kamari and Perissa.

Inland lie charming traditional villages such as Vourvoulos, to the north of Fira, and Megalohori, Pyrgos and the 'ghost village' of Exo Gonia to its south. Pyrgos, in particular, is worth visiting and a good alternative to Oia, with fabulous restaurants and stunning views (see www.santorinipyrgos.com). Ancient sites round out a comprehensive package.

◉ Sights

★ Ancient Thira ARCHAEOLOGICAL SITE
(Map p412; ☎22860 25405; http://odysseus.
culture.gr/h/3/eh351.jsp?obj_id=2454; adult/child
€4/free; ◷8am-3pm Tue-Sun) First settled by
the Dorians in the 9th century BCE, Ancient
Thira consists of Hellenistic, Roman and
Byzantine ruins and is an atmospheric and
rewarding site to visit. The ruins include
temples, houses with mosaics, an *agora*
(market), a theatre and a gymnasium. Views
are splendid. If you're driving, take the narrow, switchbacked road from Kamari for
3km. From Perissa, a hike up a dusty path
takes a bit over an hour to reach the site.

★ Art Space GALLERY
(Map p412; ☎22860 32774; www.artspace-santo
rini.com; Exo Gonia; ◷11am-sunset Apr-Oct) FREE
This atmospheric gallery is on the way to
Kamari, in Argyros Canava, one of the oldest
wineries on the island. The walls and niches of the wine caverns feature paintings and
sculptures by some 30 contemporary Greek
artists, one of them from Santorini. Winemaking is still in the owner's blood, and
part of the complex produces some stellar
vintages under the Art Space Wines label
(only available for purchase at the gallery).
Tastings (from €10) enhance the experience.

Akrotiri Lighthouse VIEWPOINT
(Map p412) If you want to watch the greatest
free show on earth (the sunset!) in seclusion,
well, you're out of luck. Word is out, and you
will be joined at the tip of this promontory
by dozens of sunset-gazers. Still, there's plenty of room for everybody and the lighthouse
lacks Oia's crowds.

Tomato Industrial Museum MUSEUM
(Map p412; ☎22860 85141; www.tomatomuseum.
gr; Vlihada; €5; ◷10am-6pm Tue-Sun) Tomato
processing was a major industry on the island before the earthquake of 1952, and this
is a unique look inside an old tomato factory
in Vlihada. The video interviews of elderly
former factory workers are interesting and
the museum is part of the cool Santorini
Arts Factory (www.santoriniartsfactory.gr),
which hosts exhibitions, concerts and theatre shows; check its programme online.

Wine Museum WINERY
(Map p412; ☎22860 31322; www.winemuseum.gr;
€10; ◷10am-5pm Apr-Oct, 9am-4.30pm Mon-Sat
Nov-Mar) At the Koutsoyannopoulos Winery
en route to Kamari, this slightly kitsch but
fun museum in a traditional *canava* (winery) depicts the traditional winemaking

process through a series of cheesy dioramas.
Admission includes tastings of four wines;
none are exceptional, though Koutsoyannopoulos Winery is the only one to produce a
very palatable Kamaritis dessert wine from
red grapes.

Ancient Akrotiri ARCHAEOLOGICAL SITE
(Map p412; ☎22860 81366; http://odysseus.
culture.gr/h/3/eh351.jsp?obj_id=2410; adult/con-
cession €12/6; ◷8am-8pm May-Sep, to 3pm Oct-
Apr) In 1967, excavations in the southwest of
Santorini uncovered an ancient Minoan city
buried deep beneath volcanic ash from the
catastrophic eruption of 1613 BCE. Housed
within a cool, protective structure, wooden
walkways allow you to pass through the city.
Peek inside three-storey buildings that survived, and see roads, drainage systems and
stashes of pottery.

🏃 Activities & Tours

There's more than just the spectacular caldera and sunset views to keep visitors busy
on Santorini. Head out to visit impressive
ancient sites, black-sand beaches, wineries
(and a brewery), take a boat tour to an active
volcanic island in the caldera or explore Santorini's underwater topography.

Navy's Waterworld Dive Center DIVING
(Map p412; ☎22860 28190; https://navyswater
world.gr; Kamari Beach; 2-tank dive €95; ◷8am-
10pm) This five-star PADI operator does a
range of diving excursions, from exploring
lava caves and wreck diving to discovery dives
for beginners and full PADI certification.

Santorini Dive Center DIVING
(Map p412; ☎22860 83190; www.divecenter.gr;
Perissa; 1-/2-tank dive €60/90; ◷9am-8pm) Reputable diving outfit in Perissa, offering standard dives as well as a range of PADI course,
and snorkelling outings (€30).

Fira to Oia Hike WALKING
(Map p412) Head north from Fira to Firostefani and Imerovigli along the caldera-edge
pathway for sensational views. It's about a
30-minute walk one way. Keep walking and
you can eventually reach Oia, but be aware
that this is no small undertaking, especially in the heat of the day. It's about 9km and
three hours' walk one way.

Santorini Brewery Company BREWERY
(Map p412; ☎22860 30268; www.santorinibrew
ingcompany.gr; Messaria–Kamari Rd; ◷11am-
5pm Mon-Sat summer, shorter hours rest of the
year) The home of the island's in-demand

Donkey beers is well worth a stop. Sample the Yellow Donkey (hoppy golden ale), Red Donkey (amber ale), the Crazy Donkey (IPA), the White Donkey (wheat with a touch of orange peel), plus the Lazy Ass lager. All are unfiltered, unpasteurised and extremely palatable. There are free tastings, plus cool merchandise.

In August, look out for the seasonal Slow Donkey, matured in oak barrels from the nearby Argyros Estate after its used them for fermenting its Vinsanto dessert wine.

⭐**Santorini MTB Adventures** CYCLING
(Map p412; ☑6980289453; www.santoriniadventures.gr; Agios Georgios; mountain bike/e-bike rental €25/50 per day) This up-and-coming operator rents out e-bikes for an ecofriendly and active way of exploring the island and also runs highly regarded tours (€120 to €150) that either take in the highlights of the south coast or truly put you through your paces if you have experience of technical downhills. Full-day cycling and sailing adventures also available.

🛏 Sleeping

Away from these main villages, the biggest concentration of midrange and budget rooms can be found in and around Kamari, Perissa and Messaria.

Zorzis Hotel BOUTIQUE HOTEL €
(Map p412; ☑22860 81104; www.santorinizorzis.com; Perissa; d incl breakfast from €99; 🅿🛜🗙) Behind a huge bloom of geraniums on Perissa's main street, Hiroko and Spiros (a Japanese-Greek couple) run an immaculate 10-room hotel. It's a pastel-coloured sea of calm (no kids), with a delightful garden, pool and an eye-catching mountain backdrop.

Karterados Caveland Hostel HOSTEL €
(Map p412; ☑22860 22122; www.cave-land.com; Karterados; dm from €39, d incl breakfast €129; ⊙Mar-Oct; 🅿🛜🗙) This fabulous, chilled-out hostel is based in an old winery complex in Karterados about 2km from central Fira (see website for directions). Dorms (four, six and 10 beds) are in the big old wine caves, all of them with creative, colourful decor and good facilities. (Warning: claustrophobes might find the tiny windows problematic.) The garden swimming pool tops it off.

Narkissos Hotel HOTEL €
(Map p412; ☑22860 34205; www.narkissoshotel.com; Kamari; s/d/tr incl breakfast €88/96/122; ⊙Apr-Nov; 🅿🛜) A decent budget option at the southern end of Kamari, close to the

beach and with well-kept rooms. Outside the summer peak, room prices tumble (€35).

Stelios Place HOTEL €
(Map p412; ☑22860 81860; www.steliosplace.com; Perissa; d/tr/q €80/100/120; 🅿@🛜🗙) This small, family-run hotel has a great position set back from the main drag in Perissa, one block from the beach. Well-equipped rooms sparkle with cleanliness, as does the swimming pool. Breakfast is available. Free airport or port transfers for those staying three nights or longer; note that off-peak rates fall to a bargain €35.

Hippocampus Hotel HOTEL €€
(Map p412; ☑22860 32050; www.hippocampushotel.gr; Kamari; d/tr/q €138/145/185; ⊙May-Oct; 🅿🛜🗙) 🌿 Just steps from Kamari's beachfront, this friendly place has a sparkling collection of rooms and studios, with added extras like hand-painted wall murals and a commitment to ecopractices.

⭐**Villa Blanca** VILLA €€€
(Map p412; ☑22860 81860; http://villablancasantorini.com; Megalohori; villa €275; ⊙Jun-Sep; 🅿🛜🛜) A superb option away from the crowds amid Megalohori's vineyards, 6km south of Fira. Villa Blanca is a luxury villa built in traditional Cycladic style, featuring two bedrooms, living room, kitchen and balcony with a lovely Jacuzzi and ocean view out to the southeast. Perfect for a family, sleeping up to five; you'll need own wheels.

🍴 Eating

Brusco CAFE €
(☑22860 30944; Pyrgos; mains from €8) In Pyrgos, Brusco offers coffee, wine and local flavours in a sweet rustic cafe-deli with plenty of outdoor space. Stop by for the warm welcome, homemade cakes (including baklava) and platters of great Santorini produce (*fava*, tomatoes, aubergines, capers and more).

⭐**Tzanakis** GREEK €€
(Map p412; ☑22860 81929; http://tavernatzanakis.com; Megalohori; mains €8-14; ⊙noon-midnight) A local institution into its third decade, this family-run taverna uses vegetables and herbs grown in its garden and meat and fish sourced from farmer and fisher friends to cook up such classics as tomato balls, courgette fritters, goat with lemon sauce, *domadakia* (stuffed vine leaves) and more.

⭐**Aroma Avlis** MODERN GREEK €€
(Map p412; ☑22860 33794; www.artemiskaramolegos-winery.com; Messaria–Kamari Rd; mains

SANTORINI'S WINES

Santorini is blessed with a dry volcanic microclimate and wine culture here goes back millennia. Santorini's vines are Europe's oldest, impervious to the *phylloxera* bug that wiped out most of the continent's vines in the late 19th century.

Grapes are grown close to the ground, in a *kouloura* (nest) of vines to make the most of the moisture and protect the grapes from fierce winds.

Santorini's most lauded wine is a crisp dry white *assyrtiko*, as well as the amber-coloured, unfortified dessert wine known as Vinsanto (that must be made from at least 51% *assyrtiko*, plus *aidani* and *athiri* in order to qualify). Both wines are made from the heritage-protected, indigenous grape variety, *assyrtiko*, as is Nykteri (*assyrtiko* made at night). *Assyrtiko* grapes are grown across the Cyclades, but the Santorini variety stands out in terms of unique flavour. You'll also come across *mavrotragano* (full-bodied red), and the medium-bodied *mandelaria* red.

Most local vineyards host tastings (for a small charge), with snacks or meals on the side. Santorini Wine Adventure (☑22860 34123; www.winetoursantorini.com; half-day tours from €120) and Santorini Wine Tour (☑22860 28358; www.santoriniwinetour.com; ☺half-day tour from €145) are two of many operators, with knowledgeable guides and tours that blend food, wine, scenery and history, but you can also explore on your own.

Of Santorini's 20 wineries, a dozen or so are open to the public. Don't miss:

Estate Argyros Winery (Map p412; ☑22860 31489; https://estateargyros.com; Messaria–Kamari Rd; 4/7 tastings €15/40; ☺10am-8pm) Terrific, internationally renowned *assyrtiko*, Nykteri and *mavrotragano*, plus exceptional Vinsanto. A short tour and snacks are included in the tastings price.

Gavalas Winery (Map p412; ☑22860 82552; www.gavalaswines.gr; Megalohori; tastings €9-24; ☺10am-8pm) Small, family-run winery with award-winning Vinsanto and opportunities to join in traditional grape-crushing in August.

Canava Roussos (Map p412; ☑22860 31278; www.canavaroussos.gr; Mesa Gonia; ☺10am-6pm May-Oct) Santorini's oldest winery's aged dessert wines are a speciality. It has an appealing outdoor tastings area under a trellis of vines.

Art Space (p423) Santorini's smallest winery combined with an art gallery.

Hatzidakis Winery (Map p412; ☑22860 32466, 6970013556; www.hatzidakiswines.gr; Pyrgos; ☺by appointment) The island's only organic winery, run by the family of a Cretan oenologist.

€13-48; ☺1-11pm) 🍴 Part of the Artemis Karamolegos winery, this terrific restaurant does wonderful things with local ingredients with brilliance and flourish. Go for the smoked white aubergine mousse, *chloro* (fresh Santorinian goat's cheese), local sausages or *orzotto* with king crab and speck from Crete. Eat on the vine-covered terrace and don't miss out on the extensive selection of local wines.

⭐**Metaxi Mas**   CRETAN €€
(Map p412; ☑22860 31323; www.santorini-metaximas.gr; Exo Gonia; mains €9-21; ☺2pm-midnight Apr-Oct) The raki flows at this convivial taverna near the church, a favourite among locals and authenticity-seeking travellers. It serves a delicious menu of local and Cretan specialities (the owner-chef is from Crete), such as grilled pork belly, oven-baked asparagus with Cretan *graviera* and more.

The wine list focuses on the best of local tipples. Enjoy sweeping views, too. Book ahead.

Fratzeskos Fish Tavern   SEAFOOD €€
(☑22860 83488; www.facebook.com/fishtavern frageskos1; Perissa; mains from €8; ☺noon-11.30pm) This superb waterfront taverna specialises in fresh fish, from grouper to sea bream, expertly grilled with the high notes of lemon making it sing of the sea right on your plate. There's lobster spaghetti for two, shrimp *saganaki* and other crowd-pleasers. Enthusiastic staff top off the experience.

Apollon Taverna   GREEK €€
(Map p412; ☑22860 85340; Perissa; mains €9-14; ☺10am-midnight) This marvellous taverna sits just across the road from the beach, about 400m along the Perissa waterfront from the bus stop. Try the mouthwatering seafood platter for two (€30) or pick from

CRUISES

Boat and catamaran cruises are a must-do activity on Santorini and are a terrific way of appreciating the island's dramatic topography and equally dramatic sunsets.

There are three types of cruises to choose from: half-day (five/six hours) boat/catamaran cruises that typically depart around 10am, half-day sunset cruises that leave at 3.30pm, and full-day (nine hour) boat cruises.

Half-day and sunset boat/catamaran cruises typically take in the caldera's volcanic islands of Nea Kameni and Palia Kameni, including a stop at the former's crater and the latter's hot springs. Catamaran cruises stop for swimming at the hot springs but don't dock at the crater, and most sail past the lighthouse and along the Red and White beaches of the south coast. Lunch and refreshments are included in the price.

Full-day tours may call at Thirasia, and/or a port below Oia.

Departures are either from Fira Skala, below Fira, Oia's Ammoudi Bay or the Vlychada marina on the south coast. Rule of thumb is: the cheaper the tour, the more crowded the boat and the less time at any one location. Quick three-hour sails around the caldera with Caldera's Boats (Map p416; ☑ 22860 24355; www.santorini-sea-excursions.com; 25is Martiou, Fira; half-/full-day cruise from €20/44) cost just €20, but it's well worth paying more for a longer tour and better service. Before booking, ask exactly what's included.

The most relaxed sailing tours are the semiprivate (or private, if you can spare the cash) small-group catamaran tours; Santorini Sailing (Map p412; ☑ 22860 21380; www.santorinisailing.com; St Gerasimos, Firostefani; per person €105-165), Sunset Oia (Map p412; ☑ 22860 72200; https://sailing-santorini.com; 5hr catamaran tour €145-190; ⊗ 9am-10pm) and Spiridakos Sailing Cruises (Map p416; ☑ 22860 23755; www.santorini-yachts.com; 25is Martiou, Fira; cruises from €95; ⊗ 8am-10pm) are among the top operators.

the likes of smoked Santorini aubergine and traditional pies from the full-on menu.

★ Selene   MODERN GREEK €€€
(☑ 22860 22249; www.selene.gr; Pyrgos; mains restaurant €32-50, bistro €14-21; ⊗ restaurant 7-11pm, bistro noon-11pm) This is one of Santorini's most celebrated restaurants. Dishes such as *pasticcio* stuffed with pork cheek and Aegean codfish with smoked aubergine are pleasing to the eye and the palate, and the wine list is superb. That said, the more moderately priced Meze & Wine Bistro downstairs is just as satisfying and creative but without the hefty price tag.

🍷 Drinking & Nightlife

Beach Bar   BAR
(Map p412; www.thebeachbar.gr; ⊗ 24hr; 🛜) Round-the-clock fun in season on the black-sand beach on the Perissa waterfront. The Beach Bar does it all, from breakfast, lunch and dinner offerings, sunbeds and umbrellas, cocktails and beers, right through to live bands and DJ sets loud enough to dislodge a filling. The water is only a step or two away once you've overheated!

★ CineKamari   CINEMA
(Map p412; ☑ 22860 33452; www.cinekamari.gr; Kamari; €10; ⊗ 9.30pm) After the

caldera sunset, this is one of the finest ways to spend a Santorini evening. On the road into Kamari, this tree-surrounded, open-air cinema screens movies in their original language throughout the summer. Pull up a deckchair, request a blanket if you're feeling chilly, and relax. Drinks and snacks available.

ANAFI   ΑΝΑΦΗ

POP 271

Though Anafi lies a mere 22km east of Santorini, its rugged, hilly landscape, dotted with prickly pears and a few hardy olive trees and overlooked by Kalamos (or Monastery Rock, 463m) – believed to be the second-largest in the Mediterranean after the Rock of Gibraltar – is among the least visited in the Cyclades. Myth has it that it once served as a refuge for the exhausted Argonauts, revealed to them by Apollo only after they'd spent hours battling a tempest. A refuge it remains – from the crowds that descend on the neighbouring islands – so if seclusion and great hiking is what you're after, you've hit the jackpot.

The port of Agios Nikolaos is on the south coast, with the main town of Hora a steep 2km by road above to the north.

◉ Sights

There is a string of lovely beaches along the south coast, starting near Agios Nikolaos. Klissidi, an 800m (10-minute) walk east of the port, is the closest and most popular. Around 2.4km (40-minute walk) further east, past the Katsouni, Phlamourou, Exo Roukounas and Mikros Roukounas coves, is the broad sweep of Roukounas, a sandy beach backed by dunes and home to the superb Roukounas taverna. Further still, the trail meanders past the delightful Katalimatsa cove and passes by three more small beaches before climbing up to the monastery from the pebble beach of Prasies.

Zoodochos Pigi Monastery MONASTERY
Incorporating the ruins of the temple of Apollo (allegedly built by the Argonauts) into its building, monastery Zoodochos Pigi is 9km from Hora by road, or reached by a 7km walk along the south-coast trail. Not open to visitors, the monastery lies in the east of the island, on the isthmus connecting Anafi to the imposing 463m Kalamos (or Monastery Rock), which has the uninhabited Kalamiotissas Monastery at its peak.

🛏 Sleeping

Most lodgings are in Hora and consist of self-catering apartments and B&Bs. There's a beach resort west of Hora and a couple of options overlooking Klissidi Beach. Many of the rooms on Hora's main pedestrian street have good views across Anafi's hills, the sea and the great summit of Kalamos. Book early for July and August.

Ostria GUESTHOUSE €
(☑ 22860 61375; studio from €30; 🛜) Run by a welcoming local couple (little English spoken), this sweet guesthouse consists of several spotless rooms with kitchenettes, with great views down to the port from the hillside from its location in the quiet, southern part of Hora. Accessible via some steps down from the end of the ring road.

⭐ Margarita's Rooms PENSION €€
(☑ 22860 61237; www.margarita-anafi.gr; d from €70; 🛜) Just above Klissidi Beach, these simple, beloved family-run rooms hark back to the Greek island life of quieter times. Nothing luxurious here, but it's an affordable island escape next to a lovely beach, with an excellent restaurant attached – Margarita's taverna. It's a tad isolated, so renting some wheels is a good idea. Port transfers included.

Apollon Village Hotel APARTMENT €€
(☑ 22860 28739; http://apollonvillagehotel.com; d/studio/bungalow/ste from €100/150/160/180; ⊙ May-Sep; ❄ 🛜) Rising in tiers above Klissidi Beach, these individual rooms, studios and apartments with glorious views are each named after a Greek god and remain outstanding value. The Blue Cafe-Bar is a cool adjunct to the hotel, with homemade sweets and pastries. It's not in Hora, so can feel a little isolated without your own wheels.

🍴 Eating

⭐ Roukounas TAVERNA €
(☑ 22860 61206; Roukounas Beach; mains €5-8; ⊙ 10am-midnight late May-Oct) A little way up from Roukounas Beach, this delightful family-run taverna hides amid a lush garden. A great place to sample simple, hearty dishes such as oven-baked lamb and rabbit casserole, as well as local cheese and seasonal greens.

⭐ Margarita's TAVERNA €
(☑ 22860 61237; www.margarita-anafi.gr; Klissidi; mains €6-12; ⊙ 9am-10pm Jun-Sep; 🛜) This standard-bearer of the 'Aegean Cuisine' label has a sunny little terrace overlooking the bay at Klissidi. Margarita's fresh-baked bread, handmade pasta and meatballs are staples; goat stew, shrimp risotto with Anafi crocus and cheese pies are all full of local flavour. There are rooms here, too.

⭐ Liotrivi TAVERNA €
(☑ 22860 61209; www.facebook.com/liotrivi.rest; mains €7-10; ⊙ noon-11pm May-Oct) A classy old-school taverna on the main street in Hora, where fresh fish is brought in from the family's boat, while the eggs, vegetables and honey come from their garden. Come into the kitchen and choose from the likes of lemon and dill rice with mussels, *mousakas* and catch of the day.

Armenaki TAVERNA €€
(☑ 22860 61234; mains €8-16; ⊙ noon-10pm Jun-Sep) Fresh fish dishes are the go-to staples at this traditional taverna in Hora, enhanced by an airy terrace, splendid views and occasional live music. Head down the small street opposite the bakery in central Hora to find it.

ℹ Getting There & Away

Anafi is remote, and reached by fewer ferry services than most of the Cyclades. In inclement weather, ferries may have trouble landing, since Anafi lacks a sheltered bay. Plan

WALKING ON ANAFI

The four main (relatively well-marked) walking trails are the following:

#1: Klisidi Beach to Zoodochos Pigi Monastery (7km, around 2½ to three hours one way) Takes in the south coast and around 10 beaches and coves, including the ancient harbour of Katalimatsa.

#2: Milies to Zoodochos Pigi Monastery via the Kastelli ruins (7.5km, around 3½ hours one way) Beginning from a farmhouse in the hamlet of Milies, this moderately tough trail passes the ruins of the ancient Kastelli and Kastelli peak (325m), from where the ancient Sacred Way leads to the former Temple of Apollo (now a monastery).

#3: Zoodochos Pigi Monastery to Moni Kalamiotissas (2.5km, around an hour one way). The island's most famous (and steepest) hike to the top of the Kalamos rock, with staggering views from the summit.

#4: Hora to Aghia Irini (7km, 2½ hours one way) A gentle ramble through the countryside, past the chapel of Stavros, and a descent to the Aghia Irini chapel through some old estates.

ahead, especially outside the high season, and consult http://ferries.gr for up-to-date ferry information.

Buy ferry tickets at **Roussou Travel** (☎ 22860 61220; ⊗ 10am-1pm & 6-8pm), either in the village or on the harbourfront, an hour before ferries are due.

Boat services from Anafi:

DESTINATION	DURATION	FARE (€)	FREQUENCY
Folegandros	5¼hrs	11	2 weekly
Ios	3½hrs	9	2 weekly
Karpathos	6¾hrs	17	2 weekly
Milos	6¼hrs	21	2 weekly
Naxos	7½hrs	13	2 weekly
Paros	7hrs	16	2 weekly
Piraeus	11½hrs	38	2 weekly
Rhodes	13½hrs	29	2 weekly
Santorini	1½hrs	8	2 weekly
Sikinos	4¼hrs	11	2 weekly
Syros	15½hrs	19.50	2 weekly

ⓘ Getting Around

The island's port is Agios Nikolaos. From here, the main village, Hora, is a 10-minute bus ride (€2) up a winding road, or a 2km hike up a less winding but steep walkway. Between May and September, free buses run from the **bus stop**, arriving at the port one hour before scheduled boat departures. Three buses daily run down to the port at 11am, 2pm and 6pm, departing from Hora for the monastery 10 minutes later and returning from the monastery at 11.25am, 2.25pm and 6.25pm (€3).

Summertime caïques serve various beaches and nearby small islands (price depends on distance and number of passengers).

In Hora, **Manos** (☎ 22860 61430; www.renta caranafi.gr) hires cars, scooters and four-wheelers for rent; some lodgings do so also.

SIKINOS ΣΙΚΙΝΟΣ

POP 300

Legend has it that Thoas, the king of Lemnos, fled to Sikinos, hidden in a trunk, to escape his island's womenfolk who rose up and slaughtered all the men. A succession of Mycenaeans, Ionians, Dorians, Venetians and Turks followed, while in the late 1930s, the island was a place of exile for communists and socialists.

With a tiny population, Sikinos is still quiet and remote, the place to come if you want to experience traditional island life at its least commercial. With a charming old town and terraced hills that make up terrific hiking terrain, Sikinos is the antithesis of neighbouring Ios.

The main clusters of habitation are the port of Alopronia and the linked inland villages of Horio and Kastro (collectively known as the Hora).

July and August see lots of Greek visitors turn up, but if you arrive before mid-May, don't expect there to be much going on.

⊙ Sights

The beach at the port of **Alopronia** is lovely – sandy, with some shade and a children's playground. It looks straight out at Santorini.

A narrow, dramatic bay with a small sandy patch, **Agios Nikolaos Beach** is a 20-minute walk through the countryside from the port. To find it, follow signs to Dialiskari. A path leads further on to Agios Georgios, or you can reach it by sealed road (7km).

Summertime caïques (about €6) run to beaches, including Maltas (Map p429) in the north (which has ancient ruins on the hill above) and Kara in the south.

★**Moni Zoödohou Pigis**   MONASTERY
(Map p429; ☑ 6975743928; ⊙ 11.30am-1.30pm Tue-Sun) **FREE** A flight of whitewashed steps leads to the fortified monastery of Moni Zoödohou Pigis, high above the Kastro. Originally built as a women's monastery in 1690, this is where the nuns and villagers would hide out during pirate attacks. The monastery has recently opened to the public, and you can go into the church and the visitors' room, or check out the amazing views. Don't miss the nuns' emergency escape route, by rope down the cliffs out the back.

Kastro   VILLAGE
A Venetian fortress that stood here in the 13th century gave Kastro its name. Today it is a charming, lived-in place, with winding alleyways between brilliant white houses. At its heart is the main square and the Church of Pantanassa. Check out the buildings surrounding the church, which were homes to the town's wealthy merchants: two-storey affairs with remnants of ornate stonework around the windows.

Moni Episkopis   MONASTERY
(Map p429) **FREE** From the saddle between Kastro and Horio, a surfaced road leads southwest for 5km to Moni Episkopis, under renovation during research time. The remains here are believed to be those of a 3rd-century CE Roman mausoleum that was transformed into a church in the 7th century and a monastery 10 centuries later. A couple of excellent hiking trails start here and one bus per day runs here on summer evenings.

🏃 Activities

Sikinos is popular with walkers, and the island has set up seven Paths of Culture, a network of well-signposted paths all over the island. Keen walkers should purchase Terrain's (http://terrainmaps.gr) excellent hiking map for Sikinos.

Manalis Winery   WINE
(Map p429; ☑ 6932272854; www.manaliswinery. gr; ⊙ 6pm-late Jun-Sep) On the road to Moni Episkopis, family-run Manalis Winery produces Sikinos wine using traditional, self-sustaining methods. The friendly owner can give you a taste and the on-site

restaurant serves traditional island dishes (mains €10 to €15). The food won't blow your mind, but the view of the vineyard and coast from the terrace will. The bus stops here summer evenings.

🛏 Sleeping

The dozen or so options in Alopronia, near the beach, range from simple pensions and self-catering studios to three-star hotels. Atmospheric Hora (Kastro) has only a couple of places to stay: a pension and a clutch of apartments. Book early for July and August.

★**Kastellos Apartments**   GUESTHOUSE €
(☑ 6972377729; www.kastellos-sikinos.gr; studios €50; ❋ 🛜) Spotless, spacious and well-equipped with little kitchenettes, these three individually designed studio apartments with bold splashes of colour are a stone's throw from the port and have tiny balconies looking out to sea. The friendly owner will help you with your luggage.

Porto Sikinos Hotel   HOTEL €€
(☑ 22860 51220; www.portosikinos.gr; Alopronia; s/d/f incl breakfast €75/90/120; ⊙ May-Oct; ❋ 🛜) The sweet rooms here are traditional tile-and-marble affairs with pastel-coloured accents and balconies. This central, whitewashed complex is the closest thing to a standard hotel on Sikinos and it's well run and appealing, with an on-site cafe.

Stegadi Apartments   APARTMENT €€
(☑ 22860 51305; www.stegadi.com; Kastro; apt €110; ❋ 🛜) Near the heart of Kastro, these four beautiful, traditional apartments sleep up to four and are individually decorated with modern furnishings and splashes of

vibrant colour. The balconies are small oases with views across to the sea.

Ostria Studios PENSION €€
(☑ 22860 51062; www.ostriastudios-sikinos.gr; Alopronia; d from €110; ✴🐾) These comfy rooms and studios are lovingly decorated. Margarita has three sets of rooms – Ostria Studios Spilia, Agnanti and Molos; Spilia is on the far side of the bay from the ferry quay. The rooms are right on the water, and you can swim below your room. They have sea-view balconies and plenty of natural light.

✕ Eating

★ **Anemelo** CAFE €
(☑ 22860 51216; Kastro; mains €5-9; ⊙ 10am-3pm & 5pm-late) This is Kastro's most atmospheric place to grab a local tea, beer or simple crêpe-and-salad lunch. Locals chat at the tables over chess games or lounge over coffee at the tables outside. Take the *tiny* spiral staircase up to the terrace for ace views. The killer Traditional Sandwich (€6) features olive paste, feta, capers and tomato.

In the evenings, this place is really hopping!

Kapari GREEK €
(☑ 22860 51070; Kastro; mains €7.50-11; ⊙ 12.30-3pm & 6pm-1am) Your go-to place if you arrive out of season or are staying at Alopronia and absolutely nothing is open. This 'Aegean Cuisine' standard bearer is on the main road in Hora, and Evgenia cooks up solid Greek staples, including her own 'beer salad' with local sausage, spicy meatballs and veal cooked in beer.

❶ Getting There & Away

Ferry tickets can be bought at the port at **Kountouris Travel** (Map p429; ☑ 22860 51232, 6981594106). Out of high season, boat services are skeletal.

Destinations are: Folegandros (€5, 45 minutes, two weekly), Ios (€4.50, 25 minutes, three weekly), Kimolos (€9, two to 2½ hours, four weekly), Milos (€12.50, 3¼ hours, three weekly), Naxos (€7, three hours, three weekly), Paros (€8, 4¼ hours, three weekly), Piraeus (€40, 10¼ hours, three weekly), Serifos (€13, 4½ hours, two weekly), Sifnos (€10.50, 4¾ hours, three weekly), Santorini (€7.50, 2¼ to 2½ hours, three weekly) and Syros (€13, 5½ to six hours, three weekly).

❶ Getting Around

The local bus meets ferry arrivals and runs between Alopronia and Horio/Kastro (€1.80) every half-hour in August, 10 times daily the rest of summer from 7.45am to 10.45pm, and less

frequently at other times. A timetable is posted at the terminus, just inland from the port. One bus daily continues from Kastro to Agios Georgios, and a 7.15pm bus runs to the Manalis Winery, making the return journey at 8.45pm.

If you're out of season and nothing is going on, talk to English-speaking Flora in the minimarket at Alopronia, and she'll help you figure out your options. Her son also runs the petrol station, so she's the person to call if it's closed.

There is a branch of **RaC** (☑ 21040 80300; www.rentacar-sikinos.gr), the Cyclades-wide agency, at the port, hiring out cars and fairly decrepit scooters; **Kostis** (☑ 6981751555) is a better bet for scooter hire.

FOLEGANDROS
ΦΟΛΕΓΑΝΔΡΟΣ

POP 760

Folegandros lies on the southern edge of the Cyclades, with the Sea of Crete sweeping away to its south. The island has a quiet beauty, amplified by the clifftop Hora, one of the most appealing villages in the Cyclades.

The hilly topography, with terraced fields sloping down to the sea, verdant countryside dotted with chapels and ruins and numerous beaches to explore – some reachable via strenuous slogs – make Folegandros a favourite with hikers. The island is barely 12km by 4km and both the little harbour of Karavostasis on the east coast and the village of Ano Meria are easily walkable from Hora.

You'll find no signs of it today, but Folegandros shoulders a somewhat dark past. The remoteness and ruggedness of the island made it a place of exile for political prisoners from Roman times to the 20th century, as late as the military dictatorship of 1967–74.

❶ Getting There & Away

Folegandros has good connections (at least from May/June to September) with Piraeus through the western Cyclades route. It has connections to Santorini and is part of an Ios–Sikinos–Folegandros link, with regular ferries passing through.

Boat services from Folegandros:

DESTINATION	DURATION	FARE (€)	FREQUENCY
Amorgos	2½hrs	70	daily
Ios	1¼-1¾hrs	6-45	2-4 daily
Kimolos	1½hrs	6	weekly
Koufonisia	3½hrs	70	daily
Milos	1hr	34-40	3 daily
Mykonos	2¾-3¾hrs	49	2 daily

Folegandros

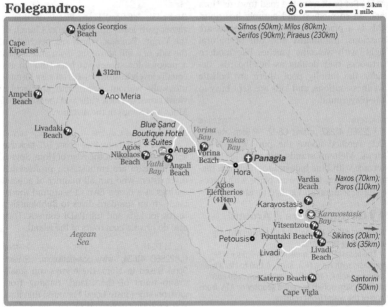

Naxos	2¾-3¼hrs	11-43	2-3 daily
Piraeus	4¼-4½hrs	63-70	2-3 daily
Santorini	45mins-3¼hrs	7-45	3-4 daily
Serifos	2½hrs	50	2 daily
Sifnos	2hrs	46-50	3 daily
Sikinos	45mins	5	2 weekly
Syros	5-6½hrs	13.50	3 weekly

🛈 Getting Around

The local bus meets all ferry arrivals and takes passengers to Hora (€1.80, 3km). From Hora there are buses to the port one hour before ferry departures. Buses from Hora run hourly in summer to Ano Meria (€1.80) and divert to Angali Beach (€2.20).

There is a **taxi service** (☑ 6944693957) on Folegandros. Fares to the port are about €7 to €10, to Ano Meria €10 and to Angali Beach €10 to €14.

You can hire cars/ATVs/motorbikes from a number of outlets in high season for about €60/40/25 per day. Rates can drop by half outside high season. **Donkey Scooters** (☑ 22860 41628; www.donkeyscooters.gr; scooter/ATV hire per day from €20/30; ⊙ 9.30am-8.30pm May-Oct) and **Tomaso** (☑ 22860 41600; www.tomaso.gr; ⊙ 9am-9pm) in Hora are good options.

In summer, small boats regularly run between beaches.

Karavostasis Καραβοστάσις

POP LESS THAN 100

Folegandros' port is centred on a pebble beach, with another – sand-and-pebble Vardia – just across the small headland. A 15-minute walk south along the coast, past the pebble coves of Vitsentzou and Pountaki, is the family-friendly beach of Livadi, with its calm waters. In high season, boats leave Karavostasis for beaches further afield, such as Katergo (also reachable by steep hike).

🛏 Sleeping & Eating

There are a dozen or so waterside lodgings here, from hotels to self-catering studios, but Folegandros' Hora is by far the most atmospheric place to stay. Book early for July and August.

Aeolos Beach Hotel HOTEL €€

(☑ 22860 41205; www.aeolos-folegandros.gr; s/d/ste from €80/100/240; ⊙ May-Sep; ❉ 🛜) Settle in right on the beach here at Aeolos. Rooms have sea or mountain views and are each unique, with varying degrees of character. There's a minimum three-night stay in July and August; breakfast costs €8.50.

⭐ Anemi LUXURY HOTEL €€€

(☑ 22860 41610; www.anemihotel.gr; d/ste incl breakfast from €385/649; ⊙ late May-Sep; ❉

� ⌨) Set back from the road towards Hora and oh so modern and entirely luxurious, this is a place for pampering. Rooms are spacious, minimalist and full of natural light, with welcome touches like modern artworks that double as headboards. Besides the infinity pool, there are holistic wellness options, and kids are kept busy in the playground.

Meltemi TAVERNA €

(☐ 22860 41287; mains €8-12; ⊙ 9am-late Apr-Oct) Perched above the port with lovely views, Meltemi stands out with its lovely terrace with blue balustrades. This is a mama's cooking, family-run place with Greek staples, seafood and grilled meats.

❶ Getting There & Around

Karavostasis is the port for all ferries arriving and leaving the island.

The local bus that meets ferries links Karavostasis with Hora (€2, 3km). A taxi to Hora will set you back €7 to €10. Alternatively, you can walk (3.5km uphill) or rent a scooter or ATV from one of the waterfront rentals.

Hora (Folegandros)
Χώρα (Φολέγανδρος)

POP 450

Sitting on a plateau that abruptly gives way to a cliff edge, this maze of tiny streets lined with houses and churches in Cycladic white and blue, draped in blazing bougainvillea, is among the most charming villages in the Cyclades.

Its pedestrianised main street meanders between the five adjacent leafy squares, where al fresco tables buzz with diners. Towards the east end of the village, pass through a low archway to enter the *kastro* neighbourhood, made up of two-storey houses and dating from when Marco Sanudo ruled the island in the 13th century.

❂ Sights & Activities

Given the tough-to-access nature of many beaches, a popular excursion is the six-hour boat trip around the island (adult/child €50/25). The price includes lunch and at least four swimming stops. The tour, booked through Diaplous Travel (p434), leaves Karavostasis at 11am.

Private and shorter boat trips can also be arranged.

★ **Panagia** CHURCH

(Map p431; ⊙ 6-9pm) From Plateia Pounta, a zigzag path leads up to the large Church of the Virgin, Panagia, which sits perched on the side of a hill above the town and acts as a magnet for sunset-watchers (though it's equally lovely at sunrise). It's an easy 15-minute walk without steps, with spectacular views down to Hora, cliffs and the islands of Milos and Sifnos in the distance.

★ **Sea U Dive Centre** DIVING

(☐ 22860 41624; https://sea-u.com; 1-/2-tank dive €55/80; ⌨) Based at the edge of Hora, Spyros and his team are enthusiastic, professional divemasters who run all manner of aquatic outings at a dozen dive sites around the island – from standard dives to Bubblemaker intros for kids and full PADI courses. They also do private boat tours of the island.

Local Path FOOD

(☐ 22860 41624; www.local-path.com; ⊙ 9am-9pm) Based in Hora, these guys run small-group tours of the island, ranging from gastronomic (Taste Local Flavours) that have you exploring Folegandros' cuisine and organic gardens, to rambles across the countryside. Book in advance; price depends on the number of participants.

🛏 Sleeping

Accommodation ranges from simple domatia to boutique hotels; in July and August, most lodgings will be full, so book well in advance. Free port transfers (3km to the port) are generally included.

★ **Ampelos** BOUTIQUE HOTEL €€

(☐ 22860 41544; http://ampelosresort.com; s/d/tr €100/110/120; ⊙ May-Oct; ❉ 715 ⌨) Theo and Areti's place is a gorgeous family-run operation with a sparkling pool, tasteful colours and lovely rooms. It's an easy six-minute stroll into the centre of Hora from just south of town. There are free port transfers, complimentary coffee, rates that halve outside the peak season and friendly smiles.

Hotel Odysseus HOTEL €€

(☐ 22860 41276; www.hotelodysseus.com; s/d/studio €100/120/155; ⊙ mid-May–Sep; ❉ 715 ⌨) Tucked away in a quiet corner of town with some dramatic views and colourful green doors, Odysseus has pretty, compact rooms with sweet terraces, and a lovely pool area that's shared with Aria Boutique Hotel next door. Low-season prices are ace (doubles €65) but breakfast is an additional €12.

BEACHES AROUND FOLEGANDROS

For Livadi Beach, 1.2km southeast of Karavostasis, take the 'bypass' road just past the Anemi Hotel and follow it around the coast. There is camping here (see www.folegandros.org).

Katergo Beach is on the southeastern tip of the island and is reached either by fairly demanding hike or by boat from Karavostasis. Boats leave regularly (weather permitting) and cost €8 return.

The sandy and pebbled Angali Beach, on the central coast opposite Hora, is a popular spot. There are some rooms here and reasonable tavernas; buses run here regularly in summer from Hora. About 750m west of Angali along a coastal footpath is Agios Nikolaos, a clothes-optional beach with a summer restaurant and taverna.

A number of beaches can be reached from where the road ends beyond Ano Meria: Livadaki Beach is a 1.5km hike from the bus stop near the church of Agios Andreas at Ano Meria. Agios Georgios Beach is north of Ano Meria and requires another demanding walk (about 40 minutes). Have tough footwear and sun protection – and, because most beaches have no shops or tavernas, make sure you take food and water.

Boats connect some west-coast beaches in high season: excursion boats make separate round trips from Angali to Agios Nikolaos (€5), and from Angali to Livadaki Beach (€10).

Folegandros Apartments APARTMENT €€
(☑ 22860 41239; www.folegandros-apartments.com; d from €135; ☺ May-Sep; ✴ 🛜 🏊) This lovely complex of studios and apartments (the largest can sleep seven) is set in well-kept gardens around a pristine pool just above Plateia Pounta in Hora. It's only a couple of minutes' stroll into the village.

Anemomilos Apartments HOTEL €€€
(☑ 22860 41309; www.anemomilosapartments.com; apt incl breakfast from €310; ☺ May-Sep; ✴ 🛜 🏊) A prime clifftop location just above Plateia Pounta in Hora grants awesome views from this stylish complex and its lovely terraces. Rooms are elegant and embellished with antiques. The clifftop pool is shaded by eucalyptus trees, and service is warm and personalised.

Blue Sand Boutique Hotel & Suites BOUTIQUE HOTEL €€€
(Map p431; ☑ 22860 41042; www.bluesand.gr; r/ste from €180/350; ☺ May-Oct; ✴ 🛜) This luxury boutique hotel sits above lovely Angali Beach, a 10-minute drive from Hora. Of the spacious and minimalist rooms decked out in creams and whites, those with sea views come with little private terraces overlooking the clear Aegean waters below. The on-site bar and restaurant is top-notch and open all day.

🍴 Eating & Drinking

Cafe Mikro CAFE €
(☑ 22860 27644; mains from €8; ☺ 9am-11pm Jun-Sep) On a tiny dead-end street off Plateia Maraki, this thimble-sized cafe is popular all day long. Come here for pancakes and coffee in the morning, or nurse a predinner Aperol spritz at sunset while cuddling up to Paoki the rescue cat.

Chic GREEK €€
(☑ 22860 41515; Piatsa; mains €7-14; ☺ 7-11pm Easter-Oct; ☑) On an enchanting little square, Chic is perfectly placed for watching the passing parade. But what's more impressive is the flavoursome food: everything is made from scratch, with the menu indicating gluten-free, dairy-free and vegan options (a rarity in Greece). Veggie dishes (featuring homegrown veggies and herbs) are plentiful; carnivores should plump for goat and lamb from the owners' farm.

Pounta TAVERNA €€
(☑ 22860 41063; www.pounta.gr; Plateia Pounta; mains €7-14; ☺ 8am-3pm & 6pm-midnight Easter–mid-Oct) A family business for over 20 years, Pounta is the work of a creative Danish-Greek couple – dishes are served on Lisbet's handmade ceramics (also for sale) in a large, lush garden. The menu ranges from breakfast yoghurt to grilled octopus by way of rabbit *stifadho* (cooked with onions and tomatoes) and baked eggplant. Right on Plateia Pounta in Hora.

★ Blue Cuisine FUSION €€€
(☑ 22860 41665; www.bluecuisine.gr; mains €14-25; ☺ 7pm-midnight) The short and sweet menu at this adventurous place near Hora's southern entrance takes you on a culinary journey, with ingredients from across

LOCAL KNOWLEDGE

WALKING ON FOLEGANDROS

Folegandros is popular with walkers, with six main, signposted walking trails, including:

#1: Hora to Agios Nikolaos Beach via Angali (4.5km, 1½ hours one way) A descent through the countryside followed by a coastal ramble.

#3: Ano Meria to Agios Georgios (2.6km, 1¼ hours) Gorgeous descent along a cobbled path from the north end of the village to the seaside chapel.

#5: Ano Meria to Livadaki Beach (5.7km, 2¼ hours) Loop hike that starts near the windmills in Ano Meria, descends to the beach and climbs steeply through the countryside to the north end of the village.

#6: Hora to Katergo Beach (6.4km, 2½ hours) Relatively demanding trail that passes by Folegandros' highest peak and Petousis village before descending steeply to the beach.

Check out the detailed information at www.folegandros.com/footpaths.asp. Terrain (http://terrainmaps.gr) produces an excellent Folegandros map.

Greece interacting in surprising combinations. Seafood meets citrus and fennel, the sharpness of pickled melon alleviates the saltiness of Cypriot *lountza* ham and smoky goat souvlaki is enhanced by the sweetness of tomato chutney. Book ahead.

Eva's Garden MEDITERRANEAN €€€
(☑22860 41110; mains €12-27; ☺7pm-midnight late May-Sep) Eva's is a sophisticated spot that puts a gourmet spin on Greek cuisine. The menu mixes classic and bold flavour combinations, with crayfish risotto and rib-eye steak sitting alongside baked onions stuffed with veal, pine nuts and raisins and octopus carpaccio. Book ahead. Turn left after Plateia Piatsa.

★**Wine Bar Merkouri** WINE BAR
(☑6977272373; www.facebook.com/merkouriwine folegandros; ☺7pm-3am) Overlooking a vineyard, this convivial spot is a must for wine lovers: there are over 40 Greek vintages by the glass. Get talking to the owner about oenology and sample some of his own wine. The dishes – such as the beef carpaccio – are as good as the tipples.

❶ Information

Travel agencies are good sources of information. There's information (and a downloadable app) at www.folegandros.com.
Diaplous Travel (☑22860 41158; www.diaploustravel.gr; Plateia Pounta; ☺9am-1.30pm & 6.30-9pm) Sells ferry tickets and arranges boat trips. The office at Karavostasis opens half an hour before ferry departures.
Folegandros Travel (☑22860 41273; www.folegandros-travel.gr; Plateia Dounavi; ☺9.30am-1pm & 6-9pm) Sells ferry tickets

and exchanges money. There's also an office at the port.

❶ Getting There & Away

The local bus meets all ferry arrivals at Karavostasis port and takes passengers to Hora (€2, 3km). From Hora buses connect with arriving ferries at least three times daily (8am, 2pm and 6.30pm) and with Ano Meria at least four times daily (8.30am, 1.10pm, 2.45pm and 8pm; calling at Angali Beach in summer). The **bus station** is at the entrance to Hora from the south, behind the post office.

There is a taxi service on Folegandros. Fares to the port are about €7 to €10, to Ano Meria €10 and to Angali Beach €10 to €14.

Donkey Scooters (p431) rents 125cc scooters and ATVs and will drop them at designated places around the island if you request it in advance.

Ano Meria Ανω Μεριά

POP 240

Ano Meria is a spread-out string of tiny hamlets that stretches along the road for several kilometres, virtually on the crest of the island. Several excellent hiking trails start here: one leads down to the Agios Georgios chapel on the north coast from Sinadisi restaurant, while Livadaki Beach can be reached either from the imposing windmills in the centre of Ano Meria or the trail that leads past the Agii Anargiri church from the far end of the village.

Buses from Hora run hourly in summer to Ano Meria (€2). Taxis cost around €10, but things are a lot easier if you explore with your own wheels.

Eating

Sinadisi TAVERNA €

(☑ 22860 41208; mains from €7; ☺ noon-10pm May-Sep) Also known as Maria's, Sinadisi is at the far end of the strung-out village, so much so that you may think you've missed it. With pale blue colours, it was originally opened in 1920 by the proprietor's grandfather. This is a great spot to try *matsata* and Greek salad with local Folegandros cheese.

★Pane e Vino ITALIAN €€

(☑ 22860 41531; www.facebook.com/PaneVino Folegandros; mains from €10; ☺ 1pm-midnight Jun-Sep; ☑) At the far end of Ano Meria, Folegandros' only Italian restaurant is run by Paolo and Flavia, an Italian couple who settled here after visiting the island for 20 years. Expect authentic pizzas, tiramisu and proper caprese salad with buffalo mozzarella.

MILOS ΜΗΛΟΣ

POP 4980

Volcanic Milos arches around a central caldera and is ringed with dramatic coastal landscapes of colourful and surreal rock formations. The island's most celebrated export, the *Venus de Milo,* is far away in the Louvre, but dozens of beaches (the most of any Cycladic island) and a series of picturesque villages contribute to its current, compelling, attractions.

The island has a fascinating history of mineral extraction dating from the Neolithic period when obsidian was exported to the Minoan world of Crete. Today Milos is the biggest source of bentonite and perlite in the EU.

A substantial western chunk of Milos (and part of the east coast) is off-limits to rental vehicles due to bad roads and a proliferation of the Milos viper, but the beaches are reachable by boat tours.

ⓘ Getting There & Away

AIR

Milos National Airport (MLO) is 4km southwest around the bay from Adamas. Sky Express (www.skyexpress.gr) and Olympic Air (www.olympicair.com) both fly here from Athens.

BOAT

Adamas, the island's main port, is on the main western Cyclades ferry route. In the high season, destinations include Piraeus (€40 to €58, 2¾ to 6½ hours, six daily), Serifos (€8 to €18, one to two hours, five daily), Sifnos (€7 to €16, one hour,

seven daily), Folegandros (€29 to €40, one hour, four daily) and Santorini (€39 to €53, two hours, four daily). Services are reduced in winter; see www.ferries.gr for detailed information.

There are also ferries from Pollonia to Kimolos.

ⓘ Getting Around

➤ Adamas is the main hub for bus services, operated by **Milos Buses** (www.milosbuses.com). In the peak season there are buses to the airport and Achivadolimni Camping (five daily), Triovasalos/Plaka/Catacombs/Trypiti (hourly), Pollonia (10 daily), Paleohori (seven daily) and Sarakiniko (four daily). In winter services reduce to four buses a day to Triovasalos/Trypiti and two to Pollonia. Check the website for detailed schedules.

➤ Cars can be hired from the airport, Adamas and Pollonia. Options include **Giourgas Rent a Car** (☑ 22870 22352; www.giourgasrent.com) and **Milos Rent** (☑ 22870 41473; www.milosrent.gr).

➤ From Adamas, **taxis** (☑ 22870 22219) charge around €13 to the airport, €8 to Plaka and €15 to Pollonia.

Adamas Αδάμας

POP 1350

Ferries to Milos are greeted by the classic Cycladic sight of a tight cluster of white houses spreading up a hill towards a picture-perfect, blue-domed church. At the base of the compact old town is a broad, attractive, waterfront promenade lined with shops, travel agencies, cafes, bars, ice-cream parlours and restaurants. A short walk in either direction will bring you to sandy beaches, or you can book a trip to otherwise inaccessible coves from the boats moored along the quay.

◉ Sights

Ecclesiastical Museum of Milos MUSEUM

(☑ 22870 22252; www.ecclesiasticalmuseum.org; ☺ 9.15am-1.15pm & 6.15-10.15pm May-Sep) FREE Housed in the venerable Holy Trinity Church, which has its roots in the 9th century, this collection has rare artefacts and icons, including works by acclaimed 17th-century Cretan father-and-son team, Emmanuel and Antonios Skordilis.

Milos Mining Museum MUSEUM

(☑ 22870 22481; www.milosminingmuseum.gr; adult/child €5/3; ☺ 10am-2pm Sun Jan-Mar, daily Apr & May, 10am-2pm & 5.30-9pm Jun-Sep, 10am-2pm Tue-Sun Oct) This mildly interesting museum details Milos' mining history, starting with the quarrying of obsidian on the island

Milos & Kimolos

in 7000 BCE. It's located on the waterfront, about 650m east of the centre.

Ask here about the Miloterranean Geo Experience (www.miloterranean.gr), a series of seven maps that outline great half-day 'geo walks' through Milos. The maps highlight the island's geology and volcanic origin, mining history and natural environment (€3 each).

🛏 Sleeping

⭐Konstantinos
HOTEL €€

(Map p436; ☑ 22870 22104; www.milos-konst antinos.gr; r from €110; ⊙ Easter-Oct; 🅿 ❄ 🛜) Sitting on its own within the fields on the eastern edge of Adamas, this friendly, family-run hotel offers spacious, stylish rooms with balconies, some of which have sea views. It's a 20-minute walk from town but they'll pick you up from the port on request. Breakfast is available for €8 extra.

Tassoula Rooms
GUESTHOUSE €€

(☑ 22870 22674; r from €86; 🅿 ❄ 🛜) Run by a friendly family, this place is good value. Some of the spacious, bright rooms have tiny balconies overlooking the flowering inner courtyard, and the owner is the epitome of helpfulness.

Aeolis Hotel
HOTEL €€

(☑ 22870 23985; www.hotel-aeolis.com; s/d from €130/148; 🅿 ❄ 🛜) Inland from the harbourfront, this sweet, neat 12-room hotel is peaceful and calm, its white rooms given a pop of colour here and there. It's open year-round, with prices diving in the low season (double €45).

Villa Helios Studios
APARTMENT €€

(☑ 22870 22258; www.studioshelios.com; apt €90-100; ⊙ May-Oct; ❄ 🛜) Rising high above the port, these five large self-catering studios are neat as a pin and decorated in an attractive traditional style, with sea-view balconies.

✖ Eating & Drinking

Artemis BAKERY €
(items €2-2.50; ⊙6am-11pm; 🖤) Set on a side street next to the main free car park, this excellent bakery serves lip-smacking *spanakopita* (spinach pie), pizza slices, sandwiches and all manner of biscuits and cakes. There are little round tables decorated with potted carnations at the front, if you want to relax somewhere over a coffee.

O! Hamos TAVERNA €€
(Map p436; ☑22870 21672; www.ohamos-milos. gr; Papikinou Beach; dishes €8.20-14; ⊙noon-11pm Apr-Oct; 🖤) Located just across from the beach, 1.2km southeast of the centre, this rustic taverna delivers a delicious array of traditional recipes, such as *pitarakia tis Giagias* (Grandma's cheese pies), *agriokatsiko sti hovoli* (slow-roasted wild goat and potatoes) and *portokaloglyko* (a cake-like orange-and-chocolate filo pie). Everything is served with warmth and flair, alongside craft beers and local wines.

Akri COCKTAIL BAR
(☑22870 22064; www.akrimilos.gr; ⊙7pm-late Easter-Oct; 🖤) Tucked up above the port, this classy little bar serves cocktails and coffee on a beautiful terrace with views over the water. In summer, themed party nights continue into the wee small hours.

❶ Information

Milos Travel (☑22870 22000; www. milostravel.gr; ⊙9am-3.30pm & 6.30-9.30pm Mon-Fri, 9am-2pm & 6.30-9.30pm Sat & Sun) Ferry tickets, excursions and car rental.

Riva Travel (☑22870 24024; www.rivatravel. gr; ⊙9am-9pm) Car hire and ferry tickets.

Tourist Information Office (☑22870 22445; www.milos.gr; ⊙9am-5pm & 7-11pm Jun-Sep) Helpful kiosk opposite the quay, with maps and general info.

❶ Getting There & Away

In the peak season there are buses to Triovasalos/Plaka/Catacombs/Trypiti (hourly), Pollonia (10 daily), Paleohori (seven daily) and Sarakiniko (four daily). In winter services reduce to four buses a day to Triovasalos/Trypiti and two to Pollonia.

Cars can be hired from various agencies around town, including Giourgas Rent a Car (p435) and Milos Rent (p435).

Plaka, Trypiti & Triovasalos
Πλάκα, Τρυπητή & Τριοβάσαλος
POP 2130

The bulk of Milos' population lives in this cluster of nearly conjoined towns in the north of the island. This was the site of the great ancient city of Melos, which lasted from around the 9th-century BCE until the 7th-century CE before falling into decline.

Charming Plaka embodies the Cycladic ideal, with its white houses and labyrinthine lanes perched along the edge of an escarpment. The courtyard of Panagia Korfiatissa church (built in 1840) offers spectacular views west over the water and gets packed out at sunset during the high season. A little further down the hill is Trypiti, a pleasant village with a backdrop of churches and windmills. Triovasalos is the workaday part of the settlement, with shops and authentic tavernas catering mainly to the local population.

◎ Sights & Activities

Ancient Theatre & Catacombs RUINS
(⊙24hr) FREE Clinging to a lonely patch of hillside just below Trypiti, this large Roman-era theatre entertained the citizens of Ancient Melos from the 1st to the 4th century CE. It was rediscovered in 1735 but only around a tenth of the original structure has been uncovered and partially restored, including part of the richly carved marble facade of the stage that once faced an audience of up to 8000 people.

The path to the theatre is well signposted, just up from the car park for the catacombs. The flattened oval area beside the road was the site of an ancient stadium. To the right of the path, look out for an info board marking the site near where, in 1820, a farmer discovered an exquisite 2m-high armless Parian marble statue of Aphrodite (c120 BCE), still standing in her own niche. She was promptly packed off to the Louvre in Paris, where she's now better known as the *Venus de Milo*. A campaign has been launched to bring her home (www.takeaphroditehome.gr).

Archaeological Museum of Melos MUSEUM
(☑22870 21620; Plaka; adult/child €2/1; ⊙9am-10pm Sun, 8.30am-4pm Mon, Wed, Thu & Sat, 2-10pm Fri) This handsome neoclassical

building contains some riveting exhibits, including a plaster cast of local lass, the *Venus de Milo,* who now resides in the Louvre (much to the consternation of her fellow islanders). The enigmatic clay goddess and perky little herd of tiny bull figurines in the adjoining rooms were already ancient when the famous statue was carved. Recovered from a shrine in Phylakopi, they date from between 1400 and 1100 BCE.

Catacombs of Melos
MONUMENT

(☑22870 21625; adult/child €4/2; ⊙9am-7pm Tue-Sun Apr-Sep, to 2pm Oct-Mar) Greece's only Christian catacombs, on the slopes below Trypiti, date from the 1st century and were the burial site for some of the earliest believers. Over 2000 people were interred within the 183m network of tunnels, which range from 1m to 5m in width and 1.6m to 2.5m in height. Entry is via a 15-minute guided tour to lit alcoves within two main chambers, explaining the workings of the ancient cemetery.

Kastro
FORTRESS

(Plaka; ⊙24hr) FREE Signs mark the path climbing to Plaka's hilltop fortress, built by the Venetians on the ancient acropolis. Little of the structure remains, but the views from the top stretch right over the island. On the way up, call into the old church of Panagia Thalassitra to admire its lovely gilded iconostasis.

Syrmata
ARCHITECTURE

Tiny, photogenic Klima clings to the beachfront cliff face below Trypiti. It offers the best example of Milos' *syrmata* (traditional fishers' huts), where the downstairs, with brightly painted doors, are used for rough-weather boat storage, and the upstairs are used for family life. The homes, most still in use today, are incorporated into the rocks. A unique experience is to rent *syrmata* for your stay; a few of these are available via home-sharing services. You'll need your own wheels.

Sea Kayak Milos
KAYAKING

(☑6946477170; www.seakayakgreece.com; Triovasalos; sea kayak trip per person €75; ⊙9am-5pm Apr-Oct) Kayaking is a superb way to explore the coastline, and Australian Rod and his team lead highly regarded day trips, with no experience required. Itineraries depend on weather conditions.

🛏 Sleeping & Eating

Studios Betty
APARTMENT €€

(☑22870 21538; www.studiosbetty-milos.com; Plaka; apt from €141; ﹡🅿) Enjoy glorious sunset views from this complex of four simple studios at Plaka's cliff edge.

Mimallis Houses
RENTAL HOUSE €€€

(☑22870 21094; www.mimallis.gr; Plaka & Klima; apt €186-290; ⊙Apr-Oct; ﹡🅿) Mimallis rents two small houses in Plaka (sleeping two), and one right on the water in Klima (sleeping up to five) – each is different, comfortable and packed with amenities. The Klima house comes with a canoe and fishing equipment, but no air-conditioning. Low-season discounts are excellent.

Vaos Windmill
RENTAL HOUSE €€€

(☑26103 21742; Trypiti; apt from €180; 🅿) A footpath behind and above Trypiti's main church leads to this windmill, converted into a two-bedroom house, sleeping up to four people. There's a fully equipped kitchen a couple of steps out the front door, and the views from the terrace are nothing short of stupendous. Booking.com handles the reservations.

Bakalikon Galanis
MEZEDHES €

(☑22870 28163; Triovasalos; dishes €4-12; ⊙11am-1am Mon-Sat) Retro shop stock (tinned goods, matchboxes, pantyhose etc) line the walls of this atmospheric *mezedhopoleio* (mezedhes bar), a local favourite. Tick off your selections on the printed menu – *saganaki* (fried cheese), *soutzouki* (spicy sausage), *siglino* (smoked pork), *kavourmas* (pork with spices) – and settle in for a long night; the kitchen closes at 1am but the venue stays open far later.

Barrielo
GREEK €€

(☑6984218360; www.barriello.com; Trypiti; mains €12-18; ⊙6.30pm-12.30am Apr-Sep, 7.30pm-1am Thu-Sat Oct-Mar; 🅿) 🍃 Every evening, diners are lured to the little square below Trypiti's church by the wafting smells of sizzling meat on the grill. It's all organic and raised on the owner's farm.

❶ Getting There & Away

In summer there are hourly buses on the Adamas–Triovasalos–Plaka–Catacombs–Trypiti route. In winter the only services are from Trypiti and Triovasalos to Adamas (four daily) and Pollonia (two daily). Most fares are €1.80.

Pollonia Πολλώνια

POP 272

Pollonia (sometimes called Apollonia), on the north coast, is a low-key fishing village with clear waters and a sandy beach. In summer it completely transforms into a chic (albeit petite) resort, with the island's best accommodation and dining options.

Activities, excursions, accommodation and ferry tickets, as well as car hire, can be booked at **Travel Me to Milos** (☑ 22870 41008; www.travelmetomilos.com).

🛏 Sleeping

Zoe
GUESTHOUSE €€

(☑ 22870 41235; www.zoe-milos.gr; r/apt from €109/154; ☉ May-Oct; ☀ 🛜) This little guesthouse has decent-sized rooms and studio apartments (with kitchenettes), all of which have balconies or terraces; some have sea views. An extensive breakfast spread is included.

Nefeli Sunset Studios
HOTEL €€€

(☑ 22870 41466; www.milos-nefelistudios.gr; r/ste from €160/220; ☉ Apr-Oct; ☀ 🛜) Whitewashed cubes combine modern design with traditional touches in this bay-front property at the northern edge of the village. All of the rooms have terraces or balconies with at least a partial sea view.

Salt
BOUTIQUE HOTEL €€€

(☑ 22870 41110; www.salt-milos.com; d/ste from €200/250; ☉ Easter-Oct; ☀ 🛜) Set on a pebbly shoreline, this upmarket hotel offers sophistication, luxury and sea views. The decor is strikingly minimal: mainly white with natural wood accents. Low-season rates drop by nearly half.

🍴 Eating

★ Enalion
GREEK €€

(☑ 22870 41415; www.enalion-milos.gr; mains €10-17; ☉ noon-midnight; 🛜 ♿) The finest Greek produce is showcased at this wonderful little restaurant. Grab a seat on the waterfront terrace and let the switched-on staff guide you through their top-notch selection of PDO (Protected Designation of Origin) olives, wine and cheese. Locally caught seafood features prominently on the menu, including a delicious *stifado* (stew) featuring octopus, tomatoes, onions, wine and Milos honey.

DON'T MISS

CRUISING MILOS

Tour boats line Adamas' waterfront in the evening, touting their daily cruises. These leave every morning (weather permitting) to explore the impressive coastline, bizarre rock formations and beaches not reachable by road. Kleftiko in Milos' southwest, with its striking rock arches and caves, is a prime destination. Some cruises also visit Kimolos and other outlying islands.

There are large and small boats, private charters, and speedboats, woodenhulled boats, catamarans and sailboats. Check out what takes your fancy. It may be worth asking about group sizes, itineraries, lunch arrangements and swimming time.

Prices generally start from about €35. Most travel agencies can book you on a cruise; note that in summer you can usually find departures from Pollonia as well.

Gialos
SEAFOOD €€

(☑ 22870 41208; www.gialos-pollonia.gr; mains €8.50-26; ☉ noon-11pm Apr-Oct; 🛜) Bustling Gialos has a creative modern menu bursting with fresh local and international flavours and techniques – everything from prawn ravioli to tuna tataki. Seafood is the focus but the meat dishes are also good, including a tender and delicious beef *tagliata* (sliced steak) marinated in olive oil and rosemary. Save room for dessert.

Armenaki
GREEK €€

(☑ 22870 41061; www.armenaki.gr; mains €9-18; ☉ noon-11pm Apr-Oct; 🛜) Armenaki is revered for its fishy business – this place is all about seafood (in fact, there's little else on the menu). Seafood in all its guises is cooked to perfection, and service is first-rate (including the filleting of fish at your table). There's an extensive wine list.

Hanabi
FUSION €€€

(☑ 22870 41180; www.facebook.com/hanabi cocktailsandsushi; mains €16-26; ☉ 11am-midnight Apr-Oct; 🛜) You'll find everything from sushi to burgers at this stylish Japanese-inspired restaurant, but the kitchen's at its best when delivering creative fusion dishes such as tagliatelle with baby vegetables, sea urchin and orange ouzo. Grab a seat on the waterside terrace and enjoy the friendly service.

ⓘ Getting There & Away

In the height of summer there are 10 buses a day to Adamas. In winter these narrow to two, but they continue on to Trypiti and Triovasalos.

Pollonia is also the main port for ferries to Kimolos.

Around Milos

◉ Sights

Phylakopi
ARCHAEOLOGICAL SITE

(Map p436; ☑ 22870 41290; adult/child €2/1; ⊘ 8am-3pm Tue, Fri & Sat Easter-Oct) This ancient Minoan town in the island's northeast (on the main road en route to Pollonia but poorly signed) was one of the earliest settlements in the Cyclades. Now it's not much more than rubble but the seaside setting is attractive, with cavelike rock formations all around.

🏖 Beaches

Milos and its offshore islets have more than 70 splendid beaches garnished in different-coloured sands and stone. You'll need to rent a vehicle to visit most of them; a 4WD or ATV is required to reach those on the rugged west coast. In the case of remote Kleftiko in the southwest, the only access is by boat (p439).

Paleohori
BEACH

One of the island's most beautiful beaches, the long arch of Paleohori is backed by banded cliffs and has tavernas, beach bars, water sports and patches of hot sand, thanks to thermal springs in the area. It's reached by a good sealed road, and buses from Adamas head here seven times a day in summer.

Sarakiniko
BEACH

Sarakiniko's meringue-like rock formations and caves attract scores of budding photographers, even in winter. The sandy beach is tiny but there's a deep channel that's perfect for swimming, and room to spread out on the rocks. It's reached by a good sealed road, with parking at the end. Buses head here from Adamas in summer (four daily).

Kyriaki
BEACH

Kyriaki is a lovely long sandy beach on the south coast, backed by otherworldly grey-, rose- and rust-coloured cliffs. There's a taverna at one end and a good restaurant up in the hills. The access road is mainly sealed; fine with a 2WD.

Plathiena
BEACH

Sitting at the end of a valley beyond Plaka in the north of the island, this pebble-strewn sandy beach is exceptionally pretty. The water is a vivid aquamarine and there are craggy limestone formations at each end. There's not much development here apart from a single flash house and a summertime beach bar. The access road is good, although there's limited parking.

Nerodafni & Trachilas
BEACH

From Firopotamas, an unsealed but well-maintained wide road (fine with a 2WD, although it gets a little bumpy towards the end) leads past active quarries to these remote pebble and rock beaches, separated from each other by a headland. Nerodafni is slightly easier to access, but Trachilas is distinguished by tiny islets with rock arches just offshore.

Mandrakia
BEACH

Village cats form the welcoming committee at this tiny fishing harbour, with brightly coloured boat sheds, cute wee cottages and a sweet little whitewashed church. There are small shingle beaches on either side and, to the east, a large expanse of rocky shelves to spread out on abutting the water.

Firopotamos
BEACH

The road is sealed all the way to Firopotamos, a picturesque little cove embraced by craggy limestone cliffs and lined with *syrmata* (boat-house dwellings). There's a lovely little blue-trimmed church on the headland and the remains of a quarry nearby, with some car parking alongside.

KIMOLOS ΚΙΜΩΛΟΣ

POP 910

Little Kimolos, perched off the northeast tip of Milos, feels like a step back in time. Few visitors take the opportunity to explore its tiny old town, sparkling bays and picturesque *syrmata* (boat houses). It's an easy day trip from Milos; consider taking a car, bike or scooter on the ferry to make it easier to get around.

◉ Sights

The boat (from Pollonia in Milos' north) docks at Psathi, where there's a gravelly beach and a smattering of cafes and tavernas. The pretty capital, Hora, is about 800m up the hill. At the centre of its network of atmospheric little lanes is the *kastro,* a crumbling square-shaped castle dating from the 14th to 16th centuries. In among the rubble is the tiny whitewashed Church of the Nativity; built in 1592, it's the oldest of Hora's 16 churches. Nearby is the petite Folk & Maritime Museum (☑ 22870 51118; ⊙ hours vary) FREE.

Caïques from Psathi buzz out to beaches, the best of which is magnificent, white-sand Prassa (also reachable along a partially sealed road). You can walk there from Hora in about an hour.

🛌 Sleeping & Eating

Domatia, tavernas, cafes and bars pepper Hora and Psathi. There's some development at the southern beaches of Aliki and neighbouring Bonatsa, as well as several boutique properties. Aria Hotels (www.ariahotels.gr) is a group with three boutique hotels and five holiday homes on Kimolos, including a converted windmill.

Meltemi Studio Rooms   HOTEL €
(☑ 22870 51360; www.kimolos-meltemi.gr; r from €55; P ❄ 🤫) This set of compact rooms is perched on the edge of Hora, with views to the sea. The in-house restaurant specialises in Kimolian cuisine.

Windmill Kimolos   BOUTIQUE HOTEL €€€
(☑ 22870 51677; www.kimoloshotel.com; r from €165; ⊙ May-Sep; P ❄ 🤫) The most atmospheric abode in Kimolos, this converted windmill looks over the island from its hilltop position. The rooms are cosy and comfortable, and there's a popular cafe and bar on-site.

Raventi   CAFE €
(☑ 22870 51212; snacks €3.50-7.50; ⊙ 9am-late; 🤫) On the beach at Psathi, this fashionable cafe has a comfy terrace and a counter full of drool-inducing cakes, tarts and ice cream, all of which are made on the premises. In the high season it also serves the likes of eggs Benedict, and stays open late for cocktails.

Kali Kardia Bohoris   TAVERNA €
(☑ 22870 51495; mains €5-8; ⊙ 6am-10pm) Set on a picturesque street leading up from the *kastro* at the centre of Hora, this humble-looking place serves good local specialities such as roast goat, cheese pies and *mousakas.*

To Kyma   TAVERNA €€
(☑ 22870 51001; mains €7-20; ⊙ noon-11pm Apr-Oct; 🤫) The name means 'The Wave' and this

taverna, right on the beach at Psathi, is good for seafood and local specialities like *ladenia* (similar to pizza, topped with tomatoes and onions).

ℹ️ Information

Kimolos Travel (☑ 22870 51219; Hora; ⊙ 9am-1pm & 4-8pm) Sells ferry tickets.

ℹ️ Getting There & Around

A small **car ferry** (☑ 6948308758; www.kimolos-link.gr; per adult/child/scooter/car €2.20/1.10/1.80/8.80) connects Pollonia (Milos) with Psathi (Kimolos) up to eight times daily in high season, three times in low season (30 minutes).

In the high season, larger long-distance ferries head to destinations including Piraeus (€36, seven hours, five weekly), Serifos (€9, two hours, daily), Sifnos (€6.50, one hour, daily), Paros (€11, 4¼ hours, three weekly) and Folegandros (€6, 1½ hours, three weekly).

Buses connect Psathi and Hora in high season only; infrequent services also visit beaches. A couple of rental agencies in Kimolos offer cars, scooters and ATVs. Otherwise **taxis** (☑ 6945464093) from Psathi charge around €5 to Hora and €10 to Prassa.

SIFNOS   ΣΙΦΝΟΣ

POP 2625

Sifnos has a dreamlike quality. Three whitewashed villages, anchored by the capital Apollonia, sit like pearls on a string along the crest of the island. The changing light kisses the landscape, and as you explore the slopes of the central mountains you'll discover abundant terraced olive groves, almond trees, oleander and aromatic herbs. Each of the island's bays offers aqua waters and breathtaking vistas.

During the Archaic period (from about the 8th century BCE), Sifnos was enriched by its gold and silver deposits, but by the 5th century BCE the mines were exhausted. Sifnos is now known for pottery, basket weaving and cookery. Visitors flock to the southern half of the island, served by good bus links, but it's worth getting your own wheels and driving to the remote beaches of the north, where the main road culminates in – you guessed it – a church.

ℹ️ Getting There & Away

Sifnos is on the Piraeus to western Cyclades ferry route, with good summer connections to destinations including Piraeus (€36 to €52, 2½ to 5½ hours, six daily), Serifos (€6.50 to €15,

Sifnos

50 minutes, four daily), Paros (€5 to €60, 50 minutes to three hours, one or two daily), Folegandros (€9 to €50, 1¾ hours, three daily) and Milos (€7 to €16, one hour, seven daily). Services reduce in winter; see www.ferries.gr for details.

❶ Getting Around

➤ Bus timetables are posted around the island, and frequent buses connect Kamares with Apollonia and Artemonas. Buses also link Apollonia with Kastro, Vathy, Faros and Platys Gialos. Fares are generally €1.80 (maximum €2.30).

➤ For car and scooter rental, try **Apollo Rental** (☑ 22840 33333; www.automotoapollo. gr; ⊗ 9am-9pm Apr-Oct) in Apollonia or **1° Moto Car Rental** (☑ 22840 33791; www. protomotocar.gr) in Kamares.

➤ There are only 10 **taxis** (☑ 6932403485, 6944761210) on Sifnos, so you're best to book in the high season. You'll find a list of taxi numbers posted at bus stops.

Kamares   Καμάρες

POP 245

Scenically hemmed in by steep mountains, the port of Kamares has a holiday atmosphere, with waterfront cafes, tavernas and shops, a good range of accommodation, and a beautiful large beach of its own. The water's very shallow, making it ideal for families

with toddlers but less so if you're after a decent swim.

🛏 Sleeping

⭐ **Morpheas Pension**   GUESTHOUSE €
(☑ 22840 33615; www.morpheas.gr; r/apt from €50/80; P ❊ 🛜) Named after the Greek god of dreams, this friendly family-run place does its best to ensure that yours will be pleasant ones. It's set back from the beach in a classic Cycladic-style building, albeit with pistachio trim rather than blue. The simple but well-kept rooms all have bathrooms, fridges and kettles, while the two one-bedroom apartments have full kitchens.

Makis Camping   CAMPGROUND €
(☑ 6945946339; www.makiscamping.gr; site per adult/child/tent €8/4/4, r from €70; ⊗ May-Nov; P ❊ 🛜) Pitch your tent behind the beach in a well-run lot with shady trees, or hire tents with mattresses for €30. There are well-equipped rooms and apartments (sleeping up to five), a cafe, barbecue, communal kitchen, minimarket and laundry.

Aglaia Studios   GUESTHOUSE €€
(☑ 22840 31513; www.aglaiastudios.gr; Agia Marina; r/apt from €77/154; ❊ 🛜) In the evenings, you can sit on your balcony and watch the lights of Kamares across the bay. By day, a few steps take you down to the swimming platform, from which you can launch yourself into the Aegean. The rooms themselves are snug and comfortable. Free port pickups are included.

Stavros Hotel   HOTEL €€
(☑ 22840 33383; www.sifnostravel.com; r from €80; ❊ 🛜) Grapevines curl over the balconies of this main street hotel that offers good service and excellent, spacious studios with kitchenettes and sea views. A bonus: flexible room configurations work to accommodate families. The info desk downstairs can help with car hire.

🍴 Eating

Absinthe   FUSION €€
(☑ 22840 31202; www.absinthe-sifnos.gr; mains €15-23; ⊗ May-Oct) On a 1st-floor terrace above the main street, Absinthe takes inspiration from the cuisine of historic Smyrna, incorporating Greek, Anatolian, Ottoman and Asian elements, and pairing them with fresh local ingredients. Smrynaian meatballs sit alongside *hünkâr beğendi* (veal stew on a spicy eggplant puree) and a standout goat coconut curry on rice.

Folie INTERNATIONAL €€

(☑22840 31183; www.foliesifnos.gr; Agia Marina; mains €4-16; ☉10am-late; 🕸) Advertising itself as an 'all-day bar restaurant', this beachside terrace allows you to slip from morning coffee to a salad lunch, a lazy sunlounger G&T and then on to dinner, and finally cocktails. The menu covers a lot of territory, too: omelettes, pancakes, pasta, risotto, burgers, tortillas, spring rolls and octopus on *fava* puree.

🛍 Shopping

Peristeriona CERAMICS

(☑22840 32121; www.handmadepotteryart.com; ☉10am-2pm & 5-9.30pm Mon-Sat, 5-9.30pm Sun) Of Sifnos' many ceramics stores, this is the most stylish. Bright glazes and rainbow stripes decorate tumblers, plates and casserole dishes, while large platters display motifs lifted from traditional fabric designs.

ℹ Information

Aegean Thesaurus (☑22840 33151; www. thesaurus.gr; ☉8.45am-8.30pm Mon-Sat, 8.45am-12.30pm & 3-5pm Sun) Books ferry tickets, tours and rental cars, and sells a €3 Sifnos welcome pack (hiking info, bus timetables, map and more).

Municipal Tourist Office (☑22840 31977; www.sifnos.gr) On the little square near the ferry dock, this office only opens in high season, and the hours vary with boat arrivals. It's helpful with ferry tickets, accommodation and bus timetables.

ℹ Getting There & Away

Kamares is Sifnos' main ferry port.

From Easter there are five buses a day to Apollonia (€1.80, 20 minutes), with services every 30 minutes in the peak season and one direct bus daily carrying on to Kastro and another to Platys Gialos (€2.30). Otherwise, change in Apollonia.

Cars, scooters and ATVs can be hired from 1° Moto Car Rental (p442), which has a booking office by the port and a main base near the beach. The nearest petrol station is in Apollonia.

Apollonia Απολλωνία

POP 869

Labyrinthine, church-studded Apollonia comes alive in high season with its parade of well-dressed Athenians strutting their stuff along Odos Prokou, known as the Steno (meaning 'narrow') because of its slenderness. Cafes, bars, clubs, shops and restaurants buzz with life.

The main vehicular road cuts right through the centre of town, but park at the large free car park downhill from the village and walk up and into the warren of streets. At the central junction you'll find all the services: banks, post office, pharmacy, bookshop, taxis and so on.

From Apollonia, the string of houses continues north into the conjoined village of Ano Petali and then to Artemonas, with its grand mansions, churches, cafes and tavernas. The 20-minute walk along the pedestrian lane heading up behind Mamma Mia restaurant offers unforgettable views over Apollonia's white houses and blue-domed churches.

🛏 Sleeping & Eating

Pension Nikoletta Geronti GUESTHOUSE €

(☑22840 31473; www.gerontisifnos.gr; Ano Petali; s/d from €50/55; 🕸🛰) Opposite Petali Village Hotel, on the walkway between Apollonia and Artemonas, is this gem of a pension, with spotless rooms, sweeping views, sweet hosts and excellent rates.

Eleonas Apartments APARTMENT €€

(☑22840 33383; www.sifnostravel.com; apt from €85; 🕸🛰) An idyllic complex tucked away in an olive grove, Eleonas offers gloriously roomy two-bedroom apartments that sleep six, with kitchen, living space and terrace. Studios are slightly smaller, but still very spacious. It feels peaceful and rural, but it's just a few minutes' walk from the Steno.

Petali Village Hotel HOTEL €€

(☑22840 33024; www.petalihotel.gr; Ano Petali; d/ste from €145/238; 🕸🛰🏊) Suspended on a walking street between Apollonia and Artemonas, this terraced array of rooms and suites has sweeping views to Apollonia and the sea, and an inviting kidney-shaped pool. Low-season discounts are decent; port pickup is offered.

Cayenne GREEK €€

(☑22840 31080; www.facebook.com/Cayenne RestaurantSifnos; mains €12-25; ☉1pm-late; 🛰✏) Shaded by a fig tree and drowning in a riot of herbs just off the Steno, this modern Greek restaurant affirms its strong commitment to Cycladic ingredients through dishes such as lemon-caper risotto, Byzantine meat patties and smoked eel with Santorini *fava* beans.

Drimoni MEDITERRANEAN €€

(☑22840 31434; www.drimoni.gr; mains €8.50-14; ☉6pm-late May-Sep; 🛰) Look out over the countryside or lounge by the pool (yes, pool!) at this bright and breezy contemporary restaurant. Chef Giorgos Patriarchis does the Sifnian culinary tradition proud with the likes of *mastelo* (goat slow-cooked in wine with rosemary and dill), imaginative salads, risottos and pastas.

ℹ️ Information

Aegean Thesaurus Travel (p443) The €3 info pack from Thesaurus Travel, on main square, is a great investment. It includes the terrain map of Sifnos, an overview of the island's walking trails, plus the current bus and ferry timetables.

Xidis Travel (📞 22840 32373; www.xidis.com. gr; ⏰ 9am-9pm) Books ferry tickets.

ℹ️ Getting There & Away

From Easter, there are buses from Apollonia to Kamares (five daily, 20 minutes), Faros (three daily, 20 minutes), Kastro (three daily, 20 minutes), Platys Gialos (four daily, 30 minutes) and Vathi (three daily, 50 minutes). Services are much more frequent in the peak season; all routes cost €1.80.

Cars can be hired from Apollo Rental (p442).

Kastro Κάστρο

POP 118

Dramatically positioned on a crag with sheer drops to the crystalline waters below and terraced valleys all around, Kastro is Sifnos' most atmospheric and magical settlement. Until 1836 it was the island's capital but now it's a sleepy place, with only a single excellent taverna and a couple of seasonal cafes as its main signs of life.

People have lived here continuously since 1000 BCE and the remains of an acropolis can still be seen at the very top, where a temple to a female goddess (Athena or Artemis, no one's sure) once stood. The Romans left behind several large stone sarcophagi, which can be easily spotted as you pick your way up through the steep lanes.

The small port and pebble beach of Seralia is nestled below.

👁️ Sights

Archaeological Museum of Sifnos MUSEUM
(📞 22840 31022; €2; ⏰ 8am-3pm Tue-Sun) This small museum in the heart of Kastro houses archaeological remains from the ancient town. It's sometimes inexplicably closed.

Church of the Seven Martyrs CHURCH
From the seaward end of town, a steep but sturdy path leads down the cliff to this tiny blue-domed church, set on its own little promontory surrounded by startlingly green water. The church is usually locked but it's

the exceptionally beautiful setting that's the draw, especially in spring when the path is lined with yellow and mauve flowers. At its base, people swim naked from the rocks.

🛏️ Sleeping & Eating

Antonis Rooms GUESTHOUSE €
(📞 22840 33708; www.sifnosholidays.gr; r from €40; ❄️ 🛜) On the road as it winds up to Kastro, these simple, spotless rooms beckon. They're terrific value, with a communal kitchen and a terrace with splendid valley views. It's open year-round.

Aris & Maria Traditional Houses APARTMENT €
(📞 22840 31161; www.arismaria-traditional.com; apt from €46; ❄️ 🛜) For an authentic Kastro experience, rent one of these six traditional Sifnian houses. Some have sea views.

Leonidas TAVERNA €€
(📞 22840 31153; www.facebook.com/leonidastavern; mains €9-15; ⏰ noon-10pm Easter-Sep; 🛜) At the northern entrance to the village, this popular place offers tasty local dishes, including Sifnian appetisers like chickpea croquettes and cheese patties with honey and sesame seeds.

ℹ️ Getting There & Away

From Easter there are buses from Apollonia to Kastro (€1.80, three daily, 20 minutes). Services are much more frequent in peak season.

Around Sifnos

On the southeast coast, the fishing hamlet of Faros has fish tavernas and a couple of nice beaches nearby, including Fasolou, reached up steps and over the headland from the bus stop.

Platys Gialos, 10km south of Apollonia, has a generous sandy beach entirely backed by tavernas, hotels and shops. Vathy, on the southwest coast, is a low-key resort village on an almost circular bay of aquamarine beauty.

👁️ Sights

Moni Chrysopigi MONASTERY
(Map p442; Chrysopigi) Perched on an islet connected to the shore by a tiny footbridge, this handsome whitewashed monastery is considered to be the protector of Sifnos. Built in 1650, it's dedicated to the Life-giving Spring, a representation of the Mother of Christ in the Orthodox tradition. Inside the darkened church there's a carved wooden iconostasis and an interesting boat-shaped

metal candelabra. Beautiful, azure Chrysopigi Beach is home to two excellent tavernas.

Acropolis of Agios Andreas
MONUMENT
(Map p442; ☑22840 31488; adult/child €2/1; ☉8.30am-3pm Tue-Sun) At the heart of the island, about 2km south of Apollonia, this well-excavated hilltop acropolis dates from the Mycenaean period (13th century BCE). Take in extensive views of interior valleys and neighbouring Paros from above the intact defensive wall. The adjacent St Andrew's Church dates from about 1700.

🛏 Sleeping & Eating

Aerides Boutique Rooms
GUESTHOUSE €€
(Map p442; ☑22840 36093; www.aerides-sifnos.com; Vathy; s/d from €59/67; 🕸🛜) Run by a friendly young couple and artfully decorated with bits of flotsam and jetsam, this converted *syrma* (boat shed) comprises four spacious rooms. The sea is right under your window.

Windmill Bella Vista
BOUTIQUE HOTEL €€
(Map p442; ☑22840 33518; www.windmillbellavista.gr; apt from €128; 🅿🕸🛜🏊) A converted Cycladic windmill is the atmospheric pick of the spacious, high-beamed apartments and studios at this small hotel, clustered around an infinity pool.

Hotel Efrosini
HOTEL €€
(☑22840 71353; www.hotel-efrosini.gr; Platys Gialos; r €80-90; ☉May-Sep; 🅿🕸🛜) This well-kept, family-run hotel is one of the best on the Platys Gialos strip. Small balconies overlook a leafy courtyard with the sea lapping just in front.

Verina Suites
APARTMENT €€€
(☑6976867641; https://verinahotelsifnos.com; Platys Gialos; d/apt from €190/220; ☉Easter-Sep; 🕸🛜🏊) Effortlessly chic, Verina rents minimalist suites and villas at outposts in Platys Gialos, Vathy and above Poulati (north of Kastro). Verina Suites lies behind the beach at Platys Gialos, but try dragging yourself from the gorgeous pool and cafe-bar area.

★ Omega 3
SEAFOOD €€
(☑22840 72014; www.facebook.com/omega3greece; Platys Gialos; mains €12-15; ☉noon-11pm Easter-Sep) The cute name (Ω3) hints at the treats on offer at this small, casual 'fish and wine bar'. There's a menu of fab fishy flavours, grabbing techniques from around the globe (sashimi, ceviche) while still staying true to its roots with marinated octopus and orzo pasta with crayfish. Showstoppers

COOKING CLASSES

A big drawcard for travellers is Sifnos' culinary heritage. The island was the birthplace of Nikolaos Tselementes (1878–1958), author of the first (and best-known) Greek cookbook, published in 1910. Since then, Sifnos has enjoyed a reputation for producing excellent chefs. Engaging cooking classes are available with Sifnos Farm Narlis (Map p442; ☑6979778283; www.sifnos-farm-narlis.com; 3hr/5hr class €70/95). Book directly, or via Aegean Thesaurus (☑22840 33151; www.thesaurus.gr; ☉9.30am-2pm & 5-8.30pm Mon-Sat).

include punchy fish soup and a fish tartare with pickled zucchini.

To Limanaki
SEAFOOD €€
(☑22840 71425; Faros; mains €14-22; ☉noon-10pm) It's well worth detouring to the village of Faros just to dine at this seafront taverna, where fisherman and owner, Giorgios, cooks up the sea's bounty using his mother's recipes. You can't go wrong with grilled catch of the day or orzo pasta with lobster.

SERIFOS ΣΕΡΙΦΟΣ
POP 1420

Serifos has a raw, rugged beauty, with steep mountains plunging to broad ultramarine bays. Relatively deserted outside the quaint hilltop capital of Hora or the dusty, Wild West–feeling port of Livadi down below, the island feels like it's gone beautifully feral. All that you find are the occasional remnants of past mining enterprises (rusting tracks, cranes) and the whoosh of the wind (which can be fierce). Rent wheels to make the most of it. Serifos is one of the few islands where locals drink the water.

In Greek mythology, Serifos is where Perseus grew up, bringing back Medusa's head to save his mother from the unwanted romantic attentions of Polydectes, and where the Cyclopes were said to live.

The island can be explored via a network of 10 signposted trails of varying lengths and difficulty; see the 'hiking' page of www.serifos-greece.com for detailed information.

❶ Getting There & Away

Serifos is on the Piraeus to western Cyclades ferry route and has reasonable summer

Serifos

population. This, along with its proximity to some excellent beaches, make it an excellent base for exploring the island.

Sights & Activities

Livadakia
BEACH

Just over the headland that rises from the ferry quay, this gorgeous tamarisk-fringed beach has a long swoop of coarse golden sand and a rustic taverna.

Ramos
BEACH

Just past Livadakia, Ramos is a small sandy beach backed with grapevines and a smattering of flash holiday apartments.

Serifos Scuba Divers
DIVING

(☑ 6932570552; www.serifosscubadivers.gr; 1-tank dive/snorkelling €50/30) This recommended scuba operator takes divers to a dozen sites around the island, including wrecks and more. Day-long snorkelling trips can be arranged in July and August, and it also rents boats and arranges adrenalin-packed flyboard sessions.

Sleeping

Alexandros-Vassilia
GUESTHOUSE €

(☑ 22810 51119; www.alexandros-vassilia.gr; Livadakia Beach; r/ste from €55/160; ⊙ Apr-Oct; ✳ ⓢ) Best known for its beachfront taverna in a flowering garden, this friendly Livadakia compound also has a big range of basic rooms and apartments. They range from decent-value economy rooms (no sea view) to family-sized, sea-view suites.

Marousa's
APARTMENT €€

(Map p446; ☑ 22810 51807; www.serifos apartments.gr; Ramos; apt from €65; ⊙ Easter-Oct; P ✳ ⓢ) Up above Ramos Beach, this inviting complex offers 11 simple but well-equipped one- and two-bedroom apartments. The handsome couple who run it put on a delicious breakfast spread including homemade jams, and olives and capers from their own garden. It's a steep 1km walk southwest of town, above Ramos Beach; best with your own wheels. The wi-fi is terrible, though.

Studios Niovi
APARTMENT €€

(Map p446; ☑ 22810 51900; www.studiosniovi.gr; apt €90-140; P ✳ ⓢ) On the furthest eastern curve of Livadi's bay, about a 15-minute walk from the centre, these immaculate apartments look over the broad expanse of the bay, bustling Livadi, towering Hora and the mountains beyond. The owner is a gem and makes a super breakfast spread. Good low-season rates.

connections. High-season services include Piraeus (€31 to €48, two to 4½ hours, five daily), Kythnos (€8, 1¼ hours, daily), Sifnos (€6.50 to €15, 50 minutes, four daily), Milos (€8 to €18, one to two hours, five daily) and Syros (€8.50, 2¼ hours, daily). See www.ferries.gr for detailed information.

❶ Getting Around

Buses connect Livadi and Hora (€1.80, hourly, 15 minutes); the timetable is posted at the bus stop by the yacht quay. In high season, a circular bus route takes in Panagia, Galani, Kendarhos and Agios Ioannis Beach (up to six daily), with a couple of daily buses to Megalo Livadi and Koutalas.

Rent cars, scooters and quads at **Blue Bird** (☑ 22810 51511; www.rentacar-bluebird. gr), **Poseidon Rent a Car** (☑ 22810 52030, 6974789706; www.serifosisland.gr/poseidon) or **Serifos Tours** (☑ 22810 51463; www.serifos tours.gr) in Livadi.

Taxis (☑ 6932431114, 6944473044) from Livadi to Hora cost €8, Psili Ammos €8, Platys Gialos €20, Sykamia €23 and Megalo Livadi €23.

Livadi
Λιβάδι

POP 605

Serifos' main port and biggest town has a large marina that's popular with touring yachties, and a surprisingly buzzy strip of waterfront tavernas and bars given its tiny

DON'T MISS

BEACHES OF SERIFOS

The island's most strikingly beautiful beach, Agios Sostis, is a 40-minute walk northeast of Livadi. It occupies a sandy spit terminating in a headland topped with a blue-vaulted church and craggy golden rock formations. On each side are gravelly golden beaches abutting crystal-clear waters, perfectly framing views of distant islands. It's best reached on foot as the access road is rough and there's only parking for a handful of cars.

Next up is pretty little Psili Ammos, tucked below the main road, offering good swimming and a couple of tavernas. Reached by a steep side road, Platys Gialos in the north has gravelly sand and a good seasonal taverna. Near the turnoff, look out for the Monastery of the Taxiarches (a title referring to the archangels Michael and Gabriel), built in 1572 and fortified to protect it from pirates and other raiders. If it's open, it's worth exploring.

Sykamia is one of the island's best beaches, with a dramatic approach along a steep, windy, sealed road through terraced hills. There's a good taverna set back from its pebble-strewn, grey-brown sands.

Tiny Megalo Livadi, on the southwest coast, is interesting for its crumbling neoclassical buildings (remnants of the mining era) and seaside tavernas but the beach is a little muddy and rocky. The cave where the Cyclops was said to dwell is near here.

The best beaches on the south coast tend to be broad and sandy, and deserted out of high season. It's a wild landscape, punctuated by derelict machinery. Three of them share a large sheltered bay: Koutalas, a small fishing village with a pebble-strewn beach; Ganema, a tamarisk-edged beach with vivid green waters giving way to deep-blue depths; and, best of all, Vagia, a horseshoe of golden sand and shingle embracing iridescent waters.

🍴 Eating & Drinking

To Bakakaki
TAVERNA €

(☑ 22810 51010; mains €8.30-10; ☺ 1pm-late; 🛜) Named after a small native frog, this chilled-out *kreatotaverna* (literally 'meat tavern') on the waterfront is known for its grilled and slow-roasted meat, but it also serves delicious traditional snacks such as *tirokafteri* (spicy cheese-and-red-pepper spread) and *sfakiopita* (cheese filo pie topped with honey).

★ Kali's
SEAFOOD €€

(☑ 22810 52301; www.kaliseafood.gr; mains €7-18; ☺ noon-11pm Mar-Oct; 🛜🅿) Slather zingy seafood spread onto bread and get messy with mussels *saganaki* (in a rich broth, with feta) and scampi on orzo (pasta) at this water's edge restaurant. Gregarious waiters play show and tell with the day's fresh fish selection, to be grilled whole. The traditional orange cake is sublime, too.

Metalleio
MEDITERRANEAN €€

(☑ 22810 51755; www.facebook.com/Metalleio; mains €10-16; ☺ 7.30pm-late Easter-Oct; 🛜) On the road behind the waterfront, Metalleio dishes up quality cuisine from a short menu emphasising local products, such as risotto with goat's cheese, veal *tagliata* (sliced steak) and ice cream with homemade sweets.

Yacht Club Serifos
BAR

(☑ 22810 51888; www.facebook.com/YachtClub Serifos; ☺ 7.30am-late; 🛜) Livadi's original waterfront cafe-bar (dating back to 1938) maintains a cheerful buzz, delivering good music, light meals, coffee and cocktails under the shade of large tamarisks. It stays open really late, too – until 5am in the peak season.

ℹ Information

Kondilis (☑ 22810 52340; www.kondilis.gr; ☺ 9am-9pm) Sells ferry tickets.

Serifos Tours (p446) Sells ferry tickets, books excursions and rents cars and bikes.

ℹ Getting There & Around

From the bus stop by the yacht quay, buses run to Hora and, less frequently, to other main villages.

Car rental agencies include Poseidon Rent A Car (p446) and Blue Bird (p446).

Hora (Serifos)
Χώρα (Σέριφος)

POP 364

This tiny town cascades down the summit of the rocky mountain above Livadi, putting it among the most dramatically striking (and loftiest) of all the Cycladic capitals. The bus terminus and main car park are on its upper side, near some windmills. From there, steps climb into the maze of Hora proper and lead to the main square, watched over by the lovely neoclassical town hall and a blue-domed church.

From the square, narrow alleys and more steps lead upwards to the ancient acropolis and the scant remnants of the 15th-century Venetian Kastro (castle), offering spectacular views over the water to distant Sifnos. Just below the summit, the barrel-vaulted Church of St John the Theologian is carved into the rock on the site of an ancient temple to Athena.

⊙ Sights

Archaeological
Collection of Serifos
MUSEUM

(☑ 22810 52611; adult/child €2/1; ⊙ 9am-4pm Wed-Mon) This modest museum displays fragments of mainly Hellenic and Roman sculpture excavated from the *kastro*. Panels in Greek and English retell the legend of Perseus, the mythic hero who washed ashore on Serifos as a baby. The building's not well signed; look for it near the upper bus stop.

⌨ Sleeping & Eating

Anemoessa Studios
APARTMENT €€

(☑ 22810 51132; www.serifos-anemoessa.gr; apt €100; ❄🅿) Six pretty, modern studios each sleep four in whitewashed Cycladic style.

Stou Stratou
CAFE €

(☑ 22810 52566; www.stoustratou.com; Plateia Agiou Athanasiou; dishes €3-10; ⊙ 9am-late Easter-Oct) Sitting postcard-pretty in the sunbaked main square, Stou Stratou has a menu full of art and poetry (literally), plus it serves good breakfasts and light snacks such as Cretan wild fennel pie or a mixed plate of cold cuts and cheese. Cocktails and coffee, too.

Aloni
TAVERNA €€

(Map p446; ☑ 22810 52603; www.facebook.com/alwni1; mains €7-15; ⊙ 7pm-late Jun-Oct, Sat & Sun Nov-May) Halfway up the hill between Livadi and Hora, signposted on the right, Aloni offers splendid panoramas and an upscale feel. Islanders rate it among Serifos' best, with local produce (roasted meat, rabbit in lemon sauce, fennel pie) proudly showcased.

ⓘ Getting There & Away

If you're coming from Livadi, consider catching the bus up and walking back down. Hourly buses (€1.80) run between Livadi and Hora in the high season; fewer in low season. A scenic 2.5km,

vehicle-free walking path (route 1A) winds down through Hora to Livadi

KYTHNOS   ΚΥΘΝΟΣ

POP 1460

Low-key Kythnos (also known as Kithnos or Thermia) is a series of rolling hills punctuated by stone huts and bisected by ancient walls, green valleys and some wonderful beaches. Port life in Merihas and village life in beautiful Hora and Dryopida remain easygoing, and foreign tourists are few, although the marina at Loutra brings with it an international buzz in summertime. Ease of access from Athens sees Greek travellers filling the island's beaches on sunny weekends.

ⓘ Getting There & Away

In the high season, ferries connect Kythnos to various destinations including Piraeus (€25, three hours, four daily), Lavrio (€16, two hours, two daily), Kea (€6.90, 1¼ hours, daily), Syros (€9, 2¼ hours, three daily) and Serifos (€8, 1¼ hours, daily). Services between the islands are reduced in winter; see www.ferries.gr for detailed information.

ⓘ Getting Around

In the high season, five buses per day run in each direction on the Merihas–Hora–Loutra and Merihas–Dryopida–Kanala routes; fares range from €1.40 to €2. In the low season, the best way to see the island is by car or scooter. Rentals are available at **Nikitos** (☑ 22810 31419; www.kythnosrentalcar.gr) and Larentzakis Antonis (p449), among other places.

Taxis (☑ 6944271609) from Merihas charge about €10 to Hora and €8 to Dryopida. A water taxi to/from the beaches in summer costs about €10.

Merihas   Μέριχας

POP 369

Little Merihas is home to much of the island's low-season life. Cafes and restaurants line the small harbour, and rooms for let dot its hills. The town beach is uninspiring but good beaches are within walking distance, north of the quay at Martinakia and Episkopi.

⊙ Sights

Episkopi
BEACH

(Map p449) This wide swathe of coarse grey sand is a 30-minute walk north of the harbour. There's a popular beach bar at one end and a tiny church at the other.

Martinakia
BEACH

Although you can swim in the centre of town, you're better off walking 10 minutes north to this pretty little cove.

🛏 Sleeping & Eating

Kontseta
APARTMENT €€

(📞 22810 33024; www.kontseta.gr; r €100-120; ☉ Apr-Oct; ❄ 🗈) Easily the nicest option in town, these modern studio apartments are a cut above, with fresh decor and fine views. They are high above the ferry quay, with steps signposted next door to the Alpha Bank.

Molos
GRILL €

(📞 22810 32455; mains €2.50-12; ☉ 2-11pm) Quick, delicious souvlaki, kebabs, burgers stuffed with cheese, grilled haloumi and salads, served from an unassuming waterfront location near where the ferries dock.

Ostria
SEAFOOD €€

(📞 22810 33017; mains €9-20; ☉ 10.30am-midnight; 🗈) Seafood is the main attraction here: grilled snapper, scorpion fish, grouper, calamari and lobster spaghetti all get the thumbs up. Stop by earlier for an omelette and coffee on the terrace overlooking the water.

❶ Information

➡ **Larentzakis Antonis** (📞 22810 32104; www.rentacarkythnos.gr; ☉ 9am-9pm) Sells ferry tickets, arranges accommodation, and hires ATVs, scooters and cars.

➡ **Anerousa Travel** (📞 22810 32372; ☉ 9am-9pm) Sells ferry tickets.

❶ Getting There & Away

Between early June and September, buses from Merihas serve Hora (15 minutes), Loutra (30 minutes), Dryopida (30 minutes) and Kanala (45 minutes) five times daily; fares range from €1.40 to €2. Agencies along the waterfront rent scooters, ATVs and cars.

Hora (Kythnos)
Χώρα (Κύθνος)

POP 561

Behind its workaday outskirts, the island's unassuming capital, Hora (also known as Kythnos or Messaria), hides a lovely network of lanes branching off a long, narrow, main alley lined with gleaming white churches, cafes, tavernas, ice-cream parlours and ceramics shops. Despite some obviously

Kythnos

tourist-focused stores, the town has held on to its inherent character as the centre of a largely agricultural community. Grannies still string out their laundry above the whitewashed lanes, farmers trot by on donkeys and, come Easter, the village kids amuse themselves on a traditional wooden swing bedecked with flowers.

🛏 Sleeping & Eating

Filoxenia Studios
APARTMENT €€

(📞 22810 31644; www.filoxenia-kythnos.gr; d €70; ❄ 🗈) These well-priced, fully equipped apartments and studios are set behind a terrace filled with palms and flowering shrubs. It's located on the square just before the pedestrian part of town.

Messaria
GREEK €€

(📞 22810 31620; www.messaria.gr; mains €8.50-11; ☉ 1-10pm; 🗈) Set on the small square at the edge of the pedestrian part of Hora, this restaurant specialises in traditional island

WORTH A TRIP

BEACHES & VILLAGES OF KYTHNOS

The island's most famous beaches are in the northwest. Apokrousi (Map p449) is a wide strip of gravelly sand with a couple of tavernas, a popular beach bar and ample parking. From Apokrousi, a rough road leads over the hill to the exquisite double bay of Kolona (Map p449), a narrow sun-blasted strip of sand anchoring a hilly headland to the main island. In summer it gets packed, and the seasonal cafe does a brisk trade. In low season it's a favourite anchorage for yachts; although the road to the spit is often gated when the cafe is closed, you can still access the first beach and swim to the spit. It's easiest to reach Kolona via water taxi from Merihas, or else by ATV or a hot 30-minute walk from Apokrousi.

At the centre of the island is Kythnos' prettiest village, Dryopida. Clinging to either side of a ravine, this picturesque collection of red-tiled roofs and winding, car-free lanes has a cluster of cafes, tavernas and small museums gathered around its impressive church.

From Dryopida, the main road runs all the way south to Agios Dimitrios, a stone-strewn, grey-sand beach with placid waters. Of the half-dozen east-coast beaches, mostly reachable by unsealed minor roads, the most accessible (and loveliest) is the sandy cove next to Kanala village. This substantial seaside settlement is also notable for its church, which contains a beloved icon of the Virgin and Child, and for the excellent traditional trattoria, Archipelagos (Map p449; ☑ 22810 32380; www.archipelagos-kythnos.gr; Kanala; mains €6.80-20; ☺ 1-10pm; ☎).

If you're after a hike, it's well worth walking the minor roads from Dryopida down to the less-visited Lefkes, Kato Livadi and Liotrivi beaches. Another worthwhile ramble is the picturesque 90-minute track from Loutra to Kastro Orias (Map p449), on Cape Kefalos. These ruins are all that remains of a medieval city of around 5000 people.

dishes, such as rooster cooked in wine, baked chickpeas and rabbit stew.

ℹ Getting There & Away

Hora is 7km from Merihas by road. During high season there are five daily buses to Merihas and Loutra (€1.40).

Loutra ———— Λουτρά

POP 81

This low-key fishing village, 3km north of Hora, sits on a windy bay, its large marina full of yachts and its harbour front lined with high-standard restaurants, cafes and bars. In summer it's a popular destination for sailing tours and the liveliest spot on the island in which to base yourself.

Maroula, a short coastal walk north, is the site of ancient Mesolithic-era graves.

🏃 Activities

Aqua Team   DIVING
(☑ 22810 31333; www.aquakythnos.gr; 1-/2-tank dive €50/90; ⊕) With more than 30 dive sites to choose from, from wrecks and caves to drift dives, Kythnos is a great destination for underwater explorers. This crew offers boat dives, snorkelling trips and diving courses, including Discover Scuba sessions for beginners.

Hot Springs   HOT SPRINGS
FREE Loutra's unusual claim to fame is its thermal waters, which bubble along a culvert to the beach where they're detained in a large rock pool before seeping out to sea. It's a popular spot for a soak, any time of the year.

🛏 Sleeping & Eating

★ Kythnos Bay Hotel   HOTEL €€
(☑ 22810 31218; www.kythnosbay.gr; r €70-80; ⊙ Easter-Sep; P ❋ ☎) Drifted in on a summer breeze, this beachy hotel is Loutra's most upmarket choice, with an elegantly bleached colour palate and artfully hung driftwood in reception. Well-equipped rooms, friendly staff and a delicious breakfast buffet compensate for the slow wi-fi.

Sofrano   INTERNATIONAL €€
(☑ 22810 31436; www.sofrano-yachtingclub.gr; mains €10-19; ⊙ 9am-late; ☎) The mainstay of the Loutra waterfront is this schmick year-round restaurant serving a good selection of traditional mezedhes, grilled fresh fish and more unusual dishes such as beef tenderloin in a spicy chocolate sauce.

ℹ Getting There & Away

In the high season there are five daily buses in each direction on the Merihas–Hora–Loutra route; fares range from €1.40 to €2.

KEA

POP 2460

Kea has plenty of natural appeal with craggy cliffs, a spectacular coastline and fertile valleys filled with orchards, olive groves and oak trees. A smattering of interesting historical sights and some excellent walking routes only add to the attraction. It's also the closest island to Attica, making it a popular weekend destination for wealthy Athenians whose modern holiday homes have sprouted in some areas – although the use of local stone and peach-coloured plaster helps them blend into the hillsides.

🛈 Getting There & Around

Kea's only mainland service is to Lavrio; boats get packed on weekends. In the off season, connections to other islands are few. High-season destinations include Lavrio (€12.40, one hour, three daily), Kythnos (€6.90, 1¼ hours, daily), Syros (€11, four hours, three weekly), Tinos (€12, 3½ hours, weekly) and Andros (€9.30, 5½ hours, weekly); see www.ferries.gr for details.

In July and August, regular buses go from Korissia to Vourkari, Otzias, Ioulida and Pisses; fewer services run out of season. Taxis (☑ 22812 00158) to Ioulida cost around €10, Otzias €8 and Pisses €25.

Leon Rent A Car (☑ 22880 21898; www. rentacarkea.gr) rents cars and scooters from an office very near the ferry terminal.

Korissia

Κορησσία

POP 711

The little port of Korissia may not be quite as picturesque as the island's capital, but it has a lively strip of waterfront bars and tavernas. The north-facing beach tends to catch the wind, but you're only about a 15-minute walk from small but popular Gialiskari Beach, backed by eucalypts.

🛏 Sleeping

Koralli Studios　　APARTMENT €€
(☑ 22880 21268; www.kea-rooms.gr; s/d from €58/63; P ❄ 🤖) These spotless, well-equipped, bougainvillea-clad studios are just 150m from the beach but they don't have the most salubrious view, overlooking a boat storage yard. The owner can meet the ferry and goes out of his way to assist his guests.

Red Tractor Farm　　FARMSTAY €€
(☑ 22880 21046; www.redtractorfarm.com; r/studio from €98/132; ❄ 🤖) 🖉 Set among vineyards and olive groves, this organic agritourism farm offers rooms, studios and whole

cottages in a range of beautiful Cycladic buildings, combining traditional and modern style and comfort. Hosts Kostis and Marcie can advise on the best hiking routes; they also produce olive oil, wine, marmalade and chutney, plus unique acorn cookies.

Aegean View　　GUESTHOUSE €€
(☑ 22880 22046; www.roomsinkea.gr; r from €71; ☺ Mar-Dec; ❄ 🤖) On the harbourfront, just metres from the ferry dock, this guesthouse has a handful of bright, modern rooms and studios with en suite bathrooms. Some have small private balconies; all share a lovely communal deck.

🍴 Eating

Rolando's　　GREEK €€
(☑ 22880 29129; mains €8-17; ☺ noon-midnight; 🤖) One of the humbler looking tavernas on the waterfront strip, Rolando's serves tasty rustic food such as meatballs, *katsiki* (kid goat), an excellent *mousakas*, fresh fish and rabbit stew.

Magazes　　MEDITERRANEAN €€
(☑ 22880 21104; www.kearestaurant.gr; mains €9-20; ☺ noon-midnight Easter-Sep; 🤖🖉) Run by Greek-Californian Stefanos, Magazes serves high-quality local dishes in a stylishly restored warehouse on the waterfront. It's recommended for its fresh seafood, including lobster pasta, and tasty vegetarian options such as zucchini fritters and stuffed eggplant.

🛈 Information

Stegadi (☑ 22880 21435; www.praktoreiokeas. gr) Sells ferry tickets and has good information on Kea's hiking trails on its website.

🛈 Getting There & Away

Korissia is the island's main ferry port. Leon Rent A Car rents vehicles from an office right by the port. Buses run to Ioulida, Otzias and Pisses several times daily.

Ioulida

Ιουλίδα

POP 633

Ioulida is Kea's gem, its pretty scramble of narrow lanes, churches and houses draping themselves across two hilltops in the island's mountainous heart. Once one of Kea's four ancient city-states, it's been the island's administrative capital since late Roman/Byzantine times. It's now a thoroughly pleasant place to wander around, with enough interesting sights, tavernas and cafes to detain you for a few hours.

Kea

0 — 5 km
0 — 2.5 miles

Lavrio (25km)
Anemousa Studios
Otzias
Kastrianis Monastery
Vourkari
Korissia
Glaliskari Beach
Ancient Lion of Kea
Kythnos (40km);
Syros (110km)
Flea
Ioulida
Spathi
Cape Spathi
570m
Pera Meria
Astras
Ellinika
Pisses
Kato Meria
Koundouros
450m
Havouna
Kampi
Karthaia
Aegean Sea
Cape Tamelos

⊙ Sights

★ Ancient Lion of Kea   MONUMENT
(Map p452) The enigmatic 8m-long Kea Lion, chiselled from schist sometime between the 9th and 6th century BCE, lies along the ridge beyond the last of Ioulida's houses. The 15-minute walk to reach it is fantastic: follow small wooden signs reading Αρχαίος Λέων from the top of the main street until the path leads you out of town. The footpath curves past a cemetery, and the lion, with its smooth-worn haunches and Cheshire-cat smile, is reached through a gate on the left.

Archaeological Museum of Kea   MUSEUM
(☑22880 22079; adult/child €2/1; ⊙8.30am-3.30pm Wed-Mon) The most intriguing artefacts displayed at this well-presented museum were ancient even before Kea's four archaic city-states were formed. The 13 terracotta figurines are the best preserved of 50 recovered from a temple at Agia Irini (Vourkari Bay), dating from between 3300 and 1100 BCE. Were they goddesses, priestesses or devotees? Nobody knows.

🛏 Sleeping

Hotel Serie   HOTEL €€
(☑22880 22355; www.serie.com.gr; r from €110; P❄🖰) Just a few minutes' walk from labyrinthine Ioulida, this compact hotel offers a cluster of light, brightly painted rooms with hilly views from the balconies.

Kea Village   HOTEL €€
(☑6972243330; www.keavillas.gr; ste from €140; ⊙Mar–mid-Nov; P❄🖰🏊) Gorgeously situated at the highest point of Ioulida, this complex with sweeping views offers a variety of suites and villas that sleep you and up to nine of your dearest friends in style. All have a veranda and either a kitchenette or a full kitchen.

🍴 Eating

★ To Steki   TAVERNA €
(☑22880 22088; www.facebook.com/tostekikea; mains €8-9.50; ⊙12.30pm-midnight daily Jun-Sep, 7pm-midnight Fri & Sat, 12.30-4pm Sun Oct-May; 🖰) Regular taverna fare is taken to the next level at this attractive place tucked beside St Spyridon's Church, with terrace seating overlooking the valley. Expect the likes of goat in lemon sauce, rabbit, mushroom pie, zucchini pie and delicious *dolmadhes* (vine leaves stuffed with rice and mince) served warm in an olive oil and lemon emulsion.

O Paparounas   TAVERNA €€
(☑22880 22583; www.facebook.com/Paparounas. Kea; mains from €8.50; ⊙10am-midnight; 🖰) Occupying a terrace on the corner of the main square, this friendly little taverna serves local favourites such as Greek salad, tabouleh, grilled sardines, fried anchovies and eat-whole fried bait fish. Local farmers drop by around 10am for their morning coffee or *raki* shot; the kitchen gets going at midday.

To Spiti Sti Hora   GREEK €€€
(☑22880 29101; www.tospitistihora.gr; mains €18-27; ⊙noon-3pm & 7-11pm Jun-Sep; 🖰) Set on a series of terraces with views over the town to the distant sea, this restaurant prepares elaborate takes on seasonal Kea dishes, with local ingredients put to excellent use. Expect the likes of goat spaghetti, cuttlefish risotto, octopus stew and awesome sunset views over Ioulida to go with your cocktails.

🍷 Drinking & Nightlife

To Panorama   CAFE
(☑22880 22341; ⊙9am-2pm Mon & Thu, 5.30-9pm Fri, 9am-9pm Sat & Sun; 🖰) Large windows and a small terrace showcase extraordinary valley views at this bright and cheery little cafe. Thankfully, the coffee's good, too – and there's a good selection of pastries, cakes, waffles, crêpes, omelettes and sandwiches, should you get peckish.

❶ Getting There & Away

During the mid-June to September high season there are regular buses (every 40 minutes) to Korissia; fewer in the off season.

Around Kea

The beach road from Korissia leads past appealing golden-sand Gialiskari Beach to the marina at Vourkari, where the waterfront is lined with yachts, restaurants, bars and fashionable cafes.

Four kilometres to the northeast, Otzias has a large, sandy beach in a lovely, almost circular bay – though it can get rather windy. From Otzias, a 12km road runs inland to Ioulida, connected to the east coast's finest beach, Spathi, via a wide but bumpy unsealed road. There's not much here aside from a large beach bar and a scattering of holiday homes, and there's not much shade.

Eight kilometres southwest of Ioulida is the unfortunately named Pisses (also spelt Poisses), a pebble-strewn sandy beach with a taverna and beach bar, backed by orchards and rugged hills. Four kilometres south along the coast is Koundouros, a playground for moneyed Athenians, with a succession of small sandy coves. A little further south, Kampi is an inviting little swimming spot with a waterfront taverna.

◉ Sights

★Karthaia   RUINS
(Map p452) From the 8th century BCE until the 7th century CE, this remote twin cove was the site of the ancient city of Karthaia, one of Kea's four historic city-states. Now the partly uncovered ruins sit in splendid isolation, only accessible by boat or on foot. Three hiking trails lead here, with the easiest being route 6: a 40-minute walk down from the parking area at the bottom of a narrow lane, signposted from the main road at Stavroudaki.

Part of the great charm of this site is that you'd be very unlucky to find more than a handful of people here – and there's a good chance you'll have it completely to yourself. The small, craggy acropolis has the remains of the Temple of Apollo Pythios on its lower level and the Temple of Athena at the top, dating from 530 to 500 BCE. Down below is a theatre that once seated 880 people, and the remains of a Roman-era bathhouse.

Kastrianis Monastery   MONASTERY
(Map p452; ⊘ sunrise-sunset Jun-Sep) From Otzias, a spectacular coastal road runs for

DIVING KEA

Kea has some of the best diving in Greece, with more than a dozen varied and challenging dive sites that include walls, ship and plane wrecks and underwater caves. Vourkari-based Kea Divers (☑ 6973430860; www.keadivers.com; Vourkari; 1/2 dives incl equipment €50/90) is a reputable scuba-diving outfit that also runs snorkelling trips.

6.5km to this clifftop, 18th-century monastery, offering extraordinary views to the surrounding islands. A peacock-blue dome caps the baby-blue church and, inside, the walls are covered with frescoes of saints.

🍴 Sleeping & Eating

Anemousa Studios   APARTMENT €€
(Map p452; ☑ 22880 21335; www.anemousa.gr; Otzias; apt from €95; ⊘ Apr-Oct; ❄ 🤶 ❄) Surrounded by well-maintained gardens, these comfortable and spacious apartments curve around an attractive pool, 50m inland from the beach in Otzias. Breakfast and drinks can be ordered from the poolside bar, and there's a BBQ, plus a playground for kids.

Seirios   SEAFOOD €€
(☑ 22880 28280; www.facebook.com/seirios.kea; Vourkari; mains €12-20; ⊘ 11am-late; 🤶) The best of Vourkari's waterfront restaurants delivers a concise but appealing seafood-focused menu including marinated anchovies and delicately battered squid, but the main focus is on whole grilled fish, presented for your appraisal.

I Strofi tou Mimi   SEAFOOD €€
(☑ 22880 21480; www.facebook.com/istrofitou mimi; Vourkari; mains €9-20; ⊘ noon-midnight daily Jun-Aug, Sat & Sun Apr, May, Sep & Oct; 🤶) On the far side of Vourkari Bay, this waterfront restaurant focuses mainly on seafood, particularly grilled fish, with a few meaty dishes offered as well. In the summer, the glassed-in terrace opens up to let in the sea breezes.

🍸 Drinking & Nightlife

Zeus Faber   BAR
(☑ 6987410707; Vourkari; ⊘ 8pm-4am; 🤶) Kea's hippest bar by far sits up above the waterfront tavernas, with a deck gazing over the water and a dimly lit interior furnished with wooden benches, driftwood, candles, old records and interesting art.

Palace of Knossos (p466)
TIMOFEEV VLADIMIR/SHUTTERSTOCK

AT A GLANCE

POPULATION
Crete/Iraklio:
634,930/140,730

CAPITAL
Iraklio (Heraklion)

**BEST CRETAN
DINING**
Peskesi (p464)

BEST FILO MASTER
Yiorgos
Hatziparaskos (p476)

BEST WINERY
Diamantakis Winery
(p470)

WHEN TO GO
Jul & Aug High
season. Queues
at big sights, busy
beaches. hot days,
balmy evenings,
warm waters.

Apr–Jun & Sep–Oct
Moderate temper-
atures, smaller
crowds. Best time for
hiking and outdoor
activities.

Nov–Mar Low
season. Sights and
restaurants scale
back hours. Beach
resorts close. Major
sights uncrowded.

Crete

Crete (Κρήτη) is the culmination of the Greek experience. There's something undeniably artistic in the way its landscape unfolds, from the sun-drenched beaches in the north to the rugged canyons spilling out at the cliff-lined southern coast. In between, valleys cradle moody villages, and round-shouldered hills are the overture to often snow-dabbed mountains. Take it all in on a driving tour, trek through Europe's longest gorge or hike to the cave where Zeus was born. Leave time to plant your footprints on a sandy beach, and boat, kayak or snorkel in the crystalline waters. Crete's natural beauty is equalled only by the richness of its history. The Palace of Knossos is but one of many vestiges of the mysterious ancient Minoan civilisation. Venetian fortresses, Turkish mosques and Byzantine churches bring history alive all over Crete, but nowhere more so than in charismatic Hania and Rethymno.

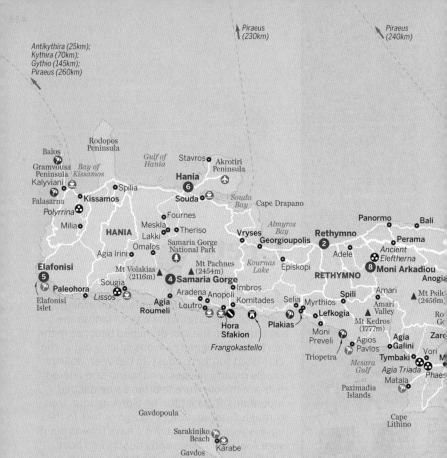

Crete Highlights

1 **Palace of Knossos** (p466) Rubbing shoulders with Europe's oldest civilisation, the ancient Minoans.

2 **Rethymno** (p474) Getting lost in the charismatic jumble of Venetian buildings sprinkled

with exotic features from the Ottoman period.

3 **Heraklion Archaeological Museum** (p459) Marvelling at the treasures unearthed during the excavation of ancient sites on the island.

4 **Samaria Gorge** (p496) Following an old riverbed to the Libyan Sea on a trek through Europe's longest canyon.

5 **Elafonisi** (p498) Counting the colours of the sea while relaxing on this

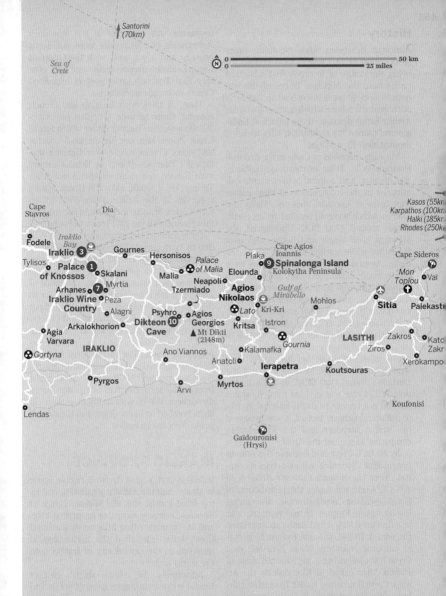

Santorini
(70km)

Sea of
Crete

0 —— 50 km
0 —— 25 miles

Cape
Stavros   Dia

Kasos (55km
Karpathos (100km
Halki (185km
Rhodes (250km

Fodele   *Iraklio*
             Bay   Cape Agios   Cape Sideros
Iraklio 3   **Gournes** **Hersonisos**   Plaka   Ioannis
Tylisos   *Palace* **9 Spinalonga Island**   Mon
Palace 1   **Skalani**   **Malia** *of Malia* **Elounda** Kolokytha Peninsula   Toplou *Vaï*
of Knossos   Myrtia   **Neapoli**
Arhanes **7**   Peza   Tzermiado   **Agios** *Gulf of*   **Sitia** Palekast
Iraklio Wine   Psyhro **Agios** **Nikolaos** *Mirabello*   Mohlos
Country Alagni   **Georgios**   *Lato* Kri-Kri
             Arkalokhorion **Dikteon 10**   **Kritsa** Istron   Zakros Kato
Agia   **Cave** ▲ Mt Dikti   **LASITHI** Ziros Zakr
Varvara   **IRAKLIO**   (2148m) **Gournia**   Xerokampo
Gortyna   Ano Viannos   *Kalamafka* *Gournia*
                                    Anatoli **Ierapetra** **Koutsouras**
Pyrgos   Koufonisi
             Arvi   **Myrtos**
Lendas

Gaïdouronisi
(Hrysi)

---

glorious pink-tinged sandy beach.

6 Hania (p486) Wandering the historic city's romantic old town and Venetian harbour.

7 Iraklio Wine Country (p470) Sampling fine

vintages on a tour of this vine-blanketed sylvan landscape.

8 Moni Arkadiou (p479) Being moved by the bloody tragedy of this isolated monastery.

9 Spinalonga Island (p504) Feeling the history of this former leper colony.

10 Dikteon Cave (p509) Making the piligrimage to the birthplace of Zeus, king of the gods.

History

Although inhabited since Neolithic times (7000–3000 BCE), Crete is most famous for being the cradle of Europe's first advanced civilisation, the Minoan. Traces of this enigmatic society were uncovered in the early 20th century, when British archaeologist Sir Arthur Evans discovered the palace at Knossos and named the civilisation after its ruler, the mythical King Minos.

Minoans migrated to Crete in the 3rd millennium BCE. Their extraordinary artistic, architectural and cultural achievements culminated in the construction of huge palace complexes at Knossos, Phaestos, Malia and Zakros, which were all levelled by an earthquake around 1700 BCE. Undeterred, the Minoans built bigger and better ones over the ruins, while settling more widely across Crete. Around 1450 BCE, the palaces were mysteriously destroyed again, possibly by a tsunami triggered by a volcanic eruption on Santorini (Thira). Knossos, the only palace saved, finally burned down around 1400 BCE.

Archaeological evidence shows that the Minoans lingered on for a few centuries in small, isolated settlements before disappearing as mysteriously as they had come. They were followed by the Mycenaeans and the Dorians (around 1100 BCE). By the 5th century BCE, Crete was divided into city-states but did not benefit from the cultural glories of mainland Greece; in fact, it was bypassed by Persian invaders and the Macedonian conqueror Alexander the Great.

By 67 BCE Crete had become the Roman province of Cyrenaica, with Gortyna its capital. After the Roman Empire's division in 395 CE, Crete fell under the jurisdiction of Greek-speaking Constantinople – the emerging Byzantine Empire. Things went more or less fine until 824, when Arabs appropriated the island. In 961, though, Byzantine general emperor Nikiforas Fokas (912–69) won Crete back following a nine-month siege of Iraklio (then called El Khandak by the Arabs). Crete flourished under Byzantine rule, but with the infamous Fourth Crusade of 1204 the maritime power of Venice received Crete as part of its 'payment' for supplying the Crusaders' fleet.

Much of Crete's most impressive surviving architecture dates from the Venetian period, which lasted until 1669 when Iraklio (then called Candia) became the last domino to fall after a 21-year Ottoman siege. Turkish rule brought new administrative organisation, Islamic culture and Muslim settlers. Cretan resistance was strongest in the mountain strongholds but all revolts were put down brutally, and it was only with the Ottoman Empire's disintegration in the late 19th century that Europe's great powers expedited Crete's sovereign aspirations.

Thus, in 1898, with Russian and French consent, Crete became a British protectorate. However, the banner under which future Greek Prime Minister Eleftherios Venizelos and other Cretan rebels were fighting was Enosis i Thanatos (Unity or Death) – unity with Greece, not mere independence from Turkey. Yet it would take the Greek army's successes in the Balkan Wars (1912–13) to turn Crete's de facto inclusion in the country into reality, with the 1913 Treaty of Bucharest.

Crete suffered tremendously during WWII, due to being coveted by Adolf Hitler for its strategic location. On 20 May 1941 a huge flock of German parachutists quickly overwhelmed the Cretan defenders. The Battle of Crete, as it would become known, raged for 10 days between German and Allied troops from Britain, Australia, New Zealand and Greece. For two days the battle hung in the balance until the Germans captured the Maleme Airfield, near Hania. The Allied forces fought a valiant rearguard action, enabling the British Navy to evacuate 18,000 of the 32,000 Allied troops. The harsh German occupation lasted throughout WWII, with many mountain villages bombed or burnt down and their occupants executed en masse.

IRAKLIO PROVINCE

Iraklio is Crete's most dynamic region, home to almost half the island's population and its top-rated tourist site, the Minoan Palace of Knossos. Priceless treasures unearthed here, and at the many other Minoan sites around Crete, have catapulted the archaeological museum in the capital city of Iraklio onto the world stage.

Admittedly, the coastal stretch east of Iraklio is one continuous band of hotels and resorts. But a few kilometres inland, villages sweetly lost in time provide pleasing contrast. Taste the increasingly sophisticated tipple produced in the Iraklio Wine Country, walk in the footsteps of painter El Greco and writer Nikos Kazantzakis, and revel in the rustic grandeur of remote mountain villages such as Zaros.

On the quieter southern coast, the ex-hippie hangout of Matala is the only developed resort, while in the charming villages the laid-back life unfolds much the way it has since time immemorial.

Iraklio   Ηράκλειο

POP 140.730

Crete's capital, Iraklio (also called Heraklion), is Greece's fifth-largest city and the island's economic and administrative hub. It's also home to Crete's blockbuster sights: the must-see Heraklion Archaeological Museum and the nearby Palace of Knossos, which both provide fascinating windows into Crete's ancient past.

Though not pretty in a conventional way, Iraklio definitely grows on you if you take the time to explore its layers and wander its backstreets. You'll discover a low-key urban sophistication with a thriving cafe and restaurant scene, good shopping and bustling nightlife. A revitalised waterfront invites strolling, and the pedestrianised historic centre is punctuated by bustling squares flanked by buildings from the time when Christopher Columbus first set sail.

◉ Sights

★ Heraklion Archaeological Museum   MUSEUM

(Map p460; www.heraklionmuseum.gr; Xanthoudidou 2; adult/concession/child €10/5/free, combined ticket with Palace of Knossos adult/concession €16/8; ⊘ 8am-8pm Mon & Wed-Sun, 10am-8pm Tue mid-Apr–Oct, 8am-4pm Nov–mid-Apr) This state-of-the-art museum is one of the largest and most important in Greece. The two-storey revamped 1930s Bauhaus building makes a gleaming showcase for artefacts spanning 5500 years from Neolithic to Roman times, including a Minoan collection of unparalleled richness. The rooms are colour coded and displays are arranged both chronologically and thematically, and presented with descriptions in English. You can follow the suggested route on p462. A visit here will greatly enhance your understanding of Crete's rich history. Don't skip it.

The museum's treasure trove includes pottery, jewellery and sarcophagi, plus famous frescoes from the sites of Knossos, Tylissos, Amnissos and Agia Triada. The pieces are grouped into comprehensive themes such as settlements, trade, death, religion and administration. Along with clear descriptions, these bring to life both the day-to-day functioning and the long-term progression of societies in Crete and beyond. Allow at least two hours for this extraordinary collection.

★ Koules Fortress   FORTRESS

(Rocca al Mare; Map p460; http://koules.efah.gr; Venetian Harbour; adult/concession €2/1; ⊘ 8am-8pm May-Sep, to 4pm Oct-Apr) After six years of restoration, Iraklio's symbol, the 16th-century fortress called Rocca al Mare by the Venetians, reopened in August 2016 with a brand-new exhibition. It tells the story of the building, zeroes in on milestones in city history, and displays ancient amphorae, Venetian cannons and other finds recovered from shipwrecks around Dia Island by Jacques Cousteau in 1976.

The presentation is insightful and atmospheric thanks to muted light filtering in through the old cannon holes. Visits conclude on the rooftop, with panoramic views over the sea and the city.

★ Historical Museum of Crete   MUSEUM

(Map p460; www.historical-museum.gr; Sofokli Venizelou 27; adult/concession €5/3; ⊘ 9am-5pm Mon-Sat, 10.30am-3pm Sun Apr-Oct, to 3.30pm daily Nov-Mar) If you're wondering what Crete's been up to for the past, say, 1700 years, a spin around this engagingly curated museum is in order. Exhibits hopscotch from the Byzantine to the Venetian and Turkish periods, culminating with WWII. Quality English labelling, interactive stations throughout and audio guides (€3) in five languages greatly enhance the experience.

The Venetian era receives special emphasis and there's even a huge model of the city c 1650 prior to the Turkish occupation. Start in the introductory room, which charts the major phases of history through maps, books, artefacts and images. First-floor highlights include the only two El Greco paintings in Crete (1569's *The Baptism of Christ* and 1570's *View of Mt Sinai and the Monastery of St Catherine*), 13th- and 14th-century frescoes, exquisite Venetian gold jewellery, and embroidered vestments. A historical exhibition charts Crete's road to independence from the Turks in the early 20th century. The most interesting rooms on the 2nd floor are the recreated study of Cretan-born author Nikos Kazantzakis and those dramatically detailing aspects of the WWII Battle of Crete in 1941, including the Cretan resistance and the role of the Allied Secret Service. The top floor features an outstanding folklore collection.

Monastery of St Peter & St Paul   RUINS

(Map p460; Sofokli Venizelou 19; admission by donation; ⊘ 10am-2.30pm May-Sep) One of Iraklio's most striking ruins, this 13th-century

Iraklio

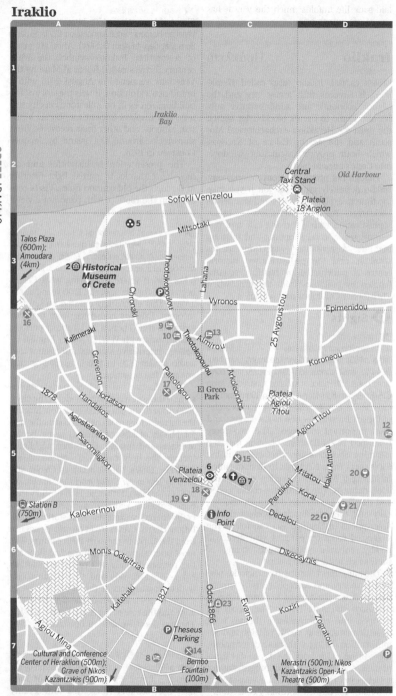

Iraklio Bay

Old Harbour

Central Taxi Stand

Plateia 18 Anglon

Sofokli Venizelou

Mitsotaki

5

Talos Plaza (600m); Amoudara (4km)

2 **Historical Museum of Crete**

Theotokopoulou

Lahana

Vyronos

Epimenidou

25 Avgoustou

Koroneou

16

Kalimeraki

Chronaki

9
10

Theotokopoulou

Almirou

13

Grevenon

Hortatson

Paleologou

17

El Greco Park

Arkoleondos

Plateia Agiou Titou

Agiou Titou

12

1878

Handakos

Agiostefaniton

Psaromiligkon

Milatou

20

Station B (750m)

Kalokerinou

Plateia Venizelou

6
4 **7**

15

18

19

Perdikari

Korai

Idaiou Antrou

Dedalou

22 **21**

i Info Point

Dikeosynis

Monis Odigitrias

Kafehaki

1821

Odos 1866

Evans

Koziri

Zografou

Agiou Mina

Cultural and Conference Center of Heraklion (500m); Grave of Nikos Kazantzakis (900m)

8

P Theseus Parking

14

Bembo Fountain (100m)

23

Merastri (500m); Nikos Kazantzakis Open-Air Theatre (500m)

Iraklio

Dominican monastery has been rebuilt and repackaged (mosque, movie theatre) numerous times throughout the centuries. Unusually located right on the sea wall, the monastery contains some beautiful 15th-century frescoes, as well as a modern mosaic exhibition by Loukas Peiniris that is well worth checking out.

Excavations in the surrounding area have uncovered graves dating to the 2nd Byzantine period. Monastery caretakers can be quite pushy for a donation.

Municipal Art Gallery   GALLERY
(Map p460; cnr 25 Avgoustou & Plateia Venizelou; ⊙9am-3pm) FREE The three-aisled 13th-century **Agios Markos Basilica** (Map p460; cnr 25 Avgoustou & Plateia Venizelou; ⊙9am-3pm) FREE was reconstructed many times and turned into a mosque by the Turks. Today it's an exhibit space showcasing the work of Greek and foreign artists.

Morosini Fountain
FOUNTAIN

(Lion Fountain; Map p460; Plateia Venizelou) Four water-spouting lions make up this charming fountain, the town's most beloved Venetian vestige. Built in 1628 by Francesco Morosini, it once supplied Iraklio with fresh water.

🏃 Activities

Dinosauria Park
AMUSEMENT PARK

(☑2810 332089; www.dinosauriapark.com; International Exhibit Centre, Gournes; adult/child €10/8; ⊙10am-6pm) Get in touch with your inner Tyrannosaurus rex at this fun and educational theme park. You enter a time tunnel (with explanations on the way) and exit into a Jurassic universe complete with moving, roaring, life-size animatronic beasts.

🛏 Sleeping

So Young Hostel
HOSTEL €

(Map p460; ☑6978871355; www.facebook.com/soyoungheraklion; Almirou 22; dm/d from €21/40; 🌼🛜) One of Iraklio's best central hostels, So Young, opened in 2018, earns high marks for its wonderful guest kitchen and even better rooftop terrace. Dorms come in both female and mixed varieties, with four-to-six- and eight-bed configurations, good mattresses and particle-board lockers. Interestingly, showers are co-ed.

Hotel Mirabello
HOTEL €

(Map p460; ☑2810 285052; www.mirabello-hotel.gr; Theotokopoulou 20; s/d from €40/50; 🌼@🛜) Despite its dated, plain-Jane looks, this friendly and low-key hotel offers excellent value for money. Assets include squeaky-clean rooms with modern bathrooms, beds with individual reading lamps, a fridge and a kettle, plus a location close to, well, everything. The nicest units have a balcony.

★ Crops Suites
APARTMENT €€

(Map p460; ☑6974320857; www.cropssuites.com; Thiseos 3; apt incl breakfast €65; 🌼🛜) Smack in the town centre, these stylish one-bedroom apartments will leave you feeling like a local hipster. Featuring canary-yellow cabinetry, plush grey sofas and light hardwoods throughout, they come with full kitchens stocked with coffee, olive oil, raki and more. Spacious balconies with city views are perfect for a glass of crisp white wine at sunset and/or a cuppa at daybreak.

★ Olive Green Hotel
HOTEL €€

(Map p460; ☑2810 302900; www.olivegreenhotel.com; cnr Idomeneos & Meramvellou; d incl breakfast €109-126; 🌼🛜) 🗘 This chic, contemporary

---

🏃 Museum Tour
Heraklion Archaeological Museum

DURATION: TWO HOURS

Start on the **ground floor**, where rooms I to III focus on the Neolithic period to the Middle Bronze Age (7000–1700 BCE), showing life in the first settlements in Crete and around Knossos. In room II, don't miss the pectoral **golden pendant with bees** from Malia, a sophisticated jeweller's masterpiece depicting two bees depositing a drop of honey into a honeycomb; the finial sceptre handle in the shape of panther; and the extensive jewellery collection. The undisputed standout in room III is the elaborately embellished **Kamares tableware** of red, black and white clay, including a 'royal dinner service' from Phaestos, but don't rush past the extraordinary painted faience miniature plaques showcasing elaborate architectural details and the wooden scale model of Phaestos.

Rooms IV to VI illustrate life in the Late Bronze Age (1700–1450 BCE). This is when Minoan culture reached its zenith, as reflected in the elaborate architecture, prolific trading practices and founding of new palaces. Not surprisingly, these are among the most visited rooms and the collection here is vast. Highlights include the **small clay house from Arhanes**, a stunning **ivory-and-crystal inlaid draughts board** and a scale model of Knossos. Most visitors home in on the **Phaistos disc**, a stunning clay piece embossed with 45 signs that has never been deciphered. Nearby, the massive **copper ingots** from Agia Triada and Zakros Palace demonstrate important units of economic exchange. Other gems include the **bull-leaping fresco** and the incredible **bull-leaper sculpture** (room VI) that show daring sporting practices of the time.

Rooms VII and VIII reveal the importance of Minoan religion and ideology, with cult objects and figurines. Don't miss the stone bull's head and the gorgeous limestone lioness vessels (said to be used for libations). Room VII houses the **chieftain's cup** from Agia Triada, which portrays two men, one holding a staff, the other a sword. In room VIII, the **snake goddesses** and **stone bull's head** (inlaid with seashell and crystal) are stunning ceremonial items from Knossos.

Ground Floor

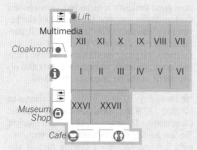

Lift

Multimedia

Cloakroom

| XII | XI | X | IX | VIII | VII |
| I | II | III | IV | V | VI |

XXVI | XXVII

Museum Shop

Cafe

First Floor

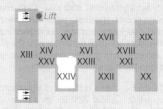

Lift

| XIII | XIV XXV | XV | XVI XXIII | XVII | XVIII XXI | XIX |
| | | XXIV | | XXII | | XX |

Rooms IX and X are dedicated to the palace of Knossos and its emergence as a centralised state (after the administrative collapse of other palaces) along with evidence of the Mycenaeans. **Linear B clay tablets** reveal the first 'Greek' script and indicate Knossos' complex administrative system and bureaucratic processes. In room X, look for the extraordinary **boar's-tusk helmet** (complete with cheek guards) and the **gold-handled swords**, displaying the importance of the aristocratic warrior status.

Rooms XI and XII highlight settlements, sanctuaries and graves of the Late Bronze Age, including fascinating visual representations of death. The extraordinary **sarcophagus** from Agia Triada (room XII) is presumed to be that of a ruler, given its detailed, honorific fresco-style scenes, including the sacrifice of a bull (you can just make out the horror in his eyes).

On the **1st floor**, room XIII showcases Minoan frescoes (1800–1350 BCE), including recreations by archaeologist **Sir Arthur Evans**, the British amateur journalist and adventurer who spent 30 years excavating the area around Knossos. The paintings, including the **Prince of the Lilies**, the **Ladies in Blue**, the **Cupbearer**, **La Parisienne** and the **Dolphin Fresco**, reflect the interest in art and nature at the time.

Rooms XV to XIX focus on the Geometric and Archaic periods (10th to 6th century BCE), the transition to the Iron Age and the formation of the first Greek cities. The **Apollonian Triad**, bronze statues from Deros, are the earliest known Greek hammered-bronze statues, while the **bronze shields of the Ideon Cave** are extravagant votive offerings to Zeus.

Rooms XX to XXII move to the Classical, Hellenistic and Roman periods (5th to 4th century BCE), where utensils, figurines and stunning mosaic floors and amphorae set the scene for the foundation of the autonomous Greek city-states, followed by civil wars and, finally, the Roman period. The huge **Phalagari hoard of silver coins** (room XXI) is thought to be a military or state fund. The cemetery finds of these periods are especially fascinating: look out for the bronze skull with the gilded clay wreath (room XXII).

Room XXIII exhibits two private collections donated to the museum.

Back on the **ground floor (part II)**, rooms XXVI and XXVII (7th to 4th century BCE) house the museum's sculpture collection. Architectural reliefs from Gortyna demonstrate the role of Crete in the development of monumental sculpture, while Roman sculptures and copies of heroes and gods of the preceding Classical era showcase art from the Roman period.

hotel is probably Iraklio's hippest digs. Clean rooms feature minimalistic white and olive-green decor, with separate shower and toilet (as opposed to the usual Greek-style all-in-one bathroom), and feature large, impressive photographs of tempting travel destinations within an hour of the city.

Guests are given a tablet to control electronic room features, and are welcomed with bread, olive-oil and raki. Club rooms are especially spacious, with espresso machines and larger terraces. Solar panels and low-impact building materials give the place an eco edge, and there's a cool cafe that spills out into the plaza.

★ **Lato Boutique Hotel** BOUTIQUE HOTEL **€€**
(Map p460; ✆2810 228103; www.lato.gr; Epimenidou 15; d incl breakfast from €80; ✱@🖅) Iraklio goes Hollywood – with all the sass but sans the attitude – at this mod boutique hotel overlooking the old harbour, recognisable by its jazzy facade. With 79 rooms, it's hardly boutique, but smallish rooms are styled with rich woods and warm reds and have pillow-top mattresses and a playful lighting scheme. A newer annexe across the street is even more modern.

Kastro Hotel HOTEL **€€**
(Map p460; ✆2810 284185; www.kastro-hotel.gr; Theotokopoulou 22; s/d/tr incl breakfast from €50/80/95; ✱🖅) Clearly, plenty of thought has gone into the design of the smartly renovated Kastro, with rooms accented in airy, seafaring colours like turquoise and aqua. Good-quality mattresses, strong hot showers, a good breakfast buffet and the rooftop terrace are all welcome aspects of this central city hotel.

✗ Eating

Phyllo Sophies CAFE **€**
(Map p460; www.phyllosophies.gr; Plateia Venizelou 33; mains €3.50-12.50; ☉6am-midnight; 🖅) With tables sprawling towards the Morosini Fountain, this is a great place to sample *bougatsa* (creamy semolina pudding wrapped in a pastry envelope and sprinkled with cinnamon and sugar). The less-sweet version is made with *myzithra* (sheep's-milk cheese).

Kritikos Fournos CAFE **€**
(Map p460; www.kritikosfournosgeuseis.gr; Plateia Kallergon 3; snacks €1-5; ☉6am-midnight; 🖅🖊) This fun cafe-bakery is a Cretan chain, and it's a dependable stop for good espresso (it opens at 6am!), baked goods, pastries and sandwiches (including tasty vegan focaccia

options) and even a craft beer or two. Perch yourself in a choice people-watching spot overlooking Lion Sq and banter with the hip, friendly staff. Signed in Greek only.

★ **Peskesi** CRETAN **€€**
(Map p460; ✆2810 288887; www.peskesicrete.gr; Kapetan Haralampi 6-8; mains €9-14; ☉1pm-2am; 🖅🖊) 🖉 It's almost impossible to overstate how good Peskesi's resurrected, slow-cooked Cretan dishes are, nor the beauty of the revamped Venetian villa in which you'll partake of them: this is Crete's finest culinary moment. Nearly everything is forged from heirloom produce and organic meats and olive oils from the restaurant's own farm.

★ **Merastri** CRETAN **€€**
(✆2810 221910; www.facebook.com/merastri; Chrisostomou 17; mains €5-13; ☉6pm-midnight Tue-Sun Jun-Aug, 6pm-midnight Tue-Sat, noon-midnight Sun Sep-May; 🖅) Enjoying one of the most authentic Cretan meals in town, served in this stunning home (a former music building), is a highlight of dining in Iraklio. The family of owners is passionate about its products (including oil and wine), and will conjure up everything from slow-cooked lamb to porterhouse steak with wine and sage.

★ **Parasties** GREEK **€€**
(Map p460; ✆2810 225009; www.parastiescrete.gr; Handakos 81; mains €9-43; ☉noon-1am; 🖅) Parasties' owner, Haris, is genuine about serving great-quality local produce and top Cretan wines. And his passion shows in his gourmet menu of inventively updated traditional fare, including a daily special. Grab a seat under an annexe with a bar, in the roomy dining area or on the side patio with sea views..

🍷 Drinking & Nightlife

★ **Xalavro** COCKTAIL BAR
(Map p460; www.facebook.com/xalavro; Milatou 10; ☉10am-3am; 🖅) This rather idyllic open-air bar gets a whole lot right, with charming servers slinging creative cocktails to a diverse crowd of holidaymakers and locals in the ruins of an archaeologically protected roofless stone house. It exudes *Ef Zin* – the Greek art of living well.

★ **Solo Brewery** MICROBREWERY
(www.solobeer.gr; Kointoirioti 35; ☉noon-5pm; 🖅) Norwegian brewer Kjetil Jikiun started Norway's first craft brewery (Nøgne Ø) before he founded Crete's first craft brewery (he's clearly a man of firsts). There's no taproom

per se, but drinking here is a worthwhile excursion for beer connoisseurs. A wealth of IPAs, stouts and porters, and hoppy saisons across five taps and numerous bottles await for makeshift front-patio consumption.

Bitters Bar
COCKTAIL BAR

(Map p460; www.thebittersbar.com; Plateia Venizelou; ☺8pm-3am Mon-Thu, to 5am Fri-Sun; 🖥) The indisputable frontrunner of Iraklio's mixology scene is this den of Prohibition-inspired decadence centred on a retail alcove just off Lion Sq. Throwback cocktails dominate the classics on the list, but let the bartenders shine with creations such as Bitters House (gin, ginger syrup, pink-grapefruit and lemon juice, cardamom bitters) and Attaboy (vodka, mango puree, lemon juice, aromatic bitters).

Crop
CRAFT BEER

(Map p460; www.crop.coffee; Aretousas 4; ☺7am-1am; 🖥) Crop divides its focus equally between two vices: caffeine and craft beer. At the time of writing it was Iraklio's only craft-focused bar, with five independent taps (including Crete's own Solo Brewing and Brewdog, and 25 or so bottled; beers cost €4 to €6). It's also a highly recommended roastery specialising in Third Wave coffee preparations such as V60 and Chemex.

☆ Entertainment

Cultural and Conference Center of Heraklion
ARTS CENTRE

(☎2810 229618; Plastira 10) This modern five-building complex, opened in 2019, is Crete's most important cultural and events venue. It includes the gorgeous 800-seat Andreas and Maria Kalokairinou Hall, designed for theatre, opera and classical music.

🛍 Shopping

★Zalo
GIFTS & SOUVENIRS

(Map p460; www.zalo.gr; Papa Aleksandrou 2; ☺9am-9pm Mon-Sat, to 4pm Sun) This recommended shop specialises in the kinds of souvenirs that won't embarrass you a year down the track: designer art prints, jewellery, notebooks, frameable postcards, funky handbags and the like, all 100% made in Greece from a network of cutting-edge, contemporary artists and designers.

Aerakis Music
MUSIC

(Map p460; ☎2810 225758; www.aerakis.net; Korai 14; ☺9am-9pm Mon-Fri, to 5pm Sat) An Iraklio landmark since 1974, this little shop stocks an expertly curated selection of Cretan and Greek music, from old and rare recordings to the latest releases, many on its own record labels, Cretan Musical Workshop and Seistron.

Iraklio Central Market
MARKET

(Map p460; Odus 1866; ☺hours vary) An Iraklio institution, if slightly touristy these days, this busy, narrow *agora* (market), along Odos 1866 between the Meidani crossroads and Plateia Kornarou, is one of the best in Crete and has everything you need to put together a delicious picnic.

ℹ Information

Info Point (Map p460; ☎28134 09777; www.heraklion.gr; Plateia Venizelou; ☺8.30am-2.30pm Mon-Fri) The municipality's official tourist-info point.

Tourist Police (☎2810 283551, emergency 171; Dikeosynis 10; ☺7am-10pm) In the suburb of Halikarnassos, near the airport.

University Hospital of Heraklion (☎28103 92111; www.pagni.gr; Stavrakia; ☺24hr) In the area of Stavrakia, some 8km south of central Iraklio, this is one of Greece's largest public hospitals and is affiliated with the adjacent school of medicine.

ℹ Getting There & Away

AIR

Nikos Kazantzakis Heraklion International Airport (HER; ☎2810 397800; www.ypa.gr/en/our-airports/kratikos-aerolimenas-hrakleioyn-kazantzakhs) About 5km east of the city centre, the airport has a bank, ATMs, duty-free shops and cafe-bars.

BOAT

The **ferry port** (☎2810 338000; www.portheraklion.gr) is 500m east of Koules Fortress and the old harbour. Iraklio is a major port for access to many of the Greek islands, though services are spotty outside high season. Tickets can be purchased online or through travel agencies, including central **Paleologos** (☎2810 346185; www.paleologos.gr; 25 Avgoustou 5; ☺9am-8pm Mon-Fri, to 3pm Sat). Daily ferries from Iraklio's port include services to Piraeus and faster catamarans to Santorini and other Cycladic islands. Ferries sail east to Rhodes via Sitia, Kasos, Karpathos and Halki

BUS

KTEL Heraklion Lassithi Bus Station (☎28102 46530; www.ktelherlas.gr; Leoforos Ikarou 9; 🖥) Near the waterfront east of Koules Fortress, this depot serves major destinations in eastern and western Crete, including Hania, Rethymno, Agios Nikolaos, Sitia and the Lassithi Plateau. Buses to Knossos leave from the adjacent local bus station.

Bus Station B (Chanioporta Station; ☑ 28102 55965; Machis Kritis 3; ☎) Just beyond Hania Gate, west of the centre, this station serves the traditional village of Anogia. There's a ticket office inside Restaurant Chanioporta across the street.

Buses to Knossos (Map p460; Plateia Eleftherias) Handy stop for bus 2 to Knossos.

LONG-DISTANCE TAXI

For destinations around Crete, you can order a cab from **Crete Taxi Services** (☑ 6970021970; www.crete-taxi.gr; ☺ 24hr) or **Crete Cab** (☑ 6955171473; www.crete.cab). There are also long-distance cabs waiting at the airport, at Plateia Eleftherias (outside the Capsis Astoria hotel) and at KTEL Heraklion Lassithi Bus Station. Sample fares for up to four people include Agios Nikolaos €84, Hersonisos €40, Malia €50, Matala €86 and Rethymno €101.

ⓘ Getting Around

TO/FROM THE AIRPORT

Bus 1 to Airport (Map p460; Plateia Eleftherias) Central stop for bus 1, linking the city with the airport.

CAR & MOTORCYCLE

Iraklio's streets are narrow and chaotic, so it's best to drop your vehicle in a car park (between €5 and €12 per day), and explore on foot; though not the cheapest option, it doesn't get much more central than **Theseus Parking** (www. facebook.com/theseusparking; Thiseos 18; 1st hour €4.80, per additional hour €.80, overnight €12). All the international car-hire companies have branches at the airport. Local outlets line the northern end of 25 Avgoustou and include **Caravel** (☑ 28103 00150; www.caravel.gr; 25 Avgoustou 39; ☺ 8am-11pm), **Hertz** (☑ 28103 00744; www.hertz.gr; 25 Avgoustou 17; ☺ 7am-9pm), **Motor Club** (☑ 28102 22408; www. motorclub.gr; Plateia 18 Anglon 1; car per day/ week incl insurance from €35/180, scooter from €25/100; ☺ 8am-10pm), **Loggetta Cars** (☑ 28102 89462; www.loggetta.gr; 25 Avgoustou 20; ☺ 9am-1.30pm & 4.30-8.30pm) and **Sun Rise** (☑ 28102 21609; www.sunrise-cars.com; 25 Avgoustou 46; ☺ 8am-9pm May-Oct, 8am-2pm & 5-9pm Mon-Sat Nov-Apr).

TAXI

There are small taxi stands all over town, but the main ones are at the Regional Bus Station, on **Plateia Eleftherias** (Map p460) and at the northern end of **25 Avgoustou** (Map p460; Venizelou). You can also phone for one on ☑ 28140 03084.

Useful taxi apps include Aegean Taxi (www. aegeantaxi.com).

Knossos   Κνωσσός

★**Palace of Knossos**   ARCHAEOLOGICAL SITE
(http://odysseus.culture.gr; Knossos; adult/concession €15/8, incl Heraklion Archaeological Museum €16/8; ☺ 8am-8pm Apr-Sep, to 7pm Oct, to 3pm Nov-Mar; 🅿; 🚌 2) Crete's most famous historical attraction is the Palace of Knossos, the grand capital of Minoan Crete, located 5km south of Iraklio. The setting is evocative and the ruins and recreations impressive, incorporating an immense palace, courtyards, private apartments, baths, lively frescoes and more. Excavation of the site started in 1878 with Cretan archaeologist Minos Kalokerinos, and continued from 1900 to 1930 with British archaeologist Sir Arthur Evans, who controversially restored parts of the site.

Evans' reconstructions bring to life the palace's most significant parts, including the columns, which are painted deep brown-red with gold-trimmed black capitals and taper gracefully at the bottom. Vibrant frescoes add dramatic flourishes. The advanced drainage system and a clever floor plan that kept rooms cool in summer and warm in winter are further evidence of Minoan society's sophistication.

There is no prescribed route for exploring the palace, but the following one takes in all the highlights. Entering from the West Court, which may have been a marketplace or the site of public gatherings, you'll note a trio of circular pits on your left. Called *kouloures*, they were used for grain storage. From here, continue counterclockwise, starting with a walk along the Processional Walkway that leads to the South Propylaion, where you can admire the Cup Bearer Fresco. From here, a staircase leads past giant storage jars to an upper floor that Evans called the Piano Nobile because it reminded him of Italian Renaissance palazzi and where he supposed the reception and staterooms were located. On your left, you can see the west magazines (storage rooms), where giant *pithoi* (clay jars) once held oil, wine and other staples.

The restored room at the northern end of the Piano Nobile houses the Fresco Gallery, with replicas of Knossos' most famous frescoes, including the *Bull Leaper*, the *Ladies in Blue* and the *Blue Bird*. The originals are now in the Heraklion Archaeological Museum (p459). From the balcony, a great view unfolds of the Central Court,

467

Palace of Knossos

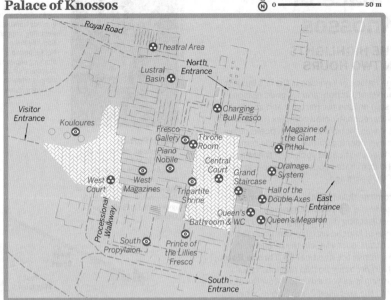

N   0 ——————— 50 m

Royal Road

Theatral Area

North Entrance

Lustral Basin

Visitor Entrance

Kouloures

Charging Bull Fresco

Fresco Gallery

Throne Room

Magazine of the Giant Pithoi

Piano Nobile

Central Court

Drainage System

West Court

West Magazines

Tripartite Shrine

Grand Staircase

Hall of the Double Axes

East Entrance

Processional Walkway

Queen's Bathroom & WC

Queen's Megaron

South Propylaion

Prince of the Lillies Fresco

South Entrance

CRETE KNOSSOS

which was hemmed in by high walls during Minoan times. Rooms facing the western side of the courtyard had official and religious purposes, while the residential quarters were on the opposite side.

Follow the stairs down to the courtyard and then turn left to peek inside the beautifully proportioned Throne Room, with its simple alabaster seat and walls decorated with frescoes of griffins (mythical beasts regarded by the Minoans as sacred). To the right of the stairs is a three-sectioned room that Evans called the Tripartite Shrine. Areas behind it yielded many precious finds, including the famous *Snake Goddess* statue.

Crossing the Central Court takes you to the east wing, where the Grand Staircase drops down to the royal apartments. Get there via the ramp off the southeastern corner, but not without first popping by the south entrance to admire a replica of the Prince of the Lilies fresco. Down below you can peek inside the queen's megaron (bedroom), with a copy of the *Dolphin* fresco, one of the most exquisite Minoan artworks. The small adjacent chamber (behind plexiglass) may have been the queen's bathroom, with some sort of toilet. Continue to the king's quarters in the Hall of the Double Axes; the latter takes its name from

the double axe marks *(labrys)* on its light well, a sacred symbol to the Minoans and the origin of the word 'labyrinth'.

Beyond, you can admire the Minoans' surprisingly sophisticated water and drainage system, pop by a stonemason's workshop and check out more giant storage jars before jogging around to the palace's north side for a good view of the partly reconstructed north entrance, easily recognised by the Charging Bull fresco. Walking towards the exit, you pass the theatral area, a series of shallow steps whose function remains unknown. It could have been a theatre where spectators watched acrobatic and dance performances, or the place where people gathered to welcome important visitors arriving by the Royal Road, which leads off to the west and was flanked by workshops and the houses of ordinary people.

Unlike at other ruins around Iraklio, visitors make their way through the site on platform walkways, which can get very crowded. This makes it all the more important to time your visit for outside the tourbus onslaught. Avoid ticket lines by buying in advance through the Archaeological Resources Fund e-Ticketing System (www. etickets.tap.gr).

Palace of Knossos

THE HIGHLIGHTS IN TWO HOURS

The Palace of Knossos is Crete's busiest tourist attraction, and for good reason. A spin around the partially and imaginatively reconstructed complex (shown here as it was thought to be at its peak) delivers an eye-opening glimpse into the remarkably sophisticated society of the Minoans, who dominated southern Europe some 4000 years ago.

From the ticket booth, follow the marked trail to the ❶ **North Entrance** where the Charging Bull fresco gives you a first taste of Minoan artistry. Continue to the Central Court and join the queue waiting to glimpse the mystical ❷ **Throne Room**, which probably hosted religious rituals. Turn right as you exit and follow the stairs up to the so-called Piano Nobile, where replicas of the palace's most famous artworks conveniently cluster in the ❸ **Fresco Room**. Walk the length of the Piano Nobile, pausing to look at the clay storage vessels in the West Magazine. Circle back and descend to the ❹ **South Portico**, beautifully decorated with the Cup Bearer fresco. Make your way back to the Central Court and head to the palace's eastern wing to admire the architecture of the ❺ **Grand Staircase** that led to what Sir Arthur Evans imagined to be the royal family's private quarters. For a closer look at some rooms, walk to the south end of the courtyard, stopping for a peek at the ❻ **Prince of the Lilies Fresco**, and head down to the lower floor. A highlight here is the ❼ **Queen's Megaron** (Evans imagined this was the Queen's chambers), playfully adorned with a fresco of frolicking dolphins. Stay on the lower level and make your way to the ❽ **Giant Pithoi**, huge clay jars used for storage.

PLANNING

To beat the crowds and avoid the heat, arrive bang on opening or two hours before closing. Budget one or two hours to explore the site thoroughly.

Fresco Room
Take in sweeping views of the palace grounds from the west wing's upper floor, the Piano Nobile, before studying copies of the palace's most famous artworks in its Fresco Room.

South Portico
Fine frescoes, most famously the Cup Bearer, embellish this palace entrance anchored by a massive open staircase leading to the Piano Nobile. The Horns of Consecration recreated nearby once topped the entire south facade.

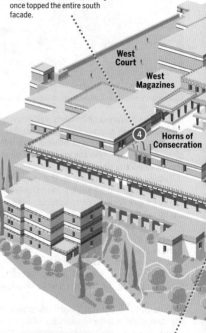

West Court

West Magazines

❹ Horns of Consecration

Prince of the Lilies Fresco
One of Knossos' most beloved frescoes was controversially cobbled together from various fragments and shows a young man adorned in lilies and peacock feathers.

Throne Room

Sir Arthur Evans, who began excavating the Palace of Knossos in 1900, imagined the mythical King Minos himself holding court seated on the alabaster throne of this beautifully proportioned room. However, the lustral basin and griffin frescoes suggest a religious purpose, possibly under a priestess.

North Entrance

Bulls held a special status in Minoan society, as evidenced by the famous relief fresco of a charging beast gracing the columned west bastion of the north palace, which harboured workshops and storage rooms.

Grand Staircase

The royal apartments in the eastern wing were accessed via this monumental staircase sporting four flights of gypsum steps supported by columns. The lower two flights are original. It's closed to the public.

Piano Nobile

③ ①

② ⑤

Central Court

Royal Apartments

⑧

⑥

⑦

Giant Pithoi

These massive clay jars are rare remnants from the Old Palace period and were used to store wine, oil and grain. The jars were transported by slinging ropes through a series of handles.

Queen's Megaron

The queen's room is among the prettiest in the residential eastern wing thanks to the playful Dolphin Fresco. The adjacent bathroom (with clay tub) and toilet are evidence of a sophisticated drainage system.

Iraklio Wine Country

Winemaking in the Iraklio Wine Country dates back to Minoan times, some 4000 years ago, as evidenced by the oldest stomping vat in the world, found at the ruins of Vathypetro. Unfortunately, today's vineyards are a lot younger, as a mighty bout of phylloxera (plant louse) in the 1970s nearly wiped out everything. But Cretan wine rebounded and today about 70% of the wine produced on the island comes from this region. Almost two dozen wineries are embedded in a harmonious landscape of round-shouldered hills, sunbaked slopes and lush valleys. Winemakers cultivate many indigenous, nearly extinct Cretan grape varietals – be sure to introduce your nose and taste buds to Kotsifali, Mandilari, Malvasia and Liatiko, among others – while many estates offer tours, wine museums and wine tastings.

Activities

★ Diamantakis Winery   WINE

(☏ 6949198350; www.diamantakiswines.gr; Kato Asites; tastings €3-5; ⊗ by appointment 9am-4pm Mon-Fri) This winery's Petali Liatiko red has a great story: it was produced as a table wine, but then experts tasted it and said, 'Whoa! Bottle this right now!' Diamantakis is one of a mere handful who make a Liatiko today, and tasting it on the extraordinary property between olive trees (there's no tasting room), surrounded by vineyards, is a remarkable experience.

★ Lyrarakis   WINE

(☏ 6981050681; www.lyrarakis.gr; Alagni; tastings €10-60; ⊗ 11am-7pm Mon-Sat Apr-Oct, by appointment rest of year) One of Crete's most visitor-friendly wineries, Lyrarakis should be your go-to if you must pick only one. It rakes in awards and is known for reviving three nearly extinct white varietals (Dafni, Plyto and Melissaki). It was also the first to

---

BEYOND KNOSSOS: CRETE'S BEST ANCIENT SITES

Phaestos (http://odysseus.culture.gr; Iraklio-Phaestos Rd; adult/concession €8/4; ⊗ 8am-8pm May-Aug, shorter hours rest of year; P) Phaestos was the second-most-important Minoan palace-city after Knossos and enjoys an awe-inspiring setting with panoramic views of the Messara Plain and Mt Psiloritis. It was built around 1700 BCE atop an older, previously destroyed palace, and laid out around a central court. In contrast to Knossos, it had fewer frescoes, as its walls were likely covered with white gypsum. Phaestos was defeated by Gortyna in the 2nd century BCE. Good English panelling and graphics stationed in key spots help demystify the ruins.

Palace of Malia (adult/concession/child €6/3/free; ⊗ 8am-8pm Tue-Sun May-Nov, to 3pm Tue-Sun Dec-Apr) The Palace of Malia, 3km east of Malia, was built at about the same time as the great Minoan palaces of Phaestos and Knossos. The First Palace dates back to around 1900 BCE and was rebuilt after the earthquake of 1700 BCE, only to be levelled again by another tremor around 1450 BCE. Most of what you see today are the remains of the Second Palace, where many exquisite Minoan artefacts, including the famous **gold bee pendant**, were found.

Gortyna (Γόρτυνα; Iraklio-Phaestos Rd; adult/concession €6/3; ⊗ 8am-8pm Apr-Oct, to 4pm Nov-Mar) Gortyna (also Gortyn or Gortys) has been inhabited since Neolithic times but reached its pinnacle after becoming the capital of Roman Crete from around 67 BCE until the Saracens raided the island in 824 CE. At its peak, as many as 100,000 people may have milled around Gortyna's streets.

There are two sections, bisected by the highway. Most people only stop long enough to investigate the fenced area on the north side of the road past the entrance. However, several more important temples, baths and other buildings are scattered south of the road.

Agia Triada (adult/concession €4/2; ⊗ 8.30am-4pm; P) In an enchanting spot 3km west of Phaestos, Agia Triada encompasses vestiges of an L-shaped royal villa, a ramp once leading out to sea, and a village with residences and stores. Built around 1550 BCE, Agia Triada succumbed to fire around 1400 BCE but was never looted. This accounts for the many Minoan masterpieces found here, most famously the Agia Triada Sarcophagus, now a star exhibit at the Heraklion Archaeological Museum (p459).

produce a single-vineyard Mandilari red (a move ridiculed as 'absurd' – but it went on to become one of its bestsellers).

Digenakis Winery WINE

(☑ 28103 22846; www.digenakis.gr; Katakouzinon 7, Kaloni; tastings €7; ⊙ by appointment 10am-5pm) Opened in 2017, this modern winery marches to a different drum, both in its design and in its winemaking. The striking edifice features poured concrete and glass, offset by colourful tapestry art. Its 2017 single-vineyard Kotsifali was produced from the fruit of 35-year-old vines – some of the few to escape the 1970s phylloxera outbreak that devastated Crete's vineyards.

Idaia Winery WINE

(☑ 2810 792156; www.idaiawine.gr; Kiparissou 90, Venerato; tasting €5; ⊙ 11am-4pm Mon-Fri, to 2pm Sat) This tiny boutique winery is hyper-focused on local varietals. Be on the lookout for its Ocean Thrapsathiri white (one of the island's best for pairing with seafood), its barrel-matured Liatiko and its sun-dried Liatiko dessert wine. The modern tasting room is small but one of the nicest.

👉 Tours

Made in Crete WINE

(☑ 6975626830; www.tours.madeincrete.com; €100) This Belgian-run agency leads the most highly recommended wine-tasting tours around Iraklio Wine Country. Tours take in two wineries as well as lunch at Bakaliko (www.bakalikocrete.com; Plateia Eleftheriou Venizelou, Arhanes; mains €7.50-9.50; ⊙ 10am-11pm Apr-Oct, 5-10pm Fri, 10am-10pm Sat & Sun Nov-Mar; 🛜) 🅿 in Arhanes. The price includes transport, tastings (olive oil in addition to wine) and lunch paired with four wines. Pierre, a former journalist and chef, leads tours in French or English.

ℹ Information

Check Wines of Crete (www.winesofcrete.gr) for tourist info. Look for the burgundy-red road signs directing you to local wineries.

ℹ Getting There & Away

The majority of wineries are within 20km of Iraklio, beginning just south of Knossos (the industry is headquartered in Peza). Besides an organised tours, having your own wheels is definitely a necessity to fully partake in a proper day of wine tasting: the wineries are spread out and not otherwise served directly by any public transport.

NIKOS KAZANTZAKIS MUSEUM

The Nikos Kazantzakis Museum (☑ 28107 41689; www.kazantzaki.gr; Myrtia; adult/concessions €5/3; ⊙ 9am-5pm daily Apr-Oct, 10am-3pm Mon-Fri & Sun Nov-Mar) is a housed in a modern building overlooking the *kafeneia*-flanked central plaza of author Nikos Kazantzakis' ancestral village, this well-curated museum zeroes in on the life, philosophy and accomplishments of Crete's most famous writer.

Watch a short documentary, then use one of the wireless audio guides (€1) to add more meaning to the exhibits, which include movie posters, letters, photographs and various personal effects.

Upstairs rooms present an overview of Kazantzakis' best-known works, including, of course, *Zorba the Greek*.

Don't miss the interesting 20-minute video (in 10 languages); ask staff to turn it on if it's not playing.

Myrtia is some 15km southeast of Iraklio.

Zaros Ζαρός

POP 2120

At the foot of Mt Psiloritis, Zaros is famous for its natural spring water, which is bottled here and sold all over Crete. But Zaros also has some fine Byzantine monasteries, excellent walking and delicious farm-raised trout, served up in tavernas around town and on emerald-green Lake Votomos (actually a reservoir). The lake is also the kick-off point for the 5km trail through the mighty Rouvas Gorge, a major lure for hikers and birders.

Part of the E4 European Path, the Rouvas Gorge hike leads to a protected swathe of forest, home to some of the oldest oak trees in Crete. It's an especially lovely walk in springtime, when hooded helleborine orchids, poppies, irises and other wildflowers give the landscape the vibrancy of an impressionist painting, but is recommended any time from April to November. It's a 10km up-and-back trek from the main trailhead at Lake Votomos north of Zaros village. The trail is mostly signed in Greek (and mostly referring to churches), but small red and white circles painted onto the rocks and trees lead the way.

🛏 Sleeping & Eating

Studios Keramos PENSION €

(☎28940 31352; www.studiokeramos-zaros.gr; s/d/tr incl breakfast €35/50/65; ❄ 🛜) Close to the village centre, this old-style pension is run by the friendly Katerina and is decorated with Cretan crafts, weaving and family heirlooms. Many of the rooms and studios pair antique beds and furniture with TV and kitchenette (the more modern four-room annexe is fine but lacks character). Katerina is up early preparing an absolutely fantastic traditional breakfast.

★ Vegera CRETAN €

(www.vegerazaros.gr; all-you-can-eat buffet €12; ⊙11am-11pm Apr–mid-Nov; 🛜🍴) The vivacious Vivi has a knack for turning farm-fresh local produce into flavourful and creative dishes based on traditional recipes. Her philosophy is to 'cook the way we cook in our house' and indeed her cute place quickly feels like home. Allow ample time to savour the generous buffet of salads, cheese and olives, cooked mains, pastries and freshly baked bread.

With advance booking, you can also take a cooking class or visit the family farm.

ℹ Getting There & Away

Zaros is about 46km southwest of Iraklio. The most scenic approach is by turning west off the main road at Agia Varvara. There's also a smaller road heading north from Kapariana just east of Mires (turn north at the small road between a bakery and Kafeneio i Zariani Strofi; look for the little sign). One daily bus heading from Iraklio's KTEL Heraklion Lassithi Bus Station to Kamares passes through Zaros (€5.20, one hour, 1.30pm). Alternatively, take one of the more frequent buses to Mires (€6, 75 minutes) and cab it to Zaros from there (around €16).

Matala Μάταλα

POP 70

In mythology, Matala is the place where Zeus swam ashore with the kidnapped Europa on his back before dragging her off to Gortyna and getting her pregnant with the future King Minos. The Minoans used Matala as their harbour for Phaestos and under the Romans it became the port for Gortyna (p470).

In more recent times, Matala became legendary thanks to the scores of hippies flocking here in the late 1960s to take up rent-free residence in cliffside caves once used as tombs by the Romans. Joni Mitchell immortalised the era in her 1971 song 'Carey'.

On summer days the village feels anything but peaceful, thanks to coachloads of day trippers. Stay overnight or visit in the low season, though, and it's still possible to discern the Matala magic: the setting along a crescent-shaped bay flanked by headlands is simply spectacular, especially at sunset.

◉ Sights

Matala Caves CAVE

(Roman Cemetery; €2; ⊙10am-7pm Mar-Oct, 8am-3pm Nov-Apr) Matala's sightseeing credentials are limited to these famous caves where hippies camped out in the 1960s and 1970s. Hewn into the porous sandstone cliffs in prehistoric times, they were actually used as tombs by the Romans.

🛏 Sleeping & Eating

Hotel Fantastic Matala HOTEL €

(☎28920 45262; www.fantastic-matala.com; s/d/tr €45/50/60; 🅿❄🛜) Quirky host Natasa (and father) woos guests with her mystical Matala magic at this budget-friendly hotel, be it via motherly doting, morning *tiropites* (cheese pies) or Greek coffee. Whatever the method, you'll feel like one of the family. Rooms, across two traditional, partly stone buildings, are smallish, with frustrating showers (those pesky curtains!), but the hospitality trumps the grumps.

Hotel Nikos HOTEL €€

(www.matala-nikos.com; s/d/q €55/65/110; 🅿❄🛜) A standout on hotel row, family-run Nikos has 17 modernised rooms, many with small kitchens, a terrace and snazzy bathrooms, on two floors flanking a flower-filled courtyard. The nicest is the top-floor room 24, with cave views. Breakfast is €7.50.

★ George's Yard GREEK €€

(☎69488 78600; mains €7.50-24.50; ⊙5-11.30pm May-Oct; 🛜) George (Giorgos) was the lone local who dug in with the invading hippies in the 1970s, coining Matala's motto: 'Today is life. Tomorrow never comes.' George is no longer with us, but his home is occupied by Greek-German couple Manolis and Yvonne, who along with their Athenian chef are aces of hospitality at Matala's best restaurant. Service and culinary creativity are next level.

★ Scala Fish Tavern SEAFOOD €€

(☎69813 88135; mains €7-19; ⊙10am-11pm Apr-Oct; 🛜) Past all the bars at the easternmost end of the beach, this dramatically perched, multitiered pit stop is Matala's best seafood restaurant. It's been in the family for over

30 years, so it's doing something right. Top marks for its fresh fish, superior service and fabulous desserts – try the *tzizkeik* (cheesecake). The cave views are especially nice at sunset. Reservations recommended.

ℹ Getting There & Away

Two KTEL buses daily leave Iraklio's KTEL Heraklion Lassithi Bus Station for Matala (€8.50, two hours, 7.30am and 12.45pm). Buses to Iraklio from Matala leave from a **stop** 800m east of the main village.

There's free roadside parking and a beach car park that charges €2.

Hersonisos   Χερσόνησος

POP 26,700

Hersonisos, about 25km east of Iraklio, has grown from a small fishing village into one of Crete's largest and busiest tourist towns and is deluged in summer. The main thoroughfare is lined with sprawling hotels, apartment buildings and a cacophonous strip of bars, cafes, tourist shops, clubs, fast-food eateries, travel agencies and quad-hire places. Its most decent stretch of sand is the quaint Sarandaris Beach.

To escape the bustle, base yourself uphill in one of three adjoining villages: Koutouloufari, Piskopiano or Old Hersonisos. Although touristy, these are nonetheless appealing and have some excellent tavernas and accommodation options.

◉ Sights & Activities

★**Lychnostatis Open Air Museum**   MUSEUM
(www.lychnostatis.gr; adult/child €6/2; ⊙9am-2pm Sun-Fri Apr-Oct) In a lovely seaside setting at Hersonisos' eastern edge, this family-operated, open-air folklore museum recreates a traditional Cretan village with commendable authenticity. The various buildings, including windmill, schoolhouse and farmer's home, were rescued around Crete and moved here. Elsewhere there are weaving workshops, ceramics and plant-dying demonstrations, olive-oil pressing and raki distilling, orchards and herb gardens, and a theatre that hosts music and dance performances.

Acqua Plus   WATER PARK
(☑28970 24950; www.acquaplus.gr; Hersonisos-Kastelli Rd; adult/child €27/17; ⊙10am-6pm May, Jun, Sep & Oct, to 7pm Jul & Aug; ⊕) Greece's oldest water park is showing its age despite an expansion and upgrade but is still good for a few hours of fun. It's divided into an adult

section, where wicked slides with names like Tsunami and Kamikaze should give adrenaline junkies a kick, and another for kids, with pools, playgrounds, an inflatable castle and gentler thrills like the 270m-long Lazy River.

🛏 Sleeping & Eating

Skip the identikit tourist tavernas in Hersonisos proper and opt for a more authentic culinary experience uphill in Koutouloufari and Piskopiano. A table full of traditional mezedhes is what's for dinner.

Balsamico Suites   APARTMENT €€
(☑28970 23323; www.balsamico-suites.gr; Old Hersonisos; ste incl breakfast from €89; P❄🖥🛜⛱) This stone complex fuses old-world charm with such mod cons as smart TVs and hairdryers. Seventeen well-proportioned suites are decked out in rich, dark wood and come with balconies.

★**Villa Ippocampi**   APARTMENT €€€
(☑28970 22316; www.ippocampi.com; 4g Seferi, Koutouloufari; apt €150-190; P❄🖥🛜⛱) This relaxing Dutch-Greek retreat exudes style and will mesmerise you from the moment you step past its lavender bushes and pool. Once you're ensconced in your apartment (all are decorated in a strong blue-and-white theme), it'll be hard to go past two choices – laze by the pool or chat to the charming owners, Lydia and Nikos.

★**David Vegera**   CRETAN €
(Piskopiano; mezedhes €4.50-10; ⊙5pm-midnight Mon-Sat; 🛜) A fabulous spot housed in a former *kafeneio* (coffee house), this place has a buzzy vibe due to the scores of Greeks and tourists who descend on it from opening time. David Vegera started this gig in 1954, and his great-grandson helps run the show today. It serves old-time mezedhes, efficiently and without fuss.

Saradari   SEAFOOD €€€
(☑28970 25375; www.saradari.com; Anissaras; mains €11-20, fish per kg €50-70; ⊙10am-midnight; 🛜) Set on the upper slopes at the eastern end of Hersonisos, Saradari has a lot going for it: top-quality cuisine, posh factor and lovely ocean view. Write off the afternoon and settle in among the beautiful people.

ℹ Getting There & Away

Buses from KTEL Heraklion Lassithi Bus Station (p465) run at least every 30 minutes to Hersonisos (€3.30, 40 minutes). Heading back, catch buses at **stop 19 (west)** (Palio EO Iraklio-Agios

Nikolaos) heading west along the main road. Buses heading east to Malia and Agios Nikolas stop at **stop 19 (east)** (Palio EO Iraklio-Agios Nikolaos) on the opposite side of the road.

There's a **taxi stand** on Sanoudaki just off the main drag. Parking uphill in Old Hersonisos, Koutouloufari and Piskopiano is mayhem, but there's a free **car park** just behind the main thoroughfare in Hersonisos proper.

RETHYMNO PROVINCE

Wild beauty Rethymno is peppered with historic sites and natural wonders. Ribbons of mountain road wind through the timeless interior, passing fields of wildflowers and traditional hamlets cradled by olive groves. Descend into the spooky darkness of grotto-like caves; explore steep, lush gorges; and rest in the shade of lofty Mt Psiloritis, Crete's highest peak. Visit enduring monasteries, Minoan tombs and Venetian strongholds. Rethymno is also a magnet for artists, while practising age-old trades with modern twists.

The eponymous capital on the northern coast is a bustle of atmosphere-soaked cobbled lanes, laden with shops, restaurants and bars and flanked by a wide, sandy beach. The southern coast is graced with bewitching beaches in seductive isolation. Weave your way through this spellbinding land from shore to shore.

Rethymno   Ρέθυμνο

POP 35,000

Basking between the commanding bastions of its 15th-century fortress and the glittering azure waters of the Mediterranean, Rethymno is one of Crete's most enchanting settlements. Its Venetian-Ottoman quarter is a lyrical maze of lanes draped in floral canopies and punctuated with graceful wood-balconied houses, ornate monuments and the occasional minaret.

Crete's third-largest centre has lively nightlife thanks to its sizable student population, some excellent restaurants and a worthwhile sandy beach right in town. The busier beaches, with their requisite resorts, line up along a nearly uninterrupted stretch all the way to Panormo, some 22km away.

◉ Sights

★ Fortezza   FORTRESS
(Map p476; adult/concession/family €4/3/10; ☉ 8am-8pm Apr-Oct, 10am-5pm Nov-Mar; ℗) Looming over Rethymno, the star-shaped Venetian fortress cuts an imposing figure with its massive walls and bastions but was nevertheless unable to stave off the Turks in 1646. Over time, an entire village took shape on the grounds, most of which was destroyed in WWII. Views over the town, the Mediterranean and mountains are fabulous up here and it's fun to poke around the ramparts, palm trees and remaining buildings, most notably the Sultan Bin Ibrahim Mosque with its huge dome.

Head inside the mosque to admire its impressive mosaic ceiling, with wonderful acoustics that are perfect for the occasional musical event held here. A few other buildings (like the twin buildings of the Bastion of Agios Nikolaos) are also used to showcase art exhibits. Pick up a free map from the ticket office, which offers useful info on the site.

Last entry is 45 minutes before closing.

★ Archaeological Museum of Rethymno   MUSEUM
(Map p476; ☑ 28310 27506; www.archmuseum reth.gr; Argiropoulon; adult/concession €2/1; ☉ 10am-6pm Wed-Mon) Set inside the atmospheric Venetian-built Church of St Francis, this well-curated museum features a stunning collection of well-preserved relics unearthed from major archaeological digs around Rethymno Province. Its collection offers a comprehensive snapshot (without leaving you overwhelmed) that predominantly covers pieces from the Minoan, Byzantine and Venetian periods. Highlights include exquisite hand-painted Minoan ceramics, a 9000-year-old limestone deity statue and a bronze lamp from the Hellenistic period (1st century BCE) depicting Dionysus riding a panther.

Venetian Harbour   LANDMARK
(Map p476) Rethymno's compact historic harbour is chock-a-block with tourist-geared fish tavernas and cafes. For a more atmospheric perspective, walk along the harbour walls, past the fishing boats to the prominent lighthouse, built in the 19th century by the Egyptians.

Agios Spyridon Church   CHAPEL
(Kefalogiannidon) FREE Built right into the cliff beneath the Venetian fortress, tiny Agios Spyridon has enough atmosphere to fill a cathedral. This Byzantine chapel is filled with richly painted icons, swinging bird candleholders and the sound of the nearby pounding surf. You'll see pairs of slippers, baby shoes and sandals in crevices in the rock wall, left as prayer offerings for the sick.

Find the chapel at the top of a staircase on the fortress' western side. Opening hours are erratic.

Museum of Contemporary Art MUSEUM
(Map p476; ☑ 28310 52530; www.cca.gr; Mesologhiou 32; adult/concession/student €3/1.50/free, Thu free; ⏱ 9am-2pm & 7-9pm Tue-Fri, 10am-3pm Sat & Sun May-Oct, reduced hours Nov-Apr) The cornerstone of the permanent collection of this well-curated modern-art museum, founded in 1992, is the oils, drawings and watercolours of local lad Lefteris Kanakakis, but over time it has amassed enough works to present the arc of creative endeavour in Greece since the 1950s. Temporary exhibits keep things dynamic. Entrance is off Mesologhiou.

Rimondi Fountain FOUNTAIN
(Map p476) Another vestige of Venetian rule is this small fountain where water spouts from three lions' heads into three basins flanked by Corinthian columns. Above the central basin you can make out the Rimondi family crest. It was built in 1626 by city rector Alvise Rimondi. Located off Paleologou.

🏃 Activities

Paradise Dive Center DIVING
(☑ 28310 26317; www.diving-center.gr; Petres Geraniou; 2 dives incl equipment from €100, open-water certification €400) Runs diving trips for all grades of diver from its base at Petres, 14km west of Rethymno. Its most popular dive is to the underwater Elephant Cave, where fossilised remains of elephants were discovered in 1999. Paradise also offers night dives and PADI courses for beginners. Book through travel agencies, by phone or via the website.

★ Happy Walker HIKING
(Map p476; ☑ 28310 52920; www.happywalker.com; Tombazi 56; guided day walks €32; ⏱ 10am-2pm Apr-Oct) In operation for over a quarter of a century, this congenial Dutch-run outfit takes up to 16 global ramblers on day hikes to gorges, ancient shepherd trails and traditional villages. It's ideal for solo travellers. Rates include transport to and from trailheads and an English-speaking guide, but coffee and a vegetarian lunch with wine are an extra €12.

Eco Events TOURS
(Map p476; ☑ 6946686857, 28310 50055; www.ecoevents.gr; Eleftheriou Venizelou 39; tours €18-70; ⏱ 10am-9pm) This outfit specialises in small-group English-language tours that get you in touch with land, people and culture. Options include the Eco Tour, on which you'll meet a baker, a weaver and a woodcarver before sampling charcoal-grilled lamb in a traditional shepherd's shelter in the mountains. Cooking classes, wine and olive-oil tastings, and hiking trips are also part of the lineup.

🛏 Sleeping

★ Rethymno Youth Hostel HOSTEL €
(Map p476; ☑ 28310 22848; www.yhrethymno.com; Tombazi 41; dm €12-14; ⏱ reception 8am-1pm & 5-11pm Sep-May, 8am-midnight Jun-Aug; 🛜) Centrally located in a quiet street, this cheerful and professionally run hostel sleeps six to 12 people in clean, well-presented dorms (one is for women only). Dorms have comfy mattresses, personalised power points and good-size lockers, and it's a nice place to relax, with a sociable patio, a bar and a flowering garden. Offers excellent travel info for Crete and beyond.

★ Atelier Frosso Bora PENSION €
(Map p476; ☑ 28310 24440; www.frosso-bora.com; Chimaras 25; d €35-60; ⏱ Mar-Nov; ❄🛜) Run by local artist Frosso Bora and located above her pottery studio, these four spotless, ambience-laden rooms with exposed stone walls, small flat-screen TVs, modern bathrooms and kitchenettes are a superb budget pick. Two units have small balconies facing the old town, while the other two sport Venetian architectural features and a beamed ceiling.

Casa Moazzo BOUTIQUE HOTEL €€
(Map p476; ☑ 28310 36235; www.casamoazzo.gr; 57 Tombazi; r incl breakfast €85-180; ❄🛜) Occupying the former home of Venetian nobles, these 10 newly renovated rooms are elegant and bright. Just a stone's throw from the harbour, they're nonetheless very private. Each room is unique, combining wallpaper, exposed stone and wooden beams for a classy Italian feel. Some have balconies, claw-foot tubs and kitchenettes, and all have king-size beds and an option for goose-down pillows.

Sohora BOUTIQUE HOTEL €€
(Map p476; ☑ 28313 00913; www.sohora.net; Plateia Iroön Politechniou 11; studios €50-70, d €60-75, apt €100; ❄🛜) Extremely comfortable and slightly quirky, the rooms with kitchenette in this 200-year-old home are named after the seasons and incorporate original architectural features alongside upcycled vintage furnishings. A solar water heater, organic bath products and a hearty, homemade breakfast (€6) provide eco-cred. Service is both friendly and professional.

Rethymno

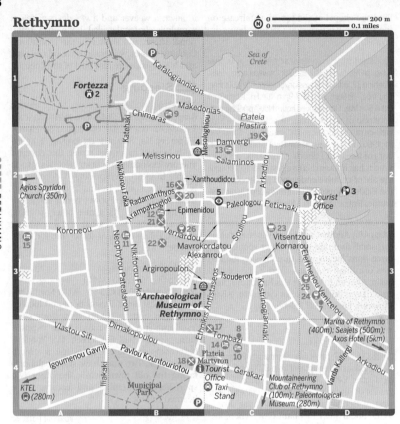

Palazzino di Corina BOUTIQUE HOTEL €€
(Map p476; ☑ 28310 21205; www.corina.gr; Damvergi 9; d €70-170; ❋ 🛜 ☷) This regal Venetian mansion is an elegant place to unpack. Fine furniture, exposed stone walls and timber vaulted ceilings create a plush period ambience. You'll also find a good dose of mod cons, including Jacuzzis. In the courtyard, a small, deep pool begs you to dive in, while the lounge is overflowing with antiques – from gramophones to sewing machines.

★**Hamam**
Oriental Suites BOUTIQUE HOTEL €€€
(Map p476; ☑ 28310 50378, 6981649377; www.hamamsuites.com; Nikiforou Foka 86; r incl breakfast €135-230) In a quiet alleyway in the old quarter is this former Venetian-Ottoman bathhouse that, after several reincarnations, has undergone an elegant refit to open as a hotel. Each of its five atmospheric rooms is unique – some feature striking mosaics, domed ceilings, original stone walls and steam rooms or

Jacuzzis – but all are lavishly decorated with period furnishings and antiques.

🍴 Eating

★**Raki Baraki** CRETAN €
(Map p476; ☑ 28310 58250; www.facebook.com/1600rakibaraki; Arampatzoglou 17; mezedhes €3.50-13; ⏲ 12.30pm-midnight; ❋ 🛜 ☷) Rustic, colourful and lively, this is a fantastic place to while away the evening over mezedhes like flavoursome grilled mushrooms with mountain herbs, warm homemade dolmadhes with yoghurt, or mussels steamed with sage. The fried filo-coated feta with marmalade is divine, as is the sheep's-milk ice cream. Comfort food at its finest.

koo koo CAFE €
(Map p476; ☑ 28310 26380; Plateia Martyron; dishes €4-6; ⏲ 7am-11pm; ❋ 🛜 ☷) The place to head if you need respite from traditional Greek food, this contemporary cafe does a menu of all-day brunch fare. Expect the likes

Rethymno

of smashed avocado on toast, crispy chicken waffles, pizza by the slice and a heap of tasty burgers. There's a welcome choice of healthy and vegetarian options, too, along with top-notch coffees, smoothies and teas.

Gaias Gefseis BAKERY €
(Map p476; ☑ 28311 00428; Ethnikis Antistaseos 15; pastries €0.50-2.50; ⊙ 7am-10pm) For *loukoumadhes* (doughnut-like concoctions drizzled with honey and cinnamon), follow your nose to Gaias Gefseis. This bakery creates some of the city's best traditional cakes and biscuits, as well as homemade sheep's-milk gelato. If your sweet tooth needs a break, there's a mammoth supply of savoury breads; try one stuffed with feta and olives.

Veneto CRETAN €€
(Map p476; ☑ 28310 56634; www.veneto.gr; Epimenidou 4; mains €15-20; ⊙ 6-11pm May-Oct; 🛜) In a 14th-century manor house that doubles as a **boutique hotel** (s €70-95, d €95-130, ste €114-148; 🌀🛜), Veneto oozes historic charm from every nook. The kitchen adds a contemporary streak to traditional Cretan recipes, with results like fish with fennel and lime or meatballs with basil sauce. The owner is a wine buff and will happily help you pick a bottle to complement your meal.

Avli CRETAN €€
(Map p476; ☑ 28310 58250; www.avli.gr; Xanthoudidou 22; mains €12-20; ⊙ 12.30-11pm; 🌀🛜) This well-established Venetian villa serves creative Cretan food with a side of romance. Farm-fresh fare steers the menu, resulting in dishes with bold flavour pairings such as *creatotouria* (ravioli filled with lamb, cheese, mint and

lime) or *fouriariko* (slow-cooked organic goat with honey and thyme). Be sure to reserve a table in the bewitching garden courtyard.

🍷 Drinking & Nightlife

Rethymno's young and restless are mostly drawn to the cafe-bars along Eleftheriou Venizelou. The area around the Rimondi Fountain and Plateia Petihaki is popular with tourists. Wander the side streets to find quieter places.

★**Monitor** BAR
(Map p476; ☑ 6974130764; www.facebook.com/monitorartcafe; Vernardou 21-23; ⊙ 10am-late) A gathering spot for Rethymno's slightly older indie crowd, this relaxed, unpretentious bar is decked out in arthouse-film posters and modern-art installations. Its atmospheric old-town setting makes it a wonderful spot for a relaxed coffee, beer or old-fashioned cocktail and a good burger. Check the Facebook page for upcoming bands, DJs and events.

Bricks Beerhouse CRAFT BEER
(Map p476; ☑ 6945297481; www.bricksbeerhouse.gr; Eleftheriou Venizelou 41; ⊙ 10am-1am mid-Apr–Oct, from 6pm Nov–mid-Apr) While Cretans are still developing a thirst for craft beer, Bricks is doing its best to convert them with its selection of 30 ales produced by Greek microbreweries, including a few local ones. You can also try a gin distilled in Irakalio that uses Cretan botanicals.

Chaplin's BAR
(Map p476; ☑ 28310 24566; Eleftheriou Venizelou 52; ⊙ 9am-4am) Rethymno's most raucous drinking spot is this smoke-filled rock bar

RETHYMNO'S FILO MASTER

Established in 1948, Yiorgos Hatzi-paraskos (Map p476; ☑ 28310 29488; Vernardou 30; pastries €2-4; ⊙ 8am-9.30pm) is one of the last traditional filo masters in all of Greece. Assisted by his wife, Katerina, and son, Paraskevas, today he still makes superfine pastry by hand in his workshop. Watch the spectacle and try some of the best baklava and *kataïfi* ('angel hair' pastry) you will ever eat.

The highlight is when they whirl the dough into a giant bubble before stretching it over a huge table.

that's been banging out tunes since the 1970s. It attracts a boozy crowd of black-clad students and older rockers propped at the bar sinking shots between beers.

Brew Your Mind COFFEE
(Map p476; ☑ 28313 01940; www.facebook.com/brewyourmind1; Arkadiou 251; ⊙ 8am-10pm; ☎) Wake up and smell the coffee at this hip microroaster that offers a pleasing array of speciality beans. Whether you're into V60, Aeropress, Chemex, syphon, cold brew, flat whites or your traditional Greek double, the baristas here have the full arsenal at their disposal to nail your next caffeine hit.

⊙ Information

You'll find a **tourist information office** (Map p476; www.rethymno.guide; Rethymno Old Port; ⊙ 9am-2.30pm Mon-Fri) at the Venetian Harbour, and a smaller **kiosk** (Map p476; www.rethymno.guide; Plateia Martyron; ⊙ 9am-2.30pm Mon-Fri) just south of Porta Guora. Both offer local maps and regional information and their website is also useful.

General Hospital of Rethymno (☑ 28313 42100; www.rethymnohospital.gr; Triandalydou 17; ⊙ 24hr) Has 24-hour accident and emergency care.

Tourist Police (☑ 28310 28156, emergency 171; Sofokli Venizelou 37; ⊙ on call 24hr) At Rethymno's marina, next to the beach.

⊙ Getting There & Away

KTEL Bus Station (☑ 28310 22785, 28310 22212; Kefalogiannidon; ☎) The bus station is at the western edge of the centre. Services are reduced at weekends and outside high season.

Seajets (☑ 21041 21001; www.seajets.gr) Ferries from Rethymno's marina depart on Tuesday and Saturday at 8am for Santorini (€69, 2¼

hours), Ios (€70, 3½ hours), Naxos (€78, four hours) and Mykonos (€74, five hours). A car is an additional €60 to €65.

West of Rethymno

Argyroupoli

POP 450

Located 25km southwest of Rethymno, Argyroupoli is built on the ruins of the ancient city of Lappa, one of the most important Roman cities in western Crete, though very few remnants of it survive. Argyroupoli's network of atmospheric cobblestone alleyways lined with Venetian-era stone houses and Byzantine churches makes it a lovely place to stroll. As it's in the foothills of the Lefka Ori (White Mountains), the town is a useful gateway to some fine hiking trails.

At the bottom of the town is a watery oasis formed by springs from the Lefka Ori that keep the temperature markedly cooler here than on the coast, making it a good place to escape the summer heat. Running through aqueducts, washing down walls, seeping from stones and pouring from spigots, the gushing springs supply water for the entire city of Rethymno.

⊙ Sights

Necropolis HISTORIC SITE
Ancient Lappa's cemetery lies north of the town and is reached via a signed 1.5km footpath from the main square. Hundreds of tombs have been cut into the rock cliffs here, especially around the Chapel of the Five Virgins. The path leads on to a plane tree that is said to be 2000 years old.

✗ Eating

★ **Garden Arkoudenas** CRETAN €€
(O Kipos Tis Arkoudenas; ☑ 28310 61607; Episkopi; mains €10-18; ⊙ 1pm-late) One of the most enjoyable places to experience traditional Cretan cuisine and hospitality is this vibrant taverna. Gregarious host Georgios (who appears in Yotam Ottolenghi's *Mediterranean Feast* documentary) will take you through the day's specials, cooked by his mother using superb organic produce sourced from their farm and the mountains.

⊙ Getting There & Away

From Monday to Friday three daily buses ply the route from Rethymno to Argyroupoli. Before you head out, be sure to check that there is in fact a return bus to Rethymno (€3.60, 40 minutes); generally, the last bus back goes at 3.30pm.

Agreco Farm

Embedded in rolling hills near the village of Adele, about 13km southeast of Rethymno, Agreco Farm (☑28310 72129; www.agreco.gr; Adelianos Kampos; tour & lunch or dinner from €38; ⊙11am-10pm May-Oct) is a replica of a 17th-century estate and a showcase of centuries-old, organic and ecofriendly farming methods. It uses mostly traditional machinery, including a donkey-driven olive press, a watermill and a wine press. Call ahead to make sure it's open. You'll also find small shops selling local produce and artwork, plus a mini-zoo featuring *kri-kri* (Cretan goats), wild boar and bantam chickens.

The farm is usually open from May to October, but private events, such as weddings or baptisms, often keep it closed to the public. Normally, farm tours culminate in a 30-course Cretan feast in the taverna. Most of the dishes are prepared with produce, dairy and meat grown on the farm.

If you're more the hands-on type, enquire in advance for upcoming farm days, when visitors are invited to participate in traditional agricultural activities. Depending on the time of year, you could find yourself shearing a sheep, milking a goat, making cheese, pressing grapes with your feet or baking bread using hand-picked, freshly stoneground flour; see the website for the schedule. This is followed by a buffet-style Harvest Festival Lunch. Reservations are essential for the farm tour and the Sunday experience.

If you're just stopping by during the day, you can do an independent tour (€5) and enjoy a drink in the *kafeneio* (coffeehouse).

East of Rethymno

Moni Arkadiou

The 16th-century Moni Arkadiou (Arkadi Monastery; ☑28310 83136; Arkadi; €3; ⊙9am-8pm Jun-Sep, to 7pm Apr, May & Oct, to 5pm Nov, to 4pm Dec-Mar), 23km southeast of Rethymno, has deep significance for Cretans. As the site where hundreds of cornered locals massacred both themselves and invading Turks, it's a stark and potent symbol of resistance and considered a catalyst in the island's struggle towards freedom from Turkish occupation.

Arkadiou's impressive Venetian church (1587) has a striking Renaissance facade

topped by an ornate triple-belled tower. The grounds include a small museum and the old wine cellar where the gunpowder was stored.

In November 1866, massive Ottoman forces arrived to crush island-wide revolts. Hundreds of Cretan men, women and children fled their villages to find shelter at Arkadiou. However, far from being a safe haven, the monastery was soon besieged by 2000 Turkish soldiers. Rather than surrender, the entrapped locals blew up stored gunpowder kegs, killing everyone, Turks included. One small girl miraculously survived and lived to a ripe old age in a village nearby. A bust of this woman and another of the abbot who lit the gunpowder are outside the monastery not far from the old windmill – now an ossuary with skulls and bones of the 1866 victims neatly arranged in a glass cabinet.

Four to five buses arrive here each weekday (two to three at weekends) from Rethymno (€3.10, 40 minutes), leaving you about 90 minutes for your visit before returning.

Ancient Eleutherna

The archaeological site of Ancient Eleutherna (☑28340 92501; http://en.mae.com.gr/archaeological-site; Eleutherna; necropolis adult/senior/student €4/2/free, with museum €6/3/free, acropolis free; ⊙necropolis 10am-6pm May-Oct, acropolis 24hr year-round) is a Dorian-built settlement that was among the most important in the 8th and 7th centuries BCE, and also experienced heydays in Hellenistic and Roman times. Excavations have been ongoing since 1985 and archaeologists continue to make new finds all the time; many are showcased at the impressive museum nearby. The 2010 discovery of the gold-adorned remains of a woman in a 2700-year-old double tomb made international news.

The museum (http://en.mae.com.gr/museum.html; Milopotamos; adult/senior/student €4/2/free, combined necropolis ticket €6/3/free, Sun free; ⊙10am-6pm Wed-Mon) is a must-see for anyone visiting the ruins of Eleutherna is the accompanying modern museum that contextualises the ancient city through the exhibition of treasures unearthed at the site over the past 30 years. Located 3km from the ruins, and set over three rooms, the beautifully curated collection covers artefacts ranging from the early Iron Age and Minoan periods to Hellenic, Roman and Byzantine eras.

Its showpiece is the bronze shield with a protruding lion's head, unearthed from the Tomb of the Warriors and dating to the 8th century BCE; it sits alongside a polished, gleaming replica of how it would have originally looked. Other artefacts excavated from the necropolis include beautiful ceramic vases and ornaments, detailed gold pendants and marble statuettes, all with exquisite artisanship and much that has retained its colour.

Margarites   Μαργαρίτες

Tiny Margarites, 26km southeast of Rethymno, is famous for its pottery, a tradition that can be traced back to Minoan times. The village has only one road, and no bank or post office, but it has more than 20 ceramics stores and studios. Most studios source their clay by hand (the area is known for its clay), and offer unique, bright and good-quality usable pieces. This is the perfect place to pick up a keepsake.

If possible, try to avoid mornings and lunchtime, when droves of tour buses flood the town. By afternoon all is calm, and you can explore the atmospheric alleyways, wander through the studios and enjoy wonderful valley views from the eucalyptus-lined taverna terraces on the main square.

Melidoni Cave

About 2km outside the village of Melidoni is the stunning cathedral-like Melidoni Cave (Gerontospilios; www.melidoni.gr; adult/child under 12yr €4/free; ⊙9am-8pm May-Sep, to 7pm Apr, Oct & Nov), an evocative underworld of stalactites and stalagmites. A place of worship since Neolithic times, it also carries heavy historical significance as the site of a massacre in 1824 during the Turkish occupation. Here 370 villagers and 30 soldiers sought refuge from the Ottoman army; after a three-month siege, the Turks lit a fire and asphyxiated the people inside, including 340 women and children.

Wear decent walking shoes, as the cave is poorly lit and the ground uneven and slippery in places. You'll need to descend 70 steps into the cave. Also bring a sweater: at 24m below ground, the temperature never gets above 18°C.

If you're out this way to the cave, tack on a visit to the nearby Paraschakis Olive Oil Factory (☑28340 22039, 6973863551; www.paraschakis.gr; Melidoni Geropotamou; ⊙9am-6pm Mon-Sat Apr-Nov) FREE for a lowdown on the production process. Its welcoming American-Greek owner, Joanna, will guide you through the evolution of olive-oil pressing, from donkey-driven methods to current-day machinery. The factory is part of a local co-op used by farmers to convert their yearly harvest into liquid gold.

Panormo   Πάνορμο
POP 880

Panormo, about 22km east of Rethymno, is one of the few relatively unspoilt beach towns on the northern coast. Despite a couple of big hotel complexes, it retains an unhurried, authentic village feel and makes for a quieter alternative to the overcrowded scene immediately east of Rethymno and at nearby Bali. In summer, concerts and other events are held in a carob mill turned cultural centre.

◉ Sights

Klados Winery   WINERY
(☑28340 51589, 6973654840; www.kladoswinery.gr; tasting 5/7 wines €3/4; ⊙10am-6pm Mon-Fri, to 3pm Sat Apr-Oct, other times by appointment) While Iraklio gets all the plaudits as Crete's main wine producer, Rethymno has the honour of being the first place in Greece to be named a 'European City of Wine', in 2018. It's fitting recognition for this winery, family-run since 1997 and known primarily for Vidiano, a dry white produced from a grape grown only in the immediate area.

Castel Milopotamo   VIEWPOINT
For wonderful views overlooking Panormo's port, head up the hill to a *tiny* segment of stone wall that remains from a 13th-century fortress. It's believed to have been built by the Genoese during their fleeting rule in 1206 before the Venetians took over.

Panormo Beach   BEACH
There's no one main beach in Panormo but a series of small, attractive coves with brown sand and a brilliant turquoise sea. The tiny swoop of sand at the harbour with its calm waters is perfect for families.

🍴 Sleeping & Eating

The touristy harbour tavernas serve standard Greek and international dishes as well as fresh fish. More traditional places can be found a block or two inland. If you have a car, try to make it out to Dalabelos Estate for lunch, a wonderful culinary experience.

Captain's House   GUESTHOUSE €
(☑28103 80833; www.captainshouse.gr; apt €40-60; ⊙Apr-Oct; ❉🤙) In a prime waterfront

location, the Captain's modern and spacious split-level apartments are an excellent choice – all are different, but each is spacious and comfortable, and catches the sea breeze. They're equipped with satellite TV, fast wi-fi and kitchenette, and some feature sea views. Staff members are friendly, and a welcoming gift of fruit and wine is a lovely touch.

★ **Idili** GUESTHOUSE €€
(📞6970994408, 28340 20240; www.idili.gr; apt €65-95; ❄ 🎵) If cookie-cutter rooms don't do it for you, you'll love the three traditionally furnished apartments in this protected stone house, which has seen incarnations as courthouse, carpenter's workshop and residence. Arches, wooden ceilings and sleeping lofts endow each unit with charm and uniqueness, while the fireplace and veranda are delightful places to unwind. The flowering garden offers a shady retreat.

★ **George & Georgia's** CRETAN €
(To Steki tou Sifaki; 📞28340 51230; mains €7-12; ⏲12.30-4pm & 7pm-late; 🍴) Husband-and-wife team George and Georgia serve up satisfying homestyle Cretan food at this cheerful, hopping place. Expect scrumptious oven-roasted dishes and flavoursome grilled fish, along with a great selection of veggie options. Find it between the waterfront and the main road, near the post office.

Angira SEAFOOD €€
(mains €7-15; ⏲noon-11pm Apr-Oct) Seafood doesn't get any fresher than at this place right at the harbour. Choose from marinated anchovies, shrimp salad or grilled fish, along with a wonderful slow-cooked lamb in wine.

❶ Getting There & Away

In high season, hourly buses go from Rethymno to Panormo (€2.60, 25 minutes). Buses stop on the main road just outside town. For car hire, try **Rent-A-Car** (www.bestcars-rental.gr; ⏲9am-2pm & 5-8pm), with branches opposite the carob factory and the Grecotel Club Marine Palace.

A **taxi** (📞28340 23000) is available for drop-offs at Rethymno (€28) or Bali (€20).

Anogia Ανώγεια
POP 2500

Perched beside Mt Psiloritis, 37km southwest of Iraklio, Anogia is a wonderful spot to slow things down and glimpse authentic rural Cretan life. It's the perfect base for excursions up to the Nida Plateau (1400m) and Zeus' cave.

DALABELOS ESTATE

Hemmed in by vines, olives and fruit trees, these 10 traditional-style houses (📞28340 22155; www.dalabelos.gr; Aggeliana; d/ste from €80/100; ❄ 🎵 🏊) have a view over rolling hills to the sea. The modern rooms have stone fireplaces, private terraces, outdoor hot tubs and beautiful bathrooms. The infinity pool and restaurant are first class, plus there are seasonal activities from olive harvesting to raki distilling, as well as hands-on Cretan cooking classes.

It's located inland, 5km south of Panormo, so it helps to have your own transport, but otherwise there are free mountain bikes. The husband-and-wife owners are exceptionally hospitable and proud Cretans, with unsurpassed passion for local food and culture. In high season there's a minimum three-night stay.

Here locals cling to time-honoured traditions, and it's the norm to see men gossiping in the *kafeneia* (coffeehouses), flicking *komboloïa* (worry beads) in their hand, and dressed in traditional black shirts with *vraka* (baggy pants) tucked into black boots. Elderly women, meanwhile, keep busy selling traditional woven blankets and embroidered textiles. The town's turbulent history – in WWII and under Ottoman rule – has instilled a legacy of rebelliousness and a determination to express an undiluted Cretan character.

The town's also famous for its stirring music and has spawned many of Crete's best-known musicians, such as Nikos Xylouris.

🛏 Sleeping & Eating

Hotel Aristea HOTEL €
(📞6972410486, 28340 31459; www.hotelaristea.gr; Michaeli Stavrakaki; d/apt from €35/85; 🅿🎵) Run by the chatty and charming Aristea, this small inn offers sweeping valley views from balconies attached to five fairly basic but spotless and comfortable enough rooms. The four split-level apartments in a next-door annexe are more modern and have kitchen and a wood-burning fireplace for those chilly mountain nights. There's also a common kitchen with full cooking facilities.

Taverna Aetos CRETAN €
(📞28340 31262; 13is Avgoustou 1944 17; grills €7-9; ⏲noon-11pm) This traditional taverna in the upper village has a giant charcoal grill out

the front and fantastic mountain views out the back. On offer are such regional specialities as *ofto* (a flame-cooked lamb or goat), and spaghetti cooked in stock with cheese.

Arodamos   CRETAN €

(☏ 28340 31100; www.arodamos.gr; Tylisos-Anogia Rd; mains €6-10.50; ☺10am-10pm; ☏) This big restaurant in a modern stone house in the upper village is highly regarded for its hearty mountain fare and gracious hospitality. Local specialities include the flame-teased lamb or goat (*ofto*) and the deceptively simple but tasty dish of spaghetti cooked in stock and topped with *anthotiros* (white cheese). If you're ordering mezedhes, be sure to get the *dakos* (Cretan rusks).

❶ Getting There & Away

From Monday to Saturday there are three daily buses from Iraklio (€4.10, one hour), and one on Sunday. From Rethymno (€6, 1¼ hours) two buses depart daily Monday to Friday.

Mt Psiloritis

At 2456m, Mt Psiloritis, also known as Mt Ida, is Crete's highest mountain. At its eastern base is the Nida Plateau (1400m), a wide, fertile expanse reached via a paved 21km-long road from Anogia. It passes several round stone *mitata* (traditional shepherds' huts used for cheesemaking and shelter) as well as the turnoff to the highly regarded (but rarely open) Skinakas Observatory.

From the Nida Plateau it's a short walk to the Ideon Cave (1538m), where according to legend the god Zeus was reared (although Dikteon Cave in Lasithi makes the same claim). Also on the plateau is Andartis, an impressive landscape sculpture honouring the WWII Cretan resistance.

◉ Sights

★ Ideon Cave   CAVE

(ℙ) **FREE** Although just a huge and fairly featureless hole in the ground, Ideon has sacred importance in mythology as the place where Zeus was reared by his mother, Rhea, to save him from the clutches of his child-devouring father, Cronos. (Some also believe it's where he died and is buried.) Ideon is on Mt Psiloritis about 15km from Anogia; it's a 1km uphill walk along a rocky path from the parking lot to the entrance.

Ideon was a place of worship from the late 4th millennium BCE onward, and many artefacts, including gold jewellery and bronze shields, statuettes and other offerings to Zeus, have been unearthed here. The rail track used for these archaeological digs is still here.

In winter (and sometimes as late as May) the cave entrance can be blocked by snow, in which case it's easy enough to climb over the fence. However, for safety reasons, avoid clambering on the snow.

❶ Getting There & Away

To reach Mt Psiloritis, you really need your own wheels. The views en route are stunning.

Buses run from Rethymno to Anogia (€6, 1¼ hours, twice daily on weekdays).

South of Rethymno

Spili   Σπήλι

POP 630

Spili is a pretty mountain village and shutterbug favourite thanks to its cobbled streets, big old plane trees and flower-festooned whitewashed houses. Most people just stop

---

CLIMBING MT PSILORITIS

The classic route to the summit of Mt Psiloritis follows the east–west E4 European Path from the Nida Plateau and in summer can be done in a round trip of about seven hours. While you don't need to be an alpine mountaineer, it's a long slog and the views from the summit may be marred by cloud cover. En route, occasional *mitata* (round, stone shepherds' huts) provide shelter should the weather turn inclement, while at the summit there's a small, twin-domed chapel. The best map is the Anavasi 1:30,000 *Psiloritis (Mt Ida)*. For trekking conditions and general advice, get in touch with the visitor centre (AKOMM; ☏ 28340 31402; www.psiloritisgeopark.gr; ☺8am-4pm Mon-Fri) in Anogia prior to departure.

If you're planning on tackling Psiloritis from a destination other than Anogia, visit www.psiloritisgeopark.gr for the comprehensive online Psiloritis Tourist Guide. Be sure to bring a warm jacket, even if the weather's fine, as conditions can change quickly.

Backcountry skiing is possible at Mt Psiloritis from December to March; contact the Cretan Ski School (www.facebook.com/skiincrete) for equipment hire, lessons and guided trips.

for lunch on a coast-to-coast trip, but it's well worth staying a day or two to explore the trails weaving through the local mountains. The rugged Kourtaliotiko Gorge, which culminates at the famous palm grove of Preveli Beach (p484), starts not far south of town.

Sights

Maravel Garden GARDENS

(☎28320 22056; www.maravelspili.gr; ⏰8am-8pm Mar-Nov) FREE On the western outskirts of town are these botanical gardens filled with an aromatic variety of plant species from Crete and across the globe. You're free to wander and check out the herbs and medicinal plants staff use to distil essential oils and produce the organic products sold in the shop. The cafe has a deck overlooking the gardens and does a menu of light meals, homemade ice cream, herbal teas and superfood smoothies.

Call in advance for tours (€5), but usually they're for groups only. The garden's **Maravel Shop** (☎28320 22056; www.shop.maravelspili.gr; ⏰9am-9pm) in town has a larger stock of its products.

Sleeping & Eating

★**Hotel Heracles** PENSION €

(☎28320 22111, 6973667495; www.heracles-hotel.eu; s/d/tr/q €35/40/45/50; ❄📶) These five balconied rooms are quiet, spotless and simply furnished, but it's the charming and softly spoken Heracles himself who makes the place so special. Intimately familiar with the area, he's happy to put you on to the right hiking trail, birdwatching site or hidden beach. Optional breakfasts (from €4.50) feature local eggs and an array of homemade marmalades.

★**Taverna Sideratico** CRETAN €

(☎28320 22916; mains €8; ⏰noon-10pm Apr-Nov; 🌿) In an appealing location away from Spili's touristy centre, this delightful taverna sits on the main road 500m south of town. There's no menu, so you'll be guided through its mouthwatering array of *mayirefta* prepared by hard-working chef-owner-farmer Nico, who sources all ingredients from the immediate area. As well as slow-cooked meat dishes, its vegetarian meals are outstanding.

Getting There & Away

Spili is on the Rethymno–Agia Galini bus route (€3.80, 30 minutes), which has up to five services daily.

Plakias Πλακιάς

POP 300

Set beside a sweeping sandy crescent and accessed via two scenic gorges – Kotsifou and Kourtaliotiko – Plakias gets swarmed with package tourists in summer (when it can be very windy) but otherwise remains a laid-back indie travellers' favourite. While the village itself isn't particularly pretty, it's an excellent launch pad for regional excursions and hikes through olive groves, along seaside cliffs and to some sparkling hidden beaches.

Sights & Activities

There are well-worn walking paths to the scenic villages of Selia, Moni Finika and Lefkogia, and a lovely walk along the Kourtaliotiko Gorge to Moni Preveli. An easy 30-minute uphill path to Myrthios begins just before the youth hostel.

Several diving operators run certification courses, as well as shore and boat dives to nearby rocky bays, caves and canyons.

Captain Lefteris Boat Cruises BOATING

(☎28320 31971, 6936806635; www.lbferries.gr; tours €15-39) In summer Baradakis Lefteris (owner-chef of the Smerna Bar) and his son Nikos run entertaining boat trips to nearby beaches such as Preveli (adult/child €15/8), Loutro (€39/20), and Agios Pavlos and Triopetra (€30/15). They also offer boat hire (€120 per day, excluding fuel).

Elena Tours TOURS

(☎6936371451, 28320 20465; tours from €45; ⏰9.30am-1.30pm & 6-9pm) Hop in Elena's minibus for an excursion into the less touristy side of the area. Hike through gorges, take boats to unheard-of beaches, visit ancient churches and meet locals in quaint villages. Each tour includes a maximum of eight people. The office is located in the centre of Plakias, just over the bridge.

Sleeping

★**Plakias Youth Hostel** HOSTEL €

(☎28320 32118; www.yhplakias.com; dm €10-12; ⏰mid-Mar–Nov; P@📶) 🌿 This charismatic pad and 'Hoscar' winner for best Greek hostel is set in an olive grove about 500m from the beach. Serene and laid-back, it fosters an atmosphere of inclusiveness and good cheer that appeals to people of all ages and nationalities. There are six eight-bed dorms with fans, communal facilities, an outdoor kitchen and an honour-system fridge with cheap beers.

Gio-Ma

PENSION €

(☑ 28320 31942, 694737793; www.gioma.gr; r from €40; ✸ 🛜) Located at the quiet end of town and fronted by a flower-filled balcony, the spacious self-contained rooms here are clean and comfortable, and feature fabulous sea views. Snag one of the upper units for post-card-perfect photos. The owners also run the waterfront taverna across the street.

Plakias Suites

APARTMENT €€

(☑ 28320 31680, 6975811559; www.plakiassuites. com; d €75-140; ⊘ Mar–mid-Nov; 🅿 ✸ 🛜) This stylish outpost has six two- and three-room apartments with contemporary aesthetics and zeitgeist-compatible touches such as large flat-screen TVs, supremely comfortable mattresses, a chic kitchen and a private balcony or patio. Staying here puts you within a whisker of the best stretch of local beach, albeit about 1km from the village centre.

✖ Eating & Drinking

Tasomanolis

SEAFOOD €€

(☑ 6979887749, 28320 31229; www.tasomanolis.gr; mains €7-16; ⊘ noon-11pm; 🛜 🍴) Tasos and his Belgian wife, Lisa, preside over this nautical-themed family taverna towards the far end of town. Park yourself on the colourful patio to tuck into classic Greek grills and inspired daily specials like anchovy bruschetta, ouzo shrimp or the daily catch with wild greens. Children's menu available.

Enquire about their boat tours (☑ 28320 31229; www.plakiasboattours.gr; cruises from €15).

Taverna Christos

CRETAN €€

(☑ 28320 31472; mains €6-17; ⊘ noon-late; 🛜) This established taverna has a romantic tamarisk-shaded terrace right next to the crashing waves, and lots of interesting dishes that you won't find everywhere, including home-smoked sea bass, black spaghetti with calamari, and lamb *avgolemono* with fresh pasta. Finish off with the orange pie.

Cozy Backyard

BAR

(⊘ 5pm-late Apr-Oct) Down a side street off the main drag is this much-loved drinking hole with an intimate bar fronted by a patio under a palm tree. Jovial staff sling drinks – including the signature Cretan Cocktail, a fruity amaretto number topped with a mini Greek flag – to a tipsy crowd of holidaymakers.

ℹ Information

Plakias has numerous ATMs along the waterfront and about town.

ℹ Getting There & Away

There are up to five buses daily to Rethymno (€5, one hour) and four to Preveli (€1.80, 30 minutes).

Myrthios   Μύρθιος

POP 100

The postcard-pretty village of Myrthios, draped across the hillside above Plakias, makes for a quieter and more traditional alternative to staying beachside. You might also be lured by great food and good deals on boutique accommodation.

★ Taverna Panorama

CRETAN €€

(☑ 28320 31450; mains €6-16; ⊘ 11am-11pm Apr–mid-Nov; 🛜) One of the oldest restaurants in the area, Panorama could not be more aptly named: on the shaded terrace, intoxicating views stretch towards the Libyan Sea. Women from the village prepare Cretan soul food here with passion and know-how, using impeccably fresh ingredients from the owner's farm. If there's freshly baked apple pie, don't miss it!

Preveli

A smooth, curving ribbon of road winds from the bottom of Kourtaliotiko Gorge towards the southern coast, soaring up to the historic Moni Preveli and plunging down to palm-studded Preveli Beach. Although home to two of the region's biggest draws and receiving a lot of visitors, Preveli retains a feeling of remoteness.

Moni Preveli

MONASTERY

(Μονή Πρεβέλης; ☑ 28320 31246; www.preveli. org; Koxaron-Moni Preveli Rd; €3; ⊘ 9am-6.30pm Apr, May, Sep & Oct, 9am-1.30pm & 3.30-7pm Jun-Aug; 🅿) Historic Moni Preveli cuts an imposing silhouette high above the Libyan Sea. Like most Cretan monasteries, it was a centre of resistance during the Turkish occupation and also played a key role in WWII, hiding trapped Allied soldiers from the Nazis until they could escape to Egypt by submarine. A small museum features exquisite icons, richly embroidered vestments and two silver candelabra presented by grateful soldiers after the war.

Preveli Beach

BEACH

(Παραλία Πρεβέλης) Also known as Palm Beach, dazzling Preveli is one of Crete's most celebrated strands. At the mouth of the Kourtaliotiko Gorge, where the Megalopotamos river empties into the Libyan Sea, the palm-lined riverbanks have freshwater pools good for a dip. The beach is backed by rugged cliffs and punctuated by a heart-shaped boulder at the water's edge.

A steep path leads down to the beach (10 minutes) from a car park (€2), 1km before Moni Preveli.

Triopetra   Τριόπετρα

Triopetra is one for those who want to avoid the package-tourist beach-resort scene and instead keep their holiday blissfully simple. On a good day, this long, brown-sand beach is a real crowd-pleaser, featuring magnificent crystal-clear waters. However, it's often blighted by winds – the only thing keeping it from appearing in any top-100 lists. Instead, the attraction here is more about the unhurried, mellow pace of life.

It's named after the three giant rocks jutting out of the sea. Other than a few tavernas and pensions scattered about, there's not much else out this way.

Pavlos' Place   PENSION €
(☑ 6945998101; www.triopetra.com.gr; d €40-45; ⊙ taverna 8am-4pm & 6-10pm Apr-Oct; ❄ 🛜) Right above Little Triopetra Beach, dreamy Pavlos is the perfect chill spot and a popular yoga retreat. Rooms are down to earth (no TV), with kitchenettes, and balconies that catch the sea breeze. The attached taverna does homegrown fare (mains €8 to €12). Wi-fi is intermittent and available in public areas only – great for that digital detox.

Agios Pavlos   Αγιος Παύλος

Cradled by cliffs, Agios Pavlos is little more than a couple of small tavernas with rooms and a beach bar set around a picture-perfect crescent with dark, coarse sand and the distinctive silhouette of Paximadia Island looming offshore. Its beauty and tranquillity have made it a popular destination for yoga retreats. A steep staircase at the bay's western end leads up Cape Melissa to some intricately pleated multihued rock formations.

Agios Pavlos Hotel   HOTEL €
(☑ 28320 71104; www.agiospavloshotel.gr; s €25-30, d €35-45, apt €45-60; ⊙ Apr-Oct; 🅿❄🛜) Hugging a rugged and remote sandy bay, this place offers small but updated rooms, some with gorgeous bay views, below a traditional taverna (☑ 28320 71104; mains €6-13; ⊙ 8am-late Apr-Oct; 🛜). Alternatively, there are larger apartments with kitchens and balconies

in a modern building about 1km uphill. At research time luxurious villas built into the natural landscape were under construction; these will have sea views and saltwater plunge pools.

Agia Galini   Αγια Γαλήνη

One of southern Crete's most touristy seaside towns, the picturesque erstwhile fishing village of Agia Galini serves as a handy base for exploring miles of remote beaches, mountain villages and nearby Minoan sights. Despite the sparkling Libyan Sea settsing, the town itself is blighted by package tourism and overdevelopment, which has diluted much of its original charm.

With ageing hotels and restaurants clinging densely to a steep hillside and hemmed in by cliffs, small beaches and a fishing harbour, the town can feel claustrophobic in high season. However, with its concentration of lively tavernas and pubs, the evenings bring a fun holiday atmosphere. While the town's pebbly beach is nothing special, the remote beaches west of here are lovely. Agia Galini all but shuts down in winter.

🍴 Sleeping & Eating

Glaros Hotel   HOTEL €€
(☑ 28320 91151; www.glaros-agiagalini.com; incl breakfast d €50-85, tr/q €91/101; ❄🛜♨) These well-maintained rooms have a modern edge in a town full of ho-hum hotels. Some rooms have balconies overlooking the pool, and there's a stylish common area and a decent buffet breakfast. Excellent, friendly service seals the deal. It's at the back of town, straight up from the harbour.

Faros Fish Tavern   SEAFOOD €€
(☑ 6944773702; mains €7-13; ⊙ 6-11pm) This no-frills family-run fish taverna is usually packed to the gills, and for good reason: the owner himself drops his nets into the Med, so you know that what's on the plate tonight was still swimming in the sea that morning. It's in the first lane coming from the port.

La Mar   CAFE
(☑ 28320 91018; ⊙ 8.30am-late Apr-Oct) Classy La Mar is the standout among the port-side terrace cafes, with tasteful decor and an interesting menu of original cocktails. Here you can opt for a Martini shaken with a local twist, infused with *malotira* (mountain tea) or olive oil, or a G&T with local gin. Otherwise, pop in for a vegan burger or other Western fare.

ⓘ Getting There & Away

In high season there are up to seven buses daily to Iraklio (€8.70, two hours), up to five to Rethymno (€6.80, 1½ hours) and to Phaestos (€2.30, 30 to 45 minutes), and around five buses to Matala (€3.60, 45 minutes), with a change in Tymbaki. Buses stop down in the village near the port.

If enough people have booked, **Galini Express** (☑ 6936923848; www.galiniexpress.com) offers direct buses to the airport in Iraklio (from €20) and Hania (from €25).

In 2019 Anendyk (www.anendyk.gr) began trialling a ferry service linking Agia Galini with Gavdos Island (two hours, one way/return €30/55) departing on Tuesday, Friday, Saturday and Sunday; check the website for the latest.

HANIA PROVINCE

The west of Crete stands apart in so many ways. A land of giant mountains, grandiose legends and memorials to great battles past, it is presided over by the romantic port city of Hania, once Venice's jewel of a capital and now filled with boutique hotels, interesting shops and some of Greece's best restaurants. The region also has the grandest gorge in Europe, impressive west-coast beaches, Europe's southernmost possession (tranquil Gavdos, a remote island nearer to Africa than to Greece), and mountain villages that are like a step back in time. The steep mountains that ripple across the west and into the southern sea guarantee that the region generally remains untouched by the excesses of tourism. If you want to see beautiful and traditional Crete, Hania and the west is definitely the place.

Hania   Χανιά

POP 54,000

Hania (also spelled Chania) is Crete's most evocative city, with its pretty Venetian quarter criss-crossed by narrow lanes and culminating at a magnificent harbour. Remnants of Venetian and Turkish architecture abound, with old townhouses now transformed into atmospheric restaurants and boutique hotels.

Although all this beauty means the old town is deluged with tourists in summer, it's still a great place to unwind. The Venetian Harbour is ideal for a stroll and a coffee or cocktail. Thanks to an active modern centre, the city retains its charm in winter. Indie boutiques and an entire lane (Skrydlof) dedicated to leather products provide good shopping, and a multitude of creative restaurants means you'll eat very well here.

◉ Sights

From Plateia 1866, the Venetian Harbour is a short walk north up Halidon. Zambeliou, once Hania's main thoroughfare, is lined with craft shops, small hotels and tavernas. The slightly bohemian Splantzia quarter, running from Plateia 1821 between Daskalogianni and Halidon, brims with atmospheric restaurants and cafes, boutique hotels and traditional shopping. The headland near the lighthouse separates the Venetian Harbour from the crowded town beach in the modern Nea Hora quarter.

★ **Venetian Harbour**   HISTORIC SITE
(Map p488) **FREE** There are few places where Hania's historic charm and grandeur are more palpable than in the old Venetian Harbour. It's lined by pastel-coloured buildings that punctuate a maze of narrow lanes lined with shops and tavernas. The eastern side is dominated by the domed Mosque of Kioutsouk Hasan, now an exhibition hall, while a few steps further east the impressively restored **Grand Arsenal** (Map p488; ☑ 28210 34200; Plateia Katehaki; ☉ varies by exhibit) houses the Centre of Mediterranean Architecture. At sunset, join locals and tourists on a stroll out to the **lighthouse** (Map p488) that stands sentinel over the harbour entrance.

★ **Hania Archaeological Museum**   MUSEUM
(Map p488; ☑ 28210 90334; http://chaniamuseum.culture.gr; Halidon 28; adult/concession/child €4/2/free; ☉ 8.30am-8pm Wed-Mon Apr-Oct, to 4pm Wed-Mon Nov-Mar) The setting alone in the beautifully restored 16th-century Venetian Church of San Francisco is reason to visit this fine collection of artefacts from Neolithic to Roman times. Late-Minoan clay baths used as coffins catch the eye, along with a large glass case with an entire herd of clay bulls (used to worship Poseidon). Other standouts include Roman floor mosaics, Hellenistic gold jewellery, clay tablets with Linear A and Linear B script, and a marble sculpture of the head of Roman emperor Hadrian.

Downstairs is a private collection of Minoan pottery, jewellery and clay models. Also particularly impressive are the statue of Diana and, in the pretty courtyard, a marble fountain decorated with lions' heads, a vestige of the Venetian tradition. A Turkish fountain is a relic from the building's days as a mosque.

The church itself was a mosque under the Turks, a movie theatre in 1913, and a WWII German munitions depot. At the time of research there were plans to move the museum to a new location due to open in mid 2021; check ahead before visiting.

★**Maritime Museum of Crete** MUSEUM
(Map p488; ☎28210 91875; www.mar-mus-crete.gr; Akti Koundourioti; adult/concession €3/2; ⏲9am-5pm May-Oct, to 3.30pm Nov-Apr) Part of the hulking Venetian-built Firkas Fortress at the western port entrance, this museum celebrates Crete's nautical tradition with model ships, naval instruments, paintings, photographs, maps and memorabilia. One room is dedicated to historical sea battles, while upstairs there's thorough documentation of the WWII-era Battle of Crete. You might be lucky enough to see artists working on new model ships in the ship workroom.

Firkas Fortress FORTRESS
(Map p488; ⏲8am-2pm Mon-Fri) The Firkas Fortress at the western tip of the harbour heads the best-preserved section of the massive fortifications that were built by the Venetians to protect the city from marauding pirates and invading Turks. The Turks invaded anyway, in 1645, and turned the fortress into a barracks and a prison. Today, parts of it house the Maritime Museum of Crete . There's a great view of the harbour from the top.

Mosque of Kioutsouk Hasan MOSQUE
(Mosque of the Janissaries; Map p488) One of the prettiest and most dominant vestiges of the Turkish era is this dusky-pink multidomed former mosque on the eastern side of the Venetian Harbour. It was built in 1645, making it the oldest Ottoman building in town. It's sometimes open for temporary art exhibits.

Byzantine & Post-Byzantine Collection MUSEUM
(Map p488; ☎28210 96046; Theotokopoulou 78; adult/concession/child €2/1/free; ⏲8am-4pm Wed-Mon) In the impressively restored Venetian Church of San Salvatore, this small but fascinating collection of artefacts, icons, jewellery and coins spans the period from 62 CE to 1913. Highlights include a segment of a mosaic floor from an early-Christian basilica, an icon of St George slaying the dragon, and a panel recently attributed to El Greco.

The building has a mixed bag of interesting architectural features from its various occupiers. A combined ticket (€6) also gives you entry to the archaeological museums of Hania and Kissamos (p492).

Venetian Fortifications FORTRESS
(Map p488) Part of a defensive system begun in 1538 by Michele Sanmichele, who also designed Iraklio's defences, Hania's massive fortifications remain impressive. Best preserved is the western wall, running from the Firkas Fortress to the **Siavo Bastion**. Entrance to the fortress is via the gates next to the Maritime Museum. The bastion offers good views of the old town.

Beaches

The town beach 2km west of the Venetian Harbour at **Nea Hora** (Akti Papanikoli) is crowded but convenient if you just want to cool off and get some rays. Koum Kapi is less used (and less clean). For better swimming, keep heading west to the beaches (in order) of **Hrysi Akti** (Nea Kydonia), **Agioi Apostoli** and **Kalamaki**, which are all served by local buses heading towards Platanias.

Activities

Trekking Plan OUTDOORS
(Map p488; ☎28210 27040, 6932417040; www.cycling.gr; Halidon 85; ⏲9am-2pm & 6-8.30pm, closed Sun Nov-Apr) Trekking Plan (operating out of the Attios travel agency) arranges hikes to Agia Irini, Samaria and Imbros Gorges; climbs of Mt Gingilos; canyoning, rappelling and rock climbing; kayaking and mountain-biking, and ski tours in winter.

Blue Adventures Diving DIVING
(Map p488; ☎28210 40608; www.blueadventures.gr; Chrysanthou Episkopou 39; 2 dives incl gear €90, snorkelling tour €50; ⏲9am-9pm Mon-Sat May-Oct) This established outfit offers a host of options, including discover courses (€85), PADI open-water certification (€460), and diving trips around Hania, including beginner dives in PADI training standards.

Sleeping

★**Cocoon City Hostel** HOSTEL €
(Map p488; ☎28210 76100; www.cocooncityhostel.com; Kydonias 145; dm from €18, d with/without bathroom from €40/35; ❄📶) Within easy reach of the bus station and the old town, this modern, spick-and-span hostel has four- and six-bed mixed dorms that come with their own light, charging point and under-bed storage. Private rooms share a bathroom, except one that comes with its own (though its proximity to the lobby cafe-bar means some noise). Helpful staff can arrange excursions to Samaria Gorge.

Hania

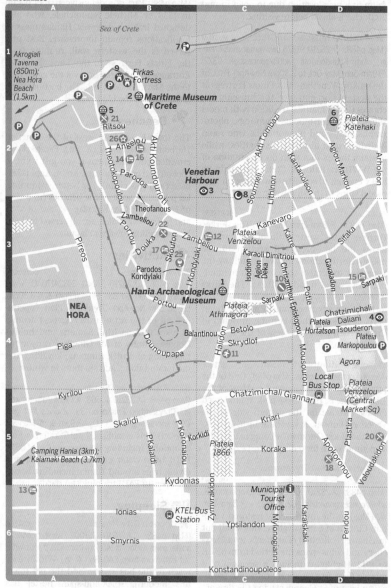

Pension Theresa　　　　　PENSION €

(Map p488; ☎ 28210 92798; www.pensiontheresa. gr; Angelou 8; s €25-30, d €40-70; ❋ ⛱) This creaky old Venetian house with a long, steep, winding staircase and antique furniture delivers eight snug rooms with character aplenty. The location is excellent, the ambience is rustic and convivial, and there are fab views from the rooftop terrace, plus a communal kitchen stocked with basic breakfast items. There's an annexe nearby with apartments suitable for families.

Delightful hosts Maria and Victor are on hand to help at any time.

Hania

◎ Top Sights
1	Hania Archaeological Museum	C3
2	Maritime Museum of Crete	B1
3	Venetian Harbour	C2

◎ Sights
4	Ahmet Aga Minaret	D4
5	Byzantine & Post-Byzantine Collection	B2
6	Grand Arsenal	D2
7	Lighthouse	B1
8	Mosque of Kioutsouk Hasan	C2
9	Venetian Fortifications	B1

✪ Activities, Courses & Tours
10	Blue Adventures Diving	C3
11	Trekking Plan	C4

⬤ Sleeping
12	Bellmondo	C3
13	Cocoon City Hostel	A6
14	Ifigenia Rooms & Studios	B2
15	Ionas Hotel	D3
16	Pension Theresa	B2
17	Serenissima	B3

✪ Eating
18	Bougatsa Iordanis	D5
19	Kouzina EPE	E3
20	Oasis	D5
21	Pulse	B2
22	Tamam Restaurant	B3
23	To Maridaki	E3

◉ Drinking & Nightlife
24	Monogram	E4
25	Sinagogi	B3

✪ Entertainment
26	Fagotto Jazz Bar	B2

are kitted out with all mod cons (including a spa bath in one) and share a rooftop terrace. Original features include a Venetian archway in the entrance and walls from the mid-16th century.

Ifigenia Rooms & Studios   GUESTHOUSE €€
(Map p488; ☑ 28210 94357; www.ifigeniastudios. gr; Gamba 23; r €50-130; ※ ⑤) This network of refurbished buildings around the Venetian Harbour has a bed for every budget, from basic rooms to luxurious bi-level suites with Jacuzzis and sea views. Most of the 25 units brim with such old-timey touches as wrought-iron canopy beds and beamed ceilings. The pricier ones have kitchens and can sleep up to four.

★**Ionas Hotel**   HOTEL €€
(Map p488; ☑ 28210 55090; www.ionashotel.com; cnr Sarpaki & Sorvolou; s/d/ste incl breakfast from €85/100/120; ※ ⑤) In the quieter Splantzia quarter, Ionas is housed in a historic building with contemporary interior design and friendly owners. The nine charming rooms

Bellmondo HOTEL €€
(Map p488; ☑28210 36217; www.belmondohotel.
com; Zambeliou 10; s/d/tr incl breakfast from
€73/90/105; ❄ ☎) With Turkish and Venetian features, including part of an old
hammam (Turkish baths) in one room, the
Bellmondo is furnished with simple wooden
pieces and offers friendly service. The nicest
rooms have balconies (for about €25 more
than the standard rate) and harbour views.

★**Serenissima** BOUTIQUE HOTEL €€€
(Map p488; ☑28210 86386; www.serenissima.gr;
Skoufon 4; d incl breakfast from €170; ❄ ☎) This
tranquil Venetian townhouse, renovated to
impeccable standards, packs plenty of design cachet into its historic walls. The elegant rooms feature the gamut of mod cons,
along with period touches such as stone
walls, wooden beams and candlelit niches.
Rates include an à la carte breakfast in the
downstairs restaurant-bar.

✗ Eating

★**Kouzina EPE** CRETAN €
(Map p488; ☑28210 42391; www.facebook.com/
kouzinaepe; Daskalogianni 25; dishes €5-10;
⊗noon-7.30pm Mon-Sat; ☎🥡) This cheery
lunch spot gets contemporary designer flair
from the cement floor and hip lighting. It
wins the area's 'local favourite' hands down,
by serving a mix of modern à la carte options
and great-value, delicious blackboard-listed
mayirefta (ready-cooked meals); you can
inspect what you're about to eat in the open
kitchen. Good veg options, too.

Bougatsa Iordanis CRETAN €
(Map p488; ☑28210 88855; www.iordanis.gr;
Apokoronou 24; bougatsa €3; ⊗6am-2pm) Locals start salivating at the mention of this
bakery dedicated since 1924 to making the
finest *bougatsa*. The flaky treat, filled with
sweet or savoury cheese, is cooked fresh in
enormous slabs, carved into bite-sized pieces and served on simple aluminium trays.
Pair it with a double Greek coffee and you're
set for the morning. There's nothing else on
the menu!

Pulse VEGAN €
(Map p488; Theotokopoulou 70; mains €9.50;
⊗noon-midnight daily May-Oct, noon-9pm Mon-
Sat Nov-Mar; 🥡) Settle in at an outdoor table with sea views for some fantastic vegan
dishes at meat-free Pulse, located at the
western end of Firkas Fortress. The mezes
boards are great for snacking on, as are the

potato cakes with chilli jam; mains include
a tasty cheeseburger and a beef-free red-
wine casserole. The *mousakas* is an absolute highlight.

Oasis FAST FOOD €
(Map p488; Vouloudakidon 2; souvlaki €2; ⊗9am-
10pm) Locals swear by the undeniably tasty
gyros (meat slivers cooked on a vertical rotisserie) and souvlaki at tiny, old-style Oasis.
There are a few seats inside, but it's mostly
a takeaway joint.

★**To Maridaki** SEAFOOD €€
(Map p488; ☑28210 08880; www.tomaridaki.gr;
Daskalogianni 33; dishes €6-13; ⊗noon-midnight
Mon-Sat) This modern seafood *mezedhopoleio* (restaurant specialising in mezedhes)
is often packed to the gills with chatty locals and tourists. Dishes straddle the line
between tradition and innovation with to-
die-for mussels *saganaki,* charcoal-grilled
fresh fish, and delicious house white wine.
The complimentary panna cotta is a worthy
finish.

Tamam Restaurant MEDITERRANEAN €€
(Map p488; ☑28210 96080; www.tamamrestaur
ant.com; Zambeliou 49; mains €7-14; ⊗noon-
midnight; ☎🥡) This stylish, convivial taverna, part of which is in a converted Turkish
bathhouse, has captured people's attention
since 1982 with strong-flavoured Cretan
dishes that often incorporate Middle Eastern spices and touches. The boneless lamb
in tomato sauce and yoghurt is a winner.
Tables spill onto the narrow alleyway.

★**Thalassino Ageri** SEAFOOD €€€
(☑28210 51136; www.thalasino-ageri.gr; Vivila-
ki 35; fish per kg €55-65; ⊗6.30pm-midnight
Mon-Sat, 12.30pm-midnight Sun Apr & May, from
7pm daily Jun-Oct) This solitary fish taverna
among the vestiges of Hania's old tanneries
in Halepa, 2km east of the centre, is one of
Crete's top restaurants. Take in the sunset
from the superb waterside setting and pe-
ruse the changing menu, dictated by the
day's catch, which is cooked over charcoal.
The fried calamari melts in your mouth.

🍷 Drinking & Nightlife

The cafe-bars around the Venetian Harbour
are nice places to sit, but they charge top
euro. For a more local vibe, head to Plateia
1821 in the Splantzia quarter, the interior
streets near Potie, or to alt-flavoured Sarpi-
dona at the eastern end of the harbour.

★ Monogram
COFFEE

(Map p488; ☑ 28215 07046; www.facebook.com/monogramchania; Daskalogianni 5; ⊘ 8am-9pm) Soak up the sun at a street-side table with music wafting from this hip corner coffee spot. Beans are sourced from around the globe, including Guatemala and Ethiopia, then roasted locally in Iraklio. It also has a large range of teas you'd be hard-pressed to find elsewhere in Greece, and a few tempting cakes.

★ Sinagogi
BAR

(Map p488; ☑ 28210 95242; Parodos Kondylaki 15; ⊘ noon-5am May-Oct; 🛜) Housed in a roofless Venetian building on a small lane next to the synagogue, this popular summer-only lounge bar with eclectic decor is a laid-back place to relax and take it all in. After dark it's bathed in a romantic glow while DJs play soft electro and bartenders whip up mojitos and daiquiris.

☆ Entertainment

★ Fagotto Jazz Bar
LIVE MUSIC

(Map p488; ☑ 28210 71877; Angelou 16; ⊘ 8.30am-2pm & 9pm-late) Established in 1978, this Hania institution in a Venetian building offers smooth jazz and blues, and occasionally live bands or DJs, in an intimate setting in a narrow lane close to the Maritime Museum. The action picks up after 10pm. It opens in the mornings as a cafe and does great breakfasts, too.

🛍 Shopping

Hania offers top shopping, especially in the backstreets. Theotokopoulou is lined with souvenir and handicraft shops. Skrydlof offers a vast array of local and imported sandals, belts and bags. Find some of the most authentic crafts in the Splantzia quarter, along Chatzimichali Daliani and Daskalogianni. The central *agora* (market hall) is touristy but still worth a wander.

ℹ Information

Free wi-fi is widely available in public spaces, including the harbour, around the central market and at Plateia 1866, as well as at most hotels, restaurants, cafes and bars.

Banks cluster around Plateia Markopoulou in the new city, but there are also ATMs in the old town on Halidon.

Alpha Bank (cnr Halidon & Skalidi; ⊘ 8am-6pm Mon-Fri, 10am-5pm Sat, ATM 24hr)

National Bank of Greece (cnr Tzanakaki & Giannari; ⊘ 8am-2pm)

WORTH A TRIP

MANOUSAKIS WINERY

The pretty Manousakis Winery (☑ 28210 78787; www.manousakiswinery.com; Vatolakkos; wine tasting from €10; ⊘ 11am-5pm Apr, to 10pm May–mid-Nov, by appointment rest of year) is a family-run business – 16km southwest of the centre of Hania – that has been around for over 25 years. Taste the Nostos wines (the rosé is made blending the *Romeiko* grape, which is indigenous to Hania), take a free 15-minute tour of the winery production, or simply settle in for lunch or dinner with a bottle on the tree-shaded terrace set among olive groves and citrus trees.

A bus from Hania stops at the main square in Vatolakkos, an eight-minute walk from the winery.

Municipal Tourist Office (Map p488; ☑ 28213 36155; Kydonias 29; ⊘ 9am-3pm Mon-Fri) Modest selection of brochures, maps and transport timetables.

Tourist Police (☑ 171, 28210 25931; ⊘ 24hr) The tourist police can assist with legal matters in multiple languages, including English, French and German.

ℹ Getting There & Away

AIR

Hania's **airport** (☑ 28210 83800; www.chania-airport.com) is 14km east of town on the Akrotiri Peninsula, and is served year-round from Athens and Thessaloniki and seasonally from throughout Europe. A taxi from the airport to anywhere in Hania costs €25. Public buses into town stop right outside the terminal (€2.50, 30 minutes) and run between 5.30am and 11pm daily.

BOAT

Hania's port is at Souda, 7km southeast of town (and the site of a NATO base). The port is linked to town by bus (€2, or €2.50 if paying onboard) and taxi (€10). Hania buses meet each boat, as do buses to Rethymno.

Anek Lines (www.anek.gr) runs an overnight ferry between Piraeus and Hania (from €38 per person, nine hours). Buy tickets online or at the port; reserve ahead for cars.

BUS

Hania's **KTEL bus station** (Map p488; ☑ info 28210 93052, tickets 28210 93306; www.e-ktel.com; Kelaidi 73-77; 🛜) has an information kiosk with helpful staff and timetables, a cafeteria, a

OFF THE BEATEN TRACK

CRETAN BREWERY

Established in 2007, **Cretan Brewery** (☎28240 31002; www.cretanbeer.gr; Zounaki; guided tour €3; ⏰10am-8pm Apr-Nov) makes Charma, the first beer to be produced in Hania and you can sample the excellent brews at the slick operation here, set up by a local. There's a covered terrace where you can enjoy the range of beers, from a blond lager to an excellent pale ale, along with seasonal brews, or opt for a tasting flight of five beers (€5). There's good beer-soaking pub grub on the menu and you can join a guided tour of the brewery; book ahead.

It's located in Zounaki village, around 25km west of the centre of Hania. The attached shop is the only place in Crete where you can buy the beer to take away.

minimarket and a left-luggage service. Check the excellent website for the current schedule.

Getting Around

Local buses are operated by **Chania Urban Buses** (☎28210 98115; http://chaniabus.gr). Zone A/B tickets cost €1.20/1.70 if bought from a kiosk or vending machine and €2/2.50 from the driver.

A handily central **bus stop** (Map p488) for Souda port, Halepa, Nea Hora and other local destinations is on Giannari, near the *agora*.

Taxi (☎28210 98700; www.chaniataxi.gr) Hania-based taxi company.

Kissamos Κίσσαμος

POP 4275

Kissamos is not a place given entirely over to tourism and exudes an unpolished, almost gritty, air compared to other north-coast towns. It's a good base for day-tripping to Balos in the Gramvousa Peninsula by cruise boat and it has an archaeological museum to keep history buffs interested. There are two beaches in town, separated by a waterfront promenade: the sandy Mavros Molos in the west and the pebbly Telonio to the east.

The largest town and capital of Kissamos province, it is referred to interchangeably as Kissamos and as Kastelli (though the official name is the former).

Sights

Archaeological Museum of Kissamos MUSEUM
(☎28220 83308; http://odysseus.culture.gr; Plateia Tzanakaki; adult/child €2/free; ⏰8.30am-6pm Wed-Mon) In an imposing two-level Venetian-Turkish building on the main square, this museum presents locally excavated treasure, including statues, jewellery, coins and a large mosaic floor from a Kissamos villa. Most items are from the Hellenistic and Roman eras, though there are also some Minoan objects. There are exhibits from Falasarna, Polyrrinia and Nopigia, too.

Sleeping

Stavroula Palace HOTEL €€
(☎28220 23620; s/d/tr incl breakfast €50/65/80; ❄📶🏊) Run by the warm and gracious Stavroula and her family, this cheery and good-value waterfront hotel has breezy, modern rooms with balconies fronting a large swimming pool and an immaculately kept garden where breakfast is served. Children's recreation area, too.

Christina Beach Hotel APARTMENT €€
(☎28220 83333; www.christina-beach.gr; studios from €40; P❄@📶🏊) This smart studio complex on the western side of Kissamos represents the upper end of accommodation in town. Right across from the water, the modern studios are large and airy, and the sandy beach is right nearby, or you can just lounge by the inviting pool.

Eating & Drinking

Taverna Sunset TAVERNA €€
(☎28220 83478; Paraliaki; mains €7-14; ⏰noon-midnight) Locals mix with in-the-know visitors at this quintessential family taverna presided over by Giannis, who's usually ensconced behind the grill coaxing meat and fish into succulent perfection. It's right on the waterfront, so you can feel the breezes coming from offshore.

★**Babel Cafe Bar** BAR
(☎28220 22045; ⏰8am-late; 📶) Not only a good choice for a quick breakfast or snack, this smart modern waterfront cafe-bar is a great place for coffee and gets lively at night with young locals. It has one of the most extensive beer and cocktail lists in town, and it's worth swinging by simply for the amazing bay views from its bustling patio.

❶ Getting There & Away

KTEL Bus Station (☑ 28210 93052; www.e-ktel.com; Kampouri)

Triton Ferries (☑ 28210 75444; www.triton ferries.gr) Triton has three ferries a week to Kythira (€15, four hours) and one to Gythio (€25, seven hours).

Around Kissamos

Balos

The rugged Gramvousa Peninsula cradles the lagoon-like sandy beach of Balos, whose shallow, shimmering turquoise waters draw huge crowds in summer. This remote stretch features on many tourist brochures for Crete, and when it's at its best it's a heavenly scene, with lapping waters shimmering with darting fish. If the tide is out, the wind is whipping up or it's overrun by visitors off the cruise ferry, it can be something of a letdown.

Balos can be accessed by a very rough, 12km dirt road, precarious at times, that begins at the end of the main street of Kalyviani village. While some cars do make the drive, a 4WD is really necessary (and note that most car-hire companies won't cover you for damage sustained on the drive to Balos). The views from the car park when you arrive are sensational. From here there's a 1km walking path down to the beach. The other option is to visit Balos on a cruise (☑ 28220 24344; www.cretandailycruises.com; adult/child €27/13; ☉ late Apr–Oct) from Kissamos, which stops first for around 90 minutes at the peninsula's offshore island Imeri Gramvousa, overlooking Balos, where you can make the sweaty climb to the ruins of a humongous Venetian fortress built to keep pirates at bay.

Note: there's no shade at Balos, but you can hire a sun-lounger and an umbrella. Toilet facilities are basic.

Falasarna   Φαλάσαρνα

This broad sweep of beach has magical-looking pink-cream sands and teal waters and is known for its stunning sunsets. Along with superb water clarity, Falasarna has wonderfully big waves: long rollers coming from the open Mediterranean. It gets busy from mid-July to mid-August, primarily with day trippers from Hania and Kissamos.

Spread your towel on the Big Beach (Megali Paralia) at the southern end or pick a spot in one of the coves separated by rocky spits further north.

Bus schedules vary seasonally (check www.e-ktel.com). In summer at least three daily buses make the trip out to Falasarna from Hania (€8.30, 1¾ hours) via Kissamos (Kasteli; €3.80, 40 minutes).

Imbros Gorge

Half the length of the more famous Samaria Gorge, 8km-long Imbros Gorge (€2; ☉ year-round) is no less beautiful and a lot less busy. Most people start in the mountain village of Imbros and hike down to the southern coastal village of Komitades. Going the other way provides a bit more of a workout, as you'll be walking up a gentle grade.

A taxi between the two villages (about €20 to €25) can be arranged by tavernas at either end. The hike takes you past 300m-high walls buttressed by cypresses, holm oaks, fig and almond trees, and redolent sage. Landmarks include a giant arch at the 2km mark (coming from the south) or the 6km mark (coming from the north) and the narrowest point of the ravine (near the 4.5km mark coming from Imbros), which is under 2m wide. The track is easy to follow, as it traces the stream bed past rockslides and caves. Sturdy shoes are essential. Allow two to three hours.

Southern Coast

Hania's rocky southern coast is punctuated by laid-back beach communities and secluded coves reachable only by boat. Samaria Gorge spills out into the village of Agia Roumeli. Along with the impenetrable geography, strong summer winds keep the area happily safe from mass tourism.

Hora Sfakion   Χώρα Σφακίων

POP 212

The more bullet holes you see in the road signs along the way, the closer you are to Hora Sfakion, long renowned in Cretan history for its streak of rebellion against foreign occupiers. But don't worry: the tiny fishing village is today an amiable and somewhat scenic place that caters well to visitors, many of whom are Samaria Gorge hikers stumbling off the Agia Roumeli boat on their way back to Hania. Most pause just long enough to catch the next bus out, but there's sufficient appeal here to tempt you to stay, from boat trips to nearby isolated beaches to hiking the Aradena Gorge.

◉ Sights & Activities

Sweetwater Beach   BEACH
(Glyka Nera) West of Hora Sfakion, lovely Sweetwater Beach is accessible by a small daily ferry (see box below), by taxi boat (one way/return €25/50) or on foot via a stony and partly vertiginous 3.5km coastal path starting at the first hairpin turn of the Anopoli road. A small cafe rents umbrellas and sun chairs.

Notos Mare Marine Adventures   DIVING
(☑ 28210 08536, 6947270106; www.notosmare. com; New Harbour; 1/2 dives €49/85; ⊙ 8am-9pm Apr-Oct) In addition to PADI certification and dives for beginners and advanced divers, this long-running professional outfit also rents boats, organises charter boat and fishing trips, and operates taxi boats 24/7 to secluded beaches along the south coast, including Sweetwater Beach, Mareme and Loutro.

🛏 Sleeping & Eating

There are tavernas lined up along the harbour, but most are fairly touristy affairs. For stunning views, check out Three Brothers (☑ 28250 91040; www.three-brothers-chora-sfakion-crete.com; Vrissi Beach; mains €7.50-18; ⊙ 9am-midnight May-Oct; 🛜), set on a hill overlooking the sea backed by cliffs. Be sure to try the local *Sfakiani pita* – this thin, circular pancake filled with sweet *myzithra* (sheep's-milk cheese) and flecked with honey makes a great breakfast when served with a bit of Greek yogurt on the side.

Xenia Hotel   HOTEL €
(☑ 28250 91490; www.sfakia-xenia-hotel.gr; Old Harbour; d incl breakfast €58; 🅿 ✳ 🛜) Well positioned overlooking the water, this hotel has been around since the early 1960s but has seen a number of upgrades, with another renovation underway at the time of writing.

See in the evening by toasting the waves on your sea-facing balcony.

ℹ Getting There & Away

KTEL buses (☑ 28210 93052; www.e-ktel.com) leave from the square up the hill above the municipal car park. Schedules change seasonally; check online. In summer there are three daily services to/from Hania (€8.30, 1¾ hours) and to/from Frangokastello (€2.30, 30 minutes).

Loutro   Λουτρό
POP 56
The pint-sized fishing village of Loutro is a tranquil crescent of flower-festooned white-and-blue buildings hugging a narrow pebbly beach between Agia Roumeli and Hora Sfakion. It's only accessible by boat and on foot and is the departure point for coastal walks to isolated beaches, such as Finix, Marmara and Sweetwater.

🛏 Sleeping & Eating

Blue House   PENSION €
(☑ 28250 91035; www.thebluehouse.gr; d incl breakfast €50-65; ✳ 🛜) Midway along the white buildings lining the port, the Blue House has spacious, well-appointed rooms with big verandas overlooking the water. The nicest rooms are in the refurbished top-floor section. The taverna downstairs serves excellent *mayirefta* (ready-cooked meals; mains €6 to €9), including delicious *bourekia* baked with zucchini, potato and goat's cheese.

Ilios   SEAFOOD €€
(☑ 28250 91160; www.iliosloutro.gr; mains €5-15; ⊙ 8am-11pm mid-Apr–Oct; 🛜) Ilios is the best spot in town for fish and seafood, though it offers a full range of Cretan classics and breakfast, too. Rooms are also available.

FERRYING AROUND THE SOUTH COAST

Hora Sfakion is the eastern terminus for the south-coast Anendyk (☑ 8am-4pm Mon-Fri 28250 91221; www.anendyk.gr; New Harbour) ferry route. Ferries run to Paleohora (€20.70), Loutro (€6, 20 minutes), Agia Roumeli (€12.50, one hour) and Sougia (€16.20). Boats make extended stops in Agia Roumeli to accommodate Samaria Gorge hikers. Ferries may be cancelled in bad weather, so be careful not to get stuck in Agia Roumeli or Loutro. There are also two to three boats per week to/from Gavdos Island via Loutro and Agia Roumeli (€21.20, four hours). Some ferries carry vehicles (to Sougia with car one way/return €29/50, to Paleohora €36.40, reservation required). There are also ferries direct to Gavdos Island from Hora Sfakion from July to early September (€21.20, 2½ hours).

Schedules vary seasonally, so always check ahead. Often boats only run as far as Agia Roumeli, where you must change for another ferry to Sougia and Paleohora.

GAVDOS ISLAND ΝΗΣΙ ΤΗΣ ΓΑΥΔΟΥ

In the Libyan Sea, 65km from Paleohora and 45km from Hora Sfakion, Gavdos is Europe's most southerly point and as much a state of mind as it is an island. It's a blissful spot with only a few rooms, tavernas and unspoilt beaches, some accessible only by foot or boat. There's little to do here except swim, walk and relax. Gavdos attracts campers, nudists and free spirits happy to trade the trappings of civilisation for an unsullied nature experience.

The island is surprisingly green, with almost 65% covered in low-lying pine and cedar trees and vegetation. Most of the electricity is supplied by generators, which are often turned off at night and in the middle of the day. Day trippers can take the Gavdos Cruises (☑ 6981920076; www.gavdos-cruises.jimdo.com; adult/child return €40/20) fast boat departing at 10.10am and returning from Gavdos at 5pm. The journey takes one hour.

❶ Information

There's no bank, ATM or post office, and many places do not accept credit cards. Bring plenty of cash. The nearest ATM is in Hora Sfakion.

Sougia Σούγια

POP 136

Sougia, 67km south of Hania and on the Hora Sfakion–Paleohora ferry route, is one of the most chilled-out and refreshingly undeveloped southern beach resorts. Cafes, bars and tavernas line a tamarisk-shaded waterfront promenade along a grey pebble-and-sand beach. Most pensions and apartments enjoy a quieter inland setting roughly 100m to 200m from the beach. There is little to do other than relax or explore the local hiking trails, including the popular Agia Irini Gorge and Lissos beach and ruins.

🏃 Activities

Sougia has a pleasant 1km-long grey sand-and-pebble beach, but its drop-off is steep, so it's not ideal for families with small children.

★ Agia Irini Gorge HIKING

(€2; ⊙ year-round) Pretty Agia Irini Gorge starts around 13km north of Sougia near the village of Agia Irini. The well-maintained, well-signposted and mostly shaded 7.5km trail (with a 500m elevation drop) follows the riverbed, is shaded by oleander, pines and other greenery, and passes caves hidden in the gorge walls. Allow around three hours to complete the hike.

It makes for a lovely, less crowded alternative to Samaria Gorge. The trail includes a few steep sections but is mostly relatively easy, with a few river crossings. There are rest stops with benches and toilets along the way, but be sure to take plenty of drinking water with you. You'll emerge at a taverna where

you can call a taxi (€15) or continue on foot for another 4.5km via a paved road to Sougia.

🍴 Sleeping & Eating

Aretousa Studios & Rooms APARTMENT €

(☑ 28230 51178; studios €55-65; ⊙ Apr-Oct; P ❄ 🛜) This lovely pension on the road to Hania, 200m from the sea, has bright and comfortably furnished studios with tile floors and balconies. There's a tranquil garden, friendly service and even a kids' playground out the back.

Polyfimos TAVERNA €

(☑ 28230 51343; www.polifimos.gr; Main Rd; mains €5-11; ⊙ 1pm-midnight Apr-Oct) Hidden in a pretty grapevine-shrouded courtyard off the Hania road, this charismatic restaurant specialises in traditional charcoal-grilled local meats, fresh fish of the day, hearty stews such as rabbit *stifadho* (cooked with onions in a tomato puree) and lamb *tsigariasto*. It's run by ex-hippie Yiannis, who also makes his own oil, wine and raki.

★ Omikron INTERNATIONAL €€

(☑ 28230 51492; Beach Rd; mains €7-12; ⊙ 8am-late Apr-Oct; 🛜 🍴) At this elegantly rustic beachfront spot with crushed pebbles underfoot, Jean-Luc Delfosse has forged his own culinary path in a refreshing change from taverna staples. From mushroom crêpes to *Flammekuche* (Alsatian-style pizza), seafood pasta to pepper steak – it's all fresh, creative and delicious.

❶ Information

There is one ATM in Sougia.

❶ Getting There & Away

At least one daily bus operates between Sougia and Hania (€7.80, 1¾ hours), with a stop in Agia

DON'T MISS

SAMARIA GORGE

Hiking the 16km-long Samaria Gorge (☑ 28210 45570; www.samaria.gr; Omalos; adult/child €5/free; ⊙ 7.30am-4pm May–mid-Oct), one of Europe's longest canyons, is high on the list of must-dos for many visitors to Crete. There's an undeniable raw beauty to the canyon, with its soaring cliffs and needlenose passageways. The hike begins at an elevation of 1230m just south of Omalos at Xyloskalo and ends in the coastal village of Agia Roumeli. It's also possible to do it the 'lazy way': hiking a shorter distance by starting at Agia Roumeli. The only way out of Agia Roumeli is by taking the boat to Sougia or Hora Sfakion, which are served by bus and taxi back to Hania.

The best time for the Samaria trek is in April and May, when wildflowers brighten the trail. Keep your eyes peeled for the endemic *kri-kri*, a shy endangered wild goat.

Hiking the Gorge

From the trailhead at Xyloskalo, a steep, serpentine stone path descends some 600m into the canyon to arrive at the simple, cypress-framed Chapel of Agios Nikolaos.

Beyond here the gorge is wide and open and not particularly scenic for the next 6km until you reach the abandoned settlement of Samaria. This is the main rest stop, with toilets, water and benches. Just south of the village is a 14th-century chapel dedicated to St Maria of Egypt, after whom the gorge is named.

Further on, the gorge narrows and becomes more dramatic until, at 11km, the walls are only 3.5m apart and you'll find the famous Sideroportes (Iron Gates), where a rickety wooden pathway leads hikers the 20m or so across the water.

The gorge ends at the 13km mark just north of the almost abandoned village of Palea (Old) Agia Roumeli. From here it's a further 3km to the seaside village of Agia Roumeli, whose fine pebble beach and sparkling water are a most welcome sight. Few people miss taking a refreshing dip or at least bathing their aching feet before they fill up at one of the seaside tavernas.

The entire trek takes about four hours (for sprinters) to six hours (for strollers). This is a rocky trail and suitable footwear is essential.

Sleeping & Eating

It is forbidden to camp (or indeed spend the night) in the gorge. Stay at Omalos at the northern end, or Agia Roumeli in the south.

There are tavernas in Omalos, including one right by the gorge entrance. When the gorge is open, stands sell souvenirs, snacks, bottled water and the like. Agia Roumeli has several tavernas. There's also a snack stall at the national-park exit selling beer, coffee and other refreshments.

Getting There & Away

Most people hike Samaria one way, going north–south on a day trip that can be arranged from every sizeable town and resort in Crete. Confirm whether tour prices include gorge admission (€5) and the boat ride from Agia Roumeli to Sougia or Hora Sfakion.

With some planning, it's possible to do the trek on your own. There are early-morning public buses to Omalos from Hania (€7.50, one hour), Sougia (€5.30, one hour) and Paleohora (€7, one hour), once or twice daily in high season. Check www.e-ktel.com for the schedule, which changes seasonally. Taxis are another option.

At the end of the trail, in Agia Roumeli, ferries operated by Anendyk (☑ 28250 91251; www.anendyk.gr) depart for Sougia (€11) and Hora Sfakion (€12.50) at 5.30pm and take 40 minutes. These are usually met by public buses back to Hania from Hora Sfakion at 6.30pm and Sougia at 6.15pm; some buses from Sougia go to Omalos.

Irini to drop off gorge hikers. The bus departing Sougia at 6.15pm waits for the Agia Roumeli boat. In summer there are also daily buses to Omalos (for Samaria Gorge; €5.30, one hour).

Local taxi drivers, including **Selino Taxi** (☑ 6940859860; www.taxi-selino.com) and **Sougia Taxi** (☑ 6970344422; www.sougiataxi.com), have a central kiosk on the waterfront.

Paleohora   Παλαιόχωρα

POP 1900

Appealing, laid-back and full of character, Paleohora lies on a narrow peninsula flanked by a long, curving, tamarisk-shaded sandy beach (Pahia Ammos) and a pebbly beach (Halikia). Shallow waters and general quietude make the village a good choice for families with small children. The most picturesque part of Paleohora is the maze of narrow streets below the castle. Tavernas spill out onto the pavement and occasional cultural happenings inject a lively ambience. In spring and autumn Paleohora attracts many walkers.

🛌 Sleeping

Joanna's Place   APARTMENT €

(☑6978583503, 28230 41801; www.joanna-place.com; studios €50-60, 2-bed apt €100-110; ☺Apr-Nov; 🅿❄🌐) This modern beige building sits in a quiet spot across from a small stone beach at the southeastern tip of the peninsula. The 16 spacious and spotless studios are outfitted with functional locally made furniture, and there's a kitchenette for preparing breakfast to enjoy on your balcony. There's also a two-bedroom apartment that will suit families.

Villa Anna   PENSION €

(☑28103 46428; www.villaanna-paleochora.com; apt €50-75; ❄🌐) Run by the warm and welcoming Anna and set in a lovely shady garden bordered by tall poplars, these well-appointed, family-friendly apartments sleep up to five. There are cots, and swings and a sandpit in the garden, and the grounds are fenced.

🍴 Eating & Drinking

To Skolio   CRETAN €

(☑28230 83001; Anydri; dishes €5-13; ☺coffee from 9am, food noon-11pm daily Easter-Oct; 🌐) Whether gorge walker or hire-car driver, do not miss the chance to dine at wonderful To Skolio, about 5km east of Paleohora. The converted red-and-white schoolhouse has cheerily painted tables on a tree-shaded cliff-side terrace with views out to sea. The daily-changing chalkboard menu of mezedhes (small dishes) incorporates the best local produce.

Third Eye   VEGETARIAN €

(☑6986793504, 28230 41234; https://thirdeye-paleochora.com; mains €6-9; ☺1-10pm; 🌐🍴) A local institution and community gathering spot since 1990, the Third Eye knew what to do with beetroot, quinoa and hummus long before meatless fare went mainstream. The globally inspired menu features delicious salads, rotating mains, and snacks such as a juicy portobello burger and caramelised-onion *fava* dip with bread. Sit on the streetside patio or in the tranquil garden.

★ Monika's Garden Wine Bar   WINE BAR

(☑28230 41150; www.facebook.com/monikas garden; Kondekaki; ☺6pm-1am Apr-Oct) One of the best spots for a drink in town, this attractive, modern wine bar with a delightful garden courtyard features more than 40 top-quality wines by the glass, all from Crete. Drop in for a tipple paired with snacks such as cheese platters and traditional *kalitsounia* (filled pastries).

ℹ Information

There's a couple of ATMs on the main drag, Eleftheriou Venizelou.

ℹ Getting There & Away

KTEL (☑28230 41914; www.e-ktel.com; Eleftherios Venizelos) runs four daily buses to Hania (€8.30, 1¾ hours) and one bus daily except Sunday at 6.15am to Omalos (€7, one hour) for

---

OFF THE BEATEN TRACK

MARVELLOUS MILIA

The isolated mountain resort village of Milia (☑28210 46774; www.milia.gr; Vlatos; cottages incl breakfast from €85; ☺year-round; 🅿🌐) is one of Crete's ecotourism trailblazers. Inspired by a back-to-nature philosophy, 16 abandoned stone farmhouses were transformed into ecocottages sleeping one to four, with only solar energy for basic needs. Milia is one of the most peaceful places to stay in Crete, but it's also worth visiting just to dine at the superb organic restaurant (mains €9-13; ☺1-8pm; 🅿🌐).

Milia makes a great base for those who wish to unwind and see the Innahorion region. The cottages have antique beds, rustic furnishings, and fireplaces or wood-burning stoves. Since it's all solar powered, it's best to shelve the laptop and hairdryer. To reach Milia, follow the signposted turnoff north of the village of Vlatos. The narrow access road becomes a drivable 3km dirt road.

PALEOHORA–SOUGIA COASTAL WALK

Following a portion of the E4 European Path, this hike connects two charming coastal towns via a 13km path that runs mostly along the coast and then heads inland from Lissos to Sougia.

From Paleohora, follow signs to the camp sites to the northeast and turn right at the sign for Anydri. After a couple of kilometres the path climbs steeply for a beautiful view back to Paleohora. You'll pass Anydri Beach and several inviting coves where people may be getting an all-over tan. Take a dip, because the path soon turns inland to pass over Cape Flomes. You'll walk along a plateau carpeted with brush that leads towards the coast and some breathtaking views over the Libyan Sea. About 10km into the hike you'll reach the Dorian site of Lissos, from where the path weaves through a pine forest before spilling out at Sougia.

Allow five to six hours for the nearly shadeless walk and take plenty of water, a hat and sunblock. From June to August it's best to start at sunrise in order to get to Sougia before the heat of the day. The boat back to Paleohora runs at around 6pm (check the schedule at www.anendyk.gr).

Samaria Gorge. Buses also stop in Sougia and, on request, at the Agia Irini Gorge trailhead. There are also Elafonisi-bound buses (€5.50, one hour).

Paleochora Taxi (6979594667, 28230 41128; www.paleochora-taxi.com; 7.30am-10pm) This professional outfit runs shuttle buses to the trailheads for Agia Irini (€19 per person) and Samaria Gorges (€25 per person including the boat ticket for the return) three times a week, departing at 7.30am.

Elafonisi   Ελαφονήσι

Tucked into Crete's southwestern corner, this symphony of fine pink-white sand, turquoise water and gentle rose dunes looks like a magical dreamscape. As the water swirls across the sands, rainbows shimmer across its surface. Off Elafonisi's long, wide strand lies Elafonisi Islet, occasionally connected by a thin, sandy isthmus, which creates a lovely double beach; otherwise, it's easily reached by wading through 50m of knee-deep water.

Elafonisi Islet is marked by low dunes and a string of semisecluded coves that attract a sprinkling of naturists. Walk the length of the beach and up to its high point for mind-blowing views of the beaches, sea and raw mountainscape. The area is part of EU environmental-protection program Natura 2000.

Alas, this natural gem is less than idyllic in high summer, when hundreds of umbrellas and sunbeds clog the sand (dash out to the island, where you can find peace). The invasion puts enormous pressure on this delicate ecosystem and on the minimal infrastructure, especially the toilets (€0.50). Come early or late in the day; better yet, stay overnight to truly sample Elafonisi's magic. Outside high season, when there's no public transport to the beach and very few tours, you may have it all to yourself. There are a few snack bars and stores at the beach entrance. Elafonisi is about 75km southwest of Hania town – reckon on 1½ to two hours for the nonstop drive.

From Paleohora, one boat (€10, one hour) and one bus (€5.50, one hour) make a daily trip out here from June to September. There's also one daily bus from Hania (€11, 2¼ hours) via Kissamos (Kastelli; €6.90, 1¼ hours) from June to September.

LASITHI PROVINCE

Crete's easternmost region is home to the island's top resorts: Agios Nikolaos smoulders with cosmopolitan cool, while just around the bay, Elounda tiptoes between luxe and relaxed. Paradoxically, this is also the wildest region, with the richest biodiversity and the least trampled ranges; it's so rugged in places that you half expect Pan to emerge, pipes in hand, from the meadows.

For the wanderer in search of adventure and gastro delights, Lasithi ticks all the boxes: cyclists head up to misty Lasithi Plateau, trekkers tackle dramatic canyons such as the famous Zakros Gorge, and foodies enjoy some of Crete's finest tavernas and restaurants. Then there are attractions like the historic monastery of Toplou, Vaï's beguiling palm-lined beach, and scores of towns and villages that maintain a rich undertow of Cretan history and spirit. And let's not forget Lasithi's rich ancient history, with Minoan and Dorian sites to explore in numerous places.

Agios Nikolaos
Αγιος Νικόλαος

POP 12,000

Lasithi's capital, Agios Nikolaos has an enviable location on hilly terrain overlooking the sensuously curving Bay of Mirabello. There's a strong local character to Agios Nikolaos that imbues it with charismatic, low-key flair. A narrow channel separates the small harbour from the circular Voulismeni Lake, whose shore is lined with cafes and restaurants.

In the daytime the city beaches, while not particularly large or pretty, lend themselves to a few hours of relaxing and taking a dip in the sea. There's also some decent shopping in the pedestrianised lane above the lake.

Agios Nikolaos truly comes into its own at night, when a lively ambience descends on the lake, harbour and beaches, and loungebars fill with stylish young Greeks and holidaymakers from the nearby resorts.

Beaches

The most central beaches are sandy Ammos (Map p500) and Kytroplatia (Map p500), but both are small and get crowded. Let your feet take you 1km north and south respectively to tree-backed Ammoudi and Almyros for longer stretches of finer sand to spread your towel. Drawing mostly a local crowd is small, pebbly Gargadoros, just before Almyros. All beaches have umbrellas and sun chairs for rent.

Activities

Sail Crete BOATING
(☑ 6937605600, 28410 24376; www.sailcrete.com; Minos Beach Art Hotel, Agios Nikolaos-Vrouchas Rd; half/full day incl snacks & drinks €900/1300) This sailing-charter outfit arranges private half- and full-day cruises to Spinalonga Island and beyond aboard the *General,* a handsome 14m catamaran, and the 12m *Jaquelina* yacht. Boats depart from the Pelagos Dive Centre at Minos Beach Art Hotel. Bring a swimsuit and towels for a cooling dip during the cruise.

Creta's Happy Divers DIVING
(☑ 28410 82546; www.happydivers.gr; Akti Koundourou 23; boat dive €50) In business since 1989, Happy Divers has a wealth of experience and knows local sites inside out. Rates include all equipment. Also offers PADI certification courses from open water to dive master.

Nostos Cruises BOATING
(Map p500; ☑ 28410 22819; www.nostoscruises.com; Rousou Koundourou 30; trips to Spinalonga with/without barbecue €25/16; ☺ 8am-9pm) Nostos Cruises runs 4½-hour boat trips to Spinalonga Island, including a swim at Kolokytha Beach, from the harbour in Agios Nikolaos on large vessels with two bars and a restaurant. Another version of this trip includes a barbecue on the beach. Fishing trips are also possible.

Pelagos Dive Centre DIVING
(☑ 28410 24376, 6937605600; http://divecrete.com; Minos Beach Art Hotel, Agios Nikolaos-Vrouchas Rd; dives incl equipment from €60, night dives €80; ☺ Apr-Nov) Just north of town, this well-established PADI centre offers dives at all levels as well as PADI courses and introductory dives for kids. It's part of the Minos Beach Art Hotel but has its own entrance in the northern section of the compound. Boat hire is also available.

Sleeping

Pension Mylos PENSION €
(Map p500; ☑ 28410 23783; http://pensionmylos.com; Sarolidi 24; s/d/tr €47/55/67; ☀ ❄ 🛜 🏠) At these prices, you know you're not getting the Ritz, but behind the faded facade lie surprisingly welcoming, though wee, rooms with bedside lamps, shiny en suites, seaward balconies and quality mattresses. The charming owner truly delivers on her tagline of 'home from home'. Fridge, TV and coffee-making service, too. Wi-fi in public areas only.

Pergola Hotel HOTEL €
(Map p500; ☑ 28410 28152; http://pergola-hotel.agios-nikolaos-crete.hotel-crete.net; Sarolidi 20; s/d/apt €32/38/65; ☺ Apr-Oct; ☀ ❄ 🛜) Though not of recent vintage, this low-key guesthouse is an excellent base of operation whose owners get an A+ for charm. Lovingly spruced-up units range from singles to family apartments with kitchen; the nicest sport four-poster beds and balconies from where you can wave at passing ships. Optional breakfast is €5.

Hotel Creta APARTMENT €€
(Map p500; ☑ 28410 28893; www.agiosnikolaoshotels.gr; Sarolidi 22; apt €70-90; ☺ late Apr-Sep; ☀ ❄ 🛜) These 23 breezy and good-value self-catering studios and apartments sleeping two to four are in a quiet location, yet just a few minutes' walk from the harbour. All have balconies, but only units on the upper floors face the sparkling bay. There's a lift, as

Agios Nikolaos

Creta's Happy Divers (150m); Toedeledokie (150m);
Ammoudi Beach (700m); Minos Beach Art Hotel (1km);
Lato Hotel (1.3km); Villa Olga (6km)

Bay of Mirabello

Port
Municipal
Tourist
Office

Voulismeni
Lake

Plateia
Venizelou

(600m)

Kytroplatia
Beach

Gargadoros Beach
(700m); Almyros
Beach (2km)

Ammos
Beach

Agios Nikolaos

well as limited parking in the surrounding streets. Optional breakfast is €8.

Minos Beach Art Hotel　　　RESORT €€€
(☑28410 22345; www.minosbeach.com; Agios Nikolaos-Vrouchas Rd; r incl breakfast from €500; ☺Apr-Oct; P❄🛜🌊) Privacy, luxury and tranquillity are taken very seriously in this sprawling resort in a superb waterfront location just north of town. Gardens dotted with conversation-sparking art lead to white-cube bungalows and villas kitted out in comfy but minimalist style. Some have private pools; the most coveted front the sea. Four restaurants, three bars, a gym and a spa invite lingering.

🍴 Eating

Creta Embassy　　　　　　　GREEK €
(Map p500; ☑28410 83153; www.cretaembassy. com; Kondylaki; mains €7-10; ☺noon-late; ❄) Eclectic curios, wooden furniture and a fairytale garden make this traditional restaurant a few steps from the lake as welcoming as a hug from an old friend. Lamb *kleftiko* (slow oven-baked), veal with lemon, casseroles,

and calamari with mouthwatering olives are among the menu stars.

★Pelagos
SEAFOOD €€

(Map p500; ☑28410 25737; Stratigou Koraka 11; mains €9-25; ⊙noon-midnight Apr-Oct; 🛜) Pelagos is not for the indecisive. First you must choose whether to sit in the elegantly rustic historic house or in the romantic garden with colourful furniture and wall fountain. Tough one – but perhaps not as tough as deciding whether to feast on fresh fish, grilled meats, inventive salads or homemade pastas. If in doubt, go for the seafood pasta.

Portes
CRETAN €€

(Map p500; ☑28410 28489; Anapafseos 2; mezedhes €2.50-7.50; ⊙12.30pm-1am; 🗷) Conversation flows as freely as the excellent house wine at this garage-sized taverna, where wooden doors, all evocatively weathered and cheerfully painted, form part of the charming backdrop to home-cooked mezedhes. Menu stars include a soulful rabbit *stifadho* (stew cooked with onions in a tomato puree) with plums and figs, and chicken with peppers and feta.

Ble Katsarolakia
GREEK €€

(Map p500; ☑28410 21955; www.blekatsarolakia.gr; Akti Koundourou 8; mains €7-16; ⊙noon-1am; 🗷🛜☑) Enjoying great views of the harbour, this effervescent restaurant, with its modern decor of exposed stone, turquoise walls and white-wood floors, offers a contemporary take on Greek cuisine, serving up tzatziki, halloumi, souvlaki, octopus and much more. It's packed with young Greeks and deservedly so. Take the lift to the top floor.

Drinking & Nightlife

The buzziest party strip is along car-free Akti Koundourou east of the harbour, whose see-and-be-seen lounge bars are busy from midmorning until the wee hours. Akti Koundourou continues north of the harbour, where a few grittier watering holes lure more low-key punters.

Toedeledokie
BAR

(☑28410 25537; www.toedeledokiecafe-bar.com; Akti Koundourou 19; ⊙9am-late; 🛜) Dutch for 'cheerio', Toedeledokie is the brainchild of Dutch artist Lucia, who supplies killer coffee, creamy milkshakes and creative toasties all day long below cheerful umbrellas on the waterfront terrace. At night, make new friends over cold beers and finely crafted cocktails and see if you can coax Lucia

into divulging tips on the area's 'secret' destinations.

Bajamar
BAR

(Map p500; ☑6973366035; Sarolidi 1; ⊙9am-2am or later) The most stylish among the harbourfront bars, Bajamar is a mellow daytime port of call for coffee, juices and snacks but is buzziest after 11pm, when the cocktails are flowing and a DJ showers shiny happy people with a high-energy mix of Latin, funk and house.

Arodo Cafe
BAR

(Map p500; ☑28410 89895; www.facebook.com/pg/arodocoffeebeerwine; Akti Koundourou 6; ⊙11am-2am; 🛜) This alt-flavoured lair buzzes with the conversation of earnest boho locals and offers a cocktail of cool tunes, a sea-facing terrace, and an eclectic selection of beer and wine. Located at the corner of Kantanoleontos. The entrance is up the steep stairs. Also serves breakfast and snacks.

Yanni's Rock Bar
BAR

(Map p500; Akti Koundourou 1; ⊙10pm-5am) The clientele is chatty, the rock music thunderous and the beer ice cold at this funky haunt that's rocked the waterfront since 1983, making it the town's oldest music bar. Its walls peppered with old Brando and Stallone photos, Yanni's oozes atmosphere from every nook and cranny and is a night owl's delight.

🛈 Information

General Hospital (☑28413 43000; cnr Knosou & Paleologou; ⊙24hr) OK for broken bones and X-rays, but for anything more serious you'll need to head to Iraklio.

Municipal Tourist Office (Map p500; ☑28410 22357; www.agiosnikolaoscrete.com; Akti Koundourou 21; ⊙9am-5pm Mon-Sat Apr-Nov, extended hours Jul & Aug; 🛜) Has helpful staff, free maps of the city and surrounds, and free bike rentals.

Tourist Police (☑28410 91409, emergency 171; Erythrou Stavrou 49)

🛈 Getting There & Away

Bus Station (☑28410 22234; Epimenidou 59) From the main bus station, about 1.5km north of the city centre, buses leave for Ierapetra (€4.10, one hour, nine daily), Iraklio (€7.70, 1½ hours, 22 daily), Kritsa (€1.80, 30 minutes, six daily), Sitia (€8.30, 1½ hours, six daily) and other destinations.

The most central **taxi rank** (Map p500; Paleologou) is behind the tourist office down by the lake. Typical fares are €14 for Elounda, €21 for Plaka,

€14 for Kritsa and €20 for Ancient Lato. There are additional ranks on Plateia Venizelou and at the main bus station.

Around Agios Nikolaos

Elounda   Ελούντα

POP 2200

Although surrounded by some of Crete's most luxurious resorts, Elounda retains a charming down-to-earth feel. Salty fishing craft bob in its little harbour, where you can board a boat to Spinalonga, a former leper colony and the area's biggest tourist attraction. Attractive shops, bars and tavernas wrap around the harbour and continue north along the sandy municipal beach and south along a paved waterfront promenade. Offshore lies the rugged Spinalonga Peninsula, linked to the mainland by a narrow causeway and home to ancient ruins, beaches and hiking trails.

🏃 Activities

Blue Dolphin Diving Centre   DIVING
(☑ 6955897711, 28410 41802; www.dive-bluedolphin.com; Ellinika; dive incl equipment €55, open-water course €390) The crystalline sea around Elounda offers excellent diving, with around 20 sites ready to be explored. Make finny friends on expeditions run by this professional and experienced PADI centre based at the Hotel Aquila Elounda Village in Ellinika, about 3.5km south of Elounda.

🛏 Sleeping

Dolphins Apartments   APARTMENT €
(☑ 28410 41641; http://dolphins.elounda-crete.hotel-crete.net; Papandreou 51; apt €50; P ❉ 🛜) These six one-bedroom apartments with pleasingly rustic furniture and tile floors pack a lot of features into a compact frame, including a kitchenette with microwave and a furnished balcony (with neat dolphin motif) overlooking the sea. It's a five-minute stroll into town along the waterfront promenade.

Corali Studios & Portobello Apartments   APARTMENT €
(☑ 28410 41712; www.coralistudios.com; Akti Poseidonos; apt €45-75; P ❉ 🛜 ⛱) Immaculately kept Corali and Portobello sit side by side amid flower-festooned gardens and overlooking the town beach. The 35 stucco-walled studios and apartments come with balcony,

kitchenette and wooden furniture painted cheerful shades of blue. All except the economy units have a sea view. Catch some rays by the good-size pool with snack bar.

★**Elounda Heights**   HOTEL €€
(☑ 6932385337; www.eloundaheights.com; Emmanouil Pouli; apt €85-115; ⊘ late Apr-Oct; P ❉ 🛜 ⛱) This hilltop hideaway run by a charming family is a class act all around. Swoon-worthy bay views unfold from your sunny studio or apartment with terrace, thoughtfully equipped kitchenette and crisp decor picking up the shades of the sea. A garden bursting with roses and oleander wraps around the units and the pool, where days start with a lavish breakfast.

Home-cooked dinners are available in the main house. No children permitted.

🍴 Eating & Drinking

★**Hope**   CRETAN €€
(To Rakadiko Tou Kamari; ☑ 6972295150; Mavrikiano; mains €6-18; ⊘ noon-11.30pm) Clinging to a steep hillside in the ancient hamlet of Mavrikiano above Elounda, Hope has been a local fixture since 1938. The terrace where fishermen once gathered nightly to suss out the next day's weather is now packed with people getting giddy on wine, raki, home-made mezedhes, succulent lamb chops and the stupendous bay view.

It's run by a charismatic couple, Dimitris and Amalia, with respect for the past *and* modern nutritional needs. If you're driving, the turnoff is about 600m north of Elounda's main square.

★**Okeanis**   MEDITERRANEAN €€
(☑ 28410 44404; Akti Poseidonos 7; mains €8.50-14; ⊘ 11.30am-4pm & 6-11pm Apr-Oct) At Okeanis, the decor, menu and service blend as perfectly as the rich oven-baked lamb with garlic and sweet wine that's a top menu pick, alongside chef Adonis' handmade stuffed ravioli and tortellini. It's all served in an elegant yet relaxed loft-style al fresco space with white furniture and leafy plants.

★**Ergospasio**   GREEK €€€
(☑ 28410 42082; www.facebook.com/pg/ergos pasio; Akti Olountos 5; mains €15-23; ⊘ noon-midnight Apr-Oct) A design feast in a converted carob factory with rave-worthy food to match. Count the fish in the sea from tables lined up along – and above – the waterfront while savouring market-fresh and skilfully executed Greek faves. If you're here at dinner

time, try lamb or chicken slow-roasted in the custom-designed *antikristo* spit grill. Also a great anytime spot for coffee or cocktails.

★**Beeraki** PUB
(☑28410 42785; Mavrikiano; ☺11am-midnight or later May-Oct) Well worth the uphill walk to the ancient village of Mavrikiano, this adorable drinking den does a roaring trade in bottled craft beers, quality local wines and expertly prepared cocktails. There's a small menu of elevated pub grub to keep your brain balanced so that you can enjoy the panoramic sea views just a little longer.

❶ **Getting There & Away**

Up to 14 buses daily shuttle between Agios Nikolaos and Elounda (€1.90, 20 minutes). The **bus stop** (Plateia Elountas) is on the main square, where you can buy tickets at the kiosk next to Nikos Taverna.

The **taxi stand** (☑28410 41151; Plateia Elounda) is also on the square. The fare to Agios Nikolaos is €14 and to Plaka €8.

Cars, motorcycles and scooters can be hired at **Olous Travel** (☑28410 41324; www.olous-travel.gr; Plateia Elountas; ☺9am-11pm) and **Elounda Travel** (☑28410 41800; www.eloundatravel.gr; Sfakianaki 3; car per day/week from €45/160; ☺8am-9pm), both with offices on, you guessed it, the main square, which also serves as a (fee-based) car park.

Plaka Πλάκα

POP 100

Wind-pounded Plaka, 5km north of Elounda, is a bijou village of attractive boutiques, a narrow pebble beach and a string of cosy tavernas hugging the waterfront. It's also the best jumping-off point for Spinalonga Island (p504). A boat co-op makes the 10-minute trip to the island twice hourly.

Kritsa Κριτσά

POP 2000

Clinging to the craggy foothills of the Dikti range, Kritsa is one of the oldest and prettiest mountain villages in eastern Crete. The upper village with its web of narrow, car-free lanes is especially atmospheric. Along the main strip, Kritsotopoulas, you'll find charming cafes, shops slinging local products and surprisingly sophisticated boutiques. Away from the village, rugged Kritsa Gorge, the romantic ruins of Ancient Lato and the church of Panagia Kera, with its stunning Byzantine frescoes, are all worth your attention.

Note that in season Kritsa is often clogged with tour buses and day trippers, so come early or late in the day to avoid the worst crowds.

◉ Sights

★**Church of Panagia Kera** CHURCH
(☑28410 51806; Eparchiotiki Odos Agios Nikolaos-Prinas; adult/concession €2/1; ☺8.30am-4pm Wed-Mon; ℙ) This tiny triple-aisled church on the main road shelters Crete's best-preserved Byzantine frescoes. The oldest in the central nave (13th century) depict scenes surrounding the life of Christ, including the Ascension in the apse, the four Gospel scenes (Presentation, Baptism, Raising of Lazarus and Entry into Jerusalem) in the dome and a superb Last Supper. The south aisle is dedicated to St Anne, mother of Mary, with depictions including her marriage and Mary's birth. The north aisle focuses on St Anthony.

The church is about 1km south of Krista – look for the parking area opposite the Paradise restaurant. After your visit, you can sit in the garden cafe and ponder it all.

★**Ancient Lato** ARCHAEOLOGICAL SITE
(Λατώ; ☑28410 22462; http://odysseus.culture.gr; adult/concession €2/1; ☺8.30am-4pm Wed-Mon) The fortified hilltop city state of Lato is one of Crete's best-preserved non-Minoan ancient sites and worth the trip for the rural serenity and stunning views down to the Bay of Mirabello alone. Founded by the Dorians in the 7th century BCE, Lato reached its heyday in the 3rd century BCE but was gradually abandoned. By the 2nd century CE its administrative centre had moved to its port in present-day Agios Nikolaos.

About 100m past the ticket gate, you enter the site via the city gate, from where a long, stepped street leads up to the agora (marketplace) past a wall with two towers, residences, and buildings that housed shops and workshops. At the top of the steps, as you approach the agora, you'll first come upon vestiges of a stoa (colonnaded portico). Immediately behind it is a rectangular temple where numerous 6th-century-BCE figurines were unearthed. The deep hole to the left of the temple was Lato's public cistern. Behind it, a monumental staircase leads up to the prytaneion (administrative centre). At its centre, a hearth that burnt 24/7 was surrounded by stepped benches where the city leaders held their meetings.

South of the agora, climb up the slope to a terrace with another sanctuary fronted by

CRETE AROUND AGIOS NIKOLAOS

a three-stepped altar. Views of the entire site are fabulous from here. Down below to your right (east) you can spot a theatral area that could seat about 350 spectators on stone benches cut into the rock and on an exedra (open portico with seats).

Nearchus, an admiral under Alexander the Great, is believed to hail from Lato, whose name derives from the goddess Leto. Legend has it that Leto's union with Zeus produced Artemis and Apollo.

There are no buses to Lato. The nearest stop is in Kritsa, from where it's a 3km walk north. The site is off the Kritsa–Lakonion Rd.

Activities

★ Kritsa Gorge   HIKING

Kritsa Gorge, signposted off the road to Ancient Lato, is one of eastern Crete's most enchanting canyons. Flanked by steep cliffs, it follows a riverbed dotted with oak and olive trees and resplendent with spring wildflowers. Sturdy shoes and reasonable fitness are essential, since the trail is stony and requires occasional bouldering and the handling of metal rails and a rope.

There are two routes. The shorter one (about 5km) follows the canyon for about 2km before heading uphill; turn right and follow the trail paralleling the gorge below back to the parking area. The longer one (about 11km) continues to the village of Tapes. Along the way you will encounter fences put there by shepherds to keep the goat herd together. Be sure to close their gates again after passing through.

The hike can be done year-round except after heavy rain. Check in Kritsa before setting out.

Eating

Taverna Platanos   CRETAN €

(☑ 28410 51230; Kritsotopoulas; mains €6.50-9.50; ☺10am-9pm) A taverna-*kafeneio* (coffeehouse) halfway along Kritzotopoula, Platanos has a pleasant setting under a giant 200-year-old plane tree and vine canopy. The tasty menu revolves around grills, *mousakas* and *stifadho*.

ⓘ Getting There & Away

Up to four buses on weekdays and three at weekends travel from Agios Nikolaos to Kritsa (€1.80). The bus stop (Olouf Palme) is in the centre of town. A taxi costs €14.

SPINALONGA

Tiny Spinalonga Island (Νήσος Σπιναλόγκα; ☑ 28410 22462; adult/concession €8/4; ☺9am-6pm) became a leper colony in 1903 and catapulted into pop-cultural consciousness thanks to Victoria Hislop's 2005 bestselling novel *The Island* and the subsequent Greek TV series spin-off *To Nisi*. Boats departing from Elounda, Plaka and Agios Nikolaos drop visitors at Dante's Gate, the 20m-long tunnel through which patients arrived. From here, a 1km trail takes you past such 'sights' (mostly ruined) as a church, the disinfection room, the hospital and the cemetery.

Before it became a leper colony the island was a stronghold of the Venetians, who built a massive fortress in 1579 to protect the bays of Elounda and Mirabello. In 1715 the island fell under Ottoman control. Spinalonga's isolated location off the northern tip of the Spinalonga Peninsula made it a good leprosy quarantine zone. Also known as Hansen's Disease, the condition causes skin lesions, nerve damage and muscle weakness and has been around since ancient times. As many as 1000 Greeks were quarantined on Spinalonga, initially in squalid and miserable conditions. This changed in 1936 with the arrival of Epaminondas Remoundakis, a law student who contracted leprosy at the age of 21, and who fought passionately for better medical care and infrastructure on the island. A cure for leprosy was finally discovered in 1948 and the last person left Spinalonga in 1957.

Thanks to Hislop's tale about her own family's connection to the island, interest in Spinalonga has skyrocketed and you're unlikely to feel lonely during your visit.

Ferries operated by local boat cooperatives depart half-hourly from Elounda (€12) and Plaka (€8), giving you as much time on the island as you need. From Agios Nikolaos, Nostos Cruises runs one daily excursion boat.

Mohlos   Μόχλος

POP 100

At the end of a narrow road winding past massive open-cast quarries, tranquil Mohlos is an off-the-radar gem along Crete's northern shore. In this pint-sized fishing village time moves as gently as the waves lapping the pebble-and-grey-sand beach. There's little to do but relax, soak up the peacefulness and enjoy a leisurely meal in one of the excellent waterfront cafes and tavernas.

In ancient times Mohlos was a thriving Early Minoan community, traces of which have been excavated on the small island that's now 200m offshore. If you want to visit, ask around in the village for someone to take you there in a boat.

★ Ta Kochilia   CRETAN €€

(☑ 28430 94432; mains €5.50-17; ◷ 10.30am-midnight; 🛜) The oldest among several waterfront tavernas, Ta Kochilia has cooked up a storm for nearly a century and is still an excellent port of call for fanciers of fish and traditional Cretan dishes.

❶ Getting There & Away

There's no public transport to Mohlos. Buses between Sitia and Agios Nikolaos can drop you at the Mohlos turnoff, from where you'll need to hitch or walk the 6km down to the village.

Sitia   Σητεία

POP 9900

Though not conventionally pretty, Sitia exudes an attractive vibe that stems from not having sold its soul to mass tourism. It's a slow-paced, friendly place where agriculture is the mainstay of the local economy.

In the tranquil old town above the fishing harbour, whitewashed buildings tumble down a hillside laced by steep staircases and accented by a ruined Venetian castle. Down below, tavernas and cafes line the bustling waterfront and wide promenade along Karamanli. A long, sandy beach skirts the bay to the east. Many visitors use Sitia as launch pad for explorations of Vaï, Moni Toplou, Zakros and other remote destinations further east, although it's well worth spending a day or two in town.

◉ Sights

Sitia Archaeological Museum   MUSEUM

(☑ 28430 23917; Piskokefalou; adult/concession €2/1; ◷ 8.30am-4pm Wed-Mon) This is a compact showcase of archaeological finds from eastern Crete spanning the arc from Neolithic to Roman times, with an emphasis on Minoan artefacts. Pride of place goes to the *Palekastro Kouros* – a statue carved from hippopotamus tusks that was once fully covered in gold leaf.

🛏 Sleeping

Hotel El Greco   HOTEL €

(☑ 28430 23133; www.elgreco-sitia.gr; Arkadiou 13; d €50; ❄ 🛜 🐾) This old-school hotel has smart and impeccably clean rooms with tiled floors, nice but dated furniture, plasma TV, fridge and balcony (most with sea views). It's a good city hotel and a convenient base for short stays.

★ Nereids Apartments   APARTMENT €€

(☑ 6944909834, 28430 26027; https://nereids.gr; Sitia-Palekastro Rd; studios €70-90; ◷ May-Oct; 🅿 ❄) One of the nicest properties in Sitia, this bungalow complex with studios and family apartments sits right across from the beach in a colourful garden brimming with jasmine and geranium. The stylish lounge-bar serves breakfast, a mean burger, crisp salads and good cocktails.

🍴 Eating & Drinking

★ Mitsakakis   CAFE €

(☑ 28430 20200; Karamanli 6; galaktoboureko €2.70; ◷ 8am-midnight; ❄ 🛜 🐾) This cafe and pastry shop is a Sitian institution (open since 1965) and famous for its sugar-rush-inducing *galaktoboureko* (custard-filled pastry), *loukoumadhes* (ball-shaped doughnuts) and *kataïfi* (angel-hair pastry).

★ Rakadiko Oinodeion   CRETAN €

(☑ 28430 26166; El Venizelou 157; mezedhes €3.50-8, mains €7.50-13; ◷ 6pm-1am; ❄ 🛜) Tops among the waterfront tavernas, this rustic family place offers a recognisable array of Greek dishes, but it's the local seasonal specials that truly shine. Among these, anything with rabbit or goat gets top marks and is best paired with the local wine. Many ingredients, including the oil, bread and raki, are produced by the Garefalakis family itself.

Nouvelle Boutique   CAFE

(☑ 6972825942; El Venizelou 161; ◷ 9am-late; 🛜) This comfy-chic local fave with huge backlit bar and stone-walled interior is a top after-dark spot, when a youthful crowd invades for funky sounds, sweet and strong drinks, dancing and the occasional band. Also a nice place for a daytime chill session.

❶ Getting There & Away

AIR

Small **Sitia Municipal Airport** (JSH; ☑ 28430 24424) is about 1km north of the town centre and handles domestic flights to Athens, Alexandroupoli, Iraklio, Kassos and Rhodes as well as seasonal charter flights from Germany and Scandinavia. A taxi into town costs €6 to €8.

BOAT

Ferries dock about 1km north of the town centre. **Anek/Aegeon Pelagos Sea Lines** (☑ Hania 28210 24000; www.anek.gr) has service to Anafi (€20, eight hours), Chalki (€20, 8½ hours), Diafani (€18, six hours), Iraklio (€16, three hours), Karpathos (€19, 4½ hours), Kasos (€12, 2¾ hours), Milos (€26, 14¼ hours), Piraeus (€44, 21½ hours), Rhodes (€28, 10½ hours) and Santorini (€28, 10 hours) on a seasonally changing schedule. Prices quoted are for deckchair seating.

BUS

Connections from Sitia's **bus station** (☑ 28430 22272, 28102 46530; http://ktelherlas.gr; Sitia-Palekastro Rd; 🛜) include four buses daily to Ierapetra (€6.90, 1¾ hours), five buses to Iraklio (€16, three hours), and six to Agios Nikolaos (€8.30, 1¾ hours). Two buses leave for Zakros on Monday, Tuesday and Friday (€4.50, one hour). No services on Sunday.

Around Sitia

Moni Toplou

In splendid isolation on a windswept plateau, 15th-century fortified Moni Toplou (Μονή Τοπλού; ☑ 28430 61226; Toplou; €3; ⏰ 8am-6pm Apr-Oct) is one of the most historically significant monasteries in Crete. Its defences were tested by everyone from pirates to crusading knights to the Turks. The church brims with superb icons, although the main magnet is the intricate *Lord Thou Art Great* icon by celebrated Cretan artist Ioannis Kornaros. It depicts scenes from the Old and New Testaments, including Noah's Ark, Jonah and the Whale, and Moses parting the Red Sea.

The name Toplou is derived from the Turkish word for cannon, which is what the monks used to defend themselves against pirates during Venetian times. The monastery was also repeatedly active in the cause of Cretan independence. Under the Turkish occupation a secret school operated on the premises, while during WWII resistance leaders ran an underground radio transmitter here. A small exhibit in the museum recalls this period with rifles, helmets and a field telephone. The adjacent main room displays engravings and icons.

Today the monastery is not only an attraction for fans of history, religion, art and architecture but also the largest landowner in the area and an active producer of award-winning wine and olive oil, which you can sample in a nearby tasting room (open 10.30am to 5pm Monday to Saturday).

Moni Toplou is about 15km east of Sitia. Buses can drop you at the junction of the Sitia–Palekastro road, from where you'll need to hitch or walk for 3.5km.

Vaï

The beach at Vaï (parking €2.50), 24km northeast of Sitia, is famous for its large grove of *Phoenix theophrasti* (Cretan date) palms. With calm, clear waters, it's one of the island's most popular strands and its tightly spaced rows of umbrellas and sunbeds often fill by 10am in July and August. Jet skis kick into gear shortly thereafter. Snack bars and a taverna provide refreshments. Two buses daily make the trip from Sitia (€3.30, one hour) between May and October.

Palekastro   Παλαίκαστρο

POP 1100

Palekastro (pah-leh-kas-tro) is an unpretentious farming village underpinned by low-key tourism. It lies in a rocky landscape interspersed with fields close to the beaches at Kouremenos (with Crete's best windsurfing), Hiona and Vaï. In the village you'll find an ATM, a petrol station and small markets.

About 1km east of town, about 150m south of Hiona Beach, is the archaeological site of Roussolakkos, where archaeologists are digging up a Minoan town and hoping for evidence of a major Minoan palace. This is where the *Palekastro Kouros* ivory figurine – now residing in the Archaeological Museum in Sitia – was found.

🍴 Eating

There are a number of earthy tavernas around the town square as well as two excellent restaurants overlooking Hiona Beach.

⭐ **Hiona Taverna**   SEAFOOD €€
(☑ 28430 61228; Hiona Beach; mains €15-25; ⏰ noon-11pm Apr-Oct; 🛜) One of two top-ranked tavernas at the northern end of Hiona Beach, this more upscale contender in a stone house is usually filled with patrons lusting after the fresh fish and seafood. Book ahead for a romantic table on the cliffs.

ℹ Getting There & Away

There are four buses per day from Sitia to Palekastro (€2.80, one hour). Buses stop in the central square.

Zakros & Kato Zakros
Ζάκρος & Κάτω Ζάκρος
POP 800

Zakros, 45km southeast of Sitia, is the starting point for the trail through Zakros Gorge. The small town has lodging, minimarkets, an ATM and a gas station but is otherwise a mere prelude to the coastal village of Kato Zakros. The 7km drive down a winding road is spectacular and delivers mesmerising views after every bend.

Shortly before reaching the village, you can see the huge jaw of Zakros Gorge breaching the cliffs in the distance. Look closely and you might also spot the ruins of the Minoan palace just up from Kato Zakros' pebbly, narrow beach and row of tavernas. Add to all this the isolated tranquillity and sense of peace, and you have the perfect recipe for escapism.

◉ Sights & Activities

★ **Zakros Palace**   ARCHAEOLOGICAL SITE
(☑ 28410 22462; Kato Zakros; adult/concession €6/3; ⊙ 8am-8pm May-Sep, to 3pm Oct-Apr) Ancient Zakros, the smallest of Crete's four Minoan palatial complexes, sat next to a harbour and was likely engaged in sea trade with the Middle East, as suggested by excavated elephant tusks and oxhide ingots. Like Knossos, Phaestos and Malia, Zakros centred on a courtyard flanked by royal apartments, shrines, ceremonial halls, storerooms and workshops. While the ruins are sparse, the remote setting makes it an attractive site to nose around. Information panels help spur your imagination.

★ **Zakros Gorge**   HIKING
(Gorge of the Dead) Zakros Gorge is also known as the Gorge of the Dead because the Minoans used to bury their dead in the caves dotting the canyon walls. This easy-to-moderate walk starts just below Zakros village and follows a dry riverbed through a narrow and soaring canyon with a riot of vegetation and wild herbs before emerging close to Zakros Palace near the taverna-flanked beach of Kato Zakros.

There are two trailheads on the road to Kato Zakros. Budget about two hours to hike down from 'Entrance A' and 1½ hours from

'Entrance B'. There may still be water in the gorge until May – check locally. A taxi back to Zakros costs about €12.

The hike is part of the 12,000km-long E4 European Path, which kicks off in Tarifa (Spain) and ends in Larnaca (Cyprus).

🛏 Sleeping & Eating

Katerina Apartments   APARTMENT €
(☑ 6974656617, 28430 26893; www.kato-zakros.gr/_en/katerina.php; Kato Zakros; apt €50-70; ⊙ Apr-Sep; 🅿 ❄ 🛜) These four stone-built studios and maisonettes sleep up to four and enjoy a lovely garden setting in the hillside at Kato Zakros. The 800m walk to the beach takes you past the trailhead for Zakros Gorge and the Minoan palace ruins. Units welcome you with family-style hominess, accented by the occasional lace doily, and a small jug of homemade raki.

★ **Stella's Traditional Apartments**   APARTMENT €€
(☑ 6976719461, 28430 23739; www.stelapts.com; Kato Zakros; studios €80-90; ⊙ mid-Mar–mid-Nov; 🅿 ❄ 🛜) Close to the mouth of Zakros Gorge, these charming self-contained studios are in a lovely garden setting and decorated with distinctive wooden furniture and other artefacts made by joint owner Elias Pagianidis. Perks range from hammocks under the trees to barbecues and an external kitchen with an honesty system for supplies. Rates include free breakfast provisions.

Elias and his wife, Stella, have excellent knowledge and experience of hiking trails in the area.

Akrogiali Taverna   CRETAN €€
(☑ 28430 26893; Kato Zakros; mains €6-19; ⊙ 8am-midnight; 🛜) The food gods have been smiling upon Kato Zakros' oldest taverna, which does a brisk trade in fresh-off-the-boat fish and Cretan classics, all prepared with locally sourced ingredients, including oil made from the owner's trees. The cheerful blue-and-white furniture and the beachfront setting add two more notches to its appeal.

ℹ Getting There & Away

Buses from a central **stop** (☑ 28102 45020; http://ktelherlas.gr; Eleftherias) link Zakros and Sitia twice on Monday, Tuesday and Friday (€4.50, one hour), continuing down to Kato Zakros in summer (June to September). A taxi from Sitia to Zakros costs about €50, while the fare between Zakros and Kato Zakros is €12. In summer there's usually one afternoon bus leaving Kato Zakros for Sitia Monday to Friday.

Ierapetra Ιεράπετρα

POP 16,150

Ierapetra is a laid-back seafront town and the commercial centre of southeastern Crete's substantial greenhouse-based agribusiness. Hot and dusty in summer, it offers a low-key, authentic Cretan experience and is also the jumping-off point for the semitropical Chrissi Island (also called Gaïdouronisi or Hrysi).

The city's grey-sand beaches are backed by tavernas and cafes where the nightlife is busy in summer. Though few visible signs remain, Ierapetra has an impressive history, with interludes as a Roman port and as a Venetian stronghold, as attested to by the harbour fortress. The narrow alleyways of the old quarter (Kato Mera) flash back to the Ottoman period.

◉ Sights & Activities

Ierapetra is the launch pad for boat trips to uninhabited Chrissi Island (Gaïdouronisi/Hrysi Island; ☑ 28420 20008; boat trip adult/child €25/12; ☺ mid-May–Oct). It is famous for its golden beaches, clear water shimmering in myriad shades of blue, cedar forest, traces of Minoan ruins, and Belegrina, a beach covered with a mountain of shells. There are usually a couple of morning boat departures that give you 4½ hours on the island. Tickets are sold online and by agents around town. Bring a picnic or buy refreshments on board. One company that will take you there is Cretan Daily Cruises (☑ 28420 20008, www.cretandailycruises.com boat trip adult/child €25/12, ☺ mid-May–Oct) their vessels carry 200-400 passengers.

Old Quarter   AREA

(Kato Mera) Inland from the fortress is the labyrinthine old quarter, where you'll see a Turkish fountain, the restored mosque (Plateia Tzami) with its minaret, Napoleon's house and several churches, including Agios Ioannis (Katsanevaki) and Agios Georgios (Agiou Georgiou).

Kales Fortress   FORTRESS

(Stratigou Samouil 10; ☺ 8am-3pm Tue-Sun) FREE Overlooking the fishing harbour, the crenellated Venetian fort dates from the 17th century but was built atop an older defensive structure reputedly built by Genoese pirates in the 13th century and destroyed by an earthquake and the Turks. There's not much to see inside, but it's fun to climb up to the ramparts and the single tower for grand views of the bay and the mountains.

🛏 Sleeping & Eating

⭐ Cretan Villa Hotel   HOTEL €

(☑ 28420 28522, 6973037671; www.cretan-villa.com; Lakerda 16; d €45-56; ❈ 🛜) A heavy wooden door gives way to a vine-shaded courtyard at this restful, friendly space that's a happy coupling of historic touches and mod cons. Beautiful rooms have stone walls, elegantly rustic furniture, stone-tiled showers, wood-beamed ceilings, small fridges and satellite TV. A central city hotel with country flair.

Coral Boutique Hotel   HOTEL €€

(☑ 28420 20444, 6977232766; www.coralhotelcrete.gr; Plateia Eleftherias 19; d €57-86) A recent facelift has turned this breezy city hotel into a cocoon of relaxed sophistication, with ultracomfy mattresses, an easy-on-the-eye palette of white and aqua tones, and accommodating staff. Breakfast is €7.50 extra but worth it.

Special   FAST FOOD €

(☑ 28420 27835; cnr Metaxaki 1 & Kothri; dishes €3.50-8; ☺ 10.30am-12.30am; ❈ 🖐) Special jazzes up Ierapetra's dining scene with quality fast food served in an upbeat, contemporary setting. The menu is a reminder of the simple goodness of charcoal-grilled souvlakia or well-prepared rotisserie *gyros* (chicken or pork), although the burgers, salads and sausages hold their own. Portions are big enough to share, and there's a kids' menu to boot.

⭐ Vira Potzi   CRETAN €€

(☑ 28420 28254; www.facebook.com/virapotzi; Stratigou Samouil 82; mains €7-14; ☺ noon-midnight Tue-Sun; ❈ 🛜🍽) Next to the Kales Fortress, this next-gen Cretan seaside tavern has an enticing menu packed with culinary twists such as grilled calamari with zucchini sticks and *fava* (bean dip) or the crowd-pleasing shrimp orzo-pasta pilaf. A classy place with nary a plastic picture menu in sight.

🍸 Drinking & Nightlife

Ierapetra has the most lively after-dark scene in the region. The waterfront tavernas often bustle until the wee hours, and if you want to bust a move on the dance floor, look for the latest music lairs in the streets behind the beachfront drag Stratigou Stamouil.

ℹ Getting There & Away

Ierapetra Bus Station (☑ 28420 28237; www.ktelherlas.gr; Lasthenous 28) KTEL operates up to eight buses per day to Iraklio (€12, 2½ hours) via Agios Nikolaos (€4.10, one hour), four to Sitia (€6.90, 1½ hours) and five to Myrtos (€2.40, 30 minutes).

Central Taxi Stand (☑ 28420 26600; cnr Kothri & Plateia Kanoupaki) The central taxi stand with fixed fares posted on a board is outside the town hall. Sample fares: Iraklio (€128), Agios Nikolaos (€50), Sitia (€83) and Myrtos (€20).

Myrtos   Μύρτος
POP 600

Tiny Myrtos, 14km west of Ierapetra, is a positively delightful lived-in community: cheerful, trim and fringed by an apron of grey pebble-and-sand beach and bright-blue water. It's also an excellent base for mountain and canyon hikes and even has a couple of minor Minoan sites. All these assets attract a devoted clientele that also cherishes its slow boho pulse, flower-festooned guesthouses, and cluster of tavernas in the village and along its languid seafront. In short, it's a traveller's jewel, the perfect antidote to noise, haste and mass tourism.

🛏️ Sleeping & Eating

⭐ **Big Blue**   APARTMENT €€
(☑ 28420 51094; www.big-blue.gr; studios €56-98; ❄🐾🛜) Modern amenities meet traditional Greece in these breezy sea-facing and self-catering studios decorated with plenty of style and imagination. Apartment 'Blue Eye', for instance, has a neat display of evil eyes (for good luck); in fact, every room is different. Private decks have expansive views, and the fragrant front garden is a good spot for sundowners.

O Platanos   CRETAN €€
(mains €7-13.50; ⊙11am-late Apr-Oct; 🛜🐾) Beneath a giant plane tree on the main street, Platanos is a focus of village social life and has live music on many summer evenings. Feast on Cretan staples such as rabbit *stifadho* (stew cooked with onions in a tomato puree), or try such homey specials as the 'pita pizza' or grandma's meatballs with yoghurt sauce.

La Sera   MEDITERRANEAN €€
(☑ 28420 51261; mains €8-16; ⊙5pm-midnight Apr-Oct; 🛜) Soft lighting, fine wine and delicious food are the hallmarks of a romantic night out in this al fresco–only lair wedged into an alley off the main drag. The compact menu includes farm-fresh salads, grilled seafood, and tender lamb chops from the local butcher, alongside wine from the renowned Lyrarakis winery (p470) in Alagni.

ℹ️ Getting There & Away

There are five buses daily from Ierapetra (€2.40, 30 minutes). A taxi costs about €20.

Lasithi Plateau

The tranquil Lasithi Plateau, 900m above sea level (bring a sweater even in summer), is a windswept expanse of green fields interspersed with almond trees and orchards. Offering a sense of secluded rural Crete, it's really more a plain than a plateau, sitting as it does in a huge depression amid the rock-studded mountains of the Dikti range. It's sparsely inhabited, with just a few villages dotted along the periphery. Most people visit on a day trip to Psyhro, the gateway to the Dikteon Cave, where – so the myth goes – Zeus was born and hidden as an infant to protect him from his voracious father.

Lasithi must have been a stunning sight in the 17th century, when it was dotted with some 20,000 windmills with white-canvas sails, put up by the Venetians for irrigation purposes. The skeletal few that remain are an iconic (and much-photographed) sight.

👁️ Sights

Dikteon Cave   CAVE
(Cave of Psyhro; ☑ 28410 22462; http://odysseus. culture.gr; Psyhro; adult/concession €6/3; ⊙8am-8pm Apr-Oct, to 3pm Nov-Mar) According to legend, Rhea hid in this cave to give birth to Zeus, far from the clutches of his offspring-gobbling father, Cronos. A slick and vertiginous staircase corkscrews into the damp dark, passing overhanging stalactites, ethereal formations and a lake. From Psyhro it's a steep 800m walk to the cave entrance, via a rocky but shaded natural trail or the sunny paved path starting near the car park.

The most famous formation is a stalactite nicknamed 'the mantle of Zeus' in a chamber on the right-hand side off the larger hall. Offerings found in the cave, including daggers, arrowheads, figures and double axes, indicate that it was a place of cult worship from Minoan to Roman times. Key items are now on display at the Archaeological Museum (p459) in Iraklio.

ℹ️ Getting There & Away

The Lasithi Plateau is not served by public buses. A taxi to Tzermiado or Psyhro costs about €60 from Iraklio and €50 from Agios Nikolaos. To cut costs, take a bus to Malia and a taxi from there (about €25).

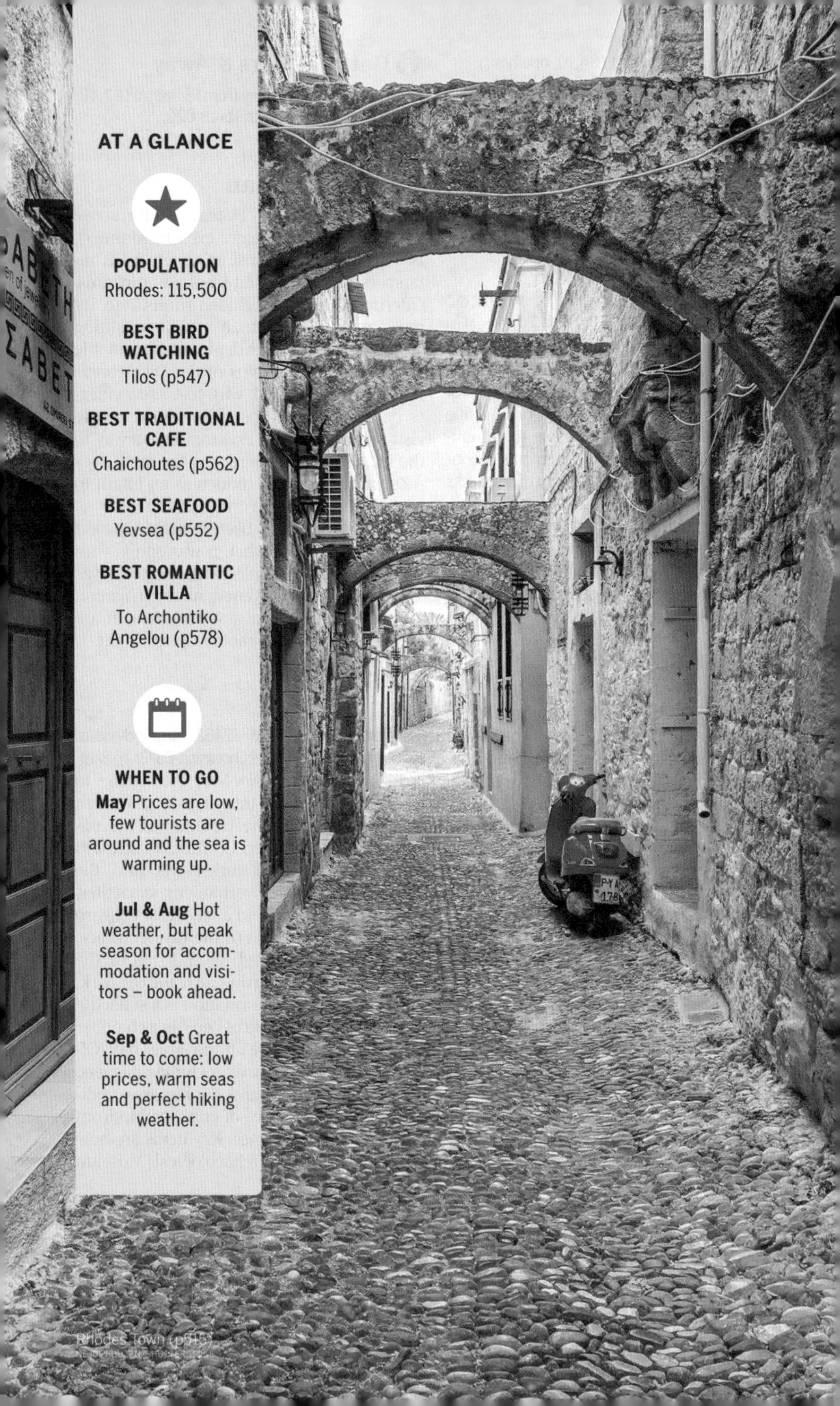

AT A GLANCE

⭐

POPULATION
Rhodes: 115,500

BEST BIRD WATCHING
Tilos (p547)

BEST TRADITIONAL CAFE
Chaichoutes (p562)

BEST SEAFOOD
Yevsea (p552)

BEST ROMANTIC VILLA
To Archontiko Angelou (p578)

📅

WHEN TO GO

May Prices are low, few tourists are around and the sea is warming up.

Jul & Aug Hot weather, but peak season for accommodation and visitors – book ahead.

Sep & Oct Great time to come: low prices, warm seas and perfect hiking weather.

Rhodes Town (p515)

Dodecanese

Ever pined for the old Greece, where timeless islands beckon modern-day adventurers just as they did Odysseus and Alexander? Enter the far-flung Dodecanese (Δωδεκάνησα) archipelago, curving through the southeastern Aegean parallel to the ever-visible shoreline of Turkey. The footprints of everyone from Greeks and Romans to crusading medieval knights, and Byzantine and Ottoman potentates to 20th-century Italian bureaucrats, are found here. Beyond better-known Rhodes and Kos, enigmatic islands beg to be explored.

Hikers and naturalists flock to Tilos, while climbers scale the limestone cliffs in Kalymnos. Aesthetes adore the neoclassical mansions of Symi, Halki and Kastellorizo, and kitesurfers blow in to Karpathos for its legendary winds.

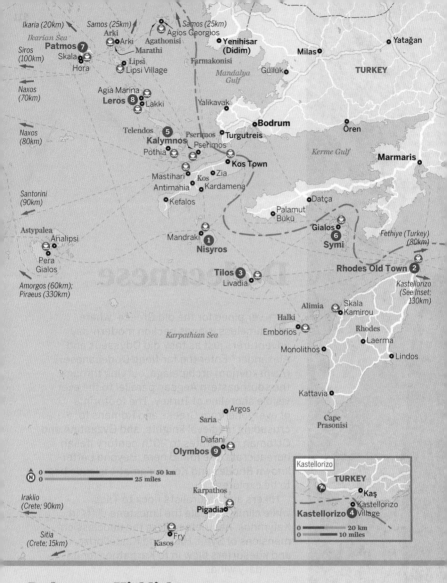

Dodecanese Highlights

① **Nisyros** (p550) Entering its fabled volcano, home to an imprisoned Titan.

② **Rhodes Old Town** (p516) Wandering beneath Byzantine arches and along ancient cobbled alleyways.

③ **Tilos** (p547) Hiking or birdwatching on this postcard-perfect island.

④ **Kastellorizo** (p540) Gasping in awe at the colour in the most dramatic of blue caves in the Mediterranean.

⑤ **Kalymnos** (p567) Testing your mettle diving for wrecks or climbing limestone cliffs.

⑥ **Symi** (p542) Being delighted as your boat pulls into the gorgeous Italianate harbour.

⑦ **Patmos** (p578) Making a pilgrimage to where St John experienced his 'Revelations'.

⑧ **Leros** (p573) Visiting Greece's most 'modern' town of Lakki.

⑨ **Olymbos** (p534) Following the winding road up to this timeless mountaintop village on Karpathos.

History

The Dodecanese islands have been inhabited since pre-Minoan times. After the death of Alexander the Great in 323 BCE, they were ruled by Ptolemy I of Egypt. The islanders later became the first Greeks to convert to Christianity, thanks to the tireless efforts of St Paul, who made two journeys to the archipelago during the 1st century, and St John the Divine, who was banished to Patmos, where he had his revelation and added a chapter to the Bible.

The early Byzantine era saw the islands prosper, but by the 7th century CE they were being plundered by a string of invaders. The Knights of St John of Jerusalem (Knights Hospitaller), who arrived during the 14th century, eventually ruled almost all the Dodecanese. Their mighty fortifications have proved strong enough to withstand time, but failed to keep out the Turks in 1522.

The Turks were in turn ousted in 1912 by the Italians, who made Italian the official language and banned the Orthodox religion. Inspired by Mussolini's vision of a vast Mediterranean empire, they also constructed public buildings in the fascist style, the antithesis of archetypal Greek architecture. More beneficially, they excavated and restored many archaeological monuments.

After the Italian surrender of 1943, the islands became a battleground for British and German forces, inflicting much suffering upon the population. The Dodecanese were formally returned to Greece in 1947.

RHODES ΡΟΔΟΣ

POP 115,500

By far the largest and historically the most important of the Dodecanese islands, Rhodes (ro-dos) abounds in beaches, wooded valleys and ancient history. Whether you're here on a culture-vulture journey through past civilisations, or simply for some laid-back beach time, buzzing nightlife, or diving in crystal-clear waters, it's all here. The atmospheric Old Town of Rhodes is a maze of cobbled streets that will spirit you back to the days of the Byzantine Empire and beyond. Further south is the picture-perfect town of Lindos. While both Lindos and Rhodes Old Town get very crowded in summer, Rhodes is large enough to allow plenty of room to breathe that pure Aegean air.

History

Although the Minoans and Mycenaeans established early outposts on Rhodes, the island only made itself felt from 1100 BCE onwards,

after the Dorians settled in Kamiros, Ialysos and Lindos. Switching allegiances like a pendulum, Rhodes was allied to Athens when the Persians were defeated in the Battle of Marathon (490 BCE), but shifted to the Persian side in time for the Battle of Salamis (480 BCE).

Following the unexpected Athenian victory at Salamis, Rhodes threw in its lot with Athens once more, joining the Delian League in 477 BCE. Following the disastrous Sicilian Expedition (416–412 BCE), Rhodes revolted against Athens and hooked up with Sparta instead, aiding it in the Peloponnesian Wars.

What's now Rhodes Town was founded in 408 BCE, when the cities of Kamiros, Ialysos and Lindos joined forces. After aligning itself with Athens again to defeat Sparta at the Battle of Knidos (394 BCE), Rhodes joined forces with Persia to fight Alexander the Great, only to attach itself to Alexander in turn when he proved invincible.

In 305 BCE Antigonus, a rival of Ptolemy, sent his formidable son, Demetrius Poliorketes – Besieger of Cities – to lay siege to Rhodes. When the city managed to repel Demetrius, it built a 32m-high bronze statue of Helios to celebrate. Known as the Colossus of Rhodes, this became one of the Seven Wonders of the Ancient World.

Rhodes now knew no bounds. It built the biggest navy in the Aegean, its port became a major Mediterranean trading centre, and the arts flourished. When Greece became the arena in which Roman generals fought for leadership of the empire, Rhodes allied itself with Julius Caesar, who had studied here in his youth. After Caesar was assassinated in 44 BCE, Cassius besieged the city, destroying its ships and carting its artworks off to Rome. Rhodes went into decline and was assimilated into the Roman Empire in 70 CE.

In due course, Rhodes joined the Byzantine province of the Dodecanese and was granted independence when the Crusaders seized Constantinople. Later, the Genoese gained control. Next to arrive, in 1309, were the Knights of St John, who ruled Rhodes for 213 years. They were ousted after two mighty sieges by the Ottomans, who were themselves kicked out by the Italians nearly four centuries later. In 1947, after 35 years of Italian occupation, Rhodes finally became part of Greece, along with the other Dodecanese islands.

ℹ Getting There & Away

AIR

Diagoras Airport (RHO; Map p514; www.rho-airport.gr) is near Paradisi on the west coast, 14km southwest of Rhodes Town.

Rhodes

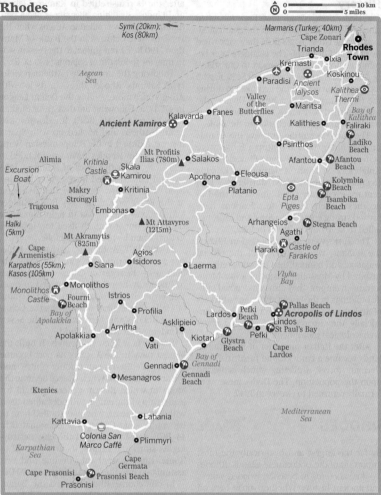

Aegean Airlines (☎ 22410 98345; https://en.aegeanair.com; Diagoras Airport) flies to Athens, Iraklio, Kastellorizo and Thessaloniki.

Olympic Air (☎ 21035 50500; www.olympicair.com) offers frequent flights to and from Athens, where you can connect to destinations throughout Greece, and also flies to Kastellorizo.

Sky Express (☎ 22410 88700; www.skyexpress.gr) offers direct flights to Iraklio on Crete, and island-hopping routes including Astypalea with stops on Leros, Kalymnos, and Kos; Kasos via Karpathos; and Limnos via Mytilini, Chios and Samos.

BOAT

International

In summer, **Marmaris Ferry** (Map p516; www.marmarisferry.com; Commercial Harbour, Old Town; one-way or day return adult/child €45/30; ⊙ Jun–mid-Oct) and **Dodecanese Flying Dolphins** (Map p516; ☎ 22410 37101; www.12fd.gr; Commercial Harbour, Old Town; one-way adult/child €40/25; ⊙ May-Oct) send daily hydrofoils and catamarans from Rhodes Town to the Turkish resorts of Bodrum, Marmaris and Fethiye.

Domestic

Rhodes Town is the main port in the Dodecanese. Three interisland ferry companies operate from immediately outside the walls of the Old Town.

The high-speed catamarans of **Dodekanisos Seaways** (Map p516; ☑ 22410 70590; www.12ne. gr/en; Kolona Harbour, Old Town) sail from Kolona Harbour.

DESTINATION	DURATION	FARE (€)	FREQUENCY
Agathonisi	5½hrs	49	2 weekly
Halki	1¼hrs	18	2 weekly
Kalymnos	3hrs	34	daily
Kastellorizo	2¼hrs	37	weekly
Kos	2½hrs	34	1-2 daily
Leros	4hrs	42	daily
Lipsi	4hrs	47	6 weekly
Nisyros	2¾hrs	7	2 weekly
Patmos	5hrs	49	daily
Samos	10hrs	59	2 weekly
Symi	50mins	19	1-2 daily
Tilos	2hrs	27	2 weekly

The cheaper, slower traditional vessels of **Blue Star Ferries** (Map p519; ☑ 22410 22461; www.bluestarferries.com; Amerikis 111, New Town; ⊗ 9am-8pm) leave from the Commercial Harbour.

DESTINATION	DURATION	FARE (€)	FREQUENCY
Astypalea	9hrs	28.50	weekly
Kalymnos	5hrs	24	5 weekly
Karpathos	3¾hrs	24.50	weekly
Kasos	5hrs	29.50	weekly
Kastellorizo	3hrs	29.50	2 weekly
Kos	3-5hrs	24.50	1-2 daily
Leros	5½hrs	32.50	4 weekly
Lipsi	7½hrs	32.50	2 weekly
Nisyros	4hrs	16	2 weekly
Patmos	6½hrs	37.50	5 weekly
Piraeus	11-17hrs	65.50	1-2 daily
Samos	6½hrs	39	weekly
Santorini	8hrs	39	2 weekly
Symi	1hr	9	3 weekly
Syros	9hrs	49	3 weekly
Tilos	2¼hrs	16	2 weekly

Two weekly **Anek Lines** (Map p516; ☑ 22410 35066; www.anek.gr/en; 5 Akti Sahtouri) ferries from the Commercial Harbour call at Halki (2 hours, €8), Diafani on Karpathos (4¼ hours, €19), Karpathos Town (5¾ hours, €21), Kasos (8 hours, €25), Anafi (13 hours, €29), Santorini (15 hours, €29), Milos (19½ hours, €39) and Piraeus (25 hours, €47).

In addition, regular ferries link the tiny port at Skala Kamirou, 45km southwest of Rhodes Town and served by hour-long connecting buses, with the island of Halki. They're operated by **Nissos Halki** (Velis Lines; Map p514; ☑ 6946519817, 6934117388; Skala Kamirou; ⊗ 2-3 daily Tue-Sun) and **Nikos Express** (☑ 6946826905; nikos_express@hotmail.com; Skala Kamirou; ⊗ 1-2 daily Wed-Sun).

Finally, operators including **Sea Dreams** (Map p519; ☑ 22410 74235; www.seadreams.gr; Lambraki 46, New Town) send daily excursion boats from Mandraki Harbour in Rhodes Town to Symi

❶ Getting Around

Bus routes radiate out from Rhodes Town to destinations all over the island. Only along the northeastern shoreline between Rhodes Town and Lindos, though, are services frequent enough to be truly convenient for visitors.

If you want to explore the island as a whole, it's best to rent a vehicle of some kind. All the major car-rental chains are represented at Rhodes airport, and plenty more car- and motorcycle-rental outlets are scattered throughout Rhodes Town and the resorts. Competition is fierce, so shop around.

And bear in mind too that if you're only visiting Rhodes for a few days, perhaps as part of an island-hopping itinerary, there's plenty to see in Rhodes Old Town without venturing further afield.

Rhodes Town   Ρόδος

POP 90,000

Rhodes Town is really two distinct and very different towns. The Old Town lies within but utterly apart from the New Town, sealed like a medieval time capsule behind a double ring of high walls and a deep moat. Few cities can boast so many layers of architectural history, with ruins and relics of the Classical, Ottoman and Italian eras entangled in a mind-boggling maze of twisting lanes.

In season, the Old Town receives a huge daily influx of day trippers and, especially, passengers from giant cruise ships. Even then, you can escape the crowds by heading away from the busy commercial streets into its hauntingly pretty cobbled alleyways. Staying a night or two, and losing yourself in the labyrinth after dark, is an experience no traveller should miss.

The New Town, meanwhile, is a modern Mediterranean resort, with decent beaches, upscale shops, lively nightlife and waterfront bars servicing the package crowd.

Rhodes Old Town

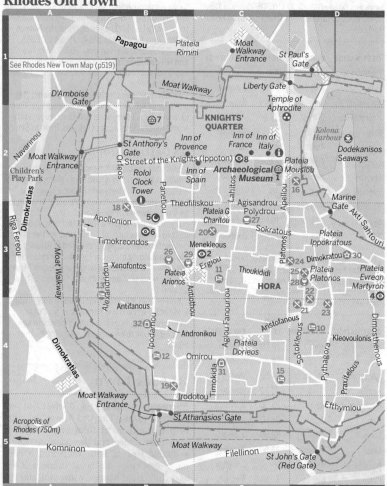

☉ Sights

☉ Old Town

A glorious mixture of Byzantine, Turkish and Italian architecture, erected on top of far more ancient and largely unidentifiable remains, the Old Town is a world of its own. In theory, it consists of three separate sections, though casual visitors seldom notice the transition from one to the next. To the north, sturdy stone mansions known as inns line the arrow-straight streets of the Knights' Quarter. These strikingly austere edifices, built to house knights from specific countries, were laid out by the medieval Knights of St John. South of that, the Hora, also known as the Turkish Quarter, occupies the central bulk of the Old Town. This tangle of cobbled alleyways is now the main commercial hub, packed with restaurants and shops interspersed between derelict mosques and Muslim monuments, and, regrettably, bursting with visitors every day in summer. The Jewish Quarter in the southeast, which lost most of its inhabitants during WWII, is now a sleepy residential district.

Visitors can walk atop the central stretch of the imposing 12m-thick ramparts that

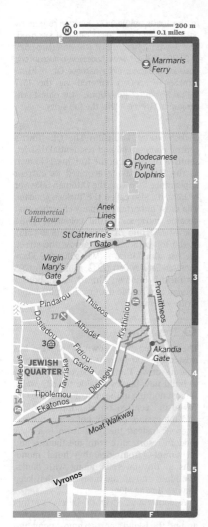

DODECANESE RHODES TOWN

still protect the landward side of the Old Town, and descend at various points into the wide, deep moat that encircles them, filled with lush gardens and perfect for a relaxed stroll.

Of the nine gateways to the Old Town, the busiest and most dramatic are the northernmost two, closest to the New Town. Liberty Gate, the nearest to Mandraki Harbour and the taxi rank, leads to a small bridge and the main tourist areas, while the atmospheric D'Amboise Gate, further inland, crosses an especially attractive section of the moat en route to the Palace of the Grand Master.

★ **Archaeological Museum**   MUSEUM
(Map p516; ☎ 22413 65257; Plateia Mousiou; adult/child €8/free, combination ticket incl Grand Master's Palace, Panagia tou Kastrou & Decorative Arts Collection €10; ☺ 8am-8pm daily Apr-Oct, to 3pm Tue-Sun Nov-Mar) A weathered, sun-kissed stone lion, visible from the street, invites visitors into the magnificent 15th-century Knights' Hospital that holds Rhodes' superb archaeology museum. Exhibits range through several upstairs galleries, and across beautiful gardens to an annexe that's open shorter

hours in summer (9am to 4.50pm). Highlights include the exquisite *Aphrodite Bathing* marble statue from the 1st century BCE, a pavilion displaying wall-mounted mosaics, and a reconstructed burial site from 1630 BCE that held a helmeted warrior alongside his horse.

Ancient treasures unearthed all over Rhodes, including some wonderful ceramics and a sleek carved dolphin, trace 7000 years of local history. The annexe is especially strong on the Mycenean era, at its peak in the 14th and 13th centuries BCE.

Palace of the Grand Master
HISTORIC BUILDING

(Map p516; ☑ 22413 65270; Ippoton; adult/child €6/free, combination ticket incl Archaeological Museum, Decorative Arts Collection & Panagia tou Kastrou €10; ⊙ 8am-8pm Apr-Oct, to 3pm Nov-Mar) From the outside, this magnificent castle-like palace looks much as it did when erected by the 14th-century Knights Hospitaller. During the 19th century, however, it was devastated by an explosion, so the interior is now an Italian reconstruction, completed in the '18th year of the Fascist Era' (1940). Dreary chambers upstairs hold haphazard looted artworks, so the most interesting sections are the twin historical museums downstairs, one devoted to ancient Rhodes and the other to the island's medieval history.

The ancient section holds some lovely pottery from the 6th century BCE, along with all sorts of everyday domestic objects and even glassware.

Street of the Knights
HISTORIC SITE

(Map p516; Ippoton; ⊙ 24hr) Austere and somewhat forbidding, the Street of the Knights (Ippoton) was home from the 14th century to the Knights Hospitaller who ruled Rhodes. The knights were divided into seven 'tongues', or languages, according to their birthplace – England, France, Germany, Italy, Aragon, Auvergne and Provence – each responsible for a specific section of the fortifications. As wall displays explain, the street holds an 'inn', or palace, for each tongue. Its modern appearance, though, owes much to Italian restorations during the 1930s.

Jewish Quarter
AREA

(Map p516) The Jewish Quarter, an enclave of narrow lanes in the Old Town's southeast corner, centres on Plateia Evreon Martyron (Square of the Jewish Martyrs). Now all too quiet and dilapidated, it was home a century ago to a population of 5500. Half fled

in the 1930s, while 1673 Jews were deported to Auschwitz in 1944; only 151 survived. The **Jewish Museum of Rhodes** (Map p516; ☑ 22410 22364; www.rhodesjewishmuseum.org; Dosiadou & Simiou; incl synagogue €4; ⊙ 10am-3pm Sun-Fri Apr-Oct), entered via the 1577 **Kahal Shalom Synagogue** – the oldest synagogue in Greece – tells the full story.

Hora
AREA

(Turkish Quarter; Map p516) The Old Town's central commercial and residential district, south of the Street of the Knights, is known as the Hora. Having acquired its current appearance following the Ottoman takeover of 1522, it's also called the Turkish Quarter. The most important of many churches that became mosques is the colourful, pink-domed **Mosque of Süleyman** (Map p516), at the top of Sokratous. Across the street, the **Muslim Library** (Map p516; ⊙ 9.30am-3pm Mon-Sat May-Oct) **FREE**, founded in 1793 by Turkish Rhodian Ahmed Hasuf, houses Persian and Arabic manuscripts plus hand-written Korans.

◉ New Town

The so-called New Town of Rhodes has existed for 500 years, since Ottoman conquerors drove the local Greek population to build new homes outside the city walls. Almost nothing in the area, north of the Old Town and centred on Mandraki Harbour and the casino, though, holds any historic interest. Instead the New Town is a busy modern resort, alive with guesthouses and restaurants, from gleaming hotel monoliths to tiny tavernas, along with banks, boutiques and all the businesses that keep Rhodes ticking along.

A continuous strip of beach, starting north of Mandraki Harbour, stretches around the island's northernmost point and down the west side of the New Town. The best spots are on the east side, known as **Elli Beach**, where there's better sand, more facilities, and, usually, calmer water.

Modern Greek Art Museum
GALLERY

(Nestoridio Melathro; Map p519; ☑ 22410 43780; www.mgamuseum.gr; Plateia Haritou, New Town; adult/child €3/free, all four sections €8; ⊙ 8am-3pm Tue-Sat) The main gallery of the four-part Modern Greek Art Museum, near the New Town's northern tip, holds paintings, engravings and sculptures by some of Greece's greatest 20th-century artists. The real highlight is the top floor, devoted to

Rhodes New Town

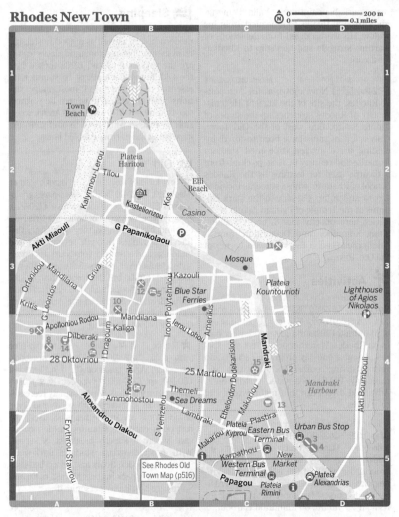

Rhodes New Town

⊙ Sights
1 Modern Greek Art Museum B2

⊛ Activities, Courses & Tours
2 Poseidon Submarine C4
3 Trident Scuba Diving School D5
4 Waterhoppers Diving School D5

🛏 Sleeping
5 Florida Hotel B3
6 Hotel Anastasia A4
7 Stay Hostel B4

🍽 Eating
8 Kerasma A4
9 Koozina A4
10 Koykos B3
11 Meltemi C3
12 Niohori B3

🍷 Drinking & Nightlife
13 Aktaion Cafe C4
14 Christos Garden A4

⊛ Entertainment
15 9D: Throne of Helios C4

the remarkable paintings of Valias Semertzidis (1911–83) thanks to a bequest from his widow. His work ranged from depictions of wartime struggle and hardship to Rhodian landscapes.

Acropolis of Rhodes ARCHAEOLOGICAL SITE
(⊘24hr) **FREE** Now known as the Acropolis of Rhodes, the site of the ancient Hellenistic city of Rhodes stretches up the slopes of Monte Smith, 1km west of the Old Town. Only a few of ruins have been restored, including an elongated, tree-lined stadium from the 2nd century BCE. Steps climb from a theatre, used for lectures by the Rhodes School of Rhetoric (whose students included Cicero and Julius Caesar), to the stark columns of the Temple of Pythian Apollo.

Get here on city bus 6, or by walking along Komninon and Diagoridon from St Athanasius Gate at the southwest corner of the Old Town.

Activities

Waterhoppers Diving School DIVING
(Map p519; ✆22410 38146; www.waterhoppers. com; Mandraki Harbour, New Town) Operating out of Mandraki Harbour and several other bases on Rhodes, Waterhoppers offers an 'experience scuba' one-day program (€93.50) and various diving courses, including two- and three-day PADI open-water certifications. Advanced divers can join night, wreck and cave dives.

Trident Scuba Diving School DIVING
(Map p519; ✆22410 29160; www.tridentdiving school.com; Mandraki Harbour, New Town; ⊕) Trident offers daily excursions to dive spots around the north of the island, plus beginner classes and two- and three-day PADI-certified courses. For more details, look for its boat, *Armonia*, on Mandraki Harbour.

Poseidon Submarine BOATING
(Map p519; ✆6945370301; www.poseidonsubma rine.com; Mandraki Harbour, New Town; adult/child €15/5; ⊘9.30am-9.30pm mid-Apr–Oct; ⊕) Despite appearances, the bright-red *Poseidon* is not a submarine, but a glass-bottomed boat. After puttering out to the point where the Colossus of Rhodes supposedly stood, for fine views back to the Old Town, it returns to Mandraki Harbour, where a diver feeds fish outside the underwater windows. It's fun for kids, with turtle sightings a possibility. Cheaper tickets online. Boats leave every hour and the trip lasts 45 minutes.

🛏 Sleeping

Although the New Town holds plenty of modern hotels, as well as a good hostel, the most memorable and romantic places to stay are the various inns and B&Bs tucked into the Old Town's back alleys. In summer it's essential to reserve ahead; most budget options close altogether in winter. Be warned, too, that most Old Town hotels aren't accessible by taxi, so you'll have to haul your luggage along the narrow, cobbled lanes.

🛏 Old Town

★**S Nikolis Hotel** HISTORIC HOTEL €€
(Map p516; ✆22410 34561; www.s-nikolis.gr; Ipodamou 61; r/ste incl breakfast from €120/220; ⊕❄☎) The life's work of builder Sotiris Nikolis and his Danish partner Marianne, this fine hotel ranges through several restored buildings and a flowery courtyard. Its dozen stylish split-level rooms feature medieval-accented quilts on dark-wood four-poster beds, marble floors, and stone and oxblood walls. Breakfast in the on-site Arxaia Agora cafe – named for the ancient marketplace that lies below – is superb.

★**Marco Polo Mansion** BOUTIQUE HOTEL €€
(Map p516; ✆22410 25562; www.marcopolo mansion.gr; Agiou Fanouriou 40; d incl breakfast €80-160, apt €130-180; ⊘Apr-Oct; ❄☎) This 15th-century pasha's house lovingly recreates an Ottoman ambience with verve and style. Some rooms are in the mansion itself, the rest open onto the stunning garden courtyard where a superb breakfast is served. With its stained-glass windows, dark-wood furniture, wooden floors and raised beds, it's like a journey back in time. Managers Efi and Spiros are hospitality personified.

The Andreas HOTEL €€
(Map p516; ✆22410 34156; www.hotelandreas. com; Omirou 28d; ste incl breakfast €100, both stes €160; ⊘Jul-Sep; ❄@☎) This former pasha's house holds just two suites, each with two bedrooms. Best is the Tower Suite where you wake in your traditional raised bed to a view of the Aegean, while the Terrace Suite has its own private sun terrace. The gardens out front and shared roof terrace are lovely spots to make conversation. Four-night minimum stay.

Hotel Cava d'Oro B&B €€
(Map p516; ✆22410 36980; www.cavadoro.com; Kisthiniou 15; s/d/tr incl breakfast €110/130/160; P❄☎) This small family-run hotel, set in

THE COLOSSUS OF RHODES

A giant bronze statue of the sun god Helios, the Colossus of Rhodes was erected to celebrate the end of an unsuccessful siege of Rhodes. It took 12 years to build, was completed in 292 BCE, and stood for less than a century, before being toppled by an earthquake in 227 BCE.

The statue was considered one of the Seven Wonders of the Ancient World. In legend, its two legs straddled the entrance to what's now Mandraki Harbour, tall enough for high-masted triremes to pass underneath. Historians suggest that given the higher sea levels back then, however, it may have stood further up the hill, on the site of the modern Palace of the Grand Master.

After remaining in ruins on the waterfront for almost 1000 years, the Colossus was broken into pieces and sold by invading Arabs to a Syrian Jew in 654 CE. He supposedly transported it abroad on the backs of 900 camels. There has long been talk of recreating a colossal statue of Helios at Mandraki Harbour, but that looks no closer to happening than ever.

a medieval storage building, offers characterful rooms of varying sizes, with canopied beds, exposed stone walls and high arching ceilings. Breakfast is served in a cool garden courtyard, and guests can even walk on a short stretch of ramparts. Unusually for the Old Town, it's possible to drive right to the front door.

St Michel Hotel HERITAGE HOTEL €€
(Map p516; ☑ 22410 25111; www.saintmichel.gr; Perikleous 68; s/d/ste €70/90/130; ※ ⑤) This 700-year-old building has half-a-dozen rooms, some large, some cramped, with choice furniture including wrought-iron four-poster beds, and tiled floors. A sense of history exudes from its stone walls and wood-beamed ceilings. The superior room has its own roof terrace.

★ **Spirit of the Knights** BOUTIQUE HOTEL €€€
(Map p516; ☑ 22410 39765; www.rhodesluxury hotel.com; Alexandridou 14; s/d incl breakfast from €180/200; ☺※⑤) With their thick rugs, dark woods, stained-glass windows and sense of tranquillity, the six opulent suites in this gorgeous boutique hotel ooze medieval atmosphere. Perfectly isolated down a side alley near the Old Town walls, it's a true work of passion and vision. As well as a fragrant garden courtyard to read in and take breakfast, there's also a library.

In Camera Art
Boutique Hotel BOUTIQUE HOTEL €€€
(Map p516; ☑ 22410 77277; www.incamera.gr; Sofokleous 35; r/ste incl breakfast from €175/250; ☺※⑤) This stunning design hotel, owned by a Greek photographer whose equipment is on show throughout, looks out on ancient ruins. It holds eight very different suites and two rooms. The three-level 'Forms of Light' suite has stained-glass windows,

beautifully finished bedrooms and two roof terraces. Two rooms have private gardens with Jacuzzis, the rest share a garden and breakfast cafe.

🛏 New Town

Stay Hostel HOSTEL €
(Map p519; ☑ 22410 24024; www.stayrhodes.com; Fanouraki 19-21, New Town; dm/r €22/69; ☺※⑤) This nicely equipped modern hostel in the New Town is by far the best budget option in Rhodes Town. As well as clean, well-maintained dorms and double rooms, where the staff even leave little gifts for guests, it has a shared kitchen downstairs, a lounge bar, a cinema room and a small rooftop gym.

Hotel Anastasia PENSION €€
(Map p519; ☑ 22410 28007; www.anastasia-hotel. com; 28 Oktovriou 46, New Town; s/d/tr incl breakfast €59/70/94; ※@⑤) The New Town's friendliest and most peaceful lodgings, in a handsome villa set well back from the busy road. The ochre-coloured rooms have wooden shutters, tiled floors and traditional furnishings; two at the front have small private balconies, oddly accessed via their bathrooms. Breakfast is served in the lush garden.

Florida Hotel HOTEL €€
(Map p519; ☑ 22410 22111; www.florida-rhodes. com; Amarandou 5, New Town; s/d/tr €43/78/97; ☺※⑤) This small, simple, modern hotel is set in a quiet little pedestrian street that's a short walk from the beach near the New Town's northern tip. The crisp, clean, whitewashed rooms have kitchenettes and air-con, and each has its own flower-bedecked terrace or balcony. Yvonne, the helpful owner, provides her own hand-drawn local maps.

DODECANESE RHODES TOWN

Eating

Old Town

To Marouli
VEGETARIAN €

(Map p516; ✆ 22413 04394; Platonos 22; mains €8-12; ⏱ noon-10pm Mon-Sat, 1-7pm Sun; ❋ 🐾 🍴) 🌱 'Marouli' means lettuce, and you can expect greens galore in this standout vegetarian restaurant. The pasta, which like the owner comes from Italy, is delicious. But then again, it's hard to choose between the vegan Thai pineapple and fried rice, or the fine salads – not to mention the 'Junk Food' such as onion rings.

Old Town Corner Bakery
BAKERY €

(Map p516; ✆ 22410 38494; Omirou 88; snacks €2-6; ⏱ 7am-7pm Mon-Sat, 8am-3pm Sun; 🐾) With jazz and the scent of aromatic arabica coffee drifting through this tiny bakery cafe, and out to a handful of tables on the street, this is an Old Town residents' favourite, just inside St Athanasios' Gate. As well as amazing pastries – dawn-fresh croissants sell out very quickly – it serves club sandwiches, apple pie and a host of healthy juices.

To Megiston
TAVERNA €

(Map p516; ✆ 22410 29127; Sofokleous 9; mains €6-23; ⏱ 10am-1.30am; ❋) Look no further for the classic Greek-holiday taverna experience: welcoming, witty waiters; retsina flowing freely; and all the classics prepared just right. People-watch al fresco, as sightseers swoon at the Ibrahim Pasha mosque opposite, and feast on the likes of *spetsofaï* (sausage stewed with chicken and peppers), lamb *kleftiko* (slow oven-baked), and succulent little Symi shrimp.

★ Marco Polo Cafe
MEDITERRANEAN €€

(Map p516; ✆ 22410 25562; www.marcopolo mansion.gr; Agiou Fanouriou 40-42; mains €15-25; ⏱ 7-11pm Apr-Oct; 🐾) 🌱 Despite being barely visible, or even signed, from the street, this irresistible dinner-only restaurant is filled nightly, with diners savouring exquisite culinary creations like sea-bream fillets on a 'risotto' of local wheat, pork loin with figs, or octopus sous vide with cream of beetroot. Linger over a romantic meal in the delightful lemon-fragrant garden courtyard.

Pizanias
SEAFOOD €€

(The Sea Star; Map p516; ✆ 22410 22117; Sofokleous 24; mains €10-17; ⏱ noon-midnight Mar-Oct; 🐾 🚻) This atmospheric restaurant, opening onto one of the Old Town's most attractive, peaceful squares, is celebrated for its fresh seafood – from boned, slow-grilled sea bream to jumbo prawns or squid stuffed with cheese. Dine beneath a canopy of trees, with the night sky shining through.

Taverna Kostas
GREEK €€

(Map p516; ✆ 22410 26217; Pythagora 62; mains €9-22; ⏱ 10am-late; ❋) Run by grandfather Kostas, this friendly Old Town taverna spreads from a simple limewashed dining room into a bright rear conservatory. Come for Greek standards done well – like dolmadhes (stuffed vine leaves) with a hint of cumin – and a succulent octopus salad.

Romios Restaurant
GREEK €€

(Map p516; ✆ 22410 25549; www.romios-rhodes. gr; Sofokleous 15; mains €9-20; ⏱ noon-midnight; ❋ 🐾) Don't be misled by the enchanted-grotto setting of canopied couches, bird-cage nooks and fairy lights. Romios (not to be confused with run-of-the-mill Romeo's, also in the Old Town) is very serious about its food, serving a classic Rhodian menu of local delicacies such as pork in chestnut sauce, veal with olives, and delicious octopus cooked with orange.

Petaladika
GREEK €€

(Map p516; ✆ 22410 27359; Menakleous 8; mains €6-20; ⏱ noon-late; ❋) Petaladika might look like just another tourist trap, tucked into a corner just off the main Old Town drag, but with its fresh white-wood interior, and chic tables and chairs out front, it's a good option. Try the deep-fried baby squid, zucchini balls and freshly grilled fish.

Mama Sofia
TAVERNA €€

(Map p516; ✆ 22410 24469; www.mamasofia.gr; Orfeos 28; mains €14-28; ⏱ 9am-late; ❋ 🐾 🚻) A spit away from the Roloi clock tower, facing the Mosque of Süleyman, Mama's has been feeding travellers quality Greek cuisine for generations. The presentation and homely service is first class, and you can expect all the usual suspects from souvlakia to octopus, *stifadho* (meat, game or seafood stewed with tomatoes) and *kleftiko* (slow oven-baked lamb or goat).

Dinoris Fish Restaurant
SEAFOOD €€€

(Map p516; ✆ 22410 25824; www.dinoris.com; Plateia Mousiou 14; mains €20-30; ⏱ noon-midnight; ❋ 🐾 🚻) Tucked just inside the walls, across from the Archaeological Museum, Dinoris is among the Old Town's fanciest and more expensive options, with romantic trimmings like lemon-painted walls, candelabra, linen tablecloths and gleaming glassware.

The menu is drenched with an oceanic array of mussels, risotto, fish soup, lobster and octopus. Some prices are per kilo; check costs before you eat.

Hatzikelis
SEAFOOD €€€

(Map p516; ☑ 22410 27215; www.hatzikelistavern.com; Alhadef 9; mains €9-45; ☉ noon-midnight; ❉ 🐾 ♿) Smart Hatzikelis has a romantic setting near the harbour, beside a ruined basilica. Lunchtime sees bargain deals to lure in day trippers; in the evening it sells the concept of choosing a whole fish, making a soup with the head and assorted shellfish, and serving the rest as a main course. With ingredients sold by weight, dinner can work out expensive.

✖ New Town

Koykos
GREEK €

(Map p519; ☑ 22410 73022; www.koukosrodos.com; Mandilana 20-22, New Town; mains €3-27; ☉ 24hr; 🐾 ♪) This inviting complex of historic homes, on a pedestrian shopping street, consists of several antique-filled rooms – cuckoo clocks feature strongly – along with pavement patio seating and a bougainvillea-draped courtyard. Best known for fabulous pies (from around €2.30), it also serves classic mezedhes (small plates), plus meat and fish dishes, and a simple coffee or sandwich.

Niohori
TAVERNA €

(Map p519; ☑ 22410 35116; I Kazouli 29, New Town; mains €7-12; ☉ 1-11pm Mon-Sat, 5-11pm Sun) It's all about the meat at this simple backstreet taverna; the owner is a butcher, with a shop across the street. Sit outside rather than the dazzling-white interior, or in the covered courtyard (really it's a garage), and tuck into steak, meatballs or veal liver with oil and oregano, occasionally seasoned with organ music from the nearby church.

★Meltemi
SEAFOOD €€

(Map p519; ☑ 22410 30480; Kountourioti 8; mains €9-22.50; ☉ 10am-late; P ❉ ♿) If you want to eat on the waterfront, Rhodes Town holds no better option than Meltemi, nestled into the sands of Elli Beach, just beyond Mandraki Harbour. The building itself may be drab, but the terrace views are magnificent, while the menu bursts with the tastes of the sea: octopus, jumbo prawns, lobster and calamari, all delivered with gusto.

Kerasma
GREEK €€

(Map p519; ☑ 22413 02410; www.kerasmarestaurant.com; George Leontos 4-6, New Town; mains €14-32; ☉ 12.15-11.30pm Mon-Sat, 6-11.30pm Sun; ❉🐾) The pick of several contemporary-styled restaurants on the New Town's fanciest dining street, Kerasma gives Greek classics a fusion twist, with dishes like grilled octopus dipped in honey with *fava*, and beef fillet with green pepper and white chocolate. An impressive cellar holds over 60 Greek wines.

Koozina
GREEK €€

(Map p519; ☑ 6943451450; George Leontos 19, New Town; mains €12-27; ☉ 1-11.30pm) The New Town sees a lot of Scandinavian visitors, and with its wooden floors and tin watering cans artfully hanging from its white walls, this open-sided place has a real sense of 'Scandi' chic. The owner prides herself on fresh-made dishes like ravioli stuffed with shrimps and scallops, and lamb shank cooked in beer.

🍷 Drinking & Nightlife

The Old Town is surprisingly short of bars. The most popular drinking venues are the broad terraces of its many tavernas, though Sofokleous holds some laid-back options, and music-oriented bars circle Plateia Arionos.

The New Town has a more active nightlife scene. Orfanidou is an out-and-out 'bar street' – read 'drunk street' – while I Dragoumi too is lined with pubs. Classier bars and cafes line the streets parallel to Mandraki Harbour.

🍶 Old Town

★Raxati Cafe
BAR

(Map p516; ☑ 22410 36365; Sofokleous 1-3; ☉ 10am-late; 🐾) This high-ceilinged, free-spirited bar and coffeehouse, close to the attractive Ibrahim Pasha mosque, is as pretty as it is friendly. Inside, the stone walls are peppered with vintage ad posters, and the back-lit bar glitters with glass spirit bottles, while cushioned benches line recycled Singer sewing machine tables outside. Snacks, cocktails, easy tunes and good conversation.

Rogmi Tou Chronou
BAR

(Map p516; ☑ 22410 25202; Plateia Arionos 4; ☉ 7pm-4am; 🐾) If Dracula developed a taste for rock music and opened a bar it might look something like this. Imagine purple velvet drapes, a handsomely crafted wooden bar lit with spirits, stained-glass windows, and the odd candle. Tables out on the square are perfect for a relaxed early-evening drink, while there's live rock later on Fridays and Saturdays.

Mevlana
CAFE

(Map p516; ☑ 6942210846; Sokratous 76; ☉ 10am-midnight; ☎) Shoppers on the Old Town's most commercialised street tend to double-take when they spot this venerable Turkish-styled cafe, with its pebble-mosaic floor, carved wooden panels, laid-back atmosphere and hookah-smoking clientele reclining on cushions. Expect a hearty welcome if you drop in for coffee or cocktails, iced tea or ice cream, juice or beer; apart from desserts, though, there's no food.

Macao Bar
BAR

(Map p516; ☑ 6936400305; www.macaobar.gr/en; Plateia Arionos; ☉ 7pm-5am; ☎) Uber-stylish Macao bar, hidden away in the heart of the Old Town, has a moody, low-lit ambience, polished concrete floors and the occasional guest DJ spinning the decks to a well-heeled crowd of fashionistas. Be sure to try the herb-flavoured cocktails (€10).

New Town

Aktaion Cafe
CAFE

(Map p519; ☑ 22410 76856; www.aktaion-rodos. gr; Plateia Eleftheria, New Town; ☉ 8am-midnight; ☎✦) The New Town's busy central rendezvous sprawls across a large open-air terrace beneath the shade of a spreading plane tree, across the street from Mandraki Harbour. Locals and day trippers alike watch the world go by, relaxing over drinks and snacks, while children head straight to the adjoining enclosed playground.

Christos Garden
BAR

(Map p519; ☑ 22410 32144; Griva 102, New Town; ☉ 10pm-late; ☎) With its grotto-like bar and pebble-mosaic courtyard, Christos offers New Town visitors a tranquil escape. During the day it doubles as an art gallery; after dark the fairy lights twinkle. Perfect for a cocktail.

☆ Entertainment

9D: Throne of Helios
FILM

(Map p519; ☑ 22410 76850; www.throneofhelios. com; 25 Martiou 2, New Town; adult/child €13/9; ☉ 10am-11pm; ☎✦) This entertaining 20-minute movie takes viewers back to the very birth of Rhodes, its 3D effects complemented by a further six dimensions (!) including shaking chairs, falling rain, snow and bubbles. The historic content is good, while amazing visuals recreate the construction of the Colossus, the creation of the medieval citadel, and more.

There's no great reason for adults to stay on for the wordless short 3D cartoon that follows the main film, but young kids will enjoy the even more vigorous special effects.

Cafe Chantant
LIVE MUSIC

(Map p516; ☑ 22410 32277; Dimokratou 3; ☉ 11pm-late Fri & Sat) Locals flock to sit at the long wooden tables here and listen to live traditional Greek music while drinking ouzo or beer. It's dark inside and you won't find snacks or nibbles, but the atmosphere is warm-hearted and friendly and the band is always lively.

🔒 Shopping

As well as a *lot* of souvenir tat, the Old Town holds plenty of shops that sell quality keepsakes: Moorish lamps, icons, classical busts, leather sandals, belts and bags, silver jewellery, olive-wood chopping boards, Rhodian wine, and thyme honey. The New Town is more prosaic, with its grocery shops, general stores and clutch of big-name fashion and style brands.

Rhodes Handmade Gallery
ARTS & CRAFTS

(Map p516; ☑ 22414 22242; Omirou 45; ☉ 9am-9pm) Best viewed by night, this Aladdin's cave of a shop conjures up thoughts of the *Arabian Nights,* with its shiny brass lamps, ornate antique rings and Eastern mosaic lights glowing like clusters of fireflies.

So Greek
FOOD & DRINKS

(Map p516; ☑ 22410 36870; https://sogreek. business.site; Ipodamou 40-42; ☉ 9am-10pm Mon-Sat) ✦ The perfect pit stop for choice gifts, So Greek sells nicely packaged Greek wine, olive oil and a wide range of homemade honey, natural cosmetics and herbs and spices.

ℹ Information

EMERGENCY & IMPORTANT NUMBERS

Emergencies & Ambulance (☑ 166)

Port Police (☑ 22410 27634; Mandraki Harbour, New Town)

Tourist Police (☑ 22410 27423; New Town; ☉ 24hr)

MEDICAL SERVICES

Euromedica General Hospital (☑ 22410 45000; www.euromedica-rhodes.gr; Koskinou) Large private health facility, in Koskinou, 9km south of the Old Town, with a 24-hour emergency department and English-speaking staff.

General Hospital Rhodes (☑ 22413 60000; Andreas Papandreou; ☉ 24hr) This public hospital, 5km southwest of the Old Town, has been hit hard by cuts in government funding. Staff shortages can result in long waits for treatment.

Rhodes Medical Care (☎22410 38008; www.rmc.gr; Krito Bldg, Ioannou Metaxa 3, New Town) Private clinic that will treat any emergency provided you have health insurance. Excellent staff and facilities.

You'll find plenty of ATMs throughout Rhodes Town, with useful ATM-equipped branches of Alpha Bank next door to the Old Town tourist office (p525) and on Plateia Kypriou in the New Town. The National Bank of Greece has a conveniently located office in the **New Town** (Plateia Kyprou, New Town), as well as a branch on Plateia Mousiou in the Old Town.

EOT (Greek Tourist Information Office; Map p519; ☎22410 44335; www.ando.gr/eot; cnr Makariou & Papagou, New Town; ⊙8.30am-2.45pm Mon-Fri) National tourism information, with brochures, maps and transport details.

Rhodes Tourism Office – New Town (Map p519; ☎22410 35495; www.rhodes.gr; Plateia Rimini, New Town; ⊙7.30am-3pm Mon-Fri) Conveniently poised between Mandraki Harbour and the Old Town, with public toilets alongside, this efficient office has helpful staff.

Rhodes Tourism Office – Old Town (Map p516; ☎22410 35945; www.rhodes.gr; cnr Platonos & Ippoton; ⊙7am-3pm Mon-Fri) Rhodes Town's most useful tourist office, housed in an ancient building at the foot of the Street of the Knights, supplies excellent street maps, some good handouts on the whole island, and various commercial brochures.

❶ Getting Around

Bicycles can be rented from **Margaritis** (☎22410 37420; www.margaritisrentals.gr; I Kazouli 17, New Town; ⊙8am-9pm) in the New Town.

Excursion boats based on the quayside at Mandraki Harbour offer day trips to towns and beaches along Rhodes' east coast, including Faliraki and Lindos.

Local buses within Rhodes Town leave from the **urban bus stop** (Map p519; Mandraki Harbour, New Town) on Mandraki Harbour. The most useful route for visitors is bus 6, which goes to the Acropolis. Buy tickets on board.

Regular buses serve the entire island on weekdays, with fewer services on Saturday and only a few on Sunday. Two bus terminals, at either end of the same short street in the New Town, serve half the island each. Schedules are posted beside the

ticket kiosks at each terminal, and also online. All tickets cost €0.20 extra when bought from the driver as you board the bus.

Eastern Bus Terminal (Map p519; ☎22410 27706; www.ktelrodou.gr; Averof, New Town) Services to Faliraki (€2.40), Tsambika Beach (€3.90), Haraki (€4.90), Lindos (€5.50), Lahania (€7.80), Kattavia (€9) and Prasonisi (€10.40).

Western Bus Terminal (Map p519; ☎22410 26300; www.desroda.gr; Averof, New Town) Very frequent buses run down the coast to the airport (€2.40). Although fewer services continue any further, daily excursion buses head to Ancient Ialysos (not Sun; €5.20), Ancient Kamiros (€5.20) and the Valley of the Butterflies (€5) while buses timed to coincide with ferry sailings connect Rhodes Town with Skala Kamirou (€4.50). Buses to Monolithos (€5) run on Monday and Friday only. One slight anomaly is that the Western Terminal also offers regular service to Kalithea Thermi (€2.40).

If you're based in Rhodes Old Town, it's worth remembering that you can't drive into the Old Town, let alone park there, so it makes sense to rent a car only for the actual day(s) you're going to use it.

Drive Rent A Car (☎22410 68243; www.driverentacar.gr; 1st Km Tsairi-Airport; ⊙8am-9pm) Sturdier, newer scooters and cars.

Margaritis (p525) Reliable cars, scooters and bicycles in the New Town.

Orion Rent a Car (☎22410 22137; www.orioncarrental.com; Leontos 38, New Town) A wide range of small and luxury cars.

As the narrow lanes of the Old Town are largely pedestrianised, taxis cannot drive to most destinations within the walls; expect to be dropped at the gate nearest your destination. A few upscale hotels will pick up guests in golf buggies.

Rhodes Town's main **taxi rank** (Map p519; Papagou, Old Town) is on the northern edge of the Old Town, just east of Plateia Rimini; a board displays set fares for specified destinations. Meters charge slightly less for journeys in Rhodes Town than for the rest of the island. Rates double between midnight and 5am.

You can also phone for a **taxi** (☎in Rhodes Town 22410 69800, outside Rhodes Town 22410 69600; www.rhodes-taxi.gr).

Northeastern Rhodes

Most of Rhodes' sandiest beaches lie along the island's northeastern coast, between Rhodes Town and Lindos. As a result, this stretch is punctuated by a long succession of resorts, filled with package holidaymakers in summer and holding endless strips of tourist bars.

One of Rhodes' loveliest (and busiest) beaches, Ladiko Beach (🅿️🚻) consists of two back-to-back coves, just past Faliraki, 16km south of Rhodes Town. The first and larger of the two is composed of sand and gravel, while the even prettier bay beyond, consisting of pebbles and also known as Anthony Quinn Beach, is better for swimming. Quinn, the star of *Zorba the Greek*, bought the beach from the Greek government in the 1960s, but according to his family the authorities failed to honour the sale.

Two more fine beaches, Kolymbia and Tsambika, stand either side of the massive Tsambika promontory 10km further south. Both are sandy but get crowded in summer. Not far beyond, the coast road curves inland, but a short detour seawards brings you to the low-key little resort of Stegna, arrayed along sandy, idyllic Stegna Beach. The spotless little Pirofani Fish Taverna (📞6972165186; Stegna; mains €7-17; ⊗10am-11pm; 🅿️🛜🚻) here makes a good lunchtime stop.

The headland that marks the start of the final curve towards Lindos, 40km south of Rhodes Town, is topped by the ruins of the 15th-century Castle of Faraklos. Once a prison for recalcitrant knights, this was the last stronghold on the island to fall to the Turks and now offers fabulous views. A footpath climbs from the appealing little resort of Haraki, immediately south, where the neat horseshoe bay is lined by a pebbly beach.

🔴 Sights

Kalithea Thermi   ARCHITECTURE
(Map p514; 📞22410 37090; www.kallitheasprings. gr; Kalithea; €3; ⊗8am-8pm Apr-Oct, to 5pm Nov-Mar; 🚻) Italian architect Pietro Lombardi constructed this opulent art deco spa, on the site of ancient thermal springs, in 1929. Its dazzling white-domed pavilions, pebble-mosaic courtyards and sweeping sea-view colonnades have appeared in movies such as *Zorba the Greek* and *The Guns of Navarone*. In peak season its small sandy bathing beach and cafe get impossibly crowded.

Epta Piges   SPRING
(Seven Springs; Map p514; Kolymbia; ⊗24hr; 🅿️🚻) **FREE** Seven natural springs at this beauty spot, in the hills 4km inland from Kolymbia, feed a river that's channelled into a narrow tunnel, exactly the size of an adult. Thrill-seeking visitors can walk a few hundred metres in pitch darkness, ankle-deep in

fast-flowing water, to reach the shaded lake at the far end.

There's also a taverna and the House of the Python gift shop, so called because it is indeed home to a colossal live snake.

ℹ️ Getting There & Away

Frequent buses from Rhodes Town's Eastern Bus Terminal (p525) ply the main road, connecting the best-known beaches. If you're happy to hike, you can walk down to much emptier strands at several points along the way.

Lindos   Λίνδος
POP 1100

With its timeless Acropolis atop a cypress-silvered hill, and sugar-cube houses tumbling towards an aquamarine bay, your first glimpse of the ancient village of Lindos is guaranteed to steal your breath away.

Close up, things can feel very different. Lindos has become a major tourist destination, its approaches plagued by circling traffic and its narrow lanes jammed solid with sightseers. Come out of season, though, or stay the night and venture out before the day trippers arrive, and you can still experience the old Lindos, a warren of alleyways where the mansions of long-vanished sea captains hold tavernas, bars and cool cafes. Coax your calves up to the Acropolis, and you'll encounter one of the finest views in Greece.

Lindos has been enjoying its wonderful setting for 3000 years, since the Dorians first settled beside this excellent harbour. Since then it has been successively overlaid with Byzantine, Frankish and Turkish structures.

🔴 Sights & Activities

⭐ **Acropolis of Lindos**   ARCHAEOLOGICAL SITE
(Map p514; 📞22440 31258; adult/concession/child €12/6/free; ⊗8am-7.40pm Apr-Oct, to 3pm Tue-Sun Nov-Mar) A short, steep-stepped footpath climbs the rocky 116m-high headland above the village to reach Lindos' beautifully preserved Acropolis. First fortified in the 6th century BCE, the clifftop is now enclosed by battlements constructed by the Knights of St John. Once within the walls, you're confronted by ancient remains that include the Temple to Athena Lindia and a 20-columned Hellenistic stoa. Silhouetted against the blue sky, the stark pillars are dazzling, while the long-range coastal views are out of this world.

Be sure to pack a hat and some water, as there's no shade at the top, and take care to protect young kids from the many dangerous drop-offs.

Donkey rides follow a longer pathway to the Acropolis from the village entrance (€8), an option that spares you a mere three minutes of exposed walking on the hillside. Animal-rights groups strongly urge visitors to consider how the donkeys are treated before deciding to ride.

★ **Lepia Dive** DIVING
(☎6937417970; www.lepiadive.com; Pefkos; ♿) Options with this brilliantly inclusive dive company include reef, wreck and cave dives, plus PADI courses for kids, beginners and advanced divers. The centre is adapted for wheelchairs, and offers expertly designed dives for people with additional needs, certified by Disabled Divers International. Free pickup.

Beaches

Lindos Main Beach BEACH
The larger of Lindos' two superb beaches stretches north along the innermost shoreline of the bay, north of the village. Known logically enough as Main Beach, it's sandy and shelves softly into the sea, making it a perfect swimming spot for kids. In summer it gets very crowded. There's free parking on the hillside just above.

Pallas Beach BEACH
Tucked just below Lindos village, pocket-sized, taverna-fringed Pallas Beach is reached by a footpath that drops down near the start of the mule trail up to the Acropolis, and can also be accessed directly from Main Beach by a narrow coastal path. Don't swim near the jetty here, which is home to sea urchins, but if it gets too crowded you can launch yourself from the rocks beyond.

St Paul's Bay BEACH
A short walk from the southern end of Lindos village, St Paul's Bay is an all-but-circular inlet that's only open to the Aegean via a slender gap in the rocks. Its tiny sheltered beach, caressed by turquoise waters, is a supremely tranquil place to swim, but does get very crowded in peak season.

Local tradition has it that St Paul sought refuge here in 57 CE, when his ship was fleeing a storm at sea.

Sleeping

Accommodation in Lindos is very limited, so be sure to book in advance. And check carefully, as most hotels that include 'Lindos' in their names and/or addresses are in fact located not in the village centre, but along the coast nearby.

F Charm Hotel BOUTIQUE HOTEL €€
(☎6944339937, 22440 32080; www.lindosfinestaying.com; Lindos VIllage; r incl breakfast from €140; ❄📶) This enclosed courtyard accommodation, next to the police station at the south end of the village, holds half-a-dozen heavenly white rooms plus two family-sized suites. All have shabby-chic distressed furniture, wood-beamed ceilings and traditional raised-platform beds with Coco-mat mattresses, plus fridge and kitchenette.

Anastasia Studios APARTMENT €€
(☎22440 31212; www.lindos-studios.gr; Lindos Village; d & tr €60; P❄📶) Focused around a geranium-filled courtyard, just in from the car park at Lindos' southern end, these six split-level apartments enjoy soaring Acropolis views. Each has a tiled floor, sofa bed, well-equipped kitchen and separate bedroom, while room 6 has its own private balcony.

★ **Melenos Lindos** BOUTIQUE HOTEL €€€
(☎22440 32222; www.melenoslindos.com; Lindos Village; ste incl breakfast from €335; ❄@📶) 🍃 This Moorish-style palace, on the mule trail above Pallas Beach, has bougainvillea walkways, pebble-mosaic floors, verandas festooned in lanterns and bauble lights that cast a glow on Ottoman furniture. Staff glide discreetly around as you soak up the stunning bay view. Rooms are lovingly re-created in traditional Lyndian style, with raised beds, wooden ceilings and private balconies, and there's a superb restaurant (p528).

Eating & Drinking

Most Lindos tavernas serve their customers on roof terraces high above the central tangle of lanes. Although these give fabulous views up to the Acropolis – illuminated at night – and over the bay, you can't necessarily tell whether there's anyone in your chosen venue until you've already committed to eat there.

Village Cafe BAKERY €
(☎22440 31559; www.villagecafelindos.com; Lindos Village; mains €8-20; ⏰8am-6.30pm Mon-Sat, to 5.30pm Sun; ❄📶♿) Near the start of the donkey path up to the Acropolis, this whitewashed bakery-cafe consists of an enticing vine-covered pebble-mosaic courtyard, shaded over to keep things cool. Drop in for hot or frozen coffee, juice or ice cream, and a mouthwatering array of breakfasts,

cheesecakes, pies, salads, wraps and sandwiches. Don't miss the delectable *bougatsa* (vanilla custard pie).

★Kalypso
TAVERNA €€

(☑ 22440 32135; www.kalypsolindos.com; Lindos VIllage; mains €10-24; ☺ 11am-midnight; ❉ ☎) This former sea captain's residence with its beautiful stone relief is perfect for lunch or dinner on the roof terrace or inside. Sea bass, octopus, *makarounes* (homemade pasta served with fresh onions and melted local cheese) and grilled lamb chops are but a few of the delights. Try the 'Kalypso bread' with feta and tomato.

Melenos
MEDITERRANEAN €€€

(☑ 22440 32222; www.melenoslindos.com; Lindos VIllage; mains €22-32; ☺ 8am-11pm; ☎) This gorgeous terrace restaurant of the Melenos luxury hotel (p527) is set high above Pallas Beach on the donkey path up to the Acropolis. Standout dishes include salmon marinated in ouzo, steamed sea bass, goats' meat pasta and steak with baby vegetables in red-wine sauce. Round things off with a sumptuous dessert.

Ambrosia
MEDITERRANEAN €€€

(☑ 22440 31804; Lindos Village; mains €14-42; ☺ lunch & dinner; ❉ ☑) Lindos' smartest stand-alone restaurant doesn't have a roof garden – its dozen linen-clad tables are in the pristine white interior visible from the lanes – so the food has to be special. And it is, whether you opt for the raw sea-bream appetiser, squid-ink pasta or lamb shank. Owner George welcomes each diner with a little glass of sparkling wine.

Captain's House
CAFE

(☑ 22440 31235; Lindos Village; snacks €5; ☺ 8am-midnight; ☎) Soaked in Lyndian atmosphere, this nautically themed, 16th-century sea captain's house is perfect for a juice or coffee on your way down from the Acropolis. Grab a pew in the pebble-mosaic courtyard and admire the fabulous carved reliefs, or peer into the ground floor, restored with period furniture to display the lifestyle of its original owners.

❶ Information

Lindos Tourist Office (☑ 22440 31900; Main Sq, Lindos Village; ☺ 9am-3pm) Small information kiosk at the main village entrance.
Island Of The Sun Travel (☑ 22440 31264; Lindos Village; ☺ 9am-11pm) Local excursions, rental cars and accommodation.

❶ Getting There & Away

Frequent buses connect the main square with the Eastern Bus Terminal (p525) in Rhodes Town, with services every half-hour at peak times (€5.50). That journey costs €65 by taxi, while a taxi to or from the airport costs €75.

Southeastern Rhodes

Immediately south of Lindos, resorts such as Pefki have been burgeoning in recent years. The further you continue down the east coast, however, traffic diminishes, villages seem to have a slower pace, and the landscape takes on an ever more windswept appearance.

Just 2km south of Lindos, sandy Pefki Beach is deservedly popular. If it's too crowded, try Glystra Beach, just down the road and a great spot for swimming.

Sleepy Gennadi consists of a cluster of coffeehouses, tavernas and whitewashed buildings, not far inland from the main road. In the opposite direction, the local beach is a long straight strand of sand and pebbles, which continues pretty much uninterrupted for the 11km south to Plimmyri. Watch for a signposted turning to Lahania, 2km inland; once there, head downhill into the centre to find an old village of winding alleyways and traditional buildings.

Beyond the signposted side road to Plimmyri, the main road heads west, leaving the coast and skirting Rhodes' southern tip. Don't miss the lonesome Colonia San Marco Caffé, 5km along. Resembling something from a spaghetti western, it holds a little espresso cafe displaying memorabilia from its days as an Italian colonial outpost. Another 3km on, sleepy Kattavia livens up at lunchtime, when neighbouring tavernas jostle to feed circle-island day trippers.

A windswept road heads off south from Kattavia, snaking for 10km – and passing a monstrous new diesel-fuelled power plant – to reach remote Cape Prasonisi, the island's southernmost point. Joined to Rhodes by a tenuously narrow sandy isthmus in summer, it's cut off completely when water levels rise in winter. The Aegean Sea meets the Mediterranean here, creating ideal wind and wave conditions for kitesurfers and windsurfers. Outfitters help with everything from rental equipment and lessons to overnight accommodation in surfer-dude-style hostels, but it all closes down in winter. To get here direct from the airport by taxi costs around €120 and takes 1½ hours.

🏃 Activities

Pro Center
Christof Kirschner   ADVENTURE SPORTS
(📞22400 91045; www.prasonisi.com; Prasonisi Beach; ⊙May-Oct; ♿) Services for windsurfers include equipment rental (from €30 per hour) and two-hour classes (from €75).

🛏 Sleeping

★Four Elements   B&B €€
(📞6939450014, 22440 46001; www.bnbthefour elements.com; Lahania; apt incl breakfast €115-180; 🅿✳@🛜♿) Four comfortable and spacious apartments, perfect for a relaxing rural holiday. All have full kitchens – one is adapted for wheelchair users – and there's a divine pool, outdoor barbecue and garden. The friendly Belgian owners run the on-site Fifth Element cafe-bar (beer being the fifth element after earth, air, fire and water).

🍴 Eating & Drinking

Taverna Platanos   TAVERNA €
(📞6944199991; www.lachaniaplatanostaverna.com; Lahania; mains €6-13.50; ⊙11am-late; 🅿✳🛜) It's worth braving Lahania's ultranarrow lanes to reach this classic village taverna, tucked behind Agios Georgios church and famed throughout the island. With its traditional decor and flower-filled patio, it's a great place to take a break. Lamb baked with lemon costs €13.50, while hearty stews are €10.50, and salads and dips less than half that.

Mama's Kitchen   GREEK €
(📞22440 43547; Gennadi; mains €7-13; ⊙breakfast, lunch & dinner; 🅿✳) In this lively and always busy taverna in the heart of Gennadi, you can check out the murals depicting ancient myths while feasting on Olympian portions of grilled meat like lamb and beef, or child-friendly pizzas.

★Colonia San Marco Caffé   CAFE
(Map p514; 📞22440 91483; Kattavia; ⊙8am-midnight; 🛜) This lonesome relic, 3km east of Kattavia, resembles something from a spaghetti western. Constructed in 1926 as the centrepiece of an Italian agricultural colony, it originally held a school and still holds a church. It's now home to a welcoming espresso cafe that, as well as selling snacks and local produce, displays memorabilia from its intriguing past.

ℹ Getting There & Away

If you don't have a rental car, local buses make a decent fallback. Regular buses (www.ktelrodou. gr) connect Rhodes Town with Pefki, Kiotari and Gennadi between around 6am and 9pm, but far fewer services continue to Lahania and Cape Prasonisi.

Western Rhodes & the Interior

Western Rhodes is redolent with the scent of pine, its hillsides shimmering with forests. More exposed than the east side, it's also windier – a boon for kitesurfers and windsurfers – so the sea tends to be rough and the beaches mostly pebbled. If you're cycling, or have a scooter or car, the hilly roads that cross the interior are well worth exploring for their wonderful scenery.

For sightseers, the most significant potential stopoffs along the west coast are the ruined ancient cities of Ialysos and, especially, Kamiros. Once you get past the airport, settlements are few and far between. Skala Kamirou, 45km southwest of Rhodes Town, is a small port served by direct ferries to the nearby island of Halki. A couple of tavernas sit by the harbour, and connecting buses link it with Rhodes Town.

The ruins of 16th-century Kritinia Castle stand proudly on a headland immediately south of Skala Kamirou. Detour off the main road for awe-inspiring views along the coast and across to Halki, in a magical setting where you half expect to encounter Romeo or Rapunzel.

Continuing south, the road turns sublimely scenic. Vast mountainous vistas open up as you approach Siana, a picturesque village below Mt Akramytis (825m), and the village of Monolithos, 5km beyond.

A spectacularly sited 15th-century castle stands 2km west, perched on a sheer-sided pinnacle. Thanks to a gap in the walls, there's free, unrestricted access; at sunset especially, the views are superb. Continue another 5km down a precipitous, winding road to reach the attractive, if gravelly, Fourni Beach (🅿).

👁 Sights

★Ancient Kamiros   ARCHAEOLOGICAL SITE
(Map p514; 📞22410 40037; www.gtp.gr/archaeo logicalsiteofkameiros; €6; ⊙8am-7.40pm May-Oct, 8.30am-3pm Nov-Apr; ♿) Cradled in a natural hillside amphitheatre 1km up from the sea, the remarkably complete ruins of ancient Kamiros stand 34km southwest of Rhodes Town. Founded in the 10th century BCE, and mentioned by Homer, Kamiros reached its peak during the 7th century BCE, but was

devastated by earthquakes in 226 BCE and 142 BCE. Visitors enjoy a real feeling of walking the streets of an ancient city, complete with baths, temples, private homes and public squares.

Monolithos Castle
CASTLE

(Map p514; ⊙24hr; P🅿) FREE Monolithos' 15th-century castle crowns an isolated pinnacle 2km west of the village towards Fourni Beach. Beside a cafe at a curve in the road, a short footpath climbs to the hole in the battlements that allows visitors unrestricted access. Only the inland side is walled; the far side is defended by sheer colossal cliffs. A little whitewashed chapel marks the summit, while another stands in ruins just below. Come if you can at sunset, when the views are magnificent.

Valley of the Butterflies
FOREST

(Petaloudes; Map p514; ☑22410 82822; €5; ⊙9am-5pm; P🅿) The so-called Valley of the Butterflies, 7km up from the west coast, and 32km southwest of Rhodes Town, is a major day-trip destination for package tourists. A narrow wooded cleft in the mountains, threaded with footpaths, it comes alive in summer – typically between around 10 June and 20 September – with colourful butterflies, drawn by the resin exuded by storax trees. That's by far the best time to visit, though the trails remain busy for most of the year.

Ancient Ialysos
ARCHAEOLOGICAL SITE

(Map p514; ☑22410 92202; www.gtp.gr/acropolisof ialysos; €6; ⊙8am-7.40pm May-Oct, 8.30am-3pm Nov-Apr; 🅿) Ancient Ialysos was one of three cities that joined to create the new city of Rhodes in 408 BCE. Its flat hilltop site, 12km southwest of Rhodes Town, can be reached by a signposted drive or a demanding but enjoyable 5km hike from nearby Ialysos, but there's surprisingly little to see. A paved walkway, lined by trees, climbs the final 100m to the Byzantine Monastery of Filerimos that now occupies the summit, alongside the ruins of a small Athena temple.

🛏 Sleeping & Eating

Hotel Thomas
HOTEL €

(☑22460 61291; Monolithos; r €44; P🅿📶) This good-value, long-standing hotel, with very welcoming owners, sits 150m down the hillside from the southwestern end of Monolithos (turn opposite the Limeri restaurant). Its good-sized, tiled-floor rooms have tiny kitchenettes, and long-range views over the olive groves to the sea. A simple breakfast costs €5.

Limeri
GREEK €

(☑22460 61227; www.limeri.gr; Monolithos; mains €6.50-13; ⊙breakfast, lunch & dinner; P📶📶) This large restaurant, beside the road as it heads out of Monolithos towards the castle, serves high-quality local food on a spacious terrace or in its cosy indoor dining room. The dolmadhes are excellent, while the hearty oven-baked lamb or goat is succulent and juicy. It also offers classy rooms (€50) and two-bedroom suites (€75).

To Stolidi Tis Psinthou
TAVERNA €€

(☑22410 50009; Psinthos; mains €9-13.50; ⊙lunch & dinner; P📶) The pick of several appealing lunch spots in the lively main square of Psinthos, 16km southeast of the Valley of the Butterflies. The wooden-beamed interior holds a colourful array of vintage bric-a-brac, and the excellent food comes in huge portions. Be sure to try high-cal, local speciality *kapamas* – meat, rice, potatoes and herbs all baked together – and the chickpea croquettes.

❶ Getting There & Away

All buses along the west coast depart from the Western Bus Terminal (p525) in Rhodes Town. Every morning, separate excursion buses serve Ialysos (not Sun), Kamiros and the Valley of the Butterflies. In addition, connecting buses carry ferry passengers between Skala Kamirou and Rhodes Town, and there's also a bus service to Monolithos, on Monday and Friday only.

HALKI
ΧΑΛΚΗ

POP 310

Thanks to the gorgeous Italianate mansions that surround its harbour, the former sponge-diving island of Halki makes an irresistible first impression. Stepping off the ferry, you enter a composite of all that's best about Greece: an old fisherman shelling prawns under a fig tree, an Orthodox priest flitting down a narrow alley, brightly painted boats bobbing along the quay. There's little to do except relax and indulge in the sleepy splendour, venturing out to tempting little beaches lapped by aquamarine waters and, in cooler months, hiking along the island's spectacular high-mountain spine to visit the island's monastery and admire the views.

❶ Getting There & Away

The Dodekanisos Seaways (p515) catamaran stops at Halki's port in Emborios on Tuesday and Thursday as it heads from Rhodes via Halki (€18,

80 minutes) to Tilos (€13, 40 minutes), Nisyros (€24, 1½ hour), Kos (€24, 1½ hour) and Kalymnos (€35, three hours) in the morning, and back to Rhodes in the evening. On those days, you can visit the island as a day trip from Rhodes. Anek Prevalis (of Anek Lines; p515) runs three days a week linking Santorini, Anafi, Kasos, Karpathos (Pigadia and Diafani) and finally, Rhodes. Once a week it heads between Halki and Iraklio on Crete (€22, 11½ hours).

Three boats, Nissos Halki (p515), Nikos Express (p515) and **Fedon** ([22460 45110), link Halki daily with the tiny port of Skala Kamirou on the west coast of Rhodes; there's an hour-long connecting bus service with Rhodes Old Town.

🛈 Getting Around

In summer, regular minibuses connect Emborios with Pondamos, Ftenagia and Kania beaches (€2 each way), while on Friday evenings there's also a round trip to Moni Agiou Ioanni monastery (€5). A summer-only excursion boat heads to the uninhabited island of Alimia (around €30).

Emborios   Εμπορειός

POP 300

Halki's one tiny town curves luxuriantly around a sheltered turquoise bay. The waterfront is a broad expanse of flagstones, almost entirely pedestrianised, populated by as many cats as humans and lined with enticing tavernas and cafes. Climbing in tiers up a low ridge, the cream, ochre, stone and rose-hued homes of 19th-century fisherfolk and sea captains form a magnificent backdrop. There's no town beach, but here and there ladders enable swimmers to enter the water.

👁 Sights

The neoclassical mansions of Emborios are a visual feast. A few have crumbled into complete ruination, but most have been restored and many now serve as rental properties.

The impressive central clock tower was donated by the expat Halki community in Florida; the clock itself hasn't worked for over 20 years. Nearby, the Church of Agios Nikolaos has the tallest belfry in the Dodecanese, incorporating stones from an ancient temple of Apollo, and has a picturesque mosaic-pebbled courtyard.

Traditional House of Chalki   HISTORIC BUILDING
([22460 45284; €2.50; ⊙11am-3pm & 6-8pm) Perched on the hillside, not far up from the harbour (signed to the right off the road to Pondamos Beach), the Traditional House of Chalki – an alternative transliteration of

Halki – is a two-storey family home, built a century ago. It's now meticulously preserved as a museum, displaying authentic furniture, tableware and costumes, old photos – and even the underwear of the owner's grandmother, neatly framed.

🛌 Sleeping

Captain's House   PENSION €
([22460 45201, 6932511762; capt50@otenet.gr; d €45; 🌊🌐) Attractive white-painted 19th-century house just up from the sea, near the church, featuring antique clocks and model schooners. Two lovely rooms have high ceilings, wood floors, air-con and good bathrooms, and the relaxing garden courtyard holds a sun terrace with great harbour views. Excellent value for money.

⭐ Aretanassa Hotel   HOTEL €€
([22460 70927; www.facebook.com/aretanassa.hotel; Harbour; incl breakfast d €105-122, tr €127; 🌊🌐🏊) This wine-coloured former sponge factory has 19 gloriously sunny, sea-facing rooms with powder-blue walls, large beds and spotless tiled floors. Nearly all rooms have balconies. There's a lovely restaurant and bar, and a sun terrace over your own azure Mediterranean swimming pool. There's also a lift and access for those with additional needs.

🍴 Eating

Magefseis   GREEK €
([22460 45065; mains €7-11; ⊙breakfast, lunch & dinner; 🍴) 🖋 Don't be misled by the commercial-looking, photo-filled menu. This place has a unique take, from the jovial owner, Christos, to the fresh fresh seafood that comes off the boats. The rest of the huge menu spans grills to the standard cooked favourites (*mousakas* etc), but you can't go wrong. Portions are not huge, but adequate.

Dimitri's Bakery   BAKERY €
(snacks €1.50-3; ⊙6am-3pm) Generations of Halki residents and visitors have stocked up on Dimitri's delicious sweet and savoury pies and pastries, available from early morning. Cheese pies. Spinach pies. Apple pies. Croissants. You get the doughy, mouthwatering picture. Don't miss the *tsoureki*, the sweet bread.

Black Sea   TAVERNA €€
([22460 45021; mains €8-15; ⊙lunch & dinner; 🌊) 🖋 Sitting peacefully on the south side of the harbour, metres from bobbing boats, this blue-hued haunt is run by a charming

DODECANESE EMBORIOS

Georgian family. It's great for fresh fish, from octopus and little shrimp to grilled bream, but the vegetable dishes, including fried mushrooms, are also delicious. Has a slightly gourmet touch that some others lack.

ℹ Information

The only ATM (located under the **post office**; ⊗9am-2.45pm Mon-Fri) is often out of action, so bring plenty of spare cash.

Zifos Travel (☑22460 45028; www.zifostravel. gr; ⊗10am-8pm) The best source of help with boat tickets and currency exchange.

ℹ Getting There & Away

All boats arrive at the island's harbour in Emborios. From here, it's an easy walk to your hotel (albeit with steps); for around €5, a baggage cart meets boats and will transport your luggage.

Around Halki

A broad concrete road crosses the low hill above Emborios Harbour to reach Pondamos Beach, the most popular of Halki's handful of tiny shingle beaches, after 500m. Beyond that, it climbs to the abandoned village of Horio, 3km along, then continues west to the hilltop monastery of Agiou Ioanni. That's a total one-way hike of 8km, recommended in the cooler months only.

Two more pebble beaches, both equipped with decent tavernas and served by buses in summer, lie within walking distance of Emborios. Ftenagia Beach is beyond the headland 500m south of the harbour, while Kania Beach is an enjoyable but unshaded 2.5km hike north, signposted off the main road halfway to Pondamos.

◉ Sights & Activities

Horio   ARCHAEOLOGICAL SITE
A stiff switchback climb along the road from Pondamos Beach leads up through Halki's fertile central valley to Horio. This picturesque ruin was originally the island's main village, hidden away to escape the eyes of roving pirates. A freshly cobbled footpath heads up to the battlements of the Knights of St John Castle that once protected it. Pass through its forbidding gateway to see a restored chapel and amazing long-range views.

Pondamos Beach   BEACH
Pretty little Pondamos Beach is lapped by the turquoise waters of a crescent bay 15 minutes' walk up and over the hill west of

Emborios. The only way to get a comfortable shaded spot is to rent a sunbed alongside Nick's Taverna (☑22460 45295; Pondamos Beach; mains €6-15; ⊗breakfast & lunch, dinner Fri only; 🖥), where separate sections serve good seafood meals, and drinks and snacks.

Chalki Dive Center   DIVING
(☑6943117220; www.chalkidive.com; Kania Beach) This new PADI-certified diving operation, the only one on Halki, gives divers the chance to explore the waters off Kania Beach. And believe us, you'll want to don the tanks and masks when you see the crystal 'H-two-Oh!' here. Prices start from €40 for advanced certified divers, to €50 for beginners. Children over eight years can dive, too (€50).

KARPATHOS ΚΑΡΠΑΘΟΣ
POP 6200
Celebrated for its wild mountains and blue coves, this long craggy island is among the least commercialised in Greece (although that is changing). Legend has it Prometheus and his Titans were born here, and with its cloud-wrapped villages and rugged beauty, there's still something undeniably primal in the air. Homer mentions it in the the *Iliad*. It's a lovely spot.

Popular with adrenaline junkies, southern Karpathos is in the spotlight each summer when it hosts an international kitesurfing competition. Meanwhile, the fierce wind that lifts the spray from the turquoise waves blows its way to the mountainous north, battering pine trees and howling past sugar-cube houses. Karpathian women at this end of the island still wear traditional garb, especially in the time-forgotten village eyrie of Olymbos, perched atop a perilous mountain ridge.

ℹ Getting There & Away

AIR
The airport at the very southern tip of Karpathos is linked by Olympic Air (p514) which has daily flights to Athens (€75, one hour).
Sky Express (p514) has daily links between Karpathos and Rhodes (€68, 40 minutes), plus Kasos (€56, 15 minutes). It also heads to Iraklio, Crete, via Rhodes (€162, two hours).

BOAT
The island's main port, Pigadia, is served by Blue Star Ferries and Anek Lines (which stops at Diafani). Blue Star (p515) has a weekly connection to/from Rhodes, Symi, Kos, Kalymnos, Leros and Patmos. Anek Lines (p515) ferries head once a

week to/from Milos (€38, 20¼ hours), Santorini (€27, 15¼ hours), Anafi (€17, 13¼ hours), Iraklio (€19, 8¼ hours), Sitia (€19, 4¾ hours) and Kasos (€8, 1¾ hours) before ending up at Karpathos en route to Rhodes. Two services also head to Santorini, and one to Crete.

Local passenger ferry, the **Kasos Princess** (☑ 6977911209; one way €10) (€10, 1½ hours), also offers day excursions to Kasos three times a week; one-way trips are permitted (but check first as regulations change).

🛈 Getting Around

TO/FROM THE AIRPORT

The airport is 14km southwest of Pigadia. A taxi will cost around €25. From Monday to Friday there is a daily bus departure to the airport from Pigadia (€3), but don't count on getting from the airport (at the time of research it departed at 7am). Given the size of the island it makes sense to rent a car. Many car-rental chains are based at the airport plus there are a couple of excellent in-town options that will arrange pickup.

BOAT

Day trips head from Pigadia up to Diafani, where they connect with buses to Olymbos, or continue north to remote beaches.

BUS

KTEL runs buses all over the island from the bus station (p537) in Pigadia, just up from the harbour. In summer, there's a daily departure to/from Apella Beach and around four weekly services to Finiki. There's a daily summer service to southern beaches though these change seasonally; check the return times before you head off. Between two and four buses a week go all the way north to Olymbos.

CAR

All major car-rental chains have outlets at the airport, and there are local agencies mainly based in Pigadia, but also in resort towns. A recommended operator is **Euromoto** (☑ 6970130912, 22450 23238; www.euromotokarpathos.com; scooter/car from €15/45) run by English-speaking George; it has four offices around the island.

TAXI

Taxi prices are posted at Pigadia's central **taxi rank** (☑ 22450 22705; Dimokratias). Fares are prohibitively high, with trips to Lefkos costing €60 and Olymbos €85.

Pigadia   Πηγάδια

POP 1690

Karpathos' capital and main ferry port, Pigadia sprawls beside a long bay in the island's southeast. Decent beaches stretch away to the north, backed by large resorts. The town lacks the photogenic good looks

and geometrically pleasing whitewashed houses of other island capitals. But it makes up for this. For here, it's about the people. It's proudly, determinedly Greek. Give it a little time and wander its harbour and among waterfront bars and backstreet bakeries. Chat to the locals who frequently

Karpathos

Karpathos Strait
Cape Paraspori
Saria
Excursion Boat
Tristomo
Cape Vroukounda
Vroukounda
Vananda Beach
Avlona
Halki (50km); Rhodes (132km)
Mt Profitis Ilias (716m)
Diafani
Olymbos
Sea of Crete
Papa Mina Bay
Agios Minas
Spoa
Mesohori
Agios Nikolaos
Roman Cistern
Apella Beach
Lefkos Beach
Apella Beach
Excursion Boat
Lefkos
Mertonas
Kyra Panagia Beach
Kali Limni (1215m)
Kato Lakos Beach
Volada
Aperi
Ahata Beach
Adia
Othos
Cape Proni
Pyles
Vrondi Bay
Menetes
Pigadia
Basilica of Agia Sophia
Finiki
Arkasa
Ammoopi
Agios Nikolaos Beach
Cape Volakas
Cape Agios Theodoros
Afiartis Bay
Cape Lingi
Cape Akrotiri
Cape Kastello
Kasos (10km); Crete (80km)

DODECANESE PIGADIA

DON'T MISS

OLYMBOS ΟΛΥΜΠΟΣ

Few moments can beat rounding a curve in the mountain road to receive your first glimpse of this mist-blown eyrie of pastel-coloured houses. Olymbos clings precariously to the summit of Mt Profitis Ilias (716m), as if flung there by a Titan's hand. Thread your way along its wind-tunnel alleys, passing old ladies in vividly coloured traditional dress, and you may feel as though you've strayed onto a film set. Some locals even speak with a dialect that still contains traces of ancient Dorian Greek.

It's considered to be the most traditional of all places in Greece; some of Olymbos' local ladies still wear their stunning hand-spun jackets and floral headgear. And the views – 'jaw-dropping' just doesn't cover it – will leave you spellbound as the earth plunges dramatically metres from your feet. Try to arrive in late afternoon or early morning to have the place to yourself.

The most memorable way of reaching Olymbos is by taking a private tour boat/water taxi to Diafani from Pigadia, then catching the connecting prearranged bus. The schedules vary according to the various taxi boats running from Pigadia's harbour, but most leave at around 8.30am and cost about €25.

There's also around three weekly summer bus services from Pigadia, departing at 8.45am or 9.15am and returning at 3.45pm. You can drive the spectacular, if winding, route (take it very slowly and keep your eyes on the road and *not* the views, however spectacular they are). Taxis from Pigadia cost €85.

Hotel Aphrodite (☏ 22450 51307; www.discoverolympos.com; d/tr €45/50; ☎) This hotel is located just beyond the central square at the far end of Olymbos. Its four rooms have seen better days (nothing has been done to them for years), but they are simple spaces with a fridge and kettle and above all – literally – they have astonishing west-facing sea views. The owners run the recommended Parthenon restaurant nearby, topped by a roof terrace.

Hotel Olymbos (☏ 22450 51009; r incl breakfast €45) Hidden away beneath the owners' excellent street-level restaurant, these two rooms have raised beds and traditional furnishings. Tread carefully; the walls are festooned in the traditional manner – with delicate decorated plates.

O Mylos (☏ 22450 51333; mains €7-14; ⊙ lunch & dinner) This wonderful spot, beside a traditional (and working) windmill, serves Karpathian dishes, some of which are cooked in a traditional oven. This means while you wrap your teeth around some of the island's best home-baked bread, or tuck into a goat stew, you can gaze across at one of Greece's finest views.

invite you to sit by them for a coffee. This place will grow on you.

🛏 Sleeping

Budget options are concentrated in the hillside streets that rise from central Pigadia, while newer and more luxurious options are resort style; these spread northwards around the curve of the bay.

Rose's Studios APARTMENT €
(☏ 22450 22284; www.rosesstudios.com; r €35; ✳☎) For ultrasimple, but good-value budget lodgings, it's well worth trudging 300m up from the port to reach these eight dated, but functional, rooms. They have

clean bathrooms, large sea-view balconies and decent fittings, including minimal kitchenettes. It's an extra €5 per day for air conditioning.

Nereides Hotel HOTEL €€
(☏ 22450 23347; www.nereideshotel.gr; Nereidon; d incl breakfast €130; P✳☎☀) This charming little hotel has been open since 2011 and everything from the paintwork to its up-to-the-minute bathrooms still gleams like new. It offers 30 stylish rooms with sea-view balconies, plus a good pool and snack bar. It's on the town's western edge and, although 10 minutes' walk from the beach, it's a good 15 minutes plus to the harbour.

Atlantis Hotel
HOTEL €€

(☑22450 22777; www.atlantishotelkarpathos.gr; incl breakfast s €65-75, d €75-88; ❄☎⊜) Long-established, family-run hotel across from the Italian-era public building just above the west end of the harbour. The pleasant, no-frills rooms are nicely maintained, though the hot water can be a bit temperamental. Although cheaper, those facing the decent-sized pool are pleasant; the lower ones have their own mini terrace. Decent breakfast.

✗ Eating

Both the quay and the pedestrian streets just behind it are lined with seafood tavernas, all-purpose brasseries, cafes and cocktail bars. Look out, too, for the Italian gelaterias on Apodimon Karpathion, parallel to the harbour.

Pantheon Cafe
CAFE €

(☑22450 22502; Papathanassiou; snacks €5-12; ⊙8am-late; ❄☎) The pick of the best-of-both-worlds cafes along this pedestrian street, with a fine old wood-panelled interior decorated in *kafeneio* style of old, and a rear balcony terrace, perched high above the harbour with fabulous views. Sure, you can get a full English breakfast (€11) but it's the salads that really hit the spot. Go for the Karpathian (€9, with cucumber, olives and local bread).

★ To Ellenikon
TAVERNA €€

(☑22450 23932; Apodimon Karpathion; mains €8-20; ⊙lunch & dinner; ❄☎♪) If you're looking for typical Karpathian food cooked the way it should be then 'the Greek' is your place. Try *saganaki* (fried cheese), meatballs, shrimp and calamari, served within the wood-accented traditional interior or outside on the narrow terrace. Also offers hefty, more 'international' dishes should you want a change. Owner, Christos, meets and greets and works the floor.

Odyssey
GREEK €€

(☑22450 23506; www.facebook.com/OdysseyRestaurantKarpathos; Harbour; mains €7-13.50) Owner Pascales comes from the region of Macedonia, so don't expect things to be served the same way here, despite their having the same menu listings. Your culinary odyssey will include delicious dolmadhes (with lemon and oil), eggplant salad that's grilled (not boiled), and pastas and grilled meats with different herbs. Mains are served with vegetables – a welcome treat.

🍷 Drinking & Nightlife

★ Caffe Karpathos
CAFE

(Angolo Italiano; ☑21022 87383; www.cafekarpathos.com; Apodimon Karpathion; ⊙7am-late; ☎) The oldest cafe on the island was once a magnet for Italians (thus the fabulous coffee served in the original Bialetti espresso pots). These days travellers and locals alike nestle into wicker chairs, with a fabulous brew or cocktail in hand, and philosophise with Michalis, the multilingual owner. Simply relax and chat, Greek style. It's a thrill in itself.

Enplo
COCKTAIL BAR

(cocktails €6; ⊙8am-late; ☎) This chilled spot on the quay offers good happy hour cocktails (from €8). Its impressive snack menu has six vegan options.

ℹ️ Information

Both the **National Bank of Greece** on Apodimon Karpathion, and **Alpha Bank**, a block higher on Dimokratias, have ATMs.

Possi Travel (☑22450 23342; 28 Oktovriou; ⊙8am-1pm & 5-8pm) The main travel agency for ferry and air tickets. The helpful staff speak excellent English.

Tourist Office (www.karpathos.org; ⊙Jul & Aug) Summer-only kiosk, in the middle of the seafront.

ℹ️ Getting There & Away

Local passenger ferry, the Kasos Princess (p533), offers day excursions to Kasos three times a week; one-way trips are permitted (but check first as regulations change).

Pigadia's bus station (p537), just up from the harbour, is served by KTEL buses, which travel infrequently to various destinations across the island. You can obtain printed schedules from the station's tiny office.

There's a taxi (p533) stand up the hill from the harbourfront; a sign shows destinations and costs.

Southern Karpathos

Thanks to their sandy beaches, several appealing villages in the southern half of Karpathos have reinvented themselves as small-scale resorts. Peaceful villages nestle amid the hills inland, an area that's crisscrossed by scenic walking tracks. Here, too, you can have a surfing lesson on the island's only surf beach, Agios Nikolaos, near Arkasa.

Menetes

Buffeted by mountain gales, the tiny village of Menetes sits high in the cliffs just above Pigadia. Climb to the church at its highest point before exploring its narrow white-washed streets.

⊙ Sights

Folklore Museum   MUSEUM
(☑ 6985847672; Menetes; ⊙ 9am-1pm & 5-8pm) **FREE** To gain entry to the ancient chapel that houses this two-room museum, you need to call ahead to Irini, custodian of the keys. Having unlocked it, she'll talk you through its haphazard treasures and point you towards the tunnels in the hillside near-by, used by German troops in WWII. Donations welcomed.

✕ Eating

★ **Dionysos Fiesta**   TAVERNA €
(☑ 22450 81269; Menetes; mains €6-10; ⊙ break-fast, lunch & dinner; ✳ 🛜) Run by the ultrafri-endly Irini, and set in a restored traditional house, in the twisting village lanes just up from the main road, this relaxed and wel-coming taverna spreads onto a raised gar-den terrace. Sit under the shade of the lemon tree and enjoy the likes of lemon chicken, artichoke omelettes and succulent Karpathian sausages.

Arkasa

Arkasa, on the southwest coast 9km from Menetes, is one of the oldest settlements on Karpathos. The original village centre, just up from the water, is now complemented by a burgeoning beach resort below. A water-side track leads 500m to the remains of the 5th-century **Basilica of Agia Sophia**, where two chapels stand amid mosaic fragments and columns, and to an ancient acropolis on the headland beyond.

The best beach hereabouts, sandy **Agios Nikolaos Beach** is accessible from the vil-lage, but you'll need to drive there.

🛏 Sleeping

★ **Glaros Studios**   APARTMENT €€
(☑ 22450 61015; www.glarosstudios-karpathos. com; Agios Nikolaos Beach, Arkasa; apt €80; ☐ 🛜) This well-managed, garden-set complex of five studios pretty much has Agios Nikola-os Beach to itself. There are spotless white studios, decorated in traditional Karpathian style with raised platform beds and small kitchenettes, plus a relaxed and good-value adjoining restaurant.

Eleni Studios   APARTMENT €€
(☑ 22450 61248; www.elenikarpathos.gr; Arkasa; studio €70, apt from €90; ☐ ✳ 🛜 ✈) On the road to Finiki and fronting the beach, Ele-ni Studios has fully equipped and very tidy powder-blue apartments with appealing bedrooms, built around a relaxing garden. There's an on-site bar, too, for sunset drinks and breakfast (extra cost), and a very tempt-ing pool. Great sea views.

Finiki

Arrayed along a neat little south-facing cres-cent bay, picturesque Finiki stands just 2km north of Arkasa. White-and-blue houses, in-terspersed with a peppering of tavernas, front its sleepy harbour and small grey-sand beach. The best local swimming is at **Agios Georgi-os Beach**, a short way south towards Arkasa.

🛏 Sleeping & Eating

★ **Arhontiko Finikes**   APARTMENT €
(☑ 22450 61473; www.hotelarhontiko.gr; Finiki; apt from €50) Clean, ultraspacious apartments with the most lovely view of the water. You can choose between contemporary decor or traditional Karpathian-style fit-outs, com-plete with a platform bed to sleep in, and wooden shelving on the walls (there's even willow pattern plates in some). There's no full-time reception; instead, the friendly Aus-tralian-Greek owners cater to your needs as required.

Marina Taverna   TAVERNA €€
(☑ 22450 61100; Finiki; mains €7-16; ⊙ breakfast, lunch & dinner; 🛜) One of the few places open all year, this laid-back taverna features an expansive terrace that surveys the gentle tur-quoise bay just metres from the waterfront. Enjoy inexpensive breakfasts, snack lunches and an enjoyable seafood-accented evening menu featuring squid, crab and grilled meats.

Lefkos

The largest and most attractive of the low-key west-coast resorts, Lefkos is 20km north of Finiki and a 5km detour down from the main road. Lefkos is here for a very good rea-son – its curving sandy beach is absolutely delightful. This is the kind of place where two weeks can vanish in gentle wanderings between beach and brunch.

🛏 Sleeping & Eating

★**Hotel Lefkorama** HOTEL €€
(☑ 6909091840, 22450 71173; www.lefkorama.gr;
d/apt €95/58; P❄🤚🛜) This gorgeous hotel
may not be on the beach, but sits instead
in its own patch of peaceful olive-groved
paradise. Recently renovated fresh white
rooms pop with colour accents. Delightful
English-speaking Sofia serves up amazing
breakfasts in the lovely garden sunroom. It's
a 2km walk from Potali Bay, and 2.5km from
Lefkos Beach, and has a handy taverna 20m
up the road.

It's also near interesting ruins of a Roman
cistern (as Sofia says, 'sure, it ain't the Parthenon, but very interesting all the same!').
Prices are significantly less outside of high
season.

Le Grand Bleu HOTEL €€
(☑ 22450 71009; www.karpathos-legrandbleu.
com; Lefkos; studio/apt €88/125; ❄🛜) Very
nicely equipped studios and two-bedroom
apartments beside the graceful main beach,
kitted out with crisp fresh linen, tasteful art
and sumptuous balconies with cushioned
armchairs. The kitchen of the highly recommended on-site taverna closes at 10pm to let
guests sleep. A gorgeous spot.

Dramountana TAVERNA €€
(☑ 22450 71373; Lefkos; mains €8-15; ⊙ 8am-late)
Part of a cluster of five almost-identical ca-
fes-tavernas with waterside tables at the
northern end of Lefkos Harbour, this all-day
cafe serves everything from fresh juices and
coffee to fish soup, grilled squid, roast lamb
and souvlakia.

ℹ Getting There & Away

The airport is situated in the far south of the
island. Finiki, Lefkos, Menetes and Arkasa are
served by KTEL buses to/from Pigadia **bus terminus** (☑ 22450 22338; M Mattheou) with one to
three buses per day, except Sundays (check this,
however, as summer services do change).

Diafani Διαφάνι
POP 250
Diafani is an intimate, wind-blasted huddle
of white houses fronted by cobalt-blue water,
with a mountain backdrop. Bar the crash of
the waves and old men playing backgammon, nothing else stirs. Most travellers simply pass through Diafani, so if you stay you'll
likely have the beaches and trails to yourself.
There's no post office or petrol station, but
there is an ATM (but no bank).

WORTH A TRIP

APELLA BEACH
• •
However determined you may be to
reach Olymbos, allow time to take
the precipitous spur road that drops
seawards from the east-coast highway
17km north of Pigadia. Here you'll find
award-winning Apella Beach (Map
p533); backed by a cascading hillside of
wildflowers, with towering cliffs to both
north and south, it is the finest beach in
the Dodecanese. It's often described as
'sandy', though it was pebbly when we
were there. Nevertheless, it's gorgeous.
There's a good taverna at road's end,
just above the beach.

🏃 Activities

Hiking
Hiking trails from Diafani village are waymarked with red or blue markers or stone
cairns. The most popular route heads inland,
straight up the valley to Olymbos. That takes
around two hours – though inevitably some
prefer to catch a bus uphill and walk back
down. Alternatively, a 4km track (50 minutes) leads north along the coast, through
the pines, to Vananda Beach, which has a
seasonal taverna.

A more strenuous three-hour walk takes
you 11km northwest to the Hellenistic site
of Vroukounda, passing the agricultural village of Avlona along the way. There are no
facilities, so carry food and water with you.

Anyone planning serious walking should
get hold of the 1:60,000 *Karpathos-Kasos*
map, published by Terrain Maps (www.
terrainmaps.gr) and available in Pigadia. Note: conditions change regularly on
these paths and each season they can get a
little straggly. Check with locals before you
head out.

Boat Trips
Boat excursions head north daily from Diafani to inaccessible beaches on Karpathos
and the nearby island of Saria.

🛏 Sleeping & Eating

Balaskas Hotel HOTEL €
(☑ 22450 51320; www.balaskashotel.com; d €40-
45; ❄🛜) You have a choice here of either
'economy' rooms (essentially pension-style
minimalism with white walls and wood
beds) or 'standard', which feature more colour and flair, with romantic mozzie nets and

wrought-iron beds. Some have kitchenettes, all have fridges.

★ **Corali** TAVERNA €
(☑ 22450 51332; mains €7-12; ☺ lunch & dinner) Run by Popi and Mihalis, this is *the* spot for fresh, tasty traditional fare. These spontaneous creatives whip up the likes of delicious *stifadho* (meat or seafood cooked with onions in a tomato puree) or eggplant. Service is slow but the quality of the food and *filoxenia* (hospitality) make up for it.

ⓘ Getting There & Away

Anek (p515) ferries call in at Diafani's small jetty twice a week en route to/from Pigadia, Halki and Rhodes, and three times weekly en route to/from Pigadia and Kasos (€4, one hour). One of these continues to, or returns from, Crete (€19, eight hours) while two other services head to/from Santorini (€27, 15½ hours). There are also day trips by boat to Pigadia in summer, as well as assorted excursions (from €10 per person).

Tourist coaches carry day trippers from the jetty up to Olymbos. Unfortunately for both locals and tourists, there's only one weekly bus to/from Pigadia, but in summer services can increase (via Olymbos).

KASOS ΚΑΣΟΣ
POP 800

Kasos, the southernmost Dodecanese island, looks like the Greece that time forgot. Deceptively inviting in summer, it can feel very isolated in winter, when it's battered by severe winds and imprisoned by huge turquoise waves. Most of its visitors are rare seabirds; most of the human returnees are Kasiots on fleeting visits. Come here, though, and you may well succumb to its tumbledown charm.

ⓘ Getting There & Away

There are daily flights (except Sundays) to/from Karpathos (€60, 10 minutes) and Rhodes (€75, one hour) with Sky Express (p514).

There's a once-a-week Blue Star Ferries (p515) service en route between Rhodes and Piraeus (via Milos (€35, 18 hours), Santorini (€27, 13½ hours) and Anafi (€23, 11½ hours); another goes to Karpathos (€8, 1½ hours) and Halki (€16, 5¾ hours). Anek Lines (p515) heads twice a week to/from Crete (€20, 6¼ hours). An excellent alternative to the ferries is the *Kasos Princess*, both an excursion boat (p538) and ferry alternative. In summer it runs daily except for Thursdays and Sundays (check ahead as schedules can change).

Fry Φρυ
POP 350

The capital, Fry (pronounced 'free'), is on the north coast. The broad gentle valley behind it is the only fertile land on Kasos, so the only other villages are dotted across the surrounding hillside. Although Fry is more of a working port than a tourist destination, the tiny old harbour at its core, known as Bouka, is impossibly photogenic. Shabby, if pretty, white houses with navy-blue trim line the quay, a few cafes sit waiting for customers, grizzled fishermen patiently mend their nets, and the white-and-pastel-blue church of Agios Spyridon surveys the scene. Even as late as June, though, Fry still has the feel of a ghost town.

The nearest beach is 10 minutes' walk east along the shoreline, in the tiny satellite port of Emborios. There are patches of gravel amid the sand, but the sea is clear and sheltered, so it's a good place for a quick dip.

⊙ Sights & Activities

Archaeological Museum MUSEUM
(☺ 9am-3pm Jul-Sep) FREE Housed in a grand 19th-century villa above the harbour, this seasonal museum displays objects pulled from ancient shipwrecks, assorted Greek oil lamps and Hellenistic finds, including inscribed stone slabs.

Excursion Boat BOATING
(Kasos Princess; ☑ 22450 41047, 6977911209; 🛥) When they can round up 10 or more passengers, two boats, *Athina* and *Kasos Princess,* offer summer excursions on Monday, Wednesday and Saturday (€15) to the uninhabited islet of Armathia, which has superb sandy beaches. The *Kasos Princess* also runs full-day trips to Pigadia on Karpathos, daily except Thursday and Sunday (€10 one way), plus it heads to Sitia, Crete, every Friday (€15 one way). Check ahead as schedules may change.

🛏 Sleeping & Eating

Amfi Rooms APARTMENT €€
(☑ 6972140910, 22450 41175; r €70; P ❋ 🛜) Set 1km up on the hill behind Fry, with a glorious view, these dark wooded and stone studios comprise a spacious all-in-one traditional raised bed, kitchenette and living area, plus a washing machine. Mosquito netting covers the windows. The owner runs Mylos (☑ 22450 41825; Plateia Iroön Kasou; mains €6.50-

Kasos

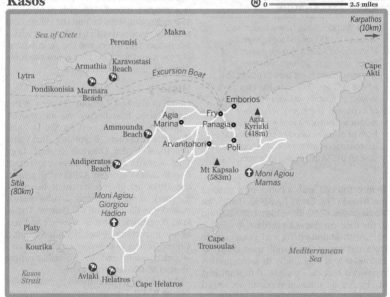

11; ⊙ lunch & dinner;) taverna and will arrange to pick you up from the airport.

Giaeli   GREEK €

(☑ 22450 41779; mains €5-9; ⊙ noon-late) The best spot to eat in Fry (and one of the best on the island), Giaeli (meaning 'traditional song') has raised the island's cuisine bar. This is traditional food but with a big difference: a gourmet twist and lovely presentation. The setting is gorgeous – in a pretty historic building or outside by the water – in the middle of Bouka Harbour.

Owner Maria also runs the gourmet canteen at Helatros Beach that's been celebrated by locals and tourists alike.

Taverna Emborios   TAVERNA €

(☑ 22450 41586; Emborios Beach; mains €8-10; ⊙ lunch & dinner Jun-Sep; 🛜) Crisp, beautifully neat beachfront restaurant (open high season only), 10 minutes' walk from Fry. The friendly owner, who lived in New York for many years, serves up wonderful local specialities, including delicious octopus, tiny home-grown olives and his own salty preserved fish. One of the best on the island.

ℹ Information

Both the Commercial Bank on the main road leading off the port, and Alpha to the right of the port facing town, have ATMs.

Kasos Maritime & Travel Agency (☑ 22450 41495; www.kassos-island.gr; Plateia Iroön Kasou) For all travel tickets.

ℹ Getting There & Away

The island's airport is 1km west of Fry. Either walk for 15 minutes along the coast road – yes, it's exposed, but you won't half feel pleased with yourself – or call a taxi. A small island bus runs from Monday to Friday; it's meant for the locals but tourists can take it, too, though keep in mind that for many elderly, it's their only means of transport.

Cars and scooters can be hired from **Oasis Rent-a-Car** (☑ 6974594486, 22450 41746; from €30).

Around Kasos

None of the beaches on Kasos offer shade. The best is the isolated pebbled cove of Helatros, near Moni Agiou Georgiou Hadion, 11km southwest of Fry, but you'll need your own transport to reach it. In the summer months it has a fabulous food canteen run by the owner of Giaeli. Otherwise, there's no facilities. There's another tiny but decent beach, Avlaki, in walking distance.

Agia Marina, 1km southwest of Fry, is a pretty village with a gleaming white-and-blue church that celebrates a festival on

KASOS MASSACRE

In 1820, under Turkish rule, Kasos was home to 11,000 inhabitants. Tragically, Mohammad Ali, the Turkish governor of Egypt, saw its large merchant fleet as an impediment to his plan to establish a base in Crete. On 7 June 1824 his men landed on Kasos and killed around 7000 of its people. The island never really recovered, but each year Kasiots return from all over the world to commemorate the massacre; white rocks spell out the year on the small peninsula beyond Fry.

17 July. You can grab a coffee or a meal at the friendly To Steki (☑ 22450 41885; Agia Marina; mains €2.50-10; ☉ 10am-late). Beyond it, the road continues to verdant Arvanitohori, with abundant fig and pomegranate trees and one of the island's most gorgeous *kafeneio*. It is also home to some prettily renovated houses. Panagia, 1km southeast of Fry, has an unusual series of six linked red-roofed, Byzantine churches; these are locked, but well worth seeing for the setting alone. Poli, 3km southeast of Fry, is the former capital, built on the ancient acropolis but there's not much here to see. For the most extraordinary views, head to Agia Kyriaki, east of Poli, as well as Moni Agiou Mamas, where a festival is held every 2 September. This area gives you a good idea of how harsh and barren the landscape is and evokes the sense of how people survived off the land in former times.

KASTELLORIZO
ΚΑΣΤΕΛΛΟΡΙΖΟ

POP 275

So close to the Turkish coast – Kaş is just 2km away – that you can almost taste the East, the tiny, far-flung island of Kastellorizo is insanely pretty. Sailing into its one village (of the same name), past the ruined castle, minaret and pastel-painted neoclassical houses huddled around the turquoise bay, is soul enriching. 'Megisti', as Kastellorizo was once called (meaning 'great'), is the largest of a small archipelago at around only 10 sq km. And while it may lack powder-fine beaches, there are bathing platforms with ladders into the ocean and satellite idylls you can reach by boat.

It's easy to get stuck on the harbour – it is a magnet indeed. However, venture up 400 zigzagging steps behind the village, and you'll be rewarded with a plateau, on which is a former monastery and the *paleokastro*, old town and fortress. Plus it has the most dramatic blue cave in the Med.

History

Home to the best harbour between Beirut and Piraeus, Kastellorizo was successively a prosperous trading port for the Dorians, Romans, Crusaders, Egyptians, Turks and Venetians. Under Ottoman control, from 1552 onwards, it had the largest merchant fleet in the Dodecanese. A 1913 revolt against the Turks briefly resulted in it becoming a French naval base, and it subsequently passed into the hands of the Italians. The island progressively lost all strategic and economic importance, especially after the 1923 Greece–Turkey population exchange. Many islanders emigrated to Australia, where around 30,000 continue to live.

After Kastellorizo suffered bombardment during WWII, English commanders ordered the few remaining inhabitants to abandon the island. Most fled to Cyprus, Palestine and Egypt and those that later returned found their houses in ruins. While the island has never regained its previous population levels – the village alone was once home to 10,000 people – more recent returnees have finally restored almost all the waterfront buildings, and Kastellorizo is looking better than it has for a century.

The island has found itself in recent years in the migration path of thousands of fleeing refugees, though numbers have recently fallen to only a few; given their grandparents' experiences as refugees, the islanders acted, not surprisingly, with great compassion.

ⓘ Getting There & Away

AIR

Olympic Air (p514) flies six times weekly (four in low season) from Rhodes to Kastellorizo (one way €80, 40 minutes).

BOAT

A very limited ferry service arrives and leaves from Kastellorizo Village's harbour. Blue Star Ferries (p515) calls in twice a week to and from Piraeus via Rhodes (€23, three to four hours). Once a week in summer, Dodekanisos Seaways (p515) sails from Rhodes to Kastellorizo and back (one way €39, 2½ hours); used as a day trip, it gives you four hours on the island.

❶ Getting Around

The main destinations for boat trips are Kaş in Turkey and the spectacular Blue Cave (€10). Try **Antonis Sea Taxi** (☑ 6977776927). Given the limited road network (which heads to the airport only), most people get around using the island's one taxi. Hiking is a popular alternative.

Kastellorizo Village
Καστελλόριζο

POP 250

Kastellorizo Village is the only settlement on the island. Its harbour is its lifeblood and where the limited action gathers: mounds of yellow nets, stretching cats, youths on mobile phones and sleepy fishermen sit outside *kafeneia* (coffee houses), backdropped by smartly shuttered, brightly coloured mansions. Make sure you explore the labyrinthine cobbled backstreets behind.

An amazing 80% of the villagers are returned Aussie expats, which adds a definite upbeat energy to the community. Come August, thousands of 'Kassies' return to see their families.

◉ Sights

Reach the hilltop settlement of Horafia, and Mandraki Bay beyond, by climbing the broad steps east of the harbour.

A coastal pathway around the headland below passes precarious steps that climb to a rock-hewn Lycian tomb from the 4th century BCE, which has an impressive Doric facade. There are several such tombs along Turkey's Anatolian coast, but they are very rare in Greece.

It's also possible to walk the 1km up to Paleokastro, the island's ancient capital. Follow the concrete steps that start just past a soldier's sentry box on the airport road. The old city's Hellenistic walls enclose a tower, a water cistern and three churches.

Alternatively, for a longer hike, you can walk up the 400 steps behind town (ask where they begin) and head to a monastery and other paths. The basic *Walking Map* by Pantazis C Houlis is available at some souvenir shops for €2. But the best way to get the local flavour is to head on a guided walk with the folk from Visit Kastellorizo (p542).

Archaeological Museum   MUSEUM
(☑ 22460 49283; €2; ⊗ 8.30am-4pm Wed-Mon; ♿) Holds an interesting assortment of ancient finds, costumes and photos relating to

BLUE CAVE MAGIC

Located on Kastellorizo's remote southeast shore, the extraordinary Blue Cave (water taxi per person €10) is famous for its mirror-like blue water. To get there, you must take one of around four competing water taxis in Kastellorizo. It's a 45-minute experience including the 15-minute journey there (and back) plus around 15 minutes in the cave itself, which is free to enter. Boats will not enter if conditions are not right. The entrance – a distance of around two metres – is so low that you must lie down in the boat.

Kastellorizo. Labels are limited but it gives a reasonable sense of the island's past.

Megisti Museum   MUSEUM
(€2; ⊗ 8.30am-4pm Tue-Sun; ♿) In a former mosque near the ferry jetty, this museum devotes itself largely to display panels telling the island's fascinating story.

**Knights of St
John Castle**   ARCHAEOLOGICAL SITE
(⊗ 24hr) FREE At the top of the hill, a rickety stairway leads to the ruins of the Knights of St John Castle, which gave the island its name – thanks to the red cliff on which it stood, this was the 'Castello Rosso'.

🛏 Sleeping

★ **Mediterraneo**   PENSION €€
(☑ 22460 49007; www.mediterraneo-kastelorizo. com; s/d/ste €70/80/180; ⊗ May-Oct; ❄🌐) If Picasso was a hotel, he'd be the Mediterraneo. With its lime, mango and smurf-blue exterior, this revamped mansion has romantic rooms tastefully scattered with art and some with traditional raised-platform beds. Take breakfast on the terrace amid a confection of fruit and homemade jams, read in the shaded arbour, or flop on loungers by the sea.

The best suite takes up the whole of the ground floor and has its own Bedouin-style sunbathing area yards from the water.

Poseidon   HOTEL €€
(☑ 6956617585, 22460 49212; www.kastelorizo-poseidon.gr; Plateia Australias; apt/ste €125/150; ❄🌐) Set in four faux-neoclassical villas, near the western corner of the harbour, Poseidon offers comfortably finished studios and apartments with grey shabby-chic furniture offset by sugar-white walls and

contemporary accessories. Apart from the decent breakfast near reception, it's largely DIY here. Given its location – close to the harbour action – it can be slightly noisy if there's music.

Megisti Hotel HOTEL €€€
(☑ 22460 49220; www.megistihotel.gr; d/ste incl breakfast €174/262; ❄@☎❄) On the harbour's western extremity, it's impossible to miss the most imposing hotel on the island. Megisti's four suites and 15 stylish rooms have rain showers, tiled floors, standard lamps, safety deposit boxes and private balconies. Outside on the chequerboard waterfront terrace, you can climb easily into the sea from Megisti's iron-hoop steps (like a giant swimming pool).

✕ Eating & Drinking

★ Radio Cafe CAFE €
(☑ 22460 49029; mains €6-9; ☉9am-late; ❄☎) This cool high-ceilinged cafe, run by Elma and Vaggelis, is close to the jetty, has art-spattered walls, outside tables and both Greek- and English-style breakfasts – from yogurt with honey and fruit salad, to fried eggs and bacon. By night it morphs into a relaxing bar. The name is a nod to the antique radios Vaggelis repairs to working condition.

★ Alexandra's TAVERNA €€
(☑ 22460 49019; mains €8.50-17; ☉lunch & dinner; ❄☎) ♪ With bouzouki music and salt breeze wafting over its thyme-topped tables, the friendliest of Kastellorizo's quayside restaurants also serves the best food. Everything from the squid-ink risotto and calamari stuffed with feta is made in-house. Mezedhes are full of vim and superfresh. Treat yourself

---

ⓘ WALKING WITH LOCALS

Run by an enthusiastic group of locals, passionate about the island, Visit Kastellorizo (☑ 6971589790, 6977092616; www.facebook.com/visitkastellorizo; per person approx €20) takes the visitor away from the tourist-focused harbour on excellent walks. On the town walk they reveal intricate details about Kastellorizo, from historic customs and current insights, to photogenic viewpoints. The tour ends at the museum. The other option is the mountain walk, which covers the ecology, nature and either the monastery or *paleokastro* (or both).

---

to lamb on the spit or whatever goat dish is being offered.

Faros Bar BAR
(mains €4.50-6; ☉9am-late; ☎) Occupying an enviable location in the former lighthouse, beyond the ferry jetty and beside the mosque, this bar offers a wonderful opportunity to swim in turquoise shallows before taking breakfast and drinking in wide-screen views of Turkey. It even has its own quayside loungers. Salads and snacks, plus cocktails, are the go here.

ⓘ Getting There & Away

Kastellorizo's tiny airport is up on the central plateau, 2.5km above the village. There's no bus, so you'll have to take the island's only taxi (p541) to and from the harbour (€5).

Ferries somehow manoeuvre themselves miraculously into Kastellorizo's small harbour.

SYMI ΣΥΜΗ

POP 2610

Beautiful Symi is guaranteed to evoke oohs and aahs from ferry passengers before they even get off the boat. The first sight of Gialos Harbour, framed against an amphitheatre of pastel-coloured houses rising on all sides, is unforgettable. It's all thanks to the Italians, who ruled the island almost a century ago and established the neoclassical architectural style that Symi has followed ever since.

Although Symi is far from small, it's mostly barren and the only settlements are Gialos, the old village of Horio, which sprawls over the hilly ridge behind, and Pedi, down in the valley beyond. One road runs all the way to the monastery at Panormitis, near Symi's southern tip. The rest of the island is largely deserted, but it's surrounded by blue coves and small beaches.

Culturally, it's a little light on (beyond a couple of museums). But nobody seems to worry; there's enough here.

History

Symi has long traditions of both sponge diving and shipbuilding and is mentioned in the *Iliad* as sending three ships to assist Agamemnon's siege of Troy. In ancient legend, Glaucus, one of the island's sons, was the master builder of *Argo*, the ship that would take Jason and his compadres to distant Colchis in search of the Golden Fleece. During Ottoman times it was granted the right to fish for sponges in Turkish waters.

DODECANESE SYMI

Symi

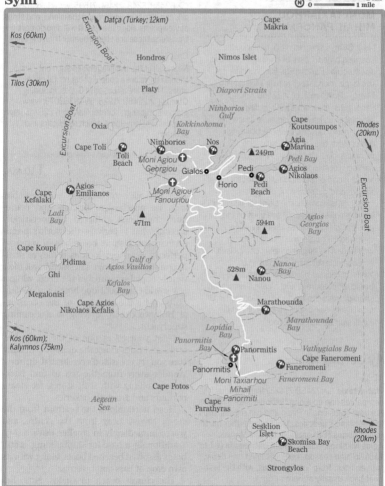

In return, Symi supplied the sultan with first-class boat builders. This exchange enriched the island – gracious mansions were built and culture and education flourished. By the early 20th century, the population was 22,500 and Symi was launching around 500 ships a year. But the Italian occupation, the advent of the steamship and the decline of the sponge industry put an end to prosperity, obliging Symi to reinvent itself as a tourist destination.

ⓘ Getting There & Away

Dodekanisos Seaways (p515) runs catamarans to and from Rhodes at least once daily (€19,

50 minutes) and also offers frequent sailings northwest, to Kos and beyond. Blue Star Ferries (p515) calls in three times weekly heading towards Rhodes (€9, one hour), and one also en route for Tilos (€10, 30 minutes), Nisyros (€13.50, 2½ hours), Kos (€14.50, four hours), Kalymnos (€20, five hours) and Piraeus (16¼ hours, €56.50). Symi fills up every morning with day trippers from Rhodes, with several Rhodes-based excursion boats complementing the high-speed catamaran.

Look out for summer day trips from Gialos to Datça in Turkey (around €45, including Turkish port taxes).

OFF THE BEATEN TRACK

MONI TAXIARHOU MIHAIL PANORMITI

Near Symi's southern tip, beyond the scented pine forests of the high interior, spectacular Panormitis Bay is home to the large monastery Moni Taxiarhou Mihail Panormiti (☑ 22460 72414; Panormitis; museum €1.50; ⊗ dawn-dusk). Monasteries have stood here since the 5th century but the present building dates from the 18th century. The principal church contains an intricately carved wooden iconostasis, frescoes and an icon of St Michael, protector of sailors and patron saint of Symi.

Pilgrims who ask the saint for a favour leave an offering; you'll see piles of these, plus prayers in bottles that have been dropped off boats and found their own way here. The large complex comprises an eccelesiastical museum and a folkloric museum, a bakery with excellent bread, a restaurant and a cafe. Visitors should dress modestly. Buses come here from Gialos, and some ferries and daily excursion boats call in, too.

ⓘ Getting Around

BOAT

Water taxis (☑ 22460 71423) from various companies line up along the inner side of Gialos Harbour (plus one in Pedi) and run regular trips to the island's beaches. Most head either north to Nimborios (€8) or south to Agia Marina, Agios Nikolaos, Nanou and Marathounda (€7 to €15). In high season there's at least one departure an hour, from 9am onwards, with the last boat back usually at 5pm or 6pm.

Larger boats offer day trips further afield to remote west-coast beaches, the monastery at Panormitis, or complete island-circuit tours (up to €40) that include a barbecue lunch.

BUS & TAXI

The island **bus** makes hourly runs between the south side of Gialos harbour and Pedi Beach, via Horio (flat fare €1.70).

Taxis (☑ 6987569469, 6974623492) depart from a rank 100m west of the bus stop. These can be pricey and have set rates between them (although run independently), and can take you to anywhere on the island where there are roads, including Panormitis, the monastery, Pedi Beach and Marathounda Beach.

Symi Tours (p545) runs twice daily trips to Panormitis Monastery.

The island's bus company, **Lakis Travel** (☑ 6945316248, 22460 71695; www.lakistravel. gr), can also take you around the island, and stops at viewpoints along the way. It will also do port transfers; these are often cheaper than the taxis.

CAR

Nearly all of the travel agencies also rent cars, though there are a couple of car rental operators. These are all based in Gialos, including **Glaros** (☑ 22460 71926, 6948362079; www. glarosrentacar.gr; scooter/car from €25/45 (high season); ⊗ 9am-9pm), which rents cars and scooters.

Gialos   Γιαλός

POP 2200

Your first view of Gialos is unforgettable, with its neoclassical biscuit- and ochre-hued buildings gathered aristocratically around what is perhaps the world's prettiest harbour. Fishing boats bob in water so perfectly clear they look as if they're floating on thin air, sponge salesmen hawk their weird-shaped treasures of the deep, while a few world-class boutique hotels and restaurants invite the attention of the occasional Hollywood star arriving in a gleaming superyacht.

Plant yourself at one of the many tavernas and cafes along the quayside, making sure you try the island's celebrated shrimps. Wander away from the sea to find backstreets spilling with fruit stores, ice-cream parlours and aromatic bakeries.

Head north along the seafront from the clock tower, away from the centre, and you're immediately in smaller Harani Bay. Traditionally a base for shipbuilding, it still holds assorted beached boats, along with its own crop of bars and tavernas.

The closest beach to Gialos, Nos, lies around the next headland, 500m north from the clock tower. Access to this narrow strip of gravel is controlled by a taverna and bar, but it's a great spot for a swim, nonetheless.

⊙ Sights & Activities

Horio   VILLAGE

Climbing calf-crunching, knee-knobbling Kali Strata, the broad stair path that sets off from the alleyways behind the harbour, will bring you in a mere 500-or-so steps to the hilltop village of Horio. En route you'll pass a bewitching succession of majestic villas built for long-gone Symi sea captains – some are utterly dilapidated, others restored to splendour.

Constructed to deter marauding pirates, Horio is an absolute warren of a place. All its tavernas and bars, though, are clustered around the top of Kali Strata. Most of the houses beyond are in ruins, and so is the Knights of St John Kastro at the very top, thanks to an explosion of German munitions during WWII. The island's Archaeological Museum is up here, too.

Archaeological Museum   MUSEUM
(€2; ⊙ 8.30am-4pm Wed-Mon) **FREE** Reopened after years of restoration, this compact museum contains some fabulous archaeological and folkloric finds, and is worth checking out.

Symi Tours   BOATING
(✓22460 71307; www.symitours.com; boat trip €40) Symi Tours organises daily excursions in the *Poseidon* to explore Symi's beautiful coves, bays and secluded beaches. Daily departures from Gialos Harbour leave at 10.30am, returning at 5pm. Find it on the south side of Gialos Harbour. The price includes a barbecue lunch.

🛏 Sleeping

★**Hotel Fiona**   HOTEL €
(✓22460 72088; www.fionahotel.com; Horio; r incl breakfast from €55; ❄ 🛜) Offering Symi's best-value accommodation, this simple but charming family-run hotel perches on the edge of Horio. Its simple but attractive rooms, kitted out with blue and white furniture, have balconies that have truly astonishing views across the harbour. There's a pleasant breakfast area downstairs and a peaceful courtyard. Simple, if adequate, buffet breakfast.

The delightful owners are elderly, so it's a little get-on-with-it-yourself experience. Turn left at the top of Kali Strata.

★**Thea Apartments**   APARTMENT €€
(✓22460 72559; www.symi-thea.gr; d/f incl breakfast €135/220) This tasteful spot oozes style. The owner's grandmother's house has been converted into studios (with sink and fridge, but no stove). Blonde-wood floors, tasteful faux-antique bedheads and yellow and olive hues combine well throughout these airy rooms. Each has a front-facing balcony. It's up the stairs directly behind the taxi rank. A simple but delicious breakfast is provided in the room.

Albatros Hotel   HOTEL €€
(✓22460 71707, 6984107939; www.albatrosymi.gr; d incl breakfast €70; ⊙ Apr-Nov; ❄🛜) With its cloud blue and aqua exterior, small and appealing Albatros has a sunny breakfast room and four whitewashed bedrooms with tiled floors, traditional wood ceilings and little balconies giving side-on sea views, plus great mattresses and memory-foam pillows. Just a block back from the harbour in the heart of Gialos, it's clean and welcoming.

★**Old Markets**   BOUTIQUE HOTEL €€€
(✓22460 71440; www.theoldmarkets.com; r/ste incl breakfast €240/495; ❄🛜▨) Symi's finest hotel stands a few steps up Kali Strata (it's unsigned). The old market space has seven stunningly individual rooms and three suites, housed over several adjoining mansions, with fabulous views across the harbour to the coloured houses beyond. All rooms enjoy a pillow library and use of an honesty bar, plus a roof terrace, pool and optional spa treatments.

🍴 Eating & Drinking

★**Meraklis**   SEAFOOD €
(✓22460 71003; www.omeraklis.com; mains €8-13; ⊙10.30am-late; 🛜) This old-school taverna, with Santorini-blue walls decked in vintage diving photos and antique mirrors, is as pretty as it is friendly. Sure, it is a tourist magnet, but it has good souvlakia, meatballs and roast lamb, not to mention fresh octopus, sea bream and Symi shrimp. Why not try the lot, with a mixed seafood plate for two (€35)?

It's hidden in a backstreet, a block behind the waterfront.

★**Tholos**   TAVERNA €€
(✓22460 72033; Harani Bay; mains €9-15; ⊙ lunch & dinner May-Oct) The name on locals' lips is Tholos and there's no more romantic restaurant in the Dodecanese than this lovely taverna, poised at the tip of Harani Bay, along the quay from Gialos. The sunset views from its waterfront tables are stupendous, and so too is the food, which includes local meats prepared to the restaurant's own recipes, such as beef in lemon sauce, as well as fresh fish.

★**Tsati**   BAR
(✓22460 72498; www.facebook.com/tsatibar; Harani Bay; ⊙11am-late; 🛜) This ultrawelcoming quayside bar, 100m along Harani Bay beyond the clock tower, has tables on a tree-shaded terrace, plus it offers stone benches carved into the sea wall. Cushioned

and whitewashed, they're perfect for a sunset cocktail, served with free snacks.

Taverna Giorgos & Maria
TAVERNA €

(☑ 22460 71984; Horio; mains €8-13; ☉ lunch & dinner; 🛜) This ultratraditional spot, at the top of the Kali Strata (steps to Hora), is especially fun in summer, when bouzouki music pipes across its breezy pebble-mosaic veranda, and the locals and tourists mingle over an ouzo. It's not fancy, but the changing menu will have everything from Symi shrimp and grilled bream, to braised rabbit and pork casserole.

Live music from 9pm on Friday and Saturday.

Secret Garden
BAR

(☑ 22460 72153; Hora; mains €5-12) 🥗 What does an owner do when his wife needs him at home if he's working too long elsewhere? Open up a business in his home (and garden), of course. This quirky spot, a bar and eatery, is housed in the owner's house. He's converted it into a fun bar-cum-restaurant. The family cooks up great meze plates, plus there's live music.

Good vegetarian options, too.

ℹ Information

Both the National Bank and Alpha Bank have ATM-equipped branches on the northern side of the harbour.

ℹ Getting There & Away

Catamarans arrive at a smaller port nearer to Gialos, while Blue Star Ferries dock at the larger port, named 'new port', around 500m northeast of town. Here, you'll find car rental agencies.

The town's public bus (p544) runs hourly between the south side of Gialos Harbour and Pedi Beach (flat fare €1.70).

Taxis (p544) depart from a rank 100m west of the bus stop and can take you to anywhere on the island where there are roads, including the major sites and beaches.

Around Symi

Apart from the monastery at Panormitis (which has two small museums), the only tourist destinations on Symi are the beaches scattered along its coastline.

Nimborius

Nimborios is a narrow, pebble beach 3km west of Gialos, reached by walking or driving all the way around the harbour and simply continuing along the exposed but beautiful shorefront road beyond. It's a peaceful spot, with an excellent little taverna that allows its customers to spend the day on sunloungers beneath the tamarisk trees alongside.

🛏 Sleeping

Niriides Apartments
APARTMENT €€

(☑ 22460 71784; www.niriideshotel.com; Nimborios; apt incl breakfast €140) Three kilometres northwest of Gialos is the quiet little village of Nimborios where you'll find Niriides Apartments, sitting by peaceful Symi Bay. Pleasant, traditional decor with kitchenettes, fridges and balconies with sea views. There's a snack bar to take breakfast at and also a library. The owners speak good English.

Pedi

Once a village, now more of a yachting marina and low-key resort, Pedi stretches along the inner end of a large bay east of Gialos, immediately below Horio. The gentle valley behind it has always been the agricultural heartland of Symi.

Two beaches, to either side of the mouth of the bay, can be reached on foot from Pedi or water taxi from Gialos; both have appealing tavernas. Agia Marina to the north is a lagoon-like little bay, facing a delightful chapel-topped islet across turquoise waters, which gets very crowded in summer. Agios Nikolaos, on the south side, is broader and sandier, with decent tree cover and idyllic swimming.

🛏 Sleeping

Pedi Beach Hotel
HOTEL €€

(☑ 22460 71981; www.pedibeachhotel.gr; Pedi; r from €117; ❄) These pleasant, simple cool-tiled rooms are fresher than a tube of toothpaste with their aquamarine-striped beds and cobalt-blue curtains, and unblemished sea-view balconies. Popular with overseas groups.

Nanou & Marathounda

Two large bays south of Pedi, Nanou and Marathounda, hold large beaches and tavernas and make great destinations for water-taxi day trips. Goat-roamed Marathounda, backed by a lush valley and also accessible via a rough road, is especially recommended.

Eating

★ Marathounda Taverna TAVERNA €€
(☎22460 71425; Marathounda; mains €10-12; ⏰10am-late) Quintessential beach taverna (a boat shed in historic times), where the island's wild goats – responsible for the delicious homemade cheese and, whisper it, the goat stew, too – sometimes nuzzle up to the tables. Be sure to sample the Symi shrimp and grilled fish, along with herbs and vegetables.

TILOS ΤΗΛΟΣ

POP 550

With its russet gold mountains, lack of people, and wildflowers blooming at every turn, Tilos has a charm that will salve your busy mind like no other island. If you're looking for a green adventure on a lost idyll, this is the place, for you can hike through meadows, mountains and valleys on shepherds' paths before flopping onto one of Tilos' many deserted beaches. And while its azure waters play host to monk seals and sea turtles, the island has a beguiling biodiversity, drawing birdwatchers and wildlife buffs from across the globe.

Best still? Locals are proud of their island and, as such, want to ensure their guests enjoy it, too. Repeat visitors, many of whom have been coming for over 30 years, are testament to the fact that *filoxenia* (hospitality) is as strong here as anywhere in Greece; this tiny place has a very big heart.

Getting There & Away

Tilos has no airport and only a minimal ferry service. The Dodekanisos Seaways (p515) catamaran stops at Tilos twice weekly, to/from Rhodes (€27, 2½ hours) and Halki (€13, 40 minutes). Check the schedules: if it heads to Nisyros, Kos and Kalymnos in the morning, and back to Rhodes in the evening, on those days, you can visit the island as a day trip from Rhodes or Halki. In addition, from Tilos, Blue Star Ferries (p515) sails twice each week to Piraeus via Nisyros, Kos and Kalymnos, and twice to Rhodes, one of which stops at Symi (€16, between two and three hours).

Getting Around

Five buses each day connect Livadia with Megalo Horio, Eristos Beach and Agios Antonios (€1.70). There is no taxi, but you can rent a car or scooter from **Drive Rent A Car** (☎6946944883, 22460 44173; www.drivetilos.gr; ⏰9am-6pm) or Stefanakis Travel (p549).

Livadia Λιβαδειά

POP 470

Livadia is a photogenic jumble of whitewashed houses huddled around the northern end of Agios Stefanos Bay. Little happens here – a cat yawns, a fisherman falls asleep over his glass of ouzo... And that's precisely its charm: tranquillity. A narrow girdle of pebbled beach, perfect for sun worshipping, stretches some 2km from the village down the turquoise-laced bay, while the village's central square is hugged by cafes, old-time tavernas and Italian-era municipal buildings.

Sights

Mikro Horio ARCHAEOLOGICAL SITE
(Map p548; ⏰24hr) When pirates prowled the Dodecanese, this medieval settlement was Tilos' main population centre. Its last inhabitants only left after WWII and it now stands empty, 45 minutes' walk up from Livadia. In various states of ruin – one house opens as a music bar in summer – it's a fascinating place to wander. Linger until the light fades and it turns downright eerie. If you can stay awake long enough, visit Mikro Horio nightclub (p549), in the middle of the village.

BIRDWATCHER'S PARADISE

The landscape of Tilos is much gentler than other Dodecanese islands. Rather than forbidding mountains, the interior is characterised by fertile valleys carved into agricultural terraces. It's crisscrossed by trails laid out by farmers that now serve as perfect footpaths. With small-scale ancient fortifications and medieval chapels scattered in profusion, Tilos makes a wonderful hiking destination.

What's more, thanks to the island's low population – and long-standing ban on hunting – it's also a favourite haunt for rare birds. More than 150 species have been recorded. Some are residential, some migratory. An estimated 46 species are threatened. As you hike, keep your eyes peeled for the Bonelli's eagle, Eleonora's falcon, long-legged buzzard, Sardinian warbler, scops owl and Mediterranean black shag.

Tilos

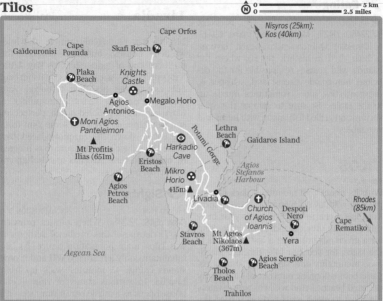

🛏 Sleeping

★Apollo Studios APARTMENT €

(☑22460 44379, 6942061912; www.apollostudios. gr; studio €50-80; ❄🔊) ✒ Fresh, well-appointed studios, run by a lovely young couple and set a few streets back from the harbour, with spotless kitchenettes, modern bathrooms, private balconies and a great communal roof terrace. It also has roomy apartments with tiled floors and sofa beds – ask for number 3 (it has a massive terrace).

Hotel Irini HOTEL €

(☑22460 44293; www.ilidirock.gr; r incl breakfast from €55; ❄🔊⛱) Irini has stunning white rooms with flat-screen TVs, shabby chic furniture, colourful quilts, tasteful ceramics, fridges and pool-facing balconies. Behind are great mountain views to admire over breakfast. Some of the rooms are slightly squishy, but there is a terrace and pool to make up for it.

★Eleni Beach Hotel HOTEL €€

(☑22460 44062; www.elenihoteltilos.gr; d incl breakfast from €80, studio €85; ❄🔊) Eleni has 35 studios and rooms, some with balconies, all with sea views. Expect comfy, spotlessly fresh interiors surrounded by a garden abloom with flowers. You'll find it 10 minutes' walk from the jetty southeast

along the promenade. Rates also include a sun lounger on the beach. Breakfast is not included in rates for studios, which have kitchenettes..

Ilidi Rock Hotel HOTEL €€

(☑22460 44293; www.ilidirock.gr; studio/apt €95/137; ❄@🔊) The 'glitziest' hotel in Tilos cascades down the cliff to two tiny aqua-marine-laced inlets, so the rooms' views are indeed ravishing. The fully equipped studios and apartments are stylishly minimalist; all have private balconies and four-poster beds The downsides (upsides for some) are the many stairs, breakfast is not included, plus 'favourite' rooms tend to get booked out by regulars.

🍴 Eating & Drinking

★Omonoia Cafe CAFE €

(☑22460 44287; breakfast €3-6, mains €8-13; ⊙8am-late; ☑) Shaded by a mature fig tree on Livadia's main square, just up from the quay, this much-loved all-day cafe is ideal for breakfast, light lunch or dinner. Its delightful elderly owners and family prepare everything from grilled meats and seafood to simple juices and salads, but you'll probably lose your heart – and your waistline – to their sponge cake.

To Mikro Kafé
CAFE €

(☑6932086094; snacks €5-7, mains €7-15; ☺noon-midnight July-Oct, 6pm-late Nov-Jun; ✳☎♪) Micro in size it may be, but there's nothing diminutive about this cosy nook's appeal. With its exposed stone walls and nautically themed decoration, Micro offers porthole windows, board games and little corners to play in while you nurse a sundowner on the beach-view patio (there's also a roof terrace). Offers salads, seafood, pies and sandwiches.

Faros Taverna
TAVERNA €€

(☑22460 44068; mains €7-12; ☺breakfast, lunch & dinner) Friendly Roula runs a tip-top taverna here that sits out on the eastern end of the beach, a half hour walk from Livadi. Expect fresh seafood and changing traditional Greek dishes (all excellent). But in truth, you'd be happy eating sand, such is the gorgeous setting, under a shady, bougainvillea-covered terrace with a view of miles of ocean and coast.

Gorgona
GREEK €€

(☑22460 70755; mains €7.50-15; ☺lunch & dinner; ☎✚) ✒ Enjoying sweeping views of Agios Stefanos Bay, this highly regarded rooftop restaurant serves olives and vegetables grown at its own farm. Following special recipes from the owner's grandmother, there's a wealth of choice from Tilos goat, lamb chops and pasta, to shrimps and octopus salad.

Mikro Horio Nightclub
BAR

(☑22460 44204, 6932086094; Mikro Horio Village; ☺11pm-late Jul-Sep; ☎) Set in the abandoned village of Mikro Horio, this place has a delightful veranda bar with amazing views of the village that is lit up atmospherically for the patrons. Night owls can make the most of the free shuttle bus (10 minutes) that runs from Livadia until 1am (later on Saturdays). The longer you stay, the louder the music.

ℹ Information

Stefanakis Travel (Tilos Travel; ☑22460 44360; www.tilos-travel.com; ☺9am-10pm) Sells ferry tickets and rents out cars and motorbikes. Also sells tickets for one-day cruises to Symi (€17) and Nisyros (€18) on the larger ferries.

Tourism Office (☺9am-2pm May-Oct) High season only, located on the beachfront centre; might have a few brochures, if you're lucky.

Megalo Horio

Megalo Horio, the tiny 'capital' of Tilos, is a hillside village where the narrow streets hold sun-blasted cubic houses and teem with battle-scarred cats. There's not much here but views and a couple of eateries, but it's a good base for walks. Ask about its small museum (Megalo Horio; ☺9am-2pm Jun-Sep) FREE that displays dwarf elephants; at the time of research, the collection was relocating to a new, modern premises by Harkadio Cave, several kilometres away.

A taxing one-hour hike from the north end of Megalo Horio takes you to the Knights Castle, passing the island's most ancient settlement en route.

TRAIL BLAZING ON TILOS

Walking is the reason many people, especially repeat visitors, come to Tilos. There are around 54km of trails in Tilos, with varying degrees of marking. Keen walkers should get their hands on the outstanding guide, *Exploring Tilos: a Walkers' Guide to the Island* by Jim Osborne (available online and in some local shops). It outlines in great detail every trail, and is a delight to follow, given the accuracy of visual cues and grading of each walk, from easy to difficult.

One well-maintained and very scenic 3km walk leads north from Livadia to Lethra Beach, an undeveloped pebble-and-sand cove with limited shade. Follow the tarmac behind the Ilidi Rock Hotel, at the northwestern end of the port, to find the start of the trail. Returning via the picturesque Potami Gorge brings you to the main island highway. (Note, however, at the time of research, part of the trail had been destroyed due to winter storms; check with other walkers before heading out.)

A longer walk leads to the small abandoned settlement of Yera and its accompanying beach at Despoti Nero. Simply follow the road south from Livadia around the bay and keep going beyond the Church of Agios Ioannis at the far eastern end. Allow half a day for the full 6km round trip.

🛏 Sleeping & Eating

Miliou Studios APARTMENT €
(☏ 6932086094, 22460 44204; www.milios-studios.gr; Megalo Horio; d/tr €40/50; ❄ 🛜) 🅿
Located in the centre of sleepy Megalo Horio, Miliou has comfortable rooms and self-catering studios with sweeping views of Eristos Bay far below. There's a supermarket close by, and free barbecue facilities in the lush grounds, plus you can also pick herbs for your own use from Miliou's organic garden.

Kastro Cafe TAVERNA €
(☏ 22460 44232; Megalo Horio; mains €8-13; ⊙ lunch & dinner) The best taverna in the village, tucked into a fairly residential area, but with a glorious hillside terrace commanding a fabulous panorama of the bay. Everything on the menu is good, from the organic spit-roasted goat and locally raised pork, to the fresh little dolmadhes and tiny red shrimps.

Northwest Tilos

The northwestern end of Tilos is home to several attractive beaches. The best for swimming is long, broad Eristos Beach, lapped by sapphire-hued waters, 2.5km south of Megalo Horio. Generally deserted but for the odd local person line-fishing, its greyish sands are fringed by tamarisk trees.

The quiet settlement of Agios Antonios, in the large bay 1.5km northwest of Megalo Horio, is a narrow strip of shingle with a taverna at either end. Much prettier Plaka Beach, in a cove another 3km west, is completely undeveloped. The water is slightly warmer, there's shade in the afternoon and, once you wade in a little, the rock shelves are good for snorkelling.

Beyond Plaka, the coast road climbs the sheer hillside, skirting 3km of alarming drop-offs to reach the cliff-edge monastery, Moni Agios Panteleimon (☏ 22420 31676).

🛏 Sleeping & Eating

Nitsa Apartments APARTMENT €
(☏ 22460 44093; www.nitsa-tilosapartments.com; Eristos Beach; apt from €50) This modern studio block, 200m inland from Eristos Beach, holds simple, nondescript two-bedroom self-catering apartments. It's attached to the all-day En Plo snack bar, which can be a good (or bad) thing if you like to indulge.

En Plo TAVERNA €€
(☏ 22460 44176; Eristos Beach; mains €8-13; ⊙ lunch & dinner; 🛜🅿) About 200m behind

the beach, this taverna has slow-cooked food like goat stew, and regulars like squid *saganaki* (stuffed with fried cheese), souvlakia and superfresh vegetables. You can enjoy your meals under the vine-shaded canopy in a pleasant garden. While it seems to have a popular following, in our opinion the price-to-quality ratio is a little out.

NISYROS ΝΙΣΥΡΟΣ

POP 950

Thanks to its lack of beaches, Nisyros is very much off the tourist radar – apart from the day trippers from nearby Kos who come to witness the magnificent volcano. Yet for those seeking an island of natural beauty, goats wandering meadows stippled with beehives, soaring mountain views over terraced fields and wildflowers, intimate Nisyros is just the ticket. Then there's hidden Byzantine churches, an extraordinary ancient wall and gourmet offerings.

The main settlement, Mandraki, is a sleepy little fishing village garlanded with cafes, while hilltop villages Nikea and Emborios are stunning. Hike among the wildflowers, head into volcano craters, or immerse yourself in agrotourism. Those who chance a visit often return, again and again.

ℹ Information

Visit www.nisyros.gr for information on sights, history and local services.

ℹ Getting There & Away

Catamarans run by Dodekanisos Seaways (p515) call in at Nisyros on Tuesday and Thursday, heading to and from Kos (€10, one to 1½ hours) and Rhodes (€27, 2¾ hours). Blue Star Ferries (p515) also stops once to twice a week in each direction, en route to either Kos (€16, 50 minutes), Kalymnos (€9.50, two to three hours), Astypalea (€12.50, 5½ hours) and Piraeus (€56.50, 13½ hours), or Tilos (€14, 40 minutes), Symi (€13.50, 2½ hours) and Rhodes (€16, three hours).

There are also links with Kos five times a week. The Panagia Spiliani (p551) sails to either Kos Town or Kardamena (around €8), while the smaller *Agios Konstantinos* runs to and from Kardamena (€8).

ℹ Getting Around

BOAT

Summer-only excursion boats leave Mandraki Harbour for the pumice-stone, sandy beach islet of Giali (€10), returning at around 6pm.

Nisyros

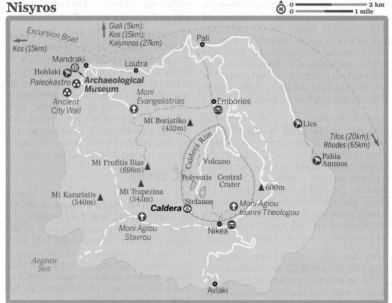

BUS

Public buses do a circuit around the island three times daily in summer, but you'll need to be clever to co-ordinate visits; catch them at the port (€2.50).

Alternatively, **Enetikon Travel** (☑ 22420 31180; www.enetikon.com; ☺ 9.30am-2pm & 6.30-9pm) runs many daily bus tours. These are largely for groups (day visitors from Kos) but independent travellers can go with a day's notice. You visit the volcano (€8), allowing around 40 minutes at the crater. Catch them outside the office at Mandraki port.

CAR & MOTORCYCLE

In Mandraki, **Diakomihalis Travel** (☑ 22420 31459; www.visitnisyros.gr; ☺ 9am-2pm & 5-9pm) offers good-value car rental and Manos (p553), just near the quay, has a wealth of scooters and cars.

TAXI

A taxi from Mandraki to the volcano costs around €25 return; call **Irini** (☑ 22420 31474).

Mandraki   Μανδράκι

POP 660

This pretty whitewashed and pastel-coloured town stretches languidly along the northern shore of Nisyros, lapped by gentle waters and lined with cafés and tavernas. Perched over the cliff is a castle and monastery. Behind

these, and just out of sight, is the incredibly well-preserved ancient city wall. Mandraki is almost completely pedestrianised, so its maze of winding backstreets and garden plots are tranquil and timeless, with a fertile valley sloping up towards the rim of the volcano behind. The ferry jetty is 500m northeast of Mandraki proper. Simply walk straight along the coast to reach the centre.

◎ Sights

The major landmark is at the far western end, where the ruins of a 14th-century Knights Castle tower atop a cliff face. Its lower levels are occupied by an equally old monastery, Moni Panagias Spilianis (Virgin of the Cave; €2; ☺ 10.30am-3pm), accessed by climbing a short but steep stairway.

With Nisyros being very short on beaches, local kids are glad of tiny but sandy Mandraki Beach, at the eastern end of town. It's a popular swimming spot, despite being sometimes covered in seaweed. There's also an exposed black-stone beach to the west, Hohlaki, reached by following a paved footpath around the headland below the monastery.

★ Archaeological Museum   MUSEUM
(Map p551; ☑ 22420 31588; €4; ☺ 8.30am-3pm Sun & Mon; ♿) This showpiece modern

museum, on Mandraki's main pedestrian street, displays a fascinating collection of Hellenistic and Roman pottery and sculpture, as well as earlier artefacts made of obsidian quarried on neighbouring Giali. The exhibits are displayed in chronological order and will help you get your head around the different historical periods, from Neolithic to Hellenic, and much more. Don't miss it.

Ancient City Wall ARCHAEOLOGICAL SITE

(Map p551; ⊙24hr) **FREE** Dating from the 4th century BCE, the ancient walls above Nisyros, accessed from the path behind the monastery and medieval castle, are one of the Aegean's best surviving fortifications from the Classical period. The massive Cyclopic stones are remarkable, as is the one standing gateway. You can climb the steps and stand on the wall itself (be aware: no barriers), a superb sunset lookout.

Paleokastro ARCHAEOLOGICAL SITE

(Map p551; ⊙24hr) **FREE** Best reached by a lovely 20-minute hike through the fields, along a trail that starts southwest of the monastery, this astonishing Mycenaean-era acropolis was founded 3000 years ago. Its restored cyclopean walls are a little newer, from the 4th century BCE – what looks like modern graffiti is in fact ancient dedications. Pass through the forbidding gateway and you can climb atop the massive blocks of volcanic rock for breathtaking views. Good explanatory signs in English are scattered throughout.

🛏 Sleeping

Hotel Porfyris HOTEL €

(☑22420 31376; www.porfyrishotel.gr; s/d incl breakfast €50/60; ❋🅿🛜) The only hotel in Mandraki town itself stands proudly on the hillside, set above a citrus orchard five minutes' walk from the sea. If you're arriving from the ferry, fork left at Piccolo Bar. Beyond the elegant marble lobby, expect simple, cosy en-suite rooms with comfy beds and terrace or balcony. There's also a welcome pool. Simple, but adequate, breakfast.

Anthousa Houses BUNGALOW €€

(☑6972947320, 6976322131; house €120) Three gorgeous traditional homes have been renovated in stunning style. Fine accents, including flagstone floors, jute rugs and polished concrete, give these a designer edge like no other, and the shabby chic furniture fills spacious areas. Quirky nooks and crannies within the sides of rock accommodate a kitchen and bathroom. The bungalows are arranged around a lush garden.

Ta Liotridia B&B €€

(☑22420 31580; www.nisyros-taliotridia.com/html/guesten.html; r incl breakfast from €140; ❋🛜) Two large and lovely B&B rooms (sleeping up to four) at the heart of the waterfront, on the upper floor of a smart wood-panelled bar of the same name (read, potential noise). Each is furnished in comfortable traditional style and has a double bed in an alcove, another box bed, polished floors, stone walls and a sea-view balcony (room 2 has the largest).

🍴 Eating

Irini TAVERNA €

(☑22420 31365; Plateia Ilikiomenis; mains €9-13; ⊙lunch & dinner; ❋🛜✏🎮) Sitting in the corner of a pebble-mosaic square in the shade of mature fig trees, with Irini Mark II diagonally opposite, Irini dishes up a mouthwatering menu of traditional fare like dolmadhes, goat in tomato sauce, souvlakia and *saganaki* (fried cheese). Try the heavenly baklava for dessert.

★Yevsea SEAFOOD €€

(Gefsea; Chevsea; ☑22420 31066; €9.50-12; ⊙lunch & dinner) Meaning 'taste', this lovely, waterfront place is set to put Nisyros on the culinary map. Run by a passionate young duo, both *Masterchef* Greece contestants (one from Nisyros whose father is a fisherman), Yevsea serves up exceptional seafood and meat dishes featuring the masterful use of local ingredients (try the unique fish soup). Whatever you do, don't miss eating here.

Loles Kores INTERNATIONAL €€

(Crazy Woman; ☑22420 31024; www.loleskores. com; mains €9-16; ⊙lunch & dinner) 🍴 This place is deceptive: you enter off the principal lane via basement stairs (with tasteful decorations of olde-world Greece), before entering a pretty, vine-covered rear terrace. The nicknamed 'Crazy Woman' conjures up gourmet delights: Greek cuisine with a gourmet touch. There's everything from the likes of *giouvarlakia* (lemon soup with meatballs) to salad with herring and pistachio. Fabulous daily specials.

🍷 Drinking & Nightlife

Mandraki's waterfront is lined with cafes and bars, with terraces perfectly aligned for watching the sun set over Kos.

★ **Oxos** CAFE
(📞 22420 31873; www.facebook.com/oxos; ⏱ 9am-midnight; 📶) At the far end of the harbour, nestled below the monastery, this gorgeous cafe-cum-bar has it all: a pretty plaza setting with tamarisk trees, a sea view, shade and tasty local treats including the likes of *pitia* (chickpea patties) and *horiatiki* (Greek salad). And the bonus? It's backed by tiny Agios Nikolaos church (pop in before you imbibe!)

Rythmos Bar BAR
(📞 22420 31463; ⏱ 9am-late; 📶) Whether you choose a seat on its sun-soaked roof terrace or within its modish interior, this is a cool spot for a midday frappé or sunset glass of vino. Curiously it draws in the old boys as well as a young crowd – and it still works! One of the few places that's open all year.

ℹ **Information**

Alpha Bank has an ATM at the harbour and a bank (no ATM) in Mandraki, and there's another ATM at the **post office** (⏱ 7am-2.30pm Mon-Fri).

ℹ **Getting There & Away**

Mandraki is your first stop for all arrivals and departures to the island. The port, 500m northeast of town, is easily walkable. There's no public transport from here, but you can rent a car from **Manos Rentals** (📞 22420 31029; www.nisyrosrentacar.gr; ⏱ 24hr), whose office is at the port.

Around Nisyros

Polyvotis Volcano

Nisyros sits on a volcanic fault line that curves around the southern Aegean. While 25,000 years have passed since the volcano that formed it last erupted, it's officially classified as dormant rather than extinct. Its summit originally stood around 850m tall, but three violent eruptions 30,000 to 40,000 years ago blew off the top 100m and caused the centre to collapse. White-and-orange pumice stones can still be seen on the northern, eastern and southern flanks of the island, while a large lava flow covers the entire southwest around Nikea.

The islanders call the volcano Polyvotis. Legend has it that during the battle between the gods and Titans, Poseidon ripped a chunk off Kos and used it to trap the giant Polyvotis deep beneath. That rock became

NISYROS UP CLOSE

Anaema (📞 6972947320, 22420 31459; www.anaema.gr; per person from €30) is a brilliant cooperative of passionate island guides who offer culturally immersive experiences. If you don't want to go it alone, you can hike the volcano (and learn fabulous things along the way), as well as partake in everything from cookery to embroidery classes and much more. Owner Haris is trying to promote tourism on the island and knows his stuff. It's based out of Diakomihalis Travel (p550).

Nisyros and the roar of the volcano is Polyvotis' angered voice.

Visitors keen to experience the power of the volcano head by bus, car or on foot into the island's hollow caldera, a vast and otherworldly plain that was home to thousands of ancient farmers. Ruined agricultural terraces climb the walls, while cows graze amid sci-fi-set rocks.

The southern end encloses several distinct craters (Map p551; adult/child €3/free; ⏱ 8.30am-8pm; P). Get there before 11am and you may have the place to yourself. A path descends into the largest crater, Stefanos, where you can examine the multicoloured 100°C fumaroles, sometimes listen to their hissing and smell the sulphurous vapours. The surface is soft and hot, making sturdy footwear essential. Don't stray too far out, as the ground is unstable and can collapse (at the time of research, the centre was roped off).

An obvious track leads to the smaller and wilder crater of Polyvotis nearby. You can't enter the caldera itself, and the fumaroles are around the edge here, so take great care.

Emborios

The village of Emborios is perched high on the jagged northern rim of the caldera, 9km up from Mandraki, and has some lovely stone houses, two restaurants and some very appealing accommodation. Many of the houses, formerly ruins, have been renovated by foreigners in recent years. These cling to the steep flanks of the rocky ridge. Apart from a few yawning cats, only around nine people live here permanently.

Sleeping & Eating

★ Melanopetra
APARTMENT €€€

(☑ 6978060289; www.melanopetra.gr; Emborios; apt €150; ❄ 🛜) With its ubiquitous white and bare-wood floors flooded in natural light, Melanopetra is pure zen minimalism. Two apartments with gorgeous bedrooms and kitchens enjoy dual views of both the caldera and Aegean on the other side. It's as if the rooms have been carved from the mountain itself with rough adobe walls and contemporary fittings.

Balcony Restaurant
GREEK €

(☑ 22420 31607; www.balkoni-nisiros.com; Emborios; mains €7; ⊗ 9am-10pm Mon-Sat; ❄ 🛜 🅿) The streetside terrace, facing Emborios' church, has a namesake balcony at the rear with an unforgettable panorama of the vast hollow crater. The owners are renowned for their produce – fresh ingredients for local meat, and some vegetable, dishes. It was here, too, in WWII where a Greek naval captain was shot; the original shattered mirror is still on display.

Apiria Taverna
TAVERNA €€

(☑ 22420 31377; Emborios; mains €9-12; ⊗ lunch & dinner; ❄ 🛜 🅿) Opening off a tiny alcove behind the church, this friendly taverna has tasteful burgundy-and-mustard walls and a few sheltered outdoor tables. It serves Nisyrian dishes, including *pitia* and lamb, pork and vegetable specialities. It's one of the few places open all year. Oh, and be sure to check out the air holes in the wall... natural heating from the volcano.

Nikea

The village of Nikea is 4km south along the crater's edge. No vehicles can penetrate this tight warren of dazzling white houses, so every visitor experiences the thrill of walking along the narrow lane from road's end to reach the tiny central square. Less a square than a circle, actually, it's among the most jaw-droppingly beautiful spots in the Dodecanese, with geometric pebble-mosaic designs in the middle and the village church standing above.

Throughout Nikea, signposted overlooks command astonishing views of the volcano, laid out far below. The challenging trail down into the crater drops from behind the Volcanological Museum.

◉ Sights

Volcanological Museum
MUSEUM

(☑ 22420 31400; Plateia Nikolaou Hartofyli, Nikea; €4; ⊗ 8am-1.30pm Mon-Sat; 🅿) Set beside the end of the road, this kid-friendly modern museum does a good job of explaining the history and mythology of the volcano and its impact on the island. There's also an interesting documentary worth a watch.

✕ Eating

Porta
CAFE €

(☑ 22420 31835; Nikea; snacks €5-8; ⊗ 9am-late; 🛜) Located in Nikea's pretty central square, Porta is a wonderfully relaxing place to enjoy a cool drink, toasted sandwich, juice or beer.

Pali

This wind-buffeted seaside village sits 5km east of Mandraki, just beyond the turnoff to the volcano. Now primarily a yachting marina, it has a handful of tavernas among the sun-beaten buildings on the quay.

The coast road continues another 5km to **Lies**, Nisyros' most usable beach. Walking 1km along a precarious track from here brings you to **Pahia Ammos**, a shadeless expanse of coarse volcanic sand.

Sleeping & Eating

Mammis' Apartments
APARTMENT €€

(☑ 22420 31453; www.mammis.com; Pali; d €60; ❄ 🛜) Set 100m up from the marina in gardens that are a riot of flowers, this peaceful complex holds 10 simple studios with kitchenettes, separate sofa beds for kids, and private balconies with sea views.

Captain's House
TAVERNA €

(☑ 22420 31016; Pali; mains €7-10; ⊗ 8am-midnight; ❄ 🛜) So close to the water that you can taste the salt, this taverna attracts yachties and wizened fishermen alike with a menu that's packed to the gills with seafood options including octopus, plus local bites including *fava* and cheeses. The owner is very knowledgeable about the island.

KOS ΚΩΣ

POP 33,400

Fringed by the finest beaches in the Dodecanese, dwarfed beneath mighty crags, and blessed with lush valleys, Kos is an island of endless treasures. Visitors soon become blasé at sidestepping the millennia-old Corinthian columns that poke through the rampant wildflowers – even in Kos Town, the lively capital, ancient Greek ruins are scattered everywhere you turn, and a mighty medieval castle still watches over the harbour.

Visitors to Kos naturally tend to focus their attention on its beaches. Beyond those near Kos Town, there are three main resort areas. Kardamena, on the south coast, is very much dominated by package tourism, but Mastihari, on the north coast, and Kamari, in the far southwest, are more appealing. Away from the resorts, the island retains considerable wilderness, with the rugged Dikeos mountains soaring to almost 850m just a few kilometres west of Kos Town.

History

So many people lived on this fertile island in Mycenaean times that Kos was rich enough to send 30 ships to the Trojan War. In 477 BCE, after suffering an earthquake and subjugation to the Persians, it joined the Delian League and again flourished. Hippocrates (460–377 BCE), the Greek physician known as the founder of medicine, was born and lived on the island. After his death, the Sanctuary of Asclepius and a medical school were built, which perpetuated his teachings and made Kos famous throughout the Greek world.

That Ptolemy II of Egypt was also born on Kos secured the island the protection of Egypt. It became a prosperous trading centre, but fell under Roman domination in 130 BCE and was administered by Rhodes from the 1st century CE onwards. Kos has shared the same ups and downs of fortune ever since, including conquest and/or occupation by the Knights, the Ottomans and the Italians and, much like Rhodes, its economy is now heavily dependent on tourism.

ⓘ Getting There & Away

AIR

Kos' **airport** (KGS; Map p556; ☑ 22420 56000; www.kosairportguide.com) is located in the middle of the island, 24km southwest of Kos Town. Aegean Airlines (https://en.aegeanair.com), Olympic Air (p514) and Sky Express (p514) offer up to four daily flights to Athens (from €60, 55 minutes). Regular flights head to Rhodes (from €100, 30 minutes) and Leros (€110, 55 minutes). Flights to some other islands, such as Naxos, go via Athens.

BOAT

Domestic

The island's main ferry port is in Kos Town, in front of the castle. Dodekanisos Seaways (p515)

runs catamarans up and down the archipelago, southeast to:

DESTINATION	DURATION	FARE (€)	FREQUENCY
Halki	2½hrs	26	2 weekly
Kalymnos	35mins	16	daily
Leros	1½hrs	23	daily
Patmos	2½hrs	31	daily
Pythagorio (Samos)	4hrs	44	3 weekly
Rhodes (via Nisyros)	1hr	16	2 weekly
Symi	1½hrs	26	2 weekly
Tilos	1½hrs	22	2 weekly

Blue Star Ferries (p515) also sails to Rhodes (€24.50, three to five hours, daily), as well as west to Astypalea (€17, 1½ hours, once weekly) and Piraeus (€45 to €56, 10 to 12 hours, daily).

In summer, the smaller and slower **Panagia Spiliani** (Map p558; ☑ 22420 31015; www.visitnisyros.gr/en; Harbour), a passenger-car ferry, also runs trips between Kos and Nisyros and from Kardamena in high season.

Elsewhere on the island, regular daily ferries also connect Mastihari with Kalymnos (€6, 50 minutes); see www.anekalymnou.gr and www.anemferries.gr. **Leros Express** (☑ 6936141900, 22470 24000; www.lerosseaways.com) also does twice weekly circuits between Leros, Kalymnos and Kos.

International

High-speed catamarans connect Kos Town with both Bodrum (two daily) and Turgutreis in Turkey (one daily). Both journeys take 30 minutes to one hour. Tickets cost €17 each way, with same-day returns €15 and longer-stay returns €30. For schedules and bookings, visit www.exas.com.

ⓘ Getting Around

TO/FROM THE AIRPORT

The airport is served by several daily **KTEL** (Map p558; ☑ 22420 22292; www.ktel-kos.gr; Kleopatras 7; ☺ information office 8am-9pm Mon-Sat Apr-Oct, to 3pm Mon-Fri Nov-Mar) buses to and from Kos Town's bus station (€3.20). It is so far from Kos Town that if you're planning to rent a car anyway, it's worth doing so when you first arrive. A recommended car hire office just outside the airport is **Auto Bank Car Rental** (☑ 22420 23397; www.autobank-kos.com).

A taxi to Kos Town costs around €37.

BICYCLE

Cycling is very popular, so you'll be tripping over bicycles for hire. Prices range from as little as €5 per day for a boneshaker, up to €20 for a decent

Kos

mountain bike. In Kos Town, **Escape Rentals** (☑ 22420 29620, 6937175860; escape.rental@ mail.gr; Vasileos Georgiou 12; bike from €5) offers a good range of bikes, including electric bikes, and reasonable rates.

Kos Mountainbike Activities (☑ 6944150129; www.kosbikeactivities.com; Psalidi; mountain bike per day €25; ☺ 9am-12.30pm & 5.30-7.30pm) offers bike rentals and guided tours.

BOAT

The massive line of boats moored in Kos Town offer excursions around Kos and to nearby islands. A 'three island' day trip to Kalymnos, Pserimos and Platy costs around €30, including lunch, while you can find day trips to Bodrum for as little as €15.

BUS

The island's main bus station is located well back from the waterfront in Kos Town. It is the base for KTEL (p555), which has services to all parts of the island, including the airport and south-coast beaches.

Kos Town   Κως

POP 17,890

A handsome harbour community, fronted by a superb medieval castle and somehow squeezed amid a mind-blowing array of ancient ruins from the Greek, Roman and Byzantine eras, Kos Town is the island's capital, main ferry port and only sizeable town. While some central streets tend to be overrun by partying tourists, most remain attractive. The square houses a fabulous museum and features some extraordinary architecture. The port is lined by cafes and tavernas and its unbroken row of excursion boats, fishing vessels and fancy yachts bob and bristle against each other along the waterfront.

Popular beaches stretch in either direction from the harbour. Long, sandy Kritika Beach, in easy walking distance of the town centre, is lined with hotels and restaurants. Southeast of the harbour the thin strip of sand known as Kos Town Beach is dotted

with parasols in summer and offers deep water for swimming.

☉ Sights

Castle of the Knights CASTLE
(Map p558; ☑ 22420 27927; Harbour) Due to damage caused by an earthquake in 2017, Kos' magnificent 15th-century castle is currently closed. Nevertheless, given its extraordinary location at the harbour entrance, it is interesting to view from the outside.

Plateia Platanou SQUARE
(Map p558) The warm, graceful charm and sedate pace of Kos Town is experienced at its best in this lovely cobblestone square, immediately south of the castle. Sitting in a cafe here, you can pay your respects to Hippocrates' plane tree (Map p558; Plateia Platanou). Hippocrates himself is said to have taught his pupils in its shade. The ancient sarcophagus beneath it was converted into a fountain by the Ottomans, while the

18th-century Mosque of Gazi Hassan Pasha (Map p558; Plateia Platanou), now sadly in disrepair, stands opposite.

Western Excavation Site ARCHAEOLOGICAL SITE
(Map p558; ☉ dawn-dusk) **FREE** This open archaeological site, south of the centre, holds ancient ruins uncovered by an earthquake in 1933. Its real treasures are the mosaics of the House of Europa (Map p558; ☉ dawn-dusk) **FREE**. The house was an opulent 2nd-century villa and the mosaics depict the abduction of Europa by Zeus in the form of a bull. Nearby, there's a section of the Decumanus Maximus (Map p558; ☉ dawn-dusk) **FREE**, the Roman city's main thoroughfare. The site also holds the Nymphaeum, a columned structure that was actually a public toilet.

There's also the Xysto, a cluster of Doric columns, and the Temple of Dionysos, dating from the 2nd century BCE. Across the street stands the Odeion, an impressive 2nd-century Roman theatre, which was built on the site of an even older Greek predecessor, and once seated around 750 spectators. In summer, performances are sometimes held here. Just east of here is the cleverly reconstructed Casa Romana.

Ancient Agora ARCHAEOLOGICAL SITE
(Map p558; ☉ dawn-dusk) **FREE** Exposed by a devastating earthquake in 1933, Kos' ancient centre – an important market, political and social hub – occupies a large area south of the castle. Back in the 4th century BCE, this was the first town ever laid out in blocks, and you can still discern the original town plan. Landmarks include a massive columned stoa, the ruins of a Shrine of Aphrodite, 2nd-century BCE Temple of Hercules, and 5th-century Christian basilica. The site is fenced, but usually open all day.

Archaeological Museum MUSEUM
(Map p558; Plateia Eleftherias; adult/child €6/free; ☉ 8am-8pm Sun & Mon) Housed in a superb example of an Italian-era building, located in the central square, the small, but excellent archaeological museum possesses a wealth of sculptures from the Hellenistic to late Roman eras, with a statue of Hippocrates and a 3rd-century-CE mosaic as the star attractions. There are information panels for many of the rooms.

Casa Romana ARCHAEOLOGICAL SITE
(The Roman House; Map p558; ☑ 22420 23234; adult €6; ☉ 8am-7.30pm Wed-Mon) Reopened to the public in 2015 after years of restoration, Casa Romana is believed to have been

Kos Town

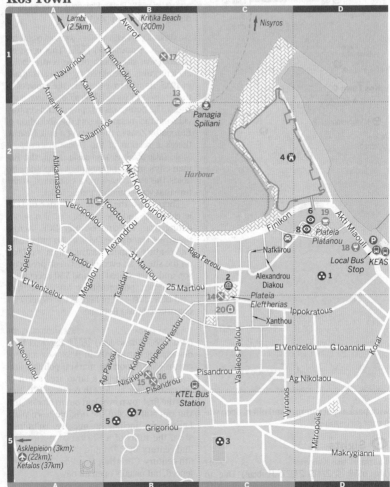

constructed during Hellenistic times and re-modelled until the 3rd century CE. In 1940, and again only recently, it was restored. The surviving structure of the house was rebuilt; it provides enormous insight into how a wealthy Koan official and his family lived. Although not advertised, listening devices have invaluable recorded information and relate to numbered exhibits.

🏖 Beaches

The nearest beach to Kos Town, crowded Lambi Beach begins just 2km northwest and has its own strip of hotels and restaurants. Further west along the coast, a long stretch of pale sand is fringed by two more resorts – Tingaki, 10km from Kos Town, and the slightly less crowded Marmari Beach beyond. You can ride your bike to all of these. Windsurfing is popular at all three beaches, while the island of Pserimos is only a few kilometres offshore and served by excursion boats from Marmari in summer.

Heading south from Kos Town along Vasileos Georgiou, on the other hand, brings you to the three busy beaches of Psalidi (3km from Kos Town), Agios Fokas (8km), and Therma Loutra (12km). At Therma Loutra, hot mineral springs warm the sea but thousands flock here (hint: it gets packed

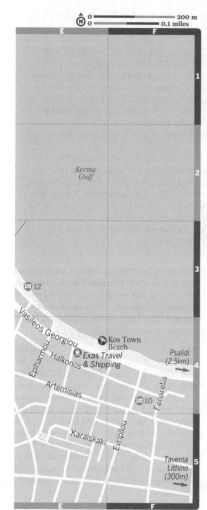

Kos Town

the delightful Afendoulis, where Alexis and his family run the most hospitable 'ship' in the Dodecanese. Sure, there may be plusher hotels in Kos, but none with the soul of this place. Expect clean rooms with small balconies, a homely lounge area (the focus of chatter and inspiration), and memorable breakfasts with homemade jams.

Kosta Palace   HOTEL €€
(Map p558; ☎22420 22855; www.kosta-palace.com; cnr Akti Kountourioti & Averof; s/d/apt €80/85/135; ❄@🞉❄) This massive harbour-front edifice, facing the castle across the port, holds 173 rooms, some with kitchenettes and private balconies. Apartments have separate rooms. There are also pools for kids and adults and a snack bar on the roof. While it's clean and functional (and good value if you nab a deal), it can be rather impersonal.

Hotel Sonia   HOTEL €€
(Map p558; ☎22420 28798; www.hotelsonia.gr; Irodotou 9; d/tr/f incl breakfast €80/95/140; ❄🞉) A block from the waterfront on a peaceful backstreet, this small hotel offers 14 sparkling rooms with tiled floors, fridges and

here so go around 6am and have the place to yourself).

🛏 Sleeping

Accommodation here runs the gamut from basic guesthouse to upscale hotel. Regardless of whether you're aiming for a beach base, it's well worth spending a couple of nights in this interesting town. For those who don't need sand, Kos makes a good base.

★**Hotel Afendoulis**   HOTEL €
(Map p558; ☎22420 25321; www.afendoulishotel.com; Evripilou 1; s/d/tr from €35/50/60; ☉Mar-Nov; ❄@🞉) Nothing is too much trouble at

ASKLEPIEION

The island's most important ancient site, Asklepieion (Map p556; ☑ 22420 28763; adult/child €8/free; ☉ 8am-7.30pm daily Apr-Oct, to 2.30pm Sun & Mon Nov-Mar) stands on a pine-covered hill 3km southwest of Kos Town, commanding lovely views across towards Turkey. A religious sanctuary devoted to Asclepius, the god of healing, it was also a healing centre and a school of medicine. It was founded in the 3rd century BCE, according to legend by Hippocrates himself, the Kos-born 'father' of modern medicine. He was already dead by then, though, and the training here simply followed his teachings.

Until the sanatorium was destroyed by an earthquake in 554 CE, people came from far and wide for treatment.

The ruins occupy three levels, with the propylaeum (approach to the main gate), Roman-era public baths and remains of guest rooms on the first level. The second holds an altar of Kyparissios Apollo, with the 1st-century-BCE Temple to Apollo to the east and the first Temple of Asclepius, built in the 4th century BCE, to the west. The remains of its successor, the once-magnificent 2nd-century-BCE Temple of Asclepius, are on the third level. Climb a little further, to the cool pine woods above, for the best views of all.

A small museum on the path down preserves ancient inscriptions. Bus 3 runs hourly from Kos Town to the site. It's also a pleasant, if uphill, bike ride.

---

smart bathrooms. Rooms 4 and 5 have the best sea views; around five rooms have balconies. If you want to, you can have breakfast outside in the rear garden. There's a decent book exchange.

Kos Aktis Art Hotel　　　　HOTEL €€€
(Map p558; ☑ 22420 47200; www.kosaktis.gr; Vasileos Georgiou 7; s/d/tr from €200/260/350; ❄️🛜) Aktis' beautiful hotels are scattered across the Dodecanese and its representative here in Kos is stunning. Bedrooms are minimalist affairs of glass, light and wood. The view of the Aegean and, by night, Bodrum glittering like a giant chandelier, is romantic. There's a gym, fine restaurant and bar. Prices vary significantly according to supply and demand and season.

✖ Eating

★ Pote Tin Kyriaki　　　　TAVERNA €
(Map p558; ☑ 6930352099; Pisandrou 9; mezedhes €2.50-8; ☉ 7pm-2am Mon-Sat) Named 'Never on Sunday' to reflect its opening hours (yes, that's its day of rest), this traditional rough-and-ready ouzerie (place that serves ouzo and light snacks) serves delicious specialities such as stuffed zucchini flowers, dolmadhes and steamed mussels. Come late, and you'll be cheek by jowl with the locals.

Aegli　　　　CAFE €
(Map p558; ☑ 22420 30016; www.aiglikos.gr; Plateia Eleftherias; snacks €4-7; ☉ breakfast, lunch & dinner) Stretching from beneath the arches of a municipal building onto the main square, this bakery-cafe is run by a cooperative

supporting low-income women and employs only female staff. The speciality is marmarites – translated as 'crumpets', but more like sourdough flatbread – with sweet or savoury toppings, but it also serves pies, juices, coffee and gigantic breakfasts (for two €20).

Elia　　　　GREEK €€
(Map p558; ☑ 22420 22133; www.elia-kos.gr; Appelou Ifestou 27; mains €9-16; ☉ 12.30pm-late; ❄️🛜✏️🍴) 🍃 With its traditional wood-beamed ceiling and partly exposed stone walls covered in murals of the gods of the pantheon, Elia is earthy and friendly, and its massive menu is fit for a hard-to-please local deity or adventurous traveller. The Mediterranean dishes span traditional Greek, such as pork and lamb stews, to marinaded chicken and vegetarian mezedhes. All fresh. All good.

Ta Votsalakia　　　　SEAFOOD €€
(Map p558; ☑ 22420 26555; Averof 10; mains €9-12, fish per kg €50; ☉ 1pm-midnight) 🍃 A lovely surprise awaits after the nondescript entrance of Ta Votsalakia. Pass the bustling kitchen and you'll be on the beach, almost netting your lunch yourself. The catch of the day is the thing to go for, but after this, choose from shrimps, mussels and seafood spaghetti. And much more. Vegetarians can munch on good mezedhes (appetisers). In-the-know locals head here.

Taverna Lithino　　　　GREEK €€
(☑ 22420 24693; www.lithino.com; Archiepiskopou Gerasimou St; mains €9-14; ☉ lunch & dinner; ✏️) This incongruous place, behind the marina

on a slightly 'busy' (for Kos) road, is worth the pilgrimage. Quality – not gourmet – Greek fare is the objective here. This means great grills, homemade mezedhes (appetisers; don't miss the meatballs) and even vegetarian dishes. There's a front and rear terrace; the latter is around a mulberry tree trunk. Friendly and family run.

 Drinking & Nightlife

Kos Town has a very lively party scene, focused a block south of the harbour and along the waterfront on Kritika Beach. Locals congregate on weekends to drink coffee and gossip in the cafes on Plateia Eleftherias (Freedom Sq).

Kaseta BAR

(Map p558; ☑ 22420 22352; www.kaseta-kos.gr; Akti Miaouli 4; ⊗ 8am-1am) For locals, this is the place to be, and to be seen. Prices are hefty (coffee is slightly more, given its location overlooking the harbour). But it's where you come to linger for a coffee by day, or a cocktail by night.

Law Court Cafe CAFE

(Map p558; Plateia Platanou; ⊗ 7.30am-late) Despite being set on Kos Town's prettiest square, facing Hippocrates' plane tree (p557), this timeless little cafe feels remote from the tourist scene. Instead, as the name suggests, it's where local lawyers and businesspeople meet to discuss the order of the day, while savouring their morning espressos.

 Shopping

For local products, the market has a fabulous selection. The Old Town is full of tourist paraphernalia; for high-street-style shops, head to the eastern end of Ioannidi and the pedestrian streets south of Ippokratous.

Dimotiki Agora MARKET

(Map p558; ☑ 22420 22900; Plateia Eleftherias; ⊗ 8am-late) 🍴 Fragrant with spices, this lively open-arched market has a cornucopia of locally made honeys, natural soaps, bonbons, sandalwood spoons, mythological curios and Kalymnian sponges.

 Getting Around

BICYCLE

Cycle lanes thread all through Kos Town, with the busiest route running along the waterfront to connect the town with Lambi to the north and Psalidi to the south. Many hotels have bikes for guests, or you can rent one from Escape Rentals (p556) or Kos Mountainbike Activities (p556).

BUS

Local buses, run by **KEAS** (Map p558; ☑ 22420 26276; fare €1.10-1.60), operate within Kos Town, the most useful being route 3 to Asklepieion; the **bus stop** (Map p558) is on Akti Miaouli.

Buses to the rest of the island, including the airport, depart from the KTEL bus station (p555). Note that Kefalos-bound buses also stop at the big roundabout near the airport entrance.

TAXI

Taxis (Map p558; ☑ 22420 22777, 22420 23333) congregate on the south side of the port.

TOURIST TRAIN

One way to get your bearings in summer is to take a 20-minute city tour on the **tourist train** (☑ 22420 26276; €5), which departs frequently from Akti Koundourioti on the harbourfront.

Around Kos

Mountain Villages

The villages scattered on the green northern slopes of the Dikeos mountains make ideal destinations for day trips.

Your first stop should be Agios Dimitrios, an abandoned village whose population left during WWII. Here, there is a stunning cafe Chaichoutes (p562) and a gorgeous village church.

Then head to the mountain village of Zia, 14km southwest of Kos Town. Formerly one of Kos' prettiest villages, it's now essentially a one-street theme park. The views down to the sea are as wonderful as ever, but coachloads of tourists are deposited every few minutes to stroll along its swathe of souvenir shops and competing tavernas.

If you continue further on, you'll reach the villages of Asfendiou and Lagoudi, where you'll be rewarded with great views and incredible churches, and most likely have them to yourself. Continuing around 5km further west you'll reach the less commercialised village of Pyli. But just before the village a left turn leads to the extensive remains of its medieval predecessor, Old Pyli, scattered amid the towering rocks and pine trees of a high and very magical hillside. The summit here is crowned by the stark ruins of Pyli Castle and the whole place is so wild you half expect Pan, god of the wild and shepherds, to pop up. A well-marked trail climbs from the roadside parking area, forking left to the castle and right to the old village, where the only building

COFFEE IN GHOSTLY HAIHOUTES

Set in a ghost village of Haihoutes (it was once a thriving village of 450 people), **Chaichoutes** (Map p556; ☑ 6932637905; snacks €5-12) is a tiny and oh so tasteful cafe has been restored and stands, along with the village church, as ongoing testament to its history. With stylish olive-green chairs and traditional tables, you can kick back with a coffee and think you were in a *kafeneio* (traditional cafe) from decades ago.

Come evening it turns into a cafe-bar, and there's sometimes live music, everything from island music to *rembetika* (blues). Be sure to check out the attached 'museum', a replica of a traditional home, plus the photos in the wee church showing life as it once was. Note: there's limited telephone reception.

still in use is the Oria Tavern hidden in the woods.

Buses connect Kos Town with Pyli itself (€2.10, two to four daily), but not Old Pyli.

✕ Eating

★ Oria Taverna
GREEK €
(Map p556; ☑ 6974408843; Old Pyli; mains €7-12; ◷ 9am-9pm; 🅿) 🥢 You'll be rewarded by making the effort to get to this idyllic taverna, only accessible by a 15-minute walk up a track. Here you'll face the 1000-year-old Pyli Castle and enjoy the best rural view on Kos over great snacks and cooling drinks. But you can't beat a sunset dinner, tucking into the seasonal, locally sourced dishes of the day.

Watermill
CAFE €
(☑ 6947412440; Zia; snacks €4-8; ◷ breakfast, lunch & dinner; 🤝🅵) 🥢 With its vine-covered arbour and relaxing patio giving stunning mountain views, this former watermill is colourful and attractive, if ultrapopular. The menu includes burgers, crêpes and fruit salad. It's worth the brief climb up the hill just to sate your thirst with its delicious homemade lemonade.

I Palia Pyli
GREEK €€
(Old Spring Water; Pyli; mains €7.50-11.50; ◷ 9am-11pm) This is one of the most understated spots on the island. Sure, it isn't fancy, just

a couple of tables out on a veranda, under a ficus tree and overlooking an historic spring on a tiny square in the village of Pyli. But it has been serving up fabulous home cooking since 1950. Try the zucchini balls, meatballs and mezedhes.

Mastihari

Hardly more than a village, this delightful old-fashioned beach resort holds everything you need for a straightforward family holiday. There's a lovely broad strip of powder-fine sand scattered with tamarisk trees, a clutch of whitewashed rental studios and small hotels, and a row of appetising waterfront tavernas and bars. There's no historic core and nothing of any architectural interest, but as a place to spend a day or a week in the sun, Mastihari has it all. You won't have it to yourself (large resorts have been constructed behind), but it's less in-your-face than some of the island's other resort villages.

Mastihari's tiny port is served by frequent **Anek** (Anekalymnou; ☑ 22420 29900; www.anekalymnou.gr) and Anem (www.anemferries.gr) ferries to Pothia on Kalymnos, as well as excursion boats to the islet of Pserimos in summer.

🛏 Sleeping & Eating

Studios Diana
APARTMENT €
(☑ 22420 59116; Mastihari; apt €40) A fabulous budget option, with clean and basic studios, all opening onto the sea, with private balconies and very tiny kitchens. Turning on the air-con costs €5 extra. Not surprisingly, Studios Diana has its regulars.

Katerina & Efi
APARTMENT €
(☑ 6937529385; efikaterina@hotmail.com; Mastihari; d/f from €45/70; 🏵🛜) This well-run budget choice, with a spiffy blue-and-white exterior, is located so close to the beach that if it were any nearer you'd have sand in your bed. The tidy rooms and kitchenettes make it great for a longer stay; it's family and pet friendly, too. Even those with a village-facing view are pleasant and sport larger terraces.

★ O Makis
SEAFOOD €
(☑ 6948668417; Mastihari; mains €6-8, fish per kg around €40) Ask any local where to eat? O Makis, of course. Don't expect linen and haute cuisine. Think better: a genuine experience. Grilled fish and seafood platters cooked by the delightful Makis, a salt-of-the-earth, friendly character that makes you

grateful to be in Greece. Go with a flexible attitude and enjoy the seafood, grills or whatever is recommended.

Kali Kardia SEAFOOD €€
(☑ 22420 59289; Mastihari; mains €7-16; ☺ breakfast, lunch & dinner) Atmospheric taverna near the harbour, with tables out on the footpath and a wooden interior that's patronised by older folk staring out to sea. Piping aromas of shrimp and souvlakia emerge from the kitchen. Mixed platters for two cost €30.

Kamari & Kefalos Bay
Καμάρι & Κέφαλος

Enormous Kefalos Bay, a 12km stretch of high-quality sand, lines the southwest shoreline of Kos. For most of its length the beach itself is continuous, but the main road runs along a crest around 500m inland, so each separate section served by signposted tracks has its own name. Backed by scrubby green hills and lapped by warm water, these are the finest and emptiest beaches on the island. Kamari, at the western extremity of this black-pebbled beach, is a low-key resort with plenty of cafes, tavernas and accommodation, as well as decent water sports. High above Kamari, perched on a bluff, the touristy village of Kefalos has a few spots to eat and stay. If you're determined to escape the crowds, continue on to the island's southern peninsula beyond.

Beaches

The most popular stretch of sand is Paradise Beach, while the least developed is Magic Beach. Exotic Beach nearby is the nudist option. Langada Beach (which you may also see referred to as Banana Beach) makes a good compromise. Sadly, Agios Stefanos Beach, at the far western end, has been ruined by a massive resort behind. Nevertheless, this small beachfront promontory has the photogenic islet of Kastri, on which is a tiny church, offshore though within swimming distance.

On the west coast, Agios Theologos Beach is backed by meadow bluffs carpeted in olive groves, and feels far removed from the resort bustle.

Sleeping & Eating

Affordable studios and apartments are the order of the day, with an emphasis on package holiday accommodation in Kamari.

Albatross Studios APARTMENT €€
(☑ 22420 71981; thealbatrossteam@gmail.com; Kamari Beach; d/apt/f €65/80/120; P ❄ 🛜 🖥) Eleven simple, spotless and identical kitchenette studios, so freshly maintained they might have been built yesterday. All have sea views, there's a swimming pool (with small pool bar), and the beach is just across the road, with the jetty a short walk away. Airport pickup for stays of three nights or more. Excellent value; prices are significantly reduced outside high season.

★ **Restaurant**
Agios Theologos TAVERNA €€
(☑ 6974503556; Agios Theologos Beach; mains €10-17; ☺ lunch & dinner, Sun only Feb-Apr; ❄ 🛜) Set in dreamy sand dunes above Agios Theologos Beach, this much-loved seasonal taverna enjoys the best sunsets in Kos. It offers everything from zesty homemade cheese, courtesy of its inquisitive goats, at its most flavoursome fried, to fresh grilled bream. There are fantastic mezedhes (appetisers), too. Pure romance.

Mylotopi GREEK €€
(☑ 22420 73000; Kefalos; snacks €4-8, mains €8-12; ☺ 9am-2pm) Mylotopi's complex comprises a bar, cafe and restaurant that has been reconstructed on a former village site (with restored windmill, thus its name). This smart stone structure sprawls across various outdoor terraces, while the interior – true to its provenance – maintains cosy nooks. It's the perfect spot to enjoy anything from a coffee and cocktail to a snack or heavier meal.

ℹ Getting There & Away

Buses to and from Kos Town (€4.80, three to six daily) stop nearby at Kamari Beach.

ASTYPALEA
ΑΣΤΥΠΑΛΑΙΑ

POP 1300

Swathed in silky aquamarine waters, far-flung, butterfly-shaped Astypalea is richly rewarding for walkers, campers and history buffs. For any island hunter, this is the ultimate escape, with mountainous meadows straight from the pages of Homer, and rugged beaches fringed in vivid blue water. Chance of sighting a mermaid: fair to middling.

Astypalea

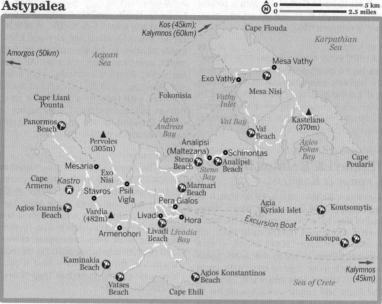

The island's main settlements, the merged villages of Pera Gialos and the hilltop Hora, are a tumble of bleached-white houses cascading down from a medieval fortress to a harbour, the former port. Although boutique hotels have been sprouting here in recent years, the tourist infrastructure – and ferry service – remains minimal, and most visitors are Greek, with the rest largely French and Italian. Fed up with the package crowds, Irish bars and fish and chips? You've come to the right place.

ⓘ Getting There & Away

AIR

Sky Express (p514) services Astypalea with several flights a week from Leros (€80, 25 minutes), Kalymnos (€62, 1¾ hours) and Kos (€74, 1¾ hours). There are also daily flights from Athens (€121, one hour). Astypalea Tours (p566) in Pera Gialos also books flights.

BOAT

Only two ferry operators serve Astypalea.

In summer, Blue Star Ferries (p515) boats arrive at the 'new port', which is rather isolated at Agios Andreas, 6.5km north of Pera Gialos. A bus is scheduled to meet each boat, as are the island's two taxis. Astypalea Tours (p566) will transfer you for €5. Outside high season, however, inconveniently, the ferry arrives in the dead of night, so book your transfer ahead if your accommodation doesn't meet you.

One ferry arrives around four times weekly, having sailed from Piraeus (€38.50, 9¾ hours) via Paros (€37, 5¼ hours) and Naxos (€20, four hours), and sets off back along the same route. The other stops once per week between Piraeus and Rhodes, calling also at Kalymnos (€14.50, two hours), Kos (€17, three hours), Tilos (€15.50, six hours) and Nisyros (€12.50, five hours).

Nisos Kalymnos (www.anekalymnou.gr) connects Pera Gialos' small harbour (sometimes referred to as the Skala Port) twice weekly with Kalymnos.

ⓘ Getting Around

Astypalea's airport is on the flat, narrow 'neck' of the island, 8km northeast of Pera Gialos. Buses connect with flights in summer, while taking either of the island's two **taxis** (📞 6976256461, 6975706365) to Pera Gialos costs around €12. From June to September, Astypalea Tours (p566) offers both airport and port shuttles (around €5 per person).

Summer buses also link Pera Gialos with Hora and Livadi to the west, and Analipsi/Maltezana to the east, stopping at beaches en route (€2).

There are several recommended vehicle-rental agencies, including **Vergoulis** (📞 22430 61351; www.vergoulis.com; per day scooters from €18, cars €45-70; ⏱ 9am-9pm) and **AstyCar** (📞 22430 62265; www.astycar.gr; scooter/car from €32/55), both based in Pera Gialos.

Pera Gialos & Hora
Πέρα Γιαλός & Χώρα

POP 1036

Astypalea's main town, Pera Gialos, lies on the southern shore of the island's western half, curving around an attractive bay that's too shallow for large interisland ferries. This compact village holds a small sand-and-pebble beach that's popular with locals. Bars and tavernas punctuate the quay, which is the preserve of old sea dogs in low season, but surprisingly lively on summer evenings.

Visitors delight in the beauty of the old settlement of Hora looming above, its white houses spilling down the hillside beneath its impressive *kastro* (castle). For the original inhabitants of Hora, however, the upward migration was prompted by the threats of marauding pirates. These days Hora is a delightful maze to explore. Stroll around the hushed tangle of streets and climb up to the fort. You can then relax in the clutch of inviting *kafeneia* (coffee houses) and tavernas alongside the restored windmills that mark the village entrance.

◎ Sights & Activities

Kastro   CASTLE
(Hora; ⊙dawn-dusk) FREE Astypalea's imposing castle was built by the Venetian Quirini family early in the 15th century. For the next 300 years, up to 4000 people lived within this ever-expanding precinct, sheltered from pirate attacks. Its last inhabitants left in 1956, after an earthquake caused the stone houses integrated into its walls to collapse. The only entrance is through a gateway that burrows beneath the Church of the Virgin of the Castle; the magical Church of Agios Georgios lies beyond.

Archaeological Museum   MUSEUM
(☑22430 61500; Pera Gialos; €2; ⊙9am-5pm Wed-Mon Jun-Sep) Pera Gialos' small archaeological museum, set back from the sea at the start of the road up to Hora, holds treasures found across the island, from earliest times up to the Middle Ages. Highlights include grave offerings from two Mycenaean chamber tombs and a little bronze Roman statue of Aphrodite.

Thalassopouli   BOATING
(☑6974436338; Pera Gialos; per person €18; ⊙Jun-Sep; ♠) Run by Captain Yiannis, *Thalassopouli* leaves Pera Gialos at 11am and returns you glowing and salty at 6pm after a day's swimming around uninhabited neighbouring islands such as Kounoupa, with its golden isthmus of sand, and Koutsomytis, outlined in purest aquamarine. Take plenty of sunscreen.

⊨ Sleeping

Reservations are essential in July and August. The finer boutique options are in Hora but there are some smart small resorts elsewhere, too.

Gyrouli Studios   APARTMENT €
(☑6946583570, 22430 61267; www.gyroulistudios.gr; Pera Gialos; from €60) These spotless studios, with kitchenettes and kind owners, are located in an ideal spot: between Hora and Pera Gialos (not too far up, nor down). Some studios are in an older style, while the newer, more modern ones would suit fussier travellers. But, hey, the view is the same. Low season prices significantly lower.

Studios Kilindra   BOUTIQUE HOTEL €€
(☑22430 61131; www.astipalea.com.gr; Hora; studio/apt/ste incl breakfast €150/160/220; ✳@🛰📶) ♨ Just below the *kastro* (castle), this enchanting boutique hotel has a swish pool with a terrace overlooking the mouthwash-green bay. The lobby is scattered with eclectic antiques as well as a grand piano, while studios and larger maisonettes fuse the contemporary with the traditional, featuring split-level floors, raised beds, sofas and kitchenettes. Massage, acupuncture and herbal treatments are also available.

★Kallichoron Art Boutique Hotel   BOUTIQUE HOTEL €€€
(☑22430 61935; www.kallichoron.gr; Hora; d incl breakfast from €150; ✳🛰📶) ♨ Eleven gorgeous rooms and two maisonettes make up Kallichoron. The bright and beautifully decorated rooms have a terrace and face directly across to Hora. The hotel has received national awards for its environmentally friendly practices and, despite the fact the rooms have small kitchenettes, it serves up scrumptious breakfasts. These 'Grandma's breakfasts' comprise more local produce than a national providore. Mooch on the terrace and stare at Hora. Or lie back and view the local artwork. Dreamy stuff.

✗ Eating

Agoni Grammi   TAVERNA €
(☑22430 62102; Hora; mains €8-15; ⊙lunch & dinner, closed Mar) It's the outdoor terrace that first catches the eye here, close to Hora's

landmark windmills, but the modern white-washed interior with its lovely open kitchen is equally appealing. As well as handmade pasta, this smart spot, one of the island's favourites, is also renowned for its fish soup and sea urchin dish.

Maïstrali TAVERNA €
(☑ 22430 61691; Pera Gialos; mains €8.50-13; ☺10am-late; ✷ 🛈 ✍) Tucked one street back from the harbour, near the stairway to heaven (well, Hora, anyway), this long-standing restaurant dishes up everything from zucchini balls, lamb chops and eggplant salad, to grilled shrimp *saganaki* (shrimp in fried cheese). It's one of the few eateries open all year.

★ **Barbarossa** TAVERNA €
(☑ 22430 61577; Hora; mains €12-15; ☺lunch & dinner; ✷ 🛈 ✍) 🍴 You can't miss this friendly taverna, serving food with soul along the main approach to Hora, with a buzzing terrace near the town hall. Menu highlights like pork fillet with prunes, mussels and grilled shrimps ensure you won't be disappointed. A favourite choice in Hora.

ⓘ Information

Alpha Bank (☑ 22430 61402; Pera Gialos; ☺8am-2pm Mon-Fri) The island's only bank, with an ATM, is on the waterfront.

Astypalea Tours (☑ 22430 61571; www.astypaleatours.gr; Pera Gialos; ☺10am-1.30pm & 5.30-8.30pm) Extremely helpful. Can book air and ferry tickets, plus boat excursions to the small islands of Kounoupa, Koutsomytis and Agia Kiriaki.

Municipal Tourist Office (☑ 22430 61412; www.visitastypalea.com; Hora; ☺6-9pm Jun-Sep) In a restored windmill, this is a high-season operation only, and can provide basic information about the island. Opening hours can be irregular, depending on staff availability.

ⓘ Getting There & Away

Local buses link Pera Gialos with Hora, Maltezana, Livadi and Agios Andreas (€2). Taxis (p564) to/from Pera Gialos or Hora and the airport cost around €12. In the summer months, Astypalea Tours (p566) offers shuttles to the airport and port (around €5 per person).

Nisos Kalymnos (www.anekalymnou.gr) connects Pera Gialos' small harbour (sometimes referred to as the Skala Port) twice weekly with Kalymnos, but major boats dock at Agios Andreas, 6.5km north of Pera Gialos.

Livadi

Astypalea's most popular beach stands at the mouth of a lush valley in the first bay south of Hora. An easy 20-minute walk down from the old town, it's also served by local buses. In summer it's effectively transformed into a buzzing little resort, with a string of hip restaurants and bars lining the waterfront.

🛏 Sleeping & Eating

Mouras Studios APARTMENT €€
(☑ 22430 61227; www.mourastudios.gr; studio from €80; ☺May–mid-Oct; ✷ 🛈) Radiating off a beachfront courtyard, these seven stunning whitewashed studios vary in size, but all have a stylish grey-and-white decor, kitchenettes and private balconies. Full-on sea views cost a few euros extra. (Note, don't confuse this with the Mouras Resort, though it is all part of the same family.)

Astropelos GREEK €€
(☑ 22430 61473; www.astropelos.com; Livadi; mains €10-20; ☺breakfast, lunch & dinner; ✷ 🛈 ✍) There's a whiff of expensive suncream about this place. But it's first-class dining by the beach, on a decked veranda with chic white tables and a gourmet menu that includes octopus salad and lobster. Vegan and vegetarian options available, too. And lounge chairs under the shade of tamarisk trees to view Hora on the hilltop horizon.

Gerani TAVERNA €€
(☑ 22430 61484; www.astypalaiagerani.gr; Livadi; mains €8-12; 🖼) An ultrafriendly, English-speaking Greek couple run this lovely spot, nestled off the main drag – look for the hanging boat and the flower boxes. It serves delicious no-nonsense, traditional Greek food. Forget the menu (although extensive) and go for the daily specials, the likes of fish soup, or ravioli stuffed with the traditional *chlori* cheese and local saffron.

West of Pera Gialos

West of Pera Gialos, you swiftly hit the Astypalea outback – gnarled, bare rolling hills, perfect for a Cyclops. There's scarcely a sealed road to speak of but, depending on the conditions (the roads are graded in preparation for summer), it's just about possible to drive. Note, however, that car rental agencies might prohibit this, except if you have a SUV or jeep. If you can, cross the western massif by heading directly inland from Hora and, from the point where the road finally peters out after 8km, where the Kastro ruins and Moni Agiou Ioanni stand proudly cheek by jowl above the shoreline, energetic walkers can hike down to Agios Ioannis Beach. Alternatively, follow the track that branches northwards shortly before road's end and you'll probably have Panormos Beach to yourself.

The rough track that winds along the southern coast west of Livadi, on the other hand, leads through mountainous meadows to several remote beaches. First along the way, reached on a brief detour (most of this on sealed road), is the pretty, tree-shaded Agios Konstantinos Beach on the south side of Livadi Bay. It's back to a dirt track to reach Kaminakia Beach in the far west, where the track reaches its terminus. Book-ended by granite boulders, Kaminakia is Astypalea's best altar to sun worshipping, with water so clear you can see the pebbles through the turquoise. Both beaches hold excellent seasonal tavernas.

In July and August, boats head out for the day from Pera Gialos to the remote western beaches of Agios Ioannis, Kaminakia and Vatses, as well as to the islets of Koutsomytis (with ethereal, emerald-green water) and Kounoupa. Contact Astypalea Tours for details.

✕ Eating

Sti Linda GREEK €
(☑ 6932610050; Kaminakia Beach; mains €5-10; ☺ Jul-Sep) 🛵 From the Stavros junction a rough track winds upwards to the shepherd's hut on the mountain spine and then an *extremely* rough track winds downwards to Kaminakia Beach, lapped by stunning turquoise water. Here you're also rewarded with a good seasonal restaurant, which rustles up hearty fish soups, oven-baked goat and homemade bread. Make it a day trip.

East of Pera Gialos

The slender isthmus that links Astypalea's two 'wings' holds some of the island's most popular beaches. Each of the three bays at Marmari, just 2km northeast of Pera Gialos, has its own pebble-and-sand beach, right beside the road. Steno Beach, another 2km along, is sandy, shady and conveniently shallow for kids. The name means 'narrow', with the isthmus being a mere 100m wide near this spot.

The only resort area away from Pera Gialos, Analipsi is a pleasantly laid-back place that spreads through a fertile valley alongside the airport, 8km northeast of Pera Gialos. Also known as Maltezana, having once been the lair of Maltese pirates, it's grown recently thanks to long Analipsi Beach to the southeast, which offers sand, pebbles, shade and clean, shallow water. Nearby the remains of the Tallaras Roman baths still hold some mosaics.

Almost no one lives on Astypalea's eastern half. The only settlement is the remote hamlet of Mesa Vathy, tucked into the shelter of an enormous bottleneck bay and home to barely half-a-dozen families. A summer yacht harbour, it doesn't have a decent beach.

⌂ Sleeping & Eating

Villa Barbara APARTMENT €
(☑ 22430 61448, 6930778530; www.villabarbara.gr; Analipsi; s/d from €45/50; ※) Set in flowering gardens, these 12 fresh blue-and-white studios have tiled floors and balconies with sea views. The ocean is less than 100m away.

★**Galini Cafe** CAFE €
(☑ 22430 61201; Exo Vathy; mains €4-8; ☺ Jun-Oct) At remote Exo Vathy hamlet you can dine at the ultracasual, fishermen-packed Galini Cafe, which offers meat and fish grills and the odd oven-baked special. You're pretty much told to grab your plates and 'come and get it' (in the Greek equivalent). It hasn't changed for decades; worth coming here for the salt-of-the-earth experience alone.

★**Astakoukos** SEAFOOD €€
(☑ 22430 64014; Sxoinontas Beach, Analipsi; mains €7-14; ☺ breakfast, lunch & dinner; 🛜🅿) While the name means 'the little lobster', there's nothing diminutive about the quality here. Hospitable John will sit you under the shaded pergola and serve up everything from his award-winning lobster and spaghetti to goat *stifhado* (goat stew with a lemon sauce). Or you can relax on the Sxoinontas Beach and order simpler snacks and refreshments. Pretty. And perfect.

KALYMNOS ΚΑΛΥΜΝΟΣ
POP 16,000

Rugged Kalymnos is characterised by its dramatic mountains that draw hardy climbers from all over the world. Its western flank is particularly spectacular with skeletal crags towering above dazzling blue waters.

Surprisingly for its rocky landscape, it cradles a couple of pretty, fertile valleys with bee boxes and olive groves. The enticing, car-free islet of Telendos is immediately offshore, a mere 10 minutes in a water taxi.

While its sponge-fishing heyday is long past, Kalymnos remains inextricably entwined with the sea, particularly in its capital and main ferry port, Pothia, where statues of Poseidon and an historic diver survey the harbour.

In recent years, the island's activities have expanded from climbing alone. Add to this diving, plus hiking and a host of interesting little museums and cultural experiences, and you begin to see why Kalymnos is now on the Greek islands must-visit list.

ⓘ Getting There & Away

AIR

Kalymnos' airport, 6km northwest of Pothia, is served by daily Sky Express (p514) flights to and from Athens (€133, one hour), Leros (€75, 15 minutes) and Kos (€75, 20 minutes). Connecting buses meet flights in summer.

BOAT

Kalymnos' main ferry port, Pothia, is linked by daily Dodekanisos Seaways (p515) catamarans running the route between Samos (€39, 3¼ hours), Ikaria (€32, 2¾ hours), Patmos (€28, 1¾ hours), Lipsi (€22, 1¼ hours), Leros (€20, 45 minutes), Kalymnos and Kos (€16, 35 minutes). A second route runs between Rhodes, Symi, Kos, Kalymnos, Leros, Lipsi and Patmos.

Blue Star Ferries (p515) connects Pothia with Piraeus (€54, 10¾ hours), plus Kos (€7.50, 45 minutes) and Rhodes (€53 to €65, 11 to 18 hours) five times weekly, and once weekly with Astypalea (€20, 3½ hours) and Symi (€29, two hours).

Anek (www.anekalymnou.gr) runs the passenger-only *Kalymnos Star* and *Kalymnos Dolphin* between Mastihari on the north shore of Kos (six daily, 45 minutes). Anem (www.anemferries.gr) offers the same trip three times a day. Several excursion boats offer day trips from Kos Town to Pothia.

In addition, the little resort of Myrties on Kalymnos' west coast is connected twice weekly with Agia Marina on Leros by Leros Express (p555).

ⓘ Getting Around

BOAT

In summer, various excursion boats run from Pothia to destinations including Kefalas Cave (around €20), the island of Pserimos and other beaches. Frequent **water taxis** (one way €2; ⊘ 8am-midnight) also connect Myrties with Telendos Islet year-round.

BUS

Buses from Pothia Harbour serve a number of the island's villages. See www.kalymnos-isl.gr.

CAR & MOTORCYCLE

Vehicle-hire companies along the harbour in Pothia include **Auto Market** (⌨ 6972834628, 22430 24202; www.kalymnoscars.gr; Pothia) and **Suzuki Rentals** (⌨ 6937980591; www.kipreosrentals.gr; Pothia). Expect to pay €20 to €40 per day for a car, and €12 to €15 for a scooter.

TAXI

Shared taxis, based at Pothia's **taxi stand** (⌨ 22430 50300; Plateia Kyprou), cost little more than buses. Private taxis cost around €10 to Myrties, €10 to the airport, €17 to Vathys and €30 to Emborios.

Pothia   Πόθια

POP 12,300

Kalymnos' capital, Pothia has a low-slung harbourfront of cream and white facades and backs up the hill in a labyrinth of streets, beneath hulking mountains. If arriving by boat, this is most likely your first taste of the island. You may find some Kalymnians a little gruff, but don't be offended – these rugged islanders have been known throughout history for their toughness and terse manner. Pothia is not a resort, and makes no attempt to be one, though for the curious traveller there's an excellent archaeological museum and a tourist office. Wander the quayside peppered with old Venetian-style mansions and sea-god statues, past nut-brown fishermen and ex-divers in *kafeneia* (coffee houses) and bars, nursing retsinas and ragged lungs.

◉ Sights & Activities

In summer boats run from Pothia to Kefalas Cave (around €20), where an impressive 103m corridor is filled with stalactites and stalagmites; and the island of Pserimos, with its big, sandy beach and tavernas. Head to the harbour to see where else they go.

Archaeological Museum   MUSEUM
(⌨ 22430 23113; adult/child €4/2; ⊘ 8.30am-4pm Wed-Mon) Kalymnos' modern Archaeological Museum is tricky to find, hidden in the backstreets behind the eastern end of Pothia's waterfront. It's worth the effort to enjoy beautifully displayed ancient artefacts dating as far back as 5300 BCE. There's some remarkable glassware and gold jewellery, but the highlight is an exquisite, larger-than-life bronze statue of a woman from

Kalymnos

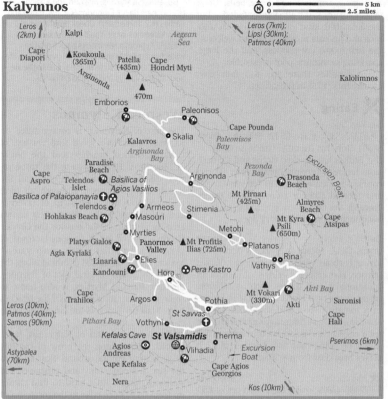

the 2nd century BCE. Swathed in a chiton (tunic), she was discovered underwater off Kalymnos in 1994.

Nautical & Folklore Museum MUSEUM
(☑ 22430 51361; €3; ☺ 9am-5pm mid-Jun–mid-Sep) On the central waterfront, this is more of a collection than a museum. The nautical section focuses on sponge fishing, displaying mighty stone weights used by ancient divers and haunting photos of their 20th-century counterparts wearing early-model diving suits. Many divers suffered terrible injuries before the bends (decompression sickness) was understood. The folklore section holds a few costumes and furniture.

🛏 Sleeping

Archontiko Hotel PENSION €
(☑ 6942838524, 22430 51344; www.apxontiko-hotel.com; s/d €35/50; ☀ 🎧) Overlooking the harbour, five minutes' walk from the ferry, this central, custard-coloured mansion is

one of the most handsome in town. The Danish manager has done a great job with 'old bones': the rooms are light and airy and oh so white. It's in the middle of the waterfront; look up for the sign. Great budget option.

Evanik Hotel HOTEL €
(☑ 22430 22057; www.evanik-hotel.gr; s/d/tr incl breakfast €35/45/60; ☀ 🎧) Beyond its smart lobby, this modern hotel, a few blocks up from the harbour and lacking views, holds 28 plush rooms of varying size, with tiled floors, Ikea-style furniture, reading lamps and immaculate en-suite bathrooms. Downstairs there's a pleasant breakfast area. Ask for a quieter room at the back.

★ Villa Melina HOTEL €€
(☑ 22430 22682; www.villa-melina.com; d/tr incl breakfast €65/70; ☀ 🎧 ☒) Set in a colourful walled garden, this rose-pink 1930s villa exudes old-world charm, its wood-panelled rooms featuring stucco ceilings, lilac walls,

mahogany armoires and huge beds. Don't expect luxury – it's all slightly faded – but the delightful, kind and gentle owner Antonios and his cats provide a homey welcome, the bathrooms are spotless, and the large, sparkling swimming pool irresistible.

For families there are also four cosy apartments (€75) in the garden.

✕ Eating

Stukas Taverna
GREEK €

(📞 6932248357; mains €6-12; ⊙ lunch & dinner; 📶📶) Run by friendly Greek-Australians, tiny Stukas has checked cloths and a wharfside terrace, serving hearty fare. Three-course set menus cost €10 for vegetarians and around €12 for fish- or meat eaters. Towards the far eastern end of the harbour, heading away from the ferry dock.

Barba Yiannis
GREEK €

(mains €8-12; ⊙ breakfast, lunch & dinner) Enjoying harbour views from its pretty decked terrace, Yiannis is a reliable spot to head for traditional Greek dishes such as *stifadho* (meat, game or seafood cooked with onions in a tomato puree) and souvlakia. There's also swordfish, shrimp *saganaki* (shrimp in fried cheese) and calamari, or whatever fish might be going that day. Another plus? It serves breakfast from 8.30am.

★ Mamouzelos
SEAFOOD €€

(📞 22430 47809; mains €12-15; fish per kg €50; ⊙ lunch & dinner) Without doubt, the best seafood-only taverna on the island. Prices here are slightly higher than your regular taverna, but you get what you pay for: the freshest of fresh fish thanks to the fishermen who save their quality catches for this place. Come with time to spare, grab a seat on the veranda. At the eastern end of the harbour.

ℹ Information

Municipal Tourist Information (📞 22430 29299; www.kalymnos-isl.gr; ⊙ 8am-3pm Mon-Fri) Has basic, if well-organised, info for buses and ferries, climbing and diving, festivals and general island practicalities. At the entrance to the ferry dock.

Tezaris Tours (📞 22430 22800; www.tezaris tours.gr; Agios Nikolaos) Arranges ferry and air tickets plus does two-hour trips of the island in minibuses.

ℹ Getting There & Away

Ferries arrive in Pothia Harbour southeast of town.

Buses serve Myrties, Masouri and Armeos (€1.50, nine daily), Emborios (€2, two daily) and Vathys (€2, three daily). Check timetables at www.kalymnos-isl.gr. You'll find the **bus stop** (Plateia Kyprou) a few blocks back from the waterfront, next to the taxi stand (p568). Private taxis cost around €10 to Myrties, €10 to the airport, €17 to Vathys and €30 to Emborios.

Western Kalymnos

The best of Kalymnos is concentrated on its west side. Here you'll find clusters of tamarisk-shaded beaches and the bluest of blue bays. Here, too, are the three resort villages of Myrties, Masouri and the less-developed Armeos, although all have morphed into one long strip of tavernas and cafes. This is the island's best-known area for climbing – famous for the Grande Grotta – attracting a seasoned crowd of global climbers that mostly congregate in Masouri, with organised climbing along the nearby cliffs. The magical islet of Telendos, opposite languid Myrties, is also home to some great climbing routes. Of the beaches here, Masouri Beach is the largest and gets crowded in summer.

The former capital of Kalymnos, Hora (Horio), stands atop the brow of the low ridge behind Pothia, around 4km up from the sea. A steep, stony and unshaded old stairway that's a little hard to find climbs up from its eastern edge to the pirate-proof village of Pera Kastro, which was inhabited until the 18th century. Beyond its forbidding walls and stern gateway, it now lies almost entirely in ruins and is overgrown with wildflowers, but amid the wreckage it's well worth seeking out nine tiny 15th-century churches that still hold stunning frescoes.

A tree-lined road drops for 2km beyond Hora to reach the pretty villages of Kandouni, Linaria and Elies within the valley of Panormos. Two neighbouring beaches are within walking distance: Linaria and the more attractive cove of Kandouni, surrounded by mountains and holding a small sandy beach where cafes, bars and hotels overlook the water.

Directly facing Telendos Islet, across 800m of generally placid sea, Myrties and Masouri have attractive beaches, with the strand at Masouri being larger and sandier. Beyond the Telendos ferry quay in Myrties, the west-coast road is a one-way loop. To continue any further north, you have

VATHYS & RINA

Follow the barren coast road northeast from Pothia, instead of heading straight over to the west coast, and, after winding for 13km along the cliffs, it enters a long, lush, east-facing valley that was historically the agricultural heartland of Kalymnos. Narrow roads here thread between citrus orchards, bordered by high stone walls known as *koumoula*.

The valley takes its name from the inland settlement of Vathys, but the attraction for visitors is the little harbour of Rina. From the sea, it's accessed by a slender twisting inlet that's more like a fjord than anything you'd expect to find on a Greek island. In summer, large excursion boats bring troupes of day trippers here from Kos for lunch, keeping a clutch of competitive quayside tavernas busy, but it's a lovely spot at quieter times. Easy walks lead to 1500-year-old chapels on the hillside to either side of the bay. This is the place to hire a kayak or stand-up paddleboard and enjoy the tranquil waters. Grab your gear from Kalymnos Kayak Centre (☑ 6972261181, 22430 31132; www.waternative.co/kalymnoskayak; Rina; kayak or SUP per hour €10) at the end of the harbour.

Inland, beyond Vathys, a windswept road switchbacks up and over the mountains to reach the island's northwest coast, providing a speedier way to reach Emborios from Pothia than the built-up route through Myrties and Masouri.

to double back and follow a largely empty stretch higher up the hillside. Only if you're heading south do you see the main commercial strip that connects the two resorts in a seamless row of restaurants, rental studios, bars, souvenir shops and minimarkets, one block up from sea level.

North of Masouri, the road becomes two-way once more and swiftly leads into Armeos, perched above the coast without a beach. Smarter and newer than its neighbours, it consists almost entirely of larger hotels and apartment complexes targeted at climbers.

North of Armeos, Kalymnos' west-coast road leaves civilisation behind. Its final stretch, skirting the deep inlet that cradles tiny Arginonda, is utterly magnificent, cut into the flanks of mighty cliffs and bordered with flowering oleander. It comes to an end 20km from Pothia at sleepy little Emborios, where sugar-white houses cluster around a long, narrow pebble beach.

For a pretty detour (and a local secret – few outsiders visit here), turn east after Skalia, to Paleonisos, and follow the winding road down to a gorgeous little cove. Here, there are several cantinas and water so calm it's like a massive swimming pool.

On the southern end of the island, southwest of Pothia, head over the steep headland to St Savvas, for some of the best views around. Behind here, the pretty Vlihadia is home to a lovely little beach strip, a couple of tavernas, and a quirky ocean-focused museum.

◎ Sights & Activities

★ St Valsamidis   MUSEUM

(Sea World Museum; Map p569; ☑ 22430 50662; www.valsamidis-museum.gr; Vlihadia; ◎ 9am-5pm) This unorthodox collection is the life's work of a local Kalymnian man, Stavros Valsamidis, who for 48 years undertook private dives, and amassed items from the ocean floor. The 17,000 objects span from archaeological amphorae (all registered), shells, corals and WWII artefacts. Prized possessions include items from the Middle East that had clearly been pillaged by pirates. Stavros is no longer alive but these days, his son promotes what Kalymnians relate to best: the sea.

Head to the cafe-bar to the left of the museum and ask for the keys if it's not open.

Kalymnos Experience   OUTDOORS

(☑ 6946302515; www.kalymnosexperience.gr; Arginonda; ◎ 8.30am-2pm & 5.30-10pm) ✎ A group of passionate, young Kalymnians recently created Kalymnos Experience to offer alternative local experiences, some of which are difficult to do on your own. Options include nature walks, yoga, rock climbing, and scuba diving, to herb walks in the mountains (ending with a practical lab to prepare your own concoctions!). There's a weekly schedule or they'll arrange... almost anything!

🛏 Sleeping

Acroyali   APARTMENT €

(☑ 22430 47521, 6938913210; www.acroyali-kalymnos.gr; Myrties; apt €60-70; ❄🛜) Run by a lookalike of the late Leonard Cohen,

Michalis, and right on the beach, Acroyali has six mint-fresh apartments spread over two floors with a large balconies. Apartments feature rustic furniture, comfy lounge, small kitchen with plenty of room to eat at the dining table, and a separate bedroom. The garden fronts onto the beach.

Myrties Boutique
Apartments APARTMENT €€
(☑ 6986285888; www.myrtiesboutiqueapartments. gr; Myrties; apt €105; ✽ ⓐ) Two colourful and comfortable rental studios, a couple of minutes' walk up from the beach, each with two rooms, sleeping up to five guests and equipped with kitchenette and broad seaview patio. They're cleaned daily and linen includes robes and beach towels.

✖ Eating & Drinking

Fatolitis Snack Bar CAFE €
(☑ 22430 47615; Masouri; snacks €3-7; ⓢ 7amlate; ⓐ) A favourite with the après-climbing gang, this lively roadside cafe has a vine-shaded terrace and cosy interior spattered with rock posters. The menu isn't great, but it's carb-focused, with the likes of waffles, omelettes and toasties. No one cares much; they're too busy swapping stories over breakfast, lunch or an evening beer.

★ Aegean Tavern GREEK €€
(☑ 22430 47146; www.aegeancuisine.org/Aigaio pelagitiko; Masouri; mains €11-19) As American trained, owner-chef George states of his produce, 'we have only the best of the best'. This means 100% Greek produce and traditional Greek cuisine. It's an upmarket experience in a stylish airy building that juts over the water, overlooking Telendos Islet. But local folk come here for the daily seafood catch that's fresh and beautifully prepared.

★ Azul Bar BAR
(☑ 22430 48269; www.facebook.com/azulkalymnos; Armeos; ⓢ 5pm-late) This rather surreal space celebrates art, wine and food. It's part home (it was a former house built in the early 1970s), part gallery, and part garden. And it's fully fun, with a quirky interior decor of clocks, books and artefacts. It has a fabulous Greek wine list, plus gourmet

---

CLIMBING, HIKING & DIVING IN PARADISE

Steep crags, stark cliffs and daredevil overhangs have turned Kalymnos into Greece's premier destination for rock climbers. It now has more than 80 designated climbing sites, holding over 3500 marked routes. Most are located above the island's west-coast road, especially around and north of Armeos – white roadside markers identify the precise spots – though several of the finest ascend the flanks of Telendos Islet, just across the water.

Climbing season runs from March to mid-November, with the busiest period from mid-September until the end of October. An annual climbing festival takes place during the first 10 days of October.

The man largely responsible for the boom is Aris Theodoropoulos, who along with Katie Roussos writes the astonishingly detailed and comprehensive *Kalymnos Rock Climbing Guidebook* and maintains the useful www.climbkalymnos.com website, which includes a climbers' forum.

Kalymnos is also increasingly popular with hikers. Established routes are detailed on the excellent 1:25,000 *Kalymnos* map published by Terrain Maps (www.terrainmaps. gr). Serious hikers may want to undertake all or part of the highly demanding, multiday Kalymnos Trail, a 100km route that circles the island and also goes around Telendos for good measure. Shorter walks head to churches and monasteries, plus you can reach the castle at Hora (p571). Less experienced climbers can make enquiries through Kalymnos Experience (p571).

Kalymnos is also becoming known as a diving island. For the beginner looking to qualify as a PADI open-water diver, as well as for the seasoned diver, there are plenty of hidden treasures in Poseidon's realm awaiting your inspection, including wreck dives, sea caves and diving with dolphins. There are several main outfits:

Diver's Island (☑ 22430 48287; www.diversisland-kalymnos.gr; Kalydna Hotel, Elies; ⊞)

Kalymnos Diving (☑ 6942062215; www.scubakalymnos.com; Agios Nikolaos, Pothia; ⓢ 8am-7pm)

Kalymnos Diving Club (☑ 6974646413; www.kalymnosdiving.com)

international treats (tapas, veggie burgers and more).

ℹ Getting There & Away

Buses serve Myrties, Masouri and Armeos (€1.50, nine daily). Two daily buses connect Emborios with Pothia.

Telendos Islet
Νήσος Τέλενδος

The bewitching islet of Telendos looms from the Aegean just off the west coast of Kalymnos. Crowned by a mountainous ridge that soars 450m high, it's thought to have been set adrift from the rest of Kalymnos by an earthquake in 554 CE. It now makes a wonderful, vehicle-free destination for a day trip or longer stay.

Daily life on Telendos focuses on the short line of tavernas, cafes and whitewashed guesthouses that stretches along the pretty waterfront to either side of the jetty. Head right to reach the ruins of the early Christian basilica of Agios Vasilios and a footpath that climbs to the similarly dilapidated basilica of Palaiopanayia. Head left, on the other hand, and you can either cross a slender ridge, rich in colourful oleander, to access windswept, fine-pebbled Hohlakas Beach or explore the islet's low-lying southern promontory, which holds some tiny early-Christian tombs now inhabited by goats, and a gloriously tranquil little swimming cove.

The cliffs along the northern flanks of Telendos hold several hugely popular rock-climbing routes, which can be accessed by walking for an hour or so along a rough, exposed footpath.

🛏 Sleeping & Eating

Hotel Porto Potha HOTEL €
(☑22430 47321, 6948884886; www.telendoshotel. gr; d incl breakfast €55; ❄🐾🛜🏊) Telendos' only hotel is located a five-minute walk out of the village heading north – look out for the smart sugar-cube complex up on the hill. Inside, rooms are adequate, and there's a large lobby where guests come to relax and watch TV over a drink. There are additional separate apartments.

★ On The Rocks PENSION €€
(☑6932978142, 22430 48260; www.telendos.org; r incl breakfast €70; ❄🏠🛜) Behind its seafront garden cafe-bar-restaurant that's strung with nautical knick-knacks, this welcoming complex is a haven for active climbers and

indolent beach bunnies alike. The spacious studios have kitchenettes, private balconies and washing machines. It's run by a friendly Greek Australian, and is 200m right from the jetty.

To Kapsouli TAVERNA €
(☑22430 47363; mains €8-15; ⏱8am-late) This claims to have been the first taverna on the island (1974) and nothing much has changed. Sitting at the waterfront tables of this impossibly picturesque little taverna, you can watch fishermen cleaning fish on the quay, straight from their boats, then dine on the freshest meat or seafood, scrutinised by a posse of purring pussycats.

Restaurant-Cafe Rita TAVERNA €
(☑22430 47914; www.telendos-rita.com; mains €8-16; ⏱breakfast, lunch & dinner; 🛜) Welcoming Rita, Petroula and Yiannis serve up a chat and reaonable meals: succulent souvlakia, lamb in lemon and garlic and hearty lamb *stifadho* (lamb cooked with onions in a tomato puree); there's a great octopus version, too. They also have a secondhand bookshop and sell crafts, as well as a few chalk-blue rooms (€30) to stay in.

ℹ Getting There & Away

Telendos is easily reached on a 10-minute water taxi (p568) from Myrties. Note: you can't take a motorbike onto the island. It's walking path territory only.

LEROS ΛΕΡΟΣ
POP 8210

Leros is said to have been the original home of Artemis the Huntress. There's certainly something alluringly untamed and beautiful about the island, which is scattered with stunning Orthodox churches, dazzling blue coves and whitewashed villages. The capital, Platanos, with its stark windmills and ancient fortress towering above, makes a striking centrepiece, while down below, the busy little harbour of Agia Marina pulses with enterprise. Leros is less about chasing activities and more about worshipping Helios, seeking out your favourite beach, sampling the delectable cuisine at a sun-kissed taverna and allowing the magic of the place to slowly unfold.

ℹ Information

There's no tourist office on the island. For information on local history and facilities, visit www.leros.org.uk or www.lerosisland.com, both private sites.

❶ Getting There & Away

AIR

Leros **airport** (Map p575; ☑22470 22777) is at the northern end of the island about 6km from Agia Marina. It's serviced by Olympic Air (p514), which offers daily flights to Athens (€80, one hour) and, in high season, thrice-weekly flights to Rhodes (€110, 1¾ hours), Kos (€177, 55 minutes) and Kastellorizo (€124, 2¾ hours).

BOAT

High-speed catamarans operated by Dodekanisos Seaways (p515) call in at Leros daily as they ply their way to and from Kos, Kalymnos, Patmos, Samos, Rhodes and other nearby islands. Generally they stop at Agia Marina on the island's east coast, but when there's bad weather they may stop at Lakki on the west coast, so always check the relevant port when you buy tickets, and double-check on the day you're due to depart and be prepared for a last-minute taxi dash across the island.

Blue Star Ferries (p515) makes late-night stops at Lakki two to three times weekly, heading towards Rhodes via Kos and Kalymnos, and towards Piraeus via Patmos and Lipsi.

Patmos Star (☑22470 32500; www.patmosstar.com) sails between Agia Marina and the islands of Lipsi and Patmos with varying frequency, increasing to daily in peak season.

Nisos Kalymnos (www.anekalymnou.gr) connects Lakki with Kalymnos to the south, and Lipsi, Patmos and assorted islets to the north, four times weekly.

Leros Express (p555) connects Agia Marina twice weekly with Lipsi, Agathonisi, Arki and Pythagorio (Samos). It also runs between Kalymnos and Kos.

❶ Getting Around

A **taxi** (☑6972014531, 6938918123) to Agia Marina from the airport will cost around €20 to €22.

Between June and September a green-and-beige-striped bus travels the full length of Leros between three and six times daily (€2 flat fare), including calling at the airport. It will usually stop anywhere if you flag it down.

Taxis (p574) are available for trips around the island, plus airport drop-off and pickup (€20 to €22).

Outlets in all resort areas rent cars, scooters and bikes; **Motoland** (☑Alinda 22470 24584, Pandeli 22470 26400; www.motoland.gr; Panteli Beach Hotel; ☺9am-7pm) in Alinda and Pandeli is recommended.

The Agios Georgios (p574) excursion boat makes assorted day trips in summer, around the island and north to islets such as Arki and Marathi, typically costing around €25.

Platanos & Agia Marina
Πλάτανος & Αγια Μαρίνα

POP 3000

Arriving at the bijou port of Agia Marina, with its yawning cats, mounds of yellow fishing nets and cluster of tavernas is a delight; the biscuit- and wine-coloured Italianate buildings are as if drawn from an artist's palette. And rising behind them are the white sugar-cube houses of Platanos, a 10-minute uphill walk. Stately mansions still pepper the slopes and the row of renovated windmills that marches up towards its imposing clifftop castle makes a magnificent spectacle.

Heading right from the ferry quay, following the shoreline for a couple of kilometres, will take you to Krithoni and Alinda.

◎ Sights & Activities

Pandeli Castle   CASTLE
(Map p575; ☑22470 23211; €1; ☺8.30am-12.30pm & 4-8pm; ⊞) A steep, stony stepped path zigzags up from Platanos to reach the hilltop ruins of Pandeli Castle. The castle's oldest, innermost sections date back 1000 years, but the outer ramparts were added by the Knights of St John during the 14th and 15th centuries. Few structures now survive, but the 360-degree views from the walls are breathtaking. You can also drive here, along an exposed road that winds up from Pandeli past the windmills, where you'll find a cafe (p576) in summertime.

Archaeological Museum   MUSEUM
(☑22470 24775; Agia Marina; €3; ☺9am-2.30pm Tue-Sun Jul-Sep; ⊞) A 19th-century building on the edge of Agia Marina, at the start of the climb up to Platanos, holds Leros' small Archaeological Museum. Well-chosen artefacts collected on and around the island trace its varied history and include ancient masks and Byzantine mosaics.

Agios Georgios   BOATING
(☑6945551731, 22470 23060; agiosgeorgios-nl54@gmail.com; cruise incl food & drink €30; ☺departs 11am) Captain Manolis and his boat leave from Agia Marina Harbour, taking in the islands of Arki, Marathi, Arhangelos, Tiganakia, Lipsi and Aspronisia,

Leros

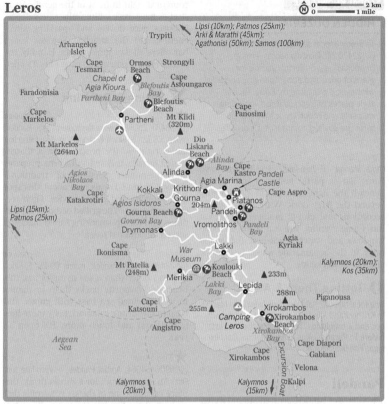

N 0 — 2 km
0 — 1 mile

Trypiti

Lipsi (10km); Patmos (25km);
Arki & Marathi (45km);
Agathonisi (50km); Samos (100km)

Arhangelos
Islet

Cape
Tesmari

Ormos
Beach

Strongyli

Chapel of
Agia Kioura

*Blefoutis
Bay*

Cape
Asfoungaros

Faradonisia

Partheni Bay

Blefoutis
Beach

Cape
Markelos

Partheni

Mt Klidi
(320m)

Cape
Panosimi

Mt Markelos
(264m)

Dio
Liskaria
Beach

*Agios
Nikolaos
Bay*

Cape
Katakrotiri

Alinda

*Alinda
Bay*

Cape
Kastro

*Pandeli
Castle*

Lipsi (15km);
Patmos (25km)

Kokkali

Agios Isidoros

Gourna Bay

Krithoni

Gourna
204m

Agia Marina

Cape Aspro

Platanos

Gourna Beach

Pandeli

Drymonas

Vromolithos

*Pandeli
Bay*

Cape
Ikonisma

*War
Museum*

Lakki

Agia
Kyriaki

Mt Patelia
(248m)

Merikia

Koulouki
Beach

*Lakki
Bay*

Lepida

233m

Kalymnos (20km);
Kos (35km)

288m

Piganousa

Cape
Katsouni

255m

Camping
Leros

Xirokambos

Xirokambos
Beach

*Xirokambos
Bay*

Cape
Angistro

Cape
Diapori

Gabiani

*Aegean
Sea*

Cape
Xirokambos

Velona

Kalymnos
(20km)

Kalymnos
(15km)

Kalpi

Excursion Boat

DODECANESE PLATANOS & AGIA MARINA

allowing you to stop and swim in the best spots (three islands per day; changes daily). Wonderful Greek cuisine served, too. Returns at 7pm.

🛏 Sleeping

There's no accommodation in Agia Marina, and little in Platanos. The closest appealing options are in Pandeli to the south, and Krithoni and Alinda to the north.

Maison des Couleurs   BOUTIQUE HOTEL €€
(📞 22470 23341; www.maisondescouleurs.com; Platanos; r incl breakfast from €130; 🖥) Maison des Couleurs is a delightfully peaceful little hotel set in a nostalgic wine-coloured villa that holds five spacious, high-ceilinged, antique-furnished rooms. Breakfast – and dinner, on request – is served on an idyllic flower-filled terrace. Look for a steep flight of yellow steps just west of the bus stop and taxi rank in Platanos.

🍴 Eating & Drinking

Some of the island's best eating is in Agia Marina and Platanos, whose excellent restaurants are putting the island well and truly on the foodie radar.

⭐ **Taverna Mylos**   SEAFOOD €€
(📞 22470 24894; www.mylosexperience.gr; Agia Marina; mains €12-18; ⊙ 1pm-late; ❄ 🖥 🅿 📶) 🌿
If there's one reason to visit Leros, it's to eat here, one of the best restaurants in the Dodecanese. Run by two passionate and knowledgeable brothers, this charming place is up there on the world's gastronomic scale. It features classic recipes with a modern twist: octopus carpaccio, peppery basil squid, and fabulous seafood pasta. And the setting? Sublime.

The wine list is one of Greece's best. It's beside an old windmill just north of the ferry dock and lapped by turquoise waves.

HIDDEN OUZERIA

To enjoy a local secret, head to O Zotos (☑ 22470 24546; www.osotos-leros.gr; Drymonas), a wonderful *ouzerie* for a glass of ouzo and accompanying snack, whatever is available that day. Tapas-style plates of fresh seafood, including mussels and much (much) more. Don't miss the stuffed calamari if it's on offer.

Faros Bar   BAR
(Agia Marina; ⊙ 7pm-late; 🛜) Tumbledown Faros Bar is partly hollowed into a cave beneath the lighthouse at the promontory beyond the ferry dock. With wall-mounted accordions and dim-lit ambience, it's great fun. Come evening, you can sit by the open windows and watch quicksilver fish swimming in the aquamarine water. Live music and DJs at weekends.

❶ Getting There & Away

One local bus (€2 flat fare) runs from Agia Marina to Krithoni and Alinda, Platanos, Lakki, Xirokambos and Vromolithos. Taxis stop at the rank just before To Paradosiakon in Agia Marina. Car hire signs line the marina.

Pandeli

The village of Pandeli, arrayed around a crescent bay 800m south of Platanos, is pretty, if crowded in summer. Overlooked by a clutch of hilltop windmills, its white houses tumble down the valley towards the sand-and-shingle beach and bobbing fishing boats in the harbour. There are some great tavernas by the water, too.

Sleeping

Studios Happiness   APARTMENT €
(☑ 22470 23498; www.studios-happiness-leros.com; Pandeli; d/studio/apt from €45/55/70; ❄🛜) Very friendly family-run place, perched in colourful gardens beside the road down into Pandeli, 50m up from the beach. Its vibrant white-and-blue studios have kitchenettes, twin beds and private balconies with great sea views. The rooms vary in size and are spotless throughout.

Panteli Beach Hotel   APARTMENT €€
(☑ 22470 26400; www.panteli-beach.gr; Pandeli; studio/apt €100/140; 🅿❄🛜) Pretty, very comfortable complex, arrayed around an open

courtyard right in front of the beach. All 14 studios have fresh white walls, safety deposit boxes, nice duvets and sparkling kitchenettes, and the attached Sorokos beach bar offers all-day sunloungers. Handily, the owner rents scooters and cars, plus it's open all year.

🍴 Eating & Drinking

★ El Greco   SEAFOOD €€
(☑ 22470 25066; www.elgrecoleros.gr; Pandeli; mains €8-12; ⊙ lunch & dinner; ❄🛜) Offering tables right on the beach or on a thatch-roofed terrace, this stylish taverna prepares up-to-the-minute versions of traditional seafood cuisine. Locals rave about this spot for its quality and genial service. Their recommendations? The grilled octopus, the sardines, and the lip-smacking salted mackerel served on buttered toast.

Taverna Psaropoula   TAVERNA €€
(☑ 22470 25200; Pandeli; mains €9-15; ⊙ lunch & dinner) Bluer than a sea nymph's iris, this beachside favourite packs them in thanks to well-executed sea bass with ginger and basil (a favourite), calamari, tasty mezedhes (appetisers) and much more. It's open all year.

★ The View   BAR
(☑ 6906454664; Apitiki, Pandeli; ⊙ 7pm-late Jun-Oct) An ethereal spot for a sunset drink, this place occupies one of the six windmills that sit high above Pandeli. It has a well-stocked bar... and, of course, The View. Service is a little slow and the food definitely isn't the magnet.

Vromolithos

Accessible only by walking or driving over the headland immediately south of Pandeli – there's no coastal footpath – Vromolithos consists of a long, narrow beach caressed by waters of a perfect shade of Aegean blue, scattered with turquoise. Forget the ugly village, this is all about the water.

🍴 Eating & Drinking

★ Dimitris O Karaflas   GREEK €€
(☑ 22470 25626; Marcopoulo, Vromolithos; mains €10-15; ⊙ noon-4pm & 6pm-late; 🛜) The sign says 'O Karaflas', but everyone knows this hilltop eyrie (enjoying one of the best views in the Dodecanese) as 'Bald Dimitri's', after its owner, the head chef. Greek music washes over the terrace, where diners feast on an

DODECANESE PANDELI

array of sea-urchin spaghetti, hearty island sausages, octopus carpaccio, steamed mussels, pork with green apples and plums, and substantial helpings of calamari.

Cafe Del Mar BAR

(☑22470 24766; Vromolithos; ⊙9am-late; 🛜) This superfriendly hillside lounge bar just above the north end of the beach has paradisiacal sea views, chilled pine-shaded patios, white sofas and deckchairs, plus cool tunes and DJs spinning the decks by night. Service can be a bit so-so (it gets busy) but call in any time for drinks and snacks. And don't miss a sunset mojito.

Lakki

Between 1912 and 1948, when the west-coast port of Lakki was a significant Italian naval base, the town was transformed beyond recognition by the construction of grandiose administrative and military buildings and homes for officers. The result is extraordinary. The prevalent architectural style, now classified as streamline moderne, started out resembling art deco and ended up distinctly more fascist. It's worth wandering the streets to view houses (those you might consider contemporary are actually from that period). Otherwise, it's a marina. It's best as a visit, not as a base.

◉ Sights

War Museum MUSEUM

(Map p575; ☑22470 22109; Merikia; €3; ⊙9.30am-1.30pm) Who remembers now that a major WWII battle was fought on this remote little island? After British troops forced the Italians to surrender in September 1943, a massive German air onslaught recaptured the island in the Battle of Leros. A network of tunnels dug by the Italians beneath the woods west of Lakki now serves as a museum, housing countless relics of the conflict. There's an explanatory video.

✖ Eating

★Bakaliko with Tsipouro GREEK €

(Groceries with Spirits; www.bakalikoleros.com; Lakki; mains €5-8; ⊙8am-10pm) Don't be fooled by the unassuming exterior, fronted with red and green wooden chairs and tables. Formerly a grocery store (that was housed across the road), this extraordinary spot is still chock-a-block with delicious food items – from cheeses to meats and useful DIY eats

– plus, it serves hearty plates of traditional cuisine for a song. Dishes change daily.

Petrino GREEK €€

(Lakki; mains €10; ⊙7am-11pm; ❄🛜) 🍷 Hands down the most succulent meat on the island is to be found at smart Petrino. Aside from delicious steaks there's octopus salad, stewed rabbit, and beef in lemon sauce. Like the architecture of Lakki, there's nothing ordinary about this place.

Xirokambos

At the southern end of Leros, Xirokambos Bay holds a pebble-and-sand beach with some good spots for snorkelling. As well as a few village houses, it's home to a good beach taverna and is served by small excursion boats from Kalymnos. Up the hill, 1km inland towards Lakki, a signposted path climbs to the ruined Paleokastro fortress, which offers tremendous views.

🛏 Sleeping & Eating

Camping Leros CAMPGROUND €

(Map p575; ☑6944238490, 22470 23372; www.campingleros.com; Xirokambos; camp sites adult/tent €8/4; ⊙Jun-Sep) Set 500m up from the beach, and 3km south of Lakki, the island's lovely campground stands in a 400-year-old olive grove and holds a welcoming cafe that puts on evening barbecues. There are plenty of pitches shaded by said olive trees. It's also a centre for scuba diving, and owner Panos offers CMAS-certified week-long open-water courses (€500).

To Aloni TAVERNA €

(☑22470 26048; Xirokambos; mains €9-15; ⊙lunch & dinner; 🅿❄🛜♿) You can't miss this prominent taverna literally so close to the sea it adds a little salt seasoning to your octopus croquettes, shrimp *saganaki* (shrimp in fried cheese), swordfish, lobster, or liver in wine sauce. Dine at tables al fresco or within its pleasant interior. Great desserts, too, if you have room.

Krithoni & Alinda
Κριθώνι & Αλιντα

POP 750

Starting just beyond the first headland north of Agia Marina, the twin resorts of Krithoni and Alinda sit next to each other on Alinda Bay, running parallel to the beach and bordered by *kafeneia* and restaurants. Leros' longest beach is at Alinda – although narrow, it's shaded and sandy with clean, shallow water. Set just back from the sea, a poignant war cemetery holds British casualties from the 1943 Battle of Leros.

For the best sun-worshipping in these parts, continue through Krithoni and Alinda to **Dio Liskaria Beach** (a few minutes' scooter ride). Bookended by rocks and with its own taverna, it's lapped by aquamarine waves.

◉ Sights

Historic & Folklore Museum MUSEUM
(☑22470 24775; Alinda; €3; ◷9am-1pm & 6-8pm Tue-Sun) Housed in an incongruous castellated villa on the seafront, this museum covers several aspects of local history. The upstairs rooms are given over largely to weapons, helmets and photos relating to WWII, while downstairs you'll find displays of traditional costumes and an emotive gallery devoted to artworks created by political prisoners incarcerated on the island during the colonels' dictatorship of the 1960s and 1970s.

🛏 Sleeping

★To Archontiko Angelou HOTEL €€
(☑6944908182, 22470 22749; www.hotel-angelou-leros.com; Alinda; r incl breakfast from €95; ⓟ🛜) ✈ Spilling with oleander and jacaranda, this incurably romantic, 19th-century rose-coloured villa, five minutes' walk from the beach, is like stepping into a vintage Italian film, with wooden floors, Viennese frescoes, antique beds and old-world-style rooms. Breakfast on the sun-dappled terrace is divine: a mouthwatering array of homemade bread, cheeses and gourmet treats. One of the finest hotels in the Dodecanese.

To Archontiko Angelou is big on healthy (and very good) eating, including vegetarian, vegan, dairy- and gluten-free dining as well.

Hotel Alinda HOTEL €€
(☑22470 23266; www.alindahotel-leros.gr; Alinda; s/d incl breakfast €40/60; 🛜) The very pleasant rooms in this beachfront hotel have private balconies, some of which look out across the leafy rear garden and others, over the coast road to the bay. They vary in size, but all are spotless with comfy beds and tea-making facilities. The charming owners also run a good on-site Greek restaurant.

History buffs will enjoy the fact that it's the oldest hotel on Leros, yet it maintains a beautifully preserved old-school, 'modern' style.

Nefeli Hotel APARTMENT €€
(☑22470 24611; www.nefelihotels.com; Krithoni; studio/apt incl breakfast from €90/125; ⓟ❄🛜) Run by friendly Eva, Nefeli has lovely sugar-white apartments with vividly coloured lavender and pink trim. These are beautifully finished spaces with stone floors, gleaming kitchens, moulded-stone couches and swallow-you-up beds. All have private balconies and there's a tempting cafe in the herb-fragrant courtyard. It's 10 minutes' walk beyond the northern edge of Agia Marina.

🍴 Eating & Drinking

Prima Plora SEAFOOD €€
(☑22470 26122; Alinda; mains €8-12; ◷lunch & dinner) While Leros offers more gourmet dining options elsewhere, this casual eatery in Alinda, with large indoor and gorgeous outdoor areas on the beach, will satisfy hungry souls craving seafood and Greek mezedhes (appetisers). The very garlicky carrot salad with a Thai zing is recommended.

Nemesis Cafe BAR
(☑22470 22070; Krithoni; ◷10am-late; 🛜) There's piping jazz and happy vibes at this well-stocked waterfront bar with a nautical theme. Perfect spot for a sundowner.

❶ Getting There & Away

The island's bus (€2 flat fare) passes through Alinda and travels the island, including to Xirokambos, Lakki and Agia Marina.

PATMOS ΠΑΤΜΟΣ

POP 3040

Patmos has a bewitchingly spiritual feel about it. That's not surprising given that it was here, in a cave, that exiled St John received the apocalyptic visions that formed sinister Revelations in the Bible. Pilgrims from around the world visit St John's cave and the island's monasteries, especially in the whitewashed, labyrinthine sanctity of hilltop Hora. Other visitors, too, from movie stars to holidaymakers, head to this hourglass-shaped island for its beautiful villages, including the picturesque harbour community of Skala, plus barely disturbed bays lined with sand and pebble beaches, and gorgeous pine- and heather-coated hillsides. The lack of an airport has protected the

Patmos

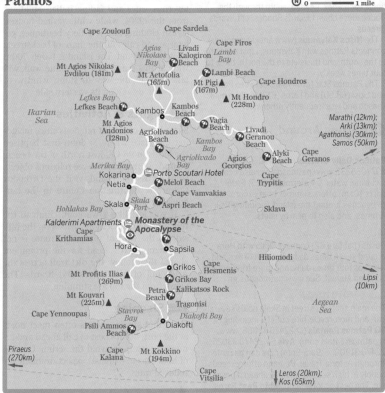

Cape Zouloufi
Cape Sardela
Cape Firos
Agios Nikolaos Bay
Livadi Kalogiron Beach
Lambi Bay
Mt Agios Nikolas Evdilou (181m)
Mt Aetofolia (165m)
Lambi Beach
Cape Hondros
Mt Pigi (167m)
Lefkes Bay
Lefkes Beach
Kambos
Kambos Beach
Mt Hondro (228m)
Ikarian Sea
Mt Agios Andonios (128m)
Agriolivado Beach
Vagia Beach
Livadi Geranou Beach
Marathi (12km); Arki (13km); Agathonisi (30km); Samos (50km)
Kambos Bay
Agriolivado Bay
Agios Georgios
Alyki Beach
Cape Geranos
Merika Bay
Kokarina
Porto Scoutari Hotel
Netia
Meloï Beach
Cape Trypitis
Skala
Skala Port
Aspri Beach
Hohlakas Bay
Cape Vamvakias
Sklava
Kalderimi Apartments
Cape Krithamias
Monastery of the Apocalypse
Hora
Sapsila
Hiliomodi
Lipsi (10km)
Mt Profitis Ilias (269m)
Grikos
Cape Hesmenis
Grikos Bay
Kalikatsos Rock
Mt Kouvari (225m)
Petra Beach
Tragonisi
Aegean Sea
Cape Yennoupas
Stavros Bay
Diakofti Bay
Psili Ammos Beach
Diakofti
Piraeus (270km)
Cape Kalana
Mt Kokkino (194m)
Cape Vitsilia
Leros (20km); Kos (65km)

0 — 2 km
0 — 1 mile

island from mass tourism; there is a calmness here that is reflected in the locals, who are as hospitable and friendly as they come.

History

St John the Divine was banished to Patmos by the pagan Roman Emperor Domitian in 95 CE. Living as a hermit in a cave above what's now Skala, St John heard the voice of God issuing from a cleft in the rock and transcribed his terrifying visions as the Book of Revelation where he 'saw a beast rise up out of the sea, having seven heads and 10 horns...'. From these events Patmos became known as the 'Holy Island' or, less appealingly, 'the island of the Apocalypse'.

Around 1000 years later, in 1088, the Byzantine Emperor Alexis I Komninos gave the Blessed Christodoulos permission to erect a monastery in John's memory. Pirate raids necessitated powerful fortifications, so the monastery took the form of a mighty hilltop castle. In the centuries that followed, Patmos

became a semi-autonomous monastic state and achieved such wealth and influence that it was able to resist Turkish oppression.

ℹ️ Information

Both www.patmos-island.com and www.patmosweb.gr provide copious information. You can also pick up a free copy of the pocket-sized *Patmos Guide* and the larger *Patmostimes Guide* in shops and hotels.

The Municipal Tourist Office (p582) has useful tips on things to see and do on the island.

ℹ️ Getting There & Away

All Patmos ferries dock in Skala. Almost daily Dodekanisos Seaways (p515) catamarans connect Patmos with Lipsi (€13.50, 1½ hours), Leros (€17, two hours), Kalymnos (€28, three hours), Kos (€15.50 to €20.50, three to four hours), Rhodes (€49, 5½ hours) and other islands to the south. Once a week there is a service between Arki (€14, 20 minutes) and Agathonisi (€16, one hour).

Blue Star Ferries (p515) also calls in several times each week, heading south through the Dodecanese chain towards Rhodes, or towards Piraeus.

The **Nisos Kalymnos** (www.anekalymnou.gr) connects Patmos with Kalymnos, Lipsi and Leros to the south, and the islets to the north, three to four times weekly.

The Patmos Star (p574) sails between Patmos and Lipsi (€8.50) and Leros (€12), daily in peak season and less frequently otherwise.

ⓘ Getting Around

BOAT

Patmos Daily Cruises (☑22470 31425, 6977035231; www.patmosdailycruises.com; incl wine, water & watermelon €25; ⊙departs 10am) offers summer boat excursions to beaches around the island, including Psili Ammos, and also to nearby islets.

BUS

Buses (flat fare €2) connect Skala with Hora around seven times daily, and with Grikos and Kambos four times daily, and more frequently in July and August. See www.patmosbus.gr.

CAR & MOTORCYCLE

The main seafront street in Skala holds several car- and motorcycle-hire outlets, including **TG Patmos Rentals** (☑22470 32066; www.tgpatmosrentals.com). **Avis** (☑22470 33025, 22470 31900; ⊙9am-9pm) cars can be rented through Astoria Travel. Demand often exceeds supply in high season, so book ahead if possible. The best scooter shop, **Moto Rent Faros** (☑22470 34400; www.patmos-motorentfaros. com; ⊙8am-8.30pm), is behind the harbour on the road to Hora, and has quick, regularly serviced bikes (plus cars).

TAXI

You can catch a **taxi** (☑22470 31225) from Skala's taxi rank, opposite the police station. Fares are around €6.50 to Grikos, €8.50 to Kampos Beach, and €12 to Lambi Beach. Add an extra €2 if you book ahead.

Skala   Σκάλα

POP 3000

Skala, Patmos' photogenic ferry port, is set on a huge bay on the eastern shore of the island. Apart from those moments when mighty cruise ships suddenly obliterate the entire harbour like a giant Monty Python foot, it's a laid-back little place. There's even a tiny patch of sandy beach – albeit covered with restaurant tables – a few hundred metres from the dock.

Skala's waterfront is an unbroken string of tavernas, cafes and fading Italian buildings from the 1930s, while whitewashed houses, stylish clothing and jewellery boutiques, geletaria, and cafes fill the maze of backstreets stretching inland. The island is barely 700m wide at this point, so a 10-minute walk will take you all the way to stony, windswept Hohlakas Beach on its western side.

⊙ Sights & Activities

Skala has a couple of religious sites, including the place where St John first baptised the locals in 96 CE, just north of the beach. To find out more and to see religious objects from across the island, visit the Orthodox Culture & Information Centre in the harbourside church.

If you feel like a workout, climb to the remains of an ancient acropolis on the hillside to the west of town. The route is not well signposted – head for the prominent chapel then follow the dirt trail across the fields full of wildflowers and lizards. The views from the top are stunning.

🛌 Sleeping

Hotel and studio owners often meet boats at the port, but it's best to call ahead and arrange a pickup to avoid the scrum. Outside of high season (August) expect dramatically reduced rates.

★**Byzance Hotel**   HOTEL €€
(☑22470 31052; www.byzancehotel.gr; d/tr from €70/90, studio/apt from €80/110; ❄🐕) This lovely, freshly renovated hotel offers light and airy rooms, each decorated in chic style. There are also studios and apartments (with kitchenettes). A pleasant roof terrace offers excellent views and breakfast is in a charming, more traditional-style dining room. Its location, a block back from the waterfront, is superb, a stone's throw from the ferry. Fabulous value.

Kalderimi Apartments   BOUTIQUE HOTEL €€
(Map p579; ☑22470 33008, 6972008757; www.kalderimi.com; apt incl breakfast €120; ⊙late May–early Oct; ❄🐕) This inland whitewashed place south of Skala on a road just past the football stadium is pure tranquillity, with a shaded courtyard overflowing with palms, bougainvillea and Moorish lanterns. The five spacious apartments (with kitchens) have a traditional feel, featuring wooden beams and stone walls. Prices are significantly lower outside high season.

Captain's House
HOTEL €€

(☑22470 31793; www.captains-house.gr; d/ste incl breakfast €70/120; ❄ ☎ ✉) This pleasant long-standing wharfside digs has white, airy rooms; five have their own sea-facing balconies. There's also a small swimming pool out back with sunloungers, along with a great front-facing breakfast terrace. It's in a fabulous location, a mere 100m walk left from the quay as you leave the ferry.

🍴 Eating

Tzivaeri
MEZEDHES €

(☑22470 31170; mezedhes €6-15, mains €8-17; ☺dinner) Skala's best option for a romantic feast spreads over a balcony terrace and elegant interior at the north end of the harbour. Cretan dishes are the raved-about 'go' here so it makes a memorable stop for Cretan-style sardines, shrimp or octopus, though you can also get a burger or souvlaki. It's the prime full-moon viewing spot, too.

★ To Tsipouradiko Mas
MEZEDHES €€

(☑22470 32803; tapas €6-15; ☺lunch & dinner) Three words: do not miss. This wonderful spot, named for small dishes (though not traditionally a *tsipouradiko*, where the spirit is served with appetisers), has tables on the beach, a can-do attitude, and some of the island's best cuisine. The caramelised octopus with *fava* is worth coming for alone. We won't say more so as not to spoil the surprise.

Pantelis
TAVERNA €€

(☑22470 31230; mains €8-16; ☺lunch & dinner) Pantelis is one of Patmos' long-standing tavernas, as the blue-and-white decor and vinyl-covered menus attest. But locals and visitors alike pack around tables on the narrow pedestrian street that runs parallel to the port. You can get standard Greek staples, but you can also be adventurous with the likes of smoky sea-urchin salad or the *fouskes* (sea figs – definitely an acquired taste).

Chiliomodi
TAVERNA €€

(☑22470 34179; mains €12; ☺lunch & dinner) Chiliomodi has been keeping locals and travellers happy for nearly three decades and, thanks to the fisherman-owner, is synonymous with the freshest of fresh mouthwatering sea bream, salted cod and various mezedhes to name a few. Its entrance is 50m along the road to Hora.

🍷 Drinking & Nightlife

★ Art Café
BAR

(☑22470 33092; ☺7pm-late; ☎) Escape the harbour hubbub by climbing to a fabulous panoramic roof terrace then blissing out over sunset cocktails (€7 to €9) amid plump pillows and white-cushioned benches. The friendly German owner also serves great homemade hummus and there's often live music in the indoor lounge below.

Arion
BAR

(☑22470 31595; snacks €3-6; ☺7.30am-late; ☎) Over 100 years old, this venerable, high-raftered, wood-panelled bar, at the heart of the waterfront, is a major local landmark and rendezvous point. Travellers generally prefer to sit outside, watching the world and the waves go by as they hook up to the wi-fi. Snacks include toasties and crêpes.

Meltemi
CAFE

(☑22470 31839; ☺9am-late; ☎) Irresistible beach bar at the far end of the harbour that curves 400m north from the ferry dock. Sit on the sand savouring a cocktail as the

---

ST JOHN THE DIVINE & THE APOCALYPSE

A great deal of confusion and uncertainty surrounds the Book of Revelation. But don't worry, it's not the end of the world. Well, maybe some of it is – the bits about the Four Horsemen of the Apocalypse, the Battle of Armageddon and the final defeat of Satan, say – but biblical scholars broadly agree that Revelation should in fact be read as a denunciation of the era in which its author lived.

St John experienced his Revelation on Patmos at the end of the 1st century CE, making it too late for him to have been either John the Evangelist, the author of the Gospel according to St John, or John the Apostle, or John the Baptist. Instead he was simply a wandering Jewish/Christian prophet of whom very little is known, though he has acquired the titles of John the Divine, John the Revelator, John the Theologian and, most simply of all, John of Patmos. His actual Revelation took the form of a letter to seven Christian churches in Asia Minor, condemning the Roman subjugation under which they then suffered and predicting an imminent apocalypse in which the Roman Empire would be swept away.

WORTH A TRIP

ISLAND ESCAPES

Three quiet, tiny islands – Agathonisi, Arki and Marathi – are not exactly on the radar of many travellers. Yet arriving at these places is pure magic. With small permanent populations, there's little to do but read, swim and explore the caves where islanders once hid from pirates... and then do it again! As for other visitors? Expect an eclectic mix of yachties, artists and the occasional backpacker.

On Agathonisi, the port village of Agios Georgios, the island's primary settlement, holds a few tavernas and simple sugar-cube pensions. There are some lovely little beaches, including Spilia Beach, 900m southwest beyond the headland, and Gaïdouravlakos, where water from one of the island's few springs meets the sea. There's also Tsangari Beach, Tholos Beach and Poros Beach, the only sandy option. You can trek 1.5km uphill to Megalo Horio, site of several summer festivals, close to the eponymous church.

Elsewhere, Arki (with around 50 inhabitants) and Marathi, just north of Patmos and Lipsi and the largest of Arki's satellite islets, are the most peaceful islets in the Dodecanese chain.

On Arki, you can poke around the Church of Metamorfosis that stands on a hill behind the settlement, or laze on several sandy coves that can be reached along a path skirting the north side of the bay. Marathi has a superb sandy beach. The old settlement, with an immaculate little church, stands on a hill above the harbour. While only several people remain on Marathi year-round, local families return each summer to reopen tavernas. If you decide to stay, take your luck at the few informal *domatia* (rooms) attached to the tavernas.

Ferries stop once a week at Arki, but not Marathi, as they sail up and down the island chain, calling at Patmos, Leros, Lipsi and Agathonisi, Samos (and back). Dodekanisos Seaways (p530) catamarans do the circuit between Arki and Patmos (€14, 20 minutes), Leros (€17, 1¼ hours), Lipsi (€13.50, 50 minutes) and Agathonisi (€14, 30 minutes). Nisos Kalymnos (www.anekalymnou.gr) starts from Kalymnos, three to four times weekly. Leros Express (p555) heads to Arki twice a week (via Patmos or Lipsi). In summer, Lipsi-based excursion boats and Patmos-based caïques offer frequent day trips (around €25) to Arki and Marathi. For Marathi, a local caïque runs from Arki several times a week.

sun sinks into the sea, or come earlier for breakfast, a midday sandwich, fruit salad or milkshake under the shade of a tamarisk tree.

ℹ Information

Apollon Travel (☑ 22470 31324; www.apollon travel.gr; ☺ 8am-11pm) and **Astoria Travel** (☑ 22470 31205; www.astoriatravel.com; ☺ 9am-late), both centrally located on the waterfront, are the best outlets for ferry tickets, along with tours, plus other practical aspects of visiting Patmos.

Municipal Tourist Office (☑ 22470 31666; ☺ 9.30am-2pm Mon-Fri, 6-9pm daily except Wed & Sun) Shares the same building as the post office and police station.

ℹ Getting There & Away

Buses leave almost hourly for Hora between around 8am and 9pm, while less regular buses

service Grikos and Kambos (flat fare €2). See www.patmosbus.gr. for seasonal schedules.

Hora $X\acute{\omega}\rho\alpha$

POP 800

With gorgeous views of the island from its hilltop eyrie, enchanting Hora is more than just a whitewashed mountain settlement. As you wander its incense-scented warren of 17th-century houses, wind gusting through the alleys, the Boschian forms of St John's demons scuttling behind in your imagination, it's easy to see why Hora draws people back again and again. Allegedly there are more monasteries per square metre here in Hora than anywhere else in the world. Aside from the sanctity of the place there are some boutiques selling fine clothes and jewellery, and a couple of interesting galleries and upscale bars.

◉ Sights

★ Monastery of the Apocalypse
MONASTERY

(Cave of the Apocalypse; Map p579; ☑22470 31398; €2; ☺8am-1.30pm daily, plus 4-7pm Tue & Sat, 4-6pm Sun) Nestled amid the pines halfway to Hora, the Monastery of the Apocalypse focuses on the cave where St John lived as a hermit and received his revelation. Pilgrims and less-than-devout cruise passengers alike stream into the chapel built over the recess to see the rocky pillow where the saint rested his head, the handhold with which he'd haul himself up from his prayers and the stone slab that served as his writing desk.

★ Monastery of St John the Theologian
MONASTERY

(☑22470 31223; €4; ☺8am-1.30pm daily, plus 4-7pm Tue & Sat, 4-6pm Sun) As this immense 11th-century monastery-cum-fortress remains active, only a small portion is open to visitors. The entrance courtyard leads to a sumptuously frescoed chapel, fronted by marble columns taken from an ancient temple. Don't expect to attend a service; daily worship is at 3am! The museum of church treasures upstairs displays the original edict establishing the monastery, signed by the Byzantine emperor in 1088.

Holy Monastery of Zoödohos Pigi
CONVENT

(☑22470 31991; ☺9am-1pm daily) FREE The Orthodox convent known as the Holy Monastery of Zoödohos Pigi is tucked away in the back alleys of Hora. You can't go beyond its pretty little courtyard, where a small church holds remarkable 17th-century frescoes. One of the 40 resident nuns will cheerfully point out Jesus on Judgement Day dispatching assorted bishops and clerics down a river of fire that flows into the maw of the beast.

⊨ Sleeping & Eating

There is one restaurant in Hora's central square, while tavernas on the approach to St John's Monastery offer spectacular views.

Archontariki
B&B €€€

(☑22470 29368; www.archontariki-patmos.gr; ste €200; ☺Easter–Oct; ✲⊛) Hidden in a little alley near the Zoödohos Pigi monastery, these heavenly suites in a 400-year-old home are equipped with every convenience, traditional furnishings and plenty of plush touches. Relaxing under the fruit trees in the cool,

quiet garden courtyard, you'll never want to leave. Suites 'Wisdom' and 'Joy' are spacious, while 'Love' and 'Hope' are smaller, traditional split-level affairs.

★ Pantheon
GREEK €

(☑22470 31226; mains €7-14; ☺5pm-midnight; ✲☑) Look for the octopus drying outside – hence its local moniker 'the octopus place'. This whitewashed belle with Aegean-blue chairs and soaring village views offers pure Greek fare at its best, including seafood, meatballs, and homemade sweets. Located in the 'restaurant strip', on the approach to the Monastery of St John the Theologian.

Jimmy's Balcony
GREEK €

(☑22470 32115; mains €9-15; ☺10am-11pm; ⊛☑) Perched above the road, on the principal lane through the village to the Monastery of the Apocalypse, the shaded terrace of this welcoming all-day cafe-restaurant commands regal views across Skala to the islands to the north. Drop in for a cooling drink, or to enjoy its decent salads, *mousakas* and veggie dishes.

Vaggelis
TAVERNA €€

(☑22470 31967; Plateia Agias Lesvias; mains €9-15; ☺lunch & dinner; ⊛⊛) With chi-chi chairs and tables, Vaggelis sits in one of the most intimate squares in the world. At the time of research it was changing ownership back to the original management; the menu is to be tested. Regardless of the cuisine, the setting is gorgeous: sit in the atmospheric square itself, or for jaw-dropping views, under the carob tree in the garden out back.

ⓘ Getting There & Away

While Hora is easily reached by road, it's much more atmospheric to hike up through the woods. Following the Byzantine footpath, signposted off the road roughly 10 minutes up from Skala, takes around 40 sweaty minutes. Allow extra time to stop off at the Monastery of the Apocalypse en route. A public bus heads to Hora around seven times daily (€2 flat fare); see www.patmosbus.gr.

North of Skala

The most popular and readily accessible beach in northern Patmos is wide, sandy **Kambos Beach**, which lies 5km northeast of Skala, just downhill from the village of Kambos. Crowded with local families in summer, it's a perfect spot for kids, with safe swimming and plenty of water-based activities.

Remoter and, with luck, quieter beaches can be reached by driving a little further. Fork inland (left) immediately after Kambos Beach and you'll soon find yourself winding down green slopes to Lambi Beach, an impressive expanse of multicoloured pebbles on the north shore. Stick to the coast road east of Kambos Beach, on the other hand, to reach Vagia Beach, a sheltered little cove that offers good snorkelling in the island's coldest though highest-visibility water, and beyond it the pebbled, tamarisk-shaded and stunningly turquoise-laced Livadi Geranou Beach, where a tiny whitewashed chapel beckons from the islet just offshore.

🏃 Activities

Kambos Beach Watersports
WATER SPORTS

(☑ 6972123541; www.patmoswatersports.com; Kambos Beach; 🚗) For over 35 years, friendly Andreas, the owner, has rented out watersports gear. You can go wakeboarding (€50 per hour) and waterskiing (€50 for 15 minutes), set loose on a pedalo or kayak (€5 for 30 minutes), get your abs going on a stand-up paddleboard or for the less athletically inclined, simply rent a sunlounger (€15 per day).

🛏 Sleeping & Eating

Porto Scoutari Hotel
HOTEL €€

(Map p579; ☑ 22470 33123; www.portoscoutari. com; d incl breakfast €100-250; 🅿🌸🛜🏊) Focused around a lavish swimming pool and spa centre, this was the first luxe hotel on the island and in many ways is still among the most unique, if just *ever*-so-slightly tired. It surveys the Aegean from a rural spot, 600m from Meloi Beach and 3km north of Skala. Enjoy palace-sized rooms with stylish antiques, spotless bathrooms, private balconies and antique beds plus, above all, stunning sea views. Check for amazing low-season rates.

George's Place
CAFE €

(☑ 22470 31881; Kambos Beach; snacks €7-12; ⏱ breakfast & lunch; 🅿🌸🛜🚗) 🌿 Superchilled, long-standing beach bar, accessed straight off Kambos Beach sand, with an enticingly shaded, sun-dappled terrace facing the peacock-blue bay. Easy tunes, wi-fi, toilets that can double as changing rooms, and a simple menu of salads, homemade pies, chocolate cake, milkshakes and pastries keep the regulars happy.

Livadi Geranou Taverna
TAVERNA €

(☑ 22470 32046; Livadi Geranou Beach; mains €9-12; ⏱ 10am-late) With its flower-bedecked terrace perched on the heather-clad hillside at road's end, a few metres above the beach, this blue-trimmed taverna draws the crowds with its heavenly sea views. Feast on a seafood spread of whitebait and octopus, or opt for a simple platter of meatballs or souvlakia.

Cafe Vagia
CAFE €

(Vagia; mains €3-6; ⏱ 9am-7pm) Located a few hundred metres above Vagia Beach, this friendly little cafe, set in garden surrounds and run by the lovely Eftichia, is great for homemade pies, salads and cakes, and a pick-me-up coffee after a morning's sun worshipping.

Lambi Fish Tavern
TAVERNA €

(☑ 22470 31490; Lambi Beach; mains €8.50-16; ⏱ lunch & dinner; 🅿🌸🚗) Idyllic 'so-this-is-island-Greece' setting with tree-shaded tables propped up amid the beach pebbles and the waves almost lapping at your feet. The reliable no-frills local menu includes salted mackerel, stuffed vine leaves, and octopus cooked in wine.

Leonidas
TAVERNA €€

(Lambi; mains €12-15; ⏱ lunch & dinner Jun-Sep; 🅿🌸🖉) 🌿 Sitting on the crest of the hill overlooking Lambi Beach, Leonidas has a flower-filled terrace with food to match the serene view. Dine on souvlakia, *stifadho* (meat, game or seafood stew) and calf's liver, as well as the catch of the day. It's open for a blink-or-you'll-miss them two or three high season months.

South of Skala

The southern half of Patmos is scattered with small, tree-filled valleys and picturesque beaches. The first settlement south of Skala is tiny, peaceful Sapsila. Grikos, 1km further along over the hill, has a sandy(ish) beach that holds a handful of tavernas and is dominated by a plush resort hotel. St John is believed to have baptised islanders here during the 1st century CE, at a spot now marked by the chapel of Agios Ioannis Theologos.

South again, Petra Beach is peaceful and has plenty of shade, while a spit leads out to the startling Kalikatsos Rock. Both a rough coastal track from the beach and a longer paved road from Hora continue as far as Diakofti, the island's southernmost community. From there, a demanding half-hour hiking trail scrambles over the rocky hillside to reach the fine, tree-shaded stretch of sand known as Psili Ammos Beach, which holds a seasonal taverna. It's bewitchingly pretty and utterly isolated; if you've got kids with you, it's safer for you to hire a boat from Skala to get here.

🛏 Sleeping & Eating

Mathios Studios   APARTMENT €€

(☑ 22470 32583; www.studiosmathios.gr; Sapsila; studio/apt €75/90; ❄ @ ☎) Located 2.5km south of Skala in sleepy Sapsila, Mathios has five studios and two apartments. All are equipped with kitchenettes. The style is rustic-chic complemented by quirky driftwood sculptures scattered about the grounds, and the balconies afford lush views of the sparkling blue bay below. The owners do their best to make you feel at home.

Patmos Aktis Suites   DESIGN HOTEL €€€

(☑ 22470 32800; www.patmosaktis.gr/en; Grikos Bay; r from €260; 🅿 ❄ ☎ ☀) Sitting incongruously upon Grikos Beach, Patmos' ultraluxe design hotel leaps from a David Hockney painting with its sleek geometric aesthetic and cube-white suites. Expect rain showers and private terraces leading to a swimming pool metres from your bed. A high-end restaurant serves up contemporary Greek food, plus facilities range from massage treatments in the sumptuous spa to a gym and boutique.

★ Ktima Petra   TAVERNA €€

(☑ 22470 33207; Petra Beach; mains €6.50-12; ⊙ lunch & dinner; 🚗) 🌿 For one of Patmos' wholesome and genuine foodie experiences, don't miss this winner, located at Petra Beach. The setting – under a shaded terrace overlooking a vegetable garden – is idyllic. The restaurant, run by two hard-working brothers, sources its vegetables from their own adjoining plots. The result? Fabulous fresh and hearty traditional Greek cuisine.

It's worth a special trip here, but is equally walkable from the nearby Grikos Beach.

Benetos   MEDITERRANEAN €€

(☑ 22470 33089; www.benetosrestaurant.com; Sapsila; mains €10-28; ⊙ 7.30pm-late Tue-Sun Jun-Sep; 🚗) 🌿 Dropping down to the sea from the coast road, a couple of kilometres southeast of Skala, this romantic boutique restaurant and tapas bar is set on a working farm. The menu draws its inspiration from all over the Mediterranean, with dishes such as stuffed zucchini blossoms with turmeric sauce, octopus confit with eggplant salad, and calamari with red-pepper sauce. It's only open for several months, however.

LIPSI   ΛΕΙΨΟΙ

POP 800

Lipsi might be tiny, at just 8km in length and with a permanent population of 800 (all of whom live in Lipsi Village), but what a powerful impact it has on the traveller, with its low-slung harbour bunched with crayon-yellow nets and the whitewashed, church-crowned village of Lipsi climbing the slope behind. If rugged hills, serene blue coves and deserted beaches are what you seek, you may have just found heaven. In the *Odyssey*, Lipsi was where the nymph Calypso waylaid Odysseus for several years. Abandon yourself to sun-worshipping and wandering the backstreets, and you may fare the same.

Check, too, the local speciality, *myzithra* cheese, made from goat's milk and seawater, and pick up a jar of distinctive thyme honey. The island even has its own winery, so enjoy a tipple.

❶ Getting There & Away

Lipsi has frequent connections with its neighbours. Dodekanisos Seaways (p515) catamarans head north to Arki (€13.50, 50 minutes), Agathonisi (€13.50, 1½ hours) and Samos (€32, two hours), and south to Patmos (€13.50, 30 minutes), Leros (€15, 30 minutes to 1½ hours), Kos (€29, two to three hours) and other islands. Twice a week, Blue Star Ferries (p515) heads to Patmos (€6.50, 30 minutes) and Leros (€7, 40 minutes). The **Nisos Kalymnos** (www. anekalymnou.gr) runs to Patmos, Leros and the islets to the north four times weekly, while the Patmos Star (p574) sails to both Patmos and Leros, daily in summer. Leros Express (p555) sails from Leros to Lipsi, Patmos, Arki, Agathonisi and Samos, plus has twice weekly trips to Kalymnos and Kos.

A small **office** (☑ 22470 41141; ⊙ 9.30am-3.30pm) on the ferry jetty sells all boat tickets.

❶ Getting Around

Ferries arrive at Lipsi's small port in front of the town. Frequent buses connect Lipsi Village with the main island beaches in summer. There is also one **taxi** (☑ 6942409679, 6942428223). Hire scooters and bicycles in Lipsi Village from **George Rental** (☑ 6942409679; www.motorentlipsi. com; bike/scooter/car per day from €7/12/35).

Lipsi

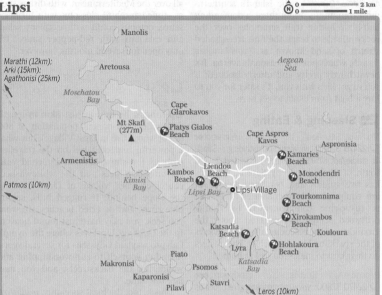

Manolis

Marathi (12km);
Arki (15km);
Agathonisi (25km)

Aretousa

*Aegean
Sea*

*Moschatou
Bay*

Cape
Glarokavos

Mt Skafi
(277m)

Platys Gialos
Beach

Cape Aspros
Kavos

Aspronisia

Cape
Armenistis

Liendou
Beach

Kamaries
Beach

Kambos
Beach

Monodendri
Beach

Patmos (10km)

*Kimisi
Bay*

Lipsi Bay

Lipsi Village

Tourkornnima
Beach

Katsadia
Beach

Xirokambos
Beach

Kouloura

Piato

Lyra

Hohlakoura
Beach

Makronisi

Psomos

*Katsadia
Bay*

Kaparonisi

Stavri

Pilavi

Leros (10km)

Lipsi Village   Λειψοί

POP 800

Hugging the deep harbour, Lipsi Village – the island's only settlement – is a cosy, intimate affair, with an atmospheric old town of blue-shuttered houses radiating up the hill in a tangle of alleyways. The harbour is the hub of the action and there's everything you need here, from an ATM and a great bakery, to delectable seafood restaurants. Be sure to visit the beautiful blue-domed church of Agios Ioannis Theologos, with its panoramic harbour-view terrace.

The closest beach to the village, Liendou Beach is a couple of minutes' walk north of the ferry port over a small headland. It's a narrow strip of sand, washed by calm, shallow water.

🏃 Activities

Rena Five Island Cruise   BOATING
(☑ 6947339141; www.facebook.com/pg/Rena5 IslandCruise; adult/child €28/14; ⊙ Jun-Oct; 🖼) Sailing since 1980, *Rena,* a traditional wooden caïque, offers summer excursions from Lipsi's smaller jetty to islets Aspronisia, Makronisi (with their sapphire waters and weird rock formations), and Tiganakia, Marathi and Arki, for a picnic and swim.

🛌 Sleeping

⭐Michalis Studios   APARTMENT €
(☑ 22470 41266, 6977906978; www.lipsimichalis. eu; studio €60-65) One of the best budget deals around, each of these simple, spacious studios comes with a kitchenette and small balcony. Rooms don't have direct sea views, but instead, face over a field and small church, and it's convenient to everything. As the island's former postmaster, the delightful and generous-hearted owner, Michalis, knows everyone and everything about the island. Italian speaking, too.

It's conveniently located next to the town's popular bakery-cafe. Prices are significantly reduced outside high season.

⭐Nefeli Hotel   APARTMENT €€
(☑ 22470 41120; www.lipsinefelihotel.com; studio/ apt incl breakfast €90/160; P ❋ 🛜) This stylish, welcoming boutique hotel sits in splendid isolation above lovely Kambos Beach, 10 minutes' walk northwest of the village. The apartments are spacious, with comfy beds, kitchenettes, sofa beds and private sea-view patios. Prepare to be lulled to sleep by the call of owls. There's also an opulent bar, lounge and dining area, bedecked in a variety of purples.

Angela Studios APARTMENT €€

(☑ 6983666611, 22470 41177; www.lipsiangela.eu; Waterfront; studio/apt from €70/80; ❄ 🛜) Angela has wrought-iron beds, sparkling kitchenettes with fridge and microwave, and a spic-'n'-span feel to the individual studios. Add to this balconies with sea views and a delicious little cafe and you need look no further. Close to the ferry dock.

✕ Eating

Kairis Lipsi Bakery Shop BAKERY €

(☑ 22470 41050; sweets €1-3; ⊘ 24hr; ❄ 🛜 💺) Chances are you'll find yourself here, at this lively bakery-gelateria-cafe, on the western side of the waterfront; it's the social hub of the island and stays open all night. It's a veritable treasure trove of fresh-baked cookies, savoury items, alcohol and some very fancy Greek sweets including baklava. Fight your way through the locals for a seat.

★Kalypso SEAFOOD €€

(☑ 22470 41241; mains €8-12; ⊘ lunch & dinner; ❄ 🛜) 🍴 Chef/owner Nicolas cooks up a culinary storm at this gorgeous spot. He uses only organic vegetables (from his own farm or personally sourced elsewhere), plus fresh fish and meat. The picks? The fish soup and the *katsikaki* (stuffed goat), though you can't go wrong. Blue and olive-green chairs dot the shaded terrace and there's a pleasant indoor area, too.

★Manolis Tastes TAVERNA €€

(☑ 22470 41065; www.manolistastes.com; mains €8-15; ⊘ noon-4pm & 5.30pm-late; 🛜) 🍴 In a handsome 19th-century neoclassical building (and former Italian Police station), Manolis Tastes has a roof terrace and upstairs lounge, and fine dining in a cream-and-wood interior. The real draw is Chef Manolis, his culinary flair recognised internationally. Mussels with ouzo, and pork with mustard and honey, are just a few of the splendid dishes served here. A must visit.

Yiannis TAVERNA €€

(☑ 22470 41395; mains €10-14; ⊘ lunch & dinner May-Oct; ❄ 🛜) This deservedly popular taverna, adorned with cobalt-and-white trim, sits to the west of the marina jetty with seating on a raised terrace next to a tiny vineyard (look out for the mural of the windmill). Try the stewed goat in red sauce and thin-sliced swordfish carpaccio.

Around Lipsi

Lipsi is remarkably green for a Dodecanese island. Walking to its further-flung beaches leads you through countryside dotted with olive groves, cypress trees and endless views. In summer, a minibus also services the main beaches.

Just 1km north of Lipsi Village, around the headland beyond Liendou Beach, **Kambos Beach** is narrower but sandier than its neighbour and somewhat shaded by tamarisk trees. The water is also deeper and rockier underfoot.

Fork inland at Kambos and a delightful 2.5km hike over the low-lying spine of the island will lead you to the shallow and child-friendly **Platys Gialos Beach**. Ringing with goat bells and shelving gently into crystal-clear water, it's home to an excellent summer-only, daytime taverna.

Just 2km south of Lipsi Village, sandy **Katsadia Beach** is wilder, especially if it's windy. There's a certain amount of shade and another good summer-only taverna, which stays open late as a bar.

The beaches at Lipsi's eastern end are harder to reach, with the roads being too rough for taxis or buses. In summer, there is a boat that can drop you off here, too.

✕ Eating

Dilaila Cafe Restaurant TAVERNA €

(☑ 22470 41041; www.dilaila.gr/en; Katsadia Beach; mains €9; ⊘ 9.30am-10pm Jun-Sep; 🅿 🛜 ✏ 💺) 🍴 Tucked behind the beach at Katsadia, this inviting restaurant with colourful decor and split levels has intimate as well as communal areas to take in the stunning sea. Dishes include lentil salad with octopus, feta in honey, pork in mustard sauce, grilled tuna and many more. It costs €4 each way in a taxi from Lipsi Village.

Platis Gialos Restaurant TAVERNA €€

(☑ 6944963303; Platys Gialos Beach; grills €10-12; ⊘ 8am-6pm Jul & Aug) Sitting on the island's best beach for swimming in unbelievable turquoise water, this pleasant little summer-only taverna has decent grilled food and fresh salads.

AT A GLANCE

POPULATION
Lesvos: 86,436

TYCOON HIDEAWAY
Inousses (p617)

BEST FESTIVALS
Panigyria (p595)

BEST MUSEUM
Chios Mastic
Museum (p619)

BEST ART HOTEL
A for Art (p644)

WHEN TO GO
Apr & May Wild red
poppies adorn the
back roads; Greek
Easter livens up
every village.

Jul & Aug Beach
bars and village
councils (in Ikaria's
case) throw wild
parties for revellers.

Oct & Nov Summer
crowds evaporate,
and hearty soups
return to the
tavernas.

Armenistis (p597)
IOANNIS MANTAS/SHUTTERSTOCK ©

Northeastern Aegean Islands

C linging to the Turkish coast, this is a bunch of radically idiosyncratic islands with landscapes and local cultures so distinct, even the smallest ones feel like proto-nations. In fact, many of them enjoyed quasi-independence at various points in time and remember it fondly.

Eccentric Ikaria is marked by jagged landscapes, pristine beaches and a famously long-lived, left-leaning population. Nearby Chios provides fertile ground for the planet's only gum-producing mastic trees. Other islands range from rambling Lesvos – producer of half the world's ouzo – to midsized islands such as semitropical Samos and workaday Limnos, and bright specks in the sea such as Inousses and Psara. Samothraki is home to the ancient Sanctuary of the Great Gods (p640), while well-watered Thasos seems an extension of the mainland.

INCLUDES

Northeastern Aegean Islands Highlights

1 Ikaria Refuelling with post-midnight coffee and spoon sweets in Hristos Rahes (p501).

2 Panagia Kakaviotissa (p636) Trekking through unearthly terrain towards a mountaintop cave chapel.

3 Potami Beach (p609) Finding a secret taverna above wooded waterfalls after lazing on a picture-perfect marble gravel beach on Samos.

4 Mytilini Town (p622) Discovering an unexpected treasure trove of top-notch 20th-century art at Teriade Museum .

5 Molyvos (p627) Sitting in Molly's Bar and watching yachts sailing through a turquoise bay.

6 Pyrgi (p619) Lodging in Mastiha House, castle-like apartments in a village that's a piece of decorative art.

7 Sanctuary of the Great Gods (p640) Contemplating the secretive cult of ancient gods who preceded the Olympians.

8 Lesvos (p621) Day-dreaming in the ancient thermal Mineral Baths of Eftalou.

ℹ️ Getting There & Away

Chios (p613), Lesvos (p621) and Samos (p603) all have international airports that receive flights from a variety of European destinations. Limnos (p633) and Ikaria (p592) are served by domestic airlines.

The island group can be accessed by ferry from the mainland ports of Piraeus and Kavala. There is also a service connecting Limnos to the port of Lavrio.

IKARIA IKAPIA

If Greek islands were humans, then magical Ikaria would be the weirdest and most charismatic. Its outlandish terrain, largely untamed by agriculture, comprises dramatic forested gorges, rocky moonscapes and hidden beaches with aquamarine waters. Ikaria's independent spirit, unique culture (characterised by dwellings pretending to be rocks), nocturnal lifestyle and rave-like *panigyria* village festivals grew out of centuries of isolated life under the constant threat of pirates and foreign invaders.

Supposedly named after mythical Icarus, said to have crashed here after flying with wax wings too close to the sun, Ikaria is also honoured as the birthplace of Dionysos, god of wine. Ikarian villages famously throw wild parties with loads of food, wine and traditional dance. The island gets packed with

Athenians and foreign visitors at the height of August's *panigyria*, but come any time to enjoy Ikaria's serenity ansd the locals' sybaritic attitude to life, which results in extraordinary longevity.

🏃 Activities

With its solitude and rugged natural beauty, Ikaria is perfect for mountain walks. The most popular starting point is Hristos Rahes, where shops sell a walking map. For inexpensive guided treks all over the island, approach Discover Ikaria (☑ 6907547342, 6974042417; www.discoverikaria.com; Hristos Rahes) or Ikarian Footprints (☑ 6974042417; https://ikarianfootprints.com).

Achievable as an independent walk, and not too hard on the bones, is the one-day circular walk along dirt roads from Kambos, south through Dafni, the remains of the 10th-century Byzantine Castle of Koskinas, and picturesque Frandato and Maratho villages.

When you reach Pigi, look for the Frandato sign; continue past it for the unusual little Byzantine Chapel of Theoskepasti, tucked into overhanging granite. You must clamber up to reach it, and duck to get inside. The rows of old monks' skulls have been retired, but the chapel makes for an unusual visit, along with nearby Moni Theoktistis, with frescoes dating from 1686.

NORTHEASTERN AEGEAN ISLANDS IKARIA

ℹ️ TURKISH CONNECTIONS

Visiting Turkey's Aegean coastal resorts and historical sites from Samos, Chios and Lesvos is easy. Visas aren't usually necessary for day trips. While boat itineraries, prices and even companies change often, the following explains how things generally work.

From **Samos**, the *Kuşadası Express* leaves daily from either Vathy or Pythagorio for the 80-minute trip to **Kuşadası** (one way/return €40/60), a coastal resort near **ancient Ephesus** (Efes). Daily excursions run from May through to October, with the option to also visit Ephesus. For tickets and information in Vathy, contact **By Ship Travel** (☑ 22730 27337; www.byshiptravel.gr; Sofouli 5; ⊙ 6am-10pm) opposite the old ferry terminal. In Pythagorio, contact **By Ship Travel** (☑ 22730 62285; Lykourgou Logotheti; ⊙ 6am-10pm May-Sep) at the main junction entering town. Additionally, a Turkish boat connects from Karlovasi in northern Samos to **Sığacık** (one way/return €30/40, five weekly), which is between Kuşadası and the airport at İzmir. None of these ferries has space for cars.

From **Chios**, daily departures year-round connect Chios Town with **Çeşme**, a port near İzmir; services are most frequent in summer and some carry vehicles on board. Boats depart morning and evening for the 40-minute journey (one way/return €20/30). Tour agencies on the seafront also sell package day trips to İzmir. Get information and tickets from **Sunrise Tours** (☑ 22710 41390; www.sunrisetours.gr; Kanari 28; ⊙ 8.30am-10pm).

From **Lesvos**, boats operated by Turkish company Turyol leave Mytilini Town for **Ayvalık** twice daily in summer and daily in winter (one way/return €15/25, 1½ hours). Thursday departures are especially popular for market day in Ayvalık. Vehicles are carried on board. Most Mytilini Town travel agencies sell Turkish tours; try **Mitilene Tours** (☑ 22510 54261; www.mitilenetours.gr; Pavlou Kountourioti 87; ⊙ 24hr) or **Tsolos Travel** (☑ 22510 25346; www.flytsolos.com; 1944 Christougennon 10; ⊙ 9am-2.15pm & 6.15-9.15pm).

Ikaria & the Fourni Islands

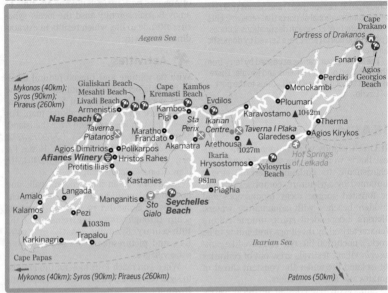

Cape Drakano

Fortress of Drakanos

Fanari

Agios Georgios Beach

Perdiki

Monokambi

Aegean Sea

Mykonos (40km); Syros (90km); Piraeus (260km)

Gialiskari Beach
Mesahti Beach
Livadi Beach
Armenistis
Nas Beach

Cape Kremasti
Kambos Beach

Evdilos

Ploumari

Kambos
Pigi
Sta Perix
Ikarian Centre

Karavostamo ▲1042m

Therma

Agios Kirykos

Taverna I Plaka
Glaredes

Taverna Platanos
Maratho
Frandato

Akamatra

Arethousa
1027m

Hot Springs of Lefkada

Agios Dimitrios
Hristos Rahes
Polikarpos

Ikaria Hrysostomos
▲

Xylosyrtis Beach

Profitis Ilias

Kastanies
981m

Plaghia

Amalo
Langada

Manganitis
Sto Gialo
Seychelles Beach

Kalamos
Pezi

▲1033m

Karkinagri
Trapalou

Ikarian Sea

Cape Papas

Mykonos (40km); Syros (90km); Piraeus (260km)

Patmos (50km)

ℹ Information

Visit Ikaria (www.visitikaria.gr/en) is a very useful online guide.

ℹ Getting There & Away

AIR

Ikaria Airport (Map p592; ☑ 22750 32216; Faros) is served by **Olympic Air** (www.olympic air.com), **Aegean Airlines** (www.aegeanair. com) and **Astra Airlines** (www.astra-airlines.gr). Tickets are available at agencies in Agios Kirykos and Evdilos, and at the **airport** (Map p592; ☑ 22750 32216; Faros).

BOAT

Ikaria finds itself at a crossing of busy routes leading to the mainland ports of Piraeus (via Cyclades) and Kavala in the north as well as to the Dodecanese Islands. Its two ports, Evdilos and Agios Kirykos, are quite far apart; make sure you know which one you need on the way in and out to avoid losing way more than your boat fare on taxis.

From Evdilos, there are daily services to Karlo-vasi, Samos (€13.50, one hour).

Nyssos Mykonos calls at Evdilos six times a week on the way to Piraeus (€31.50, 6½ hours) via the Cycladic islands of Mykonos (€20, two hours) and Syros (€23, three hours).

Once a week, the same boat leaves for Kavala (€48, 16 hours) via Chios (€18.50, 5½ hours) and Lesvos (€24, eight hours). Another weekly boat does the same route out of Agios Kirykos.

From Agios Kirykos, boats or hydrofoils run to Fourni (€7 to €14, one hour) five times a week. At least four boats or hydrofoils a week go to Patmos (€10.50 to €22, one to 1½ hours) continuing to other Dodecanese islands.

Get tickets in Agios Kirykos at **Ikariada Travel** (☑ 22750 23322; ⊙ 8.30am-5pm & 7-9pm) or **Dolihi Tours Travel Agency** (☑ 22750 23230; dolichi@otenet.gr; ⊙ 9am-3pm & 6-9pm). In Evdilos, try **Ikaria Holiday** (☑ 22750 71077, 6972221066; ⊙ 10am-10pm).

ℹ Getting Around

BOAT

In summer, a daily caïque (little boat; water taxi) goes from Agios Kirykos to Therma (€3). Another boat on Ikaria's south coast links Manganitis with the idyllic Seychelles Beach (p599), 2.5km away, for swimming and sunbathing.

BUS

In summer months, a daily bus makes the winding route from Agios Kirykos to Hristos Rahes, via Evdilos and Armenistis. It also calls at the Ikaria Airport on the way. Getting on it can be a challenge. A local bus makes the 10-minute trip to Therma every half-hour.

CAR & MOTORCYCLE

It's a good idea to hire a car or scooter for travel beyond the main towns. Hitchhiking is very common and considered safe by locals, but we don't recommend it.

Samos (20km);
Patmos (60km)

Cape Alonaki

514m
Taverna Almyra
Agios Dimitrios Beach • Hrysomilia

Fourni
Islands   Fourni
Psili Ammos   Kamari
Thymena   Beach
Thymena •   Kamari   Agios
•Fourni Korseon   Minas
Kampi
Kesiria   Elidaki Beach
Petrokopio Beach

Kasidi Beach   Vlyhada Beach
Megalos
Makronisi   Anthropofas

For cars, try Dolihi Tours Travel Agency or Ikariada Travel in Agios Kirykos; **Mav Cars** (☑ 22750 31036, 6932908944; mav-cars@hol.gr; harbour; ⊗9am-10pm) in Evdilos; and **Aventura** (☑ 22750 31140, 6972284054; aventura@otenet.gr; ⊗9am-9pm) in Evdilos and Armenistis. Most car-hire offices can arrange for airport pick-up or drop-off, too, generally at no extra charge.

Agios Kirykos
Αγιος Κήρυκος
POP 1880

Ikaria's capital is an easy-going and dependable Greek port, with clustered old streets, hotels and domatia, tasty restaurants and a lively waterfront cafe scene. Although beaches are nicer in Ikaria's north, the area's renowned hot radioactive springs, scattered along the coast, attract those with aching bodies from around Europe. The main cluster is located 2km east at Therma, which also has a nice pebble beach.

Activities

People with sore muscles and perfectly healthy pleasure seekers alike flock to hot radioactive springs in the vicinity of Agios Kirykos. Some of the springs discharge hot water into the sea, providing for a unique bathing experience. Most are located in Therma, 2km from Agios Kirykos.

★ **Spilio Hot Springs**   HOT SPRINGS
(Therma) **FREE** The best hot springs experience on Ikaria, if not in all the Aegean, is to enter the sea on the beach in Therma and swim for some 30m towards a large cave on the southern side of the bay; you'll start feeling flows of hot radon-rich water long before reaching it. Inside, there's an improvised mini-arena made of large stones.

Spilio Baths   HOT SPRINGS
(To Spilio; ☑ 22750 24048; Therma; hammam €3, Jacuzzi pool €4.50; ⊗9am-4pm) This steamy gem is an authentic thermal sauna and bath that draws on a hot underground spring. Showers and lockers are included, but bring a towel. It's past the kiosk at the end of the waterfront, to the right as you face the sea.

Hot Springs of Lefkada   HOT SPRINGS
(Map p592) **FREE** These hot sea-springs, 2.5km southwest of Agios Kirykos, are therapeutic, relaxing and free. Although it's a designated radioactive saltwater spring, in truth it's just a beautiful spot on the beach, identifiable by an irregular circle of rocks. You'll know you're in the right spot when you feel the now-it's-hot, now-it's-not intermingling of spring and seawater.

Festivals & Events

Ikaria International
Chess Tournament   SPORTS
(☑ 6978197617;   http://ikariachess.blogspot.com; ⊗Jul) This traditional annual event draws chess players of all types from around Europe and beyond. The tournament celebrated its 40th anniversary in 2017 and retains a distinctly local flavour. This battle of wits takes place in mid-July, lasting about a week.

Sleeping & Eating

Agios Kirykos has a number of fairly good hotels, but you'll find even better ones at nearby Therma, next to the beach and hot springs. The port is filled with tavernas, but some of the best eateries hide in the little lanes behind the waterfront.

★ **Pension Plumeria Flowery**   PENSION €
(☑ 22750 22742, 6945139021; www.therma-ikaria.com; Therma; r incl breakfast €50; ❅🕸) Big-hearted women run these immaculate rooms – with names such as Bougainvillea, Anemone and Hyacinth – in the centre of Therma. In addition to being as helpful as anyone possibly can be, they make great cakes for breakfast.

Pyrgos Traditional Village VILLA €€

(✆6970028000, 22750 22105; www.pyrgos-ikaria.com; r from €80; P✳🛜❄) Perched high above Agios Kirykos, this cluster of nine villas, styled as traditional stone houses, is as luxurious as it gets on this side of the island. The rooms are huge, stylishly designed and equipped with kitchenettes, even though breakfasts can be ordered.

★Tzivaeri FAST FOOD €

(✆22750 22850; snacks €2-4; ☉lunch & dinner) Best souvlaki and *gyros* (meat slithers cooked on a vertical rotisserie, eaten with pitta bread) at the port. Look for the umbrellas; it's next to Taverna Klimataria.

Taverna Klimataria TAVERNA €

(mains €6-8; ☉lunch & dinner Apr-Oct) An inviting backstreet taverna, behind the National Bank, with a lovely shaded courtyard. Strong on grilled meats and *pastitsio* (layers of buttery macaroni and seasoned minced lamb) with generous salads.

Taverna Arodou TAVERNA €€

(✆22750 22700; Xilosirtis; €6-12; ☉2pm-midnight Tue-Sun; P🛜) An excellent traditional seaside eatery overlooking the sea in the village of Xilosirtis, 5km southwest of Agios Kirykos. Strong on fresh veggies, salads and Ikarian *soufiko* (layers of baked vegetables and potatoes) on top of traditional taverna fare. They also make their own ice cream.

🍸 Drinking & Nightlife

Ambariza Bistro CAFE

(✆22750 31721; ☉9am-late) A convivial little cafe-cum-bar with some tables in a romantic bougainvillea-filled lane behind the National Bank. In addition to coffee and alcohol, it serves great desserts and breakfasts.

Akti Café-Bar BAR

(✆6945250954; ☉all day) Snappy bar at Hotel Akti (✆22750 23905; www.pensionakti.gr; r from €50; ✳🛜), with sturdy mixed drinks and decent snacks. At night you can see the twinkling lights of Fourni on the horizon.

ℹ Information

Dolihi Tours Travel Agency (p592) Full-service agency, next to Alpha Bank.

Naftiliako Praktoreio (✆22750 22426) Behind the waterfront, in the first alleyway, this helpful hole-in-the-wall specialises in ferry tickets to Fourni and Patmos, and has local tips.

Ikariada Travel (p592) Full-service waterfront travel agency next to Diagonios souvlaki shop.

ℹ Getting There & Away

Agios Kirykos is one of two major ports on the island, with ferry connections (p592) to Piraeus (Athens), other northeastern Aegean Islands and also the Dodecanese.

In summer, one or even two daily buses could be running to Evdilos and Armenistis, but don't count on that too much as it will still be a challenge getting on them.

Evdilos Εύδηλος

POP 460

Ikaria's second port, Evdilos skirts a small semicircular bay and rises in tiers up a hillside. It features stately old houses on winding streets, and a relaxed, appealing waterfront. Evdilos is 41km northwest of Agios Kirykos, to which it's connected by Ikaria's two main roads. The memorable trip takes in high mountain ridges, striking sea views and slate-roof villages.

🛏 Sleeping & Eating

Hotel Atheras HOTEL €

(✆22750 31434; www.atherashotel.gr; s/d/tr from €55/60/70; P✳🛜❄) The friendly, modern Atheras has an almost Cycladic feel due to its bright-white decor contrasting with the blue Aegean beyond. There's an outdoor bar by the pool. The hotel is in the backstreets, 200m from the port.

Kerame Studios APARTMENT €€

(✆22750 32600; www.keramehotel.gr; s/d/tr €60/70/80; P✳🛜❄) These studio apartments, located 1km before Evdilos, feature kitchens and spacious decks with views. Prices are as variable as the quarters. A breakfast cafe is built into a windmill. Kerame is the sister establishment of Hotel Atheras near the port.

★Sta Perix GREEK €

(Map p592; ✆22750 31056; Akamatra; mains €5-11; ☉lunch & dinner) Classy eatery in Akamatra, 6km south of Evdilos, well regarded for its traditional Ikarian recipes, a variety of local cheeses, and even its own wine.

RakoStroto TAVERNA €

(✆22750 32266; mains €6-10; ☉dinner) Up on the hill, at the bend in the street that connects with the main road to Kambos, this summer-only taverna occupies a kind of natural balcony with bay views. Competently made grills and vegetable dishes are served, and musicians come for impromptu concerts.

NORTHEASTERN AEGEAN ISLANDS EVDILOS

PANIGYRIA

Pagan god Dionysos may no longer reign over Ikaria's vineyards, but his legacy lives on in Christianised form in the summertime *panigyria*, all-night festival celebrations held on saints' days across the island. There's no better way to dive head first into Greek island culture than drinking, dancing and feasting while honouring a village's patron saint. Bring your wallet: *panigyria* are important fundraisers for the local community. Use this fact to explain any overindulgence as well-intended philanthropy.

Panigyria occur across the island on these dates: **Kambos** 5 May, **Armenistis** 40 days after Orthodox Easter, **Agios Isidoros** (Pezi) 24 June, **Agios Giannis** (Hristos Rahes) 24 June, **Platani** 29 June, **Karavostamo** 1 July, **Agios Kirykos & Ikarian Independence Day** 17 July, **Arethousa** 17 July, **Agios Panteleinonas** (Fidos) 27 July, **Hristos Rahes & Dafni** 6 August, **Akamatra** 15 August, **Evdilos** 15–20 August, **Agios Sofia & Monokambi** 17 September.

Drinking & Nightlife

★ Slowdown Brewery　　　　　CRAFT BEER

(☑ 22750 32463; www.facebook.com/SlowDown Brewing; ☺ 5pm-late) Its own beer production was still in the works at the time of research, but you can try seven kinds of craft beer from different parts of Greece, including the excellent Ikariotissa red ale produced on the island. They serve mouth-watering snacks, including succulent burgers.

Café-Bar Rififi　　　　　　　　CAFE

(☑ 22750 33060; Plateia Evdilou; ☺ all day; ☎) This snappy portside bar, with great pitta snacks, draught beer and good coffee, owes its name to the bank next door, with which it shares an interior wall. *Rififi* in Greek is a nickname for a bank robber, and the servers are happy to point out where the serious money is stashed.

ℹ️ Information

Ikaria Holiday (p592) Helpful full-service travel office, on the waterfront.

ℹ️ Getting There & Away

Evdilos is Ikaria's second port. **Hellenic Seaways** (https://hellenicseaways.gr) ferries connect it to other northeastern Aegean Islands and Piraeus.

One or two daily buses may or may not be running the route between Agios Kirykos and Hristos Rahes.

Aventura (p593) and Mav Cars (p593) rent cars and motorbikes.

Kambos　　　　Κάμπος

POP 250

Kambos, 3km west of Evdilos, was once mighty Oinoe (derived from the Greek word for wine), Ikaria's capital. Traces of this ancient glory remain, compliments of a ruined Byzantine palace, Ikaria's oldest church and a small museum (☑ 22750 32935; ☺ 8.30am-3pm Wed) FREE. Kambos' other main attractions are its sand-and-pebble beach and scenic hill walks. It's a very quiet place with a couple of outstanding accommodation options and some veritable tavernas, while the far more diverse nightlife scene of Evdilos is reachable on foot.

🛏️ Sleeping & Eating

★ Ikaria Utopia -
Cusco Studios　　　　　　　APARTMENT €

(☑ 6973848812, 22750 31381; http://ikariautopia. com; apt €30-55; 🅿❄☎) For musician and philosopher Christos, who runs this cluster of large and stylishly furnished apartments with huge terraces, this place seems to be an artistic as much as a business project. Perched on a hill, high above the beach, this windswept spot is a true bohemian haunt ideal for creative types in search of seclusion and inspiration.

To reach it, take a side road that branches off the main one by **Sourta-Ferta** (☑ 22750 31651; snacks €1.50-4; ☺ lunch & dinner) cafe.

Rooms Dionysos　　　　　　　　PENSION €

(☑ 6944153437, 22750 31688; www.ikaria-dion ysosrooms.com; d/tr/q from €25/35/45; 🅿☎) The many happy guests who return every year attest to the magical atmosphere of this pension run by the charismatic Vasilis 'Dionysos' Kambouris, his Australian-born wife, Demetra, and Italian-speaking brother Yiannis. Rooms are simple, with private bathrooms; rooftop beds are a summer steal at €10. There's a communal kitchen, a book exchange and you'll get great tips on exploring Ikaria.

COAST OF DIONYSOS

Dionysos, god of wine and merrymaking, may not have envisaged that planeloads of guests heading for *panigyria* festivals would be landing practically on the roof of his Ikarian cave dwelling. The island's – thankfully not so busy – airstrip is right next to the god's legendary lair and some spectacular scenery around the village of Fanari. One may only speculate what it means in terms of his relations with the island's other ancient celeb, Icarus, whose statue stands inside the airport terminal.

Lying in the lowlands next to a good pebble beach, Fanari is the starting point for a fairly easy circular trek that takes in some quirky attractions, in addition to breathtaking views of the sea and surrounding islands. You need no more than a couple of hours to do the entire route and take a dip in the sea.

On the eastern side of the village, a dirt track starts climbing up the hill before reaching a fork with a sign pointing towards the Fortress of Drakanos (Map p592; ⊙8am-3pm Tue-Sat) FREE: follow it to reach the 2500-year-old archaeological site with a name and outlook straight out of *Game of Thrones*. When Greek air-force jets fly overhead in regular drills, you may get a distinct feel that you have indeed found yourself in the land of dragons. On the way to the fortress, you may also choose to detour to the smallish Agios Georgios chapel next to the secluded beach of the same name.

From Drakanos, a well-marked trail leads through shrub-covered terrain to Iero Beach, a pleasant cove with crystal-clear water and a cave, where Dionysos cavorted with maenads and satyrs during his lifelong vacation, or so the legend says. A dirt track running along the airport fence will bring you back to Fanari, where Evon's Rooms (☑22750 32580, 6977139208; www.evonsrooms.com; Faros; studios/ste from €50/80; 🅿 ❄ @ 🛜) is a welcoming place to overnight or spend your entire holiday on Ikaria.

Popi's
TAVERNA €

(Fytema Beach; mains €5-8.50; ⊙dinner) Very traditional setting on the road halfway between Kambos and Evdilos. Excellent taverna fare, cooked and happily served by Popi.

Kalypso
GREEK €€

(☑22750 31387; Kambos; €7-15; ⊙24hr, summer only) A summer-only affair run by a Greek-Belgian couple, Kalypso is renowned for its cooking – it's all about fish here – as much as for its festive atmosphere. It's located on the beach, halfway between Kambos and Evdilos.

❶ Getting There & Away

The 2.7km to/from Evdilos can be easily done on foot, but if you have luggage, get a taxi.

Hristos Rahes
Χριστός Ραχών

POP 300

At night the heart of Ikaria beats in the cool highlands above Armenistis, where a cluster of picturesque villages, collectively known as Rahes (the main village is Hristos Rahes), come to life after dark, with children playing in the streets and adults drinking coffee or ouzo. These nocturnal habits hark back to the times when, fearing pirates based on nearby Fourni, Ikaria pretended to be an uninhabited island. An occasional roof covered with stone slabs is another vestige of that epoch, when people tried to camouflage their dwellings as piles of rocks. By day, Rahes villages serve as departure points for many exciting hikes through Ikaria's highlands, covered in pine forest and fruit orchards.

◉ Sights

★Afianes Winery
WINERY

(Map p592; ☑6977893731, 22750 40008; http://afianeswines.gr/en; ⊙noon-8pm) FREE Crowning the hill above Hristos Rahes, this small family-run winery has won several recent awards in Europe. In addition to the offered tastings and small personal tours of the operation, an exhibition room features vintage winemaking equipment, gourd vessels and 19th-century wedding dresses.

⌂ Sleeping & Eating

Estia
GUESTHOUSE €€

(☑22750 41007, 6979835757; evgeniaporis@gmail.com; r from €65; ❄ 🛜) Up the road from Hristos Rahes, this place offers simply but tastefully decorated rooms, with fully equipped kitchens and balconies that face the sea and the cascade of Rahes villages descending to Armenistis.

★ Taverna Platanos
TAVERNA €

(Map p592; ☑ 22750 42395; Agios Dimitrios; mains €5-9.50; ☺10am-2am) Nestled under the shade of a rambling plane tree, a 500m stroll from Hristos Rahes, Platanos offers authentic Ikarian dishes, including *soufiko*, a summer favourite of stewed veggies, generally featuring whatever is picked fresh that morning. Great grills, hearty salads and local wine round out the table.

★ CousinA
GREEK €

(☑ 22750 41374; mains €6-11; ☺lunch & dinner) A short walk from the main square, this tiny but outstanding eatery ventures well beyond the Ikarian mainstream, upgrading traditional Greek food to the level that would earn the acclaim of world food critics. It serves a superb aubergine salad with walnuts and *dakos* (Cretan rusks), an Ikarian version of bruschetta.

Argios Restaurant & Bar
GREEK €

(☑ 6973669492, 22750 41564; Profitis Ilias; mains €6-10; ☺lunch & dinner) Located on the 'roof' of Ikaria, up high in Profitis Ilias, a 10-minute drive from Hristos Rahes, this large terrace serves a menu that is vaguely Greek, with some international guest dishes, such as hummus with goji berries. Live and DJ music events are held in summer – look for announcements around the island.

🍷 Drinking & Nightlife

Rahati
CAFE

(☑ 22750 41512; ☺9am-late) In the main square, this cafe serves exquisite *galaktoboureko* (custard slice) and other traditional Greek desserts, as well as perhaps the best coffee on the island. Lovely chatty women rule the house.

🛍 Shopping

Women's Cooperative
MARKET

(☑ 22750 41076; ☺all day) This wonderful market-deli-bakery in the heart of Hristos Rahes sells jams, herbs and sweet treats made on the premises.

ℹ Getting There & Away

A daily bus service may or may not run to Evdilos. You may take a taxi down to Evdilos for €10, but your best bet really is to have a rented car. Many people hitchhike from Hristos Rahes and Armenistis. Hitching is never entirely safe, and we don't recommend it. Travellers who hitch should understand that they are taking a small but potentially serious risk.

Armenistis   Αρμενιστής

POP 80

Armenistis, 15km west of Evdilos, is Ikaria's humble version of a resort. It boasts two long sandy beaches separated by a narrow headland; a fishing harbour; and a web of hilly streets to explore on foot. Cafes and tavernas line the beach. Moderate nightlife livens up Armenistis in summer with a mix of locals and Greek and foreign tourists.

◉ Sights & Activities

★ Nas Beach
BEACH

(Map p592) Westward 3.5km from Armenistis lies the pebbled beach of Nas, lying below the road and the few tavernas. A nudist-friendly beach, it has an impressive location at the mouth of a forested river, behind the trace ruins of an ancient Temple of Artemis, easily viewed from Artemis Studios.

Livadi Beach
BEACH

Right next to Armenistis, a little mountain river brings some fine sand to form this picture-perfect beach. Beware the strong currents and – occasionally – high waves that make it suitable for surfing, or at least body surfing.

Mesahti Beach
BEACH

The kind of beach that makes it onto travel magazine covers, Mesahti is Ikaria's longest and arguably best organised, with gentle yellow sand, a picturesque estuary made by a mountain river on one side, sunbeds and a beach bar.

🛏 Sleeping

There are some truly wonderful places to stay in Ikaria's main tourist spot; if you plan to visit in high season, be aware that they get fully booked very early.

Artemis Studios
PENSION €

(☑ 22750 71475; www.artemis-studio.gr; Nas; d from €40; P❄🖥) This popular family-run place perched on the edge of the spectacular Chalari canyon above Nas Beach comes with its own taverna and an interesting pottery shop. Resident artists stay and work here throughout summer. Breakfast is €6 extra.

Pension Astaxi
PENSION €

(☑22750 71318, 6982446227; www.island-ikaria.com/hotels/PensionAstaxi.asp; d/tr incl breakfast from €35/50; P@🖵) This excellent, attractive budget gem is tucked back 30m from the main road, just above the Carte Postal cafe and Taverna Baido. The gracious owner, Maria, has created a relaxing and welcoming lodging, with a dozen brightly outfitted rooms with fans and balcony views to the sea.

Atsachas Rooms
HOTEL €

(☑22750 71226; www.atsachas.gr; btw Mesahti & Livadi beaches; d €40-60; ❄️🖵) On a headland between Mesahti (p597) and Livadi (p597) beaches, the Atsachas has clean, well-furnished rooms, some with fully equipped kitchens. Most have breezy sea-view balconies. The cafe spills onto a flowery garden, where a stairway descends to a nice stretch of beach.

Hotel Daidalos
HOTEL €

(☑22750 71390; www.daidaloshotel.gr; s/d incl breakfast from €40/50; ☉May-Oct; P❄️🖵🏊) You can't miss the traditional blue-and-white island colour scheme at this attractive, well-managed 25-room hotel. Rooms are large and cheerful, most with sea views, and there's a small bar off the lobby. It's 200m west of the small bridge as you enter Armenistis.

★ Koimite
GUESTHOUSE €€

(☑6974893877, 22750 71545; www.ikariarooms.gr; Armenistis; d/q from €60/110; ❄️🖵) Cascading down a rocky cliff, these pastel-coloured rooms come with balconies so huge you might be tempted to sell tickets to watch the spectacular sunset. Some rooms are equipped with kitchenettes; others have fridges. There are kerosene heaters. Supernice staff leave homemade cookies when they finish cleaning.

Erofili Beach Hotel
HOTEL €€

(☑22750 71058; www.erofili.gr; d/tr incl breakfast from €95/110; P❄️🖵🏊) Swank studio apartments and rooms, with a pool and amenities to spare. It's found just before the bridge.

🍴 Eating & Drinking

★ Thea's Restaurant & Rooms
TAVERNA €

(☑22750 71491, 6932154296; www.theasinn.com; Nas; mains €6-11; ☉lunch & dinner; 🖵) There are a few fine tavernas in Nas, but Thea's cooks, serving up outstanding mezedhes, meat grills and a perfect veggie *mousakas* (baked layers of aubergine or courgette, minced meat and

potatoes topped with cheese sauce). Good barrel wine and local *tsipouro* (distilled spirit of grape must) firewater complete the deal. An outdoor patio overlooks the sea.

Thea (aka Dorothy) also has five bright and cosy rooms (€35 including breakfast) above the restaurant.

Syntages tis Giagias
DESSERTS €

(Grandma's Recipes; ☑22750 71150; desserts €2-3; ☉lunch & dinner) Occupying a terrace on the 2nd floor of the main shopping compound in Armenistis, this small confectionery makes exemplary *galaktoboureko* (custard slice), *kataïfi* (angel-hair pastry) and ice cream with local fruit flavours. Shelves are filled with jars containing spoon sweets, such as caramelised seasonal fruit and vegetables.

Taverna Symposio
TAVERNA €

(☑6972264046; Gialiskari; mezedhes & mains €3-8.50; ☉lunch & dinner) A small taverna in tiny Gialiskari, next to Armenistis, overlooking the marina. It's known for great mezedhes and *mayirefta* (ready-cooked) dishes, and has outstanding hospitality, even by already outstanding Greek standards.

Taverna Baido
TAVERNA €

(☑6982331539; mains €6-10; ☉1.30-11.30pm) Past the bridge towards Nas, this interesting taverna is the work of Marianthi, who serves well-priced dishes using local products, fresh fish and Ikarian wine. Exceptional *soutzoukakia* (meat rissoles in tomato sauce) and *taramasalata* (a thick pink or white purée of fish roe, potato, oil and lemon juice).

Pashalia Taverna
TAVERNA €

(☑6975562415, 22750 71302; mains €4-7; ☉lunch & dinner) Meat dishes such as *katsikaki* (kid goat) or veal in a clay pot are specialities at this taverna, the first along the Armenistis harbour road. The great mezedhes and fresh fish are popular as well.

Kelaris Taverna
SEAFOOD €

(☑22750 71227; Gialiskari; mains €6-11; ☉lunch & dinner) Kelaris serves its own fresh-caught fish, cooked over coals, along with midday *mayirefta* dishes from the oven. Look for the landmark church on the point, 1.5km east of Armenistis.

★ Marymary
MEDITERRANEAN €€

(☑22750 71595; Armenistis; mains €8-12; ☉noon-midnight; 🖵) Marrying traditional island cuisine with cosmopolitan culinary fashion, this upmarket eatery in the heart

THE WILD SOUTH

You can now drive on a fairly good paved coastal road all around the island, except for a 15km section between Manganitis and Karkinagri, located in Ikaria's southwestern corner. Both are serene end-of-the-universe places, with quaint fishing ports and a few tavernas, where hikers wind up after descending from the desolate moonlike plateau south of Hristos Rahes.

Connected by a paved road to Agios Kirykos and Evdilos, Manganitis draws crowds from elsewhere on the island every lunar month in summer when the popular Sto Gialo (Map p592; ✆22750 32636; www.stogialokaneifourtouna.gr; Manganitis; ⊙10am-late) bar and restaurant holds its Full Moon Party; check out its website and advertisements around the island for other live and DJ music events. People also flock to the small and stunning Seychelles Beach (Map p592), 3km east of Manganitis. Its marble pebbles, emerald water and giant rocks polished by the waves make you feel you've been teleported into the middle of the Indian Ocean – hence the name. To access it, follow an unmarked path from the parking lot by the tunnel on the road to Manganitis, always leaning to the left side of the ravine.

Karkinagri is now connected by a brand-new road that gives mind-blowing vistas up to the tourist clusters of Nas and Armenistis in Ikaria's northwest. Life in Karkinagri revolves around the bamboo-roofed seafront patio of taverna O Karakas (Karkinagri; mains €6-9; ⊙lunch & dinner). It's the best place on the island to try the local speciality *soufiko*, a tasty vegetable stew.

East from Karkinagri, the dirt track in the direction of Manganitis is OK for a good car until Trapalou, which has a nice beach. Beyond that, the road is fairly atrocious and often gets completely blocked by falling rocks. Check with locals about its current condition.

of Armenistis has a small army of devoted regulars raving about its *mayirefta* dishes, such as rooster with homemade pasta or clay-pot stews. The sea-view terrace is inviting for sundowners and a bottle or two of local Ikarian wine.

Mythos   BAR
(⊙10am-late) Cosy, atmospheric bar managed by Dimitiros and Mariza, who deliver good drinks, fresh juices and live music in the summer. Walk down the street descending to the sea to find it.

Carte Postale   BAR
(✆22750 71031, 6981719567; ⊙10am-2am) This hip cafe-bar, 100m west of Armenistis' church, sits high over the bay. It has a mellow ambience, signalled by an eclectic music mix, from world beat to Greek fusion.

Snacks range from small pizzas and salads to breakfast omelettes and evening risotto, all managed by the welcoming Myrto; her father makes the olives.

ℹ Information

Aventura (✆22750 71117; aventura@otenet.gr; ⊙9am-9pm) Full-service travel agency located by the patisserie just before the bridge. Offers car and motorbike rentals, and is one of the few places that hires out mountain bikes. Also does airport pick-ups and drop-offs.

Dolihi Tours & Lemy Rent-a-Car
(✆6983418878, Dolihi 22750 71122, Lemy 22750 23230; lemy@otenet.gr; ⊙9am-9pm) Efficient travel agency and car hire office next to the village market. Rents cars and organises walking tours and 4WD safaris. Located 200m past the small bridge, towards Nas.

ℹ Getting There & Away

As bus services are virtually nonexistent and taxi prices are unreasonable it makes sense to rent a car, especially if your arrival/departure points on the island are the airport or Agios Kirykos. The Lemy Rent-a-Car office is 200m past the small bridge, towards Nas.

A taxi ride to Evdilos should cost around €20, but prepare to pay up to €70 if you are heading to the other side of the island.

Hitchhiking is the most common method of getting to Nas and Hristos Rahes. Hitching is never entirely safe, and we don't recommend it. Travellers who hitch should understand that they are taking a small but potentially serious risk.

Karavostamo Καραβόσταμο
POP 550

Karavostamo, 6km east of Evdilos, is one of Ikaria's largest coastal villages. From the main road, the village cascades down winding paths scattered with flowering gardens, village churches, veggie patches, chickens and goats, finally reaching a cosy square and a small fishing harbour. Here you'll find little more than a bakery, a small general store, and a few domatia, tavernas and coffeehouses where villagers congregate each evening to chat, argue, eat, play backgammon, drink and tell stories. To reach the square, take the signed road off the main road.

🎓 Courses

Ikarian Centre LANGUAGE
(Map p592; ☑ 6979024066, 22750 61140; www. ikariancentre.com; Arethousa) The Ikarian Centre is a small Greek-language school that runs intensive residential courses (usually from 10 to 20 days). It's in Arethousa, 3km up the hill from Karavostamo, where you're more likely to hear the sound of goat bells than motorbikes. The school combines an up-to-date curriculum with an unbeatable setting overlooking the Aegean, and attracts students from around Europe.

There's plenty of fun to be had, too, including trips to local eateries and surrounding sights.

🛏️ Sleeping & Eating

Despina Rooms PENSION €
(☑ 6977080808, 21066 13999; www.roomsdespina. gr; r €40-60; P ❋ 🛜) Well-appointed two-storey studios in the heart of the village, with kitchens and laundry facilities. It's about 200m from the sea and village square.

LOCAL KNOWLEDGE

A VILLAGE BAKERY

In Karavostamo, everything you need to know about island values can probably be found at the village bakery, where Stephanos Kranas bakes long loaves of bread in his wood oven, along with crunchy *paximadia* (rusks) and sweet *koulouria* (fresh pretzel-style bread).

The bakery makes deliveries each morning by motorbike to village homes. But villagers can also drop by, grab a loaf from the wicker basket on the counter and, if no one's around, leave money in a counter cup. If the bakery appears to be closed, they may simply go upstairs and knock on the owner's door to enquire if there's any bread. The system has worked for years, one reason perhaps why Ikarians don't get too excited about fluctuations in the global price of oil. Olive oil...maybe.

Taverna I Plaka TAVERNA €
(Map p592; ☑ 6972512551; Arethousa; mains €6-10; ☺ lunch & dinner) Excellent traditional taverna in Arethousa, serving traditional Greek dishes from a terrace overlooking the sea.

ℹ️ Getting There & Away

Karavostamo is a 10-minute taxi ride from Evdilos.

FOURNI ISLANDS
ΟΙ ΦΟΥΡΝΟΙ

POP 1320

The Fourni archipelago is one of Greece's great unknown island gems. Its low-lying vegetation clings to gracefully rounded hills that overlap, forming intricate bays of sandy beaches and little ports. This former pirates' lair is especially beautiful at dusk, when the setting sun turns the terrain shades of pink, violet and black.

A clue to the area's swashbuckling past can be found in the name of the archipelago's capital, Fourni Korseon. The Corsairs were French privateers with a reputation for audacity, and their name became applied generically to all pirates and rogues then roaming the eastern Aegean.

Nowadays, Fourni Korseon offers most of the area's accommodation and services, plus several beaches. Other settlements include little Hrysomilia and Kamari to the north, plus another fishing hamlet on the islet of Thymena.

👁️ Sights & Activities

Kampi BEACH
(Map p592) A short trek from the main village, this charming little bay with turquoise water has a tiny fishing port and a nice pebbly beach. A beach bar and a taverna come to life in summer. Follow a stone-paved path above the church in Fourni Korseon until you reach the windmills, then descend to the sea.

Kamari BEACH
(Map p592) A picturesque medium-sized cove protected from high waves in any weather, ideal for both swimming and snorkelling. A popular taverna is nearby in the village.

🛏️ Sleeping

⭐ **Archipelagos Hotel** HOTEL €
(☑ 22750 51250, 6973494967; www.archipelagos hotel.gr; Fourni Korseon; d incl breakfast from €50; P ❋ 🛜) This elegant and welcoming small hotel on the harbour's northern edge

comprises Fourni's most sophisticated lodgings. From the patio restaurant, set under stone arches bursting with geraniums and roses, to the well-appointed rooms and cafebar, the Archipelagos combines traditional architecture with modern luxuries.

Patras Rooms & Apartments   APARTMENT €

(☑ 22750 51268, 22750 51355; www.fourni-patras rooms.gr; Fourni Korseon; r/ste/apt from €30/ 55/60; ❋ ☎) Under the same management as To Arhontiko cafe, this merry colony of brightly coloured and individually designed studios and apartments nestles on the slope right above the port. Near the cafe, there is also a cluster of rooms that are plain, but good value for money.

Toula Studios   PENSION €

(☑ 22750 51332, 6976537948; info@fournitoulastudio.gr; Fourni Korseon; d with/without sea view €60/50; ❋ ☎) Look for the Aegean-blue balconies at this friendly seafront standby near shops and tavernas. It has clean and simple self-catering rooms with overhead fans. The rooms, 10 of which have sea views, surround a large courtyard.

Studios Nektaria   APARTMENT €

(☑ 6973097365, 22750 25134; studiosnektaria@ yahoo.gr; Fourni Korseon; tr from €35; ❋ ☎) On the harbour's far side, this is a Fourni bargain, with small, clean rooms, three of which have shaded balconies overlooking the small beach that skirts the southern end of the bay.

✖ Eating

To Arhontiko   DESSERTS €

(Fourni Korseon; desserts €2-4; ⊙ breakfast, lunch & dinner; ☎) Oranges are the reason why this seafront place is a must-visit, but To Arhontiko makes a whole range of great desserts. Come here after you've finished your lobster in a nearby taverna.

Psarotaverna O Miltos   SEAFOOD €

(☑ 22750 51407; Fourni Korseon; mains €7-10; ⊙ lunch & dinner; ☎) Fourni lobster and fresh fish are expertly prepared at this iconic waterfront taverna. Excellent mezedhes and traditional salads; fish and lobster are fairly priced by the kilo.

Taverna Almyra   TAVERNA €

(Map p592; Kamari; mains €5-9) Up in the little village of Kamari, 9km from the harbour, this relaxing waterfront taverna has subtle charm, and plenty of fresh fish and lobster.

Psarotaverna Nikos   SEAFOOD €

(Fourni Korseon; mains €7-10; ⊙ lunch & dinner; ☎) This is a very reliable seafood option, next door to sibling restaurant O Miltos. Look for daily specials on the chalkboard.

🔒 Shopping

Ka_ndilos   FOOD

(☑ 22750 51581; Fourni Korseon; ⊙ morning & evening) This wonderfully designed shop, packed with multisized jars, sells unusual homemade preserves – spoon sweets, made of all kinds of fruit and vegetables, as well as marinated products. Everything is grown here on the island and preserved the way locals do for themselves. On the main street.

ℹ Information

Fourni Fishermen & Friends (www.fourni.com) The online guide to Fourni.

ℹ Getting There & Away

Lying on major routes linking northeastern Aegean Islands to mainland ports near Athens and in northern Greece, Fourni is best connected to Agios Kirykos on Ikaria by both ferry and hydrofoil (€7 to €14, one hour, four to five weekly).

Fourni can be visited on a day trip twice a week from Samos, when *Dodekanisos Pride* calls in on the way from Pythagorio in the morning and returns by the same route in the early evening (€40 return, one hour). The same catamaran connects the archipelago with Patmos (€25, 1½ hours) and other Dodecanese islands down south.

Fourni Travel (☑ 6975576584, 22750 51019; Fourni Korseon; ⊙ 10am-2pm & 6-9pm Mon-Sat, 11.30am-7pm Sun) provides information and sells tickets. **Dodecanese Seaways** (www.12ne.gr) provides faster and more expensive catamaran services.

ℹ Getting Around

Gleaming new sealed roads, all 20km of them, connect Fourni Korseon with Hrysomilia and Kamari. Everyone seems to walk everywhere in Fourni, and then walk some more.

Rental cars are a recent addition to the Fourni transport scene. Hire a small car or scooter at **Escape Car & Bike Rental** (☑ 22750 51514; www.fourni-rentals.com; Fourni Korseon; ⊙ 8.30am-9.30pm) on the waterfront.

There's also the island's lone **taxi** (☑ 69708 79102), commanded by the ebullient Georgos.

Hitching is common and considered quite safe; however, hitchhikers should understand that they are taking a small but potentially serious risk.

Alternatively, weekly caïques (small boats) serve Hrysomilia, while another two to three go daily to Thymena.

Samos

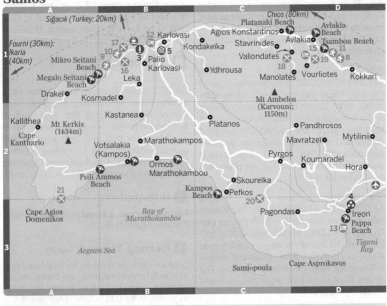

Samos

SAMOS   ΣΑΜΟΣ

POP 33.000

Lying just off the Turkish coast, Samos is one of the northeastern Aegean Islands' best-known destinations. Yet beyond its low-key resorts and the lively capital, Vathy, there are numerous off-the-beaten-track beaches and quiet spots in the cool, forested inland mountains where traditional life continues.

Famous for its sweet local wine, Samos is also historically significant. It was the legendary birthplace of Hera, and the sprawling ruins of her ancient sanctuary, the Heraion (p608), are impressive. Both the great mathematician Pythagoras and the hedonistic father of atomic theory, the 4th-century-BCE philosopher Epicurus, were born here. Samos' scientific genius is also affirmed by the astonishing 524 BCE Evpalinos Tunnel (p606), a spectacular feat of ancient engineering that stretches for more than 1km deep underground.

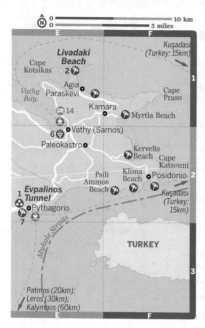

€8.50, 2½ hours) on the way to Patmos (from €9.50, 3½ hours) and Leros (from €13, six hours). The *Dodekanisos Pride* fast boat runs twice a week to Rhodes (€59, seven hours) via Fourni (€20, one hour) and Ikaria's Agios Kirykos (€25, 1½ hours) via almost every Dodecanese island.

Tickets are available from By Ship Travel (p591), which runs offices in all three ports.

❶ Getting Around

From Vathy's **bus station** (☑ 22730 27262; Themistokleous Sofouli), frequent daily buses serve Kokkari (20 minutes), Pythagorio (25 minutes), Agios Konstantinos (40 minutes), Karlovasi (one hour), the Ireon (25 minutes), Mytilinii (20 minutes) and Portrokali (20 minutes). Tickets cost €1.50 to €4 depending on distance.

From Pythagorio, five daily buses reach the Ireon (15 minutes), while four serve Mytilinii (20 minutes) and Marathokampos (one hour). Buy tickets on the buses. Services are reduced on weekends. Tickets cost €1.50 to €7 depending on distance.

In Vathy, **Pegasus Rent-a-Car** (☑ 697853 6440, 22730 24470; www.samos-car-rental.com; Themistokleous Sofouli 5) has good rates on car, 4WD and motorcycle hire.

In Pythagorio, try **John's Rentals** (☑ 22730 61405, 6977253931; www.johns-rent-a-car.gr; Lykourgou Logotheti) on the main road near the waterfront.

TO/FROM THE AIRPORT

Buses between Vathy and the airport run eight times daily, with reduced schedules during weekends. Taxis from the airport cost €25 to Vathy, or €10 to Pythagorio, from where there are local buses to Vathy.

❶ Getting There & Away

AIR

Samos' airport is 4km west of Pythagorio. **Aegean Airlines** (https://en.aegeanair.com), **Astra Airlines** (www.astra-airlines.gr), **Olympic Air** (www.olympicair.com) and **Sky Express** (www.skyexpress.gr) all serve Samos and have offices at the airport.

BOAT

Samos is home to three ports – Vathy (aka Samos), Pythagorio and Karlovasi. They provide connections to Athens and Kavala on the mainland as well as to other island groups. Karlovasi is convenient for Piraeus and Cycladic islands, while Vathy is best for Kavala and the northeastern Aegean Islands. Catamarans and regular boats out of Pythagorio are the most convenient option for the Dodecanese island group.

From Vathy, there are four boats a week to Piraeus (€41, 14 hours) via Ikaria (€10.50, three hours) and Fourni (€13.50, two hours) and two boats weekly to Kavala (€42, 18 hours) via Chios (€14, three hours), Lesvos (€19.50, seven hours) and Limnos (€31, 13 hours). On Fridays, *Blue Star 1* departs for the Dodecanese islands Kos (€37, 3½ hours) and Rhodes (€39, 6½ hours).

From Karlovasi, five boats a week travel to Piraeus (€51, eight hours) via the Cycladic islands of Mykonos (€40.50, 3½ hours) and Syros (€43.50, 4½ hours).

Originating from Pythagorio, boats and catamarans call at smaller Dodecanese islands of Agathonisi (from €8.50, 1½ hours) and Arki (from

Vathy   Βαθύ

POP 1900

The island's capital, Vathy (also called Samos) enjoys a striking setting within the fold of a deep bay, where its curving waterfront is lined with bars , cafes and restaurants. The historical quarter of Ano Vathy, filled with steep narrow streets and red-tiled 19th-century houses, brims with atmosphere. The town centre boasts two engaging museums and a striking century-old church.

Vathy has two pebble beaches, the best being Gagos Beach, about 500m north from the old quay. Along the way you'll pass a string of cool bars clinging to the town's northeastern cliff.

⊙ Sights

Vathy's attractions include the Ano Vathy old quarter (inland 1km via Sofouli), relaxing municipal gardens, Roditzes and Gagos

Vathy (Samos)

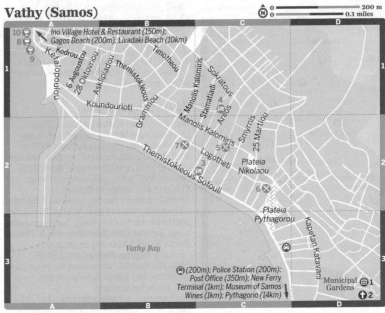

Vathy (Samos)

⊚ Sights
1	Archaeological Museum	D3
2	Church of Agios Spyridonas	D3

🛏 Sleeping
3	Hotel Aeolis	C2
4	Pension Dreams	C1

✕ Eating
5	Garden Taverna	C2

6	My Falasophy	C2
7	Pera Vrehi	B2

🍷 Drinking & Nightlife
8	Ble	A1
9	Escape Music Bar	A1
	Joy	(see 3)
10	Mezza Volta	A1

Beaches, a first-rate archaeological museum and the splendid church of **Agios Spyridonas** (Map p604; Plateia Dimarheiou; ⊙8-11am & 6.30-7.30pm).

★**Livadaki Beach**   BEACH
(Map p602) Follow the north-coast road out of Vathy for 10km and look for a signposted dirt road to the left leading to Livadaki Beach. Here, tropical azure waters lap against soft sand in a long-sheltered cove with facing islets. The water is warm and very shallow for a long way out, and Livadaki's mellow summer beach parties easily spill into it. The excellent beach bar serves snacks and drinks. For a classic taverna, get back on the main road and drive down to the hamlet of **Agia Paraskevi**, where you can enjoy a meditative lunch or dinner

with the backdrop of multicoloured boats moored in a picturesque bay.

Museum of Samos Wines   WINERY
(Map p602; ☎22730 87510, ext 548; www. samoswine.gr; €2; ⊙10am-5.30pm May-Oct; ℗) Look for this handsome stone building opposite the new ferry quay to find one of Samos' best vintners. Winery tours usually take place when you show up, and conveniently include a free tasting, with several reasonably priced wines for sale.

Archaeological Museum   MUSEUM
(Map p604; ☎22730 27469; adult/concession €4/2, 1st Sun of month Nov-Mar free; ⊙8.30am-4pm Wed-Mon) Housed in two adjacent buildings, this handsome complex displays the contents of the Heraion (p608; Sanctuary of Hera) near

Pythagorio (from Polycrates' rule in the 6th century BCE). The most famous item is the imposing *kouros* (male statue of the Archaic period). At a height of 5.5m, it's the largest-known standing *kouros*.

The collection is rounded out by many other statues, most also from the Heraion, as well as bronze sculptures, *stelae* (pillars), pottery and pieces that are unusually made of wood and are still intact.

🛏️ Sleeping & Eating

Pension Dreams   PENSION €
(Map p604; ☑ 6976425195, 22730 24350; Areos 9; d €35-40, tr €45-50; 🅿 ❈ 🛜) This small, quiet and central pension, 100m up from the waterfront, claims a hilltop view of the harbour. All seven rooms are bright and very well kept, some with large balconies and garden views. The energetic owner, Kostas, speaks English and French.

Ino Village Hotel & Restaurant   HOTEL €€
(Map p602; ☑ 22730 23241; www.inovillagehotel. com; Kalami; d incl breakfast €60-125; 🅿 ❈ 🛜 ⛱) With its courtyard pool flanked by ivy-clad, balconied white buildings, Ino Village, just 500m above Vathy, feels remote and elegant. While this mini-resort is sometimes booked by small tour groups, and can therefore feel a little impersonal, walk-in travellers are still welcome. The hotel also boasts the popular Elea restaurant and cocktail bar, which serves fine Samian wines.

Hotel Aeolis   HOTEL €€
(Map p604; ☑ 22730 28904; www.aeolis.gr; Themistokleous Sofouli 33; s/d incl breakfast €50/60; ❈ 🛜 ⛱) This central waterfront hotel attracts Athenians and foreign travellers alike, drawn by its two pools, Jacuzzi, taverna and bar. Rooms are ample and modern, all with balconies, and some overlooking the harbour. Breakfast is advertised as American as opposed to continental (read: more generous).

★ My Falasophy   MIDDLE EASTERN €
(Map p604; ☑ 22734 00835; Plateia Pythagorou; mains €4-6.5; ⊙ noon-11pm) A guest from the Levant, this little fast-food joint in the main square serves large portions of artfully prepared hummus and falafel, as well as great salads. Healthy food is complemented by freshly squeezed tropical juices.

Pera Vrehi   GREEK €
(Map p604; ☑ 22730 27965; Logotheti; salads & snacks €4-7; ⊙ 6pm-2am; 🛜 ☑) Known to

expat regulars as 'the salad place', Pera Vrehi serves large bowls of inventive salad arrangements with largely local ingredients, as well as an assortment of Greek mezedhes, such as fava-bean puree with marinated shallots. The menu is well balanced between vegetarian and carnivore food.

Garden Taverna   CAFE €€
(Map p604; ☑ 22730 24033; Manolis Kalomiris; mains €7-16; ⊙ 10am-midnight) Serves good Greek standards in a lovely garden setting. It's up to the left behind the main square.

🍷 Drinking & Nightlife

Nightlife in Vathy is more Hellenic than in the island's tourist clusters, where the scene is dominated by northern European tourists. While most cafes and bars cling to the waterfront, the coolest ones hang over the water along Kefalopoulou, 100m beyond the quay. Music and dancing is usually in full swing by midnight.

Joy   CAFE
(Map p604; ☑ 22730 89770; Themistokleous Sofouli; ⊙ 8am-midnight) The best of the waterfront cafes, serving good coffee, fresh juices and crêpes in the morning, and sandwiches, burgers, beer and wine by evening. And it delivers.

Mezza Volta   BAR
(Map p604; Kefalopoulou; ⊙ 9pm-dawn) Very popular beach bar, near the twin standbys of Ble (Map p604; Kefalopoulou 7; ⊙ 11am-4am) and Escape (Map p604; ☑ 22730 28345; Kefalopoulou 9; ⊙ 10pm-6am), with good iced drinks and snacks into the wee hours.

ℹ️ Getting There & Away

Vathy's large port handles boats to Turkey as well as domestic ferries, which connect Samos to other northeastern Aegean Islands, the Dodecanese and Piraeus.

The bus station (p603) and nearby **taxi rank** (Map p604; ☑ 22730 28404) serve as a departure point to destinations all around the island.

Pythagorio   Πυθαγόρειο
POP 1330

On the southeastern coast, opposite Turkey, pretty Pythagorio – named after the famed mathematician and philosopher Pythagoras, who was born here – has a yacht-lined harbour, and Samos' main archaeological sites, including Heraion (p608) and the extraordinary Evpalinos Tunnel. All boats

THE REFUGEE CRISIS

In 2015 the northeastern Aegean Islands hit the headlines when thousands of refugees landed on the islands' beaches, fleeing war and violence. The world watched as empathetic and concerned locals assisted the traumatised people, including children. Since then, many more refugees have arrived at Lesvos, Samos, Chios and Kos. Though refugee numbers are now at a trickle, there is a backlog in processing. While their applications for asylum are being validated and processed, the refugees are housed in several camps around the islands.

As a result of media coverage of the situation, tourism on several of the islands, particularly Lesvos and Samos, has suffered greatly. This is particularly difficult for the local people. Travellers take note: tourist infrastructure here is as strong as ever. The islands all offer wonderful accommodation, eating and cultural experiences. While it's important to stay attuned to the world news and keep alert to safety issues when planning any trip, do not overlook these wonderful islands. The world has seen how welcoming the big-hearted locals are to outsiders; deep-rooted *filoxenia* (hospitality) prevails here.

A few volunteer organisations operate on the islands trying to improve the plight of refugees in the squalid camps. **Indigo Volunteers** (https://indigovolunteers.org) is an international organisation that vets volunteers before placing them with local volunteer groups. Organisations operating on some of the islands include **Samos Volunteers** (https://samosvolunteers.org) and **Lighthouse Relief** (Lesvos; https://www.lighthouserelief.org).

departing south from Samos leave from Pythagorio, including those for day trips to Samiopoula islet. A 1.5km walk west of Pythagorio brings you to a pleasant beach with umbrellas, toilets and decent swimming.

◉ Sights & Activities

Try scuba diving with Samos Dive Center (☑ 6972997645; www.samosdiving.com; Konstantinou Kanari 1). Professional instructors lead dives in search of moray eels, sea stars, octopuses, lobsters and other critters lurking in the sponge-covered crevices around Pythagorio. A two-dive half-day for beginners costs around €50; a full-day dive, including open-water options, starts at around €85. Snorkelling (€20) is also offered.

★ Evpalinos Tunnel   ARCHAEOLOGICAL SITE
(Map p602; ☑ 22730 61400; www.eupalinostunnel.gr; adult/child €8/4; ⊙ 8.30am-3.30pm Wed-Mon May-Sep) In a word: extraordinary. In 524 BCE, when Pythagorio (then called Samos) was the island's capital and a bustling metropolis of 80,000, securing sources for drinking water became crucial. To solve the problem, ruler Polycrates ordered labourers to dig into a mountainside according to the exacting plan of his ingenious engineer, Evpalinos. Many workers died during the dangerous dig, but the result was the 1034m-long Evpalinos Tunnel. In medieval times, locals used it to hide from pirates.

The Evpalinos Tunnel is actually two tunnels: a service tunnel and a lower water conduit visible from the walkway. You enter the tunnel on narrow stairs, and it's single file from there. The first few metres are pretty tight. There are three options: a 185m section (and return), a longer version and the full 1km (you can walk back outside); guided tours take place every 20 minutes from 8.40am. Located just north of Pythagorio.

★ Archaeological
Museum of Pythagorio   MUSEUM
(☑ 22730 62813; Polykratous; adult/concession €4/2; ⊙ 8.30am-4pm Tue-Sun) One of the best museums on the islands. The exhibits in this smart space include beautifully displayed finds from Pythagorio, plus striking pottery pieces spanning the 9th century BCE through to Greece's golden age. Museum labels are in Greek and English.

Pythagorio Town Beach   BEACH
(Map p602) A short (less than 1km) walk west of Pythagorio brings you to this pristine beach with umbrellas and toilets. There's decent swimming, but pack your own food and drinks.

Castle of Lykourgos Logothetis   CASTLE
(⊙ grounds 24hr) Samians took the lead locally in the 1821 War of Independence, and this castle, built in 1824 by resistance leader Logothetis, is the major relic of that

turbulent time. It's situated on a hill at the southern end of Metamorfosis Sotiros, near the car park. The city walls once extended from here to the Evpalinos Tunnel.

Moni Panagias Spilianis MONASTERY
(Monastery of the Virgin of the Grotto; ☑22730 61361; ⊘9am-8pm) FREE About 1.5km northwest of Pythagorio, the road forks right, past traces of an ancient theatre, before reaching this grotto monastery. The walk meanders up through old olive groves; it's a welcome respite from the summer heat and gives clear views to the nearby Turkish coast.

🛏 Sleeping

Belvedere GUESTHOUSE €
(☑22730 61218; www.belvedere-samos.com; Aisopou 6; d €30-45; ❄☎) Football coach Manolis runs this immaculate, nicely furnished guesthouse in a quiet area not far from the main street and the seafront. All rooms come with balconies and a sea view. No breakfast on offer, but there is a common kitchen for self-caterers.

Pension Despina PENSION €
(☑6936930381, 22730 61677; A Nikolaou; studio/apt €35/40; ❄☎) An impeccably well-kept quiet pension on the small and central Plateia Irinis, the Despina offers attractive rooms and studios (some with kitchenettes) with overhead fans and balconies, plus a relaxing back garden. Owner Athina is very friendly. Find it on Facebook.

Samaina Hotel HOTEL €€
(☑22730 61024, 6936078159; Damous; d incl breakfast from €80; ❄☎) In a radical departure from the standard white-and-blue colour scheme, this hotel opts for a palette of autumn foliage both inside and out. Rooms feature many wooden surfaces and fittings. All come with balconies and at least some kind of sea view.

Polyxeni Hotel HOTEL €€
(☑22730 61590; www.polyxenihotel.com; s/d incl breakfast from €65/72; ❄☎) This reasonable seafront lodging is bang in the middle of the port hubbub. The several balconied harbour-view rooms are fitted with overhead fans and double-glazed windows. The garden-view rooms are the quieter ones to go for if bar and cafe noise (from below) isn't for you. Nothing special, but a decent, central bed-for-the-night choice.

🍴 Eating

Pythagorio has the most sophisticated dining scene in Samos. Be sure to head beyond the eastern side of the wharf where several attractive waterfront tavernas are out of sight.

★To Tigani tis Platias TAVERNA €
(☑6971673770; Plateia Irinis; mains €7.50-10; ⊘11am-midnight; ☎🍴) Beautiful Greek standards, popular with both locals and visitors. It's especially great for veggie choices, such as baked feta, *gigantes* (white beans) and courgette balls, all a cut above average. Meat grills here are also superb, and there's a shady setting, cheerful service and good wine.

Two Spoons DESSERTS €
(☑22730 62336; www.facebook.com/TwOSpOOns; Melissou; desserts €5-12; ⊘9am-1am; ☎) Make sure you run a marathon before coming to this place, because you'll be hard pressed to prevent yourself from gorging on profiteroles, millefeuille and pavlova. Milkshakes are also on offer and – unusually for these coffee lands – a good selection of teas. With a garden setting by the sea, this place is the definition of guilty pleasure.

Kafeneio To Mouragio CAFE €
(☑22730 62390; waterfront; mezedhes €3-6; ⊘8am-midnight; ☎) The warm ambience and predominantly Greek clientele hint at the fact that this place delivers the goods, with snacks such as chickpea croquettes and assorted mezedhes. Enjoy coffee in the morning and, later, iced ouzo, wine and beer. Customers are welcome to leave their luggage for free.

🍸 Drinking & Nightlife

Iera Odos Art Cafe BAR
(☑22730 61091; Lykourgou Logotheti; ⊘5pm-3am) Lush, decadent luxury is not what you'd expect in this corner of the Aegean, but here you are, amidst velvet cushions and lavish chandeliers, with a cocktail glass in your hand. There's also a terrace and a garden of 'magic crystals' where you can savour your drink in fresh air.

Katoi BAR
(Lykourgou Logotheti) In the main street, this smallish modern place combines the virtues of a deli and an *ouzerie* (place that sells ouzo and like snacks). Ouzo and *tsipouro* are served with local cheeses and ham (€5 for the combo), which are also available for

NORTHEASTERN AEGEAN ISLANDS PYTHAGORIO

sale from the shop inside. Fresh juices also available.

Notos BAR

(🖉 22730 62351; Tarsanas Beach; ⊙ noon-late; 🛜)
From the main road, turn right (south) at the port to find this popular late-night music bar and taverna, opposite a public car park. Live music most Tuesdays and Saturdays.

❶ Information

By Ship Travel (p591) Helpful full-service travel agency, offering car hire, accommodation, air and ferry tickets. At the junction entering town.

❶ Getting There & Away

There are five buses daily to Vathy (25 minutes) and five buses daily to Ireon (15 minutes) for Heraion (p608). A taxi between Pythagorio and the airport (4km west of town) costs €10; it's €25 to/from Vathy. **Taxis** (🖉 22730 61450) also ply the route between Pythagorio and Vathy (useful for ferry arrivals and departures) for around €20.

Around Pythagorio

Heraion ARCHAEOLOGICAL SITE

(Map p602; adult/child €6/3; ⊙ 8am-4pm Wed-Mon) It's hard to fully grasp the former magnificence of this ancient sanctuary of the goddess Hera, 4km west of Pythagorio, from these scattered ruins. The 'Sacred Way', once flanked by thousands of marble statues, led from the city to this World Heritage–listed site, built at Hera's legendary birthplace. However, enough survives to provide a glimpse of a sanctuary that was four times larger than the Parthenon.

Built in the 6th century BCE, the Heraion was constructed over an earlier Mycenaean temple. Plundering and earthquakes have left only one column standing, though extensive foundations remain. Other remains include a stoa (long colonnaded building), a 5th-century Christian basilica, and the headless, and unsettling, statues of a family, the Geneleos Group. Archaeologists continue to unearth treasures.

★ **Hotel Restaurant Cohyli** HOTEL €

(Map p602; 🖉 6977809389, 22730 95282; www.hotel-cohyli.com; Ireon; r incl breakfast from €43; 🅿 ❄ 🛜) You'll sleep and eat well at this welcoming hotel-taverna gem. Rooms are cosy and clean, and equipped with fridges and fans. When you're hungry, just relocate to the shaded courtyard next door to sample excellent mezedhes, *saganaki* (fried

cheese), fresh fish and breakfast with 'sunshine eggs'. There's a small beach across the road, and live acoustic music many summer evenings.

Northern Samos

Northern Samos is a wonderful mix of stunning sea and mountain scenery, marble gravel beaches and quirky villages favoured as a base by local and foreign artisans. The relatively remote (hence uncrowded) Potami Beach is the area's crown jewel, especially as it is a short trek away from waterfalls and pools of cool crystal water beneath the thick canopy of a broadleaf forest. Two more excellent secluded beaches can be reached by trekking from Potami.

Kokkari & Mountain Villages

From Vathy, the coast road west passes a number of beaches and resorts. The first, Kokkari (10km from Vathy), was once a fishing village, but is now a rather crowded resort. Windsurfers test the waves from its long pebble beach in summer, and the nearby beaches of Limanaki (Map p602), Tsambou (Map p602) and Livadhaki (Map p602) draw swimmers and sunbathers.

Continuing west, the landscape becomes more forested and mountainous. Take the left-hand turn-off after 5km to reach the lovely mountain village of Vourliotes. The village's multicoloured, shuttered houses cluster around a *plateia* (square). Walkers can enjoy an 8km loop trail between Vourliotes and Kokkari through olive groves and lofty woodlands – it's one of those magical *monopati* (footpath) routes where you hardly realise you've been climbing. Find the free walking map in Vourliotes.

Back on the coast road, look for the signposted turn-off for another fragrant village, Manolates, 5km further up the lower slopes of Mt Ambelos (Karvouni; 1150m). Set amid thick pine and deciduous forests, and boasting gorgeous traditional houses, Manolates is nearly encircled by mountains and offers a cooler alternative to the sweltering coast. The village is home to a fledgling artisan community, and has some excellent jewellery and souvenir shops.

Good tavernas are plentiful and, despite the more touristy patina of Manolates, both it and Vourliotes are worth visiting for a glimpse of old Samos.

Around Karlovasi

The coast road continues west from Vathy through flowery Agios Konstantinos before coming to workaday Karlovasi, Samos' third port, home to several hotels and tavernas. Rhenia Tours (☑ 22730 62280; Karlovasi; ⊘ May-Oct) is good for ferry tickets and reliable information. The town's blue-collar history is on display at the Karlovasi Folk Art Museum (Map p602; ☑ 22730 62286; Karlovasi; ⊘ 9am-1pm Tue-Sun) FREE. Once in the port, wander around and admire multiple street art (Karlovasi Port Area; Map p602) objects – the legacy of a 2017 project to enliven this slightly dilapidated area.

The old village, Palio Karlovasi, above the port is well worth the short drive up the hill. From the small car park, a 500m walk brings you to the chapel of Agia Triada, which has panoramic views.

Just 3km beyond Karlovasi lies the sand-and-pebble Potami Beach, blessed with good swimming and a reggae beach bar (p611). It's complemented by nearby forest waterfalls; head west 50m from the beach and look for the signpost on the left. Entering the forest you'll first encounter the centuries-old Metamorfosis Sotiros chapel, where the devout light candles. Continuing about 1.5km through the wooded trail along the river brings you to a river channel, where you must wade or swim before enjoying a splash under the 2m-high waterfalls. Wooden stairs going up from the canyon will bring you to the excellent Archontissa Potami Adventure Cafe (p610).

After Potami, the coastal road becomes a dirt track and a popular trail veers off towards the scenic beaches Mikro Seitani and Megalo Seitani.

★ Activities

★ Potami Beach
BEACH
(Map p602) This long, tranquil beach of marble gravel and crystal-clear water in the mouth of a mountain river is one of the island's most attractive; its beach bar is one of the best, too. Trekking up the river, you'll reach a chain of waterfalls and pools, as well as a taverna hidden in the woods.

Megalo Seitani Trek
TREKKING
(Map p602) This medium-difficulty trail branches off the main road about 1km west of Potami Beach. It follows a rugged pine-covered coastline towards the charming little

A MATTER OF MEASUREMENTS

While the obsession with the 'proper pint' may seem modern, the Ancient Greeks also fixated on measuring their alcohol. Pythagoras, a great Samian mathematician (and, presumably, drinker), created an invention that ensured party hosts and publicans could not be deceived by guests aspiring to inebriation. His creation was dubbed the *Dikiakoupa tou Pythagora* (Just Cup of Pythagoras). This mysterious, multi-holed drinking vessel holds its contents perfectly, unless filled past the engraved line, at which point the glass drains completely from the bottom, punishing the glutton!

Today, faithful reproductions, made of colourful glazed ceramic, are sold in Samos gift shops, and are tangible reminders of the Apollon Mean: 'Everything in moderation'.

cove of Micro Seitani and then continues to the long sandy beach of Megalo Seitani. It takes around two hours to reach the latter, with sweeping vistas at every step. Take water and snacks.

Tsamadou
BEACH
(Map p602) Flanked by dramatic limestone cliffs, this attractive beach is famed for its clear water and a remarkable view – with Chios and bits of the Turkish coast covering the entire horizon, it seems as if you're inside a Santorini-like giant volcanic caldera.

🛏 Sleeping

Pension Mary's House
PENSION €
(Map p602; ☑ 22730 93291; www.marys-house-samos.com; Vourliotes; d/tr €60/70; 🅿❈ 🛜) Superb location in the village, with amazing balcony views, decent furnishings, and a lovely garden and orchard setting. Follow the painted wooden signs 200m from the village square.

Hesperia Hotel
APARTMENT €
(Map p602; ☑ 22730 30706; www.hesperiahotel.gr; Karlovasi; studios/apt from €45/60; 🅿❈🛜) Run by a friendly family, these spotless apartments across from the beach get rave reviews from loyal returning guests. It's close to the ferry port.

SOUTHERN SAMOS

Driving west of Pythagorio, you enter a sparsely populated, beautiful mountainous terrain, dotted with just a few quaint fishing ports and the single fully fledged beach resort of Votsalakia. Up in the mountains, road signs point to beekeepers' huts, where the superlative but inexpensive Samian honey is on sale. But before you leave the coastal plain, make a detour to the celebrated archaeological site of the Heraion (p608), where ancient Samiots worshipped the goddess Hera.

Further west, the road starts climbing into the highlands, where mass tourism has had hardly any effect on the traditional life of mountain villages. Stop at the village of Spatharei for sweeping sea views and lunch at the quirky Shall We Go to Anna's? (Map p602; ☑22730 42141; Spatharei; €7-10; ☉9.30am-late), and look out for roadside kiosks selling honey and other local products as you drive further on beyond Pyrgos.

After Ormos Marathokambou, the road starts to descend to a cluster of tourist villages, the most crowded of them being Votsalakia (often called Kampos), with its long, sandy beach. To escape the midsummer mob, head 3km further west to the more tranquil Psili Ammos Beach or Limnionas; stay the night in domatia here and sample the fresh fish at the beach tavernas. The latter can be combined with some great snorkelling if you venture west of Limnionas towards Tavern at the End of the World (Map p602; ☑6977664437; Limnionas; €8-15; ☉10am-8pm mid-May–Sep; ☎), an aptly far-flung establishment.

Past Kampos, the rugged western route, undeveloped and tranquil, skirts Mt Kerkis (1434m) until reaching the villages of Kallithea and Drakeï, where the road abruptly ends. A walking trail is the only link between this point and Potami on the north coast.

Hikers keen on exploring the flanks of Mt Kerkis, or even reaching its peak, should enquire in Votsalakia for the trailhead, which passes the convent of Evangelistrias on the way.

Kalidon Beach Hotel HOTEL €€

(☑22730 92605; http://kalidon.gr/beach; Kokkari; d incl breakfast from €85; ✴☎) A comfortable and friendly hotel with rooms set away from Kokkari's busy main road. Breakfasts are served on a terrace. The beach is seconds away.

Virginia Apartments APARTMENT €€

(☑22730 92274, 210 777 5239; www.virginia.gr; Kokkari; apt from €130; ✴☎) On Tarsanas Beach in Kokkari, these three elegant and tastefully furnished two-room apartments are completely outfitted with modern amenities, plus hand-embroidered pillowcases, and balcony views of the small harbour and the Aegean beyond.

Kokkari Beach Hotel HOTEL €€

(☑22730 92263; www.kokkaribeach.com; Kokkari; s/d/tr incl breakfast €70/80/90; Ｐ✴☎✻) This striking upmarket establishment, 1km west of the bus stop, is set back from the road in a pastel-green-and-blue building, just opposite the beach. The airy and cool rooms are equally colourful.

 Eating

Archontissa Potami Adventure Cafe GREEK €

(Map p602; www.facebook.com/pg/ArchontissaPotamiWaterfalls; Potami; mains €8-10; ☉lunch & dinner) Its called Adventure for good reason: trekking along the creek before climbing wooden stairs on a near-vertical slope is indeed just that. But this canopy-level terrace is good enough reason to do the Potami waterfall hike. It has great food (try the goat ribs) and a fridge full of very cold drinks that you will desperately need.

Loukas Taverna TAVERNA €

(Map p602; Manolates; mains €5-8; ☉lunch & dinner) Upon entering Manolates you'll see signs, one after the other, pointing the way to this traditional eatery above the village. Proud owner Manolis serves up excellent and hearty taverna standards along with his own wines – red, white and sweet.

Café Bar Cavos CAFE €

(☑22730 92426; Kokkari; mains €6-12; ☉9am-midnight; ☎) An efficient and comfortable Kokkari harbour bar, serving good breakfasts, afternoon snacks, fresh juices and evening cocktails. Decent prices, plus free wi-fi and satellite TV for big sports events. Ask about Uli's homemade cake of the day.

Kallisti Taverna TAVERNA €
(Map p602; ✐ 22730 94661; Manolates; mains €6-9; ☺10am-11pm) This intriguing taverna on the square has numerous excellent dishes including *kleftiko* (slow oven-baked lamb with vegetables), and unusual desserts, such as a tasty orange pie.

★**Hippy's Restaurant Café** TAVERNA €€
(Map p602; ✐ 22730 67700021; Potami Beach; mains €7-15; ☺9.30am-9pm; P☎) This cool open-air cafe-bar is a family affair, combining Greek and South Seas decor with jazz, reggae, classical, trip-hop and ambient sounds. Good omelettes, pasta, grilled fresh fish and skewers are served, as well as owner Apolstolis' naturally fermented wine and assorted drinks and juices. The place has a relaxing, rambling end-of-the-road feel, with hospitality and character to spare.

AAA Restaurant GREEK €€
(✐ 22730 94472; www.aaasamos.com; Agios Konstantinos; mains €8-14; ☺2pm-11pm; ☎) Having relocated from Manolates to the main coastal road right at the turn to the village, this large restaurant offers a refined and somewhat urban take on traditional Greek cuisine. Try the slowly cooked *kleftiko* lamb.

Sophia's Place MEZEDHES €€
(✐ 22730 92561; Kokkari; mains €6.50-14; ☺11am-11pm) Excellent tiny three-table gem, with superb small plates and charming service from Sophia and friends.

O Tarsanas Restaurant TAVERNA €€
(✐ 22730 92337; Kokkari; mains €8-15; ☺5pm-midnight; ☎) Named for Kokkari's old boat-building area, this authentic old-style Greek taverna – nothing more, nothing less – does great pizzas and *mousakas*. Welcoming owner Kyriakos rolls out luscious dolmadhes and pours his own homemade wine.

Pera Vrysi TAVERNA €€
(Map p602; Vourliotes; mains €6.50-14; ☺10am-midnight Tue-Sun) This old-style Samian taverna by the spring at Vourliotes' entrance offers exceptional village cuisine in ample portions, and homemade barrel wine.

🛍 Shopping

Kerannymi JEWELLERY
(Map p602; ✐ 22730 94801; www.facebook.com/pg/kerannymi; Manolates; ☺9am-6pm) A duo or – as they call it – an alloy of female artists, Alek Lindus and Maria Karavatou produce mesmerisingly beautiful, prehistoric-looking jewellery that fuses silver with various mineral and organic materials. You can find them at work in their shop in the village square.

Genesis Pottery Shop CERAMICS
(Map p602; Manolates; ☺varies) Come to watch Giorgos spinning his wheel and making beauty out of mud. The main shop is in the main street between the parking lot and the main square.

❶ Getting There & Away

Karlovasi is the island's second port with connections to Ikaria, Fourni, other northeastern Aegean Islands and Turkey. Ferry tickets are available from local branches of **By Ship Travel** (✐ 22730 35252; Karlovasi; ☺8am-9.30pm) or Rhenia Tours (p609). Daily buses ply the route between Vathy and Karlovasi (one hour), stopping at Kokkari (20 minutes).

CHIOS ΧΙΟΣ

POP 51,930

While no Greek island is like another, Chios has one of the most distinctive faces, thanks to the unique fortress-like architecture of its villages that makes them look so different from their sugar-cube cousins on other islands. That style stems from the island's history as the ancestral home of shipping barons and the world's only commercial producer of mastic. Many of these unusual heritage buildings now serve as hotels, bringing Chios into the top league of unusual accommodation.

The island's terrain ranges from lonesome mountain crags in the north, to the citrus-grove estates of Kampos near the island's port capital in the centre, to the fertile Mastihohoria in the south, where generations of mastic growers have turned their villages into decorative art gems.

The intriguing, little-visited satellite islands of Psara and Inousses share Chios' legacy of maritime greatness.

History

As with neighbours Samos and Lesvos, geographic proximity to Turkey has brought Chios both great success and great tragedy. Under the Ottomans, Chios' monopolistic production of mastic – the sultan's favourite gum – brought Chians wealth and privilege.

Chios

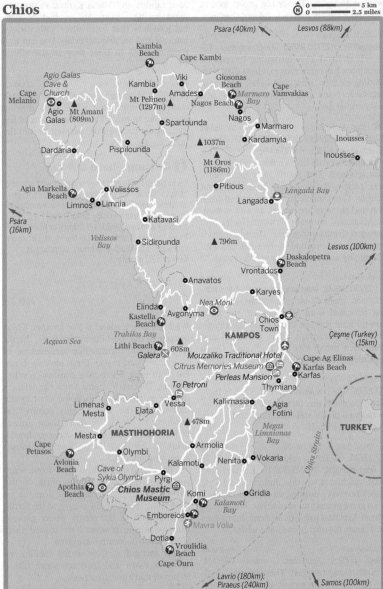

0   5 km
0   2.5 miles

Psara (40km)   *Lesvos (88km)*

Kambia Beach
Cape Kambi

Agio Galas Cave & Church
Cape Melanio
Agio Galas
Kambia
Viki
Mt Pelineo (1297m)
Amades
Giosonas Beach
Marmaro Bay
Cape Vamvakias
Nagos Beach
Nagos
Mt Amani (809m)
Spartounda
Marmaro
Kardamyla
Dardaria
Pispilounda
▲1037m
Mt Oros (1186m)
Inousses
Inousses

Agia Markella Beach
Volissos
Limnos Limnia
Pitious
Langada
Langada Bay

Psara (16km)

Katavasi

Volissos Bay
Sidirounda
▲ 796m

Lesvos (100km)

Aegean Sea

Anavatos
Daskalopetra Beach
Vrontados
Karyes

Elinda
Nea Moni
Kastella Beach
Avgonyma
Trahilos Bay
Lithi Beach
Galera
▲ 608m
Chios Town
KAMPOS

Çeşme (Turkey) (15km)

Mouzaliko Traditional Hotel
Citrus Memories Museum
Cape Ag Elinas
Karfas Beach
Karfas
Perleas Mansion
Thymiana
To Petroni
Vessa
Kallimasia
Agia Fotini

Limenas Mesta
Elata
▲ 478m
Megas Limnionas Bay

TURKEY

Mesta
MASTIHOHORIA
Armolia

Cape Petasos
Avlonia Beach
Olymbi
Kalamoti
Nenita
Vokaria

Chios Straits

Cave of Sykia Olymbi
Pyrgi
Chios Mastic Museum
Komi
Gridia

Apothia Beach
Emboreios
Kalamoti Bay
Mavra Volia

Dotia
Vroulidia Beach
Cape Oura

Lavrio (180km); Piraeus (240km)   *Samos (100km)*

However, during the 1821–29 War of Independence, thousands of Chians were slaughtered by Ottoman troops.

In 1922, a military campaign launched from Chios to reclaim lands with Greek-majority populations in Asia Minor ended disastrously, as waves of refugees from Asia Minor (Anatolia) flooded Chios and neighbouring islands. The following year saw the 'population exchange', in which two million ethnic Greeks and Turks were forced to return to the homelands of their ancestors.

ℹ️ Information

Check out www.chios.gr/en, a very comprehensive online guide to Chios run by the local branch of the Department of Tourism.

ℹ️ Getting There & Away

Chios is connected by air and also enjoys regular boat connections throughout the northeastern Aegean Islands. Between them, the ports of Chios Town in the east and Volissos in the northwest offer regular ferries to the satellite islands of Psara and Inousses, and to the lively Turkish coastal resorts just across the water.

AIR

During summer, **Aegean Air** (www.aegeanair.com), **Sky Express** (www.skyexpress.gr) and **Astra Airlines** (www.astra-airlines.gr) serve Athens and surrounding islands.

The airport is 4km from Chios Town. It is served by three buses a day departing from the **local bus station** (Map p614; ☎ 22710 22079; https://chioscitybus.gr; Plateia Vounaki; 1.50); an airport taxi costs €8.

BOAT

There are always a couple of boats moored and being loaded in the busy Chios port, which in addition to island and Greek mainland connections, links Chios with the Turkish port of Çeşme.

Up to three boats daily sail east for Piraeus (€34.50, eight to 18 hours) or north for Lesvos (€21, 2¾ hours). There are four boats a week heading for ports in Samos (€14, 3¼ hours) and Ikaria (€18.50, 5½ to 7½ hours). Kavala (€35.50, 10¼ hours) on the Macedonian mainland is served by three boats a week, going via Limnos (€24.50, seven hours).

Smaller daily local ferries provide connection with nearby islands of Inousses and Psara (€6, three hours). Additionally, *Nissos Samos* calls at these two on the way to Piraeus on Tuesdays.

Once a week, the smallish port of Chios Mesta wakes up to greet *Express Pegasus* heading for Sigri (€21, 2½ hours) on Lesvos and Agios Efstratios (€25, five hours).

In addition to regular ferry service to nearby Inousses, daily **water taxis** (☎ 6944168104, 6945361281; Langada) travel between Langada and Inousses (€65; shared between up to eight passengers).

Buy ferry tickets in Chios Town from Sunrise Tours (p591) or **Michalakis Travel** (☎ 22710 40070; Kanari 9; ⏱ 8am-10.30pm).

ℹ️ Getting Around

BUS

Chios Town's waterfront **long-distance bus station** (Map p614; ☎ 22710 27507; Neorion) is well organised, and has a cafe and coin lockers. On working days, green buses depart from here to Pyrgi (€3.10, three daily), Mesta (€4.30, three daily), Lithi Beach (€3.60, two daily), Kardamyla (€3.60, two daily) and Langada (€2, two daily). There are three buses a week serving Volissos (€4.90).

Blue city buses on Plateia Vounaki (Vounakiou Sq) also serve nearby Karfas Beach (€1.50, four daily), just south of Chios Town, and Vrontados (€1.50, six daily), just north of town. Schedules are posted at both the local bus station and the long-distance bus station.

CAR & MOTORCYCLE

Smack in the middle of the waterfront promenade, the slick **Travelshop** (☎ 22710 81500, 6934517141; www.travel-shop.gr; Leoforos Egeou 56; ⏱ 8am-9pm) has a good choice of budget vehicles, jeeps and convertibles.

TAXI

Taxis are plentiful in Chios Town; red taxis serve Chios Town only, and grey taxis are good for the rest of the island. Sample costs from Chios Town:

Chios Airport €8
Emporios €40
Langada €20
Mesta €45
Pyrgi €30

Chios Town · Χίος

POP 23,710

On the central east coast, Chios' main port and capital is home to almost half the island's inhabitants. Unlike smaller island capitals, it has a distinct urban feel. Behind the busy port area lies a quieter, intriguing old quarter, where some traditional Turkish houses and an old *hammam* (Turkish bathhouse; p615) stand enclosed by the walls of a Genoese castle. There's also a busy market area behind the waterfront, and spacious public gardens (Vounaki) where an open-air cinema operates on summer evenings. The nearest decent beach is popular Karfas, 6km south.

👁 Sights

⭐ **Korais Library & Philip Argenti Museum** · MUSEUM
(Map p614; ☎ 22710 44246; www.koraeslibrary.gr; Korai 3; €2; ⏱ 7am-3pm Mon-Sat) On the upper floor of the remarkable Korais Library, the Philip Argenti Museum contains a 19th-century birthing chair, along with shepherds' tools, embroidery, traditional costumes and portraits of the wealthy Argenti family. The place is a touching tribute to Greek cultural renaissance figure

Chios Town

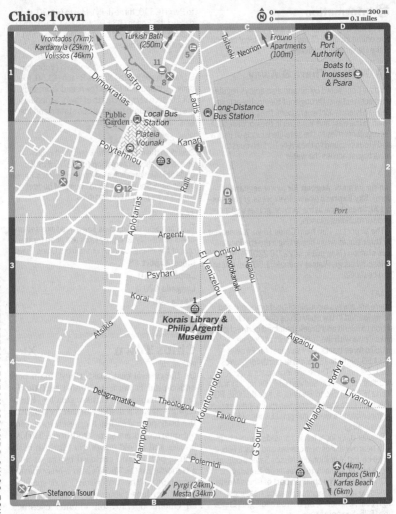

Chios Town

◎ Top Sights
1 Korais Library & Philip Argenti
   Museum...B3

◎ Sights
2 Archaeological Museum.......................D5
3 Byzantine Museum...............................B2

🛏 Sleeping
4 Homeric Poems.....................................A2
5 Porta di Marina.....................................B1
6 Rooms Alex...D4

✗ Eating
7 Hotzas Taverna.....................................A5
8 Kafenes..B1
9 Kechribari Ouzerie...............................A2
10 Pastards..D4

🍷 Drinking & Nightlife
11 Civitas Dimitris Cafe...........................B1
12 Kubrick..B2

🛍 Shopping
13 Mastihashop..C2

Adamantios Korais, who set up the library in 1792 and replenished it after the massacre of Chios. Philip Argenti was a French-born benefactor and researcher of Chian history. The library holds medicinal texts from the 15th century.

Turkish Bath
HISTORIC BUILDING

(☑22710 44238; Navarchou Nikodimou 1; ☉8.30am-4pm Wed-Mon) `FREE` With its bubble-like cupolas pierced to let in gentle shafts of light, this classic early-18th-century *hammam* (Turkish bath) was built as a charitable institution by the Ottomans for the Turkish population of the *kastro*. After the Turks were expelled in 1922, the building fell into disrepair, but was restored as a museum in 2011. Sadly, it no longer performs its original function.

Archaeological Museum
MUSEUM

(Map p614; ☑22710 44239; Mihalon 10; €2; ☉8.30am-4pm Wed-Mon) Along with prehistoric and Archaic treasures from the excavations of the British School at Emporios, this collection includes impressive Neolithic and Classical finds (coins, sculptures and pottery) from Agios Galas and Fana.

Byzantine Museum
MUSEUM

(Map p614; ☑22710 26866; Plateia Vounaki; €4; ☉8.30am-4pm Wed-Mon) Housed in a 19th-century Ottoman mosque, the Medjitie Djami, this museum contains relics from the Byzantine, post-Byzantine, Genoese and Islamic periods, including old cannons, fine icons, and Jewish, Muslim and Armenian tombstones.

🛏 Sleeping

There's a good selection of hotels in Chios Town, but those on the waterfront can be noisy. The *kastro* area is the quietest part of the centre.

Porta di Marina
APARTMENT €

(Map p614; ☑6948077911; Zachariou 4-6; apt €60; ❄🗡) What were once the actual gates of the Genovese-built castle now contain two large and fully equipped apartments, complete with a washing machine and a bathtub – a delight for those who have been on the road for some time. The place is a short walk from the port, but very quiet at night.

Frourio Apartments
APARTMENT €

(☑22710 42476, 6945408464; www.chiosfrourio.gr; Kalothetou 10; s/d/tr/q from €50/60/70/80; ❄🗡) After the hustle and bustle of traffic-filled Chios Town, it is a pleasure to find yourself in the serene neighbourhood inside the *kastro*, where the greatest noise is produced by singing canaries and church bells. There's enough equipment in the large modern apartments to sustain a nuclear winter. Crucially, that includes a washing machine.

Rooms Alex
PENSION €

(Map p614; ☑6979535256; roomsalex@hotmail.gr; Livanou 29; r €30) Host and former sea captain Alex Stoupas' handmade model ships decorate each of the simple but clean rooms here. The *kapetanios* (captain) is '100% helpful', as he'll happily tell you; he picks up guests from the ferry and speaks English, French and Spanish.

★ Homeric Poems
APARTMENT €€

(Map p614; ☑6907339239; Kontoleontos 3; d/tr €80/90; ❄🗡) Two studios in a late-19th-century captain's house are furnished as a fancy boutique hotel, with comfy beds, couches and too many multi-coloured pillows to count. Bric-a-brac and myriad jars filled with fragrances make the place feel like a curiosity shop from a children's movie and the magician-like owner, Angelika, adds to the effect.

🍴 Eating & Drinking

Although filled with Turkish day-trippers, waterfront tavernas are not necessarily tourist traps. Better places hide away from the main action. A little square at the beginning of Frourio inside the *kastro* is a particularly nice and peaceful spot to enjoy a meal.

Pastards
ITALIAN €

(Map p614; ☑22710 81466; Livanou 13; mains €7-10; ☉1pm-1am; 🗡) In a welcome departure from the island-taverna routine, this place serves homemade pastas, risottos and risonis, all with a strong locavore element, featuring items such as various types of Greek cheese and *loukanika* (pork sausages). Chios beer and good local wine are also on offer.

Kafenes
TAVERNA €

(Map p614; ☑22710 42242; Agiou Georgiou Frouriou 12; mains €5-8; ☉10am-midnight; 🗡) In a cute little square within the castle walls, this welcoming and efficient taverna receives a batch of fresh catch from the port in the morning and proceeds from there. Try the salted lakedra fish, the owner's speciality.

Hotzas Taverna TAVERNA €
(Map p614; ☑ 22710 42787; Kondyli 3; mains €5.50-9; ☺ 7pm-midnight; 🛜🍴) This comfortable, attractive taverna above Chios Town serves fine Greek standards with a twist, such as lamb kebab with yoghurt and rocket; white beans with tomato and mandarin; and dolmadhes with lemon. Everything is *herisia* (handmade), from the pasta to the dessert.

★**Kechribari Ouzerie** GREEK €€
(Map p614; ☑ 6942425459; Agion Anargyron 7; set meal €15; ☺ 12.30-5pm) This cosy gem of an *ouzerie* offers a variety of small plates in addition to excellent fish, mussels, baked potatoes and grilled meats. The choice is between two set menus featuring meat or fish; beyond that, you don't know exactly what you'll get. But indeed that's part of the appeal.

Civitas Dimitris Cafe CAFE
(Map p614; ☑ 22710 81565; Frourio 1; ☺ 8.30am till late; 🛜) Owner Dimitris is good to have a chat with and get travel tips from. He makes fresh orange juice from blood oranges and flavours Greek coffee with mastic. Fresh lemonades and an interesting selection of Greek wines are also on offer, as is the 'mastic submarine' – a typical Chios sweet.

Kubrick BAR
(Map p614; ☑ 22711 02744; Anelastou 14; ☺ 8am-4am; 🛜) It's kind of apt that a favourite bohemian hang-out in this citrus region is themed around the director of *A Clockwork Orange*. Looking sombrely from a mural on the side of a stylish wooden bar, a bearded Stanley Kubrick observes Vergina (Macedonian craft beer) taps and the island's cool kids passing their time in mellow conversations over cocktails and coffee.

🔒 Shopping

Mastihashop COSMETICS
(Map p614; ☑ 22710 81600; www.mastihashop.com; Aigaiou 36; ☺ 8.30am-10pm) Efficient and attractive shop with a range of mastic-based products such as lotions, toothpastes, soaps and condiments. Ask for a sample of pure mastic to chew on.

ℹ Information

Chios Tourist Office (Map p614; ☑ 22713 51776; www.chios.gr; Kanari 18; ☺ 7am-3pm & 6-10pm) Island transport and accommodation info, plus an assortment of brochures advertising local travel-related businesses.

Port Authority (Map p614; ☑ 22710 44432; Neorion)

ℹ Getting There & Away

Chios Town is the island's main transport hub (p613), where boats arrive and planes land. Buses depart for destinations around the island from the long-distance bus station (p613) near the port. The local bus station (p613) in Plateia Vounaki serves destinations in the large suburban area of Kampos. Taxis are available for hire at the **taxi rank** (Map p614; ☑ 22710 41111; Plateia Vounaki) nearby.

Northern Chios

Northern Chios is rocky and sparsely populated, compared with the agricultural south. A string of fishing villages, with picturesque ports and fish tavernas, lines the northeastern coast. On the western side, the scenic Volissos and Avgonyma peer into the deep blue of the Aegean from their mountaintop positions. Avgonyma's abandoned village and the sombre Nea monastery serve as reminders of the 1822 massacre – the greatest catastrophe the island has ever experienced.

⊙ Sights

Roughly 4km north of Chios Town, Vrontados is the site of Homer's legendary stone chair, the Daskalopetra (in Greek, 'teacher's stone'), a rock pinnacle near the sea that's an obvious choice for holding class.

Further north, Langada is a relaxed cove of pine trees, homes, domatia and tavernas, and a launching point for water taxis to nearby Inousses.

The main villages of Marmaro and Kardamyla follow as you head north, containing the ancestral homes of many wealthy ship-owning families. At Nagos, the road continues northwest, skirting Mt Pelineo (1297m), then winding its way through Kambia, high on a ridge overlooking the sea. In the northwest, wild camping is allowed around Agio Galas, also home to Agio Galas Cave, the island's largest, if not the most impressive.

A road leading west from Chios Town will bring you to Avgonyma, a scenic mountaintop village and convenient base for exploring desolate historic sites – including the 'ghost village' of Anavatos, and the tragic Nea Moni monastery – that witnessed some of the most catastrophic events in the island's history.

North of Avgonyma lies Volissos, Homer's legendary birthplace, now crowned with the impressive ruins of its hilltop Genoese fort. Down below, the tiny port of Limnia is flanked by a couple of pretty coves with

INOUSSES, THE TYCOON HIDEAWAY & PSARA, ISLAND OF HEROES

Just northeast of Chios Town, serene Inousses is the ancestral home of nearly a third of Greece's shipping barons (the *arhontes*), whose wealthy descendants return here annually for summer vacations from their homes overseas. Although Inousses is little visited, it does get lively in summer, with an open-air cinema, friendly residents and a buzzing night-time waterfront. The island's port attests to its seafaring identity. Arriving by ferry, you'll see a small, green, sculpted mermaid watching over the harbour. In the port, the striking statue of Mitera Inoussiotissa (Mother of Inoussa), a village woman waving goodbye to seafaring men, is incredibly photogenic at sunset.

In July and August, agencies such as Sunrise Tours (p591) run day trips to Inousses (€20 to €50), which is how most people come to the island. Otherwise you can use water taxis (p613) out of Langada or consider staying overnight. The latter is easier said than done: the only reliable accommodation option is – quite aptly – a luxurious shipowner's villa and three cheaper flats that go under the collective brand of Evgenikon (www.evgenikon.com).

Celebrated Psara is one of maritime Greece's true oddities. A tiny speck in the sea 16km northwest of Chios, this island of scrub vegetation, wandering goats and weird red-rock formations looms inordinately large in modern lore. The Psariot clans became wealthy through shipping, and their participation in the 1821–29 War of Independence is etched into modern Greek history, particularly the daring exploits of Konstantinos Kanaris (1793–1877), whose heroic stature propelled him, six times, to the position of prime minister.

Psara's main cultural attraction, the Monastery of Kimisis Theotokou, 12km north of Psara town, is a smallish chapel surrounded by protective walls. In all, there are 67 chapels across the island, each cared for by a local family.

The incongruous Psara Glory leaves Chios Town in the late afternoon on working days and returns early next morning (€12 return, three hours). The larger Express Pegasus frequently calls at Psara on the way to Limnos and the mainland port of Lavrio, or as it returns to Chios.

pebble beaches. It has a few tavernas and domatia.

Driving 5km northeast will get you to Moni Agias Markellas, named for Chios' patron saint. From Volissos the coastal road continues south until Elinda, then heads eastward towards Chios Town.

Anavatos
VILLAGE

At the end of a silent stretch of road that branches off the main road near Avgonyma, this solemn site serves as a reminder of the island's brutal history. The abandoned village of grey-stone houses and narrow stepped pathways is perched on a precipitous cliff over which villagers hurled themselves to avoid capture during Turkish reprisals in 1822. Nowadays, it's referred to as the 'ghost village'.

Agio Galas Cave & Church
CAVE

(Map p612; ☑22740 22004; admission €5) Only a small section of the island's largest cave is accessible, but the main reason to drive all the way to the northern tip of Chios is the 12th-century cave church of Agio Galas just above the official cave entrance. Local woodcarvers populated the exquisite wooden altar with whimsical creatures barely compatible

with Christian doctrine – mermaids, dragons and a character reminiscent of Dionysos, all of them looking heavily pregnant, even the dragons.

There are no specific hours, but the family that operates it is always around.

Nea Moni
MONASTERY

(New Monastery; Map p612; ☉9am-1pm & 4-7pm) FREE At the island's centre, Nea Moni is a World Heritage–listed 11th-century Byzantine monastery. Once one of Greece's richest monasteries, it attracted pre-eminent Byzantine artists to create the mosaics in its *katholikon* (principal church). Disastrously, during the Greek War of Independence (1821–29), the Turks torched the monastery and massacred its monks. Their skulls are now kept in a glass cabinet inside a chapel to the left of the main entrance. Another catastrophe occurred in 1881 when an earthquake demolished the *katholikon* dome. Nea Moni is now a convent.

🛏 Sleeping & Eating

Avgonyma is perhaps the most romantic place to overnight in northern Chios. You'll find domatia in Volissos, Langada and Kardamyla.

Spitakia   APARTMENT €
(☑ 22710 81200; missetzi@spitakia.gr; Avgonyma;
r from €45; P ✳ 🕾) These traditional studios
and cottages, spread across a striking village of medieval stone houses surrounded
by olive and pine forests, feature modern
kitchenettes and sublime sea views.

Zorbas Apartments   PENSION €
(☑ 6936775999, 22740 21436; www.chioszorbas.
gr; Limnia; d/q €50/60; ✳ 🕾) Well-furnished,
if slightly fading, sea-facing apartments
are equipped with kitchenettes and are
spacious enough to keep an elephant inside – especially the two-storey quadruples
intended for families. Excellent breakfasts
cost an extra €8 per person, and the owner,
Yannis Zorbas, leads undemanding hikes to
Volissos castle and adjacent beaches.

★ Taverna Fabrika   TAVERNA €
(☑ 6976255829, 22740 22045; fabrika_chios@
yahoo.com; Volissos; mains €6-8.50; ⊙ lunch &
dinner; P) This cheerful traditional eatery
nestled in the trees of Volissos occupies
a century-old olive-and-flour mill, where
some of the vintage equipment is displayed.
Top off excellent grills, *mayirefta* (ready-
cooked meals) and good barrel wine with
homemade custard or sweet *loukoumadhes* (ball-shaped doughnuts served with
honey and cinnamon). Above the taverna
are six handsome rooms, with fireplaces
and wi-fi (triples €50).

El Sueño   GREEK €
(☑ 22740 22122; Limnos Beach; €7-11; ⊙ 10am-
11pm) Veering from the taverna mainstream, this beach cafe features a good
variety of salads and unusual appetisers,
such as spicy mussels with beer and ginger,
as well as standard Greek seafood and meat
dishes.

★ Pyrgos   TAVERNA €€
(☑ 22710 42175; www.chiospyrgosrooms.gr; Avgonyma; mains €8-15; ⊙ breakfast, lunch & dinner)
Excellent setting, service and food. This
traditional hilltop stone taverna serves up
superb mezedhes plus spit-roasted lamb
and pork. Upstairs are five classy rooms
(from €40) with names such as Mary, Irene
and Ben.

❶ Getting There & Away

Don't rely on buses for any travel beyond Langada. Services are extremely infrequent. The best
way to enjoy this part of the island is to travel by
car or bike.

Southern Chios

Southern Chios' mastic- and citrus-growing
villages are easily the most important reason
to visit the island. Though it does grow elsewhere in the Aegean, the mastic tree of Chios
has for centuries been the sole commercial
producer of mastic gum. The tree thrives
in a fertile, reddish territory known as the
Mastihohoria (mastic villages). This region
of rolling hills, criss-crossed with elaborate stone walls running through olive and
mastic groves, is highly atmospheric. The
stunning medieval villages, each uniquely
designed, were built as fortresses protecting
farmers from invaders and pirates. There is
more defensive architecture in the maze-like
suburbs on the southern outskirts of Chios
Town, where rich citrus growers have been
building their summer residences amidst
orange-tree orchards since the 14th century.
A few of these mansions have now been converted into atmospheric hotels.

◉ Sights

◉ Mastihohoria

As you drive south out of Chios Town, you'll
immediately find yourself in the barely navigable stone-wall maze of Kampos. Behind
those forbidding walls hide lush citrus orchards and lavish mansion houses where
wealthy Genoese and Greek merchant
families summered from the 14th century
onwards. Some of them are now converted into atmospheric boutique hotels, while
others are crumbling. The nearby Karfas
Beach, also the nearest to Chios Town, is
OK for a swim, but has a bit of a dreary
urban feel.

The sun-dried hills further south are covered in mastic plantations, which gave the
island its fame and determined its at-times
tragic plight. The sad and dramatic story of
mastic production in Chios is recognised in
the Chios Mastic Museum, halfway between
Pyrgi and Emborios, which was the Mastihohoria's port back when mastic producers
were high rollers.

Today Emborios is much quieter, though
it does boast Mavra Volia Beach (p620),
named for its black volcanic pebbles. Domatia and tavernas are available, and the
archaeological ruins of an early Bronze Age
temple to Athena are signed nearby. About
3.5km north, Komi is a larger yet fairly laid-
back tourist village that comes with a long

sandy beach and a good restaurant scene, which only springs to life in the summer months.

The west-coast workaday port of **Limenas Mesta** (also called Limenas) is home to a couple of decent port tavernas and is a short drive from Mesta. It sees an occasional ferry heading for Sigri in Lesvos and Agios Efstratios.

Around 3km southeast of Mesta, **Olymbi** is a mastic-producing village characterised by its defensive architecture, similar to that of Mesta. A well-maintained 3km trail connects Olymbi and Mesta. A popular side trip takes you 5km south to the splendid Cave of Sykia Olymbi.

Some 10km north of Pyrgi, **Vessa** is another fortress village that hasn't really found itself on the tourist trail, although it has a couple of well-appointed domatia. Another 7km north, the port of **Lithi** has a nice sandy beach with sunbeds and several quality tavernas.

★**Chios Mastic Museum** MUSEUM
(Map p612; ☑ 22710 72212; www.piop.gr; Rachi Site; regular/concession €4/2; ☉ 10am-6pm Wed-Mon, to 5pm winter) Brave new architecture arrives in Chios in the form of this airy hilltop structure that casts a curious glance on mastic gardens and ancient stone houses in the valley below, like a prodigious urban teenager on a visit to the land of their ancestors. The state-of-the-art museum narrates the sad and moving story of mastic production through a succession of images and sounds, including heartbreaking songs about mastic 'tears', which is what the farmers dubbed the fruits of their toil.

The museum has its own mastic garden and a good souvenir shop. It's located halfway between Pyrgi and Mavro Volia Beach.

Citrus Memories Museum MUSEUM
(Map p612; ☑ 22710 31513; www.citrus-chios.gr; Kampos; ☉ 10am-9pm Jun-Sep, to 6pm Oct-May) FREE This museum has attractive and well-signed historical displays of Kampos-area citrus, the Chian mandarin in particular. Also has a shaded courtyard cafe with – *voila!* – fresh orange juice.

Cave of Sykia Olymbi CAVE
(Map p612; ☑ 22710 93364; €5; ☉ 11am-6pm May-Nov) This 150-million-year-old cavern was discovered accidentally in 1985. It's 57m deep and filled with multicoloured stalactites and other rock formations that have

whimsical names such as the Pipe Organ, Cacti and Jellyfish.

The cave is illuminated with floodlights, and connected via a series of platforms and staircases – be prepared for some climbing. A steady temperature of 18°C is maintained, and humidity is a moist 95%. Guided tours are mandatory and run every 30 minutes.

The cave is signposted as 'Olympi Cave'.

◉ Pyrgi & Mesta

The Ottoman rulers' penchant for mastic made the Mastihohoria (mastic villages) wealthy for centuries. Some architectural wonders remain in the villages of Pyrgi and Mesta.

The Mastihohoria's largest village, **Pyrgi** (24km southwest of Chios Town) looks like a magic jewellery box, with its facades decorated in intricate grey-and-white patterns, some geometric and others based on flowers, leaves and animals. The technique, called *xysta,* uses equal amounts of cement, volcanic sand and lime as well as bent forks and a fine eye.

Pyrgi's central square is flanked by tavernas, shops and the little 12th-century **Church of Agios Apostolos** (Pyrgi; ☉ 8am-3pm Tue-Sun). East of the square, note the house with a plaque attesting to its former occupant – one Christopher Columbus, who was also a fan of mastic gum, though he apparently preferred it as a sealant in boat construction. Should you wish to stay, the castle-like apartments at Mastiha House offer fantastic value for money.

Mesta, 9.5km from Pyrgi, is a truly memorable village, and one of Greece's most unusual. Its appealing stone alleyways, intertwined with flowers and intricate balconies, are completely enclosed by thick defensive walls – the work of Chios' former Genoese rulers, who built this fortress town in the 14th century to keep out pirates and would-be invaders. It's an ingenious example of medieval defensive architecture, featuring a double set of walls, four gates and a pentagonal structure, with the larger of the impressive **Churches of the Taxiarhes** (Mesta) at the centre.

Mesta's rooftops are interconnected, and if you have the right guide you can actually walk across the entire town this way. You can have one of Mesta's stone houses for yourself for a few nights: Medieval Castle Suites is one of several operators. To remind yourself that the residents of these fortified villages are actually farmers, drop by Despina Karavella to stock up on fruit and vegetable preserves, as well as home-made booze.

A car-free village, this is a relaxing and romantic place where children can run around safely. Mesta also makes a good base for hill-walking, exploring southern beaches and caves, and participating in cultural and ecotourism activities.

🏃 Activities & Tours

Mavra Volia   BEACH
(Map p612; Emborios) Shaped as a perfect crescent, the island's most celebrated beach is made of stark black pebbles, giving it a darkly mysterious look. There are no facilities, except a kiosk selling drinks. A couple of ancient ruins in the vicinity draw archaeology buffs.

⭐ **Masticulture**
Ecotourism Activities   ECOTOUR
(☑ 22710 76084, 6976113007; www.masticulture. com; tours from €18) ✒ To participate in traditional cultural activities such as Chian farming, contact Vassilis and Roula, who provide unique ecotourism opportunities that introduce visitors to the local community, its history and culture. Activities include mastic-cultivation tours, stargazing, and bicycle and sea-kayak outings. They can help find area accommodation and offer tips for visiting nearby Psara Island.

🛏 Sleeping & Eating

⭐ **Mastiha House**   PENSION €
(☑ 6944604870, 22710 72900; www.mastiha house.gr; Pyrgi; d/tr €54/67; ❄ 🛜) Fluent English-speaker Kaliopi runs these tastefully designed, luxurious castle-like apartments. All have sky-high ceilings, balconies facing a narrow street of Pyrgi's trademark painted stone houses, and kitchenettes – crucially equipped with a blender for making frappés.

To Petroni   GUESTHOUSE €
(Map p612; ☑ 22710 73320; Vessa; r from €40; ❄ 🛜) Ultimate rural getaway in a traditional house resembling a castle tower, with vaulted ceilings and Gothic windows in well-appointed rooms. Breakfast (€6) is served in the garden. The village taverna is nearby, and the popular Lithi Beach is a short drive away.

⭐ **Medieval**
Castle Suites   ACCOMMODATION SERVICES €€
(☑ 22710 76025; www.medievalcastlesuites.com; Mesta; d/tr from €95/120; ❄ 🛜) The Castle Suites is a collection of 20 rooms spread throughout the village, all with traditional stone touches and modern bathrooms; a few have fireplaces and even computers. Rooms vary considerably in size and proximity to the square.

Mouzaliko Traditional Hotel   GUESTHOUSE €€
(Map p612; ☑ 6974057299, 22710 31624; http:// mouzalikohotel.gr; Zanis & Marias Chalkousi 52, Kampos; r incl breakfast €50-80; ❄ 🛜) If you wonder what might be hiding behind the tall stone walls of Kampos, here's your chance to find out. Rooms in this typically introverted stone mansion all face the handsome courtyard, where the Greek–Quebecoise owners serve hearty breakfasts with yummy honey buns. A citrus version of a Chekhovian cherry orchard, also inside the enclosure, adds to the idyll.

Perleas Mansion   HISTORIC HOTEL €€
(Map p612; ☑ 22710 32217; www.perleas.gr; Vitiadou, Kampos; s/d/tr incl breakfast from €103/117/144; P ❄ 🛜) The restored Perleas Mansion offers seven elegant well-appointed apartments, and a restaurant serving traditional Greek cuisine. The relaxing estate, built in 1640, exemplifies high Genoese architecture.

Galera   TAVERNA €
(Map p612; ☑ 22710 73285; Lithi; €5-10; ⊗ 9am-midnight; 🛜) This beach taverna in Lithi marries Greek and Italian rural standards, with seafood spaghetti a definite highlight. Pizza made with Greek salad ingredients is also pretty delightful.

Despina Karavella   FOOD & DRINKS
(☑ 22710 76065, 6977353451; Mesta; ⊗ 9am-7pm) Drop by this gem of a shop in Mesta to taste homemade sweet wine and *tsipouro* or stock up on spoon sweet preserves made from citrus types you've likely never heard of. A couple of suites upstairs go for €50 to €60 per night.

ℹ Getting There & Away

From Mesta and Pyrgi there are three buses daily to Chios Town. English-speaking Dimitris Kokkinos provides a **taxi** (☑ 6972543543) service. Sample fares from Mesta include: **Chios Town** €45, **Olympi** €5, and **Pyrgi** €20.

LESVOS ΛΕΣΒΟΣ

POP 86,436

Greece's third-largest island (and one of the best organised), Lesvos is marked by long sweeps of rugged desert-like western plains that give way to sandy beaches and salt marshes in the centre. To the east are thickly forested mountains and dense olive groves – around 11 million olive trees are cultivated here.

The port and capital, Mytilini Town, is a lively place year-round, filled with exemplary *ouzeries* and reasonable accommodation, while the north-coast town of Molyvos (aka Mithymna) is an aesthetic treat, with old stone houses clustered on winding lanes overlooking the sea. The island's therapeutic hot springs gush with some of the warmest mineral waters in Europe.

Despite its undeniable tourist appeal, Lesvos' chief livelihood is agriculture. Its olive oil is highly regarded, and the island's farmers produce around half the ouzo sold worldwide.

History

Lesvos' great cultural legacy stretches from the 7th-century-BCE musical composer Terpander to 20th-century figures such as Nobel Prize–winning poet Odysseus Elytis and primitive painter Theophilos. Ancient philosophers Aristotle and Epicurus also led a philosophical academy here. Most famous, however, is Sappho, one of Ancient Greece's greatest poets. Her sensuous, passionate poetry has fuelled a modern-day following and draws lesbians from around the world to the village of Skala Eresou, where she was born (c 630 BCE).

ℹ Getting There & Away

AIR

The **airport** (Mitiline Airport; Map p622; ☑ 22510 61212, 22510 38700; www.mjt-airport. gr/en) is 8km south of Mytilini Town. A taxi to town costs €10 and a bus €1.60.

Aegean Airlines (https://en.aegeanair.com), **Olympic Air** (www.olympicair.com), **Sky Express** (www.skyexpress.gr), **Astra Airlines** (www.astra-airlines.gr) and **Air Minoan** (www.minoanair.com/en) have offices at the airport. Mytilini Town travel agents also sell tickets.

BOAT

Mytilini is a busy port with frequent connections to the Greek mainland as well as Ayvalyk in Turkey.

Up to three boats daily head for Piraeus (€38.50, 11¼ hours) via Chios (€21, 3¼ hours). Services to Kavala (€30.50, seven hours) via Limnos (€21, four hours) run three days a week. Four boats a week depart for ports located on Samos (€19.50, 5¼ hours) and Ikaria (€24, eight hours).

The smallish southern port of Sigri, 27km from Skala Eresou, comes to life once a week, when *Nissos Chios* sets off for Piraeus (€20, 7½ hours) via the equally obscure port of Mesta on Chios (€21, 2½ hours).

In Mytilini Town, buy ferry tickets from Mitilene Tours (p591) and Tsolos Travel (p591).

ℹ Getting Around

BUS

Mytilini Town's **long-distance bus station** (KTEL; ☑ 22510 28873; www.ktel-lesvou.gr; El Venizelou) is near Agias Irinis Park. From here buses depart for Molyvos, Eresou and other popular destinations around the island. Services are typically reduced to one per day on Saturdays and there are none at all on Sundays. Uniquely for this island group, the local branch of the national bus operator runs a website where you can check routes and schedules, at www.ktel-lesvou.gr.

DESTINATION	DURATION	FARE (€)	FREQUENCY
Agiasos	45mins 3.20	3.20	3 daily
Molyvos (Mithymna) via Petra	1½hrs	7.50	2 daily
Plomari	1¼hrs	5	3 daily
Sigri	2½hrs	11.40	2 weekly
Skala Eresou via Eresos	2½hrs	11.20	2 daily
Vatera via Polyhnitos	1½hrs	6.80	2 daily

CAR & MOTORCYCLE

Local companies **Discover Rent-a-Car** (☑ 6936057676, 22510 20391; www.discover1. gr; Aristarhou 1; ☻ 8am-10pm) and **Billy's Rentals** (☑ 22510 20006, 6944759716; www. billys-rentacar.com; Pavlou Kountourioti 87; ☻ 7.30am-10pm) have newish cars and flexible service. Billy's also has motorbikes, as do others along Pavlou Kountourioti in Mytilini Town. In Molyvos, hire vehicles from **Kosmos Rent-a-Car** (☑ 22530 71710; www.lesvosrentals.com; ☻ 8am-8.30pm).

Lesvos (Mytilini)

Limnos (110km);
Kavala (210km)

Aegean Sea

Cape Molyvos
Skala
Sikameneas 19 ⊗ 14 Cape
Korakas
4 Mt
Molyvos (Mithymna) Lepetymnos Sikamenea
Eftalou (968m)
Vafios Klio
Agios Georgios Petra Kapi
Petra Petri Pelopi
Anaxos Stypsi Mantamados 5
Cape
Fournia
Lapsarna Gavathas
7
Skalohori Filia Agia Paraskevi
11 6 Andissa Kalloni
18
Sigri Vatousa 16 12
Natural History Museum
of the Lesvos Skala
1 **Petrified Forest** Kallonis
Cape 799m
Sigri Parakila *Gulf of*
Eresos *Kalloni*
Agra
Ahladeri
Skala Eresou
Lisvorio
Hrousas *Spa* Lisvorio
Tavari Skala Polyhnitou
Agiasos
Nifidha 3
Polyhnitos 13 *Hot Springs* Mt Olympus
of Polyhnitos (968m)
Kato
Stavros Ambeliko
Vryssa 10 Akrassi
Vatera
Drota Paleohori
Cape Drota Melinda
Agios Beach 17
Fokas Melinda Plomari
Beach

Aegean Sea

Mytilini Town

POP 29,650

Lesvos' port and capital, Mytilini (Μυτιλήνη) is a lively student town with great eating and drinking options, plus eclectic churches and grand 19th-century mansions and museums. Its remarkable, world-class Teriade Museum boasts paintings by Picasso, Chagall and Matisse, along with home-grown painter Theophilos. The island is known in equal parts for its poets and painters and for its olive oil and ouzo.

Ferries dock at the northeastern end of the curving waterfront thoroughfare, Pavlou Kountourioti, where most of the action is centred. Handmade ceramics, jewellery and traditional products are sold on and around the main shopping street Ermou, and there are many fine *ouzeries* and student-filled bars to enjoy.

◉ Sights & Activities

The small olive-groved peninsula south of Mytilini has several attractions. Following the coast road 7km south, opposite the airport you'll find the long, pebbled Neapoli Beach; it hosts a few chilled-out beach bars, popular with students, and usually pulsates with reggae and Greek sounds.

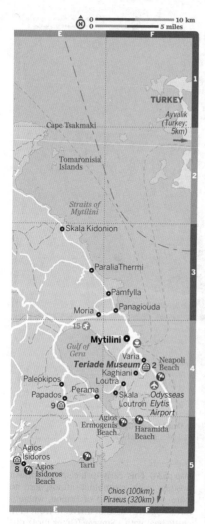

N 0 —————— 10 km
0 —————— 5 miles

Lesvos (Mytilini)

Lesvos-born artist and critic Stratis Elefthe-riadis, who brought the work of primitive painter and Lesvos native Theophilos to in-ternational attention. Located in Varia, 4km south of Mytilini.

Fortress FORTRESS
(Kastro; Map p624; €2; ⊙ 8.30am-4pm Wed-Mon) Mytilini's imposing early-Byzantine fortress was renovated in the 14th century by Geno-ese overlord Francisco Gatelouzo, and then the Turks enlarged it again. Flanked by pine trees, it's popular for a stroll, with some good views included.

Theophilos Museum MUSEUM
(Map p622; ☑ 22510 41644; Varia; €3; ⊙ 8.30am-2.30pm Mon-Fri) On the same site as the

Around 9km further south, the penin-sula wraps around to the popular sand-and-pebble **Agios Ermogenis Beach**, and **Haramida Beach**, which has toilets and showers under pine trees on the bluff above the beach.

★ **Teriade Museum** MUSEUM
(Map p622; ☑ 22510 23372; http://museumte riade.gr; Varia; €3; ⊙ 9am-2pm Tue-Sun) Ex-traordinary. It's worth coming to Lesvos for this alone – the Teriade Museum and its as-tonishing collection of paintings by artists including Picasso, Chagall, Miró, Le Corbu-sier and Matisse. The museum honours the

NORTHEASTERN AEGEAN ISLANDS MYTILINI TOWN

Mytilini Town

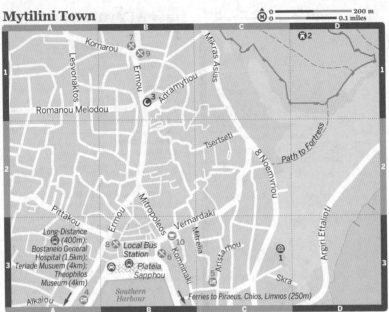

Mytilini Town

◎ Sights
1 Archaeological Museum C3
2 Fortress D1
3 Yeni Tzami B1

🛏 Sleeping
4 Hotel Lesvion A3
5 Theofilos Paradise Boutique Hotel C3

⊗ Eating
6 Cafe P B3
7 O Ermis B1
8 Taverna Kalnterimi B3
9 To Kastro B1

◎ Drinking & Nightlife
10 Mousiko Kafenio B3

NORTHEASTERN AEGEAN ISLANDS MYTILINI TOWN

Teriade Museum, this humble structure contains 86 paintings by the primitive painter Theophilos, who remains a folk hero among Greek literati. During his life he barely scratched out an existence, moving frequently and painting coffeehouse walls for his daily bread, depicting the people he met at work and at play. A year after his death in 1934, his work was exhibited at the Louvre.

Archaeological Museum   MUSEUM
(Map p624; ☎ 22510 40223; 8 Noemvriou; €4; ⊗ 8.30am-4pm Wed-Mon) This handsome refurbished museum, about 500m above the eastern quay, portrays island life during Roman times, from the 2nd century BCE to the 3rd century CE, and features extraordinary floor mosaics. You can walk around these on a protective glass surface.

Yeni Tzami   MOSQUE
(Map p624) This early-19th-century Turkish mosque, with crumbling atmosphere to spare, is near the end of Ermou, where a Turkish market used to thrive. In front of it, a little boat with a Smyrna (Greek for Izmir) port of registration sign is a touching memorial to millions who were forced to leave their homes for good in the epic exchange of populations between Greece and Turkey in 1923.

Therma Spa   HOT SPRINGS
(Map p622; http://thermaspalesvos.com/en; Km 7 Mytilini–Kalloni Rd; €8; ⊗ 9am-9pm) Hikers and cyclists can give their muscles a well-deserved rest at this renovated spa, which now combines an old Ottoman-styled indoor thermal pool with a new open-air pool next to a large sundeck facing the Bay of Gera. A range of massage and other treatments is

available (€20 to €40). There's also an on-site cafe.

Sleeping

Mytilini is filled with hotels that will suit any budget.

★Theofilos Paradise
Boutique Hotel
BOUTIQUE HOTEL €€

(Map p624; ☑ 22510 43300; www.theofilos paradise.gr; Skra 7; s/d incl breakfast from €84/112, ste from €130; P ❄ @ 🛜 ☳) This smartly restored 100-year-old mansion is elegant and good value, with modern amenities and a traditional *hammam*. The 22 swanky rooms (plus two luxe suites) are spread among three adjacent buildings surrounding an inviting courtyard.

Hotel Lesvion
HOTEL €€

(Map p624; ☑ 22510 28177; www.lesvion.gr; Pavlou Kountourioti 27a; s/d incl breakfast €47/67; ❄ 🛜) The modern and well-positioned Lesvion, smack on the harbour, has reasonable service and attractive spacious rooms, some with excellent port-view balconies. A breakfast bar overlooks the harbour.

Eating & Drinking

To Kastro
GREEK €

(Map p624; ☑ 6974925921; Ermou 326; mains €6-10; ⏱ 10am-2am) Owner George spent a large part of his life in the Netherlands – hence the proliferation of bicycles in the decor – and, more importantly, he's also a magician. He'll probably show you a trick or two while serving excellent mezedhes and mouth-watering meatballs.

Cafe P
CAFE €

(Map p624; ☑ 22510 55594; Samou 2; mains €3-7; ⏱ 11am-3am; 🛜) This hip back-alley bistro draws a crowd mostly from the university for its unusual and well-priced small plates, slight menu, eclectic music mix and all-round chilled atmosphere. Sauteed shrimps, served with a draught beer, cost around €8. Cheap daily specials, too. It's about 50m in from Plateia Sapphou (Sappho Sq). Look for a sign with the single Greek letter 'Π'.

O Ermis
TAVERNA €

(Map p624; cnr Kornarou & Ermou; mezedhes €5-9; ⏱ 10am-midnight) This no-frills taverna began life in 1800 as a cafe in the Turkish quarter, as its traditional decor reveals in faded bits and pieces. It offers good Macedonian and Limnos wines, along with generous plates of Greek kitchen standbys.

Taverna Kalnterimi
TAVERNA €

(Map p624; ☑ 22510 46577; cnr Ermou & Thasou; mains €7-10; ⏱ 11am-midnight; 🛜) This reliable alleyway cafe between Ermou and the waterfront has everything from *gavros* (marinated small fish) and grilled pork chops to *mayirefta* (ready-cooked meals) and seasonal salads. A mezedhes plate that serves four is a reasonable €15.

★Mousiko Kafenio
CAFE

(Map p624; cnr Komninaki & Vernardaki; ⏱ 7.30am-2am) This hip student favourite is filled with eclectic paintings, old mirrors and well-worn wooden fixtures, giving it a relaxed, arty vibe. Mix in some great music and it's one of the most fun places in town. Great drinks, fresh juices and coffee, and even homemade iced tea on hot summer days.

ℹ Information

Mitilene Tours (p591) Full-service agency on the east side of the port. Helps with accommodation, car rentals, and trips and tours to Turkey.

Tsolos Travel (p591) Full-service agency on the south side of the port. Sells ferry tickets to Turkey.

Zoumboulis Tours (☑ 22510 37755; Pavlou Kountourioti 69; ⏱ 8am-8pm) Sells ferry and air tickets, and runs boat trips to Turkey.

ℹ Getting There & Away

The airport (p621) is 8km south along the coast.

Mytilini is the island's main port, with connections to other northeastern Aegean Islands and Piraeus (Athens).

Mytilini's local bus station (KTEL; Map p624; ☑ 22510 46436; Pavlou Kountourioti), near Plateia Sapphou, serves in-town destinations and nearby Loutra, Skala Loutron and Tahiarhis.

The long-distance bus station (p621) is beside Irinis Park, near the domed church.

The taxi rank (Map p624) is on the western side of Plateia Sapphou.

Northern Lesvos

Home to rolling hills covered in pine and olive trees, peaceful beaches and the aesthetically harmonious town of Molyvos (also called Mithymna), northern Lesvos offers both solitude and low-key resort action. Traditional seaside hot springs and intriguing Byzantine monasteries round out the region's offerings.

⊙ Sights & Activities

⊙ Petra

Lying 5km south of Molyvos, Petra is mostly a crowded beach village. Its one cultural site, situated above the giant overhanging rock for which the village was named, is the 18th-century Panagia Glykofilousa (Church of the Sweet-Kissing Virgin), accessible on foot up 114 rock-hewn steps. Note the mysterious figurines, looking like relatives of Easter Island stone heads, on top of the main gate. It's possible to stay overnight, but the village lacks the character of Molyvos or nearby Eftalou Beach – it's barely a strip of souvenir shops and restaurants, though its small square can be relaxing. Take a look at the First Kiss Gallery (Petra; Petra; ⊙10am-noon), where local Canadian artist Paul Henry exhibits and sells his melancholic sea-themed papier-mâché sculptures.

⊙ Eftalou

Eftalou Beach (Map p622) (also called Agii Anargyri Beach), 2km northeast of Petra, is the place for solitude seekers. Backed by a cliff, the serene, narrow pebbled beach has pristine waters and also boasts the charming Mineral Baths of Eftalou. Beyond the baths, the beachfront Hrysi Akti (Map p622; ☑22530 71879; Eftalou Beach; s/d €30/35; ✺☏) offers simple rooms with bathrooms in an idyllic pebbled cove, complete with the friendly owners' small restaurant overlooking the sea.

Mineral Baths of Eftalou　　BATHHOUSE
(Map p622; ☑22530 55302; Eftalou Beach; group/private bathhouse €4/6; ⊙10am-6pm) A traditional bathhouse on the beach at Eftalou, with clear, cathartic 46.5°C (and higher!) water temperatures. The vintage Ottoman bathhouse is filled with mesmerising shafts of light piercing through the perforated cupola; an adjacent 20th-century bathhouse has private bathtubs. The springs are said to treat various ailments, from arthritis to hypertension.

⊙ Skala Sikameneas & Around

From Eftalou, a coastal road continues for 9.5km to Skala Sikameneas, an exceedingly pretty fishing port with some domatia and two popular tavernas, including I Mouria tou Mirivili. Both eating options specialise in *astakomakaronadha* (fresh lobster with

pasta). If these are overrun by day-trippers from Molyvos, take a walk to To Kyma, also on the seafront, some 800m west of the port. Just before the taverna, a signposted trail begins the ascent to the port's parent village of Sikamenea, connecting to a circular trekking route that will take you to the nearby village of Lepetymnos and back to Sikamenea in about three hours.

The nearest beach, Kagia (Map p622), is a short walk away from the port. Follow the trail cutting through the headland on the eastern side of the port. A large shady garden of Poseidon (Kagia Beach; Map p622; ☑22530 55370; Paralia Kagias; €7-13; ⊙lunch & dinner) taverna provides escape from blistering midday sun. If you wish to stay at Skala Sikameneas, Gorgona (Map p622; ☑22530 55301; www.gorgonahotel.gr; Skala Sikameneas; d from €46; ✺☏) is a good option right by the port.

At Sikamenea, the main road from Molyvos turns south towards Mantamados, home to Moni Taxiarhon monastery. Further south, Agia Paraskevi houses the excellent Museum of Industrial Olive Oil Production (Map p622; ☑22530 32300; www.piop.gr; Agia Paraskevi; regular/concession €4/2; ⊙10am-6pm Wed-Mon Mar-Oct, to 5pm Nov-Feb).

Moni Taxiarhon　　MONASTERY
(Map p622; ⊙8am-dusk) FREE Around 36km north of Mytilini Town, near Mantamados village, stands one of Lesvos' most important pilgrimage sites. An axis of Orthodoxy, myth and militarism, the grand 17th-century Moni Taxiarhon says much about the blatant lack of separation between State and Church in Greece – note the fighter plane parked out the front, reminding the faithful that the Archangel Michael is the patron saint of the Hellenic Air Force.

✕ Eating

To Kyma　　GREEK €
(Map p622; ☑22530 55302; Skala Sikameneas; €7-10; ⊙8am-late; ☏) Some 800m along the beach from Skala Sikameneas, this friendly taverna serves freshly caught fish, grilled meat and excellent vegetables, especially *gigantes* beans cooked in olive oil. Nice spot for sunset watching.

Restaurant Hrysi Akti　　TAVERNA €
(Map p622; ☑22530 71947; Eftalou Beach; mains from €5-8; ⊙8am-late; ☏) Excellent taverna fare, fresh fish and tasty grills overlooking the beach. It's part of the Hrysi Akti domatia.

I Mouria tou Mirivili TAVERNA €€
(Map p622; ☑ 22530 55319; Skala Sikameneas; €8-16; ☺ 10am-midnight; 🐾) People flock here for lobster spaghetti, but this vast taverna with tables in the shade of a mulberry tree offers an extensive list of seafood delicacies as well as great veggie snacks.

🛈 Getting There & Away

Two to three daily buses connect Molyvos with Mytilini Town (€7.50, 1½ hours). A local bus runs six times a day between Petra, Molyvos and Eftalou.

Molyvos   Μόλυμβος

POP 1500

Molyvos, also known as Mithymna, is a well-preserved Ottoman-era town of narrow cobbled lanes and stone houses with jutting wooden balconies wreathed in flowers, overlooking a sparkling pebble beach below. Its grand 14th-century Byzantine castle, some good nearby beaches and its north-central island location make it a great launch pad from which to explore Lesvos.

⊙ Sights & Activities

Beach-lovers can take an excursion boat for Skala Sikameneas village (10km) and nearby Eftalou (from €20, 10.30am daily). It's also possible to hike one way and catch the excursion boat back to Molyvos. Sunset cruises are available. Enquire at the portside Faonas Travel Agency (☑ 22530 71630; tekes@otenet.gr), inside the Sea Horse Hotel, or Lesvorama (☑ 22530 72291; www.lesvorama.gr; ☺ 9am-10pm) on the main road.

Byzantine-Genoese Castle CASTLE
(☑ 22530 71803; €2; ☺ 8.30am-4pm Wed-Mon) This handsome 14th-century castle stands guard above Molyvos. A steep climb is repaid by sweeping views over the town and sea – even across to Turkey, shimmering on the horizon. In summer the castle hosts several festivals.

Stratis Boat Trips BOATING
(☑ 6974837055; www.facebook.com/stratkab; cruises per 2/4 people €50/80) Friendly bike-riding Stratis Kapanas captains the *Escape*, a caïque (little boats) that makes for a sweet three-hour coastal cruise for up to four people, with stops for lunch and swimming. Look for his boat in front of the Sea Horse Hotel and Grand Bleu restaurant at the Old Port.

🛏 Sleeping

★**Nadia Apartments
& Studios** PENSION €
(☑ 22530 71345; www.apartmentsnadia-molivos.com; studio/apt €38/53; ❄ 🐾) On the road to Sikamenea and a short walk from the Old Town, these large motel-styled rooms surrounding an expansive shady courtyard are owned by the organised Nadia. Her trademark cakes are complimentary. It's open all year.

**Molyvos Queen
Apartments** APARTMENT €
(☑ 22530 71452; www.molyvos-queen.gr; d/tr €40/50; ❄ 🐾) Fully equipped apartments perch on the hill and offer all the mod cons, plus sea and castle views. It's located at the top of the village on the way to the castle.

Lela's Studios APARTMENT €
(☑ 6942928224, 22530 71285; www.eftalouolivegrove.com/lelas_studios.htm; studios from €40; ❄ 🐾) Two handsome studios are set in a courtyard of roses and geraniums. Each comes with a fully outfitted kitchen and sunset sea views from a relaxing stone veranda. It's located above the junction of the main road and Agora.

Marina's House PENSION €
(☑ 22530 71470; dimouks@yahoo.com; r €45; ❄ 🐾) Look for the geraniums climbing the steps of this well-managed pension 50m from the port. Rooms are spotless, bright and have small sea-facing balconies over the main road. Marina's husband, Kostas, paints icons for village shops.

Sea Horse Hotel HOTEL €€
(☑ 22530 71630; www.seahorse-hotel.com; s/d incl breakfast from €60/65; 🅿 ❄ 🐾) In the heart of the port area, you'll find these modern and comfortable rooms, all with balconies overlooking the harbour, along with the family's restaurant and travel agency. Three family-friendly studios have kitchenettes and partial sea views.

Amfitriti Hotel HOTEL €€
(☑ 22530 71741; www.amfitriti-hotel.com; s/d/tr from €45/65/80; 🅿 ❄ 🐾) Just 50m from the beach, this well-managed traditional stone hotel has modern tiled rooms and a large garden pool. Staff is friendly and helpful, and the hotel's quiet location is a plus.

✕ Eating & Drinking

★ Misirlou
INTERNATIONAL €

(☑ 22530 72388; Molyvos Harbour; mains €6-11; ☺ 1pm-midnight; 🖥) A new American-run place above the marina, Misirlou serves delicious tortilla wraps, burgers and pizzas – all using fresh local produce. In the evening, it turns into a stylish cocktail bar with an exemplary musical soundtrack.

★ Betty's
TAVERNA €

(☑ 22530 71421; 17 Noemvriou; mains €8; ☺ 9am-3pm & 6pm-late) This restored Turkish pasha's residence on the upper street, overlooking the harbour below, offers a tasty variety of *mayirefta* (ready-cooked) dishes such as *mousakas* (meat or veggie), baked fish, lamb souvlaki and *kotiropitakia* (small cheese pies), plus tasty breakfast specials.

Betty also has two spacious and well-appointed studio apartments occupying a quiet and shady corner near the restaurant.

Maistrali
TAVERNA €€

(☑ 22530 72160; Molyvos Harbour; mains €6-15; ☺ lunch & dinner) You can't eat much closer to the water than at this cosy traditional taverna at the harbour, below Molly's Bar. Roula is the owner, cook and server of well-prepared Greek standards such as *mayirefta*, along with good draught wine.

★ Molly's Bar
BAR

(☑ 22530 71772; ☺ 6pm-late; 🖥) With its painted blue stars, beaded curtains and bottles of Guinness, this whimsical British-run bar on the harbour waterfront's far eastern side is always in shipshape condition. Molly's caters to a lively local, international and expat crowd. The small balcony is perfect at sunset.

❶ Information

Molyvos Tourism Association (☑ 22510 71990; www.theotheraegean.com; Agora; ☺ 8am-3pm) Tourist office on upper Agora, near the pharmacy.

❶ Getting There & Away

At least one to two buses daily connect Molyvos with Mytilini Town (€7.50, 1½ hours).

Western Lesvos

Western Lesvos was formed by massive, primeval volcanic eruptions that fossilised trees and all other living things, making it an intriguing site for prehistoric-treasure hunters. Its striking bare landscape, broken only by craggy boulders and the occasional olive tree, is dramatically different from that of the rest of Lesvos. Heading far to the southwest, however, a grassier landscape emerges, leading to the coastal village of Skala Eresou, birthplace of one of Greece's most famous lyric poets, Sappho, who was dubbed the 10th Muse by Plato.

◉ Sights

Heading west from Skala Kallonis towards Sigri, a stark and ancient volcanic landscape awaits, home to the scattered remains of a petrified forest. A fascinating and rare monument of geological heritage, the forest is a product of intense volcanic activity in the northern Aegean during the Miocene period. Sadly, the main visitors' area in the centre of this Unesco-nominated geopark was off limits at the time of research, due to acute underfunding. Check its current status with the museum in Sigri, which has a little patch of the forest in its premises.

Sleepy Sigri is a fishing port, with narrow streets lined with pretty whitewashed houses descending towards an impressive Ottoman castle. The village has beautiful sea views, especially at sunset. The excellent sand and gravel Faneromeni Beach (Map p622) is 4km from the village.

Coming back from Sigri, stop for a lunch break or coffee at Andissa, a jovial, rustic village of narrow streets kept cool by the two enormous plane trees that stand over its square. Listen to the crickets and the banter of old-timers over a Greek coffee or frappé. Don't leave before trying the spoon sweets at To Kati Allo (p629).

★ Natural History Museum
of the Lesvos Petrified Forest
MUSEUM

(Map p622; ☑ 22530 54434; www.lesvosmuseum. gr; Sigri; €5; ☺ 9am-5pm Jul-Sep, 8.30am-4.30pm Oct-Jun; 🅿) This fascinating state-of-the-art museum chronicles what a volcano can do at a moment's notice – in this case 20 million years ago. Don't miss the interesting film and short verbal presentation. Well-signed exhibits and – crucially – the museum's own patch of the petrified forest transport visitors to when violent volcanic explosions discharged rapid flows of extremely hot ash and rock, covering the dense forest of western Lesvos, including trees, branches, root systems, leaves and fruits.

NORTHEASTERN AEGEAN ISLANDS WESTERN LESVOS

WORTH A TRIP

BIRDWATCHING

Just south of agricultural Kalloni, coastal Skala Kallonis turns from sleepy fishing village to birdwatching mecca every spring and autumn. During the spring migration, unrivalled across Europe, Lesvos' wetland reserves become home to more than 130 species of bird, from flamingos and raptors to woodpeckers and marsh sandpipers. It's a spectacular show that has grabbed the attention of European birdwatchers, who flock to the island during the peak viewing season of mid-April to mid-May, and again from mid-September to October. Skala Kallonis shares the enthusiasm, with the Pasiphae Hotel serving as an unofficial centre, where birdwatchers gather to compare notes (or brag) at the lobby bar. Bring your binoculars.

Nonexperts may find it worth stopping by a watchtower (Map p622) just off the Mytilini road on the outskirts of Kalloni to admire the flocks of flamingos that populate salt pans in springtime.

If you can't tell the difference between a blue-eyed hawker dragonfly and a crested grebe, pick up Steve Dudley's *A Birdwatching Guide to Lesvos*. Steve leads birdwatching tours around the island. There are also 50 species of butterfly and dragonfly flitting about, as well as marsh frogs filling the air with their croaky crooning.

What followed – hot fluids rich in pyrite, rising from molten magma – perfectly fossilised plant fibres. This process involved the molecule-by-molecule replacement of organic plant matter with inorganic matter. Today's petrified forest reveals structural characteristics of plants, root systems and tree trunks exactly as they existed 20 million years ago. Among the star attractions are the giant trunks of petrified sequoia trees and tiny fossils of pistachio nuts and olive leaves.

There's also a gift shop. Check website for opening hours.

Moni Ypsilou MONASTERY
(Moni Agiou Ioannou Theologou; Map p622; ☉dawn-dusk) FREE About 9km west of Andissa, the Byzantine Moni Ypsilou stands atop a solitary peak surrounded by volcanic plains. Founded in the 8th century, this storied place includes a flowering arched courtyard and a small but spectacular museum with antique icons and Byzantine manuscripts. From the top of the monastery walls, you can gaze out over the desolate ochre plains stretched out against the sea.

🍴 Sleeping & Eating

Pasiphae Hotel HOTEL €
(Map p622; ☎22530 23212; www.pasiphae.gr; Skala Kallonis; s/d incl breakfast from €40/45; P ❄ @ 🛜 🛉) A well-managed and welcoming hotel in a shady setting at Skala Kallonis, about 300m from the sea and village square. It's a favourite for returning visitors,

including the birdwatchers who gather at the lobby bar to compare notes in spring and autumn. Managed by the informative Vasillis Vogiatzis, with exceptional service and spotless rooms.

To Kati Allo CAFE €
(Something Different; Map p622; Andissa; spoon sweets €1-2, mains €6-10; ☉7am-1am) Sweet in every sense of the word, this cafe in the main square of Andissa is a wonderful place to stop for a cup of Greek coffee with a spoon sweet – a piece of caramelised seasonal fruit or vegetables, from figs to cherry tomatoes and even aubergines. Traditional taverna food is also on offer.

❶ Getting There & Away

One or two daily buses connect Skala Eresou and Sigri with Mytilini, but if you want to explore this remote part of the island, it's better to rent a car.

Skala Eresou   Σκάλα Ερεσού

POP 1560
Skala Eresou is part traditional fishing village, part laid-back bohemian beach town, and part lesbian mecca, especially during September when a lively two-week festival honours the great lyrical poet Sappho, born here in 630 BCE. The small seaside community has an easy-going, end-of-the-road ambience, with little cafes and tavernas hugging the shore and wispy tamarisk trees swaying in the breeze.

LOCAL KNOWLEDGE

SAPPHO

The classical Greek poet Sappho is re-nowned for her lyrical verse. Her words speak of passion and love for both sexes, but her emotion is balanced by clarity of language and a simple style. Though only fragments of her work remain, we do know that she married, had a daughter and was exiled for a period to Sicily, most likely for her political affiliation. Her surviving poems and love songs seem to have been addressed to an inner circle of female devotees. She was certainly an early advocate for women's voices, and hers continues to resonate.

Sights & Activities

Near the town market, the remains of the early-Christian **Basilica of Agios Andreas** include partially intact 5th-century mosaics.

Eresos
Archaeological Museum   MUSEUM
(€2; ⊙8.30am-3pm Tue-Sun) This is a modest museum, but the outside (and fenced) mosaics are of great interest. It is located on a quiet street in the southeastern part of the village, two blocks away from the sea.

Skala Eresou Circular Trail   TREKKING
A well-signposted 14km trail skirts the alluvial plain around Skala Eresou, climbing up to the top of Vigla hill by the quay, where the ancient acropolis of Skala Eresou once stood.

Festivals & Events

International Eressos
Women's Festival   LGBT
(☑22530 52130; www.womensfestival.eu; tickets €30-65; ⊙Sep) This international event with a local atmosphere involves two weeks of partying. Activities range from live music, open-air cinema, Greek dancing and poetry to beach volleyball, water sports, yoga and meditation, all in a gay-friendly atmosphere under the sun and stars.

Highlights include an LGBT film festival, live Greek, Turkish and Mediterranean folk music, 4WD safaris, an alternative fashion show (featuring festival participants), photography workshops and tattooing demonstrations. Live performances cover comedy and spoken word to burlesque and rock 'n' roll.

Sleeping

★**Heliotopos**   APARTMENT €
(☑6948510527; www.heliotoposeressos.gr; d/q €40/70; P❄🐾🛜) A leisurely 15-minute walk from the village, this lodging – set in a garden of palm trees – features five studios and three two-bedroom apartments, all with full kitchens. Free bikes are available for pedalling around.

★**Hotel Kyma**   GUESTHOUSE €
(☑22530 53555; d €45; ❄🛜) You can almost plunge into the deep blue sea from your private balcony at this lovely guesthouse perched above the narrow beach at the eastern edge of Skala Eresou. Rooms are simple yet stylish, and sunset views are to die for.

Aumkara Apartments   APARTMENT €
(☑22530 53190, 6948131032; www.aumkara.eu; d/tr/q from €40/50/60; P❄🛜) Smart spotless apartments near the centre of the village, managed by the welcoming Maria and her crew. Self-caterers will like the handy kitchenettes. Rooms range from small studios to two-bedroom apartments. About 50m from the beach.

Hotel Gallini   HOTEL €
(☑22530 53138; www.hotel-galinos.gr; Alkaiou; s/d incl breakfast from €40/50; P❄🛜) This budget gem, about 80m back from the waterfront, has tile floors and small balconies overlooking the hillside. Breakfast, with homemade jams and cheeses, is served on the flowery veranda.

Sappho the Eresia   HOTEL €€
(Sappho Hotel; ☑22530 53233; www.sapphohotel.com; waterfront; s/d/tr €45/70/85; P❄🛜) The friendly 18-room Sappho is what passes for a big hotel in laid-back Skala Eresou. Its modest position on the quieter west end of the beach is appealing, as are its overhead fans and an easy-going cafe-bar. The best rooms overlook the sea and the island of Psara. Breakfast is available for €8.

Eating & Drinking

★**Soulatso**   SEAFOOD €
(fish €6-12; ⊙lunch & dinner) This busy beachfront *ouzerie*-taverna along the boardwalk has a large outdoor patio and specialises in fresh fish, reasonably priced by the kilo; it's also known for its excellent mezedhes. Good service, ample portions and worthy wines.

Aigaio   TAVERNA €€
(Aegean; boardwalk; mains €7-13; ⊙ lunch & dinner;
🐟) Owner Theodoris spends most mornings
fishing to provide the evening's fresh fish.
Aigaio also serves very good *mayirefta* dishes and good grills, with traditional Greek
music in the background.

★ **Parasol**   BAR
(📞 22530 52050; ⊙ 9am-2am) With its orange
lanterns and super-eclectic music mix, little Parasol on the waterfront does cocktails
to match its South Seas decor. As the day
rolls on, Christos and Anastasia's made-to-
order breakfasts and cappuccinos give way
to lunch specials, fresh juices, noodles and
handmade pizza.

Notia Jazz Bar   BAR
(Plateia Anthis) Come for the drinks and stay
for the tunes at this hip music bar. There's
live jazz on summer weekends. Good cocktails, Greek wine and draught beer are on
offer at any time.

ℹ️ **Information**

The full-service **Sappho Travel** (📞 22530 52130;
www.sapphotravel.com; main square; ⊙ 9am-
2.30pm, 6-10pm) arranges car hire and accommodation, and provides information about the
International Eressos Women's Festival (p630).

ℹ️ **Getting There & Away**

One or two buses run daily between Skala Eresou
and Mytilini Town (€11.20, 2½ hours).

Southern Lesvos

Interspersed groves of olive and pine trees
mark southern Lesvos, from the flanks of Mt
Olympus (968m), the area's highest peak,
right down to the sea, where the best beaches lie. This is a hot, intensely agricultural
place where the vital olive oil, wine and ouzo
industries overshadow tourism.

◎ **Sights**

Just south of the Mytilini–Polyhnitos road,
Agiasos is the first point of interest. On
the northern side of Mt Olympus, it's a
quirky, well-kept, traditional hamlet of narrow cobbled streets where fishers sell their
morning catch from the back of old pickup trucks; village elders sip Greek coffee
in the local *kafeneia* (coffee houses); and
cheese-makers and ceramic artisans hawk
their wares. It's a relaxing, leafy place, and

boasts the exceptional Church of the Panagia Vrefokratousa.

Upon reaching Polyhnitos, famous for its
hot springs, the road turns directly south towards Vatera beach – a 10km-long stretch
of sand that remains a low-key getaway destination with a couple of tavernas and a few
domatias.

Another road from Mytilini skirts the
western shore of the Gulf of Gera before
turning to Papados, home to the Vrana
Olive-Press Museum. It continues to Plomari, the centre of Lesvos' ouzo industry.
It's an attractive, if busy, seaside village with
a large palm-lined square and waterfront
tavernas.

The popular beach settlement of Agios
Isidoros, 3km east, absorbs most of Plomari's summertime guests. Tarti, a bit further east, is less crowded. West of Plomari,
Melinda is a tranquil fishing village with a
beach, tavernas and domatia.

Church of the Panagia
Vrefokratousa   CHURCH
(Map p622; Agiasos) A pilgrimage site of national importance, this elegant walled-off
church contains a namesake icon depicting the Virgin, which is believed to make
miracles. Indeed, the recovery of a Turkish
governor in 1701, attributed to the icon, re-
lieved the village from hefty Ottoman taxes
for almost a century. On 15 August every
year, the icon is taken from the church and
carried around the village in a colourful
procession attended by thousands of religious pilgrims.

Vrana Olive-Press Museum   MUSEUM
(Map p622; 📞 22510 82007; Papados; €1; ⊙ 9am-
7pm Tue-Sun) Modestly tucked away in the
village of Papados, between Mytilini and
south-coast Plomari, this little museum
showcases 19th-century steam-powered
presses and vintage paintings of a bygone
era. It also occupies a bit of Greek literary
history – it was built by Nicholas Vranas,
grandfather of Greek Nobel Prize–winning
poet Odysseus Elytis.

Varvagianni Ouzo Museum   MUSEUM
(Map p622; 📞 22520 32741; www.barbayanni-
ouzo.com; Plomari; ⊙ 9am-4pm Mon-Fri Apr-Oct,
10am-2pm Mon-Fri Nov-Mar, by appointment Sat
& Sun) FREE Plomari is ouzo central for
Greece. This museum, where the family
has made ouzo for five generations, gives
you the chance to tour its copper distillery

and compare different ouzo tastes. When sampling ouzo, look for '100%' written on the label, indicating the quality of the distillate.

Vrisa Natural History Museum   MUSEUM

(Map p622; ☑ 22520 61890; Vrisa; €1; ☺ 9am-9pm Jun-Sep, 9.30am-3.30pm Wed-Sun Oct-May) Associated with the Museum of Palaeontology and Geology at the University of Athens, the museum displays impressive and well-signed prehistoric fossil remains from the area.

🏃 Activities

Hikers here can enjoy southern Lesvos' olive trails, which comprise paths and old local roads threading inland from Plomari and Melinda. The Melinda–Paleohori trail (1.2km, 30 minutes) follows the Selandas River for 200m before ascending to Paleohori, passing a spring with potable water along the way. The trail ends at the village's olive press.

Another appealing trail from Melinda leads to Panagia Kryfti, a cave church near a hot spring (built for two), and the nearby Drota Beach; or take the Paleohori–Rahidi trail (1km, 30 minutes), which is paved with white stone and passes springs and vineyards. Rahidi, which was only connected to electricity in 2001, has charming old houses and a coffeehouse.

Agricultural Polyhnitos, 10km north of Vatera on the road to Mytilini Town, is known for its two nearby hot springs, among the hottest in Europe. The more popular of the two, the Hot Springs of Polyhnitos, await just 1.5km east of the village. A circular trail originating from here winds through olive groves and the lands of Damandri monastery with a few heritage religious buildings along the way.

Hot Springs of Polyhnitos   HOT SPRINGS

(Polyhnitos Spa; Map p622; ☑ 22520 41229, 6977592991; Polyhnitos; €4; ☺ 2-8pm Mon-Sat, 11am-8pm Sun) Set in a pretty renovated Byzantine building, this thermal spring has some of Europe's warmest bath temperatures at 40°C (104°F). Rheumatism, arthritis, skin diseases and gynaecological problems are treated here, or visitors can simply enjoy a relaxing soak. While there, marvel at the psychedelically orange bed of the iron-rich stream that originates from the springs.

🛏 Sleeping & Eating

Pano Sto Kyma   PENSION €

(Map p622; ☑ 6942906124, 22520 33160; www.panostokyma.gr; Agios Isidoros; studios from €42; ❄ 🐾) Eleven sparkling-clean rooms come with wooden furniture painted in the lightest shade of blue – the same colour as the sea, just 30m from the front door. No breakfast is served, but village cafes open early and rooms come with kitchenettes.

Irini Studios   APARTMENT €

(Map p622; ☑ 22520 33406; Plomari; d €45; 🅿 ❄ 🐾) A comfortable budget option across the road from Varvagianni Ouzo Museum and equidistant from the centre of Plomari and Agios Isidoros Beach; you need about 30 minutes to reach either of them on foot. A complimentary bottle of ouzo will greet you upon checking in.

★ Sunset   GREEK €€

(Map p622; ☑ 22520 32740; Agios Isidoros; mains €8-16; ☺ noon-1am) Perched above the main road, this is not your average taverna but a fully fledged restaurant, with attentive service and a very competent chef-manager, Dimitris, whose advice about what's best on the day should be taken seriously. The lamb chops alone are worth the drive. Beautiful sunsets are free of charge.

To Ammoudeli   GREEK €€

(Map p622; Plomari seafront; mains €7-15; ☺ noon-late) A friendly taverna perched dramatically on the edge of a near-vertical cliff. Specialities include octopus cooked in red wine, and their trademark salad with spinach, cheese and sun-dried tomatoes.

❶ Getting There & Away

Buses link Plomari with Mytilini Town (€5, 1¼ hours, three daily), and Vatera with Mytilini Town (€6.80, 1½ hours, three daily).

LIMNOS   ΛΗΜΝΟΣ

POP 16,700

Alone in the far northern corner of the Aegean Sea, save for neighbouring Agios Efstratios, Limnos rewards those who visit with pristine scenery unspoiled by mass tourism, superb sandy beaches, a celebrated winemaking culture and a scenic capital in the shadow of a grand Venetian castle (p634).

Its rugged and treeless western part is reminiscent of the islands much further

Limnos

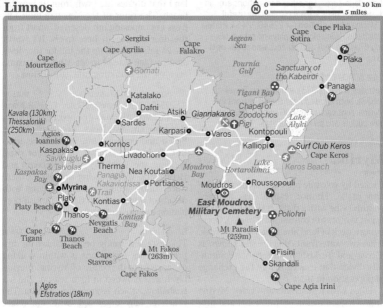

south, while the gentle agricultural lowlands of the east feel like a piece of Macedonia thrown into the sea. There are a few
notable ancient ruins to admire, more than
a few flamingos to count during winter migration and a windsurfers' haunt on a distant beach (p637) for gliding on the waves.

History

Limnos is perhaps best known as being the
central command post of the Hellenic Air
Force – the island is in an ideal position for
monitoring the Straits of the Dardanelles
leading into İstanbul. For this very reason
the island was used as the operational base
for the failed Gallipoli campaign in WWI. A
moving military cemetery (p637) for fallen
ANZAC (Australian and New Zealand Army
Corps) soldiers remains near Moudros,
where the Allied ships were based. A small
town in Victoria, Australia, bears the name
Lemnos.

❶ Getting There & Away

AIR

The airport is 22km east of Myrina, and has
offices for **Aegean Air** (www.aegeanair.com),
Sky Express (www.skyexpress.gr) and **Astra
Airlines** (www.astra-airlines.gr). Taxis to/from
Myrina cost about €25.

BOAT

Limnos is the last port of call for ferries going
north to Kavala (€16 to €27, six weekly, 4½
hours) and the first one on their way to Lesvos
(€16 to €27, three weekly, six hours) and other
northeastern Aegean Islands (and the last one on
the way back).

A helpful shortcut to Athens, four ferries a
week travel to Lavrio (€31 to €38, nine hours).

Limnos provides a lifeline to its tiny neighbour,
Agios Efstratios, with one or two services on
working days and Saturdays (€8, 1½ hours).

Ferries depart the New Port in Myrina. Buy
tickets at **Atzamis Travel** (☎ 22540 25690;
atzamisk@otenet.gr; waterfront; ☉ 8am-
10pm), **Petrides Travel** (☎ 22540 22039; www.
petridestravel.gr; Kyda-Karatza 116; ☉ 8am-
11pm) or **Aegean Travel** (☎ 22540 25936; www.
aegeantravel.eu; waterfront), all in Myrina.

For all things Agios Efstratios, enquire at
Karaiskaki Travel (☎ 22540 22900, 22540
22460; hrissa5a@otenet.gr; waterfront;
☉ varies) in Myrina.

❶ Getting Around

BUS

Limnos' bus service has one purpose: to bring
villagers to town for their morning shopping and
to get them home by lunch. From Myrina, buses
serve Moudros, via the airport (€3, 30 minutes,
five daily), with the last return bus leaving at
12.15pm. However, buses do not coordinate with

flight departures. For other destinations around the island, buses are not particularly useful.

Myrina's **bus station** (☑ 22540 22464; Plateia Eleftheriou Venizelou) displays no schedules – you'll have to deal with staffers who speak next to no English.

CAR & MOTORCYCLE

Petrides Travel (p633) and Aegean Travel (p633), both located near the waterfront in Myrina, rent cars from €30 per day. Motorcycle-hire outlets are on Kyda-Karatza.

Myrina   Μύρινα

POP 5710

Backed by volcanic rock and a craggy Venetian castle, Limnos' capital has a lively, youthful vibe with a distinct Hellenic flavour (most visitors are continental Greeks). Occupying a neck of land abutting the castle rock, it has two waterfronts that are still known as 'Greek' and 'Turkish', the legacy of a community divide that existed before the exchange of population in 1923.

Filled with restaurants and cafes, Myrina enjoys a good fusion of traditional and progressive food culture influenced by mainland urban trends. In summer, waterfront bars stay packed with students until the wee hours. Above the town, on the castle's overgrown slopes, it's a different story: here, fleet-footed deer dart about after dark, and even venture down to the *agora* (market) on winter nights.

◉ Sights & Activities

The town's beaches include the wide and sandy Rea Maditos, and the superior Romeïkos Gialos, beyond the harbour; further on, the beach becomes Riha Nera (Shallow Water), named for its gently shelving sea floor. Waterfront cafes and restaurants stay open late through summer. Five minutes south, on the road towards Thanos Beach, Platy Beach is a shallow, sandy crescent with cantinas, tavernas and a few lodgings.

From June to September, travel agencies organise round-the-island sightseeing tours by boat (half-/full day €20/25) and bus (full day €20). Boat tours stop for lunch and swimming, and take in the archaeological sites, usually ending at sunset. Bus tours can also visit the military cemeteries at Moudros (p637) and Portianos.

★ **Castle of Myrina**   CASTLE

FREE Myrina's lonely hilltop *kastro* dates from the 13th century and occupies a head-land that divides the town from its popular beach. The ruins of the Venetian-built fortress are imposing but deserted, apart from the deer that roam here freely. It's worth the 25-minute walk up the hill for the views alone, which extend to Mt Athos and, come evening, the twinkling cafe lights below.

Archaeological Museum   MUSEUM

(☑ 22540 22990; Romeïkos Gialos; €2; ⊙ 8.30am-4pm Wed-Mon) Myrina's fine neoclassical mansion-museum overlooks Romeïkos Gialos Beach and contains 8th- and 7th-century-BCE finds from Limnos' three major sites: Poliohni, the Sanctuary of the Kabeiroi and Hephaistia. Worth seeing are the earthenware lamp statuettes of sirens, along with details of the mandated Greek–Turkish population exchange of 1923.

Riha Nera   BEACH

This excellent sandy beach flanked by impressive rock formations is within walking distance from the centre of Myrina; inevitably, it gets crowded in high season. The sea is shallow, which is great for children. The beach is fully organised, with umbrellas, showers and several beach cafes.

🛏 Sleeping

Vicky Studios   APARTMENT €

(☑ 22540 22137; www.vickystudios.com; Maroulas 5; studios from €30; [P][❄][🛜]) This immaculate and friendly budget gem is a five-minute walk from shops and the beach at Riha Nera. Rooms face a lovely garden and feature kitchenettes, desks and fridges. Also has accommodation in Platy.

To Arhontiko   BOUTIQUE HOTEL €

(☑ 22540 29800; www.arxontikohotel.gr; cnr Sahtouri & Filellinon; r incl breakfast from €50; [❄][🛜]) This restored mansion (and Myrina's first hotel) dating from 1851 impresses with swanky boutique rooms, fireplaces, helpful staff, a cosy bar, classic charm throughout and a classic Greek breakfast to last the day. It's on a quiet alleyway near the *plateia* (square) of Romeïkos Gialos.

Studios Efterpi   APARTMENT €€

(☑ 6984337698, 22540 22458; www.efterpilemnos. gr; studios from €65; [❄][🛜]) Top of the hill in every sense, these tastefully furnished studios with well-equipped kitchenettes come with balconies offering views of Myrina's red-tiled roofs and the castle rock in the distance. It's a bit of a walk from the centre of Myrina, but not far from Riha Nera beach.

✕ Eating & Drinking

For a small town, Myrina has a rather energetic restaurant scene, with some good eateries at the port and more at Romeïkos Gialos, on the other side beyond the harbour.

★ Ouzeri To 11 — SEAFOOD €

(Glinou 6; seafood mezedhes €6-12; ⊙ noon-4pm & 8pm-midnight Wed-Mon) This unassuming little *ouzerie* (place that serves ouzo and light snacks) by the bus depot (p634) is the local favourite for seafood. From *kydonia* (mussels with garlic and Venus clams) to sea urchins, crayfish and more, 'To *En*-dheka' (as it's pronounced) serves all the stranger stuff, along with plenty of ouzo to help you forget what you're eating.

Grammóphōno — GREEK €

(☑ 22541 11841; Plateia Eleftheriou Venizelou 3; mains €6-10; ⊙ 10am-1am; 🐾) The traffic circle may not be the most appealing of surrounds, but this place is special thanks to its creative take on traditional taverna fare. It prides itself on various types of smoked meats, but there is more unusual stuff, such as caramelised octopus or *loukaniko* (pork sausage) with prunes.

Sinialo — GREEK €

(☑ 6947328729; Glinou; mains €6.50-9; ⊙ lunch & dinner; 🐾) A noncanonical taverna that strives to surprise you with foods that traditional establishments wouldn't feature. Shrimps in ouzo and milk sauce, fried baby octopus, croquettes with homemade cured meat, and many other unusual offerings are served in the romantic setting of a side-street patio.

O Platanos Restaurant — TAVERNA €

(Kyda-Karatza; mains €5-8; ⊙ 11am-11pm) Homemade pasta, good Limni wine and excellent *mayirefta* (ready-cooked meals) dishes with an emphasis on meat are served at this iconic place under two majestic plane trees, halfway along the main street.

Kosmos — TAVERNA €€

(Romeïkos Gialos; mains €6.50-14; ⊙ 10.30am-1am) A waterfront favourite known for well-prepared fresh fish at decent per-kilo prices. It also has postcard-worthy sunset views across the sea to Mt Athos.

Karagiozis — BAR

(Romeïkos Gialos; ⊙ 9am-5am) On a leafy terrace near the sea, Karagiozis morphs from snazzy frappé-cafe by day to a drink-till-you-drop bar under the stars. Sturdy, fair-priced drinks.

To Kelari — ALCOHOL SHOP

(☑ 22540 23261; waterfront; ⊙ 8am-1.30pm & 6-9pm) It's the kind of liquor shop you might have seen in pirate movies, with well-aged bottles covered in dust and spiderwebs, and an idiosyncratic bearded owner who makes excellent dry red, as well as *tsipouro*, at his small winery near Myrina.

ℹ Information

Aegean Travel (p633) Arranges car hire and island excursions.

Atzamis Travel (p633) Arranges ferry and air tickets, accommodation, excursions and bicycle rentals. Can arrange visits to the wetlands on Limnos' east coast.

Karaiskaki Travel (p633) Formerly known as Myrina Travel, specialises in trips to Agios Efstratios island.

Petrides Travel (p633) Helpful and informed staff arranges island sightseeing tours, boat trips, car hire, transfers and accommodation.

Pravlis Travel (☑ 22540 24617; www.pravlis.gr; ⊙ 8am-3pm & 5.30-10pm) Efficient and helpful full-service agency at the port.

ℹ Getting There & Away

Ferries arrive at the New Port on the other side of the harbour from Myrina's waterfront. Local buses depart for Moudros, the airport (p633) (22km east of Myrina) and other destinations around the island from the bus station (p634) on Plateia Eleftheriou Venizelou in the middle of town, where you will also find a **taxi rank** (☑ 22540 23820; Plateia Eleftheriou Venizelou).

Western Limnos

A densely populated area around Myrina boasts a few nice beaches and plenty of accommodation – especially at Platy, a scenic bay 2km south of the capital. The island's main road heads southeast, passing villages with quirky museums, wineries and interesting historical sites. A side road leads to the starting point of a trail, which runs through otherworldly terrain to the famous cave church of Panagia Kakaviotissa.

North of Myrina, the road left after Kaspakas village accesses the appealing Agios Ioannis Beach, set nicely beneath an overhanging volcanic slab. Hidden away in the mountainous hinterland, a cluster of villages around Sardes serves as a convenient pit stop on the way to the seldom visited sand dunes of Gomati Bay on the northern coast.

AGIOS EFSTRATIOS

You can't get any further from holidaying crowds than this little speck of land between Limnos and continental Greece. Abbreviated by locals as 'Aï-Stratis', the island attracts visitors for its isolation, remote beaches, relaxing hill walks and quiet beauty. The sparsely populated island has only a couple of domatia and tavernas, including Ai Strati (☑ 22540 93329, 6945563325; balaskajulia2000@yahoo.gr; r €30-40). The main village, also Agios Efstratios, is often just called 'the village'. Entirely rebuilt after a catastrophic earthquake that virtually flattened it in 1968, it is a serene getaway for those who need to escape from the big noisy world, and offers a chance to plunge into the microcosm of a close-knit island community.

⊙ Sights & Activities

Immediately south of Myrina, Platy is a long sandy beach with plenty of decent hotels and beach bars, but few restaurants.

Tucked into a giant rock cavity on top of a mountain, the Church of Panagia Kakaviotissa is as striking as the moonlike scenery that you'll pass through on a short trek to reach it.

Further along the southwest coast, Kontias is a charming village of windmills and stone houses, and home to the celebrated Kontias Gallery of Modern Balkan Art. Closed at the time of research, it might be open when you visit; ask locally.

From Kontias, the main road continues east to the village of Portianou. The chair Winston Churchill sat on while commanding the Allied offensive at Gallipoli is the most venerated item at the village's lovely Folklore Museum (☑ 22543 50000; www. laografiko-limnos.gr; Portianou; ⊙ 10am-2pm). Victims of Churchill's strategic gaffes lie at Portianos Military Cemetery nearby. The Old Russian Cemetery at Cape Punda (4km away) is the final resting place for more than 300 White Russians; they were interned on the islands by Allied troops, living in terrible conditions and dying of hunger and disease.

The road north passes near Savvouglu & Tsivolas winery, where you can taste the island's trademark Alexandrian muscat, before reaching a cluster of mountain villages around Sardes, which boasts an outstanding taverna. Beyond them lies a desolate coast famous for its dunes, an unusual sight for Greek islands.

Panagia Kakaviotissa Trail   TREKKING
(Map p633) A short trail leading to a locally famous cave chapel runs through a moonlike landscape of conical mountains and rock formations. Drive to the parking lot at the start of the trail or trek 5.5km from Myrina.

Gomati   BEACH
(Map p633) Tucked in the most remote corner of northwest Limnos, Gomati could be a wonderful set for a film about life on Mars thanks to its pinkish sand dunes and overall otherworldly feel. A beach bar operates here at the height of summer.

Savvouglu & Tsivolas   WINE
(Limnos Organic Wines; Map p633; http://limnos organicwines.gr; ⊙ 11am-2pm Mon-Fri, by appointment afternoons & weekends) FREE Limnos is full of wineries but this is one of the easiest to access. Off the road to Moudros, it specialises in Alexandrian muscat (white) and the local *kalabaki* red. But what earned it international acclaim is its Rodon rosé. Come for a brief tour of the facilities and an informal tasting session.

🛏 Sleeping & Eating

Panorama Plati   GUESTHOUSE €
(☑ 22540 24118, 6947718755; www.panoramaplati. com; Platy Beach; studios from €40; ❄🤶) Standing on a hillock, 500m away from Platy Beach, these tidy and well-equipped studios, complete with kitchens, indeed offer panoramic views of the scenic bay below. The charming host goes out of her way to help.

Paradise Apartments   APARTMENT €
(☑ 22540 26200, 6945443455; www.paradise limnos.gr; Platy Beach; r from €60; P❄🤶) A gleaming white block with blue doors greets you upon arrival. It's set back 150m from the beach, with palm trees and rose bushes, and has welcoming owners. Rooms are bright and spotless, all with kitchenettes.

Villa Victoria   APARTMENT €€
(☑ 6942906120, www.villa-victoria.gr; Platy Beach; d/apt €80/100; P❄🤶🏊) These attractive stone buildings are just metres from the beach, set on a rambling kid-friendly green with a pool. Rooms have smart wood-and-stone motifs, with kitchenettes. Several two-storey apartments can sleep four.

★ **Mantella Taverna** TAVERNA €
(☑ 22540 61349; Sardes; mains €5-9.50; ☺ lunch
& dinner) A popular well-managed taverna,
20 minutes' drive from Myrina in the village
of Sardes, just north of Therma. Traditional
country dishes include rooster, goat and pork
stews, along with excellent local cheeses and
crisp Limni wines. Although listed as a main
course, the sweet *moustoukoulika* pasta
makes a great calorie-bomb dessert.

O Sozos TAVERNA €
(Platy; mains €6.50-8.50; ☺ lunch & dinner) In the
main square of Platy, 2km east of Myrina, O
Sozos excels in traditional Greek fare. Specialities include *kokkaras flomaria* (rooster
served with pasta), lamb and dolmadhes.

❶ Getting There & Away

Western Limnos is best explored by car or a bike.
Platy Beach (p635) is easily accessible on foot
from Myrina.

Eastern Limnos

Eastern Limnos' flat plateaus are dotted with
wheat fields, small vineyards and sheep.
Limnos' second-largest town, Moudros, occupies the eastern side of muddy Moudros
Bay, famous for its role as the principal base
for the ill-fated Gallipoli campaign in 1915.

The rugged northeastern coast is sparsely
populated, which was not the case in Trojan
War times when Lemnians founded what's
believed to be Europe's first constituted democracy. Three large, scenic archaeological
sites in the area are related to that golden
age of Limnos. Far more recently, steady
winds have turned Keros Beach into a magnet for wind- and kitesurfers. The region also
hosts the Greek Air Force's central command,
meaning large parts are off limits to tourists.

◉ Sights & Activities

★ **East Moudros**
Military Cemetery CEMETERY
(Map p633; near Moudros) FREE As if taken
from the middle of England, this grassy
patch is dotted with memorials to 800 AN-
ZAC and other British Empire soldiers who
died of wounds in a nearby military hospital and were laid to rest here, when Limnos
served as the headquarters of the ill-fated
Gallipoli operation during WWI. In 1921 the
island also served as an internment camp
for thousands of White Russians, escaping
the Red Terror; around 20 of them are also
buried here.

The site is located right outside Moudros,
on the road to Roussopoli and Poliohni.

Chapel of Zoodochos Pigi CHURCH
(Map p633; Kotsinas) This hilltop late-Byzantine church built next to a holy-water spring
wouldn't be such an outstanding attraction if not for its scenic observation point
with a striking statue of Maroula, a fierce
sword-wielding female figure looking defiantly in the direction of nearby Turkey. A
local heroine, Maroula is said to have tak-
en her dying father's sword during the battle with the Ottomans in 1478. The site is a
short walk from the beach in Kotsinas.

Sanctuary of
the Kabeiroi ARCHAEOLOGICAL SITE
(Ta Kaviria; Map p633; €2; ☺ 8.30am-4pm Wed-
Mon) A beautifully desolate clifftop site, the
Sanctuary of the Kabeiroi lies at the northern tip of remote Tigani Bay. The worship of
the Kabeiroi gods here actually predates that
which took place on nearby Samothraki. The
major attraction is a Hellenistic sanctuary
with 11 partial columns. A trail leads down
the cliff to the legendary Cave of Philoctetes,
supposedly where the eponymous Trojan
War hero was abandoned while his gangre-
nous, snake-bitten leg healed. A marked path
from the site leads to the sea cave.

Poliohni ARCHAEOLOGICAL SITE
(Map p633; €2; ☺ 8.30am-4pm Wed-Mon) On the
southeast coast, Poliohni is considered the
first prehistoric settlement in the Aegean
and – allegedly – the first example of constituted democracy in the whole of Europe. It
has the remains of four ancient settlements,
the most significant being a pre-Mycenaean
city that predated Troy VI (1800–1275 BCE).
The site, with its tiny museum, is fascinating,
but remains are few.

Keros Beach BEACH
(Map p633) This long sandy beach, 32km from
Myrina, is high up in kitesurfers' pantheon of
beaches thanks to steady northern winds and
shallow waters, which are ideal for learning
the craft. There are several restaurants and
accommodation options in the vicinity.

🛏 Sleeping & Eating

Moudros has a couple of decent domatia.
Elsewhere, Varos Village (☑ 22540 31728;
www.varosvillage.com; ste & houses from €140;
❋ 🞔 🞮) stands out as one of the most luxurious accommodation options in the area
and on the island. Keros Beach boasts a luxurious tent camp for wind- and kitesurfers.

NORTHEASTERN AEGEAN ISLANDS EASTERN LIMNOS

There are some nice fish tavernas in Moudros, but the best one is Giannakaros.

Surf Club Keros TENTED CAMP €
(Map p633; ☑6980776064; www.surfclubkeros. com; Keros Beach, Kalliopi; tents standard/luxury from €40/90; ❄🛜) Sleep in luxurious safari tents, eat in a restaurant that gets most of its supplies from a nearby village and – most crucially – surf! That's the concept of this hedonistic tent resort doubling as a kitesurfing school on a beach famous for its steady winds and gentle surf. Seaborne stand-up paddleboard yoga classes sound especially intriguing.

Giannakaros GREEK €€
(Map p633; ☑22540 41744; Limanaki Kotsina, Kotsinas; mains €6-14; ⊗1-11pm, to 12.30am Sat & Sun) Popular with visiting Greeks and airbase personnel, this upmarket seafront taverna is heaving at weekends when it roasts a whole lamb or goat. Seafood dishes are excellent any day of the week.

🛈 Getting There & Away

Buses connect Moudros and Myrina (€3.30, 30 minutes, five daily). For other destinations, you'll need a car or a bike.

SAMOTHRAKI
ΣΑΜΟΘΡΑΚΗ

POP 2860

Emerging from obscurity as it's discovered by island hoppers, Samothraki sits alone in the northeastern corner of the Aegean, accessible only from the mainland port of Alexandroupoli. This lush, forested island boasts one of the most important archaeological sites in Greece: the ancient Thracian Sanctuary of the Great Gods (p640). Also here stands the Aegean's loftiest peak, Mt Fengari (1611m), from where, according to Homer, Poseidon, god of the sea, watched the Trojan War unfold.

Samothraki's mountainous interior, filled with massive gnarled oak and plane trees, is ideal for hiking and mountain biking, and the island's waterfalls, plunging into deep, glassy pools, provide cool relief on hot summer days. Remote southeastern beaches are pristine, while the north offers hot baths (p641) at Loutra (Therma). Inland from the main fishing port of sleepy Kamariotissa lies the former capital, Hora, bursting with flowers and handsome homes, all overlooking the distant sea.

🛈 Information

A very comprehensive guide to the island can be found at www.insamothraki.com.

🛈 Getting There & Away

SAOS Lines (www.saos.gr; ⊗varies) ferries connect Samothraki with Alexandroupoli – twice daily in summer, less frequently out of season, and varying in price (from €10 to €15.60, two hours). Rates for cars are prohibitively high at €58 (€38 on subsidised routes) and there is often not enough space. Purchase tickets at the port kiosk.

🛈 Getting Around

From Kamariotissa, there are six buses daily to Hora and Palepoli, five to Profitis Ilias via Alonia and Lakkoma, and two to Loutra.

Kyrkos Rent-a-Car (☑6972839231, 25510 41620; Kamariotissa) rents cars and small Jeeps in Kamariotissa.

There are only a couple of cabbies on the island; you can find their numbers displayed on the noticeboard by the bus stop in Kamariotissa. The longest trips cost under €20.

Kamariotissa & Around
Καμαριώτισσα

POP 960

Samothraki's port, largest town and transport hub, Kamariotissa is home to the island's main services. A nearby pebble beach has bars and decent swimming. While most visitors don't linger here, it's a likeable and attractive port filled with flowers and fish tavernas.

🛏 Sleeping

Most domatia and hotels are out of town and, unlike on many Greek isles, you won't find locals hawking rooms to arriving ferry passengers. Rooms are available at Lakkoma Beach.

Niki Beach Hotel HOTEL €
(☑25510 41545; www.nikibeach.gr; Kamariotissa; s/d/tr incl breakfast €35/55/105; ❄🛜🏊) This handsome, well-managed hotel with large modern rooms is just opposite the town beach. Balconies face the sea, while flowers and poplar trees fill an interior garden. Owners Elena and Vasillis manage to give it a boutique feel, despite the 37 rooms.

★**Hotel**
Samothraki Village HOTEL €€
(Map p639; ☑6982303396, 25510 42300; www. samothrakivillage.gr; Paleopoli; s/d/tr €65/70/90;

Samothraki

✳️📶♨️) Located 4km east of Kamariotissa on the coast road, and 1km before the Sanctuary of the Great Gods (p640), this excellent lodging consists of spacious modern rooms with sea-view balconies. There are two outdoor pools, a mini-playground for kids, a fitness centre and a *hammam*. Book ahead for free port pick-up.

🍴 Eating & Drinking

Tavernas line the waterfront in Kamariotissa. The island's best tavernas are found south of the town.

Fournello ITALIAN €
(Kamariotissa; mains €5-10; ☺ lunch & dinner) Fournello makes for a nice change of pace, serving good pizza and spaghetti. It's one of the few places where you can dine by the sea. Close to Niki Beach Hotel.

Vrahos TAVERNA €
(Map p639; 📞 25510 95264; Profitis Ilias; mains €4.50-9; ☺ lunch & dinner) This popular grill house in Profitis Ilias heaves during the weekends when a whole animal is grilled – either a goat or a sheep.

★I Synantisi TAVERNA €€
(📞 25510 41308; Kamariotissa; fish €6-12; ☺ lunch & dinner) Excellent fresh fish and *gavros* (marinated small fish) – the owner is a spear diver – as well as fine meat dishes such as roasted goat and rice pilaf. The place is cosy and welcoming, with a small open kitchen, and it often serves up *chaslamas*, a Turkish-named dessert unique to Samothraki.

Taverna Akrogiali TAVERNA €€
(Map p639; 📞 25510 95123; Lakkoma Beach; mains €6-15; ☺ lunch & dinner) A short distance from

the popular Lakkoma Beach, this is a pretty terrace filled with rose bushes and geraniums. It's a prime spot to sample Aegean fish, including some less obvious breeds.

Karnagio CAFE
(Kamariotissa waterfront) Snappy cafe for coffee and cheese pies by day, and a chill *ouzerie* for *tsipouro* and small plates at sunset.

ℹ️ Getting There & Away

Ferries depart for the mainland from the port at Kamariotissa, as do buses for Hora and Loutra.

Hora (Samothraki)
Χώρα (Σαμοθράκη)
POP 700

Set within a natural fortress of two sheer cliffs, and with a commanding view of the sea, Hora (also called Samothraki) was the obvious choice for the island's capital. In the 10th century the Byzantines built a castle on its northwestern peak, though today's substantial remains mostly date from the 15th-century Genoese rule.

Marked by twisting and colourful cobbled streets wreathed in flowers, and vintage traditional houses with terracotta roofs, Hora is perfect for enjoying a leisurely lunch or coffee, and on summer evenings there's easy-going nightlife in the small lanes and rooftop bars.

◉ Sights

Kastro CASTLE
(☺ 11am-2pm Wed & Fri-Sun) **FREE** Freshly converted into a fully fledged tourist sight complete with helpful English-language signs,

SANCTUARY OF THE GREAT GODS

About 6km northeast of Kamariotissa, Sanctuary of the Great Gods (Map p639; 📞 25510 41474; €6; ⊗ 8am-3pm) is one of Greece's most mysterious archaeological sites. The Thracians built this temple to their fertility deities around 1000 BCE. By the 5th century BCE, the secret rites and sacrifices associated with the cult had attracted famous pilgrims, including Egyptian queen Arsinou, Philip II of Macedon (father of Alexander the Great) and Greek historian Herodotus. Remarkably, the sanctuary operated until paganism was forbidden in the 4th century CE.

The principal deity, the fertility goddess Alceros Cybele (Great Mother), was later merged with the Olympian female deities Demeter, Aphrodite and Hecate. Other deities worshipped here were the Great Mother's consort, the virile young Kadmilos (god of the phallus), later integrated with the Olympian god Hermes; and the demonic Kabeiroi twins, Dardanos and Aeton, the sons of Zeus and Leda. Samothraki's great gods were venerated for their immense power – in comparison, the bickering Olympian gods were considered frivolous.

Little is known about what actually transpired here, though archaeological evidence points to two initiations, a lower and a higher. In the first, the great gods were invoked to grant the initiate a spiritual rebirth; in the second, the candidate was absolved of transgressions. This second confessional rite took place at the sacred Hieron, whose remaining columns are easily the most photographed ruin of the sanctuary.

We do know that the rituals at the sanctuary were open to all – men, women, citizens, servants and slaves – and since death was the penalty for revealing the secrets of the sanctuary, the main requirements seem to have been showing up and keeping quiet.

The Archaeological Museum at the Sanctuary of the Great Gods provides a helpful overview of the entire site. Pick up the free museum map before exploring the area. Museum exhibits include a striking marble frieze of dancing women, terracotta figurines and amphorae, jewellery, and clay lamps indicative of the nocturnal nature of the rituals. A plaster cast stands in for the celebrated Winged Victory of Samothrace (now in the Louvre), looted in 1863 by French diplomat and amateur archaeologist Charles Champoiseau.

About 75m south of the museum stands the Arisinoeion (rotunda), a gift from Queen Arisinou of Egypt. The sanctuary's original rock altar was discovered nearby. Adjacent are the rectangular Anaktoron, where lower initiations took place; the Temenos, a hall where a celebratory feast was held; and the Hieron, site of higher initiations.

Opposite the Hieron stand remnants of a theatre. Nearby, a path ascends to the Nike monument (nike means 'victory' in Greek), where once stood the magnificent Winged Victory of Samothrace, which faced northward overlooking the sea – appropriate since it was likely dedicated to the gods following a victorious naval battle.

this picturesque castle was built in 1431–33 by Genovese noble Palamede Gattilusio, who received the island in exchange for assisting the Byzantine emperor in a fratricidal war. In addition to sweeping views, the ruins feature a large stone cistern for collecting rainwater, and a murder hole for people whose company the Italian gentleman didn't enjoy.

The castle used to house a police station, which was only demolished in 2015.

Both the nobleman's and the emperor's coats of arms appear on a marble plaque at the castle entrance.

🛏 Sleeping

Hora has several domatia, but Hotel Axieros, in the heart of the village, is one of the best for value.

Hotel Axieros HOTEL €
(📞 25510 41416, 25510 41294; www.axieros.gr; d/tr/q from €50/60/65; ✳🛜) Friendly and welcoming, with handsomely furnished traditional rooms featuring well-equipped kitchenettes and views of the village.

🍴 Eating & Drinking

Cafes and tavernas are found high on the main street, where there's a small fountain with mountain-spring water.

O Lefkos Pyrgos SWEETS €
(desserts €4-6; ⊗ 9am-late Jul & Aug) The summer-only Lefkos Pyrgos is an excellent, inventive and all-natural sweets shop run by master confectioners Georgios and Dafni. Try lemonade with honey and cinnamon,

or Greek yoghurt with bitter almond, along with exotic teas, coffees and mixed drinks.

Trapeza me Thea CAFE
(⊘all day) Ex-urbanites Elias and Theodora have taken over Hora's old bank building and transformed it into a wonderful coffee shop. Take a seat on the balcony overlooking the valley below and enjoy your coffee with 'submarine' (sweet mastic paste submerged in water) or a spoon sweet.

Meltemi BAR
(☑25510 41071; ⊘8am-late) Opposite the fountain, this cool bar is managed by the gracious Panayioti, and has great views from a rooftop garden that's popular from morning until late.

❶ Getting There & Away

There are six buses daily to/from Kamariotissa (20 minutes).

Loutra Λουτρά
POP 100

Loutra (also called Therma), 14km east of Kamariotissa near the coast, is Samothraki's most popular place to stay. This relaxing village of plane and horse-chestnut trees, dense greenery and gurgling creeks comes to life at night when people of all ages gather in its outdoor cafes.

◉ Sights & Activities

Paradeisos Waterfalls WATERFALL
(Map p639) About 500m past Kafeneio Ta Therma, a lush wooded path (100m) leads to a series of rock pools and waterfalls, the most impressive being 30m in height. This is gorgeous, *Lord of the Rings*–like terrain, where gnarled 600-year-old plane trees covered in moss loom out of fog over a forest floor of giant ferns and brackish boulders. Get ready for an ice-cold dip on a hot summer's day.

Pachia Ammos Beach BEACH
(Map p639) A horseshoe-shaped sand cove with a beach bar and sunbeds, this is the best beach on the southern tip of the island. You'll need to arrange your own transport in order to get here.

Thermal Baths BATHHOUSE
(☑25513 50800; €4-6; ⊘7-10am & 6-9pm Jun-Sep) Loutra village's other name, Therma, refers to its warm, therapeutic, mineral-rich springs, reportedly able to cure everything

from skin problems to infertility. The prominent white building by the bus stop houses the official bath, though there is free bathing at two small outdoor baths 75m up the hill.

🛏 Sleeping

Aigaion PENSION €
(Map p639; ☑6986931337; Ano Karyotes; d from €40; ❄🔊) Set at the back of a shady garden, away from the main road, this family hotel has undergone a thorough renovation. Some of the old features, including doors and furniture, have been left intact, giving the place a nostalgic 1970s feel. All rooms come with balconies facing the sea and there is a common kitchen for self-caterers.

Mariva Bungalows BUNGALOW €
(☑25510 98230; www.mariva.gr; d incl breakfast €50; 🅿❄🔊) These secluded vine-covered stone bungalows, with breezy modern rooms, sit on a lush hillside near a waterfall. To reach them, turn from the coast road inland towards Loutra and follow the signs.

Hotel Orfeas HOTEL €
(☑25510 42213, 25510 98233; http://samothrakiorpheus.com; d/tr incl breakfast from €50/60; ❄🔊) Just across a leafy lane from the local stream, the Orfeas is simple, comfortable and friendly. The best rooms have balconies overlooking the stream, and the gracious owner, Christos, can offer tips on exploring the shady hills around Loutra.

★Archondissa BOUTIQUE HOTEL €€
(Map p639; ☑6942210527, 25510 98098; www.archondissa.gr; d/tr €80/95; ❄🔊) This Cycladic-styled sugar-cube cluster, located 3km east of Loutra, contains brightly coloured apartments with kilim rugs and ergonomic kitchenettes camouflaged as wardrobes. The sea is 30m away across a pretty flower garden.

🍷 Drinking & Nightlife

★Kafeneio Ta Therma CAFE
(☑6984994856; mains €3-5; ⊘8am-2am) Run by the jovial Iordanis Iordaninis for more than 20 years, this is the centre of the action in Loutra, with live music, impromptu vendors, artists and dancers in the surrounding open areas, plus coffee, beer and sweets. It's near the baths and several trails.

❶ Getting There & Away

There are four buses daily between Kamariotissa and Loutra.

THASOS ΘΑΣΟΣ

POP 13,770

One of Greece's greenest and most gentle islands, Thasos lies 10km from mainland Kavala. Its climate and vegetation make it seem like the island is an extension of northern Greece, yet it boasts enviable sandy beaches and a forested mountain interior. Quite inexpensive by Greek-island standards, it's popular with families and students from Bulgaria and the ex-Yugoslav republics. Frequent ferries from the mainland allow independent travellers to get here quickly, and the excellent bus network makes getting around easy.

The island's main draws are its natural beauty, beaches, inland villages and historical attractions. The excellent archaeological museum in the capital, Thasos (Limenas), is complemented by the Byzantine Moni Arhangelou (p647), with its stunning clifftop setting, and the Ancient Greek temple at Alyki (p646) on the serene southeast coast.

History

Over its long history, Thasos has benefited from its natural wealth. The Parians, who founded the ancient city of Thasos (Limenas) in 700 BCE, struck gold at Mt Pangaion, creating an export trade lucrative enough to subsidise a naval fleet. While the gold is long gone, Thasos' white Parian marble is still being exploited, though scarring a mountainside in the process.

🕴 Activities

The **Victoria** (☑ 6977012769; ☉ Jul & Aug) excursion boat makes full-day trips around Thasos (Limenas), with stops for swimming and lunch. It departs the Old Harbour in Limenas at 10am. Water taxis run regularly to Hrysi Ammoudia (Golden Beach) and Makryammos Beach from the Old Harbour. Excursion boats of varying sizes and alcohol content also set sail regularly from the coastal resorts. Enquire at **Visit North Greece** (☑ 25106 20566, 6942524337; www. visitnorthgreece.com; Pavlou Mela 17; ☉ 9am-9pm) or **Billias Travel Service** (☑ 25930 24003; Pavlou Mela 6) in Thasos (Limenas).

🛈 Information

Go Thasos (www.go-thassos.gr; ☉ 9am-2pm Mon-Fri) runs a comprehensive online guide to the island and a useful information office in Thasos (Limenas).

🛈 Getting There & Away

Thasos is only accessible from the mainland ports of Keramoti and Kavala. Ferries run between Keramoti and Limenas every 30 to 45 minutes (adult/car €4/18, 40 minutes), and six a day between Kavala and Skala Prinou (adult/car €5/19, 1¼ hours). Get ferry schedules at the **ticket booths** (☑ 25930 22318) in Thasos (Limenas) and the **port authority** (☑ 25930 71390; Skala Prinou).

🛈 Getting Around

BICYCLE

Basic bikes can be hired in Thasos (Limenas). Top-of-the-line models and detailed route information are available in Potos, on the southwest coast, from Velo Bike Rental (p645).

BUS

Frequent buses serve the entire island coast as well as inland villages. Buses meet arriving ferries at Skala Prinou and Thasos (Limenas), the island's transport hub. The two port towns are connected by eight daily buses (€2.10, 20 minutes).

Frequent buses run throughout the day from Thasos (Limenas) to west-coast villages such as Limenaria (€5), Potos (€5.30) and Theologos (€6.70). Buses from Limenas also reach the east-coast destinations of Hrysi Ammoudia (Golden Beach; €2.20), Skala Potamia (€1.90) via Panagia (€1.80) and Potamia (€1.80), some of them continuing to Paradise Beach (€2.80) and Alyki (€4.10).

A full circular tour (about 100km) of the island runs six to eight times daily (€10.60, 3½ hours) – three clockwise and three anticlockwise. This round-the-island ticket is valid all day, so you can jump on and off without paying extra. The **bus station** (☑ 25930 22162) on the Thasos (Limenas) waterfront provides timetables. Services are reduced during weekends.

CAR & MOTORCYCLE

Potos Car Rentals (☑ 25930 52071; www. rentacarpotos.gr; Hotel Potos, Potos) is reliable and reasonable. **Avis Rent-a-Car** (☑ 25930 22535; www.avis.gr) is in Thasos (Limenas), Potamia and Skala Prinou.

Crazy Rollers (☑ 2593071444; www. crazyrollers.gr; ☉ 9am-1pm & 5-9pm) in Skala Prinou and **Moto Zagos** (☑ 25930 53340; www. motozagos.gr; Limenaria) in Limenaria both rent motorbikes and bicycles.

TAXI

The Thasos (Limenas) **taxi rank** (☑ 6944170373, 25930 22394; waterfront) is on the waterfront, next to the main bus stop. Sample destinations and fares: Skala Prinou €20, Panagia €12, Skala Potamia €20, Alyki €40 and Potos €50.

Thasos

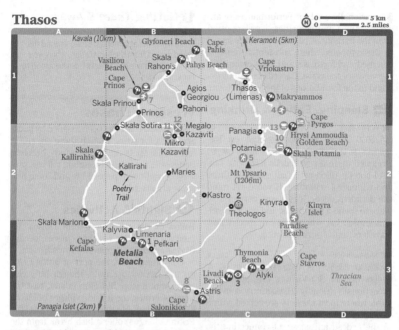

Thasos

In Potos, there's a taxi rank with listed prices beside the bus stop on the main road.

Limenas   Λιμένας

POP 2610

Limenas (also called Thasos) has the island's main services and year-round activity. It sports a picturesque fishing harbour, a sandy beach, shopping, a few ancient ruins and an archaeological museum. If you're exploring the eastern side of town, note the signpost for historical sites, beginning a five-minute walk up a shaded trail to the lovely chapel of Agioi Apostoli, where there are views over the seafront.

◉ Sights

★ Archaeological Museum   MUSEUM
(☑ 25930 22180; €2; ⊙ 8am-8pm Wed-Mon) Looking like an alien creature from the sci-fi movie *Avatar*, a 5m-tall 6th-century-BCE *kouros* (male statue of the Archaic period) carrying a ram greets visitors at this large, modern archaeological museum. Statues and other artefacts from the Classical and Roman periods are on display. The museum is located about 100m from the Old Harbour's waterfront.

Ancient Agora   RUINS
Next to the archaeological museum stand the foundation ruins of the ancient *agora,* the commercial centre in ancient times. About 100m east of the *agora,* the ancient theatre

is occasionally used for performances of ancient dramas and comedies; it's signposted from the harbour. A path connects the *agora* to the acropolis, where substantial remains of a medieval fortress stand, with commanding views of the coast. Carved rock steps descend to the foundations of the ancient town.

🛏 Sleeping, Eating & Drinking

⭐ A for Art   DESIGN HOTEL €€
(☑ 25930 58405; www.aforarthotel.gr; cnr Theogenous & 18 Oktovriou; d from €120; ❈ 🛜) Dreamed up in a psychedelic haze, this fanciful hotel is filled with Dalí-esque furniture and whimsical sculpture. If you don't mind the decadent decor, it is a very comfortable place to spend a few nights, and has an excellent garden bar where you can meet fellow travellers (and a purple flamingo).

⭐ Masabuka   GRILL €
(☑ 25930 23651; 18 Oktovriou; mains €2-4; ☺ 4pm-midnight; 🛜) Visitors rave about this exceptionally friendly 21st-century souvlaki joint, where meat skewers are served with a variety of mouth-watering dips. It's located in the pedestrianised street connecting the centre with the harbour area.

Simi   TAVERNA €€
(☑ 25930 22517; Old Harbour; mains €7-12; ☺ 9.30am-midnight; 🛜🍴) Locals agree that this year-round eatery at the Old Harbour serves Limenas' best fish, along with fine fish soup, *stifadho* (meat, game or seafood cooked with onions in a tomato puree) and grilled sardines. There's a kids' menu, good wines and spicy mezedhes, including hot peppers that can change your life.

⭐ Karnagio   BAR
(☑ 25930 23170; ☺ 8am-2am) Stroll past the Old Harbour for a quiet sunset drink at Karnagio, where outdoor seating straddles a rocky promontory lapped by waves. You can also clamber up the rocks to a small, candlelit chapel.

ℹ Information

Go Thasos (p642)

Billias Travel Service (p642) Full-service travel agency.

Visit North Greece (p642) Well-managed tour operator offering hiking, walking and cycling excursions, along with 4WD safaris and sailing trips. The helpful owners, Chrisoula and Stelios, can also handle transfers and suggest accommodation.

ℹ Getting There & Away

Ferries from Keramoti on the mainland arrive at the New Port at Limenas. Buses around the island depart from the bus station, where you can also purchase bus tickets from Keramoti to Thessaloniki.

Western Thasos

Thasos' west coast has been assailed by package tours for years, though there are still a few idyllic spots and quiet sandy beaches. Better still, the inland mountain villages preserve a traditional pace of life and some fine stone architecture.

◉ Sights & Activities

Following the coast west from Thasos (Limenas), two sandy beaches emerge: decent Glyfoneri and the superior Pahys Beach.

Continuing west, the port of Skala Prinou has ferries to Kavala, though little else to warrant a stop. But 6km inland, past the town of Prinos, the hillside villages of Mikro Kazaviti and Megalo Kazaviti (aka the Prinou villages) offer a lush break from the touristed coast, with undeniable character and a few places to stay and eat, including Menir Luxury Apartments (p645). An easy-to-follow trail network branches off from the pretty square in Megalo Kazaviti, with a sign marking the routes.

The next real point of interest, the whimsical fishing port of Skala Marion, lies further south. Its few canopied tavernas overlooking the sea are faithfully populated by village elders shuffling backgammon chips while children scamper about. The village has a few domatia and a bakery on the northern jetty. On the village's feast day (24 June), church services are followed by folk dancing around the square.

The coast road south passes more beaches until reaching Limenaria, Thasos' second-largest town, which is followed quickly by Pefkari and Potos, two fishing villages turned package resorts, both with long sandy beaches lined with cafes and tavernas.

From the Theologos–Potos corner of the main road, head southeast round the coast for views of the stunning bays. The last southwestern settlement, Astris, has a good beach with tavernas and the Astris Sun Hotel (Map p643; ☑ 25930 51281; www.astris sunhotel.gr; r from €76; ❈ 🏊).

Despite its touristy feel, Thasos' west coast offers worthwhile outdoor activities such as scuba diving, mountain biking and birdwatching. There are walking trails above the coast.

★ Metalia Beach
BEACH

(Map p643; Limenaria) Easily accessible on foot from Limenaria, this pretty cove features an elegiac retro-industrial sight in the form of a mining factory built by German entrepreneur Speidel in 1900. The ruins form an amphitheatre around the beach, with a colonial-styled green administrative building, sadly abandoned, towering above the headland.

★ Velo Bike Rental
CYCLING

(☑ 25930 52459, 6946955704; www.velobikerental. com; Potos) Hires out bikes year-round and also runs guided biking and hiking tours to Mt Ypsario. Inspired owner Yiannis Reizis also organises a number of international cycling events and races on the island.

Thassos Horse Club
HORSE RIDING

(Map p643; ☑ 6999391777; www.thassoshorse club.snadno.eu; Skala Prinou) Runs riding lessons and tailor-made horseback trips out of Skala Prinou.

Panagia Islet
BIRDWATCHING

(☑ 6973209576; www.gothassos.com; trips €25) The rocky, uninhabited Panagia Islet, southwest of Potos, is home to Greece's largest shag colony. Local environmentalist and ornithologist Yiannis Markianos at Aldebran Pension arranges birdwatching boat trips in spring and autumn, weather permitting.

Diving Club Vasiliadis
DIVING

(☑ 6944542974; www.scuba-vas.gr; Potos; ⊗ 9am-2pm & 5-8pm) Diving for beginners and open-water divers is offered in Potos by Vasilis Vasiliadis, including trips to Alyki's submerged ancient marble quarry. A one-day course for beginners costs €50.

🛏 Sleeping

Potos has some decent hotels, but Limenaria is simply a nicer place to stay.

★ Aldebran Pension
PENSION €

(☑ 25930 52494, 6973209576; www.gothassos. com; Potos; d from €55; ※ 🛜) Well-informed and attentive owners Elke and Yiannis make Aldebran the best value in southern Thasos. Along with a leafy courtyard and table tennis, it boasts modern baths, a well-equipped communal kitchen and all-day coffee and tea. Yiannis offers info on local hiking trails and more.

Villa Ioanna
APARTMENT €€

(☑ 6974466730; https://villa-ioanna.com; Potos; d/tr from €64/74; P ※ 🛜) This gentrified version of domatia has a fancy hotel quality, with an elegant subdued design that involves many wooden surfaces, ropes and bamboo stems. Comfy beds come with aromatic Coco-Mat mattresses, and are topped with an array of pillows. There are kitchenettes in each room, with complimentary coffee capsules and other breakfast supplies.

Hotel Menel – The Tree House
DESIGN HOTEL €€

(☑ 6944578954, 25930 51396; www.dhotels.gr; Limenaria; d incl breakfast from €85; ※ 🛜) This funky edifice stands out among Limenaria's seafront hotels thanks to its Scandinavian ecodesign, with a wooden facade and 16 airy modern rooms, all with sea-view balconies. A great rooftop terrace with sunbeds is a bonus.

Menir Luxury Apartments
APARTMENT €€

(Map p643; ☑ 25930 58270; www.menir-thassos. gr; Mikro Kazaviti; r incl breakfast from €90; ※ 🛜) Some of the most handsome and spacious digs in this rustic area. There are five apartments, two with spa and all with fireplaces, open year-round.

🍴 Eating

The margin between a decent taverna and a tourist trap is blurred in Potos and Limenaria, but you'll definitely not go hungry.

★ Armeno
TAVERNA €

(Skala Marion; mains €5-9; ⊗ 7am-1am) Well-regarded waterfront taverna, where you can have a look at the day's catch of fish. The organic produce here is from the gardens of the friendly Filaktaki family, who also rent rooms (☑ 6977413789, 25930 52634; Skala Marion; r from €35; ※ 🛜) and can help with local information. Located in offbeat Skala Marion.

Kazaviti Restaurant
GREEK €€

(Map p643; ☑ 6972053342; Megalo Kazaviti; €7-13; ⊗ 8am-11pm; 🛜) Set in the shade of plane trees on the beautiful square of its namesake village, this restaurant makes a conscious effort to surprise those used to (and possibly slightly tired of) the usual island taverna routine. Bean soup, lamb's head soup, liver, lamb in a pot and sundried octopus are some of the unusual and delicious menu options.

WORTH A TRIP

INLAND VILLAGES

Two interior villages warrant a day trip inland. About 6km from Skala Marion, forested Maries rewards visitors with cool highland air and a handsome monastery, Agios Taxiarchis.

Thasos' medieval and Ottoman capital, Theologos, is only accessible from Potos, where the road leads inland to the forested hamlet of 400 souls, notable for its whitewashed slate-roofed houses. Find the 1803 Church of Agios Dimitrios, distinguished by its grand slate roof, exquisite polished wood interior and white-plastered clock tower. An interesting local folklore museum (Map p643; Theologos; €2; ⊙10am-4pm) occupies the house of the island's 19th-century president. Relax at one of the local cafes or tavernas to soak it all up.

O Georgios   TAVERNA €€
(Potos; mains €6.50-13; ⊙lunch & dinner; 🛜) This traditional Greek grill house, set in a pebbled rose garden, is a local favourite away from Potos' more touristy main road. It offers friendly service and generous portions.

Psarotaverna To Limani   SEAFOOD €€
(Limenaria; mains €6.50-25; ⊙lunch & dinner) Limenaria's best seafood is served at this waterfront restaurant opposite the National Bank of Greece. Prices can be steep.

⏴ Getting There & Away

Frequent daily buses serve Potos (€5.30) and Limenaria (€5) from Limenas.

Eastern Thasos

Thasos' east-coast beaches are beautiful in summer and less crowded than the more developed west coast. The dramatic coastal landscape features thick forests that run from mountains to sea. There are fewer organised activities here, but the warm, shallow waters are excellent for families.

Tiny Alyki may be the most overlooked spot on the southeast coast. The village is great for unwinding, with a few shops, domatia and tavernas, and there are two fine sandy beach coves, separated by a small olive grove dotted with ancient ruins comprising the archaeological site of Alyki.

◉ Sights

Panagia and Potamia are 4km west of the east coast's most popular beaches: sandduned Hrysi Ammoudia (Golden Beach), tucked inside a long, curving bay; and gentle Skala Potamia, on its southern end. Both have accommodation, restaurants and a bit of nightlife.

Further south from Skala Potamia is the deservedly popular, family-friendly Paradise Beach, 2km after tiny Kinyra village.

You'll need stamina to reach the secluded Marble Beach, located at the bottom of a giant marble quarry, 6km south of Limenas, but it is one of the island's most memorable sights.

★ Archaeological Site of Alyki   ARCHAEOLOGICAL SITE
(Alyki) **FREE** Alluring and easily accessible, the island's crown gem includes the considerable and photogenic remains of an ancient temple where the gods were once invoked to protect sailors. Enter the site through the back door by following a beautiful trail that skirts the headland, passing a partially submerged marble quarry that remained operational from the 7th century BCE to the 6th century CE. The path starts at the far end of the beach lined by tavernas.

Moni Arhangelou   MONASTERY
(Map p643; ⊙9am-2pm & 5pm-sunset) **FREE** West from Alyki, past Thymonia Beach, is the clifftop Moni Arhangelou, an Athonite dependency and working convent, notable for its 400-year-old church (with some ungainly modern touches) and stellar sea views. Those improperly attired will get shawled up for entry by the friendly nuns. Archangel Michael, whose name the monastery bears, is venerated as the patron of the Greek armed forces; don't be surprised to see a room filled with sabres and uniforms attached to the main church.

From their island retreat, the nuns can observe Mt Athos, a forbidden place for women. The sacred mountain looms across the straits on Halkidiki Peninsula. About 1.5km west of the monastery, a small dirt road heads 1km to Livadi Beach, one of Thasos' most beautiful, with aquamarine waters ringed by cliffs and forests and just a few umbrellas set in the sand.

Panagia   VILLAGE
This inland village just south of Limenas is nothing if not photogenic. Its characteristic architecture includes stone-and-slate

rooftops and the elegant blue-and-white domed and icon-rich Church of the Kimisis tou Theotokou (Church of the Dormition of the Virgin). To reach this peaceful quarter, follow the sound of rushing spring water upwards along a stone path heading inland.

🏃 Activities

Paradise Beach

BEACH

(Map p643) Zanzibar-quality whitish sand, a shallow seabed and lush greenery in the background give this beautiful beach a tropical feel. There are two beach bars with sunbeds, but no showers. The beach used to attract nudists, but these days it's overrun by holidaying families from Eastern Europe.

Located 2km after tiny Kinyra village.

Marble Beach

BEACH

(Map p643) This hard-to-reach beach at the bottom of a giant quarry is entirely made of marble crumbs, making the whole place so ethereally white it feels like literal paradise. In the middle of the beach, a pine tree growing out of a marble slab makes it extremely photogenic. There's a beach bar, sunbeds and a shower. Don't trust your navigator if you drive; follow graffiti signs on the main road to find the correct turn.

Mt Ypsario

HIKING

(Map p643) Potamia makes a good jumping-off point for climbing Thasos' highest peak, Mt Ypsario (1206m). A tractor trail west from Potamia continues to the valley's end, after which arrows and cairns point the way up a steep path. The three-hour Ypsario hike is classified as moderately difficult.

🛌 Sleeping

Studios Vaso

APARTMENT €

(☑ 6946524706, 25102 33507; gemitzi.alexandra@vaso-studios.gr; Alyki; r from €55; P ❄) Heading just east of Alyki's bus stop on the main road, look for the big burst of flowers and a sign pointing up the drive to this charming set of nine self-catering domatia, run by the welcoming Vaso Gemetzi and daughter Aleka. There's a leafy courtyard. Kids stay free.

Thassos Inn

HOTEL €

(☑ 25930 61612; www.thassosinn.gr; Panagia; d from €45; P 🛜) Just follow the sound of rushing spring water to this rambling hotel by the church for great views of Panagia's slate-roofed houses. The welcoming owners, Toula and Tasos, can also advise hikers who want to stay close to the Mt Ypsario trailhead.

★ Hotel Kamelia

HOTEL €€

(Map p643; ☑ 25930 61463, 6948898767; www.hotel-kamelia.gr; s/d incl breakfast from €80/90; P ❄ 🛜) This beachfront gem is the best in town – understated, with cool jazz in the garden bar and friendly service throughout. The gracious owners, Eleni, Stavros and family, serve a fine Greek breakfast overlooking the sea and provide plenty of tips about the area. It's 500m north of the busier main beach, over a very small bridge.

Hotel Dionysos

HOTEL €€

(Map p643; ☑ 25930 61822; www.hotel-dionysos-thassos.com; Hrysi Ammoudia; s/d/tr incl breakfast from €50/70/85; P ❄ 🛜 🏊) This rambling and comfortable hilltop retreat overlooking Hrysi Ammoudia owes its appeal to energetic owners Sakis and Mary, who also ferry their guests by minivan to the beach and offer good taverna standards throughout the day from their kitchen.

🍴 Eating & Drinking

Arhontissa Alyki

GREEK €

(☑ 25930 32098; Alyki; mains €6-11; ⊗ 7am-11.30pm) The friendly Anastasios Kuzis and family run this tranquil taverna with great sea views. It serves excellent fare, with fresh fish and mezedhes among the star offerings. Find it east of the village car park, signposted up a steep drive.

Taverna Grill Elena

TAVERNA €

(☑ 25930 61709; Panagia; mains €6.50-12; ⊗ noon-midnight) This classic taverna under a shady patio off the square, run by Georgios and Elena, specialises in spit-roasted lamb and goat. Before you get to the *kokoretsi* on the spit, sample the *bougloundi* (baked feta with tomatoes and chilli) appetiser.

Limanaki

CAFE

(Map p643; ☑ 6949551875; Hrysi Ammoudia; ⊗ lunch & dinner) The words 'hip' and *'ouzerie'* seldom go together, but the understated stylishness of this terrace-bar at the northern edge of Hrysi Ammoudia (Golden Beach) succeeds. It's a pleasant place to unwind after some beach fun, with a glass of *tsipouro* and a plate of mezedhes, or simply a cup of Greek coffee.

ℹ Getting There & Away

Hrysi Ammoudia (Golden Beach; €2.20) and the villages above it are served by frequent buses from Limenas. There is also a daily service from Limenas to Alyki (€4.10).

AT A GLANCE

POPULATION
Halkida: 59,100

EVIA'S CAPITAL
Halkida

BEST FESTIVAL
Skyros Carnival
(p674)

BEST TAVERNA
O Pappous Kai Ego
(p674)

**BEST
AGROTURISMO**
Eleonas (p654)

WHEN TO GO
Feb–Apr Carnival
season keeps things
warm before spring
and Easter festivities
arrive.

Jun & Sep Perfect
temperatures, clear
skies and fewer
crowds – ideal
hiking and swimming
months.

Jul & Aug Peak sun
and beach fun (but
higher prices – book
ahead!)

Halkida (p65)

Evia & the Sporades

Evia (Εύβοια), Greece's second-largest island, is hidden in plain view, separated from the mainland by the narrow Evripos Channel at Halkida. Away from this workaday hub, the pace slows as the island morphs into hilltop monasteries, hidden bays, small vineyards, sky-reaching peaks and curious goats.

Most visitors use Evia as a jumping-off point for the four gorgeous, mountainous Sporades (Οι Σποράδες, 'scattered ones'), which feel like extensions of the forested Pelion Peninsula. Skiathos, the most developed, is graced by some of the most beautiful beaches in the Aegean. Low-key Skopelos kicks back with a sparkling-white old town, rich musical traditions and pristine pebble beaches, while secluded Alonnisos anchors a spectacular national marine park and a romantically ruined old capital. To the south, Skyros is known for its culinary and artistic heritage dating from Byzantine times.

Evia & the Sporades Highlights

1 **Skiathos** (p656) Lazing on white-sand beaches.

2 **National Marine Park of Alonnisos** (p670) Sailing between untouched islands and spotting dolphins.

3 **Skopelos Town** (p661) Drinking, dining and shopping waterside.

4 **Skyros Town** (p673) Delving into Skyros' unique

architecture and art traditions below the Venetian fortress.

5 **Skopelos Hiking** (p666) Meandering around glittering pebble bays and pine-sprinkled capes.

6 **Old Alonnisos** (p669) Wandering the alleys of this bucolic hilltop village.

7 **Skyrian Horses** (p676) Meeting rare, gentle Skyrian

horses at conservation centres.

8 **Moni Evangelistrias** (p659) Sampling monks' wine on Skiathos.

9 **Dimosari Gorge** (p655) Hiking this lush ravine in south Evia, then cooling off in the sea.

10 **Loutra Edipsou** (p654) Swimming year-round at a thermal-fed, north-Evia bay.

EVIA · ΕΥΒΟΙΑ

POP 212,000

Evia, Greece's second-largest island after Crete, remains largely off the tourist map, with most foreign visitors using it to nip off to smaller and more obviously enticing nearby islands. Take some time here, though, and you'll find it unveils glorious mountain roads, rewarding treks, rippling vineyards, major archaeological finds and plenty of uncrowded beaches – all of which of make it a popular escape for Athenians and other mainlanders. A north–south mountainous spine divides the island's eastern cliffs from the gentler and more resort-friendly west coast, with just one main road linking its distinct northern, central and southern sections.

Ferries connect Evia to the mainland, along with two bridges at humdrum capital Halkida, perched on the narrowest point of the Evripos Channel.

❶ Getting There & Away

Five ports on Evia serve the mainland. In the south, Nea Styra connects with Agia Marina and Marmari with Rafina. In the north, Loutra Edipsou has ferries to/from Arkitsa and Agiokambos to/from Glyfa, while in central Evia Eretria connects with Skala Oropou.

Kymi, on the east coast, has year-round ferries to/from the island of Skyros (€12.10, 1¾ hours, daily) and, from mid-June to mid-September, Skopelos (€20, three hours, three weekly) and Alonnisos (€20, 2¼ hours, three weekly). The northeastern port of Mantoudi serves Skiathos (€19.80, 2½ hours, one to two daily) and Skopelos (€19.80, 1½ hours, one sto two daily). All services are reduced from October to April.

Halkida has bus and train connections to the mainland.

Halkida · Χαλκίδα

POP 59,100

Mentioned in Homer's *Iliad*, once-powerful Halkida (also Halkis or Chalkis) spawned several colonies around the Mediterranean. The name derives from the bronze that was manufactured here in antiquity (*halkos* means bronze in Greek). Today there's little to detain travellers, but Evia's capital is a lively commercial centre, and the main gateway to the island, with good restaurants and accommodation. As evening approaches, the scenic waterfront promenade extending from the old bridge comes to life beside the narrow Evripos Channel, which reverses direction several times a day.

◉ Sights

To begin unravelling Halkida's diverse religious history, head up busy Kotsou from the old bridge towards the *kastro* district, where you'll find the elegant 15th-century Tzami Emir Zade (Plateia Tzami; ⊙10am-2pm Tue, Thu & Sun) – now with cartographic Evia displays – an Ottoman-era fountain and, just east, a 19th-century synagogue (Kotsou; ⊙hours vary). About 100m south of the mosque is the Byzantine church of Agia Paraskevi (Tzavara; ⊙dawn-dusk), founded around 1250. A Roman-Venetian aqueduct (Stiron; ⊙24hr) stands 2km east, just north of the bus station (you'll almost inevitably spot it as you come into town).

⫘ Sleeping & Eating

Halkida isn't a tourist hotspot, but you might need to stay over for practical reasons; there are a few comfortable budget and midrange hotels on the waterfront.

A chic, moodily lit reinvention of a handsome neoclassical building by the water, the smart bar-restaurant Pantheon 1900 (☑22210 23123; www.facebook.com/pantheon1900 restaurant; Kriezotou & Voudouri 22; mains €8-16; ⊙8am-1am; 🛜🍴) has snappy service, a buzzy atmosphere and bottles towering up to the ceiling. They stock local wines to enjoy alongside elegantly prepped Mediterranean-influenced dishes.

❶ Getting There & Away

BUS

From Halkida's **KTEL bus station** (☑22210 20400; cnr Styron & Arethousis), 2.5km east of the old bridge (taxi fare €5), buses run to/from destinations across Evia and beyond.

DESTINATION	DURATION	FARE (€)	FREQUENCY
Athens	1hr	7.50	30mins
Eretria	30mins	2.20	8-10 daily
Ioannina	7hrs	40	4 weekly
Karystos	3hrs	12.70	weekdays
Kymi & Paralia Kymis	2hrs	9.20	8-10 daily
Limni	2hrs	8.60	2-3 daily
Loutra Edipsou	3½hrs	13	daily
Mantoudi	2hrs	6	2-3 daily
Steni	45mins	3.30	4 daily
Thessaloniki	6hrs	40	daily

TRAIN

Regular trains connect Halkida with Athens (€6.50, two hours, 12 daily); for Thessaloniki, change at Inoi.

Eretria   Ερέτρια

POP 4160

Eretria, 20km southeast of Halkida, is the first place of interest on Evia for travellers coming from the mainland, with frequent ferry links to Skala Oropou. Founded around 750 BCE, it grew into a major maritime city until it was destroyed in the 1st century BCE. Today, the town has a small fishing harbour and a touristy boardwalk of lively tavernas, open-air cafes and beach bars; it is also home to some of Evia's most important archaeological remains in Ancient Eretria.

◉ Sights & Activities

Ancient Eretria   ARCHAEOLOGICAL SITE

(⊙8am-4pm Wed-Mon) **FREE** Ancient Eretria was a major maritime power with an eminent school of philosophy, and was destroyed in 87 BCE by the Roman commander Sylla. Its scant but fascinating ruins lie scattered around town; pick up a map at the Archaeological Museum. Southwest of the ancient hilltop acropolis are the remains of a 5th-century-BCE theatre and a 4th-century-BCE temple; the most fascinating site is the House of Mosaics (370 BCE), with pebble mosaics depicting mythological scenes.

**Archaeological
Museum of Eretria**   MUSEUM

(🖉22290 62206; Archaiou Theatrou & Isidos; €2; ⊙8.30am-4pm Wed-Mon) This captivating museum displays the archaeological riches unearthed in Eretria since the 19th

---

ⓘ KYMI FERRIES

A prosperous agricultural centre surrounded by vineyards and fruit orchards, the workaday east-coast hillside town of Kymi perks up at dusk when its elegant main square springs to life. The port of Paralia Kymis, 3.5km east and downhill, is the departure point for ferries to Skyros and, in summer, Alonnisos and Skopelos, with a string of waterside tavernas and cafes. Skyros Shipping Co (p661) ferries run to/from Skyros year-round (€12.10, 1¾ hours, daily) and, from mid-June to mid-September, to/from Skopelos (€20, three hours, three weekly) and Alonnisos (€20, 2¼ hours, three weekly). Buses to/from Halkida (€9.20, two hours, eight to 10 daily) coincide with ferry departures and arrivals.

---

century, with information detailed in Greek and French. The signature pieces are the 4th-century-BCE terracotta depiction of the mythical Medusa, whose tresses were turned into live serpents by the goddess Athena as revenge for Medusa's dalliance with Poseidon, and the 10th-century-BCE clay Centaur of Lefkandi, found broken in two.

Evia Adventure Tours   ADVENTURE SPORTS

(🖉6973856793; www.eviatours.com; Grand Bleu Beach Resort; ⊙9am-noon & 5-7pm Sun-Thu, 9am-noon Fri & Sat Apr-Oct) An excellent, professional adventure-activity company offering cycling trips, winery tours, guided hikes (including Dimosari Gorge and Mt Ohi in the south) and other cultural and adventure activities across Evia. The team also offers bike hire in Eretria (per day €10 to €55) and guided bike tours of Ancient Eretria (€40).

🛏 Sleeping & Eating

Diamanto Rooms   PENSION €

(🖉22290 62214; diamantorooms@gmail.com; Varvaki 2; s/d €35/45; 🌣🖥) Ten sparkling, colourful, old-fashioned budget rooms with balconies, fridges, extra blankets, a shared kitchen and a plant-wreathed entrance way, all expertly managed by friendly owner Athina. Ask for a sea-view room.

Villa Belmar   APARTMENT €€

(🖉6971588424, 6980003512; www.villabelmar. gr; 22 Aristonikou Eratonimou; studio €57-69, 1-bedroom apt €87-119; ⊙Easter-Sep; 🅿🌣🖥) Handily positioned southwest of the port, these seven stylish studios and one- to three-bedroom apartments, with a private waterfront deck and direct sea access, are managed by welcoming sisters Lina and Renia. Each rustically modern apartment has its own balcony, with views out to sea or of the palm-dotted gardens, and is decorated with beamed ceilings or colourful art.

La Cubana   GREEK €

(🖉2229061665; www.facebook.com/lacubanaresta urant; Arheou Theatrou 44; mains €6-12; ⊙noon-midnight Apr-Oct, Fri-Sun only Nov-Mar; 🖥🍴) Dine on the waterfront or in the elegant interior at this smart Greek-Cuban-owned seaside restaurant, known for its well-priced fresh fish, late-night grills, tasty seafood appetisers and good service. Veggie choices include feta-stuffed peppers and giant salads.

ⓘ Information

Info Center Evia (🖉22290 65909; www.info centerevia.gr; ⊙10am-2pm Mon-Fri)

EVIA WINERIES

Evia's increasingly popular wines highlight unique local grapes, some of which have been rescued from the brink of extinction, and several island vineyards have thrown open their doors to visitors for tours and tastings. Based in Eretria, Evia Adventure Tours (p652) runs winery-hopping excursions (from €35), while in the far south Karystos hosts a fun-filled summer wine festival (p656).

Lukas Winery (☑22290 68222; www.facebook.com/lykoswinery; Malakonta; tours €9-18; ☺10am-5pm)

Avantis Wine Estate (☑22210 55350; www.avantiswines.gr; Mytikas; tours & tastings €8-20; ☺10am-5pm Mon-Fri, 11am-4pm Sat, 11am-3pm Sun)

Vriniotis Winery (☑22260 32429, 6944694082; www.vriniotiswinery.gr; Gialtra; tours €6; ☺10am-2pm & 4-8pm Jun-Sep, by appointment Oct-May) ✎

Montofoli Estate (free Sat Jul-Sep; by appointment €8-12; ☺tours 7pm Sat Jul-Sep or by appointment)

❶ Getting There & Away

Ferries (www.ferrieseretriaoropos.gr) travel between Eretria and mainland Skala Oropou (€2, 25 minutes) half-hourly from 8.30am to 8.30pm or 9.30pm; buy tickets at the dock kiosks.

From the **KTEL bus stop** (Filosofou Menedimou), 400m northwest of the ferry dock, buses run to/from Halkida (€2.20, 30 minutes, 10 to 14 daily) and Athens (€9.70, 1½ hours, nine daily).

Steni   Στενή

POP 400

The bucolic mountain village of Steni, with its gurgling springs and shady plane and chestnut trees, 30km northeast of Halkida, is the starting point for several hiking and cycling trips, including the popular trek up Evia's tallest peak, Mt Dirfys (1743m).

From Steni, a scenic twisting mountain road continues to **Hiliadou Beach** and Kymi on the east coast.

🏃 Activities

Mt Dirfys   HIKING

Usually snow-dusted through spring, Mt Dirfys is Evia's highest mountain (1743m). From the 1120m-high **Dirfys Refuge** (☑22210 25230; www.eoschalkidas.gr; per person €12) – accessible via a winding 9km road northeast from Steni, the last 2km by dirt track – it's a steep 7km to the summit and back. Experienced hikers should allow about six hours return. A couple of trails head uphill from Steni to the refuge.

For refuge bookings and information on current hiking conditions, contact the helpful EOS-affiliated **Halkida Alpine Club** (☑22210 25279, 22210 25230; www.eoschalkidas.

gr). The Anavasi Topo 25 map, *Dirfys 5.11 1:25,000* is a handy resource.

🍴 Sleeping & Eating

⭐**Mousiko Pandoxeio**   BOUTIQUE HOTEL €€
(☑6932344755, 22280 51202; www.mousiko pandoxeio.gr; incl breakfast d €75, ste €120, q €90-105; [P][❄][🛜]) One of Evia's most wonderfully original hotels, the 'music lodge' conceals 10 individually designed, boutique-inspired, music-themed rooms, including two suites with in-room hot tubs and family pads for three to five. All are styled with custom-made music-inspired headboards and many have log fires. Owner and composer Tassos Ioannides performs regularly. On the main road at the north end of town.

Taverna Kissos   TAVERNA €€
(☑22280 51226; mains €8-14; ☺noon-late May-Sep, reduced hours Oct-Apr; [P][🛜]) One of a cluster of attractive brook-side eateries, this gentle wood-lined place serves hearty meat grills, roast mushrooms, *tyropita* (cheese pie) and generous salads of locally grown greens. Grab a table on the terrace, with river and village views.

❶ Getting There & Away

Steni has buses to/from Halkida (€3.30, 45 minutes, four daily).

Northern Evia

From Halkida a road threads 50km north into the mountainous, forested interior of northern Evia via the Derveni Gorge to the village of **Prokopi**, whose inhabitants are descended from refugees who came from

Prokopion in Turkey's Cappadocia region in 1923 and established the substantial pilgrimage church of St John the Russian (Prokopi; ☉ dawn-dusk).

At Strofylia, just north of Prokopi, the road forks northeast to the brown-sand northeast-coast beach resort of Agia Anna or southwest to picturesque Limni (which clusters around a western bay). North from Limni lie the olive-growing town of Rovies (with its crumbling medieval tower) and the well-known thermal resort of Loutra Edipsou. Northeast from Loutra Edipsou, on Evia's northernmost coast, are a string of beach-holiday spots favoured by Greeks, including Pefki.

Limni   Λίμνη

POP 1640

An attractive amphitheatre-like maze of whitewashed, rust-roofed houses and narrow lanes spilling on to a cosy harbour, the laid-back coastal town of Limni retains a small-island charm that makes it one of Evia's most appealing resorts. Slim silver-pebble beaches extend to the north and south, and there's an important 16th-century convent, Galataki, nearby. The town itself centres on its cafe- and taverna-speckled waterfront, with views across to the mainland.

◉ Sights

Moni Agios Nikolaos Galataki   CONVENT
(☎ 22270 31489; ☉ 9am-noon & 5-8pm) One of the island's oldest convents, now home to six gently welcoming nuns, the splendidly

positioned 16th-century Galataki convent lies 9km southeast of Limni. It is accessed via a narrow road that hugs a shimmering shoreline (with plenty of stops for a swim) before climbing steeply (the last sections unpaved) to hillsides that were badly damaged by fires at research time. The fine *Entry of the Righteous into Paradise* fresco adorns its *katholikon* (main church).

🛏 Sleeping & Eating

★ Eleonas   AGROTURISMO €€
(☎ 6936887902, 22270 71619; www.eleonashotel. com; Rovies; d €60-80, ste €70-90; ☉ Mar-Oct; 🅿 🛜) ⌖ Hidden amid a sea of olive trees, 12km northwest of Limni, Eleonas delights with its 10 rustic-modern balconied rooms (some with bunks) and sweeping views. Knowledgeable owner Marina (who weaves the beautiful carpets) welcomes guests with fresh lemonade and breakfasts of home-baked bread, own-grown organic olive oil and other Evia goodies. Home-cooked dinners (€18.50), yoga, hiking trips and more available.

Graegos Studios   APARTMENT €€
(☎ 22270 31117; www.graegos.com; Posidonos; apt €50-70; 🅿 ❄ 🛜) A lemon-yellow home opening through a geranium-studded courtyard, year-round Greek-German-owned Graegos has three comfortable and sprucely maintained apartments with modern kitchenettes, as well as a simple private room, at the south end of town. The front two studios have big verandas and sea views.

DON'T MISS

SPA ESCAPE

The sedate spa resort of Loutra Edipsou is the most visited spot in northern Evia, with grandiose wellness-focused hotels sprinkled along its waterfront, which gazes south towards the mainland. The therapeutic sulphur waters here bubble up at up to 80°C and have been celebrated since antiquity, though it wasn't until the mid-20th century that they enjoyed peak popularity. Famous swimmers have included Aristotle, Strabo, Plutarch, Plinius, Sylla and Churchill. Today, the town continues to draw a stream of mostly mature medical tourists, and is known for hosting the country's most up-to-date hydrotherapy and physiotherapy centres.

The showstopper property is the fabulous Thermae Sylla (☎ 22260 60100; www. thermaesylla.gr; Posidonos 2; massage or treatment €60-140; ☉ 9am-8pm) spa hotel, but there are also smaller, more affordable guesthouses and hotels, many of them with their own spas and pools.

There are several low-key waterfront eateries worth a try for mezedhes and skewered grills washed down with local wines. Loutra Edipsou has a refined and relaxed atmosphere, so nightlife usually consists of a poolside glass of wine before bed, though the waterfront has a few cafe-bars.

To Astron　　　　　　　　　　TAVERNA €
(☑ 22270 31487; dishes €4-12; ☺ noon-5pm &
7pm-midnight daily May-Sep, Sat & Sun only Oct-Apr)
The family team catches and cooks its own
fresh fish at this beautifully located seafood-
starring taverna, with check-cloth tables dotted around a shady roadside terrace, 3.5km
southeast of Limni en route to the Galataki
convent. run from tzatziki and *taramasalata* (fish-roe puree) to potato salad, and there
are plenty of meat-rich mains, too.

❶ Getting There & Away

There are two to three daily buses between Halkida and Limni (€8.60, two hours).

Southern Evia

Around 35km east of Eretria, the road
branches south at Lepoura and the north's
rich vegetation gives way to sparse, rugged
southern mountains. You'll pass Lake Dhis-
tos and plenty of wind farms, and catch
views of both coasts as the island narrows
and the road climbs spectacularly to run
along clifftops before descending to Karystos. The latter is the south's attractive
main seaside resort, with excellent hiking,
and there are interesting sights in Myli, a
well-watered village 4km inland, too. With
your own transport you can explore the
pristine, isolated Cavo d'Oro villages east
of Karystos in the southern foothills of Mt
Ohi, including pretty Platanistos (with its
waterfall and stone bridges), Potami (with
a beach and camping) and the whistling village of Antia.

Karystos　　　　　　　　　Κάρυστος

POP 5110

Set below Mt Ohi (1398m) on wide Karystos
Bay, and flanked by two sandy silver-brown
beaches, this low-key coastal resort is southern Evia's main hub, where friendly locals
enjoy life at a pace that makes you forget
how close you are to Athens. Mentioned in
Homer's *Iliad*, Karystos was a powerful city-
state during the Peloponnesian War. Today,
there's little evidence of its former status,
and the down-to-earth grid-design town is
the starting point for stunning treks up Mt
Ohi and down Dimosari Gorge, as well as a
popular weekend getaway for Athenians.

The lively Plateia Amalias faces the harbour, which glitters come evening with
lights and bobbing boats. A few white-sand-

THE WHISTLING VILLAGE OF ANTIA

Around 35km northeast of Karystos,
the 'whistling village' of Antia (pop 37) is
famous for its linguistically talented villagers who speak in *sfyria*. One of a small
global group of whistling languages, this
one was devised during Byzantine times
to warn of danger and invasion from
pirates, with each tone corresponding
to a letter of the alphabet. Until the early
1980s the language was still widely used,
but today it's mostly the old-timers who
communicate in whistles. That said, efforts are under way to save the language
from extinction. Stay tuned.

and-pebble beaches trickle southeast and
southwest around the bay.

◉ Sights & Activities

**Archaeological
Museum of Karystos**　　　　　　MUSEUM
(☑ 22240 29218; Kriezotou; €2; ☺ 8am-4pm Wed-
Mon) Karystos' small, insightful museum,
opposite the Bourtzi (Kriezotou, Waterfront;
☺ 24hr) **FREE**, highlights the region's long
history and ancient power. Displays, with
multilingual booklets, range from tiny Neolithic clay lamps found on Mt Ohi to relics
from the area's Roman quarries to a 4th-
century-CE marble Aphrodite.

★Dimosari Gorge　　　　　　HIKING
This beautiful, well-maintained 10km trail
descends northwards from the Petrokanalo
mountain shoulder (950m) through Lenosei
village to the sand-and-pebble beach of Kalli-
anos. Much of the hike follows a cobbled
path, splashing through shady creeks, ponds,
giant ferns and forest. Allow four hours (including a swim!). South Evia Tours and Evia
Adventure Tours (p652) arrange transport
and guides.

Mt Ohi　　　　　　　　　　HIKING
The summit of Mt Ohi (Profitis Ilias; 1398m),
Evia's third-highest peak, is crowned by mysterious ancient *drakospita* (dragon houses):
Stonehenge-like 7th-century-BCE dwellings
or temples, hewn from rocks weighing several tonnes and joined without mortar. From
Myli, it's a 7.6km hike to the summit (three
to four hours).

The dragon houses' commanding position
near marble quarries suggests that they were

EVIA & THE SPORADES SOUTHERN EVIA

guard posts; another theory holds that they honoured mythological deities that roamed Mt Ohi, in particular the goddess Hera.

It's possible to stay overnight at the 1000m-high refuge then hike up Mt Ohi to catch sunrise (30 minutes); contact South Evia Tours or Evia Adventure Tours (p652) for details.

🛏 Sleeping & Eating

Karystion   HOTEL €€

(☑ 22240 22391; www.karystion.gr; Kriezotou 3; incl breakfast s €36-97, d €44-105; 🅿 ❄ 🛜) With helpful multilingual staff, the in-demand Karystion sits above the beach just east of the Bourtzi (p655) castle. The modern, uncluttered, well-appointed rooms (some smarter than others) have balconies that look out on to a pine-dotted headland. Stairs lead to a small sandy beach, while perfect local-produce breakfasts are served on the shady terrace.

Montofoli Estate   VILLA €€€

(☑ 6937282347, 22240 23951; www. montofoliwines.com; villas €180-330; 🅿 ❄ 🛜 🌊) On the historical Montofoli Estate (p653), whose origins date to the Frankish era, these four character-rich, all-different villas comprise some of Evia's most inspiring accommodation. Vines and citrus trees scent the grounds, overlooked by a sea-view pool and the three main villas, which were part of a Venetian-era mansion (tiled floors, twisting staircases). The colourful Amfithea villa flaunts more contemporary style.

★ Cavo d'Oro   TAVERNA €

(☑ 22240 22326; mains €5-8; ☺ 9am-late Apr-Nov; 🛜) Join the locals at this cheery alleyway restaurant just back from the central waterfront for beautifully home-cooked Greek mainstays such as octopus in red wine sauce, creamy *spanakorizo* (spinach and rice), grilled halloumi with tomato jam, and country salads featuring local produce and olive oil. Genial owner Kyriakos is a regular at the summer wine *festival* (☺ Aug & Sep), bouzouki in hand.

❶ Getting There & Away

BOAT

There are regular ferries from Marmari (12km northwest of Karystos) to Rafina on the mainland (€9, one hour, two to six daily), and from Nea Styra (35km northwest of Karystos) to Agia Marina (€3, 45 minutes, around seven daily).

Buy tickets from dock kiosks, online or **South Evia Tours** (☑ 22240 26200; www.eviatravel.gr; Plateia Amalias; ☺ 9am-10pm)

BUS

From Karystos' **KTEL bus stop** (☑ 22240 26303; Ellinon Amerikis) opposite Agios Nikolaos church, buses run to Halkida (€12.70, three hours, 5.30am Monday to Friday) and Marmari (€2, 15 minutes, two to three daily). For Athens (€20.20, five hours), connect in Halkida.

SKIATHOS   ΣΚΙΑΘΟΣ

POP 6090

Blessed with some of the Aegean's most exquisite sandy white beaches, backed by rippling hills carpeted in scented pines and olive trees, Skiathos is the most developed of the Sporades. The beautiful beach-fringed south coast is filled with walled-in holiday villas, hotels and apartments, and from June to September, when the island fills up with sun-seeking Greeks and northern Europeans, prices soar and rooms dwindle. Seek out Skiathos' elegant monasteries, hidden-away churches and hillside hiking paths, however, and you'll still catch a glimpse of its soul.

Skiathos Town, on the southeast coast, is the attractive main port with a small cobbled old town of narrow whitewashed alleys. The only other settlement is tiny south-coast Troulos, 8km southwest.

❶ Getting There & Away

AIR

Skiathos airport (Map p657; ☑ 24270 22229) is 2km northeast of Skiathos Town. There are regular flights to/from Athens with **Olympic Air** (www.olympicair.com) and **Sky Express** (www. skyexpress.gr), as well as numerous summer charter flights to/from northern Europe.

There's no public transport to/from the airport. Taxis charge €12 to Skiathos Town. Luggage permitting, some people even walk into town.

BOAT

Skiathos' main port is Skiathos Town, which has links to Agios Konstantinos (June to September only) and Volos on the mainland, as well as to Skopelos, Alonnisos and, during summer months, Mantoudi (Evia, via Skopelos). The main companies are **Hellenic Seaways** (https:// hellenicseaways.gr), **Anes Ferries** (www.anes. gr), **Blue Star Ferries** (www.bluestarferries. com) and **Aegean Flying Dolphins** (www.aegean flyingdolphins.gr); services are scaled down between October and April. Tickets can be purchased from **Skiathos OE** (☑ 24270 22209;

Skiathos

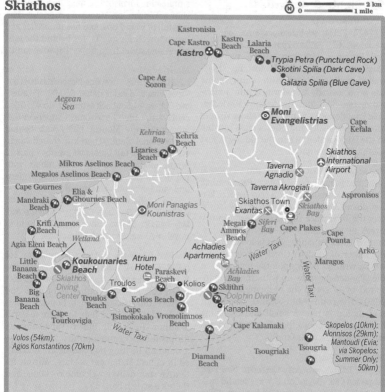

N 0 _____ 2 km
0 _____ 1 mile

Kastronisia

Cape Kastro | Kastro Beach | Lalaria Beach

Kastro

Trypia Petra (Punctured Rock)
Skotini Spilia (Dark Cave)
Galazia Spilia (Blue Cave)

Cape Ag Sozon

Aegean Sea

Moni Evangelistrias

Cape Kefala

Kehrias Bay | Kehria Beach

Ligaries Beach

Mikros Aselinos Beach

Megalos Aselinos Beach

Taverna Agnadio

Skiathos International Airport

Taverna Akrogiali

Cape Gournes

Elia & Ghournes Beach

Mandraki Beach

Moni Panagias Kounistras

Skiathos Town

Exantas

Skiathos Bay

Aspronisos

Krifi Ammos Beach

Wetland

Megali Ammos Beach | *Siferi Bay* | Cape Plakes

Cape Pounta

Agia Eleni Beach

Achladies Apartments

Water Taxi

Maragos

Arko

Little Banana Beach

Koukounaries Beach

Atrium Hotel

Paraskevi Beach | Kolios

Achladies Bay

Water Taxi

Skiathos Diving Center | Troulos

Sklithri

Dolphin Diving

Big Banana Beach

Troulos Beach

Kolios Beach

Cape Tsimokokalo | Vromolimnos Beach

Kanapitsa

Cape Tourkovigia

Water Taxi

Cape Kalamaki

Skopelos (10km); Alonnisos (29km); Mantoudi (Evia; via Skopelos; Summer Only; 50km)

Volos (54km); Agios Konstantinos (70km)

Diamandi Beach | Tsougriaki | Tsougria

www.skiathosoe.com; Papadiamanti) and other offices along the waterfront.

SeaCab (☑ 6934343287; www.seacab.gr; per person €25; ☺ May-Sep) runs hourly speedboats linking Skiathos with Skopelos (Glossa/Loutraki 10am to 8pm, Skopelos Town 9.30am to 7.30pm) from May until early October.

ⓘ Getting Around

BUS

Buses run between Skiathos Town and Koukounaries Beach (€2, 30 minutes) every 15 minutes from 7am to 11pm in July and August, with slightly reduced services the rest of the year (timetables are posted at stops); they stop at 26 numbered beach-access points along the south coast.

CAR & MOTORCYCLE

Reliable motorbike- and car-hire outlets include **Creator Tours** (Europcar; ☑ 69332382332, 24270 22385; www.creatortours.com; New Port; ☺ 9am-9pm May-Oct, reduced hours Nov-Apr) (with a Europcar concession) and **Heliotropio**

Tourism & Travel (Aegean Car and Moto Rental; ☑ 24270 22024; www.heliotropio.gr; New Port; ☺ 9am-9pm May-Oct, reduced hours Nov-Mar), both in Skiathos Town's new port.

Skiathos Town Σκιάθος

POP 4880

Extending gently across low-rise hills on the southeast coast, Skiathos Town is the island's hub and ferry harbour, with hotels, galleries, travel agents, tavernas, boutiques and bars strung along the waterfront and the cobbled pedestrian thoroughfare Papadiamanti. Away from the main drag, though, things quieten down quickly: the pedestrianised hillside old town – branching off near Tris Ierarches (Plateia Trion Ierarhon; ☺ dawn-dusk) church above the scenic old port, opposite pine-dusted Bourtzi islet – retains much of its charm and local flavour, with slim whitewashed streets, tiny squares and sky-blue doors.

⊙ Sights & Activities

Skiathitiko Spiti MUSEUM
(☑24270 21334; skiathitikospiti@gmail.com; Polytechniou; €2; ⊙10am-2pm & 6-11.30pm May-Oct) Bursting with generations' worth of Skiathos heirlooms, this handsome, stone-walled traditional early-20th-century home has been lovingly transformed into a fascinating two-floor museum by the knowledgeable Papadopoulis family, who show visitors around personally and offer a glass of wine in the back garden. It's in the old town, just south of Papadiamanti.

Papadiamantis House Museum MUSEUM
(www.papadiamantis.net; Plateia Papadiamanti; €1.50; ⊙9.30am-1.30pm & 5-8pm Tue-Sun Jun-Sep, 10am-1.30pm Tue-Sun May & Oct) Skiathos was the birthplace of famous 19th-century Greek novelist and short-story writer Alexandros Papadiamantis, who is looked on as the father of modern Greek literature, and whose writings draw upon the hard lives of the islanders he grew up with (many are inspired by or set in the old capital, Kastro; p660). His plain, whitewashed, wood-floor 1860 house is now a small and charming museum with books, paintings and photos of the author and his family.

★Argo III Yacht BOATING
(☑6932325167; www.argosailing.com; New Port; per person €85; ⊙Apr-Oct) For a splendid sailing tour of the island waters between Skiathos and Alonnisos (lunch included!), climb aboard the *Argo III,* managed by husband-and-wife team George and Dina.

Octopus Diving Centre DIVING
(☑6944168958, 24270 24549; www.odc-skiathos.com; Hotel Alkyon, New Port; s dive €50; ⊙mid-Jun–Sep) This popular husband-and-wife diving team runs a range of dives and courses, including beginner dives (€60) and PADI open-water certification (€400), as well as half-day snorkelling trips (€20). Based on their boat opposite the taxi rank, or at Hotel Alkyon.

🛏 Sleeping

Skiathos House GUESTHOUSE €
(☑6972887900, 24270 22733; www.skiathoshouse.gr; off Papadiamanti; r €40-50; ⊙Apr-Oct; ❉ 🕸) Comfortable, outstanding-value modern rooms, studios and apartments fill this lovingly restored townhouse, with a palm-shaded back garden and super-central location. Rooms come with kettles, hairdryers and

simple pine furnishings; most have little balconies. Welcoming Athenian proprietor Denis is full of island tips, and has umbrellas and beach towels for guests. It's behind the post office, one street from upper Papadiamanti.

Mouria Hotel HOTEL €€
(☑24270 21193; www.mouriahotelskiathos.com; Papadiamanti; d incl breakfast €60-90; ⊙Easter–mid-Oct; ❉🕸) Set back around a flower-filled courtyard, the handsome, super-central, efficiently run Mouria hides just behind the National Bank. There's a shared kitchen – though a full breakfast awaits – plus 12 bright, modern, blue-and-white rooms (with hairdryers and, for most, wooden balconies) and vintage photos all around.

The reliably good terrace **taverna** (☑24270 23069; mains €8-14; ⊙6pm-late mid-May–mid-Oct; 🍴) was once a regular haunt of novelist Alexandros Papadiamantis.

Bourtzi Boutique Hotel BOUTIQUE HOTEL €€€
(☑24270 21304; www.hotelbourtzi.gr; Moraitou 8, cnr Papadiamanti; r incl breakfast €110-260; ⊙May-Oct; 🅿❉🕸🏊) All straight lines and creative touches, the swish Bourtzi brings a splash of boutique flair to down-to-earth Skiathos Town, on upper Papadiamanti. Stripped-back contemporary rooms rise around an inviting pool; some are decorated in upbeat statement colours. Warmly attentive staff deliver welcome cocktails, and there's a stylish bar.

✕ Eating & Drinking

Skiathos Town is full of overpriced tourist-oriented eateries serving *etsi-ketsi* (so-so) food, but there are a few good exceptions, especially in the narrow lanes around the old port and along the waterfront past the new harbour (near the dance-until-dawn clubs).

The drink-till-you-drop scene heats up after midnight along the seafront club strip beyond the new port; most places open only from June or July to September. Late-night bars cluster on Plateia Papadiamanti, Polytechniou and Papadiamanti in town. For the beach-bar buzz, head out of town, especially to Koukounaries Beach.

★Kabourelias TAVERNA €
(☑24270 21112; Old Port; mains €7-15; ⊙11am-midnight; 🕸) Poke your nose into the open kitchen to glimpse the day's catch at this beloved, efficient, well-established old-port taverna with blue-cloth tables across from the water. Grilled octopus, *taramasalata* and halloumi dressed with lemon grace the

standout mezedhes selection; perfect fish grills and house wines complete the picture, all at deliciously down-to-earth prices. And it's open all year!

O Batis TAVERNA €
(☑6974380129, 24270 22288; Old Port; mains €4-13; ☺9am-midnight May-Sep, reduced hours Oct-Apr) This popular, long-established fish taverna on the path above the old port is a local standby for reliable and well-priced fresh fish, *gavros* (a marinated small fish) and fine mezedhes. Cosy atmosphere, warm welcome, fresh Greek ingredients and a good selection of island wines, year-round.

★ Marmita MEDITERRANEAN €€
(☑24270 21701; www.marmitaskiathos.com; 30 Evangelistrias; mains €11-18; ☺6.30-11pm late Apr-Oct; ☑) Twirls of greenery and soothing background music mingle with cheese-grater lamps, olive-oil baskets and candlelit tables in this tranquil, standout courtyard restaurant off upper Papadiamanti. From avocado-chicory salads, vegan *mousakas* (baked layers of aubergine or courgettes and potatoes) and mushroom-stuffed ravioli to succulent grilled meats and sea bass *en papillote*, Marmita's Greek-Mediterranean flavours are elegantly creative delights. Bread arrives in wooden boxes, and there are good Greek wines.

Ergon DELI €€
(☑24270 21441; www.ergonfoods.com; Papadiamanti; breakfasts €4.50-9, mains €11-19; ☺9am-midnight May–mid-Oct; ☑☑) Skiathos' upper-Papadiamanti outpost of Thessaloniki-born local-produce powerhouse Ergon is a firm favourite for third-wave coffee and internationally inspired breakfasts given a Greek twist – poached eggs with Greek yoghurt, omelettes stuffed with local cheeses, Skopelos cheese pies. It's a sleekly designed deli space where polished wood and varnished concrete offset shelves crammed with Greek wines, olive oil, ouzo and other goodies.

Taverna Akrogiali TAVERNA €€
(Map p657; ☑24270 21330; kostasgeorgoulas9@gmail.com; Paraliakos; mains €9-15; ☺noon-midnight May-Oct) In an enviable seafront perch, 300m east of the new port, Akrogiali is the town's fresh-seafood favourite. The rustic blue-and-white-themed deck, decorated with bougainvillea and potted flowers, extends out over the water, while tempting classic Greek creations include stuffed tomatoes,

grilled octopus and fried feta dressed with honey and sesame.

🛍 Shopping

★ Galerie Varsakis ANTIQUES
(☑24270 22255; www.facebook.com/galerievarsakis; Plateia Trion Ierarhon; ☺9.30am-2pm & 6-11pm Mon-Sat, 6.30-11pm Sun Apr-Oct) Crammed with handmade jewellery and unusual antiques, such as 20th-century carpets and 19th-century spinning sticks made by grooms for their intended brides, this collection rivals the best Greek folklore museums. Upstairs is a dazzling display of owner Harris Varsakis' paintings, in oil on gold leaf, begun in the 1970s and depicting Greek myths and predatory contemporary politicians.

ℹ Information

Tourist Information Kiosk (☑24270 23172; New Port; ☺Jul & Aug) By the ferry dock.

Around Skiathos

🏖 Beaches

With 65 beaches to pick from, beach-hopping on Skiathos can become a full-time occupation. Buses (€1.60 to €2) ply the beach-bejewelled south coast, stopping at 26 numbered beach-access points; the final stop is protected Koukounaries (Map p657) in the southwest, from where you can access several other lovely beaches (though the popular twin Banana (Map p657) beaches were mostly off-limits at research time due to construction work). Most south-coast beaches have sunbeds (€8), tavernas and beach bars.

The northwest coast's beaches are less crowded and more unspoilt, though subject to summer *meltemi* (dry northerly winds). There are also alluring beaches on outlying islets such as Tsougria, which you can reach by taxi boat from Skiathos Town.

◉ Sights

★ Moni Evangelistrias MONASTERY
(Map p657; museum €2; ☺9am-dusk Apr-Oct, reduced hours Nov-Mar) Centred on a triple-domed church, this historic 18th-century monastery was a hilltop refuge for freedom fighters during the War of Independence, and the Greek flag was first raised here in 1807. Today, several monks do the chores, which include wine-, marmalade- and olive-oil-making. The gift shop's vintage olive and wine presses recall an earlier era, while the

museum displays antique furniture and documents from the Balkan Wars; a cafe sits beside the vineyard. It's 5km north of Skiathos Town.

⭐ **Kastro** RUINS
(Map p657; ⊙24hr) **FREE** Perched dramatically on the island's rocky northernmost headland, 9km north of Skiathos Town, Kastro was the fortified pirate-proof capital from 1540 until it was abandoned in 1829. At its peak it held 20 churches and 500 homes; now, among the restored ruins, you'll find an old cannon, a Turkish-era mosque, several water tanks and four churches (including 17th-century Christos, home to several fine frescoes). Drive or walk down the steep sealed track, or join a boat trip from Skiathos Town.

🏃 Activities

Boat Trips

From around May to October, excursion boats make half- and full-day trips around the island (€18 to €25), usually taking in Kastro, Lalaria Beach (Map p657), Trypia Petra (Punctured Rock) and the two *spilies* (caves) of Skotini (Dark Cave) and Galazia (Blue Cave), plus a swim stop; many continue to Skopelos and, in some cases, Alonnisos. Check the individual boat signboards at the old port.

You can also hop on taxi boats from the old port to Koukounaries, Achladies Bay and Kanapitsa, as well as the offshore island of Tsougria.

Boats for private day trips are moored along the town's new port.

Diving & Snorkelling

The small islets off Skiathos' south shore make for great diving and snorkelling. Local dive schools offer beginner introductory dives (€60), open-water courses (€400) and dive trips for those already certified (€50), as well as snorkelling trips (from €20). Reputable local dive schools include Koukounaries-based Skiathos Diving Center (Map p657; ☑6977081444; www.skiathosdiving.gr; Koukounaries Beach; single dive €50; ⊙9am-7pm mid-Apr–Oct), Dolphin Diving (Map p657; ☑6944999181; www.ddiving.gr; Hotel Nostos, Tzaneria Beach; single dive €50; ⊙May-Oct), 5.5km southwest of Skiathos Town, and Theofanis and Eva of PADI-affiliated Octopus Diving Centre (p658) in Skiathos Town.

Hiking

Hiking on Skiathos gets you to places most visitors never reach. At the time of writing, 25 routes have been mapped, numbered and signposted. Long-time local resident Ortwin Widmann (☑6972705416; www.hikingskiathos.com; per person €18; ⊙May, Jun, Sep & Oct), whose excellent *Skiathos: Hiking in the Aegean Paradise* (available at local shops) outlines all walks, offers guided hikes (€18 per person) in May, June, September and October.

A particularly popular hike is the demanding 12km, four-hour loop (Route 18) from Moni Evangelistrias to Cape Kastro, returning via Agios Apostolis.

🛏️ Sleeping & Eating

Achladies Apartments APARTMENT €€
(Map p657; ☑6944232655, 24270 22486; www.achladiesapartments.com; Achladies Bay; d €65-80, tr €80-90, q €85-95; ⊙May-Sep; P🐾) Behind lime-green doors 3.5km southwest of Skiathos Town, this welcoming gem features comfortable, unfussy self-catering kitchenette rooms with balconies and ceiling fans, plus an ecofriendly tortoise sanctuary and a lovingly kept succulent garden winding down to a sandy blonde beach.

⭐ **Atrium Hotel** LUXURY HOTEL €€€
(Map p657; ☑24270 49345; www.atriumhotel.gr; Paraskevi Beach; d/ste incl breakfast from €150/160; ⊙May-Sep; P❄🐾🛜⛱) A chic fusion of monastery-inspired architecture and soothing contemporary design, courtesy of the architect owners, makes the hillside Atrium one of Skiathos' most seductive hideaways. Stone walls and hot-pink bursts of bougainvillea blend with stylishly updated white-and-wood rooms flaunting sea-view balconies and, for some, private pools or hot tubs. A taverna overlooks the pool; lavish Greek-produce breakfasts start the day.

Exantas GREEK €€
(Map p657; ☑24270 24035; www.facebook.com/exandasbarrestaurant; Megali Ammos Beach; mains €10-18; ⊙9am-11pm May-Oct; 🛜) A gorgeous rustic-chic terrace perched right above Megali Ammos' silvery sands is the setting for elegant Exantas' creative, contemporary Greek cuisine. From courgette-pesto pasta and spring rolls with watermelon dip to glammed-up *gyros* (meat slithers cooked on a vertical rotisserie), grilled Alonnisos tuna and cheese from Tinos, dishes are expertly executed and highlight local ingredients. Excellent Greek wines and cocktails round things off.

Taverna Agnadio TAVERNA €€
(Map p657; ☑24270 22016; www.facebook.com/agnadioskiathos; mains €8-15; ⊙6-11pm mid-May–

Sep) Enjoying horizon-reaching views from its lovely hillside perch, 1.5km north of Skiathos Town, deservedly popular Agnadio turns out elegantly prepped fresh seafood, grilled meats and classic island mezedhes like fried feta with sesame seeds, all accompanied by excellent wines.

SKOPELOS ΣΚΟΠΕΛΟΣ

POP 4960

Pine forests, olive groves, rippling vineyards and orchards of plums and almonds (many of which find their way into local cuisine) carpet the handsome island of Skopelos, which is notably wilder, artier and more laid-back than neighbouring Skiathos. Though famed for its starring role in the 2008 film *Mamma Mia!*, Skopelos has managed to hang on to its low-key charm. The island's sheltered southeast coast harbours a string of beautiful sand-and-pebble beaches, while the northwest coast's high jagged cliffs are exposed to the elements.

There are two settlements: the wonderfully attractive main port of Skopelos Town, on the southeast coast, and the equally delightful northwest village of Glossa, 2km north of Loutraki, the island's second port.

❶ Getting There & Away

Skopelos has two ports, Skopelos Town (p664) and Glossa/Loutraki (p665). Between them they serve Volos and Agios Konstantinos on the mainland, and the islands of Skiathos, Alonnisos and Evia (Mantoudi). From mid-June to mid-September, **Skyros Shipping Co** (☑ 22220 93465, 22220 91789; www.sne.gr; Plateia; ☺ 9am-1pm & 6-9pm) also links Skopelos Town with Kymi (Evia) and Skyros. Tickets are available online or from **Madro Travel** (☑ 24240 22300, 24240 22145; Waterfront; ☺ 9am-10pm Jun-Sep, reduced hours Oct-May) and **Dolphin Tours** (☑ 24240 23060, 6948485567; www.dolphinofskopelos. com; Waterfront; ☺ 6.30-7am, 9am-4.30pm & 6-8pm Mon-Fri, 9.30am-3pm Sat, 9.30am-3pm & 5-9pm Sun) in Skopelos Town or from **Nikos Triantafillou Agency** (☑ 6932913748, 24240 33435; www.praktorioglossas.gr; Loutraki; ☺ 7am-8.30pm) in Loutraki/Glossa.

The main companies are **Hellenic Seaways** (https://hellenicseaways.gr), **Anes Ferries** (www.anes.gr), **Blue Star Ferries** (www.blue starferries.com) and **Aegean Flying Dolphins** (www.aegeanflyingdolphins.gr). Most services are reduced between November and April.

SeaCab (p657) runs hourly speedboats linking Glossa/Loutraki (10am to 8pm) and Skopelos Town (9.30am to 7.30pm) with Skiathos, from May to early October.

❶ Getting Around

BUS

In summer there are five to 10 **buses** (Waterfront) per day from Skopelos Town to Glossa/Loutraki (€5.60, 55 minutes) and Neo Klima (Elios; €4, 45 minutes); and several more that go to Panormos (€3.50, 25 minutes), Milia (€4, 35 minutes), Agnontas (€2, 15 minutes) and Stafylos (€1.70, 15 minutes). Outside season services trickle down to two daily.

CAR & MOTORCYCLE

Reliable vehicle-hire operators include Dolphin Tours, **Magic Cars** (☑ 6973790936, 24240 23250; www.magiccars.gr; Potoki; ☺ 7am-11.30pm) and **Thalpos Holidays** (☑ 24240 29036; www.holidayislands.com; ☺ 9am-5pm Mon-Sat mid-Apr–mid-Oct).

TAXI

Taxis wait by the bus stop in Skopelos Town, charging €9 to/from Stafylos, €14 to/from Agnontas and €35 to/from Glossa.

Skopelos Town Σκόπελος

POP 3090

Skopelos Town cascades down a hillside to a semicircular southeast-coast bay in picturesque tiers of centuries-old chapels and dazzling-white houses and mansions with flower-adorned balconies and bright-blue or deep-red shutters. It's flanked at its northwest end by a ruined 13th-century Venetian kastro (☺ 24hr) **FREE** and a cluster of four gleaming whitewashed churches.

Two quays border the town's lively cafe- and boutique-lined waterfront: the old quay wraps around the northwest end of the harbour, while the new quay at the southeastern end is used by all ferries and hydrofoils.

Strolling around town and lazing at the waterside cafes might be your chief occupations here, though there are also two small museums as well as several intriguing monasteries (p665) just outside town.

◉ Sights

Vakratsa Mansion MUSEUM
(Old Skopelitan Mansion Museum; ☑ 24240 23494; €3; ☺ 10am-2pm & 6-9pm May-Sep, but hours vary) Housed in a doctor's 18th-century mansion, Vakratsa displays medical instruments, books, clothes and furniture of the era and is well worth seeing for the window it offers on to middle-class Greek life in the 19th century. It's near the middle of the waterfront, 100m inland from the Ploumisti (p664) shop, behind a tall white wall.

EVIA & THE SPORADES SKOPELOS TOWN

Skopelos

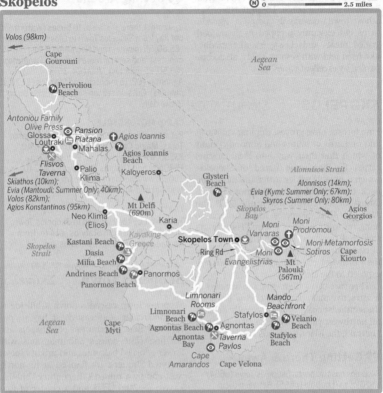

Folklore Museum

MUSEUM

(☑ 24240 23494; Hatzistamati; €3; ☺ 10am-2pm & 7-10pm Mon-Fri Jun-Sep, but hours vary) Occupying a restored 18th-century mansion, this handsome museum features a Skopelean wedding room, complete with traditional costumes and bridal bed, as well as collections of embroidery, woodcarving and other local crafts. It's just inland from the mid-waterfront and signposted.

🏃 Activities

From May to September, day-long **boat trips** (adult/child around €55/35) depart from the waterfront by 10am, usually taking in the neighbouring National Marine Park of Alonnisos (p670), with lunch and a swim. There's a good chance of spotting dolphins along the way. For bookings, contact Madro Travel (p661), Thalpos Holidays (p661) or Dolphin Tours (p661).

Several agencies in Skopelos Town, including Dolphin Tours (p661), offer *Mamma*

Mia! tours to filming locations around the island (per person €30).

SporadesSUP

WATER SPORTS

(☑ 6940448002; www.sporadessup.com; Waterfront; group class €25, 1hr rental €15, sunset tour €45; ☺ Jun-Sep) Fantastic paddleboarding excursions, including 2½-hour sunset jaunts, as well as classes and board hire.

The same on-the-ball team runs **Skopelos Dive Center** (☑ 6940448000; www.sporades diving.gr; Waterfront; single dive €50-60; ☺ May-Sep), with its own cool cafe, as well as excellent **Ikion Diving** (☑ 24240 65158, 6984181598; www.ikiondiving.gr; Waterfront, Steni Vala; single dive €50-60; ☺ May-Sep) over on Alonnisos.

Skopelos Cycling

CYCLING

(☑ 6947023145; www.facebook.com/skopelos. cycling; Old Olive Oil Factory; per 24hr €10-25; ☺ 9am-2pm & 6-10pm Mon-Sat) High-quality trekking, mountain and e-bikes are available from Panos Provias at Skopelos Cycling, who provides detailed maps and route advice, as well as original guided bike tours, including 'moon rides' (€30) and a prebreakfast e-bike trip up Mt Delphi (€50). It's opposite the post office towards the south end of town.

🛏 Sleeping

⭐ **Thea Home Hotel** PENSION €
(📞 24240 22859, 6945344428; www.theahome hotel.com; Ring Rd; incl breakfast d €45-80, studio €80-135, apt €100-150; ☺ Easter-Sep; 🛜 ♨) Perched high atop town (and well worth the steep 10-minute climb), family-owned Thea basks in fabulous views across town from its pool, rooms, verandas and apartments. The studios are stylishly contemporary, with colourful carpets and kitchenettes, while rooms have more traditional flair; most enjoy balconies. Breakfasts of Greek yoghurt and homemade pastries are served at terrace tables.

⭐ **Pension Sotos** PENSION €
(📞 24240 22549; www.skopelostravel.net/sotos; Waterfront; d €30-50, tr & q €30-45; ❄ 🛜) Each of the 12 charming pine-floored rooms at this 150-year-old waterfront home is different – an old brick oven becomes a shelf in one, others have lovely wood-beamed ceilings. Geraniums and lemon trees dot the interior courtyard and terrace, which back on to a church, and there's a communal kitchen, all managed by welcoming owner Alexandra. Secluded feel, super-central location.

Ionia Hotel HOTEL €€
(📞 24240 22568; www.ioniahotel.gr; incl breakfast s €48-85, d €55-95, tr €70-110, q €85-120; ☺ Jun-Sep; 🅿 ❄ 🛜 ♨) With rooms overlooking a calm, shady pool courtyard from private balconies, the excellently managed Ionia makes a pleasing retreat just five minutes' walk inland from the waterfront. It's a traditional-style building, spread over four floors, and Skopelos-inspired murals adorn most rooms, which are done out with a spruce rustic feel.

🍴 Eating

Juices & Books CAFE €
(www.facebook.com/juicesandbooks; Waterfront; dishes €4; ☺ 8am-1am Jul & Aug, 9am-2pm & 6pm-late May, Jun & Sep; 🖉) 🍃 A fabulous midseafront breakfast spot and bookshop, Juices & Books rustles up inventive toasted sandwiches (perhaps with avocado, creamed feta and wild fennel), home-baked cakes, Greek-yoghurt smoothies and organic coffees (dairy-free options available!), all served on stylish wooden trays and infused with Skopelos ingredients. Italian-Greek owners Tiziana

---

ANIMAL WELFARE ASSOCIATIONS

Like many other Greek Islands, the Sporades have large populations of stray cats and dogs. Several locally based charitable organisations run sterilisation, neutering, feeding and rehoming programmes. On Skiathos, the Skiathos Cat Welfare Association (www. skiathos-cats.org) accepts donations and has openings for volunteers with particular skills, as does the Skiathos Dog Shelter (www.skiathosdogshelter. com), which also welcomes visitors at its site just south of Moni Panagias Kounistras (Map p657; by donation; ☺ dawn-dusk), 4km northwest of Troulous. On Skopelos, Straycare Skopelos (straycare@yahoo.com) accepts donations and can find tasks for travellers interested in helping out.

Note that Lonely Planet does not endorse any organisation that we do not work with directly. Travellers should investigate any volunteering option thoroughly before committing to a project.

---

and Pad put an emphasis on protecting the local environment.

⭐ **To Rodi** GREEK €€
(📞 24240 24601; Chimou; mains €11-14; ☺ 7pm-midnight May-Oct, Fri-Sun only Nov-Apr; 🖉) Sprinkled with overflowing geranium pots, in the shade of a pomegranate tree, this romantic courtyard restaurant steals the show with its refined Greek cooking, elegant setting and spot-on service. Local cheeses, fresh salads and pork in citrus sauce are specialities; even the carrot salad – dressed with just olive oil and a squeeze of lemon – is beautiful. Book ahead in season.

Ta Kymata TAVERNA €€
(📞 24240 22381; Old Port; mains €7-15; ☺ noon-11pm Easter–mid-Dec; 🖉) The island's oldest tavern, at the north end of the old port, has drawn a steady local following for its hearty grills and classic *mayirefta* (ready-cooked meals) since 1896. Peek into the kitchen and pick from deliciously traditional creations like shrimp *saganaki* (fried with cheese), swordfish and lobster, along with tasty veggie options, from lemon-roasted potatoes and grilled halloumi to stuffed courgette flowers.

To Perivoli
GREEK €€

(☑24240 23758; off Plateia Platanos; mains €7-14; ☺7.30pm-midnight approx Jun-Aug) 🍴 In a graceful, secluded garden-and-terrace setting just west of Plateia Platanos, Perivoli delivers excellent Greek specialities such as cheese-stuffed courgette, seafood pasta, shrimp *saganaki* and rolled pork with *koromila* (local plums) in wine sauce, plus fine wines. Herbs and vegetables are home-grown, and service is excellent. Book ahead in summer!

🍷 Drinking & Nightlife

Some of the Sporades' most original, independent bars (both traditional and contemporary) are hidden around Skopelos Town's alleys. There are also some fun small clubs and venues staging earthy local live music, especially *rembetika* (blues songs).

★ Hidden Door
COCKTAIL BAR

(Paraporti; ☑6978252848; Chimou; ☺7pm-late May-Sep) Tucked into a moodily converted 100-year-old house where a side (hidden) door once led to the kitchen, mellow yet hugely popular Paraporti mixes Athens-worthy cocktails (€11) served at candlelit tables. It's on a lane 300m inland from the waterfront, opposite To Rodi (p663) restaurant (and signposted).

Vrachos
BAR

(www.facebook.com/vrachoscocktailbar; Old Port; ☺10am-late May-Sep) Climb the twisting whitewashed stairs just left of the town hall to find this soothing, fabulously positioned cafe-bar spread across a tree-studded terrace next to one of the island's most ancient churches. Go for the homemade rose lemonade or one of the original cocktails (€8 to €12).

★ Ouzerie Anatoli
TRADITIONAL MUSIC

(Kastro; ☺8pm-2am approx Jun-Sep) Wait until at least 11pm, then head to this breezy outdoor *ouzerie* (place that serves ouzo and light snacks), high above the north corner of the waterfront atop the *kastro*, to hear traditional *rembetika* (blues songs) sung by Georgos Xindaris, Skopelos' own exponent of the Greek blues and a bouzouki master.

🛍 Shopping

The waterfront hosts some wonderful shops selling quality ceramics, paintings, hand-made jewellery and breezy island-style fashion.

★ Ploumisti
ARTS & CRAFTS

(☑24240 22059; Waterfront; ☺10am-2pm & 6-9.30pm Easter-Sep) Owners Kostas and Voula Kalafatis have been running this wonderful shop for 40 years, stocking linen shirts and scarves, paintings, rugs and ceramics, as well as their own handmade jewellery. Kostas is a master of *rembetika* and often plays at venues around town, as well as at the Skopelos Rembetika Festival (www.rembetikoskopelosfestival.com; ☺mid-Jul).

Rodios Pottery
CERAMICS

(☑24240 23605; Potoki; ☺10.30am-2pm & 6-8.30pm May-Oct) Known for its black-clay pieces made in ancient Greek style, Rodios is one of Skopelos' original and best-known pottery-making families, now into its fourth generation and in business since 1900. It's across from the main car park; the workshop, opposite, is open year-round.

ℹ Getting There & Away

BOAT

Boat services from Skopelos Town:

DESTINATION	DURATION	FARE (€)	FREQUENCY
Alonnisos Alonnisos	30mins	6	1-2 daily
Evia (Kymi)	3hrs	20	3 weekly
Skiathos (via Glossa)	1hr	6.50	daily
Skyros	6hrs	20	3 weekly
Volos (most via Glossa)	4¼hrs	30	2 daily

Hydrofoil services go to Alonnisos (€9, 20 minutes, two daily), Skiathos (via Glossa; €18, 45 minutes, two daily) and Volos (€35, 2½ hours, two daily).

BUS

Bus services from Skopelos Town. From the bus stop (p661), just outside the ferry dock, times below are for the summer; outside the season services trickle down to two daily buses.

DESTINATION	DURATION	FARE (€)	FREQUENCY
Agnontas	15mins	2	10+ daily
Glossa/ Loutraki	55mins	5.60	5-10 daily
Milia	35mins	4	10+ daily
Neo Klima (Elios)	45mins	4	5-10 daily
Panaormos	25mins	3.50	10+ daily
Stafylos	15mins	1.70	10+ daily

Glossa & Loutraki
Γλώσσα & Λουτράκι

POP 990

Clinging to a steep far-northwest-coast hillside, Glossa, Skopelos' sleepy and scenic second settlement, is a whitewashed cluster of typically Greek homes and slim alleys fanning out from a small church square, with just a few shops, cafes and restaurants.

A 2km road winds down to the laid-back port of Loutraki ('Glossa' in ferry timetables); a shorter *kalderimi* (cobblestoned path) also connects both villages.

◉ Sights

Antoniou Family Olive Press   AGRICULTURAL CENTRE

(Map p662; ☑ 24240 33517; www.skopelosoliveoil. gr; ⊙ 10.30am-3pm & 5-7pm) **FREE** Around 800m east of Glossa, signposted just beyond a petrol station, this 130-year-old, third-generation family-owned mill produces fine extra virgin olive oil that is harvested traditionally. Visitors are welcome to tour the modern facilities (with audio guides), taste products and, of course, stock up in the shop. Call ahead.

⏟ Sleeping & Eating

Pansion Platana   PENSION €

(Map p662; ☑ 6973646702; pansionplatana@hot mail.com; Glossa; r €35-55; ⊙ May-Oct; ℗ 🛜) Just 700m east of Glossa (before you reach the petrol station), this cosy and impeccable guesthouse surrounded by greenery has jolly-coloured rooms with overhead fans, kitchenettes and balcony views down to the port of Loutraki. Welcoming Greek-Australian owner Eleni provides tea and tips.

★ **Flisvos Taverna**   TAVERNA €€

(Map p662; ☑ 24240 33856, 6974718287; www.face ook.com/flisvosrestaurant.loutraki.skopelos; Loutraki; mains €8-15; ⊙ noon-11pm late Apr-early Oct) Turquoise tablecloths match the waves washing directly below the fabulous seafront terrace at friendly Flisvos, whose simple, superb Greek cooking excels. Appetisers such as tzatziki, *taramasalata* (thick purée of fish roe, potato, oil and lemon juice), feta-courgette fritters or halloumi with a squeeze of lemon are standouts, and there's excellent fresh fish plus traditional standards like *mousakas* and *stifadho* (meat, game or seafood cooked with onions in a tomato puree).

ℹ Getting There & Away

Ferry services from Loutraki/Glossa:

DESTINATION	DURATION	FARE (€)	FREQUENCY
Agios Konstantinos (summer only)	4¼hrs	29.90	daily
Alonnisos	1½hrs	9	1-2 daily
Evia (Mantoudi)	1½hrs	19.80	daily
Skiathos	30mins	5.30	1-2 daily
Volos	3¼hrs	26.50	1-2 daily

There are also hydrofoils to Alonnisos (€11.50, one hour, two daily), Skiathos (€11, 15 minutes, two daily) and Volos (€32.50, two hours, two daily).

Around Skopelos

◉ Sights

There are more than 40 churches and monasteries sprinkled around Skopelos. Several of the most important monasteries can be visited on a scenic drive or day-long trek eastwards up Mt Palouki from Skopelos Town.

The monastery road forks 2km east of Skopelos Town. Continue straight then climb 2km east on a dirt track to reach Moni Evangelistrias (Map p662; ⊙ 9.30am-1pm & 4-8pm May-Oct), or take the right fork southwest to find Moni Metamorfosis Sotiros (Map p662; ⊙ 9am-2pm & 5-8pm approx Jun-Oct) (1.7km), Moni Varvaras (Map p662; ⊙ 9am-2pm & 5-8pm approx Jun-Oct) (4km) and Moni Prodromou (Map p662; ⊙ 8am-2pm & 4-8pm) (4.2km); at research time this road was paved until just beyond Sotiros, before becoming a (drivable) dirt track up to Prodromou. If you're hiking, it's about 1¾ hours' climb from Skopelos Town to Prodromou (6.2km), with the trail criss-crossing the main road.

Agios Ioannis   CHURCH

(Map p662; ⊙ dawn-dusk) The small, impossibly scenic cragtop chapel of Agios Ioannis, surrounded by the shimmering Aegean 5.5km east of Glossa, is famous for having played the wedding venue in the 2008 Skopelos-starring movie *Mamma Mia!* Around 200 steps climb up the cliffs.

🏖 Beaches

Most of Skopelos' best beaches lie on the sheltered southwest and west coasts; a good way to reach them is by hiring a bike from Skopelos Cycling (p662).

Velanio Beach
BEACH

(Map p662) From the eastern end of Stafylos Beach (Map p662), 5km south of Skopelos Town, a path leads over a small headland to quieter silver-sand Velanio, the island's official nudist beach and coincidentally a great snorkelling spot, with a few sunbeds and a mellow beach bar.

Agnontas Beach
BEACH

(Map p662) Pines tumble down to almost kiss the turquoise water at the lovely little southwest-coast fishing port of Agnontas, 4km west of Stafylos, which has a tiny pebble-and-sand beach overlooked by a cluster of good seafront tavernas.

Cape Amarandos
NATURAL FEATURE

(Map p662) You could easily lose an entire day picnicking and hidden-cove swimming at spectacular Cape Amarandos. It's just south of Agnontas: take the turn 75m east of town to follow a steep dust-and-rock track (4WD recommended), off which there are plenty of private rocky beach stops backed by a sea of cascading pines. Some *Mamma Mia!* opening scenes were filmed here.

At a sharp left turn 1.3km south of the original turn-off, you'll see a dramatic cleft in the rocks; follow the faint path here along the cliff to the water's edge, where a sea cave and pine shade provide a wonderfully spectacular stop.

Kastani Beach
BEACH

(Map p662) It's easy to see the temptations of Skopelos' famous '*Mamma Mia!* beach': a pine-adorned, silver-sand-and-pebble stretch at the end of a steep track 13km west of Skopelos Town, with glittering aqua-coloured water, excellent swimming and a string of sun loungers (€7). These days it's overlooked by a large beach bar (May to early October).

🏃 Activities & Tours

Skopelos' pine-sprinkled hills and pebble beaches make for wonderful hiking, especially in spring and autumn. One of the most popular hikes is the 6.2km, 1¾-hour (one way) route up the slopes of Mt Palouki (567m), taking in some of the island's most fascinating monasteries. There are also good hikes in the island's north, including the two-hour trail (about 5km) from Glossa to Agios Ioannis.

⭐ Skopelos Walks
WALKING

(☑ 6945249328; www.skopelos-walks.com; guided hikes €20-40) 🌱 If you can't tell a twin-tailed

pasha butterfly from a leopard orchid, join one of island resident Heather Parsons' guided walks. Her four-hour Coast to Coast walk follows a centuries-old *kalderimi* (cobblestoned) path across the island, ending at a beach taverna, with wonderful views to Alonnisos and Evia along the way. Her book *Skopelos Trails* contains graded trail descriptions.

Heather and a loyal band of volunteers continue to clear, signpost and GPS the trails across the island. She also offers *Mamma Mia!* jeep tours to most of the movie's filming locations and guided walks around Skopelos Town, and can arrange mountain biking.

Kayaking Greece
KAYAKING

(Map p662; ☑ 6983211298, 24240 33805; www.kayakinggreece.com; Milia Beach; ☺ May-Oct) This well-managed and experienced kayaking outfit offers everything from full-day trips (€65) and simple sunset outings (€35) to six-day adventures (€590) and customised island expeditions.

🛌 Sleeping & Eating

Limnonari Rooms
GUESTHOUSE €

(Map p662; ☑ 6946464515, 24240 23046; www.skopelos.net/limnonarirooms; Limnonari Beach; r €45-65; ☺ Mar-Nov; 🅿 🕸 🛜) Cosy, colourful decor combines with views across beautiful Limnonari Bay and its secluded white sands (Map p662) at this appealing, efficiently run 10-room guesthouse, 1.5km northwest of Agnontas. Most rooms have private balconies, original artwork and fridges. The family's garden taverna serves vegetarian *mousakas,* fish and meat grills, and homemade olives and feta, or help yourself to the shared kitchen and barbecue.

⭐ Mando Beachfront
APARTMENT €€

(Map p662; ☑ 6936131316, 24240 23917; www.mandobeachfront.com; Stafylos; incl breakfast d €60-115, tr €75-130, villa €225-300; 🅿 🕸 🛜) 🌱 Nestled above a sparkling cove on Stafylos Bay, 4.5km south of Skopelos Town, this homey, well-managed hit offers charmingly rustic rooms opening on to sea-view balconies, alongside luxe suites and villas. The outdoor communal kitchen gives way to a path down over the rocks and a platform for jumping straight into the sea, and breakfasts revolve around home-grown produce.

Taverna Pavlos
TAVERNA €€

(Map p662; ☑ 24240 22409, 6948720954; www.facebook.com/pavlosagnodasskopelos; Agnontas;

mains €9-15; ⊘ noon-10pm May-Oct, Fri-Sun only Nov-Apr) Islanders think nothing of driving over to Agnontas for beautifully prepared fresh fish and excellent mezedhes at this cheerful and beautifully positioned shaded taverna overlooking the sea. Octopus *stifadho* (cooked with onions in a tomato purée), crunchy salads and *fava* (yellow split-pea dip) are among the star offerings, and the setting is dreamy.

ALONNISOS ΑΛΟΝΝΗΣΟΣ

POP 3500

The wildest, most distant and least touristed of the inhabited Sporades, Alonnisos rises from the sea in a mountain of greenery, with stands of Aleppo pine, kermes oak, mastic and arbutus bushes, vineyards and olive and fruit trees, all threaded with perfumed patches of untamed herbs. The west and north coasts are steep and rocky, while the east is speckled with seductive aquamarine bays and pebble-and-sand beaches, all of it protected by the pristine 2260-sq-km National Marine Park of Alonnisos (p670).

The original (now-restored) hilltop capital, Old Alonnisos, was rocked by an earthquake in 1965, after which locals relocated to Patitiri, now the quaint main port and island hub. The mellow village of Steni Vala (p671), 11km northeast of Patitiri, is the only other real settlement. Things amp up a few gears in July and August, while many inhabitants decamp to Athens for the surprisingly harsh winter season.

❶ Getting There & Away

Alonnisos' main port of Patitiri has links to mainland Volos; to nearby Skopelos and Skiathos; and, from mid-June to mid-September, to Skyros and Kymi (Evia). Services are reduced from around October to April. Tickets can be purchased online or in Patitiri from **Alkyon Travel** (☑ 22350 32444; http://alkyontravel.gr; Waterfront; ⊘ 6am-8pm Apr-Oct), **Albedo Travel** (☑ 24240 65804; www.alonissosholidays. com; Waterfront; ⊘ 9.30am-2pm & 5.30-8.30pm late Apr–mid-Oct) and **Alonnisos Travel** (☑ 24240 65188, 24240 66000; www. alonnisostravel.gr; Waterfront; ⊘ 8.30am-10.30pm Apr-Oct).

❶ Getting Around

Albedo Travel and Alonnisos Travel in Patitiri are reliable car-hire outlets.

Patitiri Πατητήρι

POP 1630

Alonnisos' main town and port, Patitiri (meaning Wine Press) sits between two sandstone cliffs peppered with pine trees, at the southern end of the island's east coast. With cafes, shops, travel agents and tavernas strung out along a seafront promenade, it's a modern and not *especially* charming place, though the natural setting is alluring and there's a small pebble beach.

Two roads lead inland from the waterfront quay; the main road is at the eastern end of the harbour. There are no road signs: people simply refer to the left-hand or right-hand road.

◉ Sights

★ Alonisos Museum   MUSEUM
(☑ 24240 66250; www.alonissosmuseum.com; adult/child €4/free; ⊘ 11am-7pm May & Sep, to 8pm Jun-Aug) Patitiri's excellent town museum takes in antique nautical maps, traditional island costumes, an impressive collection of pirates' weapons and boarding equipment, and an absorbing display on wartime resistance, all with detailed multilingual info booklets. Downstairs there's a recreated farmhouse interior and artefacts relating to traditional local crafts and industries, from mining to olive-oil production. It's signposted above Bar St at the southwest end of town.

MOM   MUSEUM
(☑ 24240 66350; www.mom.gr; Waterfront; ⊘ 10am-10pm Jun-Sep) ✐ FREE Don't miss this superb 1st-floor waterfront info centre all about the rare, protected Mediterranean monk seal (p671). It has good displays, videos with English subtitles and helpful multilingual staff on hand, and the team is campaigning to reduce plastics across the local environment.

🕏 Activities & Tours

Popular excursions around the island and marine park (p670) depart from Patitiri's harbour. Knowledgeable islander Pakis Athanasiou (☑ 6978386588) (who helped establish the marine park) captains the classic *Gorgona*, whose full-day marine-park trips (€40) visit the Blue Cave on Alonnisos' northeast coast and the islets of Kyra Panagia and Peristera in the marine park, with lunch, swimming breaks and a 16th-century monastery visit; book through Albedo Travel. Alonnisos Travel offers similar trips (€45)

EVIA & THE SPORADES PATITIRI

Alonnisos

aboard the *Planitis*, and there are also speedboat marine-park excursions (€50).

🛏 Sleeping & Eating

Patitiri has a good selection of warmly hospitable hotels and pensions, as well as a campground and some surprisingly chic boutique-style picks. Book ahead in July and August.

Ilias Studios   APARTMENT €
(📞24240 65451; www.ilias-studios.gr; Pelasgon 27; apt €40-50; ☉May-Sep; ❋🐾) Just 200m inland from the port, owners Ilias and Magdalini provide a warm welcome at this

quiet, spruce blue-and-white building down a flower-fringed path. Rooms are bright and spotless, in simple contemporary style, with kitchenettes and balconies.

**★Angelo's
Apartments & Suites**   APARTMENT €€
(📞6973955267, 24240 65705; www.angelosalo nissos.com; apt €40-180; ☉Easter-early Oct) The fabulous work of an Athenian designer, this collection of contemporary, all-different apartments is spread across two buildings, one just inland from the port (with an earthier feel) and the other atop town (in bold whites). Soothing, creative styling marries

custom-made furniture (like swing chairs) with rope, bamboo, driftwood and glassed-in showers, plus attention to detail from efficient owner Angelo.

★**Hotel Liadromia**   HOTEL €€
(📋 24240 65521; www.liadromia.gr; d €50-80, studio €70-110; 🅿 ❋ 🛜) From hand-embroidered curtains to vintage furnishings, there's character to spare at Patitiri's welcoming, impeccably maintained original hotel, perched above the eastern harbour. Gracious owner Mary is full of tips and takes obvious delight in making it all work. Rooms (with balconies) are gradually being upgraded to a fresh rustic-chic look, and home-cooked breakfasts (€7.50) are served upstairs with sea views.

★**Archipelagos**   TAVERNA €
(📋 24240 65031; mains €7-11; ⊙ noon-late Apr-Dec) At this outstanding and very Greek harbourfront taverna, locals gather to order round after round of fine mezedhes, always-fresh grilled fish, lovely fresh salads (try, say, the cabbage, carrot and lemon) and local firewater favourite *tsipouro* (distilled spirit of grape must) as the night rolls on.

To Kamaki Ouzerie   TAVERNA €€
(mains €5-15; ⊙ noon-1am mid-May–mid-Oct, Fri-Sun only mid-Jan–mid-May; 🛜📋) This down-to-earth long-time local favourite, next to the National Bank on the main road, tempts with its cheerful welcome and well-priced fresh fish, tasty vegetarian plates and excellent mezedhes (potato salad, courgette fritters, zesty *fava*). Weekends often see family bouzouki sessions take over.

❶ Getting There & Away

BOAT

Ferries run to:

DESTINATION	DURATION	FARE (€)	FREQUENCY
Glossa	1½hrs	9	daily
Kymi (summer only)	2½hrs	20	3 weekly
Mantoudi (Evia)	2¾hrs	19.80	2 weekly
Skiathos	2hrs	9.50	2 daily
Skopelos Town	45mins	5.30	2-3 daily
Skyros (summer only)	5¼hrs	20	3 weekly
Volos	5hrs	30	2 daily

There are also hydrofoil services to Skiathos (€15 to €18, 1½ hours, two daily), Skopelos Town (€9.50, 20 minutes, two daily), Glossa (€11.50, one hour, two daily) and Volos (€35, 3¼ hours, two daily).

BUS

Buses run to/from Old Alonnisos (€1.70, 10 minutes) at least hourly June to September from the harbourfront bus stop, or you can hike up (2.5km, 40 minutes). Summer **beach buses** (📋 6979269099, 24240 65389; return €5-10; ⊙ Jun-Sep) leave Patitiri around 10am, returning around 4pm and serving a different point to the north each day.

TAXI

Taxis gather on the harbourfront; it's €8 to €10 to Old Alonnisos and €18 to Steni Vala.

Old Alonnisos
Παλιά Αλόννησος

POP 208

Clinging to the island's southwesternmost tip, Old Alonnisos (also Palia Alonnisos or Hora) is an enchanting hilltop village of panoramic coastal views, traditionally built homes, swirling vines and flowers, and winding, stepped, cobbled alleys branching out from a central church square. It was abandoned for Patitiri after a devastating 1965 earthquake, but has since been sensitively restored. Local families decamp here for the short summer season, when restaurants, bars, shops and hotels create a low-key buzz; at other times it's almost eerily peaceful.

◉ Sights

Church of the Birth of Christ   CHURCH
(Plateia Hristou; ⊙ hours vary) A 17th-century rough-hewn, slate-roof stone church, with its origins in the 12th century, sits on the village square; inside you'll see a tiny wooden gallery and an ornate screen depicting the lives of the Apostles.

Megalos Mourtias Beach   BEACH
(Map p668) From just east of Old Alonnisos, a steep road leads 2km downhill to popular Megalos Mourtias, a beautiful enclosed curve of pebbles with a couple of restaurants and apartments, a few sun loungers and umbrellas, and great views of Evia looming in the distance.

Mikros Mourtias Beach   BEACH
(Map p668) A 2km dirt track and a well-kept footpath lead south and downhill from the village to reach this peaceful, secluded

THE MARINE PARK

In a country not particularly noted for ecological foresight, Europe's largest marine park (2260 sq km) is a welcome innovation. National Marine Park of Alonnisos Northern Sporades (Map p668; www.alonissos-park.gr; ⊙ May-Oct) was created in 1992, its prime aim is to protect the endangered Mediterranean monk seal (p671) and several rare seabirds. In summer, boats from Alonnisos (p667) and Skopelos run full-day trips through the pristine park, whose sea floors are carpeted in oxygen-producing posidonia. The shy monk seal is rarely seen, but you may spot dolphins (three species), turtles, Eleonora's falcons or migrating whales.

The marine park is divided into two zones, A and B. Alonnisos lies within Zone B, along with the islets of Peristera and Dio Adelphi. Access to Zone A is more restricted, with boats allowed no closer than 400m to most islets; one exception is the island of Kyra Panagia, whose beautifully renovated monastery dating from 1200 is visited on most boat trips. Rocky Piperi islet is protected by a 5km radius due to its importance for monk-seal reproduction and raptor populations.

sand-and-pebble beach, which has a wild feel (no tavernas!) and a bit of a nudist scene.

🛏 Sleeping

Old Alonnisos makes a perfect spot for a secluded stay for a night or two, with a smattering of apartments and pensions offering the chance to stay in beautiful old stone buildings. Book ahead for July and August.

Chiliadromia Studios APARTMENT €
(☑ 6974532931, 24240 65814; www.chiliadromia. gr; Plateia Hristou; studio from €55; ⊙ late May-Sep; ❄ 🛜) Tucked into the heart of the old village, these homey studios with lavender trim are a wonderful budget find, featuring small balconies, comfortable check-cloth beds, well-equipped kitchens and calming modern-rustic decor (wrought-iron beds, white-and-blue colour schemes). There's a popular cafe, Piperi (☑ 24240 66384; www.facebook.com/piperibar; Plateia Hristou; ⊙ 8.30am-2.30pm & 6pm-late mid-May-Oct; 🛜), downstairs.

★ Konstantina Studios APARTMENT €€
(☑ 24240 65900, 24240 66165; www.konstantina studios.gr; d/ste/apt incl breakfast from €107/120/130; P ❄ 🛜) Among Alonnisos' most inspiring accommodation, these tranquil boutique studios amid lavender-scented gardens in the lower village are styled in calming pastels, with murals, fluffy bathrobes, fully equipped kitchens and balcony views of the southwest coast. Resourceful owner Konstantina collects guests from ferries, arranges hiking and yoga, and whips up wonderful breakfasts with homemade jams, omelettes and baked treats.

Elma's Houses APARTMENT €€
(☑ 6945466776, 24240 66108; www.elmashouses. com; studio €60-85, apt €80-120; ⊙ May-Oct; ❄ 🛜) Two traditional village houses for up to four, overlooking a flower-filled courtyard, have been charmingly restored by architect-owner Elma, with full kitchen, comfy beds and updated bathrooms. Interiors are all rugged whitewashed walls, wood-beamed ceilings and twisting staircases, while the two kitchen-equipped studios have a balcony or terrace. It's at the south/upper end of town.

🍴 Eating

★ Hayiati CAFE €
(☑ 24240 66244; www.facebook.com/melpomeni. vas; snacks €6-10; ⊙ 10.30am-late May-Sep) Gracious glykopoleio (sweets shop) by day and piano bar by night (mid-June to early September only), Hayiati delivers sweeping coastal views from its descending outdoor terraces at the south/upper end of town. Morning goodies include fresh juices and made-to-order tyropita (cheese pie); later, it's sandwiches, home-baked cakes and Greek wines.

★ Astrofegia GREEK €€
(☑ 24240 65182; www.facebook.com/astrofegia. alonissos; mains €9-15; ⊙ 7pm-midnight Jun-Sep; 🛜) There's a stunning village view from this outdoor-dining delight, with its red-check tablecloths, friendly family welcome and wandering grape vines. Choose from good house wines and expertly prepared Greek standards with a touch of creativity: rare veggie mousakas, white-wine-roasted lamb, seafood souvlakia. Or go straight for

the *galaktoboureko* (custard slice). It's up an alley from the village entrance (signposted).

Demi's　　　　　　INTERNATIONAL €€
(☑ 24240 65164; www.facebook.com/restaurants. in.alonnisos; mains €8-12; ⊗ 1-11pm, closed Mon & Tue Nov-Apr; ☑) Well-known internationally trained island chef Demi Karanastasis turns his talents to a punchy, creative Greek-international menu at this welcoming, shaded terrace restaurant near the village entrance. Dig into smartly presented classics like Alonnisos tuna, *mousakas* or fried honey-sesame feta, or perhaps taco salads and aubergine dip, or go for the daily special.

Around Alonnisos

Alonnisos' main road travels 20km northeast from Patitiri to Gerakas Bay (Map p668) at the end of the island. Several minor roads descend off it to small fishing bays and some lovely secluded beaches.

◉ Sights

Kokkinokastro Beach　　　　BEACH
(Map p668) The gorgeous golden-white pebble-and-sand arc hugging red-tinged Cape Kokkinokastro, 6km northeast of Patitiri, was the site of the ancient, now-submerged city of Ikos, whose ruined fortified wall you can still make out. Expect a few sun loungers and umbrellas and a summer beach bar beside the gentle aqua waves.

Leftos Gialos Beach　　　　BEACH
(Map p668) Washed by deep-turquoise water, this white-pebble beach 7km northeast of Patitiri is graced by a couple of lively summer tavernas and a sprinkling of sun loungers, and framed by headlands thick with pine forests.

Steni Vala　　　　　　VILLAGE
The island's third settlement, 11km northeast of Patitiri, is an attractive little fishing village and deep-water yacht port, backed by excellent seafront tavernas and simple rooms for rent.

Agios Dimitrios Beach　　　　BEACH
(Map p668) Triangular Agios Dimitrios, 5.5km northeast of Steni Vala, is one of the island's most beloved beaches, with a seasonal truck-canteen and domatia sitting opposite a graceful stretch of white pebbles and a few sunbeds. The uninhabited island of Peristera looms just across the water.

🏃 Activities

Hiking opportunities abound on Alonnisos and 14 official trails have been waymarked. Popular hikes are highlighted on the Terrain, Road Cartography and Anavasi maps of Alonnisos, and in local hiking guides such as Bente Keller's *Alonnisos on Foot*. There's also basic information at www.alonissos.gr.

A few ancient sailing vessels have been discovered at the bottom of the shallow sea around Alonnisos and efforts are under way to open these sites to guided dives. Among them is the 5th-century Peristera shipwreck – one of the Classical era's largest, with 3000 amphorae – which opened for dives in summer 2020. In the meantime, divers might spot dolphins, sea bream, groupers, octopus and more. Triton Dive Center (☑ 24240 65804;

MONKS OF THE SEA

Once populating hundreds of colonies in the Black Sea, the Mediterranean Sea and along Africa's Atlantic coast, the Mediterranean monk seal has been reduced to approximately just 500 individuals. Half of these live in the seas around Greece; others roam the waters off the Turkish and Moroccan Atlantic coasts.

One of the earth's rarest mammals, the Mediterranean monk seal is now among the 20 most endangered species worldwide. Major threats include decreasing food supplies, destruction of habitat and low pup-survival rates (driven by seals now resting in dangerous caves rather than on beaches). Thankfully, the once-common killings by fishers – who saw the seal as a pest that tore holes in nets and robbed their catch – have diminished with the recognition that protecting the seal also promotes recovery of fish stocks. Conservation efforts are rising and, in 2015, the IUCN downgraded the Mediterranean monk seal from Critically Endangered to Endangered, but there's a long way to go yet.

The seals typically eat around 35kg of fish every day, with males weighing 400kg to 500kg and females 200kg to 300kg, and live around 40 years.

For more information about monk seals and to see infrared film of their impossibly adorable pups, visit the MOM (p667) information centre in Patitiri.

www.bestdivingingreece.com; Albedo Travel, Waterfront; 2-dive trip €90; ⊙May-Sep) and Ikion Diving (p662) are respected local dive schools.

🛏️ Sleeping & Eating

4 Epoches
HOTEL €€

(📞24240 66101; www.4epochesalonnisos.com; Steni Vala; s €42-96, d €50-100, tr €70-120; ⊙May-Sep; P❄️🐾🛜🌊) Just back from Steni Vala's waterfront, this smart, efficiently operated hotel has 22 whitewashed, modern-design rooms and kitchen-equipped studios set around a cool-blue pool garden with a few palms. All rooms have terraces, while those on top floors are graced with wood-beamed ceilings. There's a roof garden plus a bar.

⭐ Ilya Suites
APARTMENT €€€

(📞6938327401; www.ilyasuites.gr; Glyfa Beach; ste €80-180, villa €200-300; ⊙May-Sep; P❄️🛜🌊) Roses, lavender and olive trees trickle down to a pebbly beach from these four low-key luxe suites and four-person villa, with sparkling views of Peristera island. From the bold white-on-white design, beamed ceilings and sleek kitchens to the sea-facing terraces and scented gardens, everything feels soothingly elegant. Yoga, hiking and diving arranged.

Dendrolimano
GREEK €€

(📞24240 65252; Votsi; mains €10-20; ⊙6pm-late May-Oct; 🅿️) With a lovely hillside terrace under the pines overlooking Votsi's azure bay, stylish Dendrolimano is known for its creatively presented Greek-Italian cuisine given an original contemporary twist – watermelon salad and squid-ink pasta with Alonnisos tuna, for example. Good wines, glorious setting.

SKYROS
ΣΚΥΡΟΣ

POP 3000

The largest of the Sporades, low-key Skyros has a more Cycladic feel than its richly forested siblings and often seems like two entirely separate islands: small shimmering bays, rolling farmland and swaths of pines (plus an air-force base) speckle the north, while the south features arid hills and a rocky shoreline. In Greek mythology, Skyros was the hiding place of the young Achilles, who is thought to have ridden a Skyrian horse into Troy: these endangered small-bodied horses can still be seen in the wild, if you're lucky.

These days, the island has a subtly fashionable yet off-radar vibe, largely thanks to

the alternative arts and wellness courses run by the British-owned Skyros Centre (📞in UK 44(0)1983 865566; www.skyros.com; off Agoras; 7-day course incl meals & accommodation from £725; ⊙Jun-Sep), but it's also increasingly popular among holidaying Greeks from Athens and Thessaloniki, as well as birdwatchers seeking the slender Eleonora's falcon. Skyros Town, perched almost magically on its high rock, is the easy-going capital.

ℹ️ Getting There & Away

AIR

From Skyros **airport** (Map p673), 11km northwest of Skyros Town, **Olympic Air** (www.olympicair. com) flies to/from Athens and **Sky Express** (www.skyexpress.gr) to/from Thessaloniki, both several times weekly.

Buses to/from Skyros Town meet flights (€2.80); taxis charge €20.

BOAT

Skyros' port is Linaria, on the west coast. Skyros Shipping Co has year-round ferries to/from Kymi on Evia (€12.10, 1¾ hours, daily); from mid-June to mid-September there are also services to/from Skopelos (€20, six hours, three weekly) and Alonnisos (€20, 5¼ hours, three weekly) .

Buy tickets online, from Skyros Shipping Co (p661) or **Skyros Travel** (📞6944884588, 22220 91600; www.skyrostravel.com; Agoras; ⊙9.30am-1.30pm & 6.30-9.30pm) in Skyros Town, or from harbour ticket kiosks in Linaria or Kymi. Skyros Travel also arranges transfers to/from Athens, via Kymi.

ℹ️ Getting Around

BICYCLE

Vagios Rent a Moto-Car (📞6986051760; www.facebook.com/rentamotocarskyros; off Agoras; ⊙9am-9pm) near the bus stop in Skyros Town and **Anemos Rent a Car-Bicycle** (📞22220 93705, 6980038667; www.anemos-skyros.gr; Molos; ⊙9am-2pm & 5-9pm) in Molos rent out bikes (€10 per day).

BUS

Buses link up with ferry arrivals/departures, running between Linaria and Skyros Town, Magazia and Molos (€2); and with flights, connecting Skyros Town and the airport (€2.80).

CAR & MOTORCYCLE

Cars and motorbikes are available in Skyros Town from **Martina's Rental** (📞6974752380, 22220 92022; www.skyroscar.gr; Machairas; ⊙9am-2pm & 6-9pm), Skyros Travel and Vagios Rent a Moto-Car, or in Magazia from **Europcar Skyros** (📞22220 92092; www.europcar.com; Magazia; ⊙8.30am-8.30pm) and in Molos from Anemos Rent a Car-Bicycle .

Skyros

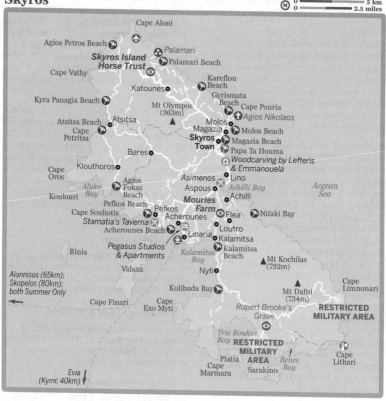

N
0 _____ 5 km
0 _____ 2.5 miles

Cape Aloni

Agios Petros Beach

Skyros Island Horse Trust

Palamari
Palamari Beach

Cape Vathy

Katounes

Kareflou Beach

Gyrismata Beach

Kyra Panagia Beach

Cape Pouria

Mt Olympos (363m)

Molos
Magazia
Skyros Town

Agios Nikolaos

Molos Beach
Magazia Beach

Papa Ta Houma

Atsitsa Beach
Cape Petritsa

Atsitsa

Bares

Woodcarving by Lefteris & Emmanouela

Cape Oros

Klouthoros

Asimenos

Lino

Aegean Sea

Alyko Bay

Agios Fokas Beach

Aspous

Achilli Bay

Achilli

Koulouri

Pefkos Beach

Mouries Farm

Cape Souliotis

Pefkos
Acherounes

Flea

Nifaki Bay

Stamatia's Taverna

Acherounes Beach

Linaria

Loutro
Kalamitsa

Rinia

Pegasus Studios & Apartments

Kalamitsa Bay

Kalamitsa Beach

Mt Kochilas (792m)

Valaxa

Nyfi

Alonnisos (65km);
Skopelos (80km);
both Summer Only

Cape Finari

Cape Exo Myti

Kolibada Bay

Mt Dafni (734m)

Cape Limnonari

Rupert Brooke's Grave

RESTRICTED MILITARY AREA

Tris Boukes Bay

RESTRICTED MILITARY AREA

Evia (Kymi; 40km)

Platia

Cape Marmara

Sarakino

Renes Bay

Cape Lithari

Skyros Town Σκύρος

POP 1660

Draped over a rocky bluff, Skyros' capital is topped by a Byzantine-Venetian fortress and laced with labyrinthine cobblestone streets that invite wandering, but were in fact designed to keep out the elements (and pirates).

A lively jumble of tavernas, bars, low-key boutiques and artisan workshops flanked by winding alleyways make up the main thoroughfare, Agoras. About 100m uphill and north from Plateia (the main square), Agoras forks left and zigzags to two small museums adjacent to Plateia Rupert Brooke, from where a wide stone path descends 1km to Magazia Beach (Map p673).

◎ Sights & Activities

★ Feel Ingreece   CULTURA TOURSL

(☏ 22220 93100; www.feelingreece.gr; off Agoras; ◷ 9.30am-2pm & 6.30-11pm) ✍ Knowledgeable Feel Ingreece owner Chrysanthi is dedicated to helping sustain Skyrian culture, with a focus on local arts and the natural environment. The team arranges hikes (with a chance of glimpsing wild Skyrian horses, €10 per person); birdwatching trips; pottery, woodcarving, cooking, embroidery and Greek dance lessons; yoga; diving; and boat trips (€50 per person) around the island's south.

★ Manos & Anastasia Faltaïts Museum   MUSEUM

(☏ 22220 91232; www.faltaits.gr; Plateia Rupert Brooke; €4, with tour €7; ◷ 10am-2pm & 6-9pm Jun-Sep, 10am-2pm Oct-May) Spread across the Faltaïts family's 19th-century mansion, this not-to-be-missed gem unravels the island's mythology and folklore in a multilevel labyrinth of Skyrian costumes, embroidery, antique furniture, ceramics, daggers, cooking pots, historical documents and vintage photographs. There's also a collection of writings by prominent journalist Konstantinos Faltaïts, the father of artist Manos who founded the museum and whose colourful and sensual paintings are displayed throughout.

Monastery of Agios Georgios
MONASTERY

(Kastro; ⊙10am-1pm & 6-8pm) Founded in 962, the working Byzantine Monastery of St George (whose bells might wake you if you're staying in town) crowns Skyros Town, within the lower walls of the Byzantine-Venetian fortress. You can visit its 17th-century chapel, which features an ornate gilded screen and faded 18th-century frescoes.

Archaeological Museum
MUSEUM

(☑22220 91327; Plateia Rupert Brooke; €2; ⊙8.30am-4pm Wed-Mon) Along with Mycenaean pottery and jewellery found near Magazia, vessels unearthed in Skyros Town and artefacts from the Bronze Age excavation at Palamari (p677) – look especially for the two-handled ceramic cups and the head of an imported early Cycladic idol – this attractive courtyard museum contains a traditional Skyrian house interior, transported in its entirety from the benefactor's home.

Skyros Carnival
CARNIVAL

(⊙Jan/Feb) In this wild pre-Lenten festival, which takes place on the last four weekends before Lent and Orthodox Easter, young men don goat masks, hairy jackets and dozens of copper goat bells. They then clank and dance through Skyros Town, each with a male partner dressed up as a Skyrian bride but also wearing a goat mask.

🍽 Sleeping & Eating

Nicolas Pension
PENSION €

(☑22220 91778; www.nicolaspension.gr; Playia; d €40-60, tr €55-75, q €65-85; 🅿❄🛜) On a quiet road on the southwest edge of town, this friendly pension is just a five-minute walk to busy Agoras. Upper-floor doubles have balconies and *kastro* views, while lower rooms open on to a shady garden; some have traditional wood-carved sleeping lofts and all are full of rustic charm, with kitchenettes.

★Nefeli Hotel
HOTEL €€

(☑22220 91964; www.skyros-nefeli.gr; d incl breakfast €89-122; 🅿❄🛜🏊) With sleekly styled or updated-Skyrian balconied rooms strung around an enormous saltwater pool looking out on the distant hilltop castle, this welcoming favourite on the southwest edge of town has a laid-back minimalist feel and a seductive boutique touch. A separate building conceals seven classically wood-carved, three-storey apartments.

★O Pappous Kai Ego
TAVERNA €

(☑22220 93200; Agoras; mains €6-9; ⊙6pm-late daily Jun-Sep, Fri & Sat only May & Oct; 🛜🌿) One generation of exquisite family recipes follows another at small, charming and elegant 'my grandfather and me'. It's known for its Skyrian dolmadhes, made with a touch of goat milk; other mezedhes, like potato salad and *fava,* are divine too.

Taverna Maryeti
GREEK €

(☑6972320265, 22220 91311; Agoras; mains €6-9; ⊙noon-late Jun-Sep, from 7pm Oct & Feb-May; 🛜🌿) The local in-town favourite for grilled fish, goat in lemon sauce, great meat grills and marvellous mezedhes, such as broccoli doused in lemon and olive oil or *fava* (yellow split-pea dip) served with fluffy bread. Look for the snug flagstone terrace and green doors on mid-Agoras.

❶ Information

Skyros Travel (p672) Helpful full-service agency for accommodation; transfers and onward travel; car and motorbike hire; boat excursions around Skyros; cooking classes; diving; hiking; and more.

❶ Getting There & Away

Buses bring you into town from Linaria (€2, 15 minutes) and the airport (€2.80, 20 minutes); taxis cost €15/20. The **bus stop** (Agoras) is at the lower/southwestern end of Agoras.

Magazia & Molos
Μαγαζιά & Μώλος

POP 400

Skirting the southern end of a long, sandy grey-brown beach beneath Skyros Town, the low-key resort of Magazia is a compact whitewashed maze of winding cobbled alleys adorned with bursts of jasmine, bougainvillea and oleander. Its original buildings were storehouses for olive oil, produce and dry goods: the name 'Magazia' comes from the Greek word for shop.

Towards the northern end of the beach and now blending with Magazia, once-sleepy Molos (Map p673) now has its own share of tavernas, bars and accommodation, along with a landmark windmill (these days a bar) and rock-hewn church. Both beaches get lively (by Skyros standards) in summer.

🍽 Sleeping

Magazia and Molos are wonderful places to stay, with an ever-expanding choice of laid-back beachside apartments, hotels and

SKYROS' ARTISANS & ARTISTIC HOMES

Skyros has a flourishing community of working artists, from potters and painters to sculptors, embroiderers and jewellery makers. The island artistry dates from Byzantine times when passing pirates collaborated with rogue residents, whose houses became virtual galleries for stolen booty looted from merchant ships, including ceramic plates and copper ornaments from Europe, the Middle East and Asia Minor. Today, similar items adorn almost every Skyrian house, shown to best advantage on locally carved wooden shelves, and the island's artisans keep traditional crafts alive.

The best places to see Skyrian domestic interiors are Skyros Town's Manos & Anastasia Faltaïts Museum (p673) and Archaeological Museum (p674), which contain atmospheric recreated homesteads and traditional 18th- and 19th-century local outfits. To see the legacy of Skyrian traditions, check out the Skyros Town workshops and showrooms of ceramicists Stamatis Ftoulis (22220 91559; Agoras; 10am-1.30pm & 7.30-9.30pm Mon-Sat May-Oct) and Olga Zacharaiki (6989992838; Plateia; 10am-2pm & 7pm-midnight); embroiderer Amerissa Panagiotou (6973397693; Agoras; 10am-2pm & 6.30-midnight May-Oct); and woodcarvers Stamatiou Andreou (22220 92827; Agoras; 10am-2pm & 5-9pm May-Oct), Yiannis Andreou (6945229135; andreouyiannis@hotmail.com; Agoras; 10am-2pm & 5-9pm May-Oct) and Yiannis Trachanas (6937215622; off Agoras; 10.30am-2pm & 7pm-midnight May-Oct). There's more fine woodcarving, plus a Skyrian homestead, at Woodcarving by Lefteris & Emmanouela (Map p673; 22220 91106; www.thesiswood.com; Lino; 10am-2pm & 7-9pm), 1km south of town. Chrysanthi Zygogianni at Feel Ingreece (p673) can fill you in on the local scene.

guesthouses to suit all budgets, many of them styled with Skyrian charm.

★ Antigoni Studios
APARTMENT €

(6945100230, 22220 91319; www.antigonistudios.com; Magazia; studio €55-115, 1-bedroom apt €80-150; P❄🛜) A subtle boho-stylish look runs through this outstanding beach-facing pick, washed in soothing blues and whites. The 20 spacious, elegantly furnished, kitchen-equipped studios are just a three-minute walk to the sea, at the southern end of Magazia. Owner Katerina is full of island tips, and some rooms are adorned with Skyrian embroidery.

★ Perigiali Hotel
HOTEL €€

(22220 92075, 6974471053; www.perigiali.com; Magazia; incl breakfast d €60-160, q €90-200; P❄🛜💺) Local embroidery and watercolours decorate whitewashed rooms at leafy Perigiali, which feels deliciously secluded despite close to Magazia Beach. The lovingly designed rooms and apartments overlook gardens of pear and apricot trees and a saltwater pool. Breakfast is a feast of local goodies, and owner Amalia is has plenty of advice.

Ammos Hotel
HOTEL €€€

(6974354181, 22220 91234; www.skyrosammos hotel.com; Magazia; incl breakfast d €72-200, q €126-235; Easter-Oct; ❄🛜💺) Set around fragrant gardens and a pool, boutique-feel Ammos has an inviting, low-key vibe to match its smartly updated cream-hued

rooms, which feature dove-grey shutters, Skyros scenes on the walls and, for some, private cabana-style terraces. Made-to-order Skyrian breakfasts start the day, and there's a summer pool bar and restaurant plus yoga and massage, all amid sparkling-white walls.

✗ Eating & Drinking

★ Stefanos Taverna
TAVERNA €

(22220 91272, 6974350372; Magazia; mains €6.50-10; 9.30am-midnight Mar-Oct; 🛜🍴) Kick back on the breezy beachside terrace at the southern end of Magazia (p673) and choose from juicy grills, baked dishes such as *yemista* (stuffed tomatoes), seriously good *saganaki* (fried cheese) drizzled with lemon, and locally sourced wild greens and fresh fish. Service nails the warm-and-efficient balance, and it's open early(ish) for breakfast omelettes and coffee.

★ Oi Istories Tou Barba
TAVERNA €

(22220 91453; Magazia; mains €6-10; noon-late Feb-Nov; 🛜🍴) Pale-blue tables and fabulous panoramas of Skyros Town mark this popular, welcoming terrace taverna overlooking the northern end of Magazia Beach (p673). Settle in for delicious fisherman's spaghetti, excellent mezedhes (tzatziki, potato salad, fried courgettes), lightly creative salads, fresh seafood and other beautifully prepared traditional plates, all in a bubbly atmosphere.

Anemomylos
BAR

(☑22220 93656; www.anemomulos.gr; Pouria; ☺9am-3am Jun-Sep, reduced hours Oct-May; ☏) Perched on the seafront by the rock-cut church of Agios Nikolaos, this chicly converted old windmill is perfect for sundowners, with wines, cocktails and light meals. Tables dot a beachside terrace and the surrounding rocks, from where you can gaze out on distant Skyros Town.

❶ Getting There & Away

Buses link Magazia and Molos with Linaria (€2, 15 minutes) and the airport (€2.80, 20 minutes), coinciding with flights and ferries; taxis charge €15 or €20 respectively.

Linaria   Λιναριά

POP 300

Skyros' mellow, fairly modern port Linaria is tucked into a small aqua bay filled with bobbing fishing boats and a few low-key tavernas and *ouzeries* (places that serve ouzo and light snacks), 10km southwest of Skyros Town. Things perk up briefly whenever the *Achilleas* ferry comes in and visitors flood the harbour, which is overlooked by a whitewashed blue-trim church.

◉ Sights

Pefkos Beach
BEACH

(Map p673) A beautiful horseshoe-shaped beach of golden-brown sand graces deep-set

Pefkos Bay, a 6km drive northwest of Linaria and home to the popular Stamatia's Taverna.

🛏 Sleeping & Eating

Lykomides
HOTEL €

(☑22220 93249, 6972694434; www.lykomides.gr; r €35-65, apt €70-120; ❉☏) Opposite the ferry dock and efficiently managed by the hospitable Soula Pappa, traditional-style Lykomides has 13 spotless, neutral-toned rooms with balconies overlooking the water. There's also a modern, all-white, kitchen-equipped apartment for up to five people.

Pegasus Studios & Apartments
APARTMENT €

(Map p673; ☑22220 91600, 6944884588; www.skyros-pegasus.gr; Acherounes; 1-bedroom apt €55-75, 2-bedroom apt €80-110; ℗☏) This cluster of comfortable, uncluttered apartments with kitchens and balconies sits amid palms, vines and grassy gardens. Rooms sleep two to five, some split-level or in classic wood-carved Skyrian style, and kayaking and cooking classes are available. It's all under the watch of Skyros expert Lefteris Trakos (p672).

★Marigo
TAVERNA €

(☑22220 96010; akamatra_makis@yahoo.gr; mains €7-12; ☺8am-late Jun-Sep, 11am-late Apr, May & Oct, 11am-late Fri-Sun Nov-Mar; ☏) Dressed in soothing greys, with fresh flowers, dangling baskets and modern-rustic style, Linaria's most elegant portside restaurant specialises in deliciously fresh seafood, home-cooked desserts

---

THE SKYRIAN HORSE: AN ENDANGERED BREED

The endangered small-bodied Skyrian horse (*Equus Cabalus Skyriano*) is valued for its intelligence, beauty and gentleness. Though common across Greece in ancient times – the horses on the Parthenon frieze are thought to be Skyrian, and Skyrian horses are said to have pulled Achilles' legendary chariot – today there are fewer than 300 of these diminutive creatures worldwide, with a small minority living on the southern slopes of Mt Kochilas on Skyros. The major challenges the horses have faced are interbreeding with donkeys and severe loss of habitat due to goat and sheep breeding.

Several Skyrians are working hard to conserve this endangered species. In 2006 Amanda Simpson and Stathis Katsarelias started the Skyros Island Horse Trust (Map p673; ☑6986051678; www.skyrosislandhorsetrust.com; Trachi; ☺by appointment) 🦮 with just three horses. Their ranch in Trachi, 10km northwest of Skyros Town, has now grown into a home for 36 horses, as they seek to re-establish a herd of pure-bred Skyrian horses and raise awareness about the species' plight. Visitors are welcome at the ranch by appointment; there are openings for volunteers, as well as plans for workshops, and donations are accepted.

You can also see Skyros horses at Mouries Farm (Map p673; ☑6947465900; www.skyrianhorses.weebly.com). Run by Marion Auffray and Manolis Trachanas, the farm is engaged in both pure-breeding and increasing awareness about the horses, with a herd of 45. It also runs a volunteer programme.

For information on breeding efforts, other Skyros farms and Skyrian horses all over Greece, check out the Skyrian Horse Society (www.skyrianhorsesociety.gr).

and Skyrian specialities such as dolmadhes, *fava* and goat in lemon sauce.

Stamatia's Taverna
TAVERNA €

(Map p673; ☑ 6972558232; www.facebook.com/sta matiaskyros; Pefkos Bay; mains €7-11; ⊙ noon-midnight Jun-Sep) Basking in views across sparkling pine-lined Pefkos Bay, with whitewashed wooden tables and a terrace enclosed by stone benches with cushions, always-a-hit Stamatia's rustles up superb daily specials and plenty of grilled fresh fish and meat.

ℹ Getting There & Away

Buses (€2, 15 minutes) to/from Skyros Town, Magazia and Molos connect with all arriving and departing ferries.

Skyros Shipping Co (p661) ferries run to/from Kymi on Evia year-round (€12.10, 1¾ hours, daily) and, from mid-June to mid-September, to/from Skopelos (€20, six hours, three weekly) and Alonnisos (€20, 5¼ hours, three weekly).

Around Skyros

◉ Sights

Palamari
ARCHAEOLOGICAL SITE

(Map p673; ⊙ 7am-3pm Mon-Fri) At the northeast end of the island, the fascinating Palamari Bronze Age excavation dates from between 2500 BCE and 1650 BCE. Paths weave through what was once a powerfully fortified prehistoric coastal settlement near the heart of early Mediterranean trade routes. The visitor centre provides an excellent introduction, and you can see more findings at Skyros Town's Archaeological Museum (p674). The site is signposted down a dirt track off the main Skyros Town–airport road, 8.5km northwest of Skyros Town.

Rupert Brooke's Grave
HISTORIC SITE

(Map p673; Tris Boukes Bay; ⊙ 24hr) The well-tended marble grave of English poet Rupert Brooke lies in a quiet roadside olive grove just inland from Tris Boukes Bay, 11km southeast of Kalamitsa. The gravestone is inscribed with Brooke's most famous sonnet, 'The Soldier'.

Paneri Winery
WINERY

(☑ 6974230437; Trachi; ⊙ by appointment) FREE Call ahead to visit this ambitious family-owned vineyard near the airport (with a winery in the works), which produces six wines including semisweets. The exact location is provided once you make an appointment. On Instagram @paneri_winery.

✕ Eating

★ Taverna Mouries
TAVERNA €

(☑ 22220 93555; Flea; mains €7-11; ⊙ noon-late May-Oct; ☑) ✔ Super-sized, deliciously traditional island cooking rooted in home-grown organic produce is the star at sprawling Mouries, whose soothing terrace sits beneath mulberry trees planted by owner Manolis' grandfather. Goat in lemon is a signature favourite, while terrific veggie bites wander from perfect salads and Skyrian feta to creamy *fava* mopped up with pillowy bread. The sight of Skyrian horses on the family's farm across the road is unforgettable, and the taverna interior is adorned with creative horse-themed artworks.

Taverna Agios Petros
TAVERNA €

(☑ 6972842116; Agios Petros Bay; mains €5-8; ⊙ 10am-late mid-Jun–mid-Sep) ✔ Just 1km inland from Agios Petros beach, in far north Skyros, this outstanding and charmingly rustic terrace taverna rests among vines and a grove of pines, and serves exclusively its own produce. The family also runs popular Amaltheia (☑ 22220 92389, 6983517459; mains €5-10; ⊙ 1-4.30pm & 7pm-midnight Mon-Sat, 1-4.30pm Sun mid-Sep–mid-Jun) in Skyros Town, with the same farm-to-table ethos.

Sunset Cafe
CAFE €

(☑ 22220 91331; www.facebook.com/atsitsa; Atsitsa; snacks €2-4; ⊙ 10am-9pm Jul-Sep) From fresh juices and hearty salads to scrumptious homemade cakes and coffees, the all-organic goodness and elevated seaside setting hit the spot at this pine-shaded boho Atsitsa cafe.

Taverna To Perasma
TAVERNA €

(☑ 22220 92911; Trachi; mains €5-9; ⊙ 10am-11pm) At the airport junction, 10.5km northwest of Skyros Town, this welcoming roadside family restaurant is decked out with Skyrian ceramics and check-print tablecloths. It's hugely popular year-round for its traditional *mayirefta* (ready-cooked meals), roast lamb, grilled meats and tasty veggie starters, all made from delicious home-grown produce.

Asimenos
SEAFOOD €€

(Map p673; ☑ 22220 93007; www.facebook.com/asimenosfishtavern; Aspous; mains €6-12; ⊙ noon-midnight May-Sep) Look for the turquoise-shutter sign and lightly stylish roof terrace, 3.5km south of Skyros Town, to find this sensational seafood taverna. The owners have their own fishing boat, so the super-fresh catch of the day is the thing here, and there are plenty of salads, wines, mezedhes and local cheeses to feast on, too.

AT A GLANCE

★

POPULATION
Corfu Town: 30,000

CAPITAL
Corfu Town (p682)

BEST WINERY
Robola Cooperative
of Kefallonia (p706)

**BEST BOUTIQUE
HOTEL**
Museum Hotel
George Molfetas
(p706)

BEST TAVERNA
Old Perithia Taverna
(p689)

📅

WHEN TO GO
May Life is still quiet
while the wildflowers
are in bloom
everywhere.

Jul Escape the heat
elsewhere in Greece
by heading to the
country's coolest
islands.

Sep Leaves change
colour, and the
robola grapes are
harvested in
Kefallonia.

Corfu (p681)
FRIMUFILMS/SHUTTERSTOCK ©

Ionian Islands

With their cooler climate, abundant olive and cypress trees, and forested mountains, the Ionian Islands (Τα Ιόνια Νησιά) are a lighter, greener variation on the Greek template. Venetian, French and British occupiers have all helped to shape the islands' architecture, culture and cuisine, and contributed to the unique feel of Ionian life.

Each island has its own distinct landscape and history. Corfu Town holds Parisian-style arcades, Venetian alleyways and Italian-inspired delicacies. Lefkada boasts some of Greece's finest turquoise-lapped beaches, while Kefallonia is adorned with vineyards and soaring mountains. Paxi's Italianate harbour villages are postcard pretty, and soulful Ithaki preserves wild terrain and a sense of myth. Zakynthos has sea caves and waters teeming with turtles, and Kythira offers alluring off-the-beaten-track walks.

Ionian Islands Highlights

❶ Corfu Town
(p682) Exploring world-class museums, fortresses and restaurants, as well as Venetian, French and British architecture.

❷ Paxi (p693)
Hopping from one gorgeous harbour to another on this tiny pastoral island.

❸ Fiskardo
(p709) Savouring the flavours in the waterfront restaurants of Kefallonia's best-preserved historic village.

❹ Kefallonia
(p702) Diving and kayaking in the myriad magnificent bays that pepper the island's coastline and hiking through gorgeous forests in the hills.

❺ Beaches
(p701) Ranking your favourite strips of sand, from the busiest on Corfu and Zakynthos to the quieter joys of Paxi and Lefkada's west coast.

❻ Ithaki (p711)
Walking in the footsteps of epic poet Homer.

❼ Kythira (p719)
Discovering tiny villages, waterfalls and remote coves.

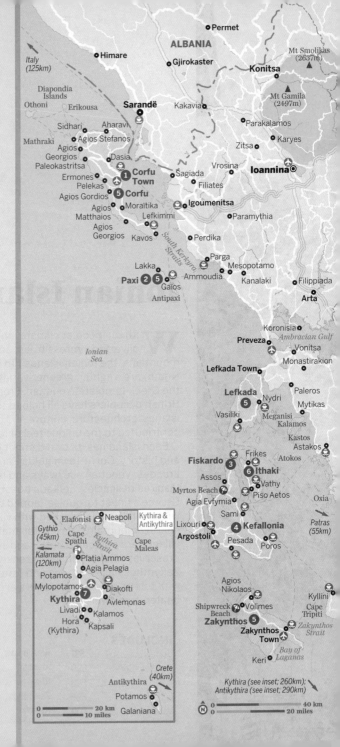

History

The origin of the name 'Ionian' is obscure but may derive from the goddess Io. A paramour of Zeus, she passed through what's now known as the Ionian Sea while fleeing the wrath of Hera.

According to the writings of Homer, the Ionian Islands were important during Mycenaean times, but to date only tombs, not villages or palaces, have been identified. By the 8th century BCE the islands belonged to mighty city state Corinth, but Corfu staged a successful revolt a century later. The Peloponnesian Wars (431–404 BCE) left Corfu as little more than a staging post for whoever happened to be controlling Greece.

By the end of the 3rd century BCE, the Romans ruled the Ionians. Antony and Cleopatra dined on Paxi the night before the Battle of Actium (31 BCE), and the emperor Nero holidayed on Corfu in the 1st century CE. Later, the islands suffered waves of invaders: the Byzantine Empire, Venice, Napoleon (in 1797), Russia (from 1799 to 1807), and then Napoleon again.

In 1815 the Ionians became a British protectorate. Although the British improved infrastructure, developed agriculture and industry, and even taught the Corfiots cricket, nationalists campaigned against their oppressive rule, and by 1864 Britain had relinquished the islands to Greece.

WWII was rough on the Ionians, under occupation first by the Italians and then by the Germans. Further mass emigration followed devastating earthquakes in 1948 and 1953. But by the 1960s foreign holidaymakers were visiting in increasing numbers, and tourism has flourished ever since.

CORFU   KEPKYPA

POP 102,070

From the writings of Gerald and Lawrence Durrell to the place where the shipwrecked Odysseus was soothed and sent on his way home, Corfu has been portrayed as an idyll for centuries. Today this reputation has led to parts of the island being defiled by mass tourism, but despite this, the Corfu of literature does still exist. All you need to do is sail around the corner, walk over the next headland or potter about the rugged interior and a place of bountiful produce, cypress-studded hills, vertiginous villages, and sandy coves lapped by cobalt-blue waters awaits.

Since the 8th century BCE the island the Greeks call Kerkyra has been prized for its untamed beauty and strategic location. Ancient armies fought to possess it, while in the early days of modern Greece it was a beacon of learning. Corfiots remain proud of their intellectual and artistic roots.

❶ Getting There & Away

AIR

Both **easyJet** (www.easyjet.com) and **Ryanair** (www.ryanair.com) offer direct flights in summer between Corfu and the UK, and several other European destinations, while **British Airways** (www.ba.com) also flies from the UK to Corfu. Between May and October, many charter flights come from northern Europe and the UK.

Aegean Airlines (https://en.aegeanair.com) has direct flights to Athens and European destinations.

Sky Express (www.skyexpress.gr) operates a thrice-weekly island-hopping route to Preveza, Kefallonia and Zakynthos. It flies twice weekly to Thessaloniki.

Taxis between the airport and Corfu Town cost around €10, while local bus 15 runs to both Plateia G Theotoki (Plateia San Rocco) in town and the Neo Limani (New Port) beyond.

BOAT

Ferries depart from the Neo Limani (New Port), northwest of Corfu Town's Old Town. Ticket agencies line Ethnikis Antistaseos, facing the Neo Limani.

ANEK/Superfast Lines (www.anek.gr) ferries and/or **Minoan Lines** (www.minoan.gr) connect Corfu with Bari (around €60, eight hours, two weekly) and Ancona (around €85, 14½ hours, one to two daily) in Italy, and Igoumenitsa, where you can pick up other connections.

Ferry services from Corfu Town include **Igoumenitsa** (€12, 1¼ hours, hourly), **Paxi** (Gaïos; high-speed service) with **Ilida** (☑ Corfu 26610 49800, Paxi 26620 32401; Ethnikis Antistaseos 1; €25, 55 to 90 minutes, three to eight daily, mid-March to mid-October), and **Paxi** (Gaïos; slower service) on the **Kamelia Lines** (☑ 26620 32131; www.kamelialines.gr; *Despina* ferry; €20, 90 minutes, one to three daily, April to October; advance bookings essential).

Ferries also sail to **Igoumenitsa** from Lefkimmi (€8, one hour 10 minutes, six daily). There are no ferries sail directly to Zakynthos; fly with **Sky Express** instead.

Some international ferries from Corfu also call in at Igoumenitsa (on the Greek mainland) and Kefallonia. For schedules, see https://travel.viva.gr. If you're heading to Patra, you must catch the ferry to Igoumenitsa first and then get a connecting bus.

BUS

Green Buses (www.greenbuses.gr) goes to Athens (€48.40, 8½ hours, three daily; one via Lefkimmi), Thessaloniki (€38.50, eight hours, twice daily) and Larissa (€30.40, 5½ hours, daily except Sunday). You can also just take one of the

Corfu

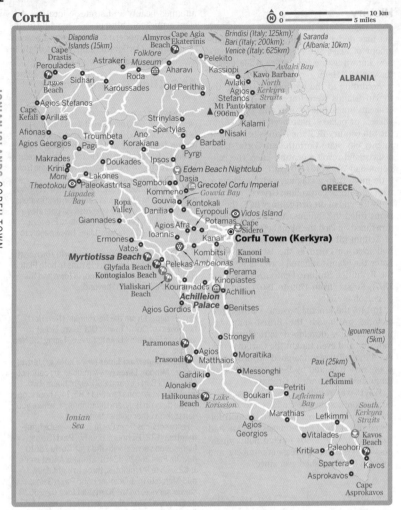

N

0 _____ 10 km
0 _____ 5 miles

Diapondia
Islands (15km)
Cape Agia
Almyros Ekaterinis
Beach
Brindisi (Italy; 125km);
Bari (Italy; 200km);
Venice (Italy; 625km)
Saranda
(Albania; 10km)

Cape
Drastis
Peroulades
Astrakeri
Folklore
Museum
Pelekito
Avlaki Bay

Lagos
Beach
Sidhari
Roda
Aharavi
Kassiopi
Kavo Barbaro
ALBANIA

Agios Stefanos
Karoussades
Old Perithia
Avlaki
North
Kerkyra
Straits

Cape
Kefali
Arillas
Agios
Stefanos
Mt Pantokrator
(906m)

Afionas
Strinylas
Spartylas
Kalami

Agios Georgios
Troumbeta
Pagi
Ano
Korakiana
Nisaki

Makrades
Doukades
Pyrgi
Barbati

Krini
Moni
Theotokou
Lakones
Paleokastritsa
Sgombou
Dasia
Ipsos
Edem Beach Nightclub

Liapades
Bay
Ropa
Valley
Kommeno
Grecotel Corfu Imperial
Gouvia Bay

Giannades
Danilia
Gouvia
Kontokali

Ermones
Agios Afra
Ioannis
Evropouli
Potamas
Vidos Island
Cape
Sidero

Vatos
Kanali
Corfu Town (Kerkyra)

Myrtiotissa Beach
Pelekas
Ambelonas
Kombitsi
Kanoni
Peninsula

Glyfada Beach
Kontogialos Beach
Yialiskari
Beach
Kouramades
Achillion
Perama
Kinopiastes

Agios Gordios
Achilleion
Palace
Benitses

Igoumenitsa
(5km)

Paramonas
Strongyli

Prasoudi
Agios
Matthaios
Moraïtika
Paxi (25km)

Gardiki
Messonghi
Cape
Lefkimmi

Alonaki
Petriti

Halikounas
Beach
Lake
Korission
Boukari
Lefkimmi
Bay
South
Kerkyra
Straits

Ionian
Sea
Marathias
Lefkimmi

Agios
Georgios
Vitalades
Kavos
Beach

Kritika
Paleohori

Spartera
Kavos

Asprokavos

Cape
Asprokavos

GREECE

many daily ferries to the mainland and catch the bus of your choice from there.

ℹ Getting Around

BUS

Long-distance Green Buses radiate out from Corfu Town's **long-distance bus station** (☏ 26610 28900; https://greenbuses.gr; Lefkimmis 13) in the New Town. Fares cost €1.50 to €4.80; services are reduced on Saturday, and may be nonexistent on Sundays and holidays.

CAR & MOTORCYCLE

Car- and motorbike-hire outlets (Alamo, Hertz, Europcar etc) abound at the airport, in Corfu Town and at the resorts. Prices start at around €50 per day.

Corfu Town   Κέρκυρα

POP 30,000

Imbued with Venetian grace and elegance, historic Corfu Town (also known as Kerkyra) stands halfway down the island's east coast. The name Corfu, meaning 'peaks', refers to its twin hills, each topped by a massive fortress built to withstand Ottoman sieges. Sitting between the two, the Old Town is a tight-packed warren of winding lanes, some bursting with fine restaurants, lively bars and intriguing shops, others timeless back alleys where washing lines stretch from balcony to balcony. It also holds some majestic architecture, including the splendid Liston arcade, and high-class museums, along with no fewer than 39 churches.

During the day, cruise passengers and day-trippers bustle through the streets; come evening, the bustle continues around the bar areas. When it comes to drinking, dining and dancing, this is the hottest spot in the Ionian Islands.

◉ Sights

The Old Town's most eye-catching feature is the grand French-built Liston (Map p684) arcade, facing the Old Fort across the lawns of the Spianada (Map p684) and lined with packed cafes. At its northern end, the neoclassical Palace of St Michael & St George contains the excellent Corfu Museum of Asian Art. Head inland and you can lose yourself for a happy hour or two amid the maze-like alleyways, seeking out sumptuous Orthodox churches or cosy cafes as the mood takes you.

Continue southwest, skirting the mighty Neo Frourio (New Fort; p685), to reach the New Town, busy with everyday shops and services and centring on Plateia G Theotoki (also known as Plateia San Rocco). To the south, around the curving Bay of Garitsa, the ruin-strewn Mon Repos Estate (p686) marks the site of the ancient settlement of Palaeopolis.

Palace of St Michael & St George PALACE
(Map p684; ✆26610 48690; adult/child €6/3/free; ⊗8am-8pm Apr-Oct, 9am-4pm Tue-Sun Nov-Mar) Beyond the northern end of the Spianada , the smart Regency-style Palace of St Michael and St George was built by the British from 1819 onwards, to house the high commissioner and the Ionian Parliament. It's now home to the prestigious Corfu Museum of Asian Art (the entry fee covers both this museum and the palace). Two municipal art galleries, I (entry €3) and II (⊗10am-4pm Tue-Sun) FREE, are housed in one annexe, and its small formal gardens make a pleasant refuge.

★Corfu Museum of Asian Art MUSEUM
(Map p684; ✆26610 30443; www.matk.gr; Palace of St Michael & St George; adult/concession/child incl palace entry €6/3/free; ⊗8am-8pm Apr-Oct, 9am-4pm Tue-Sun Nov-Mar) Home to stunning artefacts ranging from prehistoric bronzes to works in onyx and ivory, this excellent museum occupies the central portions of the Palace of St Michael and St George. One gallery provides a chronological overview of

Chinese ceramics, and showcases remarkable jade carvings and snuff bottles. The India section opens with Alexander the Great, 'When Greece Met India', and displays fascinating Graeco-Buddhist figures, including a blue-grey schist Buddha. A Japanese section incorporates magnificent samurai armour and Noh masks.

Municipal Art Gallery I GALLERY
(Map p684; ✆26610 48690; www.artcorfu.com; Palace of St Michael & St George; adult/child €3/free; ⊗10am-4pm Tue-Sun) Make the effort to find this gallery – it's entered from the exterior or on the eastern side of the Palace of St Michael and St George. You'll be rewarded with a handful of high-quality Byzantine icons, including 16th-century works by the Cretan Damaskinos, plus a more extensive array of canvases by Corfiot painters. Look out for the work of Italian-influenced 19th-century father-and-son artists Spyridon and Pavos Prossalendis.

★Palaio Frourio FORTRESS
(Old Fort; Map p684; ✆26610 48310; adult/concession/child €6/3/free; ⊗8am-8pm Apr-Oct, 8.30am-3pm Nov-Mar) The rocky headland that juts east from Corfu Town is topped by the Venetian-built 14th-century Palaio Frourio. Before that, already enclosed within massive stone walls, it cradled the entire Byzantine city. A solitary bridge crosses its seawater moat.

Only parts of this huge site, which also holds later structures from the British era, are accessible to visitors; wander up to the lighthouse on the larger of the two hills for superb views. A gatehouse contains the small Byzantine Collection of Corfu, while the temple-like Church of St George stands on a large terrace to the south. Note that in season the queues for entry can be very long.

Corfu Living History HOUSE
(Casa Parlante; Map p684; ✆26610 49190; www.casaparlante.gr; N Theotoki 16; adult/child €7/5; ⊗10am-6pm) This town house has been remodelled to illustrate the daily lives of a fictitious merchant family from the mid-19th century. Enthusiastic guides make the whole experience fun and informative, while in each room waxworks undertake small, endlessly repeated movements. The tour is enlivened by the free glass of 19th-century-style rose liquor visitors get to try.

Vidos Island ISLAND
(Map p682) Hourly boats from the Old Port make the 10-minute crossing to tiny, thickly wooded Vidos Island (€4 return), immediately

Corfu Old Town

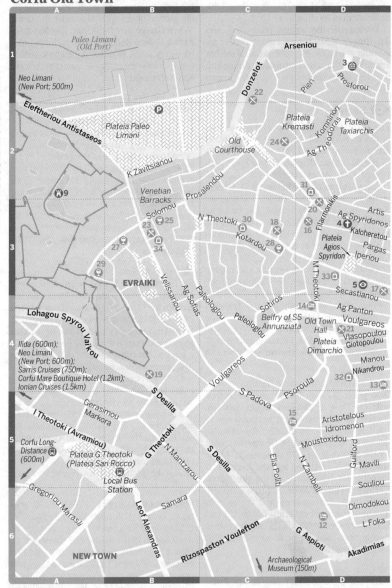

offshore. The island is the final resting place of thousands of Serbian soldiers killed during WWII. There's a monument to them here and also some abandoned buildings once used by the scouts. There's a taverna at the jetty, but the big attraction is to walk the 600m across the island to reach a couple of attractive beaches.

Archaeological Museum
MUSEUM

(☏ 26610 30680; www.amcorfu.gr; Vraïla 1; adult/concession/child €6/3/free; ☺ 8am-8pm Thu-Tue) Built in the 1960s, Corfu Town's Archaeological Museum has finally reopened after nearly a decade of renovations. The result of this work is a modern and well-lit museum

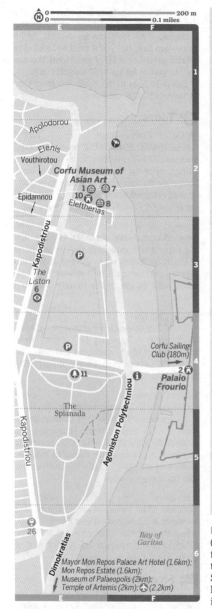

(although some of the English labelling is a bit hit and miss) housing some 16,000 pieces found around Corfu. The highlight of the fine collection is a massive gorgon pediment (590–580 BCE) from the Temple of Artemis (Kanoni Peninsula) on the nearby Kanoni Peninsula.

Neo Frourio　　　　　　　　FORTRESS

(New Fort; Map p684; ⊙9am-3.30pm) **FREE** The forbidding Neo Frourio is in fact only a little younger than the Old Fort across town. Surrounded by massive walls that crown the low hill at the western edge of the Old Town, it too dates from the Venetian era. Climbing the stairway at the western end of Solomou brings you to the entrance, where dank tunnels and passages lead through the walls. The ramparts beyond enjoy wonderful views.

Antivouniotissa Museum　　　　MUSEUM

(Byzantine Museum; Map p684; ☑26610 38313; www.antivouniotissamuseum.gr; adult/concession/

child €4/2/free; ⊙8am-3pm Tue-Sun) Home to an outstanding collection of Byzantine and post-Byzantine icons and artefacts, the exquisite, timber-roofed Church of Our Lady of Antivouniotissa has a double role as church and museum. It stands atop a short, broad stairway that climbs from shore-front Arseniou, and frames views out towards wooded Vidos Island (p683).

Church of Agios Spyridon   CHURCH
(Map p684; Agios Spyridonos; ⊙8am-9pm) Pilgrims and day-trippers alike throng this Old Town landmark. As well as magnificent frescoes, the small 16th-century basilica holds the remains of Corfu's patron saint, Spyridon, a 4th-century Cypriot shepherd. His body, brought here from Constantinople in 1453, lies in an elaborate silver casket, and is paraded through the town on festival days.

Mon Repos Estate   PARK
(Kanoni Peninsula; ⊙8am-3pm Tue-Sun) FREE This park-like wooded estate 2km around the bay south of the Old Town was the site of Corfu's most important ancient settlement, Palaeopolis. More recently, in 1921, the secluded neoclassical villa that now holds the Museum of Palaeopolis (☑26610 32783; adult/concession €4/2) was the birthplace of Prince Philip of Greece, who went on to marry Britain's Princess Elizabeth (now the current Queen). Footpaths lead through the woods to ancient ruins, including those of a Doric temple atop a small coastal cliff.

It takes half an hour to walk to Mon Repos from town, or you can catch bus 2a from the Spianada (€1.20, every 20 minutes). Bring a picnic and plenty of water; there are no shops nearby.

★ Achilleion Palace   HISTORIC BUILDING
(Map p682; ☑26610 56245; www.achilleion-corfu.gr; Gastouri; adult/concession €8/6; ⊙8am-8pm Apr-Nov, to 4pm Dec-Mar) Set atop a steep coastal hill 12km south of Corfu Town, the Achilleion Palace was built during the 1890s as the summer palace of Austria's empress Elisabeth, the niece of King Otto of Greece. The palace's two principal features are its intricately decorated central staircase, rising in geometrical flights, and its sweeping garden terraces, which command eye-popping views.

There's surprisingly little to see inside, other than mementos of Elisabeth, who was assassinated in Genoa in 1898, and of the German kaiser Wilhelm II, who bought the palace in 1907 and added its namesake statue of Achilles Triumphant.

It's well worth getting an audio guide; the descriptions of various statues, paintings and background are excellent for context. Audio guides are free, but you'll need to hand over official government ID of some kind. You can use the guides for up to 50 minutes only.

Bus N-10 runs to the Achilleion from Corfu Town (€1.70, 20 minutes).

☞ Tours

★ Corfu Walking Tours   WALKING
(☑6932894466, 6945894450; www.corfuwalkingtours.com; €64-78) Walking tours with expert guides, covering the Old Town (€64, three hours) or further afield, including popular options oriented towards eating or wine tasting (from €68), and customised hiking trips.

Corfu Walks & Hikes   HIKING
(www.walking-corfu.blogspot.co.uk) Guided hiking expeditions exploring the wilder parts of Corfu, including up to the top of Mt Pantokrator and along the hills around Paleokastritsa, with an eye to the island's flora and fauna.

Ionian Cruises   CRUISE
(☑26610 38690; www.ionian-cruises.com; Ethnikis Antistaseos 4; ⊙7am-8pm) Day cruises from the New Port to the mainland and Sivota Islands (€27), south to Paxi and Antipaxi (€28) or across to Albania (€53).

Sarris Cruises   CRUISE
(☑26610 25317; www.sarriscruises.gr; Mouriki 1) Day trips from the New Port include an excursion to the ancient World Heritage–listed ruins at Butrinti in Albania (€59; passports required), and a boat trip taking in Paxi, the Blue Caves and Antipaxi (€40) – go on a calm day. Transfers included.

Trailriders   HORSE RIDING
(☑69466 53317; www.trailriderscorfu.com; Ano Korakiana; ⊙10am-noon & 4-6pm Mon-Fri) Horse riding through the olive groves around the village of Ano Korakiana, 18km northwest of Corfu Town. Book in advance.

⌂ Sleeping

As many island visitors head straight to the beaches and resorts, Corfu Town holds fewer accommodation options than you might expect. Those that do exist tend to be relatively pricey, even in low season.

★ Bella Venezia   BOUTIQUE HOTEL €€
(Map p684; ☑26610 46500; www.bellavenezia hotel.com; N Zambeli 4; d incl breakfast from €130;

❄ ☎) Enter this historic neoclassical villa, set in a peaceful central street, and you'll be seduced by its charm. It features an elegant lobby with candelabras, velvet chairs and a piano. The plush, high-ceilinged rooms (some with balconies) have fine city or garden views, while the garden breakfast area is delightful. The cheaper loft rooms have horizontal windows but no outlook.

★**Puppet Guest House** GUESTHOUSE €€
(Map p684; ☑ 26610 40707; www.facebook.com/ Puppet.corfu; Evaggelistrias 1; d incl breakfast €125; ❄ ☎) Above a slightly eccentric bar full of string puppets, this wonderful guesthouse has big, bright rooms and fairy-tale decor and art that certainly grab the attention! Some of the rooms have balconies overlooking the pretty town-hall square and a sea of terracotta rooftops. A great breakfast is included, as is engrossing conversation with the genial owner.

★**Locandieta Guest House** GUESTHOUSE €€
(Map p684; ☑ 26610 39035; www.locorfu.com; Ioanni Gennata 8; s/d incl breakfast €100/120; ❄ ☎) This beautiful, cosy guesthouse just back from the Spianada (p683) is stuffed with arty touches, including staircases adorned with driftwood and rough-textured beach rocks in the bathrooms. A superb breakfast is included and the reception area even has a genuine water well. The owner is a fantastic host. Advance reservations are vital.

Mayor Mon Repos
Palace Art Hotel HOTEL €€
(☑ 26610 32783; www.mayormonrepospalace.com; Dimokratias; d incl breakfast from €127; ❄ ☎ ≋) A classy, modern resort hotel, with its own spa, bistro and bar, at the southern end of the long, curving Bay of Garitsa. All the cool, contemporary cream-toned rooms have balconies, and many face directly out to sea. It's a 20-minute walk from the Old Town and a few hundred metres north of Mon Repos Estate.

Corfu Mare Boutique Hotel HOTEL €€€
(☑ 26610 31011; www.corfumare.gr; Nikolau Zervou 5; d/ste incl breakfast €286/470; ❄ ☎ ≋) This eye-wateringly expensive but palatial villa-like hotel, just up from the New Port, is open to adults only. While it's larger than 'boutique' might suggest, it's every bit as stylish and modern. Each room has its own tasteful decor, with huge prints and striking wallpaper on themes such as pop art and art deco. There's also bar, restaurant and pool.

Siorra Vittoria BOUTIQUE HOTEL €€€
(Map p684; ☑ 26610 36300; www.siorravittoria. com; Stefanou Padova 36; d incl breakfast from €185; P ❄ ☎) Expect luxury and style at this quiet 19th-century Old Town mansion, where restored traditional architecture meets modern amenities; marble bathrooms, crisp linens and genteel service make for a relaxed stay. Breakfast is served in your room or beneath an ancient magnolia in the peaceful garden.

 Eating

Corfiot cuisine shows the delicious influence of many cultures, especially Italian. Solid, but few outstanding, restaurants and tavernas are scattered throughout the Old Town.

★**Pane & Souvlaki** GRILL €
(Map p684; ☑ 26610 20100; www.panesouvlaki. com; Guilford 77; mains €6-13.50; ☺ noon-1am) Arguably the Old Town's best-value budget option (the locals rave), with outdoor tables on the town-hall square, this quick-fire restaurant does exactly what its name suggests, serving up three skewers of chicken or pork with chunky chips, dipping sauce and warm pitta in individual metal trays. The salads and burgers are good, too.

Chrisomalis TAVERNA €
(Map p684; ☑ 26610 30342; N Theotoki 6; mains €7-13; ☺ noon-midnight) Going strong since 1904, this traditional little taverna was a haunt of the Durrell family and actor Anthony Quinn, and there are old pictures on the wall of Gerald and Lawrence Durrell with the owner. Follow your nose to the traditional grill for souvlaki, pork chops and swordfish. Warm service and pavement tables make it ideal for people-watching.

Oinos kai Geuseis MEDITERRANEAN €€
(Map p684; ☑ 26610 8335; Mitropoleos 22; tapas €4-8; ☺ 6pm-midnight) Sip a glass of wine and look forward to tucking into tasty treats such as shrimps with feta or fried fish marinated in sweet and sour sauce at this exciting new bar-restaurant serving what the owners describe as Greek 'tapas'. Ideal place for an *apéro* with friends.

Salto Wine Bar MEDITERRANEAN €€
(Map p684; ☑ 26613 02325; www.saltowinebar. gr; Donzelot 23; mains €9-18; ☺ 6.30pm-12.30am Mon-Sat, 12.30-4.30pm & 6.30pm-12.30am Sun; ❄) This small, bright and modern wine bar and bistro down on the waterfront is causing waves among foodies in Corfu. With a menu

strong on Italian influences and grilled meats, the place was a favourite for the cast and crew of hit UK TV series *The Durrells*.

Estiatorio Bellissimo
MEDITERRANEAN €€

(Map p684; ☑ 26610 41112; Plateia Limonia; mains €8-18; ◷10am-midnight) The Old Town holds few nicer spots for an al-fresco evening than this casual but stylish restaurant that spreads across a peaceful pedestrian square. It's renowned for its pizzas but also excels in Corfiot specialities such as *pastitsadha kokora* – chicken in red sauce, 'with a lot of cheese' – plus crêpes and salads.

Anthos
SEAFOOD €€

(Map p684; ☑ 26610 32252; www.facebook.com/anthosrestaurant; Maniarizi-Arlioti 15; mains €10-21; ◷noon-midnight Mon-Sat, 6pm-midnight Sun; ☎) Much-loved little back-alley restaurant with a handful of outdoor tables. Most diners are here for the seafood, savouring dishes such as squid carpaccio, octopus with *fava*-bean mousse, and grilled sea bass, but it also serves standard Greek meat favourites.

To Tavernaki tis Marinas
TAVERNA €€

(Map p684; ☑ 26611 00792; Velissariou 35; mains €8-15; ◷noon-11.30pm) The stone walls, hardwood floors and cheerful staff lift the ambience of this taverna. Check the daily specials, or choose anything from *mousakas* (baked layers of aubergine or courgette, minced meat and potatoes topped with cheese sauce), sardines-in-the-oven or steak. Accompany it all with a dram of ouzo or *tsipouro* (a distilled spirit similar to raki).

★Fishalida
SEAFOOD €€€

(Map p684; ☑ 26614 01213; Spirou Vlaikou 1; mains €12-20; ◷11am-midnight; ✦) Right next to the market and a fishmongers, this is an easygoing, youthful place to eat inventive and truly superb seafood such as prawn tortellini with wild-mushroom sauce or the unexpectedly delightful octopus with hummus. There's a light-filled interior or you can eat outside at one of the couple of tables. Advance bookings almost essential.

★Venetian Well
INTERNATIONAL €€€

(Map p684; ☑ 26615 50955; www.venetianwell.gr; Plateia Kremasti; mains €16-24; ◷7-11.30pm Mon-Sat; ✦☎) Corfu Town's finest special-occasion restaurant has a beautifully faded square to itself, hidden away near the cathedral and complete with a genuine Venetian well. The exquisite contemporary approach to cuisine adorns local meats, fish and vegetables with all sorts of foams, mousses and

gels; even if you can't always tell what you're eating, it's invariably delicious.

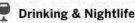

Drinking & Nightlife

Perhaps the best place to kick-start the evening is on the stylish Liston arcade; after that, the choices are legion.

For dance venues, head after 11pm to Corfu's disco strip, starting west beyond the New Port, along Ethnikis Antistaseos; take a taxi, as it's a busy, unlit road without walkways. A €10 or so admission fee usually includes one drink.

★Firi Firi – The Beer House
BAR

(Map p684; ☑ 26610 33953; www.facebook.com/FiriFiriCorfu; Solomou 1; ◷6pm-2am Tue-Sun; ☎) Sample local and imported beers, either inside the custard-coloured villa at the foot of the steps leading up to the Neo Frourio (p685) or at the terraced tables beside the neighbouring church; if you find it hard to leave, it grills up some decent dishes, too.

★Antonis Toursas Juice Bar
JUICE BAR

(Map p684; ☑ 26610 22550; Solomou 28; juices €2.50-3; ◷8am-10pm) Brilliant little juice bar that has boxes of fruit piled up outside like a fruit shop (which it also is). Pick your five a day and get them blended straight up into a juice to enjoy at the small bar.

★Mikro Café
BAR

(Map p684; ☑ 26610 31009; N Theotoki 42; ◷9am-midnight) You can smell the coffee beans roasting from 25m down the street, and whether your favoured beverage comes from these beans or is something a little more alcoholic, the Old Town holds no finer spot for drinking and people-watching than the delightful, multilevel, vine-shaded terrace of the convivial 'little café'.

54 Dreamy Nights
CLUB

(☑ 6940645436; www.54dreamynights.com; Ethnikis Antistaseos 54; ◷10pm-late; ☎) Gleaming, bright-white nightspot, west along the New Port, with a minimalist aesthetic, spectacular night shows and a retractable roof. Open-air DJ parties and live gigs by big-name Greek music stars attract up to 3000 clubbers.

Polytechno
BAR

(Map p684; ☑ 26610 27794; www.facebook.com/pg/polytechnocorfu; Sholemvorgou 39; ◷8.30pm-late; ☎) Bar and venue for performance art and experimental music. In-the-know patrons reach it by turning left along the hillside footpath at the top of the steps up from Solomou, below the Neo Frourio.

OLD PERITHIA

Falling away from the northern slope of Mt Pantokrator is a rugged land of tumbling valleys, beautiful cypress forests and mountain meadows where the only noise is goat bells. It's a magical part of the island that's well worth sacrificing some beach time to explore.

The remote village of Old Perithia is an ideal place to make for in the hills. Not so long ago lack of work and opportunities meant that this village of ramshackle stone houses was almost abandoned. Today, thanks to tourism and locals being able to work from home, the village is slowly coming back to life. Several buildings have been reconstructed and there are a couple of wonderful tavernas. The Old Perithia Taverna (☑ 26630 98055; Old Perithia; mains €5-10; ⊘ 11am-8pm), which has been a family-run restaurant for 150 years, has shelves full of dusty farming implements and sepia-coloured family photographs. Almost anything you eat here is outstanding, but the courgette nuggets followed by rabbit stew washed down with rough homemade red wine might turn out to be the best meal you eat in Corfu.

When you've finished eating, lace up your hiking boots and set off along any of the many country tracks and walking trails that spiral away from the village. Note that trail information and signposting are very limited, so unless you're on a walking tour you'll probably have to make it up as you go along.

Cavalieri Hotel Rooftop Bar   BAR
(Map p684; ☑ 26610 39041; www.cavalieri-hotel. com; Kapodistriou 4; ⊘ 6.30pm-late) Rather wonderful rooftop bar that makes an ideal venue for mellow predinner drinks, with stunning views across the Spianada to the Palaio Frourio. There's the hope that you'll stay for an Italian-flavoured meal, but you don't have to.

🔒 Shopping

The Old Town is crammed with shopping opportunities. The heaviest concentration of souvenir shops, which sell everything from 'evil eye' amulets and olive-wood carvings to pashminas and perfume, is along narrow Filarmonikis between the two main churches, while N Theotoki is good for idiosyncratic boutiques.

★**Corfu Gallery**   ART
(Map p684; ☑ 26610 25796; www.corfugallery.com; N Theotoki 72; ⊘ 10am-11pm) Fabulous sculptures, paintings and objets d'art are sold at this gallery. The pieces are uniformly expensive, but you're welcome to just browse.

★**Sweet'n'Spicy Bahar**   SPICES
(Map p684; ☑ 26610 33848; www.sweetnspicy. gr; Agias Sofias 12; ⊘ 9.45am-2pm) Gloriously aromatic spice and condiment shop, run by an ever-so-enthusiastic Greek-Canadian-Lebanese woman with a palpable love for devising her own enticing mixes of Greek and imported spices.

Icon Gallery   ARTS & CRAFTS
(Map p684; ☑ 26614 00928; www.iconcraft.gr; Guilford 52; ⊘ 10am-10.30pm Mon-Sat; 🛜) True to

its name, this hole-in-the-wall boutique sells stunning icons, handmade by an artists' co-op, as well as fine heraldic art and antiques. Some of the icons have a distinctly modern twist – Adam being titillated by a not-very-shy Eve, for example – that the Church surely wouldn't approve of!

Corfu Sandals   SHOES
(Map p684; ☑ 26610 47301; www.facebook.com/ corfusandals; Philhellinon 9; ⊘ 9am-11pm) This standout shoe store, on the narrow lane that holds Corfu Town's heaviest (and tackiest) concentration of souvenir shops, sells well-priced handmade leather sandals in all styles and sizes, many with ergonomic bubble soles. To find it, look out for the sandals that only a giant could wear.

Papagiorgis   FOOD & DRINKS
(Map p684; ☑ 26610 39474; www.papagiorgis. gr; N Theotoki 32; ⊘ 9am-midnight) Irresistible old-fashioned patisserie that's an Old Town landmark thanks to its 40 flavours of ice cream, plus a mouth-watering array of homemade tarts, biscuits and honey.

ℹ Information

Corfu General Hospital (☑ 26613 60400; www. gnkerkyras.gr; Kontokali) About 8km west of the town centre.

Municipal Tourist Kiosk (Map p684; www. corfu.gr; Spianada; ⊘ 8am-4pm Mon-Fri Mar-Nov) Helps with accommodation, transport and things to do around Corfu.

Tourist Police (☑ 26610 29169; I Andreadi 1) In the New Town, off Plateia G Theotoki (Plateia San Rocco).

OFF THE BEATEN TRACK

COASTAL WALK: AGIOS STEFANOS TO AVLAKI

Large parts of Corfu's coastline have been scarred by mass tourism, but fortunately there still exist some beaches without a single hotel, taverna or sunlounger. Some of the most untouched shores in all of the Ionians can be found in the very far northeast of Corfu, and only those prepared to go to the effort of walking there will get to enjoy them. Indeed, outside high summer there's a very good chance you'll have some of these beaches all to yourself. A 6.5km coastal path heads from the port village of Agios Stefanos to the long windsurfing beach of Avlaki. The walk takes 1½ hours, but bring a picnic and allow a full day so that you can enjoy the beaches.

The trail is well signposted and begins from the Eucalyptus Bar at the northern edge of Agios Stefanos. The trail follows the bay along the beach and then crosses multiple headlands and seven beaches, including Vromolimni and Akoli, both backed by small lakes. It's also worth making a short detour off the main trail to the gorgeous pebble beach of Arias, which is hemmed in by thick forest. From the turn-off for the Arias detour, the main trail then crosses straight over the peninsula to further beaches before arriving in Avlaki. However, a minor trail veers through dank, tangled forest to the headland of Kavo Barbaro, which has wanderlust-tingling views to Albania. There's a small cove beach here, as well as great snorkelling.

Unfortunately, even in this apparently untouched area the impact of humans is only too apparent in the piles of plastic waste washed up at the beaches' high-tide line. Unless you've prearranged return transport, once you reach Avlaki you'll have to retrace your steps to Agios Stefanos or take a short cut following the road over the hill (4km; one hour).

TRAVEL AGENCIES

All Ways Travel (☑ 26610 33955; www.allwaystravel.com.gr; Plateia G Theotoki 34) Helpful English-speaking staff in the New Town's main square.

Aperghi Travel (☑ 26610 48713; www.aperghitravel.gr; I Polyla 1) Handles tours and accommodation, especially for walkers on the Corfu Trail (www.thecorfutrail.com).

Pachis Travel (☑ 26610 28298; www.pachistravel.com; Guilford 7; ⊙ 9.30am-3pm & 6-8.30pm Mon-Fri, 9.30am-2pm Sat) Busy little agency that's useful for hotels, ferry and plane tickets, and excursions to Paxi.

ⓘ Getting There & Around

Corfu Town is at the centre of an efficient network of local buses, and you can get pretty much anywhere on the island from the long-distance bus station (p682) in the New Town.

Local blue buses depart from the **local bus station** (Map p684; ☑ 26610 31595; www.astikoktelkerkyras.gr; Plateia G Theotoki) in the Old Town. Journeys cost €1.20 or €1.70. Buy tickets at the booth on Plateia G Theotoki or on the bus itself. All trips are less than 30 minutes. Service is reduced at weekends.

Most Corfu Town rental companies are based along the northern waterfront.

Budget (☑ 26610 24404; www.budget.gr; Eleftheriou Antistaseos 6)

Sunrise (☑ 26610 44325; www.corfusunrise.com; Ethnikis Antistaseos 16)

Top Cars (☑ 26610 35237; www.carrentalcorfu.com; Donzelot 25)

Northern Corfu

Immediately north of Corfu Town, the coastline consists of an all-but-continuous strip of busy beach resorts, including Gouvia, Dasia, Ipsos and Pyrgi. These offer all you need for a family holiday but are otherwise unremarkable.

Continue north, though, and it's like heading 50 years back in time to the days before mass tourism struck parts of Corfu. The coastal road begins to wind and undulate around the massif formed by the island's highest peak, Mt Pantokrator (906m), and the scenery becomes ever more attractive, with olive groves dipping down to sapphire waters and hidden coves. Many of the pretty little inlets that punctuate the seafront here hold a delightful village or at least a taverna.

An enjoyable mishmash of everything from accordions and olive presses to puppets and phones, the cavernous private Folklore Museum (Map p682; ☑ 26630 63052; www.museum-acharavi.webs.com; adult/child €3/1.50; ⊙ 10am-2pm Mon-Sat) in Aharavi is a fun place to learn about Corfu's traditional way of life.

🛏 Sleeping

Northern Corfu (and the northeast in particular) is the most enticing and attractive part of the island because it's the least developed. Thus accommodation is quite limited, so you should book as far ahead as possible. Accommodation in the north is generally of a high standard.

★ **Manessis Apartments** APARTMENT €€
(☑ 6973918416; Kassiopi; 4-person apt €110; ❋ ⏾) Lovely, refurbished, bougainvillea-draped two-bedroom apartments, with sea-facing balconies, set in flower-filled gardens towards the far end of Kassiopi's picturesque harbour. The friendly and super-helpful Greek-Irish owners make sure everything goes smoothly. It's hard to find better.

Theofilos Studios & Apartments APARTMENT €€
(☑ 26630 81261; www.theofiloskassiopi.com; Kassiopi; d €80; ❋ ⏾) A block back from Kassiopi's northern beach, but still with memorable sea views, this is a super-friendly place to stay, with fairly plain but comfortable apartments (kitchenettes are very basic), and an owner who'll happily divulge tips and suggestions for things to do.

Melina Bay Hotel BOUTIQUE HOTEL €€
(☑ 26630 81030; http://melinabay.com; Kassiopi; s/d/tr €90/90/114; ❋ ⏾) Gleaming modern hotel immediately below the castle and with a drop-dead-stunning view of Kassiopi's harbourfront. The small rooms have a sailing-ship theme and excellent amenities. Book ahead.

Grecotel Corfu Imperial RESORT €€€
(Map p682; ☑ 26610 88400; www.corfuimperial.com; Kommeno; d incl breakfast from €470; ⏾ May-Oct; ❋ ⏾ ▩) One of the most lavish hotels in Greece, this place occupies a regal waterfront position at the western tip of the curving peninsula that defines Kommeno Bay. Ultra-luxurious rooms are set in pastel-toned seaview villas, plus there are three fine-dining restaurants and a spa. Normally there's a two-night minimum stay in summer; rates drop considerably in low season.

✗ Eating & Drinking

White House MEDITERRANEAN €€
(☑ 26630 91040; www.corfu-kalami.gr; Kalami; mains €10-23; ⏾ 9am-midnight) Almost a site of pilgrimage for fans of the Durrell family, this utterly ravishing waterfront restaurant in the former home of writer Lawrence Durrell has tables quayside – many diners arrive by motorboat – as well as on a vine-shaded terrace. The appetisers are predominantly Greek, the mains Italian. The food is decent but, as is to be expected, a bit overpriced.

Cavo Barbaro SEAFOOD €€
(☑ 26630 81905; Avlaki; mains €10-22; ⏾ 9.30am-11.30pm) With widescreen views of the beach, and sea breezes wafting through the garden, this pretty and very spacious restaurant makes a charming spot for a leisurely meal of octopus, calamari, *saganaki* (fried cheese), *mousakas* (baked layers of eggplant or zucchini, minced meat and potatoes topped with cheese sauce) or swordfish.

To Fagopotion TAVERNA €€
(☑ 26630 82020; Agios Stefanos; €11-19; ⏾ noon-1am) Of the procession of similar tavernas that serve up seafront dining at Agios Stefanos, Fagopotion, presided over by the genial Christos, has to be the best for its inventive Greek seafood and meat cuisine.

Edem Beach Nightclub CLUB
(Map p682; ☑ 26610 93013; www.edemclub.com; Dasia; ⏾ 11am-5am) Head for a sunset chill-out at one of Greece's top beach bars before the party starts at around 11pm. To get here from Corfu Town, catch bus 7 (€1.70, 30 minutes) from Plateia G Theotoki.

ℹ Information

San Stefano Travel (☑ 26630 51771, 26630 81335; www.san-stefano.gr; Agios Stefanos) offers all travel services, including boat rental and excursions to the Diapondia Islands and other nearby islands.

LOCAL KNOWLEDGE

THE DURRELLS
....
British writers Gerald and Lawrence Durrell lived on Corfu for the four years preceding WWII. Gerald, then a child but later a prominent naturalist, chronicled his eccentric family's island idyll in several charming and hilarious books, the most famous of which is *My Family and Other Animals*. The three houses where they lived and which featured in this book are all north of Corfu Town and are not open to visitors. The White House at Kalami, however, which was home to Lawrence and his wife Nancy while he wrote his lyrical nonfiction account of Corfu, *Prospero's Cell*, is now a lovely restaurant.

As for the hit UK TV series *The Durrells*, its principal shooting location is Danilia, a restored, once-abandoned village that is only accessible to guests of the Grecotel Corfu Imperial resort on the coast.

ⓘ Getting There & Away

Green Buses (www.greenbuses.gr) runs frequent services from Corfu Town, both anticlockwise along the northwestern coast as far as Kassiopi, and straight to Roda and its neighbouring resorts on the north coast.

To explore the region at all thoroughly, however, you'll need your own transport.

Western Corfu

Corfu's western shoreline boasts some of the island's most spectacular scenery, its prettiest villages and its finest beaches. No coastal road connects the many sandy coves that nibble into the towering cliffs along its central stretch, so sightseers must choose their targets wisely. Paleokastritsa in the north has a great beach, a beautiful monastery and fine hiking; Pelekas is a delightful hilltop village; and Agios Gordios in the south is a backpackers' haven with a long, sandy beach.

Paleokastritsa & North

The popular resort area of Paleokastritsa, 23km northwest of Corfu Town, stretches for nearly 3km through a series of small, picturesque bays. Craggy mountains swathed in cypress and olive trees tower above. The real treat comes at the resort's end, where an exquisite little beach is said to be where the weary Odysseus washed ashore. Boat trips from the jetty include Paradise Sunset (☑6972276442; per person €10-20) cruises to nearby grottoes.

Set amid splendid gardens on the rocky promontory above, an easy 10-minute walk from the beach, Moni Theotokou monastery (Map p682; ☉7am-1pm & 3-8pm) FREE dates to the 13th century. It's home to an interesting little museum (☉Apr-Oct) FREE and a shop selling oils and herbs.

A circuitous hike or drive west from Paleokastritsa will take you along a high, winding road through the unspoilt villages of Lakones and Krini. A minor track that drops west of Krini dead-ends far above the waves at a mighty isolated crag, where a broad stone stairway climbs to the impregnable Byzantine fortress of Angelokastro. Though its ramparts remain largely intact, luxuriant wildflowers now fill its interior; the views back to Paleokastritsa are unforgettable.

Further north, the coastline becomes much flatter, and the low-key resorts of Agios Georgios and Arillas line their own long beaches.

South of Paleokastritsa

South of Paleokastritsa, the pebbly beach at Ermones has become overdeveloped but retains a certain attraction. Sleepy little Pelekas, atop wooded cliffs 6km southeast, is an attractive confection of biscuit-cream-hued buildings. Kalimera Bakery (pastries from €2; ☉7am-late) sells fresh pastries, while the frog-green Witch House (☑6974525376; ☉10am-10pm), almost opposite, is perfect for offbeat gifts. Kaiser Wilhelm rode his horse to get 360-degree island views from the peak immediately above the village, now known as the Kaiser's Throne.

Sandy beaches within easy reach of Pelekas include Kontogialos (also called Pelekas) and Glyfada, both now fully fledged resorts with large hotels and other accommodation. Writer Lawrence Durrell hailed Myrtiotissa Beach (Map p682), further east, as arguably the best in the world. Now dominated by nudists, it remains relatively pristine because it's so hard to reach – it requires a long slog down a steep and only partly surfaced road (drivers should park on the hilltop).

The rambling old vineyard estate at Ambelonas (☑6932158888; http://ambelonas-corfu.gr; ☉7-11pm Wed-Fri Jun-Oct, 1-6pm Sun Dec-May), 5km east of Pelekas (and only 8km west of Corfu Town), produces enticing wares ranging from wine and vinegar to olive oil and sweets.

Continuing south, the resort of Agios Gordios is set below a stupendous verdant hillside, with a long sand-and-pebble beach that can accommodate any crowd. Another 12km south, just off the main road, the Byzantine Gardiki Castle makes an impressive spectacle but is largely ruined. Beyond it lies vast Lake Korission, which is a good bird-watching site. It's separated from the sea by a narrow spit that's fronted by long, sandy and often wind-blasted Halikounas Beach.

🛏 Sleeping

Sunrock HOSTEL €
(☑26610 94637; www.sunrockhostel.com; Kontogialos Beach; incl breakfast & dinner dm €25, r with/without bathroom €85/55; @ 🛜) 🍴 Run by the charming Magdalena, this complex, 30m from the sea, has dorms and doubles. It's faded on the outside, perhaps, but inside it's fresh and friendly. There's a great balcony for soaking up the sun, and a large bar full of travellers. Best of all, though, are the home-cooked, delicious meals made using produce from the owner's organic farm.

★ **Levant Hotel** HOTEL €€
(☑ 26610 94230; www.levantcorfu.com; Pelekas; s/d incl breakfast €80/100; ☉ May–mid-Oct; P ✳ 🛜 🏊) Neoclassical Levant sits at the top of a hill just below the Kaiser's Throne peak. It has pastel-blue rooms, wooden floors, belle époque lights and balconies, and a general feeling of countryside charm. Rounding things off is a refined restaurant serving shrimp, risotto and *stifadho* (stew) on a terrace with sublime sunset views.

★ **Hotel Zefiros** HOTEL €€
(☑ 26630 41244; www.zefiroscorfuhotel.gr; Paleokastritsa; d/tr/q from €95/120/140; ✳ 🛜) Set slightly askew of Paleokastritsa's pretty main beach, with a cool olive-grey terrace cafe at lobby level, wine-coloured Zefiros offers bright rooms with flowery stencils and balconies. Prices are reduced significantly outside high season.

Rolling Stone PENSION €€
(☑ 26610 94942; www.pelekasbeach.com; Kontogialos Beach; r/apt €70/95; @ 🛜) The most bohemian and backpacker-friendly place to stay on Kontogialos (Pelekas) Beach has two fresh, simple family apartments with bathrooms and kitchenettes, plus two ample-sized and spotless rooms. People gather to chat on the large, shaded terrace out the front, which has a small bar and a communal semioutdoor kitchen. It's a steep two-minute walk to the beach.

Kallisto Resort APARTMENT €€€
(☑ 6977443555; www.corfuresorts.gr; Kontogialos Beach; apt from €170, villas €240-480; P ✳ 🏊) Exuberant terraced gardens cascading down the hillside at the northern end of Kontogialos Beach hold apartments and villas (sleeping two to 12) that are the last word in Corfu luxury. When you're not lounging around your palatial apartment or soaking up the sea views from your terrace, take your pick from the two sparkling pools.

🍴 Eating

While the resorts have plenty of restaurants, it's worth hunting out locally popular tavernas in inland villages such as Pelekas, or the various panoramic-view options perched along the high road between Lakones and Krini.

Elia Restaurant TAVERNA €
(☑ 6980696364; www.eliamirtiotissa.com; Myrtiotissa; mains €7-14; ☉ noon-late May-Oct) An irresistible taverna, perched above the track down to breathtaking Myrtiotissa Beach,

serving an enticing menu of Corfiot specialities and much-needed cold drinks. Many of the ingredients used in the meals come from the owner's own farm.

To Stavrodromi TAVERNA €
(☑ 26610 94274; www.tostavrodromi.com; Pelekas; mains €7-12; ☉ 6-11pm) A homey dinner-only joint at the main crossroads just east of Pelekas. Delicious local specialities include Corfu's finest *kontosouvli* (spit-roast pork with paprika and onions), as well as rabbit *stifadho* and pepper steak.

★ **Alonaki Bay** TAVERNA €€
(☑ 26610 75872; Alonaki; mains €10-15; ☉ 9.30am-midnight; 🛜) Follow the dirt roads out to the headland northwest of Lake Korission to find this simple, family-run taverna, perched on dramatic cliffs. It serves a small menu of home-cooked meat and *mayirefta*, and also offers clean rooms and apartments, overlooking the garden.

Nereids TAVERNA €€
(☑ 26630 41013; Paleokastritsa; mains €12-19; ☉ 11am-midnight) Just below a huge curve in the road as you enter Paleokastritsa, this romantic spot is best experienced at night, when its terrace of ornamental rock pools and urns is softly lit. The dolmadhes (vine leaves stuffed with rice, and sometimes meat), meatballs in tomato sauce, *kleftiko* (slow-cooked meat) and *stifadho* are particularly recommended.

ℹ️ Getting There & Away

Green Buses (www.greenbuses.gr) provides a handy way to get to and from Corfu Town if you're based in, say, Paleokastritsa or Agios Gordios, but to reach outlying sights and beaches you'll need to rent a vehicle.

PAXI ΠΑΞΟΙ

POP 2300

Measuring a mere 13km from tip to toe, and spared overdevelopment by its lack of an airport, Paxi packs a lot of punch into its tiny frame. Facilities are concentrated in three delightful harbour villages tucked into its eastern shores – Lakka, Loggos and the ferry port of Gaïos. Each has its own crop of tasteful little hotels, rental apartments and seafront tavernas, and its own devoted fans.

All villages make wonderful bases for exploring the rolling hills and centuries-old olive groves of the interior, and the wilder scenery of the west coast. Unspoilt coves

Paxi & Antipaxi

can be reached by motorboat, while former mule trails lead to sheer limestone cliffs that plunge into the azure sea. Great hikes lead out to majestic **Tripitos Arch** (Map p694) in the south, and down to **Erimitis Beach** (Map p694), beneath a vast wall of crumbling rock, in the west.

ℹ Information

Helpful travel agencies include **New Plans** (Bouas Tours; ☑ 6980344759; www.newplans.gr; ☉ 9am-8pm) in Gaïos and **Sun & Sea** (☑ 26620 31162; www.paxossunandsea.com; ☉ 8.30am-2.30pm & 5.30-11pm) in Lakka.

ℹ Getting There & Away

BOAT

Busy passenger-only Ilida (p681) hydrofoils link Paxi's ferry port at Gaïos with Corfu Town (€25, 55 to 90 minutes, three to eight daily, mid-March to mid-October) and occasionally with Igoumenitsa on the Greek mainland. A slower but cheaper service on the Corfu Town route (€20, 90 minutes, one to three daily, April to October) is provided by Kamelia Lines (p681), while car ferries also link Paxi with Igoumenitsa (passenger/vehicle €11/42.30, one to three daily, April to October). Buy ferry tickets from New Plans.

Fast water taxis are available on demand; Corfu to Paxi costs €330 with **Paxos Sea Taxi** (☑ 26620 32444, 6932232072; www.paxossea taxi.com).

Regular excursion boats run from Gaïos to Antipaxi (€10 return) in summer from June onwards.

ℹ Getting Around

Buses link Gaïos and Lakka via Loggos twice daily except Sunday (€2.50); they're not convenient for day trips.

Taxis between Gaïos and Lakka or Loggos cost around €15; Gaïos' taxi rank is by the inland car park. Daily car rental with **Alfa Hire** (☑ 26620 32505; www.alfacarhirepaxos.com) starts at €35 in high season.

Many agencies rent small boats (from €50 to €100, depending on engine capacity).

Gaïos   Γαϊος
POP 500

Gaïos is a supremely peaceful harbour village. Arrayed in a lazy, gentle curve along a narrow, fjord-like channel, it's caressed by beautiful teal water and faces the wooded islet of Agios Nikolaos. A long row of rose- and biscuit-hued neoclassical villas lines the waterfront promenade, many of them housing cafes and tavernas, while yachts and excursion boats bob quayside.

🛏 Sleeping

Gaïos has hotels and studios to suit all budgets; owners usually offer ferry transfers.

Paxos Beach Hotel   HOTEL €€
(Map p694; ☑ 26620 32211; www.paxosbeach hotel.gr; incl breakfast d €105-180, ste €200-280; ❄ 🛜 ⛱) Nestling into a tiny cove a pleasant 1.5km walk southeast along the waterfront from Gaïos, this family-run hotel has its own beach, plus a jetty, a swimming pool, a tennis court and a seaside restaurant. With rooms in separate villas on the terraced hillside, you can expect a lot of steps. Ferry transfers and rental boats available.

Water Planet Rooms   APARTMENT €€
(☑ 6972111995; www.waterplanet.gr; d €60; ❄ 🛜) As much a homestay as a guesthouse, Water Planet is run by friendly and very helpful owners, with assistance from their entertaining little son. Rooms are pleasingly decorated in a sea-faring style, and there's a copious breakfast. Expect that a lot of fuss will be made of you. The owners run the adjoining dive shop.

Theklis-Clara Studios   PENSION €€
(☑ 6972923838, 26620 32313; www.theklis-studios. com; studios €110; ❄) Lovely Thekli, a freediver with her own boat, rents out four

beautiful two-person studios, furnished with shabby-chic flair, in a handsome house 100m up from the quayside. All have well-equipped kitchenettes and bathrooms, and balconies with serene sea views. Ferry transfers possible on request.

✖ Eating

★**Carnayo**   MEDITERRANEAN €€
(☑ 26620 32376; www.carnayopaxos.gr; mains €10-22; ⊘noon-4pm & 7-11pm Tue-Sun) Paxi's finest restaurant, 400m up from central Gaïos, serves local food that's head and shoulders above what's on offer at the harbourfront tavernas, for similar prices. The mixed plate of starters alone is worth a visit; mains range from slow-roasted pork to homemade burgers and crispy-skin bream. Sit in the refined dining room or the romantic garden courtyard.

Dodos   TAVERNA €€
(☑ 26620 32265; http://dodos-paxos.blogspot.co.uk; mains €7-15; ⊘noon-midnight) Presided over by the genial Dodo, this friendly little taverna is hidden in a quirky secret garden (follow the signs from the southern end of the waterfront), with seating that will remind you of rainbows. Come for traditional dishes such as lamb cooked with honey or pork stuffed with cheese, and linger for live music. Also rents simple studios (from €60).

❶ Information

Gaïos has no tourist office, but travel agencies, such as New Plans and **Paxos Magic Holidays** (☑ 26620 32269; www.paxosmagic.com), organise excursions, book tickets and arrange accommodation.

❶ Getting There & Around

Paxi's ferry port is 1km north along the paved, level waterfront from Gaïos' central square, and has connections to Corfu Town and Igoumenitsa. Excursion boats dock along the quayside in the heart of town. A water taxi from Corfu to Paxi costs €330.

You can rent a car from Alfa Hire from €35 per day.

Loggos   Λόγγος

Bookended by white cliffs and the hulk of an old olive-oil factory, breathtaking little Loggos, 6km northwest of Gaïos, consists of a cluster of pretty Venetian houses huddled around a tiny bay of crystal-clear water. Bars and restaurants overlook the sea, while wooded slopes climb steeply above. Just to

the south are a couple of pebble beaches backed by olive groves and with beautiful swimming and reasonable snorkelling. All these things make Loggos probably the most enticing of all Paxi's villages.

🛏 Sleeping & Eating

There are no hotels in Loggos, but there's a limited number of studio and apartment rentals. In most cases it's safer to book these in advance through an agency.

★**Vasilis**   MEDITERRANEAN €€
(☑ 26620 31587; www.vasilisrestaurant.com; mains €13-20; ⊘noon-midnight) The chefs at Vasilis, a low-slung terracotta cottage on the paved harbourfront, are by far the most creative in town. Well-turned-out local specialities include pan-fried cuttlefish, sea urchin, *bourdeto* (fresh fish cooked in tomato and paprika sauce) and a delicious slow-cooked rabbit in yoghurt sauce. Reserve in summer.

❶ Getting There & Away

Ideally you'd make your way to and from Loggos by yacht, but alternatively you can hire one of the motorboats of various shapes and sizes that you'll see lined up in the harbour; contact **Paxos Thalassa Travel** (☑ 26620 31662; www.paxosthalassatravel.com).

A bus travels between Gaïos and Lakka via Loggos twice daily. Its main function is to get children to and from school.

Lakka   Λάκκα

So languid it seems forever on the point of slipping into the yacht-flecked waters, Lakka is sure to slow your pulse and make you smile. Wander the quayside to savour the tempting aromas and gentle music that waft from the tavernas, or venture westward around the bay to reach sandy Harami Beach, or the lighthouse atop the headland beyond.

🤿 Activities

Paxos Oasi Sub   DIVING
(☑ 26620 33493; www.paxosoasisub.com) With clear visibility and diverse habitats, Paxos offers some great diving. This centre offers try dives (€80), snorkelling safaris (€45) and PADI open-water courses (€550).

🛏 Sleeping & Eating

Accommodation options in and around Lakka range from luxury hotels to inexpensive rental studios.

WORTH A TRIP

ANTIPAXI

The ravishing and barely inhabited little island of Antipaxi is a favourite day-trip destination from Paxi, just 2km north, and Corfu. While very few visitors stay overnight, the two superb beach coves near the island's northern tip are thronged every day in summer with boats large and small. Sandy Vrika Beach, the closest to Paxi, and longer but stonier Voutoumi Beach further south are among the best beaches in the Ionian Islands, and they hold a couple of tavernas each. Both lie cradled beneath densely wooded slopes and shelter dazzlingly clear waters.

Footpaths from both beaches and from the island's totally undeveloped harbour, 600m south of Voutoumi, climb to Antipaxi's central spine, where the 'village' of Vigla consists of a few scattered villas and no centre or commercial activity. Keep walking to reach the wilder and beachless western coast within a few minutes, or head for the lighthouse at the island's southernmost tip; take plenty of water and allow at least 1½ hours each way.

Between June and September boats to Antipaxi typically leave Gaïos on Paxi (return €10) at 10am and return around 4.30pm, with increased services in July and August. Ionian Cruises (p686) and other operators offer day trips to Paxi and Antipaxi from Corfu Town.

Yorgos Studios APARTMENT €€
(☑ 26620 31807; www.routsis-holidays.com; d €80; ❄ ☎) Immaculate, comfy and colourful two-person studios, next door to and run by travel agency Routsis Holidays, which represents several other local studios and apartments.

⭐ **Torri E Merli** BOUTIQUE HOTEL €€€
(Map p694; ☑ 26212 34123; www.torriemerli.com; ste from €420; ◷ May-Oct; 🅿 ❄ ☎ ☒) Constructed in 1750, its towers designed to repel pirates, this beautiful boutique property complements its original Venetian elements with contemporary decor – exposed-stone walls, white-wood floors – to create what's arguably the Ionians' loveliest hotel. Set in the olive groves 800m south of Lakka, it holds just seven suites, along with a restaurant and a kidney-shaped pool.

Arriva Fish Restaurant SEAFOOD €€
(☑ 26620 33041; mains €10-17; ◷ 11am-11pm) Waterfront taverna with little tables perched on the very brink of the quayside. Check out the blackboard for an amazing list of freshly caught fish and seafood, from lobster to scorpionfish, prepared every imaginable way – grilled, barbecued, or in risotto or pasta dishes. The cuttlefish with scallops is delectable.

ⓘ Information

Helpful **Routsis Holidays** (☑ 26620 31807; www. routsis-holidays.com) rents out well-appointed apartments and villas to suit all budgets, and arranges transport and excursions. Harbourside Sun & Sea (p694) also offers accommodation, as well as boat rental (from €50).

ⓘ Getting There & Away

The twice-daily bus connection between Lakka and Gaïos via Loggos is designed to get local kids to and from school, and is not convenient for visitors. A rental car is much more practical.

LEFKADA ΛΕΥΚΑΔΑ

POP 22,650

Despite being connected to the mainland by a narrow causeway, making it one of the few Greek islands that you can drive to, much of Lefkada remains surprisingly unaffected by tourism.

Laid-back Lefkada Town is a charming place to spend a day or two, while the soaring mountains of the interior still conceal timeless villages and wild olive groves, and the rugged west coast holds some amazing beaches, albeit in some cases badly damaged by recent earthquakes. Only along the east coast are there some overdeveloped enclaves; if you continue all the way south you'll find stunning little bays and inlets, as well as windy conditions that attract kitesurfers and windsurfers from all over the world.

Lefkada was originally a peninsula, not a true island. Corinthian colonisers cut a canal through the narrow isthmus that joined it to the rest of Greece in the 8th century BCE.

ⓘ Getting There & Away

AIR
Lefkada's closest airport is near Preveza (Aktion; PVK), on the mainland 20km north. **Sky Express** (www.skyexpress.gr) connects it with Corfu (€73, 30 minutes), Kefallonia (€67, 30 minutes), Zakynthos (€73, 1½ hours) and Sitia (Crete; €117,

1½ hours, June to September only). **Olympic Air** (www.olympicair.com) flies from Preveza to Athens, with connections throughout Greece. In summer, **easyJet** (www.easyjet.com) flies to Preveza from the UK, as do charter flights from all over northern Europe.

There's no direct bus between Lefkada Town and Preveza airport, but buses connect Lefkada Town with Preveza itself (€2.90, 30 minutes, six daily), from where you can take a taxi to the airport (€15). Taxis from the airport to Lefkada Town cost from €40.

BOAT

The normal port for boats to Kefallonia is Vasiliki in the far south of Lefkada. However, at the time of research the port here was closed for redevelopment and all ferries were leaving from Nydri instead. This is a bit of a drag for independent travellers, as Nydri is a brash and uninspiring package-tourism resort. It's hoped that normal services will recommence from Vasiliki by summer 2021.

Two ferry companies connect Vasiliki to Kefallonia in high season; **West Ferry** (www.westferry.gr) runs daily to Fiskardo (€10, one hour), while **Ionion Pelagos** (www.ionionpelagos.com) sails via Piso Aetos in Ithaki (€10, one hour) to Sami (€10, 1¾ hours). For bookings contact **Samba Tours** (📞 26450 31520; www.sambatours.gr).

Between July and mid-September, the **Meganisi II** (📞 26450 92528; www.ferryboatmeganisi.gr) ferry runs twice daily between Nydri and Frikes in Ithaki (€10, two hours).

BUS

Lefkada Town's **KTEL Bus Station** (📞 26450 22364; www.ktel-lefkadas.gr; Ant Tzeveleki), opposite the marina 1km from the centre, serves Athens (€33.90, 5½ hours, five daily), Patra (€17.60, three hours, two weekly), Thessaloniki (€35.40, eight hours, daily) and Igoumenitsa (€13.30, two hours, daily).

🛈 Getting Around

BUS

Frequent buses from Lefkada Town serve the island in high season; Sunday services are greatly reduced.

DESTINATION	DURATION	FARE (€)	FREQUENCY
Agios Nikitas	30mins	1.80	3 daily
Karya	30mins	1.80	6 daily
Nydri	30mins	1.80	13 daily
Vasiliki	1hr	3.70	3 daily
Vlicho	40mins	2	10 daily

CAR

Rentals start at €40 per day; there are car-, scooter- and bicycle-hire companies in Lefkada Town (p699), Nydri and Vasiliki.

It's possible to pick up a hire car at Preveza's Aktion Airport and return it in Nydri if you're catching a ferry south (or vice versa).

Lefkada Town   Λευκάδα

POP 8670

Unusually broad and flat for a Greek-island town, Lefkada's bustling capital faces the mainland across a salty lagoon. After losing its historic Venetian architecture in earthquakes in 1948 and 1953, Lefkada Town was rebuilt in a distinctively quake-proof and attractive style. It now resembles a Caribbean port, with attractive wooden buildings in faded pastel colours whose upper storeys are adorned with brightly painted corrugated iron.

A relaxed and cheerful place at the island's northeastern tip, it's one of the only larger Ionian towns not totally swamped by tourism. It's all very logically laid out, with shops and restaurants concentrated along its central pedestrian street (initially Dorpfeld, then Ioannou Mela further west); cafes and bars on the marina to the south; and banks and businesses closest to the causeway to the mainland.

👁 Sights

Moni Faneromenis   MONASTERY

(Map p698; 📞 26450 21305; ⊙ 8am-2pm & 4-8pm) **FREE** Set in beautiful hilltop gardens 3km west of town towards Agios Nikitas, Moni Faneromenis was founded in 1634 and rebuilt following a fire in 1886. The ascent is rewarded with magnificent views over town and lagoon.

Fortress of Agia Mavra   FORTRESS

(Map p698; adult/child €2/free; ⊙ 8am-3.30pm) Guarding Lefkada at the start of the causeway, 1.4km from town, the Agia Mavra fortress was constructed in the 14th century and later expanded by the Venetians. While its lichen-covered walls remain intact, surrounded by a saltwater moat, the interior now lies in ruins. You can enter the occasional bare chamber as you stroll among the wildflowers.

Archaeological Museum   MUSEUM

(📞 26450 21635; Ang Sikelianou; adult/child €2/free; ⊙ 8am-3.30pm Wed-Mon) This excellent museum, west along the waterfront in the modern cultural centre, illuminates island history from the Palaeolithic era to the Romans. Prize exhibits include terracotta ensembles from the 6th century BCE depicting a flute player surrounded by dancing nymphs, seen as evidence that a Pan cult once flourished on Lefkada.

Lefkada & Meganisi

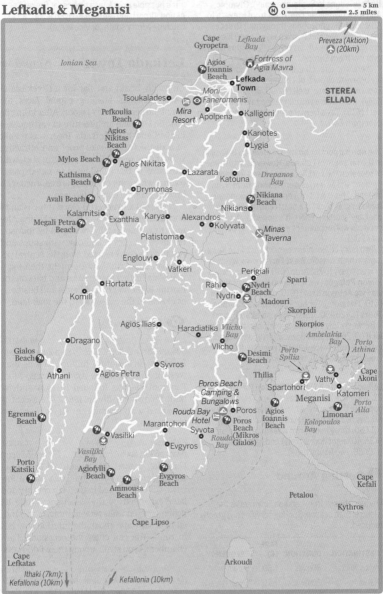

Sleeping

Several good-value hotels are located at the eastern end of town, by the causeway.

⭐ **Boschetto Hotel**   BOUTIQUE HOTEL €€
(☎ 26450 20244; www.boschettohotel.com; Dorpfeld 1; d incl breakfast from €95; ❄ 🛜) This attr-active century-old building on the seafront square holds four large, tasteful rooms and a single suite, all with wooden floors, fine linen, cosy armchairs, attractively weather-worn wooden desks, and balconies looking across the cafe below to the bright-blue waters of the lagoon. The breakfast is top notch.

Pirofani Boutique

HOTEL €€

(✉26450 25844; www.pirofanilefkada.com; Dorpfeld 10; d €120; ❄ 🕿) Very friendly and central family-run hotel that has slightly over-the-top decoration, with a few too many gold flurries, but immaculate bathrooms. The location – on the main old-town street – can't be beaten.

✖ Eating & Drinking

★ Thymari

MEDITERRANEAN €€

(✉26450 22266; www.thymari-lefkada.gr; 19 Pinelopis St; mains €15-20; ⊙7-11pm May-Oct) With tables laid out on a large, sunny terrace surrounded by flowers on a quiet neighbourhood alleyway, this is a delightful place to eat truly outstanding modern Mediterranean cuisine. Expect innovative dishes such as 'deconstructed' lasagne, and don't miss out on tasting the various olive oils. Excellent wine list. All the tables are outside, so it's not the place to head to on a wet day!

Nissi

MEDITERRANEAN €€

(✉26454 00725; www.facebook.com/nissilefkada; Plateia Ethnikis Antistaseos; mains €8-16; ⊙1pm-12.30am; ❄🕿) Memorably good Greek–Italian restaurant, as popular with locals as with tourists, with stylish, comfortable seating on the central inland square. The jet-black squid-ink risotto (€11.50), with octopus and huge grilled prawns, is an astonishing bargain.

★ Gogos Gefsis

BAR

(✉26453 00509; Ioannou Mela 149; ⊙10am-2am; 🕿) Very friendly bar-cafe on the main pedestrian street, with pavement tables plus a quirky interior kitted out like a vintage grocery. The Greek sign is fiendishly hard to read; look for the hammer-and-sickle flag flying above. While it sells a short menu of grilled snacks and cheesy shrimp, just buying a beer gets you a free hot snack.

❶ Getting Around

Rental outlets in Lefkada Town include **Green Motion** (✉26450 23581; www.greenmotion.gr; Panagou 16) for cars and **Santas** (✉26450 25250; www.ilovesantas.gr) for scooters and bikes.

Eastern Lefkada

Lefkada's east coast has experienced the island's heaviest tourist development. Head south, however, to find the unspoilt strand at lovely Poros Beach (also known as Mikros Gialos) and the relaxed and very sheltered

harbour at fjord-like Syvota, where yachts now bob alongside the fishing boats (although there's no beach here). Nydri has seen the most development; what was once a gorgeous fishing village is now a crowded strip of kiss-me-quick tourist shops, without a decent beach.

🛏 Sleeping

Poros Beach

Camping & Bungalows

CAMPGROUND €

(Map p698; ✉26450 95452; www.porosbeach.com.gr; Poros Beach; sites adult/car/tent €10/3/5, r/studios €70/80; ⊙May-Sep; 🅿❄@🕿🏊) A short walk up from perfect Poros Beach, this well-equipped campsite has a great pool, shaded olive-grove tent sites, a nice bar and a restaurant stretching across a huge wooden deck. It also offers attractive double rooms and studios – some family size.

Rouda Bay Hotel

HOTEL €€

(Map p698; ✉6932567502, 26450 95634; http://roudabay.gr; Poros Beach; d from €80; ❄🕿) Comfortable, high-standard, modern rooms and studios, right in the middle of gorgeous Poros Beach. All are capable of accommodating a family of four, and there's also a good waterfront restaurant.

✖ Eating

★ Sivota Bakery

CAFE €

(✉6972432497; Syvota; mains €6-12; ⊙7am-1am) With its harbourfront walls hung with antique bikes and carriage lamps, this cool arbour is much more cafe than bakery, serving pizzas, waffles, cocktails and wine among many other items. However, it's the breakfasts, which range from full English to a delicious melange of yoghurt, honey, fruit and granola, that are the real stars of the show.

Taberna Ionion

TAVERNA €€

(✉26650 93506; Syvota; mains €9-14; ⊙11am-midnight) On the quieter, eastern side of the port, this long-standing family-run place is a little less hectic than others, which means that staff members can pay that little extra bit of attention to diners. Expect good seafood eaten under the shade of a 'living' roof of plants.

Stavros

TAVERNA €€

(✉26450 31181; http://tavernastavros.gr; Syvota; mains €9-16; ⊙8am-midnight Easter-Oct) The pick of several similarly tempting and colourful seafood tavernas along the pretty quayside, Stavros, which has been going strong since the mid-1970s, offers a full menu of freshly

MEGANISI

The elongated island of Meganisi, off Lefkada's southeastern corner, is an easy boat ride from Nydri, on Lefkada's east coast. Most people visit on a day trip, but with its verdant hills still thick with woodland, and turquoise bays fringed by pebbled beaches with a minimum of development, the island's well worth a longer, more relaxed stay. From the ferry dock at Porto Spilia, climb the steep road or stairway to reach the narrow lanes and bougainvillea-bedecked houses of Spartohori, on the plateau above. The next inlet to the east holds pretty Vathy, Meganisi's second harbour, 1km below the village of Katomeri.

Ferries from Nydri sail to both Porto Spilia and Vathy (per person/car €1.90/12.90, 25 to 40 minutes, three to four daily); buy tickets from Borsalino Travel (see below). Local buses connect Spartohori and Vathy five to seven times daily, via Katomeri, but bringing your own vehicle is recommended.

caught fish along with local delicacies such as fish soup and leg of lamb in honey.

Minas Taverna   TAVERNA €€
(Map p698; ☑ 26450 71480; Nikiana; mains €8-18; ☺ 5pm-midnight, reduced hours in low season) Top-notch taverna with a sea-view terrace shaded by vines and a menu that serves up everything from seafood pasta to rice cooked in squid ink to grilled meat and fish. It's above the main road 5km north of Nydri, just south of Nikiana.

ⓘ Information

Borsalino Travel (☑ 26450 92528; www.borsalinotravel.gr; Nydri) For all travel arrangements, including accommodation and car rental as well as ferry and excursion tickets.

ⓘ Getting There & Away

Frequent buses link Nydri with Lefkada Town (€1.80, 30 minutes, 13 daily), but only a few continue any further south.

Vasiliki   Βασιλική

POP 395

This friendly harbour village, complete with stony beach, is one of the top places to learn windsurfing in Greece. This is thanks to a summer-only local thermal wind known to windsurfers as – of all things – Eric! This wind means it's not an ideal place for sunbathers, but a tasty clutch of eucalyptus-shaded tavernas fringing the waterfront, a number of boutique shops and an exceptional place to stay all mean that even nonwindsurfers will find something to like about Vasiliki.

🏃 Activities

Caïques take visitors to nearby beaches and coves. The big attraction for boating day trips is Egremni Beach, especially since earthquake damage means it's no longer accessible by road.

Helpful Samba Tours (p697) sells tickets for excursion boats, including to Egremni, and arranges bicycle hire.

Along the quayside, flags indicate watersports outfits; some have their own hotels for clients.

Club Vassiliki   WATER SPORTS
(☑ 26450 31588; www.clubvass.com) Long-established club specialising in learn-to-windsurf packages that include flights and accommodation. Also offers board hire, private lessons and a wide range of other activities from diving to mountain biking.

It's marketed very much at a UK audience and even has a dedicated UK phone number for queries: ☑ 0844 463 0191.

Nautilus Diving Club   DIVING
(☑ 6936181775; www.underwater.gr; ☺ May-early Oct) Very well-run dive and water-sports centre. Offers single dives (€60) and PADI open-water courses (€430), plus sea-kayak hire (per hour/half-day €15/40) and snorkelling safaris (€55), which get great feedback and take explorers of the deep blue to a hidden beach that even locals describe as being 'like the Caribbean'.

🛏 Sleeping & Eating

★ Pension Holidays   HOTEL €€
(☑ 26450 31426; d/apt €65/70; ❇ 🛜) This guesthouse has it all: immaculate, tastefully furnished double rooms and simply furnished, great-value kitchenette apartments, all with sea views and run by a family with big smiles. It's perfectly located in a quiet spot that's just around the corner beyond the main bay. One of the best guesthouses in all of the Ionian Islands.

Vasiliki Blue APARTMENT €€
(☑26450 31602; www.vasilikiblue.gr; d €75; ※ 🛜) Bright, scrupulously clean kitchenette apartments, perched on the hillside a few metres up from the harbour, with sea-view balconies draped in bougainvillea.

Vagelaras TAVERNA €€
(☑26450 31224; mains €7-16; ☺8am-midnight; 🛜) Sitting at the end of the harbour, just short of the ferry dock, this century-old taverna serves great salads, mezedhes, pasta and fresh seafood at waterfront tables.

ℹ️ Information

Samba Tours (p697) sells tickets for ferries and boat excursions, including to Egremni Beach. Also arranges car and bicycle hire and accommodation, and offers all-round assistance.

ℹ️ Getting There & Away

Three daily buses (€3.70, one hour) connect Vasiliki with Lefkada Town in high season.

Western Lefkada

On Lefkada's west coast, steep mountain slopes covered in olive trees drop dramatically to dazzling-white beaches that have long been regarded as some of the best in Greece. Tourism development remains fairly minimal and the few villages that cling precariously to this vertiginous landscape retain a slow, traditional vibe. The best-known beaches were, sadly, seriously damaged by a 2015 earthquake and can be hard to reach, but others remain intact and there's still plenty of scope for exploration.

👁️ Sights

The one resort on the west coast, the ever-expanding village of Agios Nikitas, stands 13km southwest of Lefkada Town along the coastal road. A short street of inviting tavernas leads down to a curving white-sand beach lapped by aquamarine water. Head across the headland to the west, following the footpath from the Poseidon taverna, and you'll come to broad, straight and utterly delightful Mylos Beach (Map p698). White-pebbled Pefkoulia Beach (Map p698) is a five-minute drive north, and similar Kathisma Beach (Map p698) is the same distance south.

Further south, beyond the village of Athani, where stalls sell olive oil, honey and wine, two of Lefkada's most famous beaches, Egremni Beach (Map p698) and Porto

Katsiki (Map p698), were devastated by the 2015 earthquake. Both were submerged in debris as the white cliffs that tower above them came crumbling down, though geologists believe that they will eventually be washed clean and restored to their former glory. Porto Katsiki is in slightly better shape, and remains accessible by car, but both the 720-step stairway that led to Egremni and the road by which it was reached were obliterated and are unlikely to be rebuilt. Now the only way to see what's left of Egremni, and to bathe in its magical turquoise waters, is to take a boat excursion from ports elsewhere on the island, such as Vasiliki.

🛏️ Sleeping & Eating

If you fancy basing yourself on the west coast, little Agios Nikitas has everything you need. There are also a few options in the village of Kalamitsi, a little way to the south.

In addition to the abundant eating options in Agios Nikitas, the road south – around Athani in particular – is scattered with attractive village restaurants.

⭐Mira Resort APARTMENT €€
(Map p698; ☑26450 24967, SMS only 697707 5881; www.miraresort.com; Tsoukalades; maisonettes incl breakfast from €145; ☺May-Oct; 🅿️※🛜🏊) Perfectly positioned on the mountainside 6km southwest of Lefkada Town, with panoramic views of the glittering sea, Mira has cosy and immaculate maisonettes, plus a large pool and a cafe-bar.

Hotel Agatha HOTEL €€
(☑6948620615; www.agatha-hotel.com; Agios Nikitas; studios/apt €90/100; ※🛜) Beside the coastal road, a few minutes' walk up from the eastern end of the beach, Agatha offers lovely, cool kitchenette studios and two-room apartments that are flooded with sunlight and set within pretty gardens ringing with birdsong.

Olive Tree Hotel HOTEL €€
(☑26450 97453; www.olivetreehotel.gr; Agios Nikitas; s/d/studios incl breakfast €80/90/100; ☺May-Sep; ※🛜) Brushed in the colours of olive oil, this modest hotel just above the village centre is managed by friendly Greek-Canadians. Each room has its own terrace, with side-on sea views, and there's a good buffet breakfast.

⭐Cape of Lefkatas TAVERNA €
(☑26450 33149; www.lefkatas.gr; Athani; mains €7-13; ☺1-11pm May-Sep; 🛜) 🍽️ This delightful terrace restaurant in Athani village has inspiring views down the mountainside to

the sea beyond. Join the locals sitting in the shade of a cedar tree to enjoy superb seafood, including a risotto (€13) that's so thick in creatures of the deep that it wouldn't be a surprise to find Neptune himself hidden among the rice!

T'Agnantio　　　　　　　　　TAVERNA €
(☑ 26450 97383; www.tagnantio.gr; Agios Nikitas; mains €7-15; ⊘ noon-midnight Easter-Oct) The vine-shaded terrace of Agios Nikitas' finest taverna sits in a quiet, tucked-away spot slightly up from the beach and offers sweeping views out to sea. Feast on seafood – including swordfish, shrimp and octopus – as well as souvlaki, meatballs and local cheese.

❶ Getting There & Away

Buses from Lefkada Town run to Agios Nikitas (€1.80, 30 minutes, three daily) and Kathisma Beach, and also as far south as Athani.

Central Lefkada

Replete with traditional farming villages, lush green peaks, fragrant pine trees, olive groves and vineyards, Lefkada's dramatic central spine is hugely rewarding to explore.

◉ Sights & Activities

The small village of Karya has a pretty central square with plane trees and tavernas, but it attracts crowds in high season. It's famous for its embroidery, introduced during the 19th century by a remarkable one-handed local woman, Maria Koutsochero. A small museum showcases the embroidery and traditional village life. Opening hours are flexible.

The island's highest village, Englouvi, is renowned for honey and lentils. Book ahead for a herbal walk (☑ 6934287446; www.lefkas.cc; Kolyvata) near quaint Alexandros that aims to show how easy it can be to live off the land.

There's some great walking in Lefkada's mountainous centre, but route information is hard to come by. Follow your nose down dirt roads and along goat trails.

⊨ Sleeping & Eating

Unless you find a rental villa in some far-flung village, the hills of the interior are more of a day-trip destination than an overnight stop.

★ **Maria's Tavern**　　　　　　　TAVERNA €
(☑ 6984056686, 26450 41228; www.facebook.com /MariasTavern; Kolyvata; mains €6-9; ⊘ 12.30-11.30pm Apr-Oct) In the hamlet of Kolyvata, which enjoys idyllic views over the hills, the gregarious Kiria Maria opens her home to culinary adventurers. Using whatever's ready in her garden, she serves fresh, perfectly cooked treats. Call ahead to check she's there.

❶ Getting There & Away

Although frequent buses can get you to Karya, for example, you'll see much more if you rent your own vehicle.

KEFALLONIA
ΚΕΦΑΛΛΟΝΙΑ

POP 35,800

Perhaps the most enticing of all the Ionian islands, magical Kefallonia is a place where it's easy to lose yourself, amid air thick with oleander and the sound of goat bells. The largest, and perhaps the most varied, of the islands, there's space to breathe here, and its convoluted coastline conceals all sorts of captivating coves and beach-lined bays lapped by gin-clear waters teeming with colourful fish. Despite the devastating earthquake of 1953 that razed much of the island's historic Venetian architecture, ravishing harbourfront villages such as Fiskardo and Assos still show off Italianate good looks, while the lush and mountainous interior, dotted with wild meadows, Mediterranean oak forests and vineyards, invites endless exploration.

❶ Getting There & Away

AIR

The **airport** (Map p703; ☑ 26710 29900; http:// kefaloniaairport.info) is 9km south of Argostoli. From May to September, **easyJet** (www.easyjet. com) flies from London and other cities, and many charter flights come from northern Europe and the UK. In addition, **Olympic Air** (www. olympicair.com) serves Athens, and **Sky Express** (www.skyexpress.gr) serves Corfu, Preveza and Zakynthos. There's no airport bus; taxis to Argostoli cost around €20.

BUS

Three daily buses from the **KTEL Bus Station** (☑ 26710 22281; www.ktelkefalonias.gr; A Tritsi 5) in Argostoli use the ferry from Poros to make the journey to Athens (€33, seven hours, three daily).

BOAT

Up to five daily **Ionian Group** (www.ioniangroup. com) ferries connect Poros with Kyllini in the Peloponnese in summer (€9, 1½ hours), where you can catch onward ferries to Zakynthos.

Ionian Pelagos (www.ionionpelagos.com) runs up to three ferries a day between Sami and Piso Aetos in Ithaki (€4, 30 minutes), with one or two

Kefallonia & Ithaki

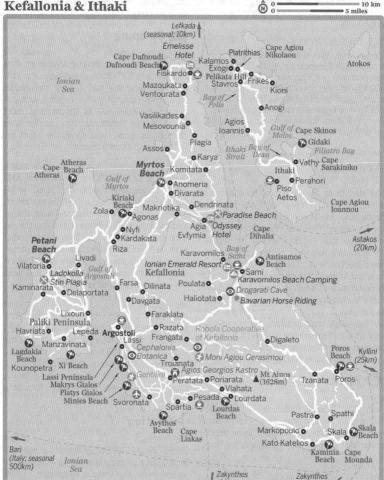

continuing to Astakos in the Peloponnese (total trip from Sami €11, three hours). It connects Sami to Vasiliki in Lefkada twice weekly in summer (€9, 1¾ hours); and also runs twice daily in summer between the remote and not readily accessible port of Pesada in southern Kefallonia and similarly isolated Agios Nikolaos in northern Zakynthos (€8, 1½ hours).

West Ferry (www.westferry.gr) runs between Fiskardo and Vasiliki (Lefkada; €9, one hour, two to three daily); buy tickets at **Nautilus Travel** (☑ 26740 41440; nautilusfiscardo@gmail.com; ⊙ 9am-1.30pm & 5-9pm) in Fiskardo.

Ertsos (☑ 26710 27301; www.ertsostravelkef alonia.com; Antoni Tritsi; ⊙ 9am-9pm) in Argostoli sells tickets for services to Ithaki and Kyllini.

Between mid-July and mid-September, **Ventouris Ferries** (http://ventourisferries.com) offers a once-weekly connection between Sami, Zakynthos, Igoumenitsa on the mainland, and Bari, Italy. Buy tickets from **Blue Sea Travel** (☑ 26740 23007; www.samistar.com; Posidonos 16, Sami). From July to mid-September **Red Star Ferries** (www.ionianislands.it) runs weekly services between Sami and Brindisi (Italy). The crossing takes 16 hours.

ⓘ Getting Around

BUS

KTEL buses (p702) connect Argostoli with all the island's major towns. In addition, one or two daily services run along the east coast, linking

Katelios with Skala, Poros, Sami, Agia Evfymia and Fiskardo. Buses run on Sunday in high season only.

CAR & MOTORCYCLE

Car- and motorbike-hire companies fill major resorts, while **Europcar** (☑ 26710 41008; www.europcar.com; ⊘ 7.30am-9pm), **Hertz** (☑ 26714 40040) and other operators have offices at the airport. Sami-based **Kefalonia2Ride** (☑ 26740 22970; www.kefalonia2ride.rentals; Maiouli 29, Sami; ⊘ 9.30am-9pm) offers scooters (from €22 per day) and ATVs.

Argostoli   Αργοστόλι

POP 9750

Shielded from the open sea, its waterfront stretching along the landward side of a short peninsula, Argostoli was once renowned for its elegant Venetian-era architecture. Almost all of that was destroyed by earthquake in 1953, but Argostoli is now a lively, forward-looking town. The main focus of activity is just inland, centred on charming, freshly pedestrianised Plateia Valianou, where locals come to chat and eat at the many restaurants. In summer, musicians stroll the streets singing *kantades* (traditional songs accompanied by guitar and mandolin). Lithostroto, the pedestrian shopping street immediately south, is lined with stylish boutiques and cafes.

◉ Sights

Makrys Gialos   BEACH

(Map p703) Blessed with enticing turquoise water, and located just 3km southwest of Argostoli, Makrys Gialos tends to be packed to the gills in summer with holidaying Brits.

Platys Gialos   BEACH

(Map p703) This little 'pocket' beach, just beyond Makrys Gialos, has plenty of shade and very clear water, as well as a few places to eat.

Cephalonia Botanica   GARDENS

(Map p703; ☑ 26710 24866; www.focas-cosmetatos.gr; ⊘ 9am-2pm) **FREE** This lovely botanical garden, designed for the study, preservation and display of the island's plants and herbs, is located 2km south of central Argostoli. It also holds a small artificial lake. Last admission is 45 minutes before closing.

Korgialenio History

& Folklore Museum   MUSEUM

(Map p705; ☑ 26710 28835; Ilia Zervou 12; €3; ⊘ 9am-2pm Mon-Sat) Dedicated to preserving Kefallonian art and culture, this fine museum houses icons, assorted furniture, clothes

and artwork from the homes of gentry and farm workers.

🛏 Sleeping

Camping Argostoli   CAMPGROUND €

(☑ 26710 23487; www.camping-argostoli.gr; sites adult/car/tent €7/3/5.50; ⊘ May-Sep; P) This pleasant, peaceful and hugely welcoming family-run campsite, 2km beyond Argostoli near the lighthouse at the northernmost point of the peninsula, can hardly have changed in years – and it's all the better for it. It also has its own tavern.

Vivian Villa   APARTMENT €

(Map p705; ☑ 26710 23396; www.kefalonia-vivianvilla.gr; Deladetsima 11; d/studios €55/60; ❈ 🛜) Tasteful guesthouse on a quiet inland street, overlooking a garden fragrant with thyme and basil. As well as hotel-style rooms, some with balconies, it offers larger apartments with well-stocked kitchenettes and separate bedrooms for the kids. Don't be surprised if the warm-hearted owner plies you with homemade cakes and lemonade.

Mouikis Hotel   HOTEL €€

(Map p705; ☑ 26710 23032; http://mouikis.com.gr; Vyronos 3; d incl breakfast from €99; ❈ 🛜) Clean, modern hotel, near the market at the southern end of the town centre, with smart, mauve-coloured rooms. Most of the small but very well-equipped rooms have balconies; some have sea views. Rates include a substantial buffet breakfast.

🍴 Eating

★ Tzivras   GREEK €

(Map p705; ☑ 26710 24259; Vandorou 1; mains €7-9; ⊘ 1-5pm) Slightly grungy and brilliantly atmospheric, this veteran restaurant a block inland from the waterfront market is where locals lunch on hearty, great-value baked standards, such as veal with okra, goat with potatoes or cod pie. Choose your meal of choice from the display counter. Everything on the menu is less than €10.

★ Ladokolla   GRILL €

(Map p705; ☑ 26710 25522; Kalypsous Vergoti; dishes €2-8; ⊘ 12.30pm-2am) Lively and hugely popular grill house, where piping-hot and irresistibly flavourful chicken, pork or lamb kebabs and pittas are served up straight onto tabletop covers (no plates). It also delivers.

Taverna Patsouras   TAVERNA €

(Map p705; ☑ 26711 02960; Antoni Tritsi; mains around €8; ⊘ noon-11pm) Since 1963 this simple place next to the fish market has been grilling and frying delicious seafood. There's no glitz or glamour; it's just down-to-earth cooking in a down-to-earth setting, and it's pretty out of this world because of it.

Kiani Akti SEAFOOD €€

(Map p705; ☑26710 26680; Antoni Tritsi; mains €8-20; ☺1pm-2am; ☜) This restaurant has a huge wooden deck on stilts stretching out into the harbour, which allows you to peer guiltily down into the water at the brothers and sisters of the fish on your plate. The wide-ranging menu includes tasty Greek appetisers, along with daily seafood specials and meaty classics.

🍷 Drinking & Nightlife

Cafes line Plateia Valianou and Lithostroto, and are buzzing by late evening. **Bass Club** (Map p705; ☑26710 25020; www.bassclub.gr; cnr S Metaxa & Vergoti; ☺noon-7am; ☜) in town draws the younger set, while club-restaurant **Katavothres** (☑26710 22221; www.katavothres. gr; Mikeli Davi 10; ☺noon-midnight Mon-Thu & Sun, 24hr Fri & Sat; ☜) at the tip of the peninsula combines strange geological formations with iconic futuristic furnishings, and hosts big-name DJs.

ℹ Information

EOT (Greek National Tourist Organisation; Map p705; ☑26710 22248; ☺7am-2.30pm Mon-Fri)

ℹ Getting There & Away

BUS

The KTEL Bus Station (p702) on Argostoli's southern waterfront is the epicentre of the island's public-transport network. Buses only run on Sundays during high season.

DESTINATION	DURATION	FARE (€)	FREQUENCY
Fiskardo	2hrs	6.40	2 daily
Lassi Peninsula	30mins	1.50	7 daily
Poros	80mins	4.50	3 daily
Sami	1hr	4	daily
Skala	65mins	4.50	2 daily

BOAT

The main ferry quay is at the northern end of the waterfront, close to the EOT information office. Car **ferries** (Map p705; person/car €2.80/4) connect Argostoli with Lixouri on the Paliki Peninsula (per person/car €2.80/4, 30 minutes, 7am to 10.30pm). Between May and September they run half-hourly from noon to 5.30pm and hourly

Argostoli

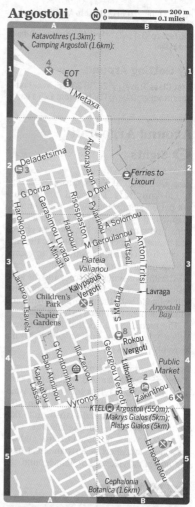

Argostoli

at other times. From October to April they run a little less frequently.

Ertsos (p703) sells tickets for services to Ithaki and Kyllini.

ℹ Getting Around

First Class Travel (📋 26710 20026; www.first classtravel.gr; D Davi) Car hire from €25 a day.

Around Argostoli

◉ Sights

Moni Agiou Gerasimou MONASTERY
(Map p703; 📋 26710 86045; Omala; ⊙9am-1pm & 3.30-8pm) FREE Dedicated to Kefallonia's patron saint, Moni Agiou Gerasimou is maintained by nuns. The large complex contains pretty gardens, a big, modern church and a small chapel, which encloses the cave to which St Gerasimos withdrew to escape the rigours of monastic life. Its interiors are filled with soot-stained frescoes and the air is heavy with incense. If you're lucky your visit will coincide with the haunting praying and singing of nuns clad head to toe in black.

The monastery is located in the Omala Valley. Take the stated opening hours with a heavenly pinch of salt.

Agios Georgios Kastro FORTRESS
(Castle of St George; Map p703; Peratata; ⊙8.30am-4pm Wed-Mon) FREE This 16th-century Venetian castle enjoys stellar views from atop a conspicuous pyramid-shaped hill 7km southeast of Argostoli. Kefallonia's capital for 200 years, it's now in ruins, and approached via a short pedestrian street from the adjoining village. Strolling around the unshaded, wildflower-strewn site takes around 20 minutes; relax afterwards over a coffee or snack in the gardens of the neighbouring Kastro Cafe or a full meal at nearby Il Borgo (📋 26710 69800; Peratata; mains €9-15; ⊙noon-midnight; 🖼).

🛏 Sleeping & Eating

★**Museum Hotel**
George Molfetas BOUTIQUE HOTEL €€€
(📋 26710 84630; www.kefaloniamuseumhotel.com; Marinaki, Faraklata; r €120-180; 🖧) One-of-a-kind boutique guesthouse with six rooms that are a monument to the art, antiques and general bric-a-brac one family can gather, and it's all been put together with the eye of a natural artist. The garden courtyard is a masterpiece of earthy oranges and big flowers, and owner Katerina is a born raconteur.

★**Gentilini Retreat** BOUTIQUE HOTEL €€€
(📋 26710 26632; www.gentiliniretreat.gr; Mitakata; d from €142) Lose yourself among swathes of olive trees at this dreamy six-room boutique guesthouse set within gentle farming countryside at the base of Mt Ainos. The individually styled rooms are redolent of country living and you get the chance to learn about Kefallonian olive-oil production while staying here. Run by the Gentilini Winery, but not on the same site, it's the perfect retreat for those after total peace.

★**Kastro Cafe** CAFE €
(📋 26710 69367; Peratata; mains €6-10; ⊙10am-7pm; 🖧) Relaxed garden cafe, just before the gateway to Agios Georgios Kastro, that's a wonderfully peaceful spot for coffee, cake, cold drinks or lunchtime snacks.

LOCAL KNOWLEDGE

IONIAN ON THE VINE

The Ionian Islands would not be the same without wine, and Kefallonia is especially famed for its vintages. The most notable derive from the unique *robola* grape (VQRPD; Vin de Qualité Produit dans une Région Déterminée), thought to have been introduced by the Venetians, while other varieties include *mavrodaphni* (AOC; Appellation d'Origine Contrôlée) and *muscat* (AOC).

Nestled at the heart of the verdant Omala Valley, in the hilly country southeast of Argostoli, the winery of the Robola Cooperative of Kefallonia (Map p703; 📋 26710 86301; www.robola.gr; Omala; ⊙9am-9pm daily Jul & Aug, to 6pm May, Jun, Sep & Oct, to 3pm Mon-Fri Nov-Apr) transforms grapes from 300 independent growers into a dry white wine of subtle yet lively flavour. Visitors can take an interesting guided tour and enjoy an all-important tasting afterwards. Smaller yet similarly distinguished Gentilini (Map p703; 📋 26710 41618; www.gentilini.gr; Minies; tastings & tour from €5; ⊙11am-8pm), 5km south of Argostoli on the airport road, has a charming setting and produces a range of superb wines, including the scintillating Classico. It also offers short tours and tastings.

Paliki Peninsula
Χερσόνησος Παλική

Anchored by the bustling gulf-side town of Lixouri, the Paliki Peninsula is an underexplored region of spectral white, cream and red clay cliffs, verdant farmland and vineyards, and hilltop villages. And beaches – oh, what beaches these are! From dreamy, perfect Petani Beach in the northwest to redsand Xi Beach in the south, there's a place to plonk a towel for everyone. Between Petani and Kounopetra in the far west, overlooking stark cliffs, azure seas and robust vineyards, the Moni Kipouria monastery was built by a lone, solitude-loving monk.

Beach

⭐ **Petani Beach**   BEACH
(Map p703) The highlight of the Paliki Peninsula is breathtaking Petani Beach, a spectacular strand of white sand and pebble that's enough to entice a jaded mermaid. In fact, it's so blissful that it's fair to call it one of the best beaches in all of Greece. Although it gets busy in summer, development remains happily minimal. Walk to the far-northern end for a little peace in high season.

🛏 Sleeping

Perdikis Travel (☑26710 91097; ptravel1@otenet.gr; Lixouri), on Lixouri's southern seafront, can help with accommodation and all travel arrangements. There's plenty of accommodation around Xi and a scattering elsewhere.

⭐ **Ksouras**   APARTMENT €€
(☑26710 97458; www.facebook.com/ksouras; Petani; d €85; ⓟ❄️🤝) Very pleasant rooms in a range of colours are on offer inside this bright-blue villa above the owners' beachfront taverna. It's a sublimely tranquil spot in the evenings, once the crowds have gone and sunset is in full swing. The taverna is open for all meals, and serves uniformly excellent and inexpensive Greek classics.

⭐ **Petani Bay Hotel**   HOTEL €€€
(☑26710 97701; www.petanibayhotel.gr; Petani; d incl breakfast €210-330; ⓟ❄️🤝🏊) Boasting one of the finest infinity pools in Greece, this adults-only boutique eyrie overlooks the cobalt-blue bay far below. There are just 13 romantic suites, with marble floors, woodblade fans and kitchenettes. It's all about peace here; the only sound is the bleating of goats and the chink of chilled wine glasses.

🍴 Eating

Lixouri's waterfront promenade, especially around the main square, is lined with lively cafes and restaurants. There are also good tavernas at Xi Beach and Petani Beach.

Mavroeidis   BAKERY €
(☑26710 91246; Lixouri; baked goods from €1.50; ☺8am-late; ❄️🤝) For over a hundred years, this large bakery-cafe in the heart of Lixouri, with outdoor tables at the inland end of the main pedestrian square, has been baking a panoply of sweet delights. Buying a coffee gets you a free taster of the island's best *amygdalopita* (sweet almond cake).

⭐ **Ladokolla Stin Plagia**   TAVERNA €€
(Map p703; ☑26710 97493; Damoulianata; mains €10-22; ☺11am-midnight; ❄️) High in the hills in the whitewashed and near-silent village of Damoulianata is this superb, family-run restaurant (the chefs are twin brothers). The menu changes according to what was available in the market or garden that day, but it's especially renowned for its meat pies and its pork cooked in honey, orange and beer.

ℹ️ Getting There & Away

It's easy to access the peninsula on the ferry (p705) from Argostoli to Lixouri (per person/car €2.80/4, 30 minutes, 7am to 10.30pm). Between May and September they run half-hourly from noon to 5.30pm and hourly at other times. From October to April they run a little less frequently.

Sami & Around   Σάμη
POP 1030

Cheerful Sami, Kefallonia's main port, stands 25km northeast of Argostoli on the other side of the island. Nestled in a bright bay and flanked by steep hills, it consists of a waterside strip that stares across to Ithaki and is loaded with tourist-oriented cafes. Nearby monasteries, castle ruins and natural features, including the much-hyped Drogarati Cave, offer enticements to linger. Quieter alternative bases with better beaches, such as Karavomilos and Agia Evfymia, line the bay as you head further north.

Agia Evfymia in particular is an attractive little port town, with some pretty cove beaches where the water glows and the snorkelling is great. On the flip side, the main road runs right past these beaches and the winds, funnelled between mountains that stand behind the town, can be strong.

WORTH A TRIP

AINOS NATIONAL PARK

Standing proud over the island is the lumbering hulk of **Mt Ainos** (1628m), most of which falls within Ainos National Park. The mountain's upper reaches are dominated by ancient, gnarled Greek fir and black pine, through which afternoon mist and cloud frequently swirl. In winter the mountain can be blanketed by snow, and at any time of year the views from close to the top (the actual summit has a crown of radio masts) are astounding.

Visitor facilities within the park are fairly undeveloped, but five **walking trails** have been established. The trails themselves are well signposted and very clear, though the trailheads are a little less obvious (a road runs right through the middle of the park and up to the summit; to find the trailheads, keep an eye out for information panels). The two most popular trails go up to the summit from opposite sides of the mountain and then loop back around to their respective starting points. Each is around 6.5km and easy, with a fairly gentle ascent. Unfortunately, in both cases the return route is back along the road, so it's best to ignore this and just retrace your steps along the footpath in the forest. Allow 1½ hours, excluding stops. If walking isn't your thing, you can drive pretty much all the way to the summit.

⊙ Sights

Drogarati Cave   CAVE
(Map p703; ☑ 26740 23302; adult/child €5/3; ☺ 10am-5pm Jun-Sep, shorter hours in low season) A popular stop for round-island coach tours, Drogarati Cave is a natural cavern hollowed into the hillside 4km south of Sami. A short, steep stairway drops from the ticket booth; once you're down, it takes 10 minutes at most to walk around the single large subterranean chamber, festooned with dripping stalactites. A couple of tavernas stand alongside.

🍴 Sleeping & Eating

Karavomilos Beach Camping   CAMPGROUND €
(Map p703; ☑ 26740 22480; www.camping-karavomilos.gr; Sami-Karavomilos Rd; adult/car/tent €9/3.50/6.50; ☺ Apr–mid-Oct; 🛜🏊) Large family-oriented campground just 800m west of central Sami, with well-shaded sites stretching back from a decent pebble beach. Good facilities include excellent washrooms, a swimming pool, a cafe and a shop.

Odyssey Hotel   HOTEL €€€
(Map p703; ☑ 26740 61089; www.hotelodyssey.gr; Agia Evfymia; d from €216; 🅿❄🛜🏊) Plush resort hotel just around the corner north of the harbour, with very comfortable balcony suites looking across to Ithaki, as well as a spa, gym, restaurant and two bars. Three-night minimum stay in high season.

Ionian Emerald Resort   HOTEL €€€
(Map p703; ☑ 26740 22708; www.ionianemerald.gr; Karavomilos; d incl breakfast from €160; ❄🛜🏊) Lavish luxury hotel with a spa and gym to complement its spacious pool area. Rooms are creamy cool, with contemporary styling, lush linens and picture windows; some are two-bedroom 'maisonettes'.

★ Paradise Beach   TAVERNA €€
(Map p703; ☑ 26740 61392; www.paradisebeachtaverna.com; Agia Evfymia; mains €7-22; ☺ noon-11pm Apr-Oct; 🛜) This much-loved taverna has a dreamy vine-shaded terrace overlooking a little beach. Thanks to its locally reared meat – in dishes such as exceptionally tender lamb chops, Kefallonian meat pie or braised rabbit – and seafood delights, it's an island institution and people even visit Kefallonia solely to eat here.

❶ Information

Blue Sea Travel (p703) offers day trips to Ithaki as well as general travel services.

❶ Getting There & Away

BOAT

Ionian Pelagos (www.ionionpelagos.com) runs up to three daily services from Sami to Piso Aetos in Ithaki (€4, 30 minutes), of which one or two continue to Astakos in the Peloponnese (€11, three hours); and two weekly sailings run in high season to Vasiliki on Lefkada (€9, 1¾ hours).

Between mid-July and mid-September, some **Ventouris Ferries** (http://ventourisferries.com) head north from Sami to Bari in Italy (€66, 18 hours) and south to Zakynthos (1½ hours).

BUS

KTEL (www.ktelkefalonias.gr) buses link Sami with Argostoli (€4, two to three daily), and also with Poros, Agia Evfymia and Fiskardo (€4.70, one hour, one or two daily). Argostoli buses usually meet ferries.

CAR

Hire cars through **Karavomilos Car Rental** (☑ 26 740 23769; http://karavomylosrentacar.gr; Sami) and scooters through Kefalonia2Ride (p704).

Fiskardo Φισκάρδο

POP 295

One of the prettiest towns in the Ionians, the little port of Fiskardo curves serenely beside coral-blue waters, gazing out towards Ithaki. Thanks to its colourful crop of Venetian villas, spared from earthquake damage because they rest on a sturdy bed of flat rock, Fiskardo is the island's most exclusive resort, home to upmarket restaurants and choice accommodation. There's no real dock or jetty here; ferries from Lefkada arrive unceremoniously at the northern end, while yachts jostle for space along the rest of the harbour. While it can get very crowded in summer, it has a cosmopolitan buzz unmatched elsewhere on the island.

⊙ Sights & Activities

There are two small pebble beaches in Fiskardo. The best is just over the headland to the east. It's backed by Venetian-style houses and olive trees, and is as nice a town beach as you could hope for. The other is just next to where the ferries dock and almost within the town centre itself, but it's only a so-so beach. Much better beaches can be found further north, where the gorgeous sand at Emblissi is shaded by olive trees, and to the south, where Foki Bay is home to an attractive taverna.

One of the more secluded beaches in the north of Kefallonia is Dafnoudi, which is around a 5km drive northwest of Fiskardo. The tiny white-pebble beach is hemmed in by forest-covered cliffs and there are absolutely no facilities or development of any type (and long may that continue!). To make the journey to Dafnoudi even more enjoyable, leave the car in Fiskardo and walk there. Using well-marked trails through forest and abandoned farmland, it's an easy 3.5km (45-minute) one-way walk.

There are also other options for some reasonable low-level walking around Fiskardo. An information panel in the car park just above town gives basic route suggestions and descriptions for three very well-marked short trips.

Fiskardo Divers DIVING

(☑ 6970206172; www.fiskardo-divers.com; 3hr beginner courses €55, 4-day PADI open-water courses €430; ☉ 9.30am-2pm & 5-7pm Mon-Sat, from 10.30am Sun) Offering trips to caves, wrecks, reefs and a downed Bristol Beaufort WWII bomber, this dive operator has won awards for its eco-credentials. It also offers beginner courses (the area's ultra-clear waters make it a perfect place to learn to dive). The waterfront shop displays marine skeletons, including a monk seal, a loggerhead turtle, a beaked whale and a shark.

🛏 Sleeping

As well as holding hotels to suit all budgets, Fiskardo and the adjacent bays are peppered with rental villas and apartments. Several are available via Ionian Villas (www.ionianvillas.co.uk).

Regina Studios APARTMENT €

(☑ 26740 41125; www.regina-studios.gr; d/tr from €55/75; ❄☎) A pink villa, beside the village car park up the steps from the waterfront, Regina offers great-value 'en-suite' economy rooms, larger studios with sea-view balconies and shared kitchens, and larger two-bedroom apartments.

Villa Romantza PENSION €€

(☑ 26740 41322; www.villa-romantza.gr; r/studios/apt €60/80/100; ❄☎) Excellent budget option, near the central car park, where simple, spacious and well-maintained rooms, studios and apartments share a communal terrace; some have two bedrooms and kitchenettes.

Emelisse Hotel RESORT €€€

(Map p703; ☑ 26740 41200; www.emelisseresort.com; Emblissi Bay; d incl breakfast from €263;

DON'T MISS

MYRTOS BEACH

From the road that zigzags down to it, you'll understand why Myrtos Beach (Map p703) is touted as one of the most breathtaking beaches in all of Greece. From afar it's certainly a stunning sight, with electric-blue waters offset by what appears to be searing-white 'sand' (in reality it's white pebbles). Unfortunately, a scrappy car park rather spoils the idyll. Even so, it's a beautiful spot and once you're in the sea it's heavenly.

The closest village is Divarata, which has a couple of tavernas, including Alexandros (☑ 26740 61777; https://alexandrosrestaurant-myrtos.gr; Divarata; mains €7-9; ☉ noon-midnight).

⊙ mid-Apr–mid-Oct; [P][✻][@][📶][🏊]) This luxury hotel is set in magnificent seclusion on a headland overlooking superb Emblissi Beach, 1.5km north of Fiskardo along the winding coastal road. Its beautifully appointed rooms are laid out on immaculately groomed terraces, leading down to a lavish swimming pool and a restaurant with fantastic views to Lefkada, Ithaki and beyond.

Fiscardonna
Luxury Suites
BOUTIQUE HOTEL €€€

([☎]26740 41289; www.fiscardonna.com; d incl breakfast €120-250; [✻][📶]) One of the few hotels in town, this five-room boutique choice, in a lovingly restored building dating to 1840, mixes the old with utterly modern technological marvels (you're unlikely to have seen door-key swipes quite like these). The result doesn't quite gel, but it's very comfortable all the same. It's in a quiet side alley just back from the waterfront.

🍴 Eating & Drinking

Café Tselenti
MEDITERRANEAN €€

([☎]26740 41344; mains €8-26; ⊙ 8am-midnight May-Oct) Owned by the Tselenti family since 1893, this popular restaurant serves Italian-influenced dishes such as a terrific linguine with prawns, mussels and crayfish, as well as local specialities such as lamb shank, beef *stifadho* (stew) and grilled swordfish. It has a romantic terrace on the village square as well as quayside tables.

If you just want a quick snack, it also does pitta *gyros* (meat slivers cooked on a vertical rotisserie; €3).

Tassia
TAVERNA €€

([☎]26740 41205; www.tassia.gr; mains €9-19; ⊙ noon-2am May-Oct) Step straight off your yacht and into a waterside seat at this taverna run by well-known Kefallonian chef Tassia, who delights diners with her homemade pies, mezedhes and courgette croquettes. Try the 'fisherman's pasta', incorporating finely chopped squid, octopus, mussels and prawns in a magical combination with a dash of cognac.

★ Irida
INTERNATIONAL €€€

([☎]26740 41343; mains €9-35; ⊙ 9am-late; [✻][📶]) Whether you dine in the shadowy boho interior with its lamp made from a deep-sea diver's mask or out on the waterfront, there's something for everyone at this 200-year-old salt store. Dishes include meatballs, stuffed aubergine, and the much pricier lobster risotto or spaghetti, and it's all scrupulously prepared and presented.

Le Passage
CAFE

([☎]26740 41505; ⊙ 9am-midnight; [📶]) Cool, very mellow quayside cafe festooned with little white lamps, and with a soothing soft-grey palette and cosy cushioned banquettes beside the water. Come early for simple breakfasts, at any hour for espresso with a smile, or in the evening for classy cocktails.

ℹ Information

Nautilus Travel (p703) and **Pama Travel** ([☎]26740 41033; www.pamatravel.com; ⊙ 9am-2pm & 5.30-9pm) can make all travel and ferry arrangements.

DON'T MISS

KEFALLONIA'S GREAT OUTDOORS

Kefallonia offers abundant and wonderful hiking, as detailed in many commercial maps and on noticeboards around the island. One gorgeous loop encompasses Agios Georgios Kastro, Moni Agiou Gerasimou, *robola*-producing vineyards and the south coast. If you fancy getting off the beaten path, it's well worth enlisting an experienced local to guide you.

Sea Kayaking Kefallonia ([☎]6934010400; www.seakayakingkefalonia-greece.com; day trips from €65) Offers a full range of day-long kayak tours, with lunch and snorkelling gear included (€65), plus some adventurous multiday excursions that see you paddling to out-of-the-way coves and beaches, and even hopping between islands. It also does certified courses.

Outdoor Kefallonia ([☎]6979987611; http://outdoorkefalonia.com) Offers all manner of trips throughout the island, from coasteering (€45), hiking (€60) and canyoning (€60) to sea kayaking (€65) and 4WD safaris (from €50).

Bavarian Horse Riding (Map p703; [☎]6977533203; www.kephalonia.com; Koulourata; 1-8hr €25-130) Ride sturdy Bavarian horses through the Kefallonian countryside. Day trips range from one to eight hours, with your choice of route. A longer trek leads across Mt Ainos and down to the sea, where you can take the horses for a swim. Multiday itineraries also possible.

WORTH A TRIP

ASSOS

It's almost hard to believe that a place as picture-perfect as Assos (population 88) can really exist. The pint-sized village is a confection of Italianate cream- and ochre-coloured houses, with a pretty crescent-shaped cove that's protected by a wooded peninsula. The fortress atop the headland makes a great hike (3.6km return), while the bay is eminently swimmable, and the water's so clear that you hardly need to put on a snorkel and mask in order to ogle the fish. Want a local secret? There's a hidden beach around the other side of the headland from the jetty at the northern end of the village, but it can only be reached by boat or a 15-minute swim!

A mouth-watering array of tasty tavernas, such as Molos (26740 51220; mains €7-14; 9.30am-late;) or Platanos (26740 51143; mains €7-15; 9am-midnight Easter-Oct;), plus a pace so slow you can palpably feel your pulse dropping, are compelling reasons to visit. Apartment Linardos (26740 51563; www.linardosapartments.gr; d/tr/q €80/90/120; May-Sep;) and Vassilis Retreat (26740 51174; www.vassilis-retreat.gr; apt €100;) are both great places to stay.

ⓘ Getting There & Away

BOAT

Two or three surprisingly large **West Ferry** (www.westferry.gr) boats arrive from and return daily to the big package-tourism resort of Nydri on the east coast of Lefkada. Buy tickets from Nautilus Travel (p703).

In the past these ferries used to sail to Vasiliki in southern Lefkada instead of Nydri, which was generally more useful for independent travellers, but at the time of research the port there was undergoing reconstruction and was closed to the ferries. It's not known whether this work was finalised after the pandemic restrictions of 2020-21. Be sure to check which port in Lefkada you'll be heading to!

BUS

KTEL (www.ktelkefalonias.gr) buses connect Fiskardo with Argostoli (€6.40, 1¾ hours, two daily), and with Sami via Agia Evfymia (€4.70, one hour, one or two daily).

ITHAKI ΙΘΑΚΗ

POP 3230

Every bit as rugged, romantic and epic as its role in Homeric legend would suggest, Ithaki is something special. The hilly, sea-girt homeland to which Odysseus struggled to return for 10 heroic years continues to charm and seduce travellers with its ancient ruins, breathtaking harbour villages and wilderness walks. Squeezed between Kefallonia and the mainland, it's the kind of island where time seems to slow down and cares slip away.

Cut almost in two by the huge gulf that shields Vathy, its main town, Ithaki effectively consists of two separate islands linked by a narrow isthmus. Vathy is the only significant settlement, but the mighty northern massif holds delightful villages such as Stavros and Anogi.

Ithaki doesn't go in for beaches the way the other Ionian islands do. It's true that there are lots of little cove beaches, but most of these are impossible to reach without a boat.

ⓘ Getting There & Away

Ionian Pelagos (www.ionionpelagos.com) runs two or three times daily in high season between Piso Aetos and Sami (Kefallonia; €4, 30 minutes), and once or twice from Piso Aetos to Astakos (on the mainland; €10, two hours 20 minutes).

Between July and mid-September, the **Meganisi II** (26740 33120; www.ferryboatmeganisi.gr) ferry runs twice daily between Frikes and Nydri on Lefkada (€8, one hour).

Buy tickets from **El Greco Tours** (26740 30000; www.elgrecotours.gr; 9am-8pm) or **Ithaca Tours** (26740 33336; www.ithacatours.gr; 9am-1pm & 2-7pm) in Vathy.

West Ferry (www.westferry.gr) has in the past connected Frikes with Fiskardo (Kefallonia) and Vasiliki (Lefkada); that service has not run in recent years, but it's worth checking the website to see whether it has resumed.

ⓘ Getting Around

Piso Aetos, the port on Ithaki's west coast, has no settlement. **Taxis** (6945700214, 6946552397) often meet boats, as does the municipal bus in high season. Bus services are very limited, though, with just two services a day running between Vathy, Stavros and Kioni, and so it's well worth renting a car – easiest in Vathy – for at least one day of your stay.

Vathy Βαθύ

POP 1820

Set around a superbly sheltered natural harbour, and fringed with sky-blue and ochre villas holding lively bars and restaurants, pretty Vathy is Ithaki's main commercial hub. The quayside buzzes with activity as small local fishing boats pootle out to sea and yachts throw anchor in the bay, while narrow lanes wriggle away inland.

◉ Sights & Activities

Other than a couple of moderately interesting museums, Vathy holds few sights to see, but there's some wonderful walking nearby. Follow the line of the harbour all the way east, until the road finally peters out, and a spectacular coastal footpath leads in another half-hour to the whitewashed waterfront chapel of Agios Andreas. Alternatively, stay on the road as it climbs away at the eastern end of the harbour; cross the brow of the hill, and you'll come to a succession of increasingly idyllic, secluded beaches – first Mnimata, then Skinos and, finally, after a total of 4km, the magnificent white sands of Gidaki (Map p703).

Albatross (☑6973467977) and Mana Korina (☑6976654351) offer boat excursions from Vathy in high season to outlying beaches and unpopulated islets. Odyssey Diving & Sea Kayaking (☑6948182655; www.outdoorithaca. com; ⊙9am-8pm mid-Apr–mid-Oct) is a very professional outfit offering an exciting array of kayaking, diving and snorkelling trips.

🛏 Sleeping & Eating

★ Perantzada 1811   BOUTIQUE HOTEL €€

(☑26740 33496; www.perantzadahotel.com; Odyssea Androutsou; d/q incl breakfast from €110/45; ⊙Easter–mid-Oct; ❋🛜⊛) Centred on a 19th-century neoclassical villa hovering above the harbour, this self-styled 'art hotel' holds large, balconied rooms as minimal as white clouds, replete with granite-and-wood bathrooms. Cheaper rooms lack sea views and share balconies, while larger suites in the new wing have baths you could free-dive in. The breakfast buffet is pure decadence, and there's an enticing infinity pool.

Hotel Familia   BOUTIQUE HOTEL €€

(☑26740 33366; www.hotel-familia.com; Odysseos 60; s/d incl breakfast from €110/125; ❋🛜) Converted from an old olive press, juxtaposing chic slate with soft tapestries and gentle lighting, this charming family-run and family-friendly boutique hotel has real wow factor. Superb value. Note that, although it's only 50m from the southwestern corner of the harbour, there are no sea views, and only one room has a courtyard.

Korina Gallery Hotel   BOUTIQUE HOTEL €€

(☑26740 33383; www.korinahotel.com; Telemachou 4; d from €70; ❋🛜⊛) This small hotel a short walk uphill from the town centre aims for an elegant, stately look, but it doesn't quite pull it off. Even so, the spacious rooms with full-length wooden shutters and paintings with filigree frames are an excellent option, with plenty of character.

★ Trehantiri   TAVERNA €

(☑26740 33444; http://trehantiri.ithakionline.com; mains €7-12; ⊙11am-11pm; ❋🛜) Traditional taverna with blue tables set up off the square in the heart of town. Every day the kitchen cooks up something different, from goat stew to stuffed tomatoes, saganaki (fried cheese) to kleftiko (slow oven-baked lamb or goat). Most of the ingredients are organically sourced. Look out for savoro (marinated local fish).

O Batis   SEAFOOD €€

(☑26740 33010; mains €8-18, lunch menu €15; ⊙11am-1am; ❋🛜) Vathy's top pick for ultra-fresh seafood sits amid similar-looking places along the harbour. Tourists flock to the waterfront tables, while local fishers, who've had quite enough sea views for one day, prefer the no-frills interior. It's one of the few places that do a set lunchtime menu (€15), which will net you a whole grilled fish plus salad and wine or beer.

Sirenes   GREEK €€

(☑26740 33001; http://sirines.eu; mains €8-15; ⊙noon-midnight; ❋🛜) A smart little restaurant a block back from the waterfront, with a cool front terrace and a swanky bar in its elegant wood-panelled dining room. Distinctive local dishes include lamb cooked in a clay pot and slow-cooked rabbit, plus there's fresh seafood.

❶ Information

El Greco Tours (p711) Ferries, car rental and accommodation.

Ithaca Tours (p711) Ferries, water taxis and accommodation, plus boat tours and rentals.

❶ Getting There & Away

Rent cars from AGS (☑26740 32702; www. agscars.com), on the western harbourfront, and bikes or scooters from **Alpha Bike & Car Hire** (☑26740 33240; www.alphacarsgreece.com; ☺9am-1pm & 5-7pm), behind Alpha Bank.

Ithaki's one bus runs twice daily between Vathy and Kioni, via Stavros and Frikes, on weekdays only (€4). Its limited schedule is not suited to day-trippers, however.

Around Ithaki

Cross the slender isthmus to reach Ithaki's northern half and you face an immediate choice of onward routes, along either flank of the island's towering (809m) central spine. Following the eastern road brings you after 5.5km to the somewhat dilapidated hilltop monastery of Katharon, which commands astonishing views back down to Vathy. Another 4km along this fabulously scenic mountain road, you'll reach sleepy Anogi, once the island's capital. Ask in the village *kafeneio* (coffee house) for the keys to the restored church of Agia Panagia, which holds incredible Byzantine frescoes.

Further north again, the east- and west-coast roads rejoin at the larger village of Stavros, above the Bay of Polis. A lovely rural walk up the nearby hillside leads to a site long known as the School of Homer (Stavros) but suggested by recent archaeological digs to be the long-lost palace of Odysseus himself. It's all in ruins, and smaller than you might expect, but wonderfully evocative nonetheless. Artefacts associated with the legendary hero are on show in Stavros' one-room archaeological museum (☑26740 31305; ☺8.30am-3.30pm Wed-Mon) FREE.

Dropping back seawards northeast of Stavros takes you to the tiny ferry port of Frikes, clasped between windswept cliffs and home to a cluster of waterfront restaurants and bars. The beautiful and sinuous coastal road beyond ends at pretty little Kioni, a hamlet of mustard-and-cream Venetian houses tumbling down to an irresistibly bijou harbour.

🏃 Tours

★**Island Walks**   WALKING
(☑6944990458; www.islandwalks.com; walks €15-18) Charming expat artist Ester runs guided walks of varying lengths all over the island. Her most popular route, the three-hour Homer Walk, winds up the hillside near Stavros to the ruins where the real Odysseus may have lived 2800 years ago, and also takes in the village museum.

OFF THE BEATEN TRACK

HIKING AROUND ANOGI

The highest village in Ithaki, Anogi (520m) is a beautiful, time-dusted place centred on its church and *kafeneio* (coffee house). The village is the starting point for a number of excellent walks. The easiest is the 6.5km, roughly two-hour return walk to the monastery of Kathara. An even better walk is the 11.5km, 4½-hour (without stops) Travel in Time hike, which winds all the way downhill to Kioni before climbing 520m back up to Anogi via a different route. Along the way hikers take in historic sites, churches and chapels, wild oak forests and soaring coastal cliffs, and get a chance to cool off with a swim on the way. For this walk, follow signs for route 12 as far as Kioni and then signs for route 12A back to Anogi.

🍴 Sleeping & Eating

Hotel Nostos   HOTEL €€
(☑26740 31644; www.hotelnostos-ithaki.gr; Frikes; s/d/f €100/135/165; ☺mid-Apr–Oct; ❄🖥🏊) The only real hotel in the northern part of Ithaki, the large, pink family-run Nostos has delightful airy rooms richly shaded in blues and with impressive photo art on the walls. The beds are unusually comfortable, the bathrooms decent and it's all set around a very inviting swimming pool. Attentive service rounds out the deal.

Kioni Apartments   APARTMENT €€
(☑26740 31144; www.ithacagreece.eu; Kioni; apt €110; ☺May-Oct; ❄🖥) A handsome Italianate building in the corner of the harbour, drowning in bougainvillea and housing welcoming apartments with wooden ceilings and large balconies. Stylish but homey, central but quiet. In a word: perfect.

Rementzo   TAVERNA €
(☑2674031719; www.ithacagreece.com/Rementzo/rementzo.html; Frikes; mains €8-15; ☺9am-midnight; ❄🖥) Right on the harbour in Frikes, this is a great place to sample traditional cuisine such as *stifadho* (stew) or fresh bream and dried apricots, as well as local speciality *savoro* (fish with vinegar, currants and garlic).

★**Yefuri**   TAVERNA €€
(☑26740 31131; www.facebook.com/Yefuri; Platrithias; mains €7-17; ☺6-11pm Tue-Sat, 11am-2pm Sun;

⊛ ⚉) This eclectic, very popular little restaurant, 2km north of Stavros, is renowned island-wide for its fresh produce and rotating Italian-influenced menu, which ranges from eggs Benedict for Sunday brunch to stir-fried chicken and roast pork for dinner.

Ithaki Restaurant GREEK €€
(✎ 26740 31081; Stavros; mains €8-15; ⏱ 11am-10pm) The best restaurant in Stavros wins big points for its expansive terrace with sunset views. The food is equally memorable: expect succulent meaty specialities such as local sausages, charcoal-grilled veal or pork, and lamb souvlaki.

ZAKYNTHOS ΖΑΚΥΝΘΟΣ

POP 40,760

Zakynthos, also known by its Italian name Zante, is an island of two stories. The southern and southeastern shorelines are dominated by heavy – and often low-quality – package tourism, although even here there are some attractive lower-key bases hiding just out of sight of the larger, run-of-the-mill resorts; examples include Keri and Limni Keriou in the remoter southwest. Once you leave the south behind, however, and set off to explore the rest of the island, you'll discover a different place altogether. It's one where plenty of forested wilderness and traditional rural villages remain, but it's the spectacular scenery of the rugged west coast, where mighty limestone cliffs plummet down to unreal turquoise waters, that's the true highlight.

ℹ Information

Isala Travel (✎ 26953 01600; www.facebook. com/pg/isalatravel; Lomvardou 30) in Zakynthos Town sells ferry tickets and offers boat excursions, vehicle hire and a wide range of island activities.

ℹ Getting There & Away

AIR

Zakynthos Airport (Map p715; ✎ 26950 29500; www.zakynthos-airport.com) is 5km southwest of Zakynthos Town.

Olympic Air (www.olympicair.com) Flies to Athens.

Sky Express (www.skyexpress.gr) Flies to Corfu via Kefallonia and Preveza.

Between May and September numerous charter flights connect Zakynthos with northern Europe and the UK.

Taxis between the airport and Zakynthos Town cost around €15.

BOAT

Ionian Group (www.ionian-group.com) runs between three and five ferries daily, depending on the season, between Zakynthos Town and Kyllini in the Peloponnese (€9.10, one hour). Occasional international ferries call in on the way to/from Igoumenitsa (on the mainland), Sami (Kefallonia), and Bari and Brindisi (Italy).

From the isolated northern port of Agios Nikolaos, **Ionian Pelagos** (www.ionionpelagos.com) ferries sail to Pesada in southern Kefallonia twice daily from mid-May to October (€8, 1½ hours); Chionis Tours (p716) sells tickets. Neither port has good bus connections, however, so most travellers find it easier and cheaper to cross to mainland Kyllini from Zakynthos Town and catch another ferry from there to Kefallonia.

Ventouris Ferries (http://ventourisferries.com) connects Zakynthos Town with Bari (Italy) in high season, with a stop in Sami (Kefallonia) en route.

BUS

The **KTEL Bus Station** (✎ 26950 22255; www. ktel-zakynthos.gr) is on the hillside bypass in Zakynthos Town, 500m from the waterfront and 15 minutes' walk southwest of Plateia Solomou. Long-distance routes include Athens (€28.60, six hours, four daily), Patra (€8.70, 3½ hours, four daily) and Thessaloniki (€54.40, 10 hours, two weekly). Budget an additional €9 for the ferry to Kyllini.

ℹ Getting Around

Zakynthos Town is the centre of an extensive local bus network.

Rental cars (from €40 per day in high season) and motorcycles are available at the airport and in larger resorts.

Europcar (✎ 26950 43313; www.europcar-greece.com; Zakynthos Airport) At the airport; office is open for all incoming flights.

Hertz (✎ 26950 24287; www.hertz.gr; Zakynthos Airport) Airport office open for all incoming flights and also in Zakynthos Town (p716).

Zakynthos Town Ζάκυνθος

POP 16,810

Sandwiched between steep wooded slopes topped by a ruined Venetian fortress and a huge harbour cradled between two long jetties, Zakynthos Town is the pulsing capital of the island. Famous for its glorious ensemble of Italianate architecture until an earthquake struck in 1953, it was subsequently reconstructed in fine style, with arcaded streets and gracious neoclassical public buildings. Recent years have seen the restoration of its showpiece waterfront square, the dazzling Plateia Solomou. The hubbub of everyday life

Zakynthos

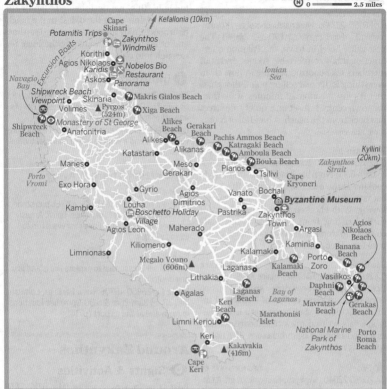

centres on the pedestrianised streets behind it, leading to smaller Plateia Agiou Markou.

You wouldn't base your whole holiday around the town's scruffy beach, but if you need to cool off with a swim, follow locals a few minutes' walk north of the centre.

◉ Sights & Activities

★ **Byzantine Museum**   MUSEUM
(Map p715; ☑ 26950 42714; Plateia Solomou; adult/child €4/free; ◷ 8am-3pm Tue-Sat) This magnificent museum of ecclesiastical art is housed in a beautifully restored building on the central waterfront plaza. Almost everything here was rescued – by volunteer sailors! – in the immediate aftermath of the 1953 earthquake, with displays including frescoes arranged in a replica of the 16th-century monastery of St Andreas.

Church of St Dionysios   CHURCH
(museum adult/child €1/free; ◷ 9am-1pm & 4.30-9pm) Devoted to Zakynthos' patron saint, the Church of St Dionysios (1948; rebuilt following the 1953 earthquake) stands at the southern end of the waterfront, near the jetty. Its interior holds opulent gilt work and impressive frescoes. The contrast between visiting tourists in shorts and praying elderly locals dressed all in black is quite startling. Around the back of the church is a museum. Exhibits include ecclesiastical trappings and vestments, including those of Dionysios himself.

Kastro   FORTRESS
(☑ 26950 48099; adult/child €4/free; ◷ 8am-2.30pm Mon & Wed-Sat) A ruined Venetian fortress sits atop the wooded slope that looms over the town centre. Reached by a steep but enjoyable 15-minute hike or a circuitous 2.5km drive, it's now essentially a peaceful forest park, enclosed within sturdy ramparts and affording tremendous views. Tumbledown churches lie scattered through the woods, along with a 19th-century British-made football pitch and a cafe.

🛏 Sleeping & Eating

Palatino Hotel
HOTEL €€

(📞26950 27780; www.palatinohotel.gr; Kolokotronis 10; d incl breakfast €70-120; 🌬🛜) The best-value hotel in town, the Palatino offers functional but comfortable rooms, and staff members take enormous pride in how clean everything is. Its real selling point, though, is that it's just a couple of minutes' walk from the town centre but set on a quiet side street just back from the beach. A handful of rooms have sea views.

To Kantouni
TAVERNA €

(📞26950 42550; Logotheton 15; mains €6-9; ⊙11am-6pm) No-frills, traditional home-style cooking is the order of the day at this small backstreet taverna that has a loyal local following. With checked tablecloths, strings of garlic hanging from the ceiling, and walls covered in replica 1930s posters, it could pass for a French bistro.

Stathmos
TAVERNA €

(📞2695 024040; Filita 42; mains €6-9; ⊙9am-11pm) A spit-and-sawdust kind of place attracting a diverse crowd of locals and in-the-know tourists, Stathmos has a list of daily specials written on a blackboard as well as a good range of island classics. The house special is rabbit stew.

⭐Prosilio
MEDITERRANEAN €€

(📞26950 22040; www.prosiliozakynthos.gr; A Latta 15; mains €9-19; ⊙6pm-late Tue-Sat summer, Fri & Sat winter; 🌬🛜) Gourmet dinner-only restaurant, with a boutique interior and a romantic garden courtyard. The hushed atmosphere may be unusual, but the service is relaxed and friendly, and if you love Greek food you're sure to relish inventive dishes such as Greek blue-crab risotto. The wine list abounds in well-priced local choices.

⭐Malanos
TAVERNA €€

(📞26950 45936; www.malanos.gr; Agiou Athanasiou, Keri; mains €9-15; ⊙noon-4pm & 7.30pm-late) This much-loved family-run taverna, set amid fields on the southern outskirts of town 2km from the centre, is renowned island wide for its huge portions of rich local favourites such as rooster, rabbit and wild boar, served at simple, plaid-clothed tables. For an authentic Greek dining experience it's unbeatable.

Ammos Taverna
TAVERNA €€

(📞26950 23753; Agiou Dionisiou 46; mains €8-15; ⊙1-11pm) In a small, tree-lined square right down at the far southern end of town and well away from the worst of the tourist hubbub, this nautical-themed, family-run taverna claims to be the oldest in the neighbourhood. Enjoy the expertly grilled sardines and other fish while watching the huge ferries pull into port.

ℹ Information

Chionis Tours (📞26950 48996; Lomvardou 8; ⊙7am-11.30pm) Useful agency for ferry tickets and other travel arrangements.

Isala Travel (p714) Ferry tickets, boat excursions, vehicle hire and a wide range of island activities. Also rents out luxury boats.

ℹ Getting There & Away

BUS

Frequent buses (€1.80) link the KTEL bus station (p714) with the resorts of Alikes, Tsilivi, Argasi, Laganas and Kalamaki. Fewer services run to inland villages.

CAR

A rental car is essential to explore the island in any depth.

Hertz (📞26950 45706; www.hertz.gr; Lomvardou 38; ⊙8am-2pm & 5.30-9pm) has locations in town and at the airport (p714).

Around Zakynthos

◉ Sights & Activities

Boat trips, run by **Karidis** (Map p715; 📞69 77275463; Agios Nikolaos) and **Potamitis Trips** (Map p715; 📞26950 31132; www.potamitisbros.gr; Cape Skinari; ⊙9am-9pm Apr-Oct), head from both Agios Nikolaos and Cape Skinari to the Blue Caves and Shipwreck Beach; smaller vessels can enter these sea-level caverns, whose water turns a translucent blue (yes, even more translucent than it normally is in the Ionians!) in the sunlight between roughly 9am and 2pm.

◉ Southern Coast

The **Vasilikos Peninsula**, poking south from the island's southeastern corner, is a little less developed than many other parts of the southern coast, though long, narrow **Banana Beach** (Map p715) on its northern side is awash with crowds, water sports and parasols. A little further along and things start to mellow out a bit. Take a side road heading west from the village of Vasilikos to find the 80-hectare **Logothetis Organic Farm** (📞26950 35106; www.oliveoilfarmshop.com; Vasilikos; ⊙10am-9pm) FREE. It produces purely organic olive oils (some flavoured with orange, lemon and other fruits) as well as olive-oil products. You can do an olive-oil tasting and watch the process of extraction. It also has accommodation (p718). Keep going right to the tip of the peninsula to reach Gerakas Beach (Map p715); a strand of fine sand that faces the Bay of Laganas, it's the best beach in the south. It's also a crucial turtle-nesting site, so visitor numbers are restricted, and all access is forbidden between dusk and dawn from May to October. Conservation advice is displayed near the access path and at the small Mediterranean Marine Life Centre (⊙9am-8pm) FREE next to the car park, where you can learn about the problems turtles face and perhaps see some at the in-house rescue and rehabilitation centre.

◉ Southwestern Coast

Beyond Laganas the rugged terrain of the far southwest starts to unfold. Follow a tiny road from the quiet village of Keri to reach lighthouse-topped Cape Keri and a high viewpoint surveying the endless cliffs that stretch away up the west coast; a converted van sells snacks. To access the parking and viewpoint here, you're expected to buy at least a drink at the van.

There's no shoreline road north, but a happily confusing tangle of highland routes threads through the wooded hill country parallel to the coast. Here and there, spur roads drop to coves such as Limnionas or climb to the clifftops, as at Kambi. Detouring inland brings you to villages such as Kiliomeno, where the Church of St Nikolaos features an unusual roofless campanile, and gorgeous Louha, a tiny, silent-at-noon village that tumbles down a valley surrounded by woodlands and pastures. There's nothing much to do here, but there are some enjoyable signed walks in the surrounding countryside and a small cafe selling snacks at the edge of the village.

◉ Northwestern Coast

The most dramatic sight along the west coast is magnificent Shipwreck Beach (Map p715; Navagio Beach). A favourite of Instagrammers travelling through the Greek islands, the beach is home to a stranded cargo ship that ran aground in the 1960s. The beach itself is only accessible on boat trips – in summer the waters immediately offshore are chock-a-block with sightseeing cruises – but you can

admire it from above, and get that all-important selfie, from a precarious lookout platform signposted between Anafonitria and Volimes. Do be careful here, though, if you're travelling with children or it's a windy day. There are no guardrails and the sheer cliff is quite unstable – it would be very easy to get blown off, and people have fallen here.

In an evocative clifftop site just south of the Shipwreck Beach turn-off, the Monastery of St George (Map p715) is well worth a visit on the way to the beach. The interior is covered in faded frescoes, and the strange tower at the centre of the complex was used by monks as a defence from pirate and Turkish attack: the monks hid inside and threw boiling olive oil over their attackers. (Today the only Turkish thing about the monastery are the free Turkish delights that are made by one of the monks and given to visitors!)

Locals sell honey and seasonal products pretty much everywhere, but Volimes, just north of the monastery and the beach, is the major sales centre for traditional products such as olive oil, tablecloths and rugs.

◉ East & North Coast

The resorts immediately north of Zakynthos Town are generally humdrum, but the further north you go the more dramatic the scenery becomes. The road narrows at the little ferry village of Agios Nikolaos, which holds a nice crop of restaurants and accommodation and has a small harbour beach as well as some pretty rocky platforms to swim off. It's a world away from the mega-resorts of the south. A nice walk (or drive) from here will bring you to the majestic headland of Cape Skinari, which marks the island's northern tip.

🛏 Sleeping

The huge curve of the Bay of Laganas, along the south coast, is lined with hotels catering to package holidaymakers, while the beach resorts immediately northwest of Zakynthos Town are a bit more sedate. More upmarket options are hidden away on the Vasilikos Peninsula in the southeast, and in Agios Nikolaos in the north.

Panorama   APARTMENT €
(Map p715; ☑26950 31013; Agios Nikolaos; studios €50; P ❄ 🛜) Excellent studios with sea views and basic kitchenettes occupy a lovely garden set back from the main road. Managed by a friendly English-speaking family, the

place is a 700m uphill walk south of Agios Nikolaos.

Logothetis Organic Farm Houses
COTTAGE €€

(📞 26950 35106; www.logothetisfarm.gr; Vasilikos; cottages from €80) Deep within an 80-hectare olive grove, the cottages here offer utter tranquillity. All are decorated in old-farmhouse style and many furnishings are homemade. Horses and goats wander freely, and horse riding and learning about olive-oil production are possible. It's perfect for families, as cottages sleep two to seven.

Joanna's Stone Villas
APARTMENT €€

(📞 26953 06787; www.joannasvillas.com; Vasilikos; d/q €124/152; ※ 🛜 🌊) Set among the olive trees a short way inland from the island's southeastern corner, these impressive apartments, maisonettes and entire villas have commanding views down to the coast, and lots of space. All have kitchens and share separate kids' and adults' pools. There's normally a three-day minimum stay.

Zakynthos Windmills
APARTMENT €€

(Map p715; 📞 26950 31132; www.potamitisbros.gr; Cape Skinari; apt from €60, windmills from €130; ※ 🛜) Two converted windmills – one dazzling white, the other with exposed-stone walls, each sleeping two guests – plus two- and four-person rooms and apartments occupy an old stone house with a fantastic clifftop location in Cape Skinari. Although there's a novelty factor to sleeping in a windmill, the rooms, which have boutique flourishes, are actually more comfortable.

⭐ Boschetto Holiday Village
VILLA €€€

(Map p715; 📞 6973743071; www.boschettovillage.gr; Agios Leon; villas €240; ※ 🛜 🌊) Fancy your own luxury stone cottage surrounded by oaks and olives that's tucked away from the rat race at the end of a long, dusty track? This place should do nicely. Each of the six villas has three bedrooms, two bathrooms, a fully fitted kitchen and a sunny terrace with private pool. Perfect for families and long country walks.

 Eating

Allegro
GREEK €

(📞 6979261627; Keri; mains €8-12; ⏱ 10am-11pm May-Oct; ※ 🛜) Don't expect to get much of a say in what you eat at this delightful, very welcoming taverna-cafe on Keri's village square. The chatty woman who runs it will likely take one look at you and decide what you're going to like. Fortunately, she's normally right! Whatever you have, it'll be good, home-cooked local food.

Cross Tavern
TAVERNA €€

(Stavros; 📞 6973334560, 26950 48481; Kambi; mains €7-16; ⏱ 10am-midnight; ※ 🛜) Perched above the west-coast cliffs at the end of the road that climbs beyond Kambi, and marked by a huge white Christian cross, this top-notch taverna extends over terraces, so diners can enjoy views so stunning they'll understand why someone built such a big cross here. The menu covers all bases, from omelettes to baked standards and grilled fish.

TURTLE TALK

The Ionian Islands are home to one of Europe's most endangered marine species, the loggerhead turtle (*Caretta caretta*). Zakynthos hosts the largest density of loggerhead nests, with up to 1300 recorded in some years along the Bay of Laganas, an area protected as the **National Marine Park of Zakynthos** (NMPZ; Map p715; 📞 26950 29870; www.nmp-zak.org).

Unfortunately, the extended tracts of clean, flat sand on which the turtles lay their eggs are also the favoured habitat of basking beach-lovers. Strict regulations are supposed to limit building, boating, fishing and water sports in designated zones, but these rules are not always obeyed. During breeding season (from May to October), nesting beaches are barred to visitors between dusk and dawn; from July onwards, as the eggs start to hatch, conservation agencies place frames with warning notes over buried nests. Many eggs are still destroyed by visitors, however, and countless hatchlings don't reach the water, having been disoriented by sunbeds, noise and lights.

Volunteers from Archelon (www.archelon.gr) and the park run education and volunteer programs, including a visitor centre at Gerakas Beach. To avoid harming turtles and nesting sites, don't use umbrellas on dry sand (use the wet part of the beach instead) and don't take boat trips in the Bay of Laganas, as these have been known to torment and even kill turtles.

Nobelos Bio Restaurant   MEDITERRANEAN €€€
(Map p715; ☑ 26950 31400; www.nobelos.gr; Agios Nikolaos; mains €22-30; ☺ 7am-midnight; ❀ 🛜) This exquisitely romantic restaurant is built into and around the rocks beside the private beach of its namesake boutique hotel. The irresistible setting is the main reason to come here, along with the sunset cocktail menu, but the Italian-Greek food is reliably good, with lots of seafood pasta options and meaty stews.

KYTHIRA   ΚΥΘΗΡΑ

POP 3973

Poised between the Aegean and Ionian Seas, the gloriously time-forgotten island of Kythira lies just 12km off the southern tip of the Peloponnese's Lakonian Peninsula. Despite its distinctly Cycladic sugar-cube architecture, both historic and modern, Kythira is officially regarded as belonging to the Ionian Islands.

With its population of fewer than 4000 spread between 40 villages, Kythira feels for much of the year like a ghost land; it's an unspoilt dreamscape of lush valleys, abrupt overgrown gorges, and flower-speckled cliffs tumbling into the vivid blue sea.

The lucky few who do make it here are invariably charmed by the island's spell and never want to leave. Do yourself a favour: however long you think you might need here, double it!

❶ Information

For more information on Kythira, visit www.kythera.gr, www.kithera.gr, www.kythira.info or www.visitkythera.com.

The free annual English-language publication *Kythera* is distributed in travel agencies, hotels and shops.

Kythira is doing admirable work to promote its **hiking trails**, with signposts added to many routes. Invaluable information, including trail guides and maps, can be found at www.kytherahiking.com, while Frank van Weerde's *Kythira on Foot: 32 Carefully Selected Walking Routes* (€10) is widely available.

❶ Getting There & Away

AIR

Kythira Airport (Map p720; ☑ 27360 33297), 10km southeast of Potamos, is connected to Athens in summer by both **Olympic Air** (www.olympicair.com; around €65, 50 minutes, one daily) and **Sky Express** (www.skyexpress.gr; €88, 50 minutes, twice daily except Tuesday

and Wednesday). **Ellinair** (http://en.ellinair.com) flies to Kythira from Thessaloniki (€89, 75 minutes, twice weekly). There are far fewer flights in low season.

BOAT

Kythira's ferry port is at sleepy little Diakofti, halfway up the east coast. Buy tickets at the port just before departure, or via Kithira Travel, with offices in **Hora (Kythira)** (☑ 27360 31390; www.kithiratravel.gr; ☺ 9am-2pm & 6-8pm Mon-Fri, 9am-2pm Sat) and in **Potamos** (☑ 27360 31848; https://kithiratravel.gr).

Boats from Neapoli in the Peloponnese come to Diakofti twice daily in summer, and once daily otherwise (€12.50, 1¼ hours); two each week continue to the even more remote island of Antikythira.

LANE Lines operates an intricate, seasonally changing schedule of ferries that connect Diakofti with Piraeus (€27, 6½ hours), Antikythira (€9.50), Kissamos (Kastelli, Crete; €22, 2½ to four hours) and Gythio (Peloponnese; €12.50, 2½ hours); in summer there are usually two weekly services to and from each of those destinations.

❶ Getting Around

Occasional buses operate in August. **Taxis** (☑ 6944305433, 6977991799) are pricey and charge around €30 between Hora (Kythira) and the airport. Your best bet is to hire a car; either pick one up at the airport, or have it dropped off at your hotel. Prices start at €30 per day.

Drakakis Tours (☑ 27360 31160; www.drakakistours.gr; Livadi; ☺ 9am-1pm & 4-8pm Mon-Sat) Rental cars, vans and 4WDs, with airport pick-up; airport transfers; buses to Athens (€45, one to two weekly); and sightseeing tours.

Panayotis Rent A Car (☑ 6944263757; www.panayotis-rent-a-car.gr; Airport; car/scooter per day from €30/15) A fleet of 120 cars – including 4WDs, small cars, motorbikes and scooters. Branches at the airport and across the island, including at Diakofti and Kapsali (call ☑ 27360 31600).

Hora (Kythira)   Χώρα
(Κύθηρα)

POP 270

Hora (also known as Kythira or Chora), the island's small capital, consists of a Cycladic-style cluster of white-and-blue cubes stretching south along a slender ridge towards a 14th-century Venetian *kastro* perched on a separate craggy hilltop. Most of the action centres on the open square at the town's northern end, while tasteful little shops, selling the likes of fine antiques and bespoke jewellery, line the way to the *kastro*.

Kythira & Antikythira

N
0 — 5 km
0 — 2.5 miles

Gythio (55km)

Neapoli (25km)

Cape Spathi

Kythira Strait

Platia Ammos

Fourni Beach

Karavas

Myrtoön Sea

Gerakari

Agia Pelagia

Agios Nikolaos

Petrouni

Lagada Beach

Stavli

Trifyllianika

Potamos

Katsoulianika

Hristoforianika

Ionian Sea

Lykodimou Beach

Logothetianika

Lianianika

Pitsinades

Vamvakaradika

Aroniadika

Kastrisianika

Frilingianika

458m

490m

Diakofti

Makronisi Island

Mitata

Kythira

Kato Hora

Mylopotamos

Viaradika

507m

389m

Cape Limnionas

Avlemonas

Skandeia

Paleopoli Beach

Cape Modoni

Fratsia

Kaladi Beach

Pitsinianika

Karvounades

Kalokerines

Goudianika

Alexandrades

Tsikalaria

Travasarianika

Kombonada Beach

Fatsadika

Skoulianika

Katouni Bridge

Sea of Crete

410m

Livadi

Kato Livadi

Kominianika

Katelouzianika

Fyri Ammos

Pourko

Strapodi

477m

Manitohori

Melidoni Beach

Kalamos

Hora (Kythira)

El Sol Hotel

Kapsali

Kastro

Vroulea

Cape Trahilos

Cape Kapello

Mediterranean Sea

Avgo/Itra

Inset: Antikythira

Diakofti (50km)

Crete (55km)

Potamos

Harhaliana

Galaniana

Antikythira

0 — 2 km
0 — 1 mile

Piraeus (230km)

Antikythira (50km; see inset); Crete (100km)

⊙ Sights

★ Kastro   FORTRESS
(Map p720; ⊙8am-sunset) **FREE** Crowning the rocky headland that soars at the southern end of Hora, this tumble-down 14th-century fortress was built by Kythira's first Venetian governor. Within its ramparts the fort is now largely in ruins, but the site is stupendous, drenched in wildflowers and commanding stunning views down to Kapsali and out as far as Antikythira. Only the underwhelming Coat of Arms Collection (adult/child €2/1; ⊙9am-2pm & 5-8pm Tue-Sun), in a former powder magazine, charges an admission fee.

As you leave, take a stroll along the adjoining eastern hillside, where several pretty little fresco-adorned chapels stand near the top of the footpath that leads to Kapsali.

Archaeological Museum of Kythira   MUSEUM
(⌨27360 39012; adult/child €4/free; ⊙8.30am-4pm Wed-Mon) Hora's impressive archaeological museum, beside the main road at the northern end of town, traces the history of 'this small island' in two rooms. Among artefacts from the ancient settlements of Palaiopolis and Palaiokastro, pride of place goes to the white-marble statue known as the Lion of Kythira.

🍴 Sleeping & Eating

Hora only has a handful of hotels, but it's the best place to stay if you're visiting Kythira in low season, and at any time of year it has a more local feeling than the nearby beach resort of Kapsali.

Hora is very short of dining options, though a couple of seasonal restaurants open in high summer.

★ Hotel Margarita   PENSION €€
(⌨27360 31711; www.hotel-margarita.com; s/d/tr incl breakfast €60/90/110; ⊙Easter-Oct; ❄📶) Set in an impeccably restored, white-walled 19th-century villa just off the main alleyway not far beyond the square, this charming French-run hotel offers 12 antique-furnished rooms accessed via a quirky old spiral staircase; note that bathrooms are very small. A wonderful terrace, used for the accomplished breakfast and afternoon drinks, affords fantastic *kastro* and sea views.

Nostos   PENSION €€
(⌨27360 31056; www.nostos-kythera.gr; d from €80; ❄📶) A delightfully old-fashioned five-room guesthouse right next to the church

(the bells start ringing around 7.30am) and below the *kastro*. Each room is different, but the unifying features are oil paintings on the walls and lots of polished-wood furnishings. Bathrooms are small. Breakfast is served in a time-warp cafe across the alleyway.

Corte O   APARTMENT €€
(⌨27360 39139; www.corteo.gr; r/2-bedroom apt incl breakfast 80/170; ⊙Apr-Oct; ❄📶) Three beautiful two-bedroom apartments set in a late-18th-century house just steps from the *kastro*. All have modern, minimal decor and full kitchens, private terraces and sea or valley views; one can be divided to create two en-suite rooms.

Zorba's   TAVERNA €
(⌨27360 31655; mains €9; ⊙7pm-midnight Tue-Sun; ❄) Nothing seems to have changed at this Hora institution for at least 60 years and it's now so retro that it could make the hipster generation giddy with excitement. Fortunately, though, the family who runs it isn't interested in such things and cares only about serving quality grilled meats, including the house special: Kythira sausages swaddled in local herbs.

🛍 Shopping

Every other shop in Hora seems to be a boutique selling designer-made jewellery and clothing.

Borse   FASHION & ACCESSORIES
(Yafanda; https://borse.gr; ⊙9am-9pm) Intriguing one-room, one-woman workshop on the pedestrian alleyway south of the main square. All the colourful and very distinctive hand-woven shoulder and clutch bags for sale are created on the loom in the middle of the floor.

Aquarium   JEWELLERY
(⌨6977287741; ⊙10am-9pm) Exquisite one-off pieces of bespoke jewellery are available in this boutique, overseen by the eponymous fish tank. It's not always open and hours vary, but it's worth persevering; if you hang around long enough the owner might come out of the next-door house. It's on the street that leads down the hill to Hora's main square.

ℹ Information

Kithira Travel (p719) Helpful staff; sells flights and boat tickets.

WORTH A TRIP

MYLOPOTAMOS

The delightful village of Mylopotamos nestles in a small valley 13km north of Hora (Kythira). The tables of charming *kafeneio* (coffee house) O Platanos (p724) fill its tiny central square, which is flanked on one side by the walled channel of a babbling stream that's populated by tame ducks and geese. As it flows northwest towards the sea, the stream cuts ever deeper into the wooded hillside, along a gorge that once held 22 watermills. Only one now survives – Mylopotamos means 'Mill on the River' – but a ravishing little footpath still follows the stream, leading through luxuriant greenery to the aquamarine pool of the Neraïda (Water Nymph) waterfall.

A separate hike, signposted along the left-hand fork in the road north of the village square, takes 15 minutes to reach the older village of Kato Hora. Make your way behind a castellated 19th-century villa here and you'll find the extraordinary ruins of Mylopotamos' Venetian-era kastro, a magical warren of abandoned churches and fortified houses, liberally overgrown with colourful flowers.

Kapsali   Καψάλι

POP 63

Down by the sea 2km east of Hora (Kythira), pretty little Kapsali was the island's main port during the Venetian era. These days, in summer at least, it's a bustling resort, with its two languidly curving bays lined by a necklace of tavernas, chic cafes and studios, and the sandy, ochre-coloured beach with its sheltered swimming. It's a superb spectacle when viewed from Hora's clifftop *kastro*.

Don't miss climbing up to the lighthouse- and church-topped low headland that separates the two bays. The views from the top are stunning.

The rocky islet offshore is known by two names. Avgo (Egg), referring to its legendary role as the birthplace of Aphrodite, and Itra (Cooking Pot), referring to its resemblance when topped by clouds to a steaming cauldron (apparently!).

🛏 Sleeping & Eating

There's a good selection of hotels and rental studios perched above the beach in Kapsali, but it all turns very quiet indeed in low season.

⭐ **El Sol Hotel**   HOTEL €€

(Map p720; ☑27360 31766; www.elsolhotels.gr; d incl breakfast €120, 5-person apt €170; P ❄ 🗢 ❄) Striking white-cube apartments, perched high above the Hora–Kapsali road, with Olympian views of the sea and across to Hora's *kastro*. Immaculate, minimalist rooms have private terraces, and there's a terrific pool, plenty of sunloungers, and a breakfast room packed with board games for rainy days (but let's hope those don't happen).

Vassili Studios   PENSION €€

(☑27360 31125; http://kithirabiz.com; d/tr incl breakfast from €65/75; P ❄ 🗢) This tree-lined complex has a perfect setting overlooking Kapsali Beach. Rooms are light and welcoming, with wooden ceilings and floors, shabby-chic furniture and wrought-iron beds; the more expensive options have bay views. It's about halfway between Kapsali and Hora.

Aphrodite Apartments   APARTMENT €€

(☑27360 31328; www.hotel-afrodite.gr; d/tr/q from €60/75/80; ❄ 🗢) On the coast road, barely a minute up from the beach, the gleaming white Aphrodite offers a choice between simple but spacious tile-floor rooms or apartments with kitchenettes and balconies. For the best views, choose the top floor. Irene and Yiannis are great hosts.

Trattamento   TAVERNA €€

(☑2736 037226; mains €9-12; ⊙noon-11pm) A newbie on the Kapsali dining scene, modern taverna Trattamento appeals as much to salt-crusted fishers as it does to holidaying city folk. The kitchen takes classic island dishes and serves them with contemporary zest. Try the cuttlefish in onion sauce.

🍷 Drinking & Nightlife

In summer, when bars and music venues open up along the waterfront, Kapsali becomes the nightlife capital of Kythira.

Fox Anglais   BAR

(☑27360 31458; ⊙noon-late Jun-Sep; 🗢) This veteran bar-club on the waterfront, with outdoor tables and a cosy interior, is the epicentre of Kythira's nightlife in summer, hosting acoustic music on the beach on Tuesday and DJs every other night.

ℹ️ Getting There & Away

While you'll need to drive to reach Kapsali from elsewhere on the island, a very pleasant (and very steep) footpath connects the bay with the village of Hora (Kythira) high above.

Potamos Ποταμός

POP 395

The attractive hillside village of Potamos, at the heart of the island, serves as Kythira's social hub. Its flower-filled central square hosts a Sunday-morning **flea market** and is great for people-watching any day of the week.

⭐**Pyrgos House** WALKING

(📋 6989863140; www.pyrgoshouse.com) Highly recommended outdoor activities, including €15 guided walks of Hora's *kastro* (10am Wednesday), a honey-bee excursion, grape gathering, olive-oil tasting and olive harvesting, cooking and dancing lessons, kayaking and exciting multiday walking holidays, among an apparently limitless array of options.

Panaretos TAVERNA €€

(📋 27360 34290; www.panaretos-kythira.gr; mains €7-14; ⊙1pm-midnight daily Mar-Oct, Thu-Sun Nov-Feb; 📶) One of five tavernas that amiably share the main village square for al fresco dining at cream-coloured tables and chairs, Panaretos excels with dishes based on home-grown produce, like wild goat with olive oil and oregano sauce or pork fillet with thyme.

⭐**Kafe Astikon** LIVE MUSIC

(📋 27360 33141; www.astikon.gr; ⊙7am-late; 📶) Very charming old cafe–music bar near the main square. The high-ceilinged and shadowy interior oozes atmosphere with its coral-green walls and its long wooden benches arranged around a makeshift stage. Expect live music (late) nightly in July and August, and impromptu jam sessions at other times. It also serves breakfast, pizza and pasta.

Agia Pelagia Αγία Πελαγία

POP 280

Kythira's northernmost resort, Agia Pelagia is a simple seafront village backed by swooping cliffs and wooded valleys. Vibrant azure waters lick against its sand-and-pebble beaches, while some magnificent volcanic beaches lie south beyond the headland. Red, pink and tawny along to **Lagada Beach**, they make a great target for coastal hikers.

🛏️ Sleeping & Eating

Hotel Pelagia Aphrodite HOTEL €€

(📋 27360 33926; www.pelagia-aphrodite.com; s/d/tr incl breakfast €90/100/140; ⊙Easter-Oct; 🅿️❄️📶) Right on the beach at the southern end of town, and run by returning Aussie-Kythirans, this lovely hotel has 13 rooms with wooden ceilings and huge, sea-facing balconies. The older rooms, whitewashed and simple, are closest to the waves, and there's a pleasant breakfast room downstairs.

⭐**Kaleris** GREEK €

(📋 27360 33461; www.facebook.com/kaleris; mains €7-11; ⊙noon-midnight Apr-Oct; 📶) Renowned for its creative cuisine, romantic little Kaleris has a waterfront pavilion and tables on the beach itself, shaded by tamarisk trees. Trust the charismatic owner, Yiannis, to advise on handwritten daily specials such as yoghurt salad with smoked aubergine, filo parcels with feta drizzled with thyme-infused honey, braised lamb shank or grilled prawns.

Around Kythira

You'll need your own transport to explore the back roads that thread between Kythira's scattered villages, which pass orchards and vineyards, olive groves and stands of cypress.

In the south, the small **Museum of Byzantine & Post-Byzantine Art** (📋 27360 31731; Kato Livadi; adult/child €2/1; ⊙8.30am-3pm Tue-Sun) in Kato Livadi, 6km north of Hora, houses icons and frescoes salvaged from churches all over the island. Spanning a shallow stream bed just north, incongruous **Katouni Bridge** (Map p720), built by the British in the 19th century, is the largest stone bridge in Greece. Head southeast, following spectacular twisty roads, to reach the mauve-grey stone beach at **Fyri Ammos**.

Avlemonas, further up the coast, is a former fishing village turned exquisite resort. A spotless vision of blue and dazzling white, with footpaths leading across the rocks to ladders that drop into the limpid turquoise waters (good snorkelling), it's basically everything the Greek island experience is supposed to be. The closest beaches lie to the west: first comes broad, pebbled **Paleopoli Beach**, then **Kaladi Beach**, in a separate cove and accessed via a staircase.

Few traces survive of ancient **Paleopoli**, just inland, but you can spend an enjoyable hour hiking up and around the hill that once held the **Temple of Aphrodite**, marking the

THE BIRTH OF APHRODITE

Kythira was famous in antiquity as the birthplace of Aphrodite. As described by Hesiod and painted by Botticelli, the goddess of love, desire and beauty rose resplendent from the foam upon a giant scallop, possibly off the islet of Avgo (Egg) off Kapsali. Confusingly, she's also said to have re-emerged near Pafos in Cyprus, so the two places haggle over the title of Love Island...

birthplace of the goddess of beauty. There's not a lot left of it today, but the quiet, barren wind- and sun-battered hilltop has its own special kind of romance.

Much more substantial ruins survive of Kythira's medieval capital, Paliohora, in the north. It's a magnificent spot, set on a craggy pinnacle at the confluence of two deep-cut gorges. In theory it was safely hidden from enemy ships, but it was destroyed by a Turkish fleet in 1537. Strewn with the tumbledown remains of chapels and mansions, the isolated hilltop can now be reached by driving a 4km dead-end road east of Potamos, the last 2km of which is unsurfaced, or following the delightful parallel hiking trail.

Kythira has a web of quiet country roads spinning out over the island, and one of the most enjoyable things to do here is to slowly drive around, going where whim and road take you (the island's so small that you won't be able to get *too* lost!). At the end of the road you might find yourself on a dramatic headland, at a tranquil beach, in a pretty village or at a half-forgotten church.

🛏 Sleeping & Eating

⭐ Maryianni
APARTMENT €€

(☎ 27360 33316; www.maryianni.gr; Avlemonas; studios €125-170; ⓟ ❋ 🕿) Rather wonderful white-and-blue studios sleeping up to four are stacked Cycladic style above the Avlemonas shoreline, with kitchens and sumptuous sea-view terraces. Even the smaller options are well above average, with boutique flourishes such as terracotta tiles, wrought-iron beds, classical art and choice furniture.

⭐ O Platanos
TAVERNA €

(☎ 27360 33397; Mylopotamos; mains €5-12; ⓧ 1pm-midnight; 🕿) The family behind this charming restaurant say that if you're searching for modern food then you're in the wrong

place, but if you prefer to savour hand-me-down recipes full of family secrets, pull up a chair here. And what recipes these are – the special is slow-cooked pork in honey that's laced with herbs and pretty much tastes of the island.

The setting is also delightful: a creaky old villa with a broad terrace shaded by plane trees and overlooking a babbling stream.

Although it's open all afternoon and evening, no food is served between about 4pm and 8pm.

⭐ Filio
TAVERNA €

(☎ 27360 31549; Kalamos; mains €8-12; ⓧ 4pm-midnight; 🕿) An acclaimed local taverna far off the beaten track, 1km beyond Kalamos en route to Fyri Ammos (look for signs), Filio offers island classics such as slow-cooked lamb in lemon sauce, aubergine stuffed with meat, and Kythiran sausages, served in a well-shaded terrace garden. The owners also rent out attractive apartments nearby.

Pierros
GREEK €

(☎ 27360 31014; Livadi; mains €6-10; ⓧ 1-4pm & 7-11pm; ❋ 🕿) For almost a century this family-run favourite has been serving no-nonsense staples such as *mousakas* (layers of eggplant or zucchini, minced meat and potatoes topped with cheese sauce), *pastitsio* (layers of macaroni and minced lamb), and baked chicken or veal. The main road through Livadi is hardly a beautiful setting, but locals drive from across the island to eat here. For an authentic Greek experience, it's hard to beat.

O Manolis
SEAFOOD €

(☎ 27360 38230; www.manolis-kythira.gr; Diakofti; mains €8-12; ⓧ 1pm-midnight May-Sep; 🕿) Locals head to this seafood specialist, its tables propped in the sand just north of the causeway in Diakofti, to savour excellent grilled fish or Italian-influenced risotto and pasta. You can watch the ferries pull into the port across the bay under the moonlight.

⭐ Skandeia
TAVERNA €€

(Map p720; ☎ 27360 33700; www.skandeia.gr; Paleopoli; mains €8-15; ⓧ 1-11pm; 🕿) A delightful family-run taverna just back from the eastern end of Paleopoli Beach, Skandeia places major emphasis on wholesome, freshly sourced local produce in preparing its definitive Greek cuisine, which ranges from lightly grilled red mullet to roasted aubergine with an aroma of wood smoke. Relax beneath the spreading elms and enjoy the Greek idyll.

Understand
Greece

History

A doorstep between Asia Minor and Europe, Greece has always been tied to the rising and waning fortunes of its neighbours. In the 5th century BCE Greece was almost devoured by the unstoppable spread of the Persian Empire, only reversed by Alexander. Later the Roman Empire overwhelmed old Hellas, but the nation revived once more under Byzantine rule. However, the Greeks' genius was their ability to adapt elements of other cultures' architecture and craft, taking it to new heights.

Early Days

The discovery of a Neanderthal skull in a cave on the Halkidiki Peninsula of Macedonia confirmed the presence of humans in Greece 700,000 years ago. People from Palaeolithic times (around 6500 BCE) left bones and tools in the Pindos Mountains, while pastoral communities emerged during Neolithic times (7000–3000 BCE), primarily in the fertile region that is now Thessaly. Agriculturally sophisticated, they grew crops, bred sheep and goats, and used clay to produce pots, vases and stylised representations of idols as figures of worship.

Artistic & Cultural Legacies

Ancient Civilisations

By 3000 BCE, Indo-European migrants had introduced the processing of bronze into Greece and from there began three remarkable civilisations: Cycladic, Minoan and Mycenaean.

Scholars divide the Cycladic civilisation into three periods: Early (3000–2000 BCE), Middle (2000–1500 BCE) and Late (1500–1100 BCE).

The Cycladic civilisation was a cluster of fishing and farming island communities with a sophisticated artistic temperament. The most striking legacy is the carving of statuettes from Parian marble – the famous Cycladic figurines. Cycladic sculptors are also renowned for their impressive, life-sized *kouroi* (marble statues).

The Minoans were Europe's first advanced civilisation, named after King Minos, the mythical ruler of Crete (and stepfather of the Minotaur). Around 1900 BCE, the splendid complex of Knossos was first built with its frescoes, ventilation shafts and sewerage systems marking an abrupt acceleration from Neolithic life. Using bronze, the Minoans were able to

TIMELINE	7000–3000 BCE	3000–1100 BCE	2000 BCE
	For 4000 years, inhabitants of the Greek peninsula live a simple agrarian life, growing crops and herding animals. Communities with housing and planned streets appear around 3000 BCE.	The discovery of blending copper and tin into a strong alloy heralds the Bronze Age. Trade gains traction; increased prosperity births the Cycladic, Minoan and Mycenaean civilisations.	Minoan civilisation reaches its peak in Crete: architectural advances lead to the first palaces in Knossos, Phaestos, Malia and Zakros, while pottery-making improves and Crete's first script emerges.

build great sea vessels and their reach extended across Asia Minor and North Africa.

The decline of the Minoan civilisation coincided with the rise of Mycenae (1600–1100 BCE), which reached its peak between 1500 and 1200 BCE with mainland city-states such as Corinth, Tiryns and Mycenae. Warrior kings, who measured their wealth in weapons, now ruled from heavily fortified palaces. Commercial transactions were documented on tablets in Linear B (a form of Greek language 500 years older than the Ionic Greek used by Homer).

Geometric & Archaic Ages

The Dorians were an ancient Hellenic people who settled in the Peloponnese by the 8th century BCE. In the 11th or 12th century BCE, these warrior-like people fanned out to occupy much of the mainland, seizing control of the Mycenaean kingdoms and enslaving the inhabitants. The following 400-year period is often referred to as Greece's dark age; however, the Dorians introduced iron and developed a new, intricate style of pottery, decorated with striking geometric designs. Significantly they were to introduce the practice of *polytheism* (the worship of many gods), paving the foundations for Zeus and his pantheon of 12 principal deities.

During the following Archaic period, about 1000–800 BCE, Greek culture developed rapidly; many of the advancements in literature, sculpture, theatre, architecture and intellectual endeavour began. This revival overlapped with the Classical period (the two eras are often classified as the Hellenic period). Advances included the Greek alphabet, the verses of Homer (the 'Odyssey' was possibly the world's first epic work of literature), and the founding of the Olympic Games and central sanctuaries such as Delphi. These common bonds gave Greeks a sense of national identity and intellectual vigour.

By about 800 BCE, Greece had been divided into a series of independent city-states, the most powerful being Argos, Athens, Corinth, Elis, Sparta and Thiva (Thebes). Most abolished monarchic rule and aristocratic monopoly, establishing a set of laws that redistributed wealth and allowed the city's citizens to regain control over their lands.

Classical Age

Greece's golden age, from the 6th to 4th centuries BCE, saw a surge in cultural creativity, increased economic reform and political prosperity. Athens reached its zenith after the monumental defeat of the Persians at the Battle of Marathon in 490 BCE, founding the Delian League, a naval alliance formed to liberate city-states still occupied by Persia. Many Aegean and Ionian city-states swore an allegiance to Athens, making an annual contribution to the treasury of ships, bringing it fantastic wealth

The Trial of Socrates by IF Stone (1989) frames in a contemporary investigative light Plato's version of events surrounding the philosopher Socrates' life and death.

HISTORY ARTISTIC & CULTURAL LEGACIES

Homer's classic work, the *Iliad*, written in the 8th century BCE, relates in poetic epithet a mythical episode of the Trojan War. Its sequel, the *Odyssey*, recounts the epic adventures of Odysseus and his companions in their journey home from the Trojan War.

c 1500 BCE	1500–1200 BCE	1400 BCE	1200–800 BCE
Santorini erupts with a cataclysmic volcanic explosion, causing a Mediterranean-wide tsunami that scholars suggest contributed to the destruction of Minoan civilisation.	The authoritarian Mycenaean culture from the Peloponnese usurps much of the Cretan and Cycladic cultures. Goldsmithing is a predominant feature of Mycenaean life.	The Mycenaeans colonise Crete, building cities such as Kydonia (Hania) and Polyrrinia. Weapons manufacturing flourishes; fine arts fall into decline. Greek gods replace worship of the Mother Goddess.	The Dorians overrun the Mycenaean cities in Crete. They reorganise the political system, dividing society into classes. A rudimentary democracy replaces monarchical government.

DEMOCRACY

The seafaring city-state of Athens was still in the hands of aristocrats when Solon, Athens' greatest reformist, was appointed chief magistrate in 594 BCE. His mandate was to defuse the mounting tensions between the haves and have-nots by cancelling all debts and liberating those who'd become enslaved because of them. Declaring all free Athenians equal by law, Solon abolished inherited privileges and restructured political power, establishing four classes based on wealth. Although only the first two classes were eligible for office, all four could elect magistrates and vote on legislation. Solon's reforms have become regarded as a blueprint of the ideological democratic system.

Greek is Europe's oldest written language, second only to Chinese in the world. It is traceable back to the Linear B script of the Minoans and Mycenaeans.

unrivalled by its poor neighbour, Sparta, and also turning it into something of an empire.

When Pericles became leader of Athens in 461 BCE, he moved the treasury from Delos to the Acropolis, reappropriating funds to construct grander temples upon it, including the majestic Parthenon, and elsewhere, including the Temple of Zeus at Olympia.

With the Aegean Sea safely under its wing, Athens began to look westward for further expansion, bringing it into conflict with the Sparta-dominated Peloponnesian League. A series of skirmishes and provocations subsequently led to the Peloponnesian Wars.

War & Conquest

The Persian Wars

Athens' rapid growth as a major city-state also meant heavy reliance on food imports from the Black Sea; and Persia's imperial expansion westward threatened strategic coastal trade routes across Asia Minor. Athens' support for a rebellion in the Persian colonies of Asia Minor sparked the Persian drive to destroy the city. Persian Emperor Darius spent five years suppressing the revolt and remained determined to succeed. A 25,000-strong Persian army reached Attica in 490 BCE, but was defeated when an Athenian force of 10,000 outmanoeuvred it at the Battle of Marathon.

Persian Fire by Tom Holland (2005) is a compelling account of the warring city-states of Athens and Sparta and how they had to finally pull together to face the Persian threat.

When Darius died in 485 BCE, his son Xerxes resumed the quest to conquer Greece with a massive land and sea invasion in 480 BCE. Some 30 city-states met in Corinth to devise a defence, forming the Hellenic League with an army and navy under Spartan command. The army held at the pass at Thermopylae, near present-day Lamia, the main passage into central Greece from the north. Despite the Greeks being greatly outnumbered, this bottleneck was easy to defend until a traitor showed the Persians another way over the mountains, from where they turned to attack the Greeks who retreated.

800–650 BCE	700–500 BCE	594 BCE	490 BCE
Independent city-states emerge in the Archaic period. Aristocrats rule these ministates while tyrants occasionally take power by force. The Greek alphabet emerges from Phoenician script.	Having originated around 1000 BCE in the Peloponnese, the Spartans come to play a decisive role in Greek history. Politically and militarily, the Spartans dominate for around 200 years.	Solon, a ruling aristocrat in Athens, introduces rules of fair play to his citizenry. His radical rule-changing – in effect creating human and political rights – is credited as being the first step to real democracy.	Athens invokes the ire of the Persians by supporting insurgencies within Persian territorial domains. Seeking revenge, the Persian King Darius sends an army to teach Greece a lesson but is defeated at Marathon.

The Greeks fell back on their second line of defence, an earthen wall across the Isthmus of Corinth, while the Persians advanced upon Athens and razed it to the ground. The Persian naval campaign, however, was not successful. By skilful manoeuvring, the smaller, more agile Greek warships trapped the larger Persian ships in the narrow waters off Salamis. Xerxes returned to Persia in disgust, leaving his general Mardonius to subdue Greece. The result was quite the reverse: a year later, the Greeks obliterated the Persian army at the Battle of Plataea.

The Peloponnesian Wars

The Peloponnesian League was a military coalition governed by the iron hand of Sparta, who maintained political dominance over the Peloponnesian region. Athens' growing imperialism threatened Spartan hegemony; the ensuing power struggle was to last almost 30 years.

Athens' support for Corcyra (present-day Corfu) against Sparta's powerful ally Corinth sparked the first Peloponnesian War (431–421 BCE). Athens knew it couldn't defeat the Spartans on land, so withdrew behind its mighty walls and blockaded the Peloponnese with its navy. Athens suffered badly during the siege; plague broke out killing a third of the population but the defences held firm. The blockade of the Peloponnese eventually began to hurt and the two cities negotiated an uneasy truce.

The truce lasted until 413 BCE, when the Spartans went to the aid of the Sicilian city of Syracuse, which the Athenians had been besieging for three years. The Spartans ended the siege, destroying the Athenian fleet and army. Athens fought on for a further nine years before it finally surrendered to Sparta in 404 BCE. Corinth urged the total destruction of Athens, but the Spartans felt honour-bound to spare the city that had saved Greece from the Persians. Instead, they crippled it by confiscating its fleet, abolishing the Delian League and tearing down the walls between the city and Piraeus.

The Rise of Macedon & Alexander the Great

By the late 4th century BCE, the Greeks were engineering their own decline. Sparta began a doomed campaign to reclaim the cities of Asia Minor from Persian rule, bringing the Persians back into Greek affairs where they found willing allies in Athens and an increasingly powerful Thebes (Thiva). The rivalry between Sparta and Thebes culminated in the decisive Battle of Leuctra in 371 BCE, where Thebes inflicted Sparta's first defeat. Spartan influence collapsed and Thebes filled the vacuum. In a surprise about-turn, Athens now allied itself with Sparta, and their combined forces battled the Theban army in the Peloponnese in 362 BCE. Thebes won the battle, but their leader was killed and Theban power soon crumbled.

HISTORY WAR & CONQUEST

In *The Peloponnesian War*, Thucydides sets out a historical narrative of the quarrels and warfare between Athens and Sparta.

The Histories, written by Herodotus in the 5th century BCE, chronicles the conflicts between the Ancient Greek city-states and Persia. The work is considered to be the first written narrative of historical events.

480 BCE	**477 BCE**	**461–32 BCE**	**413–404 BCE**
Darius' son Xerxes seeks revenge for the Marathon defeat and sacks Athens. The Greeks retaliate by smashing the Persian army at the decisive Battle of Plataea. The Persian Wars are over.	Seeking security while building a de facto empire, the Athenians establish a political and military alliance called the Delian League. Many city-states and islands join the new club.	New Athenian leader Pericles shifts power from Delos to Athens and uses the treasury wealth of the Delian League to fund massive works, including the construction of the magnificent Parthenon, an enduring legacy.	A second war between Sparta and Athens breaks out over the distant colony of Sicily, ending an eight-year truce. The Spartans break the Athenian siege and Sparta assumes total dominance.

Philip II engaged the philosopher Aristotle to tutor the teenage Alexander, who was greatly inspired by Homer's *Iliad*. Alexander retained a strong interest in the arts and culture throughout his life.

The political influence of the major city-states had by now been significantly eroded and they were unable to combat the new power in the north, Macedon (modern Macedonia), which was gathering strength under its aggressive monarch, Philip II. In 338 BCE, Philip II marched into Greece and defeated a combined army of Athenians and Thebans at the Battle of Chaeronea. Philip persuaded all the city-states (except Sparta) to swear allegiance to Macedonia by promising to campaign against Persia. Before the campaign began, Philip was assassinated and his 20-year-old son, Alexander, became king in 336 BCE.

Philip II's death sparked rebellions throughout the empire, but Alexander quickly crushed them, making an example of Thebes by razing it to the ground. Upon his black stallion he was always the first into battle ahead of his men, and was renowned for his valour, cunning and recklessness. After restoring order in Thebes, he turned his attention to the Persian Empire and marched his seasoned army of 40,000 men into Asia Minor in 334 BCE. After a few bloody battles with the Persians, Alexander succeeded in conquering Syria, Palestine and Egypt – where he was proclaimed pharaoh and founded the city of Alexandria.

Alexander continued his conquests east into what is now Uzbekistan, Balkh in Afghanistan and northern India. His ambition was to conquer the world, which he believed ended at the sea beyond India, but his now-aged soldiers grew weary and in 324 BCE forced him to return to Mesopotamia, where he settled in Babylon. The following year, at age 32, he fell ill suddenly and died. His generals swooped like vultures on the empire and, when the dust settled, Alexander's empire was carved up into fractious, independent kingdoms. Macedonia lost control of the Greek city-states to the south, which banded together into the Aetolian League, centred on Delphi, and the Achaean League, based in the Peloponnese. Athens and Sparta joined neither.

Alexander the Great is considered to be one of the best military leaders of all time. He was never beaten in battle and by the age of 30 reigned over one of the largest ancient empires, stretching from Greece to the Himalayas.

Foreign Rule

Roman Era

While Alexander the Great was forging his vast empire in the east, the Romans had been expanding theirs to the west, and now they were keen to start making inroads into Greece. After several inconclusive clashes, they defeated Macedon in 168 BCE at the Battle of Pydna.

The Achaean League was defeated in 146 BCE and the Roman consul Mummius made an example of the rebellious Corinthians by destroying their city. In 86 BCE Athens joined an ill-fated rebellion against the Romans in Asia Minor staged by the king of the Black Sea region, Mithridates VI. In retribution, the Roman statesman Sulla invaded Athens and took off with its most valuable sculptures. Greece now became the Graeco-Roman province of Achaea. Although officially under the auspices of

399 BCE	359 BCE	336–23 BCE	168 BCE–224 CE
Socrates stands trial, accused of corrupting the young with pedagogical speeches. A jury condemns him to death. Rather than appealing for voluntary exile, Socrates defiantly accepts a cup of hemlock.	In Macedonia, King Philip II seizes power. He seeks alliances with Sparta and Athens on a promise to wage war again on Persia. Following Philip's untimely murder, his son Alexander assumes leadership.	Alexander the Great creates one of the ancient world's largest empires, stretching from Greece to northwest India. He dies in 323 BCE in Babylon, aged 32.	Roman expansion includes Greek territory. First defeating Macedonia at Pydna in 168 BCE, the Romans ultimately overtake the mainland and establish the Pax Romana. It lasts 300 years.

Rome, some major Greek cities were given the freedom to self-govern to some extent. As the Romans revered Greek culture, Athens retained its status as a centre of learning. During a succession of Roman emperors, namely Augustus, Nero and Hadrian, Greece experienced a period of relative peace, the Pax Romana, which was to last until the middle of the 3rd century CE.

The Byzantine Empire & the Crusades

The Pax Romana began to crumble in 250 CE when the Goths invaded Greece, the first of a succession of invaders spurred on by the 'great migrations' of the Visigoths and then the Ostrogoths from the middle Balkans.

In 324 CE, in an effort to resolve conflict in the region, Roman Emperor Constantine I transferred the capital of the empire from Rome to Byzantium, a city on the western shore of the Bosphorus, which was renamed Constantinople (present-day İstanbul). While Rome went into terminal decline, the eastern capital began to grow in wealth and strength as a Christian state. In the ensuing centuries, Byzantine Greece faced continued pressure from the Persians and Arabs, but managed to retain its stronghold over the region.

It is ironic that the demise of the Byzantine Empire was accelerated by fellow Christians from the west – the Frankish Crusaders. The stated mission of the Crusades was to liberate the Holy Land from the Muslims, but in reality they were driven as much by greed as by religious zeal. The first three Crusades passed by without affecting the area, but the leaders of the Fourth Crusade (in the early part of the 13th century) decided that Constantinople presented richer pickings than Jerusalem and struck a deal with Venice, who had helped prop up the Christian army.

Constantinople was sacked in 1204 and much of the Byzantine Empire was partitioned into fiefdoms ruled by self-styled 'Latin' (mostly Frankish or western-Germanic) princes. The Venetians, meanwhile, had also secured a foothold in Greece. Over the next few centuries they acquired all the key Greek ports, including Methoni, Koroni and Monemvasia in the Peloponnese (then known as the Morea), and the island of Crete, and became the wealthiest and most powerful traders in the Mediterranean.

Despite this sorry state of affairs, Byzantium was not yet dead. In 1259 the Byzantine Emperor Michael VIII Palaeologos recaptured the Peloponnese and made the city of Mystras his headquarters. Many eminent Byzantine artists, architects, intellectuals and philosophers converged on the city for a final burst of Byzantine creativity. Michael VIII managed to reclaim Constantinople in 1261, but by this time Byzantium was a shadow of its former self.

63 CE	250	324	394
Christianity emerges after St Paul visits Crete and leaves his disciple, Titus, to convert the island. St Titus becomes Crete's first bishop.	The first Christian martyrs, the so-called Agii Deka (Ten Saints), are killed in the Cretan village of the same name, as Roman officials begin major Christian persecutions.	The 250 CE invasion of Greece by the Goths signals the decline of the Pax Romana and in 324 the capital of the Roman Empire is moved to Byzantium (later renamed Constantinople). Christianity gains traction.	Christianity is declared the official religion. All pagan worship of Greek and Roman gods is outlawed. Christian theology supplants classical philosophy.

Ottoman Rule

Greece is home to the oldest mosque in Europe. The Bayezit Mosque at Didymotiho was built by Ottoman Sultan Bayezit I in 1420. Damaged by fire in 2017, it is currently undergoing restoration.

Constantinople soon faced a much greater threat from the east. The Seljuk Turks, a tribe from central Asia, had first appeared on the eastern fringes of the empire in the middle of the 11th century. The Ottomans (the followers of Osman, who ruled from 1289 to 1326) supplanted the Seljuks as the dominant Turkish tribe. The Muslim Ottomans began to rapidly expand the areas under their control and by the mid-15th century were harassing the Byzantine Empire on all sides.

On 29 May 1453, Constantinople fell under Turkish Ottoman rule (referred to by Greeks as *turkokratia*). Once more Greece became a battleground, this time fought over by the Turks and Venetians. Eventually, with the exception of the Ionian Islands (where the Venetians retained control), Greece became part of the Ottoman Empire.

Ottoman power reached its zenith under Sultan Süleyman the Magnificent, who ruled from 1520 to 1566. His successor, Selim the Sot, added Cyprus to their dominions in 1570, but his death in 1574 marked an end to serious territorial expansion. Although they captured Crete in 1669 after a 25-year campaign, the ineffectual sultans that followed in the late 16th and 17th centuries saw the empire go into steady decline.

Venice expelled the Turks from the Peloponnese in a three-year campaign (1684–87) that saw Venetian troops advance as far as Athens. During this campaign, Venetian artillery struck gunpowder stored inside the ruins of the Acropolis and badly damaged the Parthenon.

The Ottomans restored rule in 1715, but never regained their former authority. By the end of the 18th century, pockets of Turkish officials and aristocrats had emerged throughout Greece as self-governing cliques that made cursory gestures of obligation to the sultan in Constantinople. Also, some Greeks had gained influence under the sultan's lax leadership or enjoyed privileged administrative status; they were influential church clerics, wealthy merchants, landowners or governors, ruling over the provincial Greek peasants. But there also existed an ever-increasing group of Greeks, including many intellectual expatriates, who aspired to emancipation.

Russia campaigned to liberate its fellow Christians in the south, and sent Russian agents to foment rebellion, first in the Peloponnese in 1770 and then in Epiros in 1786. Both insurrections were crushed ruthlessly.

Towards Independence

In 1814 businessmen Athanasios Tsakalof, Emmanuel Xanthos and Nikolaos Skoufas founded the first Greek independence party, the Filiki Eteria (Friendly Society). The underground organisation's message spread quickly. Supporters believed that armed force was the only effective means of liberation, and made generous financial contributions to the Greek fighters.

529	1204	1453	1460
Athens' cultural influence is dealt a fatal blow when Emperor Justinian outlaws the teaching of classical philosophy in favour of Christian theology, by now regarded as the ultimate form of intellectual endeavour.	Marauding Frankish Crusaders sack Constantinople. Trading religious fervour for self-interest, the Crusaders strike a blow that sets Constantinople on the road to a slow demise.	Greece becomes a dominion of the Ottoman Turks after they seize control of Constantinople, sounding the death knell for the Byzantine Empire.	By 1460 the Venetian stronghold of Morea (Peloponnese) falls to the Turks and centuries of power struggles between the Turks and Venetians follow.

On 25 March 1821, the Greeks launched the War of Independence. Uprisings broke out almost simultaneously across most of Greece and the occupied islands. The fighting was savage and atrocities were committed on both sides; in the Peloponnese, 12,000 Turkish inhabitants were killed after the capture of the city of Tripolitsa (present-day Tripoli), while the Turks retaliated with massacres in Asia Minor, most notoriously on the island of Chios.

The campaign escalated, and within a year the Greeks had captured the fortresses of Monemvasia, Navarino (modern Pylos) and Nafplio in the Peloponnese, and Messolongi, Athens and Thebes. The Greeks proclaimed independence on 13 January 1822 at Epidavros.

Regional differences over national governance escalated into civil war in 1824 and 1825. The Ottomans took advantage and by 1827 the Turks (with Egyptian reinforcements) had recaptured most of the Peloponnese, as well as Messolongi and Athens. The Western powers intervened and a combined Russian, French and British naval fleet sunk the Turkish–Egyptian fleet in the Battle of Navarino in October 1827. Sultan Mahmud II defied the odds and proclaimed a holy war, prompting Russia to send troops into the Balkans to engage the Ottoman army. Fighting continued until 1829 when, with Russian troops at the gates of Constantinople, the sultan accepted Greek independence with the Treaty of Adrianople. Independence was formally recognised in 1830.

The Modern Greek Nation

The Greeks, meanwhile, had been busy organising the independent state they had proclaimed several years earlier. In April 1827 the national Senate elected Ioannis Kapodistrias, a Corfiot and former diplomat of Russian Tsar Alexander I, as the first president of the republic. Nafplio, in the Peloponnese, was chosen as the capital.

There was, however, much dissension within Greek ranks. Kapodistrias was assassinated in 1831 after he had ordered the imprisonment of a Maniot chieftain, part of a response to undermine rising rebellion among the many parties whose authority had been weakened by the new state.

Amid the ensuing anarchy, Britain, France and Russia declared Greece a monarchy. They set on the throne a non-Greek, 17-year-old Bavarian Prince Otto, who arrived in Nafplio in January 1833. The new kingdom (established by the London Convention of 1832) consisted of the Peloponnese, Sterea Ellada, the Cyclades and the Sporades.

After moving the capital to Athens in 1834, King Otto proved to be an abrasive ruler who alienated the independence veterans by giving the most prestigious official posts to his Bavarian court. By the end of the 1850s, most of the stalwarts of the War of Independence had been replaced by a new breed of graduates from Athens University.

Eugène Delacroix' oil canvas *The Massacre at Chios* (1824) was inspired by the events in Asia Minor during Greece's War of Independence in 1821. The painting hangs in the Louvre Museum in Paris.

Poet Lord Byron was one of a large group of philhellenic volunteers who played an active role in fanning the Independence cause. Byron's war effort was cut short when he died in 1824 in Messolongi.

1684–87	1770s & 1780s	1814	1821
The Venetians expel the Turks from the Peloponnese in a campaign that sees Venetian troops advance as far as Athens.	Catherine the Great of Russia dislodges the Turks from the Black Sea coast and assigns several towns Ancient Greek names. She offers Greeks financial incentives and free land to settle the region.	The underground Hellenic Independence organisation known as the Filiki Eteria (Friendly Society) is established in the town of Odessa on the Black Sea coast. Its influence spreads throughout Greece.	On 25 March, Bishop Germanos of Patra (a member of the Filiki Eteria) signals the beginning of the War of Independence on the mainland. Greece celebrates this date as its national day of Independence.

BALKAN WARS

Although the Ottoman Empire was in its death throes at the beginning of the 20th century, it had still retained Macedonia. This was a prize coveted by the newly formed Balkan countries of Serbia and Bulgaria, as well as by Greece, and led to the outbreak of the Balkan Wars (1912 and 1913). The outcome was the Treaty of Bucharest (August 1913), which greatly expanded Greek territory (and with it, its fertile agricultural resources). Its borders now took in the southern part of Macedonia, including: Thessaloniki, the vital cultural centre strategically positioned on the Balkan trade routes; part of Thrace; another chunk of Epiros; and the northeastern Aegean Islands.

The Great Idea

Greece's foreign policy (dubbed the 'Great Idea') was to assert sovereignty over its dispersed Greek populations. Set against the background of the Crimean conflict, British and French interests were nervous at the prospect of a Greek alliance with Russia against the Ottomans, especially after 1862 when Otto was ousted in a bloodless coup.

British influence in the Ionian Islands had begun in 1815 (following a spell of political ping pong between the Venetians, Russians and French). The British did improve the islands' infrastructure and many locals adopted British customs (such as afternoon tea and cricket). But Greek independence put pressure on Britain to give sovereignty to the Greek nation, and in 1864 the British left. Meanwhile, Britain simultaneously eased on to the Greek throne the young Danish Prince William, crowned King George I in 1863. His 50-year reign eventually brought some stability to the country, beginning with a new constitution in 1864 that established the power of democratically elected representatives.

In 1881 Greece acquired Thessaly and part of Epiros as a result of a Russo-Turkish war. But Greece failed miserably when, in 1897, it tried to attack Turkey in the north in an effort to reach *enosis* (union) with Crete (who had persistently agitated for liberation from the Ottomans). The bid drained much of the country's resources and timely diplomatic intervention by the great powers prevented the Turkish army from taking Athens.

Crete was placed under international administration, but the government of the island was gradually handed over to the Greeks. In 1905 the president of the Cretan assembly, Eleftherios Venizelos, announced Crete's union with Greece, recognised by international law in 1913. Venizelos went on to become prime minister of Greece in 1910.

1822–29	1827–31	1833	1862–63
Independence is declared at Epidavros on 13 January 1822, but fighting continues for another seven years. The Ottomans capitulate and accept the terms of the Treaty of Adrianople.	Ioannis Kapodistrias is appointed prime minister of a fledgling government with its capital in the Peloponnesian town of Nafplio. Discontent ensues and Kapodistrias is assassinated.	The powers of the Triple Entente (Britain, France and Russia) decree that Greece should be a monarchy and dispatch the 17-year-old Prince Otto of Bavaria to be the first appointed monarch in modern Greece.	The monarchy takes a nosedive and King Otto is deposed in a bloodless coup. The British return the Ionian Islands (a British protectorate since 1815) to Greece in an effort to quell Greece's expansionist urges.

WWI & Smyrna

In March 1913 King George was assassinated and his son Constantine became the monarch. King Constantine, who was married to the sister of the German emperor, insisted that Greece remain neutral when WWI broke out in August 1914. As the war dragged on, the Allies (Britain, France and Russia) put increasing pressure on Greece to join forces with them against Germany and Turkey, promising concessions in Asia Minor in return. Prime Minister Venizelos favoured the Allied cause, placing him at loggerheads with the king. The king left Greece in June 1917, replaced by his second-born son, Alexander, who was more amenable to the Allies.

Greek troops served with distinction on the Allied side, but when the war ended in 1918 the promised land in Asia Minor was not forthcoming. Venizelos led a diplomatic campaign to further the case and, with Allied acquiescence, landed troops in Smyrna (present-day İzmir in Turkey) in May 1919, under the guise of protecting the half a million Greeks living in the city. With a seemingly viable hold in Asia Minor, Venizelos ordered his troops to march ahead, and by September 1921 they had advanced as far as Ankara. By this stage foreign support for Venizelos had ebbed and Turkish forces, commanded by Mustafa Kemal (later to become Atatürk), halted the offensive. The Greek army retreated but Smyrna fell in 1922, and tens of thousands of its Greek inhabitants were killed.

The outcome of these hostilities was the Treaty of Lausanne in July 1923, whereby Turkey recovered eastern Thrace and the islands of Imvros and Tenedos, while Italy kept the Dodecanese (which it had temporarily acquired in 1912 and would hold until 1947).

The treaty also called for a population exchange between Greece and Turkey to prevent future disputes. Almost 1.5 million Greeks left Turkey and almost 400,000 Turks left Greece. The exchange put tremendous strain on the Greek economy and caused great bitterness and hardship. Many Greeks abandoned a privileged life in Asia Minor for one of extreme poverty in emerging urban shanty towns in Athens and Thessaloniki.

The Republic of 1924–35

The arrival of the Greek refugees from Turkey coincided with, and compounded, a period of political instability unprecedented even by Greek standards. In 1920 King Alexander died from a monkey bite and his father Constantine was restored to the throne. But the ensuing political crisis deepened and Constantine abdicated (again) after the fall of Smyrna. He was replaced by his first son, George II, who was no match for the group of army officers who seized power after the war. A republic was proclaimed in March 1924 amid a series of coups and countercoups.

1863–64	1883	1896	1912–13
The British engineer the ascension to the Greek throne of Danish Prince William, later crowned King George I. His 50-year reign begins with a new constitution in 1864.	Greece completes construction of the Corinth Canal that cuts through the Isthmus of Corinth. The engineering feat opens a link between the Aegean and Ionian Seas.	The staging of the first modern Olympic Games in Athens marks Greece's coming of age. Winners receive a silver medal and olive crown, and second and third places receive a bronze medal and a laurel branch respectively.	The Balkan Wars erupt when Greece and Serbia initially side with Bulgaria against Turkey over Macedonia. Then Greece and Serbia fight for the same territory against Bulgaria. Greece's territory expands.

A measure of stability was attained with Venizelos' return to power in 1928. He pursued a policy of economic and educational reform, but progress was inhibited by the Great Depression. His antiroyalist Liberal Party faced a growing challenge from the monarchist Popular Party, culminating in defeat at the polls in March 1933. The new government was preparing for the restoration of the monarchy when Venizelos and his supporters staged an unsuccessful coup in March 1935. Venizelos was exiled to Paris, where he died a year later. In November 1935 King George II reassumed the throne and installed the right-wing General Ioannis Metaxas as prime minister. Nine months later, Metaxas assumed dictatorial powers with the king's consent, under the pretext of preventing a communist-inspired republican coup.

WWII

Metaxas' grandiose vision was to create a utopian Third Greek Civilisation, based on its glorious ancient and Byzantine past, but what he actually created was more like a Greek version of the Third Reich. He exiled or imprisoned opponents, banned trade unions and the recently established Kommounistiko Komma Elladas (KKE, the Greek Communist Party), imposed press censorship and created a secret police force and fascist-style youth movement. But Metaxas is best known for his reply of *ohi* (no) to Mussolini's ultimatum to allow Italians passage through Greece at the beginning of WWII, thus maintaining Greece's policy of strict neutrality. The Italians invaded Greece, but the Greeks drove them back into Albania.

Inside Hitler's Greece: The Experience of Occupation, 1941–44, by Mark Mazower (2001), is an intimate and comprehensive account of Greece under Nazi occupation and the rise of the resistance movement.

A prerequisite of Hitler's plan to invade the Soviet Union was a secure southern flank in the Balkans. The British, realising this, asked Metaxas if they could land troops in Greece. He gave the same reply as he had given the Italians, but then died suddenly in January 1941. The king replaced him with the more timid Alexandros Koryzis, who agreed to British forces landing in Greece. Koryzis committed suicide when German troops invaded Greece on 6 April 1941. The Germans vastly outnumbered the defending Greek, British, Australian and New Zealand troops, and the whole country was under German occupation within a few weeks. The civilian population suffered appallingly during the occupation, many dying of starvation. The Germans rounded up between 60,000 and 70,000 Greek Jews, at least 80% of the country's Jewish population, and transported them to death camps.

Numerous resistance movements sprang up. The dominant three were Ellinikos Laïkos Apeleftherotikos Stratos (ELAS), the left-wing Ethnikon Apeleftherotikon Metopon (EAM) and the right-wing Ethnikos Dimokratikos Ellinikos Syndesmos (EDES). These groups fought one

1914	1919–23	1924–34	1935
The outbreak of WWI sees Greece initially neutral but eventually siding with the Western Allies against Germany and Turkey on the promise of land in Asia Minor.	Greece embarks on the 'Great Idea' to unite former Hellenic regions, including those in Asia Minor. It fails and leads to a population exchange between Greece and Turkey in 1923 (aka the Asia Minor catastrophe).	Greece is proclaimed a republic and King George II leaves Greece. The Great Depression counters the nation's return to stability. Monarchists and parliamentarians under Eleftherios Venizelos tussle for control.	The monarchy is restored and King George II is reappointed to the throne. Right-wing General Ioannis Metaxas adopts the role of prime minister while introducing dictatorial measures of governance.

another with as much venom as they fought the Germans, often with devastating results for the civilian Greek population.

The Germans began to retreat from Greece in October 1944, but the communist and monarchist resistance groups continued to fight one another.

Civil War

By late 1944 the royalists, republicans and communists were polarised by interparty division and locked in a serious battle for control. The British-backed provisional government was in an untenable position: the left was threatening revolt while the British were pushing to prevent the communists from further legitimising their hold over the administration and vying to reinstate the Greek monarchy.

On 3 December 1944, the police fired on a communist demonstration in Plateia Syntagmatos (Syntagma Sq) in Athens, killing 28 people. The ensuing six weeks of fighting between the left and the right, known as the Dekemvriana (events of December), marked the first round of the Greek Civil War. British troops intervened and prevented an ELAS-EAM coalition victory.

In February 1945 formal negotiations for reconciliation between the government and the communists fell flat, and the friction continued. Many civilians on all political sides were subjected to bitter reprisals at the hands of leftist groups, the army or rogue right-wing vigilantes. The royalists won the March 1946 election (which the communists had unsuccessfully boycotted), and a plebiscite (widely reported as rigged) in September put George II back on the throne.

In October the left-wing Democratic Army of Greece (DSE) was formed to resume the fight against the monarchy and its British supporters. Under the leadership of Markos Vafiadis, the DSE swiftly occupied a large swathe of land along Greece's northern border with Albania and Yugoslavia.

In 1947 the US intervened and the civil war developed into a setting for the new Cold War theatre. Communism was declared illegal and the government introduced its notorious Certificate of Political Reliability (remaining valid until 1962), which declared that the document bearer was not a left-wing sympathiser; without this certificate Greeks could not vote and found it almost impossible to get work. US aid did little to improve the situation on the ground. The DSE continued to be supplied from the north (by Yugoslavia, Bulgaria and indirectly by the Soviets through the Balkan states) and, by the end of 1947, large chunks of the mainland were under its control as well as parts of the islands of Crete, Chios and Lesvos. The fighting dragged on until

1940	1941–44	1944–49	1967–74
On 28 October Metaxas famously rebuffs the Italian request to traverse Greece at the beginning of WWII. The Italians engage Greek forces and are driven back into Albania.	Germany invades and occupies Greece. Monarchists, republicans and communists form resistance groups that, despite infighting, drive out the Germans after three years.	The end of WWII sees Greece descend into civil war, pitching monarchists against communists. The monarchists recover in 1946, but the civil war takes its toll and many Greeks emigrate in search of a better life.	Right- and left-wing factions continue to bicker, provoking in April 1967 a right-wing military coup d'état by army generals who establish a junta. They impose martial law and abolish many civil rights.

October 1949, when Yugoslavia fell out with the Soviet Union and cut the DSE's supply lines.

The civil war left Greece politically frayed and economically shattered. More Greeks had been killed in three years of bitter civil war than in WWII, and a quarter of a million people were homeless. The sense of despair became the trigger for a mass exodus. Almost a million Greeks headed off in search of a better life elsewhere, primarily to Australia, Canada and the US.

Reconstruction

After a series of unworkable coalitions, the electoral system was changed to majority voting in 1952 – which excluded the communists from future governments. The November 1952 election was a victory for the right-wing Ellinikos Synagermos (Greek Rally). The leader, General Alexander Papagos (a former civil-war field marshal), remained in power until his death in 1955, when he was replaced by Konstandinos Karamanlis.

Greece joined NATO in 1952, and in 1953 the US was granted the right to operate sovereign bases. Intent on maintaining support for the anticommunist government, the US gave generous economic and military aid.

In 1958 Georgios Papandreou founded the broadly based Centre Union (EK), but elections in 1961 returned the National Radical Union (ERE), Karamanlis' new name for Greek Rally, to power for the third time in succession. Papandreou accused the ERE of ballot rigging, and the political turmoil that followed culminated in the murder, in May 1963, of Grigoris Lambrakis, the deputy of the communist Union of the Democratic Left (EDA). All this proved too much for Karamanlis, who resigned and went to live in Paris.

The EK finally came to power in February 1964 and Papandreou wasted no time in implementing a series of radical changes. He freed political prisoners and allowed exiles to come back to Greece, reduced income tax and the defence budget, and increased spending on social services and education.

Colonels, Monarchs & Democracy

The political right in Greece was rattled by Papandreou's tolerance of the left, and a group of army colonels, led by Georgios Papadopoulos and Stylianos Patakos, staged a coup on 21 April 1967. They established a military junta with Papadopoulos as prime minister. King Constantine tried an unsuccessful countercoup in December, after which he fled to Rome, then London.

> The 1963 political assassination of Grigoris Lambrakis is described in Vassilis Vassilikos' novel *Z*, which later became an award-winning film.

> The Green Line separating Greece and Turkey in Cyprus is a demilitarised buffer zone where the clock stopped in 1974. Greeks still peer through the barbed-wire partition to the place they were born and banished from, and are unlikely to return to live.

1974	1981	1981–90	1999
A botched plan to unite Cyprus with Greece prompts the invasion of Cyprus by Turkish troops and results in the fall of the military junta. This acts as a catalyst for the restoration of parliamentary democracy in Greece.	Greece joins the EU, effectively removing protective trade barriers and opening up the Greek economy to the wider world for the first time. The economy grows smartly.	Greece acquires its first elected socialist government (PASOK) under the leadership of Andreas Papandreou. PASOK rules for almost two decades (minus 1990–93 when the conservatives retake power).	Turkey and Greece experience powerful earthquakes within weeks of each other that result in hundreds of deaths. By pledging mutual aid and support, the two nations initiate a warming of diplomatic relations.

The colonels declared martial law, banned political parties and trade unions, imposed censorship, and imprisoned, tortured and exiled thousands of dissidents. In June 1972 Papadopoulos declared Greece a republic and appointed himself president.

On 17 November 1973, tanks stormed a building at the Athens Polytechnio (Technical University) to quell a student occupation calling for an uprising against the US-backed junta. While the number of casualties is still in dispute (more than 20 students were reportedly killed and hundreds injured), the act spelled the death knell for the junta.

The junta dictatorship collapsed. Karamanlis was invited back from self-imposed exile in Paris to take office and his New Democracy (ND) party won a large majority at the November elections in 1974, against the newly formed Panhellenic Socialist Union (PASOK), led by Andreas Papandreou (son of Georgios). A plebiscite voted 69% against the restoration of the monarchy and the ban on communist parties was lifted.

The 1980s & 1990s

When Greece became the 10th member of the EU in 1981, it was the smallest and poorest member. In October 1981 Andreas Papandreou's PASOK party was elected as Greece's first socialist government. PASOK promised ambitious social reform, to close the US air bases and to withdraw from NATO. US military presence was reduced, but unemployment was high and reforms in education and welfare were limited. Women's issues fared better: the dowry system was abolished, abortion legalised, and civil marriage and divorce were implemented.

Economic scandal, a series of general strikes and fundamental policy wrangling over the country's education system damaged PASOK, and in 1990 Konstandinos Mitsotakis led the ND back to office. Intent on redressing the country's economic problems – high inflation and high government spending – the government imposed austerity measures, including a wage freeze for civil servants and steep increases in public-utility costs and basic services.

By late 1992 corruption allegations were being levelled against the government. By mid-1993 Mitsotakis supporters had abandoned the ND for the new Political Spring party; the ND lost its parliamentary majority and an early election in October returned Andreas Papandreou's PASOK party.

Papandreou stepped down in early 1996 due to ill health and died on 26 June that year. His departure produced a dramatic change of direction for PASOK, with the party abandoning Papandreou's left-leaning politics and electing experienced economist and lawyer Costas Simitis as the new prime minister, who won a comfortable majority at the October 1996 polls.

HISTORY THE MODERN GREEK NATION

The bestseller *Eleni*, written by Nicholas Gage (1996), tells the gripping personal account of his family's life in the village of Lia, and the events leading to the execution of Gage's mother by communist guerrillas during the Greek Civil War.

2001	2004	2007	2008
Greece adopts the euro, joining the first wave of European countries to introduce the new currency on 1 January 2002.	Greece successfully hosts the 28th Summer Olympic Games but they cost €9 billion, double the original target. Greece also wins the European football championship.	Vast forest fires devastate much of the western Peloponnese as well as parts of Evia and Epiros, causing Greece's worst ecological disaster in decades. Thousands lose their homes and 66 people perish.	Police shoot and kill a 15-year-old boy in Athens following an alleged exchange between police and youths. This sparks a series of urban riots nationwide.

The 21st Century

The new millennium saw Greece join the eurozone in 2001, amid rumblings from existing members that it was not economically ready – its public borrowing was too high, as was its inflation level. In hindsight, many look back on that year and bemoan the miscalibration of the drachma against the euro, claiming Greece's currency was undervalued, and that, overnight, living became disproportionately more expensive. That said, billions of euros poured into large-scale infrastructure projects across Greece, including the redevelopment of Athens – spurred on largely by its hosting of the 2004 Olympic Games. However, rising unemployment, ballooning public debt, slowing inflation and the squeezing of consumer credit took their toll. Public opinion soured further in 2007 when the conservative government (who had come to power in 2004) was widely criticised for its handling of severe summer fires, responsible for widespread destruction throughout Greece. Nevertheless, snap elections held in September 2007 returned the conservatives, albeit with a diminished majority.

In the following years, a series of massive general strikes and blockades highlighted mounting electoral discontent. Hundreds of thousands of people protested against proposed radical labour and pension reforms and privatisation plans that analysts claimed would help curb public debt. The backlash against the government reached boiling point in December 2008, when urban rioting broke out across the country, led by youths outraged by the police shooting of a 15-year-old boy in Athens following an alleged exchange between police and a group of teenagers. Youths hurled stones and firebombs at riot police who responded with tear gas. Following a series of financial and corruption scandals, a general election held in October 2009, midway through Karamanlis' term, saw PASOK (under Georgios Papandreou) take back the reins in a landslide win against the conservatives.

The Crisis & Austerity

In 2009 a lethal cocktail of high public spending and widespread tax evasion, combined with the credit crunch of global recession, threatened to cripple Greece's economy. In 2010 Greece's fellow eurozone countries agreed to a €125 billion package (half of Greece's GDP) to get the country back on its feet, though with strict conditions – the ruling government, PASOK, still led by Georgios Papandreou, would have to impose austere measures of reform and reduce Greece's bloated deficit.

The austerity programme didn't work, Papandreou resigned in 2011 to be replaced as prime minister by Lucas Papademos – a former vice president of the European Central Bank – who lasted barely six months in the post. A second EU bailout of €130 billion brought further austerity

---

Prince Philip, Duke of Edinburgh, was part of the Greek royal family – born on Corfu as Prince Philip of Greece and Denmark in 1921. Former king of Greece, Constantine, is Prince William's godfather and Prince Charles' third cousin. Constantine and his family were exiled in London for 46 years, returning to Athens in 2013.

2008	2009	2011	2012–13
Police shoot and kill a 15-year-old boy in Athens following an alleged exchange between police and youths. This sparks a series of urban riots nationwide.	Eurozone countries approve a €110-billion rescue package for the country's economic crisis, in exchange for tougher austerity laws.	Protesters march on parliament to oppose government efforts to pass new austerity laws. Prime Minister Papandreou resigns and a coalition government is formed by Antonis Samaras of the New Democracy party.	Parliament passes a €13.5-billion austerity plan to secure a second €130-billion EU and IMF bailout. Unemployment rises to 26.8% – the highest rate in the EU.

requirements and Athens again saw major strikes aimed at the massive cuts – 22% off minimum wage, 15% off pensions and the axing of 15,000 public-sector jobs.

These were indeed brutal times for the average Greek, with wage cuts of around 30% and up to 17 'new' taxes crippling monthly income. While the EU and IMF initially predicted that Greece would return to growth in 2014, the inability for many Greeks to pay their taxes at the end of the year meant that growth was a mere 0.4%.

In January 2015 left-wing Syriza, led by Alexis Tsipras, formed a co-alition with right-wing Independent Greeks (ANEL) to win the general election with an antiausterity platform. June 2015 saw Greece become the first first-world nation to go into arrears with the EU and IMF. Attempts to negotiate a new bailout and avoid default were unsuccessful as Tsipras took the offer back to Greece and held a referendum. Over 61% of voters were not willing to accept the bailout conditions.

The week that followed was one of turmoil. Greek banks closed and began running out of cash, and stock markets around the world fell as the EU produced a detailed plan for a possible Grexit – Greece's removal from the EU. At the 11th hour, Tsipras secured an €86 billion bailout loan – but the austerity measures attached were even more vigorous than those proposed before the referendum.

Continued political turmoil over the bailout led Tsipras to resign in August 2015 and return to the polls in September. This was Greece's fourth election in just over three years. The outcome was an unexpectedly large victory for Tsipras, just six seats short of an absolute majority. Nevertheless, voter turnout was 57%, the lowest recorded in Greece.

Road to Recovery

In August 2018 Greece finally exited the €86 billion bailout programme. Under Tsipras' government unemployment had fallen, consumer spending had risen and poverty was on the decline. Even so, voters, exhausted with austerity, rejected Syriza, first in the local and European Parliament elections in May 2019, and then the general election in July. The centre-right New Democracy party, led by Kyriakos Mitsotakis, won by a landslide, giving it an outright majority of 158 seats in the Greek parliament.

In early 2020, Mitsotakis' government won general praise for its swift measures to tackle the COVID-19 pandemic: in the virus' first wave Greece suffered far fewer deaths and lower patient numbers in intensive care than other comparable European nations. The government's National Recovery and Sustainability Plan is also set to reboot the economy with an injection of €32 billion from the EU. Meanwhile, relations with neighbouring Turkey have soured over migrants crossing into Greece and clashes over rights to exploit gas reserves in the waters off Cyprus.

In February 2019 the Republic of Macedonia was renamed North Macedonia, ending a naming dispute between Greece and the Balkans state that dates back around a century and which had required negotiations at the highest level of international mediation.

2015	2016–17	2019	2021
Greece defaults on its bailout loans and is threatened with Grexit – removal from the eurozone.	A deal between the EU and Turkey closes European borders to refugees arriving in Greece, effectively trapping them in Greece or returning them to Turkey. The number of refugees in Greece reaches 62,000.	After the ruling Syriza party suffers devastating defeats in both European and local elections, it is trounced at the country's general election in July by the centre-right New Democracy party, led by Kyriakos Mitsotakis.	A military parade in Athens marks the 200th anniversary of the Greek Revolution of 1821. Other events and initiatives are held through the year in celebration of the bicentenary.

Ancient Greek Culture

When the Roman Empire assimilated Greece it did so with considerable respect and idealism. The Romans in many ways based themselves on the Ancient Greeks, absorbing their deities (and renaming them), literature, myths, philosophy, fine arts and architecture. So what made the Ancient Greeks so special? From thespians to philosophers, from monster-slewing heroes to a goddess born of sea foam, the Ancient Greeks were captivating.

The Golden Age

Exploring the World of the Ancient Greeks (2010), by archaeologists John Camp and Elizabeth Fisher, is a broad and in-depth look at how the Greeks have left their imprint on politics, philosophy, theatre, art, medicine and architecture.

In the 5th century BCE, Athens had a cultural renaissance that has never been equalled – in fact, such was the diversity of its achievements that modern classical scholars refer to it as 'the miracle'. The era started with a vastly outnumbered Greek army defeating the Persian horde in the battles of Marathon and Salamis, and ended with the beginning of the inevitable war between Athens and Sparta. It's often said that Athens' 'Golden Age' is the bedrock of Western civilisation, and had the Persians won, Europe today would have been a vastly different place. Like Paris in the 1930s, ancient Athens was a hotbed of talent. Any artist or writer worth their salt left their hometown and travelled to the great city of wisdom to share their thoughts and hear the great minds of the day express themselves.

Drama

The great dramatists such as Aeschylus, Aristophanes, Euripides and Sophocles redefined theatre from religious ritual to become a compelling form of entertainment. They were to be found at the Theatre of Dionysos at the foot of the Acropolis, and their comedies and tragedies reveal a great deal about the psyche of the Ancient Greeks.

Across the country, large open-air theatres were built on the sides of hills, designed to accommodate plays with increasingly sophisticated backdrops and props, choruses and themes, and to maximise sound so that even the people in the back row might hear the actors on stage. The dominant genres of theatre were tragedy and comedy. The first known actor was a man called Thespis, from whose name we derive the word 'thespian'.

The Greek tragedy Medea, by Euripides, is about the sun god Helios' granddaughter who takes revenge on her estranged husband Jason by killing his new wife and her own children. It was turned into a fatalistic namesake TV film by Lars von Trier in 1988.

Philosophy

While the dramatists were cutting their thespian cloth, three philosophers were introducing new trains of thought rooted in rationality and logic. Posthumously considered to be Athens' greatest, most noble citizen, Socrates (469–399 BCE) was forced to drink hemlock for allegedly corrupting the youth by asking probing, uncomfortable questions. However, before he died he established a school of hypothetical reductionism that is still used today. Two of Socrates' most famous quotes are: 'The only true wisdom consists of knowing that you know nothing' and 'The unexamined life is not worth living'.

Plato (427–347 BCE), Socrates' star student, was responsible for documenting his teacher's thoughts, and without his work in books such as the *Symposium*, they would have been lost to us. Considered an idealist, Plato wrote *The Republic* as a warning to the city-state of Athens that unless its people respected law and leadership, and educated its youth sufficiently, it would be doomed.

Plato's student Aristotle (384–322 BCE), at the end of the Golden Age, focused his gifts on astronomy, physics, zoology, ethics and politics. Aristotle was also the personal physician to Philip II, King of Macedon, and the tutor of Alexander the Great. The greatest gift of the Athenian philosophers to modern-day thought is their spirit of rational inquiry.

Sculpture

Classical sculpture began to gather pace in Greece in the 6th century BCE with the renderings of nudes in marble. Most statues were created to revere a particular god or goddess and many were robed in grandiose garments. The statues of the preceding Archaic period, known as *kouroi*, had focused on symmetry and form, but in the early 5th century BCE artists sought to create expression and animation. As temples demanded elaborate carvings, sculptors were called upon to create large reliefs upon them.

During the 5th century BCE, the craft became yet more sophisticated, as sculptors were taught to successfully map a face and create a likeness of their subject in marble busts. Perhaps the most famous Greek sculptor was Pheidias (c 480–430 BCE), whose reliefs upon the Parthenon depicting the Greek and Persian Wars – now known as the Parthenon Marbles – are celebrated as among the finest of the Golden Age.

No original works by the celebrated classical sculptor Pheidias survive, though copies were made by Roman sculptors. Pheidias' colossal chryselephantine (gold and ivory) statue of Zeus was one of the Wonders of the Ancient World.

Mythology

Ancient Greece revolved around careful worship of 12 central gods and goddesses, all of whom played a major role in the *mythos* (mythology), and none of whom can be commended for their behaviour. They frequently displayed pettiness, spitefulness, outright cruelty and low self-esteem that led to unworthy competitions with mortals that were always rigged in the gods' favour. Each city-state had its own patron god or goddess to appease and flatter, while on a personal level a farmer might make a sacrifice to the goddess Demeter to bless his crops, or a fisherman to Poseidon to bring him fish and safe passage on the waves.

ISLANDS IN MYTHOLOGY

Greece is steeped in mythology and its many islands provided dramatic settings for its legends and interactions between gods and mortals.

Myrina, Limnos Believed to have been founded by Myrina, queen of the Amazons.

Crete Zeus' mother allegedly gave birth to him in a cave to prevent him from being eaten by his father, Cronos. Crete was also home of the dreaded minotaur.

Lesvos When Orpheus was killed and dismembered by the Maenads, the waves brought his head here and it was buried near Antissa.

Kythira Aphrodite is said to have been born out of the waves surrounding Kythira.

Delos This island rose up from the waves when the goddess Leto was looking for a place to give birth to Apollo and Artemis.

Mykonos Zeus and the Titans battled it out on this island and Hercules slew the Giants here.

Rhodes The island given to Helios the sun god after Zeus' victory over the Giants.

ANCIENT GREEK CULTURE MYTHOLOGY

TOP FIVE MYTHICAL CREATURES

Of the grotesque and fantastical creatures whose stories are dear to Greek hearts, these five are the most notorious.

Medusa The snake-headed one punished by the gods for her inflated vanity. Even dead, her blood is lethal.

Cyclops A one-eyed giant. Odysseus and his crew were trapped in the cave of one such cyclops, Polyphemus.

Cerberus The three-headed dog of hell, he guards the entrance to the underworld – under his watch no one gets in or out.

Minotaur This half-man, half-bull mutant leads a life of existential angst in the abysmal labyrinth, tempered only by the occasional morsel of human flesh.

Hydra Cut one of its nine heads off and another two will grow in its place. Heracles solved the problem by cauterising each stump with his burning brand.

The Ancient Pantheon

Here's a quick guide to the 12 central gods and goddesses of Greek mythology – their Roman names are in brackets.

British actor and author Stephen Fry brings his inimitable wit to his retellings of key Greek myths and legends in *Mythos* (2017) and *Heroes* (2018).

Zeus (Jupiter) The fire-bolt-flinging king of the gods, ruler of Mt Olympus, lord of the skies and master of disguise in pursuit of mortal maidens. Wardrobe includes shower of gold, bull, eagle and swan.

Hera (Juno) Protector of women and family, the queen of heaven is both the embattled wife and sister of Zeus. She was the prototype of the jealous, domineering wife who took revenge on Zeus' illegitimate children.

Poseidon (Neptune) God of the seas, master of the mists and younger brother of Zeus. He dwelt in a glittering underwater palace.

Hades (Pluto) God of death and also brother of Zeus, he ruled the underworld, bringing in the newly dead with the help of his skeletal ferryman, Charon. Serious offenders were sent for torture in Tartarus, while heroes went to the Elysian Fields.

Athena (Minerva) Goddess of wisdom, war, science and guardian of Athens, born in full armour out of Zeus' forehead. The antithesis of Ares, Athena was deliberate and, where possible, diplomatic in the art of war. Heracles, Jason (of Jason and the Argonauts fame) and Perseus all benefited from her patronage.

Aphrodite (Venus) Goddess of love and beauty who was said to have been born of sea foam. When she wasn't cuckolding her husband, Hephaestus, she and her son Eros (Cupid) were enflaming hearts and causing trouble (cue the Trojan War).

Apollo God of music, the arts and fortune-telling, Apollo was also the god of light and an expert shot with a bow and arrow. It was his steady hand that guided Paris' arrow towards Achilles' only weak spot – his heel – thus killing him.

Artemis (Diana) The goddess of the hunt and twin sister of Apollo was, ironically, patron saint of wild animals. By turns spiteful and magnanimous, she was closely associated with the sinister Hecate, patroness of witchcraft.

Ares (Mars) God of war, bloodthirsty and lacking control. Zeus' least favourite of his progeny. Not surprisingly, Ares was worshipped by the bellicose Spartans.

Hermes (Mercury) Messenger of the gods, patron saint of travellers and the handsome one with a winged hat and sandals. He was always on hand to smooth over the affairs of Zeus, his father.

Hephaestus (Vulcan) God of artisanship, metallurgy and fire, this deformed and oft-derided son of Zeus made the world's first woman of clay, Pandora, as a punishment for man. Inside her box were the evils of mankind.

Hestia (Vesta) Goddess of the hearth, she protected state fires in city halls from which citizens of Greece could light their brands. She stayed unmarried and a virgin.

The Heroes

Some of the greatest tales of all time – and some say the wellspring of story itself – are to be found in the Greek myths. Contemporary writers continue to reinterpret these stories and characters for books and films.

Heracles (Hercules)

The most celebrated, endearing hero of ancient Greece, the son of Zeus and the mortal Alcmene. After killing his family in a fit of madness induced by the jealous Hera (sister-wife of Zeus), Heracles seeks penance by performing 12 labours set by his enemy Eurystheus, King of Mycenae. These labours included cleaning the Augean Stables in one day; slaying the arrow-feathered Stymphalian Birds; capturing the Cretan Bull; stealing the man-eating Mares of Diomedes; obtaining the Girdle of Hippolyta and the oxen of Geryon; and stealing the Apples of the Hesperides.

Theseus

The Athenian hero volunteered himself as one of seven men and maidens in the annual sacrifice to the Minotaur, the crazed half-bull, half-man offspring of King Minos of Crete. Once inside its forbidding labyrinth (from which none had returned), Theseus, aided by Princess Ariadne (who had a crush on him induced by Aphrodite's dart), loosened a spool of thread to find his way out once he'd killed the monster.

Icarus

Along with Daedalus (his father), Icarus flew off the cliffs of Crete pursued by King Minos and his troops, using wings made of feathers and wax. His father instructed him to fly away from the midday sun, but Icarus became carried away with the exhilaration of flying...the wax melted, the feathers separated and the bird-boy fell to his death.

Perseus

Perseus' impossible task was to kill the gorgon, Medusa. With a head of snakes Medusa could turn a man to stone with a single glance. Armed with an invisibility cap and a pair of flying sandals from Hermes, Perseus used his reflective shield to avoid Medusa's stare. He cut off her head and secreted it in a bag, but it was shortly unsheathed to save Andromeda, a princess bound to a rock and about to be sacrificed to a sea monster. Medusa's head turned the sea monster to stone and Perseus got the girl.

Oedipus

Oedipus was the Ancient Greeks' gift to the Freudian school of psychology. Having been abandoned at birth, Oedipus learned from the Delphic oracle that he would one day slay his father and marry his mother. On the journey back to his birthplace, Thiva (Thebes), he killed a rude stranger and then discovered the city was plagued by a murderous Sphinx (a winged lion with a woman's head). The creature gave unsuspecting travellers and citizens a riddle: if they couldn't answer it, they were dashed on the rocks. Oedipus succeeded in solving the riddle, felled the Sphinx and so gained the queen of Thiva's hand in marriage. On discovering the stranger he'd killed was his father and that his new wife was in fact his mother, Oedipus ripped out his eyes and exiled himself.

Marcel Camus' film *Black Orpheus* (1959) won an Oscar for its reimagining of the Orpheus and Eurydice tale, set in a favela in 1950s Brazil to a bossa nova soundtrack. The lovers flee a hitman and Orfeu's vindictive fiancée.

ANCIENT GREEK CULTURE MYTHOLOGY

From the Greek stories of Oedipus and the castration of Uranus by Cronos, Sigmund Freud drew the conclusion that myths often reflect strong, taboo desires that are otherwise unable to be expressed in society.

The Greek Way of Life

Recent austerity measures to tackle Greece's economic problems have taken some of the shine off Greeks' famously relaxed disposition. But it's not in the locals' nature to retreat into the gloom and their proud ways of life – which embrace family, hospitality and a rebellious, independent spirit – remain intact. Athens is bustling and it's business as usual on the Greek islands, where age-old social conventions and beliefs still hold sway.

National Psyche

Greeks have always shared good and bad times in the company of family and friends; they've danced when sad or defiant and sought solace in their country's rich culture and simple pleasures. Someone will always buy an unemployed youth a coffee, or their *yiayia* (grandmother) will give them *hatziliki* (pocket money) from her shrunken pension.

Greek values and the national character came under attack during the crisis – with locals universally characterised as lazy, leisure-loving, corrupt tax-evaders recklessly bringing Europe to the brink of economic collapse. The realities are far more complex – for every 'lazy' Greek there are hard-working people juggling two jobs to provide for their families.

Greeks pride themselves on their *filotimo*, a hard-to-translate Greek concept that underpins society's cultural norms. It encompasses personal and family honour, respect and loyalty to parents and grandparents, sacrifice and help for friends and strangers alike, pride in country and heritage, and gratitude and hospitality. Though some would argue it has been eroded, the concept remains an important part of Greek identity.

The Greeks also generously extend their *filoxenia* (hospitality). The average Greek will lavish you with free drinks, fresh cake from their kitchen and the warmth they have always been famous for. Curious by nature, as well as passionate, loyal and fiery, Greeks engage in animated personal and political discussions rather than polite small talk. Nothing is off limits for conversation, and you may find yourself quizzed on highly personal matters such as why you don't have children, why you're not married and how much you earn.

Greeks can also be fervently patriotic, nationalistic and ethnocentric. Issues are debated with strong will. Greeks are unashamed about staring and blatantly observing (and commenting on) the comings and goings of people around them. They prefer spontaneity to making plans and are notoriously unpunctual (turning up on time is referred to as 'being English').

Today's Greeks cherish the achievements of their ancient forebears, and so they should. Without the Golden Age of Ancient Greece (about 500–300 BCE), the world would arguably not have developed its classical sculpture, mathematics, geometry, philosophy, democracy, drama and politics. Not to mention the rich tapestry that Greek myths brought to the well of story and imagination. Show just a little appreciation of this to the average Greek and they will love you for it.

Showing solidarity in the face of austerity, enterprising locals in Volos have developed an alternative currency unit to the euro (the TEM), establishing a novel informal bartering system for goods and services, where participants exchange anything from olive oil to car repairs.

Social & Family Life

Greek life has always taken place in the public sphere, whether it's men talking politics at the local *kafeneio* (coffee house) or the elderly gathering in neighbourhood squares while their grandchildren play into the evening. While entertainment spending has been seriously curtailed, the gregarious Greeks nonetheless enjoy a vibrant social and cultural life and infamously lively nightlife.

Rather than living to work, Greeks work to live. People of all ages take their afternoon *volta* (outing) along seafront promenades or town centres, dressed up and refreshed from a siesta (albeit a dying institution). On weekends they flock to the beach and seaside tavernas, and summer holidays are the highlight of the year – traditionally, the capital virtually shuts down in mid-August as people take off for the islands, beach towns or their ancestral villages. A peculiarly Greek social talking point is how many swims you've had that summer.

Greek society remains dominated by the family, and while many men may appear soaked with machismo, the matriarchal domestic model is still very much commonplace, with women subtly pulling the strings in the background. These strong family ties and kinship are helping Greeks survive testing times. Greece's weak welfare system means Greeks rely on families and social groups for support. Most Greek businesses are small, family-run operations and parents strive to provide homes for their children when they get married. Greeks rarely move out of home before they marry, unless they go to university or work in another city. While this was changing among professionals and people marrying later, low wages and rising unemployment have forced many young people to stay – or return – home.

Greeks retain strong regional identities and ties to their ancestral villages. Even the country's most remote villages are bustling during holidays. Greece's large diaspora plays a significant role in the life of many islands and villages, returning each summer in droves.

Debunking the myth of the lazy Greek, OECD research suggests Greeks actually work longer hours than their European and US counterparts, though they have lower productivity and labour participation rates. Greek wages are among Europe's lowest and living costs among the highest.

The State

Personal freedom and the right to protest and protect their democratic rights are sacrosanct to Greeks. Trade-union activism, mass demonstrations and crippling general strikes are a routine part of life in Athens and other major cities, with police and property normally bearing the brunt of antiestablishment sentiment. This rebellious spirit came to the fore during antiausterity protests, as Greeks resisted economic reforms crucial to help curb Greece's soaring national debt.

SPORTING PASSIONS

If the streets are quiet, you can't get a taxi or you hear a mighty roar coming from nearby cafes, chances are there's a football (soccer) game under way. Greece's most popular spectator sport inspires local passions and often unedifying fan hooliganism.

Greece's Super League is dominated by big football clubs: Olympiakos of Piraeus and arch-rivals Panathinaikos of Athens, along with AEK Athens and Thessaloniki's PAOK. While the top clubs have won European championships, Greece has remained in the shadow of Europe's soccer heavyweights since its 2004 European Cup win; it last qualified for the European tournament in 2012.

Greece is also one of the powerhouses of European basketball. Panathinaikos has won six Euroleague championships, while Olympiakos claimed its third title in 2013. Nigerian-born Greek basketballer Giannis Antetokounmpo became the poster boy for Greece's immigrants in 2013 when he was picked for the Milwaukee Bucks in the NBA draft (having had his Greek citizenship fast-tracked).

The word *xenos* means both 'stranger' and 'guest', and Greeks see *filoxenia* (hospitality, welcome, shelter) almost as a duty and matter of personal pride and honour.

The nation's capacity to overcome its economic woes has been stifled by systemic problems with Greece's political and civil life, aspects of society that Greeks have long criticised and perpetuated. A residual mistrust of the state and its institutions is a legacy of years of foreign occupation, while political instability fostered a weak civil society based on tax evasion, political patronage and nepotism, and a black-market economy. Merit has long taken second place to political interests when allocating coveted public-sector jobs or EU funds. Making headway with Greece's bloated and inefficient bureaucracy required *meson* (the help of someone working in the system). The infamous *fakelaki* (envelope of cash) became a common way to cut red tape. At its worst, the system fed corruption and profiteering.

Aversion to the perceived over-regulated approach of Western nations is also part of the national psyche. An undercurrent of civil disobedience extends to lax attitudes to road rules or parking restrictions (you will see motorcyclists carrying their helmets as they chat on their mobile phones).

Faith & Identity

The Greek year revolves around saints' days and festivals of the Orthodox Church calendar. Easter is bigger than Christmas, and name days (celebrating your namesake saint) are more important than birthdays. Most people are named after a saint, as are boats, suburbs and train stations.

While most Greeks aren't devout, Orthodox Christianity – the official religion of Greece – remains an important part of their identity and culture. Families flock to church for lively Easter celebrations, weddings, baptisms and annual festivals, but it's largely women and the elderly who attend church services regularly.

Religious rituals are part of daily life. You will notice taxi drivers, motorcyclists and people on public transport making the sign of the cross when they pass a church; compliments to babies and adults are followed by the *'ftou ftou'* (spitting) gesture to ward off the evil eye; and people light church candles in memory of loved ones. Hundreds of privately built small chapels dot the countryside, while the tiny roadside *iconostases* (chapels) are either shrines to road-accident victims or dedications to saints.

During consecutive foreign occupations the Church was the principal upholder of Greek culture, language and traditions, and it still exerts significant social, political and economic influence, though ongoing financial and sexual scandals have taken their toll.

The Arts

Greece is revered for its artistic and cultural legacy, and the arts remain a vibrant and evolving element of Greek culture, identity and self-expression. Despite, or because of, Greece's recent economic woes, it has seen a palpable burst of artistic activity and creativity. While savage cuts in meagre state-arts funding have some sectors reeling, an alternative cultural scene is fighting back with low-budget films, artist collectives, and small underground theatres and galleries popping up in the capital.

Visual Arts

Byzantine & Renaissance Art

Until the start of the 19th century, the primary art form in Greece was Byzantine religious painting. There was little secular artistic output under Ottoman rule, during which Greece essentially missed the Renaissance.

Byzantine church frescoes and icons depicted scenes from the life of Christ and figures of the saints. The 'Cretan school' of icon painting, influenced by the Italian Renaissance and artists fleeing to Crete after the fall of Constantinople, combined technical brilliance and dramatic richness. The most famous Cretan-born Renaissance painter is El Greco ('The Greek' in Spanish), née Dominikos Theotokopoulos (1541–1614). He got his grounding in the tradition of late-Byzantine fresco painting before moving to Spain in 1577, where he lived and worked until his death.

Modern Art

Modern Greek art evolved after Independence, when painting became more secular, focusing on portraits, nautical themes and the War of Independence. Major 19th-century painters included Dionysios Tsokos, Theodoros Vryzakis, Nikiforos Lytras and Nicholas Gyzis, a leading artist of the Munich School (where many Greek artists of the day studied).

During the 20th century Greek creatives drew inspiration from worldwide movements and developments in the art world, such as the expressionist George Bouzianis, the cubist Nikos Hatzikyriakos-Ghikas and surrealist and poet Nikos Engonopoulos. Other notable Greek 20th century artists include Konstantinos Parthenis, Fotis Kontoglou, Yiannis Tsarouhis, Panayiotis Tetsis, Yannis Moralis, Dimitris Mytaras and Yiannis Kounellis, a pioneer of the Arte Povera movement.

The National Sculpture & Art Gallery in Athens has the most extensive collection of Greek 20th-century art, with significant collections at the Modern Greek Art Museum on Rhodes and the Museum of Contemporary Art on Andros.

Greece's marble sculpture tradition endures on Tinos, birthplace of renowned sculptors Dimitrios Filippotis (1839–1919) and Yannoulis Halepas (1851–1938), as well as Costas Tsoclis (b 1930), whose work is showcased in the island's Costas Tsoclis Museum.

Athens' metro stations feature an impressive showcase of Greek art from prominent artists including Yannis Gaitis (1923–84; Larisa), the sculptor Giorgos Zongolopoulos (1903–2004; Syntagma) and Alekos Fassianos (b 1935; Metaxourgio), whose work fetches record prices for a living Greek artist.

Contemporary Art Scene

Contemporary Greek art has been gaining exposure in Greece and abroad, with a growing number of Greek artists participating in international art events. The Greek arts scene has become more vibrant, less isolated and more experimental, and Athens' street art is gaining recognition.

Many Greek artists have studied and made their homes and reputations abroad, but a new wave is returning or staying put, contributing to a fresh artistic energy. Watch for work by street artists, Cacao Rocks and INO, the collages of Chryssa Romanos, painter Lucas Samaras, kinetic artist Takis, and sculptor Stephen Antonakos whose works often incorporate neon.

Greeks have had unprecedented exposure to global art through major international exhibitions held in impressive new art venues, small private galleries and artist-run initiatives such as the annual Hydra School Project. Since 2007, Biennales in Athens have put the capital on the international contemporary-arts circuit.

Modern Greek Literature

Greek literature virtually ceased under Ottoman rule, and was then stifled by conflict over language – Ancient Greek versus the vernacular *dimotiki* (colloquial language). The compromise was *katharevousa,* a conservative form of ancient Greek. (*Dimotiki* was made the country's official language in 1976.)

One of the most important works of early Greek literature is the 17th-century 10,012-line epic poem 'Erotokritos', by Crete's Vitsenzos Kornaros. Its 15-syllable rhyming verses are still recited in Crete's famous *mantinadhes* (rhyming couplets) and put to music.

Greece's most celebrated (and translated) 20th-century novelist is Nikos Kazantzakis (1883–1957), whose novels are full of drama and larger-than-life characters, such as the magnificent title character in his 1946 work *Life and Times of Alexis Zorbas* (better known as *Zorba the Greek*). Another great novelist of the time, Stratis Myrivilis (1890–1969), wrote the classics *Vasilis Arvanitis* and *The Mermaid Madonna*.

Eminent 20th-century Greek poets include Egypt-born Constantine Cavafy (1863–1933) and Nobel-prize laureates George Seferis (1900–71) and Odysseus Elytis (1911–96), awarded in 1963 and 1979 respectively.

Other local literary giants of the 20th century include Iakovos Kambanellis (1921–2011), Kostis Palamas (1859–1943), a poet who wrote the words to the *Olympic Hymn,* and poet-playwright Angelos Sikelianos (1884–1951).

British writer Patrick Michael Leigh Fermor (1915–2011) walked across Greece in his late teens, recounting the journey in *The Broken Road – Travels from Bulgaria to Mount Athos* (2013). His other classic Greek travelogues are *Mani: Travels in the Southern Peloponnese* (1958) and *Roumeli: Travels in Northern Greece* (2004).

Contemporary Writers

Greece has a prolific publishing industry but scant fiction is translated into English. Contemporary Greek writers who have made small inroads into foreign markets include Apostolos Doxiadis with his international bestseller *Uncle Petros and Goldbach's Conjecture* (2000) and award-winning children's writer Eugene Trivizas.

Greek publisher Kedros' modern-literature translation series includes Dido Sotiriou's *Farewell Anatolia* (1996), Maro Douka's *Fool's Gold* (1991) and Kostas Mourselas' bestselling *Red-Dyed Hair* (1996), which was made into a popular TV series.

The quirky, Rebus-like Inspector Haritos in Petros Markaris' popular crime series provides an enjoyable insight into crime and corruption in Athens. *Che Committed Suicide* (2010), *Basic Shareholder* (2009), *The Late Night News* (2005) and *Zone Defence* (2007) have been translated into English.

Carving a name for himself as the preeminent literary voice of contemporary Greece is Christos Ikonomou. In both his 2016 collection of short stories, *Something Will Happen, You'll See* (focusing on the lives of poor Athenians) and *Good Will Come from the Sea* (2019; four loosely connected tales set on an unnamed Greek island), the country's economic crisis provides the grim background.

Bypassing the translation issue and writing in English are Panos Karnezis whose books include *The Maze* (2004), *The Birthday Party* (2007) and *The Fugitives* (2015); and Soti Triantafyllou, author of *Poor Margo* (2001) *and Rare Earths* (2013). Other notable contemporary authors available in translation include Alexis Stamatis, who penned *Bar Flaubert* (2000) and *The Book of Rain* (2015), and Vangelis Hatziyannidis, writer of *Four Walls* (2006) and *Stolen Time* (2007).

Plays by Yiorgos Skourtis (b 1940) and Pavlos Matessis (1933–2013) have been translated and performed abroad.

Cinema

Greek movies have racked up multiple Academy Award nominations over the years, as well as two Palme d'Ors at Cannes for *Missing* (1982) and *Eternity and a Day* (1998) – the latter directed by Theo Angelopoulos (1935–2012), one of Greece's most critically acclaimed filmmakers.

The best known films about the country remain the 1964 Oscarwinner *Zorba the Greek* and *Never on a Sunday* (1960) for which Melina Mercouri won a Cannes festival award. Another classic is Nikos Koundouros' 1956 noir thriller *O Drakos* (*The Fiend of Athens*), regularly voted top Greek film of all time by the Hellenic Film Critics' Association.

In recent years, a new generation of filmmakers has been gaining international attention for what some critics have dubbed the 'weird wave' of Greek cinema. Examples including the award-winning films of Yorgos Lanthimos, some of which are in English *(Alps; The Lobster; The Killing of a Sacred Deer)* and Athina Rachel Tsangari *(Attenburg; Chevalier)*.

Ektoras Kygizos' extraordinary *Boy Eating Bird Food* (2012) is an allegory for Greece's recent economic plight, and emblematic of the small, creative collaborations largely produced in the absence of state or industry funding.

Music

Traditional Folk Music

Traditional folk music was shunned by the Greek bourgeoisie after Independence, when they looked to Europe – and classical music and opera – rather than their Eastern or 'peasant' roots.

Greece's regional folk music is generally divided into *nisiotika* (the lighter, upbeat music of the islands) and the more grounded *dimotika* of the mainland – where the *klarino* (clarinet) is prominent and lyrics refer to hard times, war and rural life. The spirited music of Crete, dominated by the Cretan *lyra* (a pear-shaped, three-string, bowed instrument) and lute, remains a dynamic musical tradition, with regular performances and recordings by new-generation exponents.

Laïka & Entehna

Laïka (popular or urban folk music) is Greece's most popular music. A mainstream offshoot of *rembetika* (blues), *laïka* emerged in the late 1950s and '60s, when clubs in Athens became bigger and glitzier, and the music more commercial. The bouzouki went electric and the sentimental tunes about love, loss, pain and emigration came to embody the nation's

Learn all about the ancient Epirotic folk music of northwestern Greece and Albania in *Lament from Epirus* (2018), an inspired travelogue by Christopher King, a Grammy winning producer and avid record collector.

REMBETIKA: THE GREEK BLUES

Known as the Greek 'blues', *rembetika* emerged in Greece's urban underground and has strongly influenced the sound of Greek popular music.

Two styles make up what is broadly known as *rembetika*. *Smyrneika* or Cafe Aman music emerged in the mid- to late-19th century in the thriving port cities of Smyrna and Constantinople, which had large Greek populations, and in Thessaloniki, Volos, Syros and Athens. With a rich vocal style, haunting *amanedhes* (vocal improvisations) and occasional Turkish lyrics, its sound had more Eastern influence. Predominant instruments were the violin, *outi* (oud), guitar, mandolin, *kanonaki* and *santouri* (a flat multistringed instrument). The second style, dominated by the six-stringed bouzouki, evolved in Piraeus.

After the influx of refugees from Asia Minor in Piraeus following the 1922 population exchange (many also went to America, where *rembetika* was recorded in the 1920s), the two styles somewhat overlapped and *rembetika* became the music of the ghettos. Infused with defiance, nostalgia and lament, the songs reflected life's bleaker themes and *manges* (streetwise outcasts) who sang and danced in the *tekedhes* (hash dens that inspired many songs).

In the mid-1930s, the Metaxas dictatorship tried to wipe out the subculture through censorship, police harassment and raids on *tekedhes*. People were arrested for carrying a bouzouki. Many artists stopped performing and recording, though the music continued clandestinely. After WWII, a new wave of *rembetika* emerged that eliminated much of its seedy side.

Rembetika legends include Markos Vamvakaris, who became popular with the first bouzouki group in the early 1930s, composer Vasilis Tsitsanis, Apostolos Kaldaras, Yiannis Papaioannou, Giorgos Mitsakis and Apostolos Hatzihristou, and the songstresses Sotiria Bellou and Marika Ninou, whose life inspired Costas Ferris' 1983 film *Rembetiko*.

Interest in genuine *rembetika* was revived in the late 1970s to early 1980s – particularly among students and intellectuals – and it continues to be rediscovered by new generations.

Rembetika ensembles perform seated in a row and traditionally play acoustically. A characteristic feature is an improvised introduction called a *taxim*.

spirit. The late Stelios Kazantzidis was the big voice of this era, along with Grigoris Bithikotsis.

Classically trained composers Mikis Theodorakis and Manos Hatzidakis led a new style known as *entehni mousiki* ('artistic' music) also known as *entehna*. They drew on *rembetika* and used instruments such as the bouzouki in more symphonic arrangements, and created popular hits from the poetry of Seferis, Elytis, Ritsos and Kavadias.

Composer Yiannis Markopoulos later introduced rural folk music and traditional string instruments such as the *lyra, santouri* and *kanonaki* into the mainstream, and brought folk performers such as Crete's legendary Nikos Xylouris to the fore.

During the junta years the music of Theodorakis and Markopoulos became a form of political expression (Theodorakis' music was banned and the composer jailed). Today, headline *laïka* performers include Yiannis Ploutarhos, Antonis Remos and Thanos Petrelis.

Athens' live-music scene includes glitzy, cabaret-style venues known as *bouzoukia* notorious for flower-throwing (plate-smashing is rare these days), expensive displays of excess and exuberant *kefi* (good spirits). Second-rate *bouzoukia* clubs are referred to as *skyladhika* (doghouses) because the crooning singers resemble a whining dog.

Contemporary & Pop Music

While few Greek performers have made it big internationally – 1970s singers Nana Mouskouri and Demis Roussos remain the best known – Greece has a strong local music scene, from traditional and pop music to Greek rock, heavy metal, rap and electronic dance.

Some of the most interesting music emerging from Greece fuses elements of folk with Western influences. One of the most whimsical examples was Greece's tongue-in-cheek 2013 Eurovision contender, in which *rembetika* (blues) veteran Agathonas Iakovidis teamed up with the ska-Balkan rhythms of Thessaloniki's kilt-wearing Koza Mostra.

Big names in popular Greek music include Dionysis Savopoulos, dubbed the Bob Dylan of Greece, and seasoned performers George Dalaras and Haris Alexiou.

Standout contemporary performers include Cypriot-born Alkinoos Ioannides, folk singer Eleftheria Arvanitaki, ethnic-jazz-fusion artists Kristi Stasinopoulou and the Cretan-inspired folk group Haïnides. Also check out Imam Baildi (www.imambaildi.com), a band who give old Greek music a modern makeover.

The local pop scene sees a steady stream of performers creating a uniquely Greek sound. Listen for Σtella (http://stellawithasigma.com), Sarah P (one half of the Athenian chillwave duo Keep Shelley), and Marina Satti (a young Greek-Sudanese singer who does a terrific dance cover of the *rembetika* 'Koupes').

Classical Music & Opera

Despite classical music and opera appealing to an (albeit growing) minority of Greeks, this field is where Greece has made the most significant international contribution, most notably composers Mikis Theodorakis and Manos Hatzidakis and opera diva Maria Callas.

Dimitris Mitropoulos led the New York Philharmonic in the 1950s, while distinguished composers include Stavros Xarhakos and the late Yannis Xenakis. Leading contemporary performers include pianist Dimitris Sgouros, tenor Mario Frangoulis and sopranos Elena Kelessidi and Irini Tsirakidou. Teodor Currentzis (b 1972) is a Greek conductor who is Artistic Director of Russia's Perm Tchaikovsky State Opera and Ballet Theatre.

The country's concert halls and major cultural festivals such as the Hellenic Festival offer rich international programs, while opera buffs have the Greek National Opera and Syros' Apollo Theatre.

Greek Dance

Greeks have danced since the dawn of Hellenism. Some folk dances derive from the ritual dances performed in ancient temples – ancient vases depict a version of the well-known *syrtos* folk dance. Dancing was later part of military education; in times of occupation it became an act of defiance and a covert way to keep fit.

Regional dances, like musical styles, vary across Greece. The slow and dignified *tsamikos* reflects the often cold and insular nature of mountain life, while the brighter islands gave rise to light, springy dances such as the *ballos* and the *syrtos*. The Pontian Greeks' vigorous and warlike dances such as the *kotsari* reflect years of altercations with their Turkish neighbours. Crete has its graceful *syrtos*, the fast and triumphant *maleviziotiko* and the dynamic *pentozali*, with its agility-testing high kicks and leaps. The so-called 'Zorba dance', or *syrtaki*, is a stylised dance for two or three dancers with arms linked on each other's shoulders, though the modern variation is danced in a long circle with an ever-quickening beat. Women and men traditionally danced separately and had their own dances, except in courtship dances such as the *sousta*.

Folk-dance groups throughout Greece preserve regional traditions. The best place to see folk dancing is at regional festivals and the Dora Stratou Dance Theatre in Athens.

Contemporary dance is gaining prominence in Greece, with leading local troupes taking their place among the international line-up at the Athens International Dance Festival.

THE ARTS GREEK DANCE

Byzantine music is mostly heard in Greek churches these days, though Byzantine choirs perform in concerts in Greece and abroad, and the music has influenced folk music.

Men dance the often spectacular solo *zeïmbekiko* – whirling, meditative improvisations with roots in *rembetika* (blues). Women do the sensuous *tsifteteli*, a svelte, sinewy show of femininity evolved from the Middle Eastern belly dance.

Architecture

Cast your eyes around most major cities and you'll find various reinterpretations of classical Greek architecture. The Renaissance was inspired by the ancient style, as was the neoclassical movement and the British Greek Revival. For those with an eye to the past, part of the allure of Greece is the sheer volume of its well-preserved buildings. Stand in the ruins of the Parthenon and with a little imagination it's easy to transport yourself back to classical 5th-century Greece.

Minoan Magnificence

Most of our knowledge of Greek architecture proper begins at around 2000 BCE with the Minoans, who were based in Crete but whose influence spread throughout the Aegean to include the Cyclades. Minoan architects are famous for having constructed technologically advanced, labyrinthine palace complexes. The famous site at Knossos is one of the largest. Usually characterised as 'palaces', these sites were in fact multifunctional settlements that were the primary residences of royalty and priests, but housed some plebs too. Large Minoan villages, such as those of Gournia and Palekastro in Crete, also included internal networks of paved roads that extended throughout the countryside to link the settlements with the palaces. More Minoan palace-era sophistication exists in Crete at Phaestos, Malia and Ancient Zakros, and at the Minoan outpost of Ancient Akrotiri on the south of Santorini.

Several gigantic volcanic eruptions rocked the region in the mid-15th century BCE, causing geological ripple effects that at the very least caused big chunks of palace to fall to the ground. The Minoans resolutely rebuilt on an even grander scale, only to have more natural disasters wipe the palaces out again. The latter effected an architectural chasm that was filled by the emerging Mycenaean rivals on mainland Greece.

Grandeur of Knossos

First discovered by a Cretan, Milos Kalokirinos, in 1878, it wasn't until 1900 that the ruins of Knossos were unearthed by Englishman Sir Arthur Evans. The elaborate palace complex at Knossos was originally formed largely as an administrative settlement surrounding the main palace, which comprised the main buildings arranged around a large central courtyard (1250 sq metres). Over time the entire settlement was rebuilt and extended. Long, raised causeways formed main corridors; narrow labyrinthine chambers flanked the palace walls (this meandering floor plan, together with the graphic ritual importance of bulls, inspired the myth of the labyrinth and the Minotaur). The compound featured strategically placed interior light wells, sophisticated ventilation systems, aqueducts, freshwater irrigation wells, and bathrooms with extensive plumbing and drainage systems. The ground levels consisted mostly of workshops, cylindrical grain silos and storage magazines.

Thanks to its restoration, today's Knossos is one of the easiest ruins for your imagination to take hold of.

According to myth, the man tasked with designing a maze to withhold the dreaded Minotaur was famous Athenian inventor Daedalus, father of Icarus. He also designed the Palace of Knossos for King Minos.

Mycenaean Engineering

The Mycenaeans had a fierce reputation as builders of massive masonry. These war-mongering people roamed southern mainland Greece, picking off the choice vantage points for their austere palaces, fenced within formidable citadels. The citadels' fortified Cyclopean-stone walls were on average an unbreachable 3m to 7m thick. The immense royal beehive tomb of the Treasury of Atreus (aka Tomb of Agamemnon) at Mycenae was constructed using tapered limestone blocks weighing up to 120 tonnes. The palace at Tiryns has stupendous corbel-vaulted galleries and is riddled with secret passageways; the incredibly well-preserved Nestor's Palace, near modern Pylos, also illustrates the Mycenaeans' structural expertise.

Classic Compositions

The classical age (5th to 4th centuries BCE) is when most Greek architectural clichés converge. This is when temples became characterised by the famous orders of columns, particularly the Doric, Ionic and Corinthian.

In the meantime, the Greek colonies of the Asia Minor coast were creating their own Ionic order, designing a column base in several tiers and adding more flutes. This more graceful order's capital (the head) received an ornamented necking, and Iktinos fused elements of its design in the Parthenon. This order is used on the Acropolis' Temple of Athena Nike and the Erechtheion, where the famous Caryatids sculptures regally stand.

Towards the tail end of the classical period, the Corinthian column was in vogue. Featuring a single or double row of ornate leafy scrolls (usually the very sculptural acanthus), the order was subsequently adopted by the Romans and used only on Corinthian temples in Athens. The Temple of Olympian Zeus, completed during Emperor Hadrian's reign, is a grand, imposing structure. Another temple design, the graceful, circular temple *tholos* (dome) style, was used for the great Sanctuary of Athena Pronaia at Delphi.

The Greek theatre design is a hallmark of the classical period (an example is the 4th-century-BCE theatre at Epidavros) and had a round stage, radiating a semicircle of steeply banked stone benches that seated many thousands. Cleverly engineered acoustics meant every spectator could monitor every syllable uttered on the stage below. Many ancient Greek theatres are still used for summer festivals, music concerts and plays.

The distinctive blue-and-white Cycladic-style architecture most associated with the Greek islands was pragmatic and functional. The cuboid flat-roofed houses, huddled together along labyrinthine alleys, were designed to guard against the elements: strong winds and pirates.

ARCHITECTURE MYCENAEAN ENGINEERING

THE COLUMNS OF ANCIENT GREECE

Columns are columns are columns, right? Recognising the differences between them is, in fact, the easiest way to differentiate between the three distinct architectural orders of Ancient Greece.

Doric The most simple of the three styles. The shaft (the main part of the column) is plain and has 20 sides, while the capital (the head) is formed in a simple circle. Also there's no base. An obvious example of this is the Parthenon.

Ionic Look out for the ridged flutes carved into the column from top to bottom. The capital is also distinctive for its scrolls, while the base looks like a stack of rings.

Corinthian The most decorative and popular of all three orders. The column is ridged; however, the distinctive feature is the capital's flowers and leaves, beneath a small scroll. The base is like that of the Ionic.

Hellenistic Citizens

In the twilight years of the classical age (from about the late 4th century BCE), cosmopolitan folks started to weary of temples, casting their gaze towards a more decadent urban style. The Hellenistic architect was in hot demand for private homes and palace makeovers as wealthy citizens, dignitaries and political heavyweights lavishly remodelled their abodes in marble, and striking mosaics were displayed as status symbols. The best Hellenistic ancient-home displays are the grand houses at Delos.

The mother of all Doric structures is the 5th-century-BCE Parthenon, the ultimate in ancient architectural bling. To this day, it's probably the most obsessively photographed and painted structure in all of Greece.

Byzantine Zeal

Church-building was particularly expressive during the time of the Byzantine Empire in Greece (from around 700 CE to the early 13th century). The original Greek Byzantine model features a distinctive cross shape – essentially a central dome supported by four arches on piers and flanked by vaults, with smaller domes at the four corners and three apses to the east. Theologian architects opted for spectacular devotional mosaics and frescoes instead of carvings for the stylistic religious interiors.

In Athens, the very appealing 12th-century Church of Agios Eleftherios incorporates fragments of a classical frieze in Pentelic marble; the charming 11th-century Church of Kapnikarea sits stranded, smack-bang in the middle of downtown Athens – its interior flooring is of coloured marble, and the external brickwork, which alternates with stone, is set in patterns. Thessaloniki's 8th-century Church of Agia Sofia, with its 30m-high dome, is a humble version of its namesake in İstanbul. There are numerous Byzantine chapels in Mystras, many of which were originally private chapels, attached to enchanting 17th- and 18th-century *arhontika* (mansions once owned by *arhons,* wealthy bourgeoisie merchants).

Frankish Keeps & Venetian Strongholds

After the sacking of Constantinople by the Crusaders in 1204, much of Greece became the fiefdoms of Western aristocrats. The Villehardouin family punctuated the Peloponnesian landscape with Frankish castles, such as at Kalamata and at Mystras, where they also built a palace that ended up as a court of the Byzantine imperial family for two centuries. When the Venetians dropped by to seize a few coastal enclaves, they built the impenetrable 16th-century Koules fortress in Iraklio, the very sturdy fortress at Methoni and the imposing 18th-century Palamidi fortress at Nafplio. The rambling defence at Acrocorinth is studded with imposing gateways, and the rock-nest protecting the enchanting Byzantine village at Monemvasia commands spectacular ocean views.

Ottoman Offerings

Interestingly, remarkably few monuments are left to catalogue after four centuries of Ottoman Turkish rule (16th to 19th centuries). Though many mosques and their minarets have sadly crumbled or are in serious disrepair, some terrific Ottoman-Turkish examples still survive. These include the prominent pink-domed Mosque of Süleyman in Rhodes Old Town. The Fethiye Mosque and Turkish Baths are two of Athens' few surviving Ottoman reminders, and the architect for the 16th-century Koursoun Tzami in Trikala also designed the Blue Mosque in İstanbul. The Turkish quarter of Varousi in Trikala, and the streets of Thessaloniki and of Didymotiho, near the Turkish border, showcase superb Turkish-designed homes with stained-glass windows, wooden overhangs on buttresses, decorated plasterwork and painted woodwork.

Several Byzantine monastic sites have made it to the Unesco World Heritage register, including the *katholikon* (main churches) of Osios Loukas, significant for their late-Byzantine multidomed style, and the 11th-century Moni Dafniou, which stands on the site of an ancient Sanctuary of Apollo.

THE CAPTAIN'S HOUSE

During the 17th century, Greek ship captains grew increasingly prosperous. Many of them poured their newfound wealth into building lofty homes that towered over the traditional village houses. These captains' houses are now dotted throughout the islands and many have been given a new lease on life as boutique hotels or restaurants.

While the size of the house often reflected the wealth of a captain, some of the smallest of these 400-year-old homes are the most grand. Captain's houses didn't need to be large as they spent so much time at sea. Whitewashed walls stretch upward to the soaring resin ceiling, often intricately painted with elaborate, colourful patterns. The windows are sea-facing and placed very high, often with wooden lofts to reach them. This was to let the heat out in summer and also so the captain's wife could watch the sea for the arrival of her husband's ship. The traditional *pyliones* (stone doorways) are hand-carved with symbolic pictures. Corn means good harvest, birds mean peace, the cross brings safety and the sunflowers sunlight. The number of ropes carved around the perimeter of the door shows how many ships the captain had.

Some of the finest examples of these houses are found in Lindos, on Rhodes.

Neoclassical Splendour

Regarded by experts as the most beautiful neoclassical building world-wide, the 1885 Athens Academy reflects Greece's post-Independence yearnings for grand and geometric forms, and Hellenistic detail. Renowned Danish architect Theophile Hansen drew inspiration from the Erechtheion to design the Academy's Ionic-style column entrance (guarded over by Apollo and Athena); the great interior oblong hall is lined with marble seating, and Austrian painter Christian Griepenkerl was commissioned to decorate its elaborate ceiling and wall paintings. In a similar vein, the Doric columns of the Temple of Hephaestus influenced Hansen's solid-marble National Library, while Christian Hansen (Hansen's brother) was responsible for the handsome but more sedate Athens University, with its clean lines.

Meticulously restored neoclassical mansions house notable museums such as the acclaimed Benaki Museum in Athens.

Many provincial towns also display beautiful domestic adaptations of neoclassicism. In Symi, the harbour at Gialos is flanked by colourful neo-classical facades (still striking even if a little derelict) and Nafplio is also embellished with neoclassical buildings.

Modern & Contemporary Ideas

Recently, Athens has embraced a sophisticated, look-both-ways architectural aesthetic to showcase its vast collection of antiquities and archaeological heritage and to beautify landscapes for pedestrian zones to improve the urban environment. Examples include the well-designed facelift of the historic centre, including its spectacular floodlighting (designed by the renowned Pierre Bideau) of the ancient promenade, and the cutting-edge spaces emerging from once-drab and derelict industrial zones, such as the Technopolis gasworks arts complex in Gazi.

The Acropolis Museum, designed by Bernard Tschumi and opened in 2009, features an internal glass *cella* (inner room) mirroring the Parthenon with the same number of columns (clad in steel) and a glass floor overlooking excavated ruins in situ.

Built for the 2004 Olympics, the Athens Olympic Complex was designed by Spanish architect Santiago Calatrava. It has a striking, ultramodern glass-and-steel roof, which is suspended by cables from

The predominant motif of late-20th-century urban Greek architecture is the *polykatoikia* (multiresidence) apartment block. In Athens alone around 35,000 five-storey cement blocks with awning-shaded balconies were erected between the 1950s and 1980s.

PROVINCIAL VARIATIONS

Considering the historical mishmash of cultural influences peppered across Greece, alongside a varying landscape, it's hardly surprising to find unique variations in architectural design.

Pyrgi See the medieval, labyrinthine, vaulted island village of Pyrgi in Chios, for its unique Genoese designs of intricate, geometric, grey-and-white facades.

Zagorohoria Gaze at the slate mansions of the Zagorohoria: schist-slab roofs, stone-slab walls and fortified courtyards.

Vathia Explore this lovely village in Lakonian Mani, home to startling meercat-esque stone tower houses with round turrets as sentry posts.

Oia Squint at the volcanic rock-hewn clifftop village of Oia in Santorini, with its dazzlingly whitewashed island streetscapes and homes.

Lefkada Town Discover the strangely attractive wooden-framed houses of Lefkada Town: the lower floors are panelled in wood, while the upper floors are lined in painted sheet metal or corrugated iron.

large arches. The laminated glass, in the shape of two giant leaves, is capable of reflecting 90% of the sunlight.

Even more impressive is the Stavros Niarchos Foundation Cultural Center (SNFCC) that, in summer, generates 100% of its energy needs from the 5400 photovoltaic panels on its roof. Designed by Pritzker Prize–winning architect Renzo Piano, the SNFCC, which opened in 2016, houses the National Library of Greece and the National Opera amid a beautiful and sustainably designed park with both city and sea views.

French firm Architecture Studio designed the Onassis Cultural Centre, a performance and exhibition space that opened in 2010. The building's facade is wrapped in strips of marble across which images can be projected.

Nature & Wildlife

Greece is an ideal location for getting up close to nature. Hike through valleys and mountains covered with wildflowers, come eye to eye with a loggerhead turtle or simply stretch out on a beach. Environmental awareness is beginning to seep into the fabric of Greek society, leading to slow but positive change. However, problems such as deforestation and soil erosion date back thousands of years. Live cultivation, goats, construction and industry have all taken their toll.

Geography & Geology

No matter where you go in Greece, it's impossible to be much more than 100km from the sea. Rugged mountains and seemingly innumerable islands dominate the landscape, which was shaped by submerging seas, volcanic explosions and mineral-rich terrain. The mainland covers 131,944 sq km, with an indented coastline stretching for 15,020km. Mountains rise over 2000m and occasionally tumble down into plains, particularly in Thessaly and Thrace. Meanwhile, the Aegean and Ionian Seas link together the country's 1400 islands, with just 169 of them inhabited. These islands fill 400,000 sq km of territorial waters.

Volcanic activity regularly hits Greece. In 1999 a 5.9-magnitude earthquake near Athens killed nearly 150 people and left thousands homeless. Since 2006 the country has had seven quakes ranging from 6.4 to 6.9 in magnitude. None caused major damage. To check out Greece's explosive past, visit the craters of Santorini, Nisyros and Polyvotis.

Greece is short on rivers, with none that are navigable, although they've become popular locations for white-water rafting. The largest rivers are the Aheloös, Aliakmonas, Aoös and Arahthos, all of which have their source in the Pindos Mountains of Epiros.

The long plains of the river valleys, and those between the mountains and the coast, form Greece's only lowlands. The mountainous terrain, dry climate and poor soil leave farmers at a loss, and less than 25% of the land is cultivated. Greece is, however, rich in minerals, with reserves of oil, manganese, bauxite and lignite.

Greek Flora

Greece is endowed with a variety of flora unrivalled in Europe. The wildflowers are spectacular, with more than 6000 species, including more than 200 varieties of orchid. They continue to thrive because most of the land is inadequate for intensive agriculture and has therefore escaped the ravages of chemical fertilisers.

The regions with the most wildflowers are the Lefka Ori (White Mountains) in Crete and the Mani area of the Peloponnese. Trees begin to blossom as early as the end of February in warmer areas and the wildflowers start to appear in March. During spring, hillsides are carpeted with flowers, which seem to sprout even from the rocks. By summer the flowers have disappeared from everywhere but the northern mountainous regions. Autumn brings a new period of blossoming.

Herbs in Cooking is an illustrative book by Maria and Nikos Psilakis that can be used as both an identification guide and a cookbook for Greek dishes seasoned with local herbs.

Greece's once lush forests have been decimated by thousands of years of clearing for grazing, boatbuilding and housing, not to mention recent severe forest fires. Northern Greece is the only region that has retained significant areas of native forest – there are mountainsides covered with dense thickets of hop hornbeam (*Ostrya carpinifolia*), noted for its lavish display of white-clustered flowers. Another common species is the Cyprus plane (*Platanus orientalis insularis*).

Watching for Wildlife
On the Ground

In areas widely inhabited by humans, you're unlikely to spot any wild animals other than the odd fox, weasel, hare or rabbit. The more remote mountains of northern Greece continue to support a wide range of wildlife, including wild dogs and shepherds' dogs, which often roam higher pastures on grazing mountains and should be given a wide berth.

The brown bear, Europe's largest land mammal, still manages to survive in very small numbers in the Pindos Mountains, the Peristeri Range that rises above the Prespa Lakes and in the mountains that lie along the Bulgarian border. It's estimated that only around 150 survive; your best bet for seeing one is at the Arcturos Bear Sanctuary (p291) in Macedonia.

NATIONAL PARKS

National parks were first established in Greece in 1938 with the creation of Mt Olympus National Park. There are now 10 national parks and two marine parks, which aim to protect Greece's unique flora and fauna.

Facilities for visitors are often basic, abundant walking trails are not always maintained and the clutch of refuges is very simple. To most, the facilities matter little when compared to nature's magnificent backdrop. It's well worth experiencing the wild side of Greece in one of these settings.

Ainos National Park (p708) The only island park, on Kefallonia, the stand of forest here is home to a single species of endemic fir and small wild horses.

Cape Sounion (p141) A cape with panoramic views and home to the Temple of Poseidon.

Iti National Park (p228) Tranquil stretches of forest, meadows and pools; home to eagles, deer and boars.

Mt Olympus National Park (p286) Home to Greece's tallest mountain, rich in flora and considered the home of the gods.

Mt Parnitha National Park (p142) Very popular wooded parkland north of Athens; home to the red deer.

National Marine Park of Alonnisos Northern Sporades (p670) Covers six islands and 22 islets in the Sporades, and is home to monk seals, dolphins and rare birdlife.

National Marine Park of Zakynthos (p718) An Ionian refuge for loggerhead turtles.

Northern Pindos National Park (p314) Excellent hiking with caves, canyons and dense forest.

Parnassos National Park (p219) Towering limestone and scenic views down to Delphi.

Prespa Lakes (p292) One of Europe's oldest lakes, steeped in wildlife and tranquillity.

Samaria Gorge (p496) Spectacular gorge in Crete and a refuge for the *kri-kri* (Cretan goat).

The protected grey wolf is officially classified as stable with an estimated 1020 surviving in the wild. It's believed up to 100 are killed annually by farmers' indiscriminate (and illegal) use of poison baits in retaliation for the occasional marauding of their flocks. The Greek government and insurance companies pay compensation for lost livestock but it doesn't appear to slow the killings. The surviving wolves live in the Pindos Mountains and the Dadia Forest Reserve area. Head to the Arcturos Wolf Sanctuary (www.arcturos.gr) in Agrapidia, near Florina, which houses wolves rescued from illegal captivity.

The golden jackal is a strong candidate for Greece's most misunderstood mammal. Although its diet is 50% vegetarian (the other 50% is made up of carrion, reptiles and small mammals), it has traditionally shouldered much of the blame for attacks on stock and has been hunted by farmers as a preventative measure. Near the brink of extinction, it was declared a protected species in 1990 and now survives only in small clusters in the Peloponnese, Phocis, Samos Island, Halkidiki and north-eastern Greece.

Once roaming across all of mainland Greece, the graceful red deer is now restricted to the Sithonia Peninsula, the Rhodope Mountain bordering Bulgaria and Mt Parnitha north of Athens. As the largest herbivore in Greece, its population is under constant threat from illegal hunters, making attempts at population redistribution unsuccessful.

Originally brought to the island of Skyros in the 5th century BCE by colonists, the diminutive Skryrian horses are an ancient breed that became wild once they had been replaced by agricultural mechanisation. You'll also see these horses featured in the Parthenon friezes. Around 190 survive on the island, approximately 70% of their global population. Mouries Farm (p676) is home to 45 Skyrian horses.

Greece has an active snake population and, in spring and summer, you will inevitably spot them on roads and pathways around the country. Fortunately, the majority are harmless, though the viper and the coral snake can cause fatalities. Lizards are in abundance too.

In the Air

Birdwatchers hit the jackpot in Greece as much of the country is on north–south migratory paths. Lesvos (Mytilini) in particular draws a regular following of birders from all over Europe, who come to spot some of more than 279 recorded species that stop at the island annually. Storks are more visible visitors, arriving in early spring from Africa and returning to the same nests year after year. These are built on electricity poles, chimney tops and church towers, and can weigh up to 50kg. Keep an eye out for them in northern Greece, especially in Thrace in Macedonia. Thrace has the richest colony of fish-eating birds in Europe, including species such as egrets, herons, cormorants and ibises, as well as the rare Dalmatian pelican. The wetlands at the mouth of the Evros River, close to the border with Turkey, are home to two easily identifiable wading birds: the avocet, which has a long curving beak, and the black-winged stilt, which has extremely long pink legs.

Upstream on the Evros River in Thrace, the dense forests and rocky outcrops of the 72-sq-km Dadia Forest Reserve play host to Europe's largest range of birds of prey. Three out of Europe's four vulture species (black, griffon and Egyptian) spend time here, as do Europe's only breeding population of black vultures.

Over 350 pairs of the rare Eleonora's falcon (60% of the world's population) nest on the island of Piperi in the Sporades and on Tilos, which is also home to the very rare Bonelli's eagle and the shy, cormorant-like Mediterranean shag.

Wildlife Websites

Pelicans and pygmy cormorants (www.spp.gr)

Birdlife (www.ornithologiki.gr)

Wildflowers (www.greek mountainflora.info)

Sea turtles (www.archelon.gr)

Under the Sea

One of Europe's most endangered marine mammals, the Mediterranean monk seal *(Monachus monachus)* ekes out an extremely precarious existence in Greece. Approximately 200 to 250 monk seals, about 50% of the world's population, are found in both the Ionian and Aegean Seas. Small colonies also live on the island of Alonnisos and there have been reported sightings on Tilos.

The waters around Zakynthos are home to the last large sea-turtle colony in Europe, that of the endangered loggerhead turtle *(Caretta caretta)*. Loggerheads also nest in smaller numbers in the Peloponnese and on Kefallonia and Crete. Greece's turtles have many hazards to dodge: entanglement in fishing nets and boat propellers, consumption of floating rubbish, and the destruction of their nesting beaches by sunloungers and beach umbrellas that threaten their eggs. It doesn't help that the turtles' nesting time coincides with the European summer-holiday season.

There is still the chance that you will spot dolphins from a ferry deck, though a number of the species, including common dolphins *(Delphinus delphis)* and Risso's dolphins *(Grampus griseus)* are now considered endangered. The main threats to dolphins are a diminished food supply and entanglement in fishing nets.

> Loggerhead-turtle hatchlings use the journey from the nest to the sea to build up their strength. Helping the baby turtles to the sea can actually lower their chances of survival.

Environmental Issues

Illegal development of mainly coastal areas, and building in forested or protected areas, has gained momentum in Greece since the 1970s. Despite attempts at introducing laws, and protests by locals and environmental groups, corruption and the lack of an infrastructure to enforce the laws means little is done to abate the land-grab. The issue is complicated by population growth and increased urban sprawl. Developments often put a severe strain on water supplies and endangered wildlife. While a few developments have been torn down, in more cases illegal buildings are legalised as they offer much-needed, affordable housing.

The lifting of the diesel ban in Athens and Thessaloniki in 2012 decreased air quality as people opted for cheaper transport. As heating oil tripled in price, people turned to burning wood, often treated, as well as garbage to keep warm. Wintertime particle pollution increased by 30% on some evenings, with lead and arsenic particles found in the air. Smog is a particular problem in Athens as the greater metropolitan area hosts over half of the country's industry, not to mention the lion's share of Greece's population. Athens has subsequently pledged to ban all diesel vehicles from its city centre by 2025.

> Greece's recycling rate is 17%, below the European Union average of 39%. In the main cities and towns, however, you will find recycling bins to dispose of paper, plastic, aluminium and other packaging.

Each year, forest fires rage across Greece, destroying many thousands of hectares, often in some of the country's most picturesque areas. During the summer of 2018 a series of wildfires across coastal areas of Attica, not far from Athens, claimed 102 lives. This was the country's worst natural disaster since wildfires destroyed large tracts of Mt Parnitha and the Peloponnese in 2007 when 63 people died.

The increasing scale of recent fires is blamed on rising Mediterranean temperatures and high winds. Many locals argue that the government is ill-prepared and that its attempts to address the annual fires are slow. Fearing they won't receive help, many locals refuse to leave areas being evacuated, preferring to take the risk and attempting to fight the flames themselves.

Survival Guide

Directory A–Z

Accessible Travel

Access for travellers with disabilities has improved somewhat in recent years, though mostly in Athens where there are more accessible sights, hotels and restaurants. Much of the rest of Greece, with its abundance of stones, marble, slippery cobbles and stepped alleys, remains inaccessible or difficult for wheelchair users. People who have visual or hearing impairments are also rarely catered to.

Careful planning before you go can make a world of difference.

Travel Guide to Greece (www. greecetravel.com/handicapped) Links to local articles, resorts and tour groups catering to tourists with physical disabilities.

DR Yachting (www.disabled sailingholidays.com) Two-day to two-week sailing trips around the Greek islands in fully accessible yachts.

Sirens Resort (www.disableds-resort.gr) Family-friendly resort with accessible apartments, tours and ramps into the sea.

Download Lonely Planet's free Accessible Travel guides from http://lptravel.to/AccessibleTravel.

Accommodation

Greece's plethora of accommodation means that, whatever your taste or budget, there is somewhere to suit your needs. All places to stay are subject to strict price controls set by the tourist police. It's difficult to generalise accommodation prices in Greece as rates depend entirely on the season and location. Don't expect to pay the same price for a double room on one of the islands as you would in central Greece or Athens.

When considering hotel prices, take note of the following points.

➡ Prices include community tax and VAT (value-added tax).

➡ An Overnight Stay Tax of between €0.50 and €4 depending on the star rating of your accommodation will also be added per night.

➡ A mandatory charge of 20% is levied for an additional bed (although this is often waived if the bed is for a child).

➡ During July and August accommodation owners will charge the maximum price, which can be as much as double the low-season price. In spring and autumn prices can drop by 20%.

➡ Also during high season there may be a two- or three-night minimum reservation policy, particularly at accommodation in the most popular islands and resorts.

➡ Rip-offs are rare; if you suspect that you have been exploited, make a report to the tourist police or the regular police, and they will act swiftly.

Camping

Camping is a decent option, especially in summer. There are almost 350 campgrounds in Greece, found on the majority of islands (with the notable exception of the Saronic Gulf Islands). Standard facilities include hot showers, kitchens, restaurants and minimarkets – and often a swimming pool.

Most camping grounds are open only between May and October, although always check ahead; in the north in particular, some don't open until June. The **Panhellenic Camping Association** (☎21036 21560; www.greece camping.gr) website lists all of its campgrounds and relevant details.

If you're camping in the height of summer, bring a silver fly sheet to reflect the heat off your tent (dark tents become sweat lodges).

Between May and mid-September the weather is warm enough to sleep out under the stars. Many campgrounds have covered areas where tourists who don't have tents can sleep in summer; you can get by with a lightweight sleeping bag. It's a good idea to have a foam pad to lie on, a waterproof cover for your sleeping bag and plenty of bug repellent.

➡ Camping fees are highest from mid-June through to the end of August.

➡ Campgrounds charge €6 to €12 per adult and €3 to €5 for children aged four to 12. There's no charge for children under four.

➡ Tent sites cost from €5 per night.

➡ You can often rent tents for around €5.

➡ Caravan sites start at around €7; car costs are typically €4 to €5.

Domatia

Once upon a time, domatia (literally 'rooms') were little more than spare rooms in the family home; nowadays, many are purpose-built appendages with fully equipped kitchens. Standards of cleanliness are generally high.

Domatia remain a popular option for budget travellers. Expect to pay from €30 to €60 for a single, and €40 to €80 for a double, depending on whether bathrooms are shared or private, the season and how long you plan to stay. Domatia are found throughout the mainland (except in large cities) and on almost every island that has a permanent population. Many domatia are open only between April and October.

From June to September, domatia owners are out in force, touting for customers. They meet buses and boats, shouting 'room, room!' and often carry photographs of their rooms. In peak season it can prove a mistake not to take up an offer – but be wary of owners who are vague about the location of their accommodation.

Hostels

The Greek Youth Hostel Organisation (https://higreece. gr) covers 18 properties across the country including guesthouses and hotels as well as traditional hostels; you don't have to be a member to stay in them but HI membership will give you a 10% discount on rates.

There are many private hostels, too. Rates vary from around €10 to €20 for a bed in a dorm. Few have curfews.

Hotels & Pensions

Hotels in Greece are divided into five categories: one to five stars. Hotels are categorised according to the size of the rooms, whether or not they have a bar, and the ratio of bathrooms to beds, rather than standards of cleanliness, comfort of beds and friendliness of staff – all elements that may be of greater relevance to guests.

5 & 4 star Full amenities, private bathrooms and constant hot water.

3 star A snack bar and rooms with private bathrooms, but not necessarily constant hot water.

2 star Generally have shared bathrooms and they may have solar-heated water, meaning hot water is not guaranteed.

1 star Shared bathrooms and hot water may cost extra.

Mountain Refuges

Mountain refuges are dotted around the Greek mainland, Crete and Evia. They range from small huts with outdoor toilets and no cooking facilities to very comfortable modern lodges. They are run by the country's various mountaineering and skiing clubs. Prices start at around €10 per person, depending on the facilities.

The EOT (Greek National Tourist Organisation; www. visitgreece.gr) publication *Greece: Mountain Refuges & Ski Centres* has details about each refuge; copies are available at all EOT branches. Also see the online maps of the Balkan Mountaineering Union (www.mountain-huts.net).

Rental Accommodation

A practical way to save money and maximise comfort is to rent a furnished apartment or villa. Many are purpose-built for tourists, while others – villas in particular – may be owners'

SLEEPING PRICE RANGES

The following price ranges refer to a double room with private bathroom in high season (May to August).

€ less than €60 (under €90 in Athens)

€€ €60–150 (€90–185 in Athens)

€€€ more than €150 (more than €185 in Athens)

PLAN YOUR STAY ONLINE

For more accommodation reviews by Lonely Planet authors, check out www.lonelyplanet.com. You'll find independent reviews, as well as recommendations on the best places to stay.

homes that they are not using. Some owners may insist on a minimum stay of a week.

Airbnb (www.airbnb.com) also has lots of rental properties listed in Greece and can be a great way to hunt down reasonable accommodation if you're planning to stay in one location for more than a couple of nights. Also check out sites such as www.mygreek-villa.com and www.prettygreekvillas.com.

Customs Regulations

There are no duty-free restrictions within the EU. Upon entering Greece from outside the EU, customs inspection is usually cursory for foreign tourists and a verbal declaration is generally all that is required. Random searches are still occasionally made for drugs. Import regulations for medicines are strict; if you are taking medication, make sure you get a statement from your doctor before you leave home. It is illegal, for instance, to take codeine into Greece without an accompanying doctor's certificate.

It is strictly forbidden in Greece to acquire and export antiquities without special permits issued by the Hellenic Ministry of Culture/General Directorate of Antiquities and Cultural Heritage (gda@culture.gr). Severe smuggling penalties might be incurred. It is an offence to remove even the smallest article from an archaeological site.

Discount Cards

Camping Card International (CCI; www.campingcardinternational.com) Gives up to 25% savings in camping fees and third-party liability insurance while in the campground. Valid in over 2500 campsites across Europe.

European Youth Card (www.eyca.org) Available for anyone up to the age of 26 or 31, depending on the country. You don't have to be a resident of Europe. It provides discounts of up to 20% at sights, shops and for some transport. Available from the website or travel agencies in Athens and Thessaloniki for €14.

International Student Identity Card (ISIC; www.isic.org) Entitles the holder to half-price admission to museums and ancient sites, and discounts at some budget hotels and hostels. Available from travel agencies in Athens. Applicants require documents proving their student status, a passport photo and €15. Available to students aged 12 to 30.

Seniors cards Card-carrying EU pensioners can claim a range of benefits such as reduced admission to ancient sites and museums, and discounts on bus and train fares.

Embassies & Consulates

All foreign embassies in Greece are in Athens and its suburbs, with a few consulates in Thessaloniki.

Albanian Embassy (☎210 687 6200; Vekiareli 7, Filothei; ⓐA7, 550 to Kollegio)

Australian Embassy (☎210 870 4000; http://greece.embassy.gov.au; Level 2, Chatzigianni Mexi 5, Hilton; Ⓜ Megaro Moussikis)

Bulgarian Embassy (☎210 674 8105; www.mfa.bg/embassies/greece; Stratigou Kallari 33a, Psyhiko; ⓐ550 to Ag Varvara)

Canadian Embassy (☎210 727 3400; www.greece.gc.ca; Ethnikis Antistaseos 48, Halandri; ⓐ10 to Serron)

Cypriot Embassy (☎210 373 4800; www.mfa.gov.cy; Xenofontos 2a, Syntagma; ⊙8am-3.30pm Mon-Fri; Ⓜ Syntagma)

French Embassy (☎210 339 1000; https://gr.ambafrance.org; Leoforos Vasilissis Sofias 7, Kolonaki; Ⓜ Syntagma)

German Embassy (☎210 728 5111; www.athen.diplo.de; Karaoli-Dimitriou 3, Kolonaki; Ⓜ Evangelismos)

Irish Embassy (☎210 723 2771; www.dfa.ie/irish-embassy/greece; Leoforos Vasileos Konstantinou 7, Pangrati; ⊙9am-1pm Mon-Fri; ⓐ2, 4, 10, 11 to Stadio, Ⓜ Akropoli, ⓐ Zappeio)

Italian Embassy (☎210 361 7260; www.ambatene.esteri.it; Sekeri 2, Kolonaki; Ⓜ Syntagma)

Netherlands Embassy (☎210 725 4900; www.nederlandwereldwijd.nl/landen/griekenland; Leoforos Vasileos Konstantinou 5, Pangrati; ⓐ2, 4, 10, 11 to Stadio, Ⓜ Akropoli, ⓐ Zappeio)

Turkish Embassy (☎210 726 3000; http://atina.be.mfa.gov.tr; Vasileos Georgiou B-8, Kolonaki; Ⓜ Syntagma) Has an additional branch in **Athens** (☎210 672 9830; http://atinapire.bk.mfa.gov.tr; Vasileos Pavlou 22, Psyhiko; ⓐ550 to Pharos) and one in **Thessaloniki** (☎2310 965 070; turkbaskon@kom.forthnet.gr; Agiou Dimitriou 151; ⊙9am-5pm Mon-Fri).

UK Embassy (☎210 727 2600; www.gov.uk/world/organisations/british-embassy-athens; Ploutarhou 1, Kolonaki; Ⓜ Evangelismos)

US Embassy (☎210 721 2951; http://gr.usembassy.gov; Vasilissis Sofias 91, Ilissia; Ⓜ Megaro Mousikis) Also has a branch in **Thessaloniki** (☎2310 242 905; https://gr.usembassy.gov; 7th fl, Tsimiski 43).

Electricity

Type C
220V/50Hz

Type F
230V/50Hz

Health

Availability &
Cost of Health Care

Although medical training is of a high standard in Greece, the public health service is badly underfunded. Hospitals can be overcrowded, hygiene is not always what it should be, and relatives are expected to bring in food for the patient –

which can be a problem for a solo traveller. Conditions and treatment are much better in private hospitals, which are expensive. All this means that a good health-insurance policy is essential.

➡ If you need an ambulance in Greece call 166 or 112.

➡ There is at least one doctor on every island, and larger islands have hospitals.

➡ Pharmacies can dispense medicines that are available only on prescription in most European countries.

➡ Consult a pharmacist for minor ailments.

Insurance

If you're an EU citizen, a European Health Insurance Card (EHIC) covers you for most medical care but not emergency repatriation or nonemergencies. Citizens from other countries should find out if there is a reciprocal arrangement for free medical care between their country and Greece. If you do need health insurance, make sure you get a policy that covers you for the worst possible scenario, such as an accident requiring an emergency flight home. Find out in advance if your insurance plan will make payments directly to providers or reimburse you later for overseas health expenditures.

Worldwide travel insurance is available at www.lonely planet.com/travel-insurance. You can buy, extend and claim online anytime – even if you're already on the road.

Environmental Hazards

➡ The only dangerous snake in Greece is the viper (also known as the common European viper). To minimise the possibilities of being bitten, always wear boots, socks and long trousers when walking through undergrowth where snakes may be present.

➡ Mosquitoes can be an annoying problem, though there is no danger of

contracting malaria. Electric mosquito-repellent devices are usually sufficient to keep the insects at bay at night. Choose accommodation that has fly screen on the windows wherever possible.

➡ The Asian tiger mosquito (*Aedes albopictus*) can be a voracious daytime biter and is known to carry several viruses, including Eastern equine encephalitis, which can affect the central nervous system and cause severe complications and death. Use protective sprays or lotion if you suspect you are being bitten during the day.

Tap Water

Tap water is drinkable and safe in most of Greece but not always in small villages and on some of the islands. Always ask locally if the water is safe, and if in doubt drink boiled or bought water. Even when water is safe, the substances and bacteria in it may be different from those you are used to, and occasionally can cause vomiting or diarrhoea. Bottled water is widely available, but think about environmental considerations when you opt for bottled over tap water.

Internet Access

Free wi-fi is available in most hotels, many cafes and some restaurants. A number of cities have free wi-fi zones in shopping and eating areas and plazas. Internet cafes have virtually disappeared – instead buy a local SIM with data to insert in your unlocked device. Some, but not all, hotels offer computers for guests to use.

Legal Matters

Arrests

It is a good idea to have your passport (or at least a copy and some ID) with you at all times in case you are stopped by the police and questioned. This is particularly true if you are travelling in border areas. Greek citizens are presumed always to have identification on them and the police presume foreign visitors do too. If you are arrested by police, insist on an interpreter (*diermi_néas*; say '*the*-lo dhi-ermi-*nea*') and/or a lawyer (*diki_góros*; say '*the*-lo dhi-ki-*go*-ro').

Drugs

Greek drug laws are among the strictest in Europe. Greek courts make no distinction between possession and pushing. Possession of even a small amount of marijuana is likely to land you in jail.

LGBT+ Travellers

Same-sex unions (but not marriages) were legally recognised in Greece in 2015 and attitudes to the LGBT+ community have grown more liberal across the country. However, the Orthodox Church plays a prominent role in shaping society's views on social issues, so you may find your sexuality being frowned upon by some locals – especially outside major cities.

Rest assured, Greece is an extremely popular destinations for LGBT+ travellers for a reason. Athens has a busy scene, but most LGBT+ travellers head for the islands. Mykonos has long been famous for its bars, beaches and general hedonism, while Skiathos also has its share of hang-outs. The island of Lesvos (Mytilini), birthplace of the lesbian poet Sappho, has become something of a place of pilgrimage for lesbians.

The Beloved Republic (http://thebelovedrepublic.com) is a company specialising in organising same-sex unions in Greece. For more info, see https://queerinthe world.com/gay-greece.

Maps

Unless you are going to hike or drive, the free maps given out by the EOT and larger hotels will probably suffice, although they are not 100% accurate.

Anavasi (www.mountains.gr) Athens-based company publishing maps with excellent coverage. Hikers should consider its *Topo* series, which has durable, waterproof paper and detailed walking trails for many of the Aegean islands.

Terrain (www.terrainmaps.gr) Maps published in Athens and offering equally good coverage. All maps can be bought online or at major bookstores in Greece.

Money

Debit and credit cards are accepted in cities, but elsewhere it's handy to have cash. Most towns have ATMs, but they may be out of order.

ATMs

There are ATMs in every town large enough to support a bank and in almost all the tourist areas. If you have MasterCard or Visa, there are plenty of places to withdraw money. Cirrus and Maestro withdrawals can be made in major towns and tourist areas.

Note that in small tourist villages, the only option may be a Euronet ATM (yellow and blue). These charge a €3.95 fee (compared to €2 to €3 at bank ATMs), and offer significantly worse exchange rates.

Be aware that many ATMs on the islands can lose their connection for a day or two at a time, making it impossible for anyone (locals included) to withdraw money. It's useful to have a backup source of money.

Automated foreign-exchange machines are common in major tourist areas. They take all major European currencies, Australian and US dollars and Japanese yen, and are useful in an emergency, although they charge a hefty commission.

Be warned that many card companies can put an automatic block on your card after your first withdrawal abroad, as an antifraud mechanism. To avoid this happening, inform your bank of your travel plans.

Cash

Nothing beats cash for convenience – or for risk. If you lose cash, it's gone for good. It's best to carry no more cash than you need for the next few days. It's also a good idea to set aside a small amount, say €100, as an emergency stash.

Note that Greek shopkeepers and small-business owners sometimes don't have small change. When buying small items it is better to tender coins or small-denomination notes.

Credit Cards

Credit cards are an accepted part of the commercial scene in Greece. In fact, since 2018 (as part of the 'management' of the financial crisis) Greeks aged below 65 and earning an income have been required by law to have a credit card. As a result, hotels and commercial ventures must be able to process them.

The main credit cards are MasterCard and Visa, both of which are widely accepted. They can also be used as cash cards to draw cash from the ATMs of affiliated Greek banks. Daily withdrawal limits are set by the issuing bank and are given in local currency only (though you may be given the opportunity to accept or decline a fixed exchange rate of your home currency).

Opening Hours

Opening hours vary throughout the year. The following are high-season hours; hours decrease significantly for shoulder and low seasons, and some places close completely. In tourist locations, some shops stay open longer year round.

Banks 8.30am–2.30pm Monday to Thursday, 8am–2pm Friday

Bars 8pm–late

Cafes 10am–midnight

Clubs 10pm–4am

Post Offices 7.30am–2pm Monday to Friday (rural); 7.30am–8pm Monday to Friday, 7.30am–2pm Saturday (urban)

Restaurants 11am–11pm

Shops 8am–2pm Monday, Wednesday and Saturday; 8am–2pm and 5pm–9pm Tuesday, Thursday and Friday

Photography

➡ Digital memory cards are readily available from camera stores.

➡ Never photograph a military installation; some are less than obvious and near to wildlife-viewing areas.

➡ Flash photography is not allowed inside churches and it's considered taboo to photograph the main altar.

➡ Greeks usually love having their photos taken, but always ask permission first.

➡ At archaeological sites you will be stopped from using a tripod as it marks you as a 'professional'.

Public Holidays

New Year's Day 1 January

Epiphany 6 January

First Sunday in Lent February

Greek Independence Day 25 March

Good Friday 22 April 2022, 14 April 2023, 3 May 2024

Orthodox Easter Sunday 24 April 2022, 16 April 2023, 5 May 2024

May Day (Protomagia) 1 May

Whit Monday (Agiou Pnevmatos) 13 June 2022, 5 June 2023, 24 June 2024

Feast of the Dormition 15 August

Ohi Day 28 October

Christmas Day 25 December

St Stephen's Day 26 December

Safe Travel

Adulterated & Spiked Drinks

Adulterated drinks (known as *bombes*) are served in some bars and clubs in Athens and at resorts known for partying. These drinks are diluted with

cheap illegal imports that leave you feeling worse for wear the next day.

At many of the party resorts catering to large budget-tour groups, spiked drinks are not uncommon; keep your hand over the top of your glass. More often than not, the perpetrators are foreign tourists rather than locals.

Tourist Police

The *touristiki_astynomia* (tourist police) work in co-operation with the regular Greek police and are found in cities and popular tourist destinations. Each tourist police office has at least one member of staff who speaks English. Hotels, restaurants, travel agencies, tourist shops, tourist guides, waiters, taxi drivers and bus drivers all come under the jurisdiction of the tourist police. If you have a complaint about any of these, report it to the tourist police and they will investigate. If you need to report a theft or loss of passport, go to the tourist police first, and they will act as interpreters between you and the regular police.

Smoking

Smoking is banned inside public places, with the penalty being fines placed on the business owners. Greece is home to some of the heaviest smokers in Europe, so enforcement is a challenge. They are often imposed in only a nominal way in remote locations where proprietors fear they would lose business.

Taxes & Refunds

Greece has some of the highest tax rates in Europe, largely due to its economic struggles. Value-added tax (VAT) is 24% for most things, although hotel accommodation, food and medicine is 13%, and for books and newspapers it's 6%. VAT is included in the price unless otherwise stated.

Telephone

The Greek telephone service is maintained by the public corporation OTE (pronounced o-*teh*; Organismos Tilepikoinonion Ellados). You may still find some public phones in central locations in cities and villages, though as people now use mobile (cell) phones, these are becoming rarities.

Note that in Greece the area code must always be dialled when making a call (ie all Greek phone numbers are 10-digit).

Mobile Phones

Local SIM cards can be used in unlocked phones. Most other phones can be set to roaming. US and Canadian phones need to have a dual- or tri-band system.

There are several mobile service providers in Greece, among which Cosmote (www.cosmote.gr), Vodafone (www.vodafone.gr) and Wind (www.wind.gr) are the best known. Of these three, Cosmote tends to have the best coverage in remote areas. All offer 4G connectivity and pay-as-you-talk services for which you can buy a rechargeable SIM card and have your own Greek mobile number. If you're buying a package, be sure to triple-check the fine print. There are restrictions on deals such as 'free minutes' only being available to phones using the same provider.

The use of a mobile phone while driving in Greece is prohibited, but the use of a Bluetooth headset is allowed.

Phonecards & Public Phones

Public phones use OTE phonecards, known as *telekarta*, not coins. These cards are available at *periptera* (street kiosks), and some corner shops and tourist shops. Public phones are easy to operate. The 'i' at the top left of the push-button dialling panel brings up the operating instructions in English.

It's also possible to use payphones with discount-card

schemes. This involves dialling an access code and then punching in your card number. The OTE version of this card is known as 'Chronokarta'. The cards come with instructions in Greek and English, and the talk time is good compared with the standard phonecard rates.

Time

Greece is two hours ahead of GMT/UTC and three hours ahead on daylight-saving time – which begins on the last Sunday in March, when clocks are put forward one hour. Daylight saving ends on the last Sunday in October.

Toilets

➡ Nearly all places have Western-style toilets, including hotels and restaurants. Public toilets at transport terminals (bus and train) sometimes have Turkish squat-style toilets.

➡ Public toilets tend to be limited to airports and bus and train stations, with the very occasional one in tourist-heavy town centres. Cafes are the best option, but in tourist-heavy places, it's polite to buy something for the privilege.

➡ The Greek plumbing system can't handle toilet paper; apparently the pipes are too narrow and anything larger than a postage stamp seems to cause a problem. Toilet paper etc must be placed in the small bin provided next to every toilet.

Tourist Information

The Greek National Tourist Organisation (www.visitgreece.gr) is known as GNTO abroad and EOT within Greece. The quality of service from office to office varies dramatically; in some you'll get information aplenty and in others you'll be hard-pressed to find anyone behind the desk. Offices can be found in major tourist locations. In some regions tourist offices are run by the local government/municipality.

Visas

Countries whose nationals can stay in Greece for up to 90 days without a visa include Australia, Canada, EU countries, Iceland, Israel, Japan, New Zealand, Norway, the UK and the USA. Other countries included are the European principalities of Monaco and San Marino, and most South American countries. The list changes though – contact Greek embassies for the latest. The Greek Ministry of Foreign Affairs publishes an updated list of countries requiring visas (www.mfa.gr/en/visas).

If you wish to stay in Greece for longer than three months within a six-month period, you will probably need a national visa (type D) from the Greek embassy in your country of residence. You cannot apply for this in Greece.

Volunteering

Hellenic Wildlife Hospital (http://ekpazp.gr) Volunteers head to Aegina (particularly during winter) to this large wildlife rehabilitation centre.

Mouries Farm (Map p673; ✆6947465900; www.skyrian horses.org; Flea; by donation; ⏱10am-1pm & 6-9pm Jul & Aug, hours vary Jun & Sep, by appointment Oct-May) ✐ Help with the breeding and care of rare Skyrian horses.

Sea Turtle Protection Society of Greece (✆210 523 1342; www.archelon.gr) Includes monitoring sea turtles in the Peloponnese.

Skopelos Walks (✆6945249328; www.skopelos-walks.com; guided hikes €20-40) ✐ Takes volunteers to help with maintaining and opening up island trails.

Skyros Island Horse Trust (Map p673; ✆6986051678; www.skyrosislandhorsetrust.com; Trachi; ⏱by appointment) ✐ A great project for volunteers to assist with programmes to preserve the endangered horses.

WWOOF (World Wide Opportunities on Organic Farms; https://wwoof.gr) Offers opportunities for volunteers at one of over 100 farms in Greece.

Women Travellers

Many women travel alone in Greece. The crime rate remains relatively low and solo travel is probably safer than in most European countries. This does not mean that you should be lulled into complacency; bag snatching and sexual assault do occur, particularly at party resorts.

The majority of Greek men treat foreign women with respect. However, smooth-talking guys aren't in the least bashful about approaching women in the street. They can be very persistent, but they are usually a hassle rather than a threat.

Work

EU nationals don't need a work permit, but do need a residency permit and a Greek tax-file number to stay longer than three months. Nationals from other countries require a work permit.

Bar & Hostel Work

Bars of the Greek islands rely on foreign workers and there are thousands of summer jobs up for grabs every year. The pay is not fantastic, but you get to spend a summer on the islands. April and May are the times to go looking. Hostels and travellers' hotels are other places that regularly employ foreign workers.

English Tutoring

If you're looking for a permanent job, the most widely available option is teaching English. A TEFL (Teaching English as a Foreign Language) certificate or a university degree is an advantage but not essential. For jobs listings check sites such as www.gooverseas.com.

You can also find a job teaching English when you are in Greece – there are language schools everywhere. Strictly speaking, you need a licence to teach in them, but many will employ teachers without one. Check the noticeboards of popular bookshops to see if anyone is looking for private tutoring.

Transport

GETTING THERE & AWAY

Greece is easy to reach by air or sea – particularly in summer when it opens its arms (and schedules) wide. Getting to or from Greece overland takes more planning but isn't impossible. Flights, cars and tours can be booked online at lonelyplanet.com/bookings.

Entering the Country

Visitors to Greece with EU passports are rarely given more than a cursory glance, but customs and police may be interested in what you are carrying. EU citizens may also enter Greece on a national identity card. Visitors from outside the EU may require a visa – check with consular authorities before you arrive.

Air

Most visitors to Greece arrive by air, which tends to be the fastest and cheapest option, if not the most environmentally friendly.

Airports & Airlines

Greece has four main international airports. Other airports across the country, including Santorini (Thira),Kalamata, Karpathos, Samos, Skiathos, Hrysoupoli/Kavala, Aktion, Kefallonia and Zakynthos, are most often used for charter flights from the UK, Germany and Scandinavia.

Eleftherios Venizelos International Airport (ATH; Map p140; ☑210 353 0000; www.aia.gr) Located 27km east Athens.

Nikos Kazantzakis International Airport (HER; ☑2810 397800; www.ypa.gr/en/our-airports/kratikos-aerolimenas-hrakleioy-n-kazantzakhs) About 5km east of Iraklio (Crete).

Diagoras Airport (RHO; Map p514; ☑22410 88700; www.rho-airport.gr) On the island of Rhodes.

Makedonia International Airport (SKG; ☑2310 985 000; www.thessalonikiairport.com) About 15km southeast of Thessaloniki.

Aegean Airlines (A3; ☑801 112 0000; https://en.aegeanair.com) and its subsidiary, **Olympic Air** (☑801 801 0101, 21035 50500; www.olympicair.com), have flights between Athens and destinations throughout Europe, as well as to Cairo, Istanbul, Tel Aviv and Toronto. They also operate flights throughout Greece, many of which transfer in Athens. Both airlines have exemplary safety records.

Tickets

If you're coming from outside Europe, consider a cheap flight to a European hub (eg London) and then an onward ticket with a budget or charter airline such as **easyJet** (☑211 198 0013; www.easyjet.com), which offers some of the cheapest tickets between Greece and the rest of Europe. Some airlines also offer cheap deals to students. If you're planning to travel between June and September, it's wise to book ahead.

CLIMATE CHANGE & TRAVEL

Every form of transport that relies on carbon-based fuel generates CO_2, the main cause of human-induced climate change. Modern travel is dependent on aeroplanes, which might use less fuel per kilometre per person than most cars but travel much greater distances. The altitude at which aircraft emit gases (including CO_2) and particles also contributes to their climate change impact. Many websites offer 'carbon calculators' that allow people to estimate the carbon emissions generated by their journey and, for those who wish to do so, to offset the impact of the greenhouse gases emitted with contributions to portfolios of climate-friendly initiatives throughout the world. Lonely Planet offsets the carbon footprint of all staff and author travel.

Land

International train travel, in particular, has become much more feasible in recent years, with speedier trains and better connections. You can now travel from London to Athens by train and ferry in less than two days. By choosing to travel on the ground instead of the air, you'll also be reducing your carbon footprint.

Border Crossings

Make sure you have all of your visas (p770) sorted out before attempting to cross land borders into or out of Greece. Before travelling, also check the status of borders with the relevant embassies.

ALBANIA

Buses between Greece and Albania are run by **Albtrans** (☑ Albania +355-42 239 203, Greece 210 520 2185; www. albtrans.net).

Kakavia The main border crossing, 56m northwest of Ioannina

Kapshtice/Krystallopigi 14km west of Kotas on the Florina–Kastoria road

Sagiada/Mavromati 30km north of Igoumenitsa

Sopik/Drymades 57km west of Konitsa and for Greek passport holders only

BULGARIA

As Bulgaria is part of the EU, crossings are usually quick and hassle-free.

Exohi A 448m-tunnel border crossing 50km north of Drama

Ormenio In northeastern Thrace

Promahonas 110km northeast of Thessaloniki

NORTH MACEDONIA

Doïrani 29km north of Kilkis

Evzoni 77km north of Thessaloniki

Niki 16km north of Florina

TURKEY

Kipi is more convenient if you're heading for İstanbul. The route through Kastanies goes via Soufli and Didymotiho in Greece, and Edirne (ancient Adrianoupolis) in Turkey.

Kastanies 132km northeast of Alexandroupoli

Kipi The main border, 46km east of Alexandroupoli

Train

The railways organisation **OSE** (Organismos Sidirodromon Ellados; ☑ 14511; www.trainose. gr) runs a daily service connecting Thessaloniki and Sofia – you'll have to transfer to a bus for the short section between Kulata on the Bulgarian side of the border and Strimon on the Greek side.

From mid-June to mid-September there is also a service between Belgrade and Thessaloniki via Skopje. In Belgrade connections are available to the rest of Europe.

INTERNATIONAL TRAIN PASSES

Greece is part of the Eurail (www.eurail.com) network. Eurail passes can only be bought by residents of non-European countries; they should be purchased before arriving in Europe, but can be bought in Europe if your passport proves that you've been there for less than six months. Greece is also part of the Interrail Pass system (www. interrail.eu), available to those who have resided in Europe for six months or more, and the Rail Plus Balkan Flexipass (www.raileurope.com), which offers unlimited travel for five, 10 or 15 days within a month. See the websites for full details of passes and prices.

Sea

Ferries can get very crowded in summer. If you want to take a vehicle across, it's wise to make a reservation beforehand. Port tax for departures to Turkey is around €10.

Another way to visit Greece by sea is to join one of the many cruises that ply the Aegean.

INTERNATIONAL FERRY ROUTES

The services indicated are for high season (July and August). For further information see www.openseas.gr.

DESTINATION	DEPARTURE POINT	ARRIVAL POINT	DURATION	FREQUENCY
Albania	Corfu	Saranda	30-70mins	3 daily
Italy	Patra	Ancona	20-22hrs	daily
Italy	Patra	Bari	16hrs	daily
Italy	Igoumenitsa	Bari	9½-11½hrs	2 daily
Italy	Patra	Brindisi	15hrs	3 weekly
Italy	Patra	Venice	31-32hrs	4-5 weekly
Turkey	Chios	Çeşme	20-30mins	6 daily
Turkey	Kos	Bodrum	45mins	daily
Turkey	Lesvos	Ayvalik	1½hrs	daily
Turkey	Rhodes	Marmaris	50mins	2 daily
Turkey	Samos	Kuşadası	1½hrs	2 daily

GETTING AROUND

Air

The vast majority of domestic mainland flights are handled by the country's national carrier **Aegean Airlines** (A3; ☑801 112 0000; https://en.aegeanair.com) and its subsidiary, **Olympic Air** (☑801 801 0101, 21035 50500; www.olympicair.com). You'll find offices wherever there are flights, as well as in other major towns. There are also a number of smaller Greek carriers, including Thessaloniki-based **Astra Airlines** (☑23104 89391; www.astra-airlines.gr) and **Sky Express** (☑21521 56510; www.skyexpress.gr).

There are discounts for return tickets for travel between Monday and Thursday, and bigger discounts for trips that include a Saturday night away. Find full details and timetables on airline websites. Viva.gr (https://travel.viva.gr) is a good website for finding cheap domestic flights as well as other travel and entertainment tickets.

The baggage allowance on domestic flights varies according to the airline and the category of ticket you've purchased, and can be scrutinised carefully at check-in. It's usually 20kg if the domestic flight is part of an international journey.

Bicycle

Cycling is not popular among Greeks – but it's gaining popularity with tourists. You'll need strong leg muscles to tackle the mountains; or you can stick to some of the flatter coastal routes. Bike lanes are rare to nonexistent; helmets are not compulsory. The main dangers are the cars on the roads – locals and tourists alike. The island of Kos is about the most bicycle-friendly place in Greece, as

is anywhere flat, such as the plains of Thessaly or Thrace.

➡ You can hire bicycles in most tourist places, but they are not as widely available as cars and motorcycles. Prices range from €10 to €15 per day, depending on the type and age of the bike.

➡ Bicycles are carried free on ferries but cannot be taken on the fast ferries (catamarans and the like; there simply isn't room to store them).

➡ You can buy decent mountain or touring bikes in Greece's major towns, though you may have a problem finding a ready buyer if you wish to on-sell it. Bike prices are much the same as across the rest of Europe: anywhere from €300 to €2000.

Boat

Greece has an extensive network of ferries – the only means of reaching many of the islands. Schedules are often subject to delays due to poor weather (note: this is a safety precaution) plus the occasional industrial action, and prices fluctuate regularly. Timetables are not announced until just prior to the season due to competition for route licences. In summer, ferries run regular services between all but the most out-of-the-way destinations; however, services seriously slow down in winter (and in some cases stop completely).

Domestic Ferry Operators

Ferry companies have local offices on many of the islands. The big companies compete for routes annually (and seem to merge and demerge regularly), so the following may have changed by the time you read this. A useful website to check is **Greek Ferries** (☑281 052 9000; www.greekferries.gr), which is also available as an app.

Aegean Flying Dolphins (www.aegeanflyingdolphins.gr) Hydrofoils between Athens, Aegina and the Sporades.

Aegean Speed Lines (www.aegeanspeedlines.gr) Super-speedy boats between Athens and the Cyclades.

Aegeon Pelagos (www.anek.gr) Subsidiary of ANEK Lines serving routes to Crete, the Cyclades and the Dodecanese.

ANEK Lines (www.anek.gr) Crete-based long-haul ferries.

ANEK/Superfast Ferries (www.superfast.com) Routes to/from Ancona, Bari, Corfu, Igoumenitsa, Patra and Venice.

ANES (www.anes.gr) Old-style ferries servicing Evia and the Sporades.

Blue Star Ferries (www.bluestarferries.com) Long-haul, high-speed ferries and Seajets catamarans between the mainland, the Cyclades, the northeastern Aegean Islands, the Sporades, Crete and the Dodecanese.

Dodekanisos Seaways (www.12ne.gr) Runs large, high-speed catamarans in the Dodecanese.

Fast Ferries (www.fastferries.com.gr) Comfortable ferries from Rafina to the Cyclades islands including Andros, Tinos, Naxos and Mykonos.

Glyfa Ferries (www.ferriesglyfa.gr) Comfortable short-haul ferry services between Glyfa on the mainland and Agiokambos in northern Evia.

Hellenic Seaways (https://hellenicseaways.gr) Offers catamarans from the mainland to the Cyclades and between the Sporades and Saronic islands.

LANE Lines (www.ferries.gr/lane) Long-haul ferries serving the Ionians, Dodecanese and Crete.

Levante Ferries (www.levanteferries.com) Large ferries serving the Ionian Islands.

Minoan Lines (www.minoan.gr) High-speed luxury ferries between Piraeus and Iraklio (Heraklion) among other destinations.

Patmos Star (www.patmos-star.com) Small, local ferry linking Patmos, Leros and Lipsi in the Dodecanese.

Ferry Routes

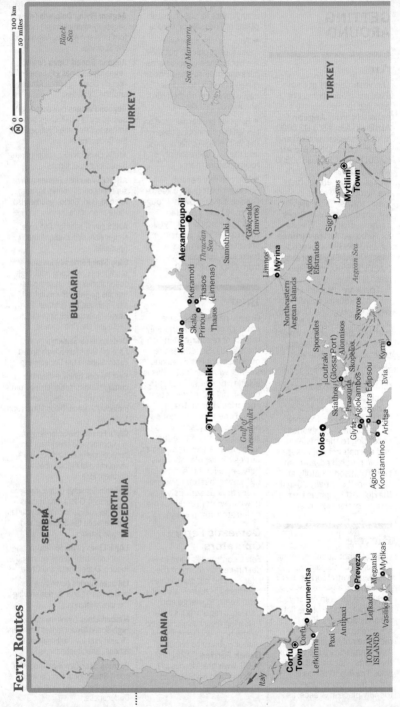

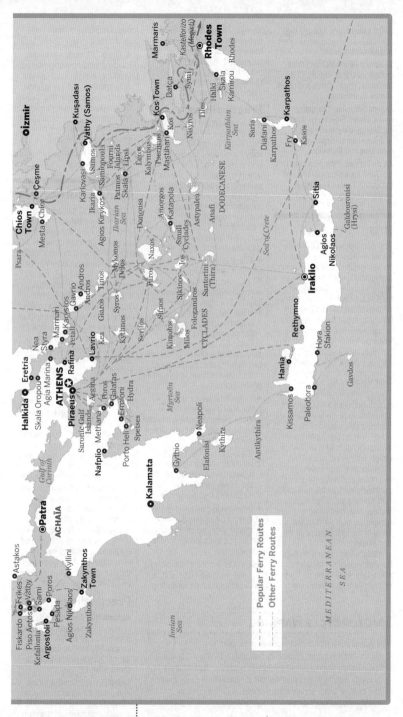

SAOS Lines (www.saos.gr) Big, slow boats between Samothraki and Alexandroupoli.

Seajets (www.seajets.gr) Catamarans calling at Athens, Crete, Santorini (Thira), Paros and many islands in between.

Skyros Shipping Company (www.sne.gr) Slow boats connecting Skyros to Kymi (Evia) and, mid-June to mid-September, to Alonnisos and Skopelos.

Zante Ferries (http://zanteferries.gr) Older ferries connecting the mainland (Piraeus) with the western Cyclades.

Bus

The bus network is comprehensive. All long-distance buses, on the mainland and the islands, are operated by regional collectives known as KTEL (www.ktelbus.com). Within towns and cities, different companies run inter urban services. The fares are fixed by the government; bus travel is reasonably priced. All have good safety records.

Services

Every prefecture on the mainland has a KTEL, which operates local services within it and to the main towns of other prefectures. With the exception of towns in Thrace, which are serviced by Thessaloniki, all major towns on the mainland have frequent connections to Athens. Corfu, Kefallonia and Zakynthos can also be reached directly from Athens by bus – often the fares include the price of the ferry ticket.

Most villages have a daily bus service of some sort, although remote areas may have only one or two buses

a week. They operate for the benefit of people going to town to shop, rather than for tourists, and consequently leave the villages very early in the morning and return early in the afternoon.

Practicalities

➡ It is important to note that big cities like Athens, Iraklio, Patra and Thessaloniki may have more than one bus station, each serving different regions. Make sure you find the correct station for your destination. In small towns and villages the 'bus station' may be no more than a bus stop outside a *kafeneio* (coffee house) or taverna that doubles as a booking office.

➡ There is no central source of bus information, and each KTEL company runs its own website, with varying amounts of info. Thessaloniki's (KTEL Makedonia) is the best, and it falls off rapidly from there. Frustratingly, KTEL bus timetables only give the end destination – check when you buy tickets at stations about intermediate town stops on a given route.

➡ In remote areas, the timetable may be in Greek only, but most booking offices have timetables in both Greek and Roman script.

➡ It's best to turn up at least 20 minutes before departure – buses have been known to leave a few minutes before their scheduled departure.

➡ When you buy a ticket, you may be allotted a seat number, printed on the ticket. In some cases locals ignore these.

➡ You can board a bus without a ticket and pay on board, but on a popular route or during

high season, you may have to stand.

➡ The KTEL buses are safe, modern and air-conditioned. In more remote, rural areas they may be older and less comfortable. Note that buses often have toilets on board that are not used; instead, on longer journeys, they must stop every 2½ hours.

➡ Smoking is prohibited on all buses in Greece.

Car & Motorcycle

In the past, Greece had a terrible reputation for road safety. In recent years, however, roads and highways have improved dramatically and European Commission statistics (2010–18) report a drop of 45% in fatalities. However, no one who has travelled on Greece's roads will be surprised to hear that the road toll of 69 deaths for every million inhabitants is still a lot higher than the EU average of 49. Overtaking is listed as the greatest cause, along with speed. Accidents can occur on single-lane roads when slower vehicles pull to the right on both sides and are overtaken at the same time, leading to head-on collisions.

Heart-stopping moments aside, your own car is a great way to explore off the beaten track. The road network has improved enormously in recent years, with a similar increase in tourist traffic, especially on the islands. This brings its own problems such as parking and congestion in island towns. There are regular (if costly) car-ferry services to almost all islands.

Practicalities

Automobile Associations Nationwide roadside assistance is provided by **ELPA** (Elliniki Leschi Aftokinitou kai Periigiseon; ☎24hr roadside assistance 10400).

Entry EU-registered vehicles enter free for up to six months without road taxes being due. A green card (international third-party insurance) is required, along with proof of date of entry (ferry ticket or your passport stamp). Non-EU-registered vehicles may be logged in your passport.

Driving licences EU driving licences are valid in Greece. Rental agencies require the corresponding driving licence for every vehicle class (eg motorcycle/moped licence for motorbikes or mopeds). Greek law requires drivers from outside the EU to have an International Driving Permit (IDP). Rental agencies will request it, as may local authorities if you're stopped. IDPs can only be obtained in person and in the country where your driving licence was issued. Carry this alongside your regular licence.

Fuel Available widely throughout the country, though service stations may be closed on weekends and public holidays. On the islands, there may be only one petrol station; check where it is before you head out. Self-service and credit-card pumps are not the norm in Greece. Petrol in Greece is among the most expensive in Europe. Petrol types include *amolyvdi* (unleaded) and *petreleo kinisis* (diesel).

Hire

CAR

➜ All the big multinational companies are represented in Athens; most have branches in major towns and popular tourist destinations. The majority of islands have at least one outlet.

➜ By Greek law, rental cars have to be replaced every 10 years. However, very often a car is quite scratched up when you get it. Be sure to take photos of all the damage.

➜ The minimum driving age is 18 years, but most car-hire firms require you to be at least 21 (or 23 for larger vehicles). In some cases, you pay extra if you're a younger driver.

➜ High-season weekly rates with unlimited mileage start at about €280 for the smallest models (eg a Fiat Seicento), dropping to about €150 per week in winter.

➜ You can often find great deals at local companies. Their advertised rates can be up to 50% cheaper than the multinationals and they are normally open to negotiation, especially if business is slow.

➜ On the islands, you can rent a car for the day for around €35 to €60, including all insurance and taxes.

➜ Always check what the insurance includes; there are often rough roads or dangerous routes that you can only tackle by renting a 4WD.

➜ It is not possible to take a car hired in Greece into another country.

➜ Unless you pay with a credit card, most hire companies will require a minimum deposit of €120 per day.

➜ Some of the international car-rental agencies have a policy that if you rent for a longer term (eg three or more days), you must prepay for a tank of gas. If you return the car with the tank full, you're entitled to a refund, but you absolutely must ask for it – there's no guarantee the prepayment will be automatically refunded.

The major car-hire companies in Greece:

Avis (www.avis.gr)

Budget (www.budget.gr)

Europcar (www.europcar-greece.gr)

MOTORCYCLE

➜ Mopeds, motorcycles, scooters and quad bikes (ATVs) are available for hire wherever there are tourists to rent them. Most machines are newish and in good condition. Nonetheless, check the brakes at the earliest opportunity.

➜ You must produce a licence that shows proficiency to ride the category of bike you wish to rent; this applies to everything from 50cc up. British citizens must obtain a Category A1 licence from the Driver & Vehicle Licensing Agency (www.dft.gov.uk/dvla) in the UK (in most other EU countries separate licences are automatically issued).

➜ Rates start from about €20 per day for a moped or 50cc motorcycle, ranging to €35 per day for a 250cc motorcycle. Out of season these prices drop considerably, so use your bargaining skills.

➜ Most motorcycle hirers include third-party insurance in the price, but it's wise to check this. This insurance will not include medical expenses.

➜ Helmets are compulsory and rental agencies are obliged to offer one as part of the hire deal.

Road Conditions

➜ Main highways in Greece have been improving steadily over the years and are now all excellent.

➜ The old highways are now quite empty of big trucks, and much nicer for driving.

➜ Some main roads retain a two-lane/hard-shoulder format, which can be confusing and even downright dangerous.

➜ Roadworks can take years and years in Greece – especially on the islands, where funding often only trickles in. In other cases, excellent new tarmac roads may have appeared that are not on any local maps.

➜ Many island roads aren't paved, which doesn't always show up clearly on GPS or online maps – take care not to get stuck down dirt tracks that aren't to be driven on.

Road Hazards

➜ Slow drivers – many of them unsure and hesitant tourists who stop suddenly on corners and other inappropriate places – can cause serious traffic events on Greece's roads.

➜ Road surfaces can change rapidly when a section of road has succumbed to subsidence or weathering. Snow and ice can be a serious challenge in winter, and drivers are advised to carry snow chains. In rural areas, look out for animals wandering on to roads.

➜ Roads passing through mountainous areas are often

ROAD DISTANCES (KM)

TRANSPORT CAR & MOTORCYCLE

	Alexandroupoli	Athens	Corinth	Edessa	Florina	Igoumenitsa	Ioannina	Kalamata	Kastoria	Kavala	Lamia	Larisa	Monemvasia	Nafplio	Patra	Pyrgos	Sparta	Thessaloniki	Trikala	Tripoli
Athens	854																			
Corinth	884	84																		
Edessa	427	569	596																	
Florina	497	592	251	353																
Igoumenitsa	816	473	393	380	353															
Ioannina	702	447	364	298	320	96														
Kalamata	1055	284	175	767	763	501	467													
Kastoria	535	489	519	108	67	286	204	690												
Kavala	177	682	655	250	320	615	525	878	358											
Lamia	643	214	244	355	360	353	263	415	274	466										
Larisa	493	361	389	218	231	309	209	561	239	323	151									
Monemvasia	1156	350	266	869	855	613	579	156	756	976	505	655								
Nafplio	947	165	63	659	664	482	427	163	582	770	307	455	215							
Patra	828	220	138	567	513	281	247	220	483	664	193	341	332	201						
Pyrgos	924	320	234	636	643	367	347	119	542	747	284	432	275	208	96					
Sparta	1025	225	145	737	759	517	483	60	660	848	385	533	96	119	236	180				
Thessaloniki	349	513	544	89	159	452	362	715	220	169	303	154	807	610	488	584	711			
Trikala	554	330	356	227	233	247	148	520	159	377	115	62	597	419	310	400	501	216		
Tripoli	964	194	110	713	681	457	430	90	639	820	324	472	157	81	176	155	61	624	466	
Volos	556	326	355	278	293	371	271	518	301	383	115	62	620	417	308	408	524	214	124	435

littered with fallen rocks, which can cause extensive damage to a vehicle's underside or throw a motorbike rider.

➡ When driving on a single carriageway, slower vehicles, including older trucks, tend to pull over to the right into the 'safety' lane, allowing drivers to pass around them. The issue is, this happens from both sides, so as a car pulls out to pass in the free space (which locals seem to wrongly consider a 'lane'), fatal head-on collisions are common.

Road Rules

➡ In Greece, as throughout continental Europe, you drive on the right and overtake on the left.

➡ Outside built-up areas, unless signed otherwise, traffic on a main road has right of way at intersections. In towns, vehicles coming from the right have right of way. This includes roundabouts – even if you're at a roundabout, you must give way to drivers coming on to the roundabout from your right.

➡ Seatbelts must be worn in front seats, and in back seats if the car is fitted with them.

➡ Children under 12 years of age are not allowed in the front seat.

➡ It is compulsory to carry a first-aid kit, fire extinguisher and warning triangle; carrying cans of petrol is prohibited.

➡ Helmets are compulsory for motorcyclists. Police will book you if you're caught without a helmet.

➡ Outside residential areas the speed limit is 120km/h on highways, 90km/h on other roads and 50km/h in built-up areas. The speed limit for motorcycles is the same as cars. Drivers exceeding the speed limit by 20% are liable to receive a fine of €40 to €120; exceeding it by 30% costs €350 plus your licence will be suspended for 60 days.

➡ A blood-alcohol content of 0.05% can incur a fine, while over 0.08% is a criminal offence.

➡ It is illegal to use a mobile phone while driving. If caught, you may be charged between €100 and €300 and have your licence suspended for 30 days.

➡ If you are involved in an accident and no one is hurt, the police are not required to write a report, but it is advisable to go to a police station and explain what happened. You may need a police report for insurance purposes. If an accident involves injury, a driver who doesn't stop and doesn't inform the police may face a prison sentence.

Hitching

Hitching is never entirely safe, and we don't recommend it. Those who hitch should understand that they are taking a potentially serious risk. Travellers who do choose to hitch will be safer if they travel in pairs; they should let someone know where they are heading. In particular, it is unwise for women to hitch alone; women are better off hitching with a male companion.

Some parts of Greece are much better for hitching than others. Getting out of major cities tends to be hard work and Athens is notoriously difficult. Hitching is much easier in remote areas and on islands with poor public transport. On country roads it is not unknown for someone to stop and ask if you want a lift, even if you haven't stuck a thumb out.

Local Transport

Bus

Most Greek towns are small enough to get around on foot. All the major towns have local buses, but they are especially useful in Athens, Patra, Kalamata and Thessaloniki.

Metro

Athens has a good underground system, and Thessaloniki is in the process of constructing one, too (expected to open in early 2023). Note that only Greek student cards are valid for a student ticket on the metro.

Taxi

Taxis are widely available in Greece, except on very small or remote islands, and are reasonably priced by European standards (especially if a few people share costs). Many taxi drivers now have sat-nav systems in their cars, so finding a destination is a breeze as long as you have the exact address.

City cabs are metered, with rates doubling between midnight and 5am. Additional costs are charged for trips from an airport or a bus, port or train station, as well as for each piece of luggage over 10kg. Before you get into the taxi, ask how much the price is likely to be. In some places, such as on islands, where tourists are shuttled around, the price is set each season.

Some taxi drivers in Athens have been known to overcharge unwary travellers. If you have a complaint about a taxi driver, take the cab number and report your complaint to the tourist police. Taxi drivers in other towns in Greece are, on the whole, friendly, helpful and honest. Useful taxi apps include Beat (www.thebeat.co/gr) and Taxiplon (www.taxiplon.gr).

Tours

Tours are worth considering if your time is limited or if you prefer to let someone else do the planning. In Athens, you'll find countless day tours, with some agencies offering two- or three-day trips to nearby sights. For something on a larger scale, try Intrepid Travel (www.intrepidtravel.com; offices in Australia, the UK and the USA): it offers, for example, a 10-day sailing tour around the Cyclades, starting and ending in Santorini and including Naxos and Mykonos (€1198), including everything except meals and flights. Encounter Greece (www.encountergreece.com) offers a plethora of tours.

More adventurous tours include guided activities such as hiking, climbing, rafting, white-water, kayaking, canoeing and canyoning. The following options are available.

Alpin Club (www.alpinclub.gr) For kayaking, rafting, canyoning and mountain biking. In Athens but operates out of Karitena in the Peloponnese.

Robinson Expeditions (www.robinson.gr) For hiking and mountain biking. Runs tours from the centre and north of Greece.

Trekking Hellas (https://trekking.gr) Runs trekking, kayaking and rafting tours from the centre and north of Greece.

Train

Trains are operated by **OSE** (Organismos Sidirodromon Ellados; ☎14511; www.trainose.gr). The railway network is extremely limited with lines closed in recent years in areas such as the Peloponnese. OSE's northern line is the most substantial. Standard-gauge services run from Athens to Dikea in the northeast via Thessaloniki and Alexandroupoli. There are also connections to Florina and the Pelion Peninsula. The Peloponnese network runs only as far as Kiato, with bus services to Plata for ferry connections.

Prices and schedules are very changeable – double-check on the OSE website. Information on departures from Athens or Thessaloniki is also available by calling 1440.

Classes

There are two types of service: regular (slow) trains that stop at all stations, and faster, modern intercity (IC) trains that link most major cities. Train fares have increased dramatically since the economic crisis; it used to be the country's cheapest form of transport, but is no longer.

Having said that, the IC trains that link the major Greek cities are an excellent way to travel and the trains are modern and comfortable, with a cafe-bar on board.

Train Passes

➡ Eurail, Interrail and Rail Plus Balkan Flexipass cards are valid in Greece, but they're generally not worth buying if Greece is the only place you plan to use them. Check if a supplement is required for IC journeys.

➡ Whatever pass you have, you must have a reservation to board the train.

➡ On presentation of ID orpassport, passengers over 65 years old are entitled to a 25% discount on all lines.

Language

The Greek language is believed to be one of the oldest European languages, with an oral tradition of 4000 years and a written tradition of approximately 3000 years. Due to its centuries of influence, Greek constitutes the origin of a large part of the vocabulary of many Indo-European languages (including English). It is the official language of Greece and co-official language of Cyprus (alongside Turkish), and is spoken by many migrant communities throughout the world.

The Greek alphabet is explained on the following page, but if you read the pronunciation guides given with each phrase in this chapter as if they were English, you'll be understood. Note that dh is pronounced as 'th' in 'there'; gh is a softer, slightly throaty version of 'g'; and kh is a throaty sound like the 'ch' in the Scottish 'loch'. All Greek words of two or more syllables have an acute accent (´), which indicates where the stress falls. In our pronunciation guides, stressed syllables are in italics.

In this chapter, masculine, feminine and neuter forms of words are included where necessary, separated with a slash and indicated with 'm', 'f' and 'n' respectively. Polite and informal options are indicated where relevant with 'pol' and 'inf'.

BASICS

Hello.	Γειά σας.	ya·sas (pol)
	Γειά σου.	ya·su (inf)
Goodbye.	Αντίο.	an·di·o

WANT MORE?

For in-depth language information and handy phrases, check out Lonely Planet's *Greek Phrasebook*. You'll find it at **shop.lonelyplanet.com**, or in your local bookstore.

Yes./No.	Ναι./Όχι.	ne/o·hi
Please.	Παρακαλώ.	pa·ra·ka·lo
Thank you.	Ευχαριστώ.	ef·ha·ri·sto
You're welcome.	Παρακαλώ.	pa·ra·ka·lo
Excuse me.	Με συγχωρείτε.	me sing·kho·ri·te
Sorry.	Συγγνώμη.	sigh·no·mi

What's your name?
Πώς σας λένε;   pos sas le·ne

My name is ...
Με λένε ...   me le·ne ...

Do you speak English?
Μιλάτε αγγλικά;   mi·la·te an·gli·ka

I don't understand.
Δεν καταλαβαίνω.   dhen ka·ta·la·ve·no

ACCOMMODATION

campsite	χώρος για κάμπινγκ	kho·ros yia kam·ping
hotel	ξενοδοχείο	kse·no·dho·khi·o
youth hostel	γιουθ χόστελ	yuth kho·stel
a ... room	ένα ... δωμάτιο	e·na ... dho·ma·ti·o
single	μονόκλινο	mo·no·kli·no
double	δίκλινο	dhi·kli·no
How much is it ...?	Πόσο κάνει ...;	po·so ka·ni ...
per night	τη βραδυά	ti·vra·dhya
per person	το άτομο	to a·to·mo
air-con	έρκοντίσιον	er·kon·di·si·on
bathroom	μπάνιο	ba·nio
fan	ανεμιστήρας	a·ne·mi·sti·ras
window	παράθυρο	pa·ra·thi·ro

DIRECTIONS

Where is ...?
Πού είναι ...; pu *i*·ne ...

What's the address?
Ποια είναι η διεύθυνση; pia *i*·ne i dhi·*ef*·thin·si

Can you show me (on the map)?
Μπορείς να μου δείξεις bo·*ris* na mu *dhik*·sis
(στο χάρτη); (sto *khar*·ti)

Turn left.
Στρίψτε αριστερά. *strips*·te a·ri·ste·*ra*

Turn right.
Στρίψτε δεξιά. *strips*·te dhe·*ksia*

at the next corner
στην επόμενη γωνία stin e·*po*·me·ni gho·*ni*·a

at the traffic lights
στα φώτα sta *fo*·ta

behind πίσω *pi*·so

far μακριά ma·kri·*a*

in front of μπροστά bro·*sta*

near (to) κοντά kon·*da*

next to δίπλα *dhi*·pla

opposite απέναντι a·*pe*·nan·di

straight ahead ολο ευθεία *o*·lo ef·*thi*·a

EATING & DRINKING

a table for ... Ενα τραπέζι *e*·na tra·*pe*·zi
για ... ya ...

(eight) o'clock στις (οχτώ) stis (okh·*to*)

(two) people (δύο) άτομα (*dhi*·o) a·to·ma

I don't eat ... Δεν τρώγω ... dhen *tro*·gho ...

fish ψάρι *psa*·ri

(red) meat (κόκκινο) (*ko*·ki·no)
κρέας *kre*·as

peanuts φυστίκια fi·*sti*·kia

poultry πουλερικά pu·le·ri·*ka*

What would you recommend?
Τι θα συνιστούσες; ti tha si·ni·*stu*·ses

What's in that dish?
Τι περιέχει αυτό το ti pe·ri·e·hi af·*to* to
φαγητό; fa·ghi·*to*

Cheers!
Εις υγείαν! is i·*yi*·an

That was delicious.
Ήταν νοστιμότατο! *i*·tan no·sti·*mo*·ta·to

Please bring the bill.
Το λογαριασμό, to lo·ghar·ya·*zmo*
παρακαλώ. pa·ra·ka·*lo*

GREEK ALPHABET

The Greek alphabet has 24 letters, shown below in their upper- and lower-case forms.
Be aware that some letters look like English letters but are pronounced very differently,
such as **B**, which is pronounced v; and **P**, pronounced r. As in English, how letters are
pronounced is also influenced by the way they are combined, for example the **ου** combination is pronounced u as in 'put', and **οι** is pronounced ee as in 'feet'.

A α	a	as in 'father'	**Ξ ξ**	x	as in 'ox'	
B β	v	as in 'vine'	**O o**	o	as in 'hot'	
Γ γ	gh	a softer, throaty 'g', or	**Π π**	p	as in 'pup'	
	y	as in 'yes'	**P ρ**	r	as in 'road',	
Δ δ	dh	as in 'there'			slightly trilled	
E ε	e	as in 'egg'	**Σ σ, ς**	s	as in 'sand'	
Z ζ	z	as in 'zoo'	**T τ**	t	as in 'tap'	
H η	i	as in 'feet'	**Y υ**	i	as in 'feet'	
Θ θ	th	as in 'throw'	**Φ φ**	f	as in 'find'	
I ι	i	as in 'feet'	**X χ**	kh	as the 'ch' in the	
K κ	k	as in 'kite'			Scottish 'loch', or	
Λ λ	l	as in 'leg'		h	like a rough 'h'	
M μ	m	as in 'man'	**Ψ ψ**	ps	as in 'lapse'	
N ν	n	as in 'net'	**Ω ω**	o	as in 'hot'	

Note that the letter **Σ** has two forms for the lower case – **σ** and **ς**. The second one is used
at the end of words. The Greek question mark is represented with the English equivalent
of a semicolon (;).

LANGUAGE KEY WORDS

Key Words

appetisers	ορεκτικά	o·rek·ti·ka
bar	μπαρ	bar
beef	βοδινό	vo·dhi·no
beer	μπύρα	bi·ra
bottle	μπουκάλι	bu·ka·li
bowl	μπωλ	bol
bread	ψωμί	pso·mi
breakfast	πρόγευμα	pro·yev·ma
cafe	καφετέρια	ka·fe·te·ri·a
cheese	τυρί	ti·ri
chicken	κοτόπουλο	ko·to·pu·lo
coffee	καφές	ka·fes
cold	κρύο	kri·o
cream	κρέμα	kre·ma
delicatessen	ντελικατέσεν	de·li·ka·te·sen
desserts	επιδόρπια	e·pi·dhor·pi·a
dinner	δείπνο	dhip·no
egg	αυγό	av·gho
fish	ψάρι	psa·ri
food	φαγητό	fa·yi·to
fork	πιρούνι	pi·ru·ni
fruit	φρούτα	fru·ta
glass	ποτήρι	po·ti·ri
grocery store	οπωροπωλείο	o·po·ro·po·li·o
herb	βότανο	vo·ta·no
high chair	καρέκλα για μωρά	ka·re·kla yia mo·ra
hot	ζεστός	ze·stos
juice	χυμός	hi·mos
knife	μαχαίρι	ma·he·ri
lamb	αρνί	ar·ni
lunch	μεσημεριανό φαγητό	me·si·me·ria·no fa·yi·to
main courses	κύρια φαγητά	ki·ri·a fa·yi·ta
market	αγορά	a·gho·ra
menu	μενού	me·nu
milk	γάλα	gha·la
nut	καρύδι	ka·ri·dhi
oil	λάδι	la·dhi
pepper	πιπέρι	pi·pe·ri
plate	πιάτο	pia·to
pork	χοιρινό	hi·ri·no
red wine	κόκκινο κρασί	ko·ki·no kra·si
restaurant	εστιατόριο	e·sti·a·to·ri·o
salt	αλάτι	a·la·ti
soft drink	αναψυκτικό	a·na·psik·ti·ko
spoon	κουτάλι	ku·ta·li
sugar	ζάχαρη	za·kha·ri
tea	τσάι	tsa·i
vegetable	λαχανικά	la·kha·ni·ka
vegetarian	χορτοφάγος	khor·to·fa·ghos
vinegar	ξύδι	ksi·dhi
water	νερό	ne·ro
white wine	άσπρο κρασί	a·spro kra·si
with/without	με/χωρίς	me/kho·ris

KEY PATTERNS

To get by in Greek, mix and match these simple patterns with words of your choice:

When's (the next bus)?
Πότε είναι (το επόμενο λεωφορείο); — po·te i·ne (to e·po·me·no le·o·fo·ri·o)

Where's (the station)?
Πού είναι (ο σταθμός); — pu i·ne (o stath·mos)

Do you have (a local map)?
Έχετε οδικό (τοπικό χάρτη); — e·he·te o·dhi·ko (to·pi·ko khar·ti)

Is there a (lift)?
Υπάρχει (ασανσέρ); — i·par·hi (a·san·ser)

Can I (try it on)?
Μπορώ να (το προβάρω); — bo·ro na (to pro·va·ro)

Could you (please help)?
Μπορείς να (βοηθήσεις, παρακαλώ); — bo·ris na (vo·i·thi·sis pa·ra·ka·lo)

Do I need (to book)?
Χρειάζεται (να κλείσω θέση); — khri·a·ze·te (na kli·so the·si)

I need (assistance).
Χρειάζομαι (βοήθεια). — khri·a·zo·me (vo·i·thi·a)

I'd like (to hire a car).
Θα ήθελα (να ενοικιάσω ένα αυτοκίνητο). — tha i·the·la (na e·ni·ki·a·so e·na af·to·ki·ni·to)

How much is it (per night)?
Πόσο είναι (για κάθε νύχτα); — po·so i·ne (yia ka·the nikh·ta)

EMERGENCIES

Help!	Βοήθεια!	vo·i·thya
Go away!	Φύγε!	fi·ye
I'm lost.	Έχω χαθεί.	e·kho kha·thi
Where's the toilet?	Πού είναι η τουαλέτα;	pu i·ne i tu·a·le·ta

Signs

ΕΙΣΟΔΟΣ	Entry
ΕΞΟΔΟΣ	Exit
ΠΛΗΡΟΦΟΡΙΕΣ	Information
ΑΝΟΙΧΤΟ	Open
ΚΛΕΙΣΤΟ	Closed
ΑΠΑΓΟΡΕΥΕΤΑΙ	Prohibited
ΑΣΤΥΝΟΜΙΑ	Police
ΓΥΝΑΙΚΩΝ	Toilets (Women)
ΑΝΔΡΩΝ	Toilets (Men)

Call ...!	Φωνάξτε ...!	fo·nak·ste ...
a doctor	ένα γιατρό	e·na yi·a·tro
the police	την αστυνομία	tin a·sti·no·mi·a

I'm ill. Είμαι άρρωστος. i·me a·ro·stos

I'm allergic to (antibiotics).
Είμαι αλλεργικός/ i·me a·ler·yi·kos/
αλλεργική a·ler·yi·ki (m/f)
(στα αντιβιωτικά) (sta an·di·vi·o·ti·ka)

SHOPPING & SERVICES

I'd like to buy ...
Θέλω ν' αγοράσω ... the·lo na·gho·ra·so ...

I'm just looking.
Απλώς κοιτάζω. ap·los ki·ta·zo

Can I see it?
Μπορώ να το δω; bo·ro na to dho

I don't like it.
Δεν μου αρέσει. dhen mu a·re·si

How much is it?
Πόσο κάνει; po·so ka·ni

It's too expensive.
Είναι πολύ ακριβό. i·ne po·li a·kri·vo

Can you lower the price?
Μπορείς να κατεβάσεις bo·ris na ka·te·va·sis
την τιμή; tin ti·mi

ATM	αυτόματη μηχανή χρημάτων	af·to·ma·ti mi·kha·ni khri·ma·ton
bank	τράπεζα	tra·pe·za
credit card	πιστωτική κάρτα	pi·sto·ti·ki kar·ta
internet cafe	καφενείο διαδικτύου	ka·fe·ni·o dhi·a·dhik·ti·u
mobile phone	κινητό	ki·ni·to
post office	ταχυδρομείο	ta·hi·dhro·mi·o
tourist office	τουριστικό γραφείο	tu·ri·sti·ko ghra·fi·o

TIME & DATES

What time is it?
Τι ώρα είναι; ti o·ra i·ne

It's (two) o'clock.
Είναι (δύο) η ώρα. i·ne (dhi·o) i o·ra

It's half past (10).
(Δέκα) και μισή. (dhe·ka) ke mi·si

morning	πρωί	pro·i
(this) afternoon	(αυτό το) απόγευμα	(af·to to) a·po·yev·ma
evening	βράδυ	vra·dhi

yesterday	χθες	hthes
today	σήμερα	si·me·ra
tomorrow	αύριο	av·ri·o

Monday	Δευτέρα	dhef·te·ra
Tuesday	Τρίτη	tri·ti
Wednesday	Τετάρτη	te·tar·ti
Thursday	Πέμπτη	pemp·ti
Friday	Παρασκευή	pa·ras·ke·vi
Saturday	Σάββατο	sa·va·to
Sunday	Κυριακή	ky·ri·a·ki

January	Ιανουάριος	ia·nu·ar·i·os
February	Φεβρουάριος	fev·ru·ar·i·os
March	Μάρτιος	mar·ti·os
April	Απρίλιος	a·pri·li·os
May	Μάιος	mai·os
June	Ιούνιος	i·u·ni·os
July	Ιούλιος	i·u·li·os
August	Αύγουστος	av·ghus·tos
September	Σεπτέμβριος	sep·tem·vri·os
October	Οκτώβριος	ok·to·vri·os
November	Νοέμβριος	no·em·vri·os
December	Δεκέμβριος	dhe·kem·vri·os

Question Words

How?	Πώς;	pos
What?	Τι;	ti
When?	Πότε;	po·te
Where?	Πού;	pu
Who?	Ποιος;	pi·os (m)
	Ποια;	pi·a (f)
	Ποιο;	pi·o (n)
Why?	Γιατί;	yi·a·ti

TRANSPORT

Public Transport

boat	πλοίο	pli·o
city bus	αστικό	a·sti·ko
intercity bus	λεωφορείο	le·o·fo·ri·o
plane	αεροπλάνο	ae·ro·pla·no
train	τρένο	tre·no

Where do I buy a ticket?
Πού αγοράζω εισιτήριο;   pu a·gho·ra·zo i·si·ti·ri·o

I want to go to ...
Θέλω να πάω στο/στη ...   the·lo na pao sto/sti...

What time does it leave?
Τι ώρα φεύγει;   ti o·ra fev·yi

Does it stop at (Iraklio)?
Σταματάει στο   sta·ma·ta·i sto
(Ηράκλειο);   (i·ra·kli·o)

I'd like to get off at (Iraklio).
Θα ήθελα να κατεβώ   tha i·the·la na ka·te·vo
στο (Ηράκλειο).   sto (i·ra·kli·o)

I'd like (a) ...	Θα ήθελα (ένα) ...	tha i·the·la (e·na) ...
1st class	πρώτη θέση	pro·ti the·si
2nd class	δεύτερη θέση	def·te·ri the·si
one-way ticket	απλό εισιτήριο	a·plo i·si·ti·ri·o
return ticket	εισιτήριο με επιστροφή	i·si·ti·ri·o me e·pi·stro·fi
cancelled	ακυρώθηκε	a·ki·ro·thi·ke
delayed	καθυστέρησε	ka·thi·ste·ri·se
platform	πλατφόρμα	plat·for·ma
ticket office	εκδοτήριο εισιτηρίων	ek·dho·ti·ri·o i·si·ti·ri·on
timetable	δρομολόγιο	dhro·mo·lo·gio
train station	σταθμός τρένου	stath·mos tre·nu

Driving & Cycling

I'd like to hire a ...	Θα ήθελα να νοικιάσω ...	tha i·the·la na ni·ki·a·so ...
4WD	ένα τέσσερα επί τέσσερα	e·na tes·se·ra e·pi tes·se·ra
bicycle	ένα ποδήλατο	e·na po·dhi·la·to
car	ένα αυτοκίνητο	e·na af·to·ki·ni·to
jeep	ένα τζιπ	e·na tzip
motorbike	μια μοτοσυκλέττα	mya mo·to·si·klet·ta

Numbers

1	ένας	e·nas (m)
	μία	mi·a (f)
	ένα	e·na (n)
2	δύο	dhi·o
3	τρεις	tris (m&f)
	τρία	tri·a (n)
4	τέσσερεις	te·se·ris (m&f)
	τέσσερα	te·se·ra (n)
5	πέντε	pen·de
6	έξη	e·xi
7	επτά	ep·ta
8	οχτώ	oh·to
9	εννέα	e·ne·a
10	δέκα	dhe·ka
20	είκοσι	ik·o·si
30	τριάντα	tri·an·da
40	σαράντα	sa·ran·da
50	πενήντα	pe·nin·da
60	εξήντα	ek·sin·da
70	εβδομήντα	ev·dho·min·da
80	ογδόντα	ogh·dhon·da
90	ενενήντα	e·ne·nin·da
100	εκατό	e·ka·to
1000	χίλιοι	hi·li·i (m)
	χίλιες	hi·li·ez (f)
	χίλια	hi·li·a (n)

Do I need a helmet?
Χρειάζομαι κράνος;   khri·a·zo·me kra·nos

Is this the road to ...?
Αυτός είναι ο   af·tos i·ne o
δρόμος για ... ;   dhro·mos ya ...

Where's a petrol station?
Πού είναι ένα πρατήριο   pu i·ne e·na pra·ti·ri·o
βενζίνας;   ven·zi·nas

(How long) Can I park here?
(Πόση ώρα) Μπορώ να   (po·si o·ra) bo·ro na
παρκάρω εδώ;   par·ka·ro e·dho

The car/motorbike has broken down (at ...).
Το αυτοκίνητο/   to af·to·ki·ni·to/
η μοτοσυκλέττα   i mo·to·si·klet·ta
χάλασε (στο ...).   kha·la·se (sto ...)

I need a mechanic.
Χρειάζομαι μηχανικό.   khri·a·zo·me mi·kha·ni·ko

I have a flat tyre.
Έπαθα λάστιχο.   e·pa·tha la·sti·cho

I've run out of petrol.
Έμεινα από βενζίνη.   e·mi·na a·po ven·zi·ni

Behind the Scenes

SEND US YOUR FEEDBACK

We love to hear from travellers – your comments keep us on our toes and help make our books better. Our well-travelled team reads every word on what you loved or loathed about this book. Although we cannot reply individually to your submissions, we always guarantee that your feedback goes straight to the appropriate authors, in time for the next edition. Each person who sends us information is thanked in the next edition – the most useful submissions are rewarded with a selection of digital PDF chapters.

Visit **lonelyplanet.com/contact** to submit your updates and suggestions or to ask for help. Our award-winning website also features inspirational travel stories, news and discussions.

Note: We may edit, reproduce and incorporate your comments in Lonely Planet products such as guidebooks, websites and digital products, so let us know if you don't want your comments reproduced or your name acknowledged. For a copy of our privacy policy visit lonelyplanet.com/privacy.

WRITER THANKS

Simon Richmond

Many thanks to the following: Steve Boyd, Valie Voutsa, Vangelis Koronakis, Yannis Bournias, Nikos Tsoniotis, Danae Zaoussis, Zora O'Neill, Harry and Jane Lushington, and Brana Vladisavljevic for hiring me for a great gig.

Andrea Schulte-Peevers

Heartfelt thank yous to Kerstin Göllrich for her patience, curiosity, stamina and awesome driving skills; Johannes Bolz for literally going the extra mile for me in the Kritsa Gorge; Konstantinos and Natalie Zivas for wonderful insider tips on Elounda and the north coast, and father Vaggelis for his kitchen wizardry; Alaska Klaus for his insights into hiking the E4; Margarita Kurowska and Jutta Berger for keeping things under control on the home front; and David for being with me in spirit.

Andy Symington

So many people in the Peloponnese were so helpful along the way that it made the trip easy. Particular thanks to Kate Armstrong, Néna Grintziá, Theo and Susanna Spiliopoulos and Chris DeLiso for providing information, and to Brana Vladislavljevic for the opportunity. Also many thanks to Richard Green for those lectures on Greece many years ago that sparked a love of the country's archaeology.

Kate Armstrong

I'd be a trillionaire for all the times I've uttered *efharisto poli* to the helpful Greeks who've opened their hearts. Especially Eleni and Yiannis (Kalymnos), Michalis of Michalis Studios (Lipsi), the Alexakis family (Alexakis Hotel; Kos), Michalis (Café Angolo Italiano; Karpathos), George (Euromoto; Karpathos), fabulous walkers Mike and John (Tilos), Tonia, Maria and Christina (Leros). Brana V, DE extraordinaire, you were the best of the LP best to work with. Finally, fellow Gemini Apostolos, without whom my Odyssey would have stalled in the Meltemi winds.

Stuart Butler

Thank you once again to my wife, Heather, and children, Jake and Grace, for putting up with me sauntering off to sunny Greece while they were stuck at home. And then I must thank them again for being the best travel partners I could ever want when they flew out to Corfu to join me towards the end of my research. Thank you also to Brana for giving me this dream gig in the first place.

Peter Dragicevich

It's always a complete delight to have company on the road, especially when it comes in the form of one of your very best friends. Thank you, David Mills, for being so diligent in assisting me in researching the Mykonos nightlife. Special thanks are also due to editor extraordinaire Brana Vladisavljevic for all of the support and opportunities you've given me over the years.

Trent Holden

First up, a huge thanks to the destination editor, Brana Vladisavljevic, not only for commissioning me on this title, but for all her work at Lonely Planet over the past 15 years. You will be missed! Also sending out my gratitude to the Cretan people who make this island so special with their humbling hospitality,good humour and willingness to help out at all times. Finally lots of love to my fiancée Kate Morgan, and to my family and friends.

Anna Kaminski
Huge thanks to Brana for entrusting me with half of the Cyclades, and to everyone who's helped me along the way. In particular: Alex in Halki (Naxos), Apostolos of Atlantis Oia in Santorini, the lifeguard who rescued me when I was swept out to sea on a paddleboard in Ios, Kostas in Folegandros, Alix and Semeli in Amorgos, Flora in Antiparos, plus all wine experts on Sikinos, Paros, Santorini and in Naxos who've contributed to my ongoing oenological education.

Vesna Maric
Many thanks to Brana Vladisavljevic, who commissioned the project – it was always an absolute joy to work with her. Thanks to Stathis Kampouridis for his generosity in Athens.

Hugh McNaughtan
I'd like to thank my long-suffering family, Brana, LP tech support and all the kind people of Macedonia who showed me such hospitality.

Kate Morgan
Huge thanks to amazing destination editor Brana for commissioning me to work on Crete, LP won't be the same without you. Thank you to Despina in Hania for all of your assistance, to the staff at the Hania tourist information office for your help and to all of the amazing Cretans I met along the way – your generosity and hospitality is unforgettable. And, as always, thank you to my fiancé Trent for being the best travel companion and for driving me all over Hania.

Isabella Noble
Efharisto to all the wonderful people who helped out on the road and back at home. Denis in Skiathos; Heather, Alexandra, Voula, Kostas, Valeria and Natasa in Skopelos; Mary, Pakis, Paul, Angela and Justine in Alonnisos; Lefteris, Katerina, Chrysanthi, Amanda and Nikos in Skyros; Marina, Giorgios and Steven in Evia. Back at home, thanks to Jack, Andrew, Papi and Sarah.

Zora O'Neill
Ευχαριστώ to Leon Vainikos, Simon Richmond, Alex Robertson-Textor and, as ever, my chauffeur, Peter Moskos. In the LP offices, huge thanks to Brana Vladisavljevic for setting Team Greece on the right track.

Leonid Ragozin
I would like to thank Christos of Ikaria Utopia for helping to get my head around new things on the island; Samos Volunteers for insights into the refugee situation; Manolis of Belvedere in Pythagario for good tips about Samos; Paulette Roberge for opening the doors of her splendid Inousses villa; dozens of other friendly and hospitable people who shared ideas and pointed me in the right direction. I also feel very grateful to Greece for its very existence – it's a great and beloved country.

Kevin Raub
Thanks to Brana Vladisavljevic and all my fellow partners in crime at LP. On the road, Kjetil Jikiun, Giorges Kteniadakis, Andria Mitsakis, Iossif Serafimidis, Dr Emmanuel Prokopkis and the nurses at Pagni, Lydia and Nikos and the brews of Kykao and Solo.

Greg Ward
Many thanks to all the wonderful people who helped me along the way, and who created so many happy memories. And thanks above all to my dear wife, Sam, for sharing such an amazing trip.

ACKNOWLEDGEMENTS

Climate map data adapted from Peel MC, Finlayson BL & McMahon TA (2007) 'Updated World Map of the Köppen-Geiger Climate Classification', *Hydrology and Earth System Sciences*, 11, 1633–44.

Cover photograph: Sanctuary of Athena Pronaia, Ancient Delphi; elgreko/Shutterstock ©

THIS BOOK

This 15th edition of Lonely Planet's *Greece* guidebook was researched and written by Simon Richmond, Andrea Schulte-Peevers, Andy Symington, Kate Armstrong, Stuart Butler, Peter Dragicevich, Trent Holden, Anna Kaminski, Vesna Maric, Hugh McNaughtan, Kate Morgan, Isabella Noble, Zora O'Neill, Leonid Ragozin, Kevin Raub and Greg Ward. This guidebook was produced by the following:

Destination Editor
Brana Vladisavljevic

Senior Product Editors
Elizabeth Jones, Sandie Kestell, Kathryn Rowan

Regional Senior Cartographer Anthony Phelan

Product Editors
Hannah Cartmel, Claire Rourke, Fergus O'Shea

Book Designers
Catalina Aragón, Jessica Rose, Mazzy Prinsep

Cartographer Alison Lyall

Assisting Editors
Janet Austin, Sarah Bailey, James Bainbridge, Judith Bamber, Samantha Cook, Michelle Coxall, Melanie Dankel, Jennifer Hattam, Rosie Nicholson, Monique Perrin, Christopher Pitts, Tamara Sheward

Assisting Cartographer
James Leversha

Cover Researcher
Gwen Cotter

Thanks to
Ronan Abayawickrema, Carolyn Boicos, Sue Burt, Hannah Cartmel, Fergal Condon, Gwen Cotter, Shona Gray, Karen Henderson, Amy Lynch, Catherine Naghten, Darren O'Connell, Charlotte Orr, Genna Patterson, Martine Power, Kirsten Rawlings, Georgia Tsarouhas, Amanda Williamson

Index

Map Pages **000**
Photo Pages **000**

Map Legend

Sights
- Beach
- Bird Sanctuary
- Buddhist
- Castle/Palace
- Christian
- Confucian
- Hindu
- Islamic
- Jain
- Jewish
- Monument
- Museum/Gallery/Historic Building
- Ruin
- Shinto
- Sikh
- Taoist
- Winery/Vineyard
- Zoo/Wildlife Sanctuary
- Other Sight

Activities, Courses & Tours
- Bodysurfing
- Diving
- Canoeing/Kayaking
- Course/Tour
- Sento Hot Baths/Onsen
- Skiing
- Snorkelling
- Surfing
- Swimming/Pool
- Walking
- Windsurfing
- Other Activity

Sleeping
- Sleeping
- Camping
- Hut/Shelter

Eating
- Eating

Drinking & Nightlife
- Drinking & Nightlife
- Cafe

Entertainment
- Entertainment

Shopping
- Shopping

Information
- Bank
- Embassy/Consulate
- Hospital/Medical
- Internet
- Police
- Post Office
- Telephone
- Toilet
- Tourist Information
- Other Information

Geographic
- Beach
- Gate
- Hut/Shelter
- Lighthouse
- Lookout
- Mountain/Volcano
- Oasis
- Park
- Pass
- Picnic Area
- Waterfall

Population
- Capital (National)
- Capital (State/Province)
- City/Large Town
- Town/Village

Transport
- Airport
- Border crossing
- Bus
- Cable car/Funicular
- Cycling
- Ferry
- Metro station
- Monorail
- Parking
- Petrol station
- S-Bahn/Subway station
- Taxi
- T-bane/Tunnelbana station
- Train station/Railway
- Tram
- U-Bahn/Underground station
- Other Transport

Routes
- Tollway
- Freeway
- Primary
- Secondary
- Tertiary
- Lane
- Unsealed road
- Road under construction
- Plaza/Mall
- Steps
- Tunnel
- Pedestrian overpass
- Walking Tour
- Walking Tour detour
- Path/Walking Trail

Boundaries
- International
- State/Province
- Disputed
- Regional/Suburb
- Marine Park
- Cliff
- Wall

Hydrography
- River, Creek
- Intermittent River
- Canal
- Water
- Dry/Salt/Intermittent Lake
- Reef

Areas
- Airport/Runway
- Beach/Desert
- Cemetery (Christian)
- Cemetery (Other)
- Glacier
- Mudflat
- Park/Forest
- Sight (Building)
- Sportsground
- Swamp/Mangrove

Note: Not all symbols displayed above appear on the maps in this book

Kate Morgan

Crete Having worked for Lonely Planet for over a decade now, Kate has been fortunate enough to cover plenty of ground working as a travel writer on destinations such as Shanghai, Japan, India, Russia, Zimbabwe, the Philippines and Phuket. She has done stints living in London, Paris and Osaka but these days is based in one of her favourite regions in the world – Victoria, Australia. In between travelling the world and writing about it, Kate enjoys spending time at home working as a freelance editor.

Isabella Noble

Evia & Sporades English-Australian on paper but Spanish at heart, Isabella has been wandering the globe since her first round-the-world trip as a one-year-old. Having grown up in a whitewashed Andalucian village, she is a Spain specialist travel journalist, but also writes extensively about India, Thailand, the UK and beyond for Lonely Planet, the *Daily Telegraph* and others. Isabella has co-written Lonely Planet guides to Spain and Andalucía, and is a *Daily Telegraph* Spain expert. She has also contributed to Lonely Planet *India*, *South India*, *Thailand*, *Thailand's Islands & Beaches*, *Southeast Asia on a Shoestring* and *Great Britain*, and authored *Pocket Phuket*. Find Isabella on Twitter and Instagram (@isabellamnoble).

Zora O'Neill

Northern Greece Zora visited Greece for the first time in 1995, and has been exploring new regions and new hiking trails ever since. A longtime Lonely Planet writer, she is also the author of *All Strangers Are Kin*, a travel memoir about studying Arabic. She lives in Queens, New York, in (not entirely coincidentally) a Greek neighbourhood, where frappés, feta and fresh herbs are plentiful.

Leonid Ragozin

Northeastern Aegean Islands Leonid studied beach dynamics at the Moscow State University, but for want of decent beaches in Russia, he switched to journalism and spent 12 years voyaging through different parts of the BBC, with a break for a four-year stint as a foreign correspondent for the Russian Newsweek. Leonid is currently a freelance journalist focusing largely on the conflict between Russia and Ukraine (both his Lonely Planet destinations), which prompted him to leave Moscow and find a new home in Rīga.

Kevin Raub

Crete Atlanta native Kevin started his career as a music journalist in New York, working for *Men's Journal* and *Rolling Stone* magazines. He ditched the rock 'n' roll lifestyle for travel writing and has written more than 95 Lonely Planet guides, focused mainly on Brazil, Chile, Colombia, USA, India, Italy and Portugal. Raub also contributes to a variety of travel magazines in both the USA and UK. Along the way, the self-confessed hophead is in constant search of wildly high IBUs in local beers. Find him at www.kevinraub.net or follow him on Twitter and Instagram (@RaubOnTheRoad).

Greg Ward

Central Greece, Rhodes Since his youthful adventures on the hippy trail to India, and living in northern Spain, Greg has written guides to destinations all over the world. As well as covering the USA from the Southwest to Hawaii, he has ranged on recent assignments from Corsica to the Cotswolds, and Dallas to Delphi. Visit his website, www.gregward.info, to see his favourite photos and memories.